SOCIAL PSYCHOLOGY

12e

SOCIAL PSYCHOLOGY

12e

David G. Myers

Hope College

Jean M. Twenge

San Diego State University

McGraw Hill Education

SOCIAL PSYCHOLOGY, TWELFTH EDITION

Published by McGraw-Hill Education, 2 Penn Plaza, New York, NY 10121. Copyright © 2017 by
McGraw-Hill Education. All rights reserved. Printed in the United States of America. Previous editions
© 2013, 2010, and 2008. No part of this publication may be reproduced or distributed in any form or by
any means, or stored in a database or retrieval system, without the prior written consent of McGraw-Hill
Education, including, but not limited to, in any network or other electronic storage or transmission, or
broadcast for distance learning.

Some ancillaries, including electronic and print components, may not be available to customers outside the
United States.

This book is printed on acid-free paper.

5 6 7 8 9 LWI 21 20 19 18

Student Edition	Instructor Review Edition
ISBN 978-0-07-786197-1	978-1-259-68063-2
MHID 0-07-786197-3	1-259-68063-0

Senior Vice President, Products & Markets: *Kurt L. Strand*
Vice President, General Manager, Products & Markets: *Michael Ryan*
Vice President, Content Design & Delivery: *Kimberly Meriwether David*
Managing Director: *William Glass*
Executive Director: *Krista Bettino*
Senior Brand Manager: *Nancy Welcher*
Director, Product Development: *Meghan Campbell*
Lead Product Developer: *Dawn Groundwater*
Marketing Managers: *Ann Helgerson, AJ Laferrera, Christina Yu*
Digital Product Analyst: *Neil Kahn*
Senior Product Developer: *Judith Kromm*
Editorial Coordinator: *Elisa Odoardi*
Director, Content Design & Delivery: *Terri Schiesl*
Program Manager: *Debra Hash*
Content Project Managers: *Sandy Wille; Amber Bettcher*
Buyer: *Laura Fuller*
Designer: *Matt Backhaus*
Content Licensing Specialists: (photo) *Shawntel Schmitt;* (text) *Beth Thole*
Cover Image: © RADEK MICA/AFP/Getty Images
Compositor: *Aptara®, Inc.*
Printer: *LSC Communications*

All credits appearing on page or at the end of the book are considered to be an extension
of the copyright page.

Library of Congress Cataloging-in-Publication Data

Myers, David G.
    Social psychology / David G. Myers, Hope College, Holland, Michigan with Jean M. Twenge,
San Diego State University.—12e [edition].
        pages cm
    ISBN 978-0-07-786197-1 (alk. paper)
    ISBN 0-07-786197-3 (alk. paper)
1. Social psychology.   I. Twenge, Jean M., 1971– II. Title.
    HM1033.M944 2016
        302—dc23   2015022159

The Internet addresses listed in the text were accurate at the time of publication. The inclusion of a website
does not indicate an endorsement by the authors or McGraw-Hill Education, and McGraw-Hill Education
does not guarantee the accuracy of the information presented at these sites.

For Kathy Adamski

With gratitude for 34 years of friendship and support

About the Authors

Since receiving his University of Iowa Ph.D., David Myers has professed psychology at Michigan's Hope College. Hope College students have invited him to be their commencement speaker and voted him "outstanding professor."

With support from National Science Foundation grants, Myers's research has appeared in some three dozen scientific books and periodicals, including *Science,* the *American Scientist, Psychological Science,* and the *American Psychologist.*

Hope College Public Relations

He has also communicated psychological science through his articles appearing in four dozen magazines, from *Today's Education* to *Scientific American,* and through his seventeen books, including *The Pursuit of Happiness and Intuition: Its Powers and Perils.*

Myers's research and writings have been recognized by the Gordon Allport Prize, by an "honored scientist" award from the Federation of Associations in the Brain and Behavioral Sciences, and by the Award for Distinguished Service on Behalf of Personality-Social Psychology.

He has chaired his city's Human Relations Commission, helped found a center for families in poverty, and spoken to hundreds of college and community groups. In recognition of his efforts to transform the way America provides assistive listening for people with hearing loss (see hearingloop.org), he has received awards from the American Academy of Audiology and the Hearing Loss Association of America.

He bikes to work year-round and plays pick-up basketball. David and Carol Myers have three children and one grandchild.

As Professor of Psychology at San Diego State University, Jean M. Twenge has authored more than 120 scientific publications on generational differences, cultural change, social rejection, gender roles, self-esteem, and narcissism. Her research has been covered in *Time, Newsweek, The New York Times, USA Today, U.S. News and World Report,* and *The Washington Post,* and she has been featured on Today, Good Morning America, CBS This Morning, Fox and Friends, NBC Nightly News, Dateline NBC, and National Public Radio.

She summarized this research for a broader audience in the books *Generation Me: Why Today's Young Americans Are More Confident, Assertive, Entitled—and More Miserable Than Ever Before* and *The Narcissism Epidemic: Living in the Age of Entitlement* (co-authored with W. Keith Campbell). She has written for general audiences on several websites and magazines, including a piece for *The Atlantic* that was nominated for a National Magazine Award. She frequently gives talks and seminars on generational differences to audiences such as college faculty and staff, military personnel, camp directors, and corporate executives.

Dr. Twenge grew up in Minnesota and Texas. She holds a B.A. and M.A. from the University of Chicago and a Ph.D. from the University of Michigan. She completed a postdoctoral research fellowship in social psychology at Case Western Reserve University. She lives in San Diego with her husband and three daughters.

Sandy Huffaker, Jr.

Brief Contents

©Donna Day/Imagestate RF

©Purestock/PunchStock RF

©Ingram Publishing RF

Table of Contents

©Somos Photography/Veer RF

©Ronnie Kaufman/Blend Images RF

Part Three: Social Relations

CHAPTER 9
Prejudice: Disliking Others   254

©Ariel Skelley/Blend Images RF

Connecting the Human Experience, Research, and Results

Social Psychology introduces students to the science of *us*; how our thoughts, feelings, and behaviors are influenced by the world we live in. In this edition, esteemed author David Myers is joined by respected psychology professor and generational differences researcher Jean Twenge in presenting an integrated learning program designed for today's students.

Written in the tradition of the liberal arts, *Social Psychology*'s style allows any student to access the rich teachings of this young and exciting science. Whether students are interested in business, teaching, law, psychology, or other areas that invite exploring our social world, the program is accessible and easy to understand.

The new edition integrates SmartBook, a personalized learning program, offering students the insight they need to study smarter and improve classroom results.

Better Data, Smarter Revision, Improved Results

Students helped inform the revision strategy:

STEP 1. Over the course of three years, data points showing concepts that caused students the most difficulty were anonymously collected from McGraw-Hill Education Connect for Social Psychology's LearnSmart® data.

STEP 2. The authors were provided with data from LearnSmart that graphically illustrated hot spots in the form of a "Heat Map" that impacted student learning (see image).

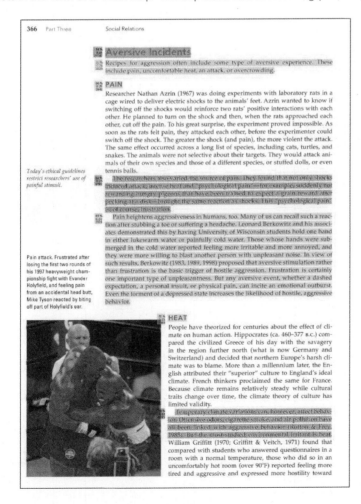

STEP 3. The authors used the Heat Map data to refine the content and reinforce student comprehension in the new edition. Additional quiz questions and assignable activities were created for use in Connect for Social Psychology to further support student success.

RESULT: With empirically based feedback at the paragraph and even at the sentence level, the authors developed the new edition using precise student data to pinpoint concepts that caused students to struggle.

LearnSmart® is an adaptive learning program designed to help students learn faster, study smarter, and retain more knowledge for greater success. Distinguishing what students know from what they don't, and focusing on concepts they are most likely to forget, LearnSmart continuously adapts to each student's needs by building an individual learning path. Millions of students have answered more than a billion questions in LearnSmart since 2009, making it the most widely used and intelligent adaptive study tool that's proven to strengthen memory recall, keep students in class, and boost grades.

SMARTBOOK®

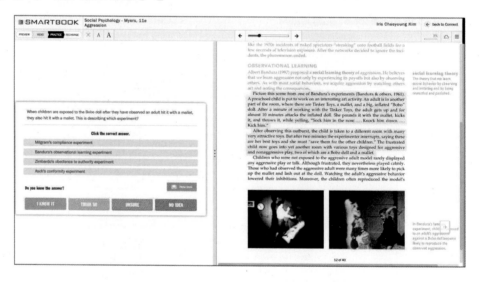

Fueled by LearnSmart, SmartBook is the first and only adaptive reading experience currently available.

- **Make It Effective.** SmartBook creates a personalized reading experience by highlighting the most impactful concepts a student needs to learn at that moment in time. This ensures that every minute spent with SmartBook is returned to the student as the most value-added minute possible.

- **Make It Informed.** Real-time reports quickly identify the concepts that require more attention from individual students—or the entire class.

Personalized Grading, On the Go, Made Easier

Connect Insight® is a one-of-kind visual analytics dashboard—now available for both instructors and students—that provides at-a-glance information regarding student performance. Designed for mobile devices, Connect Insight empowers students and helps instructors improve class performance.

- **Make it intuitive.** Instructors receive instant, at-a-glance views of student performance matched with student activity. Students can receive at-a-glance views of their own performance and how they are doing compared to the rest of the class.

- **Make it dynamic.** Connect Insight puts real-time analytics in instructors' and students' hands, so they can take action early and keep struggling students from falling behind.

- **Make it mobile.** Connect Insight is available on-demand wherever and whenever it's needed.

The **Instructor Resources** have been updated to reflect changes to the new edition; these can be accessed by faculty through Connect for Social Psychology. Resources include the test bank, instructor's manual, PowerPoint presentation, and image gallery.

Easily rearrange chapters, combine material, and quickly upload content you have written, such as your course syllabus or teaching notes, using **McGraw-Hill Education Create™**. Find the content you need by searching through thousands of leading McGraw-Hill Education textbooks. Arrange your book to fit your teaching style. Create even allows you to personalize your book's appearance by selecting the cover and adding your name, school, and course information. Order a Create book, and you will receive a complimentary print review copy in three to five business days or a complimentary electronic review copy via e-mail in about an hour. Experience how McGraw-Hill Education empowers you to teach your students your way: http://create.mheducation.com

Capture lessons and lectures in a searchable format for use in traditional, hybrid, "flipped classes" and online courses by using **Tegrity** (http://www.tegrity.com). Its personalized learning features make study time efficient, and its affordability brings this benefit to every student on campus. Patented search technology and real-time Learning Management System (LMS) integrations make Tegrity the market-leading solution and service.

McGraw-Hill Education Campus (www.mhcampus.com) provides faculty with true single sign-on access to all of McGraw-Hill Education's course content, digital tools, and other high-quality learning resources from any LMS. This innovative offering allows for secure and deep integration, enabling seamless access for faculty and students to any of McGraw-Hill Education's course solutions, such as McGraw-Hill Education Connect® (all-digital teaching and learning platform), McGraw-Hill Education Create (state-of-the-art).

Taking Sides: Clashing Views in Social Psychology

This debate-style reader both reinforces and challenges students' viewpoints on the most crucial issues social psychology today. Each topic offers current and lively pro and con essays that represent the arguments of leading scholars and commentators in their fields. *Learning Outcomes,* an *Issue Summary,* and an *Issue Introduction* set the stage for each debate topic. Following each issue is the *Exploring the Issue* section with *Critical Thinking and Reflection* questions, *Is There Common Ground?* commentary, *Additional Resources,* and *Internet References* all designed to stimulate and challenge the student's thinking and to further explore the topic. Customize this title via **McGraw-Hill Create** at http://create.mheducation.com.

Preface

What Else Is New in *Social Psychology*, Twelfth Edition?

Building on prior editions, this twelfth edition combines scientific rigor with an accessible voice. The text is updated throughout, with more than 750 new citations. From cover to cover, Myers and Twenge introduce social psychology's big ideas and apply them to everyday life by helping students think critically about their own and others' social behavior.

Chapter-by-Chapter Changes

Chapter 1   Introducing Social Psychology

- Expanded two levels of dual processing, intuitive and deliberate, to include System 1 and System 2
- New material and examples on wording of questions in surveys
- *"Random Assignment"* section moved before "Control: Manipulating Variables"
- New section titled "Replication: Are the Results Reproducible?"

Chapter 2   The Self in a Social World

- Chapter reorganized to bring together topics related to positive self-views (self-esteem, narcissism, self-serving bias) and to cover self-control separately
- New material on social comparison and self-presentation on Facebook
- New material on differences in individualism by region and class, and through cultural change
- New material on self-compassion vs. the pursuit of self-esteem
- New material on whether narcissists realize they are narcissistic

Chapter 3   Social Beliefs and Judgments

- Updated chapter opener example on same-sex marriage
- Updated coverage of System 1 and System 2 to explain unconscious, fast thinking compared with conscious, slow thinking
- Reorganized topics to bring together coverage of System 1 thinking (priming, intuitive judgments)
- Updated coverage on embodied cognition
- New Inside Story feature titled "Joseph P. Forgas: Can Bad Weather Improve Your Memory?"

Chapter 4   Behavior and Attitudes

- New research on effects of sustained role playing of "risk-glorifying" video games
- "The Foot-in-the-Door Phenomenon" section moved to Chapter 7, "Persuasion"
- New discussion about the inspiration for the cognitive dissonance theory

Chapter 5   Genes, Culture, and Gender

- New coverage of epigenetics
- Updated statistics on gender equality and gender-role attitudes
- New material on cultural similarities in emotional expression on Facebook
- New figure showing gender differences in language use on Facebook
- New material on precarious manhood
- New material on social norms across cultures
- Updated material on gender differences in sexuality

Chapter 6 Conformity and Obedience

- New coverage of acceptance
- Revised definitions and new figure illustrating the concepts acceptance, compliance, and obedience
- New material on mood linkage on Facebook
- New coverage of mass hysteria
- New examples of mass hysteria
- New material on cultural change in conformity
- Added modern interpretations of Milgram's obedience studies
- Updated and streamlined discussion of personality and conformity
- New material on pathogen prevalence and conformity
- New discussion of ways to prevent binge drinking on college campuses

Chapter 7 Persuasion

- New material on facial expressions and advertising persuasiveness
- New research on the trustworthiness of the communicator
- New examples of user-generated advertising
- New examples of fear appeals
- New discussion of consumer engagement as a key part of online advertising
- New material on persuading children toward healthier eating
- Discussion of the effects of advert-games on children

Chapter 8 Group Influence

- New discussion of social facilitation affecting home-game advantage, with a new bulleted list
- Expanded discussion of group polarization on the Internet, and introduction and example of "Dark Web" forums
- New research on creative innovation and leaders as minority influence

Chapter 9 Prejudice: Disliking Others

- Added research on microaggression
- Updated research on underreported feelings of prejudice
- Updated research on the Implicit Association Test (IAT)
- Updated data on changing gender attitudes
- New section titled "Gay-Lesbian Prejudice"
- New research on intervention for reducing implicit prejudice
- New research on values affirmation

Chapter 10 Aggression: Hurting Others

- New coverage of bullying and cyberbullying
- New information on sexual assault in the opener
- New coverage of physical aggression and social aggression
- New material on sleep and aggression
- New material on the effects of testosterone
- New material on diet and aggression
- New example of heat and aggression based on events in Ferguson, Missouri

- New material on media exposure and aggression/bullying
- New material on violent video games and aggression
- New strategies on how to reduce aggression

Chapter 11 Attraction and Intimacy: Liking and Loving Others

- Revised definitions of secure, anxious, and avoidant attachment
- Key term insecure attachment changed to anxious attachment.
- New material on mere exposure
- New research on the effects of physical attractiveness
- More thorough discussion of the correlates of avoidant attachment
- New discussion of couples' compatibility based on attachment styles

Chapter 12 Helping

- New bulleted list with examples expanding on the do-good/feel-good effect
- New bulleted list and discussion of the effect of personality on altruism, including individual differences, network of traits, and particular situations

Chapter 13 Conflict and Peacemaking

- New research citations added to "Does Contact Predict Attitudes?" section
- New research on interracial roommates, and interracial adoption
- New bulleted list and discussion of intergroup contact reducing prejudice
- More discussion of and examples of prejudice against and between Muslims

Chapter 14 Social Psychology in the Clinic

- Updated coverage on school shootings
- New bulleted list and discussion of studies comparing clinical and statistical predictions
- Updated discussion on the vicious circle of depression
- Updates in the discussion of loneliness
- New bulleted list and discussion of marital quality predicting health

Chapter 15 Social Psychology in Court

- New chapter opener, featuring events in Ferguson, MO
- New court examples, including the interrogation of Amanda Knox
- New material on false confessions
- New material on court rulings on eyewitness testimony
- New material on racial discrepancies in sentencing

Chapter 16 Social Psychology and the Sustainable Future

- Four new figures showing: (1) rise of CO_2, (2) rise in annual temperature, (3) average monthly Arctic Sea ice decline, (4) "Five Principles of Sustainable Development"
- New discussion of studies revealing spikes in *conflict* related to climate change
- New section called "Persuasion," discussing how to overcome resistance to climate science
- New Inside Story feature called "Janet Swim on Psychology's Response to Climate Change"
- New discussion about estimating income inequality gaps added to "Our Wanting to Compare" section

Acknowledgments

Although only two names appear on this book's cover, the truth is that a whole community of scholars has invested itself in it. Although none of these people should be held responsible for what we have written—nor do any of them fully agree with everything said—their suggestions made this a better book than it could otherwise have been.

This new edition still retains many of the improvements contributed by the dozens of consultants and reviewers who assisted with the first eleven editions, and now to these esteemed colleagues who contributed their wisdom and guidance for this new edition:

Daria Bakina, SUNY Oswego

Doris G. Bazzini, Appalachian State University

Steven G. Buzinski, University of North Carolina at Chapel Hill

Dr. Deborah Conway, Community College of Allegheny County

Tracey Craig, University of South Carolina, Lancaster

Michael M. Denunzio, Baruch College and The Graduate Center, CUNY

Nao Hagiwara, Virginia Commonwealth University

Mahzad Hojjat, Ph.D., University of Massachusetts Dartmouth

Lindsay J. Holland, PhD, Chattanooga State Community College

Chad Keller, Lewis and Clark Community College

Yuthika Kim, Oklahoma City Community College

Philip Lemaster, West Virginia University

Terry Miller-Herringer, California State University, Chico

Christopher Ostwinkle, Northeast Iowa Community College, Peosta

Shannon Pinegar, Ohio University

Hilmar von Strunck, Central Community College, Columbus, Nebraska

Ryan J. Winter, Florida International University

Hope College, Michigan, has been wonderfully supportive of these successive editions. Both the people and the environment have helped make the gestation of *Social Psychology* a pleasure. At Hope College, poet Jack Ridl helped shape the voice you will hear in these pages. Kathy Adamski has again assisted with obtaining much of the new research. And Kathryn Brownson did online research, edited and prepared the manuscript, managed the paper flow, and proofed the pages and art. All in all, she midwifed this book.

At San Diego State, colleagues including David Armor, Jeff Bryson, Thierry Devos, David Marx, and Radmila Prislin shared their knowledge of teaching social psychology. Social psychology friends and co-authors also provided insight, including W. Keith Campbell, Julie Exline, Benita Jackson, Tim Kasser, and Kathleen Vohs.

At McGraw-Hill, senior brand manager Nancy Welcher envisioned this new edition and its author team. Lead product developer Dawn Groundwater commissioned and oversaw its creation. With diligence and sensitivity, our editor, Sue Ewing, gently nudged and expertly guided its development. Barbara Hacha fine-tuned the final manuscript. Sandy Wille coordinated the transformation of our manuscript into your finished book. After hearing countless dozens of people say that this book's supplements have taken their teaching to a new level, we also pay tribute to the late Martin Bolt (Calvin College), for pioneering the extensive instructor's resources with their countless ready-to-use demonstration activities, and then to Jon Mueller (North Central College) as author of the instructor's resources for the eighth through tenth editions. We extend our thanks to Diane Willard (Iowa Central Community College) for updating and extending these resources. To all in this supporting cast, we are indebted. Working with all these people has made the creation of this book a stimulating, gratifying experience.

David G. Myers
davidmyers.org

Jean M. Twenge
jeantwenge.com

A Letter from the Authors

We humans have a very long history, but social psychology has a very short one—barely more than a century. Considering that we have just begun, the results are gratifying. What a feast of ideas social psychology offers! Using varied research methods, we have amassed significant insights into belief and illusion, love and hate, conformity and independence.

Much about human behavior remains a mystery, yet social psychology can now offer partial answers to many intriguing questions:

- How does our thinking—both conscious and unconscious—drive our behavior?

- What leads people sometimes to hurt and sometimes to help one another?

- What creates social conflict, and how can we transform closed fists into helping hands?

Answering these and many other questions—our mission in the pages to come—expands our self-understanding and sensitizes us to the social forces that work upon us.

We aspire to offer a text that

- is solidly scientific and warmly human, factually rigorous, and intellectually provocative,

- reveals important social phenomena, as well as how scientists discover and explain such phenomena, and

- *stimulates students' thinking*—their motivation to inquire, to analyze, to relate principles to everyday happenings.

We cast social psychology in the intellectual tradition of the liberal arts. By the teaching of great literature, philosophy, and science, liberal arts education seeks to expand our awareness and to liberate us from the confines of the present. Social psychology contributes to these goals. By focusing on humanly significant issues, we aim to offer the core content to pre-professional psychology students in ways that also are stimulating to all students. And with close-up looks at how the game is played—at the varied research tools that expose the secrets of our social nature—we hope to enable students to think smarter.

To assist the teaching and learning of social psychology is a great privilege, but also a responsibility. So please never hesitate to let us know how we are doing, and what we can do better.

David G. Myers
Hope College
www.davidmyers.org

Jean M. Twenge
San Diego State University
www.jeantwenge.com

Introducing Social Psychology

© Lifesize/Getty RF

There once was a man whose second wife was a vain and selfish woman. This woman's two daughters were similarly vain and selfish. The man's own daughter, however, was meek and unselfish. This sweet, kind daughter, whom we all know as Cinderella, learned early on that she should do as she was told, accept ill treatment and insults, and avoid doing anything to upstage her stepsisters and their mother.

But then, thanks to her fairy godmother, Cinderella was able to escape her situation for an evening and attend a grand ball, where she attracted the attention of a handsome prince. When the love-struck prince later encountered Cinderella back in her degrading home, he failed to recognize her.

Implausible? The folktale demands that we accept the power of the situation. In the presence of her oppressive stepmother, Cinderella was humble and unattractive. At the ball, Cinderella felt more beautiful—and walked and talked and smiled as if she were. In one situation, she cowered. In the other, she charmed.

The French philosopher-novelist Jean-Paul Sartre (1946) would have had no problem accepting the Cinderella premise. We humans are "first of all beings in a situation," he wrote. "We cannot be distinguished from our situations, for they form us and decide our possibilities" (pp. 59–60, paraphrased).

What is social psychology?

What are social psychology's big ideas?

How do human values influence social psychology?

I knew it all along: Is social psychology simply common sense?

Research methods: How do we do social psychology?

Postscript: Why we wrote this book

WHAT IS SOCIAL PSYCHOLOGY?

Define social psychology and explain what it does.

social psychology
The scientific study of how people think about, influence, and relate to one another.

Throughout this book, sources for information are cited parenthetically. The complete source is provided in the reference section.

Social psychology is a science that studies the influences of our situations, with special attention to how we view and affect one another. *More precisely, it is the scientific study of how people think about, influence, and relate to one another* (Figure 1).

Social psychology lies at psychology's boundary with sociology. Compared with sociology (the study of people in groups and societies), social psychology focuses more on individuals and does more experimentation. Compared with personality psychology, social psychology focuses less on individuals' differences and more on how people, in general, view and affect one another.

Social psychology is a young science. The first social psychology experiments were reported barely more than a century ago, and the first social psychology texts did not appear until approximately 1900 (Smith, 2005). Not until the 1930s did social psychology assume its current form. Not until World War II did it begin to emerge as the vibrant field it is today. And not until the 1970s and beyond did social psychology enjoy accelerating growth in Asia—first in India, then in Hong Kong and Japan, and, recently, in China and Taiwan (Haslam & Kashima, 2010).

Social psychology studies our thinking, influences, and relationships by asking questions that have intrigued us all. Here are some examples:

- *Does our social behavior depend more on the objective situations we face or how we construe them?* Our construals matter. Social beliefs can be self-fulfilling. For example, happily married people will attribute their spouse's acid remark ("Can't you ever put that where it belongs?") to something external ("He must have had a frustrating day"). Unhappily married people will attribute the same remark to a mean disposition ("Geesh, what a hostile person!") and may respond with a counterattack. Moreover, expecting hostility from their spouse, they may behave resentfully, thereby eliciting the hostility they expect.

- *Would people be cruel if ordered?* How did Nazi Germany conceive and implement the unconscionable slaughter of 6 million Jews? Those evil acts occurred partly because thousands of people followed orders. They put the prisoners on

FIGURE :: 1

Social Psychology Is . . .

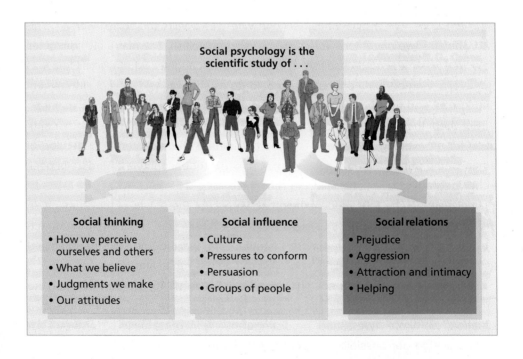

Social psychology is the scientific study of . . .

Social thinking	Social influence	Social relations
• How we perceive ourselves and others • What we believe • Judgments we make • Our attitudes	• Culture • Pressures to conform • Persuasion • Groups of people	• Prejudice • Aggression • Attraction and intimacy • Helping

trains, herded them into crowded "showers," and poisoned them with gas. How could people engage in such horrific actions? Were those individuals normal human beings? Stanley Milgram (1974) wondered. So he set up a situation in which people were ordered to administer increasing levels of electric shock to someone who was having difficulty learning a series of words. Nearly two-thirds of the participants fully complied.

- *To help? Or to help oneself?* As bags of cash tumbled from an armored truck one fall day, $2 million was scattered along a Columbus, Ohio, street. Some motorists stopped to help, returning $100,000. Judging from the $1,900,000 that disappeared, many more stopped to help themselves. (What would you have done?) When similar incidents occurred several months later in San Francisco and Toronto, the results were the same: Passersby grabbed most of the money (Bowen, 1988). What situations trigger people to be helpful or greedy? Do some cultural contexts—perhaps villages and small towns—breed less "diffusion of responsibility" and greater helpfulness?

These questions focus on how people view and affect one another. And that is what social psychology is all about. Social psychologists study attitudes and beliefs, conformity and independence, love and hate.

Tired of looking at the stars, Professor Mueller takes up social psychology.
Reprinted with permission of Jason Love at www.jasonlove.com

WHAT ARE SOCIAL PSYCHOLOGY'S BIG IDEAS?

Identify and describe the central concepts behind social psychology.

In many academic fields, the results of tens of thousands of studies, the conclusions of thousands of investigators, and the insights of hundreds of theorists can be boiled down to a few central ideas. Biology offers us natural selection and adaptation. Sociology builds on concepts such as social structure and organization. Music harnesses our ideas of rhythm, melody, and harmony.

Similarly, social psychology builds on a short list of fundamental principles that will be worth remembering long after you forget the details. Our short list of "great ideas we ought never to forget" includes these (Figure 2), each of which we will explore further in chapters to come.

We Construct Our Social Reality

People have an irresistible urge to explain behavior, to attribute it to some cause, and therefore to make it seem orderly, predictable, and controllable. You and I may *react* differently to a situation because we *think* differently. How we react to a friend's insult depends on whether we attribute it to hostility or to a bad day.

A Princeton–Dartmouth football game famously demonstrated how we construct reality (Loy & Andrews, 1981). The game lived up to its billing as a grudge match; it was rough and dirty. A Princeton All-American was gang-tackled, piled on, and finally forced out of the game with a broken nose. Fistfights erupted, with injuries on both sides. The game hardly fit the Ivy League image of gentility.

Not long afterward, two psychologists, one from each school, showed game films to students on each campus. The students played the role of scientist–observer, noting each infraction as they watched and who was responsible for it. But they could not set aside their loyalties. The Princeton students, for example, saw twice as many Dartmouth

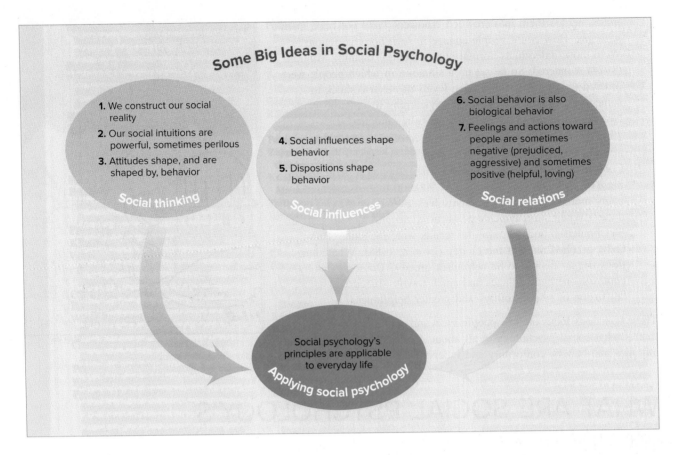

FIGURE :: 2

Some Big Ideas in Social Psychology

violations as the Dartmouth students saw. The conclusion: There *is* an objective reality out there, but we always view it through the lens of our beliefs and values.

We are all intuitive scientists. We explain people's behavior, usually with enough speed and accuracy to suit our daily needs. When someone's behavior is consistent and distinctive, we attribute that behavior to his or her personality. For example, if you observe someone who makes repeated snide comments, you may infer that this person has a nasty disposition, and then you might try to avoid the person.

Your beliefs about yourself also matter. Do you have an optimistic outlook? Do you see yourself as in control of things? Do you view yourself as relatively superior or inferior? Your answers influence your emotions and actions. *How we construe the world, and ourselves, matters.*

Our Social Intuitions Are Often Powerful but Sometimes Perilous

Our instant intuitions shape fears (Is flying dangerous?), impressions (Can I trust him?), and relationships (Does she like me?). Intuitions influence presidents in times of crisis, gamblers at the table, jurors assessing guilt, and personnel directors screening applicants. Such intuitions are commonplace.

Indeed, psychological science reveals a fascinating unconscious mind—an intuitive back-stage mind—that Freud never told us about. More than psychologists realized until recently, thinking occurs offstage, out of sight. Our intuitive capacities are revealed by studies of what later chapters will explain: "automatic processing," "implicit memory," "heuristics," "spontaneous trait inference," instant emotions, and nonverbal communication. Thinking, memory, and attitudes all operate on two levels—one conscious and deliberate, the other unconscious and automatic. Today's researchers call it "dual processing." We know more than we know we know. We think on two levels—"intuitive" and "deliberate" (Kruglanski & Gigerenzer, 2011)—some call these "System 1" and "System 2." A book title by Nobel laureate psychologist Daniel Kahneman (2011) captures the idea: We do *Thinking, Fast and Slow.*

Intuition is huge, but intuition is also perilous. For example, as we cruise through life, mostly on automatic pilot, we intuitively judge the likelihood of things by how easily various instances come to mind. We carry readily available mental images of plane crashes. Thus, most people fear flying more than driving, and many will drive great distances to avoid risking the skies. Actually, we are many times safer (per mile traveled) in a commercial plane than in a motor vehicle (in the United States, air travel was 170 times safer between 2009 and 2011, reports the National Safety Council [2014]).

Even our intuitions about ourselves often err. We intuitively trust our memories more than we should.

"He didn't actually threaten me, but I perceived him as a threat."

Social cognition matters. Our behavior is influenced not just by the objective situation but also by how we construe it.
© Lee Lorenz/The New Yorker Collection/www.cartoonbank.com

We misread our own minds; in experiments, we deny being affected by things that do influence us. We mispredict our own feelings—how bad we'll feel a year from now if we lose our job or our romance breaks up, and how good we'll feel a year from now, or even a week from now, if we win our state's lottery. And we often mispredict our own future. When selecting clothes, people approaching middle age will still buy snug ("I anticipate shedding a few pounds"); rarely does anyone say, more realistically, "I'd better buy a relatively loose fit; people my age tend to put on pounds."

Our social intuitions, then, are noteworthy for both their powers and their perils. By identifying our intuition's gifts and pitfalls, social psychologists aim to fortify our thinking. In most situations, "fast and frugal" snap judgments serve us well. But in others, in which accuracy matters—such as when needing to fear the right things and spend our resources wisely—we had best restrain our impulsive intuitions with critical thinking. *Our intuitions and unconscious information processing are routinely powerful and sometimes perilous.*

Social Influences Shape Our Behavior

We are, as Aristotle long ago observed, social animals. We speak and think in words we learned from others. We long to connect, to belong, and to be well thought of. Matthias Mehl and James Pennebaker (2003) quantified their University of Texas students' social behavior by inviting them to wear recording devices. Once every 12 minutes during their waking hours, the device would imperceptibly record for 30 seconds. Although the observation period covered only weekdays (including class time), almost 30 percent of the students' time was spent in conversation. Relationships are a big part of being human.

As social creatures, we respond to our immediate contexts. Sometimes the power of a social situation leads us to act contrary to our expressed attitudes. Indeed, powerfully evil situations sometimes overwhelm good intentions, inducing people to accept falsehoods or comply with cruelty. Under Nazi influence, many decent people became instruments of the Holocaust. Other situations may elicit great generosity and compassion. Often after major natural disasters, such as the hurricane that hit the Philippines in 2013, affected countries are overwhelmed with donated items and offers of assistance.

The power of the situation also appears in widely different views of same-sex relationships. Tell us whether you live in Africa or the Middle East (where people overwhelmingly oppose such relationships) or in western Europe, Canada, or Australia/New Zealand, and we will guess your attitude. We will become even more confident in our guess if we know your educational level, the age of your peer group, and the media you watch. Our situations matter.

Our culture helps define our situations. For example, our standards regarding promptness, frankness, and clothing vary with our culture.

- Whether you prefer a slim or a voluptuous body depends on when and where in the world you live.
- Whether you define social justice as equality (all receive the same) or as equity (those who earn more receive more) depends on whether your ideology has been shaped more by socialism or by capitalism.
- Whether you tend to be expressive or reserved, casual or formal, hinges partly on your culture and your ethnicity.
- Whether you focus primarily on yourself—your personal needs, desires, and morality—or on your family, clan, and communal groups depends on how much you are a product of modern Western individualism.

Social psychologist Hazel Markus (2005) sums it up: "People are, above all, malleable." Said differently, we adapt to our social context. *Our attitudes and behavior are shaped by external social forces.*

Personal Attitudes and Dispositions Also Shape Behavior

Internal forces also matter. We are not passive tumbleweeds, merely blown this way and that by the social winds. Our inner attitudes affect our outer behavior. Our political attitudes influence our voting behavior. Our smoking attitudes influence our susceptibility to peer pressure to smoke. Our attitudes toward the poor influence our willingness to help them. (As we will see, our attitudes also *follow* our behavior, which leads us to believe strongly in those things we have committed ourselves to or suffered for.)

Personality dispositions also affect behavior. Facing the same situation, different people may react differently. Emerging from years of political imprisonment, one person exudes bitterness and seeks revenge. Another, such as South Africa's Nelson Mandela, seeks reconciliation and unity with his former enemies. *Attitudes and personality influence behavior.*

Social Behavior Is Biologically Rooted

Twenty-first-century social psychology provides us with ever-growing insights into our behavior's biological foundations. Many of our social behaviors reflect a deep biological wisdom.

Everyone who has taken introductory psychology has learned that nature and nurture together form who we are. Just as the area of a rectangle is determined by both its length and its width, biology and experience both shape us. As *evolutionary psychologists* remind us, our inherited human nature predisposes us to behave in ways that helped our ancestors survive and reproduce. We carry the genes of those whose traits enabled them to survive and reproduce. Our behavior, too, aims to send our DNA into the future. Thus, evolutionary psychologists ask how natural selection might predispose our actions when dating and mating, hating and hurting, caring and sharing. Nature also endows us with an enormous capacity to learn and to adapt to varied environments. We are sensitive and responsive to our social context.

If every psychological event (every thought, every emotion, every behavior) is simultaneously a biological event, then we can also examine the neurobiology that underlies social behavior. What brain areas enable our experiences of love and contempt, helping and aggression, perception and belief? Do extraverts, as some research suggests, require more stimulation to keep their brain aroused? When shown a friendly face, do socially secure people, more than shy people, respond in a brain area concerned with reward? How do brain, mind, and behavior function together as one coordinated system? What does the timing of brain events reveal about how we process information? Such questions are asked by those in **social neuroscience** (Cacioppo & Cacioppo, 2013; Cikara & Van Bavel, 2014).

Social neuroscientists do not reduce complex social behaviors, such as helping and hurting, to simple neural or molecular mechanisms. Each science builds upon the principles of more basic sciences (sociology builds on psychology, which builds on biology, which builds on chemistry, which builds on physics, which builds on math). Yet each discipline also introduces new principles not predicted by the more basic sciences (Eisenberg, 2014). Thus, to understand social behavior, we must consider both under-the-skin (biological) and between-skins (social) influences. Mind and body are one grand system. Stress hormones affect how we feel and act: A dose of testosterone decreases trust, and a dose of oxytocin increases it (Bos et al., 2010). Social ostracism elevates blood pressure. Social support strengthens the disease-fighting immune system. *We are bio-psycho-social organisms.* We reflect the interplay of our biological, psychological, and social influences. That is why today's psychologists study behavior from these different levels of analysis.

> **social neuroscience**
> An interdisciplinary field that explores the neural bases of social and emotional processes and behaviors, and how these processes and behaviors affect our brain and biology.

Social Psychology's Principles Are Applicable in Everyday Life

Social psychology has the potential to illuminate your life, to make visible the subtle influences that guide your thinking and acting. It also offers many ideas about how to know ourselves better, how to win friends and influence people, how to transform closed fists into open arms.

Scholars are also applying social psychological insights. Principles of social thinking, social influence, and social relations have implications for human health and well-being, for judicial procedures and juror decisions in courtrooms, and for influencing behaviors that will enable an environmentally sustainable human future.

As but one perspective on human existence, psychological science does not answer life's ultimate questions: What is the meaning of human life? What should be our purpose? What is our ultimate destiny? But social psychology does give us a method for asking and answering some exceedingly interesting and important questions. *Social psychology is all about life—your life: your beliefs, your attitudes, your relationships.*

The rest of this chapter takes us inside social psychology. Let's first consider how social psychologists' own values influence their work in obvious and subtle ways. And then let's focus on this chapter's biggest task: glimpsing how we *do* social psychology. How do social psychologists search for explanations of social thinking, social influence, and social relations? And how might we use these analytical tools to think smarter?

Throughout this book, a brief summary will conclude each major section. We hope these summaries will help you assess how well you have learned the material in each section.

SUMMING UP: What Are Social Psychology's Big Ideas?

Social psychology is the scientific study of how people think about, influence, and relate to one another. Its central themes include the following:

- How we construe our social worlds

- How our social intuitions guide and sometimes deceive us

- How our social behavior is shaped by other people, by our attitudes and personalities, and by our biology

- How social psychology's principles apply to our everyday lives and to various other fields of study

HOW DO HUMAN VALUES INFLUENCE SOCIAL PSYCHOLOGY?

Identify the ways that values penetrate the work of social psychologists.

Social psychology is less a collection of findings than a set of strategies for answering questions. In science, as in courts of law, personal opinions are inadmissible. When ideas are put on trial, evidence determines the verdict.

But are social psychologists really that objective? Because they are human beings, don't their *values*—their personal convictions about what is desirable and how people ought to behave—seep into their work? If so, can social psychology really be scientific?

There are two general ways that values enter psychology: the obvious and the subtle.

Obvious Ways Values Enter Psychology

Values enter the picture when social psychologists *choose research topics*. These choices typically reflect social history (Kagan, 2009). Not surprisingly, the study of prejudice flourished during the 1940s as fascism raged in Europe; the 1950s, a time of look-alike fashions and intolerance of differing views, gave us studies of conformity; the 1960s saw interest in aggression increase with riots and rising crime rates; the feminist movement of the 1970s helped stimulate a wave of research on gender and sexism; the 1980s offered a resurgence of attention to psychological aspects of the arms race; and the 1990s and the early twenty-first century were marked by heightened interest in how people respond to diversity in culture, race, and sexual orientation. Susan Fiske (2011a) suggests that we can expect future research to reflect today's and tomorrow's issues, including immigration, income inequality, and aging.

Social events influence social psychologists' interests. In response to today's social issues, will immigration, aging, inequality, and racial polarization be prominent research topics in tomorrow's social psychology?
Ocean/Corbis

Values differ not only across time but also across cultures. In Europe, people take pride in their nationalities. The Scots are more self-consciously distinct from the English, and the Austrians from the Germans, than are similarly adjacent Michiganders from Ohioans. Consequently, Europe has given us a major theory of "social identity." American social psychologists have focused more on individuals—how one person thinks about others, is influenced by them, and relates to them (Fiske, 2004; Tajfel, 1981; Turner, 1984). Australian social psychologists have drawn theories and methods from both Europe and North America (Feather, 2005).

Values also influence the *types of people* who are attracted to various disciplines (Campbell, 1975a; Moynihan, 1979). At your school, do the students majoring in the humanities, the arts, the natural sciences, and the social sciences differ noticeably from one another? Do social psychology and sociology attract people who are, for example, relatively eager to challenge tradition, people more inclined to shape the future than preserve the past (Prentice, 2012)? And does social science study enhance such inclinations (Dambrun et al., 2009; Inbar & Lammers, 2012)? Such factors explain why, when psychologist Jonathan Haidt (2011) asked approximately 1,000 social psychologists at a national convention about their politics, 80 to 90 percent raised their hands to indicate they were "liberal." When he asked for those who were "conservative," only three hands raised. (Be assured that most topics covered in this text—from "How do our attitudes influence our behavior?" to "Does TV violence influence aggressive behavior?"—are not partisan.)

Finally, values obviously enter the picture as the *object* of social psychological analysis. Social psychologists investigate how values form, why they change, and how they influence attitudes and actions. None of that, however, tells us which values are "right."

Not-So-Obvious Ways Values Enter Psychology

We less often recognize the subtle ways in which value commitments masquerade as objective truth. Consider three not-so-obvious ways values enter psychology.

THE SUBJECTIVE ASPECTS OF SCIENCE

Scientists and philosophers agree: Science is not purely objective. Scientists do not simply read the book of nature. Rather, they interpret nature, using their own mental categories. Our numbers do not speak for themselves. We interpret them.

In our daily lives, too, we view the world through the lens of our preconceptions. Whether we see a moving light in the sky as a flying saucer depends on our perceptual set. While reading these words, you have been unaware that you are also looking at your nose. Your mind blocks from awareness something that is there, if only you were predisposed to perceive it. This tendency to prejudge reality based on our expectations is a basic fact about the human mind.

Because scholars in any given area often share a common viewpoint and come from the same **culture,** their assumptions may go unchallenged. What we take for granted—the shared beliefs that some European social psychologists call our **social representations** (Moscovici, 1988, 2001; Rateau et al., 2012)—are often our most important yet most unexamined convictions. Sometimes, however, someone from outside the camp will call attention to those assumptions. During the 1980s, feminists and Marxists exposed some of social psychology's unexamined assumptions. Feminist critics called attention to subtle biases—for example, the political conservatism of some scientists who favored a biological interpretation of gender differences in social behavior (Unger, 1985). Marxist critics called attention to competitive, individualist biases—for example, the assumption that conformity is bad and that individual rewards are good. Marxists and feminists, of course, make their own assumptions, as critics of academic "political correctness" are fond of noting. Social psychologist Lee Jussim (2005, 2012), for example, argues that progressive social psychologists sometimes subtly discriminate against conservative views, such as by denying group differences and assuming that stereotypes of group difference are never rooted in reality.

In the chapter on "Social Beliefs and Judgments," we discuss more ways in which our preconceptions guide our interpretations. As those Princeton and Dartmouth football fans remind us, what guides our behavior is less the situation-as-it-is than the situation-as-we-construe-it.

PSYCHOLOGICAL CONCEPTS CONTAIN HIDDEN VALUES

Implicit in our understanding that psychology is not objective is the realization that psychologists' own values may play an important part in the theories and judgments they support. Psychologists may refer to people as mature or immature, as well adjusted or poorly adjusted, as mentally healthy or mentally ill. They may talk as if they were stating facts, when they are really making *value judgments*. The following are examples:

DEFINING THE GOOD LIFE.   Values influence our idea of how best to live. The personality psychologist Abraham Maslow, for example, was known for his sensitive descriptions of "self-actualized" people—people who, with their needs for survival, safety, belonging, and self-esteem satisfied, go on to fulfill their human potential. He described, among other individuals, Thomas Jefferson, Abraham Lincoln, and Eleanor Roosevelt. Few readers noticed that Maslow, guided by his own values, selected his sample of self-actualized people himself. The resulting description of self-actualized personalities—as spontaneous, autonomous, mystical, and so forth—reflected Maslow's personal values. Had he begun with someone else's heroes—say, Napoleon, Alexander the Great, and John D. Rockefeller—his resulting description of self-actualization might have differed (Smith, 1978).

PROFESSIONAL ADVICE.   Psychological advice also reflects the advice giver's personal values. When mental health professionals advise us how to get along with our spouse

"Science does not simply describe and explain nature; it is part of the interplay between nature and ourselves; it describes nature as exposed to our method of questioning."

—Werner Heisenberg,
Physics and Philosophy, 1958

culture
The enduring behaviors, ideas, attitudes, and traditions shared by a large group of people and transmitted from one generation to the next.

social representations
A society's widely held ideas and values, including assumptions and cultural ideologies. Our social representations help us make sense of our world.

Hidden (and not-so-hidden) values seep into psychological advice. They permeate popular psychology books that offer guidance on living and loving.
Courtesy of Kathryn Brownson

or our co-workers, when child-rearing experts tell us how to handle our children, and when some psychologists advocate living free of concern for others' expectations, they are expressing their personal values. (In Western cultures, those values usually will be individualistic—encouraging what feels best for "me." Non-Western cultures more often encourage what is best for "we.") Unaware of those hidden values, many people defer to the "professional." But professional psychologists cannot answer questions of ultimate moral obligation, of purpose and direction, and of life's meaning.

FORMING CONCEPTS.   Hidden values even seep into psychology's research-based *concepts*. Pretend you have taken a personality test and the psychologist, after scoring your answers, announces: "You scored high in self-esteem. You are low in anxiety. And you have exceptional ego-strength." "Ah," you think, "I suspected as much, but it feels good to know that." Now another psychologist gives you a similar test, which asks some of the same questions. Afterward, the psychologist informs you that you seem defensive, for you scored high in "repressive coping." "How could this be?" you wonder. "The other psychologist said such nice things about me." It could be because all these labels describe the same set of responses (a tendency to say nice things about oneself and not to acknowledge problems). Shall we call it high self-esteem or defensiveness? The label reflects the judgment.

LABELING.   Value judgments, then, are often hidden within our social psychological language—but that is also true of everyday language:

- Whether we label a quiet child as "bashful" or "cautious," as "holding back" or as "an observer," conveys a judgment.
- Whether we label someone engaged in guerrilla warfare a "terrorist" or a "freedom fighter" depends on our view of the cause.
- Whether we view wartime civilian deaths as "the loss of innocent lives" or as "collateral damage" affects our acceptance of such.
- Whether we call information "propaganda" or "education" depends on our opinions.
- Whether we call public assistance "welfare" or "aid to the needy" reflects our political views.
- When "they" exalt their country and people, it is nationalism; when "we" do it, it is patriotism.
- Whether someone involved in an extramarital affair is practicing "open marriage" or "adultery" depends on one's personal values.
- "Brainwashing" is social influence we do not approve of.
- "Perversions" are sex acts we do not practice.

As these examples indicate, values lie hidden within our cultural definitions of mental health, our psychological advice for living, our concepts, and our psychological labels. Throughout this book, we call your attention to additional examples of hidden values. It's not that the implicit values are necessarily bad. It's that scientific interpretation, even at the level of labeling phenomena, is a human activity. It is therefore inevitable that prior beliefs and values will influence what social psychologists think and write.

Should we dismiss science because it has its subjective side? Quite the contrary: The realization that human thinking always involves interpretation is precisely why we need researchers with varying biases to undertake scientific analysis. By constantly checking our beliefs against the facts, we restrain our biases. Systematic observation and experimentation help us clean the lens through which we see reality.

SUMMING UP: How Do Human Values Influence Social Psychology?

- Social psychologists' values penetrate their work in obvious ways, such as their choice of research topics and the types of people who are attracted to various fields of study.

- They also do this in subtler ways, such as their hidden assumptions when forming concepts, choosing labels, and giving advice.

- This penetration of values into science is not a reason to fault social psychology or any other science. That human thinking is seldom dispassionate is precisely why we need systematic observation and experimentation if we are to check our cherished ideas against reality.

I KNEW IT ALL ALONG: IS SOCIAL PSYCHOLOGY SIMPLY COMMON SENSE?

Explore how social psychology's theories provide new insight into the human condition.

Many of the conclusions presented in this book may already have occurred to you, for social psychological phenomena are all around you. We constantly observe people thinking about, influencing, and relating to one another. It pays to discern what a facial expression predicts, how to get someone to do something, or whether to regard another as friend or foe. For centuries, philosophers, novelists, and poets have observed and commented on social behavior.

Does this mean that social psychology is just common sense in fancy words? Social psychology faces two contradictory criticisms: first, that it is trivial because it documents the obvious; second, that it is dangerous because its findings could be used to manipulate people.

In the "Persuasion" chapter we explore the second criticism. Here, let's examine the first objection.

Do social psychology and the other social sciences simply formalize what any amateur already knows intuitively? Writer Cullen Murphy (1990) took that view: "Day after day social scientists go out into the world. Day after day they discover that people's behavior is pretty much what you'd expect." Nearly a half-century earlier, historian Arthur Schlesinger, Jr. (1949), reacted with similar scorn to social scientists' studies of American World War II soldiers. Sociologist Paul Lazarsfeld (1949) reviewed those studies and offered a sample with interpretive comments:

1. Better-educated soldiers adjusted less easily than did less-educated soldiers. (Intellectuals were less prepared for battle stresses than were street-smart people.)
2. Southern soldiers coped better with the hot South Sea Island climate than did Northern soldiers. (Southerners are more accustomed to hot weather.)
3. White low-ranking soldiers were more eager for promotion than were Black low-ranking soldiers. (Years of oppression take a toll on achievement motivation.)
4. Southern Blacks preferred Southern to Northern White officers. (Southern officers were more experienced and skilled in interacting with Blacks.)

As you read those findings, did you agree that they were basically common sense? If so, you may be surprised to learn that Lazarsfeld went on to say, "*Every one of these statements is the direct opposite of what was actually found.*" In reality, the studies found that less-educated soldiers adapted more poorly. Southerners were not more likely than northerners to adjust to a tropical climate. Blacks were more eager than Whites for promotion, and so forth. "If we had mentioned the actual results of the investigation first [as Schlesinger experienced], the reader would have labeled these 'obvious' also."

One problem with common sense is that we invoke it after we know the facts. Events are far more "obvious" and predictable in hindsight than beforehand. Experiments reveal that when people learn the outcome of an experiment, that outcome suddenly seems unsurprising—much less surprising than it is to people who are simply told about the experimental procedure and the possible outcomes (Slovic & Fischhoff, 1977). After more than 800 investigations of this tendency to retrofit our prior expectations, hindsight bias has become one of psychology's best-established phenomena (Roese & Vohs, 2012).

Likewise, in everyday life we often do not expect something to happen until it does. *Then* we suddenly see clearly the forces that brought the event about and feel unsurprised. Moreover, we may also misremember our earlier view (Blank et al., 2008; Nestler et al., 2010). Errors in judging the future's foreseeability and in remembering our past combine to create **hindsight bias** (also called the *I-knew-it-all-along phenomenon*).

hindsight bias
The tendency to exaggerate, after learning an outcome, one's ability to have foreseen how something turned out. Also known as the *I-knew-it-all-along phenomenon*.

Thus, after elections or stock market shifts, most commentators find the turn of events unsurprising: "The market was due for a correction." "Republicans were bound to lose in 2012 due to demographic shifts in the population." As the Danish philosopher–theologian Søren Kierkegaard put it, "Life is lived forwards, but understood backwards."

If hindsight bias is pervasive, you may now be feeling that you already knew about this phenomenon. Indeed, almost any conceivable result of a psychological experiment can seem like common sense—*after* you know the result.

You can demonstrate the phenomenon yourself. Take a group of people and tell half of them one psychological finding and the other half the opposite result. For example, tell half as follows:

> Social psychologists have found that, whether choosing friends or falling in love, we are most attracted to people whose traits are different from our own. There seems to be wisdom in the old saying "Opposites attract."

Tell the other half:

> Social psychologists have found that, whether choosing friends or falling in love, we are most attracted to people whose traits are similar to our own. There seems to be wisdom in the old saying "Birds of a feather flock together."

Ask the people first to explain the result. Then ask them to say whether it is "surprising" or "not surprising." Virtually all will find a good explanation for whichever result they were given and will say it is "not surprising."

Indeed, we can draw on our stockpile of proverbs to make almost any result seem to make sense. If a social psychologist reports that separation intensifies romantic attraction, John Q. Public responds, "You get paid for this? Everybody knows that 'absence makes the heart grow fonder.'" Should it turn out that separation *weakens* attraction, John will say, "My grandmother could have told you, 'Out of sight, out of mind.'"

Karl Teigen (1986) must have had a few chuckles when he asked University of Leicester (England) students to evaluate actual proverbs and their opposites. When given the proverb "Fear is stronger than love," most rated it as true. But so did students who were given its reversed form, "Love is stronger than fear." Likewise, the genuine proverb "He that is fallen cannot help him who is down" was rated highly; but so too was "He that is fallen can help him who is down." Our favorites, however, were two highly rated proverbs: "Wise men make proverbs and fools repeat them" (authentic) and its made-up counterpart, "Fools make proverbs and wise men repeat them." For more dueling proverbs, see "Focus On: I Knew It All Along."

In hindsight, events seem obvious and predictable.
ScienceCartoonsPlus.com

focus
ON

Cullen Murphy (1990), managing editor of the *Atlantic*, faulted "sociology, psychology, and other social sciences for too often merely discerning the obvious or confirming the commonplace." His own casual survey of social science findings "turned up no ideas or conclusions that can't be found in *Bartlett's* or any other encyclopedia of quotations." However, to sift through competing sayings, we need research. Consider some dueling proverbs:

Is it more true that . . .

We should keep our eye on the prize.
Too many cooks spoil the broth.
The pen is mightier than the sword.

You can't teach an old dog new tricks.
Blood is thicker than water.
He who hesitates is lost.
Forewarned is forearmed.

Or that . . .

We should keep our nose to the grindstone.
Two heads are better than one.
Actions speak louder than words.
You're never too old to learn.
Many kinfolk, few friends.
Look before you leap.
Don't cross the bridge until you come to it.

The hindsight bias creates a problem for many psychology students. Sometimes results are genuinely surprising (for example, that Olympic *bronze* medalists take more joy in their achievement than do silver medalists). More often, when you read the results of experiments in your textbooks, the material seems easy, even obvious. When you later take a multiple-choice test on which you must choose among several plausible conclusions, the task may become surprisingly difficult. "I don't know what happened," the befuddled student later moans. "I thought I knew the material."

The I-knew-it-all-along phenomenon can have unfortunate consequences. It is conducive to arrogance—an overestimation of our own intellectual powers. Moreover, because outcomes seem as if they should have been foreseeable, we are more likely to blame decision makers for what are in retrospect "obvious" bad choices than to praise them for good choices, which also seem "obvious."

Starting *after* the 9/11 terror attack and working backward, signals pointing to the impending disaster seemed obvious. A U.S. Senate investigative report listed the missed or misinterpreted clues (Gladwell, 2003): The CIA knew that al Qaeda operatives had entered the country. An FBI agent sent a memo to headquarters that began by warning "the Bureau and New York of the possibility of a coordinated effort by Osama bin Laden to send students to the United States to attend civilian aviation universities and colleges." The FBI ignored that accurate warning and failed to relate it to other reports that terrorists were planning to use planes as weapons. The president received a daily briefing titled "Bin Laden Determined to Strike Inside the United States" and stayed on holiday. "The dumb fools!" it seemed to hindsight critics. "Why couldn't they connect the dots?"

But what seems clear in hindsight is seldom clear on the front side of history. The intelligence community is overwhelmed with "noise"—piles of useless information surrounding the rare shreds of useful information. Analysts must therefore be selective in deciding which to pursue, and only when a lead is pursued does it stand a chance of being connected to another lead. In the 6 years before 9/11, the FBI's counterterrorism unit could never have pursued all 68,000 uninvestigated leads. In hindsight, the few useful ones are now obvious.

We blame not only others, but also ourselves for "stupid mistakes"—perhaps for not having handled a person or a situation better. Looking back, we see how we should have handled it. "I should have known how busy I would be at the semester's end and started that paper earlier." "I should have realized sooner that he was a jerk." But sometimes we are too hard on ourselves. We forget that what is obvious to us *now* was not nearly so obvious at the time.

"It is easy to be wise after the event."

—Sherlock Holmes, in Arthur Conan Doyle's Story "The Problem of Thor Bridge"

Physicians who are told both a patient's symptoms and the cause of death (as determined by autopsy) sometimes wonder how an incorrect diagnosis could have been made. Other physicians, given only the symptoms, do not find the diagnosis nearly so obvious (Dawson et al., 1988). Would juries be slower to assume malpractice if they were forced to take a foresight rather than a hindsight perspective?

What do we conclude—that common sense is usually wrong? Sometimes it is. At other times, conventional wisdom is right—or it falls on both sides of an issue: Does happiness come from knowing the truth, or from preserving illusions? From being with others, or from living in peaceful solitude? Opinions are a dime a dozen. No matter what we find, there will be someone who foresaw it. (Mark Twain jested that the biblical Adam was the only person who, when saying a good thing, knew that nobody had said it before.) But which of the many competing ideas best fit reality? Research can specify the circumstances under which a commonsense truism is valid.

"Everything important has been said before."

—Philosopher Alfred North Whitehead, 1861–1947

The point is not that common sense is predictably wrong. Rather, common sense usually is right—*after the fact.* We therefore easily deceive ourselves into thinking that we know and knew more than we do and did. And that is precisely why we need science to help us sift reality from illusion and genuine predictions from easy hindsight.

SUMMING UP: I Knew It All Along: Is Social Psychology Simply Common Sense?

- Social psychology is criticized for being trivial because it documents things that seem obvious.

- Experiments, however, reveal that outcomes are more "obvious" *after* the facts are known.

- This *hindsight bias* (the *I-knew-it-all-along phenomenon*) often makes people overconfident about the validity of their judgments and predictions.

RESEARCH METHODS: HOW DO WE DO SOCIAL PSYCHOLOGY?

Examine the methods that make social psychology a science.

We have considered some of the intriguing questions social psychology seeks to answer. We have also seen how subjective, often unconscious, processes influence social psychologists' work. Now let's consider how social psychologists go about doing research.

Forming and Testing Hypotheses

"Nothing has such power to broaden the mind as the ability to investigate systematically and truly all that comes under thy observation in life."

—Marcus Aurelius, *Meditations*

theory

An integrated set of principles that explain and predict observed events.

As we social psychologists wrestle with human nature to pin down its secrets, we organize our ideas and findings into theories. A **theory** is *an integrated set of principles that explain and predict* observed events. Theories are a scientific shorthand.

In everyday conversation, "theory" often means "less than fact"—a middle rung on a confidence ladder from guess to theory to fact. Thus, people may dismiss Charles Darwin's theory of evolution as "just a theory." Indeed, notes Alan Leshner (2005), chief officer of the American Association for the Advancement of Science, "Evolution *is* only a theory, but so is gravity." People often respond that gravity is a fact—but the *fact* is that your keys fall to the ground when dropped. Gravity is the theoretical explanation that accounts for such observed facts.

To a scientist, facts and theories are apples and oranges. Facts are agreed-upon statements about what we observe. Theories are *ideas* that summarize and explain facts. "Science is built up with facts, as a house is with stones," wrote the French scientist Jules Henri Poincaré, "but a collection of facts is no more a science than a heap of stones is a house."

Theories not only summarize but also imply testable predictions, called **hypotheses.** Hypotheses serve several purposes. First, they allow us to *test* a theory by suggesting how we might try to falsify it. Second, predictions give *direction* to research and sometimes send investigators looking for things they might never have thought of. Third, the predictive feature of good theories can also make them *practical.* A complete theory of aggression, for example, would predict when to expect aggression and how to control it. As pioneering social psychologist Kurt Lewin declared, "There is nothing so practical as a good theory."

Consider how this works. Suppose we observe that people who loot, taunt, or attack often do so in groups or crowds. We might therefore theorize that being part of a crowd, or group, makes individuals feel anonymous and lowers their inhibitions. How could we test this theory? Perhaps we could ask individuals in groups to administer punishing shocks to a hapless victim without knowing which member of the group was actually shocking the victim. Would these individuals, as our theory predicts, administer stronger shocks than individuals acting alone?

We might also manipulate anonymity: Would people deliver stronger shocks if they were wearing masks? If the results confirm our hypothesis, they might suggest some practical applications. Perhaps police brutality could be reduced by having officers wear large name tags and drive cars identified with large numbers, or by videotaping their arrests—all of which have, in fact, become common practice in many cities.

But how do we conclude that one theory is better than another? A good theory

For humans, the most fascinating subject is people.
© Warren Miller/The New Yorker Collection/www.cartoonbank.com

- effectively *summarizes many observations,* and
- *makes clear predictions* that we can use to
  - confirm or modify the theory,
  - generate new exploration, and
  - suggest practical applications.

When we discard theories, usually it is not because they have been proved false. Rather, like old cars, they are replaced by newer, better models.

Correlational Research: Detecting Natural Associations

Let's now go backstage and see how social psychology is done. This glimpse behind the scenes should be just enough for you to appreciate findings discussed later. Understanding the logic of research can also help you think critically about everyday social events and better understand studies you see covered in the media.

Social psychological research can be *laboratory research* (a controlled situation) or **field research** (everyday situations). And it varies by method—whether **correlational** (asking whether two or more factors are naturally associated) or **experimental** (manipulating some factor to see its effect on another). If you want to be a critical reader of psychological research reported in the media, you will benefit by understanding the difference between correlational and experimental research.

Let's first consider the advantages of correlational research (often involving important variables in natural settings) and its major disadvantage (ambiguous interpretation of cause and effect). In search of possible links between socioeconomic status and health, Douglas Carroll and his colleagues (1994) ventured into Glasgow, Scotland's old graveyards and noted the life spans of 843 individuals. As an indication of status, they measured the height of the grave pillars, reasoning that height reflected cost and therefore affluence. As Figure 3 shows, status (taller grave markers) predicted longer lives.

hypothesis
A testable proposition that describes a relationship that may exist between events.

field research
Research done in natural, real-life settings outside the laboratory.

correlational research
The study of the naturally occurring relationships among variables.

experimental research
Studies that seek clues to cause–effect relationships by manipulating one or more factors (independent variables) while controlling others (holding them constant).

FIGURE :: 3

Correlating Status and Longevity

Tall grave pillars commemorated people who also tended to live longer.

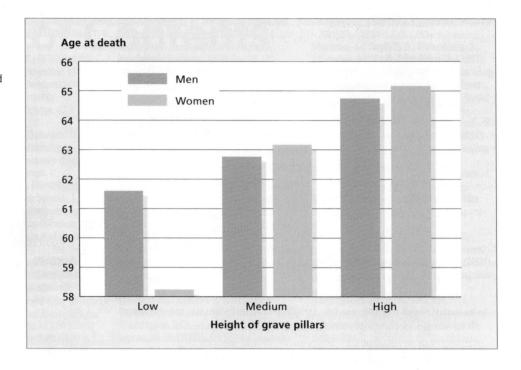

Carroll and colleagues report that other researchers, using contemporary data, have confirmed the status–longevity correlation. Scottish postal-code regions with the least overcrowding and unemployment also have the longest average lifespans. In the United States, income correlates with longevity (poor and lower-status people are more at risk for premature death). In today's Britain, occupational status correlates with longevity. One study followed 17,350 British civil service workers over 10 years. Compared with top-grade administrators, those at the professional-executive grade were 1.6 times more likely to have died. Clerical workers were 2.2 times and laborers 2.7 times more likely to have died (Adler et al., 1993, 1994). Across times and places, the status-health correlation seems reliable.

CORRELATION AND CAUSATION

The status–longevity question illustrates the most irresistible thinking error made by both amateur and professional social psychologists: When two factors such as status and health go together, it is tempting to conclude that one is causing the other. Status, we might presume, somehow protects a person from health risks. But might it be the other way around? Could it be that health promotes vigor and success? Perhaps people who live longer simply have more time to accumulate wealth (enabling them to have more expensive grave markers). Or might a third variable, such as diet, be involved (did wealthy and working-class people tend to eat differently)? In other words: correlations indicate a relationship, but that relationship is not necessarily one of cause and effect. Correlational research allows us to *predict*, but it cannot tell us whether one variable (such as social status) causes another (such as longevity).

The correlation–causation confusion is behind much muddled thinking in popular psychology. Consider another very real correlation—between self-esteem and academic achievement. Children with high self-esteem tend also to have high academic

Commemorative markers in Glasgow Cathedral graveyard.
Jon Bower/Loop Images/AGE Fotostock

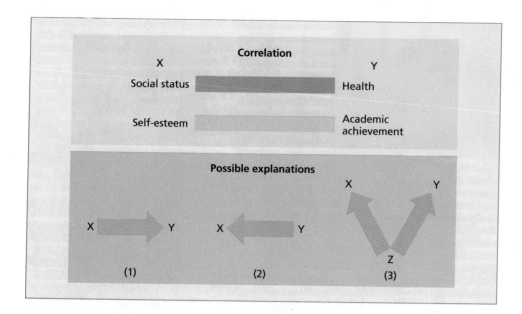

FIGURE :: 4

Correlation and Causations

When two variables correlate, any combination of three explanations is possible. Either one may cause the other, or both may be affected by an underlying "third factor."

achievement. (As with any correlation, we can also state this the other way around: High achievers tend to have high self-esteem.) Why do you suppose that is true (Figure 4)?

Some people believe a "healthy self-concept" contributes to achievement. Thus, boosting a child's self-image may also boost school achievement. Believing so, 30 U.S. states have enacted more than 170 self-esteem-promoting statutes.

But other people, including psychologists William Damon (1995), Robyn Dawes (1994), Mark Leary (2012), Martin Seligman (1994, 2002), Roy Baumeister with John Tierney (2011), and one of us (Twenge, 2013, 2014) doubt that self-esteem is really "the armor that protects kids" from underachievement (or drug abuse and delinquency). Perhaps it is the other way around: Perhaps problems and failures cause low self-esteem. Perhaps self-esteem often reflects the reality of how things are going for us. Perhaps self-esteem grows from hard-won achievements. Do well and you will feel good about yourself; goof off and fail and you will feel like a dolt. A study of 635 Norwegian schoolchildren showed that a (legitimately earned) string of gold stars by one's name on the spelling chart and accompanying praise from the admiring teacher can boost a child's self-esteem (Skaalvik & Hagtvet, 1990). Or perhaps, as in a study of nearly 6,000 German seventh-graders, the traffic between self-esteem and academic achievements runs both ways (Trautwein & Lüdtke, 2006).

It is also possible that self-esteem and achievement correlate because both are linked to underlying intelligence and family social status. That possibility was raised in a nationwide study of 1,600 young American men and another study of 715 Minnesota youngsters (Bachman & O'Malley, 1977; Maruyama et al., 1981). When the researchers mathematically removed the predictive power of intelligence and family status, the relationship between self-esteem and achievement evaporated.

Correlations quantify, with a coefficient known as r, the degree of relationship between two factors—from −1.0 (as one factor score goes up, the other goes down) through 0 to +1.0 (the two factors' scores rise and fall together). Scores on self-esteem and depression tests correlate negatively (about −.6). Identical twins' intelligence scores correlate positively (above +.8). The great strength of correlational research is that it tends to occur in real-world settings where we can examine factors such as race, gender, and social status—factors that we cannot manipulate in the laboratory. Its great disadvantage lies in the ambiguity of the results. This point is so important that even if it fails to impress people the first 25 times they hear it, it is worth repeating a twenty-sixth time: Knowing that two variables change together (correlate) enables us to predict one when we know the other, but correlation does not specify cause and effect.

Advanced correlational techniques can, however, suggest cause–effect relationships. *Time-lagged* correlations reveal the *sequence* of events (for example, by indicating whether changed achievement more often precedes or follows changed self-esteem). Researchers can also use statistical techniques that extract the influence of third variables, as when the

Even exit polls require a random (and therefore representative) sample of voters.
Steve Debenport/Getty Images

correlation between self-esteem *and* achievement evaporated after extracting intelligence and family status. As another example, the Scottish research team wondered whether the status–longevity relationship would still exist after removing the effect of cigarette smoking, which is now much less common among those of higher status. It did still exist, suggesting that some other factors, such as increased stress and decreased feelings of control, may also account for poorer people's earlier mortality.

SURVEY RESEARCH

How do we measure variables such as status and health? One way is by surveying representative samples of people. If survey researchers want to describe a whole population (which for many psychology surveys is not the aim), then they will obtain a *representative* group by taking a **random sample**—*one in which every person in the population being studied has an equal chance of inclusion.* With this procedure any subgroup of people—blondes, joggers, liberals—will tend to be represented in the survey to the extent that they are represented in the total population.

random sampling
Survey procedure in which every person in the population being studied has an equal chance of inclusion.

Whether we survey people in a city or in a whole country, 1,200 randomly selected participants will enable us to be 95 percent confident of describing the entire population with an error margin of 3 percentage points or less. Imagine a huge jar filled with beans, 50 percent red and 50 percent white. Randomly sample 1,200 of these, and you will be 95 percent certain to draw out between 47 percent and 53 percent red beans—regardless of whether the jar contains 10,000 beans or 100 million beans. If we think of the red beans as supporters of one presidential candidate and the white beans as supporters of the other candidate, we can understand why, despite skepticism about people's dishonesty or bias when answering survey questions, surveys work. Before the 2012 U.S. presidential election, pundits offered varying predictions based on their hunches. Setting aside intuition, and using aggregated survey data, statistical geek Nate Silver (2012) not only correctly predicted the national outcome, but also the presidential winner in all 50 states. When done well, self-report data from representative surveys can tell important truths. As a few drops of blood can speak for the whole body, so can a random sample speak for a population.

Bear in mind that polls do not literally *predict* voting; they only *describe* public opinion at the moment they are taken. Public opinion can shift. To evaluate surveys, we must also bear in mind four potentially biasing influences: unrepresentative samples, question order, response options, and question wording.

UNREPRESENTATIVE SAMPLES.   How closely the sample represents the population under study matters greatly. Columnist Ann Landers once accepted a letter writer's challenge to poll her readers on the question of whether women find affection more important than sex. Her question: "Would you be content to be held close and treated tenderly and forget about 'the act'?" Of the more than 100,000 women who replied, 72 percent said yes. An avalanche of worldwide publicity followed. In response to critics, Landers (1985, p. 45) granted that "the sampling may not be representative of all American women. But it does provide honest— valuable—insights from a cross section of the public. This is because my column is read by people from every walk of life, approximately 70 million of them." Still, one wonders, are the 70 million readers representative of the entire population? And are the 1 in 700 readers who took the trouble to reply to the survey representative of the 699 in 700 who did not?

The importance of representativeness was famously demonstrated in 1936 when a weekly newsmagazine, *Literary Digest,* mailed a postcard presidential election poll to 10 million Americans. Among the more than 2 million returns, Alf Landon won by a landslide over Franklin D. Roosevelt. When the actual votes were counted a few days later, Landon carried only two states. The magazine had sent the poll only to people whose names it had obtained from telephone books and automobile registrations—thus ignoring the millions of voters during the Great Depression who could afford neither a telephone nor a car (Cleghorn, 1980).

ORDER OF QUESTIONS.   Given a representative sample, we must also contend with other sources of bias, such as the order of questions in a survey. Americans' support for civil unions of gays and lesbians is higher when they are first asked their opinion of gay marriage, compared with which civil unions seem a more acceptable alternative (Moore, 2004a, 2004b).

RESPONSE OPTIONS.   Consider, too, the dramatic effects of response options. When Joop van der Plight and co-workers (1987) asked English voters what percentage of Britain's energy they wished came from nuclear power, the average preference was 41 percent. They asked other voters what percentage they wished came from (1) nuclear, (2) coal, and (3) other sources. The average preference for nuclear power among these respondents was 21 percent.

WORDING OF QUESTIONS.   The precise wording of questions may also influence answers. One poll found that only 23 percent of Americans thought their government was spending too much "on assistance to the poor." Yet 53 percent thought the government was spending too much "on welfare" (*Time,* 1994). Likewise, most people favor cutting "foreign aid" and *increasing* spending "to help hungry people in other nations" (Simon, 1996).

Survey wording is a very delicate matter. Even subtle changes in the tone of a question can have marked effects (Krosnick & Schuman, 1988; Schuman & Kalton, 1985).

SRC's Survey Services Laboratory at the University of Michigan's Institute for Social Research has interviewing carrels with monitoring stations. Staff and visitors must sign a pledge to honor the strict confidentiality of all interviews.
NORC at the University of Chicago

Some companies and institutions are seeking to "nudge" employees toward retirement savings by how they frame the options. By framing their choice as whether to opt out of an automatic savings plan, more people participate than when they must decide whether to opt in.
Photodisc/Getty Images

framing
The way a question or an issue is posed; framing can influence people's decisions and expressed opinions.

A young monk was once rebuffed when asking if he could smoke while he prayed. Ask a different question, advised a friend: Ask if you can pray while you smoke (Crossen, 1993).

"Forbidding" something may be the same as "not allowing" it. But in 1940, 54 percent of Americans said the United States should "forbid" speeches against democracy, and 75 percent said the United States should "not allow" them. Even when people say they feel strongly about an issue, a question's form and wording may affect their answer.

Sometimes even very subtle wording differences can have striking effects. Asking people, "How likely is it a randomly selected person will . . ." sounds the same as asking, "What percentage of people will . . . ." But answers will differ, because the first wording draws attention to the individual and a person's moral conscience, whereas the second draws attention to group-level influences, such as social norms (Critcher & Dunning, 2013). Likewise, saying that income inequality exists "because the rich make more money than the poor" hardly sounds different from "because the poor make less money than the rich." But if given the first wording, conservative people become more supportive of higher taxes on the rich (Chow & Galak, 2012).

Order, response, and wording effects enable political manipulators to use surveys to show public support for their views. Consultants, advertisers, and physicians can have similar disconcerting influences upon our decisions by how they **frame** our choices. No wonder the meat lobby objected to a U.S. food labeling law that required declaring ground beef, for example, as "30 percent fat," rather than "70 percent lean, 30 percent fat." To 9 in 10 college students, a condom seems effective if its protection against the AIDS virus has a "95 percent success rate." Told that it has a "5 percent failure rate," only 4 in 10 students say they find it effective (Linville et al., 1992). "Gun control" efforts gain more public support when framed as "gun safety" initiatives, such as requiring background checks (Steinhauer, 2015). Many people who don't want to be "controlled" do support "safety."

Framing research also has applications in the definition of everyday default options. Without restricting people's freedom, thoughtfully framed options can "nudge" people toward beneficial decisions (Benartzi & Thaler, 2013):

- *Opting in or out of organ donation.* In many countries, people decide, when renewing their drivers' license, whether they want to make their body available for organ donation. In countries where the default option is *yes* but one can "opt out," nearly 100 percent of people choose to be donors. In the United States, Britain, and Germany, where the default option is *no* but one can "opt in," approximately 1 in 4 choose to be donors (Johnson & Goldstein, 2003).

- *Opting in or out of retirement savings.* For many years, American employees who wanted to defer part of their compensation to a 401(k) retirement plan had to elect to lower their take-home pay. Most chose not to do so. A 2006 pension law, influenced by framing research, reframed the choice. Now companies are given an incentive to enroll their employees automatically in the plan and to allow them to opt out (and to raise their take-home pay). The choice was preserved. But one study found that with the "opt out" framing, enrollments soared from 49 to 86 percent (Rosenberg, 2010).

The lesson of framing research is told in the story of a sultan who dreamed he had lost all his teeth. Summoned to interpret the dream, the first interpreter said, "Alas! The lost teeth mean you will see your family members die." Enraged, the sultan ordered 50 lashes for this bearer of bad news. When a second dream interpreter heard the dream, he explained the sultan's good fortune: "You will outlive your whole clan!" Reassured, the sultan ordered his treasurer to go and fetch 50 pieces of gold for this bearer of good news. On the way, the bewildered treasurer observed to the second interpreter, "Your interpretation was no different from that of the first interpreter." "Ah yes," the wise interpreter replied, "but remember: What matters is not only what you say, but how you say it."

Experimental Research: Searching for Cause and Effect

The difficulty of discerning cause and effect among naturally correlated events often prompts social psychologists to create laboratory simulations of everyday processes whenever this is feasible and ethical. These simulations are akin to aeronautical wind tunnels. Aeronautical engineers do not begin by observing how flying objects perform in various natural environments. The variations in both atmospheric conditions and flying objects are too complex. Instead, they construct a simulated reality in which they can manipulate wind conditions and wing structures. Experiments have two major advantages over correlational studies: random assignment and control.

RANDOM ASSIGNMENT: THE GREAT EQUALIZER

Recall that we were reluctant, on the basis of a correlation, to assume that obesity *caused* lower status (via discrimination) or that violence viewing *caused* aggressiveness (see Table 1 for more examples). A survey researcher might measure and statistically extract other possibly pertinent factors and see if the correlations survive. But one can never control for all the factors that might distinguish obese from non-obese, and viewers of violence from non-viewers. Maybe viewers of violence differ in education, culture, intelligence—or in dozens of ways the researcher has not considered.

In one fell swoop, **random assignment** eliminates all such extraneous factors. With random assignment, each person has an equal chance of viewing the violence or the non-violence. Thus, the people in both groups would, in every conceivable way—family status, intelligence, education, initial aggressiveness, hair color—average about the same. Highly intelligent people, for example, are equally likely to appear in both groups. Because random assignment creates equivalent groups, any later aggression difference between the two groups will almost surely have something to do with the only way they differ—whether or not they viewed violence (Figure 5).

CONTROL: MANIPULATING VARIABLES

Social psychologists experiment by constructing social situations that simulate important features of our daily lives. By varying just one or two factors at a time—called **independent variables**—the experimenter pinpoints their influence. As the wind tunnel helps the aeronautical engineer discover principles of aerodynamics, so the experiment enables the social psychologist to discover principles of social thinking, social influence, and social relations.

To illustrate the laboratory experiment, consider two experiments that typify research from upcoming chapters on prejudice and aggression. Each experiment suggests possible cause–effect explanations of correlational findings.

random assignment
The process of assigning participants to the conditions of an experiment such that all persons have the same chance of being in a given condition. (Note the distinction between random *assignment* in experiments and random *sampling* in surveys. Random assignment helps us infer cause and effect. Random sampling helps us generalize to a population.)

independent variable
The experimental factor that a researcher manipulates.

TABLE :: 1 Recognizing Correlational and Experimental Research

	Can Participants Be Randomly Assigned to Condition?	Independent Variable	Dependent Variable
Are early-maturing children more confident?	No → Correlational		
Do students learn more in online or classroom courses?	Yes → Experimental	Take class online or in classroom	Learning
Do school grades predict vocational success?	No → Correlational		
Does playing violent video games increase aggressiveness?	Yes → Experimental	Play violent or nonviolent game	Aggressiveness
Do people find comedy funnier when alone or with others?	(you answer)		
Do higher-income people have higher self-esteem?	(you answer)		

FIGURE :: 5

Random Assignment

Experiments randomly assign
people either to a condition that
receives the experimental treatment or to a control condition
that does not. This gives the researcher confidence that any
later difference is somehow
caused by the treatment.

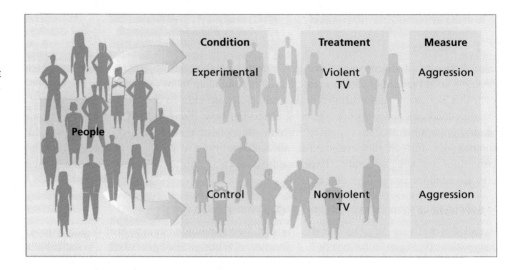

*Note: Obesity correlated with
marital status and income.*

*Whom the men were
shown—a normal or an
overweight woman—was the
independent variable.*

dependent variable
The variable being measured,
so called because it may
depend on manipulations of the
independent variable.

**CORRELATIONAL AND EXPERIMENTAL STUDIES OF PREJUDICE
AGAINST THE OBESE.**   People often perceive the obese as slow, lazy, and sloppy
(Roehling et al., 2007; Ryckman et al., 1989). Do such attitudes spawn discrimination?
In hopes of finding out, Steven Gortmaker and colleagues (1993) studied 370 obese
16- to 24-year-old women. When they restudied them 7 years later, two-thirds of the
women were still obese and were less likely to be married and earning high salaries
than a comparison group of approximately 5,000 other women. Even after correcting for
any differences in aptitude test scores, race, and parental income, the obese women's
incomes were $7,000 a year below average.

Correcting for certain other factors makes it look as though discrimination might
explain the correlation between obesity and lower status. But we cannot be sure. (Can you
think of other possibilities?) Enter social psychologists Mark Snyder and Julie Haugen
(1994, 1995). They asked 76 University of Minnesota male students to have a get-
acquainted phone conversation with 1 of 76 female students. Unknown to the women, each
man was shown a photo *said* to picture his conversational partner. Half were shown an
obese woman (not the actual partner); the other half were shown a normal-weight woman.
Later analysis of just the women's side of the conversation revealed that *they spoke less
warmly and happily if they were presumed obese.* Clearly, something in the men's tone of
voice and conversational content induced the supposedly obese women to speak in a way
that confirmed the idea that obese women are undesirable. The men's prejudice and discrimination were having an effect. Recalling the effect of the stepmother's behavior, perhaps we should call this the "Cinderella effect."

**CORRELATIONAL AND EXPERIMENTAL STUDIES OF TV VIOLENCE
VIEWING.**   As a second example of how experiments clarify causation, consider the
correlation between television viewing and children's behavior. *The more violent television
children watch, the more aggressive they tend to be.* Are children learning and reenacting
what they see on the screen? As we hope you now recognize, this is a correlational finding.
Figure 4 reminds us that there are two other cause–effect interpretations. (What are they?)

Social psychologists have therefore brought television viewing into the laboratory,
where they control the amount of violence the children see. By exposing children to violent
and nonviolent programs, researchers can observe how the amount of violence affects
behavior. Chris Boyatzis and colleagues (1995) showed some elementary schoolchildren,
but not others, an episode of the most popular—and violent—children's television program
of the 1990s, *Power Rangers.* Immediately after viewing the episode, the viewers committed seven times as many aggressive acts per 2-minute interval as the nonviewers. The
observed aggressive acts we call the **dependent variable.** Such experiments indicate that
television can be one cause of children's aggressive behavior. (More on this controversial
research topic in the "Aggression" chapter.)

So far we have seen that the logic of experimentation is simple: By creating and controlling a miniature reality, we can vary one factor and then another and discover how those factors, separately or in combination, affect people. Now let's go a little deeper and see how an experiment is done.

Every social psychological experiment has two essential ingredients. We have just considered one—*control.* We manipulate one or more independent variables while trying to hold everything else constant. The other ingredient is *random assignment.*

REPLICATION: ARE THE RESULTS REPRODUCIBLE?

A handful of unreliable findings, some from researchers who committed fraud by faking data, have raised concerns about the reproducibility of medical and psychological research. Although "mere replications" of others' research are unglamorous—they seldom make headline news—today's science is placing greater value on **replication** studies. Researchers must precisely explain their stimuli and procedures so that others can match them. And we now expect them to file their methods and their detailed data in a public, online, "open science" archive (Brandt et al., 2014; Miguel et al., 2014).

Does viewing violence on TV or in other media lead to imitation, especially among children? Experiments suggest that it does.
Bill Aron/PhotoEdit

replication
Repeating a research study, often with different participants in different settings, to determine whether a finding could be reproduced.

Additionally, teams of researchers have formed a "Reproducibility Project" and a "Many Labs Replication Project"—international collaborative efforts to replicate samples of high profile studies. In the latter project, which attempted replications of 13 studies, researchers convincingly replicated 10 findings with similar or greater effects. They replicated one with a weaker effect. And they failed to replicate two studies (Klein et al., 2014). Such replication forms an essential part of good science. Any single study provides some information—it's one estimate. Better is the aggregated data from multiple studies (Stanley & Spence, 2014). Replication = confirmation.

THE ETHICS OF EXPERIMENTATION

Our television example illustrates why experiments can raise ethical issues. Social psychologists would not, over long periods, expose one group of children to brutal violence. Rather, they briefly alter people's social experience and note the effects. Sometimes the experimental treatment is a harmless, perhaps even enjoyable, experience to which people give their knowing consent. Occasionally, however, researchers find themselves operating in a gray area between the harmless and the risky.

Social psychologists often venture into that ethical gray area when they design experiments that engage intense thoughts and emotions. Experiments do not need to have **mundane realism** (Aronson et al., 1985). That is, laboratory behavior need not be like everyday behavior, which is typically mundane, or unimportant. But the experiment *should* have **experimental realism**—it should engage the participants. Experimenters do not want participants consciously play-acting or bored, they want to engage real psychological processes. An example of such engagement would be delivering electric shocks as part of an experiment on aggression. Forcing people to choose whether to give intense or mild electric shock to someone else can be a realistic measure of aggression. It functionally simulates real aggression, much as a wind tunnel simulates atmospheric wind.

Achieving experimental realism sometimes requires deceiving people with a plausible cover story. If the person in the next room is actually not receiving the shocks, the experimenter does not want the participants to know that. That would destroy the experimental

mundane realism
Degree to which an experiment is superficially similar to everyday situations.

experimental realism
Degree to which an experiment absorbs and involves its participants.

deception
In research, an effect by which participants are misinformed or misled about the study's methods and purposes.

realism. Thus, approximately one-third of social psychological studies in past decades used **deception** (Korn & Nicks, 1993; Vitelli, 1988).

Experimenters also seek to hide their predictions lest the participants, in their eagerness to be "good subjects," merely do what is expected (or, in an ornery mood, do the opposite). Small wonder, says Ukrainian professor Anatoly Koladny, that only 15 percent of Ukrainian survey respondents declared themselves "religious" while under Soviet communism in 1990 when religion was oppressed by the government—but that 70 percent declared themselves "religious" in post-communist 1997 (Nielsen, 1998). In subtle ways, too, the experimenter's words, tone of voice, and gestures may call forth desired responses. Even search dogs trained to detect explosives and drugs are more likely to bark false alerts in places where their handlers have been misled into thinking such illegal items are located (Lit et al., 2011). To minimize such **demand characteristics**—cues that seem to "demand" certain behavior—experimenters typically standardize their instructions or even use a computer to present them.

demand characteristics
Cues in an experiment that tell the participant what behavior is expected.

Researchers often walk a tightrope in designing experiments that will be involving yet ethical. To believe that you are hurting someone, or to be subjected to strong social pressure, may be temporarily uncomfortable. Such experiments raise the age-old question of whether ends justify means. Do the risks exceed those we experience in everyday life (Fiske & Hauser, 2014)? The social psychologists' deceptions are usually brief and mild compared with many misrepresentations in real life and in some of television's reality shows. (One network reality TV series deceived women into competing for the hand of a handsome supposed millionaire, who turned out to be an ordinary laborer.)

University ethics committees review social psychological research to ensure that it will treat people humanely and that the scientific merit justifies any temporary deception or distress. Ethical principles developed by the American Psychological Association (2010), the Canadian Psychological Association (2000), and the British Psychological Society (2009) mandate investigators to

informed consent
An ethical principle requiring that research participants be told enough to enable them to choose whether they wish to participate.

- Tell potential participants enough about the experiment to enable their **informed consent.**
- Be truthful. Use deception only if essential and justified by a significant purpose and not "about aspects that would affect their willingness to participate."
- Protect participants (and bystanders, if any) from harm and significant discomfort.
- Treat information about the individual participants confidentially.
- **Debrief** participants. Fully explain the experiment afterward, including any deception. The only exception to this rule is when the feedback would be distressing, such as by making participants realize they have been stupid or cruel.

debriefing
In social psychology, the postexperimental explanation of a study to its participants. Debriefing usually discloses any deception and often queries participants regarding their understandings and feelings.

The experimenter should be sufficiently informative *and* considerate that people leave feeling at least as good about themselves as when they came in. Better yet, the participants should be compensated by having learned something (Sharpe & Faye, 2009). When treated respectfully, few participants mind being deceived (Epley & Huff, 1998; Kimmel, 1998). Indeed, say social psychology's advocates, professors provoke far greater anxiety and distress by giving and returning course exams than researchers provoke in their experiments.

Generalizing from Laboratory to Life

As the research on television and violence illustrates, social psychology mixes everyday experience and laboratory analysis. Throughout this book, we do the same by drawing our data mostly from the laboratory and our examples mostly from life. Social psychology displays a healthy interplay between laboratory research and everyday life. Hunches gained from everyday experience often inspire laboratory research, which deepens our understanding of our experience.

This interplay appears in the children's television experiment. What people saw in everyday life suggested correlational research, which led to experimental research. Network and government policymakers, those with the power to make changes, are now aware of the results. In many areas, including studies of helping, leadership style, depression, and self-efficacy, effects found in the lab have been mirrored by effects in the field, especially when the laboratory effects have been large (Mitchell, 2012). "The psychology laboratory has generally produced psychological truths rather than trivialities," note Craig Anderson and colleagues (1999).

We need to be cautious, however, in generalizing from laboratory to life. Although the laboratory uncovers basic dynamics of human existence, it is still a simplified, controlled reality. It tells us what effect to expect of variable *X,* all other things being equal—which in real life they never are. Moreover, as you will see, the participants in many experiments are college students. Although that may help you identify with them, college students are hardly a random sample of all humanity (Henry, 2008a, 2008b). And most participants are from WEIRD (*W*estern, *E*ducated, *I*ndustrialized, *R*ich, and *D*emocratic) cultures that represent but 12 percent of humanity (Henrich et al., 2010). Would we get similar results with people of different ages, educational levels, and cultures? That is always an open question.

Nevertheless, we can distinguish between the *content* of people's thinking and acting (for example, their attitudes) and the *process* by which they think and act (for example, *how* attitudes affect actions and vice versa). The content varies more from culture to culture than does the process. People from various cultures may hold different opinions yet form them in similar ways. Consider the following:

- College students in Puerto Rico have reported greater loneliness than do collegians on the U.S. mainland. Yet in the two cultures the ingredients of loneliness have been much the same—shyness, uncertain purpose in life, and low self-esteem (Jones et al., 1985).
- Ethnic groups differ in school achievement and delinquency, but the differences are "no more than skin deep," report David Rowe and colleagues (1994). To the extent that family structure, peer influences, and parental education predict achievement or delinquency for one ethnic group, they do so for other groups.

Although our behaviors may differ, we are influenced by the same social forces. Beneath our surface diversity, we are more alike than different.

SUMMING UP: Research Methods: How Do We Do Social Psychology?

- Social psychologists organize their ideas and findings into *theories*. A good theory will distill an array of facts into a much shorter list of predictive principles. We can use those predictions to confirm or modify the theory, to generate new research, and to suggest practical application.

- Most social psychological research is either *correlational* or *experimental*. Correlational studies, sometimes conducted with systematic survey methods, discern the relationship between variables, such as between amount of education and amount of income. Knowing two things are naturally related is valuable information, but it is not a reliable indicator of what is causing what—or whether a third variable is involved.

- When possible, social psychologists prefer to conduct experiments that explore cause and effect. By constructing a miniature reality that is under their control, experimenters can vary one thing and then another and discover how those things, separately or in combination, affect behavior. We *randomly assign* participants to an experimental condition, which receives the experimental treatment, or to a control condition, which does not. We can then attribute any resulting difference between the two conditions to the *independent variable* (Figure 6). By seeking to *replicate* findings, today's psychologists also assess their reproducibility.

- In creating experiments, social psychologists sometimes stage situations that engage people's emotions. In doing so, they are obliged to follow professional ethical guidelines, such as obtaining people's *informed consent*, protecting them from harm, and fully disclosing afterward any temporary deceptions. Laboratory experiments enable social psychologists to test ideas gleaned from life experience and then to apply the principles and findings to the real world.

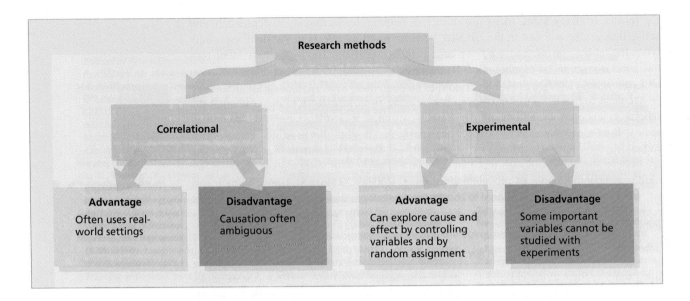

FIGURE :: 6

Two Methods of Doing Research: Correlational and Experimental

POSTSCRIPT:
Why We Wrote This Book

We conclude each chapter with a brief reflection on social psychology's human significance.

We write this text to offer social psychology's powerful, hard-wrought principles. They have, we believe, the power to expand your mind and enrich your life. If you finish this book with sharpened critical thinking skills and with a deeper understanding of how we view and affect one another—and why we sometimes like, love, and help one another and sometimes dislike, hate, and harm one another—then we will be satisfied authors and you, we trust, will be a rewarded reader.

We write knowing that many readers are in the process of defining their life goals, identities, values, and attitudes. Novelist Chaim Potok recalls being urged by his mother to forgo writing: "Be a brain surgeon. You'll keep a lot of people from dying; you'll make a lot more money." Potok's response: "Mama, I don't want to keep people from dying; I want to show them how to live" (quoted by Peterson, 1992, p. 47).

Many of us who teach and write psychology are driven not only by a love for giving psychology away but also by wanting to help students live better lives—wiser, more fulfilling, more compassionate lives. In this we are like teachers and writers in other fields. "Why do we write?" asked theologian Robert McAfee Brown. "I submit that beyond all rewards . . . *we write because we want to change things.* We write because we have this [conviction that we] can make a difference. The 'difference' may be a new perception of beauty, a new insight into self-understanding, a new experience of joy, or a decision to join the revolution" (quoted by Marty, 1988). Indeed, we write hoping to do our part to restrain intuition with critical thinking, refine judgmentalism with compassion, and replace illusion with understanding.

The Self in a Social World

Adam Lubroth/Digital Vision/Getty Images

"There are three things extremely hard, Steel, a Diamond, and to know one's self."

—*Benjamin Franklin*

This book unfolds around its definition of social psychology: the scientific study of how we *think about* (Part One), *influence* (Part Two), and *relate to* (Part Three) one another. Part Four offers additional, focused examples of how the research and the theories of social psychology are applied to real life.

Specifically, Part One examines the scientific study of how we think about one another (also called *social cognition*). Each chapter in this part confronts some overriding questions: How reasonable are our social attitudes, explanations, and beliefs? Are our impressions of ourselves and others generally accurate? How does our social thinking form? How is it prone to bias and error, and how might we bring it closer to reality?

Spotlights and illusions: What do they teach us about ourselves?

Self-concept: Who am I?

What is the nature and motivating power of self-esteem?

What is self-serving bias?

How do people manage their self-presentation?

What does it mean to have "self-control"?

Postscript: Twin truths—The perils of pride, the powers of positive thinking

At the center of our worlds, more pivotal for us than anything else, is ourselves. As we navigate our daily lives, our sense of self continually engages the world.

Consider this example: One morning, you wake up to find your hair sticking up at strange angles on your head. You can't find a hat, so you smooth down the random spikes of your hair and dash out the door to class. All morning, you are acutely self-conscious about your very bad hair day. To your surprise, your friends in class don't say anything. Are they secretly laughing to themselves about how ridiculous you look, or are they too preoccupied with themselves to notice your spiky hair?

SPOTLIGHTS AND ILLUSIONS: WHAT DO THEY TEACH US ABOUT OURSELVES?

Describe the spotlight effect and its relation to the illusion of transparency.

spotlight effect
The belief that others are paying more attention to our appearance and behavior than they really are.

Why do we often feel that others are paying more attention to us than they really are? The **spotlight effect** means seeing ourselves at center stage, thus intuitively overestimating the extent to which others' attention is aimed at us.

Timothy Lawson (2010) explored the spotlight effect by having college students change into a sweatshirt emblazoned with "American Eagle" before meeting a group of peers. Nearly 40 percent were sure the other students would remember what the shirt said, but only 10 percent actually did. Most observers did not even notice when the students changed sweatshirts after leaving the room for a few minutes. In another experiment, even noticeably embarrassing clothes, such as a T-shirt with singer Barry Manilow on it, provoked only 23 percent of observers to notice—many fewer than the 50 percent estimated by the unfortunate students sporting the 1970s soft rock warbler on their chests (Gilovich et al., 2000).

illusion of transparency
The illusion that our concealed emotions leak out and can be easily read by others.

What's true of our dorky clothes and bad hair is also true of our emotions: our anxiety, irritation, disgust, deceit, or attraction to someone else (Gilovich et al., 1998). Fewer people notice than we presume. Keenly aware of our own emotions, we often suffer an **illusion of transparency.** If we're happy and we know it, then our face will surely show it. And others, we presume, will notice. Actually, we can be more opaque than we realize. (See "Research Close-Up: On Being Nervous About Looking Nervous.")

Due to the spotlight effect, this boy might think everyone is looking at him and feel embarrassed by his grandmother's affection—even though no one really notices.
Big Cheese Photo/PunchStock

research CLOSE-UP

On Being Nervous About Looking Nervous

Have you ever felt self-conscious when approaching someone you felt attracted to, concerned that your nervousness was obvious? Or have you felt yourself trembling while speaking before an audience and presumed that everyone was noticing?

Kenneth Savitsky and Thomas Gilovich (2003) knew from their own and others' studies that people overestimate the extent to which their internal states "leak out." People asked to tell lies presume that others will detect their deceit, which feels so obvious. People asked to sample horrid-tasting drinks presume that others notice their disgust, which they can barely suppress.

Many people who give a presentation report not just feeling anxious, but anxious that others will notice their anxiety. And if they feel their knees shaking and hands trembling, their worry that others are noticing may compound and perpetuate their anxiety. This is similar to fretting about not falling asleep, which further impedes falling asleep, or feeling anxious about stuttering, which worsens the stuttering.

Savitsky and Gilovich wondered whether an "illusion of transparency" might surface among inexperienced public speakers—and whether it might disrupt their performance. To find out, they invited 40 Cornell University students to their laboratory in pairs. One person stood at the podium and spoke for 3 minutes (on a topic such as "The Best and Worst Things About Life Today") as the other sat and listened. Then the two switched positions and the other person gave a different 3-minute impromptu talk. Afterward, each rated how nervous they thought they appeared while speaking (from 0, *not at all,* to 10, *very*) and how nervous the other person seemed.

The results? People rated themselves as appearing relatively nervous (6.65, on average). But to their partner they appeared not so nervous (5.25), a difference great enough to be statistically significant (meaning that a difference this great, for this sample of people, is very unlikely to have been due to chance variation). Twenty-seven of the 40 participants (68 percent) believed that they appeared more nervous than did their partner.

To check on the reliability of their finding, Savitsky and Gilovich *replicated* (repeated) and extended the experiment by having people speak before an audience of people who weren't going to be giving speeches themselves, to rule out the possibility that this might explain the previous results. Again, speakers overestimated the transparency of their nervousness.

Savitsky and Gilovich next wondered whether informing speakers that their nervousness isn't so obvious might help them relax and perform better. They invited 77 more Cornell students to come to the lab and, after 5 minutes' preparation, give a 3-minute videotaped speech on race relations at their university. Those in one group—the *control condition*—were given no further instructions. Those in the *reassured condition* were told that it was natural to feel anxious but that "You shouldn't worry much about what other people think. . . . With this in mind you should just relax and try to do your best. Know that if you become nervous, you probably shouldn't worry about it." To those in the *informed condition* he explained the illusion of transparency. After telling them it was natural to feel anxious, the experimenter added, "Research has found that audiences can't pick up on your anxiety as well as you might expect. . . . Those speaking feel that their nervousness is transparent, but in reality their feelings are not so apparent. . . . With this in mind, you should just relax and try to do your best. Know that if you become nervous, you'll probably be the only one to know."

After the speeches, the speakers rated their speech quality and their perceived nervousness (this time using a 7-point scale) and were also rated by the observers. As Table 1 shows, those informed about the illusion-of-transparency phenomenon felt better about their speech and their appearance than did those in the control and reassurance conditions. What's more, the observers confirmed the speakers' self-assessments.

So, the next time you feel nervous about looking nervous, pause to remember the lesson of these experiments: Other people are noticing less than you might suppose.

TABLE :: 1 Average Ratings of Speeches by Speakers and Observers on a 1 to 7 Scale

Type of Rating	Control Condition	Reassured Condition	Informed Condition
Speakers' self-ratings			
Speech quality	3.04	2.83	3.50*
Relaxed appearance	3.35	2.69	4.20*
Observers' rating			
Speech quality	3.50	3.62	4.23*
Composed appearance	3.90	3.94	4.65*

*Each of these results differs by a statistically significant margin from those of the control and reassured condition.

We also overestimate the visibility of our social blunders and public mental slips. When we trigger the library alarm or accidentally insult someone, we may be mortified ("Everyone thinks I'm a jerk"). But research shows that what we agonize over, others may hardly notice and soon forget (Savitsky et al., 2001).

The spotlight effect and the related illusion of transparency are but two of many examples of the interplay between our sense of self and our social worlds. Here are a few more:

- *Social surroundings affect our self-awareness.* When we are the only member of our race, gender, or nationality in a group, we notice how we differ and how others are reacting to our difference. A White American friend once told me [DM] how self-consciously White he felt while living in a rural village in Nepal; an hour later, an African-American friend told me how self-consciously American she felt while in Africa.

- *Self-interest colors our social judgment.* When problems arise in a close relationship, we usually attribute more responsibility to our partners than to ourselves. When things go *well* at home or work or play, we see ourselves as more responsible.

- *Self-concern motivates our social behavior.* In hopes of making a positive impression, we agonize about our appearance. Like savvy politicians, we also monitor others' behavior and expectations and adjust our behavior accordingly.

- *Social relationships help define our sense of self.* In our varied relationships, we have varying selves, note Susan Andersen and Serena Chen (2002). We may be one self with Mom, another with friends, another with teachers. How we think of ourselves is linked to the person we're with at the moment. And when relationships change, our self-concepts can change as well. College students who recently broke up with a romantic partner shifted their self-perceptions and felt less certain about who they were—one reason breakups can be so emotionally distressing (Slotter et al., 2010).

As these examples suggest, the traffic between ourselves and others runs both ways. Our ideas and feelings about ourselves affect how we respond to others, and others help shape our sense of self.

No topic in psychology today is more heavily researched than the self. In 2013, the word "self" appeared in 27,729 book and article summaries in *PsycINFO* (the online archive of psychological research)—25 times more than appeared in 1970. Our sense of self organizes our thoughts, feelings, and actions and enables us to remember our past, assess our present, and project our future—and thus to behave adaptively.

In later chapters, you will see that much of our behavior is not consciously controlled but, rather, automatic and unself-conscious. However, the self does enable long-term planning, goal setting, and restraint. It imagines alternatives, compares itself with others, and manages its reputation and relationships. Moreover, as Mark Leary (2004a) noted in his aptly titled *The Curse of the Self,* the self can sometimes be an impediment to a satisfying life. That's why religious or spiritual meditation practices seek to prune the self's egocentric preoccupations, by quieting the ego, reducing its attachments to material pleasures, and redirecting it. "Mysticism," adds psychologist Jonathan Haidt (2006), "everywhere and always, is about losing the self, transcending the self, and merging with something larger than the self."

In the remainder of this chapter, we examine our self-concept (how we come to know ourselves) and the self in action (how our sense of self drives our attitudes and actions).

> "No topic is more interesting to people than people. For most people, moreover, the most interesting is the self."
> —Roy F. Baumeister,
> *The Self in Social Psychology*, 1999

SUMMING UP: Spotlights and Illusions: What Do They Teach Us About Ourselves?

- Concerned with the impression we make on others, we tend to believe that others are paying more attention to us than they are (the *spotlight effect*).

- We also tend to believe that our emotions are more obvious than they are (the *illusion of transparency*).

SELF-CONCEPT: WHO AM I?

| Understand how, and how accurately, we know ourselves and what determines our self-concept.

You have many ways to complete the sentence "I am _____." (What five answers might you give?) Your answers provide a glimpse of your **self-concept.**

At the Center of Our Worlds: Our Sense of Self

self-concept
What we know and believe about ourselves.

The most important aspect of yourself is your self. To discover where this sense of self arises, neuroscientists are exploring the brain activity that underlies our constant sense of being oneself. Most studies suggest an important role for the right hemisphere (van Veluw & Chance, 2014). Put yours to sleep (with an anesthetic to your right carotid artery) and you may have trouble recognizing your own face. One patient with right hemisphere damage failed to recognize that he owned and was controlling his left hand (Decety & Sommerville, 2003). The "medial prefrontal cortex," a neuron path located in the cleft between your brain hemispheres just behind your eyes, seemingly helps stitch together your sense of self. It becomes more active when you think about yourself (Farb et al., 2007; Zimmer, 2005).

The elements of your self-concept, the specific beliefs by which you define yourself, are your **self-schemas** (Markus & Wurf, 1987). *Schemas* are mental templates by which we organize our worlds. Our *self*-schemas—our perceiving ourselves as athletic, over-weight, smart, or anything else—powerfully affect how we perceive, remember, and evaluate other people and ourselves. If athletics is central to your self-concept (if being an athlete is one of your self-schemas), then you will tend to notice others' bodies and skills. You will quickly recall sports-related experiences. And you will welcome information that is consistent with your self-schema (Kihlstrom & Cantor, 1984). If your friend's birthday is close to yours, you'll be more likely to remember it (Kesebir & Oishi, 2010). The self-schemas that make up our self-concepts help us organize and retrieve our experiences.

self-schema
Beliefs about self that organize and guide the processing of self-relevant information.

SOCIAL COMPARISONS

How do we decide if we are rich, smart, or short? One way is through **social comparisons** (Festinger, 1954). Others help define the standard by which we define ourselves as rich or poor, smart or dumb, tall or short: we compare ourselves with them and consider how we differ. Social comparison explains why high school students tend to think of themselves as better students if their peers are only average (Marsh et al., 2000), and how self-concept can be threatened after graduation when a student who excelled in an average high school goes on to an academically selective university. The "big fish" is no longer in a small pond.

social comparison
Evaluating one's abilities and opinions by comparing oneself with others.

Much of life revolves around social comparisons. We feel handsome when others seem homely, smart when others seem dull, caring when others seem callous. More money doesn't always lead to more happiness, but having more money than those around you can (Solnick & Hemenway, 1998). When we witness a peer's performance, we cannot resist implicitly comparing ourselves (Gilbert et al., 1995). We may, therefore, privately take some pleasure in a peer's failure, especially when it happens to someone we envy and when we don't feel vulnerable to such misfortune ourselves (Lockwood, 2002; Smith et al., 1996). You might have heard the German word for this: *Schadenfreude.*

Sometimes social comparison is based on incomplete information. Have you ever been on Facebook and thought, "All of my friends are having a lot more fun than I am"? If so, you're not alone. Among students attending Utah Valley University, those who spent more time on Facebook were more likely to believe that other people were happier and had better lives than they did (Chou & Edge, 2012). Of course, it can't be true that everyone is having more fun than everyone else. More than likely, Facebook users are choosing to feature the more exciting and positive aspects of their lives. This biased social comparison might be one reason young adults who used Facebook more often were more anxious, more lonely, and less satisfied with their lives (Kross et al., 2013).

Private Pleasure in a Peer's Pratfall

In 2011, when powerful media magnates Rupert Murdoch and his son, James Murdoch, were embarrassed by illegal practices at one of their newspapers, some people felt *Schadenfreude* (a German word for the pleasure felt over someone else's misfortune).
Press Association/EPA/Newscom

"Make no comparisons!"
—King Charles I, 1600–1649

Social comparisons can also diminish our satisfaction in other ways. When we experience an increase in affluence, status, or achievement, we "compare upward"—we raise the standards by which we evaluate our attainments. When climbing the ladder of success, we tend to look up, not down; we compare ourselves with others doing even better (Gruder, 1977; Suls & Tesch, 1978; Wheeler et al., 1982). When facing competition, we often protect our shaky self-concept by perceiving the competitor as advantaged. For example, college swimmers believed that their competitors had better coaching and more practice time (Shepperd & Taylor, 1999). Even sexual activity is subject to social comparison. Adults who have sex more often are happier—you might have guessed that! But then social comparison kicks in: Even people who have a lot of sex are less happy if their peers are having more sex than they are (Wadsworth, 2014). Apparently, we judge not just how much fun we're having—but how it measures up to the fun everyone else is having.

OTHER PEOPLE'S JUDGMENTS

When people think well of us, we think well of ourselves. Children whom others label as gifted, hardworking, or helpful tend to incorporate such ideas into their self-concepts and behavior. If racial minority students feel threatened by negative stereotypes of their academic ability, or women feel threatened by low expectations for their math and science performance, they may "disidentify" with those realms. Rather than fight such prejudgments, they may identify their interests elsewhere (Steele, 2010).

The looking-glass self was how sociologist Charles H. Cooley (1902) described our use of how we think others perceive us as a mirror for perceiving ourselves. Fellow sociologist George Herbert Mead (1934) refined this concept, noting that what matters for our self-concepts is not how others actually see us but the way we *imagine* they see us. People generally feel freer to praise than to criticize; they voice their compliments and restrain their insults. We may, therefore, overestimate others' appraisal, inflating our self-images. For example, people tend to see themselves as more physically attractive than they actually are (Epley & Whitchurch, 2008).

Self and Culture

How did you complete the "I am _____" statement? Did you give information about your personal traits, such as "I am honest," "I am tall," or "I am outgoing"? Or did you also describe your social identity, such as "I am a Pisces," "I am a MacDonald," or "I am a Muslim"?

For some people, especially those in industrialized Western cultures, **individualism** prevails. Identity is self-contained. Becoming an adult means separating from parents, becoming self-reliant, and defining one's personal, **independent self.** One's identity—as a unique individual with particular abilities, traits, values, and dreams—remains fairly constant.

Western culture assumes your life will be enriched by believing in your power of personal control. Western literature, from *The Iliad* to *The Adventures of Huckleberry Finn,* celebrates the self-reliant individual. Movie plots feature rugged heroes who buck the establishment. Songs proclaim "I Gotta Be Me," declare that "The Greatest Love of All" is loving oneself (Schoeneman, 1994), or state without irony that "I Am a God" or "I Believe the World Should Revolve Around Me." Individualism flourishes when people experience affluence, mobility, urbanism, and mass media (Freeman, 1997; Greenfield, 2009; Marshall, 1997; Triandis, 1994).

Most cultures native to Asia, Africa, and Central and South America place a greater value on **collectivism,** by respecting and identifying with the group. In these cultures, people are more self-critical and focus less on positive self-views (Heine et al., 1999). Malaysians, Indians, Koreans, Japanese, and traditional Kenyans such as the Maasai, for example, are much more likely than Australians, Americans, and the British to complete the "I am" statement with their group identities (Kanagawa et al., 2001; Ma & Schoeneman, 1997). When speaking, people using the languages of collectivist countries say "I" less often (Kashima & Kashima, 1998, 2003). Compared with U.S. church websites, Korean church websites place more emphasis on social connections and participation and less on personal spiritual growth and self-betterment (Sasaki & Kim, 2011).

Of course, pigeonholing cultures as solely individualist or collectivist oversimplifies, because within any culture individualism varies from person to person (Oyserman et al., 2002a, 2002b). There are individualist Chinese and collectivist Americans, and most people behave communally at some times and individualistically at others (Bandura, 2004). Individualism–collectivism also varies across a country's political views and regions. Conservatives tend to be economic individualists ("don't tax or regulate me") and moral collectivists ("legislate against immorality"). Liberals tend to be economic collectivists (supporting national health care) and moral individualists ("keep your laws off my body"). In the United States, Native Hawaiians and people living in the deep South exhibit greater collectivism than do those in Mountain West states, such as Oregon and Montana (Plaut et al., 2002; Vandello & Cohen, 1999). The rich are more individualistic than the poor, males more than females, whites more than nonwhites, and San Franciscans more than Bostonites (Kraus et al., 2012; Markus & Conner, 2013; Plaut et al., 2012). Writes *Boston Globe* editor Brian McGrory (2004), "Boston will always have something that most other people and places don't: common ground. . . . We're a city shaped by a past that always leads to a better future . . . to tight-knit neighborhoods where the traditions are deep and the values carved into bedrock." Yet others point out the allure of the new West: "In the grimy old brick towns of the East, I sometimes feel that people have grown up history-stained. . . . In California, where the future promises continued sunniness, most of what I see is new," counters W. T. Vollman (2008). Despite individual and subcultural variations, researchers continue to regard individualism and collectivism as genuine cultural variables (Schimmack et al., 2005).

GROWING INDIVIDUALISM WITHIN CULTURES

Cultures can also change over time, and many seem to be growing more individualistic. One way to see this is using the Google Books Ngram Viewer, which shows the usage of words and phrases in the full text of 5 million books since the 1800s (try it yourself; it's online and free). In the 2000s, compared to previous decades, books published in the United States used the word "get" more and "give" less (Greenfield, 2013), and used "I," "me," and "you" more and "we" and "us" a little less (Twenge et al., 2013; see Figure 1).

Popular song lyrics also became more likely to use "I" and "me" and less likely to use "we" and "us" between 1980 and 2007 (DeWall et al., 2011), with the norm shifting from the sappy love song of the 1980s ("Endless Love," 1981) to the self-celebration of the 2000s (Justin Timberlake singlehandedly bringing "Sexy Back," 2006). These cultural

individualism
The concept of giving priority to one's own goals over group goals and defining one's identity in terms of personal attributes rather than group identifications.

independent self
Construing one's identity as an autonomous self.

collectivism
Giving priority to the goals of one's group (often one's extended family or work group) and defining one's identity accordingly.

FIGURE :: 1

In the Google Books database, American books in the 2000s (vs. those from the 1960s–1970s) used *I, me, my, mine,* and *myself* and *you, your, yours, yourself,* and *yourselves* more often.
Source: Twenge, J. M., Campbell, W. K., & Gentile, B. (2013). Changes in pronoun use in American books and the rise of individualism, 1960–2008. *Journal of Cross-Cultural Psychology, 44,* 406–415.

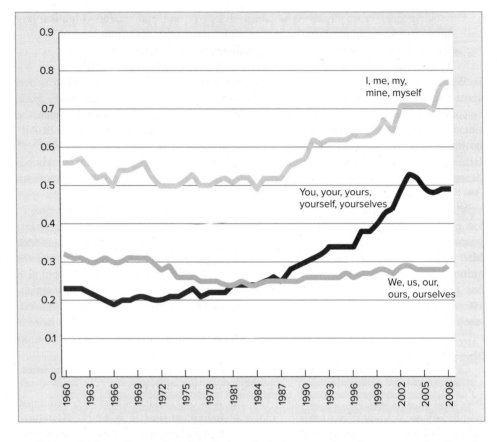

trends have had an effect on individuals, too: Today's young Americans report significantly more positive self-views than young people did in the 1960s and 1970s (Gentile et al., 2010; Twenge & Campbell, 2008; Twenge et al., 2012; but for an opposing view, see Trzesniewski & Donnellan, 2010). Chinese citizens in their early twenties are more likely than older Chinese to agree with individualistic statements, such as "make a name for yourself" and "live a life that suits your tastes" (Arora, 2005).

Even your name might show the shift toward individualism: American parents are now less likely to give their children common names and more likely to help them stand out with an unusual name. Although nearly 20 percent of boys born in 1990 received one of the 10 most common names, only 8 percent received such a common name by 2010, with the numbers similar for girls (Twenge et al., 2010). Today, you don't have to be the child of a celebrity to get a name as unique as North, Suri, or Apple.

Americans and Australians, most of whom are descended from those who struck out on their own to emigrate, are more likely than Europeans to give their children uncommon names. Parents in the western United States and Canada, descended from independent pioneers, are also more likely than those in the more established East to give their children uncommon names (Varnum & Kitayama, 2011). The more individualistic the time or the place, the more children receive unique names.

These changes demonstrate a principle that goes deeper than a name: the interaction between individuals and society. Did the culture focus on uniqueness first and cause the

In individualistic cultures, being different and standing out is seen as an asset. In collectivistic cultures, it is seen as a detriment.
Ingram Publishing/SuperStock

parents' name choices, or did individual parents decide they wanted their children to be unique, thus creating the culture? A similar chicken-and-egg question applies to song lyrics: Did a more self-focused population listen to more self-focused songs, or did listening to more self-focused songs make people more self-focused? The answer, though not yet fully understood, is probably both (Markus & Kitayama, 2010).

FIGURE :: 2

Asian and Western Thinking

When shown an underwater scene, Americans focus on the biggest fish. Asians are more likely to reference the background, such as the plants, bubbles, and rocks (Nisbett, 2003).

CULTURE AND COGNITION

In his book *The Geography of Thought* (2003), social psychologist Richard Nisbett contends that collectivism also results in different ways of thinking. When shown an animated underwater scene (Figure 2), Japanese spontaneously recalled 60 percent more background features than did Americans, and they spoke of more relationships (the frog beside the plant). Americans look more at the focal object, such as a single big fish, and less at the surroundings (Chua et al., 2005; Nisbett, 2003), a result duplicated when studies examine activation in different areas of the brain (Goh et al., 2007; Lewis et al., 2008). When shown drawings of groups of children, Japanese students took the facial expressions of all of the children into account when rating the happiness or anger of an individual child, whereas Americans focused only on the child they were asked to rate (Masuda et al., 2008). Facebook profile pictures show a similar cultural effect: U.S. students' selfies were more likely to be close-ups of their faces, whereas Taiwanese students were more likely to choose a picture with more background (Huang & Park, 2012). Nisbett and Takahiko Masuda (2003) conclude from such studies that East Asians think more holistically—perceiving and thinking about objects and people in relationship to one another and to their environment.

If you grew up in a Western culture, you were probably told to "express yourself"—through writing, the choices you make, the products you buy, and perhaps through your tattoos or piercings. When asked about the purpose of language, American students were more likely to explain that it allows self-expression, whereas Korean students focused on how language allows communication with others. American students were also more likely to see their choices as expressions of themselves and to evaluate their personal choices more favorably (Kim & Sherman, 2007). The individualized latté—"decaf, single shot, skinny, extra hot"—that seems just right at a North American coffee shop would seem strange in Seoul, note Kim and Hazel Markus (1999). In Korea, people place less value on expressing their uniqueness and more on tradition and shared practices (Choi & Choi, 2002; Figure 3). Korean advertisements tend to feature people together, whereas American advertisements highlight personal choice or freedom (Markus, 2001; Morling & Lamoreaux, 2008).

Collectivistic cultures also promote a greater sense of belonging and more integration between the self and others. When Chinese participants were asked to think about their mothers, a brain region associated with the self became activated—an area that lit up for Western participants only when they thought about themselves (Zhu et al., 2007). Interdependent selves have not one self but many selves: self-with-parents,

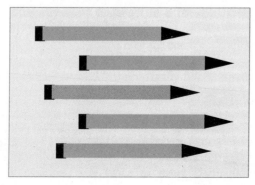

FIGURE :: 3

Which Pen Would You Choose?

When Heejung Kim and Hazel Markus (1999) invited people to choose one of these pens, 77 percent of Americans but only 31 percent of Asians chose the uncommon color (regardless of whether it was orange, as here, or green). This result illustrates differing cultural preferences for uniqueness and conformity, note Kim and Markus.

FIGURE :: 4

Self-Construal as Independent or Interdependent

The independent self acknowledges relationships with others. But the interdependent self is more deeply embedded in others (Markus & Kitayama, 1991).

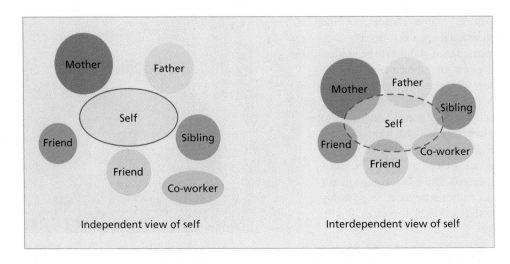

Independent view of self   Interdependent view of self

self-at-work, self-with-friends (Cross et al., 1992). As Figure 4 and Table 2 suggest, the interdependent self is embedded in social memberships. Conversation is less direct and more polite (Holtgraves, 1997), and people focus more on gaining social approval (Lalwani et al., 2006). Among Chinese students, half said they would stop dating someone if their parents disapproved, compared with less than one-third of American students (Zhang & Kline, 2009). In a collectivistic culture, the goal of social life is to harmonize with and support one's communities, not—as it is in more individualistic societies—to enhance one's individual self and make independent choices.

CULTURE AND SELF-ESTEEM

In collectivist cultures, self-esteem tends to be malleable (context-specific) rather than stable (enduring across situations). In one study, 4 in 5 Canadian students agreed that they remained essentially the same person in different situations, compared with only 1 in 3 Chinese and Japanese students (Tafarodi et al., 2004).

For those in individualistic cultures, self-esteem is more personal and less relational. If a Westerner's personal identity is threatened, she will feel angrier and sadder than when her collective identity is threatened (Gaertner et al., 1999). Unlike Japanese, who persist more on tasks when they are failing, people in individualistic countries persist more when succeeding, because success elevates self-esteem (Heine et al., 2001). Western individualists like to make comparisons with others that boost their self-esteem. Asian collectivists make comparisons (often upward, with those doing better) in ways that facilitate self-improvement (White & Lehman, 2005).

So when, do you suppose, are university students in collectivist Japan and individualist United States most likely to report positive emotions such as happiness and elation? For

"One needs to cultivate the spirits of sacrificing the *little me* to achieve the benefits of the *big me*."

—Chinese Saying

TABLE :: 2 Self-Concept: Independent or Interdependent

	Independent (Individualistic)	Interdependent (Collectivist)
Identity is	Personal, defined by individual traits and goals	Social, defined by connections with others
What matters	Me—personal achievement and fulfillment; my rights and liberties	We—group goals and solidarity; our social responsibilities and relationships
Disapproves of	Conformity	Egotism
Illustrative motto	"To thing own self be true"	"No one is an island"
Cultures that support	Individualistic Western	Collectivistic Asian and Third World

Japanese students, happiness comes with positive social engagement—with feeling close, friendly, and respectful. For American students, it more often comes with disengaged emotions—with feeling effective, superior, and proud (Kitayama & Markus, 2000). Conflict in collectivist cultures often takes place between groups; individualist cultures breed more conflict (and crime and divorce) between individuals (Triandis, 2000).

When Shinobu Kitayama (1999), after 10 years of teaching and researching in America, visited his Japanese alma mater, Kyoto University, graduate students were "astounded" when he explained the Western idea of the individualistic self. "I persisted in explaining this Western notion of self-concept—one that my American students understood intuitively—and finally began to persuade them that, indeed, many Americans do have such a disconnected notion of self. Still, one of them, sighing deeply, said at the end, 'Could this *really* be true?'" (To read more about psychological differences between cultures, see "The Inside Story: Hazel Markus and Shinobu Kitayama on Cultural Psychology.")

When East meets West, does the self-concept become more individualized? What happens when Japanese are exposed to Western advice to "believe in one's own possibilities," and to movies featuring the heroic individual police officer catching the crook *despite* others' interference? As Steven Heine and co-researchers report (1999), they become more individualistic. Being an exchange student has a similar effect: Personal self-esteem increased among Japanese exchange students after spending 7 months at the University of British Columbia. In Canada, individual self-esteem is also higher among long-term Asian immigrants than among more recent immigrants (and higher than among those living in Asia). Culture can shape self-views even in short periods of time.

Self-Knowledge

"Know thyself," admonished an ancient Greek oracle. We certainly try. We readily form beliefs about ourselves, and we in Western cultures don't hesitate to explain why we feel and act as we do. But how well do we actually know ourselves?

"There is one thing, and only one in the whole universe which we know more about than we could learn from external observation," noted C. S. Lewis (1952, pp. 18–19). "That one thing is [ourselves]. We have, so to speak, inside information; we are in the know." Indeed. Yet sometimes we *think* we know, but our inside information is wrong. That is the unavoidable conclusion of some fascinating research.

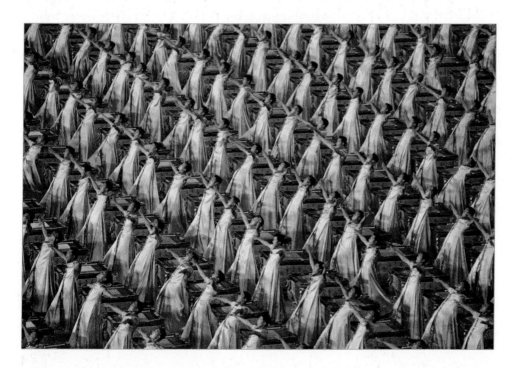

In collectivistic cultures, harmony comes from sameness and agreement.
Source: http://news.bbcimg.co.uk/media/images/58096000/jpg/_58096216_beijing_drums_getty.jpg
NICOLAS ASFOURI/Getty Images

THE inside STORY

Hazel Markus and Shinobu Kitayama on Cultural Psychology

We began our collaboration by wondering out loud. Japanese researcher Shinobu wondered why American life was so weird. American researcher Hazel countered with anecdotes about the strangeness of Japan. Cultural psychology is about making the strange familiar and the familiar strange. Our shared cultural encounters astonished us and convinced us that when it comes to psychological functioning, culture matters.

After weeks of lecturing in Japan to students with a good command of English, Hazel wondered why the students did not say anything—no questions, no comments. She assured students she was interested in ideas that were different from hers, so why was there no response? Where were the arguments, debates, and signs of critical thinking? Even if she asked a straightforward question, "Where is the best noodle shop?" the answer was invariably an audible intake of air followed by, "It depends." Didn't Japanese students have preferences, ideas, opinions, and attitudes? What is inside a head if it isn't these things? How could you know someone if she didn't tell you what she was thinking?

Shinobu was curious about why American students shouldn't just listen to a lecture and why they felt the need to be constantly interrupting each other and talking over each other and the professor. Why did the comments and questions reveal strong emotions and have a competitive edge? What was the point of this arguing? Why did intelligence seem to be associated with getting the best of another person, even within a class where people knew each other well?

Shinobu expressed his amazement at American hosts who bombard their guests with choices. Do you want wine or beer, or soft drinks or juice, or coffee or tea? Why burden the guest with trivial decisions? Surely the host knew what would be good refreshment on this occasion and could simply provide something appropriate.

Choice as a burden? Hazel wondered if this could be the key to one particularly humiliating experience in Japan. A group of eight—all native Japanese except for Hazel—was in a French restaurant, and everyone was following the universal restaurant script and studying the menu. The waiter approached and stood nearby. Hazel announced her choice of appetizer and entrée. Next was a tense conversation among the Japanese host and the Japanese guests. When the meal was served, it was not what she had ordered. Everyone at the table was served the same meal. This was deeply disturbing. If you can't choose your own dinner, how could it be enjoyable? What was the point of the menu if everybody is served the same meal?

Could a sense of sameness be a good or a desirable feeling in Japan? When Hazel walked around the grounds of a temple in Kyoto, there was a fork in the path and a sign that read: "ordinary path." Who would want to take the ordinary path? Where was the special, less-traveled path? Choosing the non-ordinary path may be an obvious course for Americans, but in this case it led to the temple dump outside the temple grounds. The ordinary path did not denote the dull and unchallenging way, but meant the appropriate and the good way.

These exchanges inspired our experimental studies and remind us that there are ways of life beyond the ones that each of us knows best. So far, most of psychology has been produced by psychologists in middle-class White American settings studying middle-class White American respondents. In other sociocultural contexts, there can be different ideas and practices about how to be a person and how to live a meaningful life, and these differences have an influence on psychological functioning. This realization fuels our continuing interest in collaboration and in cultural psychology.

Hazel Rose Markus
Stanford University
Courtesy Hazel Rose Markus

Shinobu Kitayama
University of Michigan
Courtesy Shinobu Kitayama

PREDICTING OUR BEHAVIOR

"In sooth, I know not why I am so sad."

—William Shakespeare,
The Merchant of Venice, 1596

Inevitably, dating couples tend to predict the longevity of their relationships through rose-colored glasses. Their friends and family often know better, report Tara MacDonald and Michael Ross (1997). Among University of Waterloo students, their roommates were better predictors of whether their romances would survive than they were. Medical residents weren't very good at predicting whether they would do well on a surgical skills exam, but their peers in the program predicted each other's performance with startling accuracy (Lutsky et al., 1993). Observers predicted psychology students' exam grades better than the students themselves—mostly because they relied on past performance rather than the student's hopes for acing the test (Helzer & Dunning, 2012). So if you're in love and want to know whether it will last, don't listen to your heart—ask your roommate. And if you want to predict your routine daily behaviors—how much time you will spend laughing, on the phone, or watching TV, for example—your close friends' estimates will likely prove at least as accurate as your own (Vazire & Mehl, 2008).

One of the most common errors in behavior prediction is underestimating how long it will take to complete a task (called the **planning fallacy**). The Big Dig freeway construction project in Boston was supposed to take 10 years and actually took 20 years. The Sydney Opera House was supposed to be completed in 6 years; it took 16. Less than a third of couples engaged to be married completed their wedding planning in the amount of time they anticipated, and only 4 out of 10 sweethearts bought a planned Valentine's Day gift by their self-imposed deadline (Min & Arkes, 2012). Coursework doesn't fare any better. College students writing a senior thesis paper were asked to predict when they would complete the project. On average, students finished 3 weeks later than their "most realistic" estimate—and a week later than their "worst-case scenario" estimate (Buehler et al., 2002). However, friends and teachers were able to predict how late these papers would be. Just as you should ask your friends how long your relationship is likely to survive, if you want to know when you will finish your term paper, ask your roommate or your mom. You could also do what Microsoft does: Managers automatically add 30 percent onto a software developer's estimate of completion—and 50 percent if the project involves a new operating system (Dunning, 2006).

So, how can you improve your self-predictions? The best way is to be more realistic about how long tasks took in the past. Apparently, people underestimate how long something will take because they misremember previous tasks as taking less time than they actually did (Roy et al., 2005). Another useful strategy: Estimate how long each step in the project will take. Engaged couples who described their wedding-planning steps in more detail more accurately predicted how long the process would take (Min & Arkes, 2012).

Are people equally bad at predicting how much money they will spend? Johanna Peetz and Roger Buehler (2009) found that the answer was yes. Canadian undergraduates predicted that they would spend $94 over the next week but actually spent $122. Considering

planning fallacy
The tendency to underestimate how long it will take to complete a task.

"I was hoping you could tell me something mildly favorable—yet vague enough to be believable."

Predicting behavior, even one's own, is no easy matter, which may be why some people go to psychics and tarot card readers in hope of help.
Reprinted with permission of Brett Pelham at brettpel@yahoo.com.

that they had spent $126 in the week before the study, their guess should have been more accurate. When they came back a week later, they still predicted they would spend only $85 in the coming week. Students who said they wanted to save money were more likely to predict they would spend less—but ended up spending the same amount as everyone else. U.S. homeowners renovating their kitchens planned to spend $18,658, but instead spent $38,769 (Kaheman, 2012). So just as we think we will complete tasks quickly, we think we will save our money. The difficulty lies in actually doing so. If Lao-tzu was right—"He who knows others is learned. He who knows himself is enlightened"—then most people, it would seem, are more learned than enlightened.

PREDICTING OUR FEELINGS

Many of life's big decisions involve predicting our future feelings. Would marrying this person lead to lifelong contentment? Would entering this profession make for satisfying work? Would going on this vacation produce a happy experience? Or would the likelier results be divorce, job burnout, and holiday disappointment?

Sometimes we know how we will feel—if we fail that exam, win that big game, or soothe our tensions with a half-hour jog. We know what exhilarates us and what makes us anxious or bored. Other times we may mispredict our responses. Asked how they would feel if asked sexually harassing questions on a job interview, most women studied by Julie Woodzicka and Marianne LaFrance (2001) said they would feel angry. When actually asked such questions, however, women more often experienced fear.

Studies of "affective forecasting" reveal that people have greatest difficulty predicting the *intensity* and the *duration* of their future emotions (Wilson & Gilbert, 2003). People mispredict how they would feel some time after a romantic breakup, receiving a gift, losing an election, winning a game, and being insulted (Gilbert & Ebert, 2002; Loewenstein & Schkade, 1999). Some examples:

- When young men are sexually aroused by erotic photographs, then exposed to a passionate date scenario in which their date asks them to "stop," they admit that they might not stop. If not shown sexually arousing pictures first, they are less likely to say they might be sexually aggressive. When not aroused, they easily mispredict how they will feel and act when aroused—which can lead to unexpected professions of love during lust, to unintended pregnancies, and to repeat offenses among sex abusers who have sincerely vowed "never again."
- Hungry shoppers are more likely to impulse buy ("Those doughnuts would be delicious!") than shoppers who have just enjoyed a quarter-pound blueberry muffin (Gilbert & Wilson, 2000). When you are hungry, you mispredict how gross those deep-fried doughnuts will seem when you are sated. When stuffed, you may underestimate how yummy a doughnut might be with a late-night glass of milk—a purchase whose appeal quickly fades when you've eaten one or two.
- When natural disasters such as hurricanes occur, people predict that their sadness will be greater if more people are killed. But after Hurricane Katrina struck in 2005, students' sadness was similar when it was believed that 50 people had been killed or 1,000 had been killed (Dunn & Ashton-James, 2008). What *did* influence how sad people felt? Seeing pictures of victims. No wonder poignant images of disasters on TV have so much influence on us.
- People overestimate how much their well-being would be affected both by bad events (a romantic breakup, failing to reach an athletic goal [Eastwick et al., 2007; van Dijk et al., 2008]) and good events (warmer winters, weight loss, more television channels, more free time). Even extreme events, such as winning a state lottery or suffering a paralyzing accident, impact long-term happiness less than most people suppose.

Our intuitive theory seems to be: We want. We get. We are happy. If that were true, this chapter would have fewer words. In reality, note Daniel Gilbert and Timothy Wilson (2000), we often "miswant." People who imagine an idyllic desert island holiday with sun, surf, and sand may be disappointed when they discover "how much they require daily structure, intellectual stimulation, or regular infusions of Pop Tarts." We think that if our candidate or team wins, we will be delighted for a long while. But study after study reveals our vulnerability to **impact bias**—overestimating the enduring impact of emotion-causing events. Faster than we expect, the emotional traces of such good tidings evaporate.

We are especially prone to impact bias after *negative* events. Let's make this personal. Gilbert and Wilson invite you to imagine how you might feel a year after losing your nondominant hand. Compared with today, how happy would you be?

You may have focused on what the calamity would mean: no clapping, no shoe tying, no competitive basketball, no speedy keyboarding. Although you likely would forever regret the loss, your general happiness some time after the event would be influenced by "two things: (a) the event, and (b) everything else" (Gilbert & Wilson, 2000). In focusing on the negative event, we discount the importance of everything else that contributes to happiness and thus overpredict our enduring misery. "Nothing that you focus on will make as much difference as you think," write researchers David Schkade and Daniel Kahneman (1998).

Moreover, say Wilson and Gilbert (2003), people neglect the speed and the power of their *coping mechanisms*, which include rationalizing, discounting, forgiving, and limiting emotional trauma. Because we are unaware of the speed and strength of our coping, we adapt to disabilities, romantic breakups, exam failures, layoffs, and personal and team defeats more readily than we would expect. Ironically, as Gilbert and colleagues report (2004), major negative events (which activate our psychological defenses) can be less enduringly distressing than minor irritations (which don't activate our defenses). We are, under most circumstances, amazingly resilient.

THE WISDOM AND ILLUSIONS OF SELF-ANALYSIS

To a striking extent, then, our intuitions are often dead wrong about what has influenced us and what we will feel and do. But let's not overstate the case. When the causes of our behavior are conspicuous and the correct explanation fits our intuition, our self-perceptions will be accurate (Gavanski & Hoffman, 1987). When the causes of behavior are obvious to an observer, they are usually obvious to us as well. Overall, the correlation between predicted feedings and actual feelings was .28—a modest, though far from perfect, correlation (Mathieu & Gosling, 2012).

We are unaware of much that goes on in our minds. Perception and memory studies show that we are more aware of the *results* of our thinking than of its process. Creative scientists and artists often cannot report the thought processes that produced their insights, although they have superb knowledge of the results.

Timothy Wilson (1985, 2002) offers a bold idea: Analyzing why we feel the way we do can actually make our judgments less accurate. In nine experiments, Wilson and colleagues (1989, 2008) found that the attitudes people consciously expressed toward things or people usually predicted their subsequent behavior reasonably well. Their attitude reports became useless, however, if participants were first asked to *analyze* their feelings. For example, dating couples' level of happiness with their relationship accurately predicted whether they would still be dating several months later. But participants who first listed all the reasons why their relationship was good or bad before rating their happiness were misled—their happiness ratings were useless in predicting the future of the relationship! Apparently, the process of dissecting the relationship drew attention to easily verbalized factors that were not as important as harder-to-verbalize happiness. We are often "strangers to ourselves," Wilson concluded (2002).

Such findings illustrate that we have a **dual attitude system,** say Wilson and colleagues (2000). Our automatic *implicit,* unconscious attitudes regarding someone or something often differ from our consciously controlled, *explicit* attitudes (Gawronski & Bodenhausen, 2006; Nosek, 2007). When someone says they make decisions by "trusting my gut," they're referring to their implicit attitudes (Kendrick & Olson, 2012). Although explicit attitudes may change with relative ease, notes Wilson, "implicit attitudes, like old habits, change more slowly." With repeated practice, however, new habitual attitudes can replace old ones.

impact bias
Overestimating the enduring impact of emotion-causing events.

"Weeping may tarry for the night, but joy comes with the morning."
—Psalm 30:5

dual attitude system
Differing implicit (automatic) and explicit (consciously controlled) attitudes toward the same object. Verbalized explicit attitudes may change with education and persuasion; implicit attitudes change slowly, with practice that forms new habits.

This research on the limits of our self-knowledge has two practical implications. The first is for psychological inquiry. *Self-reports are often untrustworthy.* Errors in self-understanding limit the scientific usefulness of subjective personal reports.

The second implication is for our everyday lives. Even if people report and interpret their experiences with complete honesty, that does not mean their reports are true. Personal testimonies are powerfully persuasive (as discussed in more detail in the chapter titled "Social Psychology in Court"). But they may also be wrong. Keeping this potential for error in mind can help us feel less intimidated by others and become less gullible.

SUMMING UP: Self-Concept: Who Am I?

- Our sense of self helps organize our thoughts and actions. When we process information with reference to ourselves, we remember it well (using our *self-schemas*). *Self-concept* consists of two elements: the *self-schemas* that guide our processing of self-relevant information and the *possible selves* that we dream of or dread.

- Cultures shape the self, too. Many people in *individualistic* Western cultures assume an *independent self.* Others, often in *collectivistic* cultures, assume a more

interdependent self. These contrasting ideas contribute to cultural differences in social behavior.

- Our self-knowledge is curiously flawed. We often do not know why we behave the way we do. When influences upon our behavior are not conspicuous enough for any observer to see, we, too, can miss them. The unconscious, implicit processes that control our behavior may differ from our conscious, explicit explanations of it.

WHAT IS THE NATURE AND MOTIVATING POWER OF SELF-ESTEEM?

Understand self-esteem and its implications for behavior and cognition.

Everyone desires self-esteem, which we are motivated to enhance. But can self-esteem sometimes be problematic?

self-esteem

A person's overall self-evaluation or sense of self-worth.

First, how do we decide how much self-esteem we have? Is **self-esteem** the sum of all our self-views across various domains? If we see ourselves as attractive, athletic, smart, and destined to be rich and loved, will we have high self-esteem? Yes, say Jennifer Crocker and Connie Wolfe (2001)—when we feel good about the domains (looks, smarts, or whatever) important to our self-esteem. "One person may have self-esteem that is highly contingent on doing well in school and being physically attractive, whereas another may have self-esteem that is contingent on being loved by God and adhering to moral standards." Thus, the first person will feel high self-esteem when made to feel smart and good-looking, the second person when made to feel moral.

But Jonathon Brown and Keith Dutton (1994) argue that this "bottom-up" view of self-esteem is not the whole story. The causal arrow, they believe, also goes the other way. People who value themselves in a general way—those with high self-esteem—are more likely to value their looks, abilities, and so forth. They are like new parents who, loving their infant, delight in the baby's fingers, toes, and hair: The parents do not first evaluate their infant's fingers or toes and then decide how much to value the whole baby.

Specific self-perceptions do have some influence, however. If you think you're good at math, you will be more likely to do well at math. Although general self-esteem does not predict academic performance very well, academic self-concept—whether you think you are good in school—does (Marsh & O'Mara, 2008). Of course, each causes the other: Doing well at math makes you think you are good at math, which then motivates you to do even better. If you want to encourage someone (or yourself!), it's better if your praise is specific ("You're good at math") instead of general ("You're great") and if your kind words reflect true ability and performance ("You really improved on your last test") rather than unrealistic optimism ("You can do anything"). Feedback is best when it is true and specific (Swann et al., 2007).

One intriguing study examined the effects of very general feedback on self-esteem. Imagine you're getting your grade back for the first test in a psychology class. When you see your grade, you groan—you're hovering somewhere between a D and an F. But then you get an encouraging email with some review questions for the class and this message: "Students who have high self-esteem not only get better grades, but they remain self-confident and assured. . . . Bottom line: Hold your head—and your self-esteem—high." Another group of students instead get a message about taking personal control of their performance, or receive review questions only. So which group did better on the final exam? To the surprise of the researchers, the students whose self-esteem was boosted did by far the worst on the final—in fact, they flunked it (Forsyth et al., 2007). Struggling students told to feel good about themselves, the researchers muse, may have thought, "I'm already great—why study?"

Self-Esteem Motivation

Most people are extremely motivated to maintain their self-esteem. In fact, college students prefer a boost to their self-esteem to eating their favorite food, engaging in their favorite sexual activity, seeing a best friend, drinking alcohol, or receiving a paycheck (Bushman et al., 2011). So, somewhat incredibly, self-esteem was more important than sex, pizza, and beer!

What happens when your self-esteem is threatened—for example, by a failure or an unflattering comparison with someone else? When brothers have markedly different ability levels—for example, one is a great athlete and the other is not—they report not getting along well (Tesser, 1988). Dutch university students who experienced a "double whammy"

Among sibling relationships, the threat to self-esteem is greatest for an older child with a highly capable younger brother or sister.
Fancy/Hero/Corbis/Glow Images

of low self-evaluation and negative feedback felt more Schadenfreude (joy at another's misfortune) when they watched a young woman sing horribly out of tune in an audition for the Dutch version of "American Idol" (van Dijk et al., 2012). Misery loves to laugh at others' misery.

Self-esteem threats also occur among friends, whose success can be more threatening than that of strangers (Zuckerman & Jost, 2001). Self-esteem level also makes a difference: High self-esteem people usually react to a self-esteem threat by compensating for it (blaming someone else or trying harder next time). These reactions help them preserve their positive feelings about themselves. Low self-esteem people, however, are more likely to blame themselves or give up (VanDellen et al., 2011).

What underlies the motive to maintain or enhance self-esteem? Mark Leary (1998, 2004b, 2007) believes that self-esteem is similar to a fuel gauge. Relationships enable surviving and thriving, so the self-esteem gauge alerts us to threatened social rejection, motivating us to act with greater sensitivity to others' expectations. Studies confirm that social rejection lowers self-esteem and makes people more eager for approval. Spurned or jilted, we feel unattractive or inadequate. Like a blinking dashboard light, this pain can motivate action such as self-improvement or a search for acceptance and inclusion elsewhere.

terror management theory
Proposes that people exhibit self-protective emotional and cognitive responses (including adhering more strongly to their cultural worldviews and prejudices) when confronted with reminders of their mortality.

Jeff Greenberg (2008) offers another perspective, called **terror management theory,** which argues that humans must find ways to manage their overwhelming fear of death. If self-esteem were only about acceptance, he counters, why do "people strive to be great rather than to just be accepted"? The reality of our own death, he argues, motivates us to gain recognition from our work and values. There's a worm in the apple, however: Not everyone can achieve such recognition, which is exactly why it is valuable, and why self-esteem can never be wholly unconditional (or not based on anything, such as when parents say, "You're special just for being you"). To feel our lives are not in vain, Greenberg maintains, we must continually pursue self-esteem by meeting the standards of our societies.

However, actively pursuing self-esteem can backfire. Jennifer Crocker and colleagues found that students whose self-worth was contingent on external sources (such as grades or others' opinions) experienced more stress, anger, relationship problems, drug and alcohol use, and eating disorders than did those whose sense of self-worth was rooted more in internal sources, such as personal virtues (Crocker, 2002; Crocker & Luhtanen, 2003; Crocker & Park, 2004; Crocker & Knight, 2005).

Ironically, note Crocker and Lora Park (2004), those who pursue self-esteem, perhaps by seeking to become beautiful, rich, or popular, may lose sight of what really makes them feel good about themselves. University students who tried to impress their roommates by emphasizing their good qualities and hiding their bad ones found that their roommates actually liked them *less,* which then undermined their self-esteem (Canevello & Crocker, 2011). Pursuing self-esteem, Crocker explains, is like reaching into a small hole in a barrel to grasp a delicious apple—and then getting it stuck because your hand's tight grip has made it too big for the hole (Crocker, 2011). When we focus on boosting our self-esteem, we may become less open to criticism, less likely to empathize with others, and more pressured to succeed at activities rather than enjoy them. Over time, such pursuit of self-esteem can fail to satisfy our deep needs for competence, affiliation, and autonomy. So instead of reaching for the apple and failing, Crocker observes, it's better to emulate Johnny Appleseed, who planted seeds so others could eat apples—not so he could eat them himself. This approach of compassion, she found, was actually more likely to lead to the higher self-esteem people sought. For example, college students who embraced compassionate goals toward their roommates ("I want to be supportive of my roommate") achieved better relationships with them and subsequently enjoyed higher self-esteem (Canevello & Crocker, 2011). A similar approach works for our own views of ourselves. Kristin Neff (2011) calls it self-compassion—leaving behind comparisons with others and instead treating ourselves with kindness. As an Indian proverb puts it, "There is nothing noble in being superior to some other person. The true nobility is in being superior to your previous self."

The Trade-off of Low vs. High Self-Esteem

People low in self-esteem are more vulnerable to anxiety, loneliness, and eating disorders. When feeling bad or threatened, those low in self-esteem often take a negative view of everything. They notice and remember others' worst behaviors and think their partners don't love them (Murray et al., 2002; Vorauer & Quesnel, 2013). Although people with low self-esteem do not choose less-desirable partners, they are quick to believe that their partners are criticizing or rejecting them. Perhaps as a result, those low in self-esteem are less satisfied with their relationships (Fincham & Bradbury, 1993). They may also be more likely to leave those relationships. Low-self-esteem undergraduates decided not to stay with roommates who saw them in a positive light (Swann & Pelham, 2002). Unfortunately, trying to boost low self-esteem through repeating positive phrases (such as "I'm a loveable person") backfires: It actually makes low self-esteem people feel worse (Wood et al., 2009). Those low in self-esteem also don't want to hear positive things about negative experiences (such as "at least you learned something.") Instead, they prefer understanding responses, even if they are negative (such as "that really sucks." [Marigold et al., 2014]).

© Mike Twohy/The New Yorker Collection/www.cartoonbank.com

People with low self-esteem also experience more problems in life—they make less money, abuse drugs, and are more likely to be depressed (Orth & Robins, 2013; Salmela-Aro & Nurmi, 2007). Several studies took the crucial step of following people as they grew older (called a **longitudinal study**), finding that those who had low self-esteem as teens were more likely to later be depressed, suggesting that low self-esteem causes depression instead of the other way around (Sowislo & Orth, 2013). A correlation between two variables is sometimes caused by a third factor. Maybe people low in self-esteem also faced poverty as children, experienced sexual abuse, or had parents who used drugs—all possible causes of later struggling. Sure enough, a study that controlled for these factors found that the link between self-esteem and negative outcomes disappeared (Boden et al., 2008). Low self-esteem was seemingly a symptom of an underlying disease—in this case, a tough childhood.

longitudinal study
Research in which the same people are studied over an extended period of time.

When good things happen, people with high self-esteem are more likely to savor and sustain the good feelings (Wood et al., 2003). "Believing one has more talents and positive qualities than one's peers allows one to feel good about oneself and to enter the stressful circumstances of daily life with the resources conferred by a positive sense of self," noted Shelley Taylor and co-researchers (2003b). As research on depression and anxiety suggests, self-serving perceptions can be useful. It may be strategic to believe we are smarter, stronger, and more socially successful than we are. Belief in our superiority can also motivate us to achieve—creating a self-fulfilling prophecy—and can sustain our hope through difficult times (Willard & Gramzow, 2009).

High self-esteem has other benefits—it fosters initiative, resilience, and pleasant feelings (Baumeister et al., 2003). Yet teen gang leaders, extreme ethnocentrists, terrorists, and men in prison for committing violent crimes also tend to have higher than average self-esteem (Bushman & Baumeister, 2002; Dawes, 1994, 1998). "Hitler had very high self-esteem," note Baumeister and coauthors (2003). Nor is self-esteem the key to success: Self-esteem does not cause better academic achievement or superior work performance (Baumeister et al., 2003). Can you guess which ethnic group in the United States has the lowest self-esteem? It's Asian-Americans, who achieve the most academically as students and earn the highest median income as adults. As you learned earlier, Asian cultures place more emphasis on self-improvement instead of on self-esteem, and that emphasis may pay off with better performance. "The enthusiastic claims of the self-esteem movement mostly range from fantasy to hogwash," says Baumeister (1996), who suspects he has "probably published more studies on self-esteem than anybody else. . . . The effects of self-esteem are small, limited, and not all good." Folks with high self-esteem, he reports, are more likely to be obnoxious, to interrupt, and to talk at people rather than with them (in contrast to the more shy, modest, folks with low self-esteem). "My conclusion is that self-control is worth 10 times as much as self-esteem."

NARCISSISM: SELF-ESTEEM'S CONCEITED SISTER

High self-esteem becomes especially problematic if it crosses over into narcissism, or having an inflated sense of self. Most people with high self-esteem value both individual achievement and relationships with others. Narcissists usually have high self-esteem, but they are missing the piece about caring for others (Campbell et al., 2007; Jones & Brunell, 2014). Although narcissists can be outgoing and charming early on, their self-centeredness often leads to relationship problems in the long run (Campbell, 2005). The link between narcissism and problematic social relations led Delroy Paulhus and Kevin Williams (2002) to include narcissism in "The Dark Triad" of negative traits, along with Machiavellianism (manipulativeness) and antisocial psychopathy.

In a series of experiments conducted by Brad Bushman and Roy Baumeister (1998), undergraduate volunteers wrote essays and received rigged feedback that said, "This is one of the worst essays I've read!" Those who scored high on narcissism were much more likely to retaliate, blasting painful noise into the headphones of the student they believed had criticized them. Narcissists weren't aggressive toward someone who praised them ("great essay!"). It was the insult that set them off. But what about self-esteem? Maybe only the "insecure" narcissists—those low in self-esteem—would lash out. But that's not how it turned out—instead, the students high in both self-esteem and narcissism were the most aggressive. The same was true in a classroom setting—those who were high in both self-esteem and narcissism were the most likely to retaliate against a classmate's criticism by giving him or her a bad grade (Bushman et al., 2009; Figure 5). Narcissists are especially likely to lash out when the insult is delivered publicly—and thus punctures their carefully constructed bubble of superiority. For that, someone must pay (Ferriday et al., 2011). It's true that narcissists can be charming and entertaining. But as one wit has said, "God help you if you cross them."

What about the idea that an overinflated ego is just a cover for deep-seated insecurity? Do narcissistic people actually hate themselves "deep down inside"? Recent studies show that the answer is *no*. People who score high on measures of narcissistic personality traits also score high on measures of self-esteem. In case narcissists were claiming high self-esteem just for show, researchers also asked undergraduates to play a computer game where they had to press a key as quickly as possible to match the word "me" with words such as "good," "wonderful," "great," and "right," and words such as "bad," "awful," "terrible," and "wrong." High scorers on the narcissism scale were faster than others to

"After all these years, I'm sorry to say, my recommendation is this: Forget about self-esteem and concentrate more on self-control and self-discipline. Recent work suggests this would be good for the individual and good for society."

—Roy Baumeister, 2005

FIGURE :: 5

Narcissism, Self-Esteem, and Aggression

Narcissism and self-esteem interact to influence aggression. In an experiment by Brad Bushman and colleagues (2009), the recipe for retaliation against a critical classmate required both narcissism and high self-esteem.

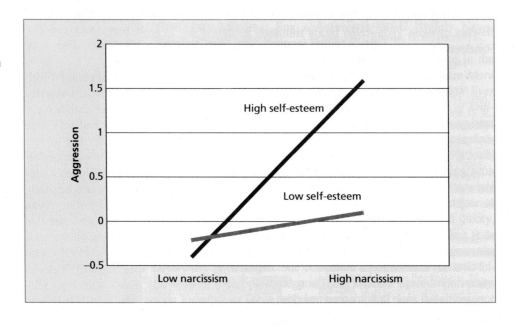

associate themselves with good words, and slower than others to pair themselves with bad words (Campbell et al., 2007). And narcissists were even faster to identify with words such as "outspoken," "dominant," and "assertive." Although it might be comforting to think that an arrogant classmate is just covering for his insecurity, chances are that deep down inside he thinks he's *awesome*.

Has the culture's growing individualism also promoted more narcissism? It appears so. Narcissism scores rose over time on college campuses from Alabama to Maryland to California (Stewart & Bernhardt, 2010; Twenge & Foster, 2008, 2010). Rising narcissism is emerging in other cultures as well, appearing among residents of China (Cai et al., 2011), South Korea (Lee et al., 2014), and New Zealand (Wilson & Sibley, 2011). Narcissism correlates with materialism, the desire to be famous, inflated expectations, fewer committed relationships and more "hooking up," more gambling, and more cheating—all of which have also risen as narcissism has increased (Twenge & Campbell, 2009). Narcissism is also linked to a lack of empathy—the ability to take someone else's perspective and be concerned about their problems—and empathy has dropped precipitously among college students. Sara Konrath and her colleagues (2011) speculate that today's generation may be so wrapped up in online interaction that their in-person interaction skills have atrophied. Or, they say, empathy might have declined because young people today are "feeling too busy on their paths to success," single-mindedly concentrating on their own achievement because the world is now so competitive. Yet, ironically, those high in narcissism and low in empathy are less—not more—successful in the long run, making lower grades in college and performing poorly at work (Judge et al., 2006; Robins & Beer, 2001).

Narcissists seem to be aware of their own narcissism. Simply asking people if they agree with the statement "I am a narcissist" predicts narcissistic behavior nearly as well as the standard 40-item measure (Konrath et al., 2014). Narcissists realize that they see themselves more positively than others see them and admit that they are arrogant and exaggerate their abilities (Carlson et al., 2011). They also recognize that they make good first impressions but are often actively disliked in the long run (Paulhus, 1998; Paulhus et al., 2013). "Early in life I had to choose between honest arrogance and hypocritical humility," observed Frank Lloyd Wright. "I chose honest arrogance and have seen no occasion to change."

Self-Efficacy

Stanford psychologist Albert Bandura (1997, 2000, 2008) captured the power of positive thinking in his research and theorizing about **self-efficacy** (how competent we feel on a task). Believing in our own competence and effectiveness pays dividends (Bandura et al., 1999; Maddux & Gosselin, 2003). Children and adults with strong feelings of self-efficacy are more persistent, less anxious, and less depressed. They also live healthier lives and are more academically successful.

In everyday life, self-efficacy leads us to set challenging goals and to persist. More than 100 studies show that self-efficacy predicts worker productivity (Stajkovic & Luthans, 1998). The results of 241 studies show that performance self-efficacy is one of the strongest predictors of students' GPAs in college (Richardson et al., 2012). When problems arise, a strong sense of self-efficacy leads people to stay calm and seek solutions rather than ruminate on their inadequacy. Competence plus persistence equals accomplishment. And with accomplishment, self-confidence grows. Self-efficacy, like self-esteem, grows with hard-won achievements.

Self-efficacy and self-esteem sound similar but are different concepts. If you believe you can do something, that's self-efficacy. If you like yourself overall, that's self-esteem. When you were a child, your parents may have encouraged you by saying things such as, "You're special!" (intended to build self-esteem) or "I know you can do it!" (intended to build self-efficacy). One study showed that self-efficacy feedback ("You tried really hard") led to better performance than self-esteem feedback ("You're really smart"). Children told they were smart were afraid to try again—maybe they wouldn't look so

self-efficacy
A sense that one is competent and effective, distinguished from self-esteem, which is one's sense of self-worth. A sharpshooter in the military might feel high self-efficacy and low self-esteem.

Someone who thinks, "If I work hard, I can swim fast" has high self-efficacy. Someone who thinks, "I am a great swimmer" has high self-esteem.
Fuse/Getty Images

smart next time. Those praised for working hard, however, knew they could exert more effort again (Mueller & Dweck, 1998). If you want to encourage someone, focus on her self-efficacy, not her self-esteem.

SUMMING UP: What Is the Nature and Motivating Power of Self-Esteem?

- *Self-esteem* is the overall sense of self-worth we use to appraise our traits and abilities. Our self-concepts are determined by multiple influences, including the roles we play, the comparisons we make, our social identities, how we perceive others appraising us, and our experiences of success and failure.

- Self-esteem motivation influences our cognitive processes: Facing failure, high-self-esteem people sustain their self-worth by perceiving other people as failing, too, and by exaggerating their superiority over others.

- Although high self-esteem is generally more beneficial than low, researchers have found that people high in both self-esteem and narcissism are the most aggressive. Someone with a big ego who is threatened or deflated by social rejection is potentially aggressive.

- *Self-efficacy* is the belief that one is effective and competent and can do something. Unlike high self-esteem, high self-efficacy is consistently linked to success.

WHAT IS SELF-SERVING BIAS?

Explain self-serving bias and its adaptive and maladaptive aspects.

Most of us have a good reputation with ourselves. In studies of self-esteem, even low-scoring people respond in the midrange of possible scores. (Someone with low self-esteem responds to statements such as "I have good ideas" with a qualifying adjective, such as "somewhat" or "sometimes.") In a study including 53 nations, the average self-esteem score was above the midpoint in every country (Schmitt & Allik, 2005). In recent samples of U.S. college students, the most common score on a self-esteem measure was the maximum—in effect, "perfect" self-esteem (Gentile et al., 2010). One of social psychology's most provocative yet firmly established conclusions is the potency of **self-serving bias**—a tendency to perceive oneself favorably.

self-serving bias
The tendency to perceive oneself favorably.

Explaining Positive and Negative Events

Many dozens of experiments have found that people accept credit when told they have succeeded. They attribute the success to their ability and effort, but they attribute failure to external factors, such as bad luck or the problem's inherent "impossibility" (Campbell & Sedikides, 1999). Similarly, in explaining their victories, athletes commonly credit themselves, but they attribute losses to something else: bad breaks, bad referee calls, or the other team's super effort or dirty play (Grove et al., 1991; Lalonde, 1992; Mullen & Riordan, 1988). And how much responsibility do you suppose car drivers tend to accept for their accidents? On insurance forms, drivers have described their accidents by writing, "An invisible car came out of nowhere, struck my car, and vanished"; "As I reached an intersection, a hedge sprang up, obscuring my vision, and I did not see the other car"; and "A pedestrian hit me and went under my car" (*Toronto News,* 1977).

> "Victory finds a hundred fathers but defeat is an orphan."
>
> —Count Galeazzo Ciano, *The Ciano Diaries,* 1938

Situations that combine skill and chance (games, exams, and job applications) are especially prone to the phenomenon. When you win at Scrabble, it's because of your verbal dexterity; when you lose, it's because "Who could get anywhere with a *Q* but no *U?*" Politicians similarly tend to attribute their wins to themselves (hard work, constituent service, reputation, and strategy) and their losses to factors beyond their control (their district's party makeup, their opponent's name, and political trends) (Kingdon, 1967). When corporate profits are up, the CEOs welcome big bonuses for their managerial skill. When profits turn to losses, well, what could you expect in a down economy? This phenomenon of **self-serving attributions** (attributing positive outcomes to oneself and negative outcomes to something else) is one of the most potent of human biases (Mezulis et al., 2004). That might be for a good reason: Making self-serving attributions activates brain areas associated with reward and pleasure (Seidel et al., 2010).

self-serving attributions
A form of self-serving bias; the tendency to attribute positive outcomes to oneself and negative outcomes to other factors.

Self-serving attributions contribute to marital discord, worker dissatisfaction, and bargaining impasses (Kruger & Gilovich, 1999). Small wonder that divorced people usually blame their partner for the breakup (Gray & Silver, 1990), or that managers often blame poor performance on workers' lack of ability or effort while workers blame external factors such as excessive workload or difficult co-workers (Imai, 1994; Rice, 1985). Small wonder, too, that people evaluate pay raises as fairer when they receive a bigger raise than most of their co-workers (Diekmann et al., 1997).

We help maintain our positive self-images by associating ourselves with success and distancing ourselves from failure. For example, "I got an A on my econ test" versus "The prof gave me a C on my history exam." Blaming failure or rejection on something external, even another's prejudice, is less depressing than seeing oneself as undeserving (Major et al., 2003). Journalists were more likely to write that "we" (people like them) had a positive outcome but "they" (those different from them) had a negative one (Sendén et al., 2014). Most people will, however, acknowledge their distant past failings—those by their "former" self, note Anne Wilson and Michael Ross (2001). Describing their old precollege selves, their University of Waterloo students offered nearly as many negative as positive statements. When describing their present selves, they offered three times more positive statements. "I've learned and grown, and I'm a better person today," most people surmise. Chumps yesterday, champs today.

Ironically, we are even biased against seeing our own bias. People claim they avoid self-serving bias themselves but readily acknowledge that others commit this bias (Pronin et al., 2002). This "bias blind spot" can have serious consequences during conflicts. If you're negotiating with your roommate over who does household chores, and you believe your

Self-serving bias at work: If his team loses the game, the player getting the penalty might blame the referee's call instead of his own lackluster play.
Brand X Pictures/PNC/PunchStock

roommate has a biased view of the situation, you're much more likely to become angry (Pronin & Ross, 2006). Apparently we see ourselves as objective and everyone else as biased. No wonder we fight, because we're each convinced we're "right" and free from bias. As the T-shirt slogan says, "Everyone is entitled to my opinion."

Is self-serving bias universal, or are people in collectivistic cultures immune? Those in collectivistic cultures do associate themselves with positive words and valued traits (Gaertner et al., 2008; Yamaguchi et al., 2007). However, in some studies, collectivists are less likely to self-enhance by believing they are better than others (Church et al., 2014; Falk et al., 2009; Heine & Hamamura, 2007), particularly in individualistic domains (Sedikides et al., 2003, 2005).

Can We All Be Better Than Average?

Self-serving bias also appears when people compare themselves with others. If the sixth-century B.C. Chinese philosopher Lao-tzu was right that "at no time in the world will a man who is sane over-reach himself, over-spend himself, over-rate himself," then most of us are a little insane. On *subjective, socially desirable,* and *common dimensions,* most people see themselves as better than the average person. Compared with people in general, most people see themselves as more ethical, more competent at their job, friendlier, more intelligent, better looking, less prejudiced, healthier, and even more insightful and less biased in their self-assessments. Even men convicted of violent crimes rated themselves as more moral, kind, and trustworthy than most people (Sedikides et al., 2014). (See "Focus On: Self-Serving Bias—How Do I Love Me? Let Me Count the Ways.")

focus ON Self-Serving Bias—How Do I Love Me? Let Me Count the Ways

"The one thing that unites all human beings, regardless of age, gender, religion, economic status, or ethnic background," notes columnist Dave Barry (1998), "is that deep down inside, we all believe that we are above average drivers." We also believe we are above average on most any other subjective and desirable trait. Among the many faces of self-serving bias are these:

- *Ethics.* Most businesspeople see themselves as more ethical than the average businessperson (Baumhart, 1968; Brenner & Molander, 1977). One national survey asked, "How would you rate your own morals and values on a scale from 1 to 100 (100 being perfect)?" Fifty percent of people rated themselves 90 or above; only 11 percent said 74 or less (Lovett, 1997).

- *Professional competence.* In one survey, 90 percent of business managers rated their performance as superior to their average peer (French, 1968). In Australia, 86 percent of people rated their job performance as above average, and only 1 percent as below average (Headey & Wearing, 1987). Most surgeons believe *their* patients' mortality rate to be lower than average (Gawande, 2002).

- *Virtues.* In the Netherlands, most high school students rate themselves as more honest, persistent, original, friendly, and reliable than the average high school student (Hoorens, 1993, 1995).

- *Intelligence.* Most people perceive themselves as more intelligent, better looking, and much less prejudiced than their average peer (*Public Opinion,* 1984; Watt & Larkin, 2010; Wylie, 1979). When someone outperforms them, people tend to think of the other as a genius (Lassiter & Munhall, 2001).

- *Parental support.* Most adults believe they support their aging parents more than do their siblings (Lerner et al., 1991).

- *Health.* Los Angeles residents view themselves as healthier than most of their neighbors, and most college students believe they will outlive their actuarially predicted age of death by approximately 10 years (Larwood, 1978; Snyder, 1978).

- *Attractiveness.* Is it your experience, as it is mine [DM], that most photos of you seem not to do you justice? One experiment showed people a lineup of faces—one their own, the others being their face morphed into those of less and more attractive faces (Epley & Whitchurch, 2008). When asked which was their actual face, people tended to identify an attractively enhanced version of their face.

- *Driving.* Most drivers—even most drivers who have been hospitalized for accidents—believe themselves to be safer and more skilled than the average driver (Guerin, 1994; McKenna & Myers, 1997; Svenson, 1981). Dave Barry was right.

Every community, it seems, is like Garrison Keillor's fictional Lake Wobegon, where "all the women are strong, all the men are good-looking, and all the children are above average." Many people believe that they will become even more above average in the future—if I'm good now, I will be even better soon, they seem to think (Kanten & Teigen, 2008). The phenomenon lurks in Freud's joke about the husband who told his wife, "If one of us dies, I shall move to Paris."

The self-serving bias is also common in marriages. In a 2008 survey, 49 percent of married men said they did half to most of the child care. But only 31 percent of wives said their husbands did this much. In the same survey, 70 percent of women said they do most of the cooking, but 56 percent of the men said *they* do most of the cooking (Galinsky et al., 2009). The general rule: Group members' estimates of how much they contribute to a joint task typically sum to more than 100 percent (Savitsky et al., 2005).

"CHANGING THE CHANNELS IS NOT PART OF SHARING THE HOUSEWORK."

Reprinted with permission of Cartoonstock. www.CartoonStock.com.

My wife and I [DM] used to pitch our laundry on the floor next to our bedroom clothes hamper. In the morning, one of us would put it in. When she suggested that I take more responsibility for this, I thought, "Huh? I already do it 75 percent of the time." So I asked her how often she thought she picked up the clothes. "Oh," she replied, "about 75 percent of the time."

Within commonly considered domains, subjective behavioral dimensions (such as "disciplined") trigger even greater self-serving bias than observable behavioral dimensions (such as "punctual"). Seventy-six percent of college students in 2009 believed they were above average in "drive to achieve" (a subjective attribute that's difficult to measure), but only 44 percent thought they were above average in the more quantifiable realm of math ability (Twenge et al., 2012). Subjective qualities give us leeway in constructing our own definition of success (Dunning et al., 1989, 1991). Rating my "athletic ability," I [JT] ponder my swimming skills, not the summer evenings I spent cowering in the softball outfield praying no one would hit the ball my way. Assessing my "leadership ability," I conjure up an image of a great leader whose style is similar to mine. By defining ambiguous criteria in our own terms, we can all see ourselves as relatively successful. In one College Entrance Examination Board survey of 829,000 high school seniors, *none* rated themselves below average in "ability to get along with others" (a subjective, desirable trait), 60 percent rated themselves in the top 10 percent, and 25 percent saw themselves among the top 1 percent! In a 2013 survey in Britain, 98 percent of 17- to 25-year-olds believed they were good drivers—even though 20 percent get into an accident within six months of passing their driving test (AFP, 2013).

Researchers have wondered: Do people really believe their above-average self-estimates? Is their self-serving bias partly a function of how the questions are phrased (Krizan & Suls, 2008)? When Elanor Williams and Thomas Gilovich (2008) had people bet real money when estimating their relative performance on tests, they found that, yes, "people truly believe their self-enhancing self-assessments."

Unrealistic Optimism

Optimism predisposes a positive approach to life. "The optimist," notes H. Jackson Brown (1990, p. 79), "goes to the window every morning and says, 'Good morning, God.' The pessimist goes to the window and says, 'Good God, morning.'"

Studies of more than 90,000 people across 22 cultures reveal that most humans are more disposed to optimism than pessimism (Fischer & Chalmers, 2008; Shepperd et al., 2013, 2015). Indeed, many of us have what researcher Neil Weinstein (1980, 1982) terms "an unrealistic optimism about future life events." In a 2006–2008 worldwide poll, most people expected their lives to improve more in the next 5 years than they did in the past 5 years (Deaton, 2009)—an especially striking expectation considering the worldwide recession that followed. Partly because of their relative pessimism about others' fates

(Hoorens et al., 2008; Shepperd, 2003), students perceive themselves as far more likely than their classmates to get a good job, draw a good salary, and own a home. They also see themselves as far *less* likely to experience negative events, such as developing a drinking problem, having a heart attack before age 40, or being fired. Adult women are much more likely to be unduly optimistic than pessimistic about their relative risk of breast cancer (Waters et al., 2011). Football fans believe their favorite team has a 70 percent chance of winning their next game (Massey et al., 2011).

Unrealistic optimism appears to be on the rise. In 2012, two-thirds of American high school seniors predicted that they would be "very good" workers as adults—the equivalent of giving themselves five stars out of five. Only half of students had such optimistic expectations in the 1970s (Twenge & Campbell, 2008). Even more striking, 56 percent of high school seniors believed that they would earn a graduate degree—even though only 9 percent were likely to actually do so (Reynolds et al., 2006). Although aiming high has benefits for success, those who aim too high may struggle with depression as they learn to adjust their goals to more realistic heights (Wrosch & Miller, 2009).

Illusory optimism increases our vulnerability. Believing ourselves immune to misfortune, we do not take sensible precautions. Sexually active undergraduate women who don't consistently use contraceptives perceived themselves, compared with other women at their university, as much *less* vulnerable to unwanted pregnancy (Burger & Burns, 1988). People trying to quit smoking who believe they are above average in willpower are more likely to keep cigarettes around and stand near others who are smoking—behaviors likely to lead to a relapse into smoking (Nordgren et al., 2009). Elderly drivers who rated themselves as "above average" were four times more likely than more modest drivers to flunk a driving test and be rated "unsafe" (Freund et al., 2005). Students who enter university with inflated assessments of their academic ability often suffer deflating self-esteem and well-being and are more likely to drop out (Robins & Beer, 2001). In perhaps the most wide-ranging example, many home buyers, mortgage lenders, and investors in the mid-2000s displayed unrealistic optimism in their belief that "housing never goes down," accumulating large amounts of debt. The eventual result was a wave of home foreclosures that spawned the 2007–2009 recession, the most severe economic downturn since the Great Depression. Even the seventeenth-century economist Adam Smith, a defender of human economic rationality, foresaw that people would overestimate their chances of gain. This "absurd presumption in their own good fortune," he said, arises from "the overweening conceit which the greater part of men have of their own abilities" (Spiegel, 1971, p. 243).

On the other hand, optimism definitely beats pessimism in promoting self-efficacy, health, and well-being (Armor & Taylor, 1996; Segerstrom, 2001). As natural optimists, most people believe they will be happier with their lives in the future—a belief that surely helps create happiness in the present (Robinson & Ryff, 1999). Pessimists even die sooner—apparently because they are more likely to suffer unfortunate accidents (Peterson et al., 2001). If our optimistic prehistoric ancestors were more likely than their pessimistic neighbors to surmount challenges and survive, then small wonder that we are disposed to optimism (Haselton & Nettle, 2006).

Yet a dash of realism—or what Julie Norem (2000) calls **defensive pessimism**—can sometimes save us from the perils of unrealistic optimism. Defensive pessimism anticipates problems and motivates effective coping. As a Chinese proverb says, "Be prepared for danger

> "Views of the future are so rosy that they would make Pollyanna blush."
>
> —Shelley E. Taylor,
> *Positive Illusions*, 1989

> "O God, give us grace to accept with serenity the things that cannot be changed, courage to change the things which should be changed, and the wisdom to distinguish the one from the other."
>
> —Reinhold Niebuhr,
> *The Serenity Prayer*, 1943

defensive pessimism
The adaptive value of anticipating problems and harnessing one's anxiety to motivate effective action.

while staying in peace." Students who exhibit excess optimism (as many students destined for low grades do) benefit from some self-doubt, which motivates study (Prohaska, 1994; Sparrell & Shrauger, 1984). Students who are overconfident tend to underprepare, whereas their equally able but less confident peers study harder and get higher grades (Goodhart, 1986; Norem & Cantor, 1986; Showers & Ruben, 1987). Viewing things in a more immediate, realistic way often helps. Students in one experiment were wildly optimistic in predicting their test performance when the test was hypothetical, but they were surprisingly accurate when the test was imminent (Armor & Sackett, 2006). Believing you're great when nothing can prove you wrong is one thing, but with an evaluation fast approaching, it's best not to look like a bragging fool.

Illusory optimism: Most couples marry feeling confident of long-term love. Actually, in individualistic cultures, half of marriages fail.
Larry Dale Gordon/Getty Images

It's also important to listen to criticism. "One gentle rule I often tell my students," writes David Dunning (2006), "is that if two people independently give them the same piece of negative feedback, they should at least consider the possibility that it might be true." So, there is a power to negative as well as positive thinking. The moral: Success in school and beyond requires enough optimism to sustain hope and enough pessimism to motivate concern.

False Consensus and Uniqueness

We have a curious tendency to enhance our self-images by overestimating or underestimating how much others think and act as we do. On matters of *opinion,* we find support for our positions by overestimating how much others agree—a phenomenon called the **false consensus effect** (Krueger & Clement, 1994b; Marks & Miller, 1987; Mullen & Goethals, 1990). Facebook users were 90 percent accurate at estimating when they agreed with their friends on political and other issues, but they were only 41 percent accurate in estimating disagreement (Goel et al., 2010). In other words, they thought their friends agreed with them more than they actually did. It goes beyond politics: When California college students thought about their favorite celebrity, they significantly underestimated how much others would express dislike for their idolized star (Bui, 2012). White Australians prejudiced against Aborigines were more likely to believe that other Whites were also prejudiced (Watt & Larkin, 2010). The sense we make of the world seems like common sense.

false consensus effect
The tendency to overestimate the commonality of one's opinions and one's undesirable or unsuccessful behaviors.

When we behave badly or fail in a task, we reassure ourselves by thinking that such lapses also are common. After one person lies to another, the liar begins to perceive the *other* person as dishonest (Sagarin et al., 1998). If we feel sexual desire toward another, we may overestimate the other's reciprocal desire. We guess that others think and act as we do: "I lie, but doesn't everyone?" If we cheat on our income taxes, smoke, or enhance our appearance, we are likely to overestimate the number of other people who do likewise. As former *Baywatch* actor David Hasselhoff said, "I have had Botox. Everyone has!" "We don't see things as they are," says a proverb. "We see things as we are."

Dawes (1990) proposes that this false consensus may occur because we generalize from a limited sample, which prominently includes ourselves. Lacking other information, why not "project" ourselves; why not impute our own knowledge to others and use our responses as a clue to their likely responses? Also, we're more likely to spend time with people who share our attitudes and behaviors and, consequently, to judge the world from the people we know. Small wonder that Germans tend to think that the typical European looks rather German, whereas the Portuguese see Europeans as looking more Portuguese (Imhoff et al., 2011).

Do you choose a designated driver when you go out? The false uniqueness effect might lead you to think this virtue of yours is exceptional, even if it is not.
ranplett/Getty Images

On matters of *ability* or when we behave well or successfully, however, a **false uniqueness effect** more often occurs (Goethals et al., 1991). We serve our self-image by seeing our talents and moral behaviors as relatively unusual. Dutch college students preferred being part of a larger group in matters of opinion such as politics (false consensus) but wanted to be part of a smaller group in matters of taste such as musical preferences (false uniqueness; Spears et al., 2009). After all, a band isn't cool anymore if too many people like it. Female college students who choose a designated driver underestimated how many other women take the same precaution (Benton et al., 2008). Thus, we may see our failings as relatively normal and our virtues as relatively exceptional.

To sum up, self-serving bias appears as self-serving attributions, self-congratulatory comparisons, illusory optimism, and false consensus for one's failings (Figure 6).

false uniqueness effect
The tendency to underestimate the commonality of one's abilities and one's desirable or successful behaviors.

Explaining Self-Serving Bias

Why do people perceive themselves in self-enhancing ways? Perhaps the self-serving bias occurs because of errors in how we process and remember information about ourselves. Comparing ourselves with others requires us to notice, assess, and recall their behavior and ours. This creates multiple opportunities for flaws in our information processing (Chambers & Windschitl, 2004). Recall that married people gave themselves credit for doing more housework than their spouses did. That might occur because we remember what we've done but not what our partner did (Ross & Sicoly, 1979). I [DM] could easily picture myself picking up the laundry off the bedroom floor, but I was less aware of the times when I absentmindedly overlooked it.

Are biased perceptions, then, simply a perceptual error, an emotion-free glitch in how we process information? Or are self-serving *motives* also involved? It's now clear from research that we have multiple motives. Questing for self-knowledge, we're motivated to *assess our competence* (Dunning, 1995). Questing for self-confirmation, we're motivated to *verify our self-conceptions* (Sanitioso et al., 1990; Swann, 1996, 1997). Questing for self-affirmation, we're especially motivated to *enhance our self-image* (Sedikides, 1993). Trying to increase self-esteem, then, helps power our self-serving bias. As social psychologist Daniel Batson (2006) surmises, "The head is an extension of the heart."

"Other sins are before our eyes; our own are behind our back."

—Seneca,
De Ira, A.D. 43

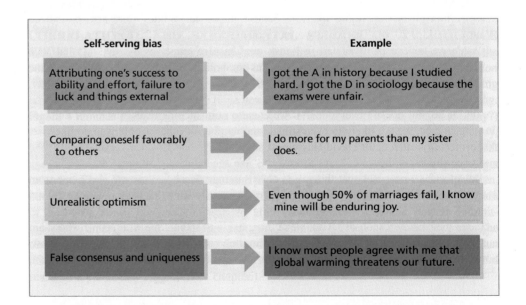

Self-serving bias	Example
Attributing one's success to ability and effort, failure to luck and things external	I got the A in history because I studied hard. I got the D in sociology because the exams were unfair.
Comparing oneself favorably to others	I do more for my parents than my sister does.
Unrealistic optimism	Even though 50% of marriages fail, I know mine will be enduring joy.
False consensus and uniqueness	I know most people agree with me that global warming threatens our future.

FIGURE :: 6

How Self-Serving Bias Works

<hr>

SUMMING UP: What Is Self-Serving Bias?

- Contrary to the presumption that most people suffer from low self-esteem or feelings of inferiority, researchers consistently find that most people exhibit a *self-serving bias.* In experiments and everyday life, we often take credit for our successes while blaming failures on the situation.

- Most people rate themselves as better than average on subjective, desirable traits and abilities.

- We exhibit unrealistic optimism about our futures.

- We overestimate the commonality of our opinions and foibles (*false consensus*) while underestimating the commonality of our abilities and virtues (*false uniqueness*).

- Such perceptions arise partly from a motive to maintain and enhance self-esteem—a motive that protects people from depression but contributes to misjudgment and group conflict.

- Self-serving bias can be adaptive in that it allows us to savor the good things that happen in our lives. When bad things happen, however, self-serving bias can have the maladaptive effect of causing us to blame others or feel cheated out of something we "deserved."

<hr>

HOW DO PEOPLE MANAGE THEIR SELF-PRESENTATION?

Identify self-presentation and understand how impression management can explain behavior.

So far, we have seen that the self is at the center of our social worlds, that self-esteem and self-efficacy pay some dividends, and that self-serving bias influences self-evaluations. Perhaps you have wondered: Are self-enhancing expressions always sincere? Do people have the same feelings privately as they express publicly? Or are they just putting on a positive face even while living with self-doubt?

Self-Handicapping

Sometimes people sabotage their chances for success by creating impediments that make success less likely. Far from being deliberately self-destructive, such behaviors typically have a self-protective aim (Arkin et al., 1986; Baumeister & Scher, 1988; Rhodewalt, 1987): "I'm really not a failure—I would have done well except for this problem." Unfortunately, this strategy usually backfires: Students who self-handicap end up with lower GPAs (Schwinger et al., 2014).

Why would people handicap themselves with self-defeating behaviors? Recall that we eagerly protect our self-images by attributing failures to external factors. Thus, *fearing failure,* people might handicap themselves by partying half the night before a job interview or playing video games instead of studying before a big exam. When self-image is tied up with performance, it can be more self-deflating to try hard and fail than to procrastinate and have a ready excuse. If we fail while handicapped in some way, we can cling to a sense of competence; if we succeed under such conditions, it can only boost our self-image. Handicaps protect both self-esteem and public image by allowing us to attribute failures to something temporary or external ("I was feeling sick"; "I was out too late the night before") rather than to lack of talent or ability.

Steven Berglas and Edward Jones (1978) confirmed this analysis of **self-handicapping.** One experiment was announced as concerning "drugs and intellectual performance." Imagine yourself in the position of their Duke University participants. You guess answers to some difficult aptitude questions and then are told, "Yours was one of the best scores seen to date!" Feeling incredibly lucky, you are then offered a choice between two drugs before answering more of these items. One drug will aid intellectual performance and the other will inhibit it. Which drug do you want? Most students wanted the drug that would supposedly disrupt their thinking, thus providing a handy excuse for doing badly.

self-handicapping

Protecting one's self-image with behaviors that create a handy excuse for later failure.

"If you try to fail, and succeed, what have you done?"

—Anonymous

Researchers have documented other ways people self-handicap. Fearing failure, people will

- reduce their preparation for important individual athletic events (Rhodewalt et al., 1984).
- give their opponent an advantage (Shepperd & Arkin, 1991).
- perform poorly at the beginning of a task to not create unreachable expectations (Baumgardner & Brownlee, 1987).
- not try as hard as they could during a tough, ego-involving task (Hormuth, 1986; Pyszczynski & Greenberg, 1987; Riggs, 1992; Turner & Pratkanis, 1993).

Impression Management

Self-serving bias, false modesty, and self-handicapping reveal the depth of our concern for self-image. To varying degrees, we are continually managing the impressions we create. Whether we wish to impress, intimidate, or seem helpless, we are social animals, playing to an audience. So great is the human desire for social acceptance that it can lead people to risk harming themselves through smoking, binge eating, premature sex, or drug and alcohol abuse (Rawn & Vohs, 2011).

Self-presentation refers to our wanting to present a desired image both to an external audience (other people) and to an internal audience (ourselves). We work at managing the impressions we create. We excuse, justify, or apologize as necessary to shore up our self-esteem and verify our self-images (Schlenker & Weigold, 1992). Just as we preserve our self-esteem, we also must make sure not to brag too much and risk the disapproval of others (Anderson et al., 2006). In one study, students who were told to "put your best face forward" actually made a more negative impression on people they just met than those who were not under self-presentational demands (Human et al., 2012). Social interaction is a careful balance of looking good while not looking *too* good. That seems to be particularly true in collectivistic cultures, where modesty is a "default strategy" to avoid offending others. When there was no risk of offense, Japanese participants self-enhanced as much as Americans (Yamagishi et al., 2012).

In familiar situations, self-presentation happens without conscious effort. In unfamiliar situations, perhaps at a party with people we would like to impress or in conversation with a crush, we are acutely self-conscious of the impressions we are creating and we are therefore less modest than when among friends who know us well (Leary et al., 1994; Tice et al., 1995). Preparing to have our photographs taken, we may even try out different faces in a mirror. We do this even though active self-presentation depletes energy, which often leads to diminished effectiveness—for example, to less persistence on a tedious experimental task or more difficulty stifling emotional expressions (Vohs et al., 2005). The upside is that self-presentation can unexpectedly improve mood. People felt significantly better than they thought they would after doing their best to "put their best face forward" and concentrate on making a positive impression on their boyfriend or girlfriend. Elizabeth Dunn and colleagues (2008) conclude that "date nights" for long-term couples work because they encourage active self-presentation, which improves mood.

Social networking sites such as Facebook provide a new and sometimes intense venue for self-presentation. They are, says communications professor

> "After losing to some younger rivals, tennis great Martina Navratilova confessed that she was "afraid to play my best. . . . I was scared to find out if they could beat me when I'm playing my best because if they can, then I am finished"
> —Frankel & Snyder, 1987

self-presentation
The act of expressing oneself and behaving in ways designed to create a favorable impression or an impression that corresponds to one's ideals.

In the age of the selfie, self-presentation can be a nearly constant concern.
Ascent Xmedia/Getty Images

Joseph Walther, "like impression management on steroids" (Rosenbloom, 2008). Users make careful decisions about which pictures, activities, and interests to highlight in their profiles. Tinkering with self-presentation online apparently has benefits: People who edit their own Facebook profile subsequently report higher self-esteem (Gentile et al., 2012; Gonzales & Hancock, 2011). Given the concern with status and attractiveness on social networking sites, it is not surprising that people high in narcissistic traits thrive on Facebook, tallying up more friends and choosing more attractive pictures of themselves (Buffardi & Campbell, 2008).

Given the concern for self-presentation, it's no wonder people will self-handicap when failure might make them look bad. It's no wonder that people take health risks—tanning their skin with wrinkle- and cancer-causing radiation; having piercings or tattoos done without proper hygiene; becoming anorexic; or yielding to peer pressures to smoke, get drunk, and do drugs (Leary et al., 1994). It's no wonder that people express more modesty when their self-flattery is vulnerable to being debunked, perhaps by experts scrutinizing their self-descriptions (Arkin et al., 1980; Riess et al., 1981; Weary et al., 1982). Professor Smith will likely express more modesty about the significance of her work when presenting it to professional colleagues than when presenting it to students—her colleagues will have the ammunition to shoot her down.

For some people, conscious self-presentation is a way of life. They continually monitor their own behavior and note how others react, then adjust their social performance to gain a desired effect. Those who score high on a scale of **self-monitoring** (who, for example, agree that "I tend to be what people expect me to be") act like social chameleons—they adjust their behavior in response to external situations (Gangestad & Snyder, 2000; Snyder, 1987). Having attuned their behavior to the situation, they are more likely to express attitudes they don't really hold and less likely to express or act on their own attitudes (Zanna & Olson, 1982). As Mark Leary (2004b) observed, the self they know often differs from the self they show. As social chameleons, those who score high in self-monitoring are also less committed to their relationships and more likely to be dissatisfied in their marriages (Leone & Hawkins, 2006). On the other hand, high self-monitors may rack up more connections online. For example, they post more on Facebook and receive more "likes" from friends (Hall & Pennington, 2013).

Those low in self-monitoring care less about what others think. They are more internally guided and thus more likely to talk and act as they feel and believe (McCann & Hancock, 1983). For example, if asked to list their thoughts about gay couples, they simply

self-monitoring
Being attuned to the way one presents oneself in social situations and adjusting one's performance to create the desired impression.

"Public opinion is always more tyrannical towards those who obviously fear it than towards those who feel indifferent to it."
—Bertrand Russell,
The Conquest of Happiness, 1930

Group identity. In Asian countries, self-presentation is restrained. Children learn to identify themselves with their groups.
Tibor Bognar/Corbis

"Hmmm... what shall I wear today...?"

© Mike Marland.

express what they think, regardless of the attitudes of their anticipated audience (Klein et al., 2004). As you might imagine, someone who is extremely low in self-monitoring could come across as an insensitive boor, whereas extremely high self-monitoring could result in dishonest behavior worthy of a con artist. Most of us fall somewhere between those two extremes.

Presenting oneself in ways that create a desired impression is a delicate balancing act. People want to be seen as capable but also as modest and honest (Carlston & Shovar, 1983). In most social situations, modesty creates a good impression and unsolicited boasting creates a bad one. Hence the false modesty phenomenon: We often display lower self-esteem than we privately feel (Miller & Schlenker, 1985). But when we have obviously done extremely well, the insincerity of a disclaimer ("I did well, but it's no big deal") may be evident. To make good impressions—to appear modest yet competent—requires social skill.

SUMMING UP: How Do People Manage Their Self-Presentation?

- As social animals, we adjust our words and actions to suit our audiences. To varying degrees, we note our performance and adjust it to create the impressions we desire.

- Sometimes people *self-handicap* with self-defeating behaviors that protect self-esteem by providing excuses for failure.

- *Self-presentation* refers to our wanting to present a favorable image both to an external audience (other people) and to an internal audience (ourselves). With regard to an external audience, those who score high on a scale of *self-monitoring* adjust their behavior to each situation, whereas those low in self-monitoring may do so little social adjusting that they seem insensitive.

WHAT DOES IT MEAN TO HAVE "SELF-CONTROL"?

Understand *self-concept* through examination of the self in action.

The self's capacity for action has limits, note Roy Baumeister and colleagues (1998, 2000; Baumeister & Tierney, 2011; Muraven et al., 1998). Consider the following:

- People who exert self-control—by forcing themselves to eat radishes rather than chocolates, or by suppressing forbidden thoughts—subsequently quit faster when given unsolvable puzzles.

- People who have tried to control their emotional responses to an upsetting movie exhibit decreased physical stamina—for example, letting go of a hand grip after less time. They also become more aggressive and are more likely to fight with their partners (DeWall et al., 2007; Finkel & Campbell, 2001).

- People who have exerted self-control on something else also become less restrained in their sexual thoughts and behaviors. When asked to express intimacy with their partner, those with depleted willpower were more likely to passionately kiss their partner and even remove some clothing right there in the lab (Gailliot & Baumeister, 2007).

- In a study of 1,112 parole board hearings in Israeli courts, judges were much less likely to grant parole to prisoners just before lunch and at the end of the day—times when they were hungry and tired, and thus depleted of the willpower necessary to go against the usual decision to deny parole and keep the prisoner incarcerated (Danziger et al., 2011). Prisoners who were lucky enough to get 9 A.M. or 1 P.M. parole hearings were much more likely to be released.

The total loss of self-control.
Andrew Olney/OJO Images/Age Fotostock

- Self-control requires energy—not just mental energy, but physical energy. In one experiment, students who drank sugar-sweetened lemonade (vs. lemonade made with artificial sweetener) were better able to control their impulses. The opposite was also true: Students asked to complete a task requiring strict attention had lower blood sugar than a control group (Gailliot et al., 2007). In other words, don't try to study, fight with your partner, or resist chocolate cake when you're hungry. This is why dessert comes at the end of the meal: If it came at the beginning, we'd eat the whole cake ourselves.

Effortful self-control depletes our limited willpower reserves. Self-control therefore operates similarly to muscular strength, conclude Baumeister and Julie Exline (2000): Both are weaker after exertion, replenished with rest, and strengthened by exercise (Muraven et al., 1999). In one experiment, college students learned a program of study skills based on planning and self-control, such as creating a study schedule and keeping a diary of their study time. Not surprisingly, these students studied for more hours than a control group who didn't learn these skills. But the students who learned how to plan reaped the benefits of increased self-control in other ways as well: They were less likely to smoke or drink alcohol, less likely to leave dirty dishes or laundry around, and more likely to eat healthier food. In other words, practicing self-control in one area improved their self-control overall (Oaten & Cheng, 2006a, b). So if you'd like to increase your willpower, don't make a long list of New Year's resolutions and tackle them all at once in January. A better strategy, the research suggests, is to start with one area and then let your increased self-control spread throughout your newly improved life. As Roy Baumeister and John Tierney write in their book *Willpower*, "The best way to reduce stress in your life is to stop screwing up" (2011, p. 238). A little self-control now means you need less self-control later.

SUMMING UP: What Does It Mean to Have "Self-Control"?

- Self-control is like a muscle: It can get tired when you use it too much. Willpower requires energy.

- But self-control can get stronger if it's used more. Improving self-control in one area leads to improvements in others.

POSTSCRIPT:
Twin Truths—The Perils of Pride, the Powers of Positive Thinking

This chapter offered two memorable truths: the truth of self-efficacy and the truth of self-serving bias. The truth concerning self-efficacy encourages us not to resign ourselves to bad situations. We need to persist despite initial failures and to exert effort without being overly distracted by self-doubts. Likewise, secure self-esteem can be adaptive. When we believe in our positive possibilities, we are less vulnerable to depression and we feel less insecure.

Thus, it's important to think positively and try hard, but not to be so self-confident that our goals are illusory or we alienate others with our narcissism. Taking self-efficacy too far leads to blaming the victim: If positive thinking can accomplish anything, then we have only ourselves to blame if we are unhappily married, poor, or depressed. For shame! If only we had tried harder, been more disciplined, less stupid. This viewpoint fails to acknowledge that bad things can happen to good people. Life's greatest achievements, but also its greatest disappointments, are born of the highest expectations.

These twin truths—self-efficacy and self-serving bias—remind us of what Pascal taught 300 years ago: No single truth is ever sufficient, because the world is complex. Any truth, separated from its complementary truth, is a half-truth.

Social Beliefs and Judgments

Jeff J Mitchell/Getty Images

There is curious power to partisanship. Consider American politics:

- When a Democrat is President, Democrats say Presidents can't do anything about high gas prices. Republicans say the same when a Republican is President. But when the President is from the opposing party, both believe Presidents *can* affect gas prices (Vedantam, 2012).
- Forty-eight percent of political liberals believed most Americans favored same-sex marriage, but only 16% of conservatives thought this was the majority opinion (Gallup, 2013).
- The taller candidate has won the U.S. Presidential election 58% of the time, and Presidents are taller than the average man (Murray & Schmitz, 2011; Stulp et al., 2013). The average male company CEO is 3 inches taller than the average man. We perceive those who look like leaders to be leaders, even if they are not.

"Motivated reasoning"—such as a gut-level liking or disliking of certain politicians—can powerfully influence how we interpret evidence and view reality. Partisanship

How do we judge our social worlds, consciously and unconsciously?

How do we perceive our social worlds?

How do we explain our social worlds?

How do our social beliefs matter?

What can we conclude about social beliefs and judgments?

Postscript: Reflecting on illusory thinking

predisposes perceptions—and perceptions predict partisanship. As an old Chinese proverb says, "Two-thirds of what we see is behind our eyes."

Such differing responses, which have been replicated in political perceptions throughout the world, illustrate how we construct social perceptions and beliefs as we

- *judge* events, informed by implicit rules that guide our snap judgments, and by our moods;
- *perceive* and recall events through the filters of our own assumptions;
- *explain* events by sometimes attributing them to the situation, sometimes to the person; and
- *expect* certain events, thereby sometimes helping bring them about.

This chapter explores how we judge, perceive, and explain our social worlds and why our expectations matter.

HOW DO WE JUDGE OUR SOCIAL WORLDS, CONSCIOUSLY AND UNCONSCIOUSLY?

Understand how judgments are influenced by both unconscious and conscious systems.

We have two brain systems, notes Nobel Prize winner Daniel Kahneman in *Thinking, Fast and Slow* (2011). **System 1** functions automatically and out of our awareness (often called "intuition" or a "gut feeling"), whereas **System 2** requires our conscious attention and effort. The big lesson of recent research: System 1 influences more of our actions than we realize.

Priming

Things we don't even consciously notice can subtly influence how we interpret and recall events. Imagine wearing earphones and concentrating on ambiguous spoken sentences such as "We stood by the bank." When a pertinent word (*river* or *money*) is simultaneously sent to your other ear, you don't consciously hear it. Yet the unheard word "primes" your interpretation of the sentence (Baars & McGovern, 1994).

Our memory system is a web of associations, and **priming** is the awakening or activating of certain associations. Experiments show that priming one thought, even without awareness, can influence another thought, or even an action (Herring et al., 2013). John Bargh has likened primes to bells that only mental butlers (who manage the small unconscious stuff) can hear. In a host of studies, priming effects surface even when the stimuli are presented subliminally—too briefly to be perceived consciously. What's out of sight may not be completely out of mind. An electric shock too slight to be felt may increase the perceived intensity of a later shock. An imperceptibly flashed word, "bread," may prime people to detect a related word, such as "butter," more quickly than they detect an unrelated word, such as "bottle" or "bubble" (Epley et al., 1999; Merikle et al., 2001). In each case, an invisible image or word primes a response to a later task. In another experiment, students were more likely to wobble on a balance beam in a room with posters of beer and vodka as opposed to apple or orange juice (Cox et al., 2014). German students who were subliminally exposed to words such as "sexuality," "sweat," "stiff," and "bed" behaved in a more gender-stereotypical way (Hundhammer & Mussweiler, 2012). These reminders of alcohol and sex primed people to behave in ways associated with alcohol and sex—even though they weren't aware they were being influenced.

System 1
The intuitive, automatic, unconscious, and fast way of thinking.

System 2
The deliberate, controlled, conscious, and slower way of thinking.

priming
Activating particular associations in memory.

Unnoticed events can also subtly prime our thinking and behavior. Rob Holland and colleagues (2005) observed that Dutch students exposed to the scent of an all-purpose cleaner were quicker to identify cleaning-related words, recalled more cleaning-related activities when describing their day, and even kept their desk cleaner while eating a crumbly cookie. Another team of Dutch psychologists found that people exposed to the scent of a cleaning product were less likely to litter (de Lange et al., 2012). And in a laboratory experiment, exposure to a fishy smell caused people to be suspicious of each other and cooperate less—priming notions of a shady deal as "fishy" (Lee & Schwarz, 2012). All these effects occurred without the participants' conscious awareness of the scent and its influence.

Prime time. Watching a scary movie can later make a creaking house sound like an intruder. Holding a warm drink or a soft ball (rather than a cold drink or hard ball) can make another person seem warmer and kinder.
Don Hammond/DesignPics

Priming experiments have their counterparts in everyday life, reports John Bargh (2006):

- Watching a scary movie alone at home can activate emotions that, without our realizing it, cause us to interpret furnace noises as a possible intruder. I [JT] experienced a version of this: Returning to my New Orleans hotel room after a "ghost tour," a shadow I hadn't noticed before looked ominous. Further inspection yielded not a ghost but an end table at a strange angle.

- Depressed moods, as this chapter explains later, prime negative associations. But put people in a *good* mood and suddenly their past seems more wonderful, their future brighter.

- For many psychology students, reading about psychological disorders primes how they interpret their own anxieties and gloomy moods. Reading about disease symptoms similarly primes medical students to worry about their congestion, fever, or headache.

Studies of how implanted ideas and images can prime our interpretations and recall illustrate one of this book's take-home lessons: *Much of our social information processing is automatic.* It is unintentional, out of sight, and happens without our conscious awareness—relying on System 1. As John Bargh and Tanya Chartrand (1999) explain, "Most of a person's everyday life is determined not by their conscious intentions and deliberate choices but by mental processes that are put into motion by features of the environment and that operate outside of conscious awareness and guidance."

Even physical sensations, thanks to our **embodied cognition,** prime our social judgments and vice versa:

embodied cognition
The mutual influence of bodily sensations on cognitive preferences and social judgments.

- After receiving a cold shoulder treatment or after assessing a cold person, people judge the room as colder than do those treated warmly or after assessing a warm person (Szymkow et al., 2013; Zhong & Leonardelli, 2008). People who hold an ice pack straight from the freezer feel more lonely than those who hold the same pack warmed to 98 degrees (Bargh & Shalev, 2012). People who ate alone judged room temperature as colder than those who ate with others (Lee et al., 2014). Social exclusion literally feels cold, and cold feels like social exclusion.

- When holding a *hard* rather than *soft* ball, people judge the same face as more likely to be Republican than Democrat, and more likely to be a physicist than a historian (Slepian et al., 2012).

- People asked to carry a basket (vs. pushing a cart) while shopping were three times more likely to impulse buy unhealthy items like candy—because, the researchers theorize, the arm flex of holding a basket mimics the motion we make when grabbing a desired object (Van Den Bergh et al., 2011).
- When sitting in a wobbly chair, people rate other couples' relationships as more unstable (Kille et al., 2013).

The bottom line: Our social cognition is embodied. The brain systems that process our bodily sensations communicate with the brain systems responsible for our social thinking.

Intuitive Judgments

What are our powers of intuition—of immediately knowing something without reasoning or analysis? Advocates of "intuitive management" believe we should tune into our hunches—to use System 1. When judging others, they say, we should plug into the non-logical smarts of our "right brain." When hiring, firing, and investing, we should listen to our premonitions. In making judgments, we should trust the force within.

Are the intuitionists right that important information is immediately available apart from our conscious analysis? Or are the skeptics correct in saying that intuition is "our knowing we are right, whether we are or not"?

Priming research hints that the unconscious indeed controls much of our behavior. When the light turns red, we react and hit the brake before consciously deciding to do so. Indeed, reflect Neil Macrae and Lucy Johnston (1998), "to be able to do just about anything at all (e.g., driving, dating, dancing), action initiation needs to be decoupled from the inefficient (i.e., slow, serial, resource-consuming) workings of the conscious mind, otherwise inaction inevitably would prevail."

THE POWERS OF INTUITION

"The heart has its reasons which reason does not know," observed seventeenth-century philosopher-mathematician Blaise Pascal. Three centuries later, scientists have proved Pascal correct. We know more than we know we know. Studies of our unconscious information processing confirm our limited access to what's going on in our minds (Bargh et al., 2012; Banaji & Greenwald, 2013; Strack & Deutsch, 2004). Our thinking is partly **automatic** (impulsive, effortless, and without our awareness—System 1) and partly **controlled** (reflective, deliberate, and conscious—System 2). Automatic, intuitive thinking occurs not "onscreen" but offscreen, out of sight, where reason does not go. Consider these examples of automatic thinking:

automatic processing
"Implicit" thinking that is effortless, habitual, and without awareness; roughly corresponds to "intuition." Also known as System 1.

controlled processing
"Explicit" thinking that is deliberate, reflective, and conscious. Also known as System 2.

- *Schemas* are mental concepts or templates that intuitively guide our perceptions and interpretations. Whether we hear someone speaking of religious *sects* or *sex* depends on how we automatically interpret the sound.
- *Emotional reactions* are often nearly instantaneous, happening before there is time for deliberate thinking. One neural shortcut takes information from the eye or the ear to the brain's sensory switchboard (the thalamus) and out to its emotional control center (the amygdala) before the thinking cortex has had any chance to intervene (LeDoux, 2002, 2014). Our ancestors who intuitively feared a sound in the bushes were usually fearing nothing. But when they were right and the sound was made by a dangerous predator, they became more likely to survive to pass their genes down to us.
- Given sufficient *expertise,* people may intuitively know the answer to a problem. Many skills, from piano playing to swinging a golf club, begin as a controlled, deliberate process and gradually become automatic and intuitive (Kruglanski & Gigerenzer, 2011). Master chess players intuitively recognize meaningful patterns that novices miss and often make their next move with only a glance at the board, as the situation cues information stored in their memory. Similarly, without knowing quite how, we recognize a friend's voice after the first spoken word of a phone conversation.

- Given but a very thin slice of someone—even just a fraction of a second glance at their photo—people's *snap judgments* can beat chance at guessing whether someone is outgoing or shy, straight or gay (Rule, 2014).

Some things—facts, names, and past experiences—we remember explicitly (consciously) using System 2. But other things—skills and conditioned dispositions—we remember *implicitly* with System 1, without consciously knowing or declaring that we know. It's true of us all but most strikingly evident in people with brain damage who cannot form new explicit memories. One such person never could learn to recognize her doctor, who would need to reintroduce himself each day. One day, the doctor affixed a tack to his hand, causing the patient to jump with pain when they shook hands. When the physician next returned, the patient still didn't explicitly recognize him. But, due to her implicit memory, she wouldn't shake his hand.

Equally dramatic are the cases of *blindsight.* Having lost a portion of the visual cortex to surgery or stroke, people may be functionally blind in part of their field of vision. Shown a series of sticks in the blind field, they report seeing nothing. After guessing whether the sticks are vertical or horizontal, the patients are astounded when told, "You got them all right." Like the patient who "remembered" the painful handshake, these people know more than they know they know.

Consider your own taken-for-granted capacity to recognize a face. As you look at it, your brain breaks the visual information into subdimensions, such as color, depth, movement, and form, and works on each aspect simultaneously before reassembling the components. Finally, using automatic processing, your brain compares the perceived image with previously stored images. Voilà! Instantly and effortlessly, you recognize your grandmother. If intuition is immediately knowing something without reasoned analysis, then perceiving is intuition par excellence.

So, many routine cognitive functions occur automatically, unintentionally, without awareness. We might remember how automatic processing helps us get through life by picturing our minds as functioning like large corporations. Our CEO—our controlled consciousness—attends to many of the most important, complex, and novel issues, while subordinates deal with routine affairs and matters requiring instant action. Like a CEO, consciousness sets goals and priorities, often with little knowledge of operational activities in the underlying departments. This delegation of resources enables us to react to many situations quickly and efficiently. The bottom line: Our brain knows much more than it tells us.

THE LIMITS OF INTUITION

We have seen how automatic, intuitive thinking can "make us smart" (Gigerenzer, 2007, 2010). Elizabeth Loftus and Mark Klinger (1992) nevertheless spoke for other cognitive scientists in having doubts about the brilliance of intuition. They reported "a general consensus that the unconscious may not be as smart as previously believed." For example, although subliminal stimuli can trigger a weak, fleeting response—enough to evoke a feeling if not conscious awareness—there is no evidence that (for example) subliminal audio recordings can "reprogram your unconscious mind" for success. In fact, a significant body of evidence indicates that they can't (Greenwald, 1992).

Social psychologists have explored not only our error-prone hindsight judgments but also our capacity for illusion—for perceptual misinterpretations, fantasies, and constructed beliefs. Michael Gazzaniga (1992, 1998, 2008) reports that patients whose brain hemispheres have been surgically separated will instantly fabricate—and believe—explanations of their own puzzling behaviors. If the patient gets up and takes a few steps after the experimenter flashes the instruction "walk" to the patient's nonverbal right hemisphere, the verbal left hemisphere will instantly provide the patient with a plausible explanation ("I felt like getting a drink").

Illusory intuition also appears in how we take in, store, and retrieve social information. As perception researchers study visual illusions for what they reveal about our normal perceptual mechanisms, social psychologists study illusory thinking for what it reveals about normal information processing. These researchers want to give us a map of everyday social thinking, with the hazards clearly marked.

As we examine these efficient thinking patterns, remember this: Demonstrations of how people create false beliefs do not prove that all beliefs are false (although to recognize falsification, it helps to know how it's done).

Overconfidence

So far we have seen that our cognitive systems process a vast amount of information efficiently and automatically. But our efficiency has a trade-off; as we interpret our experiences and construct memories, our automatic System 1 intuitions are sometimes wrong. Usually, we are unaware of our errors—in other words, we display **overconfidence.**

overconfidence phenomenon

The tendency to be more confident than correct—to overestimate the accuracy of one's beliefs.

Daniel Kahneman and Amos Tversky (1979) gave people factual statements and asked them to fill in the blanks, as in the following sentence: "I feel 98 percent certain that the air distance between New Delhi and Beijing is more than _____ miles but less than _____ miles." Most individuals were overconfident: Approximately 30 percent of the time, the correct answers lay outside the range they felt 98 percent confident about. Even when participants were offered lottery tickets for a correct answer, they were still too overconfident, identifying too narrow a range (also known as overprecision). "The consequences of overprecision are profound," note Albert Mannes and Don Moore (2013, p. 1196). "People frequently cut things too close—arriving late, missing planes, [or] bouncing checks." In thinking we know exactly how something will go, we too often miss the window.

Ironically, *incompetence feeds overconfidence.* It takes competence to recognize competence, note Justin Kruger and David Dunning (1999). Students who score the lowest on tests of grammar, humor, and logic are the most prone to overestimating their abilities. Those who don't know what good logic or grammar is are often unaware that they lack it. If you make a list of all the words you can form out of the letters in "psychology," you may feel brilliant—but then stupid when a friend starts naming the ones you missed. Deanna Caputo and David Dunning (2005) re-created this phenomenon in experiments, confirming that our ignorance of our ignorance sustains our self-confidence. Follow-up studies found that this "ignorance of one's incompetence" occurs mostly on relatively easy-seeming tasks. On more obviously difficult tasks, poor performers more often appreciate their lack of skill (Burson et al., 2006).

Robert Vallone and colleagues (1990) had college students predict in September whether they would drop a course, declare a major, elect to live off campus next year, and so forth.

The air distance between New Delhi and Beijing is 2,500 miles.

DOONESBURY   by **Garry Trudeau**

Although the students felt, on average, 84 percent sure of those self-predictions, they were wrong nearly twice as often as they expected to be. Even when feeling 100 percent sure of their predictions, they erred 15 percent of the time. Ignorance of one's incompetence helps explain David Dunning's (2005) startling conclusion from employee assessment studies that "what others see in us . . . tends to be more highly correlated with objective outcomes than what we see in ourselves." If ignorance can beget false confidence, then—yikes!—where, we may ask, are you and I unknowingly deficient?

In estimating their chances for success on a task, such as a major exam, people's confidence runs highest when the moment of truth is off in the future. By exam day, the possibility of failure looms larger and confidence typically drops (Gilovich et al., 1993; Shepperd et al., 2005). These students are not alone:

The perils of overconfidence. Before its exploded drilling platform spewed oil into the Gulf of Mexico, BP downplayed safety concerns, and then was overconfident that the spill would be modest (Mohr et al., 2010; Urbina, 2010).
U.S. Coast Guard/Handout/Getty Images News/Getty Images

- *Stockbroker overconfidence.* Investment experts market their services with the confident presumption that they can beat the stock market average, forgetting that for every stockbroker or buyer saying "Sell!" at a given price, there is another saying "Buy!" A stock's price is the balance point between those mutually confident judgments. Thus, incredible as it may seem, economist Burton Malkiel (2012) reports that mutual fund portfolios selected by investment analysts have not outperformed randomly selected stocks.

- *Political overconfidence.* Overconfident decision makers can wreak havoc. It was a confident Adolf Hitler who from 1939 to 1945 waged war against the rest of Europe. It was a confident Lyndon Johnson who in the 1960s invested U.S. weapons and soldiers in the effort to salvage democracy in South Vietnam. It was a confident George W. Bush who asserted that Iraq had weapons of mass destruction in 2003, but none were ever found.

- *Student overconfidence.* In one study, students memorizing psychology terms for a test typed in each term's definition and then predicted how much credit they expected to receive. The overconfident students—those who thought they were more accurate than they actually were—did worse on the test, mostly because they stopped studying (Dunlosky & Rawson, 2012). Why does overconfidence persist? Perhaps because we like those who are confident: Group members rewarded highly confident individuals with higher status—even when their confidence was not justified by actual ability. Overconfident individuals spoke first, talked longer, and used a more factual tone, making them appear more competent than they actually were (Anderson et al., 2012). Even when groups worked together repeatedly and learned that the overconfident individuals were not as accurate as presented, group members continued to accord them status (Kennedy et al., 2013). If confidence, but not ability, helps people become leaders, pervasive overconfidence seems less surprising—but perhaps more distressing.

CONFIRMATION BIAS

People also tend not to seek information that might disprove what they believe. P. C. Wason (1960) demonstrated this, as you can, by giving participants a sequence of three numbers—2, 4, 6—that conformed to a rule he had in mind. (The rule was simply *any*

"The wise know too well their weakness to assume infallibility; and he who knows most, knows best how little he knows."
—Thomas Jefferson, *Writings*

Regarding the atomic bomb: "That is the biggest fool thing we have ever done. The bomb will never go off, and I speak as an expert in explosives."
—Admiral William Leahy to President Truman, 1945

"When you know a thing, to hold that you know it; and when you do not know a thing, to allow that you do not know it; this is knowledge."
—Confucius, *Analects*

three ascending numbers.) To enable the participants to discover the rule, Wason invited each person to generate additional sets of three numbers. Each time, Wason told the person whether or not the set conformed to his rule. As soon as participants were sure they had discovered the rule, they were to stop and announce it.

The result? Seldom right but never in doubt: 23 of the 29 participants convinced themselves of a wrong rule. They typically formed some erroneous belief about the rule (for example, counting by two's) and then searched for *confirming* evidence (for example, by testing 8, 10, 12) rather than attempting to *disconfirm* their hunches. We are eager to verify our beliefs but less inclined to seek evidence that might disprove them, a phenomenon called the **confirmation bias.**

confirmation bias
A tendency to search for information that confirms one's preconceptions.

Confirmation bias appears to be a System 1 snap judgment, where our default reaction is to look for information consistent with our presupposition. Stopping and thinking a little—calling up System 2—makes us less likely to commit this error. For example, Ivan Hernandez and Jesse Lee Preston (2013) had college students read an article arguing for the death penalty. Those who read the article in a dark, standard font did not change their opinions. But when the words were in light gray and italics, more shifted their beliefs—probably because straining to read the words slowed down participants' thinking enough for them to consider both sides. Another cognitive complication (thinking about conflicting goals such as going to a party the night before an exam) also made students less likely to commit confirmation bias (Kleiman & Hassin, 2013). Contemplation curtails confirmation.

Confirmation bias helps explain why our self-images are so remarkably stable. In experiments at the University of Texas at Austin, William Swann and Stephen Read (1981; Swann et al., 1992a, 1992b, 2007) discovered that students seek, elicit, and recall feedback that confirms their beliefs about themselves. People seek as friends and spouses those who bolster their own self views—even if they think poorly of themselves (Swann et al., 1991, 2003).

Swann and Read (1981) compared this *self-verification* to the way a domineering person might behave at a party. When she arrives, she seeks out those whom she knows will acknowledge her dominance. In conversation, she presents her views in ways that elicit the respect she expects. After the party, she has trouble recalling conversations in which her influence was minimal and more easily recalls her persuasiveness in the conversations she dominated. Thus, her experience at the party confirms her self-image.

REMEDIES FOR OVERCONFIDENCE

What lessons can we draw from research on overconfidence? One lesson is to be wary of other people's dogmatic statements. Even when people are sure they are right, they may be wrong. Confidence and competence need not coincide.

Three techniques have successfully reduced the overconfidence bias. One is *prompt feedback* (Lichtenstein & Fischhoff, 1980). In everyday life, weather forecasters and those who set the odds in horse racing both receive clear, daily feedback. And experts in both groups do quite well at estimating their probable accuracy (Fischhoff, 1982).

When people think about why an idea *might* be true, it begins to seem true (Koehler, 1991). Thus, a third way to reduce overconfidence is to get people to think of one good reason *why* their judgments *might be wrong;* that is, force them to consider disconfirming information (Koriat et al., 1980). Managers might foster more realistic judgments by insisting that all proposals and recommendations include reasons why they might *not* work.

Still, we should be careful not to undermine people's reasonable self-confidence or to destroy their decisiveness. In times when their wisdom is needed, those lacking self-confidence may shrink from speaking up or making tough decisions. Overconfidence can cost us, but realistic self-confidence is adaptive.

Heuristics: Mental Shortcuts

With precious little time to process so much information, our cognitive system is fast and frugal. It specializes in mental shortcuts. With remarkable ease, we form impressions, make judgments, and invent explanations. We do so by using **heuristics**—simple, efficient thinking strategies. Heuristics enable us to make routine decisions with minimal effort (Shah & Oppenheimer, 2008). In most situations, our System 1 snap generalizations— "That's dangerous!"—are adaptive. The speed of these intuitive guides promotes our survival. The biological purpose of thinking is less to make us right than to keep us alive. In some situations, however, haste makes error.

heuristic
A thinking strategy that enables quick, efficient judgments.

THE REPRESENTATIVENESS HEURISTIC

University of Oregon students were told that a panel of psychologists interviewed 30 engineers and 70 lawyers and summarized their impressions in thumbnail descriptions. The following description, they were told, was drawn at random from the sample of 30 engineers and 70 lawyers:

> Twice divorced, Frank spends most of his free time hanging around the country club. His clubhouse bar conversations often center on his regrets at having tried to follow his esteemed father's footsteps. The long hours he had spent at academic drudgery would have been better invested in learning how to be less quarrelsome in his relations with other people.

Question: What is the probability that Frank is a lawyer rather than an engineer?

Asked to guess Frank's occupation, more than 80 percent of the students surmised he was one of the lawyers (Fischhoff & Bar-Hillel, 1984). Fair enough. But how do you suppose those estimates changed when the sample description was given to another group of students, modified to say that 70 percent were engineers? Not in the slightest. The students took no account of the base rate of engineers (70 percent) and lawyers (30 percent); in their minds, Frank was more *representative* of lawyers, and that was all that seemed to matter. Or consider John, a 23-year-old White man who's an atheist and abuses drugs. What kind of music does he like? Most people guessed heavy metal, even though heavy metal fans are a very small minority of the population (Lonsdale & North, 2011).

To judge something by intuitively comparing it to our mental representation of a category is to use the **representativeness heuristic.** Representativeness (typicalness) usually reflects reality. But, as we saw with "Frank" above, it doesn't always. Consider Linda, who is 31, single, outspoken, and very bright. She majored in philosophy in college. As a student, she was deeply concerned with discrimination and other social issues, and she participated in antinuclear demonstrations. Based on that description, would you say it is more likely that

representativeness heuristic
The tendency to presume, sometimes despite contrary odds, that someone or something belongs to a particular group if resembling (representing) a typical member.

a. Linda is a bank teller.
b. Linda is a bank teller and active in the feminist movement.

Most people think *b* is more likely, partly because Linda better *represents* their image of feminists (Mellers et al., 2001). But ask yourself: Is there a better chance that Linda is *both* a bank teller *and* a feminist than that she's a bank teller (whether feminist or not)? As Amos Tversky and Daniel Kahneman (1983) reminded us, the conjunction of two events cannot be more likely than either one of the events alone.

THE AVAILABILITY HEURISTIC

Consider the following: Do more people live in Iraq or in Tanzania?

You probably answered according to how readily Iraqis and Tanzanians come to mind. If examples are readily *available* in our memory—as Iraqis tend to be—then we presume that other such examples are commonplace. Usually this is true, so we are often well served by this cognitive rule, called the **availability heuristic** (Table 1). Said simply, the more easily we recall something, the more likely it seems. (*Answer: Tanzania's 52 million people greatly outnumber Iraq's 36 million. Most people, having more vivid images of Iraqi's, guess wrong.*)

But sometimes the rule deludes us. If people hear a list of famous people of one sex (Oprah Winfrey, Lady Gaga, and Hillary Clinton) intermixed with an equal-size list of

availability heuristic
A cognitive rule that judges the likelihood of things in terms of their availability in memory. If instances of something come readily to mind, we presume it to be commonplace.

TABLE :: 1 Fast and Frugal Heuristics

Heuristic	Definition	Example	But May Lead to
Representativeness	Snap judgments of whether someone or something fits a category	Deciding that Carlos is a librarian rather than a trucker because he better represents one's image of librarians	Discounting other important information
Availability	Quick judgments of likelihood of events (how available in memory)	Estimating teen violence after school shootings	Overweighting vivid instances and thus, for example, fearing the wrong things

unfamous people of the other sex (Donald Scarr, William Wood, and Mel Jasper), the famous names will later be more cognitively available. Most people will also subsequently recall having heard more women's names (McKelvie, 1995, 1997; Tversky & Kahneman, 1973). Likewise, media attention makes gays and lesbians cognitively available. Thus, the average U.S. adult in a 2011 Gallup poll estimated that 25 percent of Americans are gay or lesbian (Morales, 2011)—nearly ten times the number who, in surveys, self-identify as gay, lesbian, or bisexual (Gates, 2011).

Even fictional happenings in novels, television, and movies leave images that later penetrate our judgments (Gerrig & Prentice, 1991; Green et al., 2002; Mar & Oatley, 2008). The more absorbed and "transported" the reader ("I could easily picture the events"), the more the story affects the reader's later beliefs (Diekman et al., 2000). Readers who are captivated by romance novels, for example, may gain readily available sexual scripts that influence their own sexual perceptions, attitudes, and behaviors.

Try ordering these four cities according to their crime rates: Atlanta, Los Angeles, New York, St. Louis. If, with available images from TV crime dramas in mind, you thought New York and Los Angeles were the most crime-ridden, guess again; they each have about one-third the crime rate of Atlanta and St. Louis (FBI, 2012).

"Most people reason dramatically, not quantitatively."

—Jurist Oliver Wendell Holmes, Jr., 1841–1935

Our use of the availability heuristic highlights a basic principle of social thinking: People are slow to deduce particular instances from a general truth, but they are remarkably quick to infer general truth from a vivid instance. No wonder that after hearing and reading stories of rapes, robberies, and beatings, 9 out of 10 Canadians overestimated—usually by a considerable margin—the percentage of crimes that involved violence (Doob & Roberts, 1988). No wonder that South Africans, after a series of headline-grabbing gangland robberies and slayings, estimated that violent crime had almost doubled between 1998 and 2004, when actually it had decreased substantially (Wines, 2005). And no wonder the breakfast server at a hotel for stranded airline passengers told me [DM] that, after hearing so many vivid stories of flights delayed by weather and mechanical problems, she would *never* fly.

The availability heuristic explains why vivid, easy-to-imagine events, such as shark attacks or diseases with easy-to-picture symptoms, may seem more likely to occur than harder-to-picture events (MacLeod & Campbell, 1992; Sherman et al., 1985). Likewise, powerful anecdotes can be more compelling than statistical information. We fret over extremely rare child abduction, even if we don't buckle children in the backseat. We dread terrorism but are indifferent to global climate change—"Armageddon in slow motion." Especially after the 2011 Japanese tsunami and nuclear power catastrophe, we have feared nuclear power, with little concern for the many more deaths related to coal mining and burning (von Hippel, 2011). In short, we worry about remote possibilities while ignoring higher probabilities, a phenomenon that social scientists call our "probability neglect."

Because news footage of airplane crashes is a readily available memory for most of us—especially since September 11, 2001, and the two Malaysia Airlines crashes in 2014—we often suppose we are more at risk traveling in commercial airplanes than in cars. Actually, from 2009 to 2011, U.S. travelers were 170 times more likely to die in a car crash than on a commercial flight covering the same distance (National Safety Council, 2014). For most air travelers, the most dangerous part of the journey is the drive to the airport.

Soon after 9/11, as many people abandoned air travel and took to the roads, I [DM] estimated that if Americans flew 20 percent less and instead drove those unflown miles, we could expect an additional 800 traffic deaths in the ensuing year (Myers, 2001). A curious German researcher (why didn't I think of this?) checked that prediction against accident data, which confirmed an excess of some 350 deaths in the last 3 months of 2001 compared with the 3-month average in the preceding 5 years (Gigerenzer, 2004). The 9/11 terrorists appear to have killed more people unnoticed—on America's roads—than they did with the 266 fatalities on those four planes.

By now it is clear that our naive statistical intuitions, and our resulting fears, are driven not by calculation and reason but by emotions attuned to the availability heuristic. After this book is published, there likely will be another dramatic natural or terrorist event, which will again propel our fears, vigilance, and resources in a new direction. Terrorists, aided by the media, may again achieve their objective of capturing our attention, draining our resources, and distracting us from the mundane, undramatic, insidious risks that, over time, devastate lives, such as the rotavirus (an intestinal infection) that each day claims the equivalent of four 747s filled with children (Parashar et al., 2006). But then again, dramatic events can also serve to awaken us to real risks. That, say some scientists, is what happens when extreme weather events remind us that global climate change, by raising sea levels and spawning extreme weather, is destined to become nature's own weapon of mass destruction. For Australians and Americans, a hot day can prime people to believe more in global warming (Li et al., 2011). Even feeling hot in an *indoor* room increases people's belief in global warming (Risen & Critcher, 2011).

© Dave Coverly/Speedbump.com

"Testimonials may be more compelling than mountains of facts and figures (as mountains of facts and figures in social psychology so compellingly demonstrate)."

—Mark Snyder (1988)

Vivid, memorable—and therefore cognitively available—events influence our perception of the social world. The resulting "probability neglect" often leads people to fear the wrong things, such as fearing flying or terrorism more than smoking, driving, or climate change. If four jumbo jets filled with children crashed every day—approximating the number of childhood diarrhea deaths resulting from the rotavirus—something would have been done about it.
Source: Dave Bohn

Counterfactual Thinking

Easily imagined, cognitively available events also influence our experiences of guilt, regret, frustration, and relief. If our team loses (or wins) a big game by one point, we can easily imagine the other outcome, and thus we feel regret (or relief). Imagining worse alternatives helps us feel better. When skier Lindsay Vonn lost a World Cup slalom event by just 0.03 seconds, she was happy for her competitor but noted that "I'd rather she beat me by a second" (AP, 2012). Imagining better alternatives, and pondering what we might do differently next time, helps us prepare to do better in the future (Epstude & Roese, 2008; Scholl & Sassenberg, 2014).

counterfactual thinking
Imagining alternative scenarios and outcomes that might have happened, but didn't.

In Olympic competition, athletes' emotions after an event reflect mostly how they did relative to expectations, but also their **counterfactual thinking**—their *mentally simulating what might have been* (McGraw et al., 2005; Medvec et al., 1995). Bronze medalists (for whom an easily imagined alternative was finishing fourth—without a medal) exhibit more joy than silver medalists (who could more easily imagine having won the gold). On the medal stand, happiness is as simple as 1-3-2. Similarly, the higher a student's score within a grade category (such as B+), the *worse* they feel (Medvec & Savitsky, 1997). The B+ student who misses an A− by a point feels worse than the B+ student who actually did worse and just made a B+ by a point. In sports games or TV game shows, near misses are especially distressing when they occur near the end of the competition when there is little chance for future success (Zhang & Covey, 2014).

Such counterfactual thinking—imagining what could have been—occurs when we can easily picture an alternative outcome (Kahneman & Miller, 1986; Markman & McMullen, 2003; Petrocelli et al., 2011):

- If we barely miss a plane or a bus, we imagine making it *if only* we had left at our usual time, taken our usual route, or not paused to talk. If we miss our connection by a half hour or after taking our usual route, it's harder to simulate a different outcome, so we feel less frustration.
- If we change an exam answer, then get it wrong, we will inevitably think "If only . . ." and will vow next time to trust our immediate intuition—although, contrary to student lore, answer changes are more often from incorrect to correct (Kruger et al., 2005).

Counterfactual thinking. When *The Price is Right* contestants give the wrong answer and lose out on a prize, they likely experience counterfactual thinking—imagining what might have been.
CBS Photo Archive/Getty Images

- Students who chose a college major, but then thought about the benefits of a major they didn't choose, were less satisfied with their choice and predicted they would not perform as well (Leach & Patall, 2013).
- The team or the political candidate who barely loses will simulate over and over how they could have won (Sanna et al., 2003).

Counterfactual thinking underlies our feelings of luck. When we have barely escaped a bad event—avoiding defeat with a last-minute goal or standing near a falling icicle—we easily imagine a negative counterfactual (losing, being hit) and therefore feel "good luck" (Teigen et al., 1999). "*Bad* luck" refers to bad events that did happen but easily might not have.

The more significant and unlikely the event, the more intense the counterfactual thinking (Roese & Hur, 1997). Bereaved people who have lost a spouse or a child in a vehicle accident, or a child to sudden infant death syndrome, commonly report replaying and undoing the event (Davis et al., 1995, 1996). One friend of mine [DM] survived a head-on collision with a drunk driver that killed his wife, daughter, and mother. "For months," he recalled, "I turned the events of that day over and over in my mind. I kept reliving the day, changing the order of events so that the accident wouldn't occur" (Sittser, 1994).

Most people, however, live with more regret over things they *didn't* do than what they did, such as, "I should have told my father I loved him before he died" or "I wish I had been more serious in college" (Gilovich & Medvec, 1994; Rajagopal et al., 2006). In one survey of adults, the most common regret was not taking their education more seriously (Kinnier & Metha, 1989). Would we live with less regret if we dared more often to reach beyond our comfort zone—to venture out, risking failure, but at least having tried?

People are more often apologetic about actions than inactions (Zeelenberg et al., 1998).

Illusory Thinking

Another influence on everyday thinking is our search for order in random events, a tendency that can lead us down all sorts of wrong paths.

ILLUSORY CORRELATION

It is easy to see a correlation where none exists. When we expect to find significant relationships, we easily associate random events, perceiving an **illusory correlation.** William Ward and Herbert Jenkins (1965) showed people the results of a hypothetical 50-day cloud-seeding experiment. They told participants which of the 50 days the clouds had been seeded and which days it rained. The information was nothing more than a random mix of results: Sometimes it rained after seeding; sometimes it didn't. Participants nevertheless became convinced—in conformity with their ideas about the effects of cloud seeding—that they really had observed a relationship between cloud seeding and rain.

illusory correlation
Perception of a relationship where none exists, or perception of a stronger relationship than actually exists.

Other experiments confirm this illusory correlation phenomenon: *People easily misperceive random events as confirming their beliefs* (Crocker, 1981; Ratliff & Nosek, 2010; Trolier & Hamilton, 1986). If we believe a correlation exists, we are more likely to notice and recall confirming instances. If we believe that premonitions correlate with events, we notice and remember any joint occurrence of the premonition and the event's later occurrence. If we believe that overweight women are less happy, we perceive that we have witnessed such a correlation even when we have not (Viken et al., 2005). We ignore or forget all

The odds of winning are the same whether you choose the numbers or someone else does, but when they win, many people believe it was due to their "lucky numbers"—an example of illusory correlation.
Steve Allen/Brand X Pictures/JupiterImages

the times unusual events do not coincide. If, after we think about a friend, the friend calls us, we notice and remember that coincidence. We don't notice all the times we think of a friend without any ensuing call, or receive a call from a friend about whom we've not been thinking.

GAMBLING. Compared with those given an assigned lottery number, people who chose their own number demanded four times as much money when asked if they would sell their ticket. When playing a game of chance against an awkward and nervous person, they bet significantly more than when playing against a dapper, confident opponent (Langer, 1977). Being the person who throws the dice or spins the wheel increases people's confidence (Wohl & Enzle, 2002). In these and other ways, dozens of experiments have consistently found people acting as if they can predict or control chance events (Stefan & David, 2013).

Observations of real-life gamblers confirm these experimental findings (Orgaz et al., 2013). Dice players may throw softly for low numbers and hard for high numbers (Henslin, 1967). The gambling industry thrives on gamblers' illusions. Gamblers attribute wins to their skill and foresight. Losses become "near misses" or "flukes," or for the sports gambler, a bad call by the referee or a freakish bounce of the ball (Gilovich & Douglas, 1986).

Stock traders also like the "feeling of empowerment" that comes from being able to choose and control their own stock trades, as if their being in control can enable them to outperform the market average. One ad declared that online investing "is about control." Alas, the illusion of control breeds overconfidence and frequent losses after stock market trading costs are subtracted (Barber & Odean, 2001a, 2001b).

People like feeling in control and so, when experiencing a lack of control, will act to create a sense of predictability. In experiments, loss of control has led people to form illusory correlations in stock market information, to perceive nonexistent conspiracies, and to develop superstitions (Whitson & Galinsky, 2008).

REGRESSION TOWARD THE AVERAGE. Tversky and Kahneman (1974) noted another way by which an illusion of control may arise: We fail to recognize the statistical phenomenon of **regression toward the average.** Because exam scores fluctuate partly by chance, most students who get extremely high scores on an exam will get lower scores on the next exam. If their first score is at the ceiling, their second score is more likely to fall back ("regress") toward their own average than to push the ceiling even higher. That is why a student who does consistently good work, even if never the best, will sometimes end a course at the top of the class. Conversely, students who earn low scores on the first

regression toward the average

The statistical tendency for extreme scores or extreme behavior to return toward one's average.

Regression to the average. When we are at an extremely low point, anything we try will often seem effective. "Maybe a yoga class will improve my life." Events seldom continue at an abnormal low.
Purestock/SuperStock

exam are likely to improve. If those who scored lowest go for tutoring after the first exam, the tutors are likely to feel effective when the student improves, even if the tutoring had no effect.

Indeed, when things reach a low point, we will try anything, and whatever we try— going to a psychotherapist, starting a new diet-exercise plan, reading a self-help book—is more likely to be followed by improvement than by further deterioration. Sometimes we recognize that events are not likely to continue at an unusually good or bad extreme. Experience has taught us that when everything is going great, something will go wrong, and that when life is dealing us terrible blows, we can usually look forward to things getting better. Often, though, we fail to recognize this regression effect. We puzzle at why baseball's rookie of the year often has a more ordinary second year—did he become overconfident? Self-conscious? We forget that exceptional performance tends to regress toward normality.

By simulating the consequences of using praise and punishment, Paul Schaffner (1985) showed how the illusion of control might infiltrate human relations. He invited Bowdoin College students to train an imaginary fourth-grade boy, "Harold," to come to school by 8:30 each morning. For each school day during a 3-week period, a computer displayed Harold's arrival time, which was always between 8:20 and 8:40. The students would then select a response to Harold, ranging from strong praise to strong reprimand. As you might expect, they usually praised Harold when he arrived before 8:30 and reprimanded him when he arrived after 8:30. Because Schaffner had programmed the computer to display a random sequence of arrival times, Harold's arrival time tended to improve (to regress toward 8:30) after he was reprimanded. For example, if Harold arrived at 8:39, he was almost sure to be reprimanded, and his randomly selected next-day arrival time was likely to be earlier than 8:39. Thus, *even though their reprimands were having no effect,* most students ended the experiment believing that their reprimands had been effective.

This experiment demonstrates Tversky and Kahneman's provocative conclusion: *Nature operates in such a way that we often feel punished for rewarding others and rewarded for punishing them.* In actuality, as you probably learned in introductory psychology, positive reinforcement for doing things right is usually more effective and has fewer negative side effects.

Moods and Judgments

Social judgment involves efficient information processing. It also involves our feelings: Our moods infuse our judgments. Unhappy people—especially the bereaved or depressed—tend to be more self-focused and brooding (Myers, 1993, 2000). But there is also a bright side to sadness (Forgas, 2013). A depressed mood motivates intense thinking—a search for information that makes one's environment more memorable, understandable, and controllable.

Happy people, by contrast, are more trusting, more loving, more responsive. If people are made temporarily happy by receiving a small gift while shopping, they will report, a few moments later on an unrelated survey, that their cars and TV sets are working beautifully—better, if you took their word for it, than those belonging to folks who replied after not receiving gifts.

Moods pervade our thinking. From West Germans enjoying their team's World Cup soccer victory (Schwarz et al., 1987) to Australians emerging from a heartwarming movie (Forgas & Moylan, 1987), people seem good-hearted; life seems wonderful. When we are in a happy mood, the world seems friendlier, decisions are easier, and good news more readily comes to mind (DeSteno et al., 2000; Isen & Means, 1983; Stone & Glass, 1986).

Let a mood turn gloomy, however, and thoughts switch onto a different track. Off come the rose-colored glasses; on come the dark glasses. Now the bad mood primes our recollections of negative events (Bower, 1987; Johnson & Magaro, 1987). Our relationships seem to sour. Our self-images take a dive. Our hopes for the future dim. And other people's behavior seems more sinister (Brown & Taylor, 1986; Mayer & Salovey, 1987).

Joseph Forgas (1999, 2008, 2010, 2011) had often been struck by how people's "memories and judgments change with the color of their mood." Say you're put in a good or a

FIGURE :: 1

A temporary good or bad mood strongly influenced people's ratings of their videotaped behavior. Those in a bad mood detected far fewer positive behaviors.
Source: Forgas et al., 1984

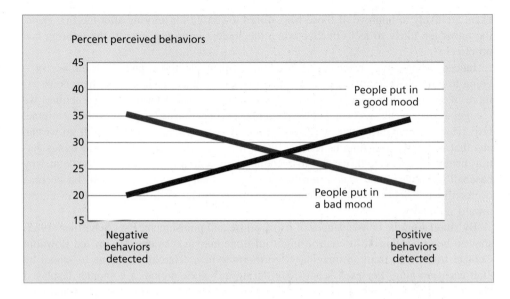

bad mood and then watch a recording (made the day before) of you talking with someone. If made to feel happy, you feel pleased with what you see, and you are able to detect many instances of your poise, interest, and social skill. If you've been put in a bad mood, viewing the same recording seems to reveal a quite different you—one who is stiff, nervous, and inarticulate (Forgas et al., 1984; Figure 1). Given how your mood colors your judgments, you feel relieved at how things brighten when the experimenter switches you to a happy mood before leaving the experiment. Curiously, note Michael Ross and Garth Fletcher (1985), we don't attribute our changing perceptions to our mood shifts. Rather, the world really seems different. (To read more about moods and memory, see "The Inside Story: Joseph P. Forgas: Can Bad Weather Improve Your Memory?")

Our moods color how we judge our worlds partly by bringing to mind past experiences associated with the mood. When we are in a bad mood, we have more depressing thoughts. Mood-related thoughts may distract us from complex thinking about something else. Thus, when emotionally aroused—when either angry or in a very good mood—we become more likely to make System 1 snap judgments and evaluate others based on stereotypes (Bodenhausen et al., 1994; Paulhus & Lim, 1994).

THE inside STORY

Joseph P. Forgas: Can Bad Weather Improve Your Memory?

I noticed some time ago that I not only get into a worse mood on cold, rainy days, but surprisingly, I also seem to remember more clearly the details of what happens on such days. Could it be that negative mood also influences how well we monitor our environment? Perhaps negative mood works like a mild alarm signal, alerting us to pay better attention to what is around us? I decided to examine this possibility in a natural experiment. We placed a number of small unusual trinkets around a Sydney suburban newsagency, and then checked how well departing customers could remember these objects when they leave the shop on cold, rainy days, or warm sunny days (Forgas, Goldenberg & Unkelbach, 2009).

My hunch was confirmed: memory for objects in the shop was significantly better when customers were in a bad mood (on unpleasant days) than on pleasant sunny days. It seems that moods subconsciously influence how closely we observe the outside around us, with negative mood improving attention and memory.

Joseph P. Forgas
The University of New South Wales,
Australia
©Joseph P. Forgas

SUMMING UP: How Do We Judge Our Social Worlds?

- We have an enormous capacity for automatic, efficient, intuitive thinking *(System 1)*. Our cognitive efficiency, although generally adaptive, comes at the price of occasional error. Because we are generally unaware of those errors entering our thinking, it is useful to identify ways in which we form and sustain false beliefs.

- Our preconceptions strongly influence how we interpret and remember events. In a phenomenon called *priming,* people's prejudgments have striking effects on how they perceive and interpret information.

- We often overestimate our judgments. This *overconfidence phenomenon* stems partly from the much greater ease with which we can imagine why we might be right than why we might be wrong. Moreover, people are much more likely to search for information that can

confirm their beliefs than for information that can disconfirm them.

- When given compelling anecdotes or even useless information, we often ignore useful base-rate information. This is partly due to the later ease of recall of vivid information (the *availability heuristic*).

- We are often swayed by illusions of correlation and personal control. It is tempting to perceive correlations where none exist *(illusory correlation)* and to think we can predict or control chance events (the *illusion of control*).

- Moods infuse judgments. Good and bad moods trigger memories of experiences associated with those moods. Moods color our interpretations of current experiences. And by distracting us, moods can also influence how deeply or superficially we think when making judgments.

HOW DO WE PERCEIVE OUR SOCIAL WORLDS?

Understand how our assumptions and prejudgments guide our perceptions, interpretations, and recall.

Our preconceptions guide how we perceive and interpret information. We construe the world through belief-tinted glasses. "Sure, preconceptions matter," people agree; yet they fail to fully appreciate the impact of their own predispositions.

Let's consider some provocative experiments. The first group examines how predispositions and prejudgments affect how we perceive and interpret information. The second group plants a judgment in people's minds *after* they have been given information to see how after-the-fact ideas bias recall. The overarching point: *We respond not to reality as it is but to reality as we construe it.*

Perceiving and Interpreting Events

Despite some startling biases and logical flaws in how we perceive and understand one another, we're mostly accurate (Jussim, 2012). Our first impressions of one another are more often right than wrong. Moreover, the better we know people, the more accurately we can read their minds and feelings.

But on occasion, our prejudgments err. The effects of prejudgments and expectations are standard fare for psychology's introductory course. Consider this phrase:

A
BIRD
IN THE
THE HAND

Did you notice anything wrong with it? There is more to perception than meets the eye*.

POLITICAL PERCEPTIONS.   The same is true of political perception. Because political perceptions are very much in the eye of the beholder, even a simple stimulus may

---

* The word "the" appears twice.

FIGURE :: 2

Pro-Israeli and pro-Arab students who viewed network news descriptions of the "Beirut massacre" believed the coverage was biased against their point of view.
Source: Data from Vallone et al., 1985.

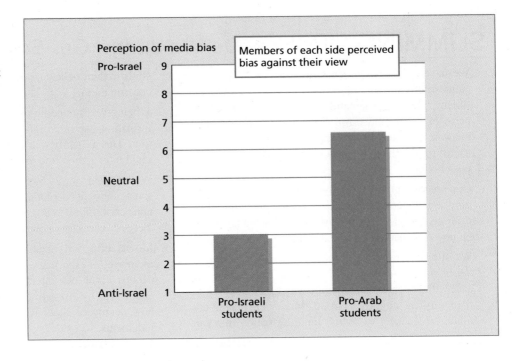

"Once you have a belief, it influences how you perceive all other relevant information. Once you see a country as hostile, you are likely to interpret ambiguous actions on their part as signifying their hostility."

—Political Scientist Robert Jervis (1985)

strike two people quite differently. An experiment by Robert Vallone, Lee Ross, and Mark Lepper (1985) revealed just how powerful preconceptions can be. They showed pro-Israeli and pro-Arab students six network news segments describing the killing of civilian refugees at two camps in Beirut, Lebanon. As Figure 2 illustrates, each group perceived the networks as hostile to its side.

The phenomenon is commonplace: Sports fans perceive referees as partial to the other side. Political candidates and their supporters nearly always view the news media as unsympathetic to their cause (Richardson et al., 2008).

It's not just fans and politicians. People everywhere perceive mediators and media as biased against their position. "There is no subject about which people are less objective than objectivity," noted one media commentator (Poniewozik, 2003). Indeed, people's perceptions of bias can be used to assess their attitudes (Saucier & Miller, 2003). Tell me where you see bias, and you will signal your attitudes.

Is that why, in politics, religion, and science, ambiguous information often fuels conflict? Presidential debates in the United States have mostly reinforced predebate opinions. By nearly a 10-to-1 margin, those who already favored one candidate or the other perceived their candidate as having won (Kinder & Sears, 1985). Thus, report Geoffrey Munro and colleagues (1997), people on both sides may become even more supportive of their respective candidates after viewing a presidential debate.

The bottom line: We view our social worlds through the spectacles of our beliefs, attitudes, and values. That is one reason our beliefs are so important; they shape our interpretation of everything else.

"I'd like your honest, unbiased and possibly career-ending opinion on something."

Some circumstances make it difficult to be unbiased.
© Alex Gregory/The New Yorker Collection/www.cartoonbank.com

Belief Perseverance

Imagine a babysitter who decides, during an evening with a crying infant, that bottle feeding produces colicky babies: "Come to think of it, cow's milk obviously suits calves better than babies." If the infant turns out to be suffering a high fever, will the sitter nevertheless persist in believing that bottle feeding causes colic (Ross & Anderson, 1982)? To find out, Lee Ross, Craig Anderson, and colleagues planted a falsehood in people's minds and then tried to discredit it.

Their research reveals that it is surprisingly difficult to demolish a falsehood after the person conjures up a rationale for it. Each experiment first *implanted a belief,* either by proclaiming it to be true or by showing the participants some anecdotal evidence. Then the participants were asked to *explain why* it is true. Finally, the researchers totally *discredited* the initial information

Partisan perceptions. Supporters of a particular candidate or cause tend to see the media as favoring the other side.
John Moore/Getty Images

by telling the participants the truth: The information was manufactured for the experiment, and half the participants in the experiment had received opposite information. Nevertheless, the false belief survived approximately 75 percent intact, presumably because the participants still retained their invented explanations for the belief. This phenomenon, called **belief perseverance,** shows that beliefs can grow their own legs and survive discrediting.

Another example: Anderson, Lepper, and Ross (1980) asked participants to decide whether individuals who take risks make good or bad firefighters. One group considered a risk-prone person who was a successful firefighter and a cautious person who was unsuccessful. The other group considered cases suggesting the opposite conclusion. After forming their theory that risk-prone people make better (or worse) firefighters, the participants wrote explanations for it—for example, that risk-prone people are brave or that cautious people have fewer accidents. After each explanation was formed, it could exist independently of the information that initially created the belief. When that information was discredited, the participants nevertheless held to their self-generated explanations and therefore continued to believe that risk-prone people really do make better (or worse) firefighters.

These experiments suggest that the more we examine our theories and explain how they *might* be true, the more closed we become to information that challenges our beliefs. When we consider why an accused person might be guilty, why an offending stranger acts that way, or why a favored stock might rise in value, our explanations may survive challenges (Davies, 1997; Jelalian & Miller, 1984).

The evidence is compelling: Our beliefs and expectations powerfully affect how we mentally construct events. Usually, we benefit from our preconceptions, just as scientists benefit from creating theories that guide them in noticing and interpreting events. But the benefits sometimes entail a cost: We become prisoners of our own thought patterns. Thus, the supposed Martian "canals" that twentieth-century astronomers delighted in spotting turned out to be the product of intelligent life—an intelligence on Earth's side of the telescope.

belief perseverance
Persistence of one's initial conceptions, such as when the basis for one's belief is discredited but an explanation of why the belief might be true survives.

"We hear and apprehend only what we already half know."
—Henry David Thoreau, 1817–1862

Constructing Memories of Ourselves and Our Worlds

Do you agree or disagree with this statement?

Memory can be likened to a storage chest in the brain into which we deposit material and from which we can withdraw it later if needed. Occasionally, something is lost from the "chest," and then we say we have forgotten.

In one survey, 85 percent of college students agreed (Lamal, 1979). As one magazine ad put it, "Science has proven the accumulated experience of a lifetime is preserved perfectly in your mind."

Actually, psychological research has proved the opposite. Our memories are not exact copies of experiences that remain on deposit in a memory bank. Rather, we construct memories at the time of withdrawal. Like a paleontologist inferring the appearance of a dinosaur from bone fragments, we reconstruct our distant past by using our current feelings and expectations to combine information fragments. Thus, we can easily (although unconsciously) revise our memories to suit our current knowledge. When one of my [DM] sons complained, "The June issue of *Cricket* never came," and was then shown where it was, he delightedly responded, "Oh good, I knew I'd gotten it."

When an experimenter or a therapist manipulates people's presumptions about their past, many people will construct false memories. Asked to imagine that, as a child, they knocked over a punch bowl at a wedding, about one-fourth will later recall the fictitious event as something that actually happened (Loftus & Bernstein, 2005). In its search for truth, the mind sometimes constructs a falsehood.

In experiments involving more than 20,000 people, Elizabeth Loftus (2003, 2007, 2011a) and collaborators have explored the mind's tendency to construct memories. In the typical experiment, people witness an event, receive misleading information about it (or not), and then take a memory test. The results find a **misinformation effect** in which people incorporate the misinformation into their memories. They recall a yield sign as a stop sign, hammers as screwdrivers, *Vogue* magazine as *Mademoiselle,* Dr. Henderson as "Dr. Davidson," breakfast cereal as eggs, and a clean-shaven man as a fellow with a mustache. Suggested misinformation may even produce false memories of supposed child sexual abuse, argues Loftus.

This process affects our recall of social as well as physical events. Jack Croxton and colleagues (1984) had students spend 15 minutes talking with someone. Those who were later informed that this person liked them recalled the person's behavior as relaxed, comfortable, and happy. Those who heard the person disliked them recalled the person as nervous, uncomfortable, and not so happy.

RECONSTRUCTING OUR PAST ATTITUDES

Five years ago, how did you feel about nuclear power? About your country's president or prime minister? About your parents? If your attitudes have changed, how much have they changed?

Experimenters have explored such questions, and the results have been unnerving. People whose attitudes have changed often insist that they have always felt much as they now feel. Carnegie Mellon University students answered a long survey that included a question about student control over the university curriculum. A week later, they agreed to write an essay opposing student control. After doing so, their attitudes shifted toward greater opposition to student control. When asked to recall how they had answered the question before writing the essay, the students "remembered" holding the opinion that they *now* held and denied that the experiment had affected them (Bem & McConnell, 1970).

After observing students similarly denying their former attitudes, researchers D. R. Wixon and James Laird (1976) commented, "The speed, magnitude, and certainty" with which the students revised their own histories "was striking." As George Vaillant (1977) noted after following adults through time, "It is all too common for caterpillars to become butterflies and then to maintain that in their youth they had been little butterflies. Maturation makes liars of us all."

The construction of positive memories brightens our recollections. Terence Mitchell, Leigh Thompson, and colleagues (1994, 1997) report that people often exhibit *rosy retrospection*—they recall mildly pleasant events more favorably than they experienced them. College students on a 3-week bike trip, older adults on a guided tour of Austria, and undergraduates on vacation all reported enjoying their experiences as they were having them. But they later recalled such experiences even more fondly, minimizing the unpleasant or boring aspects and remembering the high points. Thus, the pleasant times during which I [DM] have sojourned in Scotland, I now (back in my office, facing deadlines and interruptions) romanticize as pure bliss. The drizzle and the pesky midge bugs are but dim memories. The spectacular scenery and the fresh sea air and the favorite tea rooms are

---

"Memory isn't like reading a book: It's more like writing a book from fragmentary notes."

—John F. Kihlstrom (1994)

misinformation effect

Incorporating "misinformation" into one's memory of the event, after witnessing an event and receiving misleading information about it.

"A man should never be ashamed to own that he has been in the wrong, which is but saying in other words, that he is wiser today than he was yesterday."

—Jonathan Swift, *Thoughts on Various Subjects,* 1711

still with me. With any positive experience, some of our pleasure resides in the anticipation, some in the actual experience, and some in the rosy retrospection.

Cathy McFarland and Michael Ross (1985) found that as our relationships change, we also revise our recollections of other people. They had university students rate their steady dating partners. Two months later, they rated them again. Students who were more in love than ever had a tendency to overestimate their first impressions—it was "love at first sight." Those who had broken up were more likely to *underestimate* their earlier liking—recalling their ex as somewhat selfish and bad-tempered.

Diane Holmberg and John Holmes (1994) discovered the phenomenon also operating among 373 newlywed couples, most of whom reported being very happy. When resurveyed 2 years later, those whose marriages had soured recalled that things had always been bad. The results are "frightening," said Holmberg and Holmes: "Such biases can lead to a dangerous downward spiral. The worse your current view of your partner is, the worse your memories are, which only further confirms your negative attitudes."

It's not that we are totally unaware of how we used to feel, but when memories are hazy, current feelings guide our recall. When widows and widowers try to recall the grief they felt on their spouse's death 5 years earlier, their current emotional state colors their memories (Safer et al., 2001). When patients recall their previous day's headache pain, their current feelings sway their recollections (Eich et al., 1985). Depressed people who get Botox—which prevents them from frowning—recover from depression more quickly, perhaps because they find it more difficult to remember why they were sad (Lewis & Bowler, 2009).

> "Travel is glamorous only in retrospect."
> —Paul Theroux,
> in *The Observer*

RECONSTRUCTING OUR PAST BEHAVIOR

Memory construction enables us to revise our own histories. In one study, University of Waterloo students read a message about the benefits of toothbrushing. Later, in a supposedly different experiment, these students recalled brushing their teeth more often during the preceding 2 weeks than did students who had not heard the message (Ross et al., 1981). Likewise, judging from surveys, people report smoking many fewer cigarettes than are actually sold (Hall, 1985). And they recall casting more votes than were actually recorded (Bureau of the Census, 2012).

Social psychologist Anthony Greenwald (1980) noted the similarity of such findings in George Orwell's novel *1984*—in which it was "necessary to remember that events happened in the desired manner." Indeed, argued Greenwald, we all have "totalitarian egos" that revise the past to suit our present views. Thus, we underreport bad behavior and overreport good behavior.

> "Vanity plays lurid tricks with our memory."
> —Novelist Joseph Conrad,
> 1857–1924

Sometimes our present view is that we've improved—in which case we may misrecall our past as more unlike the present than it actually was. This tendency resolves a puzzling pair of consistent findings: Those who participate in psychotherapy and self-improvement programs for weight control, antismoking, and exercise show only modest improvement on average. Yet they often claim considerable benefit. Michael Conway and Michael Ross (1986) explain why: Having expended so much time, effort, and money on self-improvement, people may think, "I may not be perfect now, but I was worse before; this did me a lot of good."

Our social judgments are a mix of observation and expectation, reason and passion.

SUMMING UP: How Do We Perceive Our Social Worlds?

- Other experiments have planted judgments or false ideas in people's minds *after* they have been given information. These experiments reveal that as *before-the-fact judgments* bias our perceptions and interpretations, so *after-the-fact judgments* bias our recall.

- *Belief perseverance* is the phenomenon in which people cling to their initial beliefs and the reasons why a belief might be true, even when the basis for the belief is discredited.

- Far from being a repository for facts about the past, our memories are actually formed when we retrieve them, and they are subject to strong influence by the attitudes and feelings we hold at the time of retrieval.

HOW DO WE EXPLAIN OUR SOCIAL WORLDS?

> Recognize how—and how accurately—we explain others' behavior.

People make it their business to explain other people, and social psychologists make it their business to explain people's explanations.

Our judgments of people depend on how we explain their behavior. Depending on our explanation, we may judge killing as murder, manslaughter, self-defense, or heroism. Depending on our explanation, we may view a homeless person as lacking initiative or as victimized by job and welfare cutbacks. Depending on our explanation, we may interpret someone's friendly behavior as genuine warmth or as ingratiation. Attribution theory helps us make sense of how such explanations work.

Attributing Causality: To the Person or the Situation

We endlessly analyze and discuss why things happen as they do, especially when we experience something negative or unexpected (Weiner, 1985, 2008, 2010). If worker productivity declines, do we assume the workers are getting lazier? Or has their workplace become less efficient? Does a young boy who hits his classmates have a hostile personality? Or is he responding to relentless teasing? Researchers found that married people often analyze their partners' behaviors, especially their negative behaviors. Cold hostility, more than a warm hug, is likely to leave the partner wondering "Why?" (Holtzworth & Jacobson, 1988).

Spouses' answers correlate with marital satisfaction. Unhappy couples usually offer internal explanations for negative acts ("She was late because she doesn't care about me"). Happy couples more often externalize ("She was late because of heavy traffic"). Explanations for positive acts similarly work either to maintain distress ("He brought me flowers because he wants sex") or to enhance the relationship ("He brought me flowers to show he loves me") (Hewstone & Fincham, 1996; McNulty et al., 2008; Weiner, 1995).

Antonia Abbey and colleagues (1987, 1991, 2011) have repeatedly found that men are more likely than women to attribute a woman's friendliness to sexual interest. Men's misreading of women's warmth as a sexual come-on—an example of **misattribution**—can contribute to sexual harassment or even rape (Farris et al., 2008; Kolivas & Gross, 2007; Pryor et al., 1997). Many men believe women are flattered by repeated requests for dates, which women more often view as harassment (Rotundo et al., 2001).

Misattribution is particularly likely when men are in positions of power. A manager may misinterpret a subordinate woman's submissive or friendly behavior and, full of himself, see her in sexual terms (Bargh & Raymond, 1995). Men think about sex more often than do women. Men also are more likely than women to assume that others share their feelings. Thus, a man with sex on his mind may greatly overestimate the sexual significance of a woman's courtesy smile (Levesque et al., 2006; Nelson & LeBoeuf, 2002).

misattribution
Mistakenly attributing a behavior to the wrong source.

A misattribution? Date rape sometimes begins with a man's misreading a woman's warmth as a sexual come-on.
Image Source/Alamy

Such misattributions help explain the greater sexual assertiveness exhibited by men throughout the world, and the greater tendency of men in various cultures, from Boston to Bombay, to justify rape by arguing that the victim consented or implied consent (Kanekar & Nazareth, 1988; Muehlenhard, 1988; Shotland, 1989). Misattributions also help explain why, in one national survey, 23 percent of American women said they had been forced into unwanted sexual behavior, but only 3 percent of American men said they had ever forced a woman into a sexual act (Laumann et al., 1994).

Attribution theory analyzes how we explain people's behavior and what we infer from it. The variations of attribution theory share some common assumptions. Each, as Daniel Gilbert and Patrick Malone (1995) explain, "construes the human skin as a special boundary that separates one set of 'causal forces' from another. On the sunny side of the epidermis are the external or situational forces that press inward upon the person, and on the meaty side are the internal or personal forces that exert pressure outward. Sometimes these forces press in conjunction, sometimes in opposition, and their dynamic interplay manifests itself as observable behavior."

Attribution theory pioneer Fritz Heider (1958) and others after him analyzed the "commonsense psychology" of how people explain everyday events. They concluded that when we observe someone acting intentionally, we sometimes attribute that person's behavior to *internal* causes (for example, the person's disposition or mental state) and sometimes to *external* causes (for example, something about the person's situation). A teacher may wonder whether a child's underachievement is due to lack of motivation and ability (a **dispositional attribution**) or to physical and social circumstances (a **situational attribution**). Also, some of us are more inclined to attribute behavior to stable personality; others tend more to attribute behavior to situations (Bastian & Haslam, 2006; Robins et al., 2004).

INFERRING TRAITS

We often infer that other people's actions are indicative of their intentions and dispositions (Jones & Davis, 1965). If we observe Rick making a sarcastic comment to Linda, we infer that Rick is a hostile person. When are people more likely to infer that others' behavior is caused by traits? For one thing, behavior that's normal for a particular situation tells us less about the person than does behavior unusual for that situation. If Samantha is sarcastic in a job interview, a situation in which sarcasm is rare, that tells us more about Samantha than if she is sarcastic with her siblings.

The ease with which we infer traits—a phenomenon called **spontaneous trait inference**—is remarkable. In experiments at New York University, James Uleman (1989; Uleman et al., 2008) gave students statements to remember, such as "The librarian carries the old woman's groceries across the street." The students would instantly, unintentionally, and unconsciously

attribution theory
The theory of how people explain others' behavior—for example, by attributing it either to internal dispositions (enduring traits, motives, and attitudes) or to external situations.

dispositional attribution
Attributing behavior to the person's disposition and traits.

situational attribution
Attributing behavior to the environment.

spontaneous trait inference
An effortless, automatic inference of a trait after exposure to someone's behavior.

To what should we attribute a student's sleepiness? To lack of sleep? To boredom? Whether we make internal or external attributions depends on whether we notice her consistently sleeping in this and other classes, and on whether other students react as she does to this particular class.
Moodboard/Corbis

infer a trait. When later they were helped to recall the sentence, the most valuable clue word was not "books" (to cue librarian) or "bags" (to cue groceries) but "helpful"—the inferred trait that we suspect you, too, spontaneously attributed to the librarian. Just 1/10th of a second exposure to someone's face leads people to spontaneously infer some personality traits (Willis & Todorov, 2006).

An exception: Asians are less likely to attribute people's behavior to their personality traits (Na & Kitayama, 2011).

The Fundamental Attribution Error

Social psychology's most important lesson concerns the influence of our social environment. At any moment, our internal state, and therefore what we say and do, depends on the situation as well as on what we bring to the situation. In experiments, a slight difference between two situations sometimes greatly affects how people respond. As a professor, I [DM] have seen this when teaching the same class at both 8:30 A.M. and 7:00 P.M. Silent stares would greet me at 8:30; at 7:00, I had to break up a party. In each situation, some individuals were more talkative than others, but the difference between the two situations exceeded the individual differences.

Attribution researchers have found a common problem with our attributions. When explaining someone's behavior, we often underestimate the impact of the situation and overestimate the extent to which it reflects the individual's traits and attitudes. Thus, even knowing the effect of the time of day on classroom conversation, I found it terribly tempting to assume that the people in the 7:00 P.M. class were more extraverted than the "silent types" who came at 8:30 A.M. Likewise, we may infer that people fall because they're clumsy rather than because they were tripped; that people smile because they're happy rather than faking friendliness, and that people speed past us on the highway because they're aggressive rather than late for an important meeting.

fundamental attribution error

The tendency for observers to underestimate situational influences and overestimate dispositional influences upon others' behavior.

This discounting of the situation, called the **fundamental attribution error** (Ross, 1977), appears in many experiments. In the first such study, Edward Jones and Victor Harris (1967) had Duke University students read debaters' speeches supporting or attacking Cuba's leader, Fidel Castro. When told that the debater chose which position to take, the students logically assumed it reflected the person's own attitude. But what happened when the students were told that the debate coach had assigned the position? Students still inferred that the debater had the assigned leanings (Figure 3). People seemed to think, "Yeah, I know he was assigned that position, but, you know, I think he really believes it."

FIGURE :: 3

The Fundamental Attribution Error

When people read a debate speech supporting or attacking Fidel Castro, they attributed corresponding attitudes to the speechwriter, even when the debate coach assigned the writer's position.
Source: Data from Jones & Harris (1967).

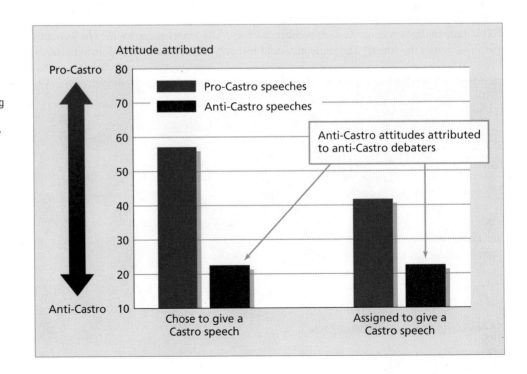

Even when people know they are *causing* someone else's behavior, they still underestimate external influences. If individuals dictate an opinion that someone else must then express, they still tend to see the person as actually holding that opinion (Gilbert & Jones, 1986). If people are asked to be either self-enhancing or self-deprecating during an interview, they are very aware of why they are acting so. But they are *un*aware of their effect on another person. If Juan acts modestly, his conversation partner Ethan is likely to exhibit modesty as well. Juan will easily understand his own behavior, but he will think that poor Ethan suffers from low self-esteem (Baumeister et al., 1988). In short, we tend to presume that others are the way they act—even when we don't make the same presumption about ourselves. Observing Cinderella cowering in her oppressive home, people (ignoring the situation) infer that she is meek; dancing with her at the ball, the prince sees a suave and glamorous person. Cinderella knows she is the same person in both situations.

When viewing a movie actor playing a "hero" or "villain" role, we find it difficult to escape the illusion that the scripted behavior reflects an inner disposition. Glenn Close, who has played villainous characters from the bunny-killing woman in *Fatal Attraction* to the unethical lawyer in the recent TV show *Damages*, is, in real life, a caring activist who co-founded a nonprofit to raise awareness of mental illness.
Desiree Navarro/Getty Images

One experiment re-created Lee Ross's firsthand experience of moving from graduate student to professor. His doctoral oral exam had proved a humbling experience as his apparently brilliant professors quizzed him on topics they specialized in. Six months later, *Dr.* Ross was himself an examiner, now able to ask penetrating questions on *his* favorite topics. Ross's hapless student later confessed to feeling exactly as Ross had a half-year before—dissatisfied with his ignorance and impressed with the apparent brilliance of the examiners.

In an experiment mimicking his student-to-professor experience, Ross set up a simulated quiz game. He randomly assigned some Stanford University students to play the role of questioner, some to play the role of contestant, and others to observe. The researchers invited the questioners to make up difficult questions that would demonstrate their wealth of knowledge. Any one of us can imagine such questions using one's own domain of competence: "Where is Bainbridge Island?" "How did Mary, Queen of Scots, die?" "Which has the longer coastline, Europe or Africa?" If even those few questions have you feeling a little uninformed, then you will appreciate the results of this experiment (Ross et al., 1977).*

Everyone had to know that the questioners would have the advantage. Yet both contestants and observers (but not the questioners) came to the erroneous conclusion that the questioners *really were* more knowledgeable than the contestants (Figure 4). Follow-up research shows that these misimpressions are hardly a reflection of low social intelligence. If anything, college students and other intelligent and socially competent people are *more* likely to make the attribution error (Bauman & Skitka, 2010; Block & Funder, 1986).

In real life, those with social power usually initiate and control conversations, which often leads underlings to overestimate their knowledge and intelligence. Medical doctors, for example, are often presumed to be experts on all sorts of questions unrelated to medicine. Similarly, students often overestimate the brilliance of their teachers. (As in the experiment, teachers are questioners on subjects of their special expertise.) When some of these students later become teachers, they are often amazed to discover that teachers are not so brilliant after all.

To illustrate the fundamental attribution error, most of us need to look no further than our own experiences. Determined to make some new friends, Nicole plasters a smile on her face and anxiously plunges into a party. Everyone else seems quite relaxed and happy

---

* Bainbridge Island is across Puget Sound from Seattle. Mary was ordered beheaded by her cousin Queen Elizabeth I. Although the African continent is more than double the area of Europe, Europe's coastline is longer. (It is more convoluted, with many harbors and inlets, a geographical fact that contributed to its role in the history of maritime trade.)

observ-
z game
n who had
role of questioner was far more
knowledgeable than the contestant. Actually, the assigned roles
of questioner and contestant
simply made the questioner
seem more knowledgeable.
The failure to appreciate this
illustrates the fundamental
attribution error.
Source: Data from Ross et al., 1977.

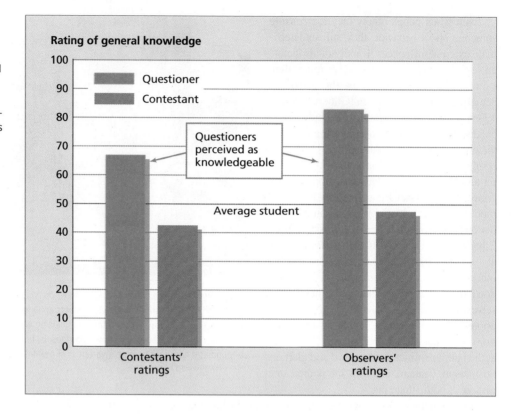

Rating of general knowledge

- Questioner
- Contestant

Questioners
perceived as
knowledgeable

Average student

Contestants'
ratings

Observers'
ratings

as they laugh and talk with one another. Nicole wonders to herself, "Why is everyone always so at ease in groups like this while I'm feeling shy and tense?" Actually, everyone else is feeling nervous, too, and making the same attribution error in assuming that Nicole and the others *are* as they *appear*—confidently convivial.

WHY DO WE MAKE THE ATTRIBUTION ERROR?

So far, we have seen a bias in the way we explain other people's behavior: We often ignore powerful situational determinants. Why do we tend to underestimate the situational determinants of others' behavior but not of our own?

People often attribute keen
intelligence to those, such as
teachers and quiz show hosts,
who test others' knowledge.
Everett Collection

PERSPECTIVE AND SITUATIONAL AWARENESS. Attribution theorists have pointed out that we observe others from a different perspective than we observe ourselves (Jones, 1976; Jones & Nisbett, 1971). When we act, the *environment* commands our attention. When we watch another *person* act, that *person* occupies the center of our attention and the environment becomes relatively invisible. If I'm mad, it's the situation that's making me angry. But someone else getting mad may seem like an ill-tempered person.

From his analysis of 173 studies, Bertram Malle (2006) concluded that the actor–observer difference is often minimal. When our action feels intentional and admirable, we attribute it to our own good reasons, not to the situation. It's only when we behave badly that we tend to display our disposition and attribute our behavior to the situation. Meanwhile, someone observing us may spontaneously infer a trait.

When people viewed a videotape of a suspect confessing during a police interview with a camera focused on the suspect, they perceived the confession as genuine. If the camera was instead focused on the detective, they perceived it as more coerced

The fundamental attribution error: observers underestimating the situation. Driving into a gas station, we may think the person parked at the second pump (blocking access to the first) is inconsiderate. That person, having arrived when the first pump was in use, attributes her behavior to the situation.
Courtesy Kathryn Brownson

(Lassiter & Irvine, 1986; Lassiter et al., 2005, 2007). The camera perspective influenced people's guilt judgments even when the judge instructed them not to allow this to happen (Lassiter et al., 2002).

In courtrooms, most confession videotapes focus on the confessor. As we might expect, noted Daniel Lassiter and Kimberly Dudley (1991), such tapes yield a nearly 100 percent conviction rate when played by prosecutors. Aware of Lassiter's research on the *camera perspective bias*, New Zealand and some parts of Canada and the United States now require that police interrogations be filmed with equal focus on the officer and the suspect.

The passage of time decreases the tendency toward the fundamental attribution error. A week after hearing someone argue a position they did not choose, people were more likely to credit the situation (Burger & Palmer, 1991). The day after a presidential election, Jerry Burger and Julie Pavelich (1994) asked voters why the election turned out as it did. Most attributed the outcome to the candidates' personal traits and positions. When they asked other voters the same question a year later, only a third attributed the verdict to the candidates. More people now credited circumstances, such as the country's good mood and the robust economy.

Consider this: Are you generally quiet, talkative, or does it depend on the situation?

"Depends on the situation" is a common answer. Likewise, when asked to predict their feelings 2 weeks after receiving grades or learning the outcome of their country's national election, people expect the situation to rule their emotions; they underestimate the importance of their own sunny or dour dispositions (Quoidbach & Dunn, 2010). But when asked to describe a friend—or to describe what they were like 5 years ago—people more often ascribe trait descriptions. *When recalling our past, we become like observers of someone else* (Pronin & Ross, 2006). For most of us, the "old you" is someone other than today's "real you." We regard our distant past selves (and our distant future selves) almost as if they were other people occupying our body.

All these experiments point to a reason for the attribution error: *We find causes where we look for them.* To see this in your own experience, consider this: Would you say your social psychology instructor is a quiet or a talkative person?

Focusing on the person. Would you infer that your professor for this course, or the professor shown here, is naturally outgoing?
Comstock Images/JupiterImages RF

"And in imagination he began to recall the best moments of his pleasant life.... But the child who had experienced that happiness existed no longer, it was like a reminiscence of somebody else."

—Leo Tolstoy,
The Death of Ivan Ilyich, 1886

Under alcohol's influence, people's attentional focus narrows and they become more likely to attribute someone's action—perhaps a bump at a bar—to intentionality (Begue et al., 2010). Thinking that a jolt or seeming insult was intentional may then trigger an aggravated reaction.

Whether conservatives or liberals offer more situational attributions depends on the topic. When explaining poverty, liberals offer stronger situational attributions. When explaining U.S. Marines' killing of Iraqi civilians, conservatives offer stronger situational attributions (Morgan et al., 2010).

You may have guessed that he or she is fairly outgoing. But consider: Your attention focuses on your instructor while he or she behaves in a public context that demands speaking. The instructor also observes his or her own behavior in many situations—in the classroom, in meetings, at home. "Me, talkative?" your instructor might say. "Well, it all depends on the situation. When I'm in class or with good friends, I'm rather outgoing. But at conferences and in unfamiliar situations I'm rather shy." Because we are acutely aware of how our behavior varies with the situation, we see ourselves as more variable than do other people (Baxter & Goldberg, 1987; Kammer, 1982; Sande et al., 1988). We think, "Nigel is uptight, but Fiona is relaxed. With me it varies."

CULTURAL DIFFERENCES. Cultures also influence attribution error (Ickes, 1980; Watson, 1982). An individualistic Western worldview predisposes people to assume that people, not situations, cause events. Internal explanations are more socially approved (Jellison & Green, 1981). "You can do it!" we are assured by the pop psychology of positive-thinking Western culture. You get what you deserve and deserve what you get.

As Western children grow up, they learn to explain other people's behavior in terms of their personal characteristics (Rholes et al., 1990; Ross, 1981). As a first-grader, one of my [DM] sons unscrambled the words "gate the sleeve caught Tom on his" into "The gate caught Tom on his sleeve." His teacher, applying Western cultural assumptions, marked that wrong. The "right" answer located the cause within Tom: "Tom caught his sleeve on the gate."

The fundamental attribution error occurs across varied cultures (Krull et al., 1999). Yet people in Eastern Asian cultures are somewhat more sensitive than Westerners to the importance of situations. Thus, when aware of the social context, they are less inclined to assume that others' behavior corresponds to their traits (Choi et al., 1999; Farwell & Weiner, 2000; Masuda & Kitayama, 2004).

Some languages promote external attributions. Instead of "I was late," Spanish idiom allows one to say, "The clock caused me to be late." In collectivistic cultures, people less often perceive others in terms of personal dispositions (Lee et al., 1996; Zebrowitz-McArthur, 1988). They are less likely to spontaneously interpret a behavior as reflecting an inner trait (Newman, 1993). When told of someone's actions, Hindus in India are less likely than Americans to offer dispositional explanations ("She is kind") and more likely to offer situational explanations ("Her friends were with her") (Miller, 1984).

The fundamental attribution error is *fundamental* because it colors our explanations in basic and important ways. Researchers in Britain, India, Australia, and the United States have found that people's attributions predict their attitudes toward the poor and the unemployed (Furnham, 1982; Pandey et al., 1982; Skitka, 1999; Wagstaff, 1983; Weiner et al., 2011). Those who attribute poverty and unemployment to personal dispositions ("They're just lazy and undeserving") tend to adopt political positions unsympathetic to such people (Figure 5). This *dispositional attribution* ascribes behavior to the person's disposition and traits. Those who make *situational attributions* ("If you or I were to live with the same overcrowding, poor education, and discrimination, would we be any better off?") tend to adopt political positions that offer more direct support to the poor. Tell me your attributions for poverty and I will guess your politics.

Can we benefit from being aware of the attribution error? I [DM] once assisted with some interviews for a faculty position. One candidate was interviewed by six of us at once; each of us had the opportunity to ask two or three questions. I came away thinking, "What a stiff, awkward person he is." The second candidate I met privately over coffee, and we immediately discovered we had a close, mutual friend. As we talked, I became increasingly impressed by what a "warm, engaging, stimulating person she is." Only later did I remember the fundamental attribution error and reassess my analysis. I had attributed his stiffness and her warmth to their dispositions; in fact, I later realized, such behavior resulted partly from the difference in their interview situations.

WHY WE STUDY ATTRIBUTION ERRORS

This chapter, like the one before it, explains some foibles and fallacies in our social thinking. Reading about these may make it seem, as one of my [DM] students put it, that "social psychologists get their kicks out of playing tricks on people." Actually, the experiments,

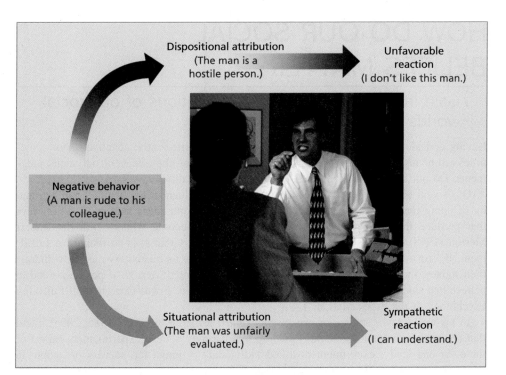

FIGURE :: 5

Attributions and
Reactions

How we explain someone's
negative behavior determines
how we feel about it.
Esbin-Anderson/The Image Works

though sometimes amusing, are not designed to demonstrate "what fools these mortals be." Their serious purpose is to reveal how we think about ourselves and others.

If our capacity for illusion and self-deception is shocking, remember that our modes of thought are generally adaptive. Illusory thinking is a by-product of our mind's strategies for simplifying complex information. It parallels our perceptual mechanisms, which generally give us useful images of the world but sometimes lead us astray.

A second reason for focusing on thinking biases such as the fundamental attribution error is humanitarian. One of social psychology's "great humanizing messages," note Thomas Gilovich and Richard Eibach (2001), is that people should not always be blamed for their problems: "More often than people are willing to acknowledge, failure, disability, and misfortune are . . . the product of real environmental causes."

A third reason for focusing on biases is that we are mostly unaware of them and can benefit from greater awareness. As with other biases, such as the self-serving bias, people see themselves as less susceptible than others to attribution errors (Pronin, 2008). You will probably find more surprises, more challenges, and more benefit in an analysis of errors and biases than you would in a string of testimonies to the human capacity for logic and intellectual achievement. That is also why world literature so often portrays pride and other human failings. Social psychology aims to expose us to fallacies in our thinking in the hope that we will become more rational, more in touch with reality, and more receptive to critical thinking.

"Most poor people are not lazy. . . . They catch the early bus. They raise other people's children. They clean the streets. No, no, they're not lazy."

—The Reverend Jesse Jackson, Address to the Democratic National Convention, July, 1988

SUMMING UP: How Do We Explain Our Social Worlds?

- *Attribution theory* involves how we explain people's behavior. *Misattribution*—attributing a behavior to the wrong source—is a major factor in sexual harassment, as a person in power (typically male) interprets friendliness as a sexual come-on.

- Although we usually make reasonable attributions, we often commit the *fundamental attribution error* when explaining other people's behavior. We attribute their behavior so much to their inner traits and attitudes that we discount situational constraints, even when those are obvious. We make this attribution error partly because when we watch someone act, that *person* is the focus of our attention and the situation is relatively invisible. When *we* act, our attention is usually on what we are reacting to—the situation is more visible.

HOW DO OUR SOCIAL BELIEFS MATTER?

| Gain insight into how our expectations of our social worlds matter.

Having considered how we explain and judge others—efficiently, adaptively, but sometimes erroneously—we conclude this chapter by pondering the effects of our social judgments. Do our social beliefs matter? Can they change reality?

Our social beliefs and judgments do matter. They influence how we feel and act, and by so doing may help generate their own reality. When our ideas lead us to act in ways that produce their apparent confirmation, they have become what sociologist Robert Merton (1948) termed **self-fulfilling prophecies**—beliefs that lead to their own fulfillment. If, led to believe that their bank is about to crash, its customers race to withdraw their money, their false perceptions may create reality, noted Merton. If people are led to believe that stocks are about to soar, they will indeed. (See "Focus On: The Self-Fulfilling Psychology of the Stock Market.")

In his well-known studies of *experimenter bias,* Robert Rosenthal (1985, 2006) found that research participants sometimes live up to what they believe experimenters expect of them. In one study, experimenters asked individuals to judge the success of people in various photographs. The experimenters read the same instructions to all their participants and showed them the same photos. Nevertheless, experimenters who expected their participants to see the photographed people as successful obtained higher ratings than did those who expected their participants to see the people as failures. Even more startling—and controversial—are reports that teachers' beliefs about their students similarly serve as

self-fulfilling prophecy
A belief that leads to its own fulfillment.

focus ON

The Self-Fulfilling Psychology of the Stock Market

On the evening of January 6, 1981, Joseph Granville, a popular Florida investment adviser, wired his clients: "Stock prices will nosedive; sell tomorrow." Word of Granville's advice soon spread, and January 7 became the heaviest day of trading in the previous history of the New York Stock Exchange. All told, stock values lost $40 billion.

Nearly a half-century ago, John Maynard Keynes likened such stock market psychology to the popular beauty contests then conducted by London newspapers. To win, one had to pick the six faces out of a hundred that were, in turn, chosen most frequently by the other newspaper contestants. Thus, as Keynes wrote, "Each competitor has to pick not those faces which he himself finds prettiest, but those which he thinks likeliest to catch the fancy of the other competitors."

Investors likewise try to pick not the stocks that touch their fancy but the stocks that other investors will favor. The name of the game is predicting others' behavior. As one Wall Street fund manager explained, "You may or may not agree with Granville's view—but that's usually beside the point." If you think his advice will cause others to sell,

you want to sell quickly, before prices drop more. If you expect others to buy, you buy now to beat the rush.

The self-fulfilling psychology of the stock market worked to an extreme on Monday, October 19, 1987, when the Dow Jones Industrial Average lost 20 percent. Part of what happens during such crashes is that the media and the rumor mill focus on whatever bad news is available to explain them. Once reported, the explanatory news stories further diminish people's expectations, causing declining prices to fall still lower. The process also works in reverse by amplifying good news when stock prices are rising.

In April of 2000, the volatile technology market again demonstrated a self-fulfilling psychology, now called "momentum investing." After 2 years of eagerly buying stocks (because prices were rising), people started frantically selling them (because prices were falling). Such wild market swings—"irrational exuberance" followed by a crash—are mainly self-generated, noted economist Robert Shiller (2005). In 2008 and 2009, the market psychology headed south again as another bubble burst.

self-fulfilling prophecies. If a teacher believes a student is good at math, will the student do well in the class? Let's examine this.

Teacher Expectations and Student Performance

Teachers do have higher expectations for some students than for others. Perhaps you have detected this after having a brother or sister precede you in school, after receiving a label such as "gifted" or "learning disabled," or after taking "honors" classes. Perhaps conversation in the teachers' lounge sent your reputation ahead of you. Or perhaps your new teacher scrutinized your school file or discovered your family's social status. It's clear that teachers' evaluations correlate with student achievement: Teachers think well of students who do well. That's mostly because teachers accurately perceive their students' abilities and achievements. "About 75 percent of the correlation between teacher expectations and student future achievement reflects accuracy," report Lee Jussim, Stacy Robustelli, and Thomas Cain (2009).

But are teachers' evaluations ever a *cause* as well as a consequence of student performance? One correlational study of 4,300 British schoolchildren suggested yes; students whose teachers expected them to perform well indeed performed well (Crano & Mellon, 1978). Not only is high performance followed by higher teacher evaluations, but the reverse is true as well—teachers' judgments predicted students' later performance even beyond their actual ability (Sorhagen, 2013).

Could we test this "teacher-expectations effect" experimentally? Imagine we gave a teacher the impression that Olivia, Emma, Ethan, and Manuel—four randomly selected students—are unusually capable. Will the teacher give special treatment to these four and elicit superior performance from them? In a now-famous experiment, Rosenthal and Lenore Jacobson (1968) reported precisely that. Randomly selected children in a San Francisco elementary school who were said (on the basis of a fictitious test) to be on the verge of a dramatic intellectual spurt did then spurt ahead in IQ score.

That dramatic result seemed to suggest that the school problems of "disadvantaged" children might reflect their teachers' low expectations. The findings were soon publicized in the national media as well as in many college textbooks. However, further analysis—which was not as highly publicized—revealed the teacher-expectations effect to be not as powerful and reliable as this initial study had led many people to believe (Jussim et al., 2009; Spitz, 1999). By Rosenthal's own count, in only approximately 4 in 10 of the nearly 500 published experiments did expectations significantly affect performance (Rosenthal, 1991, 2002). Low expectations do not doom a capable child, nor do high expectations magically transform a slow learner into a valedictorian. Human nature is not so pliable.

High expectations do, however, seem to boost low achievers, for whom a teacher's positive attitude may be a hope-giving breath of fresh air (Madon et al., 1997). How are such expectations transmitted? Rosenthal and other investigators report that teachers look, smile, and nod more at "high-potential students." Teachers also may teach more to their "gifted" students, set higher goals for them, call on them more, and give them more time to answer (Cooper, 1983; Harris & Rosenthal, 1985, 1986; Jussim, 1986).

In one study, teachers were videotaped talking to, or about, unseen students for whom they held high or low expectations. A random 10-second clip of either the teacher's voice or the teacher's face was enough to tell viewers—both children and adults—whether this was a good or a poor student and how much the teacher liked the student. (You read that right: 10 seconds.) Although teachers may think they can conceal their feelings and behave impartially toward the class, students are acutely sensitive to teachers' facial expressions and body movements (Babad, et al., 1991; Figure 6).

What about the effect of *students'* expectations upon their teachers? You no doubt begin many of your courses having heard "Professor Smith is interesting" and "Professor Jones is a bore." Robert Feldman and Thomas Prohaska (1979; Feldman & Theiss, 1982) found that such expectations can affect both student and teacher. Students who expected to be taught by an excellent teacher perceived their teacher (who was unaware of their expectations) as more competent and interesting than did students with low expectations.

Rosenthal (2008) recalls submitting a paper describing his early experiments on experimenter bias to a leading journal and to an American Association for the Advancement of Science prize competition. On the same day, some weeks later, he received a letter from the journal rejecting his paper and one from the association naming it the year's best social science research. In science, as in everyday life, some people appreciate what others do not, which is why it often pays to try and, when rebuffed, to try again.

Self-presumed expectations associated with one's gender ("women are bad at math") or race ("Blacks don't do so well on aptitude tests") can create anxiety that suppresses test scores. Remove the "stereotype threat" and performance may improve.

To judge a teacher or professor's overall warmth and enthusiasm also takes but a thin slice of behavior— mere seconds (Ambady & Rosenthal, 1992, 1993).

FIGURE :: 6

Self-Fulfilling
Prophecies

Teacher expectations
can become self-fulfilling
prophecies. But for the most
part, teachers' expectations
accurately reflect reality
(Jussim & Harber, 2005).

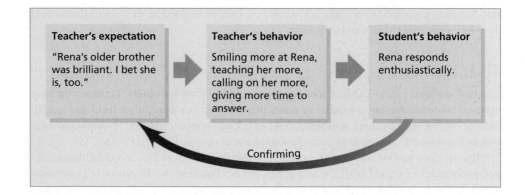

Furthermore, the students actually learned more. In a later experiment, women who were falsely told that their male instructor was sexist had a less positive experience with him, performed worse, and rated him as less competent than did women not given the expectation of sexism (Adams et al., 2006).

Were these results due entirely to the students' perceptions or also to a self-fulfilling prophecy that affected the teacher? In a follow-up experiment, Feldman and Prohaska (1979) videotaped teachers and had observers rate their performances. Teachers were judged most capable when assigned a student who nonverbally conveyed positive expectations.

To see whether such effects might also occur in actual classrooms, a research team led by David Jamieson (Jamieson et al., 1987) experimented with four Ontario high school classes taught by a newly transferred teacher. During individual interviews, they told students in two of the classes that both other students and the research team rated the teacher very highly. Compared with the control classes, students who were given positive expectations paid better attention during class. At the end of the teaching unit, they also got better grades and rated the teacher as clearer in her teaching. The attitudes that a class has toward its teacher are as important, it seems, as the teacher's attitude toward the students.

Getting from Others What We Expect

So the expectations of experimenters and teachers, although usually reasonably accurate, occasionally act as self-fulfilling prophecies. How widespread are self-fulfilling prophecies? Do we get from others what we expect of them? Studies show that our perceptions of others are more accurate than biased (Jussim, 2012). Self-fulfilling prophecies have "less than extraordinary power." Yet sometimes, self-fulfilling prophecies do operate in work settings (with managers who have high or low expectations), in courtrooms (as judges instruct juries), and in simulated police contexts (as interrogators with guilty or innocent expectations interrogate and pressure suspects; (Kassin et al., 2003; Rosenthal, 2003, 2006). Teens whose parents thought they'd tried marijuana—even though they hadn't— were more likely to subsequently try it (Lamb & Crano, 2014).

Do self-fulfilling prophecies color our personal relationships? Sometimes, negative expectations of someone lead us to be extra nice to that person, which induces him or her to be nice in return—thus *dis*confirming our expectations. But a more common finding in studies of social interaction is that, yes, we do to some extent get what we expect (Olson et al., 1996).

In laboratory games, hostility nearly always begets hostility: If someone believes an opponent will be noncooperative, the opponent often responds by becoming noncooperative (Kelley & Stahelski, 1970). Each party's perception of the other as aggressive, resentful, and vindictive induces the other to display those behaviors in self-defense, thus creating a vicious, self-perpetuating circle. In another experiment, people anticipated interacting with another person of a different race. When led to expect that the person disliked interacting with someone of their race, they felt more anger and displayed more hostility toward the person (Butz & Plant, 2006). Likewise, whether someone expects her partner to be in a bad mood or in a loving mood may affect how she relates to him, thereby inducing him to confirm her belief.

So, do intimate relationships prosper when partners idealize each other? Are positive illusions of the other's virtues self-fulfilling? Or are they more often self-defeating, by creating high expectations that can't be met? Among University of Waterloo dating couples followed by Sandra Murray and associates (1996a, 1996b, 2000), positive ideals of one's partner were good omens. Idealization helped buffer conflict, bolster satisfaction, and turn self-perceived frogs into princes or princesses. When someone loves and admires us, it helps us become more the person he or she imagines us to be.

When dating couples deal with conflicts, hopeful optimists and their partners tend to perceive each other as engaging constructively. Compared to those with more pessimistic expectations, they then feel more supported and more satisfied with the outcome (Srivastava et al., 2006). Among married couples, too, those who worry that their partner doesn't love and accept them interpret slight hurts as rejections, which motivates them to devalue the partner and distance themselves. Those who presume their partner's love and acceptance respond less defensively, read less into stressful events, and treat the partner better (Murray et al., 2003). Love helps create its presumed reality.

Several experiments conducted by Mark Snyder (1984) at the University of Minnesota show how, once formed, erroneous beliefs about the social world can induce others to confirm those beliefs, a phenomenon called **behavioral confirmation.** For example, male students talked on the telephone with women they thought (from having been shown a picture) were either attractive or unattractive. The supposedly attractive women spoke more warmly than the supposedly unattractive women. The men's erroneous beliefs had become a self-fulfilling prophecy by leading them to act in a way that influenced the women to fulfill the men's stereotype that beautiful people are desirable people (Snyder et al., 1977).

Behavioral confirmation also occurs as people interact with partners holding mistaken beliefs. People whom others believe are lonely behave less sociably (Rotenberg et al., 2002). People who believe they are accepted and liked (rather than disliked) then behave warmly—and do get accepted and liked (Stinson et al., 2009). Men whom others believe are sexist behave less favorably toward women (Pinel, 2002). Job interviewees who are believed to be warm behave more warmly.

Imagine yourself as one of the 60 young men or 60 young women in an experiment by Robert Ridge and Jeffrey Reber (2002). Each man is to interview one of the women for a teaching assistant position. Before doing so, he is told either that she feels attracted to him (based on his answers to a biographical questionnaire) or not attracted. (Imagine being told that someone you were about to meet reported considerable interest in getting to know you and in dating you, or had no interest whatsoever.) The result was behavioral confirmation: Applicants believed to feel an attraction exhibited more flirtatiousness (without being aware of doing so). Ridge and Reber believe that this process, like the misattribution phenomenon discussed previously, may be one of the roots of sexual harassment. If a woman's behavior seems to confirm a man's beliefs, he may then escalate his overtures until they become sufficiently overt for the woman to recognize and interpret them as inappropriate or harassing.

Expectations influence children's behavior, too. After observing the amount of litter in three classrooms, Richard Miller and colleagues (1975) had the teacher and others repeatedly tell one class that they should be neat and tidy. This persuasion increased the amount of litter placed in wastebaskets from 15 to 45 percent, but only temporarily. Another class, which also had been placing only 15 percent of its litter in wastebaskets, was repeatedly congratulated for being so neat and tidy. After 8 days of hearing this,

behavioral confirmation
A type of self-fulfilling prophecy whereby people's social expectations lead them to behave in ways that cause others to confirm their expectations.

"The more he treated her as though she were really very nice, the more Lotty expanded and became really very nice, and the more he, affected in his turn, became really very nice himself; so that they went round and round, not in a vicious but in a highly virtuous circle."
—Elizabeth Von Arnim,
The Enchanted April, 1922

Behavioral confirmation. If each of these people feels attracted to the other, but presumes that feeling isn't reciprocated, they may each act cool to avoid feeling rejected—and decide that the other's coolness confirms the presumption. Danu Stinson and colleagues (2009) note that such "self-protective inhibition of warmth" dooms some would-be relationships.
Chris Rout/Alamy

and still 2 weeks later, these children were fulfilling the expectation by putting more than 80 percent of their litter in wastebaskets. Tell children they are hardworking and kind (rather than lazy and mean), and they may live up to their labels. Tying the identity to the self is important: Children who were asked to be "a helper" were more likely to help in later tasks than those asked to "help" (Bryan et al., 2014). When children think of themselves as tidy and helpful, they become tidy and helpful.

Overall, these experiments help us understand how social beliefs, such as stereotypes about people with disabilities or about people of a particular race or sex, may be self-confirming. How others treat us reflects how we and others have treated them.

SUMMING UP: How Do Our Social Beliefs Matter?

- Our beliefs sometimes take on lives of their own. Usually, our beliefs about others have a basis in reality. But studies of experimenter bias and teacher expectations show that an erroneous belief that certain people are unusually capable (or incapable) can lead teachers and researchers to give those people special treatment. This may elicit superior (or inferior) performance and,

  therefore, seem to confirm an assumption that is actually false.

- Similarly, in everyday life we often get *behavioral confirmation* of what we expect. Told that someone we are about to meet is intelligent and attractive, we may come away impressed with just how intelligent and attractive he or she is.

WHAT CAN WE CONCLUDE ABOUT SOCIAL BELIEFS AND JUDGMENTS?

View human nature through cognitive social psychology.

Social cognition studies reveal that our information-processing powers are impressive for their efficiency and adaptiveness ("in apprehension how like a god!" exclaimed Shakespeare's Hamlet). Yet we are also vulnerable to predictable errors and misjudgments ("headpiece filled with straw," said T. S. Eliot). What practical lessons, and what insights into human nature, can we take home from this research?

We have reviewed reasons why people sometimes form false beliefs. We cannot easily dismiss these experiments: Most of their participants were intelligent people, often students at leading universities. Moreover, people's intelligence scores are uncorrelated with their vulnerability to many different thinking biases (Stanovich & West, 2008). One can be very smart and exhibit seriously bad judgment.

Trying hard also doesn't eliminate thinking biases. These predictable distortions and biases occurred even when payment for right answers motivated people to think optimally. As one researcher concluded, the illusions "have a persistent quality not unlike that of perceptual illusions" (Slovic, 1972).

Research in cognitive social psychology thus mirrors the mixed review given humanity in literature, philosophy, and religion. Many research psychologists have spent lifetimes exploring the awesome capacities of the human mind. We are smart enough to have cracked our own genetic code, to have invented talking computers, and to have sent people to the moon. Three cheers for human reason.

Well, two cheers—because the mind's premium on efficient judgment makes our intuition more vulnerable to misjudgment than we suspect. With remarkable ease, we form and sustain false beliefs. Led by our preconceptions, feeling overconfident, persuaded by vivid anecdotes, perceiving correlations and control even where none may exist, we construct our social beliefs and then influence others to confirm them. "The naked intellect," observed novelist Madeleine L'Engle, "is an extraordinarily inaccurate instrument."

But have these experiments just been intellectual tricks played on hapless participants, thus making them look worse than they are? Richard Nisbett and Lee Ross (1980) contended that, if anything, laboratory procedures overestimate our intuitive powers. The experiments usually present people with clear evidence and warn them that their reasoning ability is being tested. Seldom does real life say to us: "Here is some evidence. Now put on your thinking cap and answer these questions."

Often our everyday failings are inconsequential, but not always so. False impressions, interpretations, and beliefs can produce serious consequences. Even small biases can have profound social effects when we are making important social judgments: Why are so many people homeless? Unhappy? Homicidal? Does my friend love me or my money? Cognitive biases even creep into sophisticated scientific thinking. Human nature has hardly changed in the 3,000 years since the Old Testament psalmist noted that "no one can see his own errors."

Is this too cynical? Leonard Martin and Ralph Erber (2005) invite us to imagine that an intelligent being swooped down and begged for information that would help it understand the human species. When you hand it this social psychology text, the alien says "thank you" and zooms back off into space. How would you feel about having offered social psychology's analysis of human life? Joachim Krueger and David Funder (2003a, 2003b) wouldn't feel very good. Social psychology's preoccupation with human foibles needs balancing with "a more positive view of human nature," they argue.

Fellow social psychologist Lee Jussim (2005, 2012) agrees, adding, "Despite the oft demonstrated existence of a slew of logical flaws and systematic biases in lay judgment and social perception, such as the fundamental attribution error, false consensus, over-reliance on imperfect heuristics, self-serving biases, etc., people's perceptions of one another are surprisingly (though rarely perfectly) accurate." The elegant analyses of the imperfections of our thinking are themselves a tribute to human wisdom. Were one to argue that all human thought is illusory, the assertion would be self-refuting, for it, too, would be but an illusion. It would be logically equivalent to contending "All generalizations are false, including this one."

Just as medicine assumes that each body organ serves a function, behavioral scientists assume our modes of thought and behavior are adaptive. The rules of thought that produce false beliefs and deficient intuition usually serve us well. Frequently, the errors are a byproduct of our mental shortcuts that simplify the complex information we receive.

Nobel laureate psychologist Herbert Simon (1957) was among the researchers who first described the bounds of human reason. Simon contends that to cope with reality, we simplify it. Consider the complexity of a chess game: The number of possible games is greater than the number of particles in the universe. How do we cope? We adopt some simplifying rules—heuristics. These heuristics sometimes lead us to defeat. But they do enable us to make efficient snap judgments.

Illusory thinking can likewise spring from useful heuristics that aid our survival. In many ways, heuristics make us smart (Gigerenzer & Gaissmaier, 2011). The belief in our power to control events helps maintain hope and effort. If things are sometimes subject to control and sometimes not, we maximize our outcomes by positive thinking. Optimism pays dividends. We might even say that our beliefs are like scientific theories—sometimes in error, yet useful as generalizations. As social psychologist Susan Fiske (1992) says, "Thinking is for doing."

Might we reduce errors in our social thinking? In school, math teachers teach, teach, teach until the mind is finally trained to process numerical information accurately and automatically. We assume that such ability does not come naturally; otherwise, why bother with the years of training? Research psychologist Robyn Dawes (1980a, 1980b)—who was dismayed that "study after study has shown [that] people have very limited abilities to process information on a conscious level, particularly social information"—suggested that we should also teach, teach, teach how to process social information.

Richard Nisbett and Lee Ross (1980) have agreed that education could indeed reduce our vulnerability to certain types of error. They offer the following recommendations:

- Train people to recognize likely sources of error in their own social intuition.
- Set up statistics courses geared to everyday problems of logic and social judgment. Given such training, people do, in fact, reason better about everyday events (Lehman et al., 1988; Nisbett et al., 1987).

"In creating these problems, we didn't set out to fool people. All our problems fooled us, too."
—Amos Tversky (1985)

"The purposes in the human mind are like deep water, but the intelligent will draw them out."
—Proverbs 20:5

"Cognitive errors . . . exist in the present because they led to survival and reproductive advantages for humans in the past."
—Evolutionary Psychologists Martie Haselton and David Buss (2000)

"The spirit of liberty is the spirit which is not too sure that it is right; the spirit of liberty is the spirit which seeks to understand the minds of other men and women; the spirit of liberty is the spirit which weighs their interests alongside its own without bias."
—Learned Hand, "The Spirit of Liberty," 1952

- Make such teaching more effective by illustrating it richly with concrete, vivid anecdotes and examples from everyday life.
- Teach memorable and useful slogans, such as: It's an empirical question. Where did the sample come from? or You can lie with statistics, but a well-chosen example does the job better.

SUMMING UP: What Can We Conclude About Social Beliefs and Judgments?

Research on social beliefs and judgments reveals how we form and sustain beliefs that usually serve us well but sometimes lead us astray. A balanced social psychology will therefore appreciate both the powers and the perils of social thinking.

POSTSCRIPT:
Reflecting on Illusory Thinking

"Rob the average man of his life-illusion, and you rob him also of his happiness."

—Henrik Ibsen,
The Wild Duck, 1884

Is research on cognitive errors too humbling? Surely we can acknowledge the hard truth of our human limits and still sympathize with the deeper message that people are more than machines. Our subjective experiences are the stuff of our humanity—our art and our music, our enjoyment of friendship and love, our mystical and religious experiences.

The cognitive and social psychologists who explore illusory thinking are not out to remake us into unfeeling logical machines. They know that emotions enrich human experience and that intuitions are an important source of creative ideas. They add, however, the humbling reminder that our susceptibility to error also makes clear the need for disciplined training of the mind. The American writer Norman Cousins (1978) called this "the biggest truth of all about learning: that its purpose is to unlock the human mind and to develop it into an organ capable of thought—conceptual thought, analytical thought, sequential thought."

Research on error and illusion in social judgment reminds us to "judge not"—to remember, with a dash of humility, our potential for misjudgment. It also encourages us not to feel intimidated by the arrogance of those who cannot see their own potential for bias and error. We humans are wonderfully intelligent yet fallible creatures. We have dignity but not deity.

Such humility and distrust of human authority is at the heart of both religion and science. No wonder many of the founders of modern science were religious people whose convictions predisposed them to be humble before nature and skeptical of human authority (Hooykaas, 1972; Merton, 1938). Science always involves an interplay between intuition and rigorous test, between creative hunch and skepticism. To sift reality from illusion requires both open-minded curiosity and hard-headed rigor. This perspective could prove to be a good attitude for approaching all of life: to be critical but not cynical, curious but not gullible, open but not exploitable.

Behavior and Attitudes

© KidStock/Blend Images/Corbis RF

"The ancestor of every action is a thought."

—Ralph Waldo Emerson, *Essays, First Series*, 1841

How much does what we *are* (on the inside) predict what we *do* (on the outside)? Philosophers, theologians, and educators speculate about the connections between attitude and action, character and conduct, private word and public deed. Underlying most teaching, counseling, and parenting is a simple assumption: Our private beliefs and feelings determine our public behavior; so if we want to change behavior, we must first change hearts and minds.

In the beginning, social psychologists agreed: To know people's attitudes is to predict their actions. Genocidal killers and suicide terrorists have extreme attitudes that can produce extreme behavior. Countries whose people detest another country's leaders are more likely to produce terrorist acts against them (Krueger & Malečková, 2009). Hateful attitudes spawn violent behavior.

But in 1964, Leon Festinger observed that *changing* people's attitudes often hardly affects their behavior. Festinger believed the attitude-behavior relation works

How well do our attitudes predict our behavior?

When does our behavior affect our attitudes?

Why does our behavior affect our attitudes?

Postscript: Changing ourselves through action

the other way around, with our behavior as the horse and our attitudes as the cart. As Robert Abelson (1972) put it, we are "very well trained and very good at finding reasons for what we do, but not very good at doing what we find reasons for." This chapter explores the interplay of attitudes and behavior.

In social psychology, **attitudes** are defined as beliefs and feelings related to a person or an event (Eagly & Chaiken, 2005). Thus, a person may have a negative attitude toward coffee, a neutral attitude toward the French, and a positive attitude toward the next-door neighbor.

Attitudes efficiently size up the world. When we have to respond quickly to something, the way we feel about it can guide how we react. For example, a person who *believes* a particular ethnic group is lazy and aggressive may *feel* dislike for such people and therefore intend to act in a discriminatory manner. You can remember these three dimensions as the ABCs of attitudes: *A*ffect (feelings), *B*ehavior tendency, and *C*ognition (thoughts) (Figure 1).

The study of attitudes is central to social psychology and was one of its first concerns. For much of the last century, researchers wondered how much our attitudes affect our actions.

HOW WELL DO OUR ATTITUDES PREDICT OUR BEHAVIOR?

State the extent to which, and under what conditions, our inner attitudes drive our outward actions.

A blow to the supposed power of attitudes came when social psychologist Allan Wicker (1969) reviewed several dozen research studies covering a variety of people, attitudes, and behaviors. Wicker offered a shocking conclusion: People's expressed attitudes hardly predicted their varying behaviors.

- Student attitudes toward cheating bore little relation to the likelihood of their actually cheating.
- Attitudes toward the church were only modestly linked with weekly worship attendance.
- Self-described racial attitudes provided little clue to behaviors in actual situations. Many people *say* they are upset when someone makes racist remarks; yet, when they hear racism (such as someone using the N-word) respond indifferently (Kawakami et al., 2009).

The disjuncture between attitudes and actions is what Daniel Batson and his colleagues (1997, 2001, 2002; Valdesolo & DeSteno, 2007, 2008) call "moral hypocrisy" (appearing moral while avoiding the costs of being so). Their studies presented people with an appealing task with a possible $30 prize and a dull task with no rewards. The participants had to do one of the tasks and assign a supposed second participant to the other. Only 1 in 20 believed that assigning the appealing task with the reward to themselves was the more moral thing to do, yet 80 percent did so. In follow-up experiments, participants were given coins they could flip privately if they wanted. Even if they chose to flip, 90 percent

attitude
Beliefs and feelings related to a person or an event (often rooted in one's beliefs, and exhibited in one's feelings and intended behavior).

"All that we are is the result of what we have thought."
—Buddha,
Dhamma-Pada, 563 B.C.–483 B.C.

"Thought is the child of action."
—Benjamin Disraeli,
Vivian Gray, 1926

FIGURE :: 1
The ABCs of Attitudes

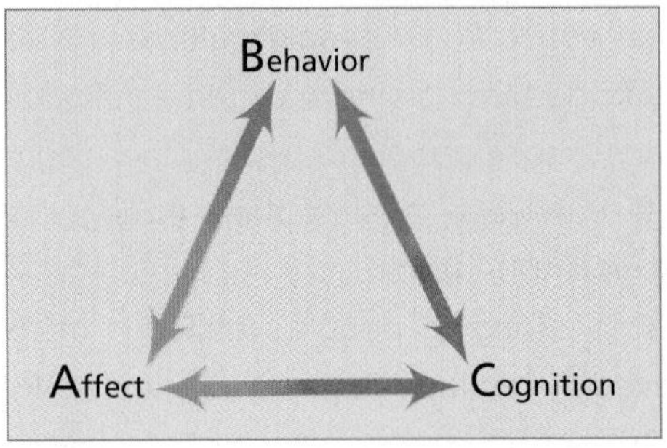

assigned themselves to the positive task! Was that because they could specify the consequences of heads and tails after the coin toss? In another experiment, Batson put a sticker on each side of the coin, indicating what the flip outcome would signify. Still, 24 of 28 people who made the toss assigned themselves to the appealing task. When morality and greed were put on a collision course, greed usually won.

If people don't walk the same line that they talk, it's little wonder that attempts to change behavior by changing attitudes often fail. Warnings about the dangers of smoking affect only minimally those who already smoke. Sex education programs have often influenced *attitudes* toward abstinence and condom use without affecting long-term abstinence and condom use *behaviors.* Whether they are "committed greens" or environmental skeptics, Australians consume about the same energy, water, and housing space (Newton & Meyer, 2013). Well-ingrained habits and practices override attitudes. We are, it seems, a population of hypocrites.

This surprising finding that what people *say* often differs from what they *do* sent social psychologists scurrying to find out why. Surely, we reasoned, convictions and feelings sometimes make a difference.

Indeed. In fact, what I [DM] am about to explain now seems so obvious that I wonder why most social psychologists (myself included) were not thinking this way before the early 1970s. I must remind myself, however, that truth seldom seems obvious until it is known.

Attitudes and behavior misaligned. After former U.S. congressman Mark Souder and staff member Tracey Jackson together recorded a pro-abstinence video, news broke that the two had been having an affair outside of their own marriages. "You'll go crazy if you don't have some sense of irony," the family values advocate told a local newspaper (Elliott, 2010).
AP Images/The Journal-Gazette/Frank Gray

> "I have opinions of my own, strong opinions, but i don't always agree with them."
> —President George H. W. Bush

When Attitudes Predict Behavior

The reason—now obvious—why our behavior and our expressed attitudes differ is that both are subject to other influences—many other influences. One social psychologist counted 40 factors that complicate the relationship between attitudes and behavior (Triandis, 1982; see also Kraus, 1995). Our attitudes do predict our behavior when these *other influences on what we say and do are minimal*, when the attitude is *specific to the behavior*, and when the *attitude is potent*.

WHEN SOCIAL INFLUENCES ON WHAT WE SAY ARE MINIMAL

Unlike a doctor measuring heart rate, social psychologists never get a direct reading on attitudes. Rather, we measure *expressed* attitudes. Like other behaviors, expressions are subject to outside influences. Sometimes, for example, we say what we think others want to hear, much as legislators may vote for a popular war or tax reduction that they privately oppose.

Today's social psychologists have some clever means at their disposal for minimizing social influences on people's attitude reports. Some of these are measures of *implicit* (unconscious) attitudes—our often unacknowledged inner beliefs that may or may not correspond to our explicit (conscious) attitudes.

The most widely used attitude measure is the **implicit association test (IAT),** which uses reaction times to measure how quickly people associate concepts (Banaji & Greenwald, 2013). One can, for example, measure implicit racial attitudes by assessing whether White people take longer to associate positive words with Black faces than with White faces. Implicit attitude researchers have offered various IAT assessments online (projectimplicit.net), from the serious (do you implicitly associate men with careers and women with home?) to the amusing (do you prefer Harry Potter or *Lord of the Rings?*). The 14+ million completed tests since 1998 have, they report, shown that

- *Implicit biases are pervasive.* For example, 80 percent of people show more implicit dislike for the elderly compared with the young.

implicit association test (IAT)
A computer-driven assessment of implicit attitudes. The test uses reaction times to measure people's automatic associations between attitude objects and evaluative words. Easier pairings (and faster responses) are taken to indicate stronger unconscious associations.

- *People differ in implicit bias.* Depending on their group memberships, their conscious attitudes, and the bias in their immediate environment, some people exhibit more implicit bias than others.
- *People are often unaware of their implicit biases.* Despite thinking themselves unprejudiced, even researchers themselves show implicit biases against some social groups.

Do implicit biases predict behavior? A review of the available research (now several hundred investigations) reveals that both explicit (self-report) and implicit attitudes help predict people's behaviors and judgments (Greenwald et al., 2015; Nosek et al., 2011). Thus, both together predict behavior better than either alone (Karpen et al., 2012; Spence & Townsend, 2007). The behavior predictions range from dental flossing to the fate of romantic relationships to suicide attempts (Lee et al., 2010; Millar, 2011; Nock et al., 2010). In one study, hiring managers received job applications matched on credential strength, but on one, the applicants' photos were digitally altered to make them appear obese. Several months later, when 153 of the managers completed an IAT, those with an implicit bias against the obese were less likely to invite the presumably obese applicants for interviews (Agerström & Rooth, 2011).

For attitudes formed early in life—such as racial and gender attitudes—implicit and explicit attitudes frequently diverge, with implicit attitudes often predicting behavior better. For example, implicit racial attitudes have successfully predicted interracial roommate relationships and willingness to penalize other-race people (Kubota et al., 2013; Towles-Schwen & Fazio, 2006). For other attitudes, such as those related to consumer behavior and support for political candidates, explicit self-reports are the better predictor.

Neuroscientists have identified brain centers that produce our automatic, implicit reactions (Stanley et al., 2008). One area deep in the brain (the amygdala, a center for threat perception) is active as we automatically evaluate social stimuli. For example, White people who show strong unconscious racial bias on the IAT also exhibit high amygdala activation when viewing unfamiliar Black faces.

A word of caution: Despite excitement over these recent studies of implicit attitudes hiding in the mind's basement, the implicit association test has detractors (Blanton et al., 2006, 2007, 2009; Oswald et al., 2013). They note that, unlike an aptitude test, the IAT is not reliable enough to assess and compare individuals. Moreover, a score that suggests bias doesn't distinguish a positive bias for one group from a negative bias against another. The critics also wonder whether compassion or guilt rather than latent hostility might slow one's speed in associating Blacks with positive words. Regardless, the existence of distinct explicit and implicit attitudes confirms one of twenty-first-century psychology's biggest lessons: our "dual processing" capacity for both *automatic* (effortless, habitual, implicit, System 1) and *controlled* (deliberate, conscious, explicit, System 2) thinking.

WHEN OTHER INFLUENCES ON BEHAVIOR ARE MINIMAL

On any occasion, it's not only our inner attitudes that guide us but also the situation we face. As we will see again and again, social influences can be enormous—enormous enough to induce people to violate their deepest convictions. So, would *averaging* across many situations enable us to detect more clearly the impact of our attitudes? Predicting people's behavior is like predicting a baseball or cricket player's hitting. The outcome of any particular turn at bat is nearly impossible to predict. But when we aggregate many times at bat, we can compare their approximate batting *averages*.

To use a research example, people's general attitude toward religion poorly predicts whether they will go to worship services during the coming week (because attendance is also influenced by the weather, the worship leader, how one is feeling, and so forth). But religious attitudes predict the total quantity of religious behaviors over time across many situations (Fishbein & Ajzen, 1974; Kahle & Berman, 1979). The findings define a *principle of aggregation:* The effects of an attitude become more apparent when we look at a person's aggregate or average behavior.

WHEN ATTITUDES ARE SPECIFIC TO THE BEHAVIOR

Other conditions further improve the predictive accuracy of attitudes. As Icek Ajzen and Martin Fishbein (1977, 2005) pointed out, when the measured attitude is a general

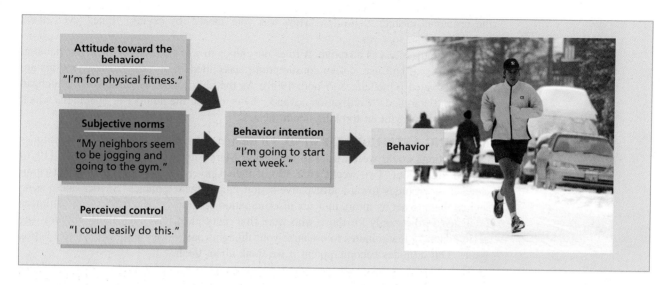

FIGURE :: 2

The Theory of Planned Behavior

Icek Ajzen, working with Martin Fishbein, has shown that one's (a) attitudes, (b) perceived social norms, and (c) feelings of control together determine one's intentions, which guide behavior. Compared with their general attitudes toward a healthy lifestyle, people's specific attitudes regarding jogging predict their jogging behavior much better.

©Kevin P Casey/Corbis News/Corbis

one—for instance, an attitude toward Asians—and the behavior is very specific—for instance, a decision whether to help a particular Asian in a particular situation—we should not expect a close correspondence between words and actions. Indeed, report Fishbein and Ajzen, in 26 out of 27 such research studies, attitudes did not predict behavior. But attitudes did predict behavior in all 26 studies they could find in which the measured attitude was directly pertinent to the situation. Thus, attitudes toward the general concept of "health fitness" poorly predict specific exercise and dietary practices. But an individual's attitudes about the costs and benefits of *jogging* are a fairly strong predictor of whether he or she *jogs* regularly.

Better yet for predicting behavior, says Ajzen and Fishbein's "theory of planned behavior," is knowing people's *intended* behaviors and their perceived self-efficacy and control (Figure 2). Moreover, several dozen experimental tests confirm that inducing new intentions induces new behavior (Bélanger-Gravel et al., 2013; Webb & Sheeran, 2006). Even asking people about their intentions to engage in a behavior often increases its likelihood (Levav & Fitzsimons, 2006). Ask people if they intend to floss their teeth in the next two weeks, and they will become more likely to do so. Ask people if they intend to vote in an upcoming election, and most will answer yes and become more likely to do so.

Further studies—more than 700 studies with 276,000 participants—confirmed that specific, relevant attitudes do predict intended and actual behavior (Armitage & Conner, 2001; Six & Eckes, 1996; Wallace et al., 2005). For example, attitudes toward condoms strongly predict condom use (Albarracin et al., 2001). And attitudes toward recycling (but not general attitudes toward environmental issues) predict intention to recycle, which predicts actual recycling (Nigbur et al., 2010; Oskamp, 1991). A practical lesson: To change habits through persuasion, we must alter people's attitudes toward *specific* practices.

So far we have seen two conditions under which attitudes will predict behavior: (1) when we minimize other influences upon our attitude statements and on our behavior, and (2) when the attitude is specifically relevant to the observed behavior. A third condition also exists: An attitude predicts behavior better when the attitude is potent.

WHEN ATTITUDES ARE POTENT

Much of our behavior is automatic. We act out familiar scripts without reflecting on what we're doing. We respond to people we meet in the hall with an automatic "Hi." We answer the restaurant cashier's question "How was your meal?" by saying, "Fine," even if we found it only so-so.

Such mindlessness is adaptive. It frees our minds to work on other things. For habitual behaviors—seat belt use, coffee consumption, class attendance—conscious intentions are hardly activated (Ouellette & Wood, 1998). As the philosopher Alfred North Whitehead (1911, p. 61) argued, "Civilization advances by extending the number of operations which we can perform without thinking about them."

BRINGING ATTITUDES TO MIND.   If we were prompted to think about our attitudes before acting, would we be truer to ourselves? Mark Snyder and William Swann (1976) wanted to find out. Two weeks after 120 of their University of Minnesota students indicated their attitudes toward affirmative-action employment policies, Snyder and Swann invited them to act as jurors in a sex-discrimination court case. The participants' attitudes predicted verdicts only for those who were first induced to remember their attitudes—by giving them "a few minutes to organize your thoughts and views on the affirmative-action issue." Our attitudes become potent *if* we think about them.

That suggests another way to induce people to focus on their inner convictions: *Make them self-aware,* perhaps by having them act in front of a mirror (Carver & Scheier, 1981). Maybe you, too, can recall suddenly being acutely aware of yourself upon entering a room with a large mirror. Making people self-aware in this way promotes consistency between words and deeds (Froming et al., 1982; Gibbons, 1978).

Edward Diener and Mark Wallbom (1976) noted that nearly all college students say that cheating is morally wrong. But will they follow the advice of Shakespeare's Polonius, "To thine own self be true"? Diener and Wallbom had University of Washington students work on an anagram-solving task (which, they were told, had predicted IQ) and told them to stop when a bell in the room sounded. Left alone, 71 percent cheated by working past the bell. Among students made self-aware—by working in front of a mirror while hearing their own tape-recorded voices—only 7 percent cheated. It makes one wonder: Would eye-level mirrors in stores make people more self-conscious of their attitudes about shoplifting?

Remember Batson's studies of moral hypocrisy? In a later experiment, Batson and his colleagues (2002) found that mirrors did bring behavior into line with espoused moral attitudes. When people flipped a coin while facing a mirror, the coin flip became scrupulously fair. Exactly half of the self-conscious participants assigned the other person to the appealing task.

FORGING STRONG ATTITUDES THROUGH EXPERIENCE.   The attitudes that best predict behavior are accessible (easily brought to mind) as well as stable (Glasman & Albarracin, 2006). And when attitudes are forged by experience, not just by hearsay, they are more accessible, more enduring, and more likely to guide actions. In one study, university students all expressed negative attitudes about their school's response to a housing shortage. But given opportunities to act—to sign a petition, solicit signatures, join a committee, or write a letter—only those whose attitudes grew from direct experience acted (Regan & Fazio, 1977).

> "Thinking is easy, acting difficult, and to put one's thoughts into action, the most difficult thing in the world."
> —German Poet Goethe, 1749–1832

> "Without doubt it is a delightful harmony when doing and saying go together."
> —Montaigne, *Essays,* 1588

> "It is easier to preach virtue than to practice it."
> —La Rochefoucauld, *Maxims,* 1665

SUMMING UP: How Well Do Our Attitudes Predict Our Behavior?

- How do our inner *attitudes* (evaluative reactions toward some object or person, often rooted in beliefs) relate to our external behavior? Although popular wisdom stresses the impact of attitudes on behavior, in fact, attitudes are often poor predictors of behaviors. Moreover, changing people's attitudes typically fails to produce much change in their behavior. These findings inspired social psychologists to find out why we so often fail to play the game we talk.

- The answer: Our expressions of attitudes and our behaviors are each subject to many influences. Our attitudes will predict our behavior (1) if these "other influences" are minimized, (2) if the attitude corresponds very closely to the predicted behavior (as in voting studies), and (3) if the attitude is potent (because something reminds us of it, or because we acquired it by direct experience). Under these conditions, what we think and feel predicts what we do.

WHEN DOES OUR BEHAVIOR AFFECT OUR ATTITUDES?

| Summarize evidence that we can act ourselves into a way of thinking.

So, to some extent, our attitudes matter. We can think ourselves into a way of acting. Now we turn to a more startling idea: that *behavior determines attitudes*. It's true that we sometimes stand up for what we believe. But it's also true that we come to believe in what we stand up for. Social-psychological theories inspired much of the research that underlies that conclusion. Instead of beginning with these theories, however, let's first see what there is to explain. As we engage evidence that behavior affects attitudes, speculate *why* this is and then compare your ideas with social psychologists' explanations.

Consider the following incidents:

- Sarah is hypnotized and told to take off her shoes when a book drops on the floor. Fifteen minutes later a book drops, and Sarah quietly slips out of her loafers. "Sarah," asks the hypnotist, "why did you take off your shoes?" "Well . . . my feet are hot and tired," Sarah replies. "It has been a long day." The act produces the idea.

- George has electrodes temporarily implanted in the brain region that controls his head movements. When neurosurgeon José Delgado (1973) stimulates the electrodes by remote control, George always turns his head. Unaware of the remote stimulation, he offers a reasonable explanation for his head turning: "I'm looking for my slipper." "I heard a noise." "I'm restless." "I was looking under the bed."

- Carol's severe seizures were relieved by surgically separating her two brain hemispheres. Now, in an experiment, psychologist Michael Gazzaniga (1985) flashes a picture of a nude woman to the left half of Carol's field of vision, which projects to her nonverbal right brain hemisphere. A sheepish smile spreads over her face, and she begins chuckling. Asked why, she invents—and apparently believes—a plausible explanation: "Oh—that funny machine." Frank, another split-brain patient, has the word "smile" flashed to his nonverbal right hemisphere. He obliges and forces a smile. Asked why, he explains, "This experiment is very funny."

The mental aftereffects of our behavior also appear in many social-psychological examples of self-persuasion. As we will see over and over, attitudes follow behavior.

Role Playing

The word **role** is borrowed from the theater and, as in the theater, refers to actions expected of those who occupy a particular social position. When enacting new social roles, we may at first feel phony. But our unease seldom lasts.

Think of a time when you stepped into some new role—perhaps your first days on a job or at college. That first week on campus, for example, you may have been supersensitive to your new social situation and tried valiantly to act mature and to suppress your high school behavior. At such times you may have felt self-conscious. You observed your new speech and actions because they weren't natural to you. Then something amazing happened: Your pseudo-intellectual talk no longer felt forced. The role began to fit as comfortably as your old jeans and T-shirt.

In one famous and controversial study, college men volunteered to spend time in a simulated prison constructed in Stanford's psychology department by Philip Zimbardo (1971; Haney & Zimbardo, 1998, 2009). Zimbardo wanted to find out: Is prison brutality a product of evil prisoners and malicious guards? Or do the institutional roles of guard and prisoner embitter and harden even compassionate people? Do the people make the place violent? Or does the place make the people violent?

By a flip of a coin, Zimbardo designated some students as guards. He gave them uniforms, billy clubs, and whistles and instructed them to enforce the rules. The other half,

role
A set of norms that defines how people in a given social position ought to behave.

"No man, for any considerable period, can wear one face to himself and another to the multitude without finally getting bewildered as to which may be true."
—Nathaniel Hawthorne, 1850

Guards and prisoners in the Stanford prison simulation quickly absorbed the roles they played.
©Phillip Zimbardo

the prisoners, were locked in cells and made to wear humiliating hospital-gown-like outfits. After a jovial first day of "playing" their roles, the guards and the prisoners, and even the experimenters, got caught up in the situation. The guards began to disparage the prisoners, and some devised cruel and degrading routines. The prisoners broke down, rebelled, or became apathetic. There developed, reported Zimbardo (1972), a "growing confusion between reality and illusion, between role-playing and self-identity. . . . This prison which we had created . . . was absorbing us as creatures of its own reality." Observing the emerging social pathology, Zimbardo ended the planned two-week simulation after only six days.

Critics have questioned the spontaneity and reliability of Zimbardo's observations (Griggs, 2014). Moreover, the point is not that we are powerless to resist imposed roles. In Zimbardo's prison simulation, in Abu Ghraib Prison (where guards degraded Iraq war prisoners), and in other atrocity-producing situations, some people become sadistic and others do not (Haslam & Reicher, 2007, 2012; Mastroianni & Reed, 2006; Zimbardo, 2007). Salt dissolves in water and sand does not. So also, notes John Johnson (2007), when placed in a rotten barrel, some people become bad apples and others do not. Behavior is a product of both the individual person and the situation, and the prison study appears to have attracted volunteers who were prone to aggressiveness (McFarland & Carnahan, 2009).

The deeper lesson of the role-playing studies is not that we are powerless machines. Rather, it concerns how what is unreal (an artificial role) can subtly morph into what is real. In a new career—as teacher, soldier, or businessperson, for example—we enact a role that shapes our attitudes. In one study, military training toughened German males' personalities. Compared to a control group, they were less agreeable, even 5 years after leaving the military (Jackson et al., 2012). And in one national study of U.S. adolescents, sustained role playing of "risk-glorifying" video games was followed by increased risky and deviant real-life behaviors (Hull et al., 2014). The moral: When we act like those around us, we slightly change our former selves into being more like them.

Imagine playing the role of slave—not just for six days but for decades. If a few days altered the behavior of those in Zimbardo's "prison," imagine the corrosive effects of decades of subservient behavior. The master may be even more profoundly affected,

After the degradation of Iraqi prisoners, Philip Zimbardo (2004a, 2004b) noted "direct and sad parallels between similar behavior of the 'guards' in the Stanford Prison Experiment." Such behavior, he contends, is attributable to a toxic situation that can make good people into perpetrators of evil. "It's not that we put bad apples in a good barrel. We put good apples in a bad barrel. The barrel corrupts anything that it touches."
Courtesy of Washington Post/Getty Images News/Getty Images

because the master's role is chosen. Frederick Douglass, a former slave, recalls his new owner's transformation as she absorbed her role:

> My new mistress proved to be all she appeared when I first met her at the door—a woman of the kindest heart and finest feelings. . . . I was utterly astonished at her goodness. I scarcely knew how to behave towards her. She was entirely unlike any other white woman I had ever seen. . . . The meanest slave was put fully at ease in her presence, and none left without feeling better for having seen her. Her face was made of heavenly smiles, and her voice of tranquil music. But, alas! this kind heart had but a short time to remain such. The fatal poison of irresponsible power was already in her hands, and soon commenced its infernal work. That cheerful eye, under the influence of slavery, soon became red with rage; that voice, made all of sweet accord, changed to one of harsh and horrid discord; and that angelic face gave place to that of a demon. (Douglass, 1845, pp. 57–58)

"Good God! He's giving the white-collar voter's speech to the blue collars."

Saying becomes believing: In expressing our thoughts to others, we sometimes tailor our words to what we think the others will want to hear, and then come to believe our own words.
© Joseph Farris/The New Yorker Collection/www.cartoonbank.com

Saying Becomes Believing

People often adapt what they say to please their listeners. They are quicker to tell people good news than bad, and they adjust their message toward their listener's views (Manis et al., 1974; Tesser et al., 1972; Tetlock, 1983). When induced to give spoken or written support to something they doubt, people will often feel bad about their deceit. Nevertheless, they begin to believe what they are saying (*assuming* they weren't bribed or coerced into doing so). When there is no compelling external explanation for one's words, saying becomes believing (Klaas, 1978).

Tory Higgins and his colleagues (Higgins & McCann, 1984; Higgins & Rholes, 1978) illustrated how saying becomes believing. They had university students read a personality description of someone and then summarize it for someone else, who was believed either to like or to dislike that person. The students wrote a more positive description when the recipient liked the person. Having said positive things, they also then liked the person more themselves. Asked to recall what they had read, they remembered the description as more positive than it was. In short, people tend to adjust their messages to their listeners, and, having done so, to believe the altered message.

Evil and Moral Acts

The attitudes-follow-behavior principle also works with immoral acts. Evil sometimes results from gradually escalating commitments. A trifling evil act erodes one's moral sensitivity, making it easier to perform a worse act. To paraphrase La Rochefoucauld's 1665 book of *Maxims,* it is not as difficult to find a person who has never succumbed to a given temptation as to find a person who has succumbed only once. After telling a "white lie" and thinking, "Well, that wasn't so bad," the person may go on to tell a bigger lie.

Harmful acts change us in other ways, too. We tend not only to hurt those we dislike but also to dislike those we hurt. Harming an innocent victim—by uttering hurtful comments or delivering electric shocks—typically leads aggressors to disparage their victims, thus helping them justify their cruel behavior (Berscheid et al., 1968; Davis & Jones, 1960; Glass, 1964). This is especially so when we are coaxed rather than coerced, and thus feel responsible for our act.

The attitudes-follow-behavior phenomenon appears in wartime. Prisoner-of-war camp guards would sometimes display good manners to captives in their first days on the job. Soldiers ordered to kill may initially react with revulsion to the point of sickness over their act. But not for long (Waller, 2002). Eventually, they will denigrate their enemies with nicknames. People tend to humanize their pets and dehumanize their enemies.

Attitudes also follow behavior in peacetime. A group that holds another in slavery will likely come to perceive the slaves as having traits that justify their oppression. Prison staff who participate in executions experience "moral disengagement" by coming to believe (more strongly than other prison staff) that their victims deserve their fate (Osofsky et al., 2005).

"Our self-definitions are not constructed in our heads; they are forged by our deeds."
—Robert McAfee Brown, *Creative Dislocation: The Movement of Grace,* 1980

Cruel acts, such as the 1994 Rwandan genocide, tend to breed even crueler and more hate-filled attitudes. "At first, killing was obligatory," explained one participant in the Rwandan genocide. "Afterward, we got used to it. We became naturally cruel. We no longer needed encouragement or fines to kill, or even orders or advice" (quoted by Hatzfeld, 2005, p. 71).

AP Images/Sayyid Azim

Actions and attitudes feed each other, sometimes to the point of moral numbness. The more one harms another and adjusts one's attitudes, the easier it becomes to do harm. Conscience is corroded.

To simulate the "killing begets killing" process, Andy Martens and his collaborators (2007, 2010, 2012) asked University of Arizona students to kill some bugs. They wondered: Would killing a few bugs in a "practice" trial increase students' willingness to kill more bugs later? To find out, they asked some students to look at one small bug in a container, then to dump it into the coffee grinding machine shown in Figure 3, and then to press the "on" button for 3 seconds. (No bugs were actually killed. An unseen stopper at the base of the insert tube prevented the bug from actually entering the killing machine, which tore bits of paper to simulate the sound of a killing.) Those who believed they killed five bugs went on to "kill" significantly more bugs during an ensuing 20-second period.

Harmful acts shape the self, but so, thankfully, do moral acts. Our character is reflected in what we do when we think no one is looking. Researchers have tested character by giving children temptations when it seems no one is watching. Consider what happens when children resist the temptation. In a dramatic experiment, Jonathan Freedman (1965) introduced elementary school children to an enticing battery-controlled robot, instructing them not to play with it while he was out of the room. Freedman used a severe threat with half the children and a mild threat with the others. Both were sufficient to deter the children.

Several weeks later a different researcher, with no apparent relation to the earlier events, left each child to play in the same room with the same toys. Three-fourths of those who had heard the severe threat now freely played with the robot; of those given the mild deterrent, only a third played with it. Apparently, the mild deterrent was strong enough to elicit the desired behavior yet mild enough to leave them with a sense of choice. Having earlier chosen consciously *not* to play with the toy, the mildly deterred children internalized their decisions. Moral action, especially when chosen rather than coerced, affects moral thinking.

FIGURE :: 3

Killing Begets Killing
Students who believed they killed several bugs by dropping them in this apparent killing machine, later killed more bugs during a self-paced killing period. (In reality, no bugs were harmed.)
Courtesy of Andy Martens, University of Canterbury

Moreover, positive behavior fosters liking for the person. Doing a favor for an experimenter or another participant, or tutoring a student, usually increases liking of the person helped (Blanchard & Cook, 1976). People who pray for a romantic partner (even in controlled experiments) thereafter exhibit greater commitment and fidelity to the partner (Fincham et al., 2010). It is a lesson worth remembering: If you wish to love someone more, act as if you do.

In 1793 Benjamin Franklin explored the idea that doing a favor engenders liking. As clerk of the Pennsylvania General Assembly, he was disturbed by opposition from another important legislator. So Franklin set out to win him over:

I did not . . . aim at gaining his favour by paying any servile respect to him but, after some time, took this other method. Having heard that he had in his library a certain very scarce and curious book I wrote a note to him expressing my desire of perusing that book and requesting he would do me the favour of lending it to me for a few days. He sent it immediately and I return'd it in about a week, expressing strongly my sense of the favour. When we next met in the House he spoke to me (which he had never done before), and with great civility; and he ever after manifested a readiness to serve me on all occasions, so that we became great friends and our friendship continued to his death. (quoted by Rosenzweig, 1972, p. 769)

"We do not love people so much for the good they have done us, as for the good we have done them."

—Leo Tolstoy,
War and Peace, 1867–1869

INTERRACIAL INTERACTION AND RACIAL ATTITUDES

If moral action feeds moral attitudes, will positive interactions between people of different races reduce racial prejudice—much as mandatory seat belt use has produced more favorable seat belt attitudes? That was part of social scientists' testimony before the U.S. Supreme Court's 1954 decision to desegregate schools. Their argument ran like this: If we wait for the heart to change—through preaching and teaching—we will wait a long time for racial justice. But if we legislate moral action, we can, under the right conditions, indirectly affect heartfelt attitudes.

That idea runs counter to the presumption that "you can't legislate morality." Yet attitude change has, as social psychologists predicted, followed desegregation. Consider:

"We become just by the practice of just actions, self-controlled by exercising self-control, and courageous by performing acts of courage."

—Aristotle

* Following the Supreme Court decision, the percentage of White Americans favoring integrated schools jumped and now includes nearly everyone.

* In the 10 years after the Civil Rights Act of 1964, the percentage of White Americans who described their neighborhoods, friends, co-workers, or other students as all-White declined by about 20 percent for each of those measures. Interracial interaction was increasing. During the same period, the percentage of White Americans who said that Blacks should be allowed to live in any neighborhood increased from 65 percent to 87 percent (*ISR Newsletter*, 1975). Attitudes were changing, too.

* More uniform national standards against discrimination were followed by decreasing differences in racial attitudes among people of differing religions, classes, and geographic regions (Greeley & Sheatsley, 1971; Taylor et al., 1978). As Americans came to act more alike, they came to think more alike.

Social Movements

We have seen that a society's laws and, therefore, its behavior can have a strong influence on its racial attitudes. A danger lies in the possibility of employing the same idea for political socialization on a mass scale. For many Germans during the 1930s, participation in Nazi rallies, displaying the Nazi flag, and especially the public greeting "Heil Hitler" established a profound inconsistency between behavior and belief. Historian Richard Grunberger (1971) reports that for those who had their doubts about Hitler, "the 'German greeting' was a powerful conditioning device. Having once decided to intone it as an outward token of conformity, many experienced . . . discomfort at the contradiction between their words and their feelings. Prevented from saying what they believed, they tried to establish their psychic equilibrium by consciously making themselves believe what they said" (p. 27).

The practice is not limited to totalitarian regimes. Political rituals—the daily flag salute by schoolchildren, singing the national anthem—use public conformity to build private patriotism. I [DM] recall participating in air-raid drills in my elementary school not far from the Boeing Company in Seattle. After we acted repeatedly as if we were the targets of Russian attack, we came to fear the Russians.

Our political rituals—the daily flag salute by schoolchildren, singing the national anthem—use public conformity to build private allegiance.
AP Images/Gary Kazanjian

Many people assume that the most potent social indoctrination comes through *brainwashing,* a term coined to describe what happened to American prisoners of war (POWs) during the 1950s Korean War. Although the "thought-control" program was not as irresistible as "brainwashing" suggests, the results still were disconcerting. Hundreds of prisoners cooperated with their captors. Twenty-one chose to remain after being granted permission to return to America. And many of those who did return came home believing that "although communism won't work in America, I think it's a good thing for Asia" (Segal, 1954).

Edgar Schein (1956) interviewed many of the POWs and reported that the captors' methods included a gradual escalation of demands. The captors always started with trivial requests and gradually worked up to more significant ones. "Thus after a prisoner had once been 'trained' to speak or write out trivia, statements on more important issues were demanded." Moreover, they always expected active participation, be it just copying something or participating in group discussions, writing self-criticism, or uttering public confessions. Once a prisoner had spoken or written a statement, he felt an inner need to make his beliefs consistent with his acts. That often drove prisoners to persuade themselves of what they had done wrong. The "start small and build" tactic was an effective application of what the "Persuasion" chapter calls "the foot-in-the-door technique," and it continues to be so today in the socialization of terrorists and torturers.

Now let us ask you, before reading further, to play theorist. Ask yourself: Why in these studies and real-life examples did attitudes follow behavior? Why might playing a role or making a speech influence your attitude?

"You can use small commitments to manipulate a person's self-image; you can use them to turn citizens into 'public servants,' prospects into 'customers,' prisoners into 'collaborators.'"

—Robert Cialdini,
Influence, 1988

SUMMING UP: When Does Our Behavior Affect Our Attitudes?

- The attitude-action relation also works in the reverse direction: We are likely not only to think ourselves into action but also to act ourselves into a way of thinking. When we act, we amplify the idea underlying what we have done, especially when we feel responsible for it. Many streams of evidence converge on this principle.

- Similarly, what we say or write can strongly influence attitudes that we subsequently hold.

- Research on the *foot-in-the-door phenomenon* reveals that committing a small act makes people more willing to do a larger one later.

- Actions also affect our moral attitudes: That which we have done, even if it is evil, we tend to justify as right.

- Similarly, our racial and political behaviors help shape our social consciousness: We not only stand up for what we believe, we also believe in what we have stood up for.

- Political and social movements may legislate behavior designed to lead to attitude change on a mass scale.

WHY DOES OUR BEHAVIOR AFFECT OUR ATTITUDES?

State the theories that seek to explain the attitudes-follow-behavior phenomenon. Discuss how the contest between these competing theories illustrates the process of scientific explanation.

We have seen that several streams of evidence merge to form a river: our actions influence our attitudes. Do these observations offer clues to *why* action affects attitude? Social psychology's detectives suspect three possible sources:

- *Self-presentation theory* assumes that for strategic reasons we express attitudes that make us appear consistent.
- *Cognitive dissonance theory* assumes that to reduce discomfort, we justify our actions to ourselves.
- *Self-perception theory* assumes that our actions are self-revealing: when uncertain about our feelings or beliefs, we look to our behavior, much as anyone else would.

Self-Presentation: Impression Management

The first explanation began as a simple idea. Who among us does not care what people think? People spend billions on clothes, diets, cosmetics, and plastic surgery—all

"I see he finally got rid of that idiotic comb-over."

because of their fretting over what others think. We see making a good impression as a way to gain social and material rewards, to feel better about ourselves, even to become more secure in our social identities (Leary, 1994, 2010, 2012).

No one wants to look foolishly inconsistent. To avoid seeming so, we express attitudes that match our actions. To appear consistent, we may automatically pretend those attitudes (Tyler, 2012). Even a little insincerity or hypocrisy can pay off in managing the impression we are making—or so self-presentation theory suggests.

Does our feigning consistency explain why expressed attitudes shift toward consistency with behavior? To some extent, yes—people exhibit a much smaller attitude change when a fake lie detector discourages them from trying to make a good impression (Paulhus, 1982; Tedeschi et al., 1987).

But there is more to attitudes than self-presentation, for people express their changed attitudes even to someone who has no knowledge of their earlier behavior. Two other theories explain why people sometimes internalize their self-presentations as genuine attitude changes.

Self-Justification: Cognitive Dissonance

One theory is that our attitudes change because we are motivated to maintain consistency among our cognitions. That is the implication of Leon Festinger's (1957) famous **cognitive dissonance** theory. The theory is simple, but its range of application is enormous, making "cognitive dissonance" part of the vocabulary of today's educated people. It assumes that we feel tension, or "dissonance", when two of our thoughts or beliefs ("cognitions") are inconsistent. Festinger argued that to reduce this unpleasant arousal, we often adjust our thinking. This simple idea, and some surprising predictions derived from it, have spawned more than 2,000 studies (Cooper, 1999).

One inspiration for the theory was a participant-observation study by Festinger and his colleagues (1956)—a study that a recent Association for Psychological Science president declared as his all-time favorite psychological study (Medin, 2011). Festinger and his collaborators read a news report of a UFO cult's expecting to be rescued by flying saucers from a cataclysmic flood anticipated on December 21, 1954. The researchers' response? They joined the group, and observed.

As December 21 approached, the most devoted followers quit their jobs and disposed of their possessions, with some even leaving their spouses. So what happened "when prophesy fails"? When December 21st passed uneventfully, the group coped with its massive dissonance not by abandoning their beliefs, but with increased fervor. Their faithfulness had, they decided,

cognitive dissonance
Tension that arises when one is simultaneously aware of two inconsistent cognitions. For example, dissonance may occur when we realize that we have, with little justification, acted contrary to our attitudes or made a decision favoring one alternative despite reasons favoring another.

persuaded God to spare the world—a message they now proclaimed boldly. In modern experiments, too, people whose confident beliefs are shaken will often respond by seeking to persuade others. "When in doubt, shout!" concluded the researchers (Gal & Rucker, 2010).

selective exposure
The tendency to seek
information and media that
agree with one's views and to
avoid dissonant information.

Another way people minimize dissonance, Festinger believed, is through **selective exposure** to agreeable information. Studies have asked people about their views on various topics, and then invited them to choose whether they wanted to view information supporting or opposing their viewpoint. Twice as many preferred supporting rather than challenging information (Fischer & Greitemeyer, 2010; Hart et al., 2009; Sweeny et al., 2010). We prefer news that affirms us over news that informs us.

People are especially keen on reading information that supports their political, religious, and ethical views—a phenomenon that most of us can illustrate from our own favorite news and blog sources. Moreover, people who have strong views on some topic—for instance, gun control, climate change, or economic policy—are prone to "identity-protective cognition" (Kahan et al., 2011, 2014). To minimize dissonance, their beliefs steer their reasoning and their evaluation of data. Shown the same data about human-caused climate change, people will read it differently depending on their preexisting views. On more practical and less values-relevant topics, "accuracy motives" drive us. Thus, we welcome a home inspection before buying or a second opinion before surgery.

Dissonance theory pertains mostly to discrepancies between behavior and attitudes. We are aware of both. Thus, if we sense an inconsistency, perhaps some hypocrisy, we feel pressure for change. That helps explain why British and U.S. cigarette smokers have been much more likely than nonsmokers to doubt that smoking is dangerous (Eiser et al., 1979; Saad, 2002).

After the 2003 Iraq War, noted the director of the Program of International Policy Attitudes, some Americans struggled to reduce their "experience of cognitive dissonance" (Kull, 2003). The war's main premise had been that Saddam Hussein, unlike most other brutal dictators, had weapons of mass destruction. As the war began, only 38 percent of Americans said the war was justified even if Iraq did not have weapons of mass destruction (Gallup, 2003). Nearly four in five Americans believed their invading troops would find such, and a similar percentage supported the just-launched war (Duffy, 2003; Newport et al., 2003).

When no such weapons were found, the war-supporting majority experienced dissonance, which was heightened by their awareness of the war's financial and human costs, by scenes of Iraq in chaos, by surging anti-American attitudes in Europe and in Muslim countries, and by inflamed pro-terrorist attitudes. To reduce their dissonance, noted the Program of International Policy Attitudes, some Americans revised their memories of their government's main rationale for going to war. The reasons now became liberating an oppressed people from tyrannical and genocidal rule and laying the groundwork for a more peaceful and democratic Middle East. Three months after the war began, the once-minority opinion became, for a time, the majority view: 58 percent of Americans now supported the war even if there were none of the proclaimed weapons of mass destruction (Gallup, 2003). "Whether or not they find weapons of mass destruction doesn't matter," suggested Republican pollster Frank Luntz (2003), "because the rationale for the war changed."

In *Mistakes Were Made (But Not By Me): Why We Justify Foolish Beliefs, Bad Decisions, and Hurtful Acts,* social psychologists Carol Tavris and Elliot Aronson (2007, p. 7) illustrate dissonance reduction by leaders of various political parties when faced with clear evidence that a decision they made or a course of action they chose turned out to be wrong, even disastrous. This human phenomenon is nonpartisan, note Tavris and Aronson: "A president who has justified his actions to himself, believing that he has *the truth,* becomes impervious to self-correction." For example, Democratic President Lyndon Johnson's biographer described him as someone who held to his beliefs, even when sinking in the quagmire of Vietnam, regardless "of the facts in the matter." And Republican president George W. Bush, in the years after launching the Iraq war, said that "knowing what I know today, I'd make the decision again" (2005), that "I've never been more convinced that the decisions I made are the right decisions" (2006), and that "this war has . . . come at a high cost in lives and treasure, but those costs are necessary" (2008).

Cognitive dissonance theory offers an explanation for such self-persuasion, and it also offers several surprising predictions. See if you can anticipate them.

INSUFFICIENT JUSTIFICATION

Imagine you are a participant in a famous experiment staged by the creative Festinger and his student J. Merrill Carlsmith (1959). For an hour, you are required to perform dull tasks, such as turning wooden knobs again and again. After you finish, the experimenter (Carlsmith) explains that the study concerns how expectations affect performance. The next participant, waiting outside, must be led to expect an *interesting* experiment. The seemingly upset experimenter, whom Festinger had spent hours coaching until he became extremely convincing, explains that the assistant who usually creates this expectation couldn't make this session. Wringing his hands, he pleads, "Could you fill in and do this?"

It's for science and you are being paid, so you agree to tell the next participant (who is actually the experimenter's accomplice) what a delightful experience you have just had. "Really?" responds the supposed participant. "A friend of mine was in this experiment a week ago, and she said it was boring." "Oh, no," you respond, "it's really very interesting. You get good exercise while turning some knobs. I'm sure you'll enjoy it." Finally, someone else who is studying how people react to experiments has you complete a questionnaire that asks how much you actually enjoyed your knob-turning experience.

Now for the prediction: Under which condition are you most likely to believe your little lie and say that the dull experiment was indeed interesting? When paid $1 for fibbing, as some of the participants were? Or when paid a then-lavish $20, as others were? Contrary to the common notion that big rewards produce big effects, Festinger and Carlsmith made an outrageous prediction: Those paid just $1 (hardly sufficient justification for a lie) would be most likely to adjust their attitudes to their actions. Having **insufficient justification** for their actions, they would experience more discomfort (dissonance) and thus be more motivated to believe in what they had done. Those paid $20 had sufficient justification for what they had done and hence should have experienced less dissonance. As Figure 4 shows, the results confirmed this intriguing prediction.*

In dozens of later experiments, this attitudes-follow-behavior effect was strongest when people felt some choice and when their actions had foreseeable consequences. One experiment had people read disparaging lawyer jokes into a recorder (for example, "How can you tell when a lawyer is lying? His lips are moving."). The reading produced more negative attitudes toward

insufficient justification
Reduction of dissonance by internally justifying one's behavior when external justification is "insufficient."

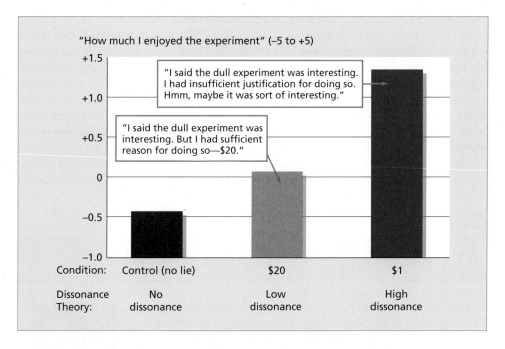

FIGURE :: 4

Insufficient Justification
Dissonance theory predicts that when our actions are not fully explained by external rewards or coercion, we will experience dissonance, which we can reduce by believing in what we have done.
Source: Data from Festinger & Carlsmith, 1959.

---

*There is a seldom-reported final aspect of this 1950s experiment. Imagine yourself finally back with the experimenter, who is truthfully explaining the whole study. Not only do you learn that you've been duped, but also the experimenter asks for the $20 back. Do you comply? Festinger and Carlsmith note that all their Stanford student participants willingly reached into their pockets and gave back the money. This is a foretaste of some quite amazing observations on compliance and conformity. As we will see, when the social situation makes clear demands, people usually respond accordingly.

Cognitive dissonance theory focuses on what induces a desired action. Research suggests that parents use "only enough" incentive to elicit desired behavior.
KidStock/Getty Images

lawyers when it was a chosen rather than a coerced activity (Hobden & Olson, 1994). Other experiments have engaged people to write essays for a measly $1.50 or so. When the essay argues something they don't believe in—for instance, a tuition increase—the underpaid writers begin to feel somewhat greater sympathy with the policy. Pretense becomes reality.

Earlier we noted how the insufficient justification principle works with punishments. Children were more likely to internalize a request not to play with an attractive toy if they were given a mild threat that insufficiently justified their compliance. When a parent says, "Clean up your room, Joshua, or else expect a hard spanking," Joshua won't need to internally justify cleaning his room. The severe threat is justification enough.

Note that cognitive dissonance theory focuses not on the relative effectiveness of rewards and punishments administered after the act but, rather, on what induces a desired action. It aims to have Joshua say, "I am cleaning up my room because I want a clean room," rather than, "I am cleaning up my room because my parents will spank me if I don't." The principle is this: *Attitudes follow behaviors for which we feel some responsibility.*

Authoritarian management will be effective, the theory predicts, only when the authority is present—because people are unlikely to internalize forced behavior. Bree, a formerly enslaved talking horse in C. S. Lewis's *The Horse and His Boy* (1974), observes, "One of the worst results of being a slave and being forced to do things is that when there is no one to force you any more you find you have almost lost the power of forcing yourself" (p. 193). Dissonance theory insists that encouragement and inducement should be enough to elicit the desired action (so that attitudes may follow the behavior). But it suggests that managers, teachers, and parents should use only enough incentive to elicit the desired behavior.

DISSONANCE AFTER DECISIONS

The emphasis on perceived choice and responsibility implies that decisions produce dissonance. When faced with an important decision—what college to attend, whom to date, which job to accept—we are sometimes torn between two equally attractive alternatives. Perhaps you can recall a time when, having committed yourself, you became painfully aware of dissonant cognitions—the desirable features of what you had rejected and the undesirable features of what you had chosen. If you decided to live on campus, you may have realized you were giving up the spaciousness and freedom of an apartment in favor of cramped, noisy dorm quarters. If you elected to live off campus, you may have realized that your decision meant physical separation from campus and friends, and having to cook and clean for yourself.

After making important decisions, you can reduce dissonance by upgrading the chosen alternative and downgrading the unchosen option. In the first published dissonance experiment

THE inside STORY

Leon Festinger on Dissonance Reduction

Following a 1934 earthquake in India, there were rumors outside the disaster zone of worse disasters to follow. It occurred to me that these rumors might be "anxiety-justifying"—cognitions that would justify their lingering fears. From that germ of an idea, I developed my theory of dissonance reduction—making your view of the world fit with how you feel or what you've done.

Leon Festinger (1920–1989)
AP Images/New School for Social Research

Big decisions can produce big dissonance when one later ponders the negative aspects of what is chosen and the positive aspects of what was not chosen.
Ariel Skelley/Getty Images

(1956), Jack Brehm brought some of his wedding gifts to his University of Minnesota lab and had women rate eight products, such as a toaster, a radio, and a hair dryer. Brehm then showed the women two objects they had rated similarly and told them they could have whichever they chose. Later, when rerating the eight objects, the women increased their evaluations of the item they had chosen and decreased their evaluations of the rejected item. It seems that after we have made our choices, the grass does not then grow greener on the other side of the fence. (Afterward, Brehm confessed he couldn't afford to let them keep what they chose.)

With simple decisions, this deciding-becomes-believing effect can breed overconfidence (Blanton et al., 2001): "What I've decided must be right." The effect can occur very quickly. Robert Knox and James Inkster (1968) found that racetrack bettors who had just put down their money felt more optimistic about their bets than did those who were about to bet. In the few moments that intervened between standing in line and walking away from the betting window, nothing had changed—except the decisive action and the person's feelings about it. There may sometimes be but a slight difference between two options, as we can recall in helping make faculty tenure decisions. The competence of one faculty member who barely makes it and that of another who barely loses seems not very different—until after the committee makes and announces the decision.

Our preferences influence our decisions, which then sharpen our preferences. This choices-influence-preferences effect occurs even after people press a button to choose what they think was a subliminally presented vacation alternative (nothing was actually shown them). They later tended to prefer the holiday that they believed they had chosen (Sharot et al., 2010, 2012). Moreover, once people chose a holiday destination, they preferred it up to three years later.

Decisions, once made, grow their own self-justifying legs of support. Often, these new legs are strong enough that when one leg is pulled away—perhaps the original one, as in the Iraq war case—the decision does not collapse. Rosalia decides to take a trip home if it can be done for an airfare under $500. It can, so she makes her reservation and begins to think of additional reasons why she will be glad to see her family. When she goes to buy the tickets, however, she learns there has been a fare increase to $575. No matter; she is now determined to go. It never occurs to people, reports Robert Cialdini (1984, p. 103), "that those additional reasons might never have existed had the choice not been made in the first place."

"Every time you make a choice you are turning the central part of you, the part of you that chooses, into something a little different from what it was before."
—C. S. Lewis,
Mere Christianity, 1942

Self-Perception

Although dissonance theory has inspired much research, an even simpler theory also explains its phenomena. Consider how we make inferences about other people's attitudes. We see how a person acts in a particular situation, and then we attribute the behavior

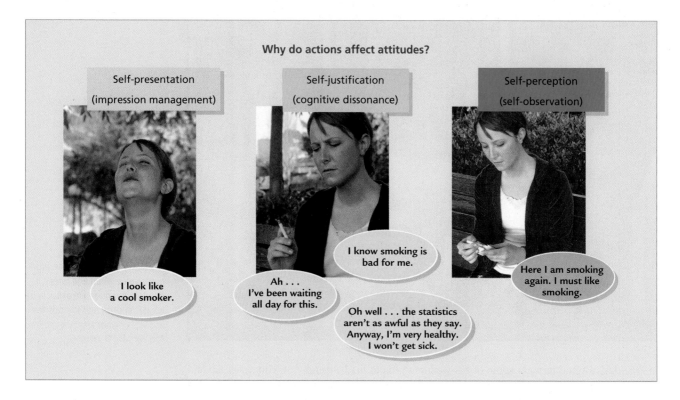

FIGURE :: 5

Three Theories Explain Why Attitudes Follow Behavior
Colin Young-Wolff/PhotoEdit

either to the person's traits and attitudes or to environmental forces. If we see parents coercing 10-year-old Brett into saying, "I'm sorry," we attribute Brett's apology to the situation, not to his personal regret. If we see Brett apologizing with no coercion, we attribute the apology to Brett himself (Figure 5).

Self-perception theory (proposed by Daryl Bem, 1972) assumes that we make similar inferences when we observe our own behavior. When our attitudes are weak or ambiguous, it's similar to someone observing us from the outside. Hearing myself talk informs me of my attitudes; seeing my actions provides clues to how strong my beliefs are. This is especially so when I can't easily attribute my behavior to external constraints. The acts we freely commit are self-revealing.

More than a century ago, psychologist William James proposed a similar self-perception process for our experienced emotion. How much our behavior guides our self-perceptions was cleverly demonstrated by researchers at Sweden's Lund University (Lind et al., 2014). They wondered: What would we experience if we said one thing but heard ourselves saying something else? Would we believe our ears? Through a headset, people heard themselves name various font colors such as "gray" when shown the word green in a gray color. But sometimes, the prankster researchers substituted the participant's own voice saying a previously recorded word, such as "green." Remarkably, two-thirds of the word switches went undetected. People experienced the inserted word as self-produced!

We infer our emotions, he suggested, by observing our bodies and our behaviors. A stimulus such as a growling bear confronts a woman in the forest. She tenses, her heartbeat increases, adrenaline flows, and she runs away. Observing all this, she then experiences fear. At a college where I [DM] am to give a lecture, I awake before dawn and am unable to get back to sleep. Noting my wakefulness, I conclude that I must be anxious. One friend of mine was shaking while standing offstage waiting to give a lecture and inferred he was really nervous. When he discovered the floor over the air-handling system was vibrating, his self-perceived nervousness vanished.

self-perception theory
The theory that when we are unsure of our attitudes, we infer them much as would someone observing us—by looking at our behavior and the circumstances under which it occurs.

"Self-knowledge is best learned, not by contemplation, but action."
—Goethe, 1749–1832

EXPRESSIONS AND ATTITUDE

You may be skeptical of the self-perception effect, as I [DM] initially was. Experiments on the effects of facial expressions suggest a way for you to experience it. When James Laird (1974, 1984) induced college students to frown while attaching electrodes to their faces— "contract these muscles," "pull your brows together"—they reported feeling angry. It's more fun to try Laird's other finding: Those induced to make a smiling face felt happier and found cartoons more humorous. Those induced to repeatedly practice happy (versus sad or angry) expressions may recall more happy memories and find the happy mood lingering (Schnall & Laird, 2003). A Japanese research team created similar expressions—and emotions—by tapping rubber bands to the sides of the face and then running them over either the top of the head (raising the cheeks into a smile) or under the chin (Mori & Mori, 2009).

Clever follow-up studies have found more examples of this **facial** (and body) **feedback effect:**

- Botox smoothes emotional wrinkles. If it's hard for us to know what the frozen-faced Botoxed are feeling, it's also hard for them to know themselves. Paralyzing the frowning muscles with Botox slows activity in people's emotion-related brain circuits and slows their reading of sadness- or anger-related sentences (Havas et al., 2010; Hennenlotter et al., 2008). Botoxing the frowning muscles decreases psychiatric patients' depressive symptoms (Wollmer et al., 2012). (Increased frowning, when facing the sun, fosters aggressive feeling [Marzoli et al., 2013].) Moreover, being unable to mimic others' expressions, it's harder for them to understand others' emotions (Neal & Chartrand, 2011). Botox messes with embodied cognition.

- When people are instructed to sit straight and push out their chest, they feel more confidence in their written ideas than when sitting slouched forward and with eyes downcast (Briñol et al., 2009).

- Even word articulation movements come tinged with emotion. In a series of experiments, both German- and English-speaking people preferred nonsense words and names spoken with inward (swallowing-like) mouth movements—for example, "BENOKA"—rather than outward (spitting-like) motions, such as "KENOBA" (Topolinski et al., 2014).

We have all experienced this phenomenon. We're feeling crabby, but then the phone rings or someone comes to the door and elicits from us warm, polite behavior. "How's everything?" "Just fine, thanks. How are things with you?" "Oh, not bad. . . ." If our crabbiness was not intense, this warm behavior may change our attitude. Putting on a happy face perks us up. It's tough to smile and feel grouchy. Motions trigger emotions.

Even your gait can affect how you feel. When you get up from reading this chapter, walk for a minute taking short, shuffling steps, with eyes downcast. It's a great way to feel depressed. "Sit all day in a moping posture, sigh, and reply to everything with a dismal voice, and your melancholy lingers," noted William James (1890, p. 463). Want to feel better? Walk for a minute taking long strides with your arms swinging and your eyes straight ahead. Want to feel powerful? Sit in an expansive posture, with your hands spread on a desk, or stand with your legs apart and hands on your hips rather than in a contracted posture (Carney et al., 2010; Park et al., 2013; Yap et al., 2013).

If our expressions influence our feelings, would imitating others' expressions help us know what they are feeling? An experiment by Katherine Burns Vaughan and John Lanzetta (1981) suggests it would. They asked Dartmouth College students to

> "I can watch myself and my actions, just like an outsider."
> —Anne Frank,
> *The Diary of a Young Girl*, 1947

facial feedback effect
The tendency of facial expressions to trigger corresponding feelings such as fear, anger, or happiness.

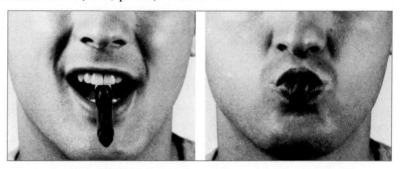

According to German psychologist Fritz Strack and colleagues (1988), people find cartoons funnier while holding a pen with their teeth (using smiling muscles) than while holding it with their lips (using muscles incompatible with smiling).
Courtesy Fritz Strack

All Nippon Airways employees, biting wooden chopsticks, beam during a smile training session. Researchers report that people who use chopsticks to activate smiling muscles during laboratory stress experiences also recover more quickly (Kraft & Pressman, 2012).
Kyodo News International, Inc.

"The free expression by outward signs of emotion intensifies it. On the other hand, the repression, as far as possible, of all outward signs softens our emotions."

—Charles Darwin,
The Expression of the Emotions in Man and Animals, 1897

observe someone receiving electric shock. They told some of the observers to make a pained expression whenever the shock came on. If, as Freud and others supposed, expressing an emotion allows us to discharge it, then the pained expression should be inwardly calming (Cacioppo et al., 1991). However, compared with other students who did not act out the expressions, these grimacing students perspired more and had faster heart rates whenever they saw the shock being delivered. Acting out the person's emotion enabled the observers to feel more empathy. And that leads to reduced prejudice after people mimic the videotaped actions of those of another race (Inzlicht et al., 2012). So, to sense how other people are feeling, let your own face and body mirror their expressions.

Actually, you hardly need to try. Observing others' faces, postures, writing styles, and voices, we naturally and unconsciously mimic (Hatfield et al., 1992; Ireland & Pennebaker, 2010). We synchronize our movements, postures, and tones of voice with theirs. Doing so helps us tune in to what they're feeling. It also makes for "emotional contagion," which helps explain why it's fun to be around happy people and depressing to be around depressed people.

Our facial expressions also influence our attitudes. In a clever experiment, Gary Wells and Richard Petty (1980) had University of Alberta students "test headphone sets" by making either vertical or horizontal head movements while listening to a radio editorial. Who most agreed with the editorial? Those who had been nodding their heads up and down. Why? Wells and Petty surmised that positive thoughts are compatible with vertical nodding and incompatible with horizontal motion. Try it yourself when listening to someone: Do you feel more agreeable when nodding rather than shaking your head? Even being seated in a left- rather than right-leaning chair has led people to lean more left in their expressed political attitudes (Oppenheimer & Trail, 2010)!

OVERJUSTIFICATION AND INTRINSIC MOTIVATIONS

Recall the insufficient justification effect: The smallest incentive that induces people to do something will most effectively get them to like it and keep on doing it. Cognitive dissonance theory explains this: When external inducements are insufficient to justify our behavior, we reduce dissonance internally by justifying the behavior.

Self-perception theory offers a different explanation: People explain their behavior by noting the conditions under which it occurs. Imagine hearing someone proclaim the wisdom of a tuition increase because they were paid $20. Surely the statement would seem more sincere if you thought the person was expressing those opinions for no pay. Perhaps we make similar inferences when observing ourselves. We observe our uncoerced action and infer our attitude.

Self-perception theory goes a step further. Contrary to the notion that rewards always increase motivation, unnecessary rewards can have a hidden cost. Rewarding people for doing what they already enjoy may lead them to attribute their action to the reward. If so, this would undermine their self-perception that they do it because they like it. Experiments confirmed this **overjustification effect** (Deci & Ryan, 1991, 2012; Lepper & Greene, 1979). Pay people for playing with puzzles, and they will later play with the puzzles less than will those who play for no pay. Promise children a reward for doing what they intrinsically enjoy (for example, playing with markers), and you will turn their play into work (Figure 6).

A folktale illustrates the overjustification effect: An old man lived alone on a street where boys played noisily every afternoon. The din annoyed him, so one day he called the boys to his door. He told them he loved the cheerful sound of children's voices and promised them each 50 cents if they would return the next day. Next afternoon the youngsters raced back and played more lustily than ever. The old man paid them and promised another reward the next day. Again they returned, whooping it up, and the man again paid them; this time 25 cents. The following day they got only 15 cents, and the man explained that his meager resources were being exhausted. "Please, though, would you come to play for 10 cents tomorrow?" The disappointed boys told the man they would not be back. It wasn't worth the effort, they said, to play all afternoon at his house for only 10 cents.

As self-perception theory implies, an *unanticipated* reward does not diminish intrinsic interest, because people can still attribute their actions to their own motivation (Bradley & Mannell, 1984; Tang & Hall, 1995). (It's like the heroine who, having fallen in love with the woodcutter, now learns that he's really a prince.) And if compliments for a good job make us feel more competent and successful, this can actually increase our intrinsic motivation. When rightly administered, rewards may also boost creativity (Eisenberger et al., 1999, 2003, 2009).

Many life tasks combine intrinsic and extrinsic rewards. A nurse takes satisfaction in caring for patients and gets paid. A student learns and gets a good grade. Ironically, report Amy Wrzesnieski, Barry Schwartz and their colleagues (2014a,b), helping people focus on the intrinsic meaning of their work boosts both their work quality and their vocational and financial success.

The overjustification effect occurs when someone offers an unnecessary reward beforehand in an obvious effort to control behavior. What matters is what a reward implies: Rewards and praise that inform people of their achievements—that make them feel, "I'm very good at this"—boost intrinsic motivation. Rewards that seek to control people and lead

"I don't sing because I am happy. I am happy because I sing."

Self-perception at work.
© Ed Frascino/The New Yorker Collection/www.cartoonbank.com

overjustification effect
The result of bribing people to do what they already like doing; they may then see their actions as externally controlled rather than intrinsically appealing.

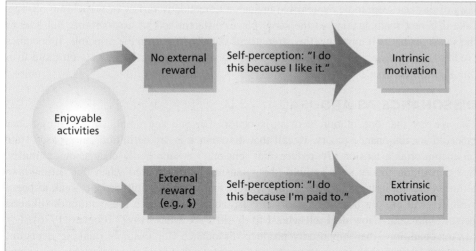

FIGURE :: 6

Intrinsic and Extrinsic Motivation
When people do something they enjoy, without reward or coercion, they attribute their behavior to their love of the activity. External rewards undermine intrinsic motivation by leading people to attribute their behavior to the incentive.

them to believe it was the reward that caused their effort—"I did it for the money"—diminish the intrinsic appeal of an enjoyable task (Rosenfeld et al., 1980; Sansone, 1986).

How then can we cultivate people's enjoyment of initially unappealing tasks? Maria may find her first piano lessons frustrating. Toshi may not have an intrinsic love of ninth-grade science. DeShawn may embark on a career not looking forward to making those first sales calls. In such cases, the parent, the teacher, or the manager should probably use some incentives to coax the desired behavior (Boggiano & Ruble, 1985; Cooke et al., 2011; Workman & Williams, 1980). After the person complies, suggest an intrinsic reason for doing so: "I'm not surprised that sales call went well, because you are so good at making a first impression."

If we provide students with just enough justification to perform a learning task and use rewards and labels to help them feel competent, we may enhance their enjoyment and their eagerness to pursue the subject on their own. When there is too much justification—as happens in classrooms where teachers dictate behavior and use rewards to control the children—student-driven learning may diminish (Deci & Ryan, 1985, 1991, 2008). My [DM's] younger son eagerly consumed 6 or 8 library books a week—until our library started a reading club that promised a party to those who read 10 books in three months. Three weeks later he began checking out only 1 or 2 books during our weekly visits. Why? "Because you only need to read 10 books, you know."

Comparing the Theories

We have seen one explanation of why our actions might only *seem* to affect our attitudes (*self-presentation* theory). And we have seen two explanations of why our actions genuinely affect our attitudes: (1) the *dissonance*-theory assumption that we justify our behavior to reduce our internal discomfort, and (2) the *self-perception*-theory assumption that we observe our behavior and make reasonable inferences about our attitudes, much as we observe other people and infer *their* attitudes.

These two explanations seem to contradict each other. Which is right? It's difficult to find a definitive test. In most instances they make the same predictions, and we can bend each theory to accommodate most of the findings we have considered (Greenwald, 1975). Self-perception theorist Daryl Bem (1972) even suggested it boils down to personal loyalties and preferences. This illustrates the human element in scientific theorizing. Neither dissonance theory nor self-perception theory has been handed to us by nature. Both are products of human imagination—creative attempts to simplify and explain what we've observed.

It is not unusual in science to find that a principle, such as "attitudes follow behavior," is predictable from more than one theory. Physicist Richard Feynman (1967) marveled that "one of the amazing characteristics of nature" is the "wide range of beautiful ways" in which we can describe it: "I do not understand the reason why it is that the correct laws of physics seem to be expressible in such a tremendous variety of ways" (pp. 53–55). Like different roads leading to the same place, different sets of assumptions can lead to the same principle. If anything, this strengthens our confidence in the principle. It becomes credible not only because of the data supporting it but also because it rests on more than one theoretical pillar.

DISSONANCE AS AROUSAL

Can we say that one of our theories is better? On one key point, strong support has emerged for dissonance theory. Recall that dissonance is, by definition, an aroused state of uncomfortable tension. To reduce that tension, we supposedly change our attitudes. Self-perception theory says nothing about tension being aroused when our actions and attitudes are not in harmony. It assumes merely that when our attitudes are weak to begin with, we will use our behavior and its circumstances as a clue to those attitudes (like the person who said, "How do I tell what I think till I see what I say?" [Forster, 1976]).

Are conditions that supposedly produce dissonance (for example, making decisions or taking actions that are contrary to one's attitudes) indeed uncomfortably arousing?

Clearly yes, providing that the behavior has unwanted consequences for which the person feels responsible (Cooper, 1999; Elliot & Devine, 1994). If, in the privacy of your room, you say something you don't believe, your dissonance will be minimal. It will be much greater if there are unpleasant results—if someone hears and believes you, if the statement causes harm and the negative effects are irrevocable, and if the person harmed is someone you like. If, moreover, you feel responsible for those consequences—if you can't easily excuse your act because you freely agreed to it and if you were able to foresee its consequences—then uncomfortable dissonance will be aroused. Such dissonance-related arousal is detectable as increased perspiration and heart rate (Cacioppo & Petty, 1986; Croyle & Cooper, 1983; Losch & Cacioppo, 1990).

After doing something undesirable or embarrassing, people can reaffirm their self-image by doing a good deed.
Ariel Skelley/Blend Images/the Agency Collection/Getty Images

Why is "volunteering" to say or do undesirable things so arousing? Because, as the **self-affirmation theory** suggests, such acts are embarrassing (Steele, 1988). They make us feel foolish. They threaten our sense of personal competence and goodness. Justifying our actions and decisions is therefore *self-affirming;* it protects and supports our sense of integrity and self-worth. When people engage in dissonance-generating actions, their thinking left frontal lobes buzz with extra arousal (Harmon-Jones et al., 2008). This is the grinding gears of belief change at work.

What do you suppose happens, then, if we offer people who have committed self-contradictory acts a way to reaffirm their self-worth, such as doing good deeds? In several experiments people whose self-concepts were restored felt much less need to justify their acts (Steele et al., 1993). People with high and secure self-esteem also engage in less self-justification (Holland et al., 2002).

So, dissonance conditions do indeed arouse tension, especially when they threaten positive feelings of self-worth. But is this arousal necessary for the attitudes-follow-behavior effect? Steele and his colleagues (1981) believe the answer is yes. When drinking alcohol reduces dissonance-produced arousal, the attitudes-follow-behavior effect disappears. In one of their experiments, they induced University of Washington students to write essays favoring a big tuition increase. The students reduced their resulting dissonance by softening their antituition attitudes—*unless* after writing the unpleasant essays they drank alcohol.

SELF-PERCEIVING WHEN NOT SELF-CONTRADICTING

Dissonance is uncomfortably arousing. That makes for self-persuasion after acting contrary to one's attitudes. But dissonance theory cannot explain attitude changes that occur without dissonance. When people argue a position that is in line with their opinion, although a step or two beyond it, procedures that eliminate arousal do not eliminate attitude change (Fazio et al., 1977, 1979). Dissonance theory also does not explain the overjustification effect, because being paid to do what you like to do should not arouse great tension. And what about situations where the action does not contradict any attitude—when, for example, people are induced to smile or grimace? Here, too, there should be no dissonance. For these cases, self-perception theory has a ready explanation.

In short, dissonance theory successfully explains what happens when we act contrary to clearly defined attitudes: We feel tension, so we adjust our attitudes to reduce it. Dissonance theory, then, explains attitude *change*. In situations where our attitudes are not well formed, self-perception theory explains attitude *formation*. As we act and reflect, we develop more readily accessible attitudes to guide our future behavior (Fazio, 1987; Roese & Olson, 1994).

self-affirmation theory
A theory that (a) people often experience a self-image threat after engaging in an undesirable behavior; and (b) they can compensate by affirming another aspect of the self. Threaten people's self-concept in one domain, and they will compensate either by refocusing or by doing good deeds in some other domain.

"Rather amazingly, 40 years after its publication, the theory of cognitive dissonance looks as strong and as interesting as ever."

—Social Psychologist Jack W. Brehm (1999)

SUMMING UP: Why Does Our Behavior Affect Our Attitudes?

Three competing theories explain why our actions affect our attitude reports.

- *Self-presentation theory* assumes that people, especially those who self-monitor their behavior hoping to create good impressions, will adapt their attitude reports to appear consistent with their actions. The available evidence confirms that people do adjust their attitude statements out of concern for what other people will think. But it also shows that some genuine attitude change occurs.

Two of these theories propose that our actions trigger genuine attitude change.

- *Dissonance theory* explains this attitude change by assuming that we feel tension after acting contrary to our attitudes or making difficult decisions. To reduce that

arousal, we internally justify our behavior. Dissonance theory further proposes that the less external justification we have for our undesirable actions, the more we feel responsible for them, and thus the more dissonance arises and the more attitudes change.

- *Self-perception theory* assumes that when our attitudes are weak, we simply observe our behavior and its circumstances, then infer our attitudes. One interesting implication of self-perception theory is the "overjustification effect": Rewarding people to do what they like doing anyway can turn their pleasure into drudgery (if the reward leads them to attribute their behavior to the reward).

- Evidence supports predictions from both theories, suggesting that each describes what happens under certain conditions.

POSTSCRIPT:
Changing Ourselves Through Action

To make anything a habit, do it.
To not make it a habit, do not do it.
To unmake a habit, do something else in place of it.
—*Greek Stoic philosopher Epictetus*

This chapter's attitudes-follow-behavior principle offers a powerful lesson for life: If we want to change ourselves in some important way, it's best not to wait for insight or inspiration. Sometimes we need to act—to begin to write that paper, to make those phone calls, to see that person—even if we don't feel like acting. Jacques Barzun (1975) recognized the energizing power of action when he advised aspiring writers to engage in the act of writing even if contemplation had left them feeling uncertain about their ideas:

> If you are too modest about yourself or too plain indifferent about the possible reader and yet are required to write, then you have to pretend. Make believe that you want to bring somebody around to your opinion; in other words, adopt a thesis and start expounding it. . . . With a slight effort of the kind at the start—a challenge to utterance—you will find your pretense disappearing and a real concern creeping in. The subject will have taken hold of you as it does in the work of all habitual writers. (pp. 173–174)

"If we wish to conquer undesirable emotional tendencies in ourselves we must . . . coldbloodedly go through the outward motions of those contrary dispositions we prefer to cultivate."

—William James, "What Is an Emotion?", 1884

This attitudes-follow-behavior phenomenon is not irrational or magical. That which prompts us to act may also prompt us to think. Writing an essay or role-playing an opposing view forces us to consider arguments we otherwise might have ignored. Also, we remember information best after explaining it in our own terms. As one student wrote me [DM], "It wasn't until I tried to verbalize my beliefs that I really understood them." As a teacher and a writer, I must therefore remind myself to not always lay out finished results. It is better to stimulate students to think through the implications of a theory, to make them active listeners and readers. Even taking notes deepens the impression. William James (1899) made the point a century ago: "No reception without reaction, no impression without correlative expression—this is the great maxim which the teacher ought never to forget."

Genes, Culture, and Gender

Royalty-Free/Digital Stock/Corbis

"By birth, the same; by custom, different."

—*Confucius,* The Analects

The preceding chapters were about how we *think about* one another. The next chapters are about how we *influence and relate to* one another. We will probe social psychology's central concern: the powers of social influence. What are these unseen social forces that push and pull us? How powerful are they? Research on social influence helps illuminate the invisible strings by which our social worlds move us about. In this chapter, we consider three related topics: genetic and evolutionary influences, cultural influences, and gender differences.

Approaching Earth from light-years away, alien scientists assigned to study the species *Homo sapiens* feel their excitement rising. Their plan: to observe two randomly sampled humans. Their first subject, Jessica, is a verbally combative trial lawyer who grew up in Nashville but moved west seeking the "California lifestyle."

How are we influenced by human nature and cultural diversity?

How are males and females alike and different?

Evolution and gender: Doing what comes naturally?

Culture and gender: Doing as the culture says?

What can we conclude about genes, culture, and gender?

Postscript: Should we view ourselves as products or architects of our social worlds?

After an affair and a divorce, Jessica is enjoying a second marriage. Friends describe Jessica as an independent thinker who is self-confident, competitive, and somewhat domineering.

Their second subject, Tomoko, lives with his wife and their two children in a rural Japanese village, a short walk from the homes of both their parents. Tomoko is proud of being a good son, a loyal husband, and a protective parent. Friends describe Tomoko as kind, gentle, respectful, sensitive, and supportive of extended family.

From their small sample of two people of different genders and cultures, what might our alien scientists conclude about human nature? Would they wonder whether the two are from different subspecies? Or would they be struck by deeper similarities beneath the surface differences?

The questions faced by our alien scientists are those faced by today's earth-bound scientists: How do we humans differ? How are we alike? In a world struggling with cultural differences, can we learn to accept our diversity, value our cultural identities, yet recognize our human kinship? We believe so. To see why, let's consider the evolutionary, cultural, and social roots of our humanity. Then let's see how each might help us understand gender similarities and differences.

HOW ARE WE INFLUENCED BY HUMAN NATURE AND CULTURAL DIVERSITY?

Summarize two perspectives on human similarities and differences: the evolutionary perspective, emphasizing human kinship, and the cultural perspective, emphasizing human diversity.

In many important ways, Jessica and Tomoko are more alike than different. As members of one great family with common ancestors, they share not only a common biology but also common behavioral tendencies. Each of them sleeps and wakes, feels hunger and thirst, and develops language through identical mechanisms. Jessica and Tomoko both prefer sweet tastes to sour and fear snakes more than sparrows. They and their kin across the globe all understand each other's frowns and smiles.

Jessica and Tomoko, and all of us everywhere, are intensely social. We join groups, conform, and recognize distinctions of social status. We return favors, punish offenses, and grieve a loved one's death. As children, beginning at about 8 months of age, we displayed fear of strangers, and as adults we favor members of our own groups. Confronted by those with dissimilar attitudes or attributes, we react warily or negatively. Anthropologist Donald Brown (1991, 2000) identified several hundred such universal behavior and language patterns. To sample among just those beginning with "v," all human societies have verbs, violence, visiting, and vowels.

Even much of our morality is common across cultures and eras. Before they can walk, babies will display a moral sense by disapproving what's wrong or naughty (Bloom, 2010). People old and young, female and male, whether living in Tokyo, Tehran, or Toledo, all say "no" when asked, "If a lethal gas is leaking into a vent and is headed toward a room with seven people, is it okay to push someone into the vent—preventing the gas from reaching the seven but killing the one?" And they are more likely to say "yes" when asked if it's okay to allow someone to fall into the vent, voluntarily sacrificing one life but saving seven (Hauser, 2006, 2009).

Our alien scientists could drop in anywhere and find humans conversing and arguing, laughing and crying, feasting and dancing, singing and worshiping. Everywhere, humans prefer living with others—in families and communal groups—to living alone. Everywhere, the family dramas that entertain us—from Greek tragedies to Chinese fiction to Mexican soap operas—portray similar plots (Dutton, 2006). Similar, too, are adventure stories in which strong and courageous men, supported by wise old people, overcome evil to the delight of beautiful women or threatened children.

Such commonalities define our shared human nature. Although differences draw our attention, we're more alike than different. We're all kin beneath the skin.

Genes, Evolution, and Behavior

The universal behaviors that define human nature arise from our biological similarity. We may say, "My ancestors came from Ireland" or "My roots are in China" or "I'm Italian," but if we trace our ancestors back 100,000 or more years, we are all Africans (Shipman, 2003). In response to climate change and the availability of food, early hominids migrated across Africa into Asia, Europe, the Australian subcontinent and, eventually, the Americas. As they adapted to their new environments, early humans developed differences that, measured on anthropological scales, are recent and superficial. Those who stayed in Africa had darker skin pigment—what Harvard psychologist Steven Pinker (2002) calls "sunscreen for the tropics"—and those who went far north of the equator evolved lighter skins capable of synthesizing vitamin D in less direct sunlight.

We were Africans recently enough that "there has not been much time to accumulate many new versions of the genes," notes Pinker (2002, p. 143). Indeed, biologists who study our genes have found that we humans—even humans as seemingly different as Jessica and Tomoko—are strikingly similar, like members of one tribe. We may be more numerous than chimpanzees, but chimps are more genetically varied.

To explain the traits of our species, and all species, the British naturalist Charles Darwin (1859) proposed an evolutionary process. Follow the genes, he advised. Darwin's idea, to which philosopher Daniel Dennett (2005) would give "the gold medal for the best idea anybody ever had," was that **natural selection** enables evolution.

The idea, simplified, is this:

- Organisms have many and varied offspring.
- Those offspring compete for survival in their environment.
- Certain biological and behavioral variations increase their chances of survival and reproduction in that environment.
- Those offspring that do survive and reproduce are more likely to pass their genes to ensuing generations.
- Thus, over time, population characteristics may change.

Natural selection implies that certain genes—those that predisposed traits that increased the odds of surviving long enough to reproduce and nurture descendants—became more abundant. In the snowy Arctic environment, for example, genes programming a thick coat of camouflaging white fur have won the genetic competition in polar bears.

Natural selection, long an organizing principle of biology, has recently become an important principle for psychology as well. **Evolutionary psychology** studies how natural selection predisposes not just physical traits suited to particular contexts—polar bears' coats, bats' sonar, humans' color vision—but also psychological traits and social behaviors that enhance the preservation and spread of one's genes (Buss, 2005, 2007, 2009). We humans are the way we are, say evolutionary psychologists, because nature selected those who had our traits—those who, for example, preferred the sweet taste of nutritious, energy-providing foods and who disliked the bitter or sour flavors of toxic foods. Those lacking such preferences were less likely to survive to contribute their genes to posterity.

As mobile gene machines, we carry not only the physical legacy but also the psychological legacy of our ancestors' adaptive preferences. We long for whatever helped our ancestors survive, reproduce, and nurture their offspring to survive and reproduce. Even negative emotions—anxiety, loneliness, depression, anger—are nature's way of motivating us to cope

natural selection
The evolutionary process by which heritable traits that best enable organisms to survive and reproduce in particular environments are passed to ensuing generations.

evolutionary psychology
The study of the evolution of cognition and behavior using principles of natural selection.

with survival challenges. "The purpose of the heart is to pump blood," notes evolutionary psychologist David Barash (2003). "The brain's purpose," he adds, is to direct our organs and our behavior "in a way that maximizes our evolutionary success. That's it."

The evolutionary perspective highlights our universal human nature. We not only share certain food preferences, but we also share answers to social questions, such as, Whom should I trust? Whom should I help? When, and with whom, should I mate? Who may dominate me, and whom may I control? Evolutionary psychologists contend that our emotional and behavioral answers to those questions are the same answers that worked for our ancestors.

And what should we fear? Mostly, we fear dangers faced by our distant ancestors. We fear foes, unfamiliar faces, and heights—and thus, possible terrorists, the ethnically different, and airplanes. We fear what's immediate and sudden more than greater, gradual harms from historically newer threats, such as smoking or climate change.

Because our social tasks are common to people everywhere, humans everywhere tend to agree on the answers. For example, all humans rank others by authority and status. And all have ideas about economic justice (Fiske, 1992). Evolutionary psychologists highlight these universal characteristics that have evolved through natural selection. Cultures, however, provide the specific rules for working out these elements of social life.

Culture and Behavior

Perhaps our most important similarity, the hallmark of our species, is our capacity to learn and adapt. Our genes enable an adaptive human brain—a cerebral hard drive that receives the culture's software. Evolution has prepared us to live creatively in a changing world and to thrive in environments from equatorial jungles to arctic ice fields. Compared with bees, birds, and bulldogs, nature has humans on a looser genetic leash. Ironically, our shared human biology enables our cultural diversity. It enables those in one **culture** to value promptness, welcome frankness, or accept premarital sex, whereas those in another culture do not. As social psychologist Roy Baumeister (2005, p. 29) observes, "Evolution made us for culture." (See "Focus On: The Cultural Animal.")

culture

The enduring behaviors, ideas, attitudes, and traditions shared by a large group of people and transmitted from one generation to the next.

focus
ON   The Cultural Animal

We are, said Aristotle, the social animal. We humans have at least one thing in common with wolves and bees: We flourish by organizing ourselves into groups and working together.

But more than that, notes Roy Baumeister, we are—as he labels us in the title of his 2005 book—*The Cultural Animal*. Humans more than other animals harness the power of culture to make life better. "Culture is a better way of being social," he writes. We have culture to thank for our communication through language, our driving safely on one side of the road, our eating fruit in winter, and our use of money to pay for our cars and fruit. Culture facilitates our survival and reproduction, and nature has blessed us with a brain that, like no other, enables culture.

Other animals show the rudiments of culture and language. Monkeys who learn new food-washing techniques then pass them to future generations. And chimps exhibit a modest capacity for language. But no species can accumulate progress across generations as smartly as humans. Your nineteenth-century ancestors had no cars, no indoor plumbing, no electricity, no air conditioning, no Internet, no smartphones, no Facebook pages, and

no Post-it notes—all things for which you can thank culture. Intelligence enables innovation, and culture enables dissemination—the transmission of information and innovation across time and place.

The division of labor is "another huge and powerful advantage of culture," notes Baumeister. Few of us grow food or build shelter, yet nearly everyone reading this book enjoys food and shelter. Indeed, books themselves are a tribute to the division of labor enabled by culture. Although only two lucky people's names go on this book's cover, the product is actually the work of a coordinated team of researchers, reviewers, assistants, and editors. Books and other media disseminate knowledge, providing the engine of progress.

"Culture is what is special about human beings," concludes Baumeister. "Culture helps us to become something much more than the sum of our talents, efforts, and other individual blessings. In that sense, culture is the greatest blessing of all. . . . Alone we would be but cunning brutes, at the mercy of our surroundings. Together, we can sustain a system that enables us to make life progressively better for ourselves, our children, and those who come after."

Evolutionary psychology incorporates environmental influences. It recognizes that nature and nurture interact in forming us. Genes are not fixed blueprints; their expression depends on the environment, much as the taste of tea is not "expressed" until meeting a hot water environment. One study of New Zealand young adults revealed a gene variation that put people at risk for depression, but only if they had also experienced major life stresses such as their parents' divorce (Caspi et al., 2003). Neither the stress nor the gene alone produced depression, but the two interacting did. Such findings have spawned the science of **epigenetics,** which considers how genes are expressed in some environments and not others.

epigenetics
A field of research exploring the expression of genes across different environments.

We humans have been selected not only for big brains and biceps but also for culture. We come prepared to learn language and to bond and cooperate with others in securing food, caring for young, and protecting ourselves. Nature therefore predisposes us to learn whatever culture we are born into. The cultural perspective highlights human adaptability. People's "natures are alike," said Confucius; "it is their habits that carry them far apart." And we are still far apart, note world culture researchers Ronald Inglehart and Christian Welzel (2005). Despite increasing education, "we are not moving toward a uniform global culture: cultural convergence is not taking place. A society's cultural heritage is remarkably enduring" (p. 46).

"Somehow the adherents of the 'nurture' side of the arguments have scared themselves silly at the power and inevitability of genes and missed the greatest lesson of all: the genes are on their side."
—Matt Ridley,
Nature via Nurture, 2003

CULTURAL DIVERSITY

The diversity of our languages, customs, and expressive behaviors confirms that much of our behavior is socially programmed, not hardwired. The genetic leash is long. As sociologist Ian Robertson (1987) has noted:

> Americans eat oysters but not snails. The French eat snails but not locusts. The Zulus eat locusts but not fish. The Jews eat fish but not pork. The Hindus eat pork but not beef. The Russians eat beef but not snakes. The Chinese eat snakes but not people. The Jalé of New Guinea find people delicious. (p. 67)

If we all lived as homogeneous ethnic groups in separate regions of the world, as some people still do, cultural diversity would be less relevant to our daily living. In Japan, where 98.5 percent of people are Japanese (CIA, 2014), internal cultural differences are minimal. In contrast, cultural differences abound in New York City, where more than one-third of the 8 million residents are foreign born.

Increasingly, cultural diversity surrounds us. More and more we live in a global village, connected to our fellow villagers by electronic social networks, jumbo jets, and international trade. The mingling of cultures is nothing new. "American" jeans were invented in 1872 by German immigrant Levi Strauss by combining Genes, the trouser style of Genoese sailors, with denim cloth from a French town (Legrain, 2003).

Confronting another culture is sometimes a startling experience. American males may feel uncomfortable when Middle Eastern heads of state greet the U.S. president with a kiss on the cheek. A German student, accustomed to speaking to "Herr Professor" only on rare occasions, considers it strange that at my [DM's] institution, most faculty office doors are open and students stop by freely. An Iranian student on her first visit to an American McDonald's restaurant fumbles around in her paper bag looking for the eating utensils until she sees the other customers eating their french fries with, of all things, their hands. In many areas of the globe, your best manners and mine are serious breaches of etiquette. Foreigners visiting Japan often struggle to master the rules of the social game—when to take off their shoes, how to pour the tea, when to give and open gifts, how to act toward someone higher or lower in the social hierarchy.

Migration and refugee evacuations are mixing cultures more than ever. "East is East and West is West, and never the twain shall meet," wrote the nineteenth-century British author Rudyard Kipling. But today, East and West, and North and South, meet all the time. Italy

"Women kiss women good night. Men kiss women good night. But men do not kiss men good night—especially in Armonk."

Although some norms are universal, every culture has its own norms—rules for accepted and expected social behavior.

© J. B. Handelsman/The New Yorker Collection/www.cartoonbank.com.

Cultures mixing. As this family (with an Asian American mother and an African American father) illustrates, immigration and globalization are bringing once-distant cultures together.
DragonImages/iStock/Getty Images

norms
Standards for accepted and expected behavior. Norms prescribe "proper" behavior. (In a different sense of the word, norms also describe what most others do—what is *normal.*)

is home to many Albanians, Germany to Turks, England—where Mohammed in its various spellings is now the most frequent name given to newborn boys (Cohen, 2011)—to Pakistanis. The result is both friendship and conflict. One in 5 Canadians and 1 in 8 Americans is an immigrant. As we work, play, and live with people from diverse cultural backgrounds, it helps to understand how our cultures influence us and how our cultures differ. In a conflict-laden world, achieving peace requires a genuine appreciation for both our genuine differences and our deep similarities.

NORMS: EXPECTED BEHAVIOR

As etiquette rules illustrate, all cultures have their accepted ideas about appropriate behavior. We often view these social expectations, or **norms,** as a negative force that imprisons people in a blind effort to perpetuate tradition. Norms do restrain and control us—so successfully and so subtly that we hardly sense their existence. Like fish in the ocean, we are all so immersed in our cultures that we must leap out of them to understand their influence. "When we see other Dutch people behaving in what foreigners would call a Dutch way," noted Dutch psychologists Willem Koomen and Anton Dijker (1997), "we often do not realize that the behavior is typically Dutch."

There is no better way to learn the norms of our native culture than to visit another culture and see that its members do things *that* way, whereas we do them *this* way. When living in Scotland, I [DM] acknowledged to my children that, yes, Europeans eat meat with the fork facing down in the left hand. "But we Americans consider it good manners to cut the meat and then transfer the fork to the right hand. I admit it's inefficient. But it's the way *we* do it."

To those who don't accept them, such norms may seem arbitrary and confining. To most in the Western world, the Muslim woman's head covering (known as the hijab) seems arbitrary and confining, but not to most in Muslim cultures. The Muslim women students in my [JT's] classes believe the hijab encourages men to see them as people rather than as sexual objects. Just as a stage play moves smoothly when the actors know their lines, so social behavior occurs smoothly when people know what to expect. Norms grease the social machinery. In unfamiliar situations, when the norms may be unclear, we monitor others' behavior and adjust our own accordingly.

Cultures vary in their norms for expressiveness, punctuality, rule breaking, and personal space. Consider the following:

INDIVIDUAL CHOICES. Cultures vary in how much they emphasize the individual self (individualistic cultures) versus others and the society (collectivistic cultures). As a result, Western (usually individualistic) countries allow people more latitude in making their own decisions. When I [JT] was in college, my Pakistani-American friend wanted to go to graduate school to study Latin. Her parents insisted she go to medical school, saying they would cut off their financial support if she did not. Having grown up in the United States, I was shocked that her parents would tell her what profession to pursue, but in collectivistic cultures this type of parental direction is widely accepted.

EXPRESSIVENESS. To someone from a relatively formal northern European culture, a person whose roots are in an expressive Latin American culture may seem "warm, charming, inefficient, and time-wasting." To the Latin American person, the northern European may seem "efficient, cold, and overconcerned with time" (Beaulieu, 2004; Triandis, 1981). And they might be right: northern Europeans walk faster on public streets than those in Latin America, and northern European bank clocks were more likely to be accurate (Levine & Norenzayan, 1999).

PUNCTUALITY. Latin American business executives who arrive late for a dinner engagement may be mystified by how obsessed their North American counterparts are with punctuality. North American tourists in Japan may wonder about the lack of eye contact from passing pedestrians. (See "Research Close-Up: Passing Encounters, East and West.")

research
CLOSE-UP

On my [DM's] Midwestern American campus and in my town, sidewalk passersby routinely glance and smile at one another. In Britain and China, where I have spent time, I have rarely observed such microinteractions. To a European, our greeting passing strangers might seem a bit silly and disrespectful of privacy; to a Midwesterner, avoiding eye contact—what sociologists have called "civil inattention"—might seem aloof.

To quantify the culture difference in pedestrian interactions, an international team led by Miles Patterson and Yuichi Iizuka (2007) conducted a simple field experiment both in the United States and in Japan with the unwitting participation of more than 1,000 pedestrians. Their procedure illustrates how social psychologists sometimes conduct unobtrusive research in natural settings (Patterson, 2008). As Figure 1 depicts, a confederate (an accomplice of the experimenter) would initiate one of three behaviors when within about 12 feet of an approaching pedestrian on an uncrowded sidewalk: (1) *avoidance* (looking straight ahead), (2) *glancing* at the person for less than a second, and (3) *looking* at the person and *smiling*. A trailing observer would then record the pedestrian's reaction. Did the pedestrian glance at the confederate? smile? nod? verbally greet the confederate? (The order of the three conditions was randomized and unknown to the trailing observer, ensuring that the person recording the data was "blind" to the experimental condition.)

As you might expect, the pedestrians were more likely to look at someone who looked at them and to smile at, nod to, or greet someone who also smiled at them. This was especially so when that someone was female rather than male. But as Figure 2 shows, the culture differences were nevertheless striking. As the research team expected, in view of Japan's greater respect for privacy and cultural reserve when interacting with outgroups, Americans were much more likely to smile at, nod to, or greet the confederate.

In Japan, they conclude, "there is little pressure to reciprocate the smile of the confederate because there is no relationship with the confederate and no obligation to respond." By contrast, the American norm is to reciprocate a friendly gesture.

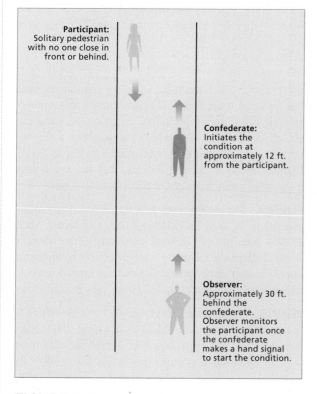

FIGURE :: 1

Illustration of Passing Encounter
Source: Patterson et al. (2007).

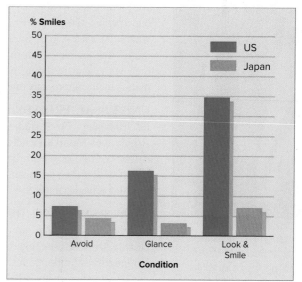

FIGURE :: 2

American and Japanese Pedestrian Responses, by Condition
Source: Adapted from Patterson et al. (2007).

RULE-BREAKING.   Norms are especially important in traditional, collectivistic cultures. In one study, Koreans (compared to Americans) were more likely to avoid co-workers who were vegetarians, a choice against the norm. To most Americans, being a vegetarian is a personal choice; to a Korean, it signals standing out from the group and is thus undesirable (Kinias et al., 2014). Many collectivistic cultures promote the belief that human suffering—such as contracting a disease—is caused by violating social norms (Sullivan et al., 2012). Collectivistic cultures are more likely to stigmatize people seen as different, whether through identity (gays and lesbians, immigrants) or behavior (heavy drinkers, drug addicts [Shin et al., 2013]).

personal space

The buffer zone we like to maintain around our bodies. Its size depends on our familiarity with whomever is near us.

"Some 30 inches from my nose, the frontier of my person goes."

—W. H. Auden, 1907–1973

PERSONAL SPACE.   **Personal space** is a sort of portable bubble or buffer zone that we like to maintain between ourselves and others. As the situation changes, the bubble varies in size. With strangers, most Americans maintain a fairly large personal space, keeping 4 feet or more between us. On uncrowded buses, or in restrooms or libraries, we protect our space and respect others' space. We let friends come closer (Novelli et al., 2010).

Individuals differ: Some people prefer more personal space than others (Perry et al., 2013). Groups differ, too: Adults maintain more distance than do children. Men keep more distance from one another than do women. For reasons unknown, cultures near the equator prefer less space and more touching and hugging. Thus, the British and the Scandinavians prefer more distance than the French and the Arabs; North Americans prefer more space than Latin Americans.

To see the effect of encroaching on another's personal space, play space invader. Stand or sit a foot or so from a friend and strike up a conversation. Does the person fidget, look away, back off, show other signs of discomfort? These are the signs of arousal noted by space-invading researchers (Altman & Vinsel, 1978).

Cultures differ not only in their norms for such behaviors, but also in the strength of their norms. One 33-nation study asked people to rate the appropriateness of various behaviors (such as eating or crying) in different situations (such as at a bank or a party). Societies with stronger, enforced norms for behaviors are "tight" cultures, more likely to have been exposed to threats such as territorial conflict or resource scarcity (Gelfand et al., 2011).

CULTURAL SIMILARITY

Thanks to human adaptability, cultures differ. Yet beneath the veneer of cultural differences, cross-cultural psychologists see "an essential universality" (Lonner, 1980). As members of one species, the processes that underlie our differing behaviors are much the same everywhere. At ages 4 to 5, for example, children across the world begin to exhibit a "theory of mind" that enables them to infer what others are thinking (Norenzayan & Heine, 2005). If they witness a toy being moved while another child isn't looking, they become able—no matter their culture—to infer that the other child will *think* it still is where it was.

UNIVERSAL FRIENDSHIP NORMS.   People everywhere have some common norms for friendship. From studies conducted in Britain, Italy, Hong Kong, and Japan, Michael Argyle and Monika Henderson (1985) noted several cultural variations in the norms that define the role of friend. For example, in Japan it's especially important not to embarrass a friend with public criticism. But there are also some apparently universal norms: respect the friend's privacy; make eye contact while talking; don't divulge things said in confidence.

By holding his hand, former President George W. Bush honored Saudi friendship norms when strolling with the late King Abdullah in 2005. Many heterosexual North American men were, however, startled by the violation of their own norm of distance from other men.
AP Images/J. Scott Applewhite

UNIVERSAL TRAIT DIMENSIONS.   Around the world, people describe others with between two and five universal personality dimensions (McCrae & Costa, 2008; Saucier et al., 2014). Evaluating others as good or bad appears across almost all cultures and languages. All cultures have norms, so all cultures evaluate how well others follow those norms (Saucier et al., 2014).

UNIVERSAL SOCIAL BELIEF DIMENSIONS.   Likewise, there are five universal dimensions of social beliefs (Leung & Bond, 2004). Across 38 countries, people varied in cynicism, social complexity, reward for application, spirituality, and fate control (Figure 4). People's adherence to these social beliefs appears to guide their living. Cynics express lower life satisfaction and favor assertive influence tactics and right-wing politics.

FIGURE :: 3

Words used to express positive emotion in (a) the U.S. and (b) India.

In a study of the language of Facebook users, positive emotion was expressed in similar ways in the U.S. (top) and India (bottom), with a few cultural differences (such as the greater use of "thanks" in India). *Source of data:* Kern & Sap, 2014.

FIGURE :: 4

Leung and Bond's Universal Social Belief Dimensions

The Big Five Social Beliefs	Sample Questionnaire Item
Cynicism	"Powerful people tend to exploit others."
Social complexity	"One has to deal with matters according to the specific circumstances."
Reward for application	"One will succeed if he/she really tries."
Spirituality	"Religious faith contributes to good mental health."
Fate control	"Fate determines one's success and failures."

In The Female Eunuch, *Germaine Greer notes how the language of affection reduces women to foods and baby animals—honey, lamb, sugar, sweetie-pie, kitten, chick.*

Those who believe in hard work ("reward for application") are inclined to invest themselves in study, planning, and competing.

UNIVERSAL STATUS NORMS.   Wherever people form status hierarchies, they also talk to higher-status people in the respectful way they often talk to strangers. And they talk to lower-status people in the more familiar, first-name way they speak to friends (Brown, 1965, 1987; Kroger & Wood, 1992). Patients call their physician "Dr. So and So"; the physician may reply using the patients' first names. Students and professors typically address one another in a similarly non-mutual way.

Most languages have two forms of the English pronoun "you": a respectful form and a familiar form (for example, *Sie* and *du* in German, *vous* and *tu* in French, *usted* and *tu* in Spanish). People typically use the familiar form with intimates and subordinates— with close friends and family members but also in speaking to children and pets. A German adolescent receives a boost when strangers begin addressing him or her as "Sie" instead of "du."

This first aspect of this universal norm—that *forms of address communicate not only social distance but also social status*—correlates with a second aspect: *Advances in intimacy are usually suggested by the higher-status person.* In Germany, where most twosomes begin a relationship with the polite, formal "you" and may eventually progress to the more intimate "Sie," someone must initiate the increased intimacy. Who do you suppose does so? On some congenial occasion, the elder or richer or more distinguished of the two is the one to say, "Let's say *du* to each other."

This norm extends beyond language to every type of advance in intimacy. It is more acceptable to borrow a pen from or put a hand on the shoulder of one's intimates and subordinates than to behave in such a casual way with strangers or superiors. Similarly, the president of my [DM's] college invites faculty to his home before they invite him to theirs. In the progression toward intimacy, the higher-status person is typically the pacesetter.

Norms—rules for accepted and expected behavior—vary by culture.
Fujifotos/The Image Works

THE INCEST TABOO.   The best-known universal norm is the taboo against incest: Parents are not to have sexual relations with their children, nor siblings with one another. Although the taboo apparently is violated more often than psychologists once believed, the norm is still universal. Every society disapproves of incest. Given the biological penalties for inbreeding (through the emergence of disorders linked to recessive genes), evolutionary psychologists can easily understand why people everywhere are predisposed against incest.

So far in this chapter, we have affirmed our biological kinship as members of one human family. We have also acknowledged our cultural diversity. And we have noted how norms vary within and across cultures. Remember that our quest in social psychology is not just to catalog differences but also to identify universal principles of behavior. Our aim is what cross-cultural psychologist Walter Lonner (1989) has called "a universalistic psychology—a psychology that is as valid and meaningful in Omaha and Osaka as it is in Rome and Botswana."

Attitudes and behaviors will always vary with culture, but the processes by which attitudes influence behavior vary much less. People in Nigeria and Japan define teen roles differently than people in Europe and North America do, but in all cultures role expectations guide social relations. English writer G. K. Chesterton had the idea nearly a century ago: When someone "has discovered why men in Bond Street wear black hats he will at the same moment have discovered why men in Timbuctoo wear red feathers."

> "I am confident that [if] modern psychology had developed in, let us say, India, the psychologists there would have discovered most of the principles discovered by the Westerners."
>
> —Cross-Cultural Psychologist John E. Williams (1993)

SUMMING UP: How Are We Influenced by Human Nature and Cultural Diversity?

- How are we humans alike, how do we differ—and why? *Evolutionary psychologists* study how *natural selection* favors behavioral traits that promote the perpetuation of one's genes. Although part of evolution's legacy is our human capacity to learn and adapt (and therefore to differ from one another), the evolutionary perspective highlights the kinship that results from our shared human nature.

- The cultural perspective highlights human diversity—the behaviors and ideas that define a group and that are transmitted across generations. The differences in attitudes and behaviors from one *culture* to another indicate the extent to which we are the products of cultural *norms* and roles. Yet cross-cultural psychologists also examine the "essential universality" of all people. For example, despite their differences, cultures have a number of norms in common, such as respecting privacy in friendships and disapproving of incest.

HOW ARE MALES AND FEMALES ALIKE AND DIFFERENT?

Describe how males and females are alike, and how they differ.

Human diversity has many obvious dimensions—height, weight, hair color, to name a few. But for people's self-concepts and social relationships, the two dimensions that matter most—and that people first attune to—are race and, especially, gender (Stangor et al., 1992). When you were born, the first thing people wanted to know about you was, "Is it a boy or a girl?" It's believed to be either one or the other, and not a matter left to choice. When a Canadian couple in 2011 vowed to keep secret the gender of their baby, "Storm," so that the child could later develop its own gender identity without having to meet gender expectations, a storm of criticism erupted (AP, 2011).

Many cultures, like North American cultures, deliver a strong message: Everyone *must* be assigned a gender. When an intersex child is born with a combination of male and female sex organs, physicians and the family traditionally have felt compelled to assign the child a gender by diminishing the ambiguity surgically. Between day and night there is dusk. Between hot and cold there is warm. But between male and female there has been, socially speaking, essentially nothing. The closest thing to an exception is *transgender* people, whose sense of being male or female differs from their birth sex (APA, 2012). A person may feel like a woman in a man's body or a man in a woman's body—and may dress or have surgery to bring their physical appearance in line with their identity.

Gender and Genes

gender

In psychology, the characteristics, whether biological or socially influenced, by which people define male and female.

Even in physical traits, individual differences among men and among women far exceed the average differences between the sexes. Don Schollander's world-record-setting 4 minutes, 12 seconds in the 400-meter freestyle swim at the 1964 Olympics trailed the times of all eight women racing in the 2012 Olympic finals for that event.

Gender refers to the characteristics people associate with male and female. What behaviors are characteristic and expected of males? Of females?

"Of the 46 chromosomes in the human genome, 45 are unisex," noted Judith Rich Harris (1998). Females and males are therefore similar in many physical traits and developmental milestones, such as the age of sitting up, teething, and walking. They also are alike in many psychological traits, such as overall vocabulary, creativity, intelligence, self-esteem, and happiness. Women and men feel the same emotions and longings, both dote on their children, and they have similar-appearing brains (although, on average, men have more neurons and women have more neural connections). Indeed, noted Janet Shibley Hyde (2005) from her review of 46 meta-analyses (each a statistical digest of dozens of studies), the common result for most variables studied is *gender similarity*. On most psychological attributes, the overlap between the sexes is larger than the difference (Carothers & Reis, 2013). Your "opposite sex" is actually your similar sex.

So shall we conclude that men and women are essentially the same, except for a few anatomical oddities that hardly matter apart from special occasions? Actually, some differences do exist, and it is these differences, not the many similarities, that capture attention and make news. In both science and everyday life, differences excite interest—enough to have stimulated some 18,000 studies comparing females and males (Ellis et al., 2008). Compared to males, the average female

- has 70 percent more fat, has 40 percent less muscle, is 5 inches shorter, and weighs 40 pounds less;
- is more sensitive to smells and sounds;
- is twice as likely to experience anxiety disorders or depression.

Compared to females, the average male is

- slower to enter puberty (by about two years) but quicker to die (by four years, worldwide);
- three times more likely to be diagnosed with ADHD (attention deficit/hyperactivity disorder), four times more likely to commit suicide, and five times more likely to be killed by lightning;
- more capable of wiggling his ears.

"There should be no qualms about the forthright study of racial and gender differences; science is in desperate need of good studies that . . . inform us of what we need to do to help underrepresented people to succeed in this society. Unlike the ostrich, we cannot afford to hide our heads for fear of socially uncomfortable discoveries."

—Developmental Psychologist Sandra Scarr (1988)

During the 1970s, many scholars worried that studies of such gender differences might reinforce stereotypes. Would gender differences be construed as women's deficits? Although the findings confirm some stereotypes of women—as less physically aggressive, more nurturing, and more socially sensitive—those traits are actually preferred by most people, whether male or female (Prentice & Carranza, 2002; Swim, 1994). Small wonder, then, that most people rate their beliefs and feelings regarding women as more *favorable* than their feelings regarding men—a phenomenon some have labeled the "women are wonderful" effect (Eagly, 1994; Haddock & Zanna, 1994).

Let's compare men's and women's social connections, dominance, aggressiveness, and sexuality. We can then consider how the evolutionary and cultural perspectives might explain them. Do gender differences reflect natural selection? Are they culturally constructed—a reflection of the roles that men and women often play and the situations in which they act? Or do genes and culture together bend the genders?

Independence Versus Connectedness

Individual men display outlooks and behavior that vary from fierce competitiveness to caring nurturance. So do individual women. Without denying that, several late-twentieth-century feminist psychologists contended that women more than men give priority to close, intimate relationships (Chodorow, 1978, 1989; Gilligan, 1982; Gilligan et al., 1990; Miller, 1986). Consider the evidence:

PLAY.   Compared to boys, girls talk more intimately and play less aggressively, noted Eleanor Maccoby (2002) from her decades of research on gender development. They also play in smaller groups, often talking with one friend. Boys more often do larger group activities (Rose & Rudolph, 2006). And as boys play with boys and girls play with girls, sex differences grow larger.

FRIENDSHIP.   As adults, women—at least in individualistic cultures—are more likely than men to describe themselves in relational terms, welcome help, experience relationship-linked emotions, and be attuned to others' relationships (Addis & Mahalik, 2003; Gabriel & Gardner, 1999; Tamres et al., 2002; Watkins et al., 1998, 2003). In conversation, men more often focus on tasks and on connections with large groups, whereas women focus on personal relationships (Tannen, 1990). On average, women are more aware of how their actions affect other people (You et al., 2011). "Perhaps because of their greater desire for intimacy," report Joyce Benenson and colleagues (2009), during their first year of college, women are twice as likely as men to change roommates.

Girls' play is often in small groups and imitates relationships. Boys' play is more often competitive or aggressive.
Kevin Dodge/Corbis RF/Corbis (top), Corbis RF/Corbis (bottom).

Women's phone conversations last longer, and girls send more than twice as many text messages as do boys (Friebel & Seabright, 2011; Lenhart, 2010; Smoreda & Licoppe, 2000). Women talk for longer when the goal is affiliation with others—though men actually talk more overall and when the goal is asserting one's opinions and giving information (Leaper & Ayres, 2007). Women spend more time sending emails, in which they express more emotion (Crabtree, 2002; Thomson & Murachver, 2001), and they spend more time on social networking sites, such as Facebook (Pryor et al., 2010).

When in groups, women share more of their lives and offer more support (Dindia & Allen, 1992; Eagly, 1987). When facing stress, men tend to respond with "fight or flight"; often, their response to a threat is combat. In nearly all studies, notes Shelley Taylor (2002), women who are under stress more often "tend and befriend"; they turn to friends and family for support. Among first-year college students, 66 percent of men, but 77 percent of women, say it is *very* important to "help others who are in difficulty" (Eagan et al., 2015).

VOCATIONS. In general, women are more interested in jobs dealing with people (teachers, doctors), and men in jobs with things (truck driver, engineer: Diekman et al., 2010; Eagly,

> "In the different voice of women lies the truth of an ethic of care."
>
> —Carol Gilligan,
> *In a Different Voice*, 1982

FIGURE :: 5

Words and phrases with the largest gender differences among more than 70,000 Facebook users

The gender difference in independence vs. connectedness is readily apparent in this natural language study, as are other differences such as men's greater propensity to swear and women's greater focus on shopping. The red clusters show the specific topics with the largest gender differences. *Source of data:* Schwartz et al., 2013.

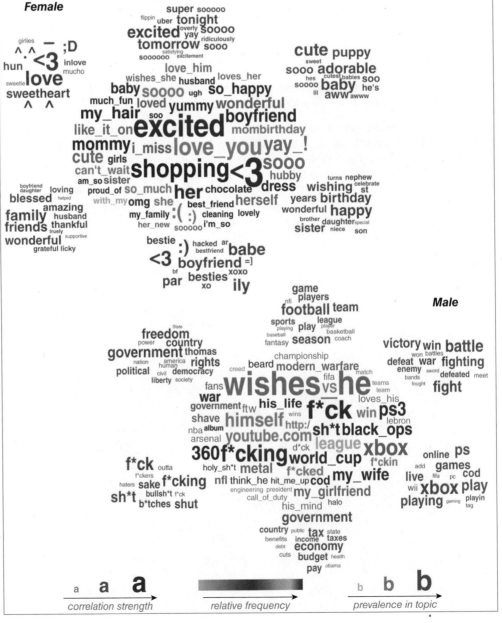

2009; Lippa, 2010; Su et al., 2009). Females are less interested in math-intensive careers than are males, even among those with a talent for math (Lubinski & Benbow, 2006). Another distinction: Men gravitate disproportionately to jobs that enhance inequalities (prosecuting attorney, corporate advertising); women gravitate to jobs that reduce inequalities (public defender, advertising work for a charity; Pratto et al., 1997). Studies of 640,000 people's job preferences reveal that men more than women value earnings, promotion, challenge, and power; women more than men value good hours, personal relationships, and opportunities to help others (Konrad et al., 2000; Pinker, 2008). Indeed, in most of the North American care-giving professions, such as social worker, teacher, and nurse, women outnumber men. Recent years have seen a few changes: Among Israeli young adults, men and women did not differ in their preferences for management careers in 2010 (vs. 1990, when men preferred these careers), but men still preferred technical careers more than women did (Gati & Perez, 2014). As of 2012, 66% of young women agreed that being successful in a high-paying career was important—higher than the 59% of young men who agreed (Patten & Parker, 2012).

FAMILY RELATIONS.   Women's connections as mothers, daughters, sisters, and grandmothers bind families (Rossi & Rossi, 1990). Following their child's birth, parents (women especially) become more traditional in their gender-related attitudes and behaviors (Ferriman et al., 2009; Katz-Wise, 2010). Women spend about twice as much time caring for children than men (Bureau of Labor Statistics, 2014). Compared with men, women buy three times as many gifts and greeting cards, write two to four times as many personal letters, and make 10 to 20 percent more long-distance calls to friends and family (Putnam, 2000). Among 500 randomly selected Facebook pages around the world, women displayed more family photos and expressed more emotion, and men were more likely to display status or risk taking (Tiffert & Vilnai-Yavetz, 2014).

SMILING.   Smiling, of course, varies with situations. Yet across more than 400 studies, women's greater connectedness has been expressed in their generally higher rate of smiling (LaFrance et al., 2003). For example, when Marianne LaFrance (1985) analyzed 9,000 college yearbook photos, she found females more often smiling. So did Amy Halberstadt and Martha Saitta (1987) in 1,100 magazine and newspaper photos and 1,300 people in shopping malls, parks, and streets. Apparently, boys learn not to smile by age 11: Boys and girls smile just as often in their elementary school pictures, but by sixth grade, girls smile significantly more than boys (Wondergem & Friedmeier, 2012).

EMPATHY.   When surveyed, women are far more likely to describe themselves as having **empathy,** or being able to feel what another feels—to rejoice with those who rejoice and weep with those who weep (O'Brien et al., 2013). To a lesser extent, the empathy difference extends to laboratory studies:

- Shown pictures or told stories, girls react with more empathy (Hunt, 1990).
- Given upsetting experiences in the laboratory or in real life, women more than men express empathy for others enduring similar experiences (Batson et al., 1996).
- Observing someone receiving pain, women's empathy-related brain circuits display elevated activity even when men's do not (Singer et al., 2006).

All these differences help to explain why, compared with male friendships, both men and women report friendships with women to be more intimate, enjoyable, and nurturing (Rubin, 1985; Sapadin, 1988). When you want empathy and understanding, someone to whom you can disclose your joys and hurts, to whom do you turn? Most men and women usually turn to women.

One explanation for this male–female empathy difference is that women tend to outperform men at reading others' emotions. In her analysis of 125 studies of men's and women's sensitivity to nonverbal cues, Judith Hall (1984, 2006) discerned that women are generally superior at decoding others' emotional messages. For example, shown a 2-second silent film clip of the face of an upset woman, women guess more accurately whether she is criticizing someone or discussing her divorce. Women also are more often strikingly better than men at recalling others' appearance (Mast & Hall, 2006).

"Contrary to what many women believe, it's fairly easy to develop a long-term, stable, intimate, and mutually fulfilling relationship with a guy. Of course this guy has to be a Labrador retriever."

—Dave Barry,
Dave Barry's Complete Guide to Guys, 1995

empathy
The vicarious experience of another's feelings; putting oneself in another's shoes.

What do you think: Should Western women become more self-reliant and more attuned to their culture's individualism? Or might women's relational approach to life help transform power-oriented Western societies (marked by high levels of child neglect, loneliness, and depression) into more caring communities?

Because they are generally empathic and skilled at reading others' emotions, girls are less vulnerable to autism, which, to Simon Baron-Cohen (2004), represents an "extreme male brain."

Finally, women are more skilled at *expressing* emotions nonverbally, says Hall. This is especially so for positive emotion, report Erick Coats and Robert Feldman (1996). They had people talk about times they had been happy, sad, and angry. When shown 5-second silent video clips of those reports, observers could much more accurately discern women's than men's emotions when recalling happiness. Men, however, were slightly more successful in conveying anger.

Social Dominance

Imagine two people: One is "adventurous, autocratic, coarse, dominant, forceful, independent, and strong." The other is "affectionate, dependent, dreamy, emotional, submissive, and weak." If the first person sounds more to you like a man and the second like a woman, you are not alone, report John Williams and Deborah Best (1990, p. 15). From Asia to Africa and Europe to Australia, people rate men as more dominant, driven, and aggressive. Moreover, studies of nearly 80,000 people across 70 countries show that men more than women rate power and achievement as important (Schwartz & Rubel, 2005).

These perceptions and expectations correlate with reality. In essentially every society, men *are* socially dominant (Pratto, 1996). As Peter Hegarty and his colleagues (2010) have observed, across time, men's names have come first: "King and Queen," "his and hers," "husband and wife," "Mr. and Mrs.," "Bill and Hillary." Shakespeare never wrote plays with titles such as *Juliet and Romeo* or *Cleopatra and Antony*.

Men also outnumber women among the most powerless, such as prisoners and the homeless (Baumeister, 2010).

As we will see, gender differences vary greatly by culture, and gender differences are shrinking in many industrialized societies as women assume more managerial and leadership positions (Koenig et al., 2011). However:

- In 2014, women were but 22 percent of the world's legislators (IPU, 2015).
- Men more than women are concerned with social dominance and are more likely to favor conservative political candidates and programs that preserve group inequality (Eagly et al., 2004; Sidanius & Pratto, 1999).
- Men are half of all jurors but 90 percent of elected jury leaders; men are also the leaders of most ad hoc laboratory groups (Colarelli et al., 2006; Davis & Gilbert, 1989; Kerr et al., 1982).
- In Britain, men hold 77 percent of top-100 corporate board positions (BIS, 2014).
- Women's wages are "between 70 and 90 percent of men's wages in a majority of countries," in 2012, reports the United Nations (2014). Only about one-fifth of this wage gap is attributable to gender differences in education, work experience, or job characteristics (World Bank, 2003).

Across many studies, people *perceive* leaders as having more culturally masculine traits—as being more confident, forceful, independent, and outspoken (Koenig et al., 2011). When writing letters of recommendation, people more often use such "agentic" adjectives when describing male candidates, and more "communal" adjectives (helpful, kind, sympathetic, nurturing, tactful) when describing women candidates (Madera et al., 2009). The net effect may be to disadvantage women applying for leadership roles.

Men's style of communicating undergirds their social power. In leadership roles, men tend to excel as directive, task-focused leaders; women excel more often in the "transformational" or "relational" leadership that is favored by more and more organizations, with inspirational and social skills that build team spirit (Pfaff et al., 2013). Men more than women place priority on winning, getting ahead, and dominating others (Sidanius et al., 1994). This may explain why people's preference for a male leader is greater for competitions between groups, such as when countries are at war, than when conflicts occur within a group (Van Vugt & Spisak, 2008).

Men's greater social power is not entirely positive, as they may fear losing it—a phenomenon known as precarious manhood (Kroeper et al., 2014; Vandello & Bosson, 2013). In many cultures, masculinity is seen as something that must be earned and defended. As Joseph Vandello and Jennifer Bosson point out, "We implore [men] to 'man up' in the face of difficulties and we question whether someone is 'man enough' for the job . . . In contrast, one rarely if ever encounters questions about whether a woman is a 'real woman' or 'woman enough.'" (2013, p. 101). Men are much more concerned about being identified as feminine than women are at being identified as masculine (Bosson & Michniewicz, 2013)—perhaps one reason why men are more likely than women to be prejudiced against gay men (Carnaghi et al., 2011; Glick et al., 2007).

Men also act more impulsively and take more risks (Byrnes et al., 1999; Cross et al., 2011; Petraitis et al., 2014). One study of data from 35,000 stockbroker accounts found that "men are more overconfident than women" and therefore made 45 percent more stock trades (Barber & Odean, 2001a). Because trading costs money, and because men's trades proved no more successful, their results underperformed the stock market by 2.65 percent, compared with women's 1.72 percent underperformance. The men's trades were riskier—and the men were the poorer for it. Even in Finland, a country with high gender equality, men take more risks in their stock market holdings (Halko et al., 2012). Men and women do not differ, however, in taking social risks, such as expressing an unpopular opinion (Harris et al., 2006).

In writing, women tend to use more communal prepositions ("with"), fewer quantitative words, and more present tense. Men use more complex language and women use more social words and pronouns (Newman et al., 2008). One computer program, which taught itself to recognize gender differences in word usage and sentence structure, successfully identified the author's gender in 80 percent of 920 British fiction and nonfiction works (Koppel et al., 2002).

In conversation, men's style reflects their concern for independence, women's for connectedness. Men are more likely to act as powerful people often do—talking assertively, interrupting intrusively, touching with the hand, staring more, smiling less (Leaper & Robnett, 2011). Stating the results from a female perspective, women's influence style tends to be more indirect—less interruptive, more sensitive, more polite, less cocky, and more qualified and hedged.

So is it right to declare (in the title words of one 1990s bestseller), *Men Are from Mars, Women Are from Venus?* Actually, note Kay Deaux and Marianne LaFrance (1998), men's and women's conversational styles vary with the social context. Much of the style we attribute to men is typical of people (men and women) in positions of status and power (Hall et al., 2006; Pennebaker, 2011). For example, students nod more when speaking with professors than when speaking with peers, and women nod more than men (Helweg-Larsen et al., 2004). Men—and people in high-status roles—tend to talk louder and to interrupt more (Hall et al., 2005). Moreover, individuals vary; some men are hesitant, some women assertive. To suggest that women and men are from different planets greatly oversimplifies.

Aggression

By **aggression,** psychologists mean behavior intended to hurt. Throughout the world, hunting, fighting, and warring are primarily male activities (Wood & Eagly, 2007). In surveys, men admit to more aggression than do women. In laboratory experiments, men indeed exhibit more physical aggression, for example, by administering what they believe are hurtful electric shocks (Knight et al., 2002). In Canada and the U.S., 8 times as many men as women are arrested for murder (Statistics Canada, 2010; FBI, 2014). Almost all suicide terrorists have been young men (Kruglanski & Golec de Zavala, 2005). So also are nearly all battlefield deaths and death row inmates.

But again the gender difference fluctuates with the context. When people are provoked, the gender gap shrinks (Bettencourt & Kernahan, 1997; Richardson, 2005). And within less assaultive forms of aggression—for instance, slapping a family member, throwing something, or verbally attacking someone—women are no less aggressive than men, and may even be more aggressive (Archer, 2000; Björkqvist, 1994; White & Kowalski, 1994). Women are also slightly more likely to commit indirect aggressive acts, such as spreading malicious gossip (Archer, 2009). But all across the world and at all ages, men much more often injure others with physical aggression.

Males are more likely than females to take risks—both physical and financial.
Ben Blankenburg/Corbis RF/Corbis

Some gender differences do not correlate with status and power. For example, women at all status levels tend to smile more (Hall et al., 2005).

aggression
Physical or verbal behavior intended to hurt someone. In laboratory experiments, this might mean delivering electric shocks or saying something likely to hurt another's feelings.

"If women were in charge of all the world's nations there would be—I sincerely believe this—virtually no military conflicts, and when there was a military conflict, everyone involved would feel just awful and there would soon be a high-level exchange of thoughtful notes . . . followed by a Peace Luncheon."
—Humorist Dave Barry, 1997

Sexuality

In their physiological and subjective responses to sexual stimuli, women and men are "more similar than different" (Griffitt, 1987). The differences lie in what happens before-hand. Consider the following:

- Imagine you were walking on campus one day when an attractive member of the other sex approaches you. "Hi, I've been noticing you around campus lately, and I find you very attractive. Would you have sex with me tonight?" he or she asks. What would you do? Not a single woman said yes, and 3 out of 4 of the men said yes (Clark & Hatfield, 1989). When asked instead if they would go on a date, about the same percentage of men and women said yes (Clark, 1990; Clark & Hatfield, 1989).

- "I can imagine myself being comfortable and enjoying 'casual' sex with different partners," agreed 48 percent of men and 12 percent of women in an Australian survey (Bailey et al., 2000). One 48-nation study showed country-by-country variation in acceptance of unrestricted sexuality, ranging from relatively promiscuous Finland to relatively monogamous Taiwan (Schmitt, 2005). But in every country studied, men expressed more desire for unrestricted sex. Likewise, when the BBC surveyed more than 200,000 people in 53 nations, men everywhere more strongly agreed that "I have a strong sex drive" (Lippa, 2008b). Men and women apparently have similar levels of self-control—but men's sexual impulses are stronger, resulting in men yielding to sexual temptation more often (Tidwell & Eastwick, 2013).

- In a survey of 3,400 randomly selected 18- to 59-year-old Americans, half as many men (25 percent) as women (48 percent) cited affection for the partner as a reason for losing their virginity. In one sample of 18- to 25-year-old college students, the average man thought about sex about once per hour, the average woman about once every two hours—though there was lots of individual variation (Fisher et al., 2011)—although one study found that they also thought about food and sleep more than women, suggesting they might just think about all needs more (Fisher et al., 2012). Men also masturbate more often than women (Peterson & Hyde, 2011).

The gender difference in sexual attitudes carries over to behavior. "With few exceptions anywhere in the world," reported cross-cultural psychologist Marshall Segall and his colleagues (1990, p. 244), "males are more likely than females to initiate sexual activity."

Compared with lesbians, gay men also report more interest in uncommitted sex, more frequent sex, more interest in pornography, more responsiveness to visual stimuli, and more concern with partner attractiveness (Peplau & Fingerhut, 2007; Rupp & Wallen, 2008; Schmitt, 2007). Forty-seven percent of lesbians in the United States are in committed relationships, double the rate for gay men (24 percent) (Doyle, 2005). Among those entering civil unions in Vermont and same-sex marriage in Massachusetts, two-thirds have been female couples (Belluck, 2008; Rothblum, 2007). "It's not that gay men are oversexed," observed Steven Pinker (1997). "They are simply men whose male desires bounce off other male desires rather than off female desires."

Indeed, not only do men fantasize more about sex, have more permissive attitudes, and seek more partners, they also are more quickly aroused, desire sex more often, masturbate more frequently, use more pornography, are less successful at celibacy, refuse sex less often, take more risks, expend more resources to gain sex, and prefer more sexual variety (Baumeister et al., 2001; Baumeister & Vohs, 2004; Petersen & Hyde, 2011). One survey asked 16,288 people from 52 nations how many sexual partners they desired in the next month. Among the unattached, 29 percent of men and 6 percent of women wanted more than one partner (Schmitt, 2003, 2005). These results were identical for straight and gay people (29 percent of gay men and 6 percent of lesbians desired more than one partner).

"Everywhere sex is understood to be something females have that males want," offered anthropologist Donald Symons (1979, p. 253). Small wonder, say Roy Baumeister and Kathleen Vohs, that cultures everywhere attribute greater value to female than male sexuality, as indicated in gender asymmetries in prostitution and courtship, where men generally offer money, gifts, praise, or commitment in implicit exchange for a woman's sexual engagement. In human sexual economics, they note, women rarely if ever pay for sex. Like labor unions opposing "scab labor" as undermining the value of their own work, most women oppose other women offering "cheap sex," which reduces the value of their own sexuality. Across 185 countries, the scarcer the available men, the *higher* is the teen pregnancy rate—because when men are scarce "women compete against each other by offering sex at a lower price in terms of commitment" (Barber, 2000; Baumeister & Vohs, 2004). When women are scarce, as is increasingly the case in China and India, the market value of their sexuality rises, and they are able to command greater commitment.

"Oh yeah, baby, I'll listen to you—I'll listen to you all night long."

© Alex Gregory/The New Yorker Collection/www.cartoonbank.com.

Sexual fantasies, too, differ between men and women (Ellis & Symons, 1990). In male-oriented erotica, women are unattached and lust driven. In romance novels, primarily read by women, a tender male is emotionally consumed by his devoted passion for the heroine. Social scientists aren't the only ones to have noticed. "Women can be fascinated by a four-hour movie with subtitles wherein the entire plot consists of a man and a woman yearning to have, but never actually having a relationship," observes humorist Dave Barry (1995). "Men HATE that. Men can take maybe 45 seconds of yearning, and they want everybody to get naked. Followed by a car chase. A movie called 'Naked People in Car Chases' would do really well among men."

Just as police detectives are more intrigued by crime than virtue, so psychological detectives are more intrigued by differences than similarities. Let us therefore remind ourselves: *Individual* differences far exceed gender differences. Females and males are hardly "opposite" sexes. Rather, they differ like two folded hands—similar but not the same, fitting together yet differing as they grasp each other.

SUMMING UP: How Are Males and Females Alike and Different?

- Boys and girls, and men and women, are in many ways alike. Yet their differences attract more attention than their similarities.

- Social psychologists have explored *gender* differences in independence versus connectedness. Women typically do more caring, express more *empathy* and emotion, and define themselves more in terms of relationships.

- Men and women also tend to exhibit differing social dominance and *aggression*. In every known culture on earth, men tend to have more social power and are more likely than women to engage in physical aggression.

- Sexuality is another area of marked gender differences. Men more often think about and initiate sex, whereas women's sexuality tends to be inspired by emotional passion.

EVOLUTION AND GENDER: DOING WHAT COMES NATURALLY?

Compare and contrast how evolutionary psychologists, and psychologists working from a sociocultural perspective, seek to explain gender variations.

Gender researcher Diane Halpern (2010) notes "consistent findings of sex differences that hold up across studies, across species, and across cultures." But why? "What do you think is the main reason men and women have different personalities, interests, and abilities?" asked a Gallup poll in 1990. "Is it mainly because of the way men and women are raised, or are the differences part of their biological makeup?" About the same percentage of respondents answered "upbringing" as said "biology."

There are, of course, certain salient biological sex differences. Men's hormones help build the muscle mass to hunt game; women's the capability to breastfeed infants. Are biological sex differences limited to such obvious distinctions in reproduction and physique? Or do men's and women's genes, hormones, and brains differ in ways that also contribute to behavioral differences?

Gender and Mating Preferences

Noting the worldwide persistence of gender differences in aggressiveness, dominance, and sexuality, evolutionary psychologist Douglas Kenrick (1987) suggested, as have many others since, that "we cannot change the evolutionary history of our species, and some of the differences between us are undoubtedly a function of that history." Evolutionary psychology predicts no sex differences in domains where the sexes faced similar adaptive challenges (Buss, 1995b, 2009). Both sexes regulate heat with sweat. The two have similar taste preferences to nourish their bodies. And they both grow calluses where the skin meets friction. But evolutionary psychology does predict sex differences in behaviors relevant to mating and reproduction.

Consider, for example, the male's greater sexual initiative. The average male produces many trillions of sperm in his lifetime, making sperm cheap compared with eggs. (If you happen to be an average man, you will make more than 1,000 sperm while reading this sentence.) Moreover, while a female brings one fetus to term and then nurses it, a male can spread his genes by fertilizing many females. Women's investment in childbearing is, just for starters, 9 months; men's investment may be 9 seconds.

Thus, say evolutionary psychologists, females invest their reproductive opportunities carefully, by looking for signs of resources and commitment. Males compete with other males for chances to win the genetic sweepstakes by sending their genes into the future, and thus look for healthy, fertile soil in which to plant their seed. Women want to find men who will help them tend the garden—resourceful and monogamous dads rather than wandering cads. Women seek to reproduce wisely, men widely. Or so the theory goes.

Moreover, evolutionary psychology suggests, physically dominant males excelled in gaining access to females, which over generations enhanced male aggression and dominance as the less-aggressive males had fewer chances to reproduce. The genes that may have helped Montezuma II to become Aztec king were also given to his offspring, along with those from many of the 4,000 women in his harem (Wright, 1998). Genghis Khan, who led invasions that brought much of Asia under his empire, is an ancestor of approximately 1 in 200 men worldwide (Zerjal, 2003). Even today, men are more aggressive toward other men when they are thinking about dating and mating (Ainsworth & Maner, 2012). And if our ancestral mothers benefited from being able to read their infants' and suitors' emotions, then natural selection may have similarly favored emotion-detecting

In species for which males provide more parental investment than females, notes evolutionary psychologist David Schmitt (2006), males have a longer-term mating strategy, are more discriminating among potential mates, and die later.

"A hen is only an egg's way of making another egg."
—Samuel Butler, 1835–1901

What attracts you to someone? Both men and women value kindness, but gender differences appear in valuing physical appearance and status.
Sam Edwards/OJO Images/AGE Fotostock

ability in females. Underlying all these presumptions is a principle: *Nature selects traits that help send one's genes into the future.*

Little of this process is conscious. Few people in the throes of passion stop to think, "I want to give my genes to posterity." Rather, say evolutionary psychologists, our natural yearnings are our genes' way of making more genes. Emotions execute evolution's dispositions, much as hunger executes the body's need for nutrients.

Medical researcher and author Lewis Thomas (1971) captured the idea of hidden evolutionary predispositions in his fanciful description of a male moth responding to a female's release of bombykol, a single molecule of which will tremble the hairs of any male within miles and send him driving upwind in ardor. But it is doubtful if the moth has an awareness of being caught in an aerosol of chemical attractant. On the contrary, he probably finds suddenly that it has become an excellent day, the weather remarkably bracing, the time appropriate for a bit of exercise of the old wings, a brisk turn upwind.

"Humans are living fossils—collections of mechanisms produced by prior selections pressures," says David Buss (1995a). And that, evolutionary psychologists believe, helps explain not only male aggression but also the differing sexual attitudes and behaviors of females and males. Although a man's interpretation of a woman's smile as sexual interest usually proves wrong, occasionally being right can have reproductive payoff.

Evolutionary psychology also predicts that men will strive to offer what women will desire—external resources and physical protection. Male peacocks strut their feathers; male humans, their abs, Audis, and assets (Sundie et al., 2011). In one experiment, teen males rated "having lots of money" as more important after they were put alone in a room with a teen female (Roney, 2003). When speed dating, women were more attracted to men with wider faces—a physical indicator of power and dominance (Valentine et al., 2014). In one Cardiff, Wales, study, men rated a woman as equally attractive whether she was at the wheel of a humble Ford Fiesta or a swanky Bentley; women found the man more attractive if seen in the luxury car (Dunn & Searle, 2010). "Male achievement is ultimately a courtship display," says Glenn Wilson (1994).

To attract men, women may balloon their breasts, Botox their wrinkles, and liposuction their fat to offer men the youthful, healthy appearance (connoting fertility) that men desire. Women's and men's mate preferences confirm these observations. Consider the following:

- Studies in 37 cultures, from Australia to Zambia, reveal that men everywhere feel attracted to women whose physical features, such as youthful faces and forms, suggest fertility. Women everywhere feel attracted to men whose wealth, power, and ambition promise resources for protecting and nurturing offspring. But there are gender similarities, too: Whether residing on an Indonesian island or in urban São Paulo, both women and men desire kindness, love, and mutual attraction.

- Men everywhere tend to be most attracted to women whose age and features suggest peak fertility. For teen boys, this is a woman several years older than themselves. For mid-20s men, it's women their own age. For older men, it's younger women; the older the man, the greater the age difference he prefers when selecting a mate (Kenrick et al., 2009). This pattern appears worldwide, in European singles ads, Indian marital ads, and marriage records from the Americas, Africa, and the Philippines (Singh, 1993; Singh & Randall, 2007). Women of all ages prefer men just slightly older than themselves. Men married to physically attractive wives reported higher marital satisfaction, whereas husbands' physical attractiveness had little impact on wives' satisfaction (Meltzer et al., 2014). Again, say the evolutionary psychologists, we see that natural selection predisposes men to feel attracted to female features associated with fertility.

- Monthly fertility also matters. Women's behaviors, scents, and voices provide subtle clues to their ovulation, which men can detect (Haselton & Gildersleeve, 2011). When at peak fertility, women express greater preference for masculine faces, greater apprehensiveness of potentially threatening men, and greater ability to detect men's sexual orientation (Gildersleeve et al., 2014). They also behave more flirtatiously with men, particularly men who are confident and socially dominant (Cantu et al., 2014).

Reflecting on those findings, Buss (1999) reports feeling somewhat astonished "that men and women across the world differ in their mate preferences in precisely the ways predicted by the evolutionists. Just as our fears of snakes, heights, and spiders provide a window for viewing the survival hazards of our evolutionary ancestors, our mating

Actor Bruce Willis is 23 years older than his wife Emma Heming.
London Entertainment/Alamy

desires provide a window for viewing the resources our ancestors needed for reproduction. We all carry with us today the desires of our successful forebears." Or as William Faulkner wrote, "The past is never dead. In fact, it's not even past." Our ancestral past lives on, in us.

Reflections on Evolutionary Psychology

Without disputing natural selection—nature's process of selecting physical and behavioral traits that enhance gene survival—critics see a problem with evolutionary explanations. Evolutionary psychologists sometimes start with a finding (such as the male-female difference in sexual initiative) and then work backward to construct an explanation for it. As biologists Paul Ehrlich and Marcus Feldman (2003) have pointed out, the evolutionary theorist can hardly lose when employing hindsight. Today's evolutionary psychology is like yesterday's Freudian psychology, say such critics: Either theory can be retrofitted to whatever happens.

The way to overcome the hindsight bias is to imagine things turning out otherwise. Let's try it. Imagine that women were stronger and more physically aggressive than men. "But of course!" someone might say, "all the better for protecting their young." And if human males were never known to have extramarital affairs, might we not see the evolutionary wisdom behind their fidelity? There is more to bringing offspring to maturity than

Outside mainstream science, other critics challenge the teaching of evolution. (See "Focus On: Evolutionary Science and Religion.")

focus
ON   Evolutionary Science and Religion

A century and a half after Charles Darwin wrote *On the Origin of Species,* controversy continues over his big idea: that every earthly creature is descended from another earthly creature. The controversy rages most intensely in the United States, where a Gallup survey reveals that half of adults do not believe that evolution accounts for "how human beings came to exist on Earth" and that 42 percent believe humans were created "within the past 10,000 years or so" (Newport, 2014). This skepticism of evolution persists despite evidence, including research showing species' genetic relatedness, which long ago persuaded 95 percent of scientists that "human beings have developed over millions of years" (Gallup, 1996).

For most scientists, mutation and natural selection explain the emergence of life, including its ingenious designs. For example, the human eye, an engineering marvel that encodes and transmits a rich stream of information, has its building blocks "dotted around the animal kingdom," enabling nature to select mutations that over time improved the design (Dennett, 2005). Indeed, many scientists are fond of quoting the famous dictum of geneticist (and Russian Orthodox Church member) Theodosius Dobzhansky, "Nothing makes sense in biology except in the light of evolution."

Alan Leshner (2005), the American Association for the Advancement of Science's executive director, laments the polarization caused by zealots at both the antiscience and the antireligious extremes. To resolve the growing science-religion tension, he believes "we must take every

opportunity to make clear to the general public that science and religion are not adversaries. They can co-exist comfortably, and both have a place and provide important benefits to society." [Republished with permission of Association for Psychological Science, from Leshner, A. I. (2005, October). "Science and religion should not be adversaries." *APS Observer* (www.psychologicalscience.org); permission conveyed through Copyright Clearance Center, Inc.]

Many scientists concur with Leshner, believing that science offers answers to questions such as "when?" and "how?" and that religion offers answers to "who?" and "why?" In the fifth century, St. Augustine anticipated today's science-affirming people of faith: "The universe was brought into being in a less than fully formed state, but was gifted with the capacity to transform itself from unformed matter into a truly marvelous array of structures and forms" (Wilford, 1999).

And the universe truly is marvelous, say cosmologists. Had gravity been a tiny bit stronger or weaker, or had the carbon proton weighed ever so slightly more or less, our universe—which is so extraordinarily right for producing life—would never have produced us. Although there are questions beyond science (why is there something rather than nothing?), this much appears true, concludes cosmologist Paul Davies (2004, 2007): Nature seems ingeniously devised to produce self-replicating, information-processing systems (us). Although we appear to have been created over eons of time, the end result is our wonderfully complex, meaningful, and hope-filled existence.

merely depositing sperm, so men and women both gain by investing jointly in their children. Males who are loyal to their mates and offspring are more likely to see their young survive to perpetuate their genes. Monogamy also increases men's certainty of paternity. (These are, in fact, evolutionary explanations—again based on hindsight—for why humans, and certain other species whose young require a heavy parental investment, tend to pair off and be monogamous).

Evolutionary psychologists argue that hindsight plays no less a role in cultural explanations: Why do women and men differ? Because their culture *socializes* their behavior! When people's roles vary across time and place, "culture" *describes* those roles better than it explains them. And far from being mere hindsight conjecture, say evolutionary psychologists, their field is an empirical science that tests evolutionary predictions with data from animal behavior, cross-cultural observations, and hormonal and genetic studies. As in many scientific fields, observations inspire a theory that generates new, testable predictions. The predictions alert us to unnoticed phenomena and allow us to confirm, refute, or revise the theory.

Critics also worry that evolutionary explanations for gang violence, homicidal jealousy, and rape might reinforce and justify male aggression as natural behaviors—and do the same for men who cheat on their wives with younger women. But remember, reply the evolutionary psychologists, evolutionary wisdom is wisdom from the past. It tells us what behaviors worked in our early history as a species. Whether such tendencies are still adaptive today—much less socially acceptable—is an entirely different question.

Evolutionary psychology's critics acknowledge that evolution helps explain both our commonalities and our differences (a certain amount of diversity aids survival). But they contend that our common evolutionary heritage does not, by itself, predict the enormous cultural variation in human marriage patterns (from one spouse to a succession of spouses to multiple wives to multiple husbands to spouse swapping). Nor does it explain cultural changes in behavior patterns over mere decades of time. The most significant trait that nature has endowed us with, it seems, is the capacity to adapt—to learn and to change. Evolution is *not* genetic determinism, say its defenders, because evolution has prepared us to adapt to varied environments (Confer et al., 2010). As everyone agrees, cultures vary and cultures change.

Gender and Hormones

If genes predispose gender-related traits, they must do so by their effects on our bodies. In male fetuses, a single gene (called testis-determining factor) directs the formation of the testicles, which begin to secrete testosterone, the male sex hormone that influences masculine appearance and other traits. Girls exposed to excess testosterone during fetal development tend to exhibit more tomboyish play behavior than other girls (Hines, 2004) and resemble males in their career preferences, with greater interest in things than people (Beltz et al., 2011). Overall, children exposed to more testosterone in the womb exhibit the psychological pattern more typical of males, including less eye contact, lower language skill, and less empathy (Auyeung et al., 2013). Other case studies have followed males born without penises who are reared as girls (Reiner & Gearhart, 2004). Despite their being put in dresses and treated as girls, most exhibit male-typical play and eventually—in most cases, with some emotional distress—come to have a male identity.

The gender gap in aggression also seems influenced by testosterone. In various animals, administering testosterone heightens aggressiveness. In humans, violent male criminals have higher than normal testosterone levels; so do National Football League players and boisterous fraternity members (Dabbs, 2000). Moreover, for both humans and monkeys, the gender difference in aggression appears early in life (before culture has much effect) and wanes as testosterone levels decline during adulthood. No one of these lines of evidence is conclusive. Taken together, they convince many scholars that sex hormones matter. But so, as we will see, does culture.

As people mature to middle age and beyond, a curious thing happens. Women become more assertive and self-confident, and men become more empathic and less domineering (Kasen et al., 2006; Pratt et al., 1990). Hormone changes are one possible explanation for

"The finest people marry the two sexes in their own person."

—Ralph Waldo Emerson, *Journals*, 1843

the shrinking gender differences. Role demands are another. Some speculate that during courtship and early parenthood, social expectations lead both sexes to emphasize traits that enhance their roles. While courting, providing, and protecting, men play up their macho sides and forgo their needs for interdependence and nurturance (Gutmann, 1977). While dating or rearing young children, young women restrain their impulses to assert and be independent. As men and women graduate from these early adult roles, they supposedly express more of their restrained tendencies. Each becomes more **androgynous**—capable of both assertiveness and nurturance.

androgynous
From *andro* (man) + *gyn* (woman)—thus mixing both masculine and feminine characteristics.

SUMMING UP: Evolution and Gender: Doing What Comes Naturally?

- Evolutionary psychologists theorize how evolution might have predisposed gender differences in behaviors such as aggression and sexual initiative. Nature's mating game favors males who take sexual initiative toward females—especially those with physical features suggesting fertility—and who seek aggressive dominance in competing with other males. Females, who have fewer reproductive chances, place a greater priority on selecting mates offering the resources to protect and nurture their young.

- Critics say that evolutionary explanations are sometimes after-the-fact conjectures that fail to account for the reality of cultural diversity; they also question whether enough empirical evidence exists to support evolutionary psychology's theories and are concerned that these theories will reinforce troublesome stereotypes.

- Although biology (for example, in the form of male and female hormones) plays an important role in gender differences, social roles are also a major influence. What's agreed is that nature endows us with a remarkable capacity to adapt to differing contexts.

CULTURE AND GENDER: DOING AS THE CULTURE SAYS?

Understand how culture's influence is vividly illustrated by differing gender roles across place and time.

Culture, as we noted earlier, is shared by a large group and transmitted across generations—ideas, attitudes, behaviors, and traditions. Like biological creatures, cultures vary and compete for resources and thus evolve over time (Mesoudi, 2009). Cultures evolve through a "culture cycle," noted Hazel Markus and Alana Conner (2011): "1) people create the cultures to which they later adapt, and 2) cultures shape people so that they act in ways that perpetuate their cultures." Humans are culturally shaped culture shapers.

We can see the shaping power of culture in ideas about how men and women should behave. And we can see culture in the disapproval they endure when they violate those expectations (Kite, 2001). In countries everywhere, girls spend more time helping with housework and child care, and boys spend more time in unsupervised play (Edwards, 1991; Kalenkoski et al., 2009; United Nations, 2010). Even in contemporary, dual-career, North American marriages, men do most of the household repairs, and women arrange the child care (Bianchi et al., 2000; Fisher et al., 2007).

Gender socialization, it has been said, gives girls "roots" and boys "wings." Such behavior expectations for males and females—of who should cook, wash dishes, hunt game, and lead companies and countries—define **gender roles.**

Does culture construct these gender roles? Or do gender roles merely reflect men's and women's natural behavior tendencies? The variety of gender roles across cultures and over time shows that culture indeed helps construct our gender roles.

"At the United Nations, we have always understood that our work for development depends on building a successful partnership with the African farmer and her husband."
—Secretary-General Kofi Annan, 2002

gender role
A set of behavior expectations (norms) for males and females.

Three months after the southeast Asian tsunami on December 26, 2004, Oxfam (2005) counted deaths in eight villages and found that female deaths were at least triple those of men. (The women were more likely to be in or near their homes, near the shore, and less likely to be at sea or away from home on errands or at work.)
AP Images/Suzanne Plunkett

Gender Roles Vary with Culture

Despite gender role inequalities, the majority of the world's people would ideally like to see more parallel male and female roles. A 2010 Pew Global Attitudes survey asked 25,000 people whether life was more satisfying when both spouses work and share child care, or when women stay home and care for the children while the husband provides. In 21 of 22 countries, most chose both spouses working.

However, large country-to-country differences exist. Pakistanis disagreed with the world majority opinion by 4 to 1, whereas the Spanish concurred by 13 to 1. When jobs are scarce, should men have more right to a job? Yes, agreed about 1 in 8 people in Britain, Spain, and the United States—and 4 in 5 people in Indonesia, Pakistan, and Nigeria (Pew, 2010).

Gender Roles Vary Over Time

In the past half-century—a thin slice of our long history—gender roles have changed dramatically. In 1938, just 1 in 5 Americans approved "of a married woman earning money in business or industry if she has a husband capable of supporting her." By 1996, 4 in 5 approved (Niemi et al., 1989; NORC, 1996). Among U.S. 12th graders in the late 1970s, 59 percent agreed that "A preschooler is likely to suffer if the mother works," but by 2013 only 21 percent agreed (Donnelly et al., 2015). In the 1960s and 1970s, U.S. books used four times as many male pronouns as female pronouns, but by 2008 the ratio had shrunk to two to one (Twenge et al., 2012).

In Western countries, gender roles are becoming more flexible. No longer is preschool teaching necessarily women's work and piloting necessarily men's work.
Spencer Grant/PhotoEdit (left), U.S. Air Force photo by Master Sgt. Alfred A Gerloff Jr. (right)

Behavioral changes have accompanied this attitude shift. In 1965 the Harvard Business School had never granted a degree to a woman. In its 2016 class, 41 percent of students were women. From 1960 to 2014, women rose from 6 percent to 47 percent of U.S. medical students and from 3 percent to 47 percent of law students (AAMC, 2014; ABA, 2014; Hunt, 2000). Role models may be a crucial catalyst for such shifts. When a law in India reserved leadership positions in some villages for women, girls became more likely to aspire to higher education and careers compared to the villages without female role models (Beaman et al., 2012).

Things have changed at home, too. In the mid-1960s American married women devoted *seven times* as many hours to housework as did their husbands (Bianchi et al., 2000). By 2013, the gender gap had shrunk, yet persisted: 19 percent of men and 49 percent of women did housework in an average day, with women averaging 2.6 hours on their housework days and men 2.1 hours on theirs (BLS, 2014). Mothers in 2011 still spent twice as much time on childcare as men did. Mothers spent three times as many hours on paid work than they did in 1965, but still worked for pay only about half as many hours as men (Pew Research, 2013).

The trends toward more gender equality appear across many cultures—for example, women are increasingly represented in the parliaments of most nations (Inglehart & Welzel, 2005; IPU, 2015). Such changes, across cultures and over a remarkably short time, signal that evolution and biology do not fix gender roles: Time also bends the genders. They may also bend cultures toward peace: Societies with more gender equality are less likely to engage in war and are less violent (Caprioli & Boyer, 2001; Melander et al., 2005).

Peer-Transmitted Culture

Cultures, like ice cream, come in many flavors. On Wall Street, men mostly wear suits, and women often wear skirts and dresses. In Scotland, many men wear pleated skirts (kilts) as formal dress. In some equatorial cultures, men and women wear virtually nothing at all. How are such traditions preserved across generations?

The prevailing assumption is what Judith Rich Harris (1998, 2007) calls *The Nurture Assumption:* Parental nurture, the way parents bring their children up, governs who their children become. On that much, Freudians and behaviorists—and your next-door neighbor— agree. Comparing the extremes of loved children and abused children suggests that parenting *does* matter. Moreover, children do acquire many of their values, including their political

Children learn many of their attitudes from their peers.
Will Hart/PhotoEdit

affiliation and religious faith, at home. But if children's personalities likewise are molded by parental example and nurture, then children who grow up in the same families should be noticeably alike, shouldn't they?

That presumption is refuted by the most astonishing, agreed-upon, and dramatic finding of developmental psychology. In the enduring words of behavior geneticists Robert Plomin and Denise Daniels (1987), "Two children in the same family [are on average] as different from one another as are pairs of children selected randomly from the population."

The evidence from studies of twins and biological and adoptive siblings indicates that genetic influences explain roughly 50 percent of individual variations in personality traits. Shared environmental influences—including the shared home influence—account for only 0 to 10 percent of their personality differences. So what accounts for the rest? Much of it is *peer influence,* Harris argues. What children and teens care about most is not what their parents think but what their friends think. Children and youth learn their culture—their games, their musical tastes, their accents, even their dirty words—mostly from peers. Most teens therefore talk, act, and dress more like their peers than their parents. In hindsight, that makes sense. It's their peers with whom they play and eventually will work and mate. Consider the following:

- Preschoolers will often refuse to try a certain food despite parents' urgings—until they are put at a table with a group of children who like it.
- Although the children of smokers are more likely to smoke, that may be because of peer influence. Such children more often have friends who model smoking, who talk about its pleasures, and who offer cigarettes.
- Young immigrant children whose families are transplanted into foreign cultures usually grow up preferring the language and norms of their new peer culture. A young child who moves with her family from China to the United States will speak English with an American accent—even if her parents never learn English or have heavy accents. Youth may "code-switch" when they step back into their homes, but their hearts and minds are with their peer groups. Likewise, deaf children of hearing parents who attend schools for the deaf usually leave their parents' culture and assimilate into deaf culture.

Therefore, if we left a group of children with their same schools, neighborhoods, and peers but switched the parents around, says Harris (1996) in taking her argument to its limits, they "would develop into the same sort of adults." Parents have an important influence, but it's substantially indirect; parents help define the schools, neighborhoods, and peers that directly influence whether their children become delinquent, use drugs, or get pregnant. Moreover, children often take their cues from slightly older children, who get their cues from older youth, who take theirs from young adults in the parents' generation.

The links of influence from parental group to child group are loose enough that the cultural transmission is never perfect. And in both human and primate cultures, change comes from the young. When one monkey discovers a better way of washing food or when people develop a new idea about fashion or gender roles, the innovation usually comes from the young and is more readily embraced by younger adults. Thus, cultural traditions continue; yet cultures change.

SUMMING UP: Culture and Gender: Doing as the Culture Says?

- The most heavily researched of roles—*gender roles*—reflect biological influence but also illustrate culture's strong impact. The universal tendency has been for males, more than females, to occupy socially dominant roles.

- Gender roles show significant variation from culture to culture and from time to time.

- Much of culture's influence is transmitted to children by their peers.

WHAT CAN WE CONCLUDE ABOUT GENES, CULTURE, AND GENDER?

Explain how biology and culture interact, and also how our individual personalities interact with our situations.

Biology *and* Culture

We needn't think of evolution and culture as competitors. Cultural norms subtly yet powerfully affect our attitudes and behavior. But they don't do so independent of biology. Everything social and psychological is ultimately biological. If others' expectations influence us, that is part of our biological programming. Moreover, what our biological heritage initiates, culture may accentuate. Genes and hormones predispose males to be more physically aggressive than females. But culture amplifies that difference through norms that expect males to be tough and females to be the kinder, gentler sex.

Biology and culture may also **interact.** Advances in genetic science indicate how experience uses genes to change the brain (Quartz & Sejnowski, 2002). Environmental stimuli can activate genes that produce new brain cell branching receptors. Visual experience activates genes that develop the brain's visual area. Parental touch activates genes that help offspring cope with future stressful events. Genes are not set in stone; they respond adaptively to our experiences.

As we mentioned earlier in the chapter, the field of *epigenetics* (meaning "in addition to" genetics) explores the mechanisms by which environments trigger genetic expression. Diet, drugs, and stress, including child abuse, can all regulate gene expression (Champagne et al., 2003; Champagne & Mashoodh, 2009; McGowan et al., 2010). Animal studies suggest that epigenetic changes can be passed down through several generations. When pregnant females are exposed to toxins or unhealthy diets, for example, the effects are seen not just in the babies but in their offspring as well (the "grandchildren") (De Assis et al., 2012). Thus far, studies on humans have focused more on how the environment changes genetic tendencies. For example, in families who fight frequently, the genetic expression of anxiety is reduced because everyone is anxious. But when families are fairly calm, only those more genetically prone to anxiety are anxious, so genetics have more influence (Jang et al., 2005). Overall, the science of epigenetics suggests that environmental factors shape lifelong biological changes, showing that nature and nurture work together—not independently.

Biology and experience also interact when biological traits influence how the environment reacts. Men, being 8 percent taller and averaging almost double the proportion of muscle mass, are bound to experience life differently from women. Or consider this: A very strong cultural norm dictates that males should be taller than their female mates. In one study, only 1 in 720 married couples in the United States violated that norm (Gillis & Avis, 1980). With hindsight, we can speculate a psychological explanation: Perhaps being taller helps men perpetuate their social power over women. But we can also speculate evolutionary wisdom that might underlie the cultural norm: If people preferred partners of their own height, tall men and short women would often be without partners. As it is, evolution dictates that men tend to be taller than women, and culture dictates the same for couples. So the height norm might well be a result of biology *and* culture.

Alice Eagly (2009) and Wendy Wood (Wood & Eagly, 2007, 2013) theorize how biology and culture interact (Figure 6). They believe that a variety of factors, including biological influences and childhood socialization, predispose a sexual division of labor. In adult life the immediate causes of gender differences in social behavior are the *roles* that reflect this sexual division of labor. Men, because of their biologically endowed strength and speed, tend to be found in roles demanding physical power. Women's capacity for childbearing and breastfeeding inclines them to more nurturant roles. Each sex

interaction

A relationship in which the effect of one factor (such as biology) depends on another factor (such as environment).

FIGURE :: 6

A Social-Role Theory of Gender Differences in Social Behavior

Various influences, including childhood experiences and factors, bend males and females toward differing roles. It is the expectations and the skills and beliefs associated with these differing roles that affect men's and women's behavior.

Source: Adapted from Eagly (1987).

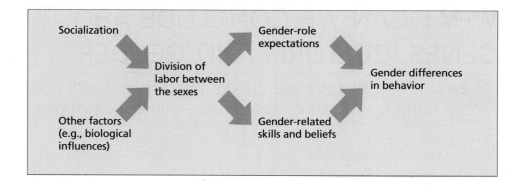

then tends to exhibit the behaviors expected of those who fill such roles and to have their skills and beliefs shaped accordingly. Nature and nurture are a "tangled web." As role assignments become more equal, Eagly predicts that gender differences "will gradually lessen."

Indeed, note Eagly and Wood, in cultures with greater equality of gender roles, the gender difference in mate preferences (men seeking youth and domestic skill, women seeking status and earning potential) is less. Likewise, as women's employment in formerly male occupations has increased, the gender difference in self-reported masculinity has decreased (Twenge, 1997). As men and women enact more similar roles, some psychological differences shrink—though they may not disappear (see "The Inside Story: Alice Eagly on Gender Similarities and Differences").

But not all, report David Schmitt and his international colleagues (2008). Across 55 nations, women report more extraversion, agreeableness, and conscientiousness. These gender differences are greatest in (surprise) prosperous, educated, egalitarian countries. In less fortunate economic and social contexts, suggests Schmitt, "the development of one's inherent personality traits is more restrained."

Although biology predisposes men to strength tasks and women to infant care, Wood and Eagly (2002) conclude that "the behavior of women and men is sufficiently malleable that individuals of both sexes are fully capable of effectively carrying out organizational roles at all levels." For today's high-status and often high-tech work roles,

THE inside STORY

Alice Eagly on Gender Similarities and Differences

I began my work on gender with a project on social influence in the early 1970s. Like many feminist activists of the day, I initially assumed that, despite negative cultural stereotypes about women, the behavior of women and men is substantially equivalent. Over the years, my views have evolved considerably. I have found that some social behaviors of women and men are somewhat different, especially in situations that bring gender roles to mind.

People should not assume that these differences necessarily reflect unfavorably on women. Women's tendencies to be more attuned to other people's concerns and to treat others more democratically are favorably evaluated and can be assets in many situations. In fact, my research

on gender stereotypes shows that, if we take both negative and positive qualities into account, the stereotype of women is currently more favorable than the stereotype of men. However, the qualities of niceness and nurturance that are important in expectations about women may decrease their power and effectiveness in situations that call for assertive and competitive behavior.

Alice Eagly
Northwestern University
Courtesy of Alice Eagly

male size and aggressiveness matter little. Moreover, lowered birthrates mean that women are less constrained by pregnancy and nursing. The end result, when combined with competitive pressures for employers to hire the best talent regardless of gender, is greater gender equality.

The Power of the Situation *and* the Person

"There are trivial truths and great truths," declared the physicist Niels Bohr. "The opposite of a trivial truth is plainly false. The opposite of a great truth is also true." This chapter teaches a great truth: *the power of the situation.* The situation would explain our behavior if we were passive, like tumbleweeds blown by the wind. But, unlike tumbleweeds, we are not just blown here and there by the situations in which we find ourselves. We act; we react. We respond, and we get responses. We can resist the social situation and sometimes even change it. That's why the power of the person is just as important, and just as true.

Food for thought: If Bohr's statement is a great truth, what is its opposite?

Perhaps stressing the power of culture leaves you somewhat uncomfortable. Do external forces determine your behavior? Most of us see ourselves as free beings, as the originators of our actions (well, at least of our good actions). We worry that cultural explanations for our actions might lead to what philosopher Jean-Paul Sartre called "bad faith"—evading responsibility by blaming something or someone for one's fate.

Actually, social control (the power of the situation) and personal control (the power of the person) no more compete with each other than do biological and cultural explanations. Social and personal explanations are both valid, for at any moment we are both the creatures and the creators of our social worlds. We may well be the products of the interplay of our genes and environment. But it is also true that the future is coming, and it is our job to decide where it is going. Our choices today determine our environment tomorrow.

"The words of truth are always paradoxical."
—Lao-Tzu,
The Simple Way, 6th Century B.C.

Social situations do profoundly influence individuals. But individuals also influence social situations. The two *interact.* Asking whether external situations or inner dispositions determine behavior is like asking whether length or width determines a room's area.

The interaction occurs in at least three ways (Snyder & Ickes, 1985).

- *A given social situation often affects different people differently.* Because our minds do not see reality identically or objectively, we respond to a situation as we construe it. And some people (groups as well as individuals) are more sensitive and responsive to social situations than others (Snyder, 1983). The Japanese, for example, are more responsive to social expectations than the British (Argyle et al., 1978).

- *People often choose their situations* (Ickes et al., 1997). Given a choice, sociable people elect situations that evoke social interaction. When you chose your college, you were also choosing to expose yourself to a specific set of social influences. Ardent political liberals are unlikely to choose to live in suburban Dallas, join the Chamber of Commerce, and watch Fox News. They are more likely to live in San Francisco or Toronto, join Greenpeace, and read the *Huffington Post*—in other words, to choose a social world that reinforces their inclinations.

- *People often create their situations.* Recall again that our preconceptions can be self-fulfilling: If we expect someone to be extraverted, hostile, intelligent, or sexy, our actions toward the person may induce the very behavior we expect. What, after all, makes a social situation but the people in it? A conservative environment is created by conservatives. What takes place in the sorority or fraternity is created by its members. The social environment is not like the weather—something that just happens to us. It is more like our homes—something we make for ourselves.

Thus, power resides both in persons and in situations. *We create and are created by our cultural worlds.*

SUMMING UP: What Can We Conclude About Genes, Culture, and Gender?

- Biological and cultural explanations need not be contradictory. Indeed, they *interact*. Biological factors operate within a cultural context, and culture builds on a biological foundation. Emerging research in the field of *epigenetics* shows that genes are expressed in some environments and not others.

- The great truth about the power of social influence is but half the truth if separated from its complementary truth: the power of the person. Persons and situations interact in at least three ways. First, individuals vary in how they interpret and react to a given situation. Second, people choose many of the situations that influence them. Third, people help create their social situations.

POSTSCRIPT:
Should We View Ourselves as Products or Architects of Our Social Worlds?

The reciprocal causation between situations and persons allows us to see people as either *reacting to* or *acting upon* their environment. Each perspective is correct, for we are both the products and the architects of our social worlds. But is one perspective wiser? In one sense, it is wise to see ourselves as the creatures of our environments (lest we become too proud of our achievements and blame ourselves too much for our problems) and to see others as free actors (lest we become paternalistic and manipulative).

Perhaps, however, we would do well more often to assume the reverse—to view ourselves as free agents and to view others as situationally influenced. We would then assume self-efficacy as we view ourselves, and we would seek understanding and social reform as we relate to others. Most religions, in fact, encourage us to take responsibility for ourselves but to refrain from judging others. Is that because our natural inclination is the opposite: to excuse our own failures while blaming others for theirs?

Conformity and Obedience

ChinaFotoPress/Getty Images

"Whatever crushes individuality is despotism, by whatever name it may be called."

—John Stuart Mill, On Liberty, 1859

"The social pressures community brings to bear are a mainstay of our moral values."

—Amitai Etzioni, The Spirit of Community, 1993

What is conformity?

What are the classic conformity and obedience studies?

What predicts conformity?

Why conform?

Who conforms?

Do we ever want to be different?

Postscript: On being an individual within community

Y ou have surely experienced the phenomenon: As a music concert finishes, the adoring fans near the front leap to their feet, applauding. The approving folks just behind them follow their example and join the standing ovation. Now the wave of people standing reaches people who, unprompted, would merely be giving polite applause from their comfortable seats. Seated among them, part of you wants to stay seated ("the concert was only okay"). But as the wave of standing people sweeps by, will you alone stay seated? It's not easy being a minority of one. Unless you heartily dislike what you've just heard, you will probably rise to your feet, at least briefly.

Such scenes of conformity raise this chapter's questions:

• Why, given our diversity, do we so often behave as social clones?

• Under what circumstances are we most likely to conform?

- Are certain people more likely than others to conform?
- Who resists the pressure to conform?
- Is conformity as bad as my image of a docile "herd" implies? Should I instead be describing their "group solidarity" and "social sensitivity"?

WHAT IS CONFORMITY?

Define conformity, and compare compliance, obedience, and acceptance.

conformity

A change in behavior or belief as the result of real or imagined group pressure.

acceptance

Conformity that involves both acting and believing in accord with social pressure.

compliance

Conformity that involves publicly acting in accord with an implied or explicit request while privately disagreeing.

obedience

A type of compliance involving acting in accord with a direct order or command.

Let us take the last question first. Is conformity good or bad? That question has no scientific answer. Conformity is sometimes bad (when it leads someone to drive drunk or to join in racist behavior), sometimes good (when it keeps people from cutting into a theater line), and sometimes inconsequential (when it directs tennis players to wear white).

In Western individualistic cultures, where submitting to peer pressure is discouraged, the word "conformity" carries a negative connotation. How would you feel if you overheard someone describing you as a "real conformist"? We suspect you would feel hurt. North American and European social psychologists, reflecting their individualistic cultures, give social influence negative labels (conformity, submission, compliance) rather than positive ones (communal sensitivity, responsiveness, cooperative team play). In Japan, going along with others is a sign not of weakness but of tolerance, self-control, and maturity (Markus & Kitayama, 1994). "Everywhere in Japan," observed Lance Morrow (1983), "one senses an intricate serenity that comes to a people who know exactly what to expect from each other."

Conformity is the overall term for acting differently due to the influence of others. Conformity is not just acting as other people act; it is also being *affected* by how they act. It is acting or thinking differently from the way you would act and think if you were alone. Thus, **conformity** is a change in behavior or belief to accord with others. If you rise to cheer a game-winning goal, drink coffee, or wear your hair in a certain style because you want to, and not due to the influence of others, you are not conforming. But if you do those things because other people did them, that's conformity.

Acceptance and compliance are two varieties of conformity (Nail et al., 2000).

Acceptance occurs when you genuinely believe in what the group has persuaded you to do—you inwardly and sincerely believe that the group's actions are right. For example, you might exercise, as millions do, because you accept that exercise is healthy. You stop at red lights because you accept that not doing so is dangerous.

In contrast, **compliance** is conforming to an expectation or a request without really believing in what you are doing. You put on the necktie or the dress, although you dislike doing so. You say you like your friends' favorite band even though you don't. You might comply primarily to reap a reward or avoid a punishment—for example, you might have followed your high school's dress code even though you thought it was dumb, because that was better than detention. In other words, compliance is an insincere, outward conformity. **Obedience,** or complying with a direct command, is a variation on compliance. If your mother tells you to clean up your room and you do, that's obedience (Figure 1).

Source: Dave Coverly, The Comic Strips

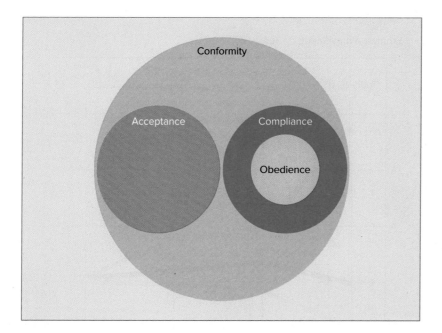

Compliance and acceptance even differ in the brain: The shorter-lived memories that underlie public compliance have a different neural basis than the memories that underlie longer-term private acceptance (Edelson et al., 2011; Zaki et al., 2011).

SUMMING UP: What Is Conformity?

Conformity—changing one's behavior or belief as a result of group pressure—comes in two forms. *Acceptance* is believing in as well as acting in accord with social pressure. *Compliance* is outwardly going along with the group while inwardly disagreeing; a subset of compliance is *obedience,* compliance with a direct command.

WHAT ARE THE CLASSIC CONFORMITY AND OBEDIENCE STUDIES?

Describe how social psychologists have studied conformity in the laboratory. Explain what their findings reveal about the potency of social forces and the nature of evil.

Researchers who study conformity and obedience construct miniature social worlds—laboratory microcultures that simplify and simulate important features of everyday social influence. Some of these studies revealed such startling findings that they have been widely replicated, making them "classic" experiments. We will consider three, each of which provides a method for studying conformity—and plenty of food for thought.

Sherif's Studies of Norm Formation

Muzafer Sherif (1935, 1937) wondered whether it was possible to observe the emergence of a social norm in the laboratory. Like biologists seeking to isolate a virus so they can experiment with it, Sherif wanted to isolate and then experiment with norm formation.

FIGURE :: 2

A Sample Group from Sherif's Study of Norm Formation

Three individuals converge as they give repeated estimates of the apparent movement of a point of light.
Source: Data from Sherif & Sherif (1969), p. 209.

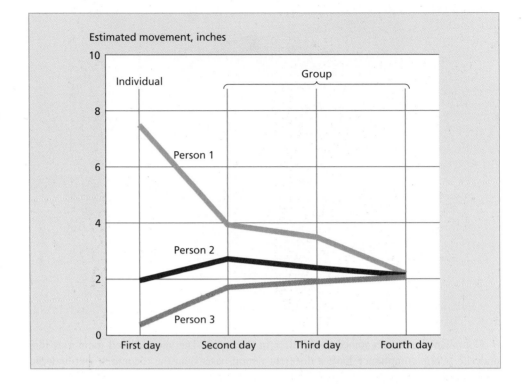

Imagine you are a participant in one of Sherif's experiments. You find yourself seated in a dark room. Fifteen feet in front of you a pinpoint of light appears. At first, nothing happens. Then for a few seconds it moves erratically and finally disappears. The experimenter asks you to guess how far it moved. The dark room gives you no way to judge distance, so you offer an uncertain "six inches." The experimenter repeats the procedure. This time you say, "Ten inches." With further repetitions, your estimates continue to average about eight inches.

The next day you return to the darkened room, joined by two other participants who had the same experience the day before. When the light goes off for the first time, the other two people offer their best guesses from the day before. "One inch," says one. "Two inches," says the other. A bit taken aback, you nevertheless say, "Six inches." With repetitions of this group experience, both on this day and for the next two days, will your responses change? The results suggest they will: Sherif's male student participants changed their estimates markedly. As Figure 2 illustrates, a group norm typically emerged. (The norm was false. Why? The light never moved! Sherif had taken advantage of an optical illusion called the **autokinetic phenomenon.)**

autokinetic phenomenon
Self *(auto)* motion *(kinetic)*. The apparent movement of a stationary point of light in the dark.

Sherif and others have used this technique to answer questions about people's suggestibility. When people were retested alone a year later, would their estimates again diverge or would they continue to follow the group norm? Remarkably, they continued to support the group norm (Rohrer et al., 1954). (Does that suggest acceptance or compliance?)

Struck by culture's seeming power to perpetuate false beliefs, Robert Jacobs and Donald Campbell (1961) studied the transmission of false beliefs in their Northwestern University laboratory. Using the autokinetic phenomenon, they had a confederate give an inflated estimate of how far the light had moved. The confederate then left the experiment and was replaced by another real participant, who was in turn replaced by a still newer member. The inflated illusion persisted (although diminishing) for five generations of participants. These people had become "unwitting conspirators in perpetuating a cultural fraud." The lesson of these experiments: Our views of reality are not ours alone.

"Why doth one man's yawning make another yawn?"

—Robert Burton,
Anatomy of Melancholy, 1621

In everyday life, the results of suggestibility are sometimes amusing. One person coughs, laughs, or yawns, and others are soon doing the same. (See "Research Close-Up: Contagious Yawning.") One person checks her cell phone and then others check theirs.

research CLOSE-UP

Contagious Yawning

Yawning is a behavior that we share with most vertebrates. Primates do it. So do cats and crocodiles and birds and turtles and even fish. But why, and when?

Sometimes, notes University of Maryland, Baltimore County, psychologist Robert Provine (2005), scientific research neglects commonplace behavior—including the behaviors he loves to study, such as laughing and yawning. To study yawning by the method of naturalistic observation, notes Provine, one needs only a stopwatch, a notepad, and a pencil. Yawning, he reports, is a "fixed action pattern" that lasts about six seconds, with a long inward breath and shorter climactic (and pleasurable) exhalation. It often comes in bouts, with just over a minute between yawns. And it is equally common among men and women. Even patients who are totally paralyzed and unable to move their body voluntarily may yawn normally, indicating that this is automatic behavior.

When do we yawn?

We yawn when we are bored or tense. When Provine asked participants to watch a TV test pattern for 30 minutes, they yawned 70 percent more often than others in a control group who watched less-boring music videos. But tension can also elicit yawning, which is commonly observed among paratroopers before their first jump, Olympic athletes before their event, and violinists waiting to go onstage. A friend says she has often been embarrassed when learning something new at work, because her anxiety about getting it right invariably causes her to have a "yawning fit."

We yawn when we are sleepy. No surprise here, except perhaps that people who kept a yawning diary for Provine recorded even more yawns in the hour after waking than in the yawn-prone hour before sleeping. Often, we awaken and yawn-stretch. And so do our dogs and cats when they rouse from slumber.

We yawn when others yawn. To test whether yawning, like laughter, is contagious, Provine exposed people to a 5-minute video of a man yawning repeatedly. Sure enough, 55 percent of viewers yawned, as did only 21 percent of those viewing a video of smiles. A yawning face acts as a stimulus that activates a yawn's fixed action pattern, even if the yawn is presented in black-and-white, upside down, or as a mid-yawn still image. The discovery of brain "mirror neurons"—neurons that rehearse or mimic witnessed actions—suggests a biological mechanism that explains why our yawns so often mirror others' yawns—and why even dogs often yawn after observing a human yawn (Joly-Mascheroni et al., 2008; Silva et al., 2012).

To see what parts of the yawning face are most potent, Provine had viewers watch a whole face, a face with the mouth masked, a mouth with the face masked, or (as a control condition) a nonyawning smiling face. As Figure 3 shows, the yawning faces triggered yawns even with the mouth masked. Thus, covering your mouth when yawning likely won't suppress yawn contagion.

Just thinking about yawning usually produces yawns, reports Provine—a phenomenon you may have noticed while reading this box. While reading Provine's research on contagious yawning, I [DM] yawned four times (and felt a little silly).

FIGURE :: 3

What Facial Features Trigger Contagious Yawns?

Robert Provine (2005) invited 4 groups of 30 people each to watch 5-minute videotapes of a smiling adult, or a yawning adult, parts of whose face were masked for two of the groups. A yawning mouth triggered some yawns, but yawning eyes and head motion triggered even more.

Source: From Provine, Robert. "Yawning." American Scientist, Volume 93, Fig. 6, page 536. Image courtesy, Dr. Robert R. Provine, Department of Psychology, University of Maryland

"I don't know why. I just suddenly felt like calling."

© Mick Stevens/The New Yorker
Collection/www.cartoonbank.com.

mass hysteria
Suggestibility to problems that spreads throughout a large group of people.

"When people are free to do as they please, they usually imitate each other."

—Eric Hoffer,
The Passionate State of Mind,
1955

Comedy-show laugh tracks capitalize on our suggestibility. Laugh tracks work especially well when we presume that the laughing audience is folks like us—"recorded here at La Trobe University" in one study by Michael Platow and colleagues (2004)—rather than a group that's unlike us. Just being around happy people can help us feel happier, a phenomenon that Peter Totterdell and his colleagues (1998) call "mood linkage." In their studies of British nurses and accountants, people within the same work groups tended to share up and down moods. People within a social network also move toward sharing similar obesity, sleep loss, loneliness, happiness, and drug use (Christakis & Fowler, 2009). An ethically controversial experiment manipulated 700,000 people's Facebook accounts, finding that when news feeds included less positive emotion, users produced fewer positive posts and more negative posts—although the effects were very small (Kramer et al., 2014). Nevertheless, friends function as a social system.

Another form of social contagion is what Tanya Chartrand and John Bargh (1999) call "the chameleon effect"—or mimicking someone else's behavior. Picture yourself in one of their experiments, working alongside a confederate who occasionally either rubbed her face or shook her foot. Would you—like their participants—be more likely to rub your face when around the face-rubber or shake your foot when around the foot-shaker? If so, it would quite likely be an automatic behavior, done without any conscious intention to conform. Studies using brain scans seem to confirm this: When women viewed avatars with happy, sad, or angry facial expressions, they unconsciously made the same expressions, and the brain regions responsible for these emotional expressions were activated (Likowski et al., 2012). Behavior synchronizing includes speaking; people tend to mirror the grammar that they read and hear (Ireland & Pennebaker, 2010). And, because our behavior influences our attitudes and emotions, our natural mimicry inclines us to feel what the other feels (Neumann & Strack, 2000).

The chameleon effect. Our natural mimicry of others' postures and language generally elicits liking—except when echoing others' negative expressions, such as anger.
From Alex (Sandy) Pentland, "To Signal Human" in *American Scientist,* May–June, 2010, p. 207. Copyright © 2010 American Scientist. Reprinted by Permission.

An experiment in the Netherlands by Rick van Baaren and his colleagues (2004) suggests that mimicry helps people look more helpful and likeable. People become more likely to help pick up dropped pens for someone whose behavior has mimicked their own. Being mimicked seems to enhance social bonds, which even leads to donating more money to a charity. In a follow-up experiment, an interviewer invited students to try a new sports drink while sometimes mirroring the student's postures and movements, with just enough delay to make it not noticeable (Tanner et al., 2008). By the experiment's end, the copied students became more likely to consume the new drink and say they would buy it. There is one exception to the imitation-fosters-fondness rule: mimicking another's anger fosters *dis*liking (Van der Velde et al., 2010).

Suggestibility can also occur on a large scale, known as **mass hysteria.** In 2006, a character on a Portuguese TV show popular with teenagers suffered from a mysterious illness involving a rash, dizziness, and difficulty breathing. Soon after the episode aired, 300 students at 14 schools reported the same symptoms. Doctors concluded that the teens, after watching the show, interpreted their previously existing minor rashes or wheezing as something serious. In August 2009, on a San Diego County freeway, a Lexus with four passengers suddenly accelerated past 100 miles per hour. The driver called 911 but was unable to stop the car's acceleration, and it crashed and burst into flames, killing all four passengers. The accident received widespread news coverage, and suddenly many people started reporting that their vehicles were accelerating out of control. In the first half of 2009 (before the accident), Toyota (who makes the Lexus) received only 9 complaints of sudden acceleration. In the first half of 2010 (after the accident), they received 651. Even complaints about non-Toyota vehicles' "unintended acceleration" tripled. Mentions of unintended acceleration of Toyotas in the media ballooned from once a month to 80 times a month. However, an investigation later determined that the Lexus that crashed, a loaner from a repair shop, had a floor mat from a larger vehicle that was too big and became lodged under the accelerator pedal. There was nothing wrong with Toyotas, no issue with the car's original floor mats, and no "demons" making the cars accelerate, as some speculated. There were no runaway cars—just runaway news coverage that led to "unintended acceleration" as an opportunity to seek fame or a convenient explanation for any driving mishap. It was all mass hysteria (Fumento, 2014).

Another disturbing case began with a mystery. One day in 2011, LeRoy, New York high school student Katie Krautwurst woke up from a nap twitching uncontrollably, her arms failing and head thrashing, and continued to twitch every few seconds. A few weeks later her best friend started twitching, too, and then more and more girls, until 18 girls at the school were affected. Parents became concerned that some contaminant at the school was causing the disorder, and two of the girls and their mothers told the *Today Show* they were desperately seeking a cure. The next day, a neurologist who had treated several of the girls offered his diagnosis: conversion disorder, or a form of mass hysteria caused when psychological stress is unconsciously expressed in physical symptoms (Dominus, 2012). It then spread as a social contagion. The case fit the usual profile for mass hysteria, which is more common in schools, especially among young women.

Suicide can also be socially contagious. When Marilyn Monroe committed suicide in August 1962, 303 more people than average took their lives that month (Stack, 2000). After Robin Williams committed suicide in 2014, calls to the National Suicide Prevention Lifeline increased (Carroll, 2014). One study found that copycat suicides were 14 times more likely when the victim was a celebrity and 87 percent more common when the coverage was on television rather than in a newspaper (Stack, 2003).

Asch's Studies of Group Pressure

Participants in Sherif's darkened-room autokinetic experiments, like those interpreting their own mysterious symptoms, faced an ambiguous reality. Consider a less ambiguous perceptual problem faced by a young boy named Solomon Asch (1907–1996). While attending the traditional Jewish Seder at Passover, Asch recalled,

> I asked my uncle, who was sitting next to me, why the door was being opened. He replied, "The prophet Elijah visits this evening every Jewish home and takes a sip of wine from the cup reserved for him."
> I was amazed at this news and repeated, "Does he really come? Does he really take a sip?"
> My uncle said, "If you watch very closely, when the door is opened you will see—you watch the cup—you will see that the wine will go down a little."
> And that's what happened. My eyes were riveted upon the cup of wine. I was determined to see whether there would be a change. And to me it seemed . . . that indeed something was happening at the rim of the cup, and the wine did go down a little. (Aron & Aron, 1989, p. 27)

Years later, social psychologist Asch recreated his boyhood experience in his laboratory. Imagine yourself as one of Asch's volunteer subjects. You are seated sixth in a row of seven people. The experimenter explains that you will be in a study of perceptual judgments, and then asks you to say which of the three lines in Figure 4 matches the standard

FIGURE :: 4

Sample Comparison from Solomon Asch's Conformity Procedure
The participants judged which of three comparison lines matched the standard.

Standard line   Comparison lines

line. You can easily see that it's line 2. So it's no surprise when the five people responding before you all say, "Line 2."

The next comparison proves as easy, and you settle in for what seems a simple test. But the third trial startles you. Although the correct answer seems just as clear-cut, the first person gives a wrong answer. When the second person gives the same wrong answer, you sit up in your chair and stare at the cards. The third person agrees with the first two. Your jaw drops; you start to perspire. "What is this?" you ask yourself. "Are they blind? Or am I?" The fourth and fifth people agree with the others. Then the experimenter looks at you. Now you are experiencing an epistemological dilemma: "What is true? Is it what my peers tell me or what my eyes tell me?"

Dozens of college students experienced that conflict in Asch's experiments. Those in a control condition who answered alone were correct more than 99 percent of the time. Asch wondered: If confederates coached by the experimenter gave identical wrong answers, would people declare what they would otherwise have denied? Although some people never conformed, three-quarters did so at least once. All told, 37 percent of the responses were conforming (or should we say *trusting* of others").

Of course, that means 63 percent of the time people did *not* conform. The experiments show that most people "tell the truth even when others do not," note Bert Hodges and Anne Geyer (2006). Despite the independence shown by many of his participants, Asch's (1955) feelings about the conformity were as clear as the correct answers to his questions: "That reasonably intelligent and well-meaning young people are willing to call white black is a matter of concern. It raises questions about our ways of education and about the values that guide our conduct."

"He who sees the truth, let him proclaim it, without asking who is for it or who is against it."
—Henry George,
The Irish Land Question, 1881

Asch's experiment was conducted in the 1950s, often considered a time of high conformity in American culture. Sure enough, fewer students in the more individualistic times of the 1970s and 1980s were willing to conform to the group judgment in experiments similar to Asch's. In addition, people in collectivistic countries were more willing to conform than those in individualistic countries, those in more recently settled frontier states less than non-frontier states, and women more conforming than men (Bond & Smith, 1996; Varnum, 2012). These are precisely the results you'd expect if culture and gender shaped conformity, with recent, individualistic cultures and maleness promoting the autonomy of the self, and established, collectivistic cultures and femaleness encouraging fitting in with the group. Nevertheless, even modern Internet-savvy citizens are not immune to conformity. Michael Rosander and Oskar Eriksson (2012) showed Internet users such questions as "In what city can you find Hollywood?" along with a graph showing most users thought

In Asch's conformity experiments, subject number 6 experienced uneasiness and conflict after hearing five people before him give a wrong answer.
From Opinions and Social Pressure, Asch, Solomon E. November 1955. Reprint with permission. Copyright © 1955 by Scientific American, a division of Nature America, Inc. All rights reserved.

it was "San Francisco" (it's Los Angeles). Fifty-three percent conformed to the incorrect "majority" answer on at least one question—less than the 75 percent who conformed in Asch's line experiment in the 1950s, but still the majority.

Asch's procedure became the standard for hundreds of later experiments. Those experiments lacked the "mundane realism" of everyday conformity, but they did have "experimental realism." People became emotionally involved in the experience. The Sherif and Asch results are startling because they involved no obvious pressure to conform—there were no rewards for "team play," no punishments for individuality. Other experiments have explored conformity in everyday situations, such as these:

Ethical note: Professional ethics usually dictate explaining the experiment afterward. Imagine you were an experimenter who had just finished a session with a conforming participant. How could you explain the deception without making the person feel gullible and dumb?

- *Dental flossing* Sarah Schmiege and her cohorts (2010) told students either that "Our studies show that [fellow] University of Colorado students your age floss approximately [X] times per week," where X was either the participant's own flossing rate, as reported in prior questioning, or five greater than that number. Those given the inflated estimate not only expressed increased intent to floss, but also flossed more over the ensuing three months.

- *Cancer screening* Monika Sieverding and her colleagues (2010) approached middle-aged German men on the street and invited them to sign up to receive information about cancer screening. If led to believe few ("only 18 percent!") of other men in Germany had undergone the screening, a similar 18 percent signed up. But 39 percent signed up after being told that most other men ("indeed 65 percent!") had been screened. Health education campaigns had best not publicize low participation rates, surmised the researchers.

- *Soccer referee decisions* In many sports, from figure skating to soccer football, referees make instantaneous decisions amid crowd noise. When rating a skating performance or deciding whether a soccer player collision merits a yellow card, does the crowd noise—which increases when an opposing player commits a seeming infraction—make a difference? To find out, Christian Unkelbach and Daniel Memmert (2010) examined 1,530 soccer matches across five seasons in Germany's premier league. On average, home teams received 1.89 yellow cards and away teams 2.35. Moreover, the difference was greater in louder soccer stadiums where fans were not separated from the field by a running track. And in laboratory experiments, professional referees who judged filmed foul scenes awarded more yellow cards when a scene was accompanied by high-volume noise.

If people are that conforming in response to such minimal pressure, how compliant will they be if they are directly coerced? Could the average North American or European be talked into committing cruel acts? We would have guessed not: Their humane, democratic, individualistic values would make them resist such pressure. Besides, the easy verbal pronouncements of those experiments are a giant step away from actually harming someone; we would never yield to coercion to hurt another. Or would we? Social psychologist Stanley Milgram wondered.

Milgram's Obedience Studies

Milgram's (1965, 1974) experiments—"the most famous, or infamous, stud[ies] in the annals of scientific psychology" (Benjamin & Simpson, 2009)—tested what happens when the demands of authority clash with the demands of conscience. "Perhaps more than any other empirical contributions in the history of social science," noted Lee Ross (1988), Milgram's obedience studies "have become part of our society's shared intellectual legacy—that small body of historical incidents, biblical parables, and classic literature that serious thinkers feel free to draw on when they debate about human nature or contemplate human history."

Although you may recall a mention of this research in a prior course, let's go backstage and examine the studies in depth. Here is the scene staged by Milgram, a creative artist who wrote stories and stage plays, and who used trial-and-error pilot testing to hone this drama for maximum impact (Russell, 2011): Two men come to Yale University's psychology laboratory to participate in a study of learning and memory. A stern experimenter in a lab coat explains that this is a pioneering study of the effect of punishment on learning. The experiment requires one of them to teach a list of word pairs to the other and to punish errors by delivering shocks of increasing intensity. To assign the roles, they draw slips out of a hat. One of the men (a mild-mannered, 47-year-old accountant who is actually the experimenter's confederate) says that his slip says "learner" and is ushered into an adjacent room. The other man (a volunteer who has come in response to a newspaper ad) is assigned to the role of "teacher." He takes a mild sample shock and then looks on as the experimenter straps the learner into a chair and attaches an electrode to his wrist.

Teacher and experimenter then return to the main room, where the teacher takes his place before a "shock generator" with switches ranging from 15 to 450 volts in 15-volt increments. The switches are labeled "Slight Shock," "Very Strong Shock," "Danger: Severe Shock," and so forth. Under the 435- and 450-volt switches appears "XXX." The experimenter tells the teacher to "move one level higher on the shock generator" each time the learner gives a wrong answer. With each flick of a switch, lights flash, relay switches click, and an electric buzzer sounds.

If the participant complies with the experimenter's requests, he hears the learner grunt at 75, 90, and 105 volts. At 120 volts the learner shouts that the shocks are painful. And at 150 volts he cries out, "Experimenter, get me out of here! I won't be in the experiment anymore! I refuse to go on!" By 270 volts his protests have become screams of agony, and his pleas to be let out continue. At 300 and 315 volts, he screams his refusal to answer. After 330 volts he falls silent. In answer to the teacher's inquiries and pleas to end the experiment, the experimenter states that the nonresponses should be treated as wrong answers. To keep the participant going, he uses four verbal prods:

Prod 1: Please continue (or Please go on).

Prod 2: The experiment requires that you continue.

Prod 3: It is absolutely essential that you continue.

Prod 4: You have no other choice; you must go on.

How far would you go? Milgram described the study to 110 psychiatrists, college students, and middle-class adults. People in all three groups guessed that they would disobey by about 135 volts; none expected to go beyond 300 volts. Recognizing that self-estimates may reflect self-serving bias, Milgram asked them how far they thought *other* people would go. Virtually no one expected anyone to proceed to XXX on the shock panel. (The psychiatrists guessed about 1 in 1,000.)

But when Milgram conducted the study with 40 men—20- to 50-year-olds with varying jobs—26 of them (65 percent) progressed all the way to 450 volts. In other words, they followed orders to hurt someone—just as Nazi soldiers did (see The Inside Story: Stanley Milgram on Obedience). Those who stopped often did so at the 150-volt point, when the learner's protestations became more compelling (Packer, 2008).

Wondering if people today would similarly obey, Jerry Burger (2009) replicated Milgram's study—though only to the 150-volt point. At that point, 70 percent of participants were still obeying, a slight reduction from Milgram's result. (In Milgram's study, most who were obedient to this point continued to the end. In fact, all who reached 450 volts complied with a command to *continue* the procedure until, after two further trials, the experimenter called a halt.) However, Berger's participants were more diverse than Milgram's—for example, half were women, unlike Milgram's initial all-male sample. Comparing Milgram's 1962 men to Berger's 2006 men, obedience at 150 volts dropped from 83 percent to 67 percent. In other words, nearly twice as many modern men (33 percent vs. 18 percent) disobeyed, but many still obeyed. Cultural change toward more individualism might have reduced obedience, but far from eliminated it. Even 54 years later, Milgram's obedience paradigm was powerful—just a little less so (Twenge, 2009).

Burger and his colleagues (2011) later analyzed their participants' spontaneous comments. Whether people stopped or obeyed was not predictable from their expressing concern for the learner's well-being, which most did, but from their voicing feelings of responsibility for their actions.

THE inside STORY

Stanley Milgram on Obedience

While working for Solomon E. Asch, I wondered whether his conformity experiments could be made more humanly significant. First, I imagined an experiment similar to Asch's, except that the group induced the person to deliver shocks to a protesting victim. But a control was needed to see how much shock a person would give in the absence of group pressure. Someone, presumably the experimenter, would have to instruct the subject to give the shocks. But now a new question arose: Just how far would a person go when ordered to administer such shocks? In my mind, the issue had shifted to the willingness of people to comply with destructive orders. It was an exciting moment for me. I realized that this simple question was both humanly important and capable of being precisely answered.

The laboratory procedure gave scientific expression to a more general concern about authority, a concern forced upon members of my generation, in particular upon Jews such as myself, by the atrocities of World War II. The impact of the Holocaust on my own psyche energized my interest in obedience and shaped the particular form in which it was examined.

Source: Abridged from the original for this book and from Milgram, 1977, with permission of Alexandra Milgram.

Stanley Milgram (1933–1984)
Stanley Milgram, 1965, from the film *Obedience*, distributed by Alexander Street Press

Having expected a low rate of obedience, Milgram was disturbed (A. Milgram, 2000). He decided to make the learner's protests even more compelling. As the learner was strapped into the chair, the teacher heard him mention his "slight heart condition" and heard the experimenter's reassurance that "although the shocks may be painful, they cause no permanent tissue damage." The learner's anguished protests were to little avail; of 40 men in this new study, 25 (63 percent) fully complied with the experimenter's demands (Figure 5). Ten later studies that included women found that women's compliance rates were similar to men's (Blass, 1999).

It's important to note that Milgram's participants did not automatically obey the experimenter—nearly all stopped and expressed concern for the learner, at which point the experimenter prompted them to continue ("You have no other choice; you must go on."). Many argued back and forth with the experimenter over several rounds. Thus, some have maintained that Milgram's study shows something more wide-ranging than mere obedience (obeying a direct order)—it challenges participants' feelings of control. In fact, many participants stopped after they argued that they *did* have a choice about whether to continue (Gibson, 2013).

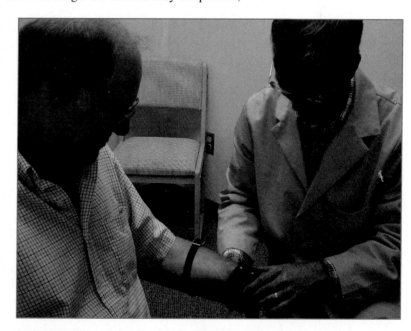

Recent replications of Milgram's obedience study have shown levels of obedience somewhat lower than in the 1960s, but two-thirds of men still administer high levels of shock.
Jerry Burger

FIGURE :: 5

The Milgram
Obedience Study
Percentage of participants
complying despite the learner's
cries of protest and failure to
respond.
Source: From Milgram, 1965.

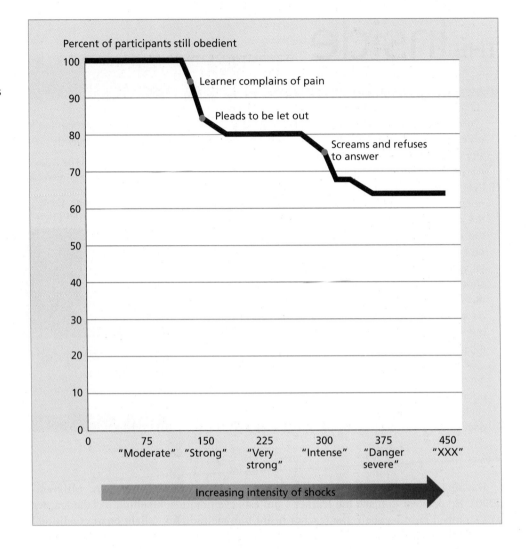

Further, notes Jerry Berger (2014), Milgram's results were not as surprising as they first seem. Four features of Milgram's study design, he argues, mirror well-documented psychological effects:

- the "slippery slope" of small requests that escalate into large ones,
- the framing of shock-giving as the social norm for the situation,
- the opportunity to deny responsibility, and
- the limited time to reflect on the decision.

All of these, in Milgram's studies and in other research, increase compliance.

The Ethics of Milgram's Studies

The obedience of his subjects disturbed Milgram. The procedures he used disturbed many social psychologists (Miller, 1986). The "learner" in these studies actually received no shock (he disengaged himself from the electric chair and turned on a tape recorder that delivered the protests). Nevertheless, some critics said that Milgram did to his participants what they assumed they were doing to their victims: He stressed them against their will. Indeed, like Nazi executioners in the early days of the Holocaust (Brooks, 2011), many of the "teachers" did experience agony. They sweated, trembled, stuttered, bit their lips, groaned, or even broke into uncontrollable nervous laughter. A *New York Times* reviewer complained that the cruelty inflicted by the studies "upon their unwitting subjects is surpassed only by the cruelty that they elicit from them" (Marcus, 1974).

Critics also argued that the participants' self-concepts may have been altered. One participant's wife told him, "You can call yourself Eichmann" (referring to Nazi death camp administrator Adolf Eichmann). CBS television depicted the results and the controversy in a two-hour dramatization. "A world of evil so terrifying no one dares penetrate its secret. Until Now!" declared a *TV Guide* ad for the program (Elms, 1995). Other scholars, after delving into Milgram's archives, report that his debriefing was less extensive and his participants' distress greater than he had suggested (Nicholson, 2011; Perry, 2013).

In his own defense, Milgram pointed to the important lessons taught by his nearly two-dozen studies with a diverse sample of more than 1,000 participants. He also reminded critics of the support he received from the participants after the deception was revealed and the study explained. When surveyed afterward, 84 percent said they were glad to have participated; only 1 percent regretted volunteering. A year later, a psychiatrist interviewed 40 of those who had suffered most and concluded that, despite the temporary stress, none was harmed.

The ethical controversy was "terribly overblown," Milgram believed:

> There is less consequence to subjects in this experiment from the standpoint of effects on self-esteem, than to university students who take ordinary course examinations, and who do not get the grades they want. . . . It seems that [in giving exams] we are quite prepared to accept stress, tension, and consequences for self-esteem. But in regard to the process of generating new knowledge, how little tolerance we show. (quoted by Blass, 1996)

Some have also pointed out that, although Milgram referred to his studies as experiments, they were not true experiments, as they did not include a control group.

What Breeds Obedience?

Milgram did more than reveal that people will obey an authority; he also examined the conditions that breed obedience. When he varied the social conditions, compliance ranged from 0 to 93 percent fully obedient. Four factors determined obedience: the victim's emotional distance, the authority's closeness and legitimacy, whether the authority was part of a respected institution, and the liberating effects of a disobedient fellow participant.

THE VICTIM'S DISTANCE

Milgram's participants acted with greatest obedience and least compassion when the "learners" could not be seen (and could not see them). When the victim was remote and the "teachers" heard no complaints, nearly all obeyed calmly to the end. That situation minimized the learner's influence relative to the experimenter's. But what if we made the learner's pleas and the experimenter's instructions more equally visible? When the learner was in the same room, "only" 40 percent obeyed to 450 volts. Full compliance dropped to a still-astonishing 30 percent when teachers were required to force the learner's hand into contact with a shock plate. In a reenacted Milgram study—with videotaped actors who were either hidden or seen on a computer screen and known to be feigning hurt—participants were, again, much less obedient when the victim was visible (Dambrun & Vatiné, 2010).

In a virtual reality re-creation of the Milgram studies, participants responded— when shocking a virtual onscreen woman—much as did Milgram's participants, with perspiration and racing heart (Slater et al., 2006).

In everyday life, too, it is easiest to abuse someone who is distant or depersonalized. People who might never be cruel to someone in person may be nasty when posting comments to anonymous people on Internet discussion boards. Throughout history, executioners have often depersonalized those being executed by placing hoods over their heads. The ethics of war allow soldiers to bomb a helpless village from 40,000 feet but not to shoot an equally helpless villager. In combat with an enemy they can see, many soldiers either do not fire or do not aim. Such disobedience is rare among those given orders to kill with the more distant artillery or aircraft weapons (Padgett, 1989). It may even be true for nuclear war

An obedient participant in Milgram's "touch" condition forces the victim's hand onto the shock plate. Usually, however, "teachers" were more merciful to victims who were this close to them.
Stanley Milgram, 1965, from the film Obedience, distributed by Alexandra Street Press

focus ON

Personalizing the Victims

Innocent victims trigger more compassion if personalized. In a week when a soon-forgotten earthquake in Iran killed 3,000 people, one small boy died, trapped in a well shaft in Italy, and the whole world grieved. Concerned that the projected death statistics of a nuclear war are impersonal to the point of being incomprehensible, international law professor Roger Fisher proposed a way to personalize the victims:

It so happens that a young man, usually a navy officer, accompanies the president wherever he goes. This young man has a black attaché case which contains the codes that are needed to fire nuclear weapons.

I can see the president at a staff meeting considering nuclear war as an abstract question. He might conclude, "On SIOP Plan One, the decision is affirmative. Communicate the Alpha line XYZ." Such jargon keeps what is involved at a distance.

My suggestion, then, is quite simple. Put that needed code number in a little capsule and implant that capsule right next to the heart of a volunteer. The volunteer will carry with him a big, heavy butcher knife as he accompanies the president. If ever the president wants to fire nuclear weapons, the only way he can do so is by first, with his own hands, killing one human being.

"George," the president would say, "I'm sorry, but tens of millions must die." The president then would have to look at someone and realize what death is—what an *innocent* death is. Blood on the White House carpet: it's reality brought home.

When I suggested this to friends in the Pentagon, they said, "My God, that's terrible. Having to kill someone would distort the president's judgment. He might never push the button."

Source: Adapted from "Preventing Nuclear War" by Roger Fisher, *Bulletin of the Atomic Scientists,* March 1981, pp. 11–17.

"Distance negates responsibility."

—Guy Davenport, "The Master Builder," 1966

Imagine you had the power to prevent either a tsunami that would kill 25,000 people on the planet's other side, a crash that would kill 250 people at your local airport, or a car accident that would kill a close friend. Which would you prevent?

(see Focus On: Personalizing the Victims). In recent years, distance from victims has further lengthened with the use of unmanned flying drones that can drop bombs, with the controller sitting at a console many miles away from the destruction and death on the ground.

As the Holocaust began, some Germans, under orders, used machine guns or rifles to kill men, women, and children standing before them. But others could not bring themselves to do so, and some who did were left shaken by the experience of face-to-face killing. That led Heinrich Himmler, the Nazi "architect of genocide," to devise a "more humane" killing, one that would visually separate the killers and their victims. The solution was the construction of concrete gas chambers, where the killers would not see or hear the human consequences of their fatal actions (Russell & Gregory, 2005).

On the positive side, people act most compassionately toward those who are personalized. That is why appeals for the unborn, for the hungry, or for animal rights are nearly always personalized with a compelling photograph or description. When queried by researchers John Lydon and Christine Dunkel-Schetter (1994), expectant women expressed more commitment to their pregnancies if they had seen ultrasound pictures of their fetuses that clearly displayed body parts.

CLOSENESS AND LEGITIMACY OF THE AUTHORITY

The physical presence of the experimenter also affected obedience. When Milgram's experimenter gave the commands by telephone, full obedience dropped to 21 percent (although many lied and said they were obeying). Other studies confirm that when the one making the command is physically close, compliance increases. Given a light touch on the arm, people are more likely to lend a dime, sign a petition, or sample a new pizza (Kleinke, 1977; Smith et al., 1982; Willis & Hamm, 1980).

The authority, however, must be perceived as legitimate. In another twist on the basic study, the researcher received a rigged telephone call that required him to leave the laboratory. He said that since the equipment recorded data automatically, the "teacher" should just go ahead. After the researcher left, an assistant (actually a second confederate), assumed command. The assistant "decided" that the shock should be increased one level for each wrong answer and instructed the teacher accordingly. Now 80 percent of the teachers refused to comply fully. The confederate, feigning disgust at this defiance, sat down in front of the shock generator and tried to take over the teacher's role. At that point most of the defiant participants protested. Some tried to unplug the generator. One large man lifted the zealous confederate from his chair and threw him across the room. This rebellion against an illegitimate authority contrasted sharply with the deferential politeness usually shown the experimenter. In a later reanalysis of the Milgram studies, Stephen Reicher and his colleagues (2012) found that participants were significantly more obedient when they identified with the researcher or the scientific community he represents. They obeyed orders because they believed they were making a contribution to science and were thus doing something worthy and noble. "Followers do not lose their moral compass so much as choose particular authorities to guide them through the dilemmas of everyday life," they noted (Reicher & Haslam, 2011, p. 61).

In one study, hospital nurses were called by an unknown physician and ordered to administer an obvious drug overdose (Hofling et al., 1966). The researchers told one group of nurses and nursing students about the experiment and asked how they would react. Nearly all said they would not have followed the order. Nevertheless, when 22 other nurses were actually given the phoned-in overdose order, all but one obeyed without delay (until being intercepted on their way to the patient). Although not all nurses are so compliant (Krackow & Blass, 1995; Rank & Jacobson, 1977), these nurses were following a familiar script: Doctor (a legitimate authority) orders; nurse obeys.

Compliance with legitimate authority was also apparent in the strange case of the "rectal ear ache" (Cohen & Davis, 1981). A doctor ordered eardrops for a patient suffering infection in the right ear. On the prescription, the doctor abbreviated "place in right ear" as "place in R ear." Reading the order, the compliant nurse put the required drops in the compliant patient's rectum.

The compliant nurse might empathize with the reported 70 fast-food restaurant managers in 30 states who, between 1995 and 2006, complied with orders from a self-described authority, usually a con man posing as a police officer (ABC News, March 2004; Snopes, 2008; Wikipedia, 2008). The supposed officer described a generic employee or customer. Once the manager had identified someone fitting the description, the authoritative-sounding caller gave an order to strip-search the person to see if he or she had stolen property. One male Taco Bell manager in Arizona pulled aside a 17-year-old female customer who fit the description and, with the caller giving orders, carried out a search that included body cavities. After forcing a 19-year-old female employee to strip against her will, a South Dakota restaurant manager explained that "I never wanted to do it. . . . I was just doing

Given orders, most soldiers will torch people's homes or kill—behaviors that in other contexts they would consider immoral.
AP Images

what he told me to do." The manager feared that disobedience might mean losing his job or going to jail, explained his defense lawyer.

In another incident, a McDonald's manager received a call from an "Officer Scott" who described an employee he said was suspected of purse stealing. The female manager brought an 18-year-old woman who fit the description into the office and followed a series of orders to have her empty her pockets and successive pieces of clothing. Over her 3½ hours of humiliating detention, the requests became progressively more bizarre, including a request for sex. The traumatized teen sued McDonald's, claiming they had not adequately forewarned staff of the scam, and was awarded $6.1 million (CNN, 2007).

INSTITUTIONAL AUTHORITY

If the prestige of the authority is that important, then perhaps the institutional prestige of Yale University legitimized the Milgram experiment commands. In postexperimental interviews, many participants said that had it not been for Yale's reputation, they would not have obeyed. To see whether that was true, Milgram moved the study to less prestigious Bridgeport, Connecticut. He set himself up in a modest commercial building as the "Research Associates of Bridgeport." When the "learner-has-a-heart-condition" study was run with the same personnel, what percentage of the men do you suppose fully obeyed? Although the obedience rate (48 percent) was still remarkably high, it was lower than the 65 percent rate at Yale. In a recent replication of Milgram's paradigm in France, a TV game show host—rather than an experimenter in a lab coat—gave the orders to shock the learner, and 81 percent obeyed to the end (Beauvois et al., 2012).

In everyday life, too, authorities backed by institutions wield social power. Robert Ornstein (1991) tells of a psychiatrist friend who was called to the edge of a cliff above San Mateo, California, where one of his patients, Alfred, was threatening to jump. When the psychiatrist's reasoned reassurance failed to dislodge Alfred, the psychiatrist could only hope that a police crisis expert would soon arrive.

Although no expert came, another police officer, unaware of the drama, happened onto the scene, took out his power bullhorn, and yelled at the assembled cliffside group: "Who's the ass who left that Pontiac station wagon double-parked out there in the middle of the road? I almost hit it. Move it *now*, whoever you are." Hearing the message, Alfred obediently got down at once, moved the car, and then without a word got into the police cruiser for a trip to a nearby hospital.

THE LIBERATING EFFECTS OF GROUP INFLUENCE

These classic experiments give us a negative view of conformity. But conformity can also be constructive. The heroic firefighters who rushed into the flaming World Trade Center towers on 9/11 were "incredibly brave," note social psychologists Susan Fiske, Lasana Harris, and Amy Cuddy (2004), but they were also "partly obeying their superiors, partly conforming to extraordinary group loyalty." Consider, too, the occasional liberating effect of conformity. Perhaps you can recall a time you felt justifiably angry at an unfair teacher but you hesitated to object. Then one or two other students spoke up about the unfair practices, and you followed their example, which had a liberating effect. Milgram captured this liberating effect of conformity by placing the teacher with two confederates who were to help conduct the procedure. During the study, both confederates defied the experimenter, who then ordered the real participant to continue alone. Did he? No. Ninety percent liberated themselves by conforming to the defiant confederates.

Reflections on the Classic Studies

The common response to Milgram's results is to note their counterparts in the "I was only following orders" defenses of Adolf Eichmann, in Nazi Germany; of American Lieutenant William Calley, who in 1968 directed the unprovoked slaughter of hundreds of Vietnamese in the village of My Lai; and of the "ethnic cleansings" occurring in Iraq, Rwanda, Bosnia, and Kosovo.

Soldiers are trained to obey superiors. Thus, one participant in the My Lai massacre recalled:

[Lieutenant Calley] told me to start shooting. So I started shooting, I poured about four clips into the group. . . . They were begging and saying, "No, no." And the mothers were hugging their children and. . . . Well, we kept right on firing. They was waving their arms and begging. (Wallace, 1969)

The "safe" scientific contexts of the obedience experiments differ from the wartime contexts. Moreover, much of the mockery and brutality of war and genocide goes beyond obedience (Miller, 2004). Some of those who implemented the Holocaust were "willing executioners" who hardly needed to be commanded to kill (Goldhagen, 1996).

The obedience studies also differ from other conformity studies in the strength of the social pressure: Obedience is explicitly commanded. Yet the Asch and the Milgram studies share four similarities:

The United States military now trains soldiers to disobey inappropriate, unlawful orders.

- They showed how compliance can take precedence over moral sense.
- They succeeded in pressuring people to go against their own consciences.
- They sensitized us to moral conflicts in our own lives.
- They affirmed two familiar social psychological principles: the link between *behavior and attitudes* and the *power of the situation.*

BEHAVIOR AND ATTITUDES

When external influences override inner convictions, attitudes fail to determine behavior. These experiments vividly illustrate that principle. When responding alone, Asch's participants nearly always gave the correct answer. It was another matter when they stood alone against a group.

In the obedience experiments, a powerful social pressure (the experimenter's commands) overcame a weaker one (the remote victim's pleas). Torn between the pleas of the victim and the orders of the experimenter, between the desire to avoid doing harm and the desire to be a good participant, a surprising number of people chose to obey.

Why were the participants unable to disengage themselves? Imagine yourself as the teacher in yet another version of Milgram's experiment (one he never conducted). Assume that when the learner gives the first wrong answer, the experimenter asks you to zap him with 330 volts. After flicking the switch, you hear the learner scream, complain of a heart disturbance, and plead for mercy. Do you continue?

We think not. Their first commitment was mild—15 volts—and it elicited no protest. By the time they delivered 75 volts and heard the learner's first groan, they already had complied 5 times, and the next request was to deliver only slightly more. By the time they delivered 330 volts, the participants had complied 22 times and reduced some of their dissonance. They were therefore in a different psychological state from that of someone beginning the experiment at that point—it was a "slippery slope" of obedience, and once they started down it was difficult to stop. In one experiment, some participants received 25 cents for a correct answer in the first round, $1 in the second, and $2.50 in the third, while others were paid $2.50 for each answer from the beginning. Those with the progressive incentives were more likely to cheat and say they got more answers correct, possibly because their infraction started out small—what's 25 cents?—and then grew (Welch et al., 2015). The same thing occurred with the fast-food restaurant managers in the strip-search scam, after they had complied with initially reasonable-seeming orders from a supposed authority. External behavior and internal disposition can feed each other, sometimes in an escalating spiral. Thus, reported Milgram (1974, p. 10):

Many subjects harshly devalue the victim as a consequence of acting against him. Such comments as, "He was so stupid and stubborn he deserved to get shocked," were common. Once having acted against the victim, these subjects found it necessary to view him as an unworthy individual, whose punishment was made inevitable by his own deficiencies of intellect and character.

"Men's actions are too strong for them. Show me a man who had acted and who had not been the victim and slave of his action."

—Ralph Waldo Emerson, *Representative Men: Goethe,* 1850

Compliance breeds acceptance. Ex-torturer Jeffrey Benzien demonstrates the "wet bag" technique of almost asphyxiating someone to South Africa's Truth and Reconciliation Commission. "I did terrible things," Benzien admitted with apologies to his victims, though he claimed only to be following orders.
Benny Gool/Capetown Independent Newspaper

During the early 1970s, Greece's military junta used this "blame-the-victim" process to train torturers (Haritos-Fatouros, 1988, 2002; Staub, 1989, 2003). There, as in the earlier training of SS officers in Nazi Germany, the military selected candidates based on their respect for and submission to authority. But such tendencies alone do not a torturer make. Thus, they would first assign the trainee to guard prisoners, then to participate in arrest squads, then to hit prisoners, then to observe torture, and only then to practice it. Step by step, an obedient but otherwise decent person evolved into an agent of cruelty. Compliance bred acceptance. If we focus on the end point—450 volts of torture administered—we are aghast at the evil conduct. If we consider how one gets there—in tiny steps—we understand.

As a Holocaust survivor, University of Massachusetts social psychologist Ervin Staub knows too well the forces that can transform citizens into agents of death. From his study of human genocide across the world, Staub (2003) shows where gradually increasing aggression can lead. Too often, criticism produces contempt, which licenses cruelty, which, when justified, leads to brutality, then killing, then systematic killing. Evolving attitudes both follow and justify actions. Staub's disturbing conclusion: "Human beings have the capacity to come to experience killing other people as nothing extraordinary" (1989, p. 13).

But humans also have a capacity for heroism. During the Nazi Holocaust, the French village of Le Chambon sheltered 5,000 Jews and other refugees destined for deportation to Germany. The villagers were mostly Protestants whose own authorities, their pastors, had taught them to "resist whenever our adversaries will demand of us obedience contrary to the orders of the Gospel" (Rochat, 1993; Rochat & Modigliani, 1995). Ordered to divulge the locations of sheltered Jews, the head pastor modeled disobedience: "I don't know of Jews, I only know of human beings." Without knowing how terrible the war would be, the resisters, beginning in 1940, made an initial commitment and then—supported by their beliefs, by their own authorities, and by one another—remained defiant until the village's liberation in 1944. Here and elsewhere, the ultimate response to Nazi occupation came early. Their initial helping heightened commitment, leading to more helping.

THE POWER OF SOCIAL NORMS

Imagine violating some minor norms: standing up in the middle of a class; singing out loud in a restaurant; playing golf in a suit. In trying to break with social constraints, we suddenly realize how strong they are.

The students in one Pennsylvania State University experiment found it surprisingly difficult to violate the social norm of being "nice" rather than confrontational—even when they were thoroughly provoked. Participants imagined themselves discussing with three others whom to select for survival on a desert island. They were asked to imagine one of the others, a man, injecting three sexist comments, such as, "I think we need more women on the island to keep the men satisfied." How would they react to such sexist remarks? Only 5 percent predicted they would ignore the comments or wait to see how others reacted. But when other students heard a male confederate actually make these comments, 55 percent (not 5 percent) said nothing (Swim & Hyers, 1999). Likewise, although people predict they would be upset by witnessing a person making a racial slur—and would avoid picking the racist person as a partner in an experiment—those actually experiencing such an event typically exhibit indifference (Kawakami et al., 2009). These experiments demonstrate the power of social norms and show how hard it is to predict behavior, even our own behavior.

"The social psychology of this century reveals a major lesson: Often it is not so much the kind of person a man is as the kind of situation in which he finds himself that determines how he will act."

—Stanley Milgram,
Obedience to Authority, 1974

How ironic that in 2011, the human struggle with confrontation should play out at Swim and Hyers' university—Penn State—in a public debate about how its revered football coach and other university officials should have responded to learning that a fellow coach had sexually abused boys. (The coaches reportedly did pass on the reports to superiors, but allowed the alleged abuser to continue using university facilities.) Commentators were outraged; they presumed that *they* themselves would have acted more strongly. These experiments remind us that *saying* what we would do in a hypothetical situation is often easier than *doing* it in a real situation.

Milgram's studies also offer a lesson about evil. In horror movies and suspense novels, evil results from a few bad apples, a few depraved killers. In real life we think of Hitler's extermination of Jews or of Osama bin Laden's terrorist plot. But evil also results from social forces—from the powerful situations that help make a whole barrel of apples go bad. The American military police, whose abuse of Iraqi prisoners at Abu Ghraib prison horrified the world, were under stress, taunted by many they had come to save, angered by comrades' deaths, overdue to return home, and under lax supervision—an evil situation that produced evil behavior (Fiske, 2004; Lankford, 2009). Situations can induce ordinary people to capitulate to cruelty.

This is especially true when, as happens often in complex societies, the most terrible evil evolves from a sequence of small evils. German civil servants surprised Nazi leaders with their willingness to handle the paperwork of the Holocaust. They were not killing Jews, of course; they were merely pushing paper (Silver & Geller, 1978). When fragmented, evil becomes easier. Milgram studied this compartmentalization of evil by involving yet another 40 men more indirectly. With someone else triggering the shock, they had only to administer the learning test. Now, 37 of the 40 fully complied.

So it is in our everyday lives: The drift toward evil usually comes in small increments, without any conscious intent to do evil. Procrastination involves a similar unintended drift, toward self-harm (Sabini & Silver, 1982). A student knows the deadline for a term paper weeks ahead. Each diversion from work on the paper—a video game here, a TV show there—seems harmless enough. Yet gradually the student veers toward not doing the paper without ever consciously deciding not to do it.

It is tempting to assume that Eichmann and the Auschwitz death camp commanders were uncivilized monsters. Indeed, their evil was fueled by virulent anti-Semitism. And the social situation alone does not explain why, in the same neighborhood or death camp, some personalities displayed vicious cruelty and others heroic kindness. Still, the commanders would not have stood out to us as monsters. After a hard day's work, they would relax by listening to Beethoven and Schubert. Of the 14 men who formulated the Final Solution leading to the Nazi Holocaust, 8 had European university doctorates (Patterson, 1996). Like most other Nazis, Eichmann himself was outwardly indistinguishable from common people with ordinary jobs (Arendt, 1963; Zillmer et al., 1995). Mohamed Atta, the leader of the 9/11 attacks, reportedly had been a "good boy" and an excellent student from a healthy family. Zacarias Moussaoui, the would-be twentieth 9/11 attacker, had

Even in an individualistic culture, few of us desire to challenge our culture's clearest social norms, as did Stephen Gough while walking the length of Britain naked (apart from hat, socks, boots, and a rucksack). Starting in June 2003, he made it to the length of Britain, from Lands' End in England's southwest to John o'Groats, in Scotland's northeast. During his 7-month, 847-mile trek he was arrested 15 times and spent about five months behind bars. "My naked activism is firstly and most importantly about me standing up for myself, a declaration of myself as a beautiful human being," Gough (2003) declared from his website.
Daily Mail/Rex/Alamy

"I would say, on the basis of having observed a thousand people . . . that if a system of death camps were set up in the United States of the sort we had seen in Nazi Germany, one would be able to find sufficient personnel for those camps in any medium-sized American town."
—Stanley Milgram, on CBS's *60 Minutes,* 1979

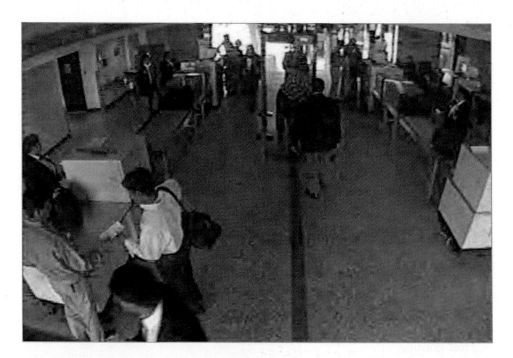

The "unexceptional" 9/11 terrorists. Hijackers Nawaf al-Hazmi (blue shirt) and Salem al-Hazmi (white shirt), both in the lower-left corner of this photo, were normal-looking, normal-acting passengers as they went through Dulles Airport security on September 11, 2001.
AP Images/APTN

been very polite when applying for flight lessons and buying knives. He called women "ma'am." The pilot of the second plane to hit the World Trade Center was said to be an amiable, "laid-back" fellow, much like the "intelligent, friendly, and 'very courteous'" pilot of the plane that dove into the Pentagon. If these men had lived next door to us, they would hardly have fit our image of evil monsters. They were "unexceptional" people (McDermott, 2005).

As Milgram noted (1974, p. 6), "The most fundamental lesson of our study is that ordinary people, simply doing their jobs, and without any particular hostility on their part, can become agents in a terrible destructive process." As Mister Rogers often reminded his preschool television audience, "Good people sometimes do bad things." Under the sway of evil forces, even nice people are sometimes corrupted as they construct moral rationalizations for immoral behavior (Tsang, 2002). So it is that ordinary soldiers may, in the end, follow orders to shoot defenseless civilians; admired political leaders may lead their citizens into ill-fated wars; ordinary employees may follow instructions to produce and distribute harmful, degrading products; and ordinary group members may heed commands to brutally haze initiates.

So, does a situational analysis of harm-doing exonerate harm-doers? Does it absolve them of responsibility? In laypeople's minds, the answer is, to some extent, yes, notes Arthur Miller (2006). But the psychologists who study the roots of evil insist otherwise. To explain is not to excuse. To understand is not to forgive. You can forgive someone whose behavior you don't understand, and you can understand someone whom you do not forgive. Moreover, adds James Waller (2002), "When we understand the ordinariness of extraordinary evil, we will be less surprised by evil, less likely to be unwitting contributors to evil, and perhaps better equipped to forestall evil." Jerry Burger's (2009) replication of the famous Milgram study excluded those familiar with it. Had such people—with the knowledge you now have—been included, might the obedience rate have been much lower (Elms, 2009)?

Finally, a comment on the experimental method used in conformity research: Conformity and obedience situations in the laboratory differ from those in everyday life. How often are we asked to judge line lengths or administer shock? But just as a match and a forest fire both burn, we assume that psychological processes in the laboratory and in everyday life are similar (Milgram, 1974). We must be careful in generalizing

TABLE :: 1 Summary of Classic Obedience Studies

Topic	Researcher	Method	Real-Life Example
Norm formation	Sherif	Assessing suggestibility regarding seeming movement of light	Interpreting events differently after hearing from others; appreciating a tasty food that others love
Conformity	Asch	Agreement with others' obviously wrong perceptual judgments	Doing as others do; fads such as tattoos
Obedience	Milgram	Complying with commands to shock another	Soldiers or employees following questionable orders

from the simplicity of a burning match to the complexity of a forest fire. Yet controlled experiments on burning matches can give us insights into combustion that we cannot gain by observing forest fires. So, too, the social-psychological experiment offers insights into behavior not readily revealed in everyday life. The experimental situation is unique, but so is every social situation. By testing with a variety of unique tasks, and by repeating experiments at different times and places, researchers probe for the common principles that lie beneath the surface diversity. For a summary of these classic obedience studies, review Table 1.

The classic conformity experiments answered some questions but raised others: Sometimes people conform; sometimes they do not. (1) *When* do they conform? (2) *Why* do people conform? Why don't they ignore the group and "to their own selves be true"? (3) Is there a type of *person* who is likely to conform? In the next section we will take these questions one at a time.

SUMMING UP: What Are the Classic Conformity and Obedience Studies?

Three classic sets of experiments illustrate how researchers have studied conformity.

- Muzafer Sherif observed that others' judgments influenced people's estimates of the movement of a point of light that actually did not move. Norms for "proper" answers emerged and survived both over long periods of time and through succeeding generations of research participants.

- Solomon Asch had people listen to others' judgments of which of three comparison lines was equal to a standard line and then make the same judgment themselves. When the others unanimously gave a wrong answer, the participants conformed 37 percent of the time.

- Stanley Milgram's studies of obedience elicited an extreme form of compliance. Under optimum conditions—a legitimate, close-at-hand commander, a remote victim, and no one else to exemplify disobedience—65 percent of his adult male participants fully obeyed instructions to deliver what were supposedly traumatizing electric shocks to a screaming, innocent victim in an adjacent room.

- These classic studies expose the potency of several phenomena. Behavior and attitudes are mutually reinforcing, enabling a small act of evil to foster the attitude that leads to a bigger evil act. The power of the situation can induce good people, faced with dire circumstances, to commit reprehensible acts (although dire situations may produce heroism in others).

WHAT PREDICTS CONFORMITY?

| Identify situations that trigger much—
and little—conformity.

Social psychologists wondered: If even Asch's noncoercive, unambiguous situation could elicit a 37 percent conformity rate, would other settings produce even more? Researchers soon discovered that conformity did grow if the judgments were difficult or if the participants felt incompetent. The more insecure we are about our judgments, the more influenced we are by others.

Group attributes also matter. Conformity is highest when the group has three or more people and is unanimous, cohesive, and high in status. Conformity is also highest when the response is public and made without prior commitment. Let's look at each of these conditions.

Group Size

In laboratory experiments, a small group can have a big effect. Asch and other researchers found that 3 to 5 people will elicit much more conformity than just 1 or 2. Increasing the number of people beyond 5 yields diminishing returns (Gerard et al., 1968; Rosenberg, 1961). In a field experiment, Milgram and his colleagues (1969) had 1, 2, 3, 5, 10, or 15 people pause on a busy New York City sidewalk and look up. As Figure 6 shows, the percentage of passersby who also looked up increased as the number looking up increased from 1 to 5 persons. Try this on your campus—get a few friends to stand with you looking up at the sky, and you'll find that almost everyone who walks by does the same. I [JT] did this with my students when I was a teaching assistant at the University of Michigan. When only one or two volunteers stood outside the classroom building, a few people glanced at them but no one looked up. But when 4 or 5 students stood outside the door, staring up at the sky, nearly every student stepping out of the building instantly lifted their head skyward. My students and I laughed so hard we embarrassed ourselves.

The way the group is "packaged" also makes a difference. Rutgers University researcher David Wilder (1977) gave students a jury case. Before giving their own judgments, the students

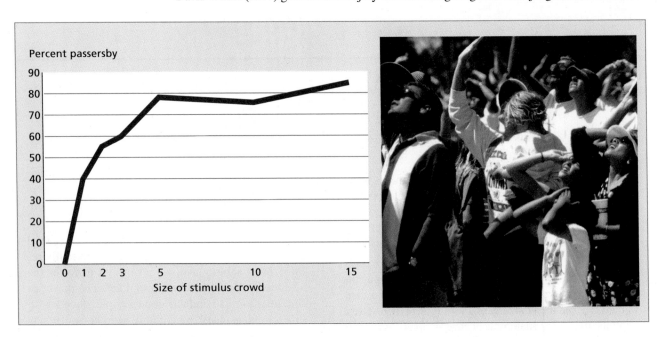

FIGURE :: 6

Group Size and Conformity

The percentage of passersby who imitated a group looking upward increased as group size increased to 5 persons.

Source: Data from Milgram, Bickman, & Berkowitz, 1969.

Jim Sugar/Documentary Value/Corbis

watched videotapes of four confederates giving their judgments. When the confederates were presented as two independent groups of two people, the participants conformed more than when the four confederates presented their judgments as a single group. Similarly, two groups of three people elicited more conformity than one group of six, and three groups of two people elicited even more. The agreement of independent small groups makes a position more credible.

Unanimity

Imagine yourself in a conformity experiment in which all but one of the people responding before you give the same wrong answer. Would the example of this one nonconforming confederate be as liberating as it was for the individuals in Milgram's obedience study? Several experiments reveal that someone who punctures a group's unanimity deflates its social power (Allen & Levine, 1969; Asch, 1955; Morris & Miller, 1975). As Figure 7 illustrates, people will usually voice their own convictions if just one other person has also differed from the majority. The participants in such experiments often later say they felt warm toward and close to their nonconforming ally. Yet they deny that the ally influenced them: "I would have answered just the same if he weren't there."

It's difficult to be a minority of one; few juries are hung because of one dissenting juror. And only 1 in 10 U.S. Supreme Court decisions during the late-twentieth century had a lone dissenter; most have been unanimous or a 5–4 split (Granberg & Bartels, 2005).

Conformity experiments teach the practical lesson that it is easier to stand up for something if you can find someone else to stand up with you. Many religious groups recognize this. Following the example of Jesus, who sent his disciples out in pairs, the Mormons send two missionaries into a neighborhood together. The support of the one comrade greatly increases a person's social courage.

Observing someone else's dissent—even when it is wrong—can increase our own independence. Charlan Nemeth and Cynthia Chiles (1988) discovered this after having people observe a lone individual in a group of four misjudge blue stimuli as green. Although the dissenter was wrong, after they had observed him the observers were more likely to exhibit their own form of independence: 76 percent of the time they correctly labeled red slides "red" even when everyone else was incorrectly calling them "orange." Participants who had no opportunity to observe the "green" dissenter conformed 70 percent of the time.

> "My opinion, my conviction, gains infinitely in strength and success, the moment a second mind has adopted it."
>
> —Novalis, Fragment

Cohesion

A minority opinion from someone outside the groups we identify with—from someone at another college or of a different religion—sways us less than the same minority opinion from someone within our group (Clark & Maass, 1988). A heterosexual arguing for gay

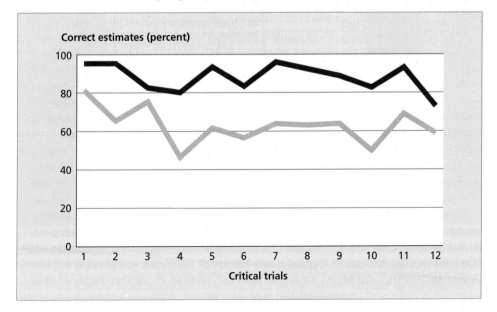

Correct estimates (percent)

Critical trials

FIGURE :: 7

The Effect of Unanimity on Conformity

When someone giving correct answers punctures the group's unanimity, individuals conform only one-fourth as often.
Source: From Asch, 1955.

It is difficult to stand alone as a minority of one. But doing so sometimes makes a hero, as was the lone dissenting jury member in the 1957 movie *12 Angry Men,* remade in 1997.
United Archives GmbH/Alamy

cohesiveness

A "we feeling"; the extent to which members of a group are bound together, such as by attraction to one another.

rights sways heterosexuals more effectively than does a homosexual. People even comply more readily with requests from those said to share their birthday, their first name, or features of their fingerprint (Burger et al., 2004; Silvia, 2005).

The more **cohesive** a group is, the more power it gains over its members. In other words, a group of your closest friends would influence you more than a group of acquaintances you don't feel very close to. In college sororities, for example, friends tend to share binge-eating tendencies, especially as they grow closer (Crandall, 1988). High school, often a time of cohesive groups, often leads students to drink as much alcohol as their peers in order to become (or stay) popular (Balsa et al., 2010). People within an ethnic group may feel a similar "own-group conformity pressure"—to talk, act, and dress just as everyone else does in their own group. In fact, Blacks who "act White" or Whites who "act Black" may be mocked by their peers for not conforming to their own ethnic group (Contrada et al., 2000).

In experiments, too, group members who feel attracted to the group are more responsive to its influence (Berkowitz, 1954; Lott & Lott, 1961; Sakurai, 1975). Fearing rejection by group members whom they like, they allow them a certain power (Hogg, 2001). In his *Essay Concerning Human Understanding,* the seventeenth-century philosopher John Locke recognized the cohesiveness factor: "Nor is there one in ten thousand who is stiff and insensible enough to bear up under the constant dislike and condemnation of his own club."

Our inclination to go with our group—to think what it thinks and do what it does—surfaced in one experiment as people reported greater liking for a piece of music that was said to be liked by people akin to themselves (but *dis*liked the music more when it was liked by someone *un*like themselves [Hilmert et al., 2006]). Likewise, when university students compare themselves with drinkers who are dissimilar from themselves, they become *less* likely to drink (Lane et al., 2011). And after observing cheating by someone wearing a T-shirt from their own university, participants in another experiment became more likely to cheat. But if the cheater wore a T-shirt from a competing university, it had the opposite effect: the participants became more honest (Gino et al., 2009). Cohesion-fed conformity also appears in college dorms, where students' attitudes become more similar to those living near them over time (Cullum & Harton, 2007).

Cohesion has tragically appeared in massacres, as men have been unwilling to separate themselves from their close comrades, even when killing was not something they would have done apart from their group. Historian Christopher Browning (1992) recalls the nearly 500-man German Reserve Police Battalion 101 being awakened in Poland one morning in July 1942. Their well-liked commander nervously explained that they had been ordered to send the male adults from the 1,800 Jews in a nearby village to a work camp, and to shoot the women, children, and elderly. With obvious discomfort over this task, he offered to let any of the older men who did not feel up to the task to step out. Only a dozen did. The rest participated, with many of them being physically sick with disgust afterwards.

In post-war testimonies from some 125 men, most of whom were middle-aged family men, anti-Semitism did not explain their actions. Rather, reported Browning, they were constrained by the power of cohesion: Don't break ranks. The men felt a "strong urge not to separate themselves from the group by stepping out" (p. 71).

Status

As you might suspect, higher-status people tend to have more impact (Driskell & Mullen, 1990). Junior group members—even junior social psychologists—acknowledge more conformity to their group than do senior group members (Jetten et al., 2006). Among 24,000 pedestrians observed in studies of jaywalking, 25 percent jaywalked when alone, which jumped to 44 percent when another person jaywalked and sunk to 17 percent when another person didn't. The nonjaywalker reduced jaywalking more when he or she was well dressed (Mullen et al., 1990). Chinese consumers who felt more powerful were less likely to conform by choosing popular products and came up with advertising slogans more focused on uniqueness (Zou et al., 2014). Even chimps are more likely to imitate the behaviors of high-ranking group members (Horner et al., 2010). Among both humans and other primates, prestige begets influence.

Milgram (1974) reported that in his obedience studies, people of lower status accepted the experimenter's commands more readily than people of higher status. After delivering 450 volts, a 37-year-old welder turned to the higher-status experimenter and deferentially asked, "Where do we go from here, Professor?" (p. 46). Another participant, a divinity school professor who disobeyed at 150 volts, said, "I don't understand why the experiment is placed above this person's life" and plied the experimenter with questions about "the ethics of this thing" (p. 48).

Public Response

One of conformity researchers' first questions was this: Would people conform more in their public responses than in their private opinions? Or would they wobble more in their private opinions but be unwilling to conform publicly, lest they appear wishy-washy?

The answer is now clear: In experiments, people conform more when they must respond in front of others rather than writing their answers privately. Asch's participants, after hearing others respond, were less influenced by group pressure if they could write answers that only the experimenter would see. Likewise, when college instructors ask controversial questions, students express more diverse opinions when answering anonymously, with clickers, than when raising hands (Stowell et al., 2010). It is much easier to stand up for what we believe in the privacy of the voting booth than before a group.

Prior Commitment

In 1980, Genuine Risk became the second filly ever to win the Kentucky Derby. In her next race, the Preakness, she came off the last turn gaining on the leader, Codex, a colt. As they came out of the turn neck and neck, Codex moved sideways toward Genuine Risk, causing her to hesitate and giving him a narrow victory. Had Codex brushed Genuine Risk? Had his jockey even whipped Genuine Risk in the face? The race referees

Prior commitment: Once they commit themselves to a position, people seldom yield to social pressure. Did Codex, the front horse closest to the inside, brush against Genuine Risk? After race referees publicly announced their decision, no amount of evidence from replays of the race could budge them.
AP Images/Ira Schwarz

huddled. After a brief deliberation they judged that no foul had occurred and confirmed Codex as the winner. The decision caused an uproar. Televised instant replays showed that Codex had indeed brushed Genuine Risk, the sentimental favorite. A protest was filed. The officials reconsidered their decision, but they did not change it.

Did their declared judgment immediately after the race affect officials' openness toward reaching a different decision later? We will never know for sure. We can, however, put people through a laboratory version of this event—with and without the immediate commitment—and observe whether the commitment makes a difference. Again, imagine yourself in an Asch-type experiment. The experimenter displays the lines and asks you to respond first. After you give your judgment and then hear everyone else disagree, the experimenter offers you an opportunity to reconsider. In the face of group pressure, do you now back down?

People almost never do (Deutsch & Gerard, 1955). After having made a public commitment, they stick to it. At most, they will change their judgments in later situations (Saltzstein & Sandberg, 1979). We may therefore expect that judges of diving or gymnastic competitions, for example, will seldom change their ratings after seeing the other judges' ratings, although they might adjust their later performance ratings.

Prior commitments restrain persuasion, too. When simulated juries make decisions, hung verdicts are more likely in cases when jurors are polled by a show of hands rather than by secret ballot (Kerr & MacCoun, 1985). Making a public commitment makes people hesitant to back down.

Smart persuaders know this. Salespeople ask questions that prompt us to make statements for, rather than against, what they are marketing. Environmentalists ask people to commit themselves to recycling, energy conservation, or bus riding. That's because behavior then changes more than when environmental appeals are heard without inviting a commitment (Katzev & Wang, 1994). Teens 14- to 17-years-old who make a public virginity-till-marriage pledge reportedly become somewhat more likely to remain sexually abstinent, or to delay intercourse, than similar teens who don't make the pledge (Bearman & Brückner, 2001; Brückner & Bearman, 2005; Uecker, 2008). (However, if they violate their pledge, they are somewhat less likely to use a condom.)

"Those who never retract their opinions love themselves more than they love truth."
—Joubert, *Pensées*

SUMMING UP: What Predicts Conformity?

- Using conformity testing procedures, experimenters have explored the circumstances that produce conformity. Certain situations appear to be especially powerful. For example, conformity is affected by the characteristics of the group: People conform most when three or more people, or groups, model the behavior or belief.
- Conformity is reduced if the modeled behavior or belief is not unanimous.

- Conformity is enhanced by group *cohesion.*
- The higher the status of those modeling the behavior or belief, the greater likelihood of conformity.
- People also conform most when their responses are public (in the presence of the group).
- A prior commitment to a certain behavior or belief increases the likelihood that a person will stick with that commitment rather than conform.

WHY CONFORM?

Identify and understand the two forms of social influence that explain why people will conform to others.

"Do you see yonder cloud that's almost in the shape of a camel?" asks Shakespeare's Hamlet of Polonius. "'Tis like a camel indeed," replies Polonius. "Methinks it is a weasel," says Hamlet a moment later. "It is backed like a weasel," acknowledges Polonius. "Or like a whale?" wonders Hamlet. "Very like a whale," agrees Polonius. Question: Why does Polonius so readily agree every time Hamlet changes his mind?

Or consider this situation: There I [DM] was, an American attending my first lecture during an extended visit at a German university. As the lecturer finished, I lifted my hands to join in the clapping. But rather than clap, the other people began rapping the tables with their knuckles. What did this mean? Did they disapprove of the speech? Surely, not everyone would be so openly rude to a visiting dignitary. Nor did their faces express displeasure. No, I realized, this must be a German ovation. So I added my knuckles to the chorus.

What prompted this conformity? Why had I not clapped even while the others rapped? Why did Polonius so readily echo Hamlet's words? There are two possibilities: A person may bow to the group (a) to be accepted and avoid rejection or (b) to obtain important information. Morton Deutsch and Harold Gerard (1955) named these two possibilities **normative influence** and **informational influence.** The first springs from our desire to be *liked,* and the second from our desire to be *right.*

Normative influence is "going along with the crowd" to avoid rejection, to stay in people's good graces, or to gain their approval. Perhaps the subordinate Polonius agreed with Hamlet, the higher-status Prince of Denmark, to curry favor. Informational influence captures how beliefs spread. Just as people look up when they see others looking up, they use the same fork others are using at a fancy dinner party.

In the laboratory and in everyday life, groups often reject those who deviate consistently (Miller & Anderson, 1979; Schachter, 1951). That's a lesson learned by a media studies professor who became an outcast while playing the online game "City of Heroes" (Vargas, 2009). The professor, with whom I [DM] empathize because we share the same name—David Myers—played by the rules but did not conform to the customs. Myers was derided with instant messages: "I hope your mother gets cancer." "EVERYONE HATES YOU." "If you kill me one more time I will come and kill you for real and I am not kidding."

As most of us know, social rejection is painful; when we deviate from group norms, we often pay an emotional price. Gerard (1999) recalls that in one of his conformity experiments, an initially friendly participant became upset, asked to leave the room, and returned looking

> sick and visibly shaken. I became worried and suggested that we discontinue the session. He absolutely refused to stop and continued through all 36 trials, not yielding to the others on a single trial. After the experiment was over and I explained the subterfuge to him, his entire body relaxed and he sighed with relief. Color returned to his face. I asked him why he had left the room. "To vomit," he said. He did not yield, but at what a price! He wanted so much to be accepted and liked by the others and was afraid he would not be because he had stood his ground against them. There you have normative pressure operating with a vengeance.

Sometimes the high price of deviation compels people to support what they do not believe in or at least to suppress their disagreement. In one experiment, participants who were ostracized by others were more likely to obey an experimenter's command to go outside in freezing weather to take 39 photographs (Riva et al., 2014). When we experience or even fear rejection, we're more likely to follow along. "I was afraid that Leideritz and others would think I was a coward," reported one German officer, explaining his reluctance to dissent from mass executions (Waller, 2002). Normative influence leads to compliance, especially for people who have recently seen others ridiculed or who are seeking to climb a status ladder (Hollander, 1958; Janes & Olson, 2000). As John F. Kennedy (1956) recalled, "'The way to get along,' I was told when I entered Congress, 'is to go along'" (p. 4).

Normative influence often sways us without our awareness. Administrators at Northern Illinois University wanted to reduce students' dangerous binge drinking at parties. At first they tried telling students to eat first, or described the consequences of binge drinking, but binge-drinking rates stayed about the same. Then they spread information about the norm, telling them that "most students drink moderately." Binge drinking was cut in half over 10 years (Haines, 1996). People follow others' lead when deciding what to eat, too.

normative influence
Conformity based on a person's desire to fulfill others' expectations, often to gain acceptance.

informational influence
Conformity occurring when people accept evidence about reality provided by other people.

"If you worry about missing the boat—remember the Titanic."
—Anonymous

In one study, customers at a bakery ate significantly more chocolates when 20 candy wrappers were left next to the bowl (Prinsen et al., 2013).

Informational influence, on the other hand, leads people to privately accept others' influence. Viewing a changing cloud shape, Polonius may actually see what Hamlet helps him see. When reality is ambiguous, as it was for participants in the autokinetic situation, other people can be a valuable source of information. The individual may reason, "I can't tell how far the light is moving. But this guy seems to know." The same is true while you're reading the restaurant reviews on Yelp or the hotel reviews on TripAdvisor: If you haven't been there before, other people's experiences can provide important information. These types of reviews are good examples of informational influence.

Your friends have extra influence on you for informational as well as normative reasons (Denrell, 2008; Denrell & Le Mens, 2007). If your friend buys a particular car and takes you to a particular restaurant, you will gain information that may lead you to like what your friend likes—even if you don't care what your friend likes. Our friends influence the experiences that inform our attitudes. However, that influence doesn't last forever: In one study, conformity to other's opinions lasted no more than three days (Huang et al., 2014).

To discover what the brain is doing when people experience an Asch-type conformity experiment, an Emory University neuroscience team put participants in a functional magnetic resonance imaging (fMRI) brain scanner while having them answer perceptual questions after hearing others' responses (Berns et al., 2005). (The task involved mentally rotating a figure to find its match among several possibilities.) When the participants conformed to a wrong answer, the brain regions dedicated to perception became active. And when they went *against* the group, brain regions associated with emotion became active. In similar experiments, brain regions associated with performance, learning, and reward became active when people conform (Hodgson et al., 2012; Shestakova et al., 2013). These results suggest that conformity may genuinely shape perceptions—people may conform because they are afraid of being wrong. Follow-up fMRI studies have identified neural activity associated with both normative influence (in a brain area that is active when people are anxious about social rejection) and with informational influence (in areas involved with one's judgments of a stimulus) (Zaki et al., 2011).

So, concern for *social image* produces *normative influence*. The desire to be *correct* produces *informational influence*. In day-to-day life, normative and informational influence often occur together. I [DM] was not about to be the only person in that German lecture hall clapping (normative influence). Yet the others' behavior also showed me the appropriate way to express my appreciation (informational influence).

Conformity experiments have sometimes isolated either normative or informational influence. Conformity is greater when people respond publicly before a group; this surely reflects normative influence (because people receive the same information whether they respond publicly or privately). On the other hand, conformity is greater when participants feel incompetent, when the task is difficult, and when the individuals care about being right—all signs of informational influence.

SUMMING UP: Why Conform?

- Experiments reveal two reasons people conform. *Normative influence* results from a person's desire for acceptance: We want to be liked. The tendency to conform more when responding publicly reflects normative influence.

- *Informational influence* results from others' providing evidence about reality. The tendency to conform more on difficult decision-making tasks reflects informational influence: We want to be right.

WHO CONFORMS?

Describe how conformity varies not only with situations but also with persons. Discuss social contexts in which personality traits shine through.

Are some people generally more susceptible (or should we say, more open) to social influence? Among your friends, can you identify some who are "conformists" and others who are "independent"? In their search for the conformer, researchers have focused on three predictors: personality, culture, and social roles.

Personality

In Milgram's time, the personality factors predicting greater conformity were unknown. As Milgram (1974) concluded: "I am certain that there is a complex personality basis to obedience and disobedience. But I know we have not found it" (p. 205). Yet individual differences clearly existed: Recall that not all of Milgram's participants obeyed the experimenter to the end. Generally speaking, people higher in agreeableness (who value getting along with others) and conscientiousness (who follow social norms for neatness and punctuality) are more likely to conform (DeYoung et al., 2002; Fürst et al., 2014; Roccas et al., 2002). People who want to please others eat more candy when a peer eats some and then hands them the bowl, apparently conforming to help the other person feel more comfortable (Exline et al., 2012). In other words, "hold the extra burgers and fries when people pleasers arrive" (Griffith, 2012). People high in openness to experience—a personality trait connected to creativity and socially progressive thinking—are less likely to conform (Jugert et al., 2009). Novelty seekers, who leap into experiences seeking stimulation, are also less likely to conform (Athota & O'Connor, 2014). Two studies found that students with a strong belief in their own free will and personal control were less likely to conform to the group (Alquist et al., 2013; Fennis & Aarts, 2012). So if you're someone who favors smooth social experiences over disagreements, follows the rules, has traditional beliefs, and doubts the existence of free will, you are more likely to conform.

An Army report on the Abu Ghraib prison abuse praised three men who, despite threats of ridicule and court-martial, stood apart from their comrades (O'Connor, 2004).

Personality effects loom larger when we note people's differing reactions to the same situation, as when one person reacts with terror and another with delight to a roller coaster ride.
Zia Soleil/Getty Images

Lt. David Sutton terminated one incident and alerted his commanders. "I don't want to judge, but yes, I witnessed something inappropriate and I reported it," said Sutton. Navy dog handler William Kimbro resisted "significant pressure" to participate in "improper interrogations." And Specialist Joseph Darby blew the whistle, giving military police the evidence that raised the alarm. Darby, called a "rat" by some, received death threats for his dissent and was given military protection. But back home, his mother joined others in applauding: "Honey, I'm so proud of you because you did the good thing and good always triumphs over evil, and the truth will always set you free" (ABC News, December 2004). In the end, both personality and the situation shape behavior.

Culture

When researchers in Australia, Austria, Germany, Italy, Jordan, South Africa, Spain, and the United States repeated the obedience experiments, how do you think the results compared with those with American participants? The obedience rates were similar, or even higher— 85 percent in Munich (Blass, 2000). As we've already noted, conformity rates are higher in collectivistic countries and more conformist times such as the 1950s (Bond & Smith, 1996).

In collectivist Japan, Western observers were struck by the absence of looting and lawlessness following the 2011 earthquake and tsunami; respect for social norms prevailed (Cafferty, 2011). In individualist countries, university students see themselves as less conforming than others in their consumer purchases and political views—as individuals amid the sheep (Pronin et al., 2007).

There may be some biological wisdom to cultural differences in conformity. Although nonconformity supports creative problem solving, groups thrive when coordinating their responses to threats. Thus, note Damian Murray and his co-workers (2011), countries that have a high risk of diseases such as malaria, typhus, and tuberculosis tend to have cultures with relatively high conformity levels. Similarly, those living in U.S. states with higher pathogen prevalence are less likely to vote for third-party candidates—a nonconformist action (Varnum, 2013). Conformity supports social norms regarding food preparation, hygiene, public health, and contact with unknown people, report the researchers. Thinking of pathogens can actually cause conformity: Students randomly assigned to see pathogen-related pictures or to talk about a time when they felt vulnerable to germs were more likely to conform to the majority's views than those who saw pictures of accidents or talked about a threat to their physical safety (Murray & Schaller, 2012; Wu & Chang, 2012). When we think about getting sick, we embrace the perceived safety of fitting in with the group.

Cultural differences also exist within social classes. For example, in five studies, Nicole Stephens and her co-researchers (2007) found that working-class people tend to prefer similarity to others, whereas middle-class people more strongly preferred to see themselves as unique. In an experiment, people chose a pen from among five green and orange pens (with three or four of one color). Of university students from working-class backgrounds, 72 percent picked one from the majority color, compared with only 44 percent of those from middle-class backgrounds. Those from working-class backgrounds also came to like their chosen pen more after seeing someone else make the same choice. They responded more positively to a friend's knowingly buying the same car they had just bought. And they were also more likely to prefer visual images that they knew others had chosen.

Social Roles

All the world's a stage,
And all the men and women merely players:
They have their exits and their entrances;
And one man in his time plays many parts.
—William Shakespeare

Role theorists have assumed, as did William Shakespeare's character Jaques in *As You Like It,* that social life is like acting on a theatrical stage, with all its scenes, masks, and scripts. And those roles have much to do with conformity. Social roles allow some freedom of interpretation to those who act them out, but some aspects of any role *must* be performed. A student must at least show up for exams, turn in papers, and maintain some minimum grade point average.

When only a few norms are associated with a social category (for example, riders on an escalator should stand to the right and walk to the left), we do not regard the position as a social role. It takes a whole cluster of norms to define a role. My [DM's] roles as a professor or as a father compel me to honor a whole set of norms. Although I may acquire my particular image by violating the least important norms (valuing efficiency, I rarely arrive early for anything), violating my role's most important norms (not showing up for class, abusing my children) could have led to my being fired or having my children removed from my care.

Roles have powerful effects. On a first date or on a new job, you may act the role self-consciously. As you internalize the role, self-consciousness subsides. What felt awkward now feels genuine.

That is the experience of many immigrants, Peace Corps workers, international students, and executives. After arriving in a new country, it takes time to learn how to talk and act appropriately in the new context—to conform, as I [DM] did with the Germans who rapped their knuckles on their desks. And the almost universal experience of those who repatriate back to their home country is reentry distress (Sussman, 2000). In ways one may not have been aware of, the process of conforming will have shifted one's behavior, values, and identity to accommodate a different place. One must "re-conform" to one's former roles before being back in sync.

As we saw earlier in this chapter, our actions depend not only on the power of the situation but also on our personalities. Not everyone responds in the same way to pressure to conform. Nevertheless, we have seen that social situations can move most "normal" people to behave in "abnormal" ways. This is clear from those experiments that put well-intentioned people in bad situations to see whether good or evil prevails. To a dismaying extent, evil wins. Nice guys often don't finish nice.

ROLE REVERSAL

Role playing can also be a positive force. By intentionally playing a new role and conforming to its expectations, people sometimes change themselves or empathize with people whose roles differ from their own.

Roles often come in pairs defined by relationships—parent and child, teacher and student, doctor and patient, employer and employee. Role reversals can help each understand the other. A negotiator or a group leader can therefore create better communication by having the two sides reverse roles, with each arguing the other's position. Or each side can be asked to restate the other party's point (to the other's satisfaction) before replying. The next time you get into a difficult argument with a friend or parent, try to restate the other person's perceptions and feelings before going on with your own. This intentional, temporary conformity may repair your relationship.

So far in this chapter, we have discussed classic studies of conformity and obedience, identified the factors that predict conformity, and considered who conforms and why. Remember that our primary quest in social psychology is not to catalog differences but to identify universal principles of behavior.

Social roles will always vary with culture, but the processes by which those roles influence behavior vary much less. People in Nigeria and Japan define teen roles differently from people in Europe and North America, but in all cultures role expectations guide the conformity found in social relations.

"Great Spirit, grant that I may not criticize my neighbor until I have walked for a moon in his moccasins."

—Native American Prayer

SUMMING UP: Who Conforms?

- People who seek to please others and are comfortable following social rules (those high in agreeableness and conscientiousness) are the most likely to conform.

- Although conformity and obedience are universal, different cultures socialize people to be more or less socially responsive.

- Social roles involve a certain degree of conformity, and conforming to expectations is an important task when stepping into a new social role.

DO WE EVER WANT TO BE DIFFERENT?

Explain what can motivate people to actively resist social pressure—by doing Z when compelled to do A.

"To do just the opposite is also a form of imitation."
—Lichtenberg, *Aphorismen*, 1764–1799

This chapter emphasizes the power of social forces. It is therefore fitting that we conclude by again reminding ourselves of the power of the person. We are not just billiard balls moving where pushed. We may act according to our own values, independently of the forces that push upon us. Knowing that someone is trying to coerce us may even prompt us to react in the *opposite* direction.

Reactance

reactance
A motive to protect or restore one's sense of freedom. Reactance arises when someone threatens our freedom of action.

Individuals value their sense of freedom and self-efficacy. When blatant social pressure threatens their sense of freedom, they often rebel. Think of Romeo and Juliet, whose love was intensified by their families' opposition. Or think of children asserting their freedom and independence by doing the opposite of what their parents ask. Savvy parents therefore offer their children limited choices instead of commands: "It's time to get clean: Do you want a bath or a shower?"

The theory of psychological **reactance**—that people act to protect their sense of freedom—is supported by experiments showing that attempts to restrict a person's freedom often produce an anticonformity "boomerang effect" (Brehm & Brehm, 1981; Nail et al., 2000; Rains, 2013). In one field experiment, many students stopped wearing a "Livestrong" wristband when geeky students started wearing the band (Berger & Heath, 2008). Likewise, rich Brits stopped wearing Burberry caps after the caps caught on among soccer hooligans (Clevstrom & Passariello, 2006).

Reactance may contribute to underage drinking. A survey of 18- to 24-year-olds by the Canadian Centre on Substance Abuse (1997) revealed that 69 percent of those over the legal drinking age (21) had been intoxicated in the past year, as had 77 percent of those *under* 21. In the United States, a survey of students on 56 campuses revealed a 25 percent rate of alcohol abstinence among students of legal drinking age (21) but only a 19 percent abstinence rate among students under 21 (Engs & Hanson, 1989). And reaching them with anti-drinking messages might not work: people with the highest risk are often the least likely to respond to programs designed to protect them, possibly due to their reactance (Noguchi et al., 2007). Reactance might also explain why most people find it so difficult to eat right and exercise. For example, 78 percent of the population does not exercise regularly. As Seppo Iso-Ahola (2013) explains, "Exercise has become a 'must' or 'should' activity that sets up a confrontation between fitness activity and freedom" (p. 100). When teens in one study were told that others believed eating fruit was healthy, they said they intended to eat less fruit. But when they heard that most other teens made an effort to eat sufficient fruit, they ate more fruit over the next two days (Stok et al., 2013). Because we know we should do it, it becomes difficult to actually do it without feeling our freedom is compromised. If we know others are doing it (normative influence again), we're more likely to do it too, due to the principles of conformity. The lesson seems to be: Do what I do, not what I say is right.

Reactance at work? Underage students have been found to drink to excess more often than students over the legal drinking age.
AP Images/Joe Hermosa

Asserting Uniqueness

Imagine a world of complete conformity, where there were no differences among people. Would such a world be a happy place? If nonconformity can create discomfort, can sameness create comfort?

People feel uncomfortable when they appear too different from others. But in individualistic Western cultures they also feel uncomfortable when they appear exactly like everyone else. That might be because nonconformity has become associated with high status. "I have a number of super-successful Silicon Valley clients who dress in ripped denim, Vans shoes, and T-shirts," business consultant Tom Searcy wrote in *CBS Moneywatch* (2011). "They are worth hundreds of millions, even more, but it's a status symbol to dress like you're homeless to attend board meetings." In a series of experiments, Silvia Bellezza and colleagues (2014) found that people wearing nonconformist clothing—such as a pair of red sneakers—were perceived by others as higher in status. And if someone copies our clothing or other aspects of our self-presentation, we're likely to be angry at the copycat (Reysen et al., 2012).

Overall, people feel better when they see themselves as moderately unique and act in ways that will assert their individuality. For example, students in one study believed that their first names were less common than their peers did—apparently people with common names wanted to believe their names—and thus, they—were more unique. Students who had considered changing their names usually choose more unique names (Kulig, 2012). In an experiment, Snyder (1980) led Purdue University students to believe that their "10 most important attitudes" were either distinct from or nearly identical to the attitudes of 10,000 other students. When they next participated in a conformity experiment, those deprived of their feeling of uniqueness were the ones most likely to assert their individuality by nonconformity. Moreover, individuals who have the highest "need for uniqueness" tend to conform the least (Imhoff & Erb, 2009).

Both social influence and the desire for uniqueness appear in popular baby names. People seeking less commonplace names often hit upon the same ones at the same time. In 2013, among the top 10 U.S. baby names for girls were Emma (#2), Isabella (#4), and Emily (#7). Those who in the 1960s broke out of the pack by naming their baby Rebecca, thinking they were bucking convention, soon discovered their choice was part of a new pack, noted Peggy Orenstein (2003). Hillary, a popular late 1980s, early 1990s name, became less original-seeming and less frequent (even among her admirers) after Hillary Clinton became well-known. Although the popularity of such names then fades, observes Orenstein, it may resurface with a future generation. Max, Rose, and Sophie sound like the roster of a retirement home—or an elementary school. These trends seem to be driven by a nonconformist urge. In one large study of names in the United States and France, when names become popular quickly, they also faded from popularity more quickly—perhaps because they were seen as fads (Berger & Le Mens, 2009).

Seeing oneself as unique also appears in people's "spontaneous self-concepts." William McGuire and his Yale University colleagues (McGuire et al., 1979; McGuire & Padawer-Singer, 1978) invited children to "tell us about yourself." In reply, the children mostly mentioned their distinctive attributes. Foreign-born children were more likely than others to mention their birthplace. Redheads were more likely than black- and brown-haired children to volunteer their hair color. Light and heavy children were the most likely to refer to their body weight. Minority children were the most likely to mention their race.

When body tattoos come to be perceived as pack behavior—as displaying conformity rather than individuality—will their popularity decline?

"When I'm in America, I have no doubt I'm a Jew, but I have strong doubts about whether I'm really an American. And when I get to Israel, I know I'm an American, but I have strong doubts about whether I'm a Jew."
—Leslie Fiedler,
Fiedler on the Roof, 1991

Asserting our uniqueness. Although not wishing to be greatly deviant, most of us express our distinctiveness through our personal styles and dress.
Igor Emmerich/Image Source

Likewise, we become more keenly aware of our gender when we are with people of the other gender (Cota & Dion, 1986). When I [DM] attended an American Psychological Association meeting with 10 others—all women, as it happened—I immediately was aware of my gender. As we took a break at the end of the second day, I joked that the line would be short at my bathroom, triggering the woman sitting next to me to notice what hadn't crossed her mind—the group's gender makeup.

The principle, says McGuire, is that "one is conscious of oneself insofar as, and in the ways that, one is different." Thus, "If I am a Black woman in a group of White women, I tend to think of myself as a Black; if I move to a group of Black men, my blackness loses salience and I become more conscious of being a woman" (McGuire et al., 1978). This insight helps us understand why White people who grow up amid non-White people tend to have a strong White identity, why gays may be more conscious of their sexual identity than straights, and why any minority group tends to be conscious of its distinctiveness and how the surrounding culture relates to it (Knowles & Peng, 2005). The majority group, being less conscious of race, may see the minority group as hypersensitive. When occasionally living in Scotland, where my [DM's] American accent marks me as a foreigner, I become conscious of my national identity and sensitive to how others react to it.

When the people of two cultures are nearly identical, they still will notice their differences, however small. Even trivial distinctions may provoke scorn and conflict. Jonathan Swift satirized the phenomenon in *Gulliver's Travels* with the story of the Little-Endians' war against the Big-Endians. Their difference: The Little-Endians preferred to break their eggs on the small end, the Big-Endians on the large end. On a world scale, the differences may not seem great between Sunni and Shia. But anyone who reads the news knows that these small differences have meant big conflicts (Rothbart & Taylor, 1992). Rivalry is often most intense when the other group closely resembles you. So, although we do not like being greatly deviant, we are, ironically, all alike in wanting to feel distinctive and in noticing how we are distinctive. (In thinking you are different, you are like everyone else.) But as research on the self-serving bias makes clear, it is not just any kind of distinctiveness we seek but distinctiveness in the right direction. Our quest is not merely to be different from the average, but *better* than average.

> "Self-consciousness, the recognition of a creature by itself as a 'self,' [cannot] exist except in contrast with an 'other,' a something which is not the self."
>
> —C. S. Lewis,
> *The Problem of Pain*, 1940

SUMMING UP: Do We Ever Want to Be Different?

- Social psychology's emphasis on the power of social pressure must be joined by a complementary emphasis on the power of the person. We are not puppets. When social coercion becomes blatant, people often experience *reactance*—a motivation to defy the coercion in order to maintain their sense of freedom.

- We are not comfortable being greatly different from a group, but neither do we want to appear the same as everyone else. Thus, we act in ways that preserve our sense of uniqueness and individuality. In a group, we are most conscious of how we differ from the others.

POSTSCRIPT:
On Being an Individual Within a Community

Do your own thing. Question authority. If it feels good, do it. Follow your bliss. Don't conform. Think for yourself. Be true to yourself. You owe it to yourself.

We hear phrases like those over and again *if* we live in an individualistic Western nation, such as those of Western Europe, Australia, New Zealand, Canada, or, especially, the United States. Our mythical cultural heroes—from Sherlock Holmes to Luke Skywalker to Neo of the *Matrix* trilogy—often stand up against institutional rules. Individualists assume the preeminence of individual rights and celebrate the one who stands against the group.

In 1831 the French writer Alexis de Tocqueville coined the term "individualism" after traveling in America. Individualists, he noted, owe no one "anything and hardly expect anything from anybody. They form the habit of thinking of themselves in isolation and imagine that their whole destiny is in their hands."

Psychologist Carl Rogers (1985) agreed: "The only question which matters is, 'Am I living in a way which is deeply satisfying to me, and which truly expresses me?'"

That is hardly the only question that matters to people in many other cultures, including those of Asia, South America, and most of Africa. Where *community* is prized, conformity is accepted. Schoolchildren often display their solidarity by wearing uniforms; many workers do the same. To maintain harmony, confrontation and dissent are muted. "The nail that stands out gets pounded down," say the Japanese. South Africans have a word that expresses human connection. *Ubuntu,* explained Desmond Tutu (1999), conveys the idea that "my humanity is caught up by, is inextricably bound up in, yours." *Umuntu ngumuntu ngabantu,* says a Zulu maxim: "A person is a person through other persons."

Amitai Etzioni (1993), a past president of the American Sociological Association, urges us toward a "communitarian" individualism that balances our nonconformist individualism with a spirit of community. Fellow sociologist Robert Bellah (1995/1996) concurs. "Communitarianism is based on the value of the sacredness of the individual," he explains. But it also "affirms the central value of solidarity . . . that we become who we are through our relationships."

As Westerners in various nations, most readers of this book enjoy the benefits of nonconformist individualism. Communitarians remind us that we also are social creatures having a basic need to belong. Conformity is neither all bad nor all good. We therefore do well to balance our "me" and our "we," our needs for independence and for attachment, our individuality and our social identity.

Persuasion

Jim West/Alamy

"To swallow and follow, whether old doctrine or new propaganda, is a weakness still dominating the human mind."

—Charlotte Perkins Gilman, *Human Work*, 1904

"Remember that to change thy mind and to follow him that sets thee right, is to be none the less a free agent."

—Marcus Aurelius Antoninus, *Meditations*, viii. 16, 121–180

What paths lead to persuasion?

What are the elements of persuasion?

How can persuasion be resisted?

Postscript: Being open but not naïve

Many of life's powers can either harm or help us. Nuclear power enables our lighting up homes or wiping out cities. Sexual power helps us express committed love or seek selfish gratification. Similarly, **persuasion**'s power enables us to promote health or to sell addiction, to advance peace or stir up hate, to enlighten or deceive. And such powers are great. Consider the following:

- *The spread of false beliefs:* About 1 in 4 Americans and 1 in 3 Europeans thinks the sun revolves around the earth (Grossman, 2014). About 1 in 5 Americans believed President Obama is a Muslim and 1 in 3 believed Obama was born outside the United States (Blanton, 2011; Pew, 2010d; Jagel, 2014). Others deny that the moon landing or the Holocaust occurred.

- *A trillion-dollar war:* The United States' invasion of Iraq was enabled by persuasive messages that led half of Americans to believe that Iraq dictator Saddam Hussein was involved in the 9/11 attacks and 4 in 5 to believe that weapons of mass destruction would be found (Duffy, 2003; Gallup Organization, 2003; Newport et al., 2003). Both beliefs were false. Shortly before the war, Americans, under the influence of their leaders and media, favored military action against Iraq by 2 to 1, whereas Europeans opposed it by the same margin (Burkholder, 2003; Moore, 2003; Pew Research Center, 2003). Depending on where they lived, people received, discussed, and believed differing information. Persuasion matters.

- *Climate change skepticism:* The scientific community, represented by various national academies of science and the Intergovernmental Panel on Climate Change, is in a virtual consensus about three facts: (1) Atmospheric greenhouse gases are accumulating; (2) diminishing sea ice and rising temperatures confirm the world's warming; and (3) this climate change will almost certainly produce rising sea levels and more extreme weather, including record floods, tornadoes, droughts, and high temperatures. Nevertheless, climate *skepticism* has grown (see Figure 1). Sixty-five percent of Americans in 2014 believed global warming had occurred, down from 75 percent in 2008. Only 36 percent saw global warming as a serious threat (Jones, 2014). In Britain, the proportion who deny climate change quadrupled between 2005 and 2013, from 4 percent to 19 percent (Poortinga, 2013). And the number of Germans fearing global warming dropped to 39 percent, from 62 percent in 2006 (Morano, 2013). Researchers wondered: Why is the scientific consensus failing to persuade and to motivate action? And what might be done?

- *Promoting healthier living:* Due partly to health-promotion campaigns, the Centers for Disease Control and Prevention reports that only 18 percent of Americans smoke cigarettes, half the rate of 40 years ago. *Statistics Canada* reports a similar smoking decline. And the rate of entering college students reporting they never drink beer has increased—from 26 percent in 1982 to 66 percent in 2014 (Eagan et al., 2015; Pryor & et al., 2007).

As the previous examples show, efforts to persuade are sometimes diabolical, sometimes controversial, and sometimes beneficial. Persuasion is neither inherently good nor bad. A message's purpose and content elicits judgments of good or bad. The bad we call "propaganda." The good we call "education." Education is more factually based and less

persuasion
The process by which a message induces change in beliefs, attitudes, or behaviors.

"Speech has power. Words do not fade. What starts out as a sound ends in a deed."
—Rabbi Abraham Heschel, 1961

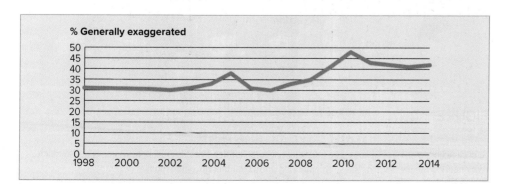

FIGURE :: 1

Americans' views of global warming, 1998–2014.

Compared to the late 1990s and early 2000s, more Americans now believe that the seriousness of global warming has been "generally exaggerated."

Persuasion is everywhere. When we approve of it, we may call it "education."

Mick Sinclair/Alamy

"Ads are propaganda by definition. We are in the persuasion business, the propaganda business."

—A U.S. Presidential Candidate's Staff Executive, 2011 (Quoted by Edsall, 2011).

A fanatic is one who can't change his mind and won't change the subject."

—Winston Churchill, 1954

central route to persuasion

Occurs when interested people focus on the arguments and respond with favorable thoughts.

coercive than propaganda. Yet generally we call it "education" when we believe it, "propaganda" when we don't (Lumsden et al., 1980).

Persuasion, whether it's education or propaganda, is everywhere—at the heart of politics, marketing, dating, parenting, negotiation, religion, and courtroom decision making. Social psychologists therefore seek to understand what leads to effective, long-lasting attitude change. What factors affect persuasion? As persuaders, how can we most effectively "educate" others?

Imagine that you are a marketing or advertising executive. Or imagine that you are a preacher, trying to increase love and charity among your parishioners. Or imagine that you want to reduce climate change, encourage breast-feeding, or campaign for a political candidate. What could you do to make yourself and your message persuasive? And if you are wary of being influenced, to what tactics should you be alert?

To answer such questions, social psychologists usually study persuasion the way some geologists study erosion—by observing the effects of various factors in brief, controlled experiments.

WHAT PATHS LEAD TO PERSUASION?

Identify two paths leading to influence. Describe the type of cognitive processing each involves—and its effects.

Persuasion entails clearing several hurdles (see Figure 2). Any factors that help people clear the persuasion hurdles will increase persuasion. For example, if an attractive source increases your attention to a message, the message should have a better chance of persuading you.

The Central Route

Richard Petty and John Cacioppo (Cass-ee-OH-poh) (1986; Petty et al., 2009) and Alice Eagly and Shelly Chaiken (1993, 1998) took this one step further. They theorized that persuasion is likely to occur via one of two routes. When people are motivated and able to think about an issue, they are likely to take the **central route to persuasion**—focusing on the arguments.

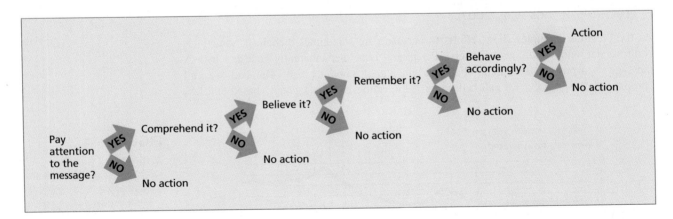

FIGURE :: 2

The Hurdles of the Persuasion Process

To elicit action, a persuasive message must clear several hurdles. What is crucial, however, is not so much remembering the message itself as remembering one's own thoughts in response.

Source: Adapted from W. J. McGuire. "An Information-Processing Model of Advertising Effectiveness," in *Behavioral and Management Sciences in Marketing,* H. L. Davis & A. J. Silk, Eds. Copyright © 1978. Reprinted by permission of John Wiley & Sons.

If those arguments are strong and compelling, persuasion is likely. If the message offers only weak arguments, thoughtful people will notice that the arguments aren't very compelling and will counterargue.

The Peripheral Route

Sometimes the strength of the arguments doesn't matter. Sometimes we're not motivated or able to think carefully. If we're distracted, uninvolved, or just plain busy, we may not take the time to reflect on the message's content. Rather than analyzing whether the arguments are compelling, we might follow the **peripheral route to persuasion**—focusing on cues that trigger automatic acceptance without much thinking. In these situations, easily understood familiar statements are more persuasive than novel statements with the same meaning. Thus,

Peripheral route processing. "Product placements" on TV and in movies aim to influence implicit attitudes.
Disney ABC Television Group/Modern Family

for uninvolved or distracted people, "Don't put all your eggs in one basket" has more impact than "Don't risk everything on a single venture" (Howard, 1997).

Smart advertisers adapt ads to their consumers' thinking. They do so for good reason. Much of consumer behavior—such as a spontaneous decision to buy ice cream of a particular brand—is made without thinking (Dijksterhuis et al., 2005). Something as minor as German music may lead customers to buy German wine, whereas those hearing French music reach for French wine (North et al., 1997). Billboards and television commercials—media that consumers are able to take in for only brief amounts of time—often use the peripheral route, with visual images as peripheral cues. Instead of providing arguments in favor of smoking, cigarette ads associate the product with images of beauty and pleasure. So do soft-drink ads that declare "America Is Beautiful" with images of happy people and fun outdoor activities. On the other hand, magazine prescription drug ads (which interested, logical consumers may pore over for some time) seldom feature Hollywood stars or great athletes. Instead, they offer customers information on benefits and side effects.

These two routes to persuasion—one explicit and reflective, the other more implicit and automatic—were a forerunner to today's "dual processing" models of the human mind. Central route processing often swiftly changes explicit attitudes. Peripheral route processing more slowly builds implicit attitudes through repeated associations between an attitude object and an emotion (Jones et al., 2009; Petty & Brinõl, 2008; Walther et al., 2011).

Different Paths for Different Purposes

The ultimate goal of the advertiser, the preacher, and even the teacher is not just to have people pay attention to the message and move on. Typically, the goal is behavior change (buying a product, loving one's neighbor, or studying more effectively). Are the two routes to persuasion equally likely to fulfill that goal? Petty and colleagues (1995, 2009) note that central route processing can lead to more enduring change than the peripheral route. When people are thinking carefully, they rely not only on the strength of persuasive appeals but on their own thoughts in response. It's not so much the arguments that are persuasive as the way they get people thinking. And when people think deeply rather than superficially, any changed attitude will more likely persist, resist attack, and influence behavior (Petty et al., 1995, 2009; Verplanken, 1991).

None of us has the time to thoughtfully analyze all issues. Often we take the peripheral route, by using simple rule-of-thumb heuristics, such as "trust the experts" or "long messages are credible" (Chaiken & Maheswaran, 1994). Residents of my [DM's] community

peripheral route to persuasion
Occurs when people are influenced by incidental cues, such as a speaker's attractiveness.

"All effective propaganda must be limited to a very few points and must harp on these in slogans until the last member of the public understands."
—Adolf Hitler,
Mein Kampf, 1926

once voted on a complicated issue involving the legal ownership of our local hospital. I didn't have the time or the interest to study that question myself (I had this book to write). But I noted that referendum supporters were all people I either liked or regarded as experts. So I used a simple heuristic—friends and experts can be trusted—and voted accordingly. We all make snap judgments using such heuristics: If a speaker is articulate and appealing, has apparently good motives, and has several arguments (or better, if the different arguments come from different sources), we usually take the easy peripheral route and accept the message without much thought.

Central route appeals seem to have dwindled in recent years, most likely because advertisers have found that peripheral, emotion-based appeals are more effective across a variety of products. In one study, researchers recorded viewers' facial expressions while they watched recent TV commercials. These facial expressions—particularly those indicating happiness—were better predictors of product sales than viewers' survey responses about how persuasive they found the ad, how closely the ad was linked to the brand, or how the ad conveyed the brand's key message (Wood, 2012). Emotion, not reason, sold the goods.

SUMMING UP: What Paths Lead to Persuasion?

- Sometimes *persuasion* occurs as people focus on arguments and respond with favorable thoughts. Such systematic, or *central route,* persuasion occurs when people are naturally analytical or involved in the issue.

- When issues don't engage systematic thinking, persuasion may occur through a faster, *"peripheral route,"* as people use heuristics or incidental cues to make snap judgments.

- Central route persuasion, being more thoughtful and less superficial, is more durable and more likely to influence behavior.

WHAT ARE THE ELEMENTS OF PERSUASION?

Describe how the factors that compose persuasion affect the likelihood that we will take either the central or the peripheral route to persuasion.

Among the ingredients of persuasion explored by social psychologists are these four: (1) the communicator, (2) the message, (3) how the message is communicated, and (4) the audience. In other words, *who* says *what*, by what *method*, to *whom*?

Who Says? The Communicator

Imagine the following scene: I. M. Wright, a middle-aged American, is watching the evening news. In the first segment, a small group of radicals is shown burning an American flag. As they do, one shouts through a bullhorn that whenever any government becomes oppressive, "it is the Right of the People to alter or to abolish it. . . . It is their right, it is their duty, to throw off such government!" Angered, Mr. Wright mutters to his wife, "It's sickening to hear them spouting that Communist line." In the next segment, a presidential candidate speaking before an antitax rally declares, "Thrift should be the guiding principle in our government expenditure. It should be made clear to all government workers that corruption and waste are very great crimes." An obviously pleased Mr. Wright relaxes and smiles: "Now that's the kind of good sense we need. That's my kinda guy." Effective persuaders know how to convey a message effectively.

Now switch the scene. Imagine Mr. Wright hearing the same revolutionary line about "the Right of the People" at a July 4 oration of the Declaration of Independence (from which the line comes) and hearing a Communist speaker read the thrift sentence from *Quotations from Chairman Mao Zedong* (from which it comes). Would he now react differently?

Social psychologists have found that who is saying something does affect how an audience receives it. In one experiment, when the Socialist and Liberal leaders in the Dutch parliament argued identical positions using the same words, each was most effective with members of his own party (Wiegman, 1985). People are more willing to agree with statements made by leaders in the political party they identify with (Verkuyten & Maliepaard, 2013). It's not just the message that matters, but also who says it. What makes one communicator more persuasive than another?

"*If I seem excited, Mr. Bolling, it's only because I know that I can make you a very rich man.*"

Effective persuaders know how to convey a message effectively.
© Charles Barsotti/The New Yorker Collection/www.cartoonbank.com.

CREDIBILITY

Any of us would find a statement about the benefits of exercise more believable if it came from the Royal Society or National Academy of Sciences rather than from a tabloid newspaper. But the effects of source **credibility** (perceived expertise and trustworthiness) diminish after a month or so. If a credible person's message is persuasive, its impact may fade as its source is forgotten or dissociated from the message. And the impact of a noncredible person may correspondingly increase over time if people remember the message better than the reason for discounting it (Kumkale & Albarracin, 2004; Pratkanis et al., 1988). This delayed persuasion, after people forget the source or its connection with the message, is called the **sleeper effect.**

credibility
Believability. A credible communicator is perceived as both expert and trustworthy.

sleeper effect
A delayed impact of a message that occurs when an initially discounted message becomes effective, such as we remember the message but forget the reason for discounting it.

PERCEIVED EXPERTISE. How do you become an authoritative "expert"? One way is to begin by saying things the audience agrees with, which makes you seem smart. One reason the "scientific consensus" about climate change fails to persuade is that people count as "expert" someone whose conclusions support their own preexisting values and views. Researchers have observed this "congenial views seems more expert" phenomenon on topics ranging from climate change to nuclear waste to gun laws (Kahan et al., 2010). It also helps to be seen as *knowledgeable* on the topic. A message about toothbrushing from "Dr. James Rundle of the Canadian Dental Association" is more convincing than the same message from "Jim Rundle, a local high school student who did a project with some of his classmates on dental hygiene" (Olson & Cal, 1984). Celebrity communicators are more persuasive when they are perceived as expert users of the product—when they are not, these appeals are very ineffective (Rossiter & Smidts, 2012).

SPEAKING STYLE. Another way to appear credible is to *speak confidently and fluently.* Whether pitching a business plan or giving advice, a charismatic, energetic, confident-seeming person who speaks fluently (without saying "you know" or "uh") is often more convincing (Moore & Swift, 2011; Pentland, 2010). Speakers who stumble over their words or say "you know" and "uh" are perceived as less credible, which then leads people to question their message, which then makes them less likely to accept what the speaker is saying (Carpenter, 2012). Bonnie Erickson and collaborators (1978) had University of North Carolina students evaluate courtroom testimony given in a straightforward manner or in a more hesitant, disfluent way. For example:

Question: Approximately how long did you stay there before the ambulance arrived?

Answer: *[Straightforward]* Twenty minutes. Long enough to help get Mrs. David straightened out.

[Hesitating] Oh, it seems like it was about uh, 20 minutes. Just long enough to help my friend Mrs. David, you know, get straightened out.

"Believe an expert."
—Virgil,
Aeneid, 19 B.C.

The students found the straightforward, fluent witnesses much more competent and credible.

On the other hand, it's not good to speak too much and not listen. Telemarketers who take this approach are less successful. The best approach? A balance between talking and listening (Grant, 2013).

PERCEIVED TRUSTWORTHINESS.   We are more willing to listen to a communicator we trust. Imagine trying to choose a laundry detergent. Online, you read (as did the participants in one experiment) a glowing description of the detergent written by a consumer protection board that collected information on the quality and affordability of products. Alternatively, you read that the description came from the detergent company, which recently changed the brand name after a product recall. In both direct survey responses and implicit judgments, participants preferred the detergent more when the information came from a trustworthy source (Smith et al., 2013). In another experiment, participants primed with trust-related words were more likely to follow the communicator's recommendation to use less tap water (Légal et al., 2012). Online reviews of products are seen as more trustworthy if they are negative—at least for practical products such as cameras (Hong & Park, 2012; Sen & Lerman, 2007). Apparently, we're more willing to believe that negative comments are honest than positive comments.

Trustworthiness is also higher if the audience believes the *communicator is not trying to persuade them.* Researchers showed British adults fake newspaper articles suggesting either that most scientists just want to inform the public about climate change, or that most scientists aim to persuade the public and governments to take action to stop climate change. Those who heard scientists aim only to inform were more likely to report more trust in climate scientists and say they would take action to help the environment by reducing water use or joining community environmental activities (Rabinovich et al., 2012). If you want to persuade someone, start with information, not arguments.

Another effective strategy is to have someone else convey your expertise. In one study, customers calling a real estate agency were told, truthfully, "I'm going to put you through to Peter. He is our head of sales and has 20 years of experience selling properties in this area." Compared to a simple call transfer, 20 percent more customers came in for in-person meetings and 15 percent more decided to use the agency (Martin et al., 2014).

Some television ads are obviously constructed to make the communicator appear both expert and trustworthy. A drug company may peddle its pain reliever using a speaker in a white lab coat, who declares confidently that most doctors recommend the product's key ingredient (which is merely aspirin). Given such peripheral cues, people who don't care enough to analyze the evidence may automatically infer that the product is special.

Thus, communicators gain credibility if they appear to be expert and trustworthy (Pornpitakpan, 2004). When we know in advance that a source is credible, we think more favorable thoughts in response to the message. If we learn the source *after* a message generates favorable thoughts, high credibility strengthens our confidence in our thinking, which also strengthens the persuasive impact of the message (Briñol et al., 2002, 2004; Tormala et al., 2006).

Is there any way to overcome people's resistance to communicators they don't trust? One study told students a supermarket chain whose manager cared only about making money was planning to target them with emails and texts. Not surprisingly, students were resistant to hearing anything from such a distrusted source. But if they then received 15 humorous texts (for example, "There are 10 types of people that understand binary. Those that do and those that don't"), their negative views of the distrusted brand disappeared (Strick et al., 2012). Humor can distract from distrust.

One thing that—surprisingly—does *not* improve persuasion is direct eye contact between the communicator and the audience. German students watched videos of speakers advocating opinions they disagreed with. They were asked to keep their gaze fixed on either the speaker's eyes or mouth. Those who focused on the eyes were less likely to change their attitudes toward the speaker's. The same result occurred in a correlational study: Students who chose to look at a speaker's eyes were less persuaded by her arguments (Chen et al., 2013).

TABLE :: 1 Six Persuasion Principles

In his book *Influence: Science and Practice,* persuasion researcher Robert Cialdini (2008) illustrates six principles that underlie human relationships and human influence. (This chapter describes the first two.)

Principle	Application
Authority: People defer to credible experts.	Establish your expertise; identify problems you have solved and people you have served.
Liking: People respond more affirmatively to those they like.	Win friends and influence people. Create bonds based on similar interest, praise freely.
Social proof: People allow the example of others to validate how to think, feel, and act.	Use "peer power"—have respected others lead the way.
Reciprocity: People feel obliged to repay in kind what they've received.	Be generous with your time and resources. What goes around, comes around.
Consistency: People tend to honor their public commitments.	Instead of telling restaurant reservation callers "Please call if you change your plans," ask, "Will you call if you change your plans?" and no-shows will drop.
Scarcity: People prize what's scarce.	Highlight genuinely exclusive information or opportunities.

ATTRACTIVENESS AND LIKING

Most of us deny that endorsements by star athletes and entertainers affect us. We know that stars are seldom knowledgeable about the products they endorse. Besides, we know the intent is to persuade us; we don't just accidentally eavesdrop on Taylor Swift discussing clothes or fragrances. Such ads are based on another characteristic of an effective communicator: **attractiveness.**

We may think we are not influenced by attractiveness or likability, but researchers have found otherwise. We're more likely to respond to those we like, a phenomenon well known to those organizing charitable solicitations and candy sales. Sure, Girl Scout cookies are tasty, but a lot fewer people would buy them if they were sold by unattractive middle-aged men instead of cute little girls. Even a mere fleeting conversation with someone is enough to increase our liking for that person and our responsiveness to his or her influence (Burger et al., 2001). Our liking may open us up to the communicator's arguments (central route persuasion), or it may trigger positive associations when we see the product later (peripheral route persuasion). As with credibility, the liking-begets-persuasion principle suggests applications (Table 1).

Attractiveness comes in several forms. *Physical attractiveness* is one. Arguments, especially emotional ones, are often more influential when they come from people we consider beautiful (Chaiken, 1979; Dion & Stein, 1978; Pallak et al., 1983). Most people understand that attractiveness matters most when people are making superficial judgments. In experiments, people exploit opportunities to use attractive communicators with audiences less inclined to think analytically (Vogel et al., 2010).

Similarity also makes for attractiveness. We tend to like people who are like us. We also are influenced by them, a fact that was harnessed by a successful antismoking campaign that featured youth appealing to other youth through ads that challenged the tobacco

attractiveness

Having qualities that appeal to an audience. An appealing communicator (often someone similar to the audience) is most persuasive on matters of subjective preference.

Attractive communicators, such as Rihanna endorsing her perfume, often trigger peripheral route persuasion. We associate their message or product with our good feelings toward the communicator, and we approve and believe.
AP Images/Press Association

Are ads made by consumers, such as this one for Doritos, more persuasive? If viewers of the ad see the ad creator as similar to them, yes.
Minneapolis Star Tribune/ZUMAPRESS/Newscom

industry about its destructiveness and its marketing practices (Krisberg, 2004). People who *act* as we do, subtly mimicking our postures, are likewise more influential. Thus, salespeople are sometimes taught to "mimic and mirror": If the customer's arms or legs are crossed, cross yours; if she smiles, smile back. (See "Research Close-Up: Experimenting with a Virtual Social Reality.")

You might have seen some consumer-generated ads online or on TV. For example, since 2006, Doritos has asked consumers to make their own 30-second commercials, and the winning ad is shown during the Super Bowl. Do these types of ads work? If people see the ad creator as a "regular guy"—someone just like them—they might. Sure enough, one experiment found that consumer-generated ads were more effective when the ad creator was seen as similar to the participant (Thompson & Malaviya, 2013).

What Is Said? The Message Content

It matters not only who says something but also *what* that person says. If you were to help organize an appeal to get people to vote for school taxes or to stop smoking or to give money to world hunger relief, you might wonder how best to persuade.

- Is a logical message more persuasive—or one that arouses emotion?
- How should you present your message?
- Should the message express your side only, or should it acknowledge and refute the opposing views?
- If people are to present both sides—say, in successive talks at a community meeting or in a political debate—is there an advantage to going first or last?
- How much information should you include?

Let's take these questions one at a time.

REASON VERSUS EMOTION

"The truth is always the strongest argument."

—Sophocles,
Phaedra, 496–406 B.C.

"Opinion is ultimately determined by the feelings and not the intellect."

—Herbert Spencer,
Social Statics, 1851

Suppose you were campaigning in support of world hunger relief. Would you best itemize your arguments and cite an array of impressive statistics? Or would you be more effective presenting an emotional approach—perhaps the compelling story of one starving child? In my [DM's] community, supporters of a proposed antidiscrimination ordinance protecting gay people wondered: To what extent might opinions be swayed by reason and evidence related to sexual orientation, and to what extent by emotion? Is what matters more *what* people know or their feelings toward *whom* they know? Of course, an argument can be both reasonable and emotional. You can marry passion and logic. Still, which is *more* influential—reason or emotion? Was Shakespeare's Lysander right: "The will of man is by his reason sway'd"? Or was Lord Chesterfield's advice wiser: "Address yourself generally to the senses, to the heart, and to the weaknesses of mankind, but rarely to their reason"?

The answer: It depends on the audience. Well-educated or analytical people are responsive to rational appeals (Cacioppo et al., 1983, 1996; Hovland et al., 1949). Thoughtful, involved audiences often travel the **central route** to persuasion; they are more responsive to reasoned arguments. Uninterested audiences more often travel the **peripheral route;** they are more affected by their liking of the communicator (Chaiken, 1980; Petty et al., 1981).

To judge from interviews before major elections, many voters are uninvolved. As we might therefore expect, Americans' voting preferences have been more predictable from emotional reactions to the candidates than from their beliefs about the candidates' traits and likely behaviors (Abelson et al., 1982). What matters is not just candidates' positions (which candidate embodies your views) but their likeability (who you want to spend time with).

research CLOSE-UP

University of California, Santa Barbara, social psychologist Jim Blascovich developed a new interest soon after walking into a colleague's virtual reality lab. Wearing a headset, Blascovich found himself facing a plank across a virtual deep pit. Although he knew that the room had no pit, he couldn't suppress his fear and bring himself to walk the plank.

The experience triggered a thought: Might social psychologists have a use for virtual environments? The experimental power of virtual human interaction is shown in an experiment by Blascovich's former associate, Jeremy Bailenson, in collaboration with graduate student Nick Yee. At Stanford University's Virtual Human Interaction Lab, 69 student volunteers fitted with a 3D virtual-reality headset found themselves across the table from a virtual human—a computer-generated man or woman who delivered a 3-minute pitch for a university security policy that required students to carry an ID at all times.

The digital person featured realistic-looking lips that moved, eyes that blinked, and a head that swayed. For half the participants, those movements mimicked, with a 4-second delay, the student's movements. If the student tilted her head and looked up, the digital chameleon would do the same. Earlier experiments with real humans had found that such mimicry fosters liking, by suggesting empathy and rapport. In Bailenson and Yee's (2005) experiment, students with a mimicking rather than a non-mimicking digital companion similarly liked the partner more. They also found the mimicker more interesting, honest, and persuasive; they paid better attention to it (looking away less often); and they were somewhat more likely to agree with the message.

For Blascovich and Bailenson (2011), such studies illustrate the potential of virtual social realities. Creating stimuli that imply others' presence costs less, requires less effort, and provides more experimental control than creating stimuli with others' actual presence. People, even trained confederates, are difficult to control. Digital people can be perfectly controlled. And exact replications become possible.

Experimenting with a virtual social reality. In an experiment by Jeremy Bailenson and Nick Yee, a person whose expressions and movements echoed one's own was both liked and persuasive.
Shawnee Baughman

It also matters how people's attitudes were formed. When people's initial attitudes are formed primarily through the peripheral route, they are more persuaded by later peripheral, emotional appeals; when their initial attitudes are formed primarily through the central route, they are more persuaded by later information-based, central route arguments (Edwards, 1990; Fabrigar & Petty, 1999). New emotions may sway an emotion-based attitude. But to change an information-based attitude, more information may be needed.

THE EFFECT OF GOOD FEELINGS. Messages also become more persuasive through association with good feelings, such as what often accompanies munching food or hearing pleasant music. Receiving money or free samples often induces people to donate

"If the jury had been sequestered in a nicer hotel, this would probably never have happened."

Good feelings help create positive attitudes.

© Frank Cotham/The New Yorker Collection/www.cartoonbank.com.

money or buy something (Cialdini, 2008). That might be why so many charities include address labels, stickers, and even coins in their mailings.

Good feelings often enhance persuasion, partly by enhancing positive thinking and partly by linking good feelings with the message (Petty et al., 1993). People who are in a good mood view the world through rose-colored glasses. But they also make faster, more impulsive decisions; they rely more on peripheral cues (Bodenhausen, 1993; Braverman, 2005; Moons & Mackie, 2007). Unhappy people ruminate more before reacting, so they are less easily swayed by weak arguments. (They also *produce* more cogent persuasive messages [Forgas, 2007].) Thus, if you can't make a strong case, you might want to put your audience in a good mood and hope they'll feel good about your message without thinking too much about it.

Knowing that humor can put people in a good mood, a Dutch research team led by Madelijn Strick (Strick et al., 2009) invited people to view ads in the vicinity of either funny cartoons (Figure 3) or the same cartoons altered to be unfunny. Their finding: Products associated with humor were better liked, as measured by an implicit attitude test, and were more often chosen.

THE EFFECT OF AROUSING FEAR.   Messages can also be effective by evoking negative emotions. When persuading people to cut down on smoking, get a tetanus shot, or drive carefully, a fear-arousing message can be potent (de Hoog et al., 2007; Muller & Johnson, 1990). By requiring cigarette makers to include graphic representations of the hazards of smoking on each pack of cigarettes, more than three dozen governments have assumed—correctly, it turns out—that showing cigarette smokers the horrible things that can happen to smokers adds to persuasiveness (O'Hegarty et al., 2007; Peters et al., 2007; Stark et al., 2008). Eight percent of Canadian youth said that the graphic warnings made smoking seem less attractive (Environics Research Group, 2006). When Australia added graphic images of sick and dying

FIGURE :: 3

In experiments at Radboud University Nijmegen, humor enhanced people's liking for products such as these.

smokers to cigarette packages in 2012, smoking rates fell nearly 5 percent (Innis, 2014). At least for now, a judge has blocked the graphic warnings from being placed on cigarette packages in the United States. (AP, 2012).

But how much fear should you arouse? Should you evoke just a little fear, lest people become so frightened that they tune out your painful message? Or should you try to scare the daylights out of them? Experiments show that, often, the more frightened and vulnerable people feel, the more they respond (de Hoog et al., 2007; Robberson & Rogers, 1988; Tannenbaum, 2013). However, there are exceptions: People who read apocalyptic warnings about global warming reacted defensively by denying the existence of global warming. The researchers concluded that the apocalyptic message went too far in challenging participants' beliefs that the world is stable, orderly, and just (Feinberg & Willer, 2011).

The effectiveness of fear-arousing communications has been applied in ads discouraging not only smoking but also risky sexual behaviors and drinking and driving. When Claude Levy-Leboyer (1988) found that attitudes toward alcohol and drinking habits among French youth were changed effectively by fear-arousing pictures, the French government incorporated such pictures into its TV spots.

One effective antismoking ad campaign offered graphic "truth" ads. In one, vans pull up outside an unnamed corporate tobacco office. Teens pile out and unload 1,200 body bags covering two city blocks. As a curious corporate suit peers out a window above, a teen shouts into a loudspeaker: "Do you know how many people tobacco kills every day? . . . We're going to leave these here for you, so you can see what 1,200 people actually look like" (Nicholson, 2007). Unlike teens who viewed a simultaneous cerebral Philip Morris ad (lecturing, "Think. Don't Smoke"), those viewing the more dramatic and edgy ad became significantly less inclined to smoke (Farrelly et al., 2002, 2008).

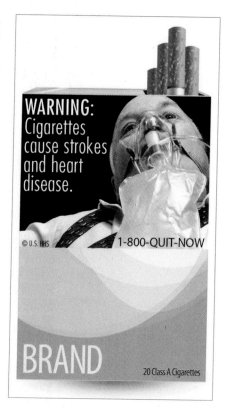

A proposed U.S. cigarette warning, shown here, uses fear arousal. In 2011, a judge blocked the requirement for such warnings.
AP Images/U.S. Food and Drug Administration

Fear-arousing communications have also been used to increase breast cancer detection behaviors, such as getting mammograms or doing breast self-exams. Sara Banks, Peter Salovey, and colleagues (1995) had women aged 40–66 years who had not obtained mammograms view an educational video on mammography. Of those who received a positively framed message (emphasizing that getting a mammogram can save your life through early detection), only half got a mammogram within 12 months. Of those who received a fear-framed message (emphasizing that not getting a mammogram can cost you your life), two-thirds got a mammogram within 12 months. People who see ultraviolent photographs of sun damaged faces—showing all of the freckles and spots destined to appear as they age—are significantly more likely to use sunscreen. Here, the intervention focuses not just on the fear of getting cancer, but the fear of looking unattractive (Williams et al., 2013).

Playing on fear works best if a message leads people not only to fear the severity and likelihood of a threatened event but also to perceive a solution and feel capable of implementing it (Devos-Comby & Salovey, 2002; Maddux & Rogers, 1983; Ruiter et al., 2001). Many ads designed to reduce sexual risks will aim both to arouse fear—"AIDS kills"—and to offer a protective strategy: Abstain, wear a condom, or save sex for a committed relationship.

These types of appeals tell people not just to be scared, but to do something about it, increasing their sense of efficacy (Ruiter et al., 2014). Andrea Morales, Eugenia Wu, and Gavan Fitzsimons (2012) theorized that fear appeals can be ineffective because they do not present a solution; in contrast, an element of disgust inspires an immediate solution of rejection and revulsion. Sure enough, they found that an ad using disgusting images (such as an anti-meth ad with a picture of someone with open sores on his face) worked better than one just arousing fear (such as a picture of a coffin).

Appeals can also focus on what you can gain by using the preventative product ("If you wear sunscreen, you'll have attractive skin") instead of one focusing on what you lose ("If you don't wear sunscreen, you'll have unattractive skin;" O'Keefe & Jensen, 2011). Gain-framed messages focus on the advantages of healthy behavior (not smoking, exercising, wearing sunscreen) are more effective than those framed in terms of loss (Gallagher & Updegraff, 2012). The principle applies in other realms as well: A global climate change article that ends by discussing possible solutions is more persuasive than one describing

Al Gore to presenters of his climate change film: "You're telling some not only inconvenient truths but hard truths, and it can be scary as hell. You're not going to get people to go with you if you scare them with fear."
—Quoted by Pooley (2007)

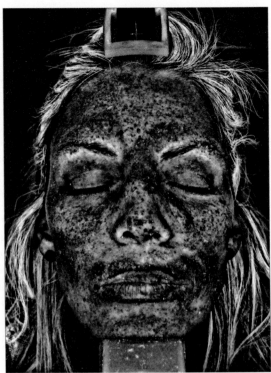

People who see ultraviolet filtered photographs showing skin damage caused by the sun are more likely to use sunscreen.
National News/ZUMA Press/Newscom

future catastrophic consequences (Feinberg & Willer, 2010). Gain messages are especially effective when they appeal to consumers' individual needs; for example, participants high in anxiety were most persuaded by a (fake) cell phone ad with the slogan "Stay safe and secure with the XPhone" (Hirsh et al., 2012).

Humor can also mitigate some negative effects of fear appeals. Imagine seeing an ad for sunscreen with a picture of a young man with facial scars from skin cancer surgery and the suggestion "Always keep it handy at beaches, pools, and parks"—an ad that manages to be scary and boring at the same time. When used in an experiment, it also wasn't very persuasive. But what if it included cartoon panels featuring people squirting sunscreen in each other's faces and spraying it on a snowman? The ad's humor defused the defensiveness the participants felt when reading the fearful skin cancer information, and this ad combining fear and humor was the most persuasive (Mukherjee & Dube, 2012).

MESSAGE CONTEXT

The context of your message—especially what immediately precedes it—can make a big difference in how persuasive it is. In one study, a confederate approached a passerby at a Polish train station and said, "Excuse me . . . Haven't you lost your wallet?" Everyone immediately checked their pockets or bags to find, to their relief, that their wallet was still in place. The confederate then explained she was selling Christmas cards for a charity, ending with "It's sublime to help people who are helpless!" Nearly 40 percent bought the cards, compared to only 10 percent who heard the appeal but had not felt the relief of still having their wallets. The researchers named this highly effective approach fear-then-relief (Dolinski & Szczuka, 2012).

Other persuasion techniques rely on the size of the request being made. Experiments suggest that if you want people to do a big favor for you, you should get them to do a small favor first. In the best-known demonstration of this **foot-in-the-door phenomenon,** researchers posing as volunteers asked Californians to permit the installation of huge, poorly lettered "Drive Carefully" signs in their front yards. Only 17 percent consented. Others were first

foot-in-the-door phenomenon
The tendency for people who have first agreed to a small request to comply later with a larger request.

approached with a small request: Would they display three-inch "Be a safe driver" window signs? Nearly all readily agreed. When approached two weeks later to allow the large, ugly signs in their front yards, 76 percent consented (Freedman & Fraser, 1966). Or imagine being a young woman walking down the street in France. You're approached by a young man who says, "Hello, I'm sorry to bother you but I was wondering if you were busy now. If not, we could have a drink together if you have some time." Only 3 percent said yes. But if he first asked them for a light for his cigarette or for directions, five times as many (15 percent) assented (Gueguen et al., 2008). Small requests can lead to bigger choices. (Hopefully, being aware of such persuasion tactics will make you less vulnerable to them.)

In this and many of the 100+ other foot-in-the-door experiments, the initial compliance—wearing a lapel pin, giving directions, signing a petition—was voluntary (Burger & Guadagno, 2003). When people commit themselves to public behaviors and perceive those acts to be their own doing, they come to believe more strongly in what they have done.

Social psychologist Robert Cialdini is a self-described "patsy." "For as long as I can recall, I've been an easy mark for the pitches of peddlers, fund-raisers, and operators of one sort or another." To better understand why one person says yes to another, he spent three years as a trainee in sales, fund-raising, and advertising organizations, discovering how they exploit "the weapons of influence." He also put those weapons to the test in simple experiments. In one, Cialdini and his collaborators (1978) explored a variation of the foot-in-the-door phenomenon by experimenting with the **lowball technique.** After the customer agrees to buy a new car because of its bargain price and begins completing the sales forms, the salesperson removes the price advantage by charging for options or by checking with a boss who disallows the deal because "we'd be losing money." Folklore has it that more lowballed customers now stick with the higher-priced purchase than would have agreed to it at the outset. Airlines and hotels use the tactic by attracting inquiries with great deals available on only a few seats or rooms; then, when those aren't available, they hope the customer will agree to a higher-priced option. Later experiments found that this works only if people verbally commit to their choice. For example, students were called and asked to donate $5 to a scholarship fund for poor students. Forty-two percent agreed. Other students were lowballed: They were at first told that if they made the donation they would receive a coupon for a free smoothie at Jamba Juice. If they agreed, the caller then said they just found out they had run out of coupons—but would the student still be willing to donate? Seventy-eight percent said yes. But if the students heard that the coupons were gone before they had a chance to say whether they would donate, only 16 percent agreed (Burger & Cornelius, 2003).

Marketing researchers and salespeople have found that the lowball technique works even when we are aware of a profit motive (Cialdini, 1988). A harmless initial commitment—returning a postcard for more information and a "free gift," agreeing to listen to an investment possibility—often moves us toward a larger commitment. Because salespeople sometimes exploited the power of those small commitments by trying to hold people to purchase agreements, many states now have laws that allow customers a few days to think over their purchases and cancel. To counter the effect of these laws, many companies use what the sales-training program of one company calls "a very important psychological aid in preventing customers from backing out of their contracts" (Cialdini, 1988, p. 78). They simply have the customer, rather than the salesperson, fill out the agreement. Having written it themselves, people usually live up to their commitment.

The foot-in-the-door phenomenon is a lesson worth remembering. Someone trying to seduce us—financially, politically, or sexually—will often sneak their foot in the door to create a momentum of compliance. The practical lesson: Before agreeing to a small request, think about what may follow.

And think, too, about what you might do next if you refuse a large request, known as the **door-in-the-face technique.** When Cialdini and his colleagues (1975) asked some of their Arizona State University students to chaperone delinquent children on a zoo trip, only 32 percent agreed to do so. With other students, though, the questioner asked if the students would commit 2 years as volunteer counselors to delinquent children. All refused (the equivalent of shutting a door in a salesperson's face). The questioner then counteroffered by asking

lowball technique
A tactic for getting people to agree to something. People who agree to an initial request will often still comply when the requester ups the ante. People who receive only the costly request are less likely to comply with it.

door-in-the-face technique
A strategy for gaining a concession. After someone first turns down a large request (the door-in-the-face), the same requester counteroffers with a more reasonable request.

if they would take the children on the zoo trip, saying, in effect, "OK, if you won't do that, would you do just this much?" With this technique, nearly twice as many—56 percent—agreed to help. If students were first asked to participate in a long-term blood donor program and then to donate blood that day, they were more likely to comply than if they were simply asked to give blood (Guéguen, 2014). Or consider finishing a meal in a restaurant when the server suggests dessert. When you say no, she offers coffee or tea. Customers first offered dessert were more likely to say yes to the next offer (Guéguen et al., 2011).

ONE-SIDED VERSUS TWO-SIDED APPEALS

Supporters of my [DM's] community's gay rights initiative faced a strategic question: Should they acknowledge and seek to refute each of the opposition's arguments? Or would that likely backfire, by planting ideas that people would remember long after forgetting the discounting? Again, common sense offers no clear answer. Acknowledging the opposing arguments might confuse the audience and weaken the case. On the other hand, a message might seem fairer and be more disarming if it recognizes the opposition's arguments.

Carol Werner and colleagues (2002) showed the disarming power of a simple two-sided message in an experiment on aluminum-can recycling. Signs added to wastebaskets in a University of Utah classroom building said, for example, "No Aluminum Cans Please!!!!! Use the Recycler Located on the First Floor, Near the Entrance." When a final persuasive message acknowledged and responded to the main counterargument—"It May Be Inconvenient. But It Is Important!!!!!!!!!!!"—recycling reached 80 percent (double the rate before any message, and more than in other message conditions).

In simulated trials, a defense case becomes more credible when the defense brings up damaging evidence before the prosecution does (Williams et al., 1993). Thus, a political candidate speaking to a politically informed group, or a community group advocating for or against gay rights, would indeed be wise to respond to the opposition. So, *if your audience will be exposed to opposing views, offer a two-sided appeal.*

Different people travel different avenues to persuasion. For optimists, positive persuasion works best ("The new plan reduces tuition in exchange for part-time university service"). For pessimists, negative persuasion is more effective ("All students will have to work part-time for the university, lest they pay out-of-state tuition") (Geers et al., 2003). We might wish that persuasion variables had simple effects. (It would make this an easier chapter to study.) Alas, most variables, note Richard Petty and Duane Wegener (1998), "have complex effects—increasing persuasion in some situations and decreasing it in others."

As students and scientists, we cherish "Occam's razor"—seeking the simplest possible principles. But if human reality is complex, well, our principles will need to have some complexity—to acknowledge interaction effects—as well.

PRIMACY VERSUS RECENCY

Imagine that you are a consultant to a politician who must soon debate another politician over a ballot proposition on bilingual education. Three weeks before the vote, each politician is to appear on the nightly news and present a prepared statement. By the flip of a coin, your side receives the choice of whether to speak first or last. Knowing that you are a former social psychology student, everyone looks to you for advice.

You mentally scan your old books and lecture notes. Would first be better? People's preconceptions control their interpretations. Moreover, a belief, once formed, is difficult to discredit, so going first could give voters ideas that would favorably bias how they perceive and interpret the second speech. Besides, people may pay more attention to what comes first. Then again, people remember recent things better. Might it really be more effective to speak last?

Your first line of reasoning predicts what is most common, a **primacy effect:** Information presented early is most persuasive. First impressions are important. For example, can you sense a difference between these two descriptions?

- John is intelligent, industrious, impulsive, critical, stubborn, and envious.
- John is envious, stubborn, critical, impulsive, industrious, and intelligent.

"Opponents fancy they refute us when they repeat their own opinion and pay no attention to ours."

—Goethe,
Maxims and Reflections, 1829

When Solomon Asch (1946) gave these sentences to college students in New York City, those who read the adjectives in the intelligent-to-envious order rated the person more positively than did those given the envious-to-intelligent order. The earlier information seemed to color their interpretation of the later information, producing the primacy effect.

Some other primacy effect examples:

- Students who read positive TripAdvisor.com reviews of a hotel before the negative reviews liked the hotel more than those who read the negative reviews first (Coker, 2012).
- In political polls and in primary election voting, candidates benefit from being listed first on the ballot (Moore, 2004b).
- Super Bowl viewers were more likely to remember brands when the commercial advertising was first in the block of commercials (Li, 2010).
- Norman Miller and Donald Campbell (1959) gave Northwestern University students a condensed transcript from an actual civil trial. They placed the plaintiff's testimony and arguments in one section and those for the defense in another. The students read both sections. When they returned a week later to declare their opinions, most sided with the information they had read first.

primacy effect
Other things being equal, information presented first usually has the most influence.

What about the opposite possibility? Would our better memory of recent information ever create a **recency effect?** We have all experienced what the book of Proverbs observed: "The one who first states a case seems right, until the other comes and cross-examines." We know from our experience (as well as from memory experiments) that today's events can temporarily outweigh significant past events. Today's blizzard makes long-term global warming seem less a threat, just as today's sweltering heat makes it seem more a threat.

recency effect
Information presented last sometimes has the most influence. Recency effects are less common than primacy effects.

To test for a possible recency effect, Miller and Campbell gave another group of students a section of testimony to read. A week later, the researchers had them read another section and then immediately state their opinions. The results were the reverse of the other experiment—a recency effect. Apparently the first section of arguments had largely faded from memory in the ensuing week.

Forgetting creates the recency effect (1) when enough time separates the two messages *and* (2) when the audience commits itself soon after the second message. When the two messages are back-to-back, followed by a time gap, the primacy effect usually occurs (Figure 4). This is especially so when the first message stimulates thinking (Haugtvedt & Wegener, 1994). What advice would you now give to the political debater?

Dana Carney and Mahzarin Banaji (2008) discovered that order can also affect simple preferences. When encountering two people or products, people tend to prefer the first presented option. For example, when offered two similar-looking pieces of bubble gum, one placed after the other on a white clipboard, 62 percent, when asked to make a snap judgment, chose the first-presented piece. Across four experiments, the findings were consistent: "First is best."

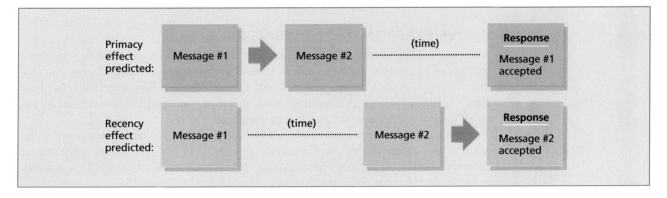

FIGURE :: 4

Primacy Effect Versus Recency Effect

When two persuasive messages are back-to-back and the audience then responds at some later time, the first message has the advantage (primacy effect). When the two messages are separated in time and the audience responds soon after the second message, the second message has the advantage (recency effect).

In 2012, the U.S. Republican Party convention was immediately followed by the Democratic Party convention, after which there was a 2-month time gap before the election. If experiments on primacy and recency are applicable, which party would benefit most from this timing?
Left: Joe Raedle/Getty Images; *Right:* ZUMA Press, Inc. / Alamy

In answer to the list of questions at the beginning of this section, the best advice for persuasion is the following:

- Use logic or emotion, depending on the audience and the message.
- Ask a small favor before making a big request.
- Offer two-sided messages that challenge arguments against your message.
- Go first or last for best results.

How Is It Said? The Channel of Communication

channel of communication

The way the message is delivered—whether face-to-face, in writing, on film, or in some other way.

For persuasion, there must be communication. And for communication, there must be a **channel:** a face-to-face appeal, a written sign or document, a media advertisement.

Commonsense psychology places faith in the power of written words. How do we try to get people to attend a campus event? We post notices. How do we get drivers to slow down and keep their eyes on the road? We put "Drive Carefully" messages on billboards. How do we discourage students from dropping trash on campus? We post antilitter messages on campus bulletin boards.

ACTIVE EXPERIENCE OR PASSIVE RECEPTION?

Are spoken appeals more persuasive? Not necessarily. Those of us who speak publicly, as teachers or persuaders, often become so enamored of our spoken words that we overestimate their power. Ask college students what aspect of their college experience has been most valuable or what they remember from their first year, and few, we are sad to say, recall the brilliant lectures that we faculty remember giving.

Written and visual appeals are both passive, and thus have similar hurdles to overcome. Many are relatively ineffective. For example, only 1 out of 1,000 online ads result in someone clicking on the link. Yet the ads do have an effect: When a website was advertised, traffic increased 65% over the week (Fulgoni & Mörn, 2009).

With such power, can the media help a wealthy political candidate buy an election? In the United States, the candidate with more money wins 91 percent of the time. Winning candidates for Congress outspent their opponents 2 to 1—$2.3 million compared to $1.1 million (Lowery, 2014). Advertising exposure helps make an unfamiliar candidate into a familiar one. Mere exposure to unfamiliar stimuli breeds liking. Moreover, *mere repetition* can make things believable (Dechêne et al., 2010; Moons et al., 2009).

Researcher Hal Arkes (1990) calls such findings "scary." As political manipulators know, believable lies can displace hard truths. Repeated clichés can cover complex realities. Even repeatedly saying that a consumer claim is *false* can, when the discounting is presented amid other true and false claims, lead older adults later to misremember it as *true* (Skurnik et al., 2005). As they forget the discounting, their lingering familiarity with the claim can make it seem believable. In the political realm, even correct information may fail to discount implanted misinformation (Bullock, 2006; Nyhan & Reifler, 2008). Thus, in the 2012 U.S. presidential election, false rumors—that Obama was born outside the United States, that Mitt Romney didn't pay taxes for 10 years—resisted efforts at disconfirmation, which sometimes helped make the falsehood seem familiar and thus true. Overall, retractions of previously provided information rarely work—people tend to remember the original story, not the retraction (Ecker et al., 2011; Lewandowsky et al., 2012). In the romantic comedy *When Harry Met Sally*, Harry says he'll take back a statement that offended Sally. "You can't take it back—it's already out there," Sally replies. Courtroom lawyers understand this, which is why they will take the risk of saying something that might be retracted, knowing the jury will remember it anyway. If you're trying to counteract a falsehood, research suggests you should provide an alternative story that's simple—and repeat it several times (Ecker et al., 2011; Schwarz et al., 2007).

Mere repetition of a statement also serves to increase its fluency—the ease with which it spills off our tongue—which increases believability (McGlone & Tofighbakhsh, 2000). Other factors, such as rhyming, further increase fluency and believability. "Haste makes waste" may say essentially the same thing as "rushing causes mistakes," but it seems more true. Whatever makes for fluency (familiarity, rhyming) also makes for credibility.

Because passively received appeals are sometimes effective and sometimes not, can we specify in advance the issues most amenable to persuasion? There is a simple rule: The more familiar people are with an issue, the less persuadable they are. On minor issues, such as which brand of aspirin to buy, it's easy to demonstrate the media's power. On more familiar and important issues, such as attitudes about a lengthy and controversial war, persuading people is like trying to push a piano uphill. It is not impossible, but one shove won't do it.

Active experience also strengthens attitudes. When we act, we amplify the idea behind what we've done, especially when we feel responsible. What is more, attitudes more often endure and influence our behavior when rooted in our own experience. Compared with attitudes formed passively, experience-based attitudes are more confident, more stable, and less vulnerable to attack. That's one reason why so many companies now aim to advertise through consumer-generated ads, viral videos, Facebook pages, Twitter feeds, and online games—consumers who have interactive experiences with brands and products are more engaged than those who merely see or hear advertisements (Huang et al., 2013). Someone who shares a viral video with others will remember the experience much longer than someone who saw the same video as a TV commercial. Interactive websites also seem to be more effective. In one study, Dutch students viewed one of two websites for the fictional company HappyBev: one that simply displayed its corporate message and another that allowed users to comment on the message and then displayed those comments. Those who appreciated the interactivity of the comment-enabled site saw the company as more credible and identified with it more (Eberle et al., 2013).

PERSONAL VERSUS MEDIA INFLUENCE

Persuasion studies demonstrate that the major influence on us is not the media but our contact with people. Modern selling strategies seek to harness the power of word-of-mouth personal influence through "viral marketing," "creating a buzz," and "seeding" sales (Walker, 2004). The *Harry Potter* series was not expected to be a best seller (the first book in the series had a first printing of 500 copies). It was kids talking to other kids that made it so.

During the 2010 midterm elections, people who saw photos of their friends voting on Facebook were more likely to vote (Bond et al., 2012). A few months before a fall 1998 election, researchers sent people to knock on doors personally and encourage people to vote. It worked: nearly 60 percent voted, compared to only 45 percent of those not contacted (Gerber & Green, 1999). In Kenya, untreated tap water causes disease and death, especially among children. Yet few families treated their water until a nonprofit

"Ah, that is always the way with you men; you believe nothing the first time, and it is foolish enough to let mere repetition convince you of what you consider in itself unbelievable."

—George MacDonald, *Phantastes,* 1858

"You do realize, you will never make a fortune out of writing children's books?"

—J. K. Rowling's Literary Agent before Release of *Harry Potter and the Sorcerer's Stone,* 1998

organization enlisted one person in each community to refill the communal chlorine tank and teach everyone about the importance of treating their water (Coster, 2014). Personal contact persuades.

In a field experiment, researchers tried to reduce the frequency of heart disease among middle-aged adults in three small California cities. To check the relative effectiveness of personal and media influence, they interviewed and medically examined 1,200 participants before the project began and at the end of each of the following 3 years. Residents of Tracy, California, received no persuasive appeals other than those occurring in their regular media. In Gilroy, California, a 2-year multimedia campaign used TV, radio, newspapers, and direct mail to teach people about coronary risk and what they could do to reduce it. In Watsonville, California, this media campaign was supplemented by personal contacts with two-thirds of those participants whose blood pressure, weight, and age put them in a high-risk group. Using behavior-modification principles, the researchers helped the Watsonville participants set specific goals and reinforced their successes (Farquhar et al., 1977; Maccoby, 1980; Maccoby & Alexander, 1980).

As Figure 5 shows, after 1, 2, and 3 years, the high-risk participants in Tracy (the control town) were at about as much at risk as before. High-risk participants in Gilroy, which was deluged with media appeals, improved their health habits and decreased their risk somewhat. Those in Watsonville, who received personal contacts as well as the media campaign, changed most.

MEDIA INFLUENCE: THE TWO-STEP FLOW.   Although face-to-face influence is usually greater than media influence, we should not underestimate the media's power. Those who personally influence our opinions must get their ideas from some source, and often their sources are the media. Elihu Katz (1957) observed that many of the media's effects operate in a **two-step flow of communication:** from media to opinion leaders to everyone else. In any large group, it is these *opinion leaders* and trendsetters—"the influentials"—that marketers and politicians seek to woo (Keller & Berry, 2003). Opinion leaders are individuals perceived as experts. They may include talk show hosts and editorial columnists; doctors, teachers, and scientists; and people in all walks of life who have made it their business to absorb information and to inform their friends and family. If I [DM] want to evaluate computer equipment, I defer to the opinions of my sons, who get many of their ideas from what they read online. Sell them and you will sell me.

two-step flow of communication

The process by which media influence often occurs through opinion leaders, who in turn influence others.

FIGURE :: 5

Percentage change from baseline (0) in coronary risk after 1, 2, or 3 years of health education.
Source: Data from Maccoby (1980).

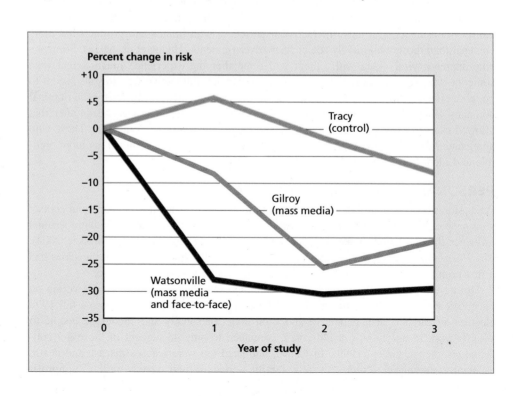

The two-step flow of information influences the drugs your doctor describes, reports a Stanford School of Business research team (Nair et al., 2008). Doctors look to opinion leaders within their social network—often a university hospital-based specialist—when deciding what drugs to favor. For more than 9 in 10 doctors, this influence comes through personal contact. The largest drug companies know that opinion leaders drive sales, and therefore they target about one-third of their marketing dollars on these influential people.

The two-step flow model reminds us that media influences penetrate the culture in subtle ways. Even if the media had little direct effect on people's attitudes, they could still have a major indirect effect. Those rare children who grow up without watching television do not grow up beyond television's influence. Unless they live as hermits, they will join in TV-imitative play on the schoolground. They will ask their parents for the TV-related toys their friends have. They will beg or demand to watch their friends' favorite programs, and they will do so when visiting friends' homes. Parents can just say no, but they cannot switch off television's influence.

COMPARING MEDIA.   Lumping together all media, from mass mailings to television to social networking, oversimplifies. Studies comparing different media find that the more lifelike the medium, the more persuasive its message. Thus, the order of persuasiveness seems to be: live (face-to-face), videotaped, audiotaped, and written.

However, messages are best *comprehended* and *recalled* when written. Comprehension is one of the first steps in the persuasion process (recall Figure 2). So Shelly Chaiken and Alice Eagly (1976) reasoned that if a message is difficult to comprehend, persuasion should be greatest when the message is written, because readers will be able to work through the message at their own pace. The researchers gave University of Massachusetts students easy or difficult messages in writing, on audiotape, or on videotape. Figure 6 displays their results: Difficult messages were indeed most persuasive when written; easy messages, when videotaped. The TV medium takes control of the pacing of the message away from the recipients. By drawing attention to the communicator and away from the message itself, TV also encourages people to focus on peripheral cues, such as the communicator's attractiveness (Chaiken & Eagly, 1983).

THE INFLUENCE OF ADULTS ON CHILDREN.   Communication flows from adults to children—although as most parents and teachers can tell you, getting them to listen is not always easy. Your parents likely taught you which foods are healthy and which aren't. But how effective were their appeals? In one experiment, children read one of three versions of a story about a girl who ate wheat crackers—one in which she "felt strong and healthy," another in which she "thought the crackers were yummy, and she was happy," and a third with no additional description. The children then had the opportunity to eat some of the crackers. Guess who ate the most? The children who read that another child

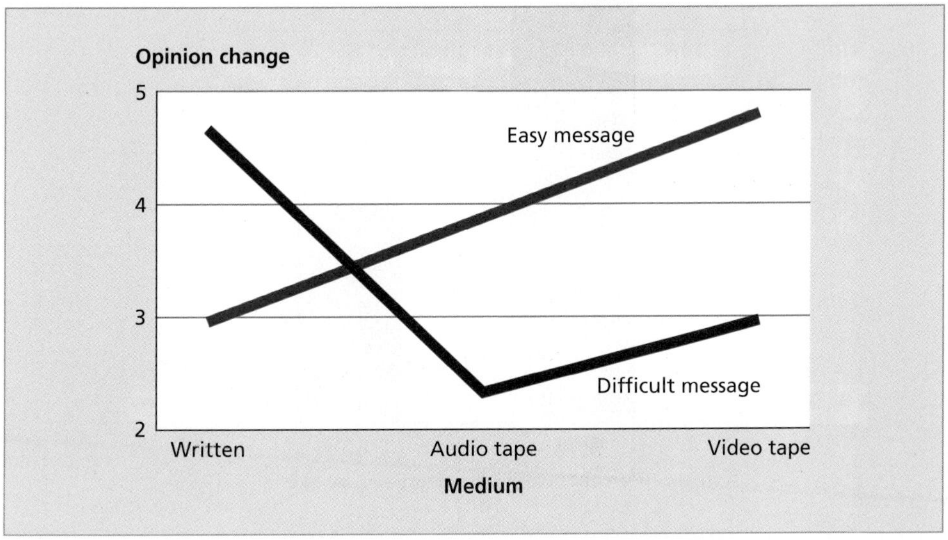

In study after study, most people agree that mass media influence attitudes—other people's attitudes, but not their own (Duck et al., 1995).

FIGURE :: 6

Easy-to-understand messages are most persuasive when videotaped. Difficult messages are most persuasive when written. Thus, the difficulty of the message interacts with the medium to determine persuasiveness.
Source: Data from Chaiken & Eagly (1976).

ate them—and nothing else. Those who heard they were yummy ate fewer, and those who heard they were healthy ate less than half as many. The same was true for younger children given messages about carrots (Maimaran & Fishbach, 2014). The lesson: When you're trying to get children to eat healthy food, just give it to them, and forget about saying anything else. If you have to say something, say it's yummy, not healthy.

To Whom Is It Said? The Audience

Persuasion varies with who . . . says what . . . by what medium . . . to whom. Let's consider two audience characteristics: age and thoughtfulness.

HOW OLD ARE THEY?

As evident during the 2012 U.S. presidential campaign—with Mitt Romney the decided favorite of older voters and Barack Obama of younger voters—people's social and political attitudes correlate with their age. Social psychologists offer two possible explanations for age differences:

- A *life cycle explanation:* Attitudes change (for example, become more conservative) as people grow older.
- A *generational explanation:* Attitudes do *not* change; older people largely hold onto the attitudes they adopted when they were young. Because these attitudes are different from those being adopted by young people today, a generation gap develops. (Figure 7 offers one example of a large generation gap.).

The evidence mostly supports the generational explanation. In surveys and resurveys of groups of younger and older people over several years, the attitudes of older people usually show less change than do those of young people. As David Sears (1979, 1986) put it, researchers have "almost invariably found generational rather than life cycle effects."

The teens and early twenties are important formative years (Koenig et al., 2008; Krosnick & Alwin, 1989). Attitudes are changeable then, and the attitudes formed tend to stabilize through middle adulthood. Gallup interviews of more than 120,000 people suggest that political attitudes formed at age 18—relatively Republican-favoring during the popular Reagan era, and more Democratic-favoring during the unpopular George W. Bush era—tend to last (Silver, 2009). Young adulthood is also the time when people are more susceptible to joining cults—entities also influenced by several other elements of persuasion (See Focus On: Cults and Persuasion).

FIGURE :: 7

A generation gap in 2014 U.S. attitudes regarding same-sex marriage, as reported by Gallup. A "life cycle" explanation of generational differences in attitudes suggests that people become more conservative with age. A "generational explanation" suggests that each generation tends to hold on to attitudes formed during the adolescent and early adult years. Adapted from http://www.gallup.com/poll/169640/sex-marriage-support-reaches-newhigh.aspx.

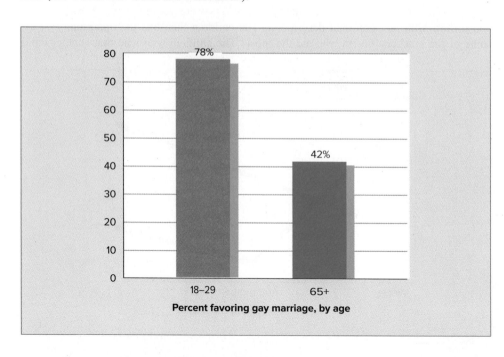

Percent favoring gay marriage, by age

focus
ON   Cults and Persuasion

On March 22, 1997, Marshall Herff Applewhite and 37 of his disciples decided the time had come to shed their bodies—mere "containers"—and be whisked up to a UFO trailing the Hale-Bopp Comet, en route to heaven's gate. So they put themselves to sleep by mixing phenobarbital into pudding or applesauce, washing it down with vodka, and then fixing plastic bags over their heads so they would suffocate in their slumber. Previous years saw other cults gather followers, often to fatal ends, including David Koresh's Waco compound that burned to the ground in 1993 and the Unification Church disciples of Jim Jones who killed themselves with cyanide-laced Kool-Aid in 1978.

What persuades people to leave behind their former beliefs and join a cult? Many people might guess that cult members are gullible, unbalanced people, but the social psychological principles of persuasion offer a different perspective—suggesting that the same strategies used by politicians and advertisers work, with larger consequences, in recruiting people to cults. Consider the following:

- Unification Church recruiters would invite people to a dinner and then to a weekend of warm fellowship and discussions of philosophies of life. At the weekend retreat, they would encourage the attendees to join them in songs, activities, and discussion. Potential converts were then urged to sign up for longer training retreats. The pattern in cults is for the activities to become gradually more arduous, culminating in having recruits solicit contributions and attempt to convert others. In other words, they used the foot-in-the-door technique.

- Successful cults typically have a charismatic leader—someone who attracts and directs the members. As in experiments on persuasion, a credible communicator is someone the audience perceives as expert and trustworthy—for example, as "Father" Moon.

Jim Jones used "psychic readings" to establish his credibility. Newcomers were asked to identify themselves as they entered the church before services. Then one of his aides would quickly call the person's home and say, "Hi. We're doing a survey, and we'd like to ask you some questions." During the service, one ex-member recalled, Jones would call out the person's name and say:

> Have you ever seen me before? Well, you live in such and such a place, your phone number is such and such, and in your living room you've got this, that, and the other, and on your sofa you've got such and such a pillow. . . . Now do you remember me ever being in your house? (Conway & Siegelman, 1979, p. 234)

- The audience matters. Potential converts are often at turning points in their lives, facing personal crises, or vacationing or living away from home. They have needs; the cult offers them an answer (Lofland & Stark, 1965; Singer, 1979). Gail Maeder joined Heaven's Gate after her T-shirt shop had failed. David Moore joined when he was 19, just out of high school, and searching

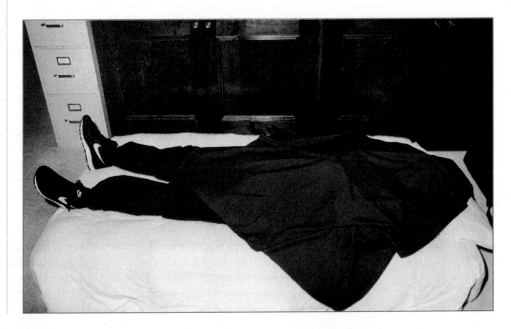

One of 37 suicide victims seeking heaven's gate.
AP Images/HO

for direction. Times of social and economic upheaval are especially conducive to someone who can make apparent simple sense out of the confusion (O'Dea, 1968; Sales, 1972).

Most of those who have carried out suicide bombings in the Middle East (and other places such as Bali, Madrid, and London) were, likewise, young men at the transition between adolescence and adult maturity. Like cult recruits, they come under the influence of authoritative, religiously oriented communicators.

These compelling voices indoctrinate them into seeing themselves as "living martyrs" whose fleeting moment of self-destruction will be their portal into bliss and heroism. To overcome the will to survive, each candidate makes public commitments—creating a will, writing good-bye letters, making a farewell video—that create a psychological point of no return (Kruglanski & Golec de Zavala, 2005). All of this typically transpires in the relative isolation of small cells, with group influences that fan hatred for the enemy.

Young people might therefore be advised to choose their social influences—the groups they join, the media they imbibe, the roles they adopt—carefully. James Davis (2004) discovered, for example, that Americans reaching age 16 during the 1960s have, ever since, been more politically liberal than average. Much as tree rings can, years later, reveal the telltale marks laid down by a drought, so attitudes decades later may reveal the events, such as the Vietnam War and civil rights era of the 1960s, that shaped the adolescent and early twenties mind. For many people, these years are a critical period for the formation of attitudes and values.

Vermont's Bennington College provides a striking example from earlier decades. During the late 1930s and early 1940s, Bennington students—women from privileged, conservative families—encountered a free-spirited environment led by a left-leaning young faculty. One of those professors, social psychologist Theodore Newcomb, later denied that the faculty was trying to make "good little liberals" out of their students. Yet the students became much more liberal than was typical of those from their social backgrounds. Moreover, attitudes formed at Bennington endured. A half-century later, the Bennington women, now 70ish, voted Democratic by a three-to-one margin in the 1984 presidential election, whereas other college-educated women who were in their seventies were voting Republican by a three-to-one margin (Alwin et al., 1991). The views embraced at an impressionable time had survived a lifetime of wider experience.

Adolescent and early adult experiences are formative partly because they make deep and lasting impressions. When Howard Schuman and Jacqueline Scott (1989) asked people to name the one or two most important national or world events of the previous half-century, most recalled events from their teens or early twenties. For those who experienced the Great Depression or World War II as 16- to 24-year-olds, those events overshadowed the civil rights movement and the Kennedy assassination of the early 1960s, the Vietnam War and moon landing of the late 1960s, and the women's movement of the 1970s—all of which were imprinted on the minds of those who experienced them as 16- to 24-year-olds. We may therefore expect that today's young adults will include events such as the 2007–2009 economic recession or the capture of Osama Bin Laden as memorable turning points.

That is not to say that older adults are inflexible. People born in the 1930s (often known as the Silent Generation for their conservative outlook) grew in their approval of modern cultural ideas such as premarital sex and working mothers as they aged from their 40s to their 70s (Donnelly et al., 2015; Twenge et al., 2015). Given the cultural shift toward more sexual freedom and more equal gender roles between the 1970s and the 2010s, these middle-aged people had apparently changed with the times. Few of us are utterly uninfluenced by changing cultural norms. Moreover, near the end of their lives, older adults may again become more susceptible to attitude change, perhaps because of a decline in the strength of their attitudes (Visser & Krosnick, 1998). Or perhaps, as some research suggests, resistance to attitude change peaks in midlife because that's when people tend to occupy higher power social roles, which call forth resoluteness (Eaton et al., 2009).

WHAT ARE THEY THINKING?

The crucial aspect of central route persuasion is not the message but the responses it evokes in a person's mind. Our minds are not sponges that soak up whatever pours over them. If a message summons favorable thoughts, it persuades us. If it provokes us to think of contrary arguments, we remain unpersuaded.

FOREWARNED IS FOREARMED—IF YOU CARE ENOUGH TO COUNTER-ARGUE.   What circumstances breed counterargument? One is knowing that someone is going to try to persuade you. If you had to tell your family that you wanted to drop out of school, you would likely anticipate their pleading with you to stay. So you might develop a list of arguments to counter every conceivable argument they might make—and you'd then be less likely to be persuaded by them (Freedman & Sears, 1965). In courtrooms, too, defense attorneys sometimes forewarn juries about prosecution evidence to come. With mock juries, such "stealing thunder" neutralizes its impact (Dolnik et al., 2003).

DISTRACTION DISARMS COUNTERARGUING.   Persuasion is also enhanced by a distraction that inhibits counterarguing (Festinger & Maccoby, 1964; Keating & Brock, 1974; Osterhouse & Brock, 1970). Participants who read a message while also watching a video (the common modern experience known as "multitasking") were less likely to counterargue (Jeong & Hwang, 2012). Political ads often use this technique. The words promote the candidate, and the visual images keep us occupied so we don't analyze the words. Distraction is especially effective when the message is simple (Harkins & Petty, 1982; Regan & Cheng, 1973). Sometimes, though, distraction precludes our processing an ad. That helps explain why ads viewed during violent or sexual TV programs are so often forgotten and ineffective (Bushman, 2005, 2007).

UNINVOLVED AUDIENCES USE PERIPHERAL CUES.   Recall the two routes to persuasion—the central route of systematic thinking and the peripheral route of heuristic cues. Like a road that winds through a small town, the central route has starts and stops as the mind analyzes arguments and formulates responses. Like the freeway that bypasses the town, the peripheral route speeds people to their destination. Analytical people—those with a high **need for cognition**—enjoy thinking carefully and prefer central routes (Cacioppo et al., 1996). People who like to conserve their mental resources—those with a low need for cognition—are quicker to respond to such peripheral cues as the communicator's attractiveness and the pleasantness of the surroundings. In one study, students

"To be forewarned and therefore forearmed . . . is eminently rational if our belief is true; but if our belief is a delusion, this same forewarning and forearming would obviously be the method whereby the delusion rendered itself incurable."

—C. S. Lewis,
Screwtape Proposes a Toast, 1965

need for cognition
The motivation to think and analyze. Assessed by agreement with items such as "The notion of thinking abstractly is appealing to me" and disagreement with items such as "I only think as hard as I have to."

Are you more focused on the information on this website or its design? Your answer might depend on how interested you are in visiting San Francisco.
NetPhotos / Alamy

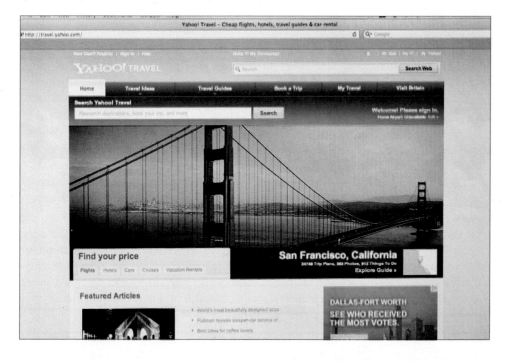

were asked to imagine they were planning a spring break trip and were trying to decide on a destination. They then looked at the tourism websites of the five most-visited U.S. cities (Los Angeles, New York, San Francisco, Orlando, and Miami). Students who were more interested in a particular destination were more persuaded by the focus on the information provided on the website (the central route), while those who were less interested focused more on the website's design (the peripheral route [Tang et al., 2012]).

This simple theory—that *what we think in response to a message is crucial,* especially if we are motivated and able to think about it—has generated many predictions, most of which have been confirmed (Axsom et al., 1987; Haddock et al., 2008; Harkins & Petty, 1987). Many experiments have explored ways to stimulate people's thinking,

- by using *rhetorical questions;*
- by presenting *multiple speakers* (for example, having each of three speakers give one argument instead of one speaker giving three);
- by making people *feel responsible* for evaluating or passing along the message;
- by *repeating* the message; or
- by getting people's *undistracted attention.*

The consistent finding with each of these techniques: *Stimulating thinking makes strong messages more persuasive and* (because of counterarguing) *weak messages less persuasive.*

The theory also has practical implications. Effective communicators care not only about their images and their messages but also about how their audience is likely to react. The best instructors get students to think actively. They ask rhetorical questions, provide intriguing examples, and challenge students with difficult problems. Such techniques foster the central route to persuasion. In classes in which the instruction is less engaging, you can still provide your own central processing. If you think about the material and elaborate on the arguments, you are likely to do better in the course.

SUMMING UP: What Are the Elements of Persuasion?

- What makes persuasion effective? Researchers have explored four factors: the communicator (who says it), the message (what is said), the *channel* (how it is said), and the audience (to whom it is said).

- *Credible* communicators tend to be persuasive. People who speak unhesitatingly, who talk fast, and who look listeners straight in the eye seem more credible. So do people who argue against their own self-interest. An *attractive* communicator is especially effective on matters of taste and personal values.

- Associating a message with good feelings makes it more convincing. People often make quicker, less reflective judgments while in good moods. Fear-arousing messages can also be effective, especially if the recipients feel vulnerable but can take protective action.

- People are more likely to do a small favor if they are asked to do a big favor first (the *door-in-the-face technique*) and are more likely to agree to a big favor if they agree to a small favor first (the *foot-in-the-door phenomenon*). A variation on the foot-in-the door phenomenon is the *lowball technique,* in which a salesperson offers a low price, elicits a commitment from the buyer, and then increases the price.

- How discrepant a message should be from an audience's existing opinions depends on the communicator's credibility. And whether a one- or two-sided message is more persuasive depends on whether the audience already agrees with the message, is unaware of opposing arguments, and is unlikely later to consider the opposition.

- When two sides of an issue are included, the *primacy effect* often makes the first message more persuasive. If a time gap separates the presentations, the more likely result will be a *recency effect* in which the second message prevails.

- Another important consideration is how the message is communicated. Usually, face-to-face appeals work best. Print media can be effective for complex messages. The mass media can be effective when the issue is minor or unfamiliar, and when the media reach opinion leaders.

- Finally, it matters who receives the message. The age of the audience makes a difference; young people's attitudes are more subject to change. What does the audience think while receiving a message? Do they think favorable thoughts? Do they counterargue? Were they forewarned?

HOW CAN PERSUASION BE RESISTED?

Identify some tactics for *resisting* influence. How might we prepare people to resist unwanted persuasion?

Martial arts trainers devote as much time teaching defensive blocks, deflections, and parries as they do teaching attack. "On the social influence battlefield," note Brad Sagarin and colleagues (2002), researchers have focused more on persuasive attack than on defense. Being persuaded comes naturally, Daniel Gilbert and colleagues (1990, 1993) report. It is easier to accept persuasive messages than to doubt them. To *understand* an assertion (say, that lead pencils are a health hazard) is to *believe* it—at least temporarily, until one actively undoes the initial, automatic acceptance. If a distracting event prevents the undoing, the acceptance lingers.

Still, blessed with logic, information, and motivation, we do resist falsehoods. If the repair person's uniform and the doctor's title have intimidated us into unthinking agreement, we can rethink our habitual responses to authority. We can seek more information before committing time or money. We can question what we don't understand.

Strengthening Personal Commitment

The "Conformity" chapter presented another way to resist: Before encountering others' judgments, make a public commitment to your position. Having stood up for your convictions, you will become less susceptible (or, should we say, less "open") to what others have to say. In mock civil trials, straw polls of jurors can foster a hardening of expressed positions, leading to more deadlocks (Davis et al., 1993).

DEVELOPING COUNTERARGUMENTS

There is a second reason a mild attack might build resistance. Like inoculations against disease, even weak arguments will prompt counterarguments, which are then available for a stronger attack. William McGuire wondered: Could we inoculate people against persuasion much as we inoculate them against a virus? Is there such a thing as **attitude inoculation?** He found that there was: When participants were "immunized" by writing an essay refuting a mild attack on a belief, they were better able to resist a more powerful attack later (McGuire, 1964).

Robert Cialdini and colleagues (2003) agree that appropriate counterarguments are a great way to resist persuasion. But they wondered how to bring them to mind in response to an opponent's ads. The answer, they suggest, is a "poison parasite" defense—one that combines a poison (strong counterarguments) with a parasite (retrieval cues that bring those arguments to mind when seeing the opponent's ads). In their studies, participants

attitude inoculation
Exposing people to weak attacks upon their attitudes so that when stronger attacks come, they will have refutations available.

A "poison parasite" ad.
Rachel Epstein / The Image Works

who viewed a familiar political ad were least persuaded by it when they had earlier seen counterarguments overlaid on a replica of the ad. Seeing the ad again thus also brought to mind the puncturing counterarguments. Antismoking ads have effectively done this, for example, by re-creating a "Marlboro Man" commercial set in the rugged outdoors but now showing a coughing, decrepit cowboy.

Real-Life Applications: Inoculation Programs

Could attitude inoculation work outside the laboratory by preparing people to resist unwanted persuasion? Applied research on smoking prevention and consumer education offers encouraging answers.

INOCULATING CHILDREN AGAINST PEER PRESSURE TO SMOKE

Consider how laboratory research findings can lead to practical applications. One research team had high school students "inoculate" seventh-graders against peer pressures to smoke (McAlister et al., 1980). The seventh-graders were taught to respond to advertisements with counterarguments. They also acted in role plays in which, after being called "chicken" for not taking a cigarette, they answered with statements such as "I'd be a real chicken if I smoked just to impress you." After several of these sessions during the seventh and eighth grades, the inoculated students were half as likely to begin smoking as were uninoculated students at another middle school—one that had an identical parental smoking rate (Figure 8).

Other research teams have confirmed that inoculation procedures, sometimes supplemented by other life-skill training, reduce teen smoking (Botvin et al., 1995, 2008; Evans et al., 1984; Flay et al., 1985). Most newer efforts emphasize strategies for resisting social pressure. One study exposed sixth- to eighth-graders to antismoking films or to information about smoking, together with role plays of student-generated ways of refusing a cigarette (Hirschman & Leventhal, 1989). A year and a half later, 31 percent of those who watched the antismoking films had taken up smoking. Among those who role-played refusing, only 19 percent had begun smoking.

Antismoking and drug education programs apply other persuasion principles, too. They use attractive peers to communicate information. They trigger the students' own cognitive processing ("Here's something you might want to think about"). They get the students to make a public commitment (by making a rational decision about smoking and then announcing it, along with their reasoning, to their classmates). Some of these smoking-prevention programs require only 2–6 hours of class, using prepared printed materials or

FIGURE :: 8

The percentage of cigarette smokers at an "inoculated" middle school was much less than at a matched control school using a more typical smoking education program. *Source:* Data from McAlister et al. (1980), Telch et al. (1981).

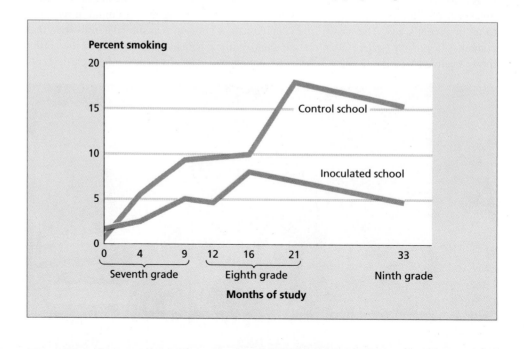

videotapes. Today, any school district or teacher wanting to use the social psychological approach to smoking prevention can do so easily, inexpensively, and with the hope of significant reductions in future smoking rates and associated health costs. These appeals and others seem to have worked: Only 14 percent of 12th graders in the United States reported smoking tobacco cigarettes in the last month in 2014, down from 38 percent in 1976. The new concern is e-cigarettes, which 18 percent of 12th graders used in the last month in 2014 (Johnston et al., 2015).

INOCULATING CHILDREN AGAINST THE INFLUENCE OF ADVERTISING

Belgium, Denmark, Greece, Ireland, Italy, and Sweden all restrict advertising that targets children (McGuire, 2002). In the United States, notes Robert Levine in *The Power of Persuasion: How We're Bought and Sold,* the average child sees more than 10,000 commercials a year. "Two decades ago," he notes, "children drank twice as much milk as soda. Thanks to advertising, the ratio is now reversed" (2003, p. 16).

Hoping to restrain advertising's influence, researchers have studied how to immunize young children against the effects of television commercials. Their research was prompted partly by studies showing that children, especially those under age 8 years, (1) have trouble distinguishing commercials from programs and fail to grasp their persuasive intent, (2) trust television advertising rather indiscriminately, and (3) desire and badger their parents for advertised products (Adler et al., 1980; Feshbach, 1980; Palmer & Dorr, 1980). Children, it seems, are an advertiser's dream: gullible, vulnerable, and an easy sell.

Armed with these findings, citizens' groups have given the advertisers of such products a chewing out (Moody, 1980): "When a sophisticated advertiser spends millions to sell unsophisticated, trusting children an unhealthy product, this can only be called exploitation." In "Mothers' Statement to Advertisers" (Motherhood Project, 2001), a broad coalition of women echoed this outrage:

> For us, our children are priceless gifts. For you, our children are customers, and childhood is a "market segment" to be exploited. . . . The line between meeting and creating consumer needs and desire is increasingly being crossed, as your battery of highly trained and creative experts study, analyze, persuade, and manipulate our children. . . . The driving messages are "You deserve a break today," "Have it your way," "Follow your instincts. Obey your thirst," "Just Do It," "No Boundaries," "Got the Urge?" These [exemplify] the dominant message of advertising and marketing: that life is about selfishness, instant gratification, and materialism.

"In general, my children refuse to eat anything that hasn't danced on television."
—Erma Bombeck

"When it comes to targeting kid consumers, we at General Mills follow the Procter and Gamble model of 'cradle to grave.' . . . We believe in getting them early and having them for life."
—Wayne Chilicki, General Mills (Quoted by Motherhood Project, 2001)

Children are the advertiser's dream. Researchers have therefore studied ways to inoculate children against the more than 10,000 ads they see each year, many as they are glued to a TV set.
BananaStock/Punchstock

Children may not realize that online games are actually advertisements—or that cereal with the word "fruit" in its name doesn't actually contain any fruit.

With much advertising moving online, new concerns arise. For example, young children may not recognize that online games they play (such as "Treasure Map Hunt" for Fruit Loops cereal or "Happy Sounds" on the MacDonald's website) are actually advertising—often for unhealthy food (An & Kang, 2013). In one experiment, 7- and 8-year-old children who played these "advergames" were more likely to choose foods higher in sugar and fat than those who did not play the games (Mallinckrodt & Mizerski, 2007).

On the other side are the commercial interests. They claim that ads allow parents to teach their children consumer skills and, more important, finance children's television programs. In the United States, the Federal Trade Commission has been in the middle, pushed by research findings and political pressures while trying to decide whether to place new constraints on TV ads for unhealthy foods and for R-rated movies aimed at underage youth.

Meanwhile, researchers have found that inner-city seventh-graders who are able to think critically about ads—who have "media resistance skills"—also better resist peer pressure as eighth-graders and are less likely to drink alcohol as ninth-graders (Epstein & Botvin, 2008). Researchers have also wondered whether children can be taught to resist deceptive ads. In one such effort, Los Angeles–area elementary schoolchildren received three half-hour lessons in analyzing commercials. The children were inoculated by viewing ads and discussing them. For example, after viewing a toy ad, they were immediately given the toy and challenged to make it do what they had just seen in the commercial (Feshbach, 1980; S. Cohen, 1980). Such experiences helped breed a more realistic understanding of commercials.

Consumer advocates worry that inoculation may be insufficient. Better to clean the air than to wear gas masks. It is no surprise, then, that parents resent it when advertisers market products to children, then place them on lower store shelves where kids will see them, pick them up, and nag and whine for them. For that reason, urges the "Mothers' Code for Advertisers," there should be no advertising in schools, no targeting children under 8 years, no product placements in movies and programs targeting children and adolescents, and no ads directed at children and adolescents "that promote an ethic of selfishness and a focus on instant gratification" (Motherhood Project, 2001).

Implications of Attitude Inoculation

The best way to build resistance to brainwashing probably is not just stronger indoctrination into one's current beliefs. If parents are worried that their children might start smoking, they might better teach their children how to counter persuasive appeals about smoking.

For the same reason, religious educators should be wary of creating a "germ-free ideological environment" in their churches and schools. People who live amid diverse views become more discerning and more likely to modify their views only in response to credible arguments (Levitan & Visser, 2008). Also, a challenge to one's views, if refuted, is more likely to solidify one's position than to undermine it, particularly if the threatening material can be examined with like-minded others (Visser & Mirabile, 2004). Cults apply this principle by forewarning members of how families and friends will attack the cult's beliefs. When the expected challenge comes, the member is armed with counterarguments.

SUMMING UP: How Can Persuasion Be Resisted?

- How do people resist persuasion? A prior public commitment to one's own position, stimulated perhaps by a mild attack on the position, breeds resistance to later persuasion.

- A mild attack can also serve as an *inoculation,* stimulating one to develop counterarguments that will then be available if and when a strong attack comes.

- This implies, paradoxically, that one way to strengthen existing attitudes is to challenge them, although the challenge must not be so strong as to overwhelm them.

POSTSCRIPT:
Being Open but Not Naïve

As recipients of persuasion, our human task is to live in the land between gullibility and cynicism. Some people say that being persuadable is a weakness. "Think for yourself," we are urged. But is being closed to informational influence a virtue, or is it the mark of a fanatic? How can we live with humility and openness to others and yet be critical consumers of persuasive appeals?

To be open, we can assume that every person we meet is, in some ways, our superior. Each person we encounter has some expertise that exceeds our own and thus has something to teach us. As we connect, we can hope to learn from this person and to reciprocate by sharing our knowledge.

Group Influence

Purestock/Superstock

"Never doubt that a small group of thoughtful, committed citizens
can change the world."

—Anthropologist Margaret Mead

Nearing the end of her daily run, a tired Tawna does a slow jog home. The next
day conditions are identical, except that two friends run with her. Tawna runs
her route 2 minutes faster. She wonders, "Did I run faster just because Gail and
Sonja went along?"

At almost every turn, we are involved in groups. Our world contains not only
7.1 billion individuals but also 195 nation-states, 4 million local communities, 20 million
economic organizations, and hundreds of millions of other formal and informal
groups—couples having dinner, roommates hanging out, business teams plotting
strategy. How do such groups influence individuals?

Group interactions often have dramatic effects. Intellectuals hang out with other
intellectuals, strengthening intellectual interests. Deviant youth hang out with other
deviant youth, sometimes amplifying one another's antisocial tendencies. But *how*

do these groups affect attitudes? And which influences lead groups to make smart and dumb decisions?

Individuals also influence their groups. As the 1957 classic film *12 Angry Men* opens, 12 wary murder trial jurors file into the jury room. They are close to agreement and eager for a quick verdict convicting a teenage boy of knifing his father. But one maverick, played by Henry Fonda, refuses to vote guilty. As the heated deliberation proceeds, the jurors change their minds one by one until they reach a unanimous verdict: "Not guilty." In real trials, a lone individual seldom sways the entire group. Yet history is made by minorities that sway majorities. What helps make a minority—or a leader—persuasive?

We will examine these intriguing phenomena of group influence one at a time. But first things first: What is a group and why do groups exist?

WHAT IS A GROUP?

The answer to this question seems self-evident—until several people compare their definitions. Are jogging partners a group? Are airplane passengers a group? Is a group those who identify with one another, who sense they belong together? Is a group those who share common goals and rely on one another? Does a group form when individuals become organized? When their relationships with one another continue over time? These are among the social psychological definitions of a group (McGrath, 1984).

Group dynamics expert Marvin Shaw (1981) argued that all groups have one thing in common: Their members interact. Therefore, he defines a **group** as two or more people who interact and who influence one another. A pair of jogging companions, then, would indeed constitute a group. Different groups help us meet different human needs—to *affiliate* (to belong to and connect with others), to *achieve,* and to gain a social *identity* (Johnson et al., 2006). Unlike the great apes, we humans are "the cooperative animal" (Tomasello, 2014). From our early ancestors to the present, we have intentionally collaborated to forage and hunt.

group
Two or more people who, for longer than a few moments, interact with and influence one another and perceive one another as "us."

By Shaw's definition, students working individually in a computer room would not be a group. Although physically together, they are more a collection of individuals than an interacting group (though each may be part of a group with dispersed others in an online chat room). The distinction between unrelated individuals in a computer lab and interacting individuals sometimes blurs. People who are merely in one another's presence do sometimes influence one another. At a football game, they may perceive themselves as "us" fans in contrast with "them"—the opposing fans.

In this chapter, we consider three effects of others' mere presence: *social facilitation, social loafing,* and *deindividuation.* These three phenomena can occur with minimal interaction (in what we call "minimal group situations"). Then we consider three examples of social influence in interacting groups: *group polarization, groupthink,* and *minority influence.*

SUMMING UP: What Is a Group?

- A *group* exists when two or more people interact for more than a few moments, affect one another in some way, and think of themselves as "us."

SOCIAL FACILITATION: HOW ARE WE AFFECTED BY THE PRESENCE OF OTHERS?

Describe how we are affected by the mere presence of another person—by people who are not competing, do not reward or punish, and in fact do nothing except be present as a passive audience or as **co-actors.**

co-actors

Co-participants working individually on a noncompetitive activity.

social facilitation

(1) Original meaning: the tendency of people to perform simple or well-learned tasks better when others are present. (2) Current meaning: the strengthening of dominant (prevalent, likely) responses in the presence of others.

The Mere Presence of Others

More than a century ago, Norman Triplett (1898), a psychologist interested in bicycle racing, noticed that cyclists' times were faster when they raced together than when each one raced alone against the clock. Before he peddled his hunch (that others' presence boosts performance), Triplett conducted one of social psychology's first laboratory experiments. Children told to wind string on a fishing reel as rapidly as possible wound faster when they worked with competing co-actors than when they worked alone. "The bodily presence of another contestant . . . serves to liberate latent energy," concluded Triplett.

A modern reanalysis of Triplett's data revealed that the difference did not reach statistical significance (Stroebe, 2012; Strube, 2005). But ensuing experiments did find that others' presence improves the speed with which people do simple multiplication problems and cross out designated letters. It also improves accuracy on simple motor tasks, such as keeping a metal stick in contact with a dime-sized disk on a moving turntable (F. H. Allport, 1920; Dashiell, 1930; Travis, 1925). This **social facilitation** effect also occurs with animals. In the presence of others of their species, ants excavate more sand, chickens eat more grain, and sexually active rat pairs mate more often (Bayer, 1929; Chen, 1937; Larsson, 1956).

But wait: Other studies revealed that on some tasks the presence of others *hinders* performance. In the presence of others, cockroaches, parakeets, and green finches learn mazes more slowly (Allee & Masure, 1936; Gates & Allee, 1933; Klopfer, 1958). This disruptive effect also occurs with people. Others' presence diminishes efficiency at learning nonsense syllables, completing a maze, and performing complex multiplication problems (Dashiell, 1930; Pessin, 1933; Pessin & Husband, 1933).

Saying that others' presence sometimes facilitates performance and sometimes hinders it is about as satisfying as the typical Scottish weather forecast—predicting that it might be sunny but then again it might rain. By 1940, social facilitation research ground to a halt, and it lay dormant for 25 years until awakened by the touch of a new idea.

Social psychologist Robert Zajonc (1923–2008, pronounced *Zy-ence,* rhymes with *science*) wondered whether these seemingly contradictory findings could be reconciled. As often happens at creative moments in science, Zajonc (1965) used one field of research to illuminate another. The illumination came from a well-established experimental psychology principle: Arousal enhances whatever response tendency is dominant. Increased arousal enhances performance on easy tasks for which the most likely—"dominant"—response is correct. People solve easy anagrams, such as *akec,* fastest when aroused. On complex tasks, for which the correct answer is not dominant,

Social facilitation: Do you ride faster when bicycling with others?
Bob Winsett/Corbis

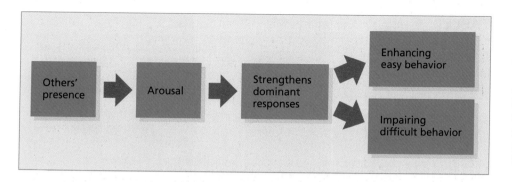

FIGURE :: 1

The Effects of Social Arousal

Robert Zajonc reconciled apparently conflicting findings by proposing that arousal from others' presence strengthens dominant responses (the correct responses only on easy or well-learned tasks).

increased arousal promotes *incorrect* responding. On more difficult anagrams, such as *theloacco,* people do worse when aroused.

Could this principle solve the mystery of social facilitation? It seemed reasonable to assume that others' presence will arouse or energize people (Mullen et al., 1997); most of us can recall feeling tense or excited in front of an audience. If social arousal facilitates dominant responses, it should *boost performance on easy tasks* and *hurt performance on difficult tasks.*

With that explanation, the confusing results made sense. Winding fishing reels, doing simple multiplication problems, and eating were all easy tasks, with well-learned or naturally dominant responses. Sure enough, having others around boosted performance.

Learning new material, doing a maze, and solving complex math problems were more difficult tasks with initially less probable correct responses. In these cases, the presence of others increased the number of *incorrect* responses on these tasks.

So, the same general rule—*arousal facilitates dominant responses*—worked in both cases (Figure 1). Suddenly, what had looked like contradictory results no longer seemed contradictory.

Zajonc's solution, so simple and elegant, left other social psychologists thinking what Thomas H. Huxley thought after first reading Darwin's *On the Origin of Species:* "How extremely stupid not to have thought of that!" It seemed obvious—once Zajonc had pointed it out. Perhaps, however, the pieces fit so neatly only through the spectacles of hindsight. Would the solution survive direct experimental tests?

After almost 300 studies of more than 25,000 people, the solution has survived (Bond & Titus, 1983; Guerin, 1993, 1999). Social arousal facilitates dominant responses, whether right or wrong. For example, Peter Hunt and Joseph Hillery (1973) found that in others' presence, students took less time to learn a simple maze and more time to learn a complex one (just as the cockroaches did!). And James Michaels and collaborators (1982) found that good pool players in a student union (who had made 71 percent of their shots while being unobtrusively observed) did even better (80 percent) when four observers came up to watch them play. Poor shooters (who had previously averaged 36 percent) did even worse (25 percent) when closely observed.

Athletes, actors, and musicians perform well-practiced skills, which helps explain why they often perform best when energized by the responses of a supportive audience. Studies of more than a quarter million college and professional athletic events worldwide reveal that home teams win approximately 6 in 10 games [Table 1]. Moreover, further analyses indicate that the home advantage is amazingly constant over time and across sport. NBA basketball teams, NHL hockey teams, and international soccer football league teams have won more home games every year, without exception (Moskowitz & Wertheim, 2011).

Social facilitation—a home audience energizing performance on well-learned skills—is an obvious explanation of the home advantage. Can you imagine other possible contributing factors? Mark Allen and Mark Jones (2014) include these possibilities:

- *Officiating bias:* In one analysis of 1,530 German soccer football matches, referees awarded an average 1.80 yellow cards to home teams and 2.35 to away teams (Unkelbach & Memmert, 2010).

- *Travel fatigue:* When flying to the East coast, West coast NFL football teams do better in night games than when playing 1 P.M. games.

"Mere social contact begets . . . a stimulation of the animal spirits that heightens the efficiency of each individual workman."

—Karl Marx,
Das Kapital, 1867

"Discovery consists of seeing what everybody has seen and thinking what nobody had thought."

—Albert von Szent-Györgyi,
The Scientist Speculates, 1962

TABLE :: 1 Home Advantage in Major Team Sports

Sport	Games Studied	Percentage of Home Games Won
Baseball	120,576	55.6
American football	11,708	57.3
Ice hockey	50,739	56.5
Basketball	30,174	63.7
Soccer	40,380	67.4

Source: Jeremy Jamieson (2010).

- *Familiarity with the home context*, which, depending on the locale, may include cold, rain, or high altitude. Even in the absence of a crowd (for safety reasons), Italian soccer football teams perform better in their home stadiums (van de Ven, 2011).
- *Crowd noise disruption* may disrupt visiting players' hearing plays or shooting free throws.

Crowding: The Presence of Many Others

So people do respond to others' presence. But does the presence of observers always arouse people? In times of stress, a supportive friend can be comforting. Nevertheless, with others present, people perspire more, breathe faster, tense their muscles more, and have higher blood pressure and a faster heart rate (Geen & Gange, 1983; Moore & Baron, 1983). Even a supportive audience may elicit poorer performance on challenging tasks (Butler & Baumeister, 1998). Having your entire extended family at your first piano recital probably won't boost your performance.

The effect of others' presence increases with their number (Jackson & Latané, 1981; Knowles, 1983). Sometimes the arousal and self-conscious attention created by a large audience interferes even with well-learned, automatic behaviors, such as speaking. Given *extreme* pressure, we're vulnerable to "choking." Stutterers tend to stutter more in front of larger audiences than when speaking to just one or two people (Mullen, 1986b). Over 28 years of major tournaments, professional golfers' scores have tended to be worse in the final day's round than on the previous day, especially so for golfers close to the tournament lead (Wells & Skowronski, 2012).

Being *in* a crowd also intensifies positive or negative reactions. When they sit close together, friendly people are liked even more, and *un*friendly people are *dis*liked even more (Schiffenbauer & Schiavo, 1976; Storms & Thomas, 1977). In experiments with Columbia University students and with Ontario Science Center visitors, Jonathan Freedman and co-workers (1979, 1980) had people listen to a humorous tape or watch a movie with other participants. When they all sat close together, an accomplice could more readily induce the individuals to laugh and clap. As theater directors and sports fans know, and as researchers have confirmed, a "good house" is a full house (Aiello et al., 1983; Worchel & Brown, 1984).

Perhaps you've noticed that a class of 35 students feels more warm and lively in a room that seats just 35 than when spread around a room that seats 100. When others are close by, we are more likely to notice and join in their laughter or clapping. But crowding also enhances arousal, as Gary Evans (1979) found. He tested 10-person groups of University of Massachusetts students, either in a room 20 by 30 feet or in one 8 by 12 feet. Compared with those in the large room, those densely packed had higher pulse rates and blood pressure (indicating arousal). On difficult tasks they made more errors, an effect of crowding replicated by Dinesh Nagar and Janak Pandey (1987) with university students in India. Crowding, then, has a similar effect to being observed by a crowd: it enhances arousal, which facilitates dominant responses.

Heightened arousal in crowded homes also tends to increase stress. Crowding produces less distress in homes divided into many spaces, however, enabling people to withdraw in privacy (Evans et al., 1996, 2000).

Why Are We Aroused in the Presence of Others?

What you do well, you will be energized to do best in front of others (unless you become hyper-aroused and self-conscious)—and choke. What you find difficult may seem impossible in the same circumstances. What is it about other people that creates arousal? Evidence supports three possible factors (Aiello & Douthitt, 2001; Feinberg & Aiello, 2006): evaluation apprehension, distraction, and mere presence.

A good house is a full house, as James Maas's Cornell University introductory psychology students experienced in this 2000-seat auditorium. If the class had 100 students meeting in this large space, it would feel much less energized.
Courtesy, Mike Okoniewski

EVALUATION APPREHENSION

Nickolas Cottrell surmised that observers make us apprehensive because we wonder how they are evaluating us. To test whether **evaluation apprehension** exists, Cottrell and associates (1968) blindfolded observers, supposedly in preparation for a perception experiment. In contrast to the effect of the watching audience, the mere presence of these blindfolded people did *not* boost well-practiced responses.

evaluation apprehension
Concern for how others are evaluating us.

Other experiments confirmed that the enhancement of dominant responses is strongest when people think they are being evaluated. In one experiment, individuals running on a jogging path sped up as they came upon a woman seated on the grass—*if* she was facing them rather than sitting with her back turned (Worringham & Messick, 1983).

The self-consciousness we feel when being evaluated can also interfere with behaviors that we perform best automatically (Mullen & Baumeister, 1987). If self-conscious basketball players analyze their body movements while shooting critical free throws, they are more likely to miss. We perform some well-learned behaviors best without overthinking them.

DRIVEN BY DISTRACTION

Glenn Sanders, Robert Baron, and Danny Moore (1978; Baron, 1986) carried evaluation apprehension a step further. They theorized that when we wonder how co-actors are doing or how an audience is reacting, we become distracted. This *conflict* between paying attention to others and paying attention to the task overloads our cognitive system, causing arousal. We are "driven by distraction." This arousal comes not just from the presence of another person but also from other distractions, such as bursts of light (Sanders, 1981a,b).

MERE PRESENCE

Zajonc, however, believed that the mere presence of others produces some arousal even without evaluation apprehension or arousing distraction. Recall that facilitation effects also occur with nonhuman animals. This hints at an innate social arousal mechanism common to much of the zoological world. (Animals probably are not consciously worrying about how other animals are evaluating them.) At the human level, most runners are energized when running with someone else, even one who neither competes nor evaluates. University rowing team members, perhaps aided by an endorphin boost from the communal activity, tolerate twice as much pain after rowing together rather than solo (Cohen et al., 2009).

This is a good time to remind ourselves that a good theory is a scientific shorthand: It simplifies and summarizes a variety of observations. Social facilitation theory does this well. It is a simple summary of many research findings. A good theory also offers clear predictions that (1) help confirm or modify the theory, (2) guide new exploration, and (3) suggest practical applications. Social facilitation theory has definitely generated the first two types of prediction: (1) The basics of the theory (that the presence of others is arousing and that this social arousal enhances dominant responses) have been confirmed, and (2) the theory has brought new life to a long-dormant field of research.

FIGURE :: 2

In the "open-office plan," people work in the presence of others. Increasingly, office environments provide their workers with "collaborative spaces" (Arieff, 2011).

AP Images/dycj

Are there (3) some practical applications? We can make some educated guesses. As Figure 2 shows, many new office buildings have replaced private offices with large, open areas divided by low partitions. Might the resulting awareness of others' presence help boost the performance of well-learned tasks but disrupt creative thinking on complex tasks? Can you think of other possible applications?

SUMMING UP: Social Facilitation: How Are We Affected by the Presence of Others?

- Social psychology's most elementary issue concerns the mere presence of others. Some early experiments on this question found that performance improved with observers or *co-actors* present. Others found that the presence of others can hurt performance. Robert Zajonc reconciled those findings by applying a well-known principle from experimental psychology: Arousal facilitates dominant responses. Because the presence of others is arousing, the presence of observers or co-actors boosts performance on easy tasks (for which the correct response is dominant) and hinders performance on difficult tasks (for which incorrect responses are dominant).

- Being in a crowd, or in crowded conditions, is similarly arousing and facilitates dominant responses. That helps explain the home-field advantage in sports.

- But why are we aroused by others' presence? Experiments suggest that the arousal stems partly from *evaluation apprehension* and partly from distraction—a conflict between paying attention to others and concentrating on the task. Other experiments, including some with animals, suggest that the presence of others can be arousing even when we are not evaluated or distracted.

SOCIAL LOAFING: DO INDIVIDUALS EXERT LESS EFFORT IN A GROUP?

Assess the level of individual effort we can expect from members of work groups. In a team tug-of-war, will eight people on a side exert as much force as the sum of their best efforts in individual tugs-of-war? If not, why not?

Social facilitation usually occurs when people work toward individual goals and when their efforts, whether winding fishing reels or solving math problems, can be individually evaluated. These situations parallel some everyday work situations. But what about those in which people pool their efforts toward a *common* goal and where individuals are *not* accountable for their efforts? A team tug-of-war provides one such example. Organizational fund-raising—using candy sale proceeds to pay for the class trip—provides another. So does a class group project on which all students get the same grade. On such "additive tasks"—tasks where the group's achievement depends on the sum of the individual efforts—will team spirit boost productivity? Will bricklayers lay bricks faster when working as a team than when working alone? One way to attack such questions is with laboratory simulations.

Many Hands Make Light Work

Nearly a century ago, French engineer Max Ringelmann (reported by Kravitz & Martin, 1986) found that the collective effort of tug-of-war teams was but half the sum of the individual efforts. Contrary to the presumption that "in unity there is strength," this suggested that group members may actually be *less* motivated when performing additive tasks. Maybe, though, poor performance stemmed from poor coordination—people pulling a rope in slightly different directions at slightly different times. A group of Massachusetts researchers led by Alan Ingham (1974) cleverly eliminated that problem by making individuals think others were pulling with them, when in fact they were pulling alone. Blindfolded participants were assigned the first position in the apparatus shown in Figure 3 and told, "Pull as hard as you can." They pulled 18 percent harder when they knew they were pulling alone than when they believed that behind them two to five people were also pulling.

Researchers Bibb Latané, Kipling Williams, and Stephen Harkins (1979; Harkins et al., 1980) kept their ears open for other ways to investigate this diminished effort, which they labeled **social loafing.** They observed that the noise produced by six people shouting or clapping "as loud as you can" was less than three times that produced by one person alone. Like the tug-of-war task, however, noisemaking is vulnerable to group inefficiency. So Latané and associates followed Ingham's example by leading their Ohio State University participants to believe others were shouting or clapping with them, when in fact they were doing so alone.

Their method was to blindfold six people, seat them in a semicircle, and have them put on headphones, over which they were blasted with the sound of people shouting or clapping. People could not hear their own shouting or clapping, much less that of others. On various trials they were instructed to shout or clap either alone or along with the group. People who were told about this experiment guessed the participants would shout louder when with others, because they would be less inhibited (Harkins, 1981). The actual result? Social loafing: When the participants believed five others were also either shouting or clapping, they produced one-third *less* noise than when they thought themselves alone. Social loafing occurred even when the participants were

social loafing
The tendency for people to exert less effort when they pool their efforts toward a common goal than when they are individually accountable.

FIGURE :: 3

The Rope-Pulling Apparatus
People in the first position pulled less hard when they thought people behind them were also pulling.
Source: Data from Ingham, Levinger, Graves, & Peckham, 1974. Photo by Alan G. Ingham.
Courtesy of Alan G. Ingham

FIGURE :: 4

Effort Decreases as Group Size Increases
A statistical digest of 49 studies, involving more than 4000 participants, revealed that effort decreases (loafing increases) as the size of the group increases. Each dot represents the aggregate data from one of these studies.
Source: Williams et al, 1992.

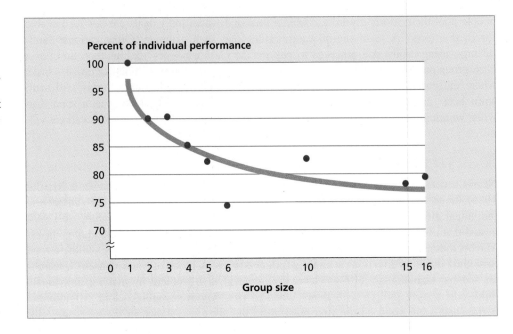

high school cheerleaders who believed themselves to be cheering together rather than alone (Hardy & Latané, 1986).

Curiously, those who clapped both alone and in groups did not view themselves as loafing; they perceived themselves as clapping equally in both situations. This parallels what happens when students work on group projects for a shared grade. Williams reports that all agree loafing occurs—but no one admits to doing the loafing.

John Sweeney (1973), a political scientist interested in the policy implications of social loafing, observed the phenomenon in a cycling experiment. University of Texas students pumped exercise bicycles more energetically (as measured by electrical output) when they knew they were being individually monitored than when they thought their output was being pooled with that of other riders. In the group condition, people were tempted to **free-ride** on the group effort.

free riders
People who benefit from the group but give little in return.

In this and 160 other studies (Karau & Williams, 1993; Figure 4), we see a twist on one of the psychological forces that makes for social facilitation: evaluation apprehension. In the social loafing experiments, individuals believed they were evaluated only when they acted alone. The group situation (rope pulling, shouting, and so forth) *decreased* evaluation apprehension. When people are not accountable and cannot evaluate their own efforts, responsibility is diffused across all group members (Harkins & Jackson, 1985; Kerr & Bruun, 1981). By contrast, the social facilitation experiments *increased* exposure to evaluation. When made the center of attention, people self-consciously monitor their behavior (Mullen & Baumeister, 1987). So, when being observed *increases* evaluation concerns, social facilitation occurs; when being lost in a crowd *decreases* evaluation concerns, social loafing occurs (Figure 5).

To motivate group members, one strategy is to make individual performance identifiable. Some football coaches do this by filming and evaluating each player individually. Whether in a group or not, people exert more effort when their outputs are individually identifiable: University swim team members swim faster in intrasquad relay races when someone monitors and announces their individual times (Williams et al., 1989).

Social Loafing in Everyday Life

How widespread is social loafing? In the laboratory, the phenomenon occurs not only among people who are pulling ropes, cycling, shouting, and clapping but also among those who are pumping water or air, evaluating poems or editorials, producing ideas, typing, and detecting signals. Do these consistent results generalize to everyday worker productivity?

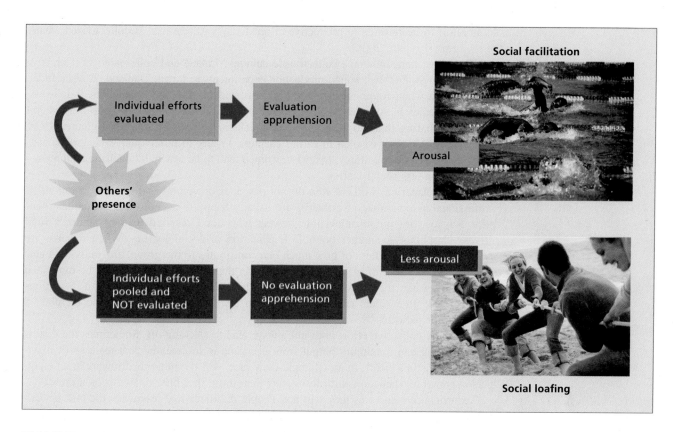

FIGURE :: 5

Social Facilitation or Social Loafing?

When individuals cannot be evaluated or held accountable, loafing becomes more likely. An individual swimmer is evaluated on her ability to win the race. In tug-of-war, no single person on the team is held accountable, so any one member might relax or loaf.

Simmers: Royalty-Free/Corbis; *Tug-of-war:* Thinkstock Images/Getty Images

In one small experiment, assembly-line workers produced 16 percent more product when their individual output was identified, even though they knew their pay would be unaffected (Faulkner & Williams, 1996). Consider the example of workers in a pickle factory who were supposed to put only the big pickles into jars. But because the jars were then merged (and their individual work unchecked), the workers just stuffed in any size pickle. Williams, Harkins, and Latané (1981) note that research on social loafing suggests "making individual production identifiable, and raises the question: 'How many pickles could a pickle packer pack if pickle packers were only paid for properly packed pickles?'"

Researchers have also found evidence of social loafing in varied cultures, particularly by assessing agricultural output in formerly communist countries. On their collective farms under communism, Russian peasants worked one field one day, another field the next, with little direct responsibility for any given plot. For their own use, they were given small private plots. One analysis found that the private plots occupied 1 percent of the agricultural land, yet produced 27 percent of the Soviet farm output (H. Smith, 1976). In communist Hungary, private plots accounted for only 13 percent of the farmland but produced one-third of the output (Spivak, 1979). When China began allowing farmers to sell food grown in excess of that owed to the state, food production jumped 8 percent per year—2.5 times the annual increase in the preceding 26 years (Church, 1986).

Teamwork at the Charles River regatta in Boston. Social loafing occurs when people work in groups but without individual accountability—unless the task is challenging, appealing, or involving and the group members are friends.

Joel Rogers/Encyclopedia/Corbis

In an effort to tie rewards to productive effort, today's Russia has "decollectivized" many of its farms (Kramer, 2008).

What about noncommunist collectivistic cultures? Latané and co-researchers (Gabrenya et al., 1985) repeated their sound-production experiments in Japan, Thailand, Taiwan, India, and Malaysia. Their findings? Social loafing was evident in all those countries, too. Seventeen later studies in Asia reveal that people in collectivistic cultures do, however, exhibit less social loafing than do people in individualistic cultures (Karau & Williams, 1993; Kugihara, 1999). As we noted in earlier chapters, loyalty to family and work groups runs strong in collectivistic cultures. Likewise, women tend to be less individualistic than men— and to exhibit less social loafing.

In North America, workers who do not pay dues or volunteer time to their unions or professional associations nevertheless are usually happy to accept the associations' benefits. So, too, are public television viewers who don't respond to their station's fund drives. This hints at another possible explanation of social loafing. When rewards are divided equally, regardless of how much one contributes to the group, any individual gets more reward per unit of effort by free-riding on the group. So people may be motivated to slack off when their efforts are not individually monitored and rewarded. Situations that welcome free riders can therefore be, in the words of one commune member, a "paradise for parasites."

But surely collective effort does not always lead to slacking off. Sometimes the goal is so compelling and maximum output from everyone is so essential that team spirit maintains or intensifies effort. In an Olympic crew race, will the individual rowers in an eight-person crew pull their oars with less effort than those in a one- or two-person crew?

The evidence assures us they will not. People in groups loaf less when the task is *challenging, appealing,* or *involving* (Karau & Williams, 1993; Tan & Tan, 2008). On challenging tasks, people may perceive their efforts as indispensable (Harkins & Petty, 1982; Kerr, 1983; Kerr et al., 2007). When swimming the last leg of a relay race with a medal at stake, swimmers tend to swim even faster than in individual competition (Hüffmeier et al., 2012).

Groups also loaf less when their members are *friends* or they feel identified with or indispensable to their group (Davis & Greenlees, 1992; Gockel et al., 2008; Karau & Williams, 1997; Worchel et al., 1998). Even just expecting to interact with someone again serves to increase effort on team projects (Groenenboom et al., 2001). Collaborate on a class project with others whom you will be seeing often and you will probably feel more motivated than you would if you never expected to see them again. Cohesiveness intensifies effort.

These findings parallel those from studies of everyday work groups. When groups are given challenging objectives, when they are rewarded for group success, and when there is a spirit of commitment to the "team," group members work hard (Hackman, 1986). Keeping work groups small can also help members believe their contributions are indispensable (Comer, 1995). Although social loafing is common when group members work without individual accountability, many hands need not always make light work.

SUMMING UP: Social Loafing: Do Individuals Exert Less Effort in a Group?

- Social facilitation researchers study people's performance on tasks where they can be evaluated individually. However, in many work situations, people pool their efforts and work toward a common goal without individual accountability.

- Group members often work less hard when performing such "additive tasks." This finding parallels everyday situations in which diffused responsibility tempts individual group members to *free-ride* on the group's effort.

- People may, however, put forth even more effort in a group when the goal is important, rewards are significant, and team spirit exists.

DEINDIVIDUATION: WHEN DO PEOPLE LOSE THEIR SENSE OF SELF IN GROUPS?

Define "deindividuation" and identify circumstances that trigger it.

In April 2003, in the wake of American troops entering Iraq's cities, looters—"liberated" from the scrutiny of Saddam Hussein's police—ran rampant. Hospitals lost beds. The National Library lost tens of thousands of old manuscripts and lay in smoldering ruins. Universities lost computers, chairs, even lightbulbs. The National Museum in Baghdad lost 15,000 precious objects (Burns, 2003a, 2003b; Lawler, 2003c; Polk & Schuster, 2005). "Not since the Spanish conquistadors ravaged the Aztec and Inca cultures has so much been lost so quickly," reported *Science* (Lawler, 2003a). "They came in mobs: A group of 50 would come, then would go, and another would come," explained one university dean (Lawler, 2003b).

Such reports—and those of the 2011 arson and looting that occurred in London and the 2014 looting in Ferguson, Missouri—had the rest of the world wondering: What happened to the looters' sense of morality? Why did such behavior erupt? And why was it not anticipated?

Their behavior even left many of the rioters later wondering what possessed them. In court, some of the arrested rioters seemed bewildered by their behavior (Smith, 2011). The mother of one of them, a recent university graduate, explained that her daughter had been sobbing in her bedroom since her arrest over a stolen television. "She doesn't even know why she took it. She doesn't need a telly." An engineering student, arrested after looting a supermarket while he was walking home, was said by his lawyer to having "got caught up in the moment" and was now "incredibly ashamed" (Somaiya, 2011).

Doing Together What We Would Not Do Alone

Social facilitation experiments show that groups can arouse people, and social loafing experiments show that groups can diffuse responsibility. When arousal and diffused responsibility combine, and normal inhibitions diminish, the results may be startling. People may commit acts that range from a mild lessening of restraint (throwing food in the dining hall, snarling at a referee, screaming during a rock concert) to impulsive self-gratification (group vandalism, orgies, thefts) to destructive social explosions (police brutality, riots, lynchings).

These unrestrained behaviors have something in common: They are somehow provoked by the power of a group. Groups can generate a sense of excitement, of being caught up in something bigger than one's self. It is hard to imagine a single rock fan screaming deliriously at a private rock concert, or a single police officer beating a defenseless offender or suspect. It's in group situations that people are more likely to abandon normal restraints, to forget their individual identity, to become responsive to group or crowd norms—in a word, to become what Leon Festinger, Albert Pepitone, and Theodore Newcomb (1952) labeled **deindividuated.** What circumstances elicit this psychological state?

GROUP SIZE

A group has the power not only to arouse its members but also to render them unidentifiable. The snarling crowd hides the snarling basketball fan. A lynch mob enables its members to

deindividuation
Loss of self-awareness and evaluation apprehension; occurs in group situations that foster responsiveness to group norms, good or bad.

Deindividuation: During England's 2011 riots and looting, rioters were disinhibited by social arousal and by the anonymity provided by darkness and their hoods and masks. Later, some of those arrested expressed bewilderment over their own behavior.
AP Images/Lewis Whyld

believe they will not be prosecuted; they perceive the action as the *group's*. Looters, made faceless by the mob, are freed to loot. One researcher analyzed 21 instances in which crowds were present as someone threatened to jump from a building or a bridge (Mann, 1981). When the crowd was small and exposed by daylight, people usually did not try to bait the person with cries of "Jump!" But when a large crowd or the cover of night gave people anonymity, the crowd usually did bait and jeer.

Lynch mobs produce a similar effect: The bigger the mob, the more its members lose self-awareness and become willing to commit atrocities, such as burning, lacerating, or dismembering the victim (Mullen, 1986a).

In each of these examples, from sports crowds to lynch mobs, evaluation apprehension plummets. People's attention is focused on the situation, not on themselves. And because "everyone is doing it," all can attribute their behavior to the situation rather than to their own choices.

ANONYMITY

How can we be sure that crowds offer anonymity? We can't. But we can experiment with anonymity to see if it actually lessens inhibitions. Philip Zimbardo (1970, 2002) got the idea for such an experiment from his undergraduate students, who questioned how good boys in William Golding's *Lord of the Flies* could so suddenly become monsters after painting their faces. To experiment with such anonymity, he dressed New York University women in identical white coats and hoods, rather like Ku Klux Klan members (Figure 6). Asked to deliver electric shocks to a woman, they pressed the shock button twice as long as did women who were unconcealed and wearing large name tags. Even dimmed lighting or wearing sunglasses increases people's perceived anonymity, and thus their willingness to cheat or behave selfishly (Zhong et al., 2010).

The Internet offers similar anonymity. Millions of those who were aghast at the looting by the Baghdad mobs were on those very days anonymously pirating music tracks using file-sharing software. With so many doing it, and with so little concern about being caught, downloading someone's copyrighted property and then offloading it to an MP3 player just didn't seem terribly immoral. Internet bullies who would never say, "Get a life, you phony," to someone's face will hide behind their anonymity. Facebook, to its credit, requires people to use their real names, which constrains the bullying, hate-filled, and inflammatory comments.

On several occasions, anonymous online bystanders have egged on people threatening suicide, sometimes with live video feeding the scene to scores of people. Online communities "are like the crowd outside the building with the guy on the ledge," noted one analyst of technology's social effects (quoted by Stelter, 2008). Sometimes a caring person tried to talk the person down, while others, in effect, chanted, "Jump, jump." "The anonymous nature of these communities only emboldens the meanness or callousness of the people on these sites."

FIGURE :: 6

In Philip Zimbardo's deindividuation research, anonymous women delivered more shock to helpless victims than did identifiable women.
Courtesy, Philip Zimbardo

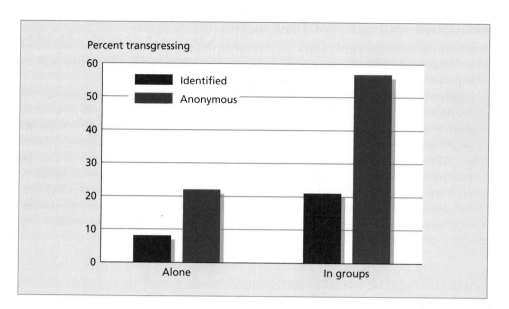

FIGURE :: 7

Children were more likely to transgress by taking extra Halloween candy when in a group, when anonymous, and, especially, when deindividuated by the combination of group immersion and anonymity.
Source: Data from Diener et al. (1976).

Testing deindividuation on the streets, Patricia Ellison, John Govern, and their colleagues (1995) had a driver stop at a red light and wait for 12 seconds whenever she was followed by a convertible or a 4 × 4 vehicle. While enduring the wait, she recorded any horn-honking (a mild aggressive act) by the car behind. Compared with drivers of convertibles and 4 × 4s with the car tops down, those who were relatively anonymous (with the tops up) honked one-third sooner, twice as often, and for nearly twice as long. Anonymity feeds incivility.

A research team led by Ed Diener (1976) cleverly demonstrated the effect both of being in a group and of being physically anonymous. At Halloween, they observed 1,352 Seattle children trick-or-treating. As the children, either alone or in groups, approached 1 of 27 homes scattered throughout the city, an experimenter greeted them warmly, invited them to "take *one* of the candies," and then left the candy unattended. Hidden observers noted that children in groups were more than twice as likely to take extra candy as were solo children. Also, children who had been asked their names and where they lived were less than half as likely to transgress as those who were left anonymous. As Figure 7 shows, the transgression rate varied dramatically with the situation. When they were deindividuated both by group immersion and by anonymity, most children stole extra candy.

Those studies make us wonder about the effect of wearing uniforms. Preparing for battle, warriors in some tribal cultures (like some rabid sports fans) depersonalize themselves with body and face paints or special masks. After the battle, some cultures kill, torture, or mutilate any remaining enemies; other cultures take prisoners alive. Robert Watson (1973) scrutinized anthropological files and discovered this: The cultures with depersonalized warriors were also the cultures that brutalized their enemies. In Northern Ireland, 206 of 500 violent attacks studied by Andrew Silke (2003) were conducted by attackers who wore masks, hoods, or other face disguises. Compared with undisguised attackers, these anonymous attackers inflicted more serious injuries, attacked more people, and committed more vandalism.

Does becoming physically anonymous *always* unleash our worst impulses? Fortunately, no. In all these situations, people were responding to clear antisocial cues. Robert Johnson and Leslie Downing (1979) point out that the Klan-like outfits worn by Zimbardo's participants may have been stimulus cues for hostility. In an experiment at the University of Georgia, women put on nurses' uniforms before deciding how much shock someone should receive. When those wearing the nurses' uniforms were made anonymous, they became *less* aggressive in administering shocks. From their analysis of 60 deindividuation studies, Tom Postmes and Russell Spears (1998; Reicher et al., 1995) concluded that being anonymous makes one less self-conscious, more group-conscious, and *more responsive to situational cues,* whether negative (Klan uniforms) or positive (nurses' uniforms).

AROUSING AND DISTRACTING ACTIVITIES

Aggressive outbursts by large groups are often preceded by minor actions that arouse and divert people's attention. Group shouting, chanting, clapping, or dancing serve both to hype people up and to reduce self-consciousness.

Experiments have shown that activities such as throwing rocks and group singing can set the stage for more disinhibited behavior (Diener, 1976, 1979). There is a self-reinforcing pleasure in acting impulsively while seeing others do likewise. When we see others act as we are acting, we think they feel as we do, which reinforces our own feelings (Orive, 1984). Moreover, impulsive group action absorbs our attention. When we yell at the referee, we are not thinking about our values; we are reacting to the immediate situation. Later, when we stop to think about what we have done or said, we sometimes feel chagrined. Sometimes. At other times we *seek* deindividuating group experiences—dances, worship experiences, team sports—where we can enjoy intense positive feelings and closeness to others.

Diminished Self-Awareness

Group experiences that diminish self-consciousness tend to disconnect behavior from attitudes. Research by Ed Diener (1980) and Steven Prentice-Dunn and Ronald Rogers (1980, 1989) revealed that unself-conscious, deindividuated people are less restrained, less self-regulated, more likely to act without thinking about their own values, and more responsive to the situation. These findings complement and reinforce the experiments on **self-awareness.**

Self-awareness is the opposite of deindividuation. Those made self-aware, by acting in front of a mirror or a TV camera, exhibit *increased* self-control, and their actions more clearly reflect their attitudes. In front of a mirror, people taste-testing cream cheese varieties eat less of the high-fat variety (Sentyrz & Bushman, 1998).

People made self-aware are also less likely to cheat (Beaman et al., 1979; Diener & Wallbom, 1976). So are those who generally have a strong sense of themselves as distinct and independent (Nadler et al., 1982). In Japan, where people more often imagine how they might look to others, the presence of a mirror had no effect on cheating (Heine et al., 2008). The principle: People who are self-conscious, or who are temporarily made so, exhibit greater consistency between their words outside a situation and their deeds in it.

We can apply those findings to many situations in everyday life. Circumstances that decrease self-awareness, as alcohol consumption does, *increase* deindividuation (Hull et al., 1983). Deindividuation *decreases* in circumstances that increase self-awareness: mirrors and cameras, small towns, bright lights, large name tags, undistracted quiet, individual clothes and houses (Ickes et al., 1978). When a teenager leaves for a party, a parent's parting advice could well be "Have fun, and remember who you are." In other words, enjoy being with the group, but be self-aware; maintain your personal identity; be wary of deindividuation.

"Attending a service in the Gothic cathedral, we have the sensation of being enclosed and steeped in an integral universe, and of losing a prickly sense of self in the community of worshipers."
—Yi-Fu Tuan, 1982

self-awareness
A self-conscious state in which attention focuses on oneself. It makes people more sensitive to their own attitudes and dispositions.

SUMMING UP: Deindividuation: When Do People Lose Their Sense of Self in Groups?

- When high levels of social arousal combine with diffused responsibility, people may abandon their normal restraints and lose their sense of individuality.

- Such *deindividuation* is especially likely when people are in a large group, are physically anonymous, and are aroused and distracted.

- The resulting diminished *self-awareness* and self-restraint tend to increase people's responsiveness to the immediate situation, be it negative or positive. Deindividuation is less likely when self-awareness is high.

GROUP POLARIZATION: DO GROUPS INTENSIFY OUR OPINIONS?

Describe and explain how interaction with like-minded people tends to amplify preexisting attitudes.

Many conflicts grow as people on both sides talk mostly with like-minded others. Which effect—good or bad—does group interaction more often have? Police brutality and mob violence demonstrate its destructive potential. Yet support-group leaders, management consultants, and educational theorists proclaim group interaction's benefits, and social and religious movements urge their members to strengthen their identities by fellowship with like-minded others.

Studies of people in small groups have produced a principle that helps explain both bad and good outcomes: Group discussion often strengthens members' initial inclinations. The unfolding of this research on **group polarization** illustrates the process of inquiry—how an interesting discovery often leads researchers to hasty and erroneous conclusions, which get replaced with more accurate conclusions. This is a scientific mystery I [DM] can discuss firsthand, having been one of the detectives.

group polarization
Group-produced enhancement of members' preexisting tendencies; a strengthening of the members' average tendency, not a split within the group.

The Case of the "Risky Shift"

More than 300 studies began with a surprising finding by James Stoner (1961), then an MIT graduate student. For his master's thesis in management, Stoner tested the commonly held belief that groups are more cautious than individuals. He posed decision dilemmas in which the participant's task was to advise imagined characters how much risk to take. Put yourself in the participant's shoes: What advice would you give the character in this situation?[1]

Helen is a writer who is said to have considerable creative talent but who so far has been earning a comfortable living by writing cheap westerns. Recently she has come up with an idea for a potentially significant novel. If it could be written and accepted, it might have considerable literary impact and be a big boost to her career. On the other hand, if she cannot work out her idea or if the novel is a flop, she will have expended considerable time and energy without remuneration.

Imagine that you are advising Helen. Please check the *lowest* probability that you would consider acceptable for Helen to attempt to write the novel.

Helen should attempt to write the novel if the chances that the novel will be a success are at least

_____ 1 in 10
_____ 2 in 10
_____ 3 in 10
_____ 4 in 10
_____ 5 in 10
_____ 6 in 10
_____ 7 in 10
_____ 8 in 10
_____ 9 in 10
_____ 10 in 10 (Place a check here if you think Helen should attempt the novel only if it is certain that the novel will be a success.)

After making your decision, guess what this book's average reader would advise.

Having marked their advice on a dozen items, five or so individuals would then discuss and reach agreement on each item. How do you think the group decisions compared with the average decision before the discussions? Would the groups be likely to take greater risks, be more cautious, or stay the same?

To everyone's amazement, the group decisions were usually riskier. This "risky shift phenomenon" set off a wave of group risk-taking studies. These revealed that risky shift occurs not only when a group decides by consensus; after a brief discussion, individuals, too, will alter their decisions. What is more, researchers successfully repeated Stoner's finding with people of varying ages and occupations in a dozen nations.

[1] This item, constructed for my [DM's] own research, illustrates the sort of decision dilemma posed by Stoner.

During discussion, opinions converged. Curiously, however, the point toward which they converged was usually a lower (riskier) number than their initial average. Here was an intriguing puzzle. The small risky shift effect was reliable, unexpected, and without any immediately obvious explanation. What group influences produce such an effect? And how widespread is it? Do discussions in juries, business committees, and military organizations also promote risk taking? Does this explain why teenage reckless driving, as measured by death rates, nearly doubles when a 16- or 17-year-old driver has two teenage passengers rather than none (Chen et al., 2000)? Does it explain stock bubbles, as people discuss why stocks are rising, thus creating an informational cascade that drives stocks even higher (Sunstein, 2009)?

After several years of study, my [DM's] colleagues and I discovered that the risky shift was not universal. We could write decision dilemmas on which people became more *cautious* after discussion. One of these featured "Roger," a young married man with two school-age children and a secure but low-paying job. Roger can afford life's necessities but few of its luxuries. He hears that the stock of a relatively unknown company may soon triple in value if its new product is favorably received or decline considerably if it does not sell. Roger has no savings. To invest in the company, he is considering selling his life insurance policy.

Can you see a general principle that predicts both the tendency to give riskier advice after discussing Helen's situation and more cautious advice after discussing Roger's? If you are like most people, you would advise Helen to take a greater risk than Roger, even before talking with others. It turns out there is a strong tendency for discussion to accentuate these initial leanings. Thus, groups discussing the "Roger" dilemma became more risk-averse than they were before discussion (Myers, 2010).

Do Groups Intensify Opinions?

Realizing that this group phenomenon was not a consistent shift toward increased risk, we reconceived the phenomenon as a tendency for group discussion to *enhance* group members' initial leanings. This idea led investigators to propose what French researchers Serge Moscovici and Marisa Zavalloni (1969) called group polarization: *Discussion typically strengthens the average inclination of group members.*

GROUP POLARIZATION EXPERIMENTS

This new view of the group-induced changes prompted experimenters to have people discuss attitude statements that most of them favored, or that most of them opposed. Would talking in groups enhance their shared initial inclinations? In groups, would risk takers take bigger risks, bigots become more hostile, and givers become more generous? That's what the group polarization hypothesis predicts (Figure 8).

Dozens of studies confirm group polarization.

- Moscovici and Zavalloni (1969) observed that discussion enhanced French students' initially positive attitude toward their president and negative attitude toward Americans.

FIGURE :: 8

Group Polarization
The group polarization hypothesis predicts that discussion will strengthen an attitude shared by group members.

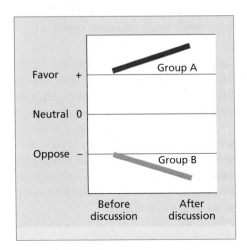

- Mititoshi Isozaki (1984) found that Japanese university students gave more pronounced judgments of "guilty" after discussing a traffic case. When jury members are inclined to award damages, the group award similarly tends to exceed that preferred by the median jury member (Sunstein, 2007a).

- Markus Brauer and co-workers (2001) found that French students' dislike for certain other people was exacerbated after discussing their shared negative impressions.

Another research strategy has been to pick issues on which opinions are divided and then isolate people who hold the same view. Does discussion with like-minded people strengthen shared views? Does it magnify the attitude gap that separates the two sides?

George Bishop and I [DM] wondered. So we set up groups of relatively prejudiced and unprejudiced high school students and asked them to respond—before and after discussion—to issues involving racial attitudes, such as property rights versus open housing (Myers & Bishop, 1970). We found that the discussions among like-minded students did indeed increase the initial gap between the two groups (Figure 9). Moreover, report Jessica Keating and her collaborators (2013), people are unaware of the phenomenon in their own lives. When small groups of like-minded people discussed whether Barack Obama or George W. Bush was the better president, participants underestimated how much the discussion polarized their attitudes (they misremembered their earlier attitudes).

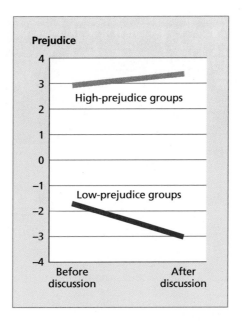

FIGURE :: 9

Discussion increased polarization between homogeneous groups of high- and low-prejudice high school students. Talking over racial issues increased prejudice in a high-prejudice group and decreased it in a low-prejudice group.
Source: Data from Myers & Bishop (1970).

Studies in Britain and Australia confirm that group discussion can magnify both negative and positive tendencies. When people share negative impressions of a group, such as an immigrant group, discussion supports their negativity and increases their willingness to discriminate (Smith & Postmes, 2011). And when people share concern about an injustice, discussion amplifies their moral concern (Thomas & McGarty, 2009).

GROUP POLARIZATION IN EVERYDAY LIFE

In everyday life, people associate mostly with others whose attitudes are similar to their own. (See the Attraction chapter, or just look at your own circle of friends.) Does everyday group interaction with like-minded friends intensify shared attitudes? Do the nerds become nerdier, the jocks jockier, and the rebels more rebellious?

It happens. The self-segregation of boys into all-male groups and of girls into all-female groups increases their initially modest gender differences, notes Eleanor Maccoby (2002). Boys with boys become gradually more competitive and action oriented in their play and fictional fare. Girls with girls become more relationally oriented.

On U.S. federal appellate court cases, judges appointed by Republican presidents tend to vote like Republicans and judges appointed by Democratic presidents tend to vote like Democrats. No surprise there. But such tendencies are accentuated when among like-minded judges, report David Schkade and Cass Sunstein (2003). "A Republican appointee sitting with two other Republicans votes far more conservatively than when the same judge sits with at least one Democratic appointee. A Democratic appointee, meanwhile, shows the same tendency in the opposite ideological direction."

GROUP POLARIZATION IN SCHOOLS.   Another real-life parallel to the laboratory phenomenon is what education researchers have called the "accentuation" effect: Over time, initial differences among groups of college students become accentuated. If the first-year students at college X are initially more intellectual than the students at college Y, that gap is likely to increase by the time they graduate. Likewise, compared with fraternity and sorority members, independents tend to have more liberal political attitudes, a difference that grows with time in college (Pascarella & Terenzini, 1991). Researchers believe this results partly from group members reinforcing shared inclinations.

GROUP POLARIZATION IN COMMUNITIES.   Polarization also occurs in communities, as people self-segregate. "Crunchy places . . . attract crunchy types and become crunchier," observes David Brooks (2005). "Conservative places . . . attract conservatives

"What explains the rise of fascism in the 1930s? The emergence of student radicalism in the 1960s? The growth of Islamic terrorism in the 1990s? . . . The unifying theme is simple: *When people find themselves in groups of like-minded types, they are especially likely to move to extremes.* [This] is the phenomenon of *group polarization.*"

—Cass Sunstein,
Going to Extremes, 2009

Groups often exceed individuals. A gang is more dangerous than the sum of its parts, much as "the pack is greater than the wolf." Creatas/PunchStock

In two trials, South African courts reduced sentences after learning how social psychological phenomena, including deindividuation and group polarization, led crowd members to commit murderous acts (Colman, 1991). What do you think: Should courts consider social psychological phenomena as possible extenuating circumstances?

and become more so." Neighborhoods can become echo chambers, with opinions ricocheting off kindred-spirited friends.

Show social psychologists a like-minded group that interacts mostly among themselves and they will show you a group that may become more extreme. One experiment assembled small groups of Coloradoans in liberal Boulder and conservative Colorado Springs. The discussions increased agreement within small groups about global warming, affirmative action, and same-sex unions. Nevertheless, those in Boulder generally converged further left and those in Colorado Springs further right (Schkade et al., 2007).

With communities serving as political echo chambers, the United States is increasingly polarized. The percentage of landslide counties—those voting 60 percent or more for one presidential candidate—nearly doubled between 1976 and 2008 (Bishop, 2008). The percentage of entering collegians declaring themselves as politically "middle of the road" dropped from 60 percent in 1983 to 46 in 2013, with corresponding increases in those declaring themselves on the right or the left (Eagan et al., 2014; Pryor et al., 2007).

In laboratory studies, the competitive relationships and mistrust that individuals often display when playing games with one another often worsen when the players are groups (Winquist & Larson, 2004). During actual community conflicts, like-minded people associate increasingly with one another, amplifying their shared tendencies. Gang delinquency emerges from a process of mutual reinforcement within neighborhood gangs, whose members share attributes and hostilities (Cartwright, 1975). If "a second out-of-control 15-year-old moves in [on your block]," surmises David Lykken (1997), "the mischief they get into as a team is likely to be more than merely double what the first would do on his own. . . . A gang is more dangerous than the sum of its individual parts." Indeed, "unsupervised peer groups" are "the strongest predictor" of a neighborhood's crime victimization rate, report Bonita Veysey and Steven Messner (1999). Moreover, experimental interventions that take delinquent adolescents and group them with other delinquents—no surprise to any group polarization researcher—increase the rate of problem behavior (Dishion et al., 1999).

GROUP POLARIZATION ON THE INTERNET. From the invention of the printing press to the increasing number of cable channels to the Internet, the amount of available information has mushroomed. Where once people shared the same information from a few networks and national news magazines and newspapers, today we choose from a myriad of sources. With so many choices, we naturally "selectively expose" ourselves to like-minded media. We enjoy media feeds that support our views and slam those we despise. (Tell us which media you read and we'll guess your political ideology.)

As people selectively read blogs and visit chat rooms, does the Internet herd them into "tribes of common thought"? Do the Internet's segregated communities amplify social fragmentation and political polarization? The Internet's countless virtual groups enable peacemakers and neo-Nazis, geeks and goths, conspiracy schemers and cancer survivors to isolate themselves with like-minded others and find support for their shared concerns, interests, and suspicions (Gerstenfeld et al., 2003; McKenna & Bargh, 1998, 2000; Sunstein, 2001, 2009).

Research confirms that most of us read blogs that reinforce rather than challenge our views, and those blogs link mostly to like-minded blogs—connecting liberals with liberals, conservatives with conservatives—like having conversations with the bathroom mirror (Lazer et al., 2009). The net result is that in today's world, political polarization—despising people of opposing political views—has become considerably more intense than racial polarization (Iyengar & Westwood, 2014). More information deepens rather than moderates partisan divisions. E-mail, Google, and chat rooms "make it much easier for small groups to rally like-minded people, crystallize diffuse hatreds, and mobilize lethal force," observed Robert Wright (2003). Peacemakers become more pacifistic and militia members more terror prone. According to one analysis, terrorist websites—which grew from a dozen in 1997 to some 4,700 at the end of 2005—increased more than four times faster than the total number of websites (Ariza, 2006). Moreover, the longer people spend in segregated "Dark Web" forums, the more violent their messages (Chen, 2012). The Boston Marathon bombers Tamerland and Dozhokhar Tsarnaev, reportedly were "self-radicalized" through their Internet exposure (Wilson et al., 2013).

GROUP POLARIZATION IN TERRORIST ORGANIZATIONS.   From their analysis of terrorist organizations throughout the world, Clark McCauley and Mary Segal (1987; McCauley, 2002) note that terrorism does not erupt suddenly. Rather, it arises among people whose shared grievances bring them together and fans their fire. As they interact in isolation from moderating influences, they become progressively more extreme. The social amplifier brings the signal in more strongly. The result is violent acts that the individuals, apart from the group, would never have committed.

For example, the September 11, 2001, terrorists were bred by a long process that engaged the polarizing effect of interaction among the like-minded. The process of becoming a terrorist, noted a National Research Council panel, isolates individuals from other belief systems, dehumanizes potential targets, and tolerates no dissent (Smelser & Mitchell, 2002). Group members come to categorize the world as "us" and "them" (Moghaddam, 2005; Qirko, 2004). Ariel Merari (2002), an investigator of Middle Eastern and Sri Lankan suicide terrorism, believes the key to creating a terrorist suicide is the group process. "To the best of my knowledge, there has not been a single case of suicide terrorism which was done on a personal whim."

According to one analysis of terrorists who were members of the Salafi Jihad—an Islamic fundamentalist movement, including al Qaeda—70 percent joined while living as expatriates. After moving to foreign places in search of jobs or education, they became keenly mindful of their Muslim identity and often gravitated to mosques and moved in with other expatriate Muslims, who sometimes recruited them into cell groups that provided "mutual

focus ON   Group Polarization

Shakespeare portrayed the polarizing power of the like-minded group in this dialogue of Julius Caesar's followers:

Antony: Kind souls, what weep you when you but behold Our Caesar's vesture wounded? Look you here. Here is himself, marr'd, as you see, with traitors.

First Citizen: O piteous spectacle!

Second Citizen: O noble Caesar!

Third Citizen: O woeful day!

Fourth Citizen: O traitors, villains!

First Citizen: O most bloody sight!

Second Citizen: We will be revenged!

All: Revenge! About! Seek! Burn! Fire! Kill! Slay! Let not a traitor live!

Source: From *Julius Caesar* by William Shakespeare, Act III, Scene ii, lines 199–209.

emotional and social support" and "development of a common identity" (Sageman, 2004). One of the Islamic State's senior militants reports that his movement was born inside an American prison in Iraq: "If there was no American prison in Iraq, there would be no IS now. [The prison] was a factory. It made us all. It built our ideology. . . . We had so much time to sit and plan. It was the perfect environment" (quoted by Chulov, 2014).

Massacres, similarly, are group phenomena. The violence is enabled and escalated by the killers egging one another on, noted Robert Zajonc (2000), who knew violence as a survivor of a World War II Warsaw air raid that killed both his parents (Burnstein, 2009). It is difficult to influence someone once "in the pressure cooker of the terrorist group," noted Jerrold Post (2005) after interviewing many accused terrorists. "In the long run, the most effective antiterrorist policy is one that inhibits potential recruits from joining in the first place."

Explaining Group Polarization

Why do groups adopt stances that are more exaggerated than that of their average individual member? Researchers hoped that solving the mystery of group polarization might provide some insights into group influence. Solving small puzzles sometimes provides clues for solving larger ones.

Among several proposed theories of group polarization, two have survived scientific scrutiny. One deals with the *arguments* presented during a discussion and is an example of *informational influence* (influence that results from accepting evidence about reality). The other concerns how members of a group view themselves vis-à-vis the other members, an example of *normative influence* (influence based on a person's desire to be accepted or admired by others).

INFORMATIONAL INFLUENCE

According to the best-supported explanation, group discussion elicits a pooling of ideas, most of which favor the dominant viewpoint. Some discussed ideas are common knowledge to group members (Gigone & Hastie, 1993; Larson et al., 1994; Stasser, 1991). Other ideas may include persuasive arguments that some group members had not previously considered. When discussing Helen the writer, someone may say, "Helen should go for it, because she has little to lose. If her novel flops, she can always go back to writing cheap westerns." Such statements often entangle information about the person's *arguments* with cues concerning the person's *position* on the issue. But when people hear relevant arguments without learning the specific stands other people assume, they still shift their positions (Burnstein & Vinokur, 1977; Hinsz et al., 1997). *Arguments,* in and of themselves, matter.

But there's more to attitude change than merely hearing someone else's arguments. *Active participation* in discussion produces more attitude change than does passive listening. Participants and observers hear the same ideas. But when participants express them in their own words, the verbal commitment magnifies the impact. The more group members repeat one another's ideas, the more they rehearse and validate them (Brauer et al., 1995).

People's minds are not just blank tablets for persuaders to write upon. With central route persuasion, what people think in response to a message is crucial. Indeed, just thinking about an issue for a couple of minutes can strengthen opinions (Tesser et al., 1995). (Perhaps you can recall your feelings becoming polarized as you merely ruminated about someone you disliked, or liked.)

NORMATIVE INFLUENCE

A second explanation of polarization involves comparison with others. As Leon Festinger (1954) argued in his influential theory of **social comparison,** we humans want to evaluate our opinions and abilities by comparing our views with others'. We are most persuaded by people in our "reference groups"—groups we identify with (Abrams et al., 1990; Hogg et al., 1990). Moreover, we want people to like us, so we may express stronger opinions after discovering that others share our views.

When we ask people (as we asked you earlier) to predict how others would respond to items such as the "Helen" dilemma, they typically exhibit **pluralistic ignorance:** They don't

"If you have an apple and I have an apple and we exchange apples, then you and I will still each have one apple. But if you have an idea and I have an idea and we exchange these ideas, then each of us will have two ideas."
—Charles F. Brannan, Secretary of Agriculture, 1949

social comparison
Evaluating one's opinions and abilities by comparing oneself with others.

pluralistic ignorance
A false impression of what most other people are thinking or feeling, or how they are responding.

realize how strongly others support the socially preferred tendency (in this case, writing the novel). A typical person will advise writing the novel even if its chance of success is only 4 in 10 but will estimate that most other people would require 5 or 6 in 10. (This finding is reminiscent of the self-serving bias: People tend to view themselves as better-than-average embodiments of socially desirable traits and attitudes.) When the discussion begins, most people discover they are not outshining the others as they had supposed. In fact, others are ahead of them, having taken an even stronger position in favor of writing the novel. No longer restrained by a misperceived group norm, they are liberated to voice their preferences more strongly.

Perhaps you can recall a time when you and someone else wanted to date each other but each of you feared to make the first move, presuming the other was not interested. Such pluralistic ignorance impedes the start-up of relationships (Vorauer & Ratner, 1996).

Or perhaps you can recall when you and others were guarded and reserved in a group, until someone broke the ice and said, "Well, to be perfectly honest, I think. . . ." Soon you were all surprised to discover strong support for your shared views. Sometimes when a professor asks if anyone has any questions, no one will respond, leading each student to infer that he or she is the only one confused. All presume that 'fear of embarrassment explains their own silence but that everyone else's silence means they understand the material.

Social comparison theory prompted experiments that exposed people to others' positions but not to their arguments. This is roughly the experience we have when reading the results of an opinion poll or of exit polling on election day. When people learn others' positions—without prior commitment and without discussion or sharing of arguments—will they adjust their responses to maintain a socially favorable position? As Figure 10 illustrates, they will. This comparison-based polarization is usually less than that produced by a lively discussion. Still, it's surprising that instead of simply conforming to the group average, people often go it one better.

Merely learning others' choices also contributes to the bandwagon effect that creates blockbuster songs, books, and movies. One experiment engaged 14,341 Internet participants in listening to and, if they wished, downloading previously unknown songs (Salganik et al., 2006). The researchers randomly assigned some participants to a

Pluralistic ignorance. Sometimes a false presumption of another's disinterest may prevent two people with a mutual romantic interest from connecting.
Digital Vision/Punchstock

FIGURE :: 10

On "risky" dilemma items (such as the case of Helen), mere exposure to others' judgments enhanced individuals' risk-prone tendencies. On "cautious" dilemma items (such as the case of Roger), exposure to others' judgments enhanced their cautiousness.
Source: Data from Myers (1978).

Risk

10-in-10
9-in-10   Cautious items
8-in-10
7-in-10
6-in-10
5-in-10
4-in-10
3-in-10   Risky items
2-in-10
1-in-10
        No exposure   Exposure

Mere exposure to others' judgments

JUST A NORMAL DAY AT THE NATION'S MOST IMPORTANT FINANCIAL INSTITUTION...

An *Economist* cover about a stock market crash.
Reprinted by permission of Kevin Kal Kallaugher, *The Economist*, Kaltoons.com

condition that disclosed previous participants' download choices. Among those given that information, popular songs became more popular and unpopular songs became less popular.

Group polarization research illustrates the complexity of social-psychological inquiry. Much as we like our explanations of a phenomenon to be simple, one explanation seldom accounts for all the data. Because people are complex, more than one factor frequently influences an outcome. In group discussions, persuasive arguments predominate on issues that have a factual element ("Is she guilty of the crime?"). Social comparison sways responses on value-laden judgments ("How long a sentence should she serve?") (Kaplan, 1989). On the many issues that have both factual and value-laden aspects, the two factors work together. Discovering that others share one's feelings (social comparison) unleashes arguments (informational influence) supporting what everyone secretly favors.

SUMMING UP: Group Polarization: Do Groups Intensify Our Opinions?

- Potentially positive and negative results arise from group discussion. While trying to understand the curious finding that discussion increased risk taking, investigators discovered that discussion actually tends to strengthen whatever is the initially dominant point of view, whether risky or cautious.

- In everyday situations, too, group interaction tends to intensify opinions. This *group polarization* phenomenon provided a window through which researchers could observe group influence.

- Experiments confirmed two group influences: informational and normative. The information gleaned from a discussion mostly favors the initially preferred alternative, thus reinforcing support for it.

GROUPTHINK: DO GROUPS HINDER OR ASSIST GOOD DECISIONS?

Describe when and why group influences often hinder good decisions. Describe also when groups promote good decisions and how we can lead groups to make optimal decisions.

Do the social psychological phenomena we have been considering occur in sophisticated groups such as corporate boards or a president's cabinet? Is there likely to be self-justification? Self-serving bias? A cohesive "we feeling" promoting conformity and stifling dissent? Public commitment producing resistance to change? Group polarization?

Social psychologist Irving Janis (1971, 1982) wondered whether such phenomena might help explain good and bad group decisions made by some twentieth-century American presidents and their advisers. To find out, he analyzed the decision-making procedures behind several major fiascos:

- *Pearl Harbor.* In the weeks before the December 1941 attack that brought the United States into World War II, military commanders in Hawaii received a stream of information about Japan's preparations for an attack on the United States somewhere in the Pacific. Military intelligence then lost radio contact with Japanese aircraft carriers, which had begun moving straight for Hawaii. Air reconnaissance could have spotted the carriers or at least provided a few minutes' warning. But complacent commanders decided against such precautions. The result: No alert was sounded until the attack on a virtually defenseless base was under way. The loss: 18 ships, 170 planes, and 2,400 lives.

- *The Bay of Pigs Invasion.* In 1961, President John Kennedy and his advisers tried to overthrow Fidel Castro by invading Cuba with 1,400 CIA-trained Cuban exiles. Nearly all the invaders were soon killed or captured, the United States was humiliated, and Cuba allied itself more closely with the former U.S.S.R. After learning the outcome, Kennedy wondered aloud, "How could we have been so stupid?"

- *The Vietnam War.* From 1964 to 1967, President Lyndon Johnson and his "Tuesday lunch group" of policy advisers escalated the war in Vietnam on the assumption that U.S. aerial bombardment, defoliation, and search-and-destroy missions would bring North Vietnam to the peace table with the appreciative support of the South Vietnamese populace. They continued the escalation despite warnings from government intelligence experts and nearly all U.S. allies. The resulting disaster cost more than 58,000 American and 1 million Vietnamese lives, polarized Americans, drove the president from office, and created huge budget deficits that helped fuel inflation in the 1970s.

Janis believed those blunders were bred by the tendency of decision-making groups to suppress dissent in the interest of group harmony, a phenomenon he called **groupthink**. (See "The Inside Story: Irving Janis on Groupthink.") In work groups, team spirit is good for morale and boosts productivity (Mellers et al., 2014; Mullen & Copper, 1994). A shared group identity motivates people to persist on a project (Haslam et al., 2014). But when making decisions, close-knit groups may pay a price. Janis believed that the soil from which groupthink sprouts includes

groupthink
"The mode of thinking that persons engage in when concurrence-seeking becomes so dominant in a cohesive in-group that it tends to override realistic appraisal of alternative courses of action."
—Irving Janis (1971)

- an amiable, *cohesive* group;
- relative *isolation* of the group from dissenting viewpoints; and
- a *directive leader* who signals what decision he or she favors.

When planning the ill-fated Bay of Pigs invasion, for example, the newly elected President Kennedy and his advisers enjoyed a strong esprit de corps. Arguments critical of the plan were suppressed or excluded, and the president soon endorsed the invasion.

Symptoms of Groupthink

From historical records and the memoirs of participants and observers, Janis identified eight groupthink symptoms. The symptoms are a collective form of dissonance reduction as group members, when facing a threat, try to maintain their positive group feeling (Turner & Pratkanis, 1994; Turner et al., 1992).

The first two groupthink symptoms lead group members to *overestimate their group's might and right.*

- *An illusion of invulnerability.* The groups Janis studied all developed an excessive optimism that blinded them to warnings of danger. Told that his forces had lost radio contact with the Japanese carriers, Admiral Kimmel, the chief naval officer at Pearl Harbor, joked that maybe the Japanese were about to round Honolulu's Diamond Head. They actually were, but Kimmel's laughing at the idea dismissed the very possibility of its being true.

THE inside STORY

The idea of *groupthink* hit me while reading Arthur Schlesinger's account of how the Kennedy administration decided to invade the Bay of Pigs. At first, I was puzzled: How could bright, shrewd people like John F. Kennedy and his advisers be taken in by the CIA's stupid, patchwork plan? I began to wonder whether some kind of psychological contagion had interfered, such as social conformity or the concurrence-seeking that I had observed in cohesive small groups. Further study (initially aided by my daughter Charlotte's work on a high school term paper) convinced me that subtle group processes had hampered their carefully appraising the risks and debating the issues. When I then analyzed other U.S. foreign policy fiascos and the Watergate cover-up, I found the same detrimental group processes at work.

Irving Janis (1918–1990)
Courtesy of Irving Janis

- *Unquestioned belief in the group's morality.* Group members assume the inherent morality of their group and ignore ethical and moral issues. The Kennedy group knew that adviser Arthur Schlesinger, Jr., and Senator J. William Fulbright had moral reservations about invading a small, neighboring country. But the group never entertained or discussed those moral qualms.

Group members also become *closed-minded.*

- *Rationalization.* The groups discount challenges by collectively justifying their decisions. President Johnson's Tuesday lunch group spent far more time rationalizing (explaining and justifying) than reflecting upon and rethinking prior decisions to escalate. Each initiative became an action to defend and justify.

- *Stereotyped view of opponent.* Groupthinkers consider their enemies too evil to negotiate with or too weak and unintelligent to defend themselves against the planned initiative. The Kennedy group convinced itself that Castro's military was so weak and his popular support so shallow that a single brigade could easily overturn his regime.

Finally, the group suffers from pressures toward *uniformity.*

- *Conformity pressure.* Group members rebuffed those who raised doubts about the group's assumptions and plans, at times by personal sarcasm. Once, when President Johnson's assistant Bill Moyers arrived at a meeting, the president derided him with, "Well, here comes Mr. Stop-the-Bombing." Faced with such ridicule, most people fall into line.

Self-censorship contributes to an illusion of unanimity.
© Henry Martin/The New Yorker Collection/www.cartoonbank.com

Groupthink on a *Titanic* scale. Despite four messages of possible icebergs ahead, Captain Edward Smith—a directive and respected leader—kept his ship sailing at full speed into the night. There was an illusion of invulnerability (many believed the ship to be unsinkable). There was conformity pressure (crew mates chided the lookout for not being able to use his naked eye and dismissed his misgivings). And there was mindguarding (a *Titanic* telegraph operator failed to pass the last and most complete iceberg warning to Captain Smith).
20TH Century Fox/Paramount/The Kobal Collection/Art Resource

- *Self-censorship.* To avoid uncomfortable disagreements, members withheld or discounted their misgivings. In the months following the Bay of Pigs invasion, Arthur Schlesinger (1965, p. 255) reproached himself "for having kept so silent during those crucial discussions in the Cabinet Room, though my feelings of guilt were tempered by the knowledge that a course of objection would have accomplished little save to gain me a name as a nuisance." It's not just politicians. Both online and in person, people are less willing to share their view when they think others disagree (Hampton et al., 2014).

- *Illusion of unanimity.* Self-censorship and pressure not to puncture the consensus create an illusion of unanimity. What is more, the apparent consensus confirms the group's decision. This appearance of consensus was evident in the Pearl Harbor, Bay of Pigs, and Vietnam fiascos and in other fiascos before and since. Albert Speer (1971), an adviser to Adolf Hitler, described the atmosphere around Hitler as one where pressure to conform suppressed all deviation. The absence of dissent created an illusion of unanimity:

  > In normal circumstances people who turn their backs on reality are soon set straight by the mockery and criticism of those around them, which makes them aware they have lost credibility. In the Third Reich there were no such correctives. . . . No external factors disturbed the uniformity of hundreds of unchanging faces, all mine. (p. 379)

- *Mindguards.* Some members protect the group from information that would call into question the effectiveness or morality of its decisions. Before the Bay of Pigs invasion, Robert Kennedy took Schlesinger aside and told him, "Don't push it any further." Secretary of State Dean Rusk withheld diplomatic and intelligence experts' warnings against the invasion. They thus served as the president's "mindguards," protecting him from disagreeable facts rather than physical harm.

People "are never so likely to settle a question rightly as when they discuss it freely."
—John Stuart Mill, *On Liberty,* 1859

Groupthink symptoms can produce a failure to seek and discuss contrary information and alternative possibilities (Figure 11). When a leader promotes an idea and when a group insulates itself from dissenting views, groupthink may produce defective decisions (McCauley, 1989).

British psychologists Ben Newell and David Lagnado (2003) believe groupthink symptoms may have also contributed to the Iraq War. They and others contended that both Saddam Hussein and George W. Bush surrounded themselves with like-minded advisers and intimidated opposing voices into silence. Moreover, they each received filtered information that mostly supported their assumptions—Iraq's expressed assumption that the

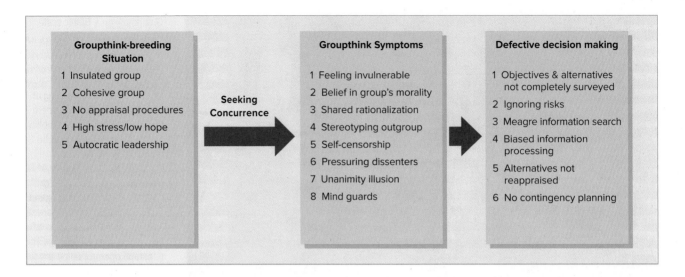

FIGURE :: 11

Theoretical Analysis of Groupthink
Source: Adapted from Janis & Mann (1977, p. 132).

invading force could be resisted; and the United States' assumption that Iraq had weapons of mass destruction, that its people would welcome invading soldiers as liberators, and that a short, peaceful occupation would soon lead to a thriving democracy.

Critiquing Groupthink

Despite the power and fame of the groupthink concept, some researchers have been skeptical (Fuller & Aldag, 1998; t'Hart, 1998). The evidence was retrospective, so Janis could pick supporting cases. Follow-up experiments have, however, supported aspects of Janis's theory:

- Directive leadership is indeed associated with poorer decisions, because subordinates sometimes feel too weak or insecure to speak up (Granstrom & Stiwne, 1998; McCauley, 1998).
- Groups do prefer supporting over challenging information (Schulz-Hardt et al., 2000).
- When members look to a group for acceptance, approval, and social identity, they may suppress disagreeable thoughts (Hogg & Hains, 1998; Turner & Pratkanis, 1997).
- Groups that make smart decisions have widely distributed conversation, with socially attuned members who take turns speaking (Woolley et al., 2010).
- Groups with diverse perspectives outperform groups of like-minded experts (Nemeth & Ormiston, 2007; Page, 2007). Engaging people who think differently from you can make you feel uncomfortable. But compared with comfortably homogeneous groups, diverse groups tend to produce more ideas and greater creativity.
- Group success depends both on what group members know and how effectively they can share that information (Bonner & Baumann, 2012). In discussion, unshared information often gets suppressed as discussion focuses on what group members all know already (Sunstein & Hastie, 2008).

Yet friendships need not breed groupthink (Esser, 1998; Mullen et al., 1994). In a secure, highly cohesive group (say, a family), committed members will often care enough to voice disagreement (Packer, 2009). The norms of a cohesive group can favor either consensus, which can lead to groupthink, or critical analysis, which prevents it (Postmes et al., 2001). When academic colleagues in a close-knit department share their draft manuscripts with one another, they *want* critique: "Do what you can to save me from my own mistakes." In a free-spirited atmosphere, cohesion can enhance effective teamwork, too.

Moreover, when Philip Tetlock and colleagues (1992) looked at a broader sample of historical episodes, it became clear that even good group procedures sometimes yield

"Truth springs from argument amongst friends."

—Philosopher David Hume, 1711–1776

ill-fated decisions. As President Carter and his advisers plotted their humiliating attempt to rescue American hostages in Iran in 1980, they welcomed different views and realistically considered the perils. Had it not been for a helicopter problem, the rescue might have succeeded. (Carter later reflected that had he sent in one more helicopter, he would have been reelected president.) Sometimes good groups suffer bad outcomes.

Preventing Groupthink

Flawed group dynamics help explain many failed decisions; sometimes too many cooks spoil the broth. However, given open leadership, a cohesive team spirit can improve decisions. Sometimes two or more heads are better than one.

In search of conditions that breed good decisions, Janis also analyzed two successful ventures: the Truman administration's formulation of the Marshall Plan for getting Europe back on its feet after World War II and the Kennedy administration's successful challenge of the Soviet Union's 1962 attempt to install missile bases in Cuba. Janis's (1982) recommendations for preventing groupthink incorporate many of the effective group procedures used in both cases:

- *Be impartial*—do not endorse any position. Don't start group discussions by having people state their positions; doing so suppresses information sharing and degrades the quality of decisions (Mojzisch & Schulz-Hardt, 2010).
- *Encourage critical evaluation;* assign a "devil's advocate." Better yet, welcome the input of a genuine dissenter, which does even more to stimulate original thinking and to open a group to opposing views, report Charlan Nemeth and colleagues (2001a,b).
- *Occasionally subdivide the group,* then reunite to air differences.
- *Welcome critiques* from outside experts and associates.
- Before implementing, call a *"second-chance" meeting* to air any lingering doubts.

When such steps are taken, group decisions may take longer to make, yet ultimately prove less defective and more effective.

> "One of the dangers in the White House, based on my reading of history, is that you get wrapped up in groupthink and everybody agrees with everything and there's no discussion and there are no dissenting views. So I'm going to be welcoming a vigorous debate inside the White House."
>
> —Barack Obama, at a December 1, 2008, Press Conference

Group Problem Solving

Not every group decision is flawed by groupthink. Under some conditions, two or more heads really are better than one. In work settings such as operating rooms and executive boardrooms, team decisions surpass individual decisions when the discussion values each person's skills and knowledge and draws out their varied information (Mesmer-Magnus & DeChurch, 2009).

Patrick Laughlin and John Adamopoulos (1980; Laughlin, 1996; Laughlin et al., 2003) have shown the wisdom of groups with various intellectual tasks. Consider one of their analogy problems:

Assertion is to *disproved* as *action* is to
   a. *hindered*
   b. *opposed*
   c. *illegal*
   d. *precipitate*
   e. *thwarted*

Most college students miss this question when answering alone, but answer correctly (thwarted) after discussion. Moreover, Laughlin finds that if just two members of a six-person group are initially correct, two-thirds of the time they convince all the others. If only one person is correct, this "minority of one" almost three-fourths of the time fails to convince the group. And when given tricky logic problems, three, four, or five heads are better than two (Laughlin et al., 2006).

Studies of the accuracy of eyewitness reports of a videotaped crime or job interview confirm that several heads can be better than one (Hinsz, 1990; Warnick & Sanders, 1980). Interacting groups of eyewitnesses gave accounts that were much more accurate than those provided by the average isolated individual. Two heads are better than one even for simple perceptual judgments made by similarly capable people (Bahrami et al., 2010; Ernst, 2010). When unsure of what they've seen, sports referees are smart to confer before making their call.

Several heads critiquing one another can also allow the group to avoid some forms of cognitive bias and produce higher quality ideas (McGlynn et al., 1995; Wright et al., 1990). In science, the benefits of diverse minds collaborating has led to more and more "team science"—to an increasing proportion of scientific publication, especially highly cited publication, by multi-author teams (Cacioppo, 2007). Teams also have surpassed individuals in predicting world political events (Mellers et al., 2014).

But contrary to the popular idea that face-to-face brainstorming generates more creative ideas than do the same people working alone, researchers agree it isn't so (Paulus et al., 1995, 2000, 2011; Stroebe & Diehl, 1994). And contrary to the popular idea that brainstorming is most productive when the brainstormers are admonished "not to criticize," encouraging people to debate stimulates ideas and extends creative thinking beyond the brainstorming session (Nemeth et al., 2004).

People *feel* more productive when generating ideas in groups (partly because people disproportionately credit themselves for the ideas that come out). But time and again researchers have found that people working alone usually will generate *more* good ideas than will the same people in a group (Nijstad et al., 2006; Rietzschel et al., 2006). Large brainstorming groups are especially inefficient. Better to have people generate ideas individually, then stimulate each other in small groups (Paulus & Korde, 2014). In accord with social loafing theory, large groups cause some individuals to free-ride on others' efforts. They cause others to feel apprehensive about voicing oddball ideas. And they cause "production blocking"—losing one's ideas while awaiting a turn to speak (Nijstad & Stroebe, 2006).

As James Watson and Francis Crick demonstrated in discovering DNA, challenging two-person conversations can effectively engage creative thinking. Watson later recalled that he and Crick benefited from *not* being the most brilliant people seeking to crack the genetic code. The most brilliant researcher "was so intelligent that she rarely sought advice" (quoted by Cialdini, 2005). If you are (and regard yourself as) the most gifted person, why seek others' input? Like Watson and Crick, psychologists Daniel Kahneman and the late Amos Tversky similarly collaborated in their exploration of intuition and its influence on economic decision making. (See "The Inside Story: Behind a Nobel Prize" shown below.)

> "Iron sharpens iron, and one person sharpens the wits of another."
> —Proverbs 27:17

> "If you want to go quickly, go alone. If you want to go far, go together."
> —African Proverb

THE inside STORY

Behind a Nobel Prize: Two Minds Are Better Than One

In the spring of 1969, Amos Tversky, my younger colleague at the Hebrew University of Jerusalem, and I met over lunch and shared our own recurrent errors of judgment. From there were born our studies of human intuition.

I had enjoyed collaboration before, but this was magical. Amos was very smart, and also very funny. We could spend hours of solid work in continuous mirth. His work was always characterized by confidence and by a crisp elegance, and it was a joy to find those characteristics now attached to my ideas as well. As we were writing our first paper, I was conscious of how much better it was than the more hesitant piece I would have written by myself.

All our ideas were jointly owned. We did almost all the work on our joint projects while physically together, including the drafting of questionnaires and papers. Our principle was to discuss every disagreement until it had been resolved to our mutual satisfaction.

Some of the greatest joys of our collaboration—and probably much of its success—came from our ability to elaborate on each other's nascent thoughts: If I expressed a half-formed idea, I knew that Amos would be there to understand it, probably more clearly than I did, and that if it had merit, he would see it.

Amos and I shared the wonder of together owning a goose that could lay golden eggs—a joint mind that was better than our separate minds. We were a team, and we remained in that mode for well over a decade. The Nobel Prize was awarded for work that we produced during that period of intense collaboration.

Daniel Kahneman
Princeton University,
Nobel Laureate, 2002
Courtesy of Daniel Kahneman

Sometimes too many talented people hurts team performance. In the laboratory and in professional sports, talented team members enhance performance—unless a "too-much-talent effect," with too many prima donnas, detracts from team coordination (Swaab et al., 2014). Sometimes a team of superstars fails to fulfill expectations. The too-much-talent effect appears mostly in sports such as basketball, when team members work together, rather than in sports such as baseball, where play requires less continual coordination.

However, Vincent Brown and Paul Paulus (2002) have identified three ways to enhance group brainstorming:

- *Combine group and solitary brainstorming.* Group brainstorming is most productive when it *precedes* solo brainstorming. With new categories primed by the group brainstorming, individuals' ideas can continue flowing without being impeded by the group context that allows only one person to speak at a time. Creative work teams also tend to be small and to alternate working alone, working in pairs, and meeting as a circle (Paulus & Coskun, 2012).

- *Have group members interact by writing.* Another way to take advantage of group priming, without being impeded by the one-at-a-time rule, is to have group members write and read, rather than speak and listen. Moreover, when leaders urge people to generate lots of ideas (rather than just good ideas), they generate both more ideas *and* more good ideas (Paulus et al., 2011). So whatever comes to mind, put it down.

- *Incorporate electronic brainstorming.* There is a potentially more efficient way to avoid the verbal traffic jams of traditional group brainstorming in larger groups: Let individuals produce and read ideas on networked computers.

So, when group members freely combine their creative ideas and varied insights, the frequent result is not groupthink but group problem solving. The wisdom of groups is evident in everyday life as well as in the laboratory:

- *Weather forecasting.* "Two forecasters will come up with a forecast that is more accurate than either would have come up with working alone," reported Joel Myers (1997), president of the largest private weather forecasting service. In 2010, scientists' predictions of the summer's minimum Arctic sea ice ranged from 2.5 million to 5.6 million square kilometers. The average prediction—4.8 million— almost exactly matched the actual result (Wiltze, 2010).

- *Google.* Google has become a dominant search engine by harnessing what James Surowiecki (2004) calls *The Wisdom of Crowds.* Google interprets a link to Page X as a vote for Page X, and weights most heavily links from pages that are themselves highly ranked.

- *The "crowd within."* Likewise, the average of different guesses from the same persons tends to surpass the person's individual guesses (Herzog & Hertwig, 2009). Edward Vul and Harold Pashler (2008) discovered this when asking people to guess the correct answers to factual questions such as "What percentage of the world's airports are in the United States?" Then the researchers asked their participants to make a second guess, either immediately or 3 weeks later. The result? "You can gain about 1/10th as much from asking yourself the same question twice as you can from getting a second opinion from someone else, but if you wait 3 weeks, the benefit of re-asking yourself the same question rises to 1/3 the value of a second opinion."

- *Prediction markets.* In U.S. presidential elections since 1988, the final public opinion polls have provided a good gauge to the election result. An even better predictor, however, has been the Iowa Election Market. Taking everything (including polls) into account, people buy and sell shares in candidates.

- *Combining expert predictions.* In one study conducted in 2010, people worldwide estimated the odds of 199 events, such as Italy's leader leaving office before January 1, 2012. When forecasters were trained to be wary of cognitive biases and shared information in teams—especially elite teams of previously successful "superforecasters"—they excelled (Mellers et al., 2014; Mannes et al., 2014).

Thus, we can conclude that when information from many, diverse people is combined, all of us together can become smarter than almost any of us alone. We're in some ways like a flock of geese, no one of which has a perfect navigational sense. Nevertheless, by staying close to one another, a group of geese can navigate accurately. The flock is smarter than the bird.

SUMMING UP: Groupthink: Do Groups Hinder or Assist Good Decisions?

- Analysis of several international fiascos indicates that group cohesion can override realistic appraisal of a situation. This is especially true when group members strongly desire unity, when they are isolated from opposing ideas, and when the leader signals what he or she wants from the group.

- Symptomatic of this overriding concern for harmony, labeled *groupthink,* are (1) an illusion of invulnerability, (2) rationalization, (3) unquestioned belief in the group's morality, (4) stereotyped views of the opposition, (5) pressure to conform, (6) self-censorship of misgivings, (7) an illusion of unanimity, and (8) "mindguards" who protect the group from unpleasant information. Critics have noted that some aspects of Janis's groupthink model (such as

directive leadership) seem more implicated in flawed decisions than others (such as cohesiveness).

- Both in experiments and in actual history, however, groups sometimes decide wisely. These cases suggest ways to prevent groupthink: upholding impartiality, encouraging "devil's advocate" positions, subdividing and then reuniting to discuss a decision, seeking outside input, and having a "second-chance" meeting before implementing a decision.

- Research on group problem solving suggests that groups can be more accurate than individuals; groups also generate more and better ideas if the group is small or if, in a large group, individual brainstorming follows the group session.

THE INFLUENCE OF THE MINORITY: HOW DO INDIVIDUALS INFLUENCE THE GROUP?

Explain when—and how—individuals influence their groups. Identify what makes some individuals effective.

Each chapter in this social influence unit concludes with a reminder of our power as individuals. We have seen that

- cultural situations mold us, but we also help create and choose these situations.
- pressures to conform sometimes overwhelm our better judgment, but blatant pressure motivates reactance as we assert our individuality and freedom.
- persuasive forces are powerful, but we can resist persuasion by making public commitments and by anticipating persuasive appeals.

This chapter has emphasized group influences on the individual, so we conclude by seeing how individuals can influence their groups.

In the film *12 Angry Men,* a lone juror eventually wins over 11 others. In a jury room, that's a rare occurrence. Yet in most social movements, a small minority will sway, and then eventually become, the majority. "All history," wrote Ralph Waldo Emerson, "is a record of the power of minorities, and of minorities of one." Think of Copernicus and Galileo, of Martin Luther King, Jr., of Susan B. Anthony, of Nelson Mandela. The American civil rights movement was ignited by the refusal of one African American woman, Rosa Parks, to relinquish her seat on a bus in Montgomery, Alabama. Technological history has also been made by innovative minorities. As Robert Fulton developed his steamboat—"Fulton's Folly"—he endured constant derision: "Never did a single encouraging remark, a bright hope, a warm wish, cross my path" (Cantril & Bumstead, 1960). Indeed, if minority viewpoints never prevailed, history would be static and nothing would ever change.

What makes a minority persuasive? What might Arthur Schlesinger have done to get the Kennedy group to consider his doubts about the Bay of Pigs invasion? Experiments initiated by Serge Moscovici in Paris identified several determinants of minority influence: *consistency, self-confidence,* and *defection.*

Note: "Minority influence" refers to minority opinions, not to ethnic minorities.

Consistency

More influential than a minority that wavers is a minority that sticks to its position. Moscovici and associates (1969; Moscovici, 1985) found that if a minority of participants consistently judges blue slides as green, members of the majority will occasionally agree. But if the minority wavers, saying "blue" to one-third of the blue slides and "green" to the rest, virtually no one in the majority will ever agree with "green."

Experiments show—and experience confirms—that nonconformity, especially persistent nonconformity, is often painful, and that being a minority in a group can be unpleasant (Levine, 1989; Lücken & Simon, 2005). That helps explain a *minority slowness effect*—a tendency for people with minority views to express them less quickly than do people in the majority (Bassili, 2003). If you set out to be Emerson's minority of one, prepare yourself for ridicule—especially when you argue an issue that's personally relevant to the majority and when the group wants to settle an issue by reaching consensus (Kameda & Sugimori, 1993; Kruglanski & Webster, 1991; Trost et al., 1992).

Even when people in the majority know that the disagreeing person is factually or morally right, they may still, if refusing to change, dislike the person (Chan et al., 2010). When Charlan Nemeth (1979, 2011) planted a minority of two within a simulated jury and had them oppose the majority's opinions, the duo was inevitably disliked. Nevertheless, the majority acknowledged that the persistence of the two did more than anything else to make them rethink their positions. Compared to majority influence that often triggers unthinking agreement, minority influence stimulates a deeper processing of arguments, often with increased creativity (Kenworthy et al., 2008; Martin et al., 2007, 2008). Deviant (minority) views may get you disliked, especially if you are on the fringe of a group, but they can also increase creative innovation (Rijnbout & McKimmie, 2012).

Some successful companies have recognized that minority perspectives can feed creativity and innovation. 3M, which has been famed for valuing "respect for individual initiative," has welcomed employees spending time on wild ideas. The Post-it note's adhesive was a failed attempt by Spencer Silver to develop a super-strong glue. Art Fry, after having trouble marking his church choir hymnal with pieces of paper, thought, "What I need is a bookmark with Spence's adhesive along the edge." Even so, this was a minority view that eventually won over a skeptical marketing department (Nemeth, 1997).

"If the single man plant himself indomitably on his instincts, and there abide, the huge world will come round to him."
—Ralph Waldo Emerson, *Nature, Address, and Lectures: The American Scholar,* 1849

Over a period of time, a few people at 3M were consistent, self-confident, and persistent about the usefulness of the glue used on Post-it notes. These are three factors that may influence a majority group.
BananaStock/Jupiterimages

Self-Confidence

Consistency and persistence convey self-confidence. Furthermore, Nemeth and Joel Wachtler (1974) reported that any behavior by a minority that conveys self-confidence—for example, taking the head seat at the table—tends to raise self-doubts among the majority. By being firm and forceful, the minority's apparent self-assurance may prompt the majority to reconsider its position. This is especially so on matters of opinion ("from which country should Italy import most of its raw oil?"), rather than fact ("from which country does Italy import most of its raw oil?" [Maass et al., 1996]).

Defections from the Majority

A persistent minority punctures any illusion of unanimity. When a minority consistently doubts the majority wisdom, majority members become freer to express their own doubts and may even switch to the minority position. But what about a lone defector, someone who initially agreed with the majority but then reconsidered and dissented? In research with University of Pittsburgh students, John Levine (1989) found that a minority person who had defected from the majority was even more persuasive than a consistent minority voice. Nemeth's jury-simulation experiments found that—not unlike the *12 Angry Men* scenario—once defections begin, others often soon follow, initiating a snowball effect.

There is a delightful irony in this new emphasis on how individuals can influence the group. Until recently, the idea that the minority could sway the majority was itself a minority view in social psychology. Nevertheless, by arguing consistently and forcefully, Moscovici, Nemeth, Maass, and others convinced the majority of group influence researchers that minority influence is a phenomenon worthy of study. And the way that several of these minority influence researchers came by their interests should, perhaps, not surprise us. Anne Maass (1998) became interested in how minorities could effect social change after growing up in postwar Germany and hearing her grandmother's personal accounts of fascism. Charlan Nemeth (1999) developed her interest while she was a visiting professor in Europe "working with Henri Tajfel and Serge Moscovici. The three of us were 'outsiders'—I an American Roman Catholic female in Europe, they having survived World War II as Eastern European Jews. Sensitivity to the value and the struggles of the minority perspective came to dominate our work."

Is Leadership Minority Influence?

leadership
The process by which certain group members motivate and guide the group.

In 1910, the Norwegians and the English engaged in an epic race to the South Pole. The Norwegians, effectively led by Roald Amundsen, made it. The English, ineptly led by Robert Falcon Scott, did not; Scott and three team members died. Amundsen illustrated the power of **leadership,** the process by which individuals mobilize and guide groups.

task leadership
Leadership that organizes work, sets standards, and focuses on goals.

Some leaders are formally appointed or elected; others emerge informally as the group interacts. What makes for good leadership often depends on the situation. The best person to lead the engineering team may not make the best leader of the sales force. Some people excel at **task leadership**—at organizing work, setting standards, and focusing on goal

Participative management, illustrated in this "quality circle," requires democratic rather than autocratic leaders.
Jose Luis Pelaez Inc./Blend Images LLC

focus
ON   Transformational Community Leadership

As a striking example of transformational (consistent, self-confident, inspirational) leadership, consider Walt and Mildred Woodward. During World War II and in the two decades after, they owned and edited the newspaper on Bainbridge Island, Washington. It was from Bainbridge that, on March 30, 1942, the first of nearly 120,000 West Coast people of Japanese descent were relocated to internment camps. With 6 days' notice and under armed guard, they boarded a ferry and were sent away, leaving behind on the dock tearful friends and neighbors (one of whom was their insurance agent, my [DM's] father). "Where, in the face of their fine record since December 7 [Pearl Harbor Day], in the face of their rights of citizenship, in the face of their own relatives being drafted and enlisting in our Army, in the face of American decency, is there any excuse for this high-handed, much-too-short evacuation order?" editorialized the Woodwards (1942) in their *Bainbridge Review*. Throughout the war, the Woodwards, alone among West Coast newspaper editors, continued to voice opposition to the internment. They also recruited their former part-time employee, Paul Ohtaki, to write a weekly column bringing news of the incarcerated islanders. Stories by Ohtaki and others of "Pneumonia Hits 'Grandpa Koura'" and "First Island Baby at Manzanar Born" reminded those back home of their absent neighbors and prepared the way for their eventual welcome home—a contrast to the prejudice that greeted their return to other West Coast communities where newspapers supported the internment and fostered hostility toward the Japanese.

After enduring some vitriolic opposition, the Woodwards lived to be honored for their courage, which was dramatized in the book and movie *Snow Falling on Cedars.* At the March 30, 2004, groundbreaking for a national memorial on the ferry departure site, former internee and Bainbridge Island Japanese American Community president Frank Kitamoto declared that "this memorial is also for Walt and Millie Woodward, for Ken Myers, for Genevive Williams . . . and the many others who supported us," and who challenged the forced removal at the risk of being called unpatriotic. "Walt Woodward said if we can suspend the Bill of Rights for Japanese Americans it can be suspended for fat Americans or blue-eyed Americans." Reflecting on the

In March of 1942, 274 Bainbridge Islanders became the first of some 120,000 Japanese Americans and Japanese immigrants interned during World War II. Sixty-two years later, ground was broken for a national memorial (*Nidoto Nai Yoni*—Let It Not Happen Again), remembering the internees and the transformational leaders who supported them and prepared for their welcome home.
Historical/Corbis

Woodwards' transformational leadership, cub reporter Ohtaki (1999) observed that "on Bainbridge Island there was none of the hostility to the returning Japanese that you saw in other places, and I think that's in large part because of the Woodwards." When, later, he asked the Woodwards, "Why did you do this, when you could have dropped it and not suffered the anger of some of your readers?" they would always answer, "It was the right thing to do."

---

attainment. Others excel at **social leadership**—at building teamwork, mediating conflicts, and being supportive.

Task leaders generally have a directive style—one that can work well if the leader is bright enough to give good orders (Fiedler, 1987). Being goal oriented, such leaders also keep the group's attention and effort focused on its mission. Experiments show that the combination

social leadership
Leadership that builds teamwork, mediates conflict, and offers support.

of specific, challenging goals and periodic progress reports helps motivate high achievement (Locke & Latham, 1990, 2002, 2009). Men who have the traits associated with ancestral male leadership—fitness, height, masculine (wide) faces—tend to be perceived as dominant leaders and to succeed as CEOs (Blaker et al., 2013; Wong et al., 2011).

Social leaders generally have a democratic style—one that delegates authority, welcomes input from team members, and, as we have seen, helps prevent groupthink. Data amassed from 118 studies reveal that women are much more egalitarian than men; they are more opposed to social hierarchies (Lee et al., 2011). Many experiments reveal that social leadership is good for morale. Group members usually feel more satisfied when they participate in making decisions (Spector, 1986; Vanderslice et al., 1987). Given control over their tasks, workers also become more motivated to achieve (Burger, 1987).

The once-popular "great person" theory of leadership—that all great leaders share certain traits—has fallen into disrepute. Effective leadership styles, we now know, are less about the big "I" than the big "we." Effective leaders represent, enhance, and champion a group's identity (Haslam et al., 2010). Effective leadership also varies with the situation. Subordinates who know what they are doing may resent working under task leadership, whereas those who don't may welcome it. Recently, however, social psychologists have again wondered if there might be qualities that mark a good leader in many situations (Hogan et al., 1994). British social psychologists Peter Smith and Monir Tayeb (1989) report that studies done in India, Taiwan, and Iran have found that the most effective supervisors in coal mines, banks, and government offices scored high on tests of *both* task and social leadership. They are actively concerned with how work is progressing *and* sensitive to the needs of their subordinates.

Studies also reveal that many effective leaders of laboratory groups, work teams, and large corporations exhibit the behaviors that help make a minority view persuasive. Such leaders engender trust by *consistently* sticking to their goals. And they often exude a *self-confident* charisma that kindles the allegiance of their followers (Bennis, 1984; House & Singh, 1987). Effective leaders typically have a compelling *vision* of some desired state of affairs, especially during times of collective stress (Halevy et al., 2011). They also have an ability to *communicate* that vision to others in clear and simple language, and enough optimism and faith in their group to *inspire* others to follow. Socially dominant, influential individuals also seem competent (whether they are or not) because they act as if they were—by talking a lot (Anderson & Kilduff, 2009).

In one analysis of 50 Dutch companies, the highest morale was at firms with chief executives who most inspired their colleagues "to transcend their own self-interests for the sake of the collective" (de Hoogh et al., 2004). Leadership of this kind—**transformational leadership**—motivates others to identify with and commit themselves to the group's mission. Transformational leaders—many of whom are charismatic, energetic, self-confident extraverts—articulate high standards, inspire people to share their vision, and offer personal attention (Bono & Judge, 2004). In organizations, the frequent result of such leadership is a more engaged, trusting, and effective workforce (Turner et al., 2002).

transformational leadership

Leadership that, enabled by a leader's vision and inspiration, exerts significant influence.

Transformational leadership: Charismatic, energetic, self-confident people will sometimes change organizations or societies by inspiring others to embrace their vision. Martin Luther King, Jr. was this type of leader.

Lei Yixin/U.S. National Park Service

To be sure, groups also influence their leaders. Sometimes those at the front of the herd have simply sensed where it is already heading. Political candidates know how to read the opinion polls. Someone who typifies the group's views is more likely to be selected as a leader; a leader who deviates too radically from the group's standards may be rejected (Hogg et al., 1998). Smart leaders usually remain with the majority and spend their influence prudently. In rare circumstances, the right traits matched with the right situation yield history-making greatness, notes Dean Keith Simonton (1994). To have a Winston Churchill or, a Thomas Jefferson, a Napoleon or an Adolf Hitler, an Abraham Lincoln or a Martin Luther King, Jr., takes the right person in the right place at the right time. When an apt combination of intelligence, skill, determination, self-confidence, and social charisma meets a rare opportunity, the result is sometimes a championship, a Nobel Prize, or a social revolution.

SUMMING UP: The Influence of the Minority: How Do Individuals Influence the Group?

- Although a majority opinion often prevails, sometimes a minority can influence and even overturn a majority position. Even if the majority does not adopt the minority's views, the minority's speaking up can increase the majority's self-doubts and prompt it to consider other alternatives, often leading to better, more creative decisions.

- In experiments, a minority is most influential when it is consistent and persistent in its views, when its actions convey self-confidence, and after it begins to elicit some defections from the majority. Such minority influence can enable creative motivation.

- Through their *task* and *social leadership,* formal and informal group leaders exert disproportionate influence. Those who consistently press toward their goals and exude a self-confident charisma often engender trust and inspire others to follow.

POSTSCRIPT:
Are Groups Bad for Us?

A selective reading of this chapter could, we must admit, leave readers with the impression that, on balance, groups are bad. In groups we become more aroused, more stressed, more tense, more error-prone on complex tasks. Submerged in a group that gives us anonymity, we have a tendency to loaf or have our worst impulses unleashed by deindividuation. Police brutality, lynchings, gang destruction, and terrorism are all group phenomena. Discussion in groups often polarizes our views, enhancing mutual racism or hostility. It may also suppress dissent, creating a homogenized groupthink that produces disastrous decisions. No wonder we celebrate those individuals—minorities of one—who, alone against a group, have stood up for truth and justice. Groups, it seems, are ba-a-a-d.

All that is true, but it's only half the truth. The other half is that, as social animals, we are group-dwelling creatures. Like our distant ancestors, we depend on one another for sustenance, support, and security. Moreover, when our individual tendencies are positive, group interaction accentuates our best. In groups, runners run faster, audiences laugh louder, and givers become more generous. In self-help groups, people strengthen their resolve to stop drinking, lose weight, and study harder. In kindred-spirited groups, people expand their spiritual consciousness. "A devout communing on spiritual things sometimes greatly helps the health of the soul," observed fifteenth-century cleric Thomas à Kempis, especially when people of faith "meet and speak and commune together."

Depending on which tendency a group is magnifying or disinhibiting, groups can be very, very bad or very, very good. So we had best choose our groups wisely and intentionally.

Prejudice

DISLIKING OTHERS

CHAPTER

9

Jim West/Alamy

"Prejudice. A vagrant opinion without visible means of support."

—Ambrose Bierce, *The Devil's Dictionary*, 1911

We have now explored how we *think about* (Part One) and how we *influence* one another (Part Two). In these chapters, we consider how we *relate* to one another (Part Three). Our feelings and actions toward people are sometimes negative, sometimes positive. Why do we dislike, even despise, one another? Why and when do we hurt one another? Why do we like or love particular people? When will we offer help to friends or strangers? We also consider how social conflicts develop and how they can be justly and amicably resolved.

Prejudice comes in many forms—for our own group and against some other group. Researchers, as we will see, have explored race, gender, and sexual orientation prejudice, but also prejudices involving:

- *Religion.* In the aftermath of 9/11 and the Iraq and Afghanistan wars, Americans with a strong national identity expressed the most disdain for Arab immigrants

(Lyons et al., 2010). If told a job applicant is Muslim, many managers have not been inclined to hire or pay well (Park et al., 2009). In Europe, most non-Muslims express concern about "Islamic extremism" (Pew, 2011). Middle Eastern Muslims have reciprocated the negativity toward "greedy" and "immoral" Westerners and frequently report not believing that Arabs carried out the 9/11 attacks (Wike & Grim, 2007; Pew, 2011).

- *Obesity.*   Fat isn't fun. One analysis of 2.2 million social media posts containing "obese" or "fat" revealed a stream of shaming and flaming—insults, criticisms, and derogatory jokes (Chou et al., 2014). When seeking love and employment, overweight people—especially White women—face slim prospects. Overweight people marry less often, gain entry to less-desirable jobs, and make less money (Swami et al., 2008). For example, they seldom (relative to their numbers in the general population) become the CEOs of large corporations or get elected to office (Roehling et al., 2008, 2009, 2010). Weight discrimination, in fact, exceeds racial or gender discrimination and occurs at every employment stage—hiring, placement, promotion, compensation, discipline, and discharge (Roehling, 2000). Just reading such findings about weight stigma can, paradoxically, have negative effects. In one experiment, some women were randomly assigned to read a news article about the job market problems faced by those overweight. After reading the article, women who perceived themselves as overweight consumed more calories and felt less capable of controlling their eating (Major et al., 2014).

- *Age.*   People's perceptions of the elderly—as generally kind but frail, incompetent, and unproductive—predispose patronizing behavior. Baby-talk speech, for example, leads elderly people to feel less competent and act less capably (Bugental & Hehman, 2007).

- *Immigrants.*   A fast-growing research literature documents anti-immigrant prejudice among Germans toward Turks, the French toward North Africans, the British toward West Indians and Pakistanis, and Americans toward Latin American immigrants, especially unauthorized immigrants (Murray & Marx, 2013; Pettigrew, 2006). As we will see, the same factors that feed racial and gender prejudice also feed dislike of immigrants (Pettigrew et al., 2008; Zick et al., 2008).

WHAT IS THE NATURE AND POWER OF PREJUDICE?

Understand the nature of prejudice and the differences between prejudice, stereotypes, and discrimination.

Prejudice, stereotyping, discrimination, racism, sexism—the terms often overlap. Let's clarify them.

Defining Prejudice

Each of the situations just described involved a negative evaluation of some group. And that is the essence of **prejudice:** a preconceived negative judgment of a group and its individual members. (Some prejudice definitions include *positive* judgments, but nearly all uses of "prejudice" refer to *negative* ones—what Gordon Allport termed in his classic book, *The Nature of Prejudice,* "an antipathy based upon a faulty and inflexible generalization" [1954, p. 9].)

Prejudice is an attitude—a combination of feelings, inclinations to act, and beliefs. It can be easily remembered as the ABCs of attitudes: *a*ffect (feelings), *b*ehavior tendency (inclination to act), and *c*ognition (beliefs). A prejudiced person may *dislike* those different from self and *behave* in a discriminatory manner, *believing* them ignorant and dangerous.

The negative evaluations that mark prejudice often are supported by negative beliefs, called **stereotypes.** To stereotype is to generalize. To simplify the world, we generalize: The British are reserved. Americans are outgoing. Professors are absentminded. The elderly are frail.

Such generalizations can be more or less true (and are not always negative). The elderly *are* generally more frail. "Stereotypes," note Lee Jussim, Clark McCauley, and Yueh-Ting Lee (1995), "may be positive or negative." People may stereotype those of African heritage as superior athletes, Asians as high-achieving scientists (Kay et al., 2013). Such stereotypes often arise from the occupational roles we observe people playing (Koenig & Eagly, 2014). And stereotypes may be accurate or inaccurate. People perceive Australians as having a wilder culture than Britons—and they do use more profanity in their millions of Facebook posts (Kramer & Chung, 2011). An accurate stereotype may even be desirable. We call it "sensitivity to diversity" or "cultural awareness in a multicultural world." To stereotype the British as more concerned about punctuality than Mexicans is to understand what to expect and how to get along with others in each culture. "Accuracy dominates bias," notes Lee Jussim (2012). "The social perception glass (of people judging others) is about 90 percent full."

The 10 percent problem with stereotypes arises when they are *overgeneralized* or just plain wrong, as when liberals and conservatives overestimate the extremity of the others' views (Graham et al., 2012). To presume that most American welfare clients are African American is to overgeneralize, because it just isn't so. To presume that single people are less conscientious and more neurotic than partnered people, as did people in one German study, was wrong, because it just wasn't so (Greitemeyer, 2009c). To presume that people with disabilities are incompetent and asexual, as did Oregonians in another study, misrepresents reality (Nario-Redmond, 2010). To stigmatize the obese as slow, lazy, and undisciplined is inaccurate (Puhl & Heuer, 2009, 2010). To presume that Muslims are terrorists, priests are pedophiles, and evangelicals hate homosexuals overgeneralizes from the worst examples of each.

Prejudice is a negative *attitude;* **discrimination** is negative *behavior.* Discriminatory behavior often has its source in prejudicial attitudes (Dovidio et al., 1996; Wagner et al., 2008). Such was evident when researchers analyzed the responses to 1,115 identically worded emails sent to Los Angeles area landlords regarding vacant apartments. Encouraging replies came back to 89 percent of notes signed "Patrick McDougall," to 66 percent from "Said Al-Rahman," and to 56 percent from "Tyrell Jackson" (Carpusor & Loges, 2006). Other researchers have followed suit. When 4,859 U.S. state legislators received emails shortly before the 2008 election asking how to register to vote, "Jake Mueller" received more replies than "DeShawn Jackson," though fewer from minority legislators (Butler & Broockman, 2011). Likewise, Jewish Israeli students were less likely to alert the sender to a misaddressed email that came from an Arab name and town ("Muhammed Yunis of Ashdod") rather than from one of their own group ("Yoav Marom of Tel Aviv") (Tykocinski & Bareket-Bojmel, 2009).

However, attitudes and behavior are often loosely linked. Prejudiced attitudes need not breed hostile acts, nor does all oppression spring from prejudice. **Racism** and **sexism** are institutional practices that discriminate, even when there is no prejudicial intent. There can be racism without racists and sexism without sexists. Consider: If word-of-mouth hiring practices in an all-White business have the effect of excluding potential non-White employees, the practice could be called racism—even if an employer intended no discrimination. Much discrimination reflects no intended harm; it's simply favoritism toward people like oneself (Greenwald & Pettigrew, 2014).

Consider this: When job ads for male-dominated vocations feature words associated with male stereotypes ("We are a dominant engineering firm seeking individuals who can perform in a competitive environment"), and job ads for female-dominated vocations feature the opposite ("We seek people who will be sensitive to clients' needs and can develop warm client relationships"), the result may be institutional sexism. Without intending any prejudice, the gendered wording helps sustain gender inequality (Gaucher et al., 2011).

Prejudice: Implicit and Explicit

Prejudice illustrates our *dual attitude* system. As hundreds of studies using the Implicit Association Test (IAT) have shown, we can have different explicit (conscious) and implicit (automatic) attitudes toward the same target (Benaji & Greenwald, 2013). The test, which has been taken more than 16 million times, assesses "implicit cognition"—what you know without knowing that you know. It does so by measuring people's speed of associations. Much as we more quickly associate a hammer with a nail than with a pail, so the test can measure how speedily we associate "White" with "good" versus "Black" with "good." Thus, people may retain from childhood a habitual, automatic fear or dislike of people for whom they now express respect and admiration. Although explicit attitudes may change dramatically with education, implicit attitudes may linger, changing only as we form new habits through practice (Kawakami et al., 2000).

A raft of experiments—by researchers at the University of Wisconsin, Yale, Harvard, Indiana University, the University of Colorado, the University of Washington, the University of Virginia, and New York University converge in pointing to one of recent social psychology's big lessons: *prejudiced and stereotypic evaluations can occur outside people's awareness.* Some of these studies briefly flash words or faces that "prime" (automatically activate) stereotypes for some racial, gender, or age group. Without their awareness, the participants' activated stereotypes may then bias their behavior. Having been primed with images associated with African Americans, for example, they may then react with more hostility to an experimenter's (intentionally) annoying request.

Critics contend that the Implicit Association Test lacks sufficient validity to assess or label individuals (Blanton et al., 2006, 2009; Oswald et al., 2013). The test is more appropriate for research, which has shown, for example, that implicit biases help predict behaviors ranging from acts of friendliness to work evaluations. In the 2008 U.S. presidential election, both implicit and explicit prejudice predicted voters' support for Barack Obama, and his election in turn led to some reduction in both explicit and implicit prejudice (Bernstein et al., 2010; Goldman, 2012; Payne et al., 2010; Stephens-Davidowitz, 2014).

Keeping in mind the distinction between conscious, explicit prejudice and unconscious, implicit prejudice, let's examine two common forms of prejudice: racial prejudice and gender prejudice.

Racial Prejudice

In the context of the world, every race is a minority. Non-Hispanic Whites, for example, are only one-fifth of the world's people and will be one-eighth within another half-century. Thanks to mobility and migration over the past two centuries, the world's races now intermingle, in relations that are sometimes hostile, sometimes amiable.

By permission Dave Coverly and Creators Syndicate, Inc.

"Although our [conscious] minds are in the right places, and we may truly believe we are not prejudiced, our hearts aren't quite there yet."

—Prejudice Researcher, John Dovidio, *Time*, 2009

To a molecular biologist, skin color is a trivial human characteristic, one controlled by a minuscule genetic difference. Moreover, nature doesn't cluster races in neatly defined categories. It is people, not nature, who label Barack Obama, the son of a White woman, as "Black."

IS RACIAL PREJUDICE DISAPPEARING?

Which is right: people's perceptions of high prejudice in others, or their perceptions of low prejudice in themselves? And is racial prejudice becoming a thing of the past?

Explicit prejudicial attitudes can change very quickly.

- In 1942, most Americans agreed, "There should be separate sections for Negroes on streetcars and buses" (Hyman & Sheatsley, 1956). Today the question would seem bizarre, because such blatant prejudice has nearly disappeared.
- In 1942, fewer than a third of all Whites (only 1 in 50 in the South) supported school integration; by 1980, support for it was 90 percent.
- "It's all right for Blacks and Whites to date each other," agreed 48 percent of Americans in 1987 and 86 percent in 2012 (Pew, 2012). "Marriage between Blacks and Whites" was approved by 4 percent of Americans in 1958 and 87 percent in 2013 (Newport, 2013).

Considering what a thin slice of history is covered by the years since 1942, or even since slavery was practiced, the changes are dramatic. In Britain, overt racial prejudice, as expressed in opposition to interracial marriage or having an ethnic minority boss, has similarly plummeted, especially among younger adults (Ford, 2008).

African Americans' attitudes also have changed since the 1940s, when Kenneth Clark and Mamie Clark (1947) demonstrated that many African Americans held anti-Black prejudices. In making its historic 1954 decision declaring segregated schools unconstitutional, the Supreme Court found it noteworthy that when the Clarks gave African American children a choice between Black dolls and White dolls, most chose the White. In studies from the 1950s through the 1970s, Black children were increasingly likely to prefer Black dolls. And adult Blacks came to view Blacks and Whites as similar in such traits as intelligence, laziness, and dependability (Jackman & Senter, 1981; Smedley & Bayton, 1978). Even in the twenty-first century, Black South African children in a multiracial school, when shown pictures of children and asked to point to who they'd like, have expressed a preference for a White child (Shutts et al., 2011).

Shall we conclude, then, that racial prejudice is extinct in countries such as the United States, Britain, and Canada? Not if we consider the 5,796 reported hate crime incidents during 2012 (FBI, 2013). Not if we consider the 4 percent of American Whites who, as Figure 1 shows, would not vote for a Black presidential candidate. Not if we consider the 6 percent greater support that Obama would likely have received in 2008, according to one statistical analysis of voter racial and political attitudes, if there had been no White racial prejudice (Fournier & Tompson, 2008). And not if we consider that people tend to underreport their negative stereotypes and feelings (Bergsieker et al., 2012).

So, how great is the progress toward racial equality? In the United States, Whites have tended to contrast the present with the oppressive past, perceiving swift and radical progress. Blacks have tended to contrast the present with their ideal world, which has not yet been realized, and perceive somewhat less progress (Eibach & Ehrlinger, 2006).

SUBTLE RACIAL PREJUDICE

Despite lingering animosities, the bigger problem in today's world is not overt, conscious prejudice. Most people support racial equality and deplore discrimination. Yet 3 in 4 people who take the Implicit Association Test display an automatic, unconscious White preference (Banaji & Greenwald, 2013). Modern prejudice also appears subtly, in our preferences for what is familiar, similar, and comfortable (Dovidio et al., 1992; Esses et al., 1993a; Gaertner & Dovidio, 2005).

Some experiments have assessed people's *behavior* toward Blacks and Whites. Whites are equally helpful to any person in need—except when the needy person is remote (for instance, a wrong-number caller with an apparent Black accent who needs a message

Psychologists usually capitalize Black and White to emphasize that these are socially applied race labels, not literal color labels for persons of African and European ancestry.

"Explicit bias is infrequent; implicit bias is pervasive."

—Mahzarin Banaji and Anthony Greenwald, *Blindspot: Hidden Biases of Good People,* 2013

FIGURE :: 1

Changing Racial Attitudes of White Americans from 1958 to 2012

Abraham Lincoln's ghostly embrace of Barack Obama visualized the Obama mantra: "Change we can believe in." Two days later, Obama stood on steps built by the hands of slaves, placed his hand on a Bible last used in Lincoln's own inauguration, and spoke "a most sacred oath"—in a place, he reflected, where his "father less than 60 years ago might not have been served at a local restaurant."
Source: Data from Gallup Polls (brain.gallup.com).
AP Images/Charles Dharapak

relayed). Likewise, when asked to use electric shocks to "teach" a task, White people have given no more (if anything, less) shock to a Black than to a White person—except when they were angered or when the recipient couldn't retaliate or know who did it (Crosby et al., 1980; Rogers & Prentice-Dunn, 1981). Subtle prejudice may also be expressed as "microaggressions," such as race-related traffic stops or a reluctance to sit on a bus or train next to a person of another race (Wang et al., 2011.)

Thus, prejudiced attitudes and discriminatory behavior surface when they can hide behind the screen of some other motive. In Australia, Britain, France, Germany, and the Netherlands, blatant prejudice has been replaced by subtle prejudice (exaggerating ethnic differences, feeling less admiration and affection for immigrant minorities, rejecting them for supposedly nonracial reasons) (Pedersen & Walker, 1997; Tropp & Pettigrew, 2005a). Some researchers call such subtle prejudice "modern racism" or "cultural racism."

We can also detect bias in behavior:

- To test for possible labor market discrimination, M.I.T. researchers sent 5,000 résumés out in response to 1,300 varied employment ads (Bertrand & Mullainathan, 2003). Applicants who were randomly assigned White names (Emily, Greg) received one callback for every 10 résumés sent. Those given Black names (Lakisha, Jamal) received one callback for every 15 résumés sent.

- Other experiments have submitted fictitious pairs of women's resumes to 613 Austrian clerical openings, and pairs of men's resumes to 1,714 Athens, Greece, openings and 1,769 American job openings (Drydakis, 2009; Tilcsik, 2011; Weichselbaumer, 2003). By random assignment, one applicant in each pair acknowledged, among other activities, volunteering in a gay-lesbian organization. In response, callbacks were much less likely to the gay-involved applicants. In the American experiment, for example, 7.2 percent of applicants whose activities included being "Treasurer, Gay and Lesbian Alliance," received replies, as did 11.5 percent of those associated with a different left-seeming group ("Treasurer, Progressive and Socialist Alliance").

Although prejudice dies last in socially intimate contacts, interracial marriage has increased in most countries, and 87 percent of Americans now approve of "marriage between Blacks and Whites"—a sharp increase from the 4 percent who approved in 1958 (Newport, 2013).
Darren Greenwood/DesignPics

- In one analysis of traffic stops, African Americans and Latinos were four times more likely than Whites to be searched, twice as likely to be arrested, and three times more likely to be handcuffed and to have excessive force used against them (Lichtblau, 2005). In an Australian study with more than 1500 observations, bus drivers allowed 72 percent of White people to board with an empty fare card and no cash to board, but only 36 percent of dark-skinned people (Mujcic & Frijters, 2014).

Modern prejudice even appears as a race sensitivity that leads to exaggerated reactions to isolated minority persons—overpraising their accomplishments, overcriticizing their mistakes, and failing to warn Black students, as they would White students, about potential academic difficulty (Crosby & Monin, 2007; Fiske, 1989; Hart & Morry, 1997; Hass et al., 1991).

It also appears as patronization. For example, Kent Harber (1998) gave White students at Stanford University a poorly written essay to evaluate. When the students thought the writer was Black, they rated it *higher* than when they were led to think the author was White, and they rarely offered harsh criticisms. The evaluators, perhaps wanting to avoid the appearance of bias, patronized the Black essayists with lower standards. Such "inflated praise and insufficient criticism" may hinder minority student achievement, Harber noted. In follow-up research, Harber and his colleagues (2010) found that Whites concerned about appearing biased not only rate and comment more favorably on weak essays attributed to Black students, they also recommend less time for skill development. To protect their own self-image as unprejudiced, they bend over backward to give positive and unchallenging feedback.

AUTOMATIC RACIAL PREJUDICE

Does automatic (implicit) prejudice, like explicit prejudice, matter? Critics note that unconscious *associations* may only indicate cultural assumptions, perhaps without *prejudice* (which involves negative feelings and action tendencies). Or perhaps people's knee-jerk responses relate to familiarity, or to actual race differences (Tetlock, 2007). But some studies find that implicit bias can leak into behavior. Those who display implicit prejudice on the IAT—by taking longer to identify positive words such as *peace* and *paradise* as "good" when associated with Black rather than White faces—also have been observed to judge White job applicants more favorably and recommend better treatment for White emergency room patients more often than Black patients:

- In a Swedish study, a measure of implicit biases against Arab-Muslims predicted the likelihood of 193 corporate employers not interviewing applicants with Muslim names (Rooth, 2007).
- In a medical study of 287 physicians, those exhibiting the most implicit racial bias were the least likely to recommend clot-busting drugs for a Black patient described as complaining of chest pain (Green et al., 2007).
- The more people's implicit prejudice, the quicker they are to perceive anger in Black faces (Figure 2).

In some situations, automatic, implicit prejudice can have life or death consequences. In separate experiments, Joshua Correll and his co-workers (2002, 2007; Sadler et al., 2012) and Anthony Greenwald and his co-workers (2003) invited people to press buttons quickly to "shoot" or "not shoot" men who suddenly appeared onscreen holding either a gun or a harmless object such as a flashlight or a bottle. The participants (both Blacks and Whites, in one of the studies) more often mistakenly shot harmless targets who were Black. (Follow-up computerized simulations revealed that it's Black *male* suspects—not females, whether Black or White—that are more likely to be associated with threat and to be shot [Plant et al., 2011].)

Other studies have found that when primed with a Black rather than a White face, people think guns: They more quickly recognize a gun and they more often mistake a tool, such as a wrench, for a gun (Payne, 2001, 2006; Judd et al., 2004). Even when race does not bias perception, it may bias reaction—as people require less evidence before firing (Klauer & Voss, 2008). In a Department of Justice analysis of 59 Philadelphia Police shootings of unarmed suspects (such as when reaching for a cell phone), Black suspects

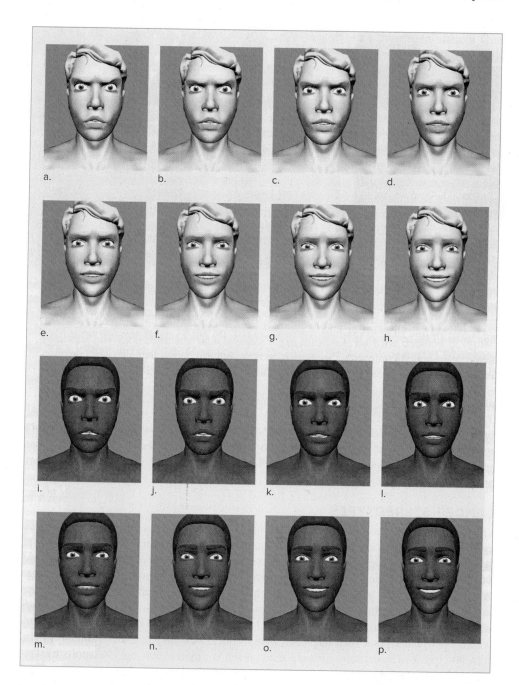

Facing Prejudice
Where does the anger disappear? Kurt Hugenberg and Galen Bodenhausen (2003) showed university students a movie of faces morphing from angry to happy. Those who had scored as most prejudiced (on an implicit racial attitudes test) perceived anger lingering more in ambiguous Black than White faces.

were victimized by officers of both races more than twice as often as White suspects (Fachner & Carter, 2015). When people are fatigued or feeling threatened by a dangerous world, they become even more likely to mistakenly shoot a minority person (Ma et al., 2013; Miller et al., 2012). Brain activity in the amygdala, a region that underlies fear and aggression, facilitates such automatic responding (Eberhardt, 2005; Harris & Fiske, 2006). These studies help explain why in 1999, Amadou Diallo (a Black immigrant in New York City) was shot 41 times by police officers for removing his wallet from his pocket.

Even the social scientists who study prejudice seem vulnerable to automatic prejudice, note Anthony Greenwald and Eric Schuh (1994). They analyzed biases in authors' citations of social science articles by people with selected non-Jewish names (Erickson, McBride, etc.) and Jewish names (Goldstein, Siegel, etc.). Their analysis of nearly 30,000 citations, including 17,000 citations of prejudice research, found something remarkable: Compared with Jewish authors, non-Jewish authors had 40 percent higher odds of citing non-Jewish names. (Greenwald and

Automatic prejudice. When Joshua Correll and his colleagues invited people to react quickly to people holding either a gun or a harmless object, race influenced perceptions and reactions.
Courtesy of Josh Correll

Google's diversity training workshops aim to inform people about and restrain the implicit biases uncovered by social psychologists (Manjoo, 2014).

Schuh could not determine whether Jewish authors were overciting their Jewish colleagues or whether non-Jewish authors were overciting their non-Jewish colleagues, or both.)

Gender Prejudice

How pervasive is prejudice against women? In another chapter we examined gender-role norms—people's ideas about how women and men *ought* to behave. Here we consider gender *stereotypes*—people's beliefs about how women and men *do* behave. Norms are *pre*scriptive; stereotypes are *de*scriptive.

GENDER STEREOTYPES

From research on stereotypes, two conclusions are indisputable: Strong gender stereotypes exist, and, as often happens, members of the stereotyped group accept them. Men and women agree that you *can* judge the book by its sexual cover. In one survey, Mary Jackman and Mary Senter (1981) found that gender stereotypes were much stronger than racial stereotypes. For example, only 22 percent of men thought the two sexes equally "emotional." Of the remaining 78 percent, those who believed females were more emotional outnumbered those who thought males were more emotional by 15 to 1. And what did the women believe? To within 1 percentage point, their responses were identical. A Gallup poll found similar results, with 90 percent of Americans agreeing that women are more emotional (Newport, 2001).

"All the pursuits of men are the pursuits of women also, and in all of them a woman is only a lesser man."
—Plato,
Republic, 360 B.C.

Remember that stereotypes are generalizations about a group of people and may be true, false, or overgeneralized from a kernel of truth. In another chapter we noted that the average man and woman do differ somewhat in social connectedness, empathy, social power, aggressiveness, and sexual initiative (though not in intelligence). Do we then conclude that gender stereotypes are accurate? Sometimes stereotypes exaggerate differences. But not always, observed Janet Swim (1994). She found that Pennsylvania State University students' stereotypes of men's and women's restlessness, nonverbal sensitivity, aggressiveness, and so forth were reasonable approximations of actual gender differences.

Gender stereotypes have persisted across time and culture. Averaging data from 27 countries, John Williams and his colleagues (1999, 2000) found that people everywhere perceive women as more agreeable, and men as more outgoing. The persistence and omnipresence of gender stereotypes have led some evolutionary psychologists to believe they reflect innate, stable reality (Lueptow et al., 1995).

Stereotypes (beliefs) are not prejudices (attitudes). Stereotypes may support prejudice. Yet one might believe, without prejudice, that men and women are "different yet equal." Let us therefore see how researchers probe for gender prejudice.

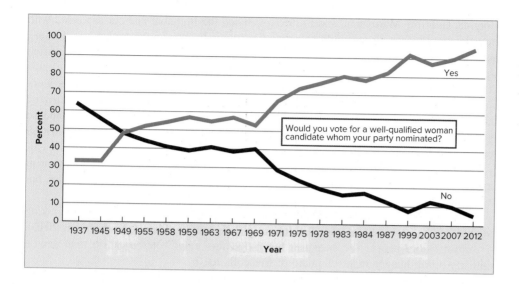

FIGURE :: 3

Changing Gender
Attitudes from 1958
to 2012
Source: Data from Gallup Polls.

SEXISM: BENEVOLENT AND HOSTILE

Judging from what people tell survey researchers, attitudes toward women have changed as rapidly as racial attitudes. As Figure 3 shows, the percentage of Americans willing to vote for a female presidential candidate has roughly paralleled the increased percentage willing to vote for a Black candidate. In 1967, 56 percent of first-year American college students agreed that "the activities of married women are best confined to the home and family"; by 2002, only 22 percent agreed (Astin et al., 1987; Sax et al., 2002). Thereafter, the home–family question no longer seemed worth asking.

Alice Eagly and her associates (1991) and Geoffrey Haddock and Mark Zanna (1994) also report that people don't respond to women with gut-level negative emotions as they do to certain other groups. Most people *like* women more than men. They perceive women as more understanding, kind, and helpful. Eagly (1994) dubbed this *favorable* stereotype the *women-are-wonderful effect.*

But gender attitudes often are ambivalent, reported Peter Glick, Susan Fiske, and their colleagues (1996, 2007, 2011) from their surveys of 15,000 people in 19 nations. Gender attitudes frequently mix a *benevolent sexism* ("Women have a superior moral sensibility") with *hostile sexism* ("Once a man commits, she puts him on a tight leash"). Moreover, in one 57-nation study, hostile sexists beliefs ("On the whole, men make better political leaders than women do") predicted increased future gender inequality (Brandt, 2011). Hostile sexism is overtly negative. Benevolent sexism, though sounding positive ("women deserve protection"), may still impede gender equity.

GENDER DISCRIMINATION

Being male isn't all roses. Compared to women, men are three times more likely to commit suicide and be murdered. They are nearly all the battlefield and death row casualties. They die five years sooner. And males are most of those with intellectual disability or autism, as well as students in special education programs (Baumeister, 2007; S. Pinker, 2008).

One publicized finding of discrimination against women came from a 1968 study in which women students were given several short articles and asked them to judge the value of each. Sometimes a given article was attributed to a male author (for example, John T. McKay) and sometimes to a female author (for example, Joan T. McKay). In general, the articles received lower ratings when attributed to a female. That's right: Women discriminated against women.

Eager to demonstrate the subtle reality of gender discrimination, I [DM] obtained the materials in 1980 and repeated the experiment with my own students. They (women and men) showed no such tendency to deprecate women's work. So Janet Swim, Eugene

> "Women are wonderful primarily because they are [perceived as] so nice. [Men are] perceived as superior to women in agentic [competitive, dominant] attributes that are viewed as equipping people for success in paid work, especially in male-dominated occupations."
>
> —Alice Eagly (1994)

Borgida, Geoffrey Maruyama, and I (1989) searched the literature and corresponded with investigators to learn all we could about studies of gender bias in the evaluation of men's and women's work. To our surprise, the biases that occasionally surfaced were as often against men as women. But the most common result across 104 studies involving almost 20,000 people was *no difference*. On most comparisons, judgments of someone's work were unaffected by whether the work was attributed to a female or a male. Summarizing other studies of people's evaluations of women and men as leaders, professors, and so forth, Alice Eagly (1994) concluded, "Experiments have *not* demonstrated any *overall* tendency to devalue women's work."

Is gender bias fast becoming extinct in Western countries? Has the women's movement nearly completed its work? As with racial prejudice, blatant gender prejudice is dying, but subtle bias lives.

Violate gender stereotypes, and people may react. People take notice of a cigar-smoking woman and a tearful man, and denigrate a White rapper (Phelan & Rudman, 2010). A woman whom people see as power hungry suffers more voter backlash than does a similarly power-hungry man (Okimoto & Brescoll, 2010).

In the world beyond democratic Western countries, gender discrimination is not subtle. Women's 20 percent literacy rate is nearly double men's (UNESCO, 2013). And worldwide, some 30 percent of women have experienced intimate partner violence (Devries et al., 2013). Such tendencies are especially likely among men who objectify women by implicitly associating them with animals or objects (Rudman & Mescher, 2012).

But the biggest violence against women may occur prenatally. Around the world, people tend to prefer having baby boys. In the United States, in 1941, 38 percent of expectant parents said they preferred a boy if they could have only one child; 24 percent preferred a girl; and 23 percent said they had no preference. In 2011, the answers were virtually unchanged, with 40 percent still preferring a boy (Newport, 2011). With the widespread use of ultrasound to determine the sex of a fetus and the growing availability of abortion, these preferences are, in some countries, affecting the number of boys and girls. In China, where 95 percent of orphanage children are girls (Webley, 2009), 111 boys have been born for every 100 girls; in India, the ratio has been 112 to 100 (CIA, 2014). In China, the 32 million "missing women" has created an excess of 32 million under-20 males. These are tomorrow's "bare branches"—bachelors who will have trouble finding mates (Hvistendahl, 2009, 2010, 2011; Zhu et al., 2009). This female shortage also contributes to increased violence, crime, prostitution, and trafficking of women (Brooks, 2012). In response, China has made sex-selective abortions a criminal offense.

Aggregate data from Google searches reveal parents' hopes for their children are also not gender neutral (Stephens-Davidowitz, 2014). Many parents seem eager to have smart sons and slender, beautiful daughters. You can see this for yourself. Google (with quotation marks) and note the number of results:

- "Is my daughter"
- "Is my son"
- "Is my son overweight"
- "Is my daughter overweight"

To conclude, overt prejudice against people of color and against women is far less common today than it was in the mid-twentieth century. Nevertheless, techniques that are sensitive to subtle prejudice still detect widespread bias. And in parts of the world, gender prejudice makes for misery. So, let's now consider the social, emotional, and cognitive sources of prejudice.

Gay-Lesbian Prejudice

Most of the world's gay and lesbian people cannot comfortably disclose who they are and whom they love (Katz-Wise & Hyde, 2012; United Nations, 2011). In many countries, same-sex relationships are a criminal offense. But cultures vary—from the mere 6 percent in Spain who agree that "homosexuality is morally unacceptable" to 98 percent in Ghana (Pew, 2014).

In Western countries, anti-gay prejudice, though rapidly diminishing, endures:

- *Gay marriage support is mixed but increasing.* In Western countries, support for same-sex marriage has soared over the past two decades—in the United States, for example, from 27 percent in 1996 to 55 percent in 2014. There is, however, an enormous generation gap, with 78 percent of 18- to 29-year-olds supportive, but only 42 percent of those over age 65 (McCarthy, 2014).

- *Harassment hurts.* In a National School climate survey, 8 out of 10 gay-lesbian adolescents reported experiencing sex-related harassment in the prior year (GLSEN, 2012). Nearly 6 in 10 gay and lesbian American adults report being "subject to slurs or jokes" and 3 in 10 report having been "threatened or physically attacked" (Pew, 2013). Two-thirds of British gay youth report experiencing homophobic bullying (Hunt & Jensen, 2007).

- *Rejection happens.* In national surveys, 40 percent of gay and lesbian Americans have said it would be difficult for someone in their community "to live openly as gay or lesbian" (Jones, 2012). Thirty-nine percent report having "a friend or family member" reject them because of their sexual orientation or gender identity (Pew, 2013).

So, over time "it gets better," yet nearly 9 in 10 LGBT adults in the U.S. still think that "discrimination against gays and lesbians" is a somewhat or very serious problem (Jones, 2012). And many straight folks are wary of associating with gays and lesbians, lest they be perceived as gay or lesbian (Buck et al., 2013).

But do disparaging attitudes and discriminatory practices against gay and lesbian people cause actual harm? Do they increase LGBT people's risk of ill health and psychological disorder? Consider (from U.S. research summarized by Hatzenbuehler, 2014):

- *State policies predict gay folks' health and well-being.* In U.S. states without gay-lesbian hate crime and nondiscrimination protection, LGBT people experience substantially higher mood disorder rates, even after controlling for state differences in education and income.

- *Community attitudes also predict LGBT health.* Communities where anti-gay prejudice is commonplace are communities with high rates of gay-lesbian suicide and cardiovascular death. Moreover, gay and lesbian individuals who experience discrimination are at increased risk of depression and anxiety (Schmitt et al., 2014).

- *A quasi-experiment confirms the toxicity of gay stigma.* Between 2001 and 2005, sixteen states banned same-sex marriage. In those states, gays and lesbians (but not heterosexuals) experienced a 37 percent increase in mood disorders, a 42 percent increase in alcohol use disorders, and a 248 percent increase in general anxiety disorders. In other states, gays and lesbians experienced no such increases in psychiatric disorder.

SUMMING UP: What Is the Nature and Power of Prejudice?

- *Prejudice* is a preconceived negative attitude. *Stereotypes* are beliefs about another group—beliefs that may be accurate, inaccurate, or overgeneralized but based on a kernel of truth. *Discrimination* is unjustified negative behavior. *Racism* and *sexism* may refer to individuals' prejudicial attitudes or discriminatory behavior, or to oppressive institutional practices (even if not intentionally prejudicial).

- Prejudice exists in subtle and unconscious guises as well as overt, conscious forms. Researchers have devised subtle survey questions and indirect methods for assessing people's attitudes and behavior to detect unconscious prejudice.

- Racial prejudice against Blacks in the United States was widely accepted until the 1960s; since that time it has become far less prevalent, but it still exists.

- Similarly, prejudice against women and gays and lesbians has lessened in recent decades. Nevertheless, strong gender stereotypes and a fair amount of gender bias are still found in the United States and, to a greater degree, elsewhere around the world.

WHAT ARE THE SOCIAL SOURCES OF PREJUDICE?

| Understand and examine the influences that give rise to and maintain prejudice.

Prejudice springs from several sources. It may arise from people differing in social status and their desires to justify and maintain those differences. It may also be learned from our parents as they socialize us about what differences they believe matter between people. Our social institutions, too, may maintain and support prejudice. Consider first how prejudice can function to defend one's social position.

Social Inequalities: Unequal Status and Prejudice

A principle to remember: *Unequal status breeds prejudice.* Masters view slaves as lazy, irresponsible, lacking ambition—as having exactly those traits that justify the slavery. Historians debate the forces that create unequal status. But after those inequalities exist, prejudice helps justify the economic and social superiority of those who have wealth and power. Tell us the economic relationship between two groups, and we'll predict the intergroup attitudes. Upper-class individuals are more likely than those in poverty to see people's fortunes as the outcomes they have earned, thanks to skill and effort, and not as the result of having connections, money, and good luck (Costa-Lopes et al., 2013; Kraus & Keltner, 2013).

Historical examples abound. Where slavery was practiced, prejudice ran strong. Nineteenth-century politicians justified imperial expansion by describing exploited colonized people as "inferior," "requiring protection," and a "burden" to be borne (G. W. Allport, 1958, pp. 204–205). Sociologist Helen Mayer Hacker (1951) noted how stereotypes of Blacks and women helped rationalize the inferior status of each: Many people thought both groups were mentally slow, emotional and primitive, and "contented" with their subordinate role. Blacks were "inferior"; women were "weak." Blacks were all right in their place; women's place was in the home.

Theresa Vescio and her colleagues (2005) tested that reasoning. They found that powerful men who stereotype their female subordinates give them plenty of praise, but fewer resources, thus undermining their performance. This sort of patronizing allows the men to maintain their positions of power. In the laboratory, too, patronizing benevolent sexism (statements implying that women, as the weaker sex, need support) has undermined women's cognitive performance by planting intrusive thoughts—self-doubts, preoccupations, and decreased self-esteem (Dardenne et al., 2007).

Peter Glick and Susan Fiske's distinction between "hostile" and "benevolent" sexism extends to other prejudices. We see other groups as *competent* or as *likable,* but often not as both. These two culturally universal dimensions of social perception—competence and likability (warmth)—were illustrated by one European's comment that "Germans love Italians, but don't admire them. Italians admire Germans, but don't love them" (Cuddy et al., 2009). We typically *respect* the competence of those high in status and *like* those who agreeably accept a lower status. Depending on the situation, we may seek to impress people with either our competence or warmth. When wanting to appear competent, people will often downplay their warmth. And when wanting to appear warm and likable, people will downplay their competence (Holoien & Fiske, 2013).

In the United States, report Fiske and her colleagues (1999), Asians, Jews, Germans, nontraditional women, and assertive African Americans have been respected but are not so well liked. Traditionally subordinate African Americans and Hispanics, traditional women, and people with disabilities tend to be seen as less competent but liked for their emotional, spiritual, artistic, or athletic qualities.

"Prejudice is never easy unless it can pass itself off for reason."

—William Hazlitt, 1778–1830, "On Prejudice"

Some people, more than others, notice and justify status differences. Those high in **social dominance orientation** tend to view people in terms of hierarchies. They like their own social groups to be high status—they prefer being on the top. Being in a dominant, high-status position also tends to promote this orientation (Guimond et al., 2003). Jim Sidanius, Felicia Pratto, and their colleagues (Levin et al., 2011; Pratto et al., 1994; Sidanius et al., 2004) argue that this desire to be on top leads people high in social dominance to embrace prejudice and to support political positions that justify prejudice. Indeed, people high in social dominance orientation often support policies that maintain hierarchies, such as tax cuts for the well-off. They prefer professions, such as politics and business, that increase their status and maintain hierarchies. They avoid jobs, such as social work, that, by virtue of their aid to disadvantaged groups, undermine hierarchies. And they express more negative attitudes toward minority persons who exhibit strong racial identities (Kaiser & Pratt-Hyatt, 2009). Status breeds prejudice, especially for people high in social dominance orientation.

social dominance orientation
A motivation to have one's group dominate other social groups.

Socialization

Prejudice springs from unequal status and from other social sources, including our acquired values and attitudes. The influence of family socialization appears in children's prejudices, which often mirror those perceived in their mothers (Castelli et al., 2007). Even children's implicit racial attitudes reflect their parents' explicit prejudice (Sinclair et al., 2004). Our families and cultures pass on all kinds of information—how to find mates, drive cars, and divide the household labors, and whom to distrust and dislike. Parental attitudes assessed shortly after their babies are born predict their children's attitudes 17 years later (Fraley et al., 2012).

THE AUTHORITARIAN PERSONALITY

In the 1940s, University of California, Berkeley, researchers—two of whom had fled Nazi Germany—set out on an urgent research mission: to uncover the psychological roots of the poisonous right-wing anti-Semitism that caused the slaughter of millions of Jews in Nazi Germany. In studies of American adults, Theodor Adorno and his colleagues (1950) discovered that hostility toward Jews often coexisted with hostility toward other minorities. In those who were strongly prejudiced, prejudice appeared to be not specific to one group but an entire way of thinking about those who are "different." These judgmental, **ethnocentric** people shared certain tendencies: an intolerance for weakness, a punitive attitude, and a submissive respect for their group's authorities, as reflected in their agreement with such statements as "Obedience and respect for authority are the most important virtues children should learn." Adorno and his colleagues (1950) surmised that these tendencies define an **authoritarian personality** that is prone to prejudice and stereotyping. Still today, prejudices coexist: antigay, anti-immigrant, anti-Black, anti-Muslim, and anti-women sentiments often live inside the same skin (Akrami et al., 2011; Zick et al., 2008).

ethnocentric
Believing in the superiority of one's own ethnic and cultural group, and having a corresponding disdain for all other groups.

authoritarian personality
A personality that is disposed to favor obedience to authority and intolerance of outgroups and those lower in status.

More recent inquiry into authoritarian people's early lives has revealed that, as children, they often faced harsh discipline. Extremism, on both the political left and the right, shares some common themes, such as catastrophizing, desiring vengeance, dehumanizing the enemy, and seeking a sense of control (Kay & Eibach, 2013; Saucier et al., 2009). Moreover, people on both the left and right express similar intolerance of groups with values and beliefs unlike their own (Brandt et al., 2014; Toner et al., 2013).

Research into authoritarianism also suggests that the insecurity of authoritarian individuals predisposes them toward an excessive concern with power and status and an inflexible right-wrong way of thinking that makes ambiguity difficult to tolerate. Authoritarian people therefore tend to be submissive to those with power over them and aggressive or punitive toward those whom they consider lower in status than themselves (Altemeyer, 1988, 1992). "My way or the highway." Authoritarians' feelings of moral superiority may go hand in hand with brutality toward perceived inferiors.

RELIGION AND RACIAL PREJUDICE

Consider those who benefit from social inequalities while avowing that "all are created equal." They need to justify keeping things the way they are. And what could be a more powerful justification than to believe that God has ordained the existing social order? For all sorts of cruel deeds, noted William James, "piety is the mask" (1902, p. 264).

In almost every country, leaders invoke religion to sanctify the present order. The use of religion to support injustice helps explain a consistent pair of findings concerning North American Christianity: (1) White church members have expressed more racial prejudice than nonmembers, and (2) those professing fundamentalist beliefs have expressed more prejudice than those professing progressive beliefs (Hall et al., 2010; Johnson et al., 2011).

Knowing the correlation between two variables—religion and prejudice—tells us nothing about their causal connection. Consider three possibilities:

- There may be *no causal connection.* Perhaps people with less education are both more fundamentalist and more prejudiced. (In one study of 7,070 Brits, those scoring high on IQ tests at age 10 expressed more nontraditional and antiracist views at age 30 [Deary et al., 2008].)

- Perhaps *prejudice causes religion,* by leading some people to create religious ideas to support their prejudices. People who feel hatred may use religion, even God, to justify their contempt for the other.

- Perhaps *religion causes prejudice,* such as by leading people to believe that because all individuals possess free will, impoverished minorities have themselves to blame for their status, and gays and lesbians chose their orientation.

If indeed religion causes prejudice, then more religious church members should also be more prejudiced. But three other findings consistently indicate otherwise.

- Among church members, faithful church attenders were, in 24 out of 26 comparisons, less prejudiced than occasional attenders (Batson & Ventis, 1982).

- Gordon Allport and Michael Ross (1967) compared "intrinsic" and "extrinsic" religiosity. They found that those for whom religion is an intrinsic end in itself (those who agree, for example, with the statement "My religious beliefs are what really lie behind my whole approach to life") express *less* prejudice than those for whom religion is more a means to other ends (who agree "A primary reason for my interest in religion is that my church is a congenial social activity"). Faced with reminders of their mortality, such as people experience during terrorist threats, intrinsic religiosity also has predicted decreased outgroup hostility among American Christians and Jews, Iranian Muslims, and Polish Christians (De Zavala et al., 2012). And those who scored highest on Gallup's "spiritual commitment" index were more welcoming of a person of another race moving in next door (Gallup & Jones, 1992).

- Protestant ministers and Roman Catholic priests gave more support to the U.S. civil rights movement than did laypeople (Fichter, 1968; Hadden, 1969). In Germany, 45 percent of clergy in 1934 had aligned themselves with the Confessing Church, which was organized to oppose Nazi influence on the German Protestant Church (Reed, 1989).

What, then, is the relationship between religion and racial prejudice? The answer we get depends on *how* we ask the question. If we define religiousness as church membership or willingness to agree at least superficially with traditional religious beliefs, then the more religious people have been the more racially prejudiced. Bigots often rationalize bigotry with religion. But if we assess depth of religious commitment in any of several other ways, then the very devout are less prejudiced—hence the religious roots of the modern civil rights movement, among whose leaders were many ministers and priests. It was Thomas Clarkson and William Wilberforce's faith-inspired values

("Love your neighbor as yourself") that, two centuries ago, motivated their successful campaign to end the British Empire's slave trade and the practice of slavery. As Gordon Allport concluded, "The role of religion is paradoxical. It makes prejudice and it unmakes prejudice" (1958, p. 413).

CONFORMITY

Once established, prejudice is maintained largely by inertia. If prejudice is socially accepted, many people will follow the path of least resistance and conform to the fashion. They will act not so much out of a need to hate as out of a need to be liked and accepted. Thus, people become more likely to favor (or oppose) discrimination after hearing someone else do so, and they are less supportive of women after hearing sexist humor (Ford et al., 2008; Zitek & Hebl, 2007).

During the 1950s, Thomas Pettigrew (1958) studied Whites in South Africa and the American South. His discovery: Those who conformed most to other social norms were also most prejudiced; those who were less conforming mirrored less of the surrounding prejudice.

The price of nonconformity was painfully clear to the ministers of Little Rock, Arkansas, where the U.S. Supreme Court's 1954 school desegregation decision was implemented. Most ministers privately favored integration but feared that advocating it openly would decrease membership and financial contributions (Campbell & Pettigrew, 1959). Or consider the Indiana steelworkers and West Virginia coal miners of the same era. In the mills and the mines, the workers accepted integration. In the neighborhoods, the norm was rigid segregation (Minard, 1952; Reitzes, 1953). Prejudice was clearly not a manifestation of "sick" personalities but simply of the social norms.

Conformity also maintains gender prejudice. "If we have come to think that the nursery and the kitchen are the natural sphere of a woman," wrote George Bernard Shaw in an 1891 essay, "we have done so exactly as English children come to think that a cage is the natural sphere of a parrot—because they have never seen one anywhere else." Children who *have* seen women elsewhere—children of employed women—have expressed less stereotyped views of men and women (Hoffman, 1977). Women students exposed to female science, technology, engineering, and mathematics (STEM) experts likewise express more positive implicit attitudes toward STEM studies and display more effort on STEM tests (Stout et al., 2011).

In all this, there is a message of hope. If prejudice is not deeply ingrained in personality, then as fashions change and new norms evolve, prejudice can diminish. And so it has.

"We have just enough religion to make us hate, but not enough to make us love one another."

—Jonathan Swift, *Thoughts on Various Subjects,* 1706

"Use your White Privilege, Luke."

Benjamin Schwartz, The New Yorker Collection/The Cartoon Bank

Institutional Supports

Social institutions (schools, government, media, families) may bolster prejudice through overt policies such as segregation, or by passively reinforcing the status quo. Until the 1970s many banks routinely denied mortgages to unmarried women and to minority applicants, with the result that most homeowners were White married couples. Similarly, political leaders may both reflect and reinforce prevailing attitudes.

Schools tend to reinforce dominant cultural attitudes. An analysis of stories in 134 children's readers written before 1970 found that male characters outnumbered female characters three to one (Women on Words and Images, 1972). Who was portrayed as showing initiative, bravery, and competence? Note the answer in this excerpt from the classic *Dick and Jane* children's reader: Jane, sprawled out on the sidewalk, her roller skates beside her, listens as Mark explains to his mother:

"She cannot skate," said Mark.
"I can help her.
"I want to help her.
"Look at her, Mother.
"Just look at her.
"She's just like a girl.
"She gives up."

Institutional supports for prejudice, like that reader, are often unintended and unnoticed. Not until the 1970s, when changing ideas about males and females brought new perceptions of such portrayals, was this blatant (to us) stereotyping widely noticed and changed.

Unintended bias: Is lighter skin "normal"?
Chris Smith/PhotoEdit

What contemporary examples of institutionalized biases still go unnoticed? Here is one that most of us failed to notice, although it was right before our eyes: By examining 1,750 photographs of people in magazines and newspapers, Dane Archer and his associates (1983) discovered that about two-thirds of the average male photo, but less than half of the average female photo, was devoted to the face. As Archer widened his search, he discovered that such "face-ism" is common. He found it in the periodicals of 11 other countries, in 920 portraits gathered from the artwork of six centuries, and in the amateur drawings of students at the University of California, Santa Cruz. Follow-up studies have confirmed the face-ism phenomenon in magazines (including the feminist *Ms.* magazine) and in website photos of male and female politicians even in countries with gender equality (Konrath et al., 2012; Nigro et al., 1988).

The researchers suspect that the visual prominence given the faces of men and the bodies of women both reflects and perpetuates gender bias. In research in Germany, Norbert Schwarz and Eva Kurz (1989) confirmed that people whose faces are prominent in photos seem more intelligent and ambitious.

Films and television programs also embody and reinforce prevailing cultural attitudes. The muddle-headed, wide-eyed African American butlers and maids in 1930s movies helped perpetuate the stereotypes they reflected. Today people find such images offensive, yet even a modern TV comedy skit of a crime-prone African American can later make another African American who is accused of assault seem more guilty (Ford, 1997). Violent rap music from Black artists leads both Black and White listeners to stereotype Blacks as having violent dispositions (Johnson et al., 2000). Sexual rap music depictions of promiscuous Black females reduce listeners' support for Black pregnant women in need (Johnson et al., 2009). And frowning and other negative nonverbal behaviors—which are more prevalent toward Black than White TV characters—likewise increase viewers' racial bias, without their awareness (Weisbuch et al., 2009).

SUMMING UP: What Are the Social Sources of Prejudice?

- The social situation breeds and maintains prejudice in several ways. A group that enjoys social and economic superiority will often use prejudicial beliefs to justify its privileged position.

- Children are also brought up in ways that foster or reduce prejudice. The family, religious communities, and the broader society can sustain or reduce prejudices.

- Social institutions (government, schools, media) also support prejudice, sometimes through overt policies and sometimes through unintentional inertia.

WHAT ARE THE MOTIVATIONAL SOURCES OF PREJUDICE?

Identify and examine the motivational sources of prejudice.

Various kinds of motivations underlie the hostilities of prejudice. Motivations can also lead people to avoid prejudice.

Frustration and Aggression: The Scapegoat Theory

Pain and frustration (from the blocking of a goal) feed hostility. When the cause of our frustration is intimidating or unknown, we often redirect our hostility. This phenomenon of "displaced aggression" (scapegoating) contributed to the lynchings of African Americans in the South after the Civil War. Between 1882 and 1930, more lynchings occurred in years when cotton prices were low and economic frustration was therefore presumably high (Hepworth & West, 1988; Hovland & Sears, 1940). Hate crimes seem not to have fluctuated with unemployment in recent decades (Falk et al., 2011; Green et al., 1998). However, when living standards are rising, societies tend to be more open to diversity and to the passage and enforcement of antidiscrimination laws (Frank, 1999). Ethnic peace is easier to maintain during prosperous times.

Targets for displaced aggression vary. Following their defeat in World War I and their country's subsequent economic chaos, many Germans saw Jews as villains. Long before Hitler came to power, one German leader explained: "The Jew is just convenient. . . . If there were no Jews, the anti-Semites would have to invent them" (quoted by G. W. Allport, 1958, p. 325). In earlier centuries people vented their fear and hostility on witches, whom they sometimes burned or drowned in public. Scapegoats provide a handy explanation for bad events (Rothschild et al., 2012).

More recently, Americans who reacted to 9/11 with more anger than fear expressed greater intolerance toward immigrants and Middle Easterners (Skitka et al., 2004). As twenty-first century Greece sank into economic misery, rage against foreign immigrants increased (Becatoros, 2012). Even threats from distant groups, such as terrorist acts, can heighten local prejudices (Bouman et al., 2014; Greenaway et al., 2014). Passions provoke prejudice. By contrast, individuals who experience no negative emotional response to social threats—namely, children with the genetic disorder called Williams syndrome—display a notable lack of racial stereotypes and prejudice (Santos et al., 2010). No passion, no prejudice.

Competition is an important source of frustration that can fuel prejudice. When two groups compete for jobs, housing, or social prestige, one group's goal fulfillment can become the other group's frustration. Thus, the **realistic group conflict theory** suggests that prejudice arises when groups compete for scarce resources (Maddux et al., 2008; Pereira et al., 2010; Sassenberg et al., 2007). In evolutionary biology, Gause's law states that maximum competition will exist between species with identical needs.

Consider how this has played out across the world:

- In Western Europe, economically frustrated people express relatively high levels of blatant prejudice toward ethnic minorities (Pettigrew et al., 2008, 2010).
- In Canada, opposition to immigration since 1975 has gone up and down with the unemployment rate (Palmer, 1996).
- In the United States, concerns about immigrants taking jobs are greatest among those with the lowest incomes (AP/Ipsos, 2006; Pew, 2006).
- In South Africa, dozens of African immigrants were killed by mobs and 35,000 people were hounded from squatter camps by poor South Africans who resented the economic competition. "These foreigners have no IDs, no papers, and yet they get the jobs," said one unemployed South African, noting that "They are willing to work for 15 rand [about $2] a day" (Bearak, 2010). When interests clash, prejudice may result.

Social Identity Theory: Feeling Superior to Others

Humans are a social species. Our ancestral history prepares us to feed and protect ourselves—to live—in groups. Humans cheer for their groups, kill for their groups, die for their groups. Evolution prepares us, when encountering strangers, to make a quick judgment: friend or foe? Those from our group, those who look like us, even those who *sound* like us—with accents like our own—we instantly tend to like (Gluszek & Dovidio, 2010; Kinzler et al., 2009).

Not surprisingly, as noted by social psychologists John Turner (1981, 2000), Michael Hogg (1992, 2010, 2014), and their colleagues, we also define ourselves by our groups. Self-concept—our sense of who we are—contains not just a *personal identity* (our sense of our personal attributes and attitudes) but also a **social identity** (Chen et al., 2006; Haslam, 2014). Fiona identifies herself as a woman, an Aussie, a Labourite, a University of New South Wales student, a MacDonald family member. We carry such social identities like playing cards, playing them when appropriate. Prime American students to think of themselves as "Americans," and they will display heightened anger and disrespect toward Muslims; prime their "student" identity, and they will instead display heightened anger toward police (Ray et al., 2008).

Working with the late British social psychologist Henri Tajfel, a Polish native who lost family and friends in the Holocaust and then devoted much of his career to studying ethnic hatred, Turner (1947–2011) proposed *social identity theory*. Turner and Tajfel observed that

- *We categorize:* We find it useful to put people, ourselves included, into categories. To label someone as a Hindu, a Scot, or a bus driver is a shorthand way of saying some other things about the person.

---

realistic group conflict theory

The theory that prejudice arises from competition between groups for scarce resources.

social identity

The "we" aspect of our self-concept; the part of our answer to "Who am I?" that comes from our group memberships.

- *We identify:* We associate ourselves with certain groups (our **ingroups**) and gain self-esteem by doing so.
- *We compare:* We contrast our groups with other groups (**outgroups**), with a favorable bias toward our own group.

Beginning in our preschool years, we humans naturally divide others into those inside and those outside our group (Buttelmann & Böhm, 2014; Dunham et al., 2013). We also evaluate ourselves partly by our group memberships. Having a sense of "we-ness" strengthens our self-concepts. It *feels* good. We seek not only *respect* for ourselves but also *pride* in our groups (Sani et al., 2012; Smith & Tyler, 1997). Moreover, seeing our groups as superior helps us feel even better. It's as if we all think, "I am an X [name your group]. X is good. Therefore, I am good."

Lacking a positive personal identity, people often seek self-esteem by identifying with a group. Thus, many disadvantaged youths find pride, power, security, and identity in gang affiliations. Much as dissonance motivates its reduction and insecurity feeds authoritarianism, so also uncertainty motivates people's seeking social identity. Their uncertainty subsides as they perceive who "we" and "they" are. Especially in a chaotic or an uncertain world, being part of a zealous, tightly knit group feels good; it validates who one is (Hogg, 2014). And that explains part of the appeal of extreme, radical groups in today's world.

When people's personal and social identities become *fused*—when the boundary between self and group blurs—they become more willing to fight or die for their group (Gómez et al., 2011; Swann et al., 2012, 2014a,b). Many patriotic individuals, for example, define themselves by their national identities (Staub, 1997a, 2005a). And many people at loose ends find identity in their associations with new religious movements, self-help groups, or fraternal clubs (Figure 4).

Because of our social identifications, we conform to our group norms. We sacrifice ourselves for team, family, and nation. The more important our social identity and the more strongly attached we feel to a group, the more we react prejudicially to threats from another group (Crocker & Luhtanen, 1990; Hinkle et al., 1992).

ingroup
"Us"—a group of people who share a sense of belonging, a feeling of common identity.

outgroup
"Them"—a group that people perceive as distinctively different from or apart from their ingroup.

"Whoever is dissatisfied with himself is continually ready for revenge."
—Nietzsche,
The Gay Science, 1882–1887

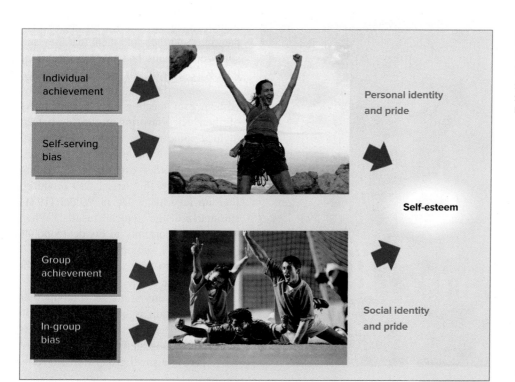

FIGURE :: 4

Personal identity and social identity together feed self-esteem.
Sam Edwards/OJO Images/AGE Fotostock; Digital Vision/PhotoDisc

INGROUP BIAS

The group definition of who you are—your gender, race, religion, marital status, academic major—implies a definition of who you are not. The circle that includes "us" (the ingroup) excludes "them" (the outgroup). The more that ethnic Turks in the Netherlands see themselves as Turks or as Muslims, the less they see themselves as Dutch (Verkuyten & Yildiz, 2007).

The mere experience of being formed into groups may promote **ingroup bias.** Ask children, "Which are better, the children in your school or the children at [another school nearby]?" Virtually all will say their own school has the better children.

INGROUP BIAS EXPRESSES AND SUPPORTS A POSITIVE SELF-CONCEPT.

Ingroup bias is one more example of the human quest for a positive self-concept. When our group has been successful, we can make ourselves feel better by identifying more strongly with it. College students whose team has just been victorious frequently report, "*We* won." After their team's defeat, students are more likely to say, "*They* lost." Basking in the reflected glory of a successful ingroup is strongest among those who have just experienced an ego blow, such as learning they did poorly on a "creativity test" (Cialdini et al., 1976). We can also bask in the reflected glory of a friend's achievement—except when the friend outperforms us on something pertinent to our identity (Tesser et al., 1988). If you think of yourself as an outstanding psychology student, you will likely take more pleasure in a friend's excellence in mathematics.

"There is a tendency to define one's own group positively in order to evaluate oneself positively."
—John C. Turner (1984)

INGROUP BIAS FEEDS FAVORITISM.

We are so group conscious that, given any excuse to think of ourselves as a group, we will do so—and we will then exhibit ingroup bias. Even forming conspicuous groups on no logical basis—for instance, merely by composing groups X and Y with the flip of a coin—will produce some ingroup bias (Billig & Tajfel, 1973; Brewer & Silver, 1978; Locksley et al., 1980). In Kurt Vonnegut's novel *Slapstick,* computers gave everyone a new middle name; all "Daffodil-11s" then felt unity with one another and distance from "Raspberry-13s." The self-serving bias rides again, enabling people to achieve a more positive social identity: "We" are better than "they," even when "we" and "they" are defined randomly!

In experiments, Tajfel and Michael Billig (1974; Tajfel, 1970, 1981, 1982) further explored how little it takes to provoke favoritism toward *us* and unfairness toward *them.* In

Basking in reflected glory. After Jamaican-Canadian sprinter Ben Johnson won the Olympic 100-meter race, Canadian media described his victory as that of a "Canadian." After Johnson's gold medal was taken away because of steroid use, Canadian media then emphasized his "Jamaican" identity (Stelzl et al., 2008).
AP Images/Dieter Endlicher

one study, Tajfel and Billig had individual British teenagers evaluate modern abstract paintings and then told them that they and some other teens had favored the art of Paul Klee over that of Wassily Kandinsky, while others favored Kandinsky. Finally, without ever meeting the other members of their Klee-favoring group, each teen divided some money among members of the Klee- and Kandinsky-favoring groups. In this and other experiments, defining groups even in this trivial way produced ingroup favoritism. David Wilder (1981) summarized the typical result: "When given the opportunity to divide 15 points [worth money], subjects generally award 9 or 10 points to their own group and 5 or 6 points to the other group."

We are more prone to ingroup bias when our group is small and differs in status relative to the outgroup (Ellemers et al., 1997; Moscatelli et al., 2014). When we're part of a small group surrounded by a larger group, we are more conscious of our group membership. When our ingroup is the majority, we think less about it. To be a foreign student, to be gay or lesbian, or to be of a minority race or gender is to feel one's social identity more keenly and to react accordingly.

MUST INGROUP LIKING FOSTER OUTGROUP DISLIKING?   Does ingroup bias reflect liking for one's ingroup, dislike for the outgroup, or both? Does ethnic pride cause prejudice? Does a strong feminist identity lead feminists to dislike nonfeminists? Does loyalty to a particular fraternity or sorority lead its members to deprecate independents and members of other fraternities and sororities? Or do people merely favor their own group without any animosity toward others?

Experiments support both liking for the ingroup and dislike for the outgroup. Love and hate are sometimes opposite sides of the same coin. If you love the Boston Red Sox, you may hate the New York Yankees. A patriot's love of tribe or country motivates dying to defend it against enemies. To the extent that we see virtue in *us,* we likely see evil in *them.* Moreover, outgroup stereotypes prosper when people feel their ingroup identity most keenly (Wilder & Shapiro, 1991).

We also ascribe uniquely human emotions (love, hope, contempt, resentment) to ingroup members, and are more reluctant to see such human emotions in outgroup members (Demoulin et al., 2008; Leyens et al., 2003, 2007). There is a long history of denying human attributes to outgroups—a process called "infrahumanization." European explorers pictured many of the peoples they encountered as savages ruled by animal instinct. "Africans have been likened to apes, Jews to vermin, and immigrants to parasites," noted Australian social psychologists Stephen Loughman and Nick Haslam (2007). We humanize pets and dehumanize outgroups.

Yet ingroup bias and discrimination result less from outgroup hostility than from ingroup favoritism (Balliet et al., 2014; Greenwald & Pettigrew, 2014). Bias is less a matter of dislike toward those who are different than of networking and mutual support among those in one's group. Even when there is no "them" (imagine yourself bonding with a handful of fellow survivors on a deserted island), one can come to love "us" (Gaertner et al., 2006). So it seems that positive feelings for our own groups need not be mirrored by equally strong negative feelings for outgroups.

NEED FOR STATUS, SELF-REGARD, AND BELONGING

Status is relative: To perceive ourselves as having status, we need people below us. Thus, one psychological benefit of prejudice, or of any status system, is a feeling of superiority. Most of us can recall a time when we took secret satisfaction in another's failure—perhaps seeing a sibling punished or a classmate failing a test. In Europe and North America, prejudice is often greater among those low or slipping on the socioeconomic ladder and among those whose positive self-image is threatened (Lemyre & Smith, 1985; Pettigrew et al., 1998; Thompson & Crocker, 1985). In one study, members of lower-status sororities were more disparaging of competing sororities than were members of higher-status sororities (Crocker et al., 1987). If our status is secure—if we feel "authentic pride" that's rooted in accomplishment, not just self-aggrandizement—we have less need to feel superior, and we express less prejudice (Ashton-James & Tracy, 2012).

In study after study, thinking about your own mortality—by writing a short essay on dying and the emotions aroused by thinking about death—provokes enough insecurity to intensify ingroup favoritism and outgroup prejudice (Greenberg et al., 1990, 2013; Schimel et al. 1999). One study found that among Whites, thinking about death can even promote liking for racists who argue for their group's superiority (Greenberg et al., 2001, 2008). With death on their minds, people exhibit **terror management.** They shield themselves from the threat of their own death by derogating those whose challenges to their worldviews further arouse their anxiety. When people are already feeling vulnerable about their mortality, prejudice helps bolster a threatened belief system. Thinking about

"Father, mother, and me, sister and auntie say all the people like us are We, and every one else is they. And they live over the sea, while we live over the way. But would you believe it? They look upon we as only a sort of they!"
—Rudyard Kipling, 1926 (Quoted by Mullen, 1991)

"By exciting emulation and comparisons of superiority, you lay the foundation of lasting mischief; you make brothers and sisters hate each other."
—Samuel Johnson, Quoted in James Boswell's *Life of Samuel Johnson,* 1791

terror management
According to "terror management theory," people's self-protective emotional and cognitive responses (including adhering more strongly to their cultural worldviews and prejudices) when confronted with reminders of their mortality.

"It's not enough that we succeed. Cats must also fail."

death can also heighten communal feelings, such as ingroup identification, togetherness, and altruism (McGregor et al., 2001; Sani et al., 2009).

Reminding people of their death can also affect support for important public policies. Before the 2004 presidential election, giving people cues related to death—including asking them to recall their emotions related to the 9/11 attack, or subliminally exposing them to 9/11 related pictures—increased support for President George W. Bush and his antiterrorism policies (Landau et al., 2004). In Iran, reminders of death increased college students' support for suicide attacks against the United States (Pyszczynski et al., 2006).

All this suggests that a man who doubts his own strength and independence might, by proclaiming women to be weak and dependent, boost his masculine image. Indeed, when Washington State University men viewed young women's videotaped job interviews, men with low self-acceptance disliked strong, nontraditional women. Men with high self-acceptance preferred them (Grube et al., 1982). Experiments confirm the connection between self-image and prejudice: Affirm people and they will evaluate an outgroup more positively; threaten their self-esteem and they will restore it by denigrating an outgroup (Fein & Spencer, 1997; Spencer et al., 1998).

Despising outgroups strengthens the ingroup. School spirit is seldom so strong as when the game is with the archrival. The sense of comradeship among workers is often highest when they all feel a common antagonism toward management. To solidify the Nazi hold over the Germany people, Hitler threatened them with the "Jewish menace."

When the need to belong is met, people become more accepting of outgroups, report Mario Mikulincer and Phillip Shaver (2001). They subliminally primed some Israeli students with words that fostered a sense of belonging (*love, support, hug*) and primed others with neutral words. The students then read an essay that was supposedly written by a fellow Jewish student and another by an Arab student. When primed with neutral words, the Israeli students evaluated the supposed Israeli student's essay as superior to the supposed Arab student's essay. When the participants were primed with a sense of belonging, that bias disappeared.

Motivation to Avoid Prejudice

Motivations not only lead people to be prejudiced but also to avoid prejudice. But try as we might to suppress unwanted thoughts—thoughts about food, thoughts about romance with a friend's partner, judgmental thoughts about another group—they sometimes refuse to go away (Macrae et al., 1994; Wegner & Erber, 1992). This is especially so for older adults, and people under alcohol's influence who lose some of their ability to inhibit unwanted thoughts and therefore to suppress old stereotypes (Bartholow et al., 2006; von Hippel et al., 2000). Patricia Devine and her colleagues (1989, 2012; Forscher & Devine, 2014) report that people low and high in prejudice sometimes have similar automatic prejudicial responses. The result: Unwanted (dissonant) thoughts and feelings often persist. Breaking the prejudice habit is not easy.

In real life, a majority person's encountering a minority person may trigger a knee-jerk stereotype. Those with accepting and those with disapproving attitudes toward homosexuals may both feel uncomfortable sitting with a gay male on a bus seat (Monteith, 1993). Encountering an unfamiliar Black male, people—even those who pride themselves on not being prejudiced—may respond warily. Seeking not to appear prejudiced, they may divert their attention away from the person (Richeson & Trawalter, 2008).

In one experiment by E. J. Vanman and colleagues (1990), White people viewed slides of White and Black people, imagined themselves interacting with them, and rated their probable liking of the person. Although the participants saw themselves liking the Black more than the White persons, their facial muscles told a different story. Instruments revealed that when a Black face appeared, there tended to be more frowning muscular activity than smiling. An emotion processing center in the brain also becomes more active as a person views an unfamiliar person of another race (Hart et al., 2000).

Researchers who study stereotyping contend, however, that prejudicial reactions are not inevitable (Crandall & Eshelman, 2003; Kunda & Spencer, 2003). The motivation to avoid prejudice can lead people to modify their thoughts and actions. Aware of the gap between how they *should* feel and how they *do* feel, self-conscious people will feel guilt and try to inhibit their prejudicial response (Bodenhausen & Macrae, 1998; Dasgupta & Rivera, 2006; Zuwerink et al., 1996). Even automatic prejudices subside, note Devine and her colleagues (2005), when people's motivation to avoid prejudice is internal (because they believe prejudice is wrong) rather than external (because they don't want others to think badly of them).

The moral: Overcoming what Devine calls "the prejudice habit" isn't easy. But it can be done. One team of 24 researchers held a "research contest" that compared 17 interventions for reducing implicit prejudice among more than 17,000 individuals (Lai et al., 2014). Eight of the interventions proved effective, especially giving people experiences with vivid, positive examples of Black people who countered stereotypes. In another study, Devine and her colleagues (2012) raised the awareness and concern of willing volunteers and training them to replace biased with unbiased knee-jerk responses. Throughout the two-year study follow-up period, participants in the experimental intervention condition displayed reduced implicit prejudice. If you find yourself reacting with knee-jerk presumptions or feelings, don't despair; that's not unusual. It's what you do with that awareness that matters. Do you let those feelings hijack your behavior? Or do you compensate by monitoring and correcting your behavior in future situations?

SUMMING UP: What Are the Motivational Sources of Prejudice?

- People's motivations affect prejudice. Frustration breeds hostility, which people sometimes vent on scapegoats and sometimes express more directly against competing groups.

- People also are motivated to view themselves and their groups as superior to other groups. Even trivial group memberships lead people to favor their group over others. A threat to self-image heightens such *ingroup* favoritism, as does the need to belong.

- On a more positive note, if people are motivated to avoid prejudice, they can break the prejudice habit.

WHAT ARE THE COGNITIVE SOURCES OF PREJUDICE?

Describe the different cognitive sources of prejudice.

How does the way we think about the world influence our stereotypes? And how do our stereotypes affect our everyday judgments? Stereotyped beliefs and prejudiced attitudes exist not only because of socialization and because they displace hostilities, but also as by-products of normal thinking processes. Stereotypes spring less from malice of the heart than from the machinery of the mind. Like perceptual illusions, which are by-products of our knack for interpreting the world, stereotypes can be by-products of how we simplify our complex worlds.

Categorization: Classifying People into Groups

One way we simplify our environment is to *categorize*—to organize the world by clustering objects into groups (Macrae & Bodenhausen, 2000, 2001). A biologist classifies plants and animals. A human classifies people. Having done so, we think about them more easily. If persons in a group share some similarities—if most MENSA members are smart, and most basketball players are tall—knowing their group memberships can provide useful information with minimal effort (Macrae et al., 1994). Stereotypes sometimes offer "a beneficial ratio of information gained to effort expended" (Sherman et al., 1998). Stereotypes represent cognitive efficiency. They are energy-saving schemes for making speedy judgments and predicting how others will think and act. We judge people in outgroups more quickly; when assessing ingroup individuals, we take longer to form impressions (Vala et al., 2012). Thus, stereotypes and outgroup bias may have served ultimate, evolutionary functions, by enabling our ancestors to cope and survive (Navarrete et al., 2010).

SPONTANEOUS CATEGORIZATION

We find it especially easy and efficient to rely on stereotypes when we are

- pressed for time (Kaplan et al., 1993);
- preoccupied (Gilbert & Hixon, 1991);
- tired (Bodenhausen, 1990; Ghumman & Barnes, 2013);
- emotionally aroused (Esses et al., 1993b; Stroessner & Mackie, 1993); or
- too young to appreciate diversity (Biernat, 1991);

Ethnicity and sex are powerful ways of categorizing people. Imagine Julius, a 45-year-old African American real-estate agent in Atlanta. We suspect that your image of "Black male" predominates over the categories "middle-aged," "businessperson," and "American southerner."

Experiments expose our spontaneous categorization of people by race. Much as we organize what is actually a color continuum into what we perceive as distinct colors, such as red, blue, and green, so our "discontinuous minds" (Dawkins, 1993) cannot resist categorizing people into groups. We label people of widely varying ancestry as simply "Black" or "White," as if such categories were black and white. When individuals view different people making statements, they often forget who said what but remember the race of the person who made each statement (Hewstone et al., 1991; Stroessner et al., 1990; Taylor et al., 1978). By itself, such categorization is not prejudice, but it does provide a foundation for prejudice.

PERCEIVED SIMILARITIES AND DIFFERENCES

Picture the following objects: apples, chairs, pencils.

There is a strong tendency to see objects within a group as being more uniform than they really are. Were your apples all red? Your chairs all straight-backed? Your pencils all yellow? Once we classify two days in the same month, they seem more alike, temperature-wise, than the same interval across months. People guess the 8-day average temperature difference between, for instance, November 15 and 23 to be less than the 8-day difference between November 30 and December 8 (Krueger & Clement, 1994a).

It's the same with people. When we assign people to groups—athletes, drama majors, math professors—we are likely to exaggerate the similarities within the groups and the differences between them (S. E. Taylor, 1981; Wilder, 1978). We assume that other groups are more homogeneous than our own. Mere division into groups can create an **outgroup homogeneity effect**—a sense that *they* are "all alike" and different from "us" and "our" group (Ostrom & Sedikides, 1992). Consider:

outgroup homogeneity effect
Perception of outgroup members as more similar to one another than are ingroup members. Thus "they are alike; we are diverse."

- Many non-Europeans see the Swiss as a fairly homogeneous people. But to the people of Switzerland, the Swiss are diverse, encompassing French-, German-, Italian-, and Romansh-speaking groups.

- Many non-Latino Americans lump "Latinos" together. Mexican Americans, Cuban Americans, and Puerto Ricans—among others—see important differences (Huddy & Virtanen, 1995).
- Sorority sisters perceive the members of any other sorority as less diverse than the members of their own (Park & Rothbart, 1982).

We also generally like people we perceive as similar to us and dislike those we perceive as different, so the result is ingroup bias (Byrne & Wong, 1962; Rokeach & Mezei, 1966; Stein et al., 1965).

To a human cartoonist, all penguins look alike. To a penguin, they differ.
Source: © Dave Coverly. Speedbump.com

In general, the greater our familiarity with a social group, the more we see its diversity (Brown & Wootton-Millward, 1993; Linville et al., 1989). The less our familiarity, the more we stereotype.

Perhaps you have noticed: *They*—the members of any racial group other than your own—even *look* alike. Many people can recall embarrassing ourselves by confusing two people of another racial group, prompting the person we've misnamed to say, "You think we all look alike." Experiments in the United States, Scotland, and Germany reveal that people of other races do in fact *seem* to look more alike than do people of one's own race (Chance & Goldstein, 1981, 1996; Ellis, 1981; Meissner & Brigham, 2001; Sporer & Horry, 2011). When White students are shown faces of a few White and a few Black individuals and then asked to pick those individuals out of a photographic lineup, they show an **own-race bias:** They more accurately recognize the White faces than the Black ones, and they often falsely recognize Black faces never before seen.

As Figure 5 illustrates, Blacks more easily recognize another Black than they do a White (Bothwell et al., 1989). Hispanics, Blacks, and Asians all recognize faces from their own races better than from one another's (Gross, 2009). Likewise, British South Asians are quicker than White Brits to recognize South Asian faces (Walker & Hewstone, 2008). And 10- to 15-year-old Turkish children are quicker than Austrian children to recognize Turkish faces (Sporer et al., 2007). Even infants as young as 9 months display better own-race recognition of faces (Kelly et al., 2005, 2007).

"Women are more like each other than men [are]."
—Lord (not Lady) Chesterfield

own-race bias

The tendency for people to more accurately recognize faces of their own race. (Also called the *cross-race effect* or *other-race effect*.)

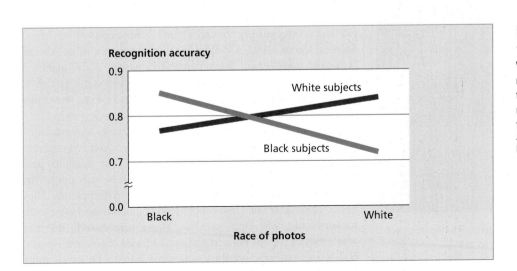

FIGURE :: 5

The Own-Race Bias
White subjects more accurately recognize the faces of Whites than of Blacks; Black subjects more accurately recognize the faces of Blacks than of Whites.
Source: From P. G. Devine & R. S. Malpass, 1985.

It's true outside the laboratory as well, as Daniel Wright and his colleagues (2001) found after either a Black or a White researcher approached Black and White people in South African and English shopping malls. When later asked to identify the researcher from lineups, people better recognized those of their own race.

It's not that we cannot perceive differences among faces of another group. Rather, when looking at a face from another racial group we often attend, first, to group ("that man is Black") rather than to individual features. When viewing someone of our own group, we are less attentive to the race category and more attentive to individual details such as the eyes (Kawakami et al., 2014; Shriver et al., 2008; Van Bavel & Cunningham, 2012; Young et al., 2010).

Our attending to someone's being in a different social category also contributes to a parallel *own-age bias*—the tendency for both children and older adults to more accurately identify faces from their own age groups (Rhodes & Anastasi, 2012; Wright & Stroud, 2002; He et al., 2011). (Perhaps you have noticed that senior citizens look more alike than do your fellow students?)

Distinctiveness: Perceiving People Who Stand Out

In other ways, too, our normal social perceptions breed stereotypes. Distinctive people and vivid or extreme occurrences often capture attention and distort judgments.

DISTINCTIVE PEOPLE

Have you ever found yourself in a situation where you were the only person of your gender, race, or nationality? If so, your difference from the others probably made you more noticeable and the object of more attention. A Black person in an otherwise White group, a man in an otherwise female group, or a woman in an otherwise male group seems more prominent and influential and to have exaggerated good and bad qualities (Crocker & McGraw, 1984; S. E. Taylor et al., 1979). When someone in a group is made conspicuous, we tend to see that person as causing whatever happens (Taylor & Fiske, 1978). If we are positioned to look at Joe, even if Joe is merely an average group member, Joe will seem to have a greater-than-average influence on the group.

Distinctive people, such as Houston Rockets 7'6" former player Yao Ming, draw attention.
AP Images/Eugene Hoshiko

Have you noticed that people also define you by your most distinctive traits and behaviors? Tell people about someone who is a skydiver and a tennis player, report Lori Nelson and Dale Miller (1995), and they will think of the person as a skydiver. Asked to choose a gift book for the person, they will pick a skydiving book over a tennis book. A person who has both a pet snake and a pet dog is seen more as a snake owner than a dog owner.

People also take note of those who violate expectations (Bettencourt et al., 1997). "Like a flower blooming in winter, intellect is more readily noticed where it is not expected," reflected Stephen Carter (1993, p. 54) on his own experience as an African American intellectual. Such perceived distinctiveness makes it easier for highly capable job applicants from low-status groups to get noticed, although they also must work harder to prove that their abilities are genuine (Biernat & Kobrynowicz, 1997).

Ellen Langer and Lois Imber (1980) cleverly demonstrated the attention paid to distinctive people. They asked Harvard students to watch a video of a man reading. The students paid closer attention when they were led to think he was out of the ordinary—a cancer patient, a homosexual, or a millionaire. They noticed characteristics that other viewers ignored, and their evaluation of him was more extreme. Those who thought the man was a cancer patient noticed distinctive facial characteristics and bodily movements and thus perceived him to be much more "different from most people" than did the other viewers. The extra attention we pay to distinctive people creates an illusion that they differ from others more than they really do. If people thought you had the IQ of a genius, they would probably notice things about you that otherwise would pass unnoticed.

DISTINCTIVENESS FEEDS SELF-CONSCIOUSNESS. When surrounded by Whites, Blacks sometimes detect people reacting to their distinctiveness. Many report being stared or glared at, being subject to insensitive comments, and receiving bad service (Swim et al., 1998). Whites, when alone amid those of another race, may be similarly sensitive to others' reactions. Sometimes, however, we misperceive others as reacting to our distinctiveness. Researchers Robert Kleck and Angelo Strenta (1980) discovered this when they led Dartmouth College women to feel disfigured. The women thought the purpose of the experiment was to assess how someone would react to a facial scar created with theatrical makeup; the scar was on the right cheek, running from the ear to the mouth. Actually, the purpose was to see how the women themselves, when made to feel deviant, would perceive others' behavior toward them. After applying the makeup, the experimenter gave each woman a small hand mirror so she could see the authentic-looking scar. When she put the mirror down, he then applied some "moisturizer" to "keep the makeup from cracking." What the "moisturizer" really did was remove the scar.

The scene that followed was poignant. A young woman, feeling terribly self-conscious about her supposedly disfigured face, talked with another woman who saw no such disfigurement and knew nothing of what had gone on before. If you have ever felt similarly self-conscious—perhaps about a physical handicap, acne, even just a bad hair day—then perhaps you can sympathize with the self-conscious woman. Compared with women who were led to believe their conversational partners merely thought they had an allergy, the "disfigured" women became acutely sensitive to how their partners were looking at them. They rated their partners as more tense, distant, and patronizing. Observers who later analyzed videotapes of how the partners treated "disfigured" persons could find no such differences in treatment. Self-conscious about being different, the "disfigured" women had misinterpreted mannerisms and comments they would otherwise not have noticed.

Self-conscious interactions between a majority and a minority person can therefore feel tense even when both are well intentioned (Devine et al., 1996). Tom, who is known to be gay, meets tolerant Bill, who is straight and wants to respond without prejudice. But feeling unsure of himself, Bill holds back a bit. Tom, expecting negative attitudes from most people, misreads Bill's hesitancy as hostility and responds with a seeming chip on his shoulder.

Anyone can experience this phenomenon. Majority group members (in one study, White residents of Manitoba) often have beliefs—"meta-stereotypes"—about how minorities stereotype them (Vorauer et al., 1998). Even relatively unprejudiced Canadian Whites, Israeli Jews, or American Christians may sense that outgroup minorities stereotype them as prejudiced, arrogant, or patronizing. If George worries that Gamal perceives him as "your typical educated racist," he may be self-consciously on guard when talking with Gamal.

STIGMA CONSCIOUSNESS.   People vary in **stigma consciousness**—in how much they expect others to stereotype them. Gays and lesbians, for example, differ in how much they suppose others "interpret all my behaviors" in terms of their homosexuality (Lewis et al., 2006; Pinel, 1999, 2004).

Seeing oneself as a victim of pervasive prejudice has its ups and downs (Branscombe et al., 1999; Dion, 1998). The downside is that those who perceive themselves as frequent victims live with the stress of presumed stereotypes and antagonism, and therefore experience lower well-being. While living in Europe, stigma-conscious Americans—Americans who perceive Europeans as resenting them—live more fretfully than those who feel accepted.

The upside is that perceptions of prejudice buffer individual self-esteem. If someone is nasty, "Well, it's not directed at me personally." Moreover, perceived prejudice and discrimination enhance our feelings of social identity and prepare us to join in collective social action.

stigma consciousness
A person's expectation of being victimized by prejudice or discrimination.

VIVID CASES

Our minds also use distinctive cases as a shortcut to judging groups. Are the Japanese good baseball players? "Well, there's Ichiro Suzuki and Junichi Tazawa and Koji Uehara. Yeah, I'd say so." Note the thought processes at work here: Given limited experience with a particular social group, we recall examples of it and generalize from those (Sherman, 1996). Moreover, encountering an example of a negative stereotype (for instance, a hostile Black) can prime the stereotype, leading us to minimize contact with the group (Henderson-King & Nisbett, 1996).

Such generalizing from a single case can cause problems. Vivid instances, though more available in memory, seldom represent the larger group. Exceptional athletes, though distinctive and memorable, are not the best basis for judging the distribution of athletic talent among an entire group.

Those in a numerical minority, being more distinctive, also may be numerically overestimated by the majority. What proportion of your country's population would you say is Muslim? People in non-Muslim countries often overestimate this proportion. (In the United States, Muslims are only about 1 percent of the population, but Americans believe 15 percent of U.S. residents are Muslim.)

Consider a 2011 Gallup survey, in which the average American guessed that 25 percent of people are exclusively homosexual (Morales, 2011). The best evidence suggests that about 3 percent of men and 1 or 2 percent of women have a same-sex orientation (Chandra et al., 2011; Herbenick et al., 2010).

Myron Rothbart and his colleagues (1978) showed how distinctive cases also fuel stereotypes. They had University of Oregon students view 50 slides, each of which stated a man's height. For one group of students, 10 of the men were slightly over 6 feet (up to 6 feet, 4 inches). For other students, these 10 men were well over 6 feet (up to 6 feet, 11 inches). When asked later how many of the men were over 6 feet, those given the moderately tall examples recalled 5 percent too many. Those given the extremely tall examples recalled 50 percent too many. In a follow-up experiment, students read descriptions of the actions of 50 men, 10 of whom had committed either nonviolent crimes, such as forgery, or violent crimes, such as rape. Of those shown the list with the violent crimes, most overestimated the number of criminal acts. Vivid cases distort judgments and create stereotypes.

DISTINCTIVE EVENTS FOSTER ILLUSORY CORRELATIONS

Stereotypes assume a correlation between group membership and individuals' presumed characteristics ("Italians are emotional," "Jews are shrewd," "Accountants are perfectionists"). Often, people's stereotypes are accurate (Jussim, 2012). But sometimes our attentiveness to unusual occurrences creates illusory correlations. Because we are sensitive to distinctive events, the co-occurrence of two such events is especially noticeable—more noticeable than each of the times the unusual events do *not* occur together.

In a classic experiment, David Hamilton and Robert Gifford (1976) demonstrated illusory correlation. They showed students slides in which various people, members of "Group A" or "Group B," were said to have done something desirable or undesirable. For example, "John, a member of Group A, visited a sick friend in the hospital." Twice as many statements described members of Group A as Group B. But both groups did nine desirable acts for every four undesirable behaviors. Since both Group B and the undesirable acts were less frequent, their co-occurrence—for example, "Allen, a member of Group B, dented the fender of a parked car and didn't leave his name"—was an unusual combination that caught people's attention. The students therefore overestimated the frequency with which the "minority" group (B) acted undesirably, and they judged Group B more harshly.

Remember, Group A members outnumbered Group B members two to one, and Group B members committed undesirable acts in the same *proportion* as Group A members (thus, they committed only half as many). Moreover, the students had no preexisting biases for or against Group B, and they received the information more systematically than daily experience ever offers it. Although researchers debate why it happens, they agree that illusory correlation occurs and provides yet another source for the formation of racial stereotypes

(Berndsen et al., 2002). Thus, the features that most distinguish a minority from a majority are those that become associated with it (Sherman et al., 2009). Your ethnic or social group may be like other groups in most ways, but people will notice how it differs.

In experiments, even single co-occurrences of an unusual act by someone in an atypical group—"Ben, a Jehovah's Witness, owns a pet sloth"—can embed illusory correlations in people's minds (Risen et al., 2007). This enables the mass media to feed illusory correlations. When a self-described homosexual person murders or sexually abuses someone, homosexuality is often mentioned. When a heterosexual does the same, the person's sexual orientation is seldom mentioned. Such reporting adds to the illusion of a large correlation between (1) violent tendencies and (2) homosexuality or mental hospitalization.

Unlike the students who judged Groups A and B, we often have preexisting biases. David Hamilton's further research with Terrence Rose (1980) revealed that our preexisting stereotypes can lead us to "see" correlations that aren't there. The researchers had University of California at Santa Barbara students read sentences in which various adjectives described the members of different occupational groups ("Juan, an accountant, is timid and thoughtful"). In actuality, each occupation was described equally often by each adjective; accountants, doctors, and salespeople were equally often timid, wealthy, and talkative. The students, however, *thought* they had more often read descriptions of timid accountants, wealthy doctors, and talkative salespeople. Their stereotyping led them to perceive correlations that weren't there, thus helping to perpetuate the stereotypes.

Likewise, guess what happened when Vaughn Becker and his colleagues (2010) invited university students to view a White and a Black face—one angry, one not—for one-tenth of a second (as in Figure 6). The participants' subsequent recollections of what they had viewed revealed racial bias. "White anger flowed to neutral Black faces (34 percent likelihood) more readily than Black anger flowed to neutral White faces (19 percent likelihood)."

Attribution: Is It a Just World?

In explaining others' actions, we frequently commit the fundamental attribution error: We attribute others' behavior so much to their inner dispositions that we discount important situational forces. The error occurs partly because our attention focuses on the person, not on the situation. A person's race or sex is vivid and gets attention; the situational forces working upon that person are usually less visible. Slavery was often overlooked as an explanation for slave behavior; the behavior was instead attributed to the slaves' own nature. Until recently, the same was true of how we explained the perceived differences between women and men. Because gender-role constraints were hard to see, we attributed men's and women's behavior solely to their presumed innate dispositions. The more people assume that human traits are fixed dispositions, the stronger are their stereotypes and the greater their acceptance of racial inequities (Levy et al., 1998; Williams & Eberhardt, 2008).

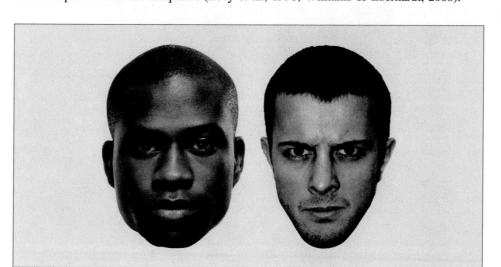

FIGURE :: 6

Ingroup biases influence perceptions. When briefly shown two faces, one neutral, one angry, people more often misrecalled the Black rather than the White face as angry (Becker et al., 2010).
Blend Image/Getty Images; Cordelia Molloy/Science Source

GROUP-SERVING BIAS

Thomas Pettigrew (1979, 1980) showed how attribution errors bias people's explanations of group members' behaviors. We grant members of our own group the benefit of the doubt: "She donated because she has a good heart; he refused because he's using every penny to help support his mother." When explaining acts by members of other groups, we more often assume the worst: "She donated to gain favor; he refused because he's selfish." In one classic study, the light shove that Whites perceived as mere "horsing around" when done by another White became a "violent gesture" when done by a Black (Duncan, 1976).

Positive behavior by outgroup members is more often dismissed. It may be seen as a "special case" ("He is certainly bright and hardworking—not at all like other . . ."), as owing to luck or some special advantage ("She probably got admitted just because her med school had to fill its quota for women applicants"), as demanded by the situation ("Under the circumstances, what could the cheap Scot do but pay the whole check?"), or as attributable to extra effort ("Asian students get better grades because they're so compulsive").

group-serving bias
Explaining away outgroup members' positive behaviors; also attributing negative behaviors to their dispositions (while excusing such behavior by one's own group).

Disadvantaged groups and groups that stress modesty (such as the Chinese) exhibit less of this **group-serving bias** (Fletcher & Ward, 1989; Heine & Lehman, 1997; Jackson et al., 1993). By contrast, immodest groups that are invested in their own greatness (that display "collective narcissism") react to threats with group-serving bias and hostility (de Zavala et al., 2013). Social psychologists Jacquie Vorauer and Stacey Sasaki (2010, 2011) note that multiculturalism's focus on differences, which can be positive in the absence of conflict (making intergroup exchanges seem interesting and stimulating), sometimes comes at a cost. When there is conflict or threat, a focus on differences can foster group-level attributions and increased hostility.

The group-serving bias can subtly color our language. A team of University of Padua (Italy) researchers led by Anne Maass (1995 et al., 1999) has found that positive behaviors by another ingroup member are often described as general dispositions (for example, "Karen is helpful"). When performed by an outgroup member, the same behavior is often described as a specific, isolated act ("Carmen opened the door for the man with the cane"). With

Just-world thinking? Some people argued against giving legal rights to American prisoners in the Guantanamo Bay detention camp that housed alleged combatants from Afghanistan and Iraq. One argument was that these people would not be confined there if they had not done horrendous things, so why allow them to argue their innocence in U.S. courts?
AP Images/Lynne Sladky

TABLE :: 1 How Self-Enhancing Social Identities Support Stereotypes

	Ingroup	Outgroup
Attitude	Favoritism	Denigration
Perceptions	Heterogeneity (we differ)	Homogeneity (they're alike)
Attributions for negative behavior	To situations	To dispositions

negative behavior, the specificity reverses: "Eric shoved her" (an isolated act by an ingroup member) but "Enrique was aggressive" (an outgroup member's general disposition).

Earlier we noted that blaming the victim can justify the blamer's own superior status (Table 1). Blaming occurs as people attribute an outgroup's failures to its members' flawed dispositions, notes Miles Hewstone (1990): "They fail because they're stupid; we fail because we didn't try." If women, Blacks, or Jews have been abused, they must somehow have brought it on themselves. When the British made a group of German civilians walk through the Bergen-Belsen concentration camp at the close of World War II, one German responded: "What terrible criminals these prisoners must have been to receive such treatment." (Such group-serving bias illustrates the motivations that underlie prejudice, as well as the cognition. Motivation and cognition, emotion and thinking, are inseparable.)

THE JUST-WORLD PHENOMENON

In a series of experiments, Melvin Lerner and his colleagues (Lerner, 1980; Lerner & Miller, 1978) discovered that merely *observing* another innocent person being victimized is enough to make the victim seem less worthy.

Lerner (1980) noted that such disparaging of hapless victims results from the need to believe that "I am a just person living in a just world, a world where people get what they deserve." From early childhood, he argues, we are taught that good is rewarded and evil punished. Hard work and virtue pay dividends; laziness and immorality do not. From this it is but a short leap to assuming that those who flourish must be good and those who suffer must deserve their fate.

Numerous studies have confirmed this **just-world phenomenon** (Hafer & Rubel, 2015). Imagine that you, along with some others, are participating in one of Lerner's studies— supposedly on the perception of emotional cues (Lerner & Simmons, 1966). One of the participants, a confederate, is selected by lottery to perform a memory task. This person receives painful shocks whenever she gives a wrong answer. You and the others note her emotional responses.

"For if [people were] to choose out of all the customs in the world such as seemed to them the best, they would examine the whole number, and end by preferring their own."

—Greek Historian Herodotus, *The Histories*, Book III, 440 B.C.

just-world phenomenon
The tendency of people to believe that the world is just and that people therefore get what they deserve and deserve what they get.

The just-world phenomenon.
© Robert Mankoff/The New Yorker Collection/www.cartoonbank.com

The classic illustration of "just-world thinking" comes from the Old Testament story of Job, a good person who suffers terrible misfortune. Job's friends surmise that, this being a just world, Job must have done something wicked to elicit such terrible suffering.

After watching the victim receive these apparently painful shocks, the experimenter asks you to evaluate her. How would you respond? With compassionate sympathy? We might expect so. As Ralph Waldo Emerson wrote, "The martyr cannot be dishonored." On the contrary, in these experiments the martyrs *were* dishonored. When observers were powerless to alter the victim's fate, they often rejected and devalued the victim. Juvenal, the Roman satirist, anticipated these results: "The Roman mob follows after Fortune . . . and hates those who have been condemned." And the more ongoing the suffering, as with Jews even after the Holocaust, the greater the dislike of the victims (Imhoff & Banse, 2009).

Linda Carli and her colleagues (1989, 1999) reported that the just-world phenomenon colors our impressions of rape victims. Carli had people read detailed descriptions of interactions between a man and a woman. In one scenario, a woman and her boss meet for dinner, go to his home, and each have a glass of wine. Some read this scenario with a happy ending: "Then he led me to the couch. He held my hand and asked me to marry him." In hindsight, people find the ending unsurprising and admire the man's and woman's character traits. Others read the same scenario with a terrible ending: "But then he became very rough and pushed me onto the couch. He held me down on the couch and raped me." Given this ending, people see the rape as inevitable and blame the woman for provocative behavior that seems faultless in the first scenario.

This line of research suggests that people are indifferent to social injustice not because they have no concern for justice but because they see no injustice. Those who assume a just world believe that:

- rape victims must have behaved seductively (Borgida & Brekke, 1985),
- battered spouses must have provoked their beatings (Summers & Feldman, 1984),
- poor people don't deserve better (Furnham & Gunter, 1984),
- sick people are responsible for their illnesses (Gruman & Sloan, 1983).

When researchers activate the concept of *choice* by having people record others' choices, participants (in the United States) display less empathy for disadvantaged individuals, engage in more victim-blaming, and show reduced support for social policies such as affirmative action (Savani et al., 2011). These beliefs have, if anything, grown even stronger: College students in the 2000s were more likely to endorse just-world beliefs than those in the 1970s— an effect the study authors attribute to growing income inequality (Malahy et al., 2009).

Such beliefs enable successful people to reassure themselves that they, too, deserve what they have. The wealthy and healthy can see their own good fortune, and others' misfortune, as justly deserved. Linking good fortune with virtue and misfortune with moral failure enables the fortunate to feel pride and to avoid responsibility for the unfortunate.

"If you don't have a job and you're not rich, blame yourself!"
—U.S. Presidential Candidate Herman Cain, 2011

People loathe a loser even when the loser's misfortune quite obviously stems substantially from bad luck. Children, for example, tend to view lucky others—such as someone who has found money on a sidewalk—as more likely than unlucky children to do good things and be a nice person (Olson et al., 2008). Adults *know* that gambling outcomes are just good or bad luck and should not affect their evaluations of the gambler. Still, they can't resist playing Monday-morning quarterback—judging people by their results. Ignoring the fact that reasonable decisions can bring bad results, they judge losers as less competent (Baron & Hershey, 1988). Lawyers and stock market investors may similarly judge themselves by their outcomes, becoming smug after successes and self-reproachful after failures. Talent and initiative matter. But the just-world assumption discounts the uncontrollable factors that can derail good efforts even by talented people.

Just-world thinking also leads people to justify their culture's familiar social systems (Jost et al., 2009; Kay et al., 2009; Osborne & Sibley, 2013). The way things are, we're inclined to think, is the way things essentially are and ought to be (Brescoll et al., 2013). Such natural conservatism makes it difficult to pass new social policies, such as voting rights laws or tax or health care reform. But after a new policy is in place, our "system justification" works to sustain it. Thus, Canadians mostly approve of their government policies, such as national health care, strict gun control, and no capital punishment, whereas Americans likewise mostly support differing policies to which they are accustomed.

SUMMING UP: What Are the Cognitive Sources of Prejudice?

- Recent research shows how the stereotyping that underlies prejudice is a by-product of our thinking—our ways of simplifying the world. Clustering people into categories exaggerates the uniformity within a group and the differences between groups.

- A distinctive individual, such as a lone minority person, has a compelling quality that makes us aware of differences that would otherwise go unnoticed. The occurrence of two distinctive events (for example, a minority person committing an unusual crime) helps create an illusory correlation between people and behavior. Attributing others' behavior to their dispositions can lead to the *group-serving bias:* assigning outgroup members' negative behavior to their natural character while explaining away their positive behaviors.

- Blaming the victim results from the common presumption that because this is a *just world,* people get what they deserve.

WHAT ARE THE CONSEQUENCES OF PREJUDICE?

Identify and understand the consequences of prejudice.

How can stereotypes create their own reality? How can prejudice impede performance? Prejudice has consequences as well as causes.

Self-Perpetuating Prejudgments

Prejudice involves preconceived judgments. Prejudgments are inevitable: None of us is a dispassionate bookkeeper of social happenings, tallying evidence for and against our biases. And prejudgments matter.

Prejudgments guide our attention and our memories. People who accept gender stereotypes often misrecall their own school grades in stereotype-consistent ways. For example, women often recall receiving worse math grades and better arts grades than were actually the case (Chatard et al., 2007).

Moreover, after we judge an item as belonging to a category such as a particular race or sex, our memory for it later shifts toward the features we associate with that category. In one experiment, Belgian university students viewed a face that was a blend of 70 percent of the features of a typical male and 30 percent female (or vice versa). Later, those shown the 70 percent male face recalled seeing a male (as you might expect), but also misrecalled the face as being even more prototypically male (as, say, the 80 percent male face shown in Figure 7).

Prejudgments are self-perpetuating. Whenever a group member behaves as expected, we duly note the fact; our prior belief is confirmed. When a group member violates our expectation, we may interpret or explain away the behavior as due to special circumstances (Crocker et al., 1983).

Perhaps you can recall a time when, try as you might, you could not overcome someone's opinion of you, when no matter what you did you were misinterpreted. Misinterpretations are likely when someone *expects* an unpleasant encounter with you (Wilder & Shapiro, 1989). William Ickes and his colleagues (1982) demonstrated this in an experiment with pairs of college-age men. As the men arrived, the experimenters falsely forewarned one member of each pair that the other person was "one of the *unfriendliest* people I've talked to lately." The two were then introduced and left alone together for five minutes. Students in another experimental condition were led to think the other participant was exceptionally *friendly.*

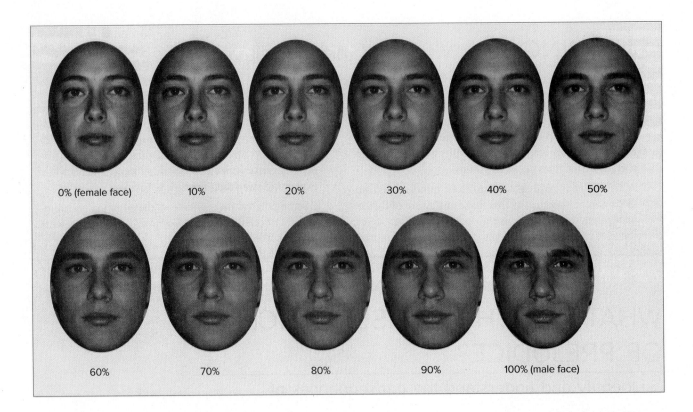

0% (female face)   10%   20%   30%   40%   50%

60%   70%   80%   90%   100% (male face)

FIGURE :: 7

Categorization Influences Memories

Shown a face that was 70 percent male, people usually classified the person as a male, and then recollected the face as more male-typical than it was (Huart et al., 2005).

Huart Johanne Corneille Olivier Becquart Emilie

Those who expected him to be *un*friendly went out of their way to be friendly, and their friendly behavior elicited a warm response. But unlike the positively biased students, their expecting an unfriendly person led them to attribute this reciprocal friendliness to their own "kid-gloves" treatment of him. They afterward expressed more mistrust and dislike for the person and rated his behavior as less friendly. Despite their partner's actual friendliness, the negative bias induced these students to "see" hostilities lurking beneath his "forced smiles." They would never have seen it if they hadn't believed it.

We do notice information that is strikingly inconsistent with a stereotype, but even that information has less impact than we might expect. When we focus on an atypical example, we can salvage the stereotype by splitting off a new category (Brewer & Gaertner, 2004; Hewstone, 1994; Kunda & Oleson, 1995, 1997). The positive image that British schoolchildren form of their friendly school police officers (whom they perceive as a special category) doesn't improve their image of police officers in general (Hewstone et al., 1992). This **subtyping**—seeing people who deviate as exceptions—helps maintain the stereotype that police officers are unfriendly and dangerous. High-prejudice people tend to subtype *positive* outgroup members (seeing them as atypical exceptions); low-prejudice people more often subtype *negative* outgroup members (Riek et al., 2013).

A different way to accommodate the inconsistent information is to form a new stereotype for those who don't fit. Recognizing that the stereotype does not apply for everyone in the category, homeowners who have "desirable" Black neighbors can form a new and different stereotype of "professional, middle-class Blacks." This **subgrouping**—forming a subgroup stereotype—tends to lead to modest change in the stereotype as the stereotype becomes more differentiated (Richards & Hewstone, 2001). Subtypes are *exceptions* to the group; subgroups are acknowledged as a *part* of the overall diverse group.

subtyping

Accommodating individuals who deviate from one's stereotype by thinking of them as "exceptions to the rule."

subgrouping

Accommodating individuals who deviate from one's stereotype by forming a new stereotype about this subset of the group.

Discrimination's Impact: The Self-Fulfilling Prophecy

Attitudes may coincide with the social hierarchy not only as a rationalization for it but also because discrimination affects its victims. "One's reputation," wrote Gordon Allport, "cannot be hammered, hammered, hammered into one's head without doing something to one's character" (1958, p. 139). If we could snap our fingers and end all discrimination, it would be naive for the White majority to say to Blacks, "The tough times are over, folks! You can now all be attaché-carrying executives and professionals." When the oppression ends, its effects linger, like a societal hangover.

In *The Nature of Prejudice,* Allport catalogued 15 possible effects of victimization. Allport believed these reactions were reducible to two basic types—those that involve *blaming oneself* (withdrawal, self-hate, aggression against one's own group) and those that involve *blaming external causes* (fighting back, suspiciousness, increased group pride). If victimization takes a toll—for instance, higher crime rates—people can use the result to justify the discrimination: "If we let those people in our nice neighborhood, property values will plummet."

Does discrimination indeed affect its victims? Social beliefs *can* be self-confirming, as demonstrated in a clever pair of experiments by Carl Word, Mark Zanna, and Joel Cooper (1974). In the first experiment, Princeton University White male volunteers interviewed White and Black research assistants posing as job applicants. When the applicant was Black, the interviewers sat farther away, ended the interview 25 percent sooner, and made 50 percent more speech errors than when the applicant was White. Imagine being interviewed by someone who sat at a distance, stammered, and ended the interview rather quickly. Would it affect your performance or your feelings about the interviewer?

To find out, the researchers conducted a second experiment in which trained interviewers treated people as the interviewers in the first experiment had treated either the White or the Black applicants. When videotapes of the interviews were later rated, those who were treated like the Blacks in the first experiment seemed more nervous and less effective. Moreover, the interviewees could themselves sense a difference; those treated the way the Blacks had been treated judged their interviewers to be less adequate and less friendly. The experimenters concluded that part of "the 'problem' of Black performance resides . . . within the interaction setting itself." As with other self-fulfilling prophecies, prejudice affects its targets.

Stereotype Threat

Just being sensitive to prejudice is enough to make us self-conscious when living as a numerical minority—perhaps as a Black person in a White community or as a White person in a Black community. As with other circumstances that siphon off our mental energy and attention, the result can be diminished mental and physical stamina (Inzlicht et al., 2006, 2012). Placed in a situation where others expect you to perform poorly, your anxiety may also cause you to confirm the belief. I [DM] am a short guy in my early 70s. When I join a pickup basketball game with bigger, younger players, I presume that they expect me to be a detriment to their team, and that tends to undermine my confidence and performance. Claude Steele and his colleagues call this phenomenon **stereotype threat**—a self-confirming apprehension

When people violate our stereotypes, we salvage the stereotype by splitting off a new subgroup stereotype, such as "senior Olympians."
Mike Brown/The Commercial Appeal/AP Images

"It is understandable that the suppressed people should develop an intense hostility towards a culture whose existence they make possible by their work, but in whose wealth they have too small a share."
—Sigmund Freud, *The Future of an Illusion,* 1927

"If we foresee evil in our fellow man, we tend to provoke it; if good, we elicit it."
—Gordon Allport, *The Nature of Prejudice,* 1958

stereotype threat
A disruptive concern, when facing a negative stereotype, that one will be evaluated based on a negative stereotype. Unlike self-fulfilling prophecies that hammer one's reputation into one's self-concept, stereotype threat situations have immediate effects.

that one will be evaluated based on a negative stereotype (Steele, 2010; Steele et al., 2002; see also reducingstereotypethreat.org).

In several experiments, Steven Spencer, Claude Steele, and Diane Quinn (1999) gave a very difficult math test to men and women students who had similar math backgrounds. When told that there were *no* gender differences on the test and no evaluation of any group stereotype, the women's performance consistently equaled the men's. Told that there *was* a gender difference, the women dramatically confirmed the stereotype (Figure 8). Frustrated by the extremely difficult test questions, they apparently felt added apprehension, which undermined their performances. For female engineering students, interacting with a sexist man likewise undermines test performance (Logel et al., 2009). Even before exams, stereotype threat can also hamper women's learning math rules and operations (Rydell et al., 2010).

Might racial stereotypes be similarly self-fulfilling? Steele and Joshua Aronson (1995) gave difficult verbal abilities tests to Whites and Blacks. Blacks underperformed Whites only when taking the tests under conditions high in stereotype threat. A similar stereotype threat effect has occurred with Hispanic Americans (Nadler & Clark, 2011).

Jeff Stone and his colleagues (1999) report that stereotype threat affects athletic performance, too. Blacks did worse than usual when a golf task was framed as a test of "sports intelligence," and Whites did worse when it was a test of "natural athletic ability." "When people are reminded of a negative stereotype about themselves—'White men can't jump' or 'Black men can't think'—it can adversely affect performance," Stone (2000) surmised. The same is true for people with disabilities, for whom concern about others' negative stereotypes can hinder achievement (Silverman & Cohen, 2014).

If you tell students they are at risk of failure (as is often suggested by minority support programs), the stereotype may erode their performance, says Steele (1997). It may cause them to "disidentify" with school and seek self-esteem elsewhere (Figure 9, and see "The Inside Story, Claude Steele on Stereotype Threat"). Indeed, as African American students move from eighth to tenth grade, there has been a weakening connection between their school performance and self-esteem (Osborne, 1995). Moreover, students who are led to think they have benefited from gender- or race-based preferences in gaining admission to a college or an academic group tend to underperform those who are led to feel competent (Brown et al., 2000).

Better, therefore, to challenge students to believe in their potential, observes Steele. In another of his research team's experiments, Black students responded well to criticism of their writing when also told, "I wouldn't go to the trouble of giving you this feedback if I didn't think, based on what I've read in your letter, that you are capable of meeting the higher standard that I mentioned" (Cohen et al., 1999).

"Math class is tough!"

—"Teen talk" Barbie Doll (Later Removed from the Market)

FIGURE :: 8

Stereotype Vulnerability and Women's Math Performance

Steven Spencer, Claude Steele, and Diane Quinn (1999) gave equally capable men and women a difficult math test. When participants were led to believe there were gender differences on the test, women scored lower than men. When the threat of confirming the stereotype was removed (when gender differences were not expected), women did just as well as men.

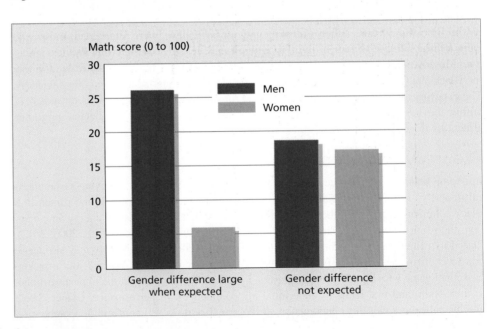

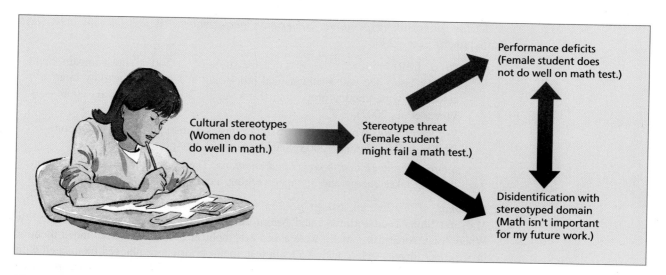

FIGURE :: 9

Stereotype Threat

Threat from facing a negative stereotype can produce performance deficits and disidentification.

"Values affirmation"—getting people to affirm who they are—also helps (Walton, 2014). A Stanford research team invited African American seventh graders to write about their most important values several times. Compared to their peers, they earned higher grades over the next 2 years (Cohen et al., 2006, 2009). Ensuing studies have extended the values affirmation effect (such as by getting people to recall times they felt successful or proud) to populations ranging from female college physics students to soup kitchen clients (Bowen et al., 2013; Hall, et al., 2014; Miyake et al., 2010; Sherman et al., 2013).

THE inside STORY

Claude Steele on Stereotype Threat

During a committee meeting on campus diversity at the University of Michigan in the late 1980s, I noticed an interesting fact: At every ability level (as assessed by SAT scores), minority students were getting lower college grades than their nonminority counterparts. Soon, Steven Spencer, Joshua Aronson, and I found that this was a national phenomenon; it happened at most colleges and it happened to other groups whose abilities were negatively stereotyped, such as women in advanced math classes. This underperformance wasn't caused by group differences in preparation. It happened at all levels of preparation (as measured by SATs).

Eventually, we produced this underperformance in the laboratory by simply having motivated people perform a difficult task in a domain where their group was negatively stereotyped. We also found that we could eliminate this underperformance by making the same task irrelevant to the stereotype, by removing the "stereotype threat," as we had come to call it. This latter finding spawned more research: figuring out how to reduce stereotype threat and its ill effects. Through this work, we have gained an appreciation for two big things: first, the importance of life context in shaping psychological functioning, and second, the importance of social identities such as age, race, and gender in shaping that context.

Claude Steele
Stanford University
Courtesy of Claude Steele

How does stereotype threat undermine performance? It does so in three ways (Schmader et al., 2008):

- *Stress.* fMRI brain scans suggest that the stress of stereotype threat impairs brain activity associated with mathematical processing and increases activity in areas associated with emotion processing (Derks et al., 2008; Krendl et al., 2008; Wraga et al., 2007).
- *Self-monitoring.* Worrying about making mistakes disrupts focused attention (Keller & Dauenheimer, 2003; Seibt & Forster, 2004).
- *Suppressing unwanted thoughts and emotions.* The effort required to regulate one's thinking takes energy and disrupts working memory (Bonnot & Croizet, 2007).

If stereotype threats can disrupt performance, could positive stereotypes enhance it? Margaret Shih, Todd Pittinsky, and Nalini Ambady (1999) confirmed that possibility. When Asian American females were asked biographical questions that reminded them of their gender identity before taking a math test, their performance plunged (compared with a control group). When similarly reminded of their Asian identity, their performance rose. Negative stereotypes disrupt performance, and positive stereotypes, it seems, facilitate performance (Rydell et al., 2009).

Do Stereotypes Bias Judgments of Individuals?

Yes, stereotypes bias judgments, but here is some good news: First, *our stereotypes mostly reflect* (though sometimes distort) *reality.* As multiculturalism recognizes, people differ— and can perceive and appreciate those differences. "Stereotype accuracy is one of the largest effects in all of social psychology," argues Lee Jussim (2012).

Second, *people often evaluate individuals more positively than the individuals' groups* (Miller & Felicio, 1990). Anne Locksley, Eugene Borgida, and Nancy Brekke found that after someone knows a person, "stereotypes may have minimal, if any, impact on judgments about that person" (Borgida et al., 1981; Locksley et al., 1980, 1982). They discovered this by giving University of Minnesota students anecdotal information about recent incidents in the life of "Nancy." In a supposed transcript of a telephone conversation, Nancy told a friend how she responded to three different situations (for example, being harassed by a seedy character while shopping). Some of the students read transcripts portraying Nancy responding assertively (telling the seedy character to

People sometimes maintain general prejudices (such as against gays and lesbians) without applying their prejudice to particular individuals whom they know and respect, such as Ellen DeGeneres.
Handout/Getty Images

leave); others read a report of passive responses (simply ignoring the character until he finally drifts away). Still other students received the same information, except that the person was named "Paul" instead of Nancy. A day later the students predicted how Nancy (or Paul) would respond to other situations.

Did knowing the person's gender have any effect on those predictions? None at all. Expectations of the person's assertiveness were influenced solely by what the students had learned about that individual the day before. Even their judgments of masculinity and femininity were unaffected by knowing the person's gender. Gender stereotypes had been left on the shelf; the students evaluated Nancy and Paul as individuals.

Given (1) general (base-rate) information about a group and (2) trivial but vivid information about a particular group member, the vivid information usually overwhelms the effect of the general information. This is especially so when the person doesn't fit our image of the typical group member (Fein & Hilton, 1992; Lord et al., 1991). For example, imagine yourself being told how most people in a conformity experiment actually behaved and then viewing a brief interview with one of the supposed participants. Would you, like the typical viewer, guess the person's behavior solely from the interview? Would you ignore the base-rate information on how most people actually behaved?

People often believe stereotypes, yet ignore them when given personalized, anecdotal information. Thus, many people believe "politicians are crooks" but "our Senator Jones has integrity." No wonder many people have a low opinion of politicians yet usually vote to reelect their own representatives. These findings resolve a puzzling set of findings considered early in this chapter. We know that gender stereotypes are strong, yet they have little effect on people's judgments of work attributed to a man or a woman. Now we see why. People may have strong gender stereotypes, but ignore them when judging a particular individual.

STRONG STEREOTYPES MATTER

However, stereotypes, when *strong,* do color our judgments of individuals (Krueger & Rothbart, 1988). When researchers had students estimate the heights of individually pictured men and women, they judged the individual men as taller than the women—even when their heights were equal, even when they were told that sex didn't predict height in this sample, and even when they were offered cash rewards for accuracy (Nelson et al., 1990).

In a follow-up study, University of Michigan students viewed photos of other students from the university's engineering and nursing schools, along with descriptions of each student's interests (Nelson et al., 1996). Even when informed that the sample contained an equal number of males and females from each school, a description attached to a female face was judged more likely to come from a nursing student. Thus, even when a strong gender stereotype is known to be irrelevant, it has an irresistible force.

Outside the laboratory, strong stereotypes affect everyday experience. For example, men who endorse "hostile sexism" behave more negatively toward their female partners and experience less relationship satisfaction (Hammond & Overall, 2013).

STEREOTYPES BIAS INTERPRETATION

Stereotypes also color how we interpret events, note David Dunning and David Sherman (1997). If people are told, "Some felt the politician's statements were untrue," they will infer that the politician was lying. If told, "Some felt the physicist's statements were untrue," they infer only that the physicist was mistaken. When told two people had an altercation, people perceive it as a fistfight if told it involved two lumberjacks, but as a verbal spat if told it involved two marriage counselors. A person concerned about her physical condition seems vain if she is a model but health conscious if she is a triathlete. Like a prison guiding and constraining its inmates, conclude Dunning and Sherman, the "cognitive prison" of our stereotypes guides and constrains our impressions.

Sometimes we make judgments or begin interacting with someone with little to go on but our stereotype. In such cases, stereotypes can strongly bias our interpretations and memories of people. For example, Charles Bond and his colleagues (1988) found that after getting to know their patients, White psychiatric nurses put Black and White patients in physical restraints equally often. But they restrained *incoming* Black patients more often than their White counterparts. With little else to go on, stereotypes mattered.

Stereotypes can also operate subtly. In an experiment by John Darley and Paget Gross (1983), Princeton University students viewed a videotape of a fourth-grade girl, Hannah. The tape depicted her either in a depressed urban neighborhood, supposedly the child of lower-class parents, or in an affluent suburban setting, the child of professional parents. Asked to guess Hannah's ability level in various subjects, both groups of viewers refused to use Hannah's class background to prejudge her ability level; each group rated her ability level at her grade level.

Other students also viewed a second videotape, showing Hannah taking an oral achievement test in which she got some questions right and some wrong. Those who had previously been introduced to professional-class Hannah judged her answers as showing high ability and later recalled her getting most questions right; those who had met lower-class Hannah judged her ability as below grade level and recalled her missing almost half the questions. But remember: The second videotape was *identical* for the two groups. So, when stereotypes are strong and the information about someone is ambiguous (unlike the cases of Nancy and Paul), stereotypes can *subtly* bias our judgments of individuals.

Finally, we evaluate people more extremely when their behavior violates our stereotypes (Bettencourt et al., 1997). A woman who rebukes someone cutting in front of her in a movie line ("Shouldn't you go to the end of the line?") may seem more assertive than a man who reacts similarly (Manis et al., 1988). Aided by the testimony of social psychologist Susan Fiske and her colleagues (1991), the U.S. Supreme Court saw such stereotyping at work when Price Waterhouse, one of the nation's top accounting firms, denied Ann Hopkins's promotion to partner. Among the 88 candidates for promotion, Hopkins, the only woman, was number one in the amount of business she brought in to the company and, according to testimony, was hardworking and exacting. But others testified that Hopkins needed a "course at charm school," where she could learn to "walk more femininely, talk more femininely, dress more femininely. . . ." After reflecting on the case and on stereotyping research, the Supreme Court in 1989 decided that encouraging men, but not women, to be aggressive, is to act "on the basis of gender":

> We sit not to determine whether Ms. Hopkins is nice, but to decide whether the partners reacted negatively to her personality because she is a woman. . . . An employer who objects to aggressiveness in women but whose positions require this trait places women in an intolerable Catch 22: out of a job if they behave aggressively and out of a job if they don't.

SUMMING UP: What Are the Consequences of Prejudice?

- Prejudice and stereotyping have important consequences, especially when strongly held, when judging unknown individuals, and when deciding policies regarding whole groups.

- Once formed, stereotypes tend to perpetuate themselves and resist change. They also create their own realities through self-fulfilling prophecies.

- Prejudice can also undermine people's performance through *stereotype threat*, by making people apprehensive that others will view them stereotypically.

- Stereotypes, especially when strong, can predispose how we perceive people and interpret events.

POSTSCRIPT:
Can We Reduce Prejudice?

Social psychologists have been more successful in explaining prejudice than in alleviating it. Because the waters of prejudice are fed by many streams, no simple remedy exists. Nevertheless, we can now anticipate techniques for reducing prejudice:

- If unequal status breeds prejudice, we can seek to create cooperative, equal-status relationships.
- If prejudice rationalizes discriminatory behavior, we can mandate nondiscrimination.
- If social institutions support prejudice, we can pull out those supports (for example, with media that model interracial harmony).

- If outgroups seem more homogeneous than they really are, we can make efforts to personalize their members.
- If our automatic prejudices lead us to feel guilt, we can use that guilt to motivate ourselves to break the prejudice habit.

Since the end of World War II in 1945, a number of those antidotes have been applied, and racial, gender, and sexual orientation prejudices have indeed diminished. Social-psychological research also has helped break down discriminatory barriers. The social psychologist Susan Fiske (1999), who testified on behalf of Ann Hopkins, the Price Waterhouse executive denied promotion to partner, later wrote:

> We risked a lot by testifying on Ann Hopkins's behalf, no doubt about it . . . As far as we knew, no one had ever introduced the social psychology of stereotyping in a gender case before. . . . If we succeeded, we would get the latest stereotyping research out of the dusty journals and into the muddy trenches of legal debate, where it might be useful. If we failed, we might hurt the client, slander social psychology, and damage my reputation as a scientist. At the time I had no idea that the testimony would eventually make it successfully through the Supreme Court.

It now remains to be seen whether, during this century, progress will continue, or whether, as could easily happen in a time of increasing population and competition for diminishing resources, antagonisms will increase.

Aggression

HURTING OTHERS

CHAPTER

10

AP Images/Pat Roque

"Our behavior toward each other is the strangest, most unpredictable, and most unaccountable of all the phenomena with which we are obliged to live. In all of nature, there is nothing so threatening to humanity as humanity itself."

—Lewis Thomas (1981)

During the past century, some 250 wars killed 110 million people, enough to populate a "nation of the dead" with more than the combined population of France, Belgium, the Netherlands, Denmark, Finland, Norway, and Sweden. The tolls came not only from the two world wars but also from genocides, including the 1915 to 1923 genocide of 1 million Armenians by the Ottoman Empire, the slaughter of some 250,000 Chinese in Nanking after it had surrendered to Japanese troops in 1937, the 1.5 million Cambodians murdered between 1975 and 1979, the murder of 1 million in Rwanda in 1994, and the approximately 300,000 killed in Darfur between 2003 and 2010 (Dutton et al., 2005; Sternberg, 2003). As Hitler's genocide of millions of Jews, Stalin's killing of millions of Russians, Mao's genocide of millions of Chinese, and the deaths of millions of Native Americans from the time of Columbus through the nineteenth century make plain, the human potential for extraordinary cruelty crosses cultures.

Even outside of war, human beings have an extraordinary capacity for harming one another. Mass shootings at schools, campuses, and movie theaters over the past few years have brought public attention to gun violence. Between 1981 and 2010, 112,375 infants, children, and teens were killed by guns in the United States, 25,000 more deaths than among soldiers in Korea, Vietnam, Iraq, and Afghanistan combined (Brock et al., 2013). 14,827 people were murdered in the United States in 2012; 84,376 were forcibly raped; and an incredible 760,739—three quarters of a million people—were shot, stabbed, or assaulted with another weapon (FBI, 2013). These numbers may be only the tip of the iceberg, because many rapes and assaults are not reported. An extensive, anonymous survey found that nearly 1 in 5 women in the United States say they have been sexually assaulted, and 1 out of 4 have been hit, beaten, or slammed against something by an intimate partner (Black et al., 2011). Worldwide, 30 percent of women have experienced violence at the hands of an intimate partner (WHO, 2014).

Less severe, but still harmful, aggression is even more common. One study found that 90 percent of young couples are verbally aggressive toward each other, including yelling, screaming, and insults (Munoz-Rivas et al., 2007). In a survey of children across 35 countries, more than 1 out of 10 reported being bullied at school (Craig & Harel, 2004). Half of Canadian middle- and high-school students said they had been bullied online in the previous three months. Their experiences included being called names, having rumors spread about them, or having their private pictures distributed without their consent (Mishna et al., 2010) Seventy-five percent of children and adolescents have experienced **cyberbullying,** defined as intentional and repeated aggression via email, texts, social networking sites, and other electronic media (Katzer et al., 2009). Cyberbullying often results in negative outcomes such as depression, fear, drug abuse, dropping out of school, poor physical health, and suicide—even years after the bullying occurred (Kowalski et al., 2014; Ortega et al., 2012; Sigurdson et al., 2014).

Are we like the mythical Minotaur—half human, half beast? What explains that midsummer day in 1941 when the non-Jewish half of the Polish town of Jebwabne murdered the other half in a macabre frenzy of violence, leaving only a dozen or so survivors among the 1,600 Jews (Gross, 2001)? Why would a college student broadcast his gay roommate's sexual encounter, driving him to suicide, as happened at Rutgers University in 2010? Why would middle school students bully 13-year-old Hailee Lamberth so cruelly and relentlessly ("Why don't you die?") that she committed suicide in December 2013 (Wagner, 2014)? Why, in 2011, would a gunman in peaceful Norway bomb government buildings and then shoot and kill 69 people, mostly teenagers? Why would a gunman kill 20 first graders and 6 teachers at Connecticut's Sandy Hook Elementary in 2012? What explains such monstrous behavior? In this chapter we ask these questions:

- Is aggression biologically predisposed, or do we learn it?
- What circumstances prompt hostile outbursts?
- Do the media influence aggression?
- How might we reduce aggression?

First, however, we need to clarify the term "aggression."

"Every gun that is made, every warship launched, every rocket fired signifies, in the final sense, a theft from those who hunger and are not fed, those who are cold and are not clothed."

—President Dwight Eisenhower, Speech to the American Society of Newspaper Editors, 1953

cyberbullying
Bullying, harassing, or threatening someone using electronic communication such as texting, online social networks, or email.

"Is there any way of delivering mankind from the menace of war?"

—Albert Einstein, Letter to Sigmund Freud, 1932

WHAT IS AGGRESSION?

Define aggression and describe its different forms.

The original Thugs, members of a sect in northern India, were aggressing when between 1550 and 1850 they strangled more than 2 million people, they claimed in the service of the goddess Kali. But people also use "aggressive" to describe a dynamic salesperson. Social psychologists distinguish such self-assured, energetic, go-getting behavior from behavior that hurts, harms, or destroys. The former is assertiveness, the latter aggression.

To a social psychologist, **aggression** is physical or verbal behavior intended to cause harm. This definition excludes unintentional harm, such as auto accidents or sidewalk collisions; it also excludes actions that may involve pain as an unavoidable side effect of helping someone, such as dental treatments or—in the extreme—assisted suicide. It includes kicks and slaps, threats and insults, even gossip or snide "digs." It includes ugly confrontational rudeness, such as giving the finger to another driver or yelling at someone who is walking too slow (Park et al., 2014). It includes decisions during experiments about how much to hurt someone, such as how much electric shock to impose. It also includes destroying property, lying, and other behavior that aims to hurt. As these examples illustrate, aggression includes both **physical aggression** (hurting someone's body) and **social aggression** (such as bullying and cyberbullying, insults, harmful gossip, or social exclusion that hurts feelings; Dehue et al., 2008). Social aggression can have serious consequences, with victims suffering from depression and sometimes—as happened in several well-publicized cases—committing suicide. Bullying researchers Dan Olweus and Kyrre Breivik (2013) describe the consequences of bullying as "the opposite of well-being."

Psychologists also make a distinction between **hostile aggression** (which springs from anger and aims to injure) and **instrumental aggression** (which aims to injure, too—but is committed in the pursuit of another goal). Both physical and social aggression can be either hostile or instrumental. For example, bullying can be hostile (one teen is angry at another for stealing her boyfriend) or instrumental (a high school student believes she can become popular by rejecting an unpopular girl [Juvonen & Graham, 2014; Prinstein & Cillessen, 2003]).

Most terrorism is instrumental aggression. "What nearly all suicide terrorist campaigns have in common is a specific secular and strategic goal," concludes Robert Pape (2003) after studying all suicide bombings from 1980 to 2001. That goal is "to compel liberal democracies to withdraw military forces from territory that the terrorists consider to be their homeland." Terrorism is rarely committed by someone with a psychological pathology, note Arie Kruglanski and his colleagues (2009); instead, terrorists seek personal significance through, for example, attaining hero or martyr status. Terrorism is also a strategic tool used during conflict. In explaining the aim of the 9/11 attacks, Osama bin Laden noted that for a cost of only $500,000 they inflicted $500 billion worth of damage to the American economy (Zakaria, 2008).

Most wars are instrumental aggression. In 2003, American and British leaders justified attacking Iraq not as a hostile effort to kill Iraqis but as an instrumental act of liberation and of self-defense against presumed weapons of mass destruction. Adolescents who bully others—either verbally or physically—are also engaged in instrumental aggression, because they often seek to demonstrate their dominance and high status. In the strange hierarchy of adolescence, being mean and disliked can sometimes make you popular and revered (Salmivalli, 2009).

Most murders are hostile aggression. Approximately half erupt from arguments, and others result from romantic triangles or from brawls that involve the influence of alcohol or drugs (Ash, 1999). Such murders are impulsive, emotional outbursts, which helps explain why data from 110 nations show that a death penalty has not resulted in fewer homicides (Costanzo,

aggression
Physical or verbal behavior intended to hurt someone.

physical aggression
Hurting someone else's body.

social aggression
Hurting someone else's feelings or threatening their relationships. Sometimes called relational aggression, it includes cyberbullying and some forms of in-person bullying.

hostile aggression
Aggression that springs from anger; its goal is to injure.

instrumental aggression
Aggression that aims to injure, but only as a means to some other end.

"Of course, we'll never actually use it against a potential enemy, but it will allow us to negotiate from a position of strength."

Source: John Ruge

1998; Wilkes, 1987). Some murders and many other violent acts of retribution and sexual coercion, however, are instrumental (Felson, 2000). Most of Chicago's more than 1,000 murders carried out by organized crime during the prohibition era and the years following were cool and calculated.

Humanity has armed its capacity for destruction without comparably arming its capacity for the inhibition of aggression.

WHAT ARE SOME THEORIES OF AGGRESSION?

Understand and evaluate the important theories of aggression.

In analyzing the causes of aggression, social psychologists have focused on three big ideas: biological influences, frustration, and learned behavior.

Aggression as a Biological Phenomenon

Philosophers have debated whether our human nature is fundamentally that of a benign, contented, "noble savage" or that of a brute. The first view, argued by the eighteenth-century French philosopher Jean-Jacques Rousseau (1712–1778), blames society, not human nature, for social evils. The second idea, associated with the English philosopher Thomas Hobbes (1588–1679), credits society for restraining the human brute. In the twentieth century, the "brutish" view—that aggressive drive is inborn and thus inevitable—was argued by Sigmund Freud, the founder of psychoanalysis, in Vienna, and Konrad Lorenz, an animal behavior expert, in Germany.

INSTINCTIVE BEHAVIOR AND EVOLUTIONARY PSYCHOLOGY

Freud speculated that human aggression springs from a self-destructive impulse. It redirects toward others the energy of a primitive death urge (the "death instinct"). Lorenz, an animal behavior expert, saw aggression as adaptive rather than self-destructive. The two agreed that aggressive energy is **instinctive** (innate, unlearned, and universal). If not discharged, it supposedly builds up until it explodes or until an appropriate stimulus "releases" it, like a mouse releasing a mousetrap.

instinctive behavior
An innate, unlearned behavior pattern exhibited by all members of a species.

The idea that aggression is an instinct collapsed as the list of supposed human instincts grew to include nearly every conceivable human behavior. Nearly 6,000 supposed instincts were enumerated in one 1924 survey of social science books (Barash, 1979). The social scientists had tried to *explain* social behavior by *naming* it. It's tempting to play this explaining-by-naming game: "Why do sheep stay together?" "Because of their herd instinct." "How do you know they have a herd instinct?" "Just look at them: They're always together!"

The idea that aggression is instinctive also fails to account for the variations in aggressiveness from person to person and culture to culture. How would a shared human instinct for aggression explain the difference between the peaceful Iroquois before White invaders came and the hostile Iroquois after the invasion (Hornstein, 1976)? Although aggression is biologically influenced, the human propensity to aggress does not qualify as instinctive behavior.

Male aggression can be heightened in the context of dating and mating.
© Valua Vitaly/Shutterstock.com

Throughout much of human history, men especially have found aggression adaptive, note evolutionary psychologists such as John Archer (2006) and Francis McAndrew (2009). Purposeful aggression improved the odds of survival and reproduction. The losers, notes McAndrew, "ran the risk of genetic annihilation." Aggression often occurs when males are competing with other males. In one study, men primed to think about mating delivered louder and longer bursts of painful noise against another man who provoked them. But mating-primed men were

not more aggressive toward women, and mating-primed women were not more aggressive at all (Ainsworth & Maner, 2012).

Men may also become aggressive when their social status is challenged. "Violence committed against the right people at the right time was a ticket to social success," McAndrew observes. Consider professional basketball player Charles Barkley, who was drinking in a bar in 1997 when a man threw a glass of water at him. Barkley promptly hurled the man through a plate-glass window—even though Barkley was not hurt by the water, even though the man might have retaliated, and even though Barkley was arrested within minutes of the assault. Nevertheless, witnesses praised Barkley in news reports, seemingly impressed by his aggression. When Barkley was asked if he regretted throwing the man through the window, he replied, "I regret we weren't on a higher floor" (Griskevicius et al., 2009).

Apparently, Barkley was not an isolated example. Across three experiments, college men motivated to increase their status were more aggressive toward others in face-to-face confrontations (Griskevicius et al., 2009). Status-based aggression also helps explain why aggression is highest during adolescence and early adulthood, when the competition for status and mates is the most intense. Although violence is less rewarded than it once was, young men scuffling for status and mates are still very much in evidence at many bars and campuses around the world.

NEURAL INFLUENCES

Because aggression is a complex behavior, no one spot in the brain controls it. But researchers have found brain neural systems in both animals and humans that facilitate aggression. When the scientists activate these brain areas, hostility increases; when they deactivate them, hostility decreases. Docile animals can thus be provoked into rage, and raging animals into submission.

In one experiment, researchers placed an electrode in an aggression-inhibiting area of a domineering monkey's brain. A smaller monkey, given a button that activated the electrode, learned to push it every time the tyrant monkey became intimidating. Brain activation works with humans, too. After receiving painless electrical stimulation in her amygdala (a brain core area involved with emotion), one woman became enraged and smashed her guitar against the wall, barely missing her psychiatrist's head (Moyer, 1976, 1983).

Does this mean that violent people's brains are in some way abnormal? To find out, Adrian Raine and his colleagues (1998, 2000, 2005, 2008) used brain scans to measure brain activity in murderers and to measure the amount of gray matter in men with antisocial conduct disorder. They found that the prefrontal cortex, which acts like an emergency brake on deeper brain areas involved in aggressive behavior, was 14 percent less active than normal in murderers (excluding those who had been abused by their parents) and 15 percent smaller in the antisocial men. Another study found that more aggressive and violent men had smaller amygdalas (Pardini et al., 2014). As other studies of murderers and death-row inmates confirm, abnormal brains can contribute to abnormally aggressive behavior (Davidson et al., 2000; Lewis, 1998; Pincus, 2001). Situational factors can also play a role: Sleep deprivation reduces activity in the prefrontal cortex, an area of the brain responsible for self-control. In individuals prone to violence and aggression, poor sleep can lead to violence and aggression (Kamphuis et al., 2012). Even in a sample of 425 normal German college students, those who slept for fewer hours were more physically and verbally aggressive (Randler & Vollmer, 2013).

GENETIC INFLUENCES

Heredity influences the neural system's sensitivity to aggressive cues. It has long been known that animals can be bred for aggressiveness. Sometimes this is done for practical purposes (the breeding of fighting cocks). Sometimes breeding is done for research. Finnish psychologist Kirsti Lagerspetz (1979) took normal albino mice and bred the most aggressive ones together; she did the same with the least aggressive ones. After repeating the procedure for 26 generations, she had one set of fierce mice and one set of placid mice.

Aggressiveness also varies among individuals (Asher, 1987; Bettencourt et al., 2006; Denson et al., 2006; Olweus, 1979). Our temperaments—how intense and reactive we are—are partly brought with us into the world, influenced by our sympathetic nervous system's reactivity (Kagan, 1989; Wilkowski & Robinson, 2008). A person's temperament, observed in infancy, usually endures (Larsen & Diener, 1987; Wilson & Matheny, 1986).

A 3-year-old who exhibits little conscientiousness and self-control is more vulnerable to substance abuse and arrest by age 32 (Moffitt et al., 2011). A child who is nonaggressive at age 8 will very likely still be a nonaggressive person at age 48 (Huesmann et al., 2003). Thus, identical twins, when asked separately, are more likely than fraternal twins to agree on whether they have "a violent temper" or have gotten into fights (Rowe et al., 1999; Rushton et al., 1986). Of convicted criminals who are twins, fully half of their identical twins (but only one in five fraternal twins) also have criminal records (Raine, 1993, 2008).

In a study examining 12.5 million residents of Sweden, those with a genetic sibling convicted of a violent crime were 4 times as likely to be convicted themselves. Rates were much lower for adopted siblings, suggesting a strong genetic component and a more modest environmental influence (Frisell et al., 2011). Recent research has identified a specific gene (MAOA-L) linked to aggression; some even call it the "warrior gene" or the "violence gene." In several studies, people with the gene showed more activation in the self-control center of their brains after being rejected or insulted, suggesting they were struggling to control their anger (Denson et al., 2009; Eisenberger et al., 2007). They were also more likely to act aggressively when provoked (McDermott et al., 2009). Long-term studies following several hundred New Zealand children reveal that a recipe for aggressive behavior combines the MAOA-L gene with childhood maltreatment (Caspi et al., 2002; Moffitt et al., 2003). Neither "bad" genes nor a "bad" environment alone predispose later aggressiveness and antisocial behavior; rather, genes predispose some children to be more sensitive and responsive to maltreatment. Nature and nurture interact.

BIOCHEMICAL INFLUENCES

Blood chemistry also influences neural sensitivity to aggressive stimulation.

ALCOHOL.   Both laboratory experiments and police data indicate that alcohol unleashes aggression when people are provoked (Bushman, 1993; Taylor & Chermack, 1993; Testa, 2002). Consider the following:

- When asked to think back on relationship conflicts, intoxicated people administer stronger shocks and feel angrier than do sober people during lab experiments (MacDonald et al., 2000).

- In nearly half of homicides in Australia between 2000 and 2006, the perpetrator had been drinking (Dearden & Payne, 2009). In crime data from the 1950s to the 2000s, 57 percent of homicides in the United States and 73 percent of homicides in Russia involved alcohol (Landberg & Norstrom, 2011). Thirty-seven percent of U.S. rapes and sexual assaults involved alcohol (NCADD, 2014). Four in 10 prisoners convicted of a violent crime were drinking when they committed murder, assault, robbery, or sexual assault (Karberg & James, 2005).

- College students followed for 2 months using electronic diaries showed a clear pattern: Those who drank alcohol were more likely to act aggressively toward their dating partners. With each drink, rates of abuse went up (Moore et al., 2011).

- Heavy men who drank alcohol were significantly more aggressive after drinking alcohol, but alcohol had little effect on women's or smaller men's aggression. Alcohol, note the researchers, seemed to encourage "heavy men to 'throw their weight around' and intimidate others by behaving aggressively" (DeWall et al., 2010). Apparently, people really are wise to avoid the "big, drunk guy" in the bar.

Alcohol enhances aggressiveness by reducing people's self-awareness, by focusing their attention on a provocation, and by people's mentally associating alcohol with aggression

Alcohol and sexual assault. One in five college-age women experiences a sexual assault, and many of these crimes involve alcohol.
Zuma/Zuma Wire Service/Alamy

(Bartholow & Heinz, 2006; Giancola & Corman, 2007; Ito et al., 1996). Alcohol also predisposes people to interpret ambiguous acts (such as a bump in a crowd) as provocations (Begue et al., 2010). Alcohol deindividuates, and it disinhibits.

Some violent sex offenders, wishing to free themselves of persistent, damaging impulses and to reduce their prison terms, have requested castration. Should their requests be granted? If so, and if they are deemed no longer at risk to commit sexual violence, should their prison terms be reduced or eliminated?

TESTOSTERONE. Hormonal influences appear to be much stronger in other animals than in humans. But human aggressiveness does correlate with the male sex hormone testosterone. Consider the following:

- Drugs that diminish testosterone levels in violent human males will subdue their aggressive tendencies.
- After men reach age 25, their testosterone levels and rates of violent crime decrease together.
- Testosterone levels are higher among prisoners convicted of planned and unprovoked violent crimes compared with those convicted of nonviolent crimes (Dabbs, 1992; Dabbs et al., 1995, 1997, 2001).
- Among the normal range of boys and men, those with high testosterone levels are more prone to delinquency, hard drug use, and aggressive responses to provocation (Archer, 1991; Barzman et al., 2013).
- One study reduced young men's testosterone to a common baseline by administering a hormone suppressor. When the suppressor was discontinued and testosterone gradually increased, the men's brains reacted increasingly strongly toward pictures of angry faces (Goetz et al., 2014).
- College students reporting higher levels of anger after being ostracized had higher levels of testosterone in their saliva (Peterson & Harmon-Jones, 2012).
- After handling a gun, men's testosterone levels rise; and the more their testosterone rises, the more aggressive they are toward others (Klinesmith et al., 2006).
- In men, testosterone during development increases the facial width-to-height ratio. Sure enough, men with relatively wider faces display more aggression in the laboratory. The same is true in the hockey rink, where collegiate and professional hockey players with relatively wide faces spend more time in the penalty box (Carré & McCormick, 2008). Other people also correctly guessed that wide-faced men would be more aggressive, and they were less likely to trust them (Carré et al., 2009; Stirrat & Perrett, 2010).

"We could avoid two-thirds of all crime simply by putting all able-bodied young men in cryogenic sleep from the age of 12 through 28."

—David Lykken,
The Antisocial Personalities, 1995

Young, male, and restless. In the 2011 riots that swept English cities, those arrested overwhelmingly shared one genetic characteristic—a Y chromosome—and were testosterone-fueled teens or people in their early 20s (*The Guardian,* 2011).
AP Images/Matt Dunham

Testosterone, said James Dabbs (2000), "is a small molecule with large effects." Injecting a man with testosterone won't automatically make him aggressive, yet men with low testosterone are somewhat less likely to react aggressively when provoked (Geen, 1998). Testosterone is roughly like battery power. Only if the battery levels are very low will things noticeably slow down.

POOR DIET. When British researcher Bernard Gesch first tried to study the effect of diet on aggression, he stood in front of hundreds of inmates at an English prison—but no matter how loudly he talked, none of them would listen. Finally, he talked privately to the "daddy"—the inmates' "tough guy" leader—and 231 inmates signed on to receive nutritional supplements or a placebo. Prisoners who got the extra nutrition were involved in 35 percent fewer violent incidents (Gesch et al., 2002). Such programs may eventually help people outside of prison as well, because many people have diets deficient in important nutrients, such as omega-3 fatty acids (found in fish and important for brain function) and calcium (which guards against impulsivity).

British actor Jamie Waylett, best known for playing Draco Malfoy's aggressive sidekick Vincent Crabbe in the Harry Potter movies, exemplifies the association between wide faces and aggressive behavior. The association held true in real life: In 2012, Waylett was sentenced to two years in jail for participating in the 2011 London riots.
AP Images/Press Association/Dominic Lipinski

In another study, researchers surveyed Boston public high school students about their diets and their aggressive or violent actions. Those who drank more than five cans of nondiet soda a week were more likely to have been violent toward peers, siblings, or dating partners and more likely to have carried a weapon, such as a gun or knife. This was true even after the researchers accounted for eight other possible factors (Solnick & Hemenway, 2012). Another correlational study found that men and women who consumed more trans fat—also known as hydrogenated oils—were more aggressive, even after adjusting for third factors (Golomb et al., 2012). Thus, perhaps surprisingly, there may have been at least some truth to the classic "Twinkie Defense," in which an accused murderer's attorneys argued he had been eating a junk food diet of Twinkies and Coca-Cola. The upshot: To lower aggression, eat a diet high in omega-3 fatty acids, low in trans fat, and without sweetened drinks.

BIOLOGY AND BEHAVIOR INTERACT.   The traffic between biology and behavior flows both ways. For example, higher levels of testosterone may cause dominant and aggressive behavior, but dominant and aggressive behavior can also lead to higher testosterone levels (Mazur & Booth, 1998). After a World Cup soccer match or a big basketball game between archrivals, testosterone levels rise in the winning fans and fall in the losing fans (Bernhardt et al., 1998). Similar results occurred among men who voted for the winning U.S. presidential candidate in 2008 (Barack Obama) versus the losing candidate (John McCain) (Stanton et al., 2009). The phenomenon also occurs in the laboratory, where socially anxious men exhibit a pronounced drop in their testosterone level after losing a rigged face-to-face competition (Maner et al., 2008). Testosterone surges, plus celebration-related drinking, probably explain the finding of Cardiff University researchers that fans of *winning* rather than losing soccer and rugby teams commit more postgame assaults (Sivarajasingam et al., 2005).

So, neural, genetic, and biochemical influences predispose some people to react aggressively to conflict and provocation. But is aggression so much a part of human nature that it makes peace unattainable? The American Psychological Association and the International Council of Psychologists endorse a statement on violence developed by scientists from a dozen nations (Adams, 1991): "It is scientifically incorrect [to say that] war or any other violent behavior is genetically programmed into our human nature [or that] war is caused by 'instinct' or any single motivation." Thus, there are, as we will see, ways to reduce human aggression.

Aggression as a Response to Frustration

Frustration-triggered aggression sometimes appears as road rage. Road rage is fed by perceptions of hostile intentions from other drivers, as when one is cut off in traffic (Britt & Garrity, 2006).
O. Burriel/Science Source

frustration-aggression theory
The theory that frustration triggers a readiness to aggress.

frustration
The blocking of goal-directed behavior.

displacement
The redirection of aggression to a target other than the source of the frustration. Generally, the new target is a safer or more socially acceptable target.

It is a warm evening. Tired and thirsty after two hours of studying, you borrow some change from a friend and head for the nearest soft-drink machine. As the machine devours the change, you can almost taste the cold, refreshing cola. But when you push the button, nothing happens. You push it again. Then you flip the coin return button. Still nothing. Again, you hit the buttons. You slam the machine. Alas, no money and no drink. You stomp back to your studies, empty-handed and shortchanged. Should your roommate beware? Are you now more likely to say or do something hurtful?

One of the first psychological theories of aggression, the popular **frustration-aggression theory,** answered yes (Dollard, 1939). **Frustration** is anything (such as the malfunctioning vending machine) that blocks us from attaining a goal. Frustration grows when our motivation to achieve a goal is very strong, when we expected gratification, and when the blocking is complete. When Rupert Brown and his colleagues (2001) surveyed British ferry passengers heading to France, they found more aggressive attitudes on a day when French fishing boats blockaded the port, preventing their travel. Blocked from obtaining their goal, the passengers became more likely (in responding to various vignettes) to agree with an insult toward a French person who had spilled coffee. College students who were frustrated by losing a multiplayer video soccer game blasted their opponents with longer and louder bursts of painful noise (Breuer et al., 2014). Cyberbullying is often rooted in frustration, such as after a breakup. Some cyberbulliers direct their aggression against the person now dating their ex-partner. One woman described her experience this way: "A girl was upset that I was dating her ex-boyfriend. She would harass me with text messages telling me I was a bad friend and a slut. Then, she turned to Facebook and started posting between her and her friend bad things about me and said my boyfriend was cheating. This went on for a good six months" (Rafferty & Vander Ven, 2014).

The aggressive energy need not explode directly against its source. Most people learn to inhibit direct retaliation, especially when others might disapprove or punish; instead, we *displace,* or redirect, our hostilities to safer targets. **Displacement** occurs in an old anecdote about a man who, humiliated by his boss, berates his wife, who yells at their son, who kicks the dog, which bites the mail carrier (who goes home and berates his wife . . .). In experiments and in real life, displaced aggression is most likely when the target shares some similarity to the instigator and does some minor irritating act that unleashes the displaced aggression (Marcus-Newhall et al., 2000; Miller et al., 2003; Pedersen et al., 2000, 2008). When someone is harboring anger from a prior provocation, even a trivial offense may elicit an explosive overreaction (as you may realize if you have ever yelled at your roommate after losing money in a malfunctioning vending machine).

In one experiment, Eduardo Vasquez and his co-researchers (2005) provoked some University of Southern California students (but not others) by having an experimenter insult their performance on an anagram-solving test. Shortly afterward, the students had to decide how long another supposed student should be required to immerse his or her hand in painful cold water while completing a task. When the supposed student committed a trivial offense—by giving a mild insult—the previously provoked participants responded punitively, by recommending a longer cold-water treatment than did the unprovoked participants. This phenomenon of displaced aggression helps us understand, notes Vasquez, why a previously provoked and still-angry person might respond to mild highway offenses with road rage, or react to spousal criticism with spouse abuse. It also helps explain why frustrated Major League Baseball pitchers, in one analysis of nearly 5 million at-bats from 74,197 games since 1960, were most likely to hit batters after the batter hit a home run the last time at bat, or after the previous batter did so (Timmerman, 2007).

Outgroup targets are especially vulnerable to displaced aggression (Pedersen et al., 2008). Opposites attack. Various commentators have observed that the understandably intense American anger over 9/11 contributed to the eagerness to attack Iraq. Americans were looking for an outlet for their rage and found one in an evil tyrant, Saddam Hussein, who was once their ally. The actual reason for the Iraq war, noted Thomas Friedman (2003), "was that after 9/11 America needed to hit someone in the Arab-Muslim world. . . . We hit Saddam for one simple reason: because we could, and because he deserved it, and because he was right in the heart of that world." One of the war's advocates, Vice President Richard Cheney (2003), seemed to concur. When asked why most others in the world disagreed with America's war, he replied, "They didn't experience 9/11."

Note that frustration-aggression theory is designed to explain hostile aggression, not instrumental aggression.

FRUSTRATION-AGGRESSION THEORY REVISED

Laboratory tests of the frustration-aggression theory have produced mixed results: Sometimes frustration increased aggressiveness, sometimes not. For example, if the frustration was understandable—if, as in one experiment, a confederate disrupted a group's problem solving because his hearing aid malfunctioned (rather than just because he wasn't paying attention)—frustration led to irritation, not aggression (Burnstein & Worchel, 1962).

Leonard Berkowitz (1978, 1989) realized that the original theory overstated the frustration-aggression connection, so he revised it. Berkowitz theorized that frustration produces aggression only when people become upset—for instance, when someone who frustrated them could have chosen to act otherwise, leading to feelings of anger (Averill, 1983; Weiner, 1981). For example, many people are frustrated in their goals while playing sports, but they usually aren't aggressive unless they are angered by a deliberate, unfair act by an opposing player.

A frustrated person is especially likely to lash out when aggressive cues pull the cork, releasing bottled-up anger (Figure 1). Sometimes the cork will blow without such cues. But, as we will see, cues associated with aggression amplify aggression (Carlson et al., 1990).

RELATIVE DEPRIVATION

Frustration is not only caused by complete deprivation; more often, *frustration arises from the gap between expectations and attainments.* The most economically frustrated people may not be the impoverished residents of African shantytowns, who might know no other way of life, but middle-class Americans who aspire to be rich—or at least upper-middle class. When your expectations are fulfilled by your attainments, and when your desires are reachable at your income, you feel satisfied rather than frustrated (Solberg et al., 2002). A study across 31 countries found that both individual economic deprivation and lower gross national income predicted higher levels of violence against intimate partners (Sabina, 2013). Among college students, those who reported experiencing stress during an economic recession were more aggressive, and those randomly assigned to watch a news story about the poor economy reported feeling more hostile (Barlett & Anderson, 2014).

Frustration is often compounded when we compare ourselves with others. Workers' feelings of well-being depend on whether their compensation compares favorably with that of others in their line of work (Yuchtman, 1976). A raise in salary for a city's police officers, while temporarily lifting their morale, may deflate that of the firefighters.

Such feelings, called **relative deprivation,** explain why happiness tends to be lower and crime rates higher in communities and nations with large income inequality (Hagerty, 2000;

relative deprivation
The perception that one is less well off than others with whom one compares oneself.

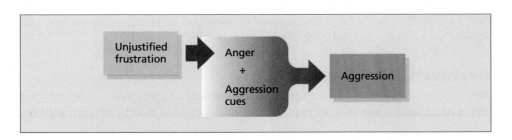

FIGURE :: 1

A Simplified Synopsis of Leonard Berkowitz's Revised Frustration-Aggression Theory

Kawachi et al., 1999). And it explains why the former East Germans revolted against their communist regime: They had a higher standard of living than some Western European countries, but a frustratingly lower one than their West German neighbors (Baron et al., 1992).

The term *relative deprivation* was coined by researchers studying the satisfaction felt by American soldiers in World War II (Merton & Kitt, 1950; Stouffer et al., 1949). Ironically, those in the Air Corps felt *more* frustrated about their own rate of promotion than those in the military police, for whom promotions were actually slower. The Air Corps' promotion rate was rapid, and most Air Corps personnel probably perceived themselves as better than the average Air Corps member (the self-serving bias). Thus, their aspirations soared higher than their achievements. The result? Frustration.

One possible source of such frustration today is the affluence depicted in television programs and commercials. In cultures where television is a universal appliance, it helps turn absolute deprivation (lacking what others have) into relative deprivation (feeling deprived). Karen Hennigan and her co-workers (1982) analyzed crime rates in American cities around the time television was introduced. In 34 cities where television ownership became widespread in 1951, the 1951 larceny theft rate (for crimes such as shoplifting and bicycle stealing) took an observable jump. In 34 other cities, where a government freeze had delayed the introduction of television until 1955, a similar jump in the theft rate occurred—in 1955.

Aggression as Learned Social Behavior

Theories of aggression based on instinct and frustration assume that hostile urges erupt from inner emotions, which naturally "push" aggression from within. Social psychologists also contend that learning "pulls" aggression out of us.

THE REWARDS OF AGGRESSION

By experience and by observing others, we learn that aggression often pays. Experiments have transformed animals from docile creatures into ferocious fighters. Severe defeats, on the other hand, create submissiveness (Ginsburg & Allee, 1942; Kahn, 1951; Scott & Marston, 1953).

People can also learn the rewards of aggression. A child who successfully intimidates other children by being aggressive will likely become increasingly aggressive (Patterson et al., 1967). Aggressive hockey players—the ones sent most often to the penalty box for rough play—score more goals than nonaggressive players (McCarthy & Kelly, 1978a,b). Canadian teenage hockey players whose fathers applaud physically aggressive play show the most aggressive attitudes and style of play (Ennis & Zanna, 1991). In the waters off Somalia, paying ransom to hijackers of ships—a reported $150 million in 2008 (BBC, 2008)—rewarded the pirates, thus fueling further hijackings. In such cases, aggression is instrumental in achieving certain rewards.

The same is true of terrorist acts, which enable powerless people to garner widespread attention. "The primary targets of suicide-bombing attacks are not those who are injured but those who are made to witness it through media coverage," note Paul Marsden and Sharon Attia (2005). Terrorism's purpose is, with the help of media amplification, to terrorize. "Kill one, frighten ten thousand," asserts an ancient Chinese proverb. Deprived of what Margaret Thatcher called "the oxygen of publicity," terrorism would surely diminish, concluded Jeffrey Rubin (1986). It's like the 1970s incidents of naked spectators "streaking" onto football fields for a few seconds of television exposure. After the networks decided not to air the incidents, the phenomenon ended.

social learning theory
The theory that we learn social behavior by observing and imitating and by being rewarded and punished.

OBSERVATIONAL LEARNING

Albert Bandura (1997) proposed a **social learning theory** of aggression. He believes that we learn aggression not only by experiencing its payoffs but also by observing others.

In Bandura's famous experiment, children exposed to an adult's aggression against a Bobo doll became likely to reproduce the observed aggression.
Courtesy of Albert Bandura

As with most social behaviors, we acquire aggression by watching others act and noting the consequences.

Picture this scene from one of Bandura's experiments (Bandura et al., 1961). A preschool child is put to work on an interesting art activity. An adult is in another part of the room, where there are Tinker Toys, a mallet, and a big, inflated "Bobo" doll. After a minute of working with the Tinker Toys, the adult gets up and for almost 10 minutes attacks the inflated doll. She pounds it with the mallet, kicks it, and throws it, while yelling, "Sock him in the nose. . . . Knock him down. . . . Kick him."

After observing this outburst, the child is taken to a different room with many very attractive toys. But after two minutes the experimenter interrupts, saying these are her best toys and she must "save them for the other children." The frustrated child now goes into yet another room with various toys designed for aggressive and nonaggressive play, two of which are a Bobo doll and a mallet.

Children who were not exposed to the aggressive adult model rarely displayed any aggressive play or talk. Although frustrated, they nevertheless played calmly. Those who had observed the aggressive adult were many times more likely to pick up the mallet and lash out at the doll. Watching the adult's aggressive behavior lowered their inhibitions. Moreover, the children often reproduced the model's specific acts and said her words. Observing aggressive behavior had both lowered their inhibitions and taught them ways to aggress.

Bandura (1979) believes that everyday life exposes us to aggressive models in the family, in one's subculture, and, as we will see, in the mass media.

THE FAMILY. Physically aggressive children tend to have had physically punitive parents, who disciplined them by modeling aggression with screaming, slapping, and beating (Patterson et al., 1982). These parents often had parents who were themselves physically punitive (Bandura & Walters, 1959; Straus & Gelles, 1980). Such punitive behavior may escalate into abuse, and although most abused children do not become criminals or abusive parents, 30 percent do later abuse their own children—4 times the rate of the general population (Kaufman & Zigler, 1987; Widom, 1989). Even more mild physical punishment, such as spanking, is linked to later aggression (Gershoff, 2002). Violence often begets violence.

THE CULTURE. The social environment outside the home also provides models. In communities where "macho" images are admired, aggression is readily transmitted to new generations (Cartwright, 1975; Short, 1969). The violent subculture of teenage gangs, for instance, provides its junior members with aggressive models. Among Chicago adolescents who are otherwise equally at risk for violence, those who have observed gun violence were twice as likely to be violent (Bingenheimer et al., 2005).

The broader culture also matters. Men from cultures that are nondemocratic, high in income inequality, focused on teaching men to be warriors, and have gone to war are more likely to behave aggressively than those from cultures with the opposite characteristics (Bond, 2004).

A peaceable kingdom. In 2008, a man was convicted of murder in Scotland's Orkney Islands—only the second murder conviction since the 1800s.
Stephen Whitehorn/AA World Travel/Topfoto/The Image Works

Richard Nisbett (1990, 1993) and Dov Cohen (1996, 1998) explored the effect of a subculture on attitudes toward violence. They report that the American South, settled by Scots-Irish sheep herders ever wary of threats to their flocks, has a "culture of honor," which maintains that insults deserve retaliation (Henry, 2009). After squeezing by another man in a hallway and hearing him mutter an insult, White Southern men expressed more aggressive thoughts and experienced a surge in testosterone. White Northern men were more likely to find the encounter funny (Cohen et al., 1996). To the present day, American cities populated by southerners have higher than average White homicide rates (Vandello et al., 2008). More students in "culture of honor" states bring weapons to school, and these states have had three times as many school shootings as others (Brown et al., 2009).

People learn aggressive responses both by experience and by observing aggressive models. But when will aggressive responses actually occur? Bandura (1979) contended that aggressive acts are motivated by a variety of aversive experiences—frustration, pain, insults (Figure 2). Such experiences arouse us emotionally. But whether we act aggressively depends on the consequences we anticipate. Aggression is most likely when we are aroused and it seems safe and rewarding to aggress.

FIGURE :: 2

The Social Learning View of Aggression

The emotional arousal stemming from an aversive experience motivates aggression. Whether aggression or some other response actually occurs depends on what consequences we have learned to expect.
Source: Based on Bandura, 1979, 1997.

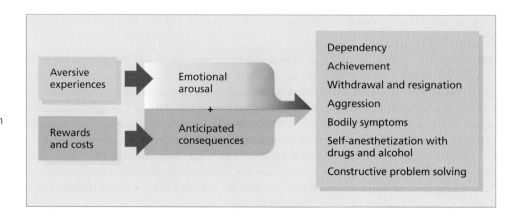

SUMMING UP: What Are Some Theories of Aggression?

- *Aggression* (defined as behavior intended to cause harm) can be *physical* (hurting someone's body) or *social* (hurting their feelings or status). *Social aggression* includes bullying and *cyberbullying* (bullying carried out online or through texting).

- *Aggression* (either physical or social) can be *hostile aggression,* which springs from emotions such as anger, and *instrumental aggression,* which aims to injure as a means to some other end.

- There are three broad theories of aggression. The first, the *instinct* view, most commonly associated with Sigmund Freud and Konrad Lorenz, contended that aggressive energy will accumulate from within, like water accumulating behind a dam. Although the available evidence offers little support for that view, it is true that aggression is biologically influenced by heredity, blood chemistry, and the brain.

- According to the second view, *frustration* causes anger and hostility. Given aggressive cues, that anger may provoke aggression. Frustration stems not from deprivation itself but from the gap between expectations and achievements.

- The *social learning* view presents aggression as learned behavior. By experience and by observing others' success, we sometimes learn that aggression pays. Social learning enables family and subcultural influences on aggression, as well as media influences (which we will discuss in the next section).

WHAT ARE SOME INFLUENCES ON AGGRESSION?

Identify the influences on aggression and describe how they work.

Consider some specific influences: aversive incidents, arousal, the media, and group context.

Aversive Incidents

Recipes for aggression often include some type of aversive experience. These include pain, uncomfortable heat, an attack, or overcrowding.

PAIN

Researcher Nathan Azrin (1967) was doing experiments with laboratory rats in a cage wired to deliver electric shocks to the animals' feet. Azrin wanted to know if switching off the shocks would reinforce two rats' positive interactions with each other. He planned to turn on the shock and then, when the rats approached each other, cut off the pain. To his great surprise, the experiment proved impossible. As soon as the rats felt pain, they attacked each other, before the experimenter could switch off the shock. The greater the shock (and pain), the more violent the attack. The same effect occurred across a long list of species, including cats, turtles, and snakes. The animals were not selective about their targets. They would attack animals of their own species and those of a different species, or stuffed dolls, or even tennis balls.

The researchers also varied the source of pain. They found that not only shocks induced attack; intense heat and "psychological pain"—for example, suddenly not rewarding hungry pigeons that have been trained to expect a grain reward after pecking at a disk—brought the same reaction as shocks. This "psychological pain" is, of course, frustration.

Pain heightens aggressiveness in humans, too. Many of us can recall such a reaction after stubbing a toe or suffering a headache. Leonard Berkowitz and his associates demonstrated this by having University of Wisconsin students hold one hand in either lukewarm water or painfully cold water. Those whose hands were submerged in the cold water

Today's ethical guidelines restrict researchers' use of painful stimuli.

Pain attack. Frustrated after losing the first two rounds of his 1997 heavyweight championship fight with Evander Holyfield, and feeling pain from an accidental head butt, Mike Tyson reacted by biting off part of Holyfield's ear.
AP Images/Jack Smith

reported feeling more irritable and more annoyed, and they were more willing to blast another person with unpleasant noise. In view of such results, Berkowitz (1983, 1989, 1998) proposed that aversive stimulation rather than frustration is the basic trigger of hostile aggression. Frustration is certainly one important type of unpleasantness. But any aversive event, whether a dashed expectation, a personal insult, or physical pain, can incite an emotional outburst. Even the torment of a depressed state increases the likelihood of hostile, aggressive behavior.

HEAT

Temporary climate variations can affect behavior. Offensive odors, cigarette smoke, and air pollution have all been linked with aggressive behavior (Rotton & Frey, 1985). But the most-studied environmental irritant is heat. William Griffitt (1970; Griffitt & Veitch, 1971) found that compared with students who answered questionnaires in a room with a normal temperature, those who did so in an uncomfortably hot room (over 90 degrees F) reported feeling more tired and aggressive and expressed more hostility toward a stranger. Follow-up experiments revealed that heat also triggers retaliation in response to an attack or injury (Bell, 1980; Rule et al., 1987) and that heat leads to aggression only after sensitive people are socially rejected (Fay & Maner, 2014).

Does uncomfortable heat increase aggression in the real world as well as in the laboratory? Consider the following:

- In heat-stricken Phoenix, Arizona, the drivers of cars without air-conditioning were more likely to honk at a stalled car (Kenrick & MacFarlane, 1986).
- In an analysis of 57,293 Major League Baseball games since 1952, batters were more likely to be hit by a pitch during hot weather—nearly 50% more likely when the temperature was 90 degrees or above (versus 59 degrees or below) and when three of the pitcher's teammates had previously been hit (Larrick et al., 2011). This wasn't due to reduced accuracy: Pitchers had no more walks or wild pitches. They just clobbered more batters.
- Studies in six cities have found that when the weather is hot, violent crimes are more likely (Anderson & Anderson, 1984; Cohn, 1993; Cotton, 1981, 1986; Harries & Stadler, 1988; Rotton & Cohn, 2004).
- Across the Northern Hemisphere, it is not only hotter days that have more violent crimes, but also hotter seasons of the year, hotter summers, hotter years, hotter cities, and hotter regions (Anderson & Delisi, 2010). Anderson and his colleagues project that if a 4-degree-Fahrenheit (about 2 degrees C) global warming occurs, the United States alone will see at least 50,000 more serious assaults annually.

"I pray thee, good Mercutio, let's retire; The day is hot, the Capulets abroad, And, if we meet, we shall not 'scape a brawl, For now, these hot days, is the mad blood stirring."

—Shakespeare,
Romeo and Juliet

Do these real-world findings show that heat discomfort directly fuels aggressiveness? Although the conclusion appears plausible, these *correlations* between temperature and aggression don't prove it. People certainly could be more irritable in hot, sticky weather. And in the laboratory, hot temperatures do increase arousal and hostile thoughts and feelings (Anderson et al., 1999). Other factors may contribute, though. Perhaps hot summer evenings drive people into the streets, where other influences may well take over. Then again (researchers have debated this), there may come a point where stifling heat suppresses violence—when it's too hot to do anything, much less hurt someone (Bell, 2005; Bushman et al., 2005a,b; Cohn & Rotton, 2005).

ATTACKS

Being attacked or insulted is especially conducive to aggression. Several experiments confirm that intentional attacks breed retaliatory attacks. In most of these experiments, one

Ferguson, Missouri, August 2014. Riots and looting occur more often during hot summer weather.
Scott Olson/Getty Images

person competes with another in a reaction-time contest. After each test trial, the winner chooses how much shock to give the loser. Actually, each person is playing a programmed opponent who steadily escalates the amount of shock. Do the real participants respond charitably? Hardly. Extracting "an eye for an eye" is the more likely response (Ohbuchi & Kambara, 1985).

Arousal

So far, we have seen that various aversive stimulations can arouse anger. Do other types of arousal, such as during exercise or sexual excitement, have a similar effect? Imagine that Lourdes, having just finished a stimulating short run, comes home to discover that her date for the evening has called and left word that he has made other plans. Will Lourdes be more likely to explode in fury after her run than if she discovered the same message after awakening from a nap? Or, because she has just exercised, will her aggression be exorcised? To discover the answer, consider how we interpret and label our bodily states.

In a famous experiment, Stanley Schachter and Jerome Singer (1962) found we can experience an aroused bodily state in different ways. They aroused University of Minnesota men by injecting them with adrenaline. The drug produced body flushing, heart palpitation, and more rapid breathing. When forewarned that the drug would produce those effects, the men felt little emotion, even when sitting next to either a hostile or a euphoric person. Of course, they could readily attribute their bodily sensations to the drug. Schachter and Singer led another group of men to believe the drug produced no such side effects. Then they, too, were placed in the company of either a hostile or a euphoric person. How did they feel and act? They were angry with the hostile person and amused by the euphoric person. The principle seemed to be: *A state of arousal can be interpreted in different ways depending on the context.*

Other experiments indicate that arousal is not as emotionally undifferentiated as Schachter believed. Yet being physically stirred up does intensify just about any emotion (Reisenzein, 1983). For example, people find radio static unpleasant, *especially* when they are aroused by bright lighting (Biner, 1991). People who have just pumped an exercise bike or watched a film of a rock concert find it easy to misattribute their arousal to a provocation and then retaliate with heightened aggression (Zillmann et al., 1988). Although common sense might lead us to assume that Lourdes's run would have drained her aggressive tensions, it's more likely she would react with more anger and aggression. As these studies show, *arousal fuels emotions.*

FIGURE :: 3

Elements of Hostile Aggression

An aversive situation can trigger aggression by provoking hostile cognitions, hostile feelings, and arousal. These reactions make us more likely to perceive harmful intent and to react aggressively.

Source: Simplified from Anderson, Deuser, & DeNeve, 1995.

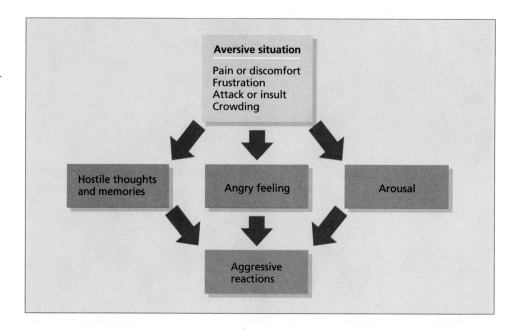

Sexual arousal and other forms of arousal, such as anger, can therefore amplify one another (Zillmann, 1989). Love is never so passionate as after a fight or a fright—one reason why it's so popular to take a hot date to a horror movie. In the laboratory, erotic stimuli are more arousing to people who have just been frightened. Similarly, the arousal of a roller-coaster ride may spill over into romantic feeling for one's partner.

A frustrating or insulting situation heightens arousal. When it does, the arousal, combined with hostile thoughts and feelings, may form a recipe for aggressive behavior (Figure 3).

Aggression Cues

As we noted when considering the frustration-aggression hypothesis, violence is more likely when aggressive cues release pent-up anger. Leonard Berkowitz (1968, 1981, 1995) and others found that the sight of a weapon is such a cue. In one experiment, children who had just played with toy guns became more willing to knock down another child's blocks. In another, angered University of Wisconsin men gave more electric shocks to their tormenter when a rifle and a revolver (supposedly left over from a previous experiment) were nearby than when badminton rackets had been left behind (Berkowitz & LePage, 1967). Guns prime hostile thoughts and punitive judgments (Anderson et al., 1998; Dienstbier et al., 1998). What's within sight is within mind. This is especially so when a weapon is perceived as an instrument of violence rather than a recreational item. For hunters, seeing a hunting rifle does not prime aggressive thoughts, although it does for nonhunters (Bartholow et al., 2004).

Berkowitz was not surprised that in the United States, a country with about 300 million privately owned guns, half of all murders are committed with handguns, or that handguns in homes are far more likely to kill household members than intruders. "Guns not only permit violence," he reported, "they can stimulate it as well. The finger pulls the trigger, but the trigger may also be pulling the finger."

Berkowitz was further unsurprised that countries that ban handguns have lower murder rates. Compared with the United States, Britain has one-fourth as many people and one-sixteenth as many murders. When Washington, D.C., adopted a law restricting handgun possession, the number of gun-related murders and suicides each abruptly dropped about 25 percent. No changes occurred in other methods of murder and suicide, and nearby cities did not show any changes in gun crimes (Loftin et al., 1991). When Australia instituted stricter gun laws and bought back 700,000 guns after a 1996 mass shooting, gun-related murders fell 59 percent, and no mass shootings have occurred since (Howard, 2013). In the United States in 2013, the five states with the highest per capita gun deaths were

Alaska, Louisiana, Alabama, Mississippi, and Wyoming—all states with higher gun ownership rates and less restrictive gun laws (VPC, 2015).

Researchers also have examined risks of violence in homes with and without guns. This is controversial research because such homes may differ in many ways. One study sponsored by the Centers for Disease Control compared gun owners and nonowners of the same gender, race, age, and neighborhood. The ironic and tragic result was that those who kept a gun in the home (often for protection) were 2.7 times as likely to be murdered—nearly always by a family member or a close acquaintance (Kellermann, 1997; Kellermann et al., 1993). A meta-analysis found that those with guns in their homes were three times more likely to be murdered and twice as likely to commit suicide (Anglemyer et al., 2014). Even after controlling for gender, age, and race, people with guns at home were 41 percent more likely to be murdered and 3 times as likely to commit suicide (Wiebe, 2003). A gun in the home is 12 times more likely to kill a household member than an intruder (Narang et al., 2010). A gun in the home has often meant the difference between a fight and a funeral, or between suffering and suicide.

Guns not only serve as aggression cues but also put psychological distance between aggressor and victim. As Milgram's obedience studies taught us, remoteness from the victim facilitates cruelty. A knife can kill someone, but a knife attack requires a great deal more personal contact than pulling a trigger from a distance (Figure 4).

2014 Gallup survey of Americans: "Do you think having a gun in the house makes it a safer place to be or a more dangerous place to be?"
Safer: 63%
More dangerous: 30%
Depends, or no opinion: 6%

Media Influences: Pornography and Sexual Violence

Pornography is now a bigger business in the United States than professional football, basketball, and baseball combined, thanks to some $13 billion a year spent on the industry's cable and satellite networks, theaters and pay-per-view movies, and in-room hotel movies, phone sex, sex magazines, and Internet sites (D'Orlando, 2011). The easy availability of pornography on the Internet has accelerated its popularity. In a recent survey of 18- to 26-year-old American men, 87 percent said they viewed pornography at least once a month, and nearly half used it at least once a week . However, only 31 percent of women reported viewing pornography at all (Carroll et al., 2008). Pornography use is more common among men who are younger, less religious, and who have had more sexual partners. Men's pornography use in the United States increased between 1993 and 2010 (Wright, 2013). Social psychological research on pornography has focused mostly on depictions of sexual violence, which is commonplace in popular recent adult videos (Sun et al., 2008). A typical sexually violent episode finds a man forcing himself upon a woman. She at first

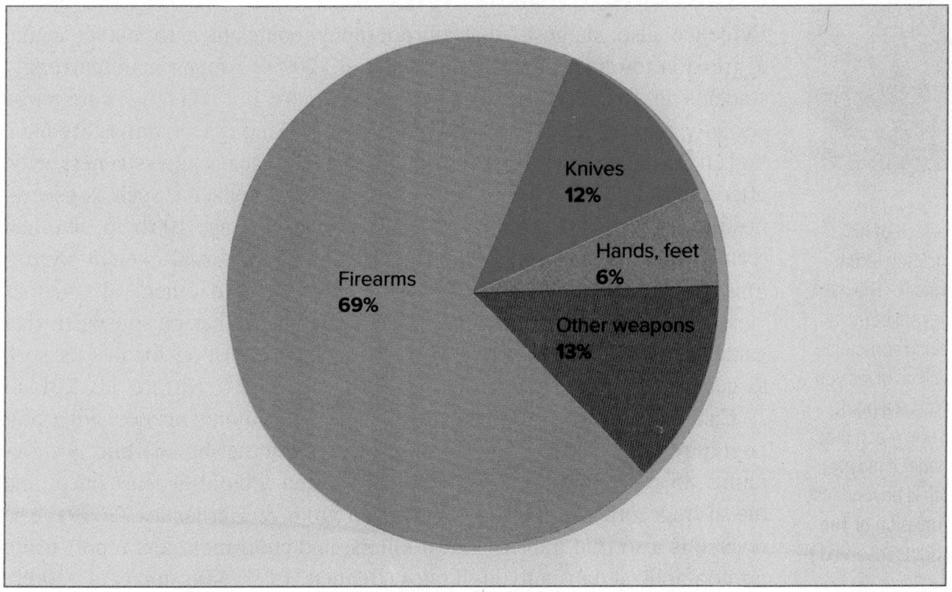

FIGURE :: 4

Weapons Used to Commit Murder in the United States in 2013
Source: FBI Uniform Crime Reports.

resists and tries to fight off her attacker. Gradually she becomes sexually aroused, and her resistance melts. By the end she is in ecstasy, pleading for more. We have all viewed or read nonpornographic versions of this sequence: She resists, he persists. Dashing man grabs and forcibly kisses protesting woman. Within moments, the arms that were pushing him away are clutching him tight, her resistance overwhelmed by her unleashed passion. The problem, of course, is that women do not actually respond this way to rape.

Social psychologists report that viewing such fictional scenes of a man overpowering and arousing a woman can (a) distort men's (and possibly women's) perceptions of how women actually respond to sexual coercion and (b) increase men's aggression against women.

DISTORTED PERCEPTIONS OF SEXUAL REALITY

"Pornography that portrays sexual aggression as pleasurable for the victim increases the acceptance of the use of coercion in sexual relations."

—Social Science Consensus at Surgeon General's Workshop on Pornography and Public Health (Koop, 1987)

Does viewing sexual violence reinforce the "rape myth"—that some women would welcome sexual assault and that "no doesn't really mean no"? Researchers have observed a correlation between the amount of TV viewing and rape myth acceptance (Kahlor & Morrison, 2007). To explore the relationship experimentally, Neil Malamuth and James Check (1981) showed University of Manitoba men either two nonsexual movies or two movies depicting a man sexually overcoming a woman. A week later, when surveyed by a different experimenter, those who saw the films with mild sexual violence were more accepting of violence against women. This was especially true if they were aroused by the films (Hald & Malamuth, 2015).

Other studies confirm that exposure to pornography increases acceptance of the rape myth (Oddone-Paolucci et al., 2000). For example, while spending three evenings watching sexually violent movies, men became progressively less bothered by the raping and slashing (Mullin & Linz, 1995). Compared with men not exposed to the films, the men expressed less sympathy for domestic violence victims and rated the victims' injuries as less severe—even three days later. In fact, noted the researchers, what better way for an evil character to get people to react calmly to the torture and mutilation of women than to show a gradually escalating series of such films (Donnerstein et al., 1987)?

Note that the sexual message (that many women enjoy being "taken") was subtle and unlikely to elicit counterarguing. Given frequent media images of women's resistance melting in the arms of a forceful man, we shouldn't be surprised that even women often believe that some *other* woman might enjoy being sexually overpowered—though virtually none think it of themselves (Malamuth et al., 1980).

Did Ted Bundy's (1989) comments on the eve of his execution for a series of rape-murders acknowledge pornography's toll or make it a handy excuse? "The most damaging kinds of pornography [involve] sexual violence. Like an addiction, you keep craving something that is harder, harder, something which, which gives you a greater sense of excitement. Until you reach a point where the pornography only goes so far, you reach that jumping off point where you begin to wonder if maybe actually doing it would give you that which is beyond just reading it or looking at it." (Used with permission of The Associated Press, Copyright © 2015. All rights reserved.)
Bettmann/Corbis

AGGRESSION AGAINST WOMEN

Evidence also suggests that pornography contributes to men's actual aggression toward women (Kingston et al., 2009). Among male university students in Brazil, those who consumed more pornography were more sexually aggressive (D'Abreu & Krahé, 2014). Among U.S. university men, high pornography consumption has predicted sexual aggressiveness even after controlling for other predictors of antisocial behavior, such as general hostility (Vega & Malamuth, 2007). Boys and girls age 10 to 15 who had seen movies, magazines, or websites with violent sexual content were 6 times more likely to be sexually aggressive toward others (defined as "kissed, touched, or done anything sexual with another person when that person did not want you to do so"), even after adjusting for factors such as gender, aggressive traits, and family background (Ybarra et al., 2011).

Canadian and American sexual offenders commonly acknowledge pornography use. Among 155 men arrested for Internet-based child pornography, 85 percent admitted they had molested a child at least once, and the average offender had 13 victims (Bourke & Hernandez, 2009). The reverse is also true: rapists, serial killers, and child molesters report using pornography at unusually high rates (Bennett, 1991; Kingston et al., 2008).

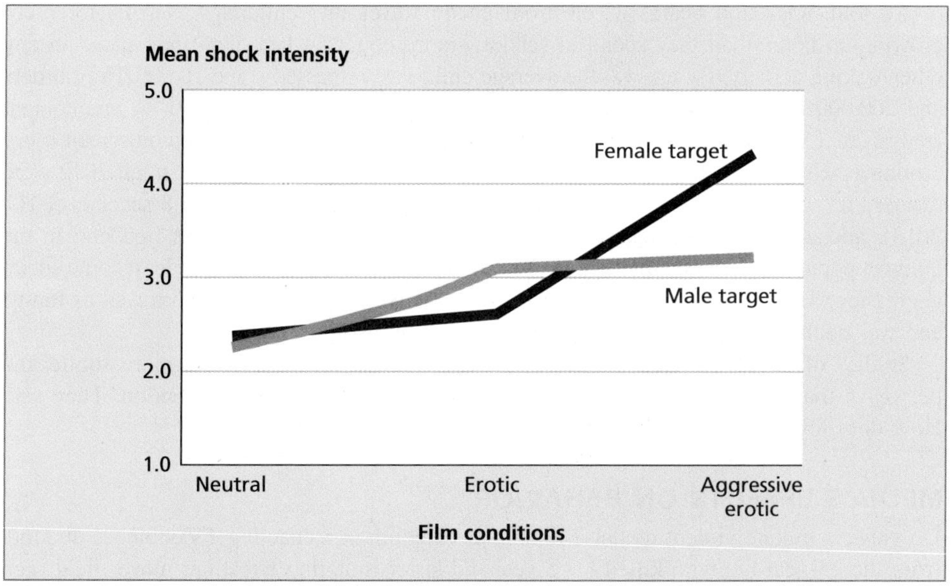

FIGURE :: 5

After viewing an aggressive-erotic film, college men delivered stronger shocks than before, especially to a woman. *Source:* Data from Donnerstein, 1980.

But perhaps pornography doesn't actually cause violence; instead, violent men like violent pornography. To rule out this explanation, it is necessary to perform an experiment—for example, to randomly assign some people to watch pornography. In one such experiment, 120 University of Wisconsin men watched a neutral, an erotic, or an aggressive-erotic (rape) film. Then the men, supposedly as part of another experiment, "taught" a male or female confederate some nonsense syllables by choosing how much shock to administer for incorrect answers. The men who had watched the rape film administered markedly stronger shocks (Figure 5), particularly to women, and particularly when angered (Donnerstein, 1980). A consensus statement by 21 leading social scientists summed up the results of experiments in this area: "Exposure to violent pornography increases punitive behavior toward women" (Koop, 1987).

If the ethics of conducting such experiments trouble you, rest assured that these researchers appreciate the controversial and powerful experience they are giving participants. Only after giving their knowing consent do people participate. Moreover, after the experiment, researchers effectively debunk any myths the films communicated (Check & Malamuth, 1984). Another experiment avoided the ethical dilemma by asking college students who usually consumed pornography to abstain from consumption for a month. Compared with those who instead gave up a favorite food, those who had dialed back on their porn consumption were less aggressive (Lambert et al., 2011).

Repeated exposure to erotic films featuring quick, uncommitted sex also tends to

- *decrease attraction for one's partner;*
- *increase acceptance of extramarital sex and of women's sexual submission to men;*
- *increase men's perceiving women in sexual terms.*

(Source: *Myers, 2000a*)

Media Influences: Television and the Internet

We have seen that watching an aggressive model attack a Bobo doll can unleash children's aggressive urges and teach them new ways to aggress. We have also seen that after viewing movies depicting sexual violence, many angry men will act more violently toward women. Does everyday television viewing have any similar effects?

Today, in much of the industrialized world, nearly all households (99.2 percent in Australia, for example) have a TV set. The average U.S. home in 2009 had 3 TV sets, which helps explain why parents and children often give differing reports of what the children are watching (Nielsen, 2010). In some households these days, each member of the family has his or her own computer tablet, making it even more difficult for parents to monitor children's media use.

In the average U.S. home, the TV is on 7 hours a day, with individual teens averaging about 3 hours and adults 6 hours (Nielsen, 2011). Teens make up some of the difference by watching video on their phones more often. Thanks to digital video recorders (DVRs) that allow people to "time shift" their TV watching, Americans in 2011 watched more TV than ever before (Nielsen, 2011).

"The average U.S. household has more televisions (2.93) than people (2.6)."
—Nielsen, 2010

All told, television beams its electromagnetic waves into children's eyeballs for more growing-up hours than they spend in school—more hours, in fact, than they spend in any other waking activity. By age 18, the average child has witnessed some 16,000 TV murders and 200,000 other violent acts (Senate Committee on the Judiciary, 1999). In one content analysis of TV dramas airing in 2012–2013, a gun, knife, or sword appeared on screen every 3 minutes. Children watching four episodes of the show "Criminal Minds" in fall 2012 were exposed to nearly 53 acts of violence per episode—one every minute and 8 seconds (PTC, 2013). Social aggression (such as bullying and social exclusion) is just as frequent; in the 50 most popular TV shows among 2- to 11-year-olds, 92 percent featured at least some social aggression. This bullying often came from an attractive perpetrator, was portrayed as funny, and was neither rewarded nor punished (Martins & Wilson, 2012a).

Studies of television viewing and aggression aim to identify effects more subtle and pervasive than the occasional "copycat" murders that capture public attention. They ask: How does television affect viewers' *behavior* and viewers' *thinking?*

MEDIA'S EFFECTS ON BEHAVIOR

"One of television's great contributions is that it brought murder back into the home where it belongs. Seeing a murder on television can be good therapy. It can help work off one's antagonisms."

—Alfred Hitchcock

Do viewers imitate violent models? Examples of children reenacting TV violence abound, from the 13-year-old who killed his 5-year-old sister imitating wrestling moves he'd seen on TV (AP, 2013) to an Indian boy who died when his brothers imitated a hanging they'd seen in a cartoon (Indo-Asian News Service, 2013).

CORRELATING MEDIA VIEWING AND BEHAVIOR. Stories of TV-inspired violence are not scientific evidence. Researchers therefore use correlational and experimental studies to examine the effects of viewing violence. One technique, commonly used with schoolchildren, correlates their TV watching with their aggressiveness. The frequent result: The more violent the content of the child's TV viewing, the more aggressive the child (Eron, 1987; Turner et al., 1986). For example, a longitudinal study of 1,715 German adolescents found that those who viewed more violent media were more aggressive two years later, even with important other factors controlled (Krahé et al., 2012). The relationship is modest but consistently found in North America, Europe, and Australia. And it extends to social aggression. British girls who watched more shows featuring gossiping, backbiting, and social exclusion more often displayed such behavior (Coyne & Archer, 2005), as did elementary school girls in Illinois who watched shows featuring social aggression (Martins & Wilson, 2012b).

Can we conclude, then, that a diet of violent TV fuels aggression? Perhaps you are already thinking that because this is a correlational study, the cause-effect relation could also work in the opposite direction. Maybe aggressive children prefer aggressive programs. Or maybe some underlying third factor, such as lower intelligence, predisposes some children to prefer both aggressive programs and aggressive behavior.

Researchers have developed two ways to test these alternative explanations. They reduce hidden third factors by statistically pulling out their influence. For example, William Belson (1978; Muson, 1978) studied 1,565 London boys. Compared with those who watched little violence, those who watched a great deal (especially realistic rather than cartoon violence) admitted to 50 percent more violent acts during the preceding six months. Belson also examined 22 likely third factors, such as family size. The "heavy violence" and "light violence" viewers still differed after these third factors were included. Belson surmised that the heavy viewers were indeed more violent *because* of their TV exposure.

Similarly, Leonard Eron and Rowell Huesmann (1980, 1985) found that violence viewing among 875 8-year-olds correlated with aggressiveness even after statistically pulling out several obvious possible third factors. Moreover, when they restudied those individuals as 19-year-olds, they discovered that viewing violence at age 8 modestly predicted aggressiveness at age 19, but that aggressiveness at age 8 did *not* predict viewing violence at age 19. Aggression followed viewing, not the reverse. Moreover, by age 30, those who had watched the most violence in childhood were more likely than others to have been convicted of a crime. Another longitudinal study followed 1,037 New Zealand children from age 5 to age 26. Children and teens who spent more time watching TV were more likely to become

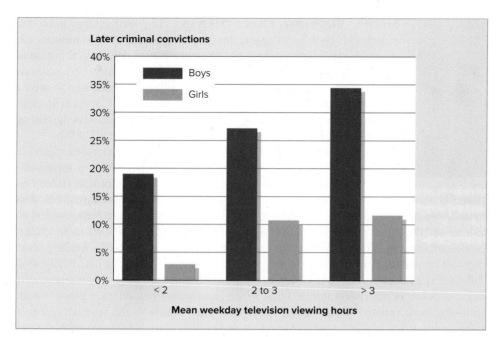

TV Viewing and Later Criminal Behavior

Television viewing between ages 5 and 15 predicted having a criminal conviction by age 26.

young adults convicted of crimes, diagnosed with antisocial personality disorder, and high in aggressive personality traits. This was true even when the researchers controlled for possible third variables such as sex, IQ, socioeconomic status, previous antisocial behavior, and parenting style (Robertson et al., 2013; see Figure 6). Researchers are *not* saying that everyone who watches violent media becomes aggressive in real life—instead, they find it is one of several risk factors for aggressive behavior, combined with family troubles, gender, and being the victim of someone else's aggression. Even taking these factors into account, though, exposure to violent media is a significant predictor (Gentile & Bushman, 2012).

Many people now spend more screen time in front of their computers than in front of the television. In many ways, the Internet allows an even greater variety of options for viewing violence than television does, including violent videos, violent pictures, and hate-group websites (Donnerstein, 2011). It also allows people to create and distribute violent media themselves, and to bully others through email, instant messaging, or on social networking websites (Donnerstein, 2011). In a survey of European adolescents, one-third reported seeing violent or hateful content online (Livingstone & Haddon, 2009). Among U.S. youth, those who frequently visited violent websites were 5 times more likely to report engaging in violent behavior (Ybarra et al., 2008). Even books influence people: Middle-school students who read more books featuring aggression and violence were more likely to behave aggressively (Stockdale et al., 2013).

Other studies have confirmed these results in various ways, finding the following:

- Eight-year-olds' violence viewing predicted spouse abuse as an adult (Huesmann et al., 1984, 2003).
- Adolescents' violence viewing predicted engaging in assault, robbery, and threats of injury (Johnson et al., 2002).
- Elementary schoolchildren's violent media exposure predicted how often they got into fights 2 to 6 months later (Gentile et al., 2004).

In all these studies, the investigators were careful to adjust for likely "third factors," such as intelligence or hostility. Nevertheless, an infinite number of possible third factors could be creating a merely coincidental relation between viewing violence and practicing aggression. Fortunately, the experimental method can control these extraneous factors. If we randomly assign some people to watch a violent film and others a nonviolent film, any later aggression difference between the two groups will be due to the only factor that distinguishes them: what they watched.

Watching violent media leads to social and physical aggression in real life.

©Gorkem Demir/Shutterstock.com

"Then shall we simply allow our children to listen to any story anyone happens to make up, and so receive into their minds ideas often the very opposite of those we shall think they ought to have when they are grown up?"

—Plato,
The Republic, 360 B.C.

MEDIA VIEWING EXPERIMENTS. The trailblazing Bobo-doll experiments by Albert Bandura and Richard Walters (1963) sometimes had young children view the adult pounding the inflated doll on film instead of observing it live—with much the same effect. Then Leonard Berkowitz and Russell Geen (1966) found that angered college students who viewed a violent film acted more aggressively than did similarly angered students who viewed nonaggressive films. More than 100 studies confirm the finding that viewing violence amplifies aggression (Anderson et al., 2003).

In one experiment, female college students were randomly assigned to watch portions of a physically aggressive film *(Kill Bill)*, a relationally aggressive film *(Mean Girls),* or a nonaggressive control film *(What Lies Beneath)*. Compared to the control group, those who watched the aggressive films were more aggressive toward an innocent person, blasting her headphones with loud, uncomfortable noise. They were also more subtly aggressive, giving negative evaluations to another participant (actually a confederate) who annoyed them (Coyne et al., 2008). Reading about physical or relational aggression produced the same results (Coyne et al., 2012). Dolf Zillmann and James Weaver (1999) similarly exposed men and women, on four consecutive days, to violent or nonviolent feature films. When participating in a different project on the fifth day, those exposed to the violent films were more hostile to the research assistant. Fifth graders who watched a tween sitcom featuring social aggression (compared with those watching a control show) were more likely to agree that a student from a different group should be excluded from joining their team for a school competition (Mares & Braun, 2013).

The aggression provoked in these experiments is not assault and battery; it's more on the scale of a shove in the lunch line, a cruel comment, or a threatening gesture. Nevertheless, the convergence of evidence is striking. "The irrefutable conclusion," said a 1993 American Psychological Association youth violence commission, is "that viewing violence increases violence." This is especially so among people with aggressive tendencies and when an attractive person commits justified, realistic violence that goes unpunished and that shows no pain or harm (Comstock, 2008; Gentile et al., 2007; Zillmann & Weaver, 2007). That description is, of course, consistent with much of the violence shown on TV and in movies.

If increased exposure to media violence causes aggression, would less exposure lead to less aggression? One group of researchers found that the answer was yes. German middle school students were randomly assigned to either a control group or an intervention group encouraged to reduce their media use and critically question it. Among those already high in aggressive behavior, the intervention group later reported less aggressive behavior than the control group (Moller et al., 2012).

All in all, conclude researchers Brad Bushman and Craig Anderson (2001), the evidence for media effects on aggression is now "overwhelming." The research base is large, the methods diverse, and the overall findings consistent, agreed a National Institute of Mental Health task force of leading media violence researchers (Anderson et al., 2003). "Our in-depth review . . . reveals unequivocal evidence that exposure to media violence can increase the likelihood of aggressive and violent behavior in both immediate and long-term contexts." This conclusion has been questioned by some critics (Elson & Ferguson, 2014), but is endorsed by the researchers with the most expertise in the field (Bushman & Huesmann, 2014) and a broad consensus of media researchers, pediatricians, and parents (Bushman et al., 2015) Some compare the denial of the effects of violent media to the initial skepticism around the idea that smoking causes lung disease (Anderson et al., 2015).

WHY DOES MEDIA VIEWING AFFECT BEHAVIOR?. Given the convergence of correlational and experimental evidence, researchers have explored *why* viewing violence has this effect. Consider three possibilities (Geen & Thomas, 1986). One is the *arousal* it produces (Mueller et al., 1983; Zillmann, 1989). As we noted earlier, arousal tends to spill over: One type of arousal energizes other behaviors.

Other research shows that viewing violence *disinhibits*. In Bandura's experiment, the adult's punching of the Bobo doll seemed to make outbursts legitimate and to lower the children's inhibitions. Viewing violence primes the viewer for aggressive behavior by activating violence-related thoughts (Berkowitz, 1984; Bushman & Geen, 1990; Josephson, 1987). Listening to music with sexually violent lyrics seems to have a similar effect (Barongan & Hall, 1995; Johnson et al., 1995; Pritchard, 1998).

Media portrayals also evoke *imitation*. The children in Bandura's experiments reenacted the specific behaviors they had witnessed. The commercial television industry is hard pressed to dispute that television leads viewers to imitate what they have seen: Its advertisers model consumption. Are media executives right, however, to argue that TV merely holds a mirror to a violent society, that art imitates life, and that the "reel" world therefore shows us the real world? Actually, on TV programs, acts of assault outnumber affectionate acts four to one. In other ways as well, television models an unreal world.

But there is good news here, too. If the ways of relating and problem solving modeled on television do trigger imitation, especially among young viewers, then TV modeling of **prosocial behavior** should be socially beneficial. A character who helps others (like Dora or Doc McStuffins) should teach children prosocial behavior.

MEDIA'S EFFECTS ON THINKING

We have focused on television's effect on behavior, but researchers have also examined the cognitive effects of viewing violence: Does prolonged viewing *desensitize* us to cruelty? Does prime time crime give us mental *scripts* for how to act? Does it distort our *perceptions* of reality? Does it *prime* aggressive thoughts?

DESENSITIZATION.   Repeat an emotion-arousing stimulus, such as an obscene word, over and over. What happens? The emotional response will "extinguish." After witnessing thousands of acts of cruelty, there is good reason to expect a similar emotional numbing. The most common response might well become, "Doesn't bother me at all." Such a response is precisely what Barbara Krahé and her colleagues (2010) observed when they measured the physiological arousal of 303 college students who watched a clip from a violent movie. Regular viewers of violence on TV and movies showed a lessened response, compared to infrequent viewers, reacting to violence with a shrug rather than concern.

In a clever experiment, Brad Bushman and Craig Anderson (2009) had a young woman with a taped-up ankle drop her crutches while outside a movie theater and then struggle to retrieve them. Moviegoers who had just seen a violent film *(The Ruins)* took longer to help than those who had just seen a nonviolent film *(Nim's Island)*. When the woman dropped her crutches *before* the movie, however, there was no difference in helping—suggesting it was the violent film itself, and not the type of people who watch violent films, that desensitized moviegoers to her dilemma.

SOCIAL SCRIPTS.   When we find ourselves in new situations, uncertain how to act, we rely on **social scripts**—culturally provided mental instructions for how to act. After so many action films, youngsters may acquire a script that is played when they face real-life conflicts. Challenged, they may "act like a man" by intimidating or eliminating the threat. Likewise, after witnessing innumerable sexual innuendoes and acts on TV and in music lyrics—mostly involving impulsive or short-term relationships—youths may acquire sexual scripts they later enact in real-life relationships (Escobar-Chaves & Anderson, 2008; Fischer & Greitemeyer, 2006; Kunkel, 2001). Thus, the more sexual content that adolescents view (even when controlling for other predictors of early sexual activity), the more likely they are to perceive their peers as sexually active, to develop sexually permissive attitudes, and to experience early intercourse (Escobar-Chaves et al., 2005; Martino et al., 2005). Media portrayals implant social scripts.

ALTERED PERCEPTIONS.   Does television's fictional world also mold our conceptions of the real world? George Gerbner and his University of Pennsylvania associates (1979, 1994) suspected this is television's most potent effect. Their surveys of both adolescents and adults showed that heavy viewers (4 hours a day or more) are more likely than light viewers (2 hours or fewer) to exaggerate the frequency of violence in the world around them and to fear being personally assaulted. Similar feelings of vulnerability have been expressed by South African women after viewing violence against women (Reid & Finchilescu, 1995). A national survey

prosocial behavior
Positive, constructive, helpful social behavior; the opposite of antisocial behavior.

"Fifty years of research on the effect of TV violence on children leads to the inescapable conclusion that viewing media violence is related to increases in aggressive attitudes, values, and behaviors."
—John P. Murray (2008)

social scripts
Culturally provided mental instructions for how to act in various situations.

"The more fully that any given generation was exposed to television in its formative years, the lower its civic engagement [its rate of voting, joining, meeting, giving, and volunteering]."
—Robert Putnam,
Bowling Alone, 2000

THIS MODERN WORLD by TOM TOMORROW

(Dan Perkins/THIS MODERN WORLD)

People who watch many hours of television may develop an altered perception that the world is a dangerous place.
© 2009 Tom Tomorrow. Reprinted with permission of Dan Perkins.

"What sense does it make to forbid selling to a 13-year-old a magazine with an image of a nude woman, while protecting the sale to that 13-year-old of an interactive video game in which he actively, but virtually, binds and gags the woman, then tortures and kills her?"
—U.S. Supreme Court Justice Stephen Breyer, in Dissent, 2011

of American 7- to 11-year-old children found that heavy viewers were more likely than light viewers to admit fears "that somebody bad might get into your house" or that "when you go outside, somebody might hurt you" (Peterson & Zill, 1981). For those who watch much television, the world becomes a scary place. Media portrayals shape perceptions of reality.

COGNITIVE PRIMING. Research also reveals that watching violent television primes aggression-related ideas (Bushman, 1998). After viewing violence, people offer more hostile explanations for others' behavior (was the shove intentional?). They interpret spoken homonyms with the more aggressive meaning (interpreting "punch" as a hit rather than a drink). And they recognize aggressive words more quickly. Media portrayals prime thinking.

Another Media Influence: Video Games

The scientific debate over the effects of media violence "is basically over," contend Douglas Gentile and Craig Anderson (2003; Anderson & Gentile, 2008). Researchers are now shifting their attention to video games, which are extremely popular among teens and can be extremely violent. Educational research shows that "video games are excellent teaching tools," note Gentile and Anderson. "If health video games can successfully teach health behaviors, and flight simulator video games can teach people how to fly, then what should we expect violent murder-simulating games to teach?"

Since the first video game in 1972, we have moved from electronic ping-pong to splatter games (Anderson et al., 2007). In a 2008 poll, 97 percent of 12- to 17-year-olds said they play video games. Half had played a video game the day before. Many of these games were violent—half of the teens said they played first-person shooter games, such as *Halo* or *Counter-Strike,* and 2 out of 3 played action games that often involve violence, such as *Grand Theft Auto* (Pew Research Center, 2008). Younger children are also playing violent games: In one survey of fourth-graders, 59 percent of girls and 73 percent of boys reported that their favorite games were violent ones (Anderson, 2003, 2004).

In the popular *Grand Theft Auto: San Andreas,* youth are invited to play the role of a psychopath, notes Gentile (2004). "You can run down pedestrians with the car, you can do carjackings, you can do drive-by shootings, you can run down to the red-light district, pick up a prostitute, have sex with her in your car, and then kill her to get your money back." In effective 3D graphics, you can knock people over, stomp on them until they cough up blood, and watch them die.

Effects of Video Games

Concerns about violent video games heightened after teen assassins in several mass shootings enacted the horrific violence they had so often played onscreen. Adam Lanza, who shot 20 first-graders and 6 teachers at Sandy Hook Elementary in Connecticut in 2012, spent many hours playing the warfare game *Call of Duty* (Kleinfield et al., 2013). In 2013, an 8-year-old boy shot and killed a 90-year-old woman after playing *Grand Theft Auto IV* (Stegall, 2013). People wondered: What do youth learn from endless hours of role-playing attacking and dismembering people? And was anything accomplished when some

Norwegian stores responded to the 2011 killing of teens by a game-addicted shooter by pulling violent games from their shelves (Anderson, 2011)?

Most smokers don't die of lung cancer. Most abused children don't become abusive. And most people who spend hundreds of hours rehearsing human slaughter live gentle lives. This enables video-game defenders, like tobacco and TV interests, to say their products are harmless. "There is absolutely no evidence, none, that playing a violent game leads to aggressive behavior," contended Doug Lowenstein (2000), president of the Interactive Digital Software Association.

Gentile and Anderson offer some reasons why violent game playing *might* have a more toxic effect than watching violent television. With game playing, players

- identify with, and play the role of, a violent character;
- actively rehearse violence, instead of passively watching it;
- engage in the whole sequence of enacting violence—selecting victims, acquiring weapons and ammunition, stalking the victim, aiming the weapon, pulling the trigger;
- are engaged with continual violence and threats of attack;
- repeat violent behaviors over and over;
- are rewarded for violent acts.

For such reasons, military organizations often prepare soldiers to fire in combat by engaging them with attack-simulation games.

But do people who play violent video games go on to behave aggressively outside the game? "I play violent video games," some may protest, "And I'm not aggressive." As columnist Roger Simon (2011) wrote about research showing that media violence leads to real-life aggression, "Such claims bewilder me. I grew up playing with toy guns and have never shot anybody (though I know plenty who deserve it)." The problem with this common argument is that one isolated example proves nothing—it's not a scientific study. A better approach is to examine large samples of people to find out if, on average, violent video games increase aggression.

Research doing just that shows that playing violent video games does, on average, increase aggressive behavior, thoughts, and feelings outside the game. Combining data from 381 studies with 130,296 participants, Craig Anderson and his colleagues (2010) found a clear effect: Violent video-game playing increased aggression—for children, adolescents, and young adults; in North America, Japan, and Western Europe; and across three research designs (correlational, experimental, and longitudinal). That means violent video games caused aggression even when participants were randomly assigned to play them (vs. a nonviolent game), which rules out the possibility that (for example) aggressive people like to play aggressive games. In one experiment, for example, French university students were randomly assigned to play either a violent video game (*Condemned 2, Call of Duty 4, The Club*) or a nonviolent video game (*S3K Superbike, Dirt 2,* or *Pure*) for 20 minutes each day for 3 days. Those randomly assigned to play a violent game blasted longer and louder unpleasant noise into the headphones of an innocent person than those who played the nonviolent game, with their aggression increasing each day they played the violent game (Hasan et al., 2013). Longitudinal studies, which follow people over time, produce similar results: among German adolescents, today's violent game playing predicted later aggression, but today's aggression did not predict future violent game playing (Moller & Krahé, 2008). The same was true for Canadian adolescents followed for four years (Willoughby et al., 2012).

Playing violent video games has an array of effects, including the following:

- *Increases in aggressive behaviors:* After violent game play, children and youth play more aggressively with their peers, get into more arguments with their teachers, and participate in more fights. The effect occurs inside and outside the laboratory, across self-reports, teacher reports, and parent reports, and for the reasons illustrated in Figure 7. Even among young adolescents usually low in hostility, 10 times more of the heavy violent gamers got into fights compared with their

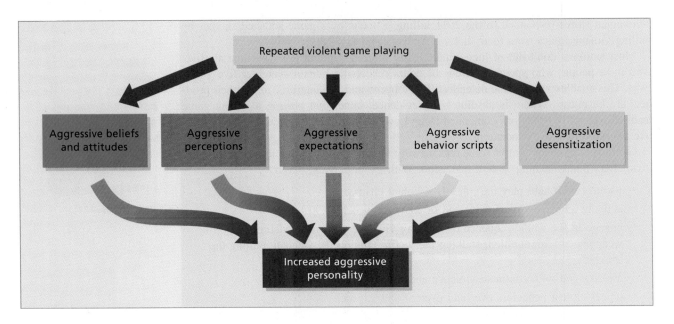

FIGURE :: 7

Violent Video-Game Influences on Aggressive Tendencies
Source: Adapted from Craig A. Anderson and Brad J. Bushman (2001).

nongaming counterparts. And after they started playing the violent games, previously nonhostile kids became more likely to have fights (Gentile et al., 2004). In Japan, too, playing violent video games early in a school year predicts physical aggressiveness later in the year, even after controlling for gender and prior aggressiveness (Anderson et al., 2008).

- *Increases in aggressive thoughts.* After playing a violent game, students became more likely to guess that a man whose car was just rear-ended would respond aggressively by using abusive language, kicking out a window, or starting a fight (Bushman & Anderson, 2002). Those who played violent games were also more likely to have a hostile attribution bias—they expected other people to act aggressively when provoked, and the greater this bias, the more aggressively they behaved themselves. Those who play violent games, conclude the researchers, see the world through "blood-red tinted glasses" (Hasan et al., 2012).

- *Increases in aggressive feelings,* including hostility, anger, or revenge. Students who played a violent video game had more aggressive thoughts and feelings than those who watched a recording of someone else playing the same game or watched a violent film, suggesting that violent video games heighten aggression even more than other violent media—most likely because people actually act aggressively when they play video games instead of acting as passive observers (Lin, 2013). Those randomly assigned to play a violent video game also reported feeling less happy than those who played prosocial or neutral games (Saleem et al., 2012).

- *Habituation in the brain.* Compared with those who did not play violent games, frequent gamers' brains reacted less strongly to negative images. Apparently, their brains have become habituated to violence, numbing their reactions (Montag et al., 2012).

- *Greater likelihood of carrying a weapon.* Among 9- to 18-year-olds in a U.S. national longitudinal study, those who played violent video games in the past year were 5 times more likely to carry a weapon to school, even when adjusted for third factors (Ybarra et al., 2014).

- *Decreases in self-control and increases in antisocial behavior.* High school students who played a violent video game (compared with a control group who played a nonviolent game) ate 4 times more M&M's out of a bowl next to the computer, suggesting lowered self-control. They were also more likely to steal, taking more raffle tickets for attractive prizes than they actually earned (Gabbiadini et al., 2014). A correlational study found that youth who played violent video games were more likely to have stolen, vandalized property, or sold drugs (DeLisi et al., 2013).

- *Decreases in helping others and in empathy for others.* Students randomly assigned to play a violent or nonviolent video game later overheard a loud fight that ended with one person writhing on the floor in pain from a sprained ankle. Students who had just played a violent game took more than 1 minute on average to come to the person's aid, almost 4 times as long as those who had played a nonviolent game (Bushman & Anderson, 2009).

After violent video-game playing, people become more likely to exploit rather than to trust and cooperate with a partner (Sheese & Graziano, 2005). They also become *desensitized* to violence, showing decreased brain activity associated with emotion (Bartholow et al., 2006; Carnagey et al., 2007). Tobias Greitemeyer and Neil McLatchie (2011) explored a specific kind of desensitization: seeing other people as less human. Among British university students, those randomly assigned to play a violent game were more likely to describe in nonhuman terms someone who had insulted them. And the less human they saw the person, the more aggressive they were. In another study, students who played a violent game saw *themselves* as less human as well (Bastian et al., 2012). The intense violence of video games may also make real-life aggression (such as shoving) seem less harmful in comparison. Thus, when someone claims that playing violent video games does not make them more aggressive, that might be because their perception of what counts as "aggressive" no longer includes less severe, but still harmful, acts (Greitemeyer, 2014).

Moreover, the more violent the games that are played, the bigger the effects. The bloodier the game (for example, the higher the blood-level setting in one experiment with *Mortal Combat* players) the greater the gamer's after-game hostility and arousal (Barlett et al., 2008). More-realistic games—showing violence more likely to happen in real life—also produced more aggressive feelings than less-realistic games (Bartlett & Rodeheffer, 2009). Although much remains to be learned, these studies challenge the **catharsis** hypothesis— the idea that violent games allow people to safely express their aggressive tendencies and "get their anger out" (Kutner & Olson, 2008). Practicing violence breeds rather than releases violence, say catharsis critics. Yet the idea that games might relieve angry feelings is one of the main draws of violent video games for angry people (Bushman & Whitaker, 2010). Unfortunately, say critics, this strategy is likely to backfire, leading to more anger and aggression.

In 2005, California State Senator Leland Yee proposed a law banning the sale of violent video games to those under 18. The bill was signed into law, but video game manufacturers immediately sued, and it never went into effect. The U.S. Supreme Court heard the case in 2010, and more than 100 social scientists signed a statement in support of the law, writing that "Overall, the research data conclude that exposure to violent video games causes an increase in the likelihood of aggressive behavior." In 2011, the Supreme Court struck down the law, primarily citing the First Amendment's guarantee of free speech but also expressing doubts that the research showed "a direct causal link between playing violent video games and actual harm to minors" (Scalia, 2011).

Christopher Ferguson and John Kilburn (2010) signed a statement to the Supreme Court criticizing the California law. They point out that from 1996 to 2006, when violent video game sales were increasing, real-life youth violence was decreasing. Ferguson and Kilburn also argue that the effects of violent video games on aggression are small—only some people who play violent video games will act aggressively in real life. In return, Craig Anderson and his colleagues (2010) argue that the violent gaming effect is larger than the toxic effects of asbestos or the effect of secondhand smoke on lung cancer. Not everyone exposed to asbestos or secondhand smoke will develop cancer, they point out, but they

catharsis
Emotional release. The catharsis view of aggression is that the aggressive drive is reduced when one "releases" aggressive energy, either by acting aggressively or by fantasizing aggression.

Is violent video game-playing cathartic? toxic? or neutral? Experiments offer some answers.
Andrew Lichtenstein/The Image Works

are still considered public health dangers. Other critics point out that most experiments on violent video games have not used control games similar in competitiveness or pace of action, creating the possibility that these factors increase aggression rather than the violence in the games per se (Adachi & Willoughy, 2011).

In addition, video games are not all bad—not all of them are violent, and even the violent games improve hand-eye coordination, reaction time, spatial ability, and selective attention (Dye et al., 2009; Sanchez, 2012; Wu et al., 2012). Moreover, game playing is focused fun that helps satisfy basic needs for a sense of competence, control, and social connection (Przyblski et al., 2010). No wonder an experiment that randomly assigned 6- to 9-year-old boys to receive a game system found them spending an average of 40 minutes a day on it over the next few months. The downside: They spent less time on schoolwork, resulting in lower reading and writing scores than the control group that did not get a game system (Weis & Cerankosky, 2010).

What about playing prosocial games in which people help each other—the conceptual opposite of violent games? In three studies with children and adults in Singapore, Japan, and the United States, those who played prosocial video games helped others, shared, and cooperated more in real-life situations (Gentile et al., 2009). German students randomly assigned to play a prosocial (vs. neutral) game were less physically and socially aggressive toward someone who had insulted them (Greitemeyer et al., 2012). As Douglas Gentile and Craig Anderson (2011) conclude, "Video games are excellent teachers." Educational games teach children reading and math, prosocial games teach prosocial behavior, and violent games teach violence, they note. We do what we're taught to do, whether that's to help or to hurt.

As a concerned scientist, Craig Anderson (2003, 2004) (see "The Inside Story, Craig Anderson on Video-Game Violence") therefore encourages parents to discover what their kids are ingesting and to ensure that their media diet, as least in their own home, is healthy. Parents may not be able to control what their child watches, plays, and eats in someone else's home. Nor can they control the media's effect on their children's peer culture. (That is why advising parents to "just say no" is naive.) But parents can oversee consumption in their own home and provide increased time for alternative activities. Networking with other parents can build a kid-friendly neighborhood. And schools can help by providing media-awareness education.

"It is hard to measure the increasing acceptance of brutality in American life, but its evidence is everywhere, starting with the video games of killing that are a principal entertainment of boys."

—Susan Sontag,
Regarding the Torture of Others, 2004

THE inside STORY

Understanding the clearly harmful effects being documented by TV/film violence researchers, I was disturbed as I noticed the increasing violence in video games. With one of my graduate students, Karen Dill, I therefore began correlational and experimental investigations that intersected with growing public concern and led to my testifying before a U.S. Senate subcommittee and consulting for a wide array of government and public policy groups, including parent and child advocacy organizations.

Although it is gratifying to see one's research have a positive impact, the video-game industry has gone to great lengths to dismiss the research, much as 30 years ago cigarette manufacturers ridiculed basic medical research by asking how many Marlboros a lab rat had to smoke before contracting cancer. I also get some pretty nasty mail from gamers, and the volume of requests for information led me to offer resources and answers at www.psychology.iastate.edu/faculty/caa.

Many people believe that the best way to enhance understanding of a complicated topic is to find people who will give opposite views and give each "side" equal time. Media violence news stories typically give equal time to industry representatives and their preferred "experts" along with reassuring words from a carefree 4-year-old, which can leave the impression that we know less than we do. If all the experts in a given area agree, does this idea of "fairness" and "balance" make sense? Or should we expect that legitimate experts will have published peer-reviewed original research articles on the issue at hand?

Craig A. Anderson
Iowa State University
Courtesy of Iowa State University

Group Influences

We have considered what provokes *individuals* to aggress. If frustrations, insults, and aggressive models heighten the aggressive tendencies of isolated people, such factors are likely to prompt the same reaction in groups. As a riot begins, aggressive acts often spread rapidly after the "trigger" example of one antagonistic person. Seeing looters freely helping themselves to TV sets, normally law-abiding bystanders may drop their moral inhibitions and imitate.

Groups can amplify aggressive reactions partly by diffusing responsibility. Decisions to attack in war typically are made by strategists remote from the front lines. They give orders, but others carry them out. Does such distancing make it easier to recommend aggression?

In one experiment, students either *shocked* someone or simply *advised* someone else how much shock to administer. When the recipient had not done anything to provoke the aggressor, characteristic of most victims of mass aggression, the advisers recommended more shock than given by the frontline participants, who felt more directly responsible for any hurt (Gaebelein & Mander, 1978).

Diffusion of responsibility increases not only with distance but also with numbers. Brian Mullen (1986) analyzed information from 60 lynchings between 1899 and 1946 and made an interesting discovery: The greater the number of people in a lynch mob, the more vicious the murder and mutilation.

Through social "contagion," groups magnify aggressive tendencies, much as they polarize other tendencies. Examples are youth gangs, soccer fans, rapacious soldiers, urban rioters, and what

Social contagion. When 17 juvenile, orphaned male bull elephants were relocated during the mid-1990s to a South African park, they became an out-of-control adolescent gang and killed 40 white rhinoceros. In 1998, concerned park officials relocated 6 older, stronger bull elephants into their midst. The result: The rampaging soon quieted down (Slotow et al., 2000). One of these dominant bulls, at left, faces down several of the juveniles.
Gus van Dyk

Scandinavians call "mobbing"—schoolchildren in groups repeatedly harassing or attacking an insecure, weak schoolmate (Lagerspetz et al., 1982). Mobbing is a group activity.

Youths sharing antisocial tendencies and lacking close family bonds and expectations of academic success may find social identity in a gang. As group identity develops, conformity pressures and deindividuation increase (Staub, 1996). Self-identity diminishes as members give themselves over to the group, often feeling a satisfying oneness with the others. The frequent result is social contagion—group-fed arousal, disinhibition, and polarization. As gang expert Arnold Goldstein (1994) observed, until gang members marry out, age out, get a job, go to prison, or die, they hang out. They define their turf, display their colors, challenge rivals, and sometimes commit delinquent acts and fight over drugs, territory, honor, women, or insults.

The twentieth-century massacres that claimed more than 150 million lives were "not the sums of individual actions," noted Robert Zajonc (2000). *"Genocide is not the plural of homicide."* Massacres are *social* phenomena fed by "moral imperatives"—a collective mentality (including images, rhetoric, and ideology) that mobilizes a group or a culture for extraordinary actions. The massacres of Rwanda's Tutsis, of Europe's Jews, and of America's native population were collective phenomena requiring widespread support, organization, and participation. Before launching the genocidal initiative, Rwanda's Hutu government and business leaders bought and distributed 2 million Chinese machetes. Over 3 months, the Hutu attackers reportedly would get up, eat a hearty breakfast, gather together, and then go hunt their former neighbors who had fled. They would hack to death anyone they found, then return home, wash, and socialize over a few beers (Dalrymple, 2007; Hatzfeld, 2007).

Experiments in Israel by Yoram Jaffe and Yoel Yinon (1983) confirm that groups can amplify aggressive tendencies. In one, university men angered by a supposed fellow participant retaliated with decisions to give much stronger shocks when in groups than when alone. In another experiment (Jaffe et al., 1981), people decided, either alone or in groups, how much punishing shock to give someone for incorrect answers on a task. As Figure 8 shows, individuals gave progressively more of the assumed shock as the experiment proceeded, and group decision making magnified this individual tendency. When circumstances provoke an individual's aggressive reaction, the addition of group interaction will often amplify it. (See "Research Close-Up: When Provoked, Are Groups More Aggressive Than Individuals?")

Perhaps you can remember a time in middle school or high school when you or someone you knew was bullied—either verbally or physically. Much of the time, other students watch bullying as it happens, or even join in. These bystanders can play an active role in the aggressive act of bullying—for example, by contributing to the humiliation by laughing or cheering (Salmivalli et al., 1999). Or they may defend the victim. An effective antibullying program used in Finland found that when bystanders stop rewarding bullies with positive feedback and status, bullying declined (Karna et al., 2011).

> "The worst barbarity of war is that it forces men collectively to commit acts against which individually they would revolt with their whole being."
>
> —Ellen Key,
> *War, Peace, and the Future,* 1916

FIGURE :: 8

Group-Enhanced Aggression

When individuals chose how much shock to administer as punishment for wrong answers, they escalated the shock level as the experiment proceeded. Group decision making further polarized this tendency.
Source: Data from Jaffe et al., 1981.

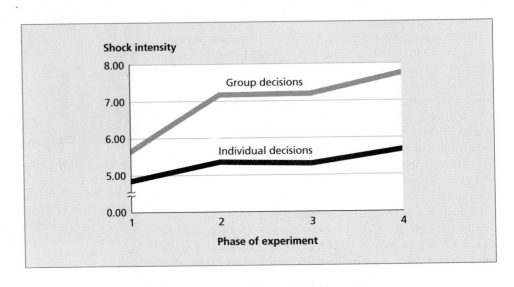

research
CLOSE-UP

When Provoked, Are Groups More Aggressive Than Individuals?

Aggression researchers are noted for their creative methods for measuring aggression, which in various experiments has involved such tactics as administering shock, blasting sound, and hurting people's feelings. Holly McGregor and her colleagues (1998) took their cue from a cook's arrest for assault after lacing two police officers' food with Tabasco sauce, and from child abuse cases in which parents have force-fed hot sauce to their children. This inspired the idea of measuring aggression by having people decide how much hot sauce someone else must consume.

That is what Bruce Meier and Verlin Hinsz (2004) did when comparing aggressive behavior by groups and individuals. They told participants, either as individuals or in groups of three, that they were studying the relationship between personality and food preferences, and that they would be tasting and rating hot sauce. The experimenter explained that he needed to remain blind as to how much hot sauce each individual or group would be consuming and so needed the participants to choose the portion. After having the participants sample the intense hot sauce

using a wooden stick, the experimenter left to collect the hot sauce that another individual or group had supposedly selected. He returned with a cup filled with 48 grams of the sauce, which each participant expected later to consume. The participants, in turn, were now to spoon as much or as little hot sauce as they wished into a cup for the supposed other people to consume. (In reality, no participant was forced to consume anything.)

The striking result, seen in Figure 9, was that groups retaliated by dishing out 24 percent more hot sauce than did individuals, and that group targets were given 24 percent more than were individuals. Thus, given toxic circumstances, interaction with a group (as a source or target) amplifies individual aggressive tendencies. This finding was particularly evident in the intergroup condition. Group members, after each receiving a nasty 48 grams of hot sauce, retaliated by dishing out 93 grams of hot sauce for each member of the group that had given them hot sauce. Apparently, surmised Meier and Hinsz, groups not only respond more aggressively to provocation but also perceive more hostility from other groups than they do from individuals.

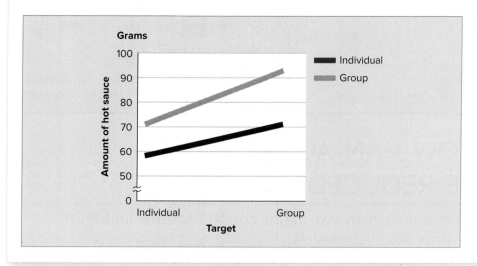

FIGURE :: 9

Mean Amount of Hot Sauce Dished Out (grams)
Source: Meier & Hinsz, 2004.

Aggression studies provide an apt opportunity to ask how well social psychology's laboratory findings generalize to everyday life. Do the circumstances that trigger someone to deliver electric shock or allocate hot sauce really tell us anything about the circumstances that trigger verbal abuse or a punch in the face? Craig Anderson and Brad Bushman (1997; Bushman & Anderson, 1998) note that social psychologists have studied aggression in both the laboratory and everyday worlds, and the findings are strikingly consistent. In *both* contexts, increased aggression is predicted by the following:

- Being male
- Aggressive or anger-prone personalities
- Alcohol use

- Violence viewing
- Anonymity
- Provocation
- The presence of weapons
- Group interaction

The laboratory allows us to test and revise theories under controlled conditions. Real-world events inspire ideas and provide the venue for applying our theories. Aggression research illustrates how the interplay between studies in the controlled lab and the complex real world advances psychology's contribution to human welfare. Hunches gained from everyday experience inspire theories, which stimulate laboratory research, which then deepens our understanding and our ability to apply psychology to real problems.

SUMMING UP: What Are Some Influences on Aggression?

- Many factors exert influence on aggression. One factor is aversive experiences, which include not only frustrations but also discomfort, pain, and personal attacks, both physical and verbal.

- Arousal from almost any source, even physical exercise or sexual stimulation, can be transformed into other emotions, such as anger.

- Aggression cues, such as the presence of a gun, increase the likelihood of aggressive behavior.

- Viewing violence (1) breeds a modest increase in aggressive behavior, especially in people who are provoked, (2) desensitizes viewers to aggression, and (3) alters their perceptions of reality. These findings parallel the results of research on the effects of viewing violent pornography, which can increase men's aggression

against women and distort their perceptions of women's responses to sexual coercion.

- Television permeates the daily life of millions of people and portrays considerable violence. Correlational and experimental studies converge on the conclusion that heavy exposure to televised violence correlates with aggressive behavior.

- Playing violent video games may increase aggressive thinking, feelings, and behavior even more than television or movies do, because the experience involves much more active participation than those other media.

- Much aggression is committed by groups. Circumstances that provoke individuals may also provoke groups. By diffusing responsibility and polarizing actions, group situations amplify aggressive reactions.

HOW CAN AGGRESSION BE REDUCED?

Examine how we might counteract the factors that provoke aggression.

Can we reduce aggression? Here we look at how theory and research suggest ways to control it.

Catharsis?

"Youngsters should be taught to vent their anger," surmised advice columnist Ann Landers (1969). If a person "bottles up his rage, we have to find an outlet. We have to give him an opportunity of letting off steam," asserted psychiatrist Fritz Perls (1973). After violent video games were implicated in a 2012 mass shooting, one defender of the games wrote, "Could it be that violent video games are an important outlet for aggression? That, on the whole, these games and 'play violence' let us express anger and aggression in a safe way?" (Gilsdorf, 2013). Such statements assume the "hydraulic model," which implies accumulated aggressive energy, like dammed-up water, needs a release.

The concept of catharsis is usually credited to Aristotle. Although Aristotle said nothing about aggression, he did argue that we can purge emotions by experiencing them and that viewing the classic tragedies therefore enabled a catharsis (purging) of pity and fear. To have an emotion excited, he believed, is to have that emotion released (Butcher, 1951). The catharsis hypothesis has been extended to include the emotional release supposedly obtained not only by observing drama but also through our recalling and reliving past events, through our expressing emotions, and through our actions.

Does venting your anger online reduce or increase aggression? Studies find it increases it.
© Lisa S./Shutterstock.com

Assuming that aggressive action or fantasy drains pent-up aggression, some therapists and group leaders have encouraged people to ventilate suppressed aggression by acting it out—by whopping one another with foam bats or beating a bed with a tennis racket while screaming. If led to believe that catharsis effectively vents emotions, people will react more aggressively to an insult as a way to improve their mood (Bushman et al., 2001). Some psychologists, believing that catharsis is therapeutic, advise parents to encourage children's release of emotional tension through aggressive play. As you saw earlier, it is also a common argument to defend violent video games. But does catharsis work? Do those who vent their anger become less aggressive—or more aggressive?

In laboratory tests of catharsis, angered participants hit a punching bag while either ruminating about someone who angered them or thinking about becoming physically fit. A third group did not hit the punching bag. When given a chance to administer loud blasts of noise to the person who angered them, people in the punching bag plus rumination condition felt angrier and were most aggressive. Moreover, doing nothing at all more effectively reduced aggression than did "blowing off steam" by hitting the bag (Bushman, 2002). Venting anger caused more aggression, not less.

Real-life experiments have produced similar results. One study examined Internet users who frequently visit "rant" sites where people are encouraged to express their anger. Did the opportunity to express their hostility reduce it? No. Their hostility and anger increased and their happiness decreased (Martin et al., 2013). Expressing hostility bred more hostility. Several studies have found that Canadian and American spectators of football, wrestling, and hockey games exhibit *more* hostility after viewing the event than before (Arms et al., 1979; Goldstein & Arms, 1971; Russell, 1983). Instead of reducing their anger, viewing these aggressive sports instead increased their anger. As Brad Bushman (2002) notes, "Venting to reduce anger is like using gasoline to put out a fire."

Cruel acts beget cruel attitudes. Furthermore, little aggressive acts can breed their own justification. People derogate their victims, rationalizing further aggression.

Retaliation may, in the short run, reduce tension and even provide pleasure (Ramirez et al., 2005). But in the long run it fuels more negative feelings. When people who have been provoked hit a punching bag, even when they believe it will be cathartic, the effect is the opposite—leading them to exhibit *more* cruelty, report Bushman and his colleagues (1999, 2000, 2001). "It's like the old joke," reflected Bushman (1999). "How do you get to Carnegie Hall? Practice, practice, practice. How do you become a very angry person? The answer is the same. Practice, practice, practice."

"He who gives way to violent gestures will increase his rage."
—Charles Darwin,
The Expression of the Emotions in Man and Animals, 1872

Should we therefore bottle up anger and aggressive urges? Silent sulking is hardly more effective, because it allows us to continue reciting our grievances as we conduct conversations in our heads. Bushman and his colleagues (2005) experimented with the toxic effect of such rumination. After being provoked by an obnoxious experimenter with insults such as, "Can't you follow directions? Speak louder!" half were given a distraction (by being asked to write an essay about their campus landscape), and half were induced to ruminate (by writing an essay about their experiences as a research participant). Next, they were mildly insulted by a supposed fellow participant (actually a confederate), to whom they responded by prescribing a hot sauce dose this person would have to consume. The distracted participants, their anger now abated, prescribed only a mild dose. The still-seething ruminators displaced their aggressive urge and prescribed twice as much.

Fortunately, there are nonaggressive ways to express our feelings and to inform others how their behavior affects us. Across cultures, those who reframe accusatory "you" messages as "I" messages—"I feel angry about what you said," or, "I get irritated when you leave dirty dishes"—communicate their feelings in a way that better enables the other person to make a positive response (Kubany et al., 1995). We can be assertive without being aggressive.

A Social Learning Approach

If aggressive behavior is learned, then there is hope for its control. Let us briefly review factors that influence aggression and speculate how to counteract them.

Aversive experiences such as frustrated expectations and personal attacks predispose hostile aggression. So it is wise to refrain from planting false, unreachable expectations in people's minds. Anticipated rewards and costs influence instrumental aggression. This suggests that we should reward cooperative, nonaggressive behavior.

In experiments, children become less aggressive when caregivers ignore their aggressive behavior and reinforce their nonaggressive behavior (Hamblin et al., 1969). Punishing the aggressor is less consistently effective. Threatened punishment deters aggression only under ideal conditions: when the punishment is strong, prompt, and sure; when it is combined with reward for the desired behavior; and when the recipient is not angry (R. A. Baron, 1977).

Moreover, there are limits to punishment's effectiveness. Most homicides are impulsive, hot aggression—the result of an argument, an insult, or an attack. If mortal aggression were cool and instrumental, we could hope that waiting until it happens and severely punishing the criminal afterward would deter such acts. In that world, states that impose the death penalty might have a lower murder rate than states without the death penalty. But in our world of hot homicide, that is not so (Costanzo, 1998). As John Darley and Adam Alter (2009) note, "A remarkable amount of crime is committed by impulsive individuals, frequently young males, who are frequently drunk or high on drugs, and who often are in packs of similar and similarly mindless young men." No wonder, they say, that trying to reduce crime by increasing sentences has proven so fruitless, whereas on-the-street policing that produces more arrests has produced encouraging results, such as a 50 percent drop in gun-related crimes in some cities.

Thus, we must *prevent* aggression before it happens. We must teach nonaggressive conflict-resolution strategies. When psychologists Sandra Jo Wilson and Mark Lipsey (2005) assembled data from 249 studies of school violence prevention programs, they found encouraging results, especially for programs focused on selected "problem" students. After being taught problem-solving skills, emotion-control strategies, and conflict resolution techniques, the typical 20 percent of students engaging in some violent or disruptive behavior in a typical school year was reduced to 13 percent. Children whose parents were more permissive (and thus rarely set limits on behavior and did not enforce rules) grew into more aggressive adolescents (Ehrenreich et al., 2014), suggesting that more authoritative parenting can prevent aggression. (But not overly harsh parenting—spanking and other forms of physical punishment can also cause aggression: Gershoff, 2002). Bullying (including cyberbullying) is reduced when parents or teachers monitor children closely (Campbell, 2005; Wingate et al., 2013) and when children are educated about what behaviors are considered bullying (Mishna, 2004). Other programs focus on teaching empathy and encourage children not to ignore bullying (Noble, 2003).

To foster a gentler world, we could model and reward sensitivity and cooperation from an early age, perhaps by training parents how to discipline without violence. Training programs encourage parents to reinforce desirable behaviors and to frame statements positively ("When you finish cleaning your room, you can go play," rather than, "If you don't clean your room, you're grounded"). One "aggression-replacement program" has kept many juvenile offenders and gang members from being

Educating children about bullying and monitoring them more closely can help reduce cyberbullying.
© SpeedKingz/Shutterstock.com

arrested again by teaching the youths and their parents communication skills, training them to control anger, and raising their level of moral reasoning (Goldstein et al., 1998).

If observing aggressive models lowers inhibitions and elicits imitation, we might also reduce brutal, dehumanizing portrayals in media—steps comparable to those already taken to reduce racist and sexist portrayals. We can also inoculate children against the effects of media violence. Wondering if the TV networks would ever "face the facts and change their programming," Eron and Huesmann (1984) taught 170 Oak Park, Illinois, children that television portrays the world unrealistically, that aggression is less common and less effective than TV suggests, and that aggressive behavior is undesirable. (Drawing upon attitude research, Eron and Huesmann encouraged children to draw these inferences themselves and to attribute their expressed criticisms of television to their own convictions.) When restudied two years later, these children were less influenced by TV violence than were untrained children. In a more recent study, Stanford University used 18 classroom lessons to persuade children to simply reduce their TV watching and video game-playing (Robinson et al., 2001). They reduced their TV viewing by a third—and the children's aggressive behavior at school dropped 25 percent compared with children in a control school. Even music can help reduce aggression when it models the right attitude: German students who were randomly assigned to hear prosocial music like "We Are the World" and "Help" behaved less aggressively than those who heard neutral music (Greitemeyer, 2011). Other ideas for how to prevent aggression come from studies of differences among people. For example, people who are sensitive to disgust are less aggressive (Pond et al., 2012), suggesting that emphasizing the disgusting aspects of violence might help prevent aggression. People who see moral rules as negotiable (agreeing, for example, "Cheating is appropriate behavior because no one gets hurt") are more aggressive (Gini et al., 2014), suggesting that teaching some non-negotiable rules and moral reasoning ("It's never okay to hit," "Cheating hurts everyone") might reduce aggressive behavior.

Suggestions such as these can help us minimize aggression. But given the complexity of aggression's causes and the difficulty of controlling them, who can feel the optimism expressed by Andrew Carnegie's forecast that in the twentieth century, "To kill a man will be considered as disgusting as we in this day consider it disgusting to eat one." Since Carnegie uttered those words in 1900, some 200 million human beings have been killed. It is a sad irony that although today we understand human aggression better than ever before, humanity's inhumanity endures.

Culture Change and World Violence

Nevertheless, cultures can change. "The Vikings slaughtered and plundered," notes science writer Natalie Angier. "Their descendants in Sweden haven't fought a war in nearly 200 years." Indeed, as psychologist Steven Pinker (2011) documents, all forms of violence—including wars, genocide, and murders—are less common in recent years than in past eras. We've graduated from plundering neighboring tribes to economic interdependence, from a world in which Western European countries initiated two new wars per year over 600 years to, for the past seven decades, zero wars. Surprisingly, to those of us who love modern British murder mysteries, "a contemporary Englishman has about a 50-fold less chance of being murdered than his compatriot in the Middle Ages," notes Pinker. In all but one western democracy, the death penalty has been abolished. And the sole exception—the United States—no longer practices it for witchcraft, counterfeiting, and horse theft. In fact, the United States has seen declines in, or the disappearance of, aggressive and violent acts such as

- lynchings,
- hate crimes,
- rapes,
- corporal punishment, and
- antigay attitudes and intimidation.

We can, Pinker concludes, be grateful "for the institutions of civilization and enlightenment [economic trade, education, government policing and justice] that have made it possible."

SUMMING UP: How Can Aggression Be Reduced?

- How can we minimize aggression? Contrary to the *catharsis* hypothesis, expressing aggression by catharsis tends to breed further aggression, not reduce it.

- The social learning approach suggests controlling aggression by counteracting the factors that provoke it: by reducing aversive stimulation, by rewarding and modeling nonaggression, and by eliciting reactions incompatible with aggression.

POSTSCRIPT:
Reforming a Violent Culture

In 1960, the United States (apologies to readers elsewhere, but we Americans do have a special problem with violence) had 3.3 police officers for every reported violent crime. In 1993 we had 3.5 crimes for every police officer (Walinsky, 1995). Since then, the crime rate has lessened, but it remains unacceptably high. Still, my [DM's] small campus, which required no campus police in 1960, now employs 6 full-time and 7 part-time officers, and offers a nightly shuttle service to transport students around campus.

Americans' ideas for protecting ourselves abound:

- Buy a gun for self-protection. (We have . . . about 300 million guns . . . which puts one at tripled risk of being murdered, often by a family member, and at doubled risk of suicide [Anglemyer et al., 2014].) In assaults where someone had some chance to resist, those who had a gun were more than 5 times more likely to be shot (Branas et al., 2009). Safer nations, such as Canada and Britain, mandate domestic disarmament.

- Build more prisons. (We have, but until recently crime continued to escalate. Moreover, the social and fiscal costs of incarcerating more than 2 million people, mostly men, are enormous.)

- Impose a "three strikes and you're out" requirement of lifetime incarceration for those convicted of three violent crimes. (But are we really ready to pay for all the new prisons—and prison hospitals and nursing homes—we would need to house and care for aging former muggers? Prisons in cash-strapped California, where three strikes has been the law since the 1990s, are perpetually overcrowded.)

- Deter brutal crime and eliminate the worst offenders as some countries do—by executing the offenders. To show that killing people is wrong—kill people who kill people. (But nearly all the cities and states with the dozen highest violent-crime rates already have the death penalty. Because most homicide is impulsive or under the influence of drugs or alcohol, murderers rarely calculate consequences.)

An alternative approach is suggested by a story about the rescue of a drowning person from a rushing river. Having successfully administered first aid, the rescuer spots another struggling person and pulls her out, too. After a half dozen repetitions, the rescuer suddenly turns and starts running away while the river sweeps yet another floundering person into view. "Aren't you going to rescue that fellow?" asks a bystander. "Heck no," the rescuer shouts. "I'm going upstream to find out what's pushing all these people in."

To be sure, we need police, prisons, and social workers, all of whom help us deal with the social pathologies that plague us. It's fine to swat the mosquitoes but better if we can drain the swamps—by infusing our culture with nonviolent ideals, challenging the social toxins that corrupt youth, and renewing the moral roots of character.

Attraction and Intimacy

LIKING AND LOVING OTHERS

Image100/Corbis

"The best and most beautiful things in the world cannot be seen nor even touched, but just felt in the heart."

—Letter from 11-year-old Helen Keller, 1891

Our lifelong dependence on one another puts relationships at the core of our existence. In your beginning, there very likely was an attraction—the attraction between a particular man and a particular woman. Aristotle called humans "the social animal." Indeed, we have what today's social psychologists call a **need to belong**—to connect with others in enduring, close relationships.

Social psychologists Roy Baumeister and Mark Leary (1995; Leary, 2010) illustrate the power of social attachments:

- For our ancestors, mutual attachments enabled group survival. When hunting game or erecting shelter, 10 hands were better than 2.

- The bonds of love can lead to children, whose survival chances are boosted by the nurturing of two bonded parents who support each other.

What leads to friendship and attraction?

What is love?

What enables close relationships?

How do relationships end?

Postscript: Making love

need to belong

A motivation to bond with others in relationships that provide ongoing, positive interactions.

- For children and their caregivers, social attachments enhance survival. Suddenly separated from each other, parent and toddler may both panic until reunited in a tight embrace. When reared instead under extreme neglect or in institutions without belonging to anybody, children become pathetic, anxious creatures.

- Relationships consume much of life. How much of your waking life is spent talking with people? One sampling of 10,000 tape recordings of half-minute slices of university students' waking hours (using belt-worn recorders) found them talking to someone 28 percent of the time—and that doesn't count the time they spent listening to someone (Mehl & Pennebaker, 2003).

- When not face-to-face, the world's 7 billion people connect by voice and texting through their nearly 7 billion cell-phone subscriptions (International Telecommunication Union, 2014) or through social networks such as Facebook. In the United States, 94 percent of entering college students use social networking sites, with 27 percent spending 6 or more hours a week on them (Eagan et al., 2014). Half of 14- to-17-year-olds send 100 or more texts a day (Lenhart, 2012); 87 percent text at least once a day (Thompson, 2014). Our need to belong motivates our investment in being continuously connected.

- For people everywhere, actual and hoped-for close relationships can dominate thinking and emotions. Finding a supportive person in whom we can confide, we feel accepted and prized. Falling in love, we feel irrepressible joy. When relationships with partners, family, and friends are healthy, self-esteem—a barometer of our relationships—rides high (Denissen et al., 2008). Longing for acceptance and love, we spend billions on cosmetics, clothes, and diets. Even seemingly dismissive people relish being accepted (Carvallo & Gabriel, 2006).

- Exiled, imprisoned, or in solitary confinement, people ache for their own people and places. Rejected, we are at risk for depression (Nolan et al., 2003). Time passes more slowly and life seems less meaningful (Twenge et al., 2003). When queried 3 months after arriving on a large university campus, many international students, like some homesick domestic students, report declining feelings of well-being (Cemalcilar & Falbo, 2008).

- For the jilted, the widowed, and the sojourner in a strange place, the loss of social bonds triggers pain, loneliness, or withdrawal. Losing a close relationship, adults feel jealous, distraught, or bereaved, as well as mindful of death and life's fragility. After relocating, people—especially those with the strongest need to belong—typically feel homesick (Watt & Badger, 2009).

- Reminders of death in turn heighten our need to belong, to be with others, and to hold close those we love (Mikulincer et al., 2003; Wisman & Koole, 2003). Facing the terror of 9/11, millions of Americans called and connected with loved ones. Likewise, the shocking death of a classmate, a co-worker, or a family member brings people together, their differences no longer mattering.

"There's no question in my mind about what stands at the heart of the communication revolution—the human desire to connect."

—Josh Silverman, President of Skype, 2009

We are, indeed, social animals. We need to belong. As with other motivations, we pursue belonging when we don't have it, and seek less when our needs are fulfilled (DeWall et al., 2009, 2011). When we do belong—when we feel supported by close, intimate relationships—we tend to be healthier and happier. Satisfy the need to belong in balance with two other human needs—to feel *autonomy* and *competence*—and the typical result is a deep sense of well-being (Deci & Ryan, 2002; Milyavskaya et al., 2009; Sheldon & Niemiec, 2006). Happiness is feeling connected, free, and capable.

Social psychologist Kipling Williams (2001, 2007, 2009, 2011) has explored what happens when our need to belong is thwarted by *ostracism* (acts of excluding or ignoring). Humans in all cultures, whether in schools, workplaces, or homes, use ostracism to regulate social behavior. Some of us know what it is like to be shunned—to be avoided, met with averted eyes, or given the silent treatment. The silent treatment is "emotional abuse" and "a terrible, terrible weapon to use," say those who have experienced it from a family member or a co-worker. In experiments, people who are left out of a simple game of ball tossing feel deflated and stressed. Ostracism hurts, and the social pain is keenly felt—more than those who are not ostracized ever know (Nordgren et al., 2011). Ostracism may be even worse than bullying: Bullying, though extremely negative, at least acknowledges someone's existence and importance, whereas ostracism treats a person as if she doesn't exist at all (Williams & Nida, 2009). In one study, children who were ostracized but not bullied felt worse than those who were bullied but not ostracized (Carpenter et al., 2012). If only we better empathized with those rejected, there might be less tolerance of ostracism.

Sometimes deflation turns nasty, as when people lash out at the very people whose acceptance they desire (Reijntjes et al., 2011) or engage in self-defeating behavior. In several experiments, students randomly assigned to be rejected by their peers (versus those who were accepted) became more likely to engage in self-defeating behaviors (such as procrastinating by reading magazines) and less able to regulate their behavior (such as eating cookies; Baumeister et al., 2005; Twenge et al., 2002). Apparently the stereotype of someone eating lots of ice cream after a breakup isn't far off.

This might result from a self-control breakdown: Ostracized people show deficits in brain mechanisms that inhibit unwanted behavior (Otten & Jonas, 2013). Outside of the laboratory, rejected children were, two years later, more likely to have self-regulation issues, such as not finishing tasks and not listening to directions (Stenseng et al., 2014). In lab experiments, socially rejected people also became more likely to disparage or blast unpleasant noise at someone who had insulted them, were less likely to help others, and were more likely to cheat and steal (Kouchaki & Wareham, 2015; Poon et al., 2013; Twenge et al., 2001, 2007). If a small laboratory experience of being "voted off the island" could produce such aggression, noted the researchers, one wonders what aggressive and antisocial tendencies "might arise from a series of important rejections or chronic exclusion."

Williams and Steve Nida (2011) were surprised to discover that even "cyber-ostracism" by faceless people whom one will never meet still takes a toll. (Perhaps you have experienced this when feeling ignored in a chat room or when your email is not answered.) The researchers had more than 5,000 participants from dozens of countries play a Web-based game of throwing a ball with two others (actually computer-generated fellow players). Those ostracized by the other players experienced poorer moods and became more likely to

> "A man's Social Self is the recognition he gets from his mates. . . . If no one turned round when we entered, answered when we spoke, or minded what we did, but if every person . . . acted as if we were non-existing things, a kind of rage and impotent despair would ere long well up in us."
>
> —William James, *Principles of Psychology,* 1890

A recipe for violence: A review of 126 school shootings in 13 countries found that 88 percent of the shooters experienced social rejection or social conflict at school (Sommer et al., 2014). In a chilling video made before he killed 7 people near the University of California, Santa Barbara, in 2014, Elliot Rodger described his rejection by women.
Robyn Beck/AFP/Getty Images

conform to others' wrong judgments on a subsequent perceptual task. Exclusion hurts longest for anxious people (Zadro et al., 2006). It hurts more for younger than older adults (Hawkley et al., 2011). And it hurts no less when it comes from a group that the rest of society spurns—Australian KKK members in one experiment (Gonsalkorale & Williams, 2006).

Williams and his psychology faculty colleagues at the University of Toledo (2001) found ostracism stressful even when each was ignored for an agreed-upon day by the unresponsive four others. Contrary to their expectations that this would be a laughter-filled role-playing game, the simulated ostracism disrupted work, interfered with pleasant social functioning, and "caused temporary concern, anxiety, paranoia, and general fragility of spirit." To thwart our deep need to belong is to unsettle our life.

Ostracized people exhibit heightened activity in a brain cortex area that also activates in response to physical pain (Figure 1). Ostracism's social pain, much like physical pain, increases aggression (Riva et al., 2011). Hurt feelings are also embodied in a depressed heart rate (Moor et al., 2010). Heartbreak makes for heart brake.

Indeed, the pain of social rejection is so real in the brain that a pain-relieving Tylenol can reduce hurt feelings (DeWall et al., 2010), as can sending a light electrical current to the brain region in which rejection is felt (Riva et al., 2012). Ostracism's opposite—feeling love—activates brain reward systems. When looking at their beloved's picture, university students feel markedly less pain when immersing their hands in cold water (Younger et al., 2010). Ostracism is a real pain, and love is a natural painkiller.

Asked to recall a time when they were socially excluded—perhaps left alone in the dorm when others went out—people in one experiment even perceived the room temperature as five degrees colder than did those asked to recall a social acceptance experience (Zhong & Leonardelli, 2008). Such recollections come easily: People remember and relive past social pain more easily than past physical pain (Chen et al., 2008). The effect moves the other way as well: Students who were ordered to ostracize others were just as distressed as those who were ostracized (Legate et al., 2013) and felt less human (Bastian et al., 2012).

Roy Baumeister (2005) finds a silver lining in the rejection research. When recently excluded people experience a safe opportunity to make a new friend, they "seem willing and even eager to take it." They become more attentive to smiling, accepting faces (DeWall et al., 2009). An exclusion experience also triggers increased mimicry of others' behavior in an unconscious attempt to build rapport (Lakin et al., 2008). And at a societal level, notes Baumeister (2005), meeting the need to belong should pay dividends.

> My colleagues in sociology have pointed out that minority groups who feel excluded show many of the same patterns that our laboratory manipulations elicit: high rates of aggression and antisocial behavior, decreased willingness to cooperate and obey rules, poorer intellectual performance, more self-destructive acts, short-term focus, and the like. If we could promote a more inclusive society, in which more people feel themselves accepted as valued members, some of these tragic patterns might be reduced.

Given the dramatic effects of rejection in experiments, what do you expect are the long-term effects of chronic rejection?

FIGURE :: 1

The Pain of Rejection

Naomi Eisenberger, Matthew Lieberman, and Kipling Williams (2003) reported that social ostracism evokes a brain response similar to that triggered by physical pain.

©2003 American Association for the Advancement of Science.

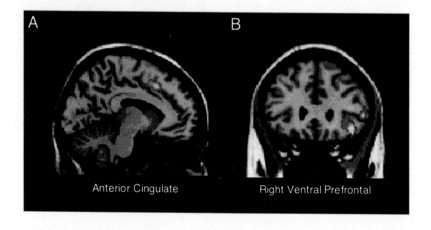

WHAT LEADS TO FRIENDSHIP AND ATTRACTION?

Explain how proximity, physical attractiveness, similarity, and feeling liked nurture liking and loving.

What predisposes one person to like, or to love, another? Few questions about human nature arouse greater interest. The ways affections flourish and fade form the stuff and fluff of soap operas, popular music, novels, and much of our everyday conversation. Long before I [DM] knew there was a field such as social psychology, I had memorized Dale Carnegie's recipe for *How to Win Friends and Influence People.*

So much has been written about liking and loving that almost every conceivable explanation—and its opposite—has already been proposed. For most people—and for you—what factors nurture liking and loving?

- Does absence make the heart grow fonder? Or is someone who is out of sight also out of mind?
- Do likes attract? Or opposites?
- How much do good looks matter?
- What has fostered your close relationships?

Let's start with those factors that lead to friendship and then consider those that sustain and deepen a relationship.

Proximity

One powerful predictor of whether any two people are friends is sheer **proximity.** Proximity can also breed hostility; most assaults and murders involve people who live close to each other. But much more often, proximity prompts liking. Mitja Back and his University of Leipzig colleagues (2008) confirmed this by randomly assigning students to seats at their first class meeting and then having each make a brief self-introduction to the whole class. One year after this one-time seating assignment, students reported greater friendship with those who happened to be seated next to or near them during that first class gathering. In baseball, umpires are less likely to call a strike on batters they have stood closer to throughout the game (Mills, 2014).

Though it may seem trivial to those pondering the mysterious origins of romantic love, sociologists long ago found that most people marry someone who lives in the same neighborhood, or works at the same company or job, or sits in the same class, or visits the same favorite place (Bossard, 1932; Burr, 1973; Clarke, 1952; McPherson et al., 2001). In a Pew survey (2006) of people married or in long-term relationships, 38 percent met at work or at school, and some of the rest met when their paths crossed in their neighborhood, church, or gym or while growing up. Look around. If you marry, it may well be to someone who has lived or worked or studied within walking distance.

INTERACTION

Even more significant than geographic distance is "functional distance"—how often

"I cannot tell how my ankles bend, nor whence the cause of my faintest wish, nor the cause of the friendship I emit, nor the cause of the friendship I take again."
—Walt Whitman, *Song of Myself,* 1855

"I do not believe that friends are necessarily the people you like best, they are merely the people who got there first."
—Sir Peter Ustinov, *Dear Me,* 1979

proximity
Geographical nearness. Proximity (more precisely, "functional distance") powerfully predicts liking.

Close relationships with friends and family contribute to health and happiness.
Tony Freeman/PhotoEdit

"Sometimes I think you only married me because I lived next door!"

© Carolita Johnson/The New Yorker Collection/www.cartoonbank.com

people's paths cross. We become friends with those who use the same entrances, parking lots, and recreation areas. Randomly assigned college roommates who interact frequently are far more likely to become good friends than enemies (Newcomb, 1961). At the college where I [DM] teach, men and women once lived on opposite sides of the campus. Unsurprisingly, cross-sex friendships were uncommon. Now that they live in gender-integrated residence halls and share common sidewalks, lounges, and laundry facilities, friendships between men and women are far more frequent. Interaction enables people to explore their similarities, to sense one another's liking, to learn more about each other, and to perceive themselves as part of a social unit (Arkin & Burger, 1980). In one study, strangers liked each other more the longer they talked (Reis et al., 2011).

So if you're new in town and want to make friends, try to get an apartment near the mailboxes, a desk near the coffeepot, a parking spot near the main buildings, or a room in a dormitory with shared bathroom facilities (Easterbrook & Vignoles, 2015). Such is the architecture of friendship.

"When I'm not near the one I love, I love the one I'm near."

—E. Y. Harburg,
Finian's Rainbow,
London: Chappell Music, 1947

The chance nature of such contacts helps explain a surprising finding. Consider this: If you had an identical twin who became engaged to someone, wouldn't you (being in so many ways similar to your twin) expect to share your twin's attraction to that person? But no, reported researchers David Lykken and Auke Tellegen (1993); only half of identical twins recall really liking their twin's selection, and only 5 percent said, "I could have fallen for my twin's fiancé." Romantic love is often rather like ducklings' imprinting, surmised Lykken and Tellegen. With repeated exposure to and interaction with someone, our infatuation may fix on almost anyone who has roughly similar characteristics and who reciprocates our affection.

Why does proximity breed liking? One factor is availability; obviously, there are fewer opportunities to get to know someone who attends a different school or lives in another town. But there is more to it. Most people like their roommates, or those one door away, better than those two doors away. Those just a few doors away, or even a floor below, hardly live at an inconvenient distance. Moreover, those close by are potential enemies as well as friends. So why does proximity encourage affection more often than animosity?

ANTICIPATION OF INTERACTION

Proximity enables people to discover commonalities and exchange rewards. But merely

Feeling close to those close by: People often become attached to, and sometimes fall in love with, familiar co-workers.
©BananaStock Ltd.

anticipating interaction also boosts liking. John Darley and Ellen Berscheid (1967) discovered this when they gave University of Minnesota women ambiguous information about two other women, one of whom they expected to talk with intimately. Asked how much they liked each one, the women preferred the person they expected to meet. Expecting to date someone also boosts liking (Berscheid et al., 1976). Even voters on the losing side of an election will find their opinions of the winning candidate—whom they are now stuck with—rising (Gilbert et al., 1998).

The phenomenon is adaptive. Anticipatory liking—expecting that someone will be pleasant and compatible—increases the chance of forming a rewarding relationship (Klein & Kunda, 1992; Knight & Vallacher, 1981; Miller & Marks, 1982). How good that we are biased to like those we often see, for our lives are filled with relationships with people whom we may not have chosen but with whom we need to have continuing interactions—roommates, siblings, grandparents, teachers, classmates, co-workers. Liking such people is surely conducive to better relationships and to happier, more productive living.

MERE EXPOSURE

Proximity leads to liking not only because it enables interaction and anticipatory liking but also for a simpler reason: More than 200 experiments reveal that, contrary to an old proverb, familiarity does not breed contempt. Rather, it fosters fondness (Bornstein, 1989, 1999). **Mere exposure** to all sorts of novel stimuli—nonsense syllables, Chinese calligraphy characters, musical selections, faces—boosts people's ratings of them. Do the supposed Turkish words *nansoma, saricik,* and *afworbu* mean something better or something worse than the words *iktitaf, biwojni,* and *kadirga?* University of Michigan students tested by Robert Zajonc (1968, 1970) preferred whichever of these words they had seen most frequently. The more times they had seen a meaningless word or a Chinese ideograph, the more likely they were to say it meant something good (Figure 2).

mere-exposure effect
The tendency for novel stimuli to be liked more or rated more positively after the rater has been repeatedly exposed to them.

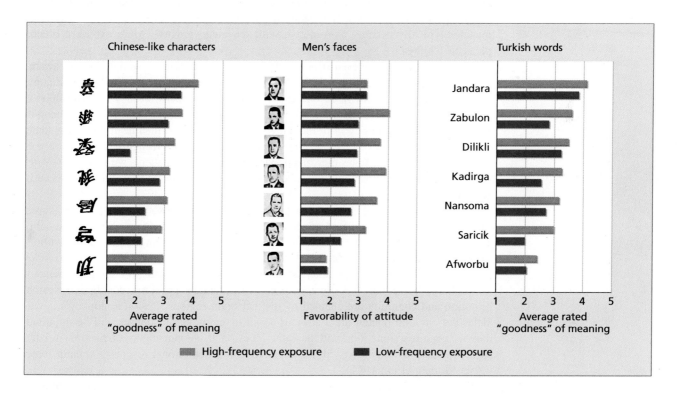

FIGURE :: 2

The Mere-Exposure Effect

Students rated stimuli—a sample of which is shown here—more positively after being shown them repeatedly.
Source: From Zajonc (1968).

I've [DM] tested this idea with my own students. Periodically flash certain nonsense words on a screen. By the end of the semester, students will rate those "words" more positively than other nonsense words they have never before seen. When hurricanes do significant damage—and thus the hurricane name is mentioned frequently—babies are more likely to receive names starting with that letter, presumably due to mere exposure (Berger et al., 2012).

Or consider this: What are your favorite letters of the alphabet? People of differing nationalities, languages, and ages prefer the letters appearing in their own names and those that frequently appear in their own languages (Hoorens & Nuttin, 1993; Hoorens et al., 1990; Kitayama & Karasawa, 1997; Nuttin, 1987). French students rate capital W, the least frequent letter in French, as their least favorite letter. In a stock market stimulation study, American business students preferred to buy stocks that shared the same first letter as their name (Knewtson & Sias, 2010). Japanese students prefer not only letters from their names but also numbers corresponding to their birth dates. Consumers prefer products whose prices remind them of their birthdates ($49.15 for a birthday on the 15th) and their names (fifty-five dollars for a name starting with F). The preference persists even when the price is higher (Coulter & Grewal, 2014). This "name letter effect" reflects more than mere exposure, however—see "Focus On: Liking Things Associated with Oneself."

How much do you like your name? In six studies, Jochen Gebauer and colleagues (2008) report that liking of one's own name is a reliable indicator of both implicit and explicit self-esteem.

The mere-exposure effect violates the commonsense prediction of boredom—*decreased interest*—regarding repeatedly heard music or tasted foods (Kahneman & Snell, 1992). Unless the repetitions are incessant ("Even the best song becomes tiresome if heard too often," says a Korean proverb), familiarity usually doesn't breed contempt, it increases liking. When completed in 1889, the Eiffel Tower in Paris was mocked as grotesque (Harrison, 1977). Today, it is the beloved symbol of Paris.

So, do visitors to the Louvre in Paris really adore the *Mona Lisa* for the artistry it displays, or are they simply delighted to find a familiar face? It might be both: To know her is to like her. Eddie Harmon-Jones and John Allen (2001) explored this phenomenon experimentally. When they showed people a woman's face, their cheek (smiling) muscles typically became more active with repeated viewings. Mere exposure breeds pleasant feelings.

Mere exposure has an even stronger effect when people receive stimuli without awareness (Bornstein & D'Agostino, 1992; Hansen & Wänke, 2009; Kunst-Wilson & Zajonc, 1980; Willems et al., 2010). In one experiment, women heard music in one headphone and words in the other; they were asked to repeat the words out loud, focusing attention toward the words and away from the tunes. Later, when the women heard the tunes interspersed among similar ones not previously played, they did not recognize them. Nevertheless, they *liked best* the tunes they had previously heard. Even patients with amnesia—who can consciously recall very little of what they experience—prefer faces they saw recently (Marin-Garcia et al., 2013).

Note that conscious judgments about the stimuli in these experiments provided fewer clues to what people had heard or seen than did their instant feelings. You can probably recall immediately and intuitively liking or disliking something or someone without consciously knowing why. Zajonc (1980) argues that *emotions are often more instantaneous than thinking*. Zajonc's rather astonishing idea—that emotions are semi-independent of thinking ("affect may precede cognition")—has found support in recent brain research. Emotion and cognition are enabled by distinct brain regions. Lesion a monkey's amygdala (the emotion-related brain structure) and its emotional responses will be impaired, but its cognitive functions will be intact. Lesion its hippocampus (a memory-related structure) and its cognition will be impaired, but its emotional responses remain intact (Zola-Morgan et al., 1991).

The mere-exposure effect has "enormous adaptive significance," notes Zajonc (1998). It is a "hardwired" phenomenon that predisposes our attractions and attachments. It helped our ancestors categorize things and people as either familiar and safe or unfamiliar and possibly dangerous. The more two strangers interact, the more attractive they tend to find each other

We humans love to feel good about ourselves, and generally we do. Not only are we prone to self-serving bias, we also exhibit what Brett Pelham, Matthew Mirenberg, and John Jones (2002) call *implicit egotism:* We like what we associate with ourselves.

That includes the letters of our name and also the people, places, and things that we unconsciously connect with ourselves (Jones et al., 2002; Koole et al., 2001). If a stranger's or politician's face is morphed to include features of our own, we like the new face better (Bailenson et al., 2009; DeBruine, 2004). We are also more attracted to people whose arbitrary experimental code number resembles our birth date, and we are even disproportionately likely to marry someone whose first or last name resembles our own, such as by starting with the same letter (Jones et al., 2004).

Such preferences appear to subtly influence other major life decisions as well, including our locations and careers. Philadelphia, which has more people than Jacksonville, has 2.2 times as many men named Jack. But it has 10.4 times as many people named Philip. Likewise, Virginia Beach has a disproportionate number of people named Virginia.

Does this merely reflect the influence of one's place when naming one's baby? Are people in Georgia, for example, more likely to name their babies George or Georgia? That may be so, but it doesn't explain why states tend to have a relative excess of people whose *last* names are similar to the state names. California, for example, has a disproportionate number of people whose names begin with Cali (as in Califano). Likewise, Toronto has a marked excess of people whose names begin with Tor.

Compared to the national average, St. Louis has 49 percent more men named Louis. People named Hill, Park, Beach, Lake, or Rock are disproportionately likely to live in cities with names (such as Park City) that include their names. "People are attracted to places that resemble their names," surmise Pelham, Mirenberg, and Jones (2002).

Weirder yet—we are not making this up—people seem to prefer careers related to their names. Across the United States, Jerry, Dennis, and Walter are equally popular names (0.42 percent of people carry each of these names). Yet America's dentists are almost twice as likely to be named Dennis as Jerry or Walter. There also are 2.5 times as many dentists named Denise as there are with the equally popular names Beverly or Tammy. People named George or Geoffrey are overrepresented among geoscientists (geologists, geophysicists, and geochemists). And in the 2000 presidential campaign, people with last names beginning with B and G were disproportionately likely to contribute to the campaigns of Bush and Gore, respectively.

The implicit egotism phenomenon does have its skeptics. Uri Simonsohn (2011a,b) acknowledges that implicit egotism occurs in the laboratory, and he was able to replicate the associations between people's names, occupations, and places. But he argues that "reverse causality" sometimes is the explanation. For example, streets are often named after their residents, and towns are often named after their founders (Williams founded Williamsburg). And founders' descendants may stick around. In reply, Pelham and Mauricio Carvallo (2011) grant that some of the effects—especially for career choice—are modest. But they contend that implicit egotism is a real, though subtle, unconscious judgmental bias.

Reading about implicit egotism-based preferences gives me [DM] pause: Has this anything to do with why I enjoyed that trip to Fort Myers? Why I've written about moods, the media, and marriage? Why I collaborated with Professor Murdoch? If so, does this also explain why it was Suzie who sold seashells by the seashore?

(Reis et al., 2011). The mere-exposure effect colors our evaluations of others: We like familiar people (Swap, 1977). "If it's familiar, it has not eaten you yet," Zajonc used to say (Bennett, 2010). It works the other way around, too: People we like (for example, smiling rather than unsmiling strangers) seem more familiar (Garcia-Marques et al., 2004).

Mere exposure's negative side is our wariness of the unfamiliar—which may explain the automatic, unconscious prejudice people often feel when confronting those who are different. Infants as young as 3 months exhibit an own-race preference: If they are being raised by others of their race, they prefer to gaze at faces of their own familiar race (Bar-Haim et al., 2006; Kelly et al., 2005, 2007).

The mere-exposure effect. If she is like most of us, German chancellor Angela Merkel may prefer her familiar mirror-image (left), which she sees each morning while brushing her teeth, to her actual image (right).
AP Images/MICHAEL SOHN

We even like ourselves better the way we're used to seeing ourselves. In a delightful experiment, researchers showed women pictures of themselves and their mirror images. Asked which picture they liked better, most preferred their mirror image—the image they were used to seeing in the mirror. (No wonder our photographs never look quite right.) When close friends of the women were shown the same two pictures, they preferred the true picture—the image *they* were used to seeing (Mita et al., 1977). Now that we see our own selfie photos so frequently, do you think the results would be different?

Advertisers and politicians exploit this phenomenon. When people have no strong feelings about a product or a candidate, repetition alone can increase sales or votes (McCullough & Ostrom, 1974; Winter, 1973). After endless repetition of a commercial, shoppers often have an unthinking, automatic, favorable response to the product. Students who saw pop-up ads for brand-name products on web pages had a more positive attitude toward the brand, even when they didn't remember seeing the ads (Courbet et al., 2014). If candidates are relatively unknown, those with the most media exposure usually win (Patterson, 1980; Schaffner et al., 1981). Political strategists who understand the mere-exposure effect have replaced reasoned argument with brief ads that hammer home a candidate's name and sound-bite message.

The respected chief of the Washington State Supreme Court, Keith Callow, learned this lesson when in 1990 he lost to a seemingly hopeless opponent, Charles Johnson. Johnson, an unknown attorney who handled minor criminal cases and divorces, filed for the seat on the principle that judges "need to be challenged." Neither man campaigned, and the media ignored the race. On election day, the two candidates' names appeared without any identification—just one name next to the other. The result: a 53 percent to 47 percent Johnson victory. "There are a lot more Johnsons out there than Callows," offered the ousted judge afterward to a stunned legal community. Indeed, the state's largest newspaper counted 27 Charles Johnsons in its local phone book. There was Charles Johnson, the local judge. And, in a nearby city, there was television anchorman Charles Johnson, whose broadcasts were seen on statewide cable TV. Forced to choose between two unknown names, many voters preferred the comfortable, familiar name of Charles Johnson.

Physical Attractiveness

What do (or did) you seek in a potential date? Sincerity? Character? Humor? Good looks? Sophisticated, intelligent people are unconcerned with such superficial qualities as good looks; they know "beauty is only skin deep" and "you can't judge a book by its cover." At least, they know that's how they *ought* to feel. As Cicero counseled, "Resist appearance."

The belief that looks are unimportant may be another instance of how we deny real influences upon us, for there is now a file cabinet full of research studies showing that appearance matters. The consistency and pervasiveness of this effect is astonishing. Good looks are an asset.

"We should look to the mind, and not to the outward appearances."

—Aesop, *Fables*

ATTRACTIVENESS AND DATING

Like it or not, a young woman's physical attractiveness is a moderately good predictor of how frequently she dates, and a young man's attractiveness is a modestly good predictor of how frequently he dates (Berscheid et al., 1971; Reis et al., 1980, 1982; Walster et al., 1966). However, women more than men say they would prefer a mate who's homely and warm over one who's attractive and cold (Fletcher et al., 2004). In a worldwide BBC Internet survey of nearly 220,000 people, men more than women ranked attractiveness as important in a mate, whereas women more than men assigned importance to honesty, humor, kindness, and dependability (Lippa, 2007). In a longitudinal study following heterosexual married couples for four years, the wife's physical attractiveness predicted the husband's marital satisfaction better than the husband's physical attractiveness predicted the wife's satisfaction. In other words, attractive wives led to happier husbands, but attractive husbands had less effect on wives' happiness (Meltzer et al., 2014). Gay men and lesbian women display these sex differences as well, with gay and straight men both valuing appearance more than lesbian or straight women do (Ha et al., 2012).

Do such self-reports imply, as many have surmised, that women are better at following Cicero's advice? Or that nothing has changed since 1930, when the English philosopher Bertrand Russell (1930, p. 139) wrote, "On the whole women tend to love men for their character while men tend to love women for their appearance"? Or does it merely reflect the fact that men more often do the inviting? If women were to indicate their preferences among various men, would looks be as important to them as looks are to men?

To determine whether men are indeed more influenced by looks, researchers have provided heterosexual male and female students with information about someone of the other sex, including the person's picture. Or they have briefly introduced a man and a woman and later asked each about their interest in dating the other. In such experiments, men have put somewhat more value on opposite-sex physical attractiveness, as they do in

Attractiveness and dating. For Internet dating customers, looks are part of what is offered and sought.

PhotoDisc/Getty Images RF

FIGURE :: 3

What Women and Men Report Finding Most Attractive

Source: Fox News/Opinion Dynamics Poll of registered voters, 1999.

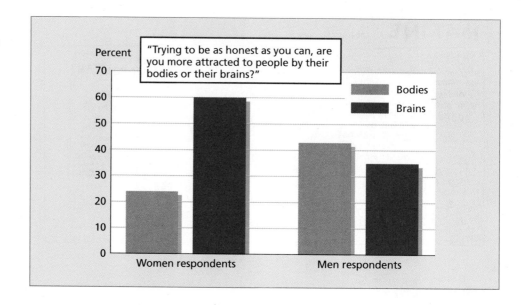

"Trying to be as honest as you can, are you more attracted to people by their bodies or their brains?"

■ Bodies
■ Brains

Women respondents   Men respondents

"Personal beauty is a greater recommendation than any letter of introduction."

—Aristotle,
Diogenes Laertius

opinion polls (Figure 3; [Feingold, 1990, 1991; Sprecher et al., 1994a]). Perhaps sensing this, women worry more about their appearance and constitute 90 percent of American cosmetic surgery patients (American Society for Aesthetic Plastic Surgery, 2014). Women also better recall others' appearance, as when asked, "Was the person on the right wearing black shoes?" or when asked to recall someone's clothing or hair (Mast & Hall, 2006).

Do women respond to men's looks? In one classic study, Elaine Hatfield and co-workers (1966) matched 752 University of Minnesota first-year students for a "Welcome Week" matching dance. The researchers gave each student personality and aptitude tests but then matched the couples randomly. On the night of the dance, the couples danced and talked for 2½ hours and then took a brief intermission to evaluate their dates. How well did the personality and aptitude tests predict attraction? Did people like someone better who was high in self-esteem, or low in anxiety, or different from themselves in outgoingness? The researchers examined a long list of possibilities. But so far as they could determine, only one thing mattered: how physically attractive the person was (as previously rated by the researchers). The more attractive a woman was, the more the man liked her and wanted to date her again. And the more attractive the man was, the more the woman liked him and wanted to date him again. Pretty pleases.

Recent studies have gathered data from speed-dating evenings, during which people interact with a succession of potential dates for only a few minutes each and later indicate which ones they would like to see again (mutual "yeses" are given contact information). The procedure is rooted in research showing that we can form durable impressions of others based on seconds-long "thin slices" of their social behavior (Ambady et al., 2000). In speed-dating research, men (vs. women) thought they would care more about a potential date's physical attractiveness; but when it came time to decide whom to date, a prospect's attractiveness was similarly important to both men and women (Eastwick & Finkel, 2008a,b).

A recent meta-analysis (statistical digest) of 97 studies found that men and women placed about the same, fairly high importance on physical attractiveness and about the same, lower importance on earning prospects (Eastwick et al., 2014). As you saw earlier, other studies have found otherwise. Thus, whether men value physical attractiveness more than women is debated, but the overall importance of physical attractiveness in dating is fairly large—especially when dates stem from first impressions. However, once people have gotten to know each other over months or years through jobs or friendships, they focus more on each person's unique qualities rather than their physical attractiveness and status. In several studies examining liking over time among friends, the more time that went by, the more the friends diverged over who was most attractive as a mate. In other words, there's someone for everyone—once you get to know them (Eastwick & Hunt, 2014). Pretty pleases, but perhaps only for a puny period.

Looks even influence voting, or so it seems from a study by Alexander Todorov and colleagues (2005; Todorov, 2011). They showed Princeton University students photographs of the two major candidates in 95 U.S. Senate races since 2000 and in 600 U.S. House of Representatives races. Based on looks alone, the students (who preferred competent-looking over more baby-faced candidates) correctly guessed the winners of 72 percent of the Senate and 67 percent of the House races. Follow-up studies have confirmed the finding that voters prefer competent-looking candidates (Antonakis & Dalgas, 2009; Chiao et al., 2008). But gender also mattered: Men were more likely to vote for physically attractive female candidates, and women were more likely to vote for approachable-looking male candidates. Likewise, heterosexual people display a positive bias toward attractive job candidates and university applicants—*if* they are of the other sex (Agthe et al., 2011).

THE MATCHING PHENOMENON

Not everyone can end up paired with someone stunningly attractive. So how do people pair off? Judging from research by Bernard Murstein (1986) and others, they get real. They pair off with people who are about as attractive as they are. Studies have found a strong correspondence between the rated attractiveness of husbands and wives, of dating partners, and even of those within particular fraternities (Feingold, 1988; Montoya, 2008). People tend to select as friends, and especially to marry, those who are a "good match" not only to their level of intelligence, popularity, and self-worth but also to their level of attractiveness (McClintock, 2014; Taylor et al., 2011).

Experiments confirm this **matching phenomenon.** When choosing whom to approach, knowing the other is free to say yes or no, people often approach and invest more in pursuing someone whose attractiveness roughly matches their own (Berscheid et al., 1971; van Straaten et al., 2009). They seek out someone who seems desirable, but they are mindful of the limits of their own desirability. Good physical matches may be conducive to good relationships, reported Gregory White (1980) from a study of UCLA dating couples. Those who were most similar in physical attractiveness were most likely, 9 months later, to have fallen more deeply in love.

Perhaps this research prompts you to think of happy couples who differ in perceived "hotness." In such cases, the less-attractive person often has compensating qualities. Each partner brings assets to the social marketplace, and the value of the respective assets creates an equitable match. Personal advertisements and self-presentations to online dating services exhibit this exchange of assets (Cicerello & Sheehan, 1995; Hitsch et al., 2006; Koestner & Wheeler, 1988; Rajecki et al., 1991). Men typically offer wealth or status and seek youth and attractiveness; women more often do the reverse: "Attractive, bright woman, 26, slender, seeks warm, professional male." Men who advertise their income and education, and women who advertise their youth and looks, receive more responses to their ads (Baize & Schroeder, 1995). The asset-matching process helps explain why beautiful young women often marry older men of higher social status (Elder, 1969; Kanazawa & Kovar, 2004). The richer the man, the younger and more beautiful the woman.

THE PHYSICAL-ATTRACTIVENESS STEREOTYPE

Does the attractiveness effect spring entirely from sexual attractiveness? Clearly not, as researchers discovered when they used a makeup artist to give an otherwise attractive accomplice a scarred, bruised, or birthmarked face. Glasgow train commuters of both sexes avoided sitting next to the apparently facially disfigured accomplice (Houston & Bull, 1994). Moreover, much as adults are biased toward attractive adults, young children are biased toward attractive children (Dion & Berscheid, 1974; Langlois et al., 2000). Judging by how long they gaze at someone, even 3-month-old infants prefer attractive faces (Langlois et al., 1987).

"If you would marry wisely, marry your equal."
—Ovid, 43 B.C.–A.D. 17

matching phenomenon
The tendency for men and women to choose as partners those who are a "good match" in attractiveness and other traits.

"Love is often nothing but a favorable exchange between two people who get the most of what they can expect, considering their value on the personality market."
—Erich Fromm,
The Sane Society, 1955

Asset matching. High-status Rolling Stones guitarist Keith Richards has been married to supermodel Patti Hansen, 19 years his junior, since 1983.
D Dipasupil/Getty Images

Adults show a similar bias when judging children. Missouri fifth-grade teachers were given identical information about a boy or a girl but with the photograph of an attractive or an unattractive child attached. The teachers perceived the attractive child as more intelligent and successful in school (Clifford & Walster, 1973). Imagine being a playground supervisor having to discipline an unruly child. Might you, like the women studied by Karen Dion (1972), show less warmth and tact to an unattractive child? The sad truth is that most of us assume that homely children are less able and socially competent than their beautiful peers (see "The Inside Story: Ellen Berscheid on Attractiveness").

What is more, we assume that beautiful people possess certain desirable traits. Other things being equal, we guess beautiful people are happier, sexually warmer, and more outgoing, intelligent, and successful—although not more honest (Eagly et al., 1991; Feingold, 1992b; Jackson et al., 1995). In one study, students judged attractive women as more agreeable, open, outgoing, ambitious, and emotionally stable (Segal-Caspi et al., 2012). We are more eager to bond with attractive people, which motivates our projecting

THE inside STORY

Ellen Berscheid on Attractiveness

I vividly remember the afternoon I began to appreciate the far-reaching implications of physical attractiveness. Graduate student Karen Dion (now a professor at the University of Toronto) learned that some researchers at our Institute of Child Development had collected popularity ratings from nursery school children and taken a photo of each child. Although teachers and caregivers of children had persuaded us that "all children are beautiful" and no physical-attractiveness discriminations could be made, Dion suggested we instruct some people to rate each child's looks and that we correlate these with popularity. After doing so, we realized our long shot had hit home: Attractive children were popular children. Indeed, the

effect was far more potent than we and others had assumed, with a host of implications that investigators are still tracing.

Ellen Berscheid
University of Minnesota
Courtesy of Ellen Berscheid

desirable attributes such as kindness and reciprocal interest into them (Lemay et al., 2010). When attractive CEOs of companies appear on television, the stock price of their companies rise—but being quoted in a newspaper, without a photo, has no effect (Halford & Hsu, 2014).

Added together, the findings define a **physical-attractiveness stereotype:** What is beautiful is good. Children learn the stereotype quite early—often through stories told to them by adults. "Disney movies promote the stereotype that what is beautiful is good," report Doris Bazzini and colleagues (2010) from an analysis of human characters in 21 animated films. Snow White and Cinderella are beautiful—and kind. The witch and the stepsisters are ugly—and wicked. "If you want to be loved by somebody who isn't already in your family, it doesn't hurt to be beautiful," surmised one 8-year-old girl. Or as one kindergarten girl put it when asked what it means to be pretty, "It's like to be a princess. Everybody loves you" (Dion, 1979).

If physical attractiveness is that important, then permanently changing people's attractiveness should change the way others react to them. But is it ethical to alter someone's looks? Such manipulations are performed millions of times a year by cosmetic surgeons and orthodontists. With teeth straightened and whitened, hair replaced and dyed, face lifted, fat liposuctioned, and breasts enlarged, lifted, or reduced, most self-dissatisfied people do express satisfaction with the results of their procedures, though some unhappy patients seek out repeat procedures (Honigman et al., 2004).

To examine the effect of such alterations on others, Michael Kalick (1977) had Harvard students rate their impressions of eight women based on profile photographs taken before or after cosmetic surgery. Not only did they judge the women as more physically attractive after the surgery but also as kinder, more sensitive, more sexually warm and responsive, more likable, and so on.

FIRST IMPRESSIONS. To say that attractiveness is important, other things being equal, is not to say that physical appearance always outranks other qualities. Some people more than others judge people by their looks (Livingston, 2001). Moreover, attractiveness most affects first impressions. But first impressions are important—and have become more so as societies become increasingly mobile and urbanized and as contacts with people become more fleeting (Berscheid, 1981). Your Facebook self-presentation starts with your face. In speed-dating experiments, the attractiveness effect is strongest when people's choices are superficially made—when meeting lots of people quickly (Lenton & Francesconi, 2010). That helps explain why attractiveness better predicts happiness and social connections for those in urban rather than rural settings (Plaut et al., 2009).

Though interviewers may deny it, attractiveness and grooming affect first impressions in job interviews—especially when the evaluator is of the other sex (Agthe et al., 2011; Cash & Janda, 1984; Mack & Rainey, 1990; Marvelle & Green, 1980). People rate new products more favorably when they are associated with attractive inventors (Baron et al., 2006). Such impressions help explain why attractive people and tall people have more prestigious jobs and make more money (Engemann & Owyang, 2003; Persico et al., 2004).

Patricia Roszell and colleagues (1990) looked at the incomes of Canadians whom interviewers had rated on a 1 (homely) to 5 (strikingly attractive) scale. They found that for each additional scale unit of rated attractiveness, people earned, on average, an additional $1,988 annually. Irene Hanson Frieze and associates (1991) did the same analysis with 737 MBA graduates after rating them on a similar 1-to-5 scale, using student yearbook photos. For each additional scale unit of rated attractiveness, men earned an added $2,600 and women earned an added $2,150. In *Beauty Pays,* economist Daniel Hamermesh (2011) argues that, for a man, good looks have the earnings effect of another year and a half of schooling.

The speed with which first impressions form, and their influence on thinking, helps explain why pretty prospers. Even a .013-second exposure—too brief to discern a face—is enough to enable people to guess a face's attractiveness (Olson & Marshuetz, 2005). Moreover, when categorizing subsequent words as either good or bad, an attractive flashed

physical-attractiveness stereotype
The presumption that physically attractive people possess other socially desirable traits as well: What is beautiful is good.

"Even virtue is fairer in a fair body."
—Virgil,
Aeneid, 1st Century B.C.

face predisposes people to categorize good words faster. Pretty is perceived promptly and primes positive processing.

IS THE "BEAUTIFUL IS GOOD" STEREOTYPE ACCURATE?   Do beautiful people indeed have desirable traits? For centuries, those who considered themselves serious scientists thought so when they sought to identify physical traits (shifty eyes, a weak chin) that would predict criminal behavior. On the other hand, was Leo Tolstoy correct when he wrote that it's "a strange illusion . . . to suppose that beauty is goodness"? Despite others' perceptions, physically attractive people do not differ from others in basic personality traits such as agreeableness, openness, extraversion, ambition, or emotional stability (Segal-Caspi et al., 2012). However, there is some truth to the stereotype. Attractive children and young adults are somewhat more relaxed, outgoing, and socially polished (Feingold, 1992b; Langlois et al., 2000). In one study, 60 University of Georgia men called and talked for 5 minutes with each of three women students. Afterward, the men and women rated the most attractive of their unseen telephone partners as somewhat more socially skillful and likable (Goldman & Lewis, 1977). The same is true online: Even when they hadn't seen the men's photos, women rated the text of attractive men's dating website profiles as more desirable and confident. What is beautiful is good, even online (Brand et al., 2012). Physically attractive individuals tend also to be more popular, more outgoing, and more gender typed—more traditionally masculine if male, more feminine if female (Langlois et al., 1996).

These small average differences between attractive and unattractive people probably result from self-fulfilling prophecies. Attractive people are valued and favored, so many develop more social self-confidence. (Recall from an earlier chapter an experiment in which men evoked a warm response from unseen women they *thought* were attractive.) By that analysis, what's crucial to your social skill is not how you look but how people treat you and how you feel about yourself—whether you accept yourself, like yourself, and feel comfortable with yourself.

WHO IS ATTRACTIVE?

We have described attractiveness as if it were an objective quality like height, which some people have more of, some less. Strictly speaking, attractiveness is whatever the people of any given place and time find attractive. This, of course, varies. The beauty standards by which Miss Universe is judged hardly apply to the whole planet. People in various places and times have pierced noses, lengthened necks, dyed hair, whitened teeth, painted skin, gorged themselves to become voluptuous, starved to become thin, and bound themselves with leather corsets to make their breasts seem small—or used silicone and padded bras to make them seem big. For cultures with scarce resources and for poor or hungry people, plumpness seems attractive; for cultures and individuals with abundant resources, beauty more often equals slimness (Nelson & Morrison, 2005). Moreover, attractiveness influences life outcomes less in cultures where relationships are based more on kinship or social arrangement than on personal choice (Anderson et al., 2008). Despite such variations, there remains "strong agreement both within and across cultures about who is and who is not attractive," note Judith Langlois and colleagues (2000).

To be really attractive is, ironically, to be *perfectly average* (Rhodes, 2006). Researchers have digitized multiple faces and averaged them using a computer. Inevitably, people find the composite faces more appealing than almost all the actual faces (Langlois & Roggman, 1990; Langlois et al., 1994; Perrett, 2010; Figure 4). Across 27 nations, an average leg-length-to-body ratio looks more attractive than very short or long legs (Sorokowski et al., 2011). With both humans and animals, averaged looks best embody prototypes (for your typical man, woman, dog, or whatever) and thus are easy for the brain to process and categorize, notes Jamin Halberstadt (2006). Let's face it: Perfectly average is easy on the eyes (and brain).

Computer-averaged faces and bodies also tend to be perfectly *symmetrical*—another characteristic of strikingly attractive (and reproductively successful) people (Brown et al., 2008;

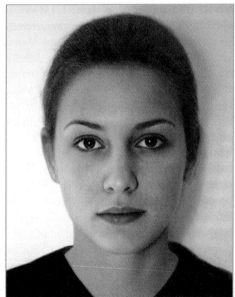

FIGURE :: 4

Who's the Fairest of Them All?

Each year's selection of "Miss Germany" provides one country's answer. A University of Regensburg student research team, working with a German television channel, offered an alternative. Christoph Braun and his compatriots (Gruendl, 2005) photographed the twenty-two 2002 "Queen of Beauty" finalists, without makeup and with hair tied back, and then created a "Virtual Miss Germany" that was the blended composite of them all. When adults in a local shopping mall were shown the finalists and the Virtual Miss Germany, they easily rated Virtual Miss Germany as the most attractive of them all. Although the winning real Miss Germany may have been disappointed by the news that everyone preferred her virtual competitor to herself, she can reassure herself that she will never meet her virtual competitor.

Oliver Bodmer/Action Press/ZUMAPRESS.com; Courtesy of Braun

Gangestad & Thornhill, 1997). If you could merge either half of your face with its mirror image—thus forming a perfectly symmetrical new face—you would boost your looks (Penton-Voak et al., 2001; Rhodes, 2006; Rhodes et al., 1999). With a few facial features excepted (Said & Todorov, 2011), averaging a number of such attractive, symmetrical faces produces an even better looking face.

Standards of beauty differ from culture to culture. Yet some people are considered attractive throughout most of the world.

2009 Jupiterimages Corporation/Jupiterimages; John Lund/Getty Images; Courtesy of Catherine Karnow; Marc Romanelli/Getty Images

EVOLUTION AND ATTRACTION. Psychologists working from the evolutionary perspective explain the human preference for attractive partners in terms of reproductive strategy. They assume that beauty signals biologically important information: health, youth, and fertility. And so it does. Men with attractive faces have higher quality sperm. Women with hourglass figures have more regular menstrual cycles and are more fertile (Gallup et al., 2008). Over time, men who preferred fertile-looking women out-reproduced those who were as happy to mate with postmenopausal females. That biological outcome of human history, David Buss (1989) believes, explains why males in 37 cultures—from Australia to Zambia—did indeed prefer youthful female characteristics that signify reproductive capacity.

Evolutionary psychologists also assume that evolution predisposes women to favor male traits that signify an ability to provide and protect resources. In screening potential mates, report Norman Li and fellow researchers (2002), men require a modicum of physical attractiveness, women require status and resources, and both welcome kindness and intelligence. Women's emphasis on men's physical attractiveness may also depend on their goals: Those focused on short-term relationships prefer more symmetrical and thus attractive men, whereas those focused on the long term find this less important, perhaps because physical attractiveness may come with more negative qualities such as infidelity (Quist et al., 2012).

Evolutionary psychologists have also explored men's and women's response to other cues to reproductive success. Judging from glamour models and beauty pageant winners, men everywhere have felt most attracted to women whose waists are 30 percent narrower than their hips—a shape associated with peak sexual fertility (Karremans et al., 2010; Perilloux et al., 2010; Platek & Singh, 2010). Circumstances that reduce a woman's fertility—malnutrition, pregnancy, menopause—also change her shape.

When judging males as potential marriage partners, women, too, prefer a male waist-to-hip ratio suggesting health and vigor. They rate muscular men as sexier, and muscular men do feel sexier and report more lifetime sex partners (Frederick & Haselton, 2007). This makes evolutionary sense, notes Jared Diamond (1996): A muscular hunk was more likely than a scrawny fellow to gather food, build houses, and defeat rivals. But today's women prefer men with high incomes even more (Singh, 1995).

During ovulation, women show heightened preference for men with more masculine faces, voices, and bodies (Gallup & Frederick, 2010; Gangestad et al., 2004; Macrae et al., 2002). They show increased accuracy in judging male sexual orientation (Rule et al., 2011). And they show increased wariness of out-group men (McDonald et al., 2011). One study found that, when ovulating, young women tend to wear and prefer more revealing outfits than when infertile (Durante et al., 2008). In another study, ovulating lap dancers averaged $70 in tips per hour—double the $35 of those who were menstruating (Miller et al., 2007).

We are, evolutionary psychologists suggest, driven by primal attractions. Like eating and breathing, attraction and mating are too important to leave to the whims of culture.

SOCIAL COMPARISON. Although our mating psychology has biological wisdom, attraction is not all hardwired. What's attractive to you also depends on your comparison standards.

To men who have recently been gazing at centerfolds, average women or even their own wives tend to seem less attractive (Kenrick et al., 1989). Viewing pornographic films simulating passionate sex similarly decreases satisfaction with one's own partner (Zillmann, 1989). Being sexually aroused may *temporarily* make a person of the other sex seem more attractive. But the lingering effect of exposure to perfect "10s," or of unrealistic sexual depictions, is to make one's own partner seem less appealing—more like a "6" than an "8."

It works the same way with our self-perceptions. After viewing a very attractive person of the same gender, people rate themselves as being *less* attractive than after viewing a homely person (Brown et al., 1992; Thornton & Maurice, 1997). Men's self-rated desirability is also deflated by exposure to more dominant, successful men. Thanks to modern media, we may see in an hour "dozens of individuals who are more attractive and more successful than any of our ancestors would have seen in a year, or even a lifetime," noted Sara Gutierres and her co-researchers (1999). Moreover, we often see slim, wrinkle-free, photoshopped people who don't exist. Such extraordinary comparison standards trick us into devaluing our potential mates and ourselves and spending billions on cosmetics, diet aids, and plastic surgery. But even after another 9.5 million annual cosmetic procedures, there may be no net gain in human satisfaction. If others get their teeth straightened, capped, and whitened, and you don't, the social comparison may leave you more dissatisfied with your normal, natural teeth than you would have been if you were surrounded by peers whose teeth were also natural.

THE ATTRACTIVENESS OF THOSE WE LOVE.   Let's conclude our discussion of attractiveness on an upbeat note. First, a 17-year-old girl's facial attractiveness is a surprisingly weak predictor of her attractiveness at ages 30 and 50. Sometimes an average-looking adolescent, especially one with a warm, attractive personality, becomes a quite attractive middle-aged adult (Zebrowitz et al., 1993, 1998).

Second, not only do we perceive attractive people as likable, but also we perceive likable people as attractive. Perhaps you can recall individuals who, as you grew to like them, became more attractive. Their physical imperfections were no longer so noticeable. Alan Gross and Christine Crofton (1977; see also Lewandowski et al., 2007) had students view someone's photograph after reading a favorable or an unfavorable description of the person's personality. Those portrayed as warm, helpful, and considerate also *looked* more attractive. Democrats rated fellow Democrat Barack Obama as more physically attractive than Republicans did; Republicans rated fellow Republican Sarah Palin more physically attractive than Democrats did (Kniffin et al., 2014). It may be true, then, that "handsome is as handsome does," and that "what is good is beautiful." Discovering someone's similarities to us also makes the person seem more attractive (Beaman & Klentz, 1983; Klentz et al., 1987).

Moreover, love sees loveliness: The more in love a woman is with a man, the more physically attractive she finds him (Price et al., 1974). And the more in love people are, the less attractive they find all others of the opposite sex (Johnson & Rusbult, 1989; Simpson et al., 1990). "The grass may be greener on the other side," note Rowland Miller and Jeffry Simpson (1990), "but happy gardeners are less likely to notice." Beauty really *is*, to some extent, in the eye of the beholder.

Similarity Versus Complementarity

From our discussion so far, one might surmise Leo Tolstoy was entirely correct: "Love depends . . . on frequent meetings, and on the style in which the hair is done up, and on the color and cut of the dress." Given time, however, other factors influence whether acquaintance develops into friendship.

DO BIRDS OF A FEATHER FLOCK TOGETHER?

Of this much we may be sure: Birds that flock together are of a feather. Friends, engaged couples, and spouses are far more likely than randomly paired people to share common attitudes, beliefs, and values. Furthermore, the greater the similarity between husband and wife, the happier they are and the less likely they are to divorce (Byrne, 1971; Caspi & Herbener, 1990). Dating couples with more similar political and religious attitudes were more likely to still be together after 11 months (Bleske-Rechek et al., 2009). Such correlational

Henry James's description of novelist George Eliot (the pen name of Mary Ann Evans): "She is magnificently ugly—deliciously hideous. She has a low forehead, a dull grey eye, a vast pendulous nose, a huge mouth, full of uneven teeth. . . . Now in this vast ugliness resides a most powerful beauty which, in a very few minutes, steals forth and charms the mind, so that you end as I ended, in falling in love with her."
Granger Collection

findings are intriguing. But cause and effect remain an enigma. Does similarity lead to liking? Or does liking lead to similarity?

LIKENESS BEGETS LIKING. To discern cause and effect, we experiment. Imagine that at a campus party Lakesha gets involved in a long discussion of politics, religion, and personal likes and dislikes with Les and Lon. She and Les discover they agree on almost everything, she and Lon on few things. Afterward, she reflects: "Les is really intelligent . . . and so likable. I hope we meet again." In experiments, Donn Byrne (1971) and his colleagues captured the essence of Lakesha's experience. Over and over again, they found that the more similar someone's attitudes are to your own, the more you will like the person. Recent studies have replicated these effects, finding that students like others with similar attitudes (Montoya & Horton, 2012; Reid et al., 2013). Likeness produces liking not only for college students but also for children and the elderly, for people of various occupations, and for those in various cultures.

The likeness-leads-to-liking effect has been tested in real-life situations:

- At two of Hong Kong's universities, Royce Lee and Michael Bond (1996) found that roommate friendships flourished when roommates shared values and personality traits, but more so when they *perceived* their roommates as similar. Perceived similarity also mattered more than actual similarity during speed-dating (Tidwell et al., 2013). Reality matters, but perception matters more.

- In various settings, people entering a room of strangers sit closer to those like themselves (Mackinnon et al., 2011). People with glasses sit closer to others with glasses. Long-haired people sit closer to people with long hair. Dark-haired people sit closer to people with dark hair (even after controlling for race and sex).

- Eleven-month-old infants were more likely to choose a stuffed animal that pretended to eat the same food or wore the same color mittens that they did. This suggests that the preference for similar others develops very early, even before babies can talk (Mahajan & Wynn, 2012).

- People like not only those who think as they do but also those who act as they do. Subtle mimicry fosters fondness. Have you noticed that when someone nods his or her head as you do and echoes your thoughts, you feel a certain rapport and liking? That's a common experience, report Rick van Baaren and colleagues (2003a,b), and one result is higher tips for Dutch restaurant servers who mimic their customers by merely repeating their order. Natural mimicry increases rapport, note Jessica Lakin and Tanya Chartrand (2003), and desire for rapport increases mimicry.

- Whether in China or the Western world, similar attitudes, traits, and values help bring couples together and predict their satisfaction (Chen et al., 2009; Gaunt, 2006; Gonzaga et al., 2007). Speed-daters are drawn to those who share their speaking style (Ireland et al., 2011). Even morning and evening types tend to find one another (Randler & Kretz, 2011). The online dating site eHarmony.com claims to match singles using the similarities that mark happy couples (Carter & Snow, 2004; Warren, 2005), and the dating app Tinder matches couples based on similar Facebook profiles.

So similarity breeds content. Birds of a feather *do* flock together. Surely you have noticed this upon discovering a person who shares your ideas, values, and desires; a special someone who likes the same foods, the same activities, the same music you do. (When liking the same music as another, people infer similar values as well [Boer et al., 2011].)

DISSIMILARITY BREEDS DISLIKE. We have a bias—the false consensus bias—toward assuming that others share our attitudes. We also tend to see those we like as being like us (Castelli et al., 2009). Getting to know someone—and discovering that the person is actually dissimilar—tends to decrease liking (Norton et al., 2007). If those dissimilar attitudes pertain to our strong moral convictions, we dislike and distance ourselves from them all the more (Skitka et al., 2005). People in one political party often are not so much fond of fellow party members as they are disdainful of the opposition (Hoyle, 1993; Rosenbaum, 1986).

In general, dissimilar attitudes depress liking more than similar attitudes enhance it (Singh & Ho, 2000; Singh & Teob, 1999). Within their own groups, where they expect similarity, people find it especially difficult to like someone with dissimilar views (Chen & Kenrick, 2002). That perhaps explains why dating partners and roommates become more similar over time in their emotional responses to events and in their attitudes (Anderson et al., 2003; Davis & Rusbult, 2001). "Attitude alignment" helps promote and sustain close relationships, a phenomenon that can also lead partners to overestimate their attitude similarities (Kenny & Acitelli, 2001; Murray et al., 2002).

Whether people perceive those of another race as similar or dissimilar influences their racial attitudes. Whenever one group regards another as "other"—as creatures that speak differently, live differently, think differently—the potential for conflict is high. In fact, except for intimate relationships such as dating, the perception of like minds is more important for attraction than like skins. In one study, liberals expressed dislike of conservatives and conservatives of liberals, but race did not affect liking (Chambers et al., 2012).

"Cultural racism" persists, argues social psychologist James Jones (1988, 2003, 2004), because cultural differences are a fact of life. Black culture tends to be present-oriented, spontaneously expressive, spiritual, and emotionally driven. White culture tends to be more future-oriented, materialistic, and achievement driven. Rather than trying to eliminate such differences, says Jones, we might better appreciate what they "contribute to the cultural fabric of a multicultural society." There are situations in which expressiveness is advantageous and situations in which future orientation is advantageous. Each culture has much to learn from the other. In countries such as Canada, Britain, and the United States, where migration and differing birthrates make for growing diversity, educating people to respect and enjoy those who differ is a major challenge. Given increasing cultural diversity and given our natural wariness of differences, this may be the major social challenge of our time.

DO OPPOSITES ATTRACT?

Are we not also attracted to people who in some ways *differ* from ourselves? We are physically attracted to people whose scent suggests dissimilar enough genes to prevent inbreeding (Garver-Apgar et al., 2006). But what about attitudes and behavioral traits?

Researchers have explored that question by comparing not only friends' and spouses' attitudes and beliefs but also their ages, religions, races, smoking behaviors, economic levels, educations, height, intelligence, and appearance. In all these ways and more, similarity still prevails (Buss, 1985; Kandel, 1978). Smart birds flock together. So do rich birds, Protestant birds, tall birds, pretty birds.

Still we resist: Are we not attracted to people whose needs and personalities complement our own? Would a sadist and a masochist find true love? The *Reader's Digest* has told us that "opposites attract.... Socializers pair with loners, novelty-lovers with those who dislike change, free spenders with scrimpers, risk-takers with the very cautious" (Jacoby, 1986). Sociologist Robert Winch (1958) reasoned that the needs of an outgoing and domineering person would naturally complement those of someone who is shy and submissive. The logic seems compelling, and most of us can think of couples who view their differences as complementary: "My husband and I are perfect for each other. I'm Aquarius—a decisive person. He's Libra—can't make decisions. But he's always happy to go along with arrangements I make."

Despite the popular theory that opposites (for example, quiet and loud people) complement each other (complementarity), *similar* people are more likely to be romantically attracted to one another.
Sunshine Pics/Alamy

Given the idea's persuasiveness, the inability of researchers to confirm it is astonishing. For example, most people feel attracted to expressive, outgoing people (Friedman et al., 1988; Watson et al., 2014). Would this be especially so when one is down in the dumps? Do depressed people seek those whose gaiety will cheer them up? To the contrary, it is nondepressed people who most prefer the company of happy people (Locke & Horowitz, 1990; Rosenblatt & Greenberg, 1988, 1991; Wenzlaff & Prohaska, 1989). When you're feeling blue, another's bubbly personality can be aggravating. The contrast effect that makes average people feel homely in the company of beautiful people also makes sad people more conscious of their misery in the company of cheerful people.

Some **complementarity** may evolve as a relationship progresses. Yet people seem slightly more prone to like and to marry those whose needs, attitudes, and personalities are *similar* (Botwin et al., 1997; Buss, 1984; Rammstedt & Schupp, 2008; Watson et al., 2004). Perhaps one day we will discover some ways in which differences commonly breed liking. Dominance/submissiveness may be one such way (Dryer & Horowitz, 1997; Markey & Kurtz, 2006). But as a general rule, opposites do not attract.

Liking Those Who Like Us

Liking is usually mutual. Proximity and attractiveness influence our initial attraction to someone, and similarity influences longer term attraction as well. If we have a deep need to belong and to feel liked and accepted, would we not also take a liking to those who like us? Are the best friendships mutual admiration societies? Indeed, one person's liking for another does predict the other's liking in return (Kenny & Nasby, 1980; Montoya & Insko, 2008).

But does one person's liking another *cause* the other to return the appreciation? People's reports of how they fell in love suggest so (Aron et al., 1989). Discovering that an appealing someone really likes you seems to awaken romantic feelings. Experiments confirm it: Those told that certain others like or admire them usually feel a reciprocal affection (Berscheid & Walster, 1978). And all the better, one speed-dating experiment suggests, when someone likes *you* especially (Eastwick et al., 2007). A dash of uncertainty can also fuel desire. Thinking that someone probably likes you—but you aren't sure—tends to increase your thinking about, and feeling attracted to, another (Whitechurch et al., 2011).

And consider this finding: Students like another student who says eight positive things about them better than one who says seven positive things and one negative thing (Berscheid et al., 1969). We are sensitive to the slightest hint of criticism. Writer Larry L. King speaks for many in noting, "I have discovered over the years that good reviews strangely fail to make the author feel as good as bad reviews make him feel bad."

Whether we are judging ourselves or others, negative information carries more weight because, being less usual, it grabs more attention (Yzerbyt & Leyens, 1991). People's votes are more influenced by their impressions of presidential candidates' weaknesses than by their impressions of strengths (Klein, 1991), a phenomenon quickly grasped by those who design negative campaigns. It's a general rule of life: Bad is stronger than good (Baumeister et al., 2001). (See "Focus On: Bad Is Stronger Than Good.")

Our liking for those we perceive as liking us was recognized long ago. Observers from the ancient philosopher Hecato ("If you wish to be loved, love") to Ralph Waldo Emerson ("The only way to have a friend is to be one") to Dale Carnegie ("Dole out praise lavishly") anticipated the findings. What they did not anticipate was the precise conditions under which the principle works.

ATTRIBUTION

As we've seen, flattery *will* get you somewhere. But not everywhere. If praise clearly violates what we know is true—if someone says, "Your hair looks great," when we haven't washed it in 3 days—we may lose respect for the flatterer and wonder whether the

---

complementarity

The popularly supposed tendency, in a relationship between two people, for each to complete what is missing in the other.

"The average man is more interested in a woman who is interested in him than he is in a woman with beautiful legs."

—Actress Marlene Dietrich, 1901–1992

"If 60,000 people tell me they loved a show, then one walks past and says it sucked, that's the comment I'll hear."

—Musician Dave Matthews, 2000

focus
ON   Bad Is Stronger Than Good

Dissimilar attitudes, we have noted, turn us off to others more than similar attitudes turn us on. And others' criticism captures our attention and affects our emotions more than does their praise. Roy Baumeister, Ellen Bratslavsky, Catrin Finkenauer, and Kathleen Vohs (2001) say this is just the tip of an iceberg: "In everyday life, bad events have stronger and more lasting consequences than comparable good events." Consider the following:

- Destructive acts harm close relationships more than constructive acts build them. (Cruel words linger after kind ones have been forgotten.)

- Bad moods affect our thinking and memory more than do good moods. (Despite our natural optimism, it's easier to recall past bad emotional events than good ones.)

- There are more words for negative than positive emotions, and people asked to think of emotion words mostly come up with negative words. (*Sadness, anger,* and *fear* are the three most common.)

- Bad events tend to evoke more misery than good events evoke joy. (In one analysis by Randy Larsen [2009], negative emotional experiences exceeded the intensity of positive emotional experiences by a factor that, coincidentally, equaled pi: 3.14.)

- Single bad events (traumas) have more lasting effects than single very good events. (A death triggers more search for meaning than does a birth.)

- Routine bad events receive more attention and trigger more rumination than do routine good events. (Losing money upsets people more than gaining the same amount of money makes them happy.)

- Income losses have a bigger influence on life satisfaction and depression vs. happiness than do income gains (Boyce et al., 2013).

- Very bad family environments override the genetic influence on intelligence more than do very good family environments. (Bad parents can make their genetically bright children less intelligent; good parents are less able to make their unintelligent children smarter.)

- A bad reputation is easier to acquire, and harder to shed, than a good one. (A single act of lying can destroy one's reputation for integrity.)

- Poor health decreases happiness more than good health increases it. (Pain produces misery far more than comfort produces joy.)

The power of the bad prepares us to deal with threats and protects us from death and disability. For survival, bad can be more bad than good is good. The importance of the bad is one likely reason why the first century of psychology focused so much more on the bad than on the good. From its start through 2014, PsycINFO (a guide to psychology's literature) had 23,951 articles mentioning anger, 171,609 mentioning anxiety, and 199,595 mentioning depression. There were 10 articles on these topics for every 1 dealing with the positive emotions of joy (7,121), life satisfaction (10,992), or happiness (12,452). Similarly, "fear" (56,656 articles) has triumphed over "courage" (2,892). The strength of the bad is "perhaps the best reason for a positive psychology movement," Baumeister and colleagues surmise. To overcome the strength of individual bad events, "human life needs far more good than bad."

---

compliment springs from ulterior motives (Shrauger, 1975). Thus, we often perceive criticism to be more sincere than praise (Coleman et al., 1987). In fact, when someone prefaces a statement with "To be honest," we know we are about to hear a criticism.

Laboratory experiments reveal something we've noted in previous chapters: Our reactions depend on our attributions. Do we attribute the flattery to **ingratiation**—to a self-serving strategy? Is the person trying to get us to buy something, to acquiesce sexually, to do a favor? If so, both the flatterer and the praise lose appeal (Gordon, 1996; Jones, 1964). But if there is no apparent ulterior motive, then we warmly receive both flattery and flatterer.

Aronson (1988) speculated that constant approval can lose value. When a husband says for the five-hundredth time, "Gee, honey, you look great," the words carry far less impact than were he now to say, "Gee, honey, you look awful in that dress." A loved one you've doted on is hard to reward but easy to hurt. This suggests that an open, honest

ingratiation
The use of strategies, such as flattery, by which people seek to gain another's favor.

"It takes your enemy and your friend, working together, to hurt you to the heart; the enemy to slander you and the friend to get the news to you."

—Mark Twain,
Pudd'nhead Wilson's New Calendar, 1897

"Well—and I'm not just saying this because you're my husband—it stinks."

The wife's comment may not show ingratiation toward her husband, but it does demonstrate authenticity.
© Robert Mankoff/The New Yorker Collection/www.cartoonbank.com

relationship—one where people enjoy one another's esteem and acceptance yet are honest—is more likely to offer continuing rewards than one dulled by the suppression of unpleasant emotions, one in which people try only, as Dale Carnegie advised, to "lavish praise." Aronson (1988) put it this way:

> As a relationship ripens toward greater intimacy, what becomes increasingly important is authenticity—our ability to give up trying to make a good impression and begin to reveal things about ourselves that are honest even if unsavory. . . . If two people are genuinely fond of each other, they will have a more satisfying and exciting relationship over a longer period of time if they are able to express both positive and negative feelings than if they are completely "nice" to each other at all times. (p. 323)

In most social interactions, we self-censor our negative feelings. Thus, note William Swann and colleagues (1991), some people receive no corrective feedback. Living in a world of pleasant illusion, they continue to act in ways that alienate their would-be friends. A true friend is one who can let us in on bad news—nicely.

Someone who really loves us will be honest with us but will also tend to see us through rose-colored glasses. The happiest dating and married couples (and those who became happier with time) were those who idealized each other, who even saw their partners more positively than their partners saw themselves (Murray & Holmes, 1997; Murray et al., 1996a,b). When we're in love, we're biased to find those we love not only physically attractive but also socially attractive, and we're happy to have our partners view us with a similar positive bias (Boyes & Fletcher, 2007). Moreover, the most satisfied married couples tend to have idealized one another as newlyweds and to approach problems without immediately criticizing their partners and finding fault (Karney & Bradbury, 1997; Miller et al., 2006; Murray et al., 2011). Honesty has its place in a good relationship, but so does a presumption of the other's basic goodness.

> "No one is perfect until you fall in love with them."
>
> —Andy Rooney

Relationship Rewards

Asked why they are friends with someone or why they were attracted to their partners, most people can readily answer. "I like Carol because she's warm, witty, and well-read." What that explanation leaves out—and what social psychologists believe is most important—is ourselves. Attraction involves the one who is attracted as well as the attractor. Thus, a more psychologically accurate answer might be, "I like Carol because of how I feel when I'm with her." We are attracted to those we find it satisfying and gratifying to be with. Attraction is in the eye (and brain) of the beholder.

reward theory of attraction

The theory that we like those whose behavior is rewarding to us or whom we associate with rewarding events.

The point can be expressed as a simple **reward theory of attraction:** Those who reward us, or whom we associate with rewards, we like. If a relationship gives us more rewards than costs, we will like it and will want it to continue. Canadian children randomly assigned to perform three acts of kindness (versus visit three places) became more socially accepted and were less likely to be bullied—they gained friends as they helped others (Layous et al., 2012). In his 1665 book of *Maxims*, La Rochefoucauld conjectured, "Friendship is a scheme for the mutual exchange of personal advantages and favors whereby self-esteem may profit."

We not only like people who are rewarding to be with but also, according to the second version of the reward principle, like those we *associate* with good feelings. Conditioning creates positive feelings toward things and people linked with rewarding events (Byrne & Clore, 1970; De Houwer et al., 2001; Lott & Lott, 1974). When, after a strenuous week, we relax in front of a fire, enjoying good food, drink, and music, we will likely feel a special warmth toward those around us. We are less likely to take a liking to someone we meet while suffering a splitting headache.

Experiments confirm this phenomenon of liking—and disliking—by association (Hofmann et al., 2010). When an experimenter was friendly, participants chose to interact with someone who looked similar to her, but if she was unfriendly, they avoided the similar-looking woman (Lewicki, 1985). Elaine Hatfield and William Walster (1978) found a practical tip in these research studies: "Romantic dinners, trips to the theatre, evenings at home together, and vacations never stop being important. . . . If your relationship is to survive, it's important that you *both* continue to associate your relationship with good things."

This simple theory of attraction—we like those who reward us and those we associate with rewards—helps us understand why people everywhere feel attracted to those who are warm, trustworthy, and responsive (Fletcher et al., 1999; Regan, 1998; Wojciszke et al., 1998). The reward theory also helps explain some of the influences on attraction:

The reward theory of attraction suggests that when we associate our partners with pleasant activities, relationships last.
Ryan McVay/Getty Images

- *Proximity* is rewarding. It costs less time and effort to receive friendship's benefits with someone who lives or works close by.

- We like *attractive* people because we perceive that they offer other desirable traits and because we benefit by associating with them.

- If others have *similar* opinions, we feel rewarded because we presume that they like us in return. Moreover, those who share our views help validate them. We especially like people if we have successfully converted them to our way of thinking (Lombardo et al., 1972; Riordan, 1980; Sigall, 1970).

- We like to be liked and love to be loved. Thus, liking is usually *mutual.* We like those who like us.

SUMMING UP: What Leads to Friendship and Attraction?

- The best predictor of whether any two people are friends is their sheer *proximity* to each other. Proximity is conducive to repeated *exposure* and interaction, which enables us to discover similarities and to feel each other's liking.

- A second determinant of initial attraction is physical attractiveness. Both in laboratory studies and in field experiments involving blind dates, college students tend to prefer attractive people. In everyday life, however, people tend to choose someone whose attractiveness roughly *matches* their own (or who, if less attractive, has other compensating qualities). Positive

attributions about attractive people define a *physical-attractiveness stereotype*—an assumption that what is beautiful is good.

- Liking is greatly aided by similarity of attitudes, beliefs, and values. Likeness leads to liking; opposites rarely attract.

- We are also likely to develop friendships with people who like us.

- According to the *reward theory of attraction,* we like people whose behavior we find rewarding, or whom we associate with rewarding events.

WHAT IS LOVE?

Describe the varieties and components of love.

Loving is more complex than liking and thus more difficult to measure, more perplexing to study. People yearn for it, live for it, die for it.

Most attraction researchers have studied what is most easily studied—responses during brief encounters between strangers. The influences on our initial liking of another—proximity, attractiveness, similarity, being liked, and other rewarding traits—also influence our long-term, close relationships. The impressions that dating couples quickly form of each other therefore provide a clue to their long-term future (Berg, 1984; Berg & McQuinn, 1986). Indeed, if North American romances flourished *randomly,* without regard to proximity and similarity, then most Catholics (being a minority) would marry Protestants, most Blacks would marry Whites, and college graduates (also a minority) would be as apt to marry high school dropouts as to marry fellow graduates.

So first impressions are important. Nevertheless, long-term loving is not merely an intensification of initial liking. Social psychologists therefore study enduring, close relationships.

Passionate Love

The first step in scientifically studying romantic love, as in studying any variable, is to decide how to define and measure it. We have ways to measure aggression, altruism, prejudice, and liking—but how do we measure love?

"How do I love thee? Let me count the ways," wrote Elizabeth Barrett Browning. Social scientists have counted various ways. Psychologist Robert Sternberg (1998) views love as a triangle consisting of three components: passion, intimacy, and commitment (Figure 5).

Some elements of love are common to all loving relationships: mutual understanding, giving and receiving support, enjoying the loved one's company. Some elements are distinctive. If we experience passionate love, we express it physically, we expect the relationship to be exclusive, and we are intensely fascinated with our partner. You can see it in our eyes.

Zick Rubin (1973) confirmed this. He administered a love scale to hundreds of University of Michigan dating couples. Later, from behind a one-way mirror in a laboratory waiting room, he clocked eye contact among "weak-love" and "strong-love" couples (mutual gaze conveys liking and averted eye gaze conveys ostracism [Wirth et al., 2010]).

FIGURE :: 5

Robert Sternberg's (1988) Conception of Kinds of Loving as Combinations of Three Basic Components of Love

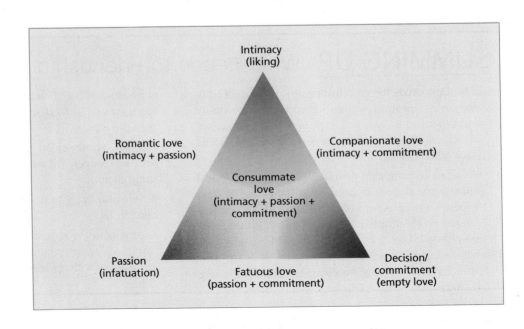

So Rubin's result will not surprise you: The strong-love couples gave themselves away by gazing long into each other's eyes. When talking, they also nod their head, smile naturally, and lean forward (Gonzaga et al., 2001). When observing speed-daters, it takes but a few seconds to make a reasonably accurate guess as to whether one person is interested in another (Place et al., 2009).

Researchers report that sustained eye contact, nodding, and smiling are indicators of passionate love.
Courtesy of Joe Polillio

Passionate love is emotional, exciting, intense. Elaine Hatfield (1988) defined it as *"a state of intense longing for union with another"* (p. 193). If reciprocated, one feels fulfilled and joyous; if not, one feels empty or despairing. Like other forms of emotional excitement, passionate love involves a roller coaster of elation and gloom, tingling exhilaration and dejected misery. "We are never so defenseless against suffering as when we love," observed Freud. Passionate love preoccupies the lover with thoughts of the other.

Passionate love is what you feel when you not only love someone but also are "in love" with him or her. As Sarah Meyers and Ellen Berscheid (1997) note, we understand that someone who says, "I love you, but I'm not in love with you," means to say, "I like you. I care about you. I think you're marvelous. But I don't feel sexually attracted to you." I feel friendship but not passion.

passionate love
A state of intense longing for union with another. Passionate lovers are absorbed in each other, feel ecstatic at attaining their partner's love, and are disconsolate on losing it.

two-factor theory of emotion
Arousal $\times$ its label = emotion.

A THEORY OF PASSIONATE LOVE

To explain passionate love, Hatfield notes that a given state of arousal can be steered into any of several emotions, depending on how we attribute the arousal. An emotion involves both body and mind—both arousal and the way we interpret and label that arousal. Imagine yourself with pounding heart and trembling hands: Are you experiencing fear, anxiety, joy? Physiologically, one emotion is quite similar to another. You may therefore experience the arousal as joy if you are in a euphoric situation, anger if your environment is hostile, and passionate love if the situation is romantic. In this view, passionate love is the psychological experience of being biologically aroused by someone we find attractive.

If indeed passion is a revved-up state that's labeled "love," then whatever revs one up should intensify feelings of love. In several experiments, college men aroused by reading or viewing erotic materials had a heightened response to a woman—for example, by scoring much higher on a love scale when describing their girlfriend (Carducci et al., 1978; Dermer & Pyszczynski, 1978). Proponents of the **two-factor theory of emotion,** developed by Stanley Schachter and Jerome Singer (1962), argue that when the revved-up men responded to a woman, they easily misattributed some of their own arousal to her.

According to the two-factor theory of emotion, emotional arousal caused by an exciting experience such as an amusement park ride may be confused for sexual attraction.
Mike Kemp/Getty Images

FIGURE :: 6

This Is Your Brain on Love

MRI scans from young adults intensely in love revealed areas, such as the caudate nucleus, that became more active when gazing at the loved-one's photo (but not when gazing at the photo of another acquaintance). *Source:* Aron et al., 2005.

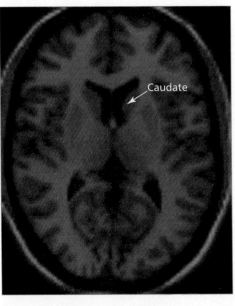

Caudate

"The 'adrenaline' associated with a wide variety of highs can spill over and make passion more passionate. (Sort of a 'Better loving through chemistry' phenomenon.)"

—Elaine Hatfield and Richard Rapson (1987)

According to this theory, being aroused by *any* source should intensify passionate feelings—provided that the mind is free to attribute some of the arousal to a romantic stimulus. In a dramatic and famous demonstration of this phenomenon, Donald Dutton and Arthur Aron (1974) had an attractive young woman approach individual young men as they crossed a narrow, wobbly, 450-foot-long suspension walkway hanging 230 feet above British Columbia's rocky Capilano River. The woman asked each man to help her fill out a class questionnaire. When he had finished, she scribbled her name and phone number and invited him to call if he wanted to hear more about the project. Most accepted the phone number, and half who did so called. By contrast, men approached by the woman on a low, solid bridge rarely called. Once again, physical arousal accentuated romantic responses.

Scary movies, roller-coaster rides, and physical exercise have the same effect, especially to those we find attractive (Foster et al., 1998; White & Kight, 1984). The effect holds true with married couples, too. Those who do exciting activities together report the best relationships. And after doing an arousing rather than a mundane laboratory task (roughly the equivalent of a three-legged race on their hands and knees), couples also reported higher satisfaction with their overall relationship (Aron et al., 2000). Adrenaline makes the heart grow fonder.

As this suggests, passionate love is a biological as well as a psychological phenomenon. Research by social psychologist Arthur Aron and colleagues (2005) indicates that passionate love engages dopamine-rich brain areas associated with reward (Figure 6).

Love is also a social phenomenon. Love is more than lust, notes Ellen Berscheid (2010). Supplement sexual desire with a deepening friendship and the result is romantic love. Passionate love = lust + attachment.

VARIATIONS IN LOVE: CULTURE AND GENDER

There is always a temptation to assume that most others share our feelings and ideas. We assume, for example, that love is a precondition for marriage. Most cultures—89 percent in one analysis of 166 cultures—do have a concept of romantic love, as reflected in flirtation or couples running off together (Jankowiak & Fischer, 1992). But in some cultures, notably those practicing arranged marriages, love tends to follow rather than to precede marriage. Even many people in the United States disconnected love and marriage just a half-century ago: In the 1960s, only 24 percent of college women and 65 percent of college men considered love to be the basis of marriage. In more recent years, nearly all college students believe this (Reis & Aron, 2008).

Do males and females differ in how they experience passionate love? Studies of men and women falling in and out of love reveal some surprises. Most people, including the writer of the following letter to a newspaper advice columnist, suppose that women fall in love more readily:

Dear Dr. Brothers:
    Do you think it's effeminate for a 19-year-old guy to fall in love so hard it's like the whole world's turned around? I think I'm really crazy because this has happened several times now and love just seems to hit me on the head from nowhere. . . . My father says this is the way girls fall in love and that it doesn't happen this way with guys—at least it's not supposed to. I can't change how I am in this way but it kind of worries me.—P.T. (quoted by Dion & Dion, 1985)

P.T. would be reassured by the repeated finding that it is actually men who tend to fall in love more readily (Ackerman et al., 2011; Dion & Dion, 1985). Men also seem to fall out of love more slowly and are less likely than women to break up a premarital romance. Surprisingly to most people, in heterosexual relationships, it's men, not women, who most often are first to say "I love you" (Ackerman et al., 2011).

Once in love, however, women are typically as emotionally involved as their partners, or more so. They are more likely to report feeling euphoric and "giddy and carefree," as if they were "floating on a cloud." Women are also somewhat more likely than men to focus on the intimacy of the friendship and on their concern for their partner. Men are more likely than women to think about the playful and physical aspects of the relationship (Hendrick & Hendrick, 1995).

Companionate Love

Although passionate love burns hot, like a relationship booster rocket, it eventually simmers down once the relationship reaches a stable orbit. The high of romance may be sustained for a few months, even a couple of years. But no high lasts forever. "When you're in love it's the most glorious two-and-a-half days of your life," jested comedian Richard Lewis. The novelty, the intense absorption in the other, the tingly thrill of the romance, the giddy "floating on a cloud" feeling fades. After 2 years of marriage, spouses express affection about half as often as when they were newlyweds (Huston & Chorost, 1994). About 4 years after marriage, the divorce rate peaks in cultures worldwide (Fisher, 1994). If a close relationship is to endure, it will settle to a steadier but still warm afterglow called **companionate love.** The passion-facilitating hormones (testosterone, dopamine, adrenaline) subside, while the hormone oxytocin supports feelings of attachment and trust (Taylor et al., 2010).

companionate love
The affection we feel for those with whom our lives are deeply intertwined.

Unlike the wild emotions of passionate love, companionate love is lower key; it's a deep, affectionate attachment. It activates different parts of the brain (Aron et al., 2005). And it is just as real. Nisa, a !Kung San woman of the African Kalahari Desert, explains: "When two people are first together, their hearts are on fire and their passion is very great. After a while, the fire cools and that's how it stays. They continue to love each other, but it's in a different way—warm and dependable" (Shostak, 1981).

The flow and ebb of romantic love follows the pattern of addictions to coffee, alcohol, and other drugs (Burkett & Young, 2012). At first, a drug gives a big kick, a high. With repetition, opponent emotions gain strength and tolerance develops. An amount that once was highly stimulating no longer gives a thrill. Stopping the substance, however, does not return you to where you started. Rather, it triggers withdrawal symptoms—malaise, depression, the blahs. The same often happens in love. The passionate high is fated to become lukewarm. The no-longer-romantic relationship becomes taken for granted—until it ends. Then the jilted lover, the widower, the divorcé, are surprised at how empty life now seems without the person they long ago stopped feeling passionately attached to. Having focused on what was not working, they stopped noticing what was (Carlson & Hatfield, 1992).

The cooling of passionate love over time and the growing importance of other factors, such as shared values, can be seen in the feelings of those who enter

Unlike passionate love, companionate love can last a lifetime.
AP Images/Jae C. Hong

FIGURE :: 7

Romantic Love Between Partners in Arranged or Love Marriages in Jaipur, India

Source: Data from Gupta & Singh (1982).

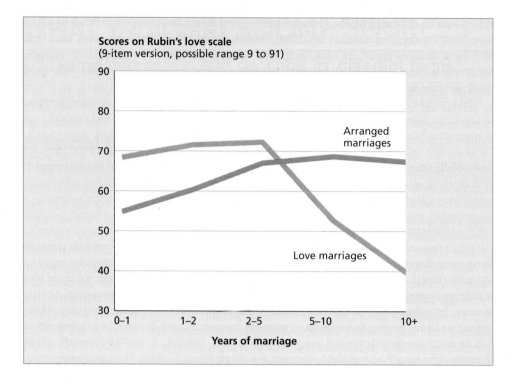

arranged versus love-based marriages in India. Those who married for love reported diminishing feelings of love after a 5-year newlywed period. By contrast, those in arranged marriages reported *more* love after 5 years (Gupta & Singh, 1982; Figure 7; for other data on the seeming success of arranged marriages, see J. E. Myers et al., 2005, Thakar & Epstein, 2011, and Yelsma & Athappilly, 1988).

The cooling of intense romantic love often triggers a period of disillusion, especially among those who believe that romantic love is essential both for a marriage and for its continuation. Compared with North Americans, Asians tend to focus less on personal feelings and more on the practical aspects of social attachments (Dion & Dion, 1988; Sprecher & Toro-Morn, 2002; Sprecher et al., 1994b). Thus, they are less vulnerable to disillusionment. Asians are also less prone to the self-focused individualism that in the long run can undermine a relationship and lead to divorce (Dion & Dion, 1991; Triandis et al., 1988).

The decline in intense mutual fascination may be natural and adaptive for species survival. The result of passionate love is often children, whose survival is aided by the parents' waning obsession with each other (Kenrick & Trost, 1987). Nevertheless, for those married more than 20 years, some of the lost romantic feeling is often renewed as the family nest empties and the parents are once again free to focus their attention on each other (Hatfield & Sprecher, 1986; White & Edwards, 1990). "No man or woman really knows what love is until they have been married a quarter of a century," said Mark Twain. If the relationship has been intimate, mutually rewarding, and rooted in a shared life history, companionate love deepens.

"Grow old along with me! The best is yet to be."

—Robert Browning, "Rabbi ben Ezra," in *Dramatis Personae*, 1864.

SUMMING UP: What Is Love?

- Researchers have characterized love as having components of intimacy, passion, and commitment. *Passionate love* is experienced as a bewildering confusion of ecstasy and anxiety, elation and pain. The *two-factor theory of emotion* suggests that in a romantic context, arousal from any source, even painful experiences, can be steered into passion.

- In the best of relationships, the initial passionate high settles to a steadier, more affectionate relationship called *companionate love*.

WHAT ENABLES CLOSE RELATIONSHIPS?

Explain how attachment styles, equity, and self-disclosure influence the ups and downs of our close relationships.

Attachment

Love is a biological imperative. We are social creatures, destined to bond with others. Our need to belong is adaptive. Cooperation promotes survival. In solo combat, our early ancestors were not the toughest predators; but as hunter–gatherers, and in fending off predators, they gained strength from numbers. Because group dwellers survived and reproduced, we today carry genes that predispose us to form such bonds.

Researchers have found that different forms of a particular gene predict mammalian pair bonding. In the mouselike prairie vole, and in humans, injections of hormones such as oxytocin (which is released in females during nursing and during mating) and vasopressin produce good feelings that trigger male–female bonding (Donaldson & Young, 2008; Young, 2009). In humans, genes associated with vasopressin activity predict marital stability (Walum et al., 2008). Such is the biology of enduring love.

Our dependence as infants strengthens our human bonds. Soon after birth we exhibit various social responses—love, fear, anger. But the first and greatest of these is love. As babies, we almost immediately prefer familiar faces and voices. We coo and smile when our parents give us attention. By approximately 8 months, we crawl toward mother or father and typically let out a wail when separated from them. Reunited, we cling. By keeping infants close to their caregivers, strong social attachment serves as a powerful survival impulse.

Deprived of familiar attachments, sometimes under conditions of extreme neglect, children may become withdrawn, frightened, silent. After studying the mental health of abandoned children for the World Health Organization, psychiatrist John Bowlby (1980, p. 442) reflected, "Intimate attachments to other human beings are the hub around which a person's life revolves. . . . From these intimate attachments [people draw] strength and enjoyment of life."

Attachment, especially to caretakers, is a powerful survival impulse.
Elizabeth Crews/The Image Works

Researchers have compared attachment and love in various close relationships—between parents and children, between friends, and between spouses or lovers (Davis, 1985; Maxwell, 1985; Sternberg & Grajek, 1984). Some elements are common to all loving attachments: mutual understanding, giving and receiving support, valuing and enjoying being with the loved one. The same brain areas associated with maternal attachment are also activated when adults think about their romantic partner (Acevedo et al., 2012). Passionate love is, however, spiced with some added features: physical affection, an expectation of exclusiveness, and an intense fascination with the loved one.

Passionate love is not just for lovers. The intense love of parent and infant for each other qualifies as a form of passionate love. Year-old infants, like young adult lovers, welcome physical affection, feel distress when separated, express intense affection when reunited, and take great pleasure in the significant other's attention and approval (Shaver & Mikulincer, 2011). Of course, infants vary in how they relate to caregivers, and so do adults in how they relate to their romantic partners. This made Phillip Shaver and Cindy Hazan (1993, 1994) wonder whether infant attachment styles might carry over to adult relationships.

ATTACHMENT STYLES

secure attachment
Attachments rooted in trust and marked by intimacy.

Approximately 7 in 10 infants, and nearly that many adults, exhibit **secure attachment** (Baldwin et al., 1996; Jones & Cunningham, 1996; Mickelson et al., 1997). When placed as infants in a strange situation (usually a laboratory playroom), they play comfortably in their mother's presence, happily exploring this strange environment. If she leaves, they become distressed; when she returns, they run to her, hold her, then relax and return to exploring and playing (Ainsworth, 1973, 1979). This trusting attachment style, many researchers believe, forms a working model of intimacy—a blueprint for one's adult intimate relationships, in which underlying trust sustains relationships through times of conflict (Miller & Rempel, 2004; Oriña et al., 2011; Salvatore et al., 2011). Securely attached adults find it easy to get close to others and don't fret about getting too dependent or being abandoned. As lovers, they enjoy sexuality within the context of a secure, committed relationship. And their relationships tend to be satisfying and enduring (Feeney, 1996; Feeney & Noller, 1990; Simpson et al., 1992).

avoidant attachment
Attachments marked by discomfort over, or resistance to, being close to others. An insecure attachment style.

Approximately 2 in 10 infants and adults exhibit **avoidant attachment,** one of the two types of insecure attachment. Although internally aroused, avoidant infants reveal little distress during separation and little clinging upon reunion. Avoiding closeness, avoidant adults tend to be less invested in relationships and more likely to leave them. They also are more likely to engage in uncommitted hookups (Garneau et al., 2013) and are more likely to be sexually unfaithful to their partners in both straight (DeWall et al., 2011) and gay (Starks & Parsons, 2014) relationships. Avoidant individuals may be either *fearful* ("I am uncomfortable getting close to others") or *dismissing* ("It is very important to me to feel independent and self-sufficient" [Bartholomew & Horowitz, 1991]). More college students in the United States had a dismissing attachment style in the 2010s (vs. the 1980s), and fewer had a secure attachment style. The researchers speculate that this shift may be rooted in changing family structures and an increasing emphasis on individualism (Konrath et al., 2014).

anxious attachment
Attachments marked by anxiety or ambivalence. An insecure attachment style.

Approximately 1 in 10 infants and adults exhibit the anxiousness and ambivalence that mark **anxious attachment,** the second type of insecure attachment. In the strange situation, infants are more likely to cling anxiously to their mother. If she leaves, they cry; when she returns, they may be indifferent or hostile. As adults, insecure individuals are less trusting, more fretful of a partner's becoming interested in someone else, and therefore more possessive and jealous. They may break up repeatedly with the same person. When discussing conflicts, they get emotional and often angry (Cassidy, 2000; Simpson et al., 1996), and their self-esteem fluctuates more based on feedback from others, especially romantic partners (Hepper & Carnelley, 2012). Their eagerness to form relationships can hamper their efforts because others perceive their anxiety and the interaction becomes awkward (McClure & Lydon, 2014).

Some researchers attribute these varying attachment styles, which have been studied across 62 cultures (Schmitt et al., 2004), to parental responsiveness. Cindy Hazan (2004) sums up the idea: "Early attachment experiences form the basis of *internal working models* or characteristic ways of thinking about relationships." Thus, sensitive, responsive mothers—mothers who engender a sense of basic trust in the world's reliability—typically have securely attached infants, observed Mary Ainsworth (1979) and Erik Erikson (1963). In fact, one study of 100 Israeli grandmother–daughter–granddaughter threesomes found intergenerational consistency of attachment styles (Besser & Priel, 2005). Youths who have experienced nurturant and involved parenting tend later to have warm and supportive relationships with their romantic partners (Conger et al., 2000). However, young adults whose parents were divorced did not differ in attachment style from those whose parents were still married (Washington & Hans, 2013). Attachment styles may be partially based in inherited temperament (Gillath et al., 2008; Harris, 1998). A gene that predisposes prairie voles to cuddle and mate for life (and has the same effect on laboratory mice genetically engineered to have the gene) has varying human forms. One is more commonly found in faithful, married men, another in those who are unmarried or unfaithful (Caldwell et al., 2008; Walum et al., 2008).

Couples with an anxiously attached woman and an avoidantly attached man experience more stress.
© wavebreakmedia/Shutterstock.com

The effects of attachment can last a lifetime: In a 22-year longitudinal study, infants who were insecurely attached to their mothers became adults who struggled to feel more positive emotions (Moutsiana et al., 2014). Attachment styles also have obvious impacts on adult relationships: In an analysis of 188 studies, avoidantly attached people were less satisfied and supported in their relationships, and anxiously attached people experienced more relationship conflict (Li & Chan, 2012).

Which attachment style combinations are the best—and worst? Two securely attached partners would seem to be ideal, and pairings in which at least one partner is insecurely attached may have more issues. The most difficult pairing appears to be an anxious woman and an avoidant man; these couples showed the highest levels of stress hormone when they anticipated talking over a conflict, and found it more difficult to give and seek care from their partner (Beck et al., 2013). This makes sense: The anxious woman, uncertain of her partner's love, seeks closeness, while the avoidant man, uncomfortable with closeness, distances himself. For better or for worse, early attachment styles do seem to lay a foundation for future relationships.

Equity

If each partner pursues his or her personal desires willy-nilly, the relationship will die. Therefore, our society teaches us to exchange rewards by the **equity** principle of attraction: What you and your partner get out of a relationship should be proportional to what you each put into it (Hatfield et al., 1978). If two people receive equal outcomes, they should contribute equally; otherwise one or the other will feel it is unfair. If both feel their outcomes correspond to the assets and efforts each contributes, then both perceive equity.

equity
A condition in which the outcomes people receive from a relationship are proportional to what they contribute to it. Note: Equitable outcomes needn't always be equal outcomes.

Strangers and casual acquaintances maintain equity by exchanging benefits: You lend me your class notes; later, I'll lend you mine. I invite you to my party; you invite me to yours. Those in an enduring relationship, including roommates and those in love, do not feel bound to trade similar benefits—notes for notes, parties for parties (Berg, 1984). They feel freer to maintain equity by exchanging a variety of benefits ("When you drop by to lend me your notes, why don't you stay for dinner?") and eventually to stop keeping track of who owes whom.

LONG-TERM EQUITY

Is it crass to suppose that friendship and love are rooted in an equitable exchange of rewards? Don't we sometimes give in response to a loved one's need, without expecting anything in return? Indeed, those involved in an equitable, long-term relationship are unconcerned with short-term equity. Margaret Clark and Judson Mills (1979, 1993; Clark, 1984, 1986) have argued that people even take pains to *avoid* calculating any exchange

"Love is the most subtle kind of self-interest."
—Holbrook Johnson

benefits. When we help a good friend, we do not want instant repayment. If someone invites us for dinner, we wait before reciprocating, lest the person attribute the motive for our return invitation to be merely paying off a social debt. True friends tune into one another's needs even when reciprocation is impossible (Clark et al., 1986, 1989). Similarly, happily married people tend not to keep score of how much they are giving and getting (Buunk & Van Yperen, 1991; Clark et al., 2010). As people observe their partners being self-giving, their sense of trust grows (Wieselquist et al., 1999).

In experiments with University of Maryland students, Clark and Mills confirmed that not being calculating is a mark of friendship. Tit-for-tat exchanges boosted people's liking when the relationship was relatively formal but diminished liking when the two sought friendship. Clark and Mills surmise that marriage contracts, in which each partner specifies what is expected from the other, would more likely undermine than enhance love. Only when the other's positive behavior is voluntary can we attribute it to love.

Previously we noted an equity principle at work in the matching phenomenon: People usually bring equal assets to romantic relationships. Often, they are matched for attractiveness, status, and so forth. If they are mismatched in one area, such as attractiveness, they tend to be mismatched in some other area, such as status. But in total assets, they are an equitable match. No one says, and few even think, "I'll trade you my good looks for your big income." But especially in relationships that last, equity is the rule.

PERCEIVED EQUITY AND SATISFACTION

In one survey, "sharing household chores" ranked third (after "faithfulness" and a "happy sexual relationship") among nine things that people saw as marks of successful marriages (Pew Research Center, 2007b). Indeed, those in an equitable relationship are typically content (Fletcher et al., 1987; Hatfield et al., 1985; Van Yperen & Buunk, 1990). Those who perceive their relationship as inequitable feel discomfort: The one who has the better deal may feel guilty and the one who senses a raw deal may feel strong irritation. (Given the self-serving bias—most husbands perceive themselves as contributing more housework than their wives credit them for—the person who is "overbenefited" is less sensitive to the inequity.)

Robert Schafer and Patricia Keith (1980) surveyed several hundred married couples of all ages, noting those who felt their marriages were somewhat unfair because one spouse contributed too little to the cooking, housekeeping, parenting, or providing. Inequity took its toll: Those who perceived inequity also felt more distressed and depressed. During the child-rearing years, when wives often feel underbenefited and husbands overbenefited, marital satisfaction tends to dip. During the honeymoon and empty-nest stages, spouses are more likely to perceive equity and to feel satisfaction with their marriages (Feeney et al., 1994). When both partners freely give and receive, and make decisions together, the odds of sustained, satisfying love are good.

Perceived inequity triggers marital distress, agree Nancy Grote and Margaret Clark (2001) from their tracking of married couples over time. But they also report that the traffic between inequity and distress runs both ways: Marital distress exacerbates the perception of unfairness (Figure 8).

Self-Disclosure

Deep, companionate relationships are intimate. They enable us to be known as we truly are and to feel accepted. We discover this delicious experience in a good marriage or a close friendship—a relationship where trust displaces anxiety and where we are free to open ourselves without fear of losing the other's affection (Holmes & Rempel, 1989). Such relationships are characterized by **self-disclosure** (Derlega et al., 1993). As a relationship grows, self-disclosing partners reveal more and more of themselves to each other; their knowledge of each other penetrates to deeper levels. In relationships that flourish, much of this self-disclosure shares successes and triumphs, and mutual delight over good happenings (Gable et al., 2006). When a friend rejoices with us over good news, it not only increases our joy about the happy event but also helps us feel better about the friendship (Reis et al., 2010).

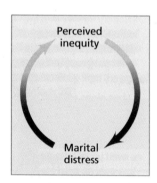

FIGURE :: 8

Perceived inequities trigger marital distress, which fosters the perception of inequities. *Source:* Adapted from Grote & Clark (2001).

self-disclosure

Revealing intimate aspects of oneself to others.

Most of us enjoy intimacy. It's gratifying to be singled out for another's disclosure. We feel pleased when a normally reserved person says that something about us "made me feel like opening up" and shares confidential information (Archer & Cook, 1986; D. Taylor et al., 1981). Not only do we like those who disclose, we also disclose to those whom we like. And after disclosing to them, we like them more (Collins & Miller, 1994). Lacking opportunities for intimate disclosure or concealing distressing information, we experience the pain of loneliness (Berg & Peplau, 1982; Solano et al., 1982; Uysal et al., 2010).

Experiments have probed both the *causes* and the *effects* of self-disclosure. When are people most willing to disclose intimate information concerning "what you like and don't like about yourself" or "what you're most ashamed and most proud of"? And what effects do such revelations have on those who reveal and receive them?

Self-disclosure is an effective way to build intimacy.
© Iakov Filimonov/Shutterstock.com

The most reliable finding is the **disclosure reciprocity** effect: Disclosure begets disclosure (Berg, 1987; Miller, 1990; Reis & Shaver, 1988). We reveal more to those who have been open with us. But intimate disclosure is seldom instant. (If it is, the person may seem indiscreet and unstable.) Appropriate intimacy progresses like a dance: I reveal a little, you reveal a little—but not too much. You then reveal more, and I reciprocate.

disclosure reciprocity
The tendency for one person's intimacy of self-disclosure to match that of a conversational partner.

For those in love, deepening intimacy is exciting. "Rising intimacy will create a strong sense of passion," note Roy Baumeister and Ellen Bratslavsky (1999). This helps explain why those who remarry after the loss of a spouse tend to begin the new marriage with an increased frequency of sex, and why passion often rides highest when intimacy is restored following severe conflict.

Some people—most of them women—are especially skilled "openers"; they easily elicit intimate disclosures from others, even from those who normally don't reveal very much of themselves (Pegalis et al., 1994; Shaffer et al., 1996). Such people tend to be good listeners. During conversation, they maintain attentive facial expressions and appear to be comfortably enjoying themselves (Purvis et al., 1984). They may also express interest by uttering supportive phrases while their conversational partner is speaking. They are what psychologist Carl Rogers (1980) called "growth-promoting" listeners—people who are genuine in revealing their own feelings, who are accepting of others' feelings, and who are empathic, sensitive, reflective listeners.

What are the effects of such self-disclosure? Humanistic psychologist Sidney Jourard (1964) argued that dropping our masks, letting ourselves be known as we are, nurtures love. He presumed that it is gratifying to open up to another and then to receive the trust another implies by being open with us. People feel better on days when they have disclosed something significant about themselves, such as their being lesbian or gay, and feel worse when concealing their identity (Beals et al., 2009). Those whose days include more deep or substantive discussions, rather than just small talk, tend to be happier. That's what Mathias Mehl and co-researchers (2010) found after equipping 70 undergraduates with recording devices that snatched 30-second conversational snippets five times each hour over 4 days.

"What is a friend? I will tell you. It is a person with whom you dare to be yourself."
—Frank Crane,
A Definition of Friendship

Having an intimate friend with whom we can discuss threats to our self-image seems to help us survive stress (Swann & Predmore, 1985). A true friendship is a special relationship that helps us cope with our other relationships. "When I am with my friend," reflected the Roman playwright Seneca, "methinks I am alone, and as much at liberty to speak anything as to think it." At its best, marriage is such a friendship, sealed by commitment.

Intimate self-disclosure is also one of companionate love's delights. The most self-revealing dating and married couples tend to enjoy the most satisfying and enduring relationships (Berg & McQuinn, 1986; Hendrick et al., 1988; Sprecher, 1987). For example, in a study of newlywed couples who were all equally in love, those who most deeply and accurately knew each other were most likely to enjoy enduring love (Neff & Karney, 2005). Married partners who most strongly agree that, "I try to share my most intimate thoughts and feelings with my partner" tend to have the most satisfying marriages (Sanderson & Cantor, 2001). For very reticent people, marriage may not be as satisfying as it is for those more willing to share their feelings (Baker & McNulty, 2010).

In a Gallup national marriage survey, 75 percent of those who prayed with their spouses (and 57 percent of those who didn't) reported their marriages as very happy (Greeley, 1991). Couples who engaged in mutual prayer felt more unity and trust with their partner (Lambert et al., 2012). Among believers, shared prayer from the heart is a humbling, intimate, soulful exposure (Beach et al., 2011). Those who pray together also more often say they discuss their marriages together, respect their spouses, and rate their spouses as skilled lovers.

Researchers have also found that women are often more willing to disclose their fears and weaknesses than are men (Cunningham, 1981). As feminist writer Kate Millett (1975) put it, "Women express, men repress." Small wonder that both men and women report friendships with women to be more intimate, enjoyable, and nurturing, and that on social networks, both males and females seem to prefer female friends (Thelwall, 2008).

Nevertheless, men today, particularly men with egalitarian gender-role attitudes, seem increasingly willing to reveal intimate feelings and to enjoy the satisfactions that accompany a relationship of mutual trust and self-disclosure. And that, say Arthur Aron and Elaine Aron (1994), is the essence of love—two selves connecting, disclosing, and identifying with each other; two selves, each retaining their individuality, yet sharing activities, delighting in similarities, and mutually supporting. The result for many romantic partners is "self–other integration": intertwined self-concepts (Slotter & Gardner, 2009; Figure 9).

That being so, might we cultivate closeness by experiences that mirror the escalating closeness of budding friendships? The Arons and their collaborators (1997) wondered. They paired volunteer students who were strangers to each other for 45 minutes. For the first 15 minutes, they shared thoughts on a list of personal but low-intimacy topics such as "When did you last sing to yourself?" The next 15 minutes were spent on more intimate topics such as "What is your most treasured memory?" The last 15 minutes invited even more self-disclosure, with questions such as "Complete this sentence: 'I wish I had someone with whom I could share . . .'" and "When did you last cry in front of another person? By yourself?"

Compared with control participants who spent the 45 minutes in small talk ("What was your high school like?" "What is your favorite holiday?"), those who experienced the escalating self-disclosure ended the hour feeling remarkably close to their conversation partners—in fact, "closer than the closest relationship in the lives of 30 percent of similar students," reported the researchers. These relationships surely were not yet marked by the loyalty and commitment of true friendship. Nevertheless, the experiment provides a striking demonstration of how readily a sense of closeness to others can grow, given open self-disclosure—which can also occur via the Internet. (See "Focus On: Does the Internet Create Intimacy or Isolation?")

FIGURE :: 9

Love: An Overlapping of Selves—You Become Part of Me, I Part of You
Source: From A. L. Weber and J. Harvey, *Perspective on Close Relationships.* Published by Allyn & Bacon, Boston, MA. Copyright © 1994 by Pearson Education.

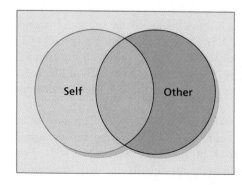

To promote self-disclosure in ongoing dating relationships, Richard Slatcher and James Pennebaker (2006) invited one member of 86 couples to spend 20 minutes on each of 3 days writing their deepest thoughts and feelings about the relationship (or, in a control condition, writing merely about their daily activities). Those who wrote about their feelings expressed more emotion to their partners in the days following. Three months later, 77 percent were still dating (compared with 52 percent in the control group).

As a reader of this college text, you are almost surely one of the world's 3 billion (as of 2015) Internet users. It took the telephone 7 decades to go from 1 percent to 75 percent penetration of North American households. Internet access reached 75 percent penetration in approximately 7 years (Putnam, 2000). You enjoy social networking, Web surfing, texting, and perhaps participating in listservs or chat rooms.

What do you think: Is computer-mediated communication within virtual communities a poor substitute for in-person relationships? Or is it a wonderful way to widen our social circles? Does the Internet do more to connect people or to drain time from face-to-face relationships? Consider the debate.

Point: The Internet, like the printing press and the telephone, expands communication, and communication enables relationships. Printing reduced face-to-face story-telling, and the telephone reduced face-to-face chats, but both enable us to communicate with people without limitations of time and distance. Social relations involve networking, and the Internet is the ultimate network. It enables efficient networking with family, friends, and kindred spirits—including people we otherwise never would have found, be they fellow MS patients, St. Nicholas collectors, or Hunger Games fans.

Counterpoint: True, but computer communication is impoverished. It lacks the nuances of eye-to-eye contact punctuated with nonverbal cues and physical touches. Outside of a few emoticons, electronic messages are devoid of gestures, facial expressions, and tones of voice. No wonder it's so easy to misread them. The absence of expressive emotion makes for ambiguous emotion.

For example, vocal nuances can signal whether a statement is serious, kidding, or sarcastic. Communicators often think their "just kidding" intent is equally clear, whether emailed or spoken. However, when emailed, the intent often isn't clear (Kruger et al., 2006). Thanks also to one's anonymity in virtual discussions, the result is sometimes a hostile "flame war."

A survey of 4,000 late-1990s Internet users found that 25 percent reported that their time online had reduced time spent in person and on the phone with family and friends (Nie & Erbring, 2000)—a number that might be considerably higher now. The Internet, like television, diverts time from real relationships. Internet discussions are not the same as in-person intimate conversations. Cybersex is artificial intimacy. Individualized web-based entertainment displaces getting together to play games. Such artificiality and isolation is regrettable because our ancestral history predisposes our needing real-time relationships, replete with smirks and smiles.

Point: But most folks don't perceive the Internet to be isolating. Two-thirds of U.S. Internet users in 2014 said online communication has strengthened their relationships with family and friends (Pew Research Center, 2014). Internet use may displace in-person intimacy, but it also displaces television watching. If one-click cyber-shopping is bad for your local bookstore, it frees time for relationships. Telecommuting does the same, enabling people to work from home and thereby spend more time with their families.

And why say that computer-formed relationships are unreal? On the Internet, your looks and location cease to matter. Your appearance, age, and race don't deter people from relating to you based on what's more genuinely important—your shared interests and values. In workplace and professional networks, computer-mediated discussions are less influenced by status and are therefore more candid and equally participatory. Computer-mediated communication fosters more spontaneous self-disclosure than face-to-face conversation (Joinson, 2001), and these disclosures are perceived as more intimate (Jiang et al., 2013).

Most Internet flirtations go nowhere. "Everyone I know who has tried online dating . . . agrees that we loathe spending (wasting?) hours gabbing to someone and then meeting him and realizing that he is a creep," observed one Toronto woman (Dicum, 2003). This experience would not surprise Eli Finkel and his fellow social psychologists (2012). Nearly a century of research on romantic compatibility leads them to conclude that the formulas of online matchmaking sites are unlikely to do what they claim. The best predictors of relationship success, such as communication patterns and other indications of compatibility, emerge only *after* people meet and get to know one another.

Nevertheless, married couples who met online were less likely to break up and more likely to be satisfied with their marriages (Cacioppo et al., 2013). Friendships and romantic relationships that form on the Internet are more likely than in-person relationships to last for at least 2 years (Bargh et al., 2002; Bargh & McKenna, 2004; McKenna & Bargh, 1998, 2000; McKenna et al., 2002). In one experiment, people disclosed more, with greater honesty and less posturing, when they met people online. They also felt more liking for people with whom they conversed online for 20 minutes than for those met for the same time face-to-face. This was true even when they unknowingly met the very same person in both contexts. People surveyed similarly feel that Internet friendships are as real, important, and close as offline relationships.

Counterpoint: The Internet allows people to be who they really are, but also to feign who they really aren't, sometimes in the interests of sexual exploitation. Internet sexual media, like other forms of pornography, may distort people's perceptions of sexual reality, decrease the attractiveness of their real-life partner, prime men to perceive women in sexual terms, make sexual coercion seem more trivial, provide mental scripts for how to act in sexual situations, increase arousal, and lead to disinhibition and imitation of loveless sexual behaviors.

Finally, suggests Robert Putnam (2000), the social benefits of computer-mediated communication are constrained by "cyberbalkanization." The Internet enables those of us with hearing loss to network, but it also enables White supremacists to find one another and thus contributes to social and political polarization.

As the debate over the Internet's social consequences continues, "the most important question," says Putnam (p. 180), will be "not what the Internet will do to us, but what we will do with it? . . . How can we harness this promising technology for thickening community ties? How can we develop the technology to enhance social presence, social feedback, and social cues? How can we use the prospect of fast, cheap communication to enhance the now fraying fabric of our real communities?"

"On the Internet, nobody knows you're a dog."

The Internet allows people to feign who they really aren't.
© Peter Steiner/The New Yorker Collection/www.cartoonbank.com

---

SUMMING UP: What Enables Close Relationships?

- From infancy to old age, attachments are central to human life. *Secure attachments,* as in an enduring marriage, mark happy lives.

- Companionate love is most likely to endure when both partners feel the partnership is *equitable,* with both

perceiving themselves receiving from the relationship in proportion to what they contribute to it.

- One reward of companionate love is the opportunity for *intimate self-disclosure,* a state achieved gradually as each partner reciprocates the other's increasing openness.

HOW DO RELATIONSHIPS END?

Summarize the factors that predict marital dissolution and describe the detachment process.

In 1971, a man wrote a love poem to his bride, slipped it into a bottle, and dropped it into the Pacific Ocean between Seattle and Hawaii. A decade later, a jogger found it on a Guam beach:

> If, by the time this letter reaches you, I am old and gray, I know that our love will be as fresh as it is today.
>
> It may take a week or it may take years for this note to find you. . . . If this should never reach you, it will still be written in my heart that I will go to extreme means to prove my love for you. Your husband, Bob.

The woman to whom the love note was addressed was reached by phone. When the note was read to her, she burst out laughing. And the more she heard, the harder she laughed. "We're divorced," she finally said, and slammed down the phone.

"When I was a young man, I vowed never to marry until I found the ideal woman. Well I found her—but alas, she was waiting for the ideal man."

—French Statesman,
Robert Schuman, 1886–1963

So it often goes. Smart brains can make dumb decisions. Comparing their unsatisfying relationship with the support and affection they imagine are available elsewhere, many relationships end. Each year, Canada and the United States record one divorce for every two marriages. As economic and social barriers to divorce weakened during the 1960s and 1970s, divorce rates rose. "We are living longer, but loving more briefly," quipped Os Guiness (1993, p. 309).

Divorce

To predict a culture's divorce rates, it helps to know its values (Triandis, 1994). Individualistic cultures (where love is a feeling and people ask, "What does my heart say?") have more divorce than do communal cultures (where love entails obligation and people ask, "What will other people say?"). Individualists marry "for as long as we both shall love," collectivists more often for life. Individualists expect more passion and personal fulfillment in a marriage, which puts greater pressure on the relationship (Dion & Dion, 1993). In one pair of surveys, "keeping romance alive" was rated as important to a good marriage by 78 percent of American women and 29 percent of Japanese women (*American Enterprise,* 1992). Eli Finkel and his colleagues (2014) argue that marriage has become more challenging in individualistic recent times as couples expect more fulfillment from marriage but invest fewer resources in it—a potentially impossible equation.

Coldness, disillusionment, and hopelessness are better predictors of divorce than arguing.
Image Source/Getty Images

Even in Western society, however, those who enter relationships with a long-term orientation and an intention to persist do experience healthier, less turbulent, and more durable partnerships (Arriaga, 2001; Arriaga & Agnew, 2001). Enduring relationships are rooted in enduring love and satisfaction, but also in fear of the termination cost, a sense of moral obligation, and inattention to possible alternative partners (Adams & Jones, 1997; Maner et al., 2009; Miller, 1997). For those determined that their marriage last, it usually does.

Those whose commitment to a union outlasts the desires that gave birth to it will endure times of conflict and unhappiness. One national survey found that 86 percent of those who were unhappily married but who stayed with the marriage were, when reinterviewed 5 years later, now mostly "very" or "quite" happy with their marriages (Popenoe, 2002). By contrast, narcissists enter relationships with less commitment and less likelihood of long-term relational success (Campbell & Foster, 2002).

Risk of divorce also depends on who marries whom (Fergusson et al., 1984; Myers, 2000a; Tzeng, 1992). People usually stay married if they

- married after age 20,
- both grew up in stable, two-parent homes,
- dated for a long while before marriage,
- are well and similarly educated,
- enjoy a stable income from a good job,
- live in a small town or on a farm,
- did not cohabit or become pregnant before marriage,
- are religiously committed,
- are of similar age, faith, and education.

None of those predictors, by itself, is essential to a stable marriage. Moreover, they are correlates of enduring marriages, not necessarily causes. But if none of those things is true for someone, marital breakdown is an almost sure bet. If all are true, they are very likely to stay together until death. The English perhaps had it right when, several centuries ago, they presumed that the temporary intoxication of passionate love was a foolish basis for permanent marital decisions. Better, they felt, to choose a mate based on stable friendship and compatible backgrounds, interests, habits, and values (Stone, 1977).

The Detachment Process

Our close relationships help define the social identity that shapes our self-concept (Slotter et al., 2010). Thus, much as we experience life's best moments when relationships begin—when having a baby, making a friend, falling in love—so we experience life's worst moments when relationships end, with death or a broken bond (Jaremka et al., 2011). Severing bonds produces a predictable sequence of agitated preoccupation with the lost partner, followed by deep sadness and, eventually, the beginnings of emotional detachment, a letting go of the old while focusing on someone new, and a renewed sense of self (Hazan & Shaver, 1994; Lewandowski & Bizzoco, 2007; Spielmann et al., 2009). Even newly separated couples who have long ago ceased feeling affection are often surprised at their desire to be near the former partner. Deep and long-standing attachments seldom break quickly; detaching is a process, not an event.

Among dating couples, the closer and longer the relationship and the fewer the available alternatives, the more painful the breakup (Simpson, 1987). Surprisingly, Roy Baumeister and Sara Wotman (1992) report that, months or years later, people recall more pain over spurning someone's love than over having been spurned. Their distress arises from guilt over hurting someone, from upset over the heartbroken lover's persistence, or from uncertainty over how to respond. Among married couples, breakup has additional costs: shocked parents and friends, guilt over broken vows, anguish over reduced household income, and possibly less time with children. Still, each year millions of couples are willing to pay such costs to extricate themselves from what they perceive as the greater costs of continuing a painful, unrewarding relationship. Such costs include, in one study of 328 married couples, a 10-fold increase in depression symptoms when a marriage is marked by discord rather than satisfaction (O'Leary et al., 1994). When, however, a marriage is "very happy," life as a whole usually seems "very happy" (Figure 10).

When relationships suffer, those without better alternatives or who feel invested in a relationship (through time, energy, mutual friends, possessions, and perhaps children) will seek alternatives to exiting the relationship. Caryl Rusbult and colleagues (1986, 1987, 1998) explored three ways of coping with a failing relationship (Table 1). Some people exhibit *loyalty*—by waiting for conditions to improve. The problems are too painful to

FIGURE :: 10

National Opinion Research Center Surveys of 30,507 Married Americans, 1972–2012

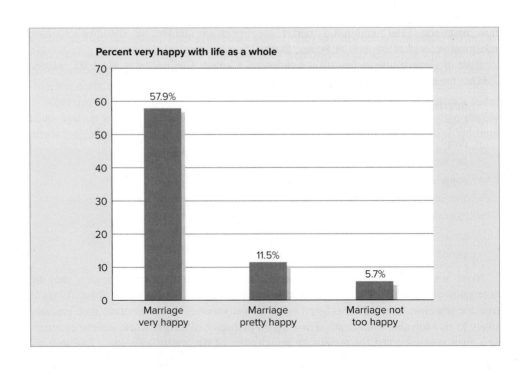

TABLE :: 1 Responses to Relationship Distress

	Passive	Active
Constructive	*Loyalty:* Await improvement	*Voice:* Seek to improve relationships
Destructive	*Neglect:* Ignore the partner	*Exit:* End the relationship

Source: Rusbult et al., 1986, 1987, 1998, 2001.

confront and the risks of separation are too great, so the loyal partner perseveres, hoping the good old days will return. Others (especially men) exhibit *neglect;* they ignore the partner and allow the relationship to deteriorate. With painful dissatisfactions ignored, an insidious emotional uncoupling ensues as the partners talk less and begin redefining their lives without each other. Still others will *voice* their concerns and take active steps to improve the relationship by discussing problems, seeking advice, and attempting to change.

Study after study—in fact, 115 studies of 45,000 couples—reveal that unhappy couples disagree, command, criticize, and put down. Happy couples more often agree, approve, assent, and laugh (Karney & Bradbury, 1995; Noller & Fitzpatrick, 1990). After observing 2,000 couples, John Gottman (1994, 1998, 2005) noted that healthy marriages were not necessarily devoid of conflict. Rather, they were marked by an ability to reconcile differences and to overbalance criticism with affection. In successful marriages, positive interactions (smiling, touching, complimenting, laughing) outnumbered negative interactions (sarcasm, disapproval, insults) by at least a 5-to-1 ratio.

It's not distress and arguments that predict divorce, add Ted Huston and colleagues (2001) from their following of newlyweds through time. (Most newlyweds experience conflict.) Rather, it's coldness, disillusionment, and hopelessness that predict a dim marital future. This is especially so, observed William Swann and associates (2003, 2006), when inhibited men are coupled with critical women.

Successful couples have learned, sometimes aided by communication training, to restrain the poisonous put-downs and gut-level reactions and to think and behave more positively (McNulty, 2010). They fight fairly (by stating feelings without insulting). They depersonalize conflict with comments such as, "I know it's not your fault" (Markman et al., 1988; Notarius & Markman, 1993; Yovetich & Rusbult, 1994). Couples randomly assigned to think less emotionally and more like an observer during fights were later more satisfied with their marriages (Finkel et al., 2013). Would unhappy relationships get better if the partners agreed to *act* more as happy couples do—by complaining and criticizing less? By affirming and agreeing more? By setting aside times to voice their concerns and doing so calmly? By praying or playing together daily? As attitudes trail behaviors, do affections trail actions?

Joan Kellerman, James Lewis, and James Laird (1989) wondered. They knew that among couples passionately in love, eye gazing is typically prolonged and mutual (Rubin, 1973). Would intimate eye gazing similarly stir feelings between those not in love (much as 45 minutes of escalating self-disclosure evoked feelings of closeness among those unacquainted students)? To find out, they asked unacquainted male–female pairs to gaze intently for 2 minutes either at each other's hands or into each other's eyes. When they separated, the eye gazers reported a tingle of attraction and affection toward each other. Simulating love had begun to stir it.

By enacting and expressing love, researcher Robert Sternberg (1988) believes the passion of initial romance can evolve into enduring love:

> "Living happily ever after" need not be a myth, but if it is to be a reality, the happiness must be based upon different configurations of mutual feelings at various times in a relationship. Couples who expect their passion to last forever, or their intimacy to remain unchallenged, are in for disappointment. . . . We must constantly work at understanding, building, and rebuilding our loving relationships. Relationships are constructions, and they decay over time if they are not maintained and improved. We cannot expect a relationship simply to take care of itself, any more than we can expect that of a building. Rather, we must take responsibility for making our relationships the best they can be.

How Do Relationships End?

vorce rates rose in the
scerned predictors of
r is an individualistic
nmitment; other factors
, values, and similarity.

- Researchers are also identifying the process through which couples either detach or rebuild their relationships. And they are identifying the positive and nondefensive communication styles that mark healthy, stable marriages.

POSTSCRIPT:
Making Love

Two facts of contemporary life seem beyond dispute: First, *close, enduring relationships are hallmarks of a happy life*. One example of a close relationship is marriage. In National Opinion Research Center surveys of 52,340 Americans since 1972, 40 percent of married adults, 23 percent of those never married, 19 percent of the divorced, and 16 percent of the separated declared their lives "very happy." Similar results come from national surveys in Canada and Europe (Inglehart, 1990).

Second, *close, enduring relationships are in decline*. Increased migration and mobility mean that more people are disconnected from extended family and childhood relationships. Compared with a half-century ago, people today more often move, live alone, divorce, and have a succession of relationships.

Given the psychological ingredients of marital happiness—kindred minds, social and sexual intimacy, equitable giving and receiving of emotional and material resources—it becomes possible to contest the French saying "Love makes the time pass and time makes love pass." But it takes effort to stem love's decay. It takes effort to carve out time each day to talk over the day's happenings. It takes effort to forgo nagging and bickering and instead to disclose and hear each other's hurts, concerns, and dreams. It takes effort to make a relationship into "a classless utopia of social equality" (Sarnoff & Sarnoff, 1989), in which both partners freely give and receive, share decision making, and enjoy life together.

By minding our close relationships, sustained satisfaction is possible, note John Harvey and Julia Omarzu (1997). Australian relationships researcher Patricia Noller (1996) concurs: "Mature love . . . love that sustains marriage and family as it creates an environment in which individual family members can grow . . . is sustained by beliefs that love involves acknowledging and accepting differences and weaknesses; that love involves an internal decision to love another person and a long-term commitment to maintain that love; and finally that love is controllable and needs to be nurtured and nourished by the lovers."

For those who commit themselves to creating an equitable, intimate, mutually supportive relationship, there may come the security, and the joy, of enduring, companionate love. This is echoed in the classic children's story *The Velveteen Rabbit*. When someone "loves you for a long, long time," explained the wise, old Skin Horse to the Velveteen Rabbit, "not just to play with, but REALLY loves you, then you become Real. . . ."

> "Does it happen all at once, like being wound up," [the rabbit] asked, "or bit by bit?"
>
> "It doesn't happen all at once," said the Skin Horse. "You become. It takes a long time. That's why it doesn't often happen to people who break easily, or have sharp edges, or who have to be carefully kept. Generally, by the time you are Real, most of your hair has been loved off, and your eyes drop out and you get loose in the joints and very shabby. But these things don't matter at all, because once you are Real you can't be ugly, except to people who don't understand."

Helping

Blend Images/Alamy

"Love cures people—both the ones who give it and the ones who receive it."

—Psychiatrist Karl Meninger, 1893–1990

On a hillside in Jerusalem, some 2000 trees form the Garden of the Righteous. Beneath each tree is a plaque with the name of those who gave refuge to one or more Jews during the Nazi Holocaust. These "righteous Gentiles" knew that if the refugees were discovered, Nazi policy dictated that host and refugee would suffer a common fate. Many did (Hellman, 1980; Wiesel, 1985).

One hero who did not survive was Jane Haining, a Church of Scotland missionary who was matron at a school for 400 mostly Jewish girls. On the eve of war, the church, fearing her safety, ordered her to return home. She refused, saying, "If these children need me in days of sunshine, how much more do they need me in days of darkness?" (Barnes, 2008; Brown, 2008). She reportedly cut up her leather luggage to make soles for her girls' shoes. In April 1944, Haining accused a cook of eating sparse food rations intended for her girls. The cook, a Nazi party member,

Why do we help?

When will we help?

Who will help?

How can we increase helping?

Postscript: Taking social psychology into life

denounced her to the Gestapo, who arrested her for having worked among the Jews and having wept to see her girls forced to wear yellow stars. A few weeks later, she was sent to Auschwitz, where she suffered the same fate as millions of Jews.

In 2013, an unnamed hero at an Oakland Raiders football game saw a woman at the edge of the seating deck 45 feet above him contemplating jumping to her death. "Don't do it," he repeatedly shouted. When she did, he lunged toward where she was about to fall, leaving him with serious injuries, but saving her life (AP, 2013).

Less dramatic acts of comforting, caring, and compassion abound: Without asking anything in return, people offer directions, donate money, give blood, volunteer time.

- Why, and when, will people help?
- Who will help?
- What can be done to lessen indifference and increase helping?

These are this chapter's primary questions.

altruism
A motive to increase another's welfare without conscious regard for one's self-interests.

Altruism is selfishness in reverse. An altruistic person is concerned and helpful even when no benefits are offered or expected in return. Jesus' parable of the Good Samaritan provides the classic illustration:

A man was going down from Jerusalem to Jericho, and fell into the hands of robbers, who stripped him, beat him, and went away, leaving him half dead. Now by chance a priest was going down that road; and when he saw him, he passed by on the other side. So likewise a Levite, when he came to the place and saw him, passed by on the other side. But a Samaritan while traveling came near him; and when he saw him, he was moved with pity. He went to him and bandaged his wounds, having poured oil and wine on them. Then he put him on his own animal, brought him to an inn, and took care of him. The next day he took out two denarii, gave them to the innkeeper, and said, "Take care of him; and when I come back, I will repay you whatever more you spend." (Luke 10:30–35, NRSV)

The Samaritan story illustrates altruism. Filled with compassion, he is motivated to give a stranger time, energy, and money while expecting neither repayment nor appreciation.

Good Samaritan, Fernand Schultz-Wettel
Permission of the Trustees of the National Gallery, London

WHY DO WE HELP?

Explain psychology's theories of what motivates helping—and the type of helping each theory seeks to explain.

Social Exchange and Social Norms

Several theories of helping agree that, in the long run, helping behavior benefits the giver as well as the receiver. One explanation assumes that human interactions are guided by "social economics." We exchange not only material goods and money but also social goods—love, services, information, status (Foa & Foa, 1975). In doing so, we aim to minimize costs and maximize rewards. **Social-exchange theory** does not contend that we consciously monitor costs and rewards, only that such considerations predict our behavior.

Suppose your campus is having a blood drive and someone asks you to participate. Might you not implicitly weigh the *costs* of donating (needle prick, time, fatigue) against those of not donating (guilt, disapproval)? Might you not also weigh the *benefits* of donating (feeling good about helping someone, free refreshments) against those of not donating (saving the time, discomfort, and anxiety)? According to social-exchange theory, such subtle calculations precede decisions to help or not.

social-exchange theory
The theory that human interactions are transactions that aim to maximize one's rewards and minimize one's costs.

REWARDS

Rewards that motivate helping may be external or internal. The New Yorker who, to prevent a train delay, jumped onto subway tracks to save a man who had fainted ("I was thinking, if he gets hit, I can't go to work"), was motivated by the external rewards of his time-and-a-half Sunday pay (Weischelbaum et al., 2010). When businesses donate money to improve their corporate images or when someone offers a ride hoping to receive appreciation or friendship, the reward is external. We give to get. Thus, we are most eager to help someone attractive to us, someone whose approval we desire (Krebs, 1970; Unger, 1979). In experiments, and in everyday life, public generosity boosts one's status, while selfish behavior can lead to punishment (Hardy & Van Vugt, 2006; Henrich et al., 2006).

Rewards may also be internal. Nearly all blood donors agree that giving blood "makes you feel good about yourself" and "gives you a feeling of self-satisfaction" (Piliavin, 2003; Piliavin et al., 1982). Indeed, "Give blood," advises an old Red Cross poster. "All you'll feel is good." Feeling good helps explain why people far from home will do kindnesses for strangers whom they will never see again.

Helping's boost to self-worth explains this *do-good/feel-good effect.* One month-long study of 85 couples found that giving emotional support to one's partner was positive for the *giver;* giving support boosted the giver's mood (Gleason et al., 2003). Jane Piliavin (2003) and Susan Andersen (1998) reviewed studies that showed that youth who engaged in community service projects, school-based "service learning," or tutoring children develop social skills and positive social values. Such youth are at markedly less risk for delinquency, pregnancy, and school dropout and are more likely to become

"Hey, there's Sara, padding her college-entrance résumé!"

© Edward Koren/The New Yorker Collection/www.cartoonbank.com

engaged citizens. Volunteering likewise benefits morale and health, especially when self-initiated rather than required (Weinstein & Ryan, 2010). Bereaved spouses recover from their depressed feelings faster when they are engaged in helping others (Brown et al., 2008, 2009). Those who do good tend to do well.

Ditto for giving money. Making donations activates brain areas linked with reward (Harbaugh et al., 2007). Generous people are happier than those whose spending is self-focused. In one experiment, people received an envelope with cash that some were instructed to spend on themselves, while others were directed to spend on other people. At the day's end, the happiest people were those assigned to the spend-it-on-others condition (Dunn et al., 2008, 2013; Geenen et al., 2014). Other research confirms that *giving increases happiness:*

- A survey of more than 200,000 people in 136 countries found that, virtually everywhere, people report feeling happier after spending money on others rather than on themselves (Aknin et al., 2013). Givers are also less prone to depression than nongivers (Smith & Davidson, 2014).
- Giving employees "prosocial bonuses"—charitable donations to spend on others, or on teammates rather than themselves—produces "happier and more satisfied employees" and higher-performing teams (Anik et al., 2013).
- Purchasing a goody bag for a sick child improved people's mood enough for others to notice their increased happiness (Aknin et al., 2014).

"Men do not value a good deed unless it brings a reward."
—Ovid,
Epistulae ex Ponto, 10 A.D.

This cost–benefit analysis can seem demeaning. In defense of the theory, however, is it not a credit to humanity that helping can be inherently rewarding? That much of our behavior is not antisocial but "prosocial"? That we can find fulfillment in the giving of love? How much worse off the human race would be if we gained pleasure only by serving ourselves.

"True," some readers may reply. "Still, reward theories imply that a helpful act is never truly altruistic—that we merely call it 'altruistic' when its rewards are inconspicuous. If we help the distressed woman so we can gain social approval, relieve our distress, prevent guilt, or boost our self-image, is it really altruistic?" That argument is reminiscent of

THE inside STORY

Dennis Krebs on Life Experience and the Study of Altruism

At age 14, I was traumatized when my family moved from Vancouver, B.C., to California. I fell from president of my junior high school to an object of social ridicule because of my clothes, accent, and behavior. The fighting skills I had acquired boxing soon generated a quite different reputation from the one I enjoyed in Canada. I sank lower and lower until, after several visits to juvenile detention homes, I was arrested and convicted for driving under the influence of drugs. I escaped from jail, hitchhiked to a logging camp in Oregon, and eventually made my way back to British Columbia. I was admitted to university on probation, graduated at the top of my class, won a Woodrow Wilson Fellowship, and was accepted to a psychology doctoral program at Harvard.

Attending Harvard required moving back to the United States. Concerned about my escapee record in California, I turned myself in and suffered through the ensuing publicity. I was pardoned, in large part because of the tremendous

support I received from many people. After 3 years at Harvard, I was hired as an assistant professor. Eventually I returned to British Columbia to chair the Psychology Department at Simon Fraser University.

Though it makes me somewhat uncomfortable, I disclose this history as a way of encouraging people with two strikes against them to remain in the game. A great deal of the energy I have invested in understanding morality has stemmed from a need to understand why I went wrong, and my interest in altruism has been fueled by the generosity of those who helped me overcome my past.

Dennis Krebs
Simon Fraser University
Courtesy of Dennis Krebs

B. F. Skinner's (1971) analysis of helping. We credit people for their good deeds, said Skinner, only when we can't explain them. We attribute their behavior to their inner dispositions only when we lack external explanations. When the external causes are obvious, we credit the causes, not the person.

There is, however, a weakness in reward theory. It easily degenerates into explaining-by-naming. If someone volunteers for the Big Sister tutor program, it is tempting to "explain" her compassionate action by the satisfaction it brings her. But such after-the-fact naming of rewards creates a circular explanation: "Why did she volunteer?" "Because of the inner rewards." "How do you know there are inner rewards?" "Why else would she have volunteered?" Because of this circular reasoning, **egoism**—the idea that self-interest motivates all behavior—has fallen into disrepute.

To escape the circularity, we must define the rewards and the costs independently of the helping behavior. If social approval motivates helping, then in experiments we should find that when approval follows helping, helping increases. And it does (Staub, 1978, 2015).

INTERNAL REWARDS

So far, we have considered external rewards that motivate helping. We also need to consider internal factors, such as the helper's emotional state or personal traits.

The benefits of helping include internal self-rewards. Near someone in distress, we may feel distress. A woman's scream outside your window arouses and distresses you. Horror movies distress us as we empathize with the frightened victims. If you cannot reduce your arousal by interpreting the scream as a playful shriek, then you may investigate or give aid, thereby reducing your distress (Piliavin & Piliavin, 1973). Altruism researcher Dennis Krebs (1975) found that Harvard University men whose physiological responses and self-reports revealed the most arousal in response to another's distress also gave the most help to the person.

GUILT. Distress is not the only negative emotion we act to reduce. Throughout recorded history, guilt has been a painful emotion that people avoid and seek to relieve. As Everett Sanderson remarked after heroically saving a child who had fallen onto subway tracks in front of an approaching train, "If I hadn't tried to save that little girl, if I had just stood there like the others, I would have died inside. I would have been no good to myself from then on."

Cultures have institutionalized ways to relieve guilt: animal and human sacrifices, offerings of grain and money, penitent behavior, confession, denial. In ancient Israel, the sins of the people were periodically laid on a "scapegoat" animal that was then led into the wilderness to carry away the people's guilt.

To examine the consequences of guilt, social psychologists have induced people to transgress: to lie, to deliver shock, to knock over a table loaded with alphabetized cards, to break a machine, to cheat. Afterward, the guilt-laden participants may be offered a way to relieve their guilt: by confessing, by disparaging the one harmed, or by doing a good deed to offset the bad one. The results are remarkably consistent: People will do whatever can be done to expunge the guilt, relieve their bad feelings, and restore their self-image.

Picture yourself as a participant in one such experiment conducted with Mississippi State University students (McMillen & Austin, 1971). You and another student, each seeking to earn credit toward a course requirement, arrive for the experiment. Soon after, a confederate enters, portraying himself as a previous participant looking for a lost book. He strikes up a conversation in which he mentions that the experiment involves taking a multiple-choice test, for which most of the correct answers are "B." After the accomplice departs, the experimenter arrives, explains the experiment, and then asks, "Have either of you been in this experiment before or heard anything about it?"

Would you lie? The behavior of those who have gone before you in this experiment—100 percent of whom told the little lie—suggests that you would. After you have taken the test (without receiving any feedback on it), the experimenter says: "You are free to leave. However, if you have some spare time, I could use your help in scoring some questionnaires."

egoism
A self-serving motive (supposedly underlying all behavior) to increase one's own welfare. The opposite of altruism, which aims to increase another's welfare.

"For it is in giving that we receive."
—Saint Francis of Assisi, 1181–1226

Schoolchildren packing toy donations for the needy. As children mature, they usually come to take pleasure in helping others.

artpipi/Getty Images

Assuming you have told the lie, do you think you would now be more or less willing to volunteer some time? On average, those who had not been induced to lie volunteered only 2 minutes of time. Those who had lied were apparently eager to redeem their self-images; on average they offered a whopping 63 minutes. One moral of this experiment was well expressed by a 7-year-old girl, who, in one of my [DM] own experiments, wrote: "Don't Lie or youl Live with gilt" (and you will feel a need to relieve it).

Our eagerness to do good after doing bad reflects our need to reduce *private* guilt and restore a shaken self-image. It also reflects our desire to reclaim a positive *public* image. We are more likely to redeem ourselves with helpful behavior when other people know about our misdeeds (Carlsmith & Gross, 1969).

All in all, guilt leads to much good. By motivating people to confess, apologize, help, and avoid repeated harm, guilt boosts sensitivity and sustains close relationships.

EXCEPTIONS TO THE FEEL-BAD/DO-GOOD SCENARIO. Among well-socialized adults, should we always expect to find the "feel-bad/do-good" phenomenon? No. One negative mood, anger, produces anything but compassion. Another exception is profound grief. People who suffer the loss of a spouse or a child, whether through death or separation, often undergo a period of intense self-preoccupation, which restrains giving to others (Aderman & Berkowitz, 1983; Gibbons & Wicklund, 1982).

In a powerful laboratory simulation of self-focused grief, William Thompson, Claudia Cowan, and David Rosenhan (1980) had Stanford University students listen privately to a taped description of a person (whom they were to imagine was their best friend) dying of cancer. The experiment focused some students' attention on their own worry and grief:

> He (she) could die and you would lose him, never be able to talk to him again. Or worse, he could die slowly. You would know every minute could be your last time together. For months you would have to be cheerful for him while you were sad. You would have to watch him die in pieces, until the last piece finally went, and you would be alone.

For others, it focused their attention on the friend:

> He spends his time lying in bed, waiting those interminable hours, just waiting and hoping for something to happen. Anything. He tells you that it's not knowing that is the hardest.

The researchers report that regardless of which tape the participants heard, they were profoundly moved and sobered by the experience, yet not the least regretful of participating (although some participants who in a control condition listened to a boring tape were regretful). Did their moods affect their helpfulness? When immediately thereafter they were given a chance to help a graduate student with her research anonymously, 25 percent of those whose attention had been self-focused helped. Of those whose attention was other-focused, 83 percent helped. The two groups were equally touched, but only the other-focused participants found helping someone especially rewarding. In short, the feel-bad/do-good effect occurs with people whose attention is on others, people for whom altruism is therefore rewarding (Barnett et al., 1980; McMillen et al., 1977). If they are not self-preoccupied by depression or grief, sad people are sensitive, helpful people.

FEEL GOOD, DO GOOD. So, are happy people unhelpful? Quite the contrary. There are few more consistent findings in psychology: Happy people are helpful people. This effect occurs with both children and adults, regardless of whether the good mood comes from a success, from thinking happy thoughts, or from any of several other positive experiences (Salovey et al., 1991). One woman recalled her experience after falling in love:

> At the office, I could hardly keep from shouting out how deliriously happy I felt. The work was easy; things that had annoyed me on previous occasions were taken in stride. And I had strong impulses to help others; I wanted to share my joy. When Mary's typewriter broke down, I virtually sprang to my feet to assist. Mary! My former "enemy"! (Tennov, 1979, p. 22)

"It's curious how, when you're in love, you yearn to go about doing acts of kindness to everybody."

—P. G. Wodehouse,
The Mating Season, 1949

In experiments on happiness and helpfulness, the person who is helped may be someone seeking a donation, an experimenter seeking help with paperwork, or a woman who drops papers. Here are three examples.

In Sydney, Australia, Joseph Forgas and colleagues (2008) had a confederate offer either a mood-boosting compliment to a Target department store salesperson or a neutral or mood-deflating comment. Moments later, a second confederate, who was "blind" to the mood-induction condition, sought the employee's help in locating a nonexistent item. Among less-experienced staff (who lacked a practiced routine for answering such requests), those receiving the mood boost made the greatest effort to help.

In Opole, Poland, Dariusz Dolinski and Richard Nawrat (1998) found that a positive mood of relief can dramatically boost helping. Imagine yourself as one of their unwitting subjects. After illegally parking your car for a few moments, you return to discover what looks like a ticket under your windshield wiper (where parking tickets are placed). Groaning inwardly, you pick up the apparent ticket and then are much relieved to discover it is only an ad (or a blood drive appeal). Moments later, a university student approaches you and asks you to spend 15 minutes answering questions—to "help me complete my M.A. thesis." Would your positive, relieved mood make you more likely to help? Indeed, 62 percent of people whose fear had just turned to relief agreed willingly. That was nearly double the number who did so when no ticketlike paper was left or when it was left on the car door (not a place for a ticket).

In the United States, Alice Isen, Margaret Clark, and Mark Schwartz (1976) had a confederate call people who had received a free sample of stationery 0 to 20 minutes earlier. The confederate said she had used her last dime to dial this (supposedly wrong) number and asked each person to relay a message by phone. As Figure 1 shows, the individuals' willingness to relay the phone message rose during the 5 minutes afterward. Then, as the good mood wore off, helpfulness dropped.

If sad people are sometimes extra helpful, how can it be that happy people are also helpful? Experiments reveal several factors at work (Carlson et al., 1988). Helping softens a bad mood and sustains a good mood. (Perhaps you can recall feeling good after giving someone directions.) A positive mood is, in turn, conducive to positive thoughts and positive self-esteem, which predispose us to positive behavior (Berkowitz, 1987; Cunningham et al., 1990; Isen et al., 1978). In a good mood—after receiving a gift or while feeling the warm glow of success—people are more likely to have positive thoughts. And positive thinkers are likely to be positive actors . . . which helps explain why, even after controlling for other demographic factors, extraordinary acts of altruism tend to come from happy

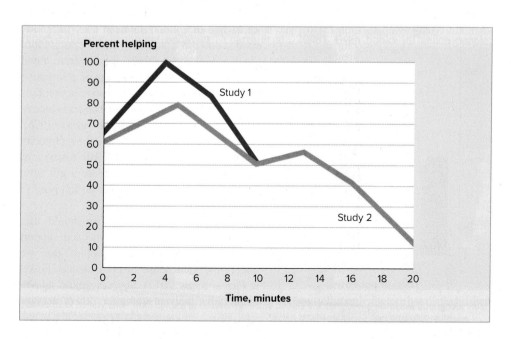

FIGURE :: 1

Percentage of Those Willing to Relay a Phone Message 0 to 20 Minutes after Receiving a Free Sample

Of control subjects who did not receive a gift, only 10 percent helped.

Source: Data from Isen et al. (1976).

places. The areas of the United States where people report the most happiness also tend to be the places with high rates of kidney donation (Brethel-Haurwitz & Marsh, 2014).

SOCIAL NORMS

Often, we help others not because we have calculated consciously that such behavior is in our self-interest but because of a subtler form of self-interest: because something tells us we *ought* to. We ought to help a new neighbor move in. We ought to return the wallet we found. We ought to protect our combat buddies from harm. Norms, the *oughts* of our lives, are social expectations. They *prescribe* proper behavior. Researchers who study helping behavior have identified two social norms that motivate altruism: the reciprocity norm and the social-responsibility norm.

reciprocity norm

An expectation that people will help, not hurt, those who have helped them.

THE RECIPROCITY NORM. One universal moral code is a **reciprocity norm:** *To those who help us, we should return help, not harm* (Gouldner, 1960). This norm is as universal as the incest taboo. We "invest" in others and expect dividends. Politicians know that the one who gives a favor can later expect a favor. Mail surveys and solicitations sometimes include a little gift of money or personalized address labels, assuming some people will reciprocate the favor. Even 21-month-old infants display reciprocity, they are more willing to help those who have tried to give them a toy (Dunfield & Kuhlmeier, 2010). The reciprocity norm also applies in marriage. At times, you may give more than you receive, but in the long run, the exchange should balance out. In all such interactions, to receive without giving in return violates the reciprocity norm.

social capital

The mutual support and cooperation enabled by a social network.

Reciprocity within social networks helps define the **social capital**—the supportive connections, information flow, trust, and cooperative actions—that keep a community healthy. Neighbors keeping an eye on one another's homes is social capital in action.

The norm operates most effectively as people respond publicly to deeds earlier done to them. In laboratory games as in everyday life, fleeting one-shot encounters produce greater selfishness than sustained relationships. But even when people respond anonymously, they sometimes do the right thing and repay the good done to them (Burger et al., 2009). In one experiment, university students more willingly made a charity pledge when it was the charity of someone who had previously bought them some candy (Whatley et al., 1999; Figure 2).

"If you don't go to somebody's funeral, they won't come to yours."

—Yogi Berra

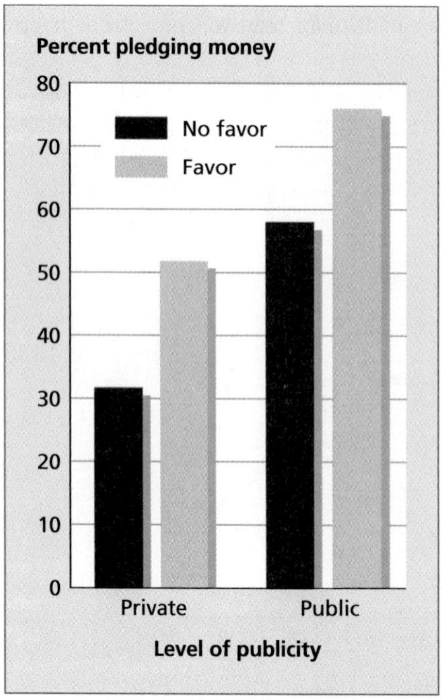

FIGURE :: 2

Private and Public Reciprocation of a Favor

People were more willing to pledge to an experimental confederate's charity if the confederate had done a small favor for them earlier, especially when their reciprocation was made known to the confederate.
Source: From Whatley et al. (1999).

When people cannot reciprocate, they may feel threatened and demeaned by accepting aid. Thus, proud, high-self-esteem people are often reluctant to seek help (Nadler & Fisher, 1986). Receiving unsolicited help can take one's self-esteem down a notch (Schneider et al., 1996; Shell & Eisenberg, 1992). Studies have found this can happen to beneficiaries of affirmative action, especially when affirmative action fails to affirm the person's competence and chances for future success (Pratkanis & Turner, 1996). Asians, for whom social ties and the reciprocity norm are stronger than for North Americans, are therefore more likely to refuse a gift from a casual acquaintance to avoid the felt need to reciprocate (Shen et al., 2011).

The practical moral is that we should offer our children and our friends needed support but not provide so much support that we undermine their sense of competence (Finkel & Fitzsimmons, 2013). Support should supplement, rather than substitute for, others' actions.

THE SOCIAL-RESPONSIBILITY NORM.   The reciprocity norm reminds us to balance giving and receiving. If the only norm were reciprocity, however, the Samaritan would not have been the Good Samaritan. In the parable, Jesus obviously had something more humanitarian in mind, something made explicit in another of his teachings: "If you love those who love you [the reciprocity norm], what right have you to claim any credit? . . . I say to you, love your enemies" (Matthew 5:46, 44).

With people who clearly are dependent and unable to reciprocate, such as children, the severely impoverished, and those with disabilities, another social norm motivates our helping. The **social-responsibility** norm decrees that people should help those who need help, without regard to future exchanges (Berkowitz, 1972; Schwartz, 1975). This social responsibility norm has a long history, as evident from archeological discoveries of 7,500-year-old skeletons of people who were severely crippled and unable to feed or care for themselves, yet able to survive, thanks to others' compassionate care (Gorman, 2012). If a person on crutches drops a book, you honor the social responsibility norm as you pick it up. In India, a relatively collectivist culture, people support the social-responsibility norm more strongly than in the individualist West (Baron & Miller, 2000). They voice an obligation to help even when the need is not life threatening or the needy person—perhaps a stranger needing a bone marrow transplant—is outside their family circle.

Even when helpers in Western countries remain anonymous and have no expectation of any reward, they often help needy people (Shotland & Stebbins, 1983). However, they usually apply the social-responsibility norm selectively to those whose need appears not to be due to their own negligence. Especially among political conservatives (Skitka & Tetlock, 1993), the norm seems to be: Give people what they deserve. If they are victims of circumstance, such as natural disaster, then by all means be compassionate (Goetz et al., 2010; Zagefka et al., 2011). If they seem to have created their own problems (by laziness, immorality, or lack of foresight, for example), then, the norm suggests, they don't deserve help.

Responses are thus closely tied to *attributions.* If we attribute the need to an uncontrollable predicament, we help. If we attribute the need to the person's choices, fairness does not require us to help; we say it's the person's own fault (Weiner, 1980). Attributions affect public policy as well as individual helping decisions.

The key, say Udo Rudolph and colleagues (2004) from their review of more than three dozen pertinent studies, is whether your attributions evoke sympathy, which in turn motivates helping (Figure 3).

Imagine yourself as one of the University of Wisconsin students receiving a call from "Tony Freeman," who explains that he is in your introductory psychology class (Barnes et al., 1979). He says that he needs help for the upcoming exam and that he has gotten your name from the class roster. "I don't know. I just don't seem to take good notes in there," Tony explains. "I know I can, but sometimes I just don't feel like it, so most of the notes I have aren't very good to study with." How sympathetic would you feel toward Tony? How much of a sacrifice would you make to lend him your notes? If you are like the students in this experiment, you would probably be much less inclined to help than if Tony had

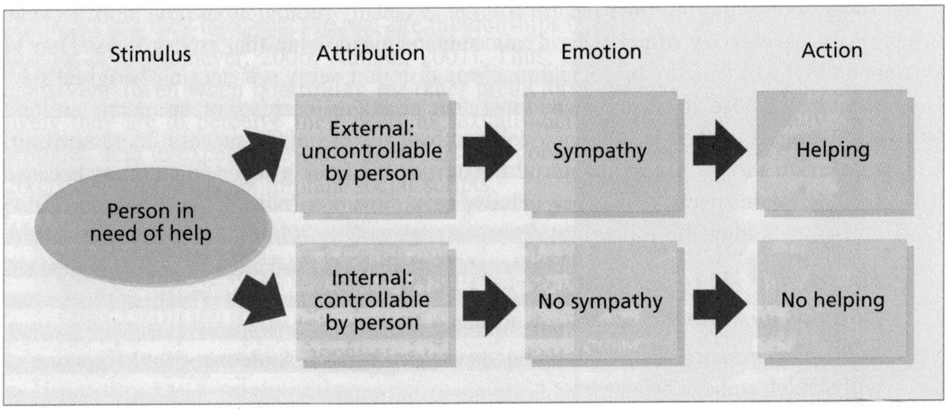

social-responsibility norm
An expectation that people will help those needing help.

FIGURE :: 3

Attributions and Helping

In this model, proposed by German researcher Udo Rudolph and colleagues (2004), helping is mediated by people's explanations of the predicament and their resulting degree of sympathy.

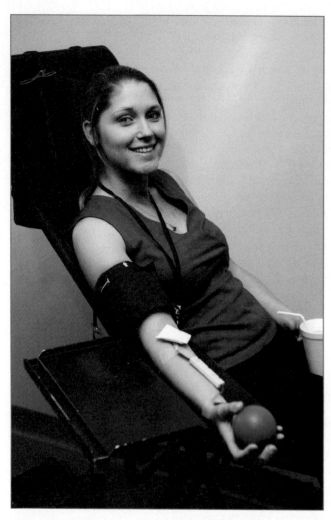

Blood donors respond to the social responsibility norm.
David H. Lewis/E-plus/Getty Images

explained that his troubles were beyond his control. Thus, the social-responsibility norm compels us to help those most in need and those most deserving.

GENDER AND RECEIVING HELP.   If, indeed, perception of another's need strongly determines one's willingness to help, will women, if perceived as less competent and more dependent, receive more help than men? That is indeed the case. Alice Eagly and Maureen Crowley (1986) located 35 studies that compared help received by male or female victims. (Virtually all the studies involved short-term encounters with strangers in need—the very situations in which people expect males to be chivalrous, note Eagly and Crowley.)

Women offered help equally to males and females, whereas men offered more help when the persons in need were females. Several experiments in the 1970s found that women with disabled cars (for example, with a flat tire) got many more offers of help than did men (Penner et al., 1973; Pomazal & Clore, 1973; West et al., 1975). Similarly, solo female hitchhikers received far more offers of help than solo males or couples (Pomazal & Clore, 1973; M. Snyder et al., 1974). Of course, men's chivalry toward lone women may have been motivated by something other than altruism. Mating motives can motivate displays of heroism (Griskevicius et al., 2007). Not surprisingly, men more frequently helped attractive than unattractive women (Mims et al., 1975; Stroufe et al., 1977; West & Brown, 1975).

Women not only receive more offers of help in certain situations but also seek more help (Addis & Mahalik, 2003). They are twice as likely to seek medical and psychiatric help. They are the majority of callers to radio counseling programs and clients of college counseling centers. They more often welcome help from friends. Arie Nadler (1991), a Tel Aviv University expert on help seeking, attributes this to gender differences in individualism versus collectivism.

Evolutionary Psychology

Another explanation of helping comes from evolutionary theory. Evolutionary psychology contends that life's essence is gene survival. Our genes drive us in adaptive ways that have maximized their chance of survival. When our ancestors died, their genes lived on, predisposing us to behave in ways that will spread them into the future.

As suggested by the title of Richard Dawkins's (1976) popular book *The Selfish Gene,* evolutionary psychology offers a humbling human image—one that psychologist Donald Campbell (1975a,b) called a biological reaffirmation of a deep, self-serving "original sin." Genes that predispose individuals to self-sacrifice in the interests of strangers' welfare would not survive in the evolutionary competition. Evolutionary success does, however, come from cooperation. And humans, are the animal kingdom's super-cooperators because we exhibit multiple mechanisms for overcoming selfishness (Nowak & Highfield, 2011; Pfaff, 2014), including the following:

- *Kin selection:* If you carry my genes, I'll favor you.
- *Direct reciprocity:* We scratch each other's backs.
- *Indirect reciprocity:* I'll scratch your back, you scratch someone's, and someone will scratch mine.
- *Group selection:* Back-scratching groups survive.

"Fallen heroes do not have children. If self-sacrifice results in fewer descendants, the genes that allow heroes to be created can be expected to disappear gradually from the population."

—E. O. Wilson,
On Human Nature (1978)

When the *Titanic* sank, 70 percent of the females and 20 percent of the males survived. The chances of survival were 2.5 times better for a first- than a third-class passenger. Yet, thanks to gender norms for altruism, the survival odds were better for third-class passengers who were women (47 percent) than for first-class passengers who were men (31 percent).
MERIE WALLACE/AFI/Getty Images

KIN SELECTION

Our genes dispose us to care for relatives. Thus, one form of self-sacrifice that *would* increase gene survival is devotion to one's children, the primal altruism with its neural systems enabling other forms of altruism (Preston, 2013). Compared with neglectful parents, parents who prioritize their children's welfare are more likely to pass their genes on. As evolutionary psychologist David Barash (1979, p. 153) wrote, "Genes help themselves by being nice to themselves, even if they are enclosed in different bodies." Genetic egoism (at the biological level) fosters parental altruism (at the psychological level). Although evolution favors self-sacrifice for one's children, children have less at stake in the survival of their parents' genes. Thus, parents will generally be more devoted to their children than their children are to them.

Other relatives share genes in proportion to their biological closeness. You share one-half your genes with your brothers and sisters, one-eighth with your cousins. **Kin selection**—favoritism toward those who share our genes—led the evolutionary biologist J. B. S. Haldane to jest that although he would not give up his life for his brother, he would sacrifice himself for *three* brothers—or for nine cousins. Haldane would not have been surprised that genetic relatedness predicts helping and that genetically identical twins are noticeably more mutually supportive than fraternal twins (Segal, 1984; Stewart-Williams, 2007). In one laboratory game experiment, identical twins were half again as likely as fraternal twins to cooperate with their twin for a shared gain when playing for money (Segal & Hershberger, 1999).

The kin selection principle implies that nature (as well as culture) programs us to care about close relatives. When Carlos Rogers of the Toronto Raptors NBA basketball team volunteered to end his career and donate a kidney to his sister (who died before she could receive it), people applauded his self-sacrificial love. But such acts for close kin are not totally unexpected. What we do not expect (and therefore honor) is the altruism of those who risk themselves to save a stranger.

We share common genes with many besides our relatives. How do we detect the people in which copies of our genes occur most abundantly? One clue lies in physical similarities. Blue-eyed people share particular genes with other blue-eyed people.

Also, in evolutionary history, genes were shared more with neighbors than with foreigners. Are we therefore biologically biased to be more helpful to those who look similar to us

kin selection
The idea that evolution has selected altruism toward one's close relatives to enhance the survival of mutually shared genes.

"Let's say you're walking by a pond and there's a drowning baby. If you said, 'I've just paid $200 for these shoes and the water would ruin them, so I won't save the baby,' you'd be an awful, horrible person. But there are millions of children around the world in the same situation, where just a little money for medicine or food could save their lives. And yet we don't consider ourselves monsters for having this dinner rather than giving the money to Oxfam. Why is that?"

—Philosopher-Psychologist Joshua Greene (Quoted by Zimmer, 2005).

and those who live near us? In the aftermath of natural disasters and other life-and-death situations, the order of who gets helped would not surprise an evolutionary psychologist: the children before the old, family members before friends, neighbors before strangers (Burnstein et al., 1994; Form & Nosow, 1958). We feel more empathy for a distressed or tortured person in our ingroup, and even *Schadenfreude* (secret pleasure at another's misfortune) for rival or outgroup members, (Batson et al., 2009; Cikara et al., 2011; Tarrant et al., 2009). Helping stays close to home.

Some evolutionary psychologists note that kin selection predisposes ethnic ingroup favoritism—the root of countless historical and contemporary conflicts (Rushton, 1991). E. O. Wilson (1978) noted that kin selection is "the enemy of civilization. If human beings are to a large extent guided . . . to favor their own relatives and tribe, only a limited amount of global harmony is possible" (p. 167).

RECIPROCITY

Genetic self-interest also predicts reciprocity. An organism helps another, biologist Robert Trivers argued, because it expects help in return (Binham, 1980). The giver expects later to be the getter. Failure to reciprocate gets punished. People despise the cheat, the turncoat, and the traitor.

Reciprocity works best in small, isolated groups in which one will often see the people for whom one does favors. Sociable female baboons—those who groom and stay in close contact with their peers—gain a reproductive advantage: Their infants more often live to see a first birthday (Silk et al., 2003). If a vampire bat has gone a day or two without food, a well-fed nestmate will regurgitate food for a meal (Wilkinson, 1990). The donor bat does so willingly, losing fewer hours till starvation than the recipient gains. But such favors occur only among familiar nestmates who share in the give-and-take. Those who always take and never give, and those who have no relationship with the donor bat, go hungry. It pays to have friends.

For similar reasons, reciprocity among humans is stronger in rural villages than in big cities. Small schools, towns, churches, work teams, and dorms are all conducive to a community spirit in which people care for one another. Compared to people in small-town or rural environments, those in big cities are less willing to relay a phone message, less likely to mail "lost" letters, less cooperative with survey interviewers, less helpful to a lost child, and less willing to do small favors (Hedge & Yousif, 1992; Steblay, 1987).

GROUP SELECTION

If individual self-interest inevitably wins in genetic competition, then why will we help strangers? Why will we help those whose limited resources or abilities preclude their reciprocating? And what causes soldiers to throw themselves on grenades? One answer, initially favored by Darwin (then discounted by selfish-gene theorists, but now back again), is *group selection:* When groups are in competition, groups of mutually supportive altruists outlast groups of nonaltruists (Krebs, 1998; McAndrew, 2002; Wilson, 2015). This is most dramatically evident with the social insects, which function like cells in a body. Bees and ants will labor sacrificially for their colony's survival.

To a much lesser extent, humans exhibit ingroup loyalty by sacrificing to support "us," sometimes against "them." We are like employees who compete with one another to move up the corporate ladder, while cooperating to enable their business to surpass competitors (Nowak, 2012). Natural selection is therefore "multilevel," say some researchers (Mirsky, 2009). It operates at *both* individual and group levels.

"Just as nature is said to abhor a vacuum, so it abhors true altruism. Society, on the other hand, adores it."

—Evolutionary Psychologist David Barash, "The Conflicting Pressures of Selfishness and Altruism," 2003

Donald Campbell (1975a,b) offered another basis for unreciprocated altruism: Human societies evolved ethical and religious rules that serve as brakes on the biological bias toward self-interest. Commandments such as "love your neighbor as yourself" admonish us to balance self-concern with concern for the group, and so contribute to the survival of the group. Richard Dawkins (1976) offered a similar conclusion: "Let us try to *teach* generosity and altruism, because we are born selfish. Let us understand what our selfish genes are up to, because we may then at least have the chance to upset their designs, something no other species has ever aspired to" (p. 3).

TABLE 1 :: Comparing Theories of Altruism

How Is Altruism Explained?

Theory	Level of Explanation	Externally Rewarded Helping	Intrinsic Helping
Social-exchange	Psychological	External rewards for helping	Distress → inner rewards for helping
Social norms	Sociological	Reciprocity norm	Social-responsibility norm
Evolutionary	Biological	Reciprocity	Kin selection

Comparing and Evaluating Theories of Helping

By now, you perhaps have noticed similarities among the social-exchange, social norm, and evolutionary views of altruism. As Table 1 shows, each proposes two types of prosocial behavior: a tit-for-tat reciprocal exchange and a more unconditional helpfulness. They do so at three complementary levels of explanation. If the evolutionary view is correct, then our genetic predispositions *should* manifest themselves in psychological and sociological phenomena.

Each theory appeals to logic. Yet each is vulnerable to charges of being speculative and after the fact. When we start with a known effect (the give-and-take of everyday life) and explain it by conjecturing a social-exchange process, a "reciprocity norm," or an evolutionary origin, we might merely be explaining-by-naming. The argument that a behavior occurs because of its survival function is hard to disprove. With hindsight it's easy to think it had to be that way. If we can explain *any* conceivable behavior after the fact as the result of a social exchange, a norm, or natural selection, then we cannot disprove the theories. Each theory's task is therefore to generate predictions that enable us to test it.

An effective theory also provides a coherent scheme for summarizing a variety of observations. On this criterion, our three altruism theories get higher marks. Each offers us a broad perspective that illuminates both enduring commitments and spontaneous help.

Genuine Altruism

My [DM's] town, Holland, Michigan, has a corporation with several thousand employees that, for most of the last half-century, annually gave away 10 percent of its pretax profits with one stipulation: The gift was always anonymous. In nearby Kalamazoo, anonymous donors in 2005 pledged to provide Michigan public university or community college costs—ranging from 65 to 100 percent depending on length of residence—for *all* the city's public school graduates. Are such anonymous benefactors—along with lifesaving heroes, everyday blood donors, and Peace Corps volunteers—ever motivated by an ultimate goal of selfless concern for others? Or is their ultimate goal some form of self-benefit, such as gaining a reward, avoiding punishment and guilt, or relieving distress?

Abraham Lincoln illustrated the philosophical issue while conversing with another passenger in a horse-drawn coach. After Lincoln argued that selfishness prompts all good deeds, he noticed a sow making a terrible noise. Her piglets had gotten into a marshy pond and were in danger of drowning. Lincoln called the coach to a halt, jumped out, ran back, and lifted the little pigs to safety. Upon his return, his companion remarked, "Now, Abe, where does selfishness come in on this little episode?" "Why, bless your soul, Ed, that was the very essence of selfishness. I should have had no peace of mind all day had I gone and left that suffering old sow worrying over those pigs. I did it to get peace of mind, don't you see?" (Sharp, cited by Batson et al., 1986). Until recently, psychologists would have sided with Lincoln.

Helpfulness so reliably makes helpers feel better that Daniel Batson (2011) devoted much of his career to discerning whether helpfulness also contains a streak of genuine altruism. Batson theorized that our willingness to help is influenced by both self-serving and selfless considerations (Figure 4). Distress over someone's suffering motivates us to relieve our upset, either by escaping the distressing situation (like the priest and the Levite)

"When people ask me how I'm doing, I say, 'I'm only as good as my most sad child.'"

—Michelle Obama,
October 24, 2008

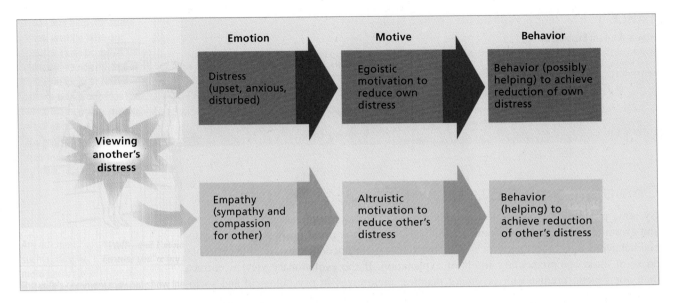

FIGURE :: 4

Egoistic and Altruistic Routes to Helping

Viewing another's distress can evoke a mixture of self-focused distress and other-focused empathy. Researchers agree that distress triggers egoistic motives. But they debate whether empathy can trigger a pure altruistic motive.
Source: Adapted from Batson, Fultz, & Schoenrade (1987).

empathy
The vicarious experience of another's feelings; putting oneself in another's shoes.

or by helping (like the Samaritan). But especially when we feel securely attached to someone, report both Batson and a team of attachment researchers led by Mario Mikulincer (2005), we also feel **empathy.** Loving parents suffer when their children suffer and rejoice over their children's joys—an empathy lacking in child abusers and other perpetrators of cruelty (Miller & Eisenberg, 1988).

"Are you all right, Mister? Is there anything I can do?"

"Young man, you're the only one who bothered to stop! I'm a millionaire and I'm going to give you five thousand dollars!"

We never know what benefits may come from helping someone in distress.
© Barney Tobey/The New Yorker Collection/www.cartoonbank.com

Might genuine altruism motivate an international health educator leading exercise with children in Uganda? Daniel Batson believes it might.
Courtesy, Laura Myers

When we feel empathy, we focus not so much on our own distress as on the sufferer. Genuine sympathy and compassion motivate us to help others for their own sakes. When we value another's welfare, perceive the person as in need, and take the person's perspective, we feel empathic concern (Batson et al., 2007).

To increase empathy, it helps to get a small dose of what another feels. A specific torture technique becomes less acceptable when people experience even a small dose of it. For example, when moderately sleep-deprived, people become more likely to say that, yes, extreme sleep deprivation is torture (Nordgren et al., 2011).

In humans, empathy comes naturally. Even day-old infants cry more when they hear another infant cry (Hoffman, 1981). In hospital nurseries, one baby's crying sometimes evokes a chorus of crying. Most 18-month-old infants, after observing an unfamiliar adult accidentally drop a marker or clothespin and have trouble reaching it, will readily help (Tomasello, 2009). Two-year-olds display arousal when observing someone who needs help (Hepach et al., 2012). And with six- to nine-year olds, the greater their empathy, the greater their helpfulness (Li et al., 2013). To some, all this suggests that humans are hardwired for empathy.

Primates, elephants, dogs, rats, and even mice also display empathy, indicating that the building blocks of altruism predate humanity (de Waal, 2014a,b; Langford et al., 2006). Chimpanzees will choose a token that gives both themselves and another chimp a food treat over a token that gratifies only themselves (Horner et al., 2011).

To separate egoistic distress reduction from empathy-based altruism, Batson's research group conducted studies that aroused empathy. Then the researchers noted whether the aroused people would reduce their own distress by escaping the situation, or whether they would go out of their way to aid the person. The results were consistent: With their empathy aroused, people usually helped.

In one of these experiments, Batson and associates (1981) had University of Kansas women observe a young woman suffering while she supposedly received electric shocks. During a pause in the experiment, the obviously upset victim explained to the experimenter that a childhood fall against an electric fence left her acutely sensitive to shocks. The experimenter suggested that perhaps the observer (the actual participant in this experiment) might trade places and take the remaining shocks for her. Previously, half of these actual participants had been led to believe the suffering person was a kindred spirit on matters of values and interests (thus arousing their empathy). Some also were led to believe that their part in the experiment was completed, so that in any case they were done observing the woman's suffering. Nevertheless, their empathy aroused, virtually all willingly offered to substitute for the victim.

Is this genuine altruism? Mark Schaller and Robert Cialdini (1988) doubted it. Feeling empathy for a sufferer makes one sad, they noted. In one of their experiments, they led people to believe that their sadness was going to be relieved by a different sort of mood-boosting experience—listening to a comedy tape. Under such conditions, people who felt empathy were not especially helpful. Schaller and Cialdini concluded that if we feel empathy but know that something else will make us feel better, we aren't as likely to help.

Everyone agrees that some helpful acts are either obviously egoistic (done to gain external rewards or avoid punishment) or subtly egoistic (done to gain internal rewards or relieve inner distress). Is there a third type of helpfulness—a genuine altruism that aims simply to increase another's welfare (producing happiness for oneself merely as a by-product)? Is empathy-based helping a source of such altruism? Cialdini (1991) and his colleagues Mark Schaller and Jim Fultz have doubted it. They note that no experiment rules out all possible egoistic explanations for helpfulness.

But other findings suggest that genuine altruism does exist: With their empathy aroused, people will help even when they believe no one will know about their helping. Their concern continues until someone *has* been helped (Fultz et al., 1986). If their efforts to help are unsuccessful, they feel bad even if the failure is not their fault (Batson & Weeks, 1996). And people will sometimes persist in wanting to help a suffering person even when they believe their own distressed mood arises from a "mood-fixing" drug (Schroeder et al., 1988).

After 25 such experiments testing egoism versus altruistic empathy, Batson (2001, 2006, 2011) and others (Dovidio, 1991; Staub, 2015; Stocks et al., 2009) believe that sometimes people do focus on others' welfare, not on their own. Batson, a former philosophy and theology student, had begun his research feeling "excited to think that if we could ascertain whether people's concerned reactions were genuine, and not simply a subtle form of selfishness, then we could shed new light on a basic issue regarding human nature" (1999a). Two decades later, he believes he has his answer. Genuine "empathy-induced altruism is part of human nature" (1999b). And that, says Batson, raises the hope—confirmed by research—that inducing empathy might improve attitudes toward stigmatized people: people with AIDS, the homeless, the imprisoned, and other minorities. (See "Focus On: The Benefits—and the Costs—of Empathy-Induced Altruism.")

"The measure of our character is what we would do if we were never found out."

—Paraphrased from
Thomas Macaulay

"As I see it, there are two great forces of human nature: self-interest, and caring for others."

—Bill Gates,
"A New Approach to Capitalism in the Twenty-First Century," 2008

focus ON

The Benefits—and the Costs—of Empathy-Induced Altruism

People do most of what they do, including much of what they do for others, for their own benefit, acknowledges altruism researcher Daniel Batson (2011). But egoism is not the whole story of helping, he believes; there is also a genuine altruism rooted in empathy, in feelings of sympathy and compassion for others' welfare. We are supremely social creatures. Consider:

Empathy-induced altruism

- *produces sensitive helping.* Where there is empathy, it's not just the thought that counts—it's alleviating the other's suffering.

- *inhibits aggression.* Show Batson someone who feels empathy for a target of potential aggression and he'll show you someone who's unlikely to favor attack—someone who's as likely to forgive as to harbor anger. In general, women report more empathic feelings than men, and they are less likely to support war and other forms of aggression (Jones, 2003).

- *increases cooperation.* In laboratory experiments, Batson and Nadia Ahmad found that people in potential conflict are more trusting and cooperative when they feel empathy for the other. Personalizing an outgroup, by getting to know people in it, helps people understand their perspective.

- *improves attitudes toward stigmatized groups.* Take others' perspective, allow yourself to feel what they feel, and you may become more supportive of others like them (the homeless, those with AIDS, or even convicted criminals).

But empathy-induced altruism comes with liabilities, notes Batson and colleagues.

- *It can be harmful.* People who risk their lives on behalf of others sometimes lose them. People who seek to do good can also do harm, sometimes by unintentionally humiliating or demotivating the recipient.

- *It can't address all needs.* It's easier to feel empathy for a needy individual than, say, for Mother Earth, whose environment is being stripped and warmed at the peril of our descendants.

- *It burns out.* Feeling others' pain is painful, which may cause us to avoid situations that evoke our empathy, or to experience "burnout" or "compassion fatigue."

- *It can feed favoritism, injustice, and indifference to the larger common good (Decety & Cowell, 2014).*

Empathy, being particular, produces partiality—toward a single child or family or pet. Moral principles, being universal, produce concern for unseen others as well. Empathy-based estate planning assigns inheritances to particular loved ones. Morality-based estate planning is more inclusive. When their empathy for someone is aroused, people will violate their own standards of fairness and justice by giving that person favored treatment (Batson et al., 1997; Oceja, 2008). Ironically, note Batson and colleagues (1999), empathy-induced altruism can therefore "pose a powerful threat to the common good [by leading] me to narrow my focus of concern to those for whom I especially care—the needing friend—and in so doing to lose sight of the bleeding crowd." No wonder charity so often stays close to home.

SUMMING UP: Why Do We Help?

- Three theories explain helping behavior. The *social-exchange theory* assumes that helping, like other social behaviors, is motivated by a desire to maximize rewards, which may be external or internal. Thus, after wrongdoing, people often become more willing to offer help. Sad people also tend to be helpful. Finally, there is a striking feel-good/do-good effect: Happy people are helpful people. Social norms also mandate helping. The *reciprocity norm* stimulates us to help those who have helped us. The *social-responsibility norm* beckons us to help needy people, even if they cannot reciprocate, as long as they are deserving. Women in crisis, partly because they may be seen as more needy, receive more offers of help than men, especially from men.

- Evolutionary psychology assumes two types of helping: devotion to kin and reciprocity. Most evolutionary psychologists, however, believe that the genes of selfish individuals are more likely to survive than the genes of self-sacrificing individuals. Thus, selfishness is our natural tendency and society must therefore teach helping.

- We can evaluate these three theories according to the ways in which they characterize prosocial behavior as based on tit-for-tat exchange and/or unconditional helpfulness. Each can be criticized for using speculative or after-the-fact reasoning, but they do provide a coherent scheme for summarizing observations of prosocial behavior.

- In addition to helping that is motivated by external and internal rewards, and the evading of punishment or distress, there appears also to be a genuine, *empathy-based altruism*. With their empathy aroused, many people are motivated to assist others in need or distress, even when their helping is anonymous or their own mood will be unaffected.

WHEN WILL WE HELP?

Identify circumstances that prompt people to help, or not to help. Explain how and why helping is influenced by the number and behavior of other bystanders, by mood states, and by traits and values.

On March 13, 1964, 28-year-old bar manager Kitty Genovese was set upon by a knife-wielding attacker as she returned from work to her Queens, New York, apartment house at 3:00 A.M. Her screams of terror and pleas for help—"Oh my God, he stabbed me! Please help me! Please help me!"—aroused some of her neighbors (38 of them, according to an initial *New York Times* report). Some supposedly came to their windows and caught fleeting glimpses as the attacker left and returned to attack again. Not until her attacker

Bystander inaction. What influences our interpretations of a scene such as this and our decisions to help or not to help?
Ed Kashi/Documentary/Corbis

finally departed did anyone call the police. Soon after, Kitty Genovese died.

Later analyses disputed the initial report that 38 witnesses observed the murder yet remained inactive (Cook, 2014; Pelonero, 2014). Nevertheless, the initial story helped inspire research on bystander inaction, which is illustrated in other incidents. Eleanor Bradley tripped and broke her leg while shopping. Dazed and in pain, she pleaded for help. For 40 minutes, the stream of sidewalk pedestrians simply parted and flowed around her. Finally, a cab driver helped her to a doctor (Darley & Latané, 1968).

Or consider how you might respond if you saw someone topple from a subway platform onto the tracks below, with a train approaching. Would you react like those on a crowded New York subway platform who, in 2012, did nothing when a man was pushed onto the tracks and then was killed by a train? Or like Wesley Autrey—who became a New York hero in 2007 when, alone on a platform with his two daughters, he saw a man have a seizure and fall onto the tracks? Autrey jumped down to position the man's body between the rails and then lay on top of him, enabling the train to screech to a halt just above them (Nocera, 2012).

Social psychologists were curious and concerned about bystanders' inaction. So they undertook experiments to identify when people will help in an emergency. Then they broadened the question to "Who is likely to help in non-emergencies—by such deeds as giving money, donating blood, or contributing time?" Let's see what they have learned, looking first at the *circumstances* that enhance helpfulness and then at the *people* who help.

Number of Bystanders

Bystander passivity during emergencies prompted social commentators to lament people's "alienation," "apathy," "indifference," and "unconscious sadistic impulses." By attributing the nonintervention to the bystanders' dispositions, we can reassure ourselves that, as caring people, we would have helped. But were the bystanders such inhuman characters?

Social psychologists Bibb Latané and John Darley (1970) were unconvinced. They staged ingenious emergencies and found that a single situational factor—the presence of other bystanders—greatly decreased intervention. By 1980, they had conducted four dozen experiments that compared help given by bystanders who perceived themselves to be either alone or with others. Given unrestricted communication among the bystanders, a person was at least as likely to be helped by a lone bystander as when observed by several bystanders (Latané & Nida, 1981; Stalder, 2008). In Internet communication, too, people are more likely to respond helpfully to a request for help (such as from someone seeking the link to the campus library) if they believe the request has come to them alone, and not to several others as well (Blair et al., 2005).

Sometimes the victim, as in the New York subway incidents, was actually less likely to get help when many people were around. When Latané, James Dabbs (1975), and 145 collaborators "accidentally" dropped coins or pencils during 1,497 elevator rides, they were helped 40 percent of the time when one other person was on the elevator and less than 20 percent of the time when there were six passengers.

Why does the presence of other bystanders sometimes inhibit helping? Latané and Darley surmised that as the number of bystanders increases, any given bystander is less likely to *notice* the incident, less likely to *interpret* the incident as a problem or an emergency, and less likely to *assume responsibility* for taking action (Figure 5).

NOTICING

Twenty minutes after Eleanor Bradley has fallen and broken her leg on a crowded city sidewalk, you come along. Your eyes are on the backs of the pedestrians in front of you

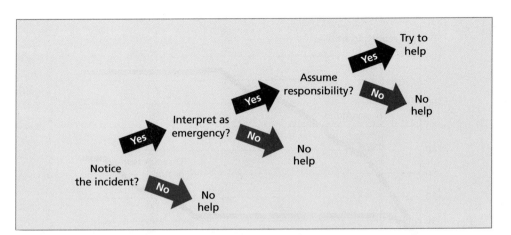

FIGURE :: 5

Latané and Darley's
Decision Tree

Only one path up the tree leads
to helping. At each fork of the
path, the presence of other
bystanders may divert a person
down a branch toward not
helping.
Source: Adapted from Darley &
Latané (1968).

(it is bad manners to stare at those you pass) and your private thoughts are on the day's events. Would you therefore be less likely to notice the injured woman than if the sidewalk were virtually deserted?

To find out, Latané and Darley (1968) had Columbia University men fill out a questionnaire in a room, either by themselves or with two strangers. While they were working (and being observed through a one-way mirror), there was a staged emergency: Smoke poured into the room through a wall vent. Solitary students, who often glanced idly about the room while working, noticed the smoke almost immediately—usually in less than 5 seconds. Those in groups kept their eyes on their work. It typically took them about 20 seconds to notice the smoke.

INTERPRETING

Once we notice an ambiguous event, we must interpret it. Put yourself in the room filling with smoke. Though worried, you don't want to embarrass yourself by appearing flustered. You glance at the others. They look calm, indifferent. Assuming everything must be okay, you shrug it off and go back to work. Then one of the others notices the smoke and, noting your apparent unconcern, reacts similarly. This is yet another example of informational influence. Each person uses others' behavior as clues to reality. Such misinterpretations can contribute to a delayed response to actual fires in offices, restaurants, and other multiple-occupancy settings (Canter et al., 1980).

The misinterpretations are fed by what Thomas Gilovich, Kenneth Savitsky, and Victoria Husted Medvec (1998) call an *illusion of transparency*—a tendency to overestimate others' ability to "read" our internal states. In their experiments, people facing an emergency presumed their concern was more visible than it was. More than we usually suppose, our concern or alarm is opaque. Keenly aware of our emotions, we presume they leak out and that others see right through us. Sometimes others do read our emotions, but often we effectively keep our cool. The result is "pluralistic ignorance"—ignorance that others are thinking and feeling what we are. In emergencies, each person may think, "I'm very concerned," but perceive others as calm—"so maybe it's not an emergency."

So it happened in Latané and Darley's experiment. When those working alone noticed the smoke, they usually hesitated a moment, then got up, walked over to the vent, felt, sniffed, and waved at the smoke, hesitated again, and then went to report it. In dramatic contrast, those in groups of 3 did not move. Among the 24 men in eight groups, only 1 person reported the smoke within the first 4 minutes (Figure 6). By the end of the 6-minute experiment, the smoke was so thick it was obscuring the men's vision and they were rubbing their eyes and coughing. Still, in only three of the eight groups did even a single person leave to report the problem.

Equally interesting, the group's passivity affected its members' interpretations. What caused the smoke? "A leak in the air conditioning." "Chemistry labs in the building." "Steam pipes." "Truth gas." Not one said, "Fire." The group members, by serving as nonresponsive models, influenced one another's interpretation of the situation.

FIGURE :: 6

The Smoke-Filled-Room Experiment

Smoke pouring into the testing room was much more likely to be reported by individuals working alone than by three-person groups.
Source: Data from Darley & Latané (1968).

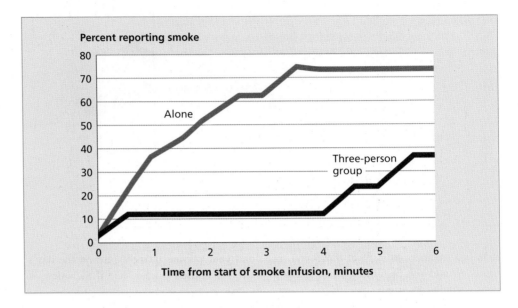

Percent reporting smoke

Alone

Three-person group

Time from start of smoke infusion, minutes

That experimental dilemma parallels real-life dilemmas we all face. Are the shrieks outside merely playful antics or the desperate screams of someone being assaulted? Is the boys' scuffling a friendly tussle or a vicious fight? Is the person slumped in the doorway sleeping, high on drugs, or seriously ill, perhaps in a diabetic coma? That surely was the question confronting those who passed by Hugo Alfredo Tale-Yax as he lay on a Queens, New York, sidewalk, facedown and bleeding to death from multiple stab wounds. A surveillance video showed that for more than an hour, people walked by the homeless man, until finally one passerby shook him and then turned him over to reveal his wounds (*New York Times,* 2010).

Unlike the smoke-filled-room experiment, each of these everyday situations involves the desperate need of another person. In such situations, a **bystander effect** occurs. The bystander effect is the finding that a person is less likely to help someone when other bystanders are present. Latané and Judith Rodin (1969) staged an experiment around a woman in distress. A female researcher set Columbia University men to work on a questionnaire and then left through a curtained doorway to work in an adjacent office. Four minutes later, she could be heard (from a tape recorder) climbing on a chair to reach some papers. This was followed by a scream and a loud crash as the chair collapsed and she fell to the floor. "Oh, my God, my foot . . . I . . . I . . . can't move it," she sobbed. "Oh . . . my ankle . . . I . . . can't get this . . . thing . . . off me." Only after 2 minutes of moaning did she manage to make it out her office door.

Seventy percent of those who were alone when they overheard the "accident" came into the room or called out to offer help. Among pairs of strangers confronting

bystander effect

The finding that a person is less likely to provide help when there are other bystanders.

John M. Darley on Bystander Reactions

Shocked by the Kitty Genovese murder, Bibb Latané and I met over dinner and began to analyze the bystanders' reactions. Being social psychologists, we thought not about the personality flaws of the "apathetic" individuals but rather about how anyone in that situation might react as did these people. By the time we finished our dinner, we had formulated several factors that together could lead to the surprising result: no one helping. Then we set about conducting experiments that isolated each factor and demonstrated its importance in an emergency situation.

John M. Darley
Princeton University
Courtesy of John M. Darley,
Princeton University

the emergency, only 40 percent of the time did either person offer help. Those who did nothing apparently interpreted the situation as a nonemergency. "A mild sprain," said some. "I didn't want to embarrass her," explained others. This again demonstrates the bystander effect. As the number of people known to be aware of an emergency increases, any given person becomes less likely to help. For the victim, there is no safety in numbers.

People's interpretations also affect their reactions to street crimes. In staging physical fights between a man and a woman, Lance Shotland and Margaret Straw (1976) found that bystanders intervened 65 percent of the time when the woman shouted, "Get away from me; I don't know you," but only 19 percent of the time when she shouted, "Get away from me; I don't know why I ever married you." Assumed spouse abuse, it seems, triggers less intervention than stranger abuse.

In such dangerous situations with a perpetrator present and intervention requiring physical risk, the bystander effect is less (Fischer et al., 2011). Indeed, sometimes bystanders provide physical support in intervening. This was dramatically evident on 9/11 as passengers, led by Todd Beamer ("Let's roll!"), collectively intervened as four al Qaeda hijackers headed United Flight 93 toward its presumed target of the U.S. Capitol.

Interpretations matter. Is this man locked out of his car or is he a burglar? Our interpretation affects our response.
Peter Dazeley/Getty Images

ASSUMING RESPONSIBILITY

Failing to notice and misinterpretation are not the bystander effect's only causes. Sometimes an emergency is obvious. According to initial reports, those who saw and heard Kitty Genovese's pleas for help correctly interpreted what was happening. But the lights and silhouetted figures in neighboring windows told them that others were also watching. That diffused the responsibility for action.

Few of us have observed a murder. But all of us have at times been slower to react to a need when others were present. Passing a stranded motorist on a busy highway, we are less likely to offer help than if on a country road. To explore bystander inaction in clear emergencies, Darley and Latané (1968) simulated the Genovese drama. They placed people in separate rooms from which the participants would hear a victim crying for help. To create that situation, Darley and Latané asked some New York University students to discuss their problems with university life over a laboratory intercom. The researchers told the students that to guarantee their anonymity, no one would be visible, nor would the experimenter eavesdrop. During the ensuing discussion, the participants heard one person, after his microphone was turned on, lapse into a seizure. With increasing intensity and speech difficulty, he pleaded for someone to help.

Of those led to believe there were no other listeners, 85 percent left their room to seek help. Of those who believed four others also overheard the victim, only 31 percent went for help. Were those who didn't respond apathetic and indifferent? When the experimenter came in to end the experiment, most immediately expressed concern. Many had trembling hands and sweating palms. They believed an emergency had occurred but were undecided whether to act.

After the smoke-filled room, the woman-in-distress, and the seizure experiments, Latané and Darley asked the participants whether the presence of others had influenced them. We know the others had a dramatic effect. Yet the participants almost invariably denied the influence. They typically replied, "I was aware of the others, but I would have reacted just the same if they weren't there." That response reinforces a familiar point: *We often do not know why we do what we do.* That is why experiments are revealing. A survey of uninvolved bystanders following a real emergency would have left the bystander effect hidden.

In the Conformity and Obedience chapter, we noted other examples of people's inability to predict their own actions. Although university students predicted they would respond with moral courage to sexist remarks, a racial slur, or a theft of someone's phone, few of their comparable classmates (when facing the actual situations) did so. Thus, it takes research to see how people in fact behave.

Responsibility diffusion. The nine paparazzi photographers on the scene immediately after the Princess Diana car accident all had cell phones. Only one called for help. Their almost unanimous explanation was that they assumed "someone else" had already called (Sancton, 1997).
Charles Platiau/Reuters/Corbis

Urban dwellers are seldom alone in public places, which helps account for why city people often are less helpful than country people. "Compassion fatigue" and "sensory overload" from encountering so many needy people further restrain helping in large cities across the world (Levine et al., 1994; Yousif & Korte, 1995). In large cities, bystanders are also more often strangers—whose increasing numbers depress helping. When by-standers are friends or people who share a group identity, increased numbers may, instead, increase helping (Levine & Crowther, 2008).

Nations, too, have often been bystanders to catastrophes, even to genocide. As 800,000 people were murdered in Rwanda, the rest of the world stood by. "With many potential actors, each feels less responsible," notes Ervin Staub (1997b). "It's not our responsibility," say the leaders of unaffected nations. Psychologist Peter Suedfeld (2000)—like Staub, a Holocaust survivor—notes that the diffusion of responsibility also helps explain "why the vast majority of European citizens stood idly by during the persecution, removal, and killing of their Jewish compatriots."

REVISITING RESEARCH ETHICS

These experiments raise an ethical issue. Is it right to force unwitting people to overhear someone's apparent collapse? Were the researchers in the seizure experiment ethical when they forced people to decide whether to interrupt their discussion to report the problem? Would you object to being in such a study? Note that it would have been impossible to get your "informed consent"; doing so would have destroyed the experiment's cover.

The researchers were always careful to debrief the laboratory participants. After explaining the seizure experiment, probably the most stressful, the experimenter gave the participants a questionnaire. One hundred percent said the deception was justified and that they would be willing to take part in similar experiments in the future. None reported feeling angry at the experimenter. Other researchers confirm that the overwhelming majority of participants in such experiments say that their participation was both instructive and ethically justified (Schwartz & Gottlieb, 1981). In field experiments, an accomplice assisted the victim if no one else did, thus reassuring bystanders that the problem was being dealt with.

Remember that the social psychologist has a twofold ethical obligation: to protect the participants and to enhance human welfare by discovering influences upon human behavior. Such discoveries can alert us to unwanted influences and show us how we might exert positive influences. The ethical principle seems to be: After protecting participants' welfare, social psychologists fulfill their responsibility to society by giving us insight into our behavior.

Helping When Someone Else Does

If observing aggressive models can heighten aggression and if unresponsive models can heighten nonresponding, then will helpful models promote helping? Imagine hearing a crash followed by sobs and moans. If another bystander said, "Uh-oh. This is an emergency! We've got to do something," would it stimulate others to help?

The evidence is clear: Prosocial models do promote altruism. In several studies,

- Los Angeles drivers were more likely to offer help to a female driver with a flat tire if a quarter mile earlier they had witnessed someone helping another woman change a tire (Bryan & Test, 1967). Bryan and Test also observed that New Jersey Christmas shoppers were more likely to drop money in a Salvation Army kettle if they had just seen someone else do the same.

- British adults were more willing to donate blood if they were approached after observing a confederate consent to donating (Rushton & Campbell, 1977).
- A glimpse of extraordinary human kindness and charity—such as we gave you in the examples of heroic altruism at this chapter's outset—often triggers what Jonathan Haidt (2003) calls *elevation*, "a distinctive feeling in the chest of warmth and expansion" that may provoke chills, tears, and throat clenching. Such elevation often inspires people to become more self-giving (Schnall et al., 2010).

Models sometimes, however, contradict in practice what they preach. Parents may tell their children, "Do as I say, not as I do." Experiments show that children learn moral judgments both from what they hear preached and from what they see practiced (Rice & Grusec, 1975; Rushton, 1975). When exposed to hypocrites, they imitate: They *say* what the model *says* and *do* what the model *does*.

Time Pressures

Darley and Batson (1973) discerned another determinant of helping in the Good Samaritan parable. The priest and the Levite were both busy, important people, probably hurrying to their duties. The lowly Samaritan surely was less pressed for time. To see whether people in a hurry would behave as the priest and the Levite did, Darley and Batson cleverly staged the situation described in the parable.

After collecting their thoughts before recording a brief extemporaneous talk (which, for half the participants, was actually on the Good Samaritan parable), Princeton Theological Seminary students were directed to a recording studio in an adjacent building. En route, they passed a man sitting slumped in a doorway, head down, coughing and groaning. Some of the students had been sent off nonchalantly: "It will be a few minutes before they're ready for you, but you might as well head on over." Of those, almost two-thirds stopped to offer help. Others were told, "Oh, you're late. They were expecting you a few minutes ago . . . so you'd better hurry." Of these, only 10 percent offered help.

Reflecting on these findings, Darley and Batson noted that the hurried participants passed on by the person in distress even when en route "to speak on the parable of the Good Samaritan, thus inadvertently confirming the point of the parable. (Indeed, on several occasions, a seminary student going to give his talk on the parable of the Good Samaritan literally stepped over the victim as he hurried on his way!)"

Are we being unfair to the seminary students, who were, after all, hurrying to *help* the experimenter? Perhaps they keenly felt the social-responsibility norm but found it pulling them two ways—toward the experimenter and toward the victim. In another enactment of the Good Samaritan situation, Batson and associates (1978) directed 40 University of Kansas students to an experiment in another building. Half were told they were late, half that they had plenty of time. Half of each of these groups thought their participation was vitally important to the experimenter; half thought it was not essential. The results: Those leisurely on their way to an unimportant appointment usually stopped to help. But people seldom stopped to help if, like the White Rabbit in *Alice's Adventures in Wonderland,* they were late for a very important date.

Can we conclude that those who were rushed were callous? Did the seminarians notice the victim's distress and then consciously choose to ignore it? No. Harried, preoccupied, rushing to help the experimenter, they (and we, too) simply did not take time to tune in to a person in need. As social psychologists have so often observed, their behavior was influenced more by context than by conviction.

Similarity

Because similarity is conducive to liking, and liking is conducive to helping, we are more empathic and helpful toward those *similar* to us (Miller et al., 2001). The similarity bias applies to both dress and beliefs. Tim Emswiller and his fellow researchers (1971) had confederates, dressed either conservatively or in counterculture garb, approach "conservative" and "hip" Purdue University students seeking a dime for a phone call. Fewer than

"We are, in truth, more than half what we are by imitation. The great point is, to choose good models and to study them with care."

—Lord Chesterfield, *Letters,* January 18, 1750

half the students did the favor for those dressed differently from themselves. Two-thirds did so for those dressed similarly. See "Research Close-Up: Ingroup Similarity and Helping."

Like similarity, familiarity breeds compassion. The more people know about disaster victims and where they live, the more they donate (Zagefka et al., 2013). No face is more familiar than one's own. That explains why, when Lisa DeBruine (2002) had McMaster University students play an interactive game with a supposed other player, they were more

research CLOSE-UP

Ingroup Similarity and Helping

Likeness breeds liking, and liking elicits helping. So, do people offer more help to others who display similarities to themselves? To explore the similarity-helping relationship, Mark Levine, Amy Prosser, and David Evans at Lancaster University joined with Stephen Reicher at St. Andrews University (2005) to study the behavior of Manchester United soccer football team fans. Taking their cue from John Darley and Daniel Batson's (1973) famous Good Samaritan experiment, they directed each newly arrived student participant to the laboratory in an adjacent building. En route, a confederate jogger—wearing a shirt from either nearby Manchester United or rival Liverpool—seemingly slipped on a grass bank just in front of them, grasped his ankle, and groaned in apparent pain. As Figure 7 shows, the Manchester fans routinely paused to offer help to their fellow Manchester supporter but usually did not offer such help to a supposed Liverpool supporter.

But, the researchers wondered, what if we remind Manchester fans of the identity they share with Liverpool supporters—as football fans rather than as detractors who

scorn football fans as violent hooligans? So they repeated the experiment, but with one difference: Before participants witnessed the jogger's fall, the researcher explained that the study concerned the positive aspects of being a football fan. Given that only a small minority of fans are troublemakers, this research aimed to explore what fans get out of their love for "the beautiful game." Now a jogger wearing a football club shirt, whether for Manchester or Liverpool, became one of "us fans." And as Figure 8 shows, the grimacing jogger was helped regardless of which team he supported—and more so than if wearing a plain shirt.

The principle in the two cases is the same, noted the researchers. People are predisposed to help their fellow group members, whether those are defined more narrowly (as "us Manchester fans") or more inclusively (as "us football fans"). If even rival fans can be persuaded to help one another by thinking about what unites them, then surely other antagonists can as well. One way to increase people's willingness to help others is to promote social identities that are inclusive rather than exclusive.

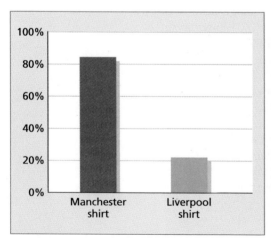

FIGURE :: 7
Percentage of Manchester United Fans Who Helped Victim Wearing Manchester or Liverpool Shirt

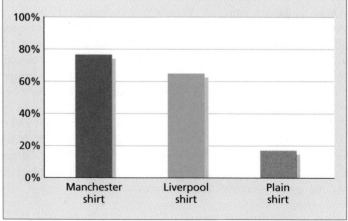

FIGURE :: 8
Common Fan Identity Condition: Percentage of Manchester United Fans Who Helped Victim Wearing Manchester or Liverpool Shirt

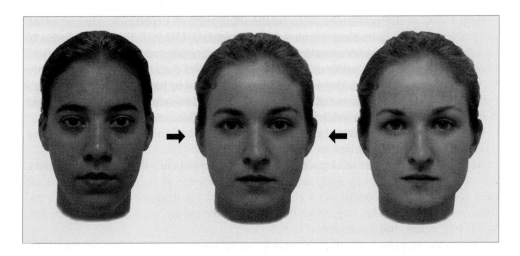

FIGURE :: 9

Similarity Breeds
Cooperation

Lisa DeBruine (2002) morphed
participants' faces (left) with
strangers' faces (right) to make
the composite center faces—
toward whom the participants
were more generous than
toward the stranger.
Courtesy of Lisa DeBruine

trusting and generous when the other person's pictured face had some features of their own face morphed into it (Figure 9). In me I trust. Even just sharing a birthday, a first name, or a fingerprint pattern leads people to respond more to a request for help (Burger et al., 2004).

Does the similarity bias extend to race? During the 1970s, researchers explored that question with confusing results:

- Some studies found a *same-race bias* (Benson et al., 1976; Clark, 1974; Franklin, 1974; Gaertner, 1973; Gaertner & Bickman, 1971; Sissons, 1981).
- Others found *no bias* (Gaertner, 1975; Lerner & Frank, 1974; Wilson & Donnerstein, 1979; Wispe & Freshley, 1971).
- Still others—especially those involving face-to-face situations—found a bias toward helping those of a *different race* (Dutton, 1971, 1973; Dutton & Lake, 1973; Katz et al., 1975).

Is there a general rule that resolves these seemingly contradictory findings?

Few people want to appear prejudiced. Perhaps, then, people favor their own race but keep that bias secret to preserve a positive image. If so, the same-race bias should appear only when people can attribute failure to help to nonrace factors. That is what happened in experiments by Samuel Gaertner and John Dovidio (1977, 1986). For example, University of Delaware White women were less willing to help a Black than a White woman in distress *if* their responsibility could be diffused among the bystanders ("I didn't help the Black woman because there were others who could"). When there were no other bystanders, the women were equally helpful to the Black and the White women. The rule seems to be: When norms for appropriate behavior are well-defined, Whites don't discriminate; when norms are ambiguous or conflicting, racial similarity may bias responses (Saucier et al., 2005).

For me [DM], the laboratory came to life one night as I walked from a dinner meeting in Washington, D.C., to my hotel. On a deserted sidewalk, a well-dressed, distraught-seeming man about my age approached me and begged for a dollar. He explained that he had just come over from London and, after visiting the Holocaust Museum, had accidentally left his wallet in a taxi. So here he was, stranded and needing a $24 taxi fare to a friend's home in suburban D.C.

"So how's one dollar going to get you there?" I asked.

"I asked people for more, but no one would help me," he nearly sobbed, "so I thought maybe if I asked for less I could collect taxi fare."

"But why not take the Metro?" I challenged.

"It stops about 5 miles from Greenbriar, where I need to go," he explained. "Oh my, how am I ever going to get there? If you could help me out, I will mail you back the money on Monday."

Here I was, as if a participant in an on-the-street altruism experiment. Having grown up in a city, and as a frequent visitor to New York and Chicago, I am accustomed to panhandling and have never rewarded it. But I also consider myself a caring person. Moreover, this fellow was unlike any panhandler I had ever met. He was dressed sharply. He was intelligent. He had a convincing story. And he looked like me! If he's lying, he's a slimeball, I said to myself, and giving him money would be stupid, naive, and rewarding slimeballism. If he's a truth-teller and I turn my back on him, then *I'm* a slimeball.

He had asked for $1. I gave him $30, along with my name and address, which he took gratefully, and disappeared into the night.

As I walked on, I began to suspect—correctly as it turned out—that I had been a patsy. Having lived in Britain, why had I not tested his knowledge of England? Why had I not taken him to a phone booth to call his friend? Why had I at least not offered to pay a taxi driver and send him on his way, rather than give him the money? And why, after a lifetime of resisting scams, had I succumbed to this one?

Sheepishly, because I like to think myself not influenced by ethnic stereotypes, I had to admit that it was not only his socially skilled, personal approach but also the mere fact of his similarity to me.

SUMMING UP: When Will We Help?

- Several situational influences work to inhibit or to encourage altruism. As the number of bystanders at an emergency increases, any given bystander is (1) less likely to notice the incident, (2) less likely to interpret it as an emergency, and (3) less likely to assume responsibility. Experiments on helping behavior pose an ethical dilemma but fulfill the researcher's mandate to enhance human life by uncovering important influences on behavior.

- When are people most likely to help? One circumstance is when they have just observed someone else helping.

- Another circumstance that promotes helping is having at least a little spare time; those in a hurry are less likely to help.

- We tend to help those whom we perceive as being similar to us.

WHO WILL HELP?

Identify some traits and values that predict helping.

We have considered internal influences on the decision to help (such as guilt and mood) and external influences as well (such as social norms, number of bystanders, time pressures, and similarity). We also need to consider the helpers' dispositions, including, for example, their personality traits, gender, and religious values.

Personality Traits

Surely some traits must distinguish the Mother Teresa types from others. Faced with identical situations, some people will respond helpfully, while others won't bother. Who are the likely helpers?

For many years, social psychologists were unable to discover a single personality trait that predicted helping with anything close to the predictive power of situational, guilt, and mood factors. Modest relationships were found between helping and certain personality variables, such as a need for social approval. But by and large, personality tests were unable to identify the helpers. Studies of rescuers of Jews in Nazi Europe reveal a similar conclusion: Although the social context clearly influenced willingness to help, there was no definable set of altruistic personality traits (Darley, 1995).

If that finding has a familiar ring, it could be from a similar conclusion by conformity researchers: Conformity, too, seemed more influenced by the situation than by measurable

"There are . . . reasons why personality should be rather unimportant in determining people's reactions to the emergency. For one thing, the situational forces affecting a person's decision are so strong."

—Bibb Latané and John Darley (1970, p. 115)

personality traits. Perhaps, though, who we are does affect what we do. Attitude and trait measures seldom predict a *specific* act, which is what most experiments on altruism measure (in contrast with the lifelong altruism of a Mother Teresa). But they predict average behavior across many situations more accurately.

Personality researchers have responded to the challenge and summarize the effect of personality on altruism in three ways:

- They have found *individual differences* in helpfulness and shown that those differences persist over time and are noticed by one's peers (Hampson, 1984; Penner, 2002; Rushton et al., 1981). In one study, five-year-olds who most readily shared their treats were, at ages 23 and 32, most socially progressive in their political views (Dunkel, 2014). Some people *are* reliably more helpful.

- Researchers are gathering clues to the *network of traits* that predispose a person to helpfulness. Those high in positive emotionality, empathy, and self-efficacy are most likely to be concerned and helpful (Eisenberg et al., 1991; Krueger et al., 2001; Walker & Frimer, 2007). Even easily embarrassed people—being socially attuned—tend to be more prosocial and generous than average (Feinberg et al., 2012).

- Personality influences how particular people react to *particular situations* (Carlo et al., 1991; Romer et al., 1986; Wilson & Petruska, 1984). Those high in self-monitoring are attuned to others' expectations and are therefore helpful *if* they think helpfulness will be socially rewarded (White & Gerstein, 1987). Others' opinions matter less to internally guided, low-self-monitoring people.

Gender

The interaction of person and situation also appears in 172 studies that have compared the helpfulness of nearly 50,000 male and female individuals. After analyzing these results, Alice Eagly and Maureen Crowley (1986) reported that when faced with potentially dangerous situations in which strangers need help (such as with a flat tire or a fall in a subway), men more often help. Eagly (2009) also reports that among recipients of the Carnegie medal for heroism in saving human life, 91 percent have been men.

Would gender norms—"women and children first"—more likely come into play in situations when people have time to reflect on social norms (as opposed to acting instinctively, on impulse)? To explore this possibility, some fiendish experimenter might wish to assign passengers to fast- or slow-sinking ships and observe behavior. Actually, note Zurich researcher Bruno Frey and his colleagues (2010), the course of human events has conducted this experiment. In 1915, a German U-boat sank the passenger liner, the *Lusitania,* in a panicked 18 minutes, with women on board being 1 percent less likely to survive than men. In 1912, the *Titanic,* carrying a similar mix of passengers, hit an iceberg and took nearly 3 hours to sink—and women were 53 percent more likely to survive than men. In this natural experiment, time enabled prosocial behavior and the activation of gender norms.

In safer situations, such as volunteering to help with an experiment or spend time with children with developmental disabilities, women are slightly more likely to help. In a 2014 national survey of 153,015 entering American collegians, 66 percent of men—and 77 percent of women—rated "helping others in difficulty" as "very important" or "essential" (Eagan et al., 2014). Women also have been as likely as, or more likely than, men to risk death as Holocaust rescuers, to donate a kidney, and to volunteer with the Peace Corps and Doctors of the World (Becker & Eagly, 2004). Thus, the gender difference interacts with (depends on) the situation. Faced with a friend's problems, women respond with greater empathy and spend more time helping (George et al., 1998).

Finally, women tend to be more generous. They are more supportive of government programs that distribute wealth and are more likely to distribute their own wealth. Indiana University's Women's Philanthropy Institute reports that: 1) single women donate more

The four chaplains' ultimate selflessness inspired this painting, which hangs in Valley Forge, Pennsylvania's Chapel of the Four Chaplains.
Lynn Burkholder/First Impressions

than single men, 2) men donate more if married to a woman, and 3) at every income level, female-headed households donate more than male-headed households (Mesch & Pactor, 2015). Small wonder, notes Adam Grant (2013), that twenty years ago, philanthropist Bill Gates rejected advice to set up a charitable foundation—until marrying, having two daughters, and recalling his mother who "never stopped pressing me to do more for others."

Religious Faith

In 1943, with Nazi submarines sinking ships faster than the Allied forces could replace them, the troop ship *SS Dorchester* steamed out of New York harbor with 902 men headed for Greenland (Elliott, 1989; Kurzman, 2004; Parachin, 1992). Among those leaving anxious families behind were four chaplains: Methodist preacher George Fox, Rabbi Alexander Goode, Catholic priest John Washington, and Reformed Church minister Clark Poling. Some 150 miles from their destination, on a moonless night, *U-boat 456* caught the *Dorchester* in its crosshairs. Within moments of the torpedo's impact, stunned men were pouring out of their bunks as the ship began listing. With power cut, the ship's radio was useless; its escort vessels, unaware of the unfolding tragedy, pushed on in the darkness. On board, chaos reigned as panicky men came up from the hold without life jackets and leapt into overcrowded lifeboats.

As the four chaplains arrived on the steeply sloping deck, they began guiding the men to their boat stations. They opened a storage locker, distributed life jackets, and coaxed the men over the side. When Petty Officer John Mahoney turned back to retrieve his gloves, Rabbi Goode responded, "Never mind. I have two pairs." Only later did Mahoney realize that the Rabbi was not conveniently carrying an extra pair; he was giving up his own.

In the icy, oil-smeared water, as Private William Bednar heard the chaplains preaching courage he found the strength to swim out from under the ship until reaching a life raft. Still on board, Grady Clark watched in awe as the chaplains handed out the last life jacket and then, with ultimate selflessness, gave away their own. As Clark slipped into the waters, he looked back at an unforgettable sight: The four chaplains were standing—their arms linked—praying, in Latin, Hebrew, and English. Other men joined them in a huddle as the *Dorchester* slid beneath the sea. "It was the finest thing I have ever seen or hope to see this side of heaven," said John Ladd, another of the 230 survivors.

Does the chaplains' heroic example rightly imply that faith promotes courage and caring? The world's four largest religions—Christianity, Islam, Hinduism, and Buddhism—all teach compassion and charity (Steffen & Masters, 2005). But do their followers walk the talk? Religiosity is a mixed bag, report Ariel Malka and colleagues (2011). It is often associated with conservative opposition to government initiatives, including support for the poor, yet it also promotes prosocial values.

Consider what happens when people are subtly "primed" with either materialistic or spiritual thoughts. With money on their minds—after unscrambling text that included words such as *salary* or after seeing a poster with currency on it—people were less helpful to a confused person and less generous when asked to donate to help needy students (Vohs et al., 2006, 2008). With God on their minds—after unscrambling sentences with words such as *spirit, divine, God,* and *sacred*—people become much more generous in their donations (Pichon et al., 2007; Schumann et al., 2014; Shariff et al., 2015). Follow-up studies have found that religious priming increases other "good" behaviors, such as persistence on an assigned task and actions consistent with one's moral beliefs (Carpenter & Marshall, 2009; Toburen & Meier, 2010). But "religion" and "God" have somewhat different priming effects. "Religion" primes helpfulness toward ingroup members and "God" toward outgroup members (Preston & Ritter, 2013).

Consider also the many studies of spontaneous helping. Confronted with a minor emergency, intrinsically religious people are only slightly more responsive (Trimble, 1993). More recently, researchers are also exploring planned helping—the sort of sustained helping provided by AIDS volunteers, Big Brother and Big Sister helpers, and supporters of campus service organizations. It is when making intentional choices about long-term helping that religious faith better predicts altruism. (Remember how the *Titanic*'s slow sinking gave time for social norms and intentions to operate.)

In studies of college students and the general public, those religiously committed have reported volunteering more hours—as tutors, relief workers, and campaigners for social justice—than have the religiously uncommitted (Benson et al., 1980; Hansen et al., 1995; Penner, 2002). Among Americans whom the Gallup Poll classifies as "engaged" with a faith community, the median person has reported volunteering 2 hours per week; the median disengaged person reported volunteering 0 hours per week (Winseman, 2005). Worldwide surveys confirm the correlation between faith engagement and volunteering. One analysis of 117,007 people responding to World Values Surveys in 53 countries reported that twice-weekly religious attenders "are more than five times more likely to volunteer" than nonattenders (Ruiter & De Graaf, 2006).

Moreover, Sam Levenson's jest—"When it comes to giving, some people stop at nothing"—is seldom true of those who are most actively religious. A massive Gallup World Poll surveyed 2,000 or more people in each of 140 countries. Despite having lower incomes, highly religious people (who reported that religion is important to their daily lives and that they had attended a religious service in the prior week) reported markedly higher than average rates of charitable giving, volunteerism, and helping a stranger in the previous month (Figure 10).

Do the religious links with planned helping extend similarly to other communal organizations? Robert Putnam (2000) analyzed national survey data from 22 types of organizations, including hobby clubs, professional associations, self-help groups, and service clubs. "It was membership in religious groups," he reports, "that was most closely associated with other forms of civic involvement, like voting, jury service, community projects, talking with neighbors, and giving to charity" (p. 67).

A newer analysis across 70 countries confirmed that "religious individuals were more likely to be members of charitable organizations" and less likely to engage in self-serving lies or fraud. But this seeming prosocial effect of religiosity was strongest "in countries in which religious behavior is a matter of personal choice" rather than imposed by strong social norms (Stavrova & Siegers, 2014).

> "Religion is the mother of philanthropy."
> —Frank Emerson Andrews, *Attitudes Toward Giving,* 1953

Ironically, lower income households are proportionately more generous. In the U.S., those with income below $50,000 give, on average, 4.2 percent of their income. Those with income above $100,000 give, on average, 2.2 percent (Center on Philanthropy, 2008; see also Piff et al., 2010).

FIGURE :: 10

Helping and Religious Engagement

Worldwide, report Gallup researchers Brett Pelham and Steve Crabtree (2008), highly religious people are—despite averaging lower incomes—more likely to report having given away money in the last month and also to report having volunteered and helped a stranger. The highly religious said religion is important in their daily life and attended a service in the last week. Less religious are all others.

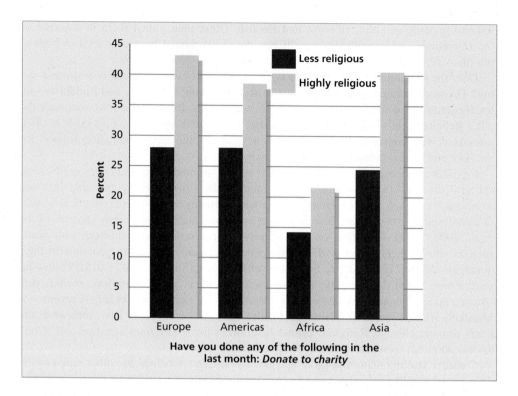

Have you done any of the following in the
last month: *Donate to charity*

SUMMING UP: Who Will Help?

- In contrast with altruism's potent situational and mood determinants, personality test scores have served as only modest predictors of helping. However, new evidence indicates that some people are consistently more helpful than others.

- The effect of personality or gender may depend on the situation. Men, for example, have been observed to help more in dangerous situations, women as volunteers.

- Religious faith predicts long-term altruism, as reflected in volunteerism and charitable contributions.

HOW CAN WE INCREASE HELPING?

Suggest how helping might be increased by reversing the factors that inhibit helping, by teaching norms of helping, and by socializing people to see themselves as helpful.

As social scientists, our goal is to understand human behavior, thus also suggesting ways to improve it. One way to promote altruism is to reverse those factors that inhibit it. Given that hurried, preoccupied people help less, can we think of ways to slow people down and turn their attention outward? If the presence of others diminishes each bystander's sense of responsibility, how can we enhance responsibility?

Reduce Ambiguity, Increase Responsibility

If Latané and Darley's decision tree (see Figure 5) describes the dilemmas bystanders face, then helping should increase if we can prompt people to correctly *interpret an incident* and to *assume responsibility*. Leonard Bickman and colleagues (Bickman, 1975, 1979; Bickman & Green, 1977) tested that presumption in a series of experiments on crime reporting. In each, they staged a shoplifting incident in a supermarket or bookstore.

In some of the stores, they placed signs aimed at sensitizing bystanders to shoplifting and informing them how to report it. The researchers found that the signs had little effect. In other cases, witnesses heard a bystander interpret the incident: "Say, look at her. She's shoplifting. She put that into her purse." (The bystander then left to look for a lost child.) Still others heard this person add, "We saw it. We should report it. It's our responsibility." Both comments substantially boosted reporting of the crime.

The potency of personal influence is no longer in doubt. New blood donors, unlike repeat donors, were usually there at someone's personal invitation (Foss, 1978). Leonard Jason and collaborators (1984) confirmed that personal appeals for blood donation are much more effective than posters and media announcements—if the personal appeals come from friends.

PERSONALIZED APPEAL

Personalized nonverbal appeals can also be effective. Mark Snyder and co-workers (1974; Omoto & Snyder, 2002) found that hitchhikers doubled their number of ride offers by looking drivers straight in the eye, and that most AIDS volunteers got involved through someone's personal influence. A personal approach, as my [DM's] panhandler knew, makes one feel less anonymous, more responsible.

To reduce anonymity, researchers have had bystanders identify themselves to one another—by name, age, and so forth—after which, they were more likely to offer aid to a sick person (Solomon & Solomon, 1978; Solomon et al., 1981). Similarly, when a female experimenter caught the eye of another shopper and gave her a warm smile before stepping on an elevator, that shopper was far more likely than other shoppers to offer help when the experimenter later said, "Damn. I've left my glasses. Can anyone tell me what floor the umbrellas are on?" Even a trivial momentary conversation with someone ("Excuse me, aren't you Suzie Spear's sister?" "No, I'm not") dramatically increased the person's later helpfulness.

Helpfulness also increases when one expects to meet the victim and other witnesses again. Using a laboratory intercom system, Jody Gottlieb and Charles Carver (1980) led University of Miami students to believe they were discussing problems of college living with other students. (Actually, the other discussants were tape-recorded.) When one of the supposed fellow discussants had a choking fit and cried out for help, she was helped most quickly by those who believed they would soon be meeting the discussants face-to-face. In short, *anything that personalizes bystanders*—a personal request, eye contact, stating one's name, anticipating interaction—increases willingness to help. In experiments, restaurant patrons have tipped more when their servers introduced themselves by name, wrote friendly messages on checks, touched guests on the arm or shoulder, and sat or squatted at the table during the service encounter (Leodoro & Lynn, 2007; Schirmer et al., 2011). In another experiment, door-to-door solicitors asking for a 1 Euro donation to a children's charity received nearly doubled compliance (96%) after first shaking the householder's hand (Guéguen, 2013).

Personal treatment makes bystanders more self-aware. And self-aware people are more attuned to their own altruistic ideals. Note that people made self-aware by acting in front of a mirror or a TV camera exhibit increased consistency between attitudes and actions. By contrast, "deindividuated" people are less responsible. Thus, circumstances that promote self-awareness—name tags, being watched and evaluated, undistracted quiet—should also increase helping.

Shelley Duval, Virginia Duval, and Robert Neely (1979) confirmed this. They showed some University of Southern California women their own images on a TV screen or had them complete biographical questionnaires just before giving them a chance to contribute time and money to people in need. Those made self-aware contributed more. Similarly, pedestrians who have just had their pictures taken by someone became more likely to help another pedestrian pick up dropped envelopes (Hoover et al., 1983). And among Italian pedestrians who had just seen themselves in a mirror, 70 percent helped a stranger by mailing a postcard, as did 13 percent of others approached (Abbate et al., 2006). Self-aware people more often live out their ideals.

Guilt and Concern for Self-Image

Previously, we noted that people who feel guilty will act to reduce guilt and restore their self-worth. Can awakening people's guilt therefore increase their desire to help?

A Reed College research team led by Richard Katzev (1978) experimented with guilt-induced helping. When visitors to the Portland Art Museum disobeyed a "Please do not touch" sign, experimenters reprimanded some of them: "Please don't touch the objects. If everyone touches them, they will deteriorate." Likewise, when visitors to the Portland Zoo fed unauthorized food to the bears, some of them were admonished with, "Hey, don't feed unauthorized food to the animals. Don't you know it could hurt them?" In both cases, 58 percent of the now guilt-laden individuals shortly thereafter offered help to another experimenter who had "accidentally" dropped something. Of those not reprimanded, only one-third helped. Guilt-laden people are helpful people.

That was my [DM's] experience recently, after passing a man struggling to get up from a busy city sidewalk as I raced to catch a train. His glazed eyes brought to mind the many drunken people I had assisted during my college days as an emergency room attendant. Or . . . I wondered after walking by . . . was he actually experiencing a health crisis? Plagued by guilt, I picked up sidewalk litter, offered my train seat to an elderly couple looking for seats together, and vowed that the next time I faced uncertainty in an unfamiliar city I would think to call 911.

Cialdini and David Schroeder (1976) offer another practical way to trigger concern for self-image: Ask for a contribution so small that it's hard to say no without feeling like a Scrooge. Cialdini (1995) discovered this when a United Way canvasser came to his door. As she solicited his contribution, he was mentally preparing his refusal—until she said magic words that demolished his financial excuse: "Even a penny will help." "I had been neatly finessed into compliance," recalled Cialdini. "And there was another interesting feature of our exchange as well. When I stopped coughing (I really had choked on my attempted rejection), I gave her not the penny she had mentioned but the amount I usually allot to legitimate charity solicitors. At that, she thanked me, smiled innocently, and moved on."

Was Cialdini's response atypical? To find out, he and Schroeder had a solicitor approach suburbanites. When the solicitor said, "I'm collecting money for the American Cancer Society," 29 percent contributed an average of $1.44 each. When the solicitor added, "Even a penny will help," 50 percent contributed, and gave an average of $1.54 each. When James Weyant (1984) repeated this experiment, he found similar results: The "even a penny will help" boosted the number contributing from 39 to 57 percent. And when 6,000 people were solicited by mail for the American Cancer Society, those asked for small amounts were more likely to give—and gave no less on average—than those asked for larger amounts (Weyant & Smith, 1987). A qualification: when previous donors are approached, bigger requests (within reason) do elicit bigger donations (Doob & McLaughlin, 1989). But with door-to-door solicitation, there is more success with requests for small contributions, which are difficult to turn down and still allow the person to maintain an altruistic self-image.

Labeling people as helpful can also strengthen a helpful self-image. After they had made charitable contributions, Robert Kraut (1973) told some Connecticut women, "You are a generous person." Two weeks later, these women were more willing than those not so labeled to contribute to a different charity.

Socializing Altruism

How might we socialize altruism? Here are five ways (Figure 11).

TEACHING MORAL INCLUSION

Rescuers of Jews in Nazi Europe, leaders of the antislavery movement, and medical missionaries shared at least one common trait: They were *morally inclusive.* Their moral concern encircled diverse people. One rescuer faked a pregnancy on behalf of a pregnant hidden Jew—thus including the soon-to-be-born child within the circle of her own children's identities (Fogelman, 1994).

Moral exclusion—omitting certain people from one's circle of moral concern—has the opposite effect. It justifies all sorts of harm, from discrimination to genocide (Opotow, 1990;

moral exclusion
The perception of certain individuals or groups as outside the boundary within which one applies moral values and rules of fairness. *Moral inclusion* is regarding others as within one's circle of moral concern.

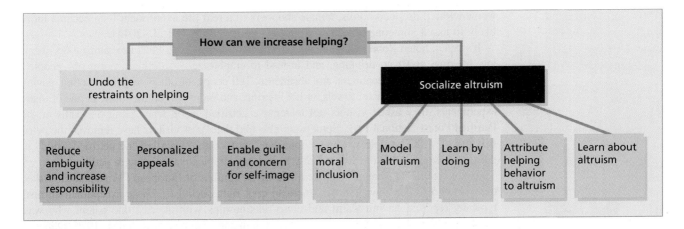

FIGURE :: 11

Practical Ways to Increase Helping

Staub, 2005a; Tyler & Lind, 1990). Exploitation or cruelty becomes acceptable, even appropriate, toward those whom we regard as undeserving or as nonpersons. The Nazis excluded Jews from their moral community. Anyone who participates in enslavement, death squads, or torture practices a similar exclusion. To a lesser extent, moral exclusion describes those of us who concentrate our concerns, favors, and financial inheritance upon "our people" (for example, our children) to the exclusion of others.

More exclusion also describes restrictions in the public empathy for the human costs of war. Reported war deaths are typically "our deaths." Many Americans, for example, know that some 58,000 Americans died in the Vietnam War (their 58,248 names are inscribed on the Vietnam War Memorial). But few Americans know that the war also left some 2 million Vietnamese dead. During the Iraq War, news of American fatalities—nearly 4,500—caused much more concern than the little-known number of Iraqi deaths, for which a low range of estimates published by leading medical journals was more than 150,000 (Alkhuzai et al., 2008).

We easily become numbed by impersonal big numbers of outgroup fatalities (Dunn & Aston-James, 2008; Slovic, 2007). People presume that they would be more upset about a hurricane that killed 5,000 rather than 50 people. But whether people heard that Hurricane Katrina claimed 50, 500, 1,000, or 5,000 lives, their sadness was unaffected by the number. Ditto for the scale of other tragedies, including a forest fire in Spain and the war in Iraq. "If I look at the mass I will never act," said Mother Teresa. "If I look at the one, I will." Shown a single victim, a 7-year-old girl named Rokia, people responded with more money for a hunger charity than when told the organization was working to save millions (Slovic & Västfjäll, 2010).

A first step toward socializing altruism is therefore to counter the natural ingroup bias favoring kin and tribe by personalizing and broadening the range of people whose well-being should concern us. Daniel Batson (1983) notes how religious teachings do this. They extend the reach of kin-linked altruism by urging "brotherly and sisterly" love toward all "children of God" in the whole human "family." As research with a new "Identification with All Humanity Scale" shows, if everyone is part of our family, then everyone has a moral claim on us (McFarland et al., 2013). The boundaries between "we" and "they" fade. Inviting advantaged people to put themselves in others' shoes, to imagine how they feel, also helps (Batson et al., 2003). To "do unto others as you would have them do unto you," one must take the others' perspective.

"We consider humankind our family."

—Parliament of the World Religions,
Towards a Global Ethic, 1993

MODELING ALTRUISM

Previously, we noted that seeing unresponsive bystanders makes us less likely to help. People reared by extremely punitive parents, as were many delinquents and chronic criminals, also show much less of the empathy and principled caring that typify altruists.

REAL-LIFE MODELING.   If, however, we see or read about someone helping, we become more likely to offer assistance. If they had earlier witnessed someone helping a woman who'd dropped books, female shoppers in a real life experiment then became more likely to assist someone who had dropped a dollar (Burger et al., 2014).

It's better, noted Robert Cialdini and co-workers (2003), *not* to publicize rampant tax cheating, littering, and teen drinking, and instead to emphasize—to define a norm of—people's widespread honesty, cleanliness, and abstinence. Tell people of others recycling, voting, paying taxes on time, reusing hotel towels, or not littering, and more will do the same. In one of many experiments, they asked visitors not to remove petrified wood from along the paths of the Petrified Forest National Park. Some were also told that "past visitors have removed the petrified wood." Other people who were told that "past visitors have left the petrified wood" to preserve the park were much less likely to pick up samples placed along a path.

Modeling effects were also apparent within the families of European Christians who risked their lives to rescue Jews and of American civil rights activists. These exceptional altruists typically reported having warm and close relationships with at least one parent who was, similarly, a strong "moralist" or committed to humanitarian causes (London, 1970; Oliner & Oliner, 1988; Rosenhan, 1970). Their families—and often their friends and churches—had taught them the norm of helping and caring for others. This "prosocial value orientation" led them to include people from other groups in their circle of moral concern and to feel responsible for others' welfare, reported altruism researcher Ervin Staub (1989, 1991, 2015).

Staub (1999) knows of what he speaks: "As a young Jewish child in Budapest I survived the Holocaust, the destruction of most European Jews by Nazi Germany and its allies. My life was saved by a Christian woman who repeatedly endangered her life to help me and my family, and by Raoul Wallenberg, the Swede who came to Budapest and with courage, brilliance, and complete commitment saved the lives of tens of thousands of Jews destined for the gas chambers. These two heroes were not passive bystanders, and my work is one of the ways for me not to be one." (See "Focus On: Behavior and Attitudes Among Rescuers of Jews.")

focus ON   Behavior and Attitudes Among Rescuers of Jews

Goodness, like evil, often evolves in small steps. The Gentiles who saved Jews often began with a small commitment—to hide someone for a day or two. Having taken that step, they began to see themselves differently, as people who help. Then they became more intensely involved. Given control of a confiscated Jewish-owned factory, Oskar Schindler began by doing small favors for his Jewish workers, who were earning him handsome profits. Gradually, he took greater and greater risks to protect them. He got permission to set up workers' housing next to the factory. He rescued individuals separated from their families and reunited loved ones. Finally, as the Russians advanced, he saved some 1,200 Jews by setting up a fake factory in his hometown and taking along his entire group of "skilled workers" to staff it.

Others, such as Raoul Wallenberg, began by agreeing to a personal request for help and ended up repeatedly risking their lives. Wallenberg became Swedish ambassador to Hungary, where he saved tens of thousands of Hungarian Jews from extermination at Auschwitz. One of those given protective identity papers was 6-year-old Ervin Staub, who became a University of Massachusetts social psychologist whose experience set him on a lifelong mission to understand why some people perpetrate evil, some stand by, and some help.

Munich, 1948. Oskar Schindler with some of the Jews he saved from the Nazis during World War II.
Source: Rappoport & Kren (1993).
Leopold Page Photographic Collection, courtesy of USHMM Photo Archives

MEDIA MODELING.   Do television's positive models promote helping, much as its aggressive portrayals promote aggression? Prosocial TV models have actually had even greater effects than antisocial models. Susan Hearold (1986) statistically combined 108 comparisons of prosocial programs with neutral programs or no program. She found that, on average, "If the viewer watched prosocial programs instead of neutral programs, he would [at least temporarily] be elevated from the 50th to the 74th percentile in prosocial behavior—typically altruism."

In one such study, researchers Lynette Friedrich and Aletha Stein (1973; Stein & Friedrich, 1972) showed preschool children *Mister Rogers' Neighborhood* episodes each day for 4 weeks as part of their nursery school program. (*Mister Rogers' Neighborhood* aimed to enhance young children's social and emotional development.) During the viewing period, children from less-educated homes became more cooperative, helpful, and likely to state their feelings. In a follow-up study, kindergartners who viewed four *Mister Rogers'* programs were able to state the show's prosocial content, both on a test and in puppet play (Friedrich & Stein, 1975; also Coates et al., 1976).

Other media also effectively model prosocial behavior, partly by increasing empathy. Recent studies from across the world show positive effects on attitudes or behavior from prosocial media, including playing prosocial video games and listening to prosocial music lyrics (Gentile et al., 2009; Greitemeyer et al., 2010; Prot et al., 2014). For example, playing *Lemmings,* where the goal is to help others, increases later real-life empathy and helping in response to another's misfortune (Greitemeyer & Osswald, 2010; Greitemeyer et al., 2010). Listening to prosocial songs, such as Michael Jackson's "Heal the World," made listeners more likely to help someone pick up dropped pencils and less likely to say harsh things about a job candidate or give someone a large dose of disliked chili sauce (Greitemeyer, 2009a,b, 2011).

> "Children can learn to be altruistic, friendly, and self-controlled by looking at television programs depicting such behavior patterns."
>
> —National Institute of Mental Health,
> *Television and Behavior,* 1982

LEARNING BY DOING

Ervin Staub (2005b, 2015) has shown that just as immoral behavior fuels immoral attitudes, helping increases future helping. Children and adults learn by doing. In a series of studies with children near age 12, Staub and his students found that after children were induced to make toys for hospitalized children or for an art teacher, they became more helpful. So were children after teaching younger children to make puzzles or use first aid.

When children act helpfully, they develop helping-related values, beliefs, and skills, notes Staub. Helping also helps satisfy their needs for a positive self-concept. On a larger scale, "service learning" and volunteer programs woven into a school curriculum have been shown to increase later citizen involvement, social responsibility, cooperation, and leadership (Andersen, 1998; Putnam, 2000). Attitudes follow behavior. Helpful actions therefore promote the self-perception that one is caring and helpful. And that compassionate positive self-perception in turn promotes further helping.

ATTRIBUTING HELPFUL BEHAVIOR TO ALTRUISTIC MOTIVES

Another clue to socializing altruism comes from research on the **overjustification effect:** When the justification for an act is more than sufficient, the person may attribute the act to the extrinsic justification rather than to an inner motive. Rewarding people for doing what they would do anyway therefore undermines intrinsic motivation. We can state the principle positively: By providing people with just enough justification to prompt a good deed (weaning them from bribes and threats), we may increase their pleasure in doing such deeds on their own.

Daniel Batson and associates (1978, 1979) put the overjustification phenomenon to work. In several experiments, they found that University of Kansas students felt most altruistic after they agreed to help someone without payment or implied social pressure. When pay had been offered or social pressures were present, people felt less altruistic after helping.

In another experiment, the researchers led students to attribute a helpful act to compliance ("I guess we really don't have a choice") or to compassion ("The guy really needs help"). Later, when the students were asked to volunteer their time to a local service agency, 25 percent of those who had been led to perceive their previous helpfulness as mere compliance now volunteered; of those led to see themselves as compassionate, 60 percent volunteered.

overjustification effect
The result of bribing people to do what they already like doing; they may then see their actions as externally controlled rather than intrinsically appealing.

The moral? When people wonder, "Why am I helping?" it's best if the circumstances enable them to answer, "Because help was needed, and *I am a caring, giving, helpful person.*"

To predispose more people to help in situations in which most don't, it can also pay to induce a tentative positive commitment, from which people may infer their own helpfulness. Delia Cioffi and Randy Garner (1998) observed that only about 5 percent of students responded to a campus blood drive after receiving an e-mail announcement a week ahead. They asked other students to reply to the announcement with a yes "if you think you probably will donate." Of those, 29 percent did reply and the actual donation rate was 8 percent. They asked a third group to reply with a no if they did *not* anticipate donating. Now 71 percent implied they might give (by not replying). Imagine yourself in this third group. Might you have decided not to say no because, after all, you *are* a caring person so there's a chance you might give? And might that thought have opened you to persuasion as you encountered campus posters and flyers during the ensuing week? That apparently is what happened, because 12 percent of these students—more than twice the normal rate—showed up to offer their blood.

Inferring that one is a helpful person seems also to have happened when Dariusz Dolinski (2000) stopped pedestrians on the streets of Wroclaw, Poland, and asked them for directions to a nonexistent "Zubrzyckiego Street" or to an illegible address. Everyone tried unsuccessfully to help. After doing so, about two-thirds (twice the number of those not given the opportunity to try to help) agreed when asked by someone 100 meters farther down the road to watch their bag or bicycle for 5 minutes.

LEARNING ABOUT ALTRUISM

Researchers have found another way to boost altruism, one that provides a happy chapter conclusion. Some social psychologists worry that as people become more aware of social psychology's findings, their behavior may change, thus invalidating the findings (Gergen, 1982). Will learning about the factors that inhibit altruism reduce their influence? Philip Zimbardo, whose "Heroism Project" aims to strengthen people's courage and compassion, contends that the first step to becoming a hero is recognizing social pressures that might deter your bystander action (Miller, 2011).

Experiments with University of Montana students by Arthur Beaman and colleagues (1978) revealed that once people understand why the presence of bystanders inhibits helping, they become more likely to help in group situations. The researchers used a lecture to inform some students how bystander inaction can affect the interpretation of an emergency and feelings of responsibility. Other students heard either a different lecture or no lecture at all. Two weeks later, as part of a different experiment in a different location, the participants found themselves walking (with an unresponsive confederate) past someone slumped over or past a person sprawled beneath a bicycle. Of those who had not heard the helping lecture, one-fourth paused to offer help; twice as many of those "enlightened" did so.

Having read this chapter, perhaps you, too, have changed. As you come to understand what influences people's responses, will your attitudes and your behavior be the same?

SUMMING UP: How Can We Increase Helping?

Research suggests that we can enhance helpfulness in three ways.

- First, we can reverse those factors that inhibit helping. We can take steps to reduce the ambiguity of an emergency, to make a personal appeal, and to increase feelings of responsibility.

- Second, we can teach altruism. Research into television's portrayals of prosocial models shows the medium's power to teach positive behavior. Children who view helpful behavior tend to act helpfully. If we want to promote altruistic behavior, we should remember the *overjustification effect:* When we coerce good deeds, intrinsic love of the activity often diminishes. If we provide people with enough justification for them to decide to do good, but not much more, they will attribute their behavior to their own altruistic motivation and henceforth be more willing to help. Learning about altruism, as you have just done, can also prepare people to perceive and respond to others' needs.

POSTSCRIPT:
Taking Social Psychology Into Life

Those of us who research, teach, and write about social psychology do so believing that our work matters. It engages humanly significant phenomena. Studying social psychology can therefore expand our thinking and prepare us to live and act with greater awareness and compassion, or so we presume.

How good it feels, then, when students and former students confirm our presumptions with stories of how they have related social psychology to their lives. As it turns out, both of us authors have had this experience. After I [JT] taught a social psychology class about this research, a student e-mailed me to say he'd seen a young woman collapse right outside the classroom. Remembering from the lecture that no one else might help, he called 911 and stayed with her. Shortly before I [DM] wrote the last paragraph, a former student, now living in Washington, D.C., stopped by. She mentioned that she recently found herself part of a stream of pedestrians striding past a man lying unconscious on the sidewalk. "It took my mind back to our social psych class and the accounts of why people fail to help in such situations. Then I thought, 'Well, if I just walk by, too, who's going to help him?'" So she made a call to an emergency help number and waited with the victim—and other bystanders who now joined her—until help arrived.

Conflict and Peacemaking

CHAPTER

13

Rafael Suanes/Newscom

"If you want peace, work for justice."

—Pope Paul VI

There is a speech that has been spoken in many languages by the leaders of many countries. It goes like this: "The intentions of our country are entirely peaceful. But other nations threaten us. Thus we must defend ourselves against attack. By so doing, we shall protect our way of life and preserve the peace" (Richardson, 1960). Almost every nation claims concern only for peace but, mistrusting other nations, arms itself in self-defense. The result is a world that has been spending nearly $5 billion per day on arms and armies while millions die of malnutrition and untreated disease (SIPRI, 2014).

The elements of such **conflict** (a perceived incompatibility of actions or goals) are similar at many levels, from nations to individuals. People in conflict perceive that one side's gain is the other's loss:

- "We want peace and security." "So do we, but you threaten us."
- "We want more pay." "We can't afford it."
- "I'd like the music off." "I'd like it on."

An organization or a relationship without conflict is probably apathetic. Conflict signifies involvement, commitment, and caring. If conflict is understood and recognized, it can end oppression and stimulate renewed relationships. Without conflict, people seldom face and resolve their problems.

Genuine **peace** is more than the suppression of open conflict, more than a fragile, superficial calm. Peace is the outcome of a creatively managed conflict. Peace is the parties reconciling their perceived differences and reaching genuine accord. "We got our increased pay. You got your increased profit. Now each of us is helping the other achieve the organization's goals."

conflict
A perceived incompatibility of actions or goals.

As civil rights leaders know, creatively managed conflicts can have constructive outcomes.
AP Images

peace
A condition marked by low levels of hostility and aggression and by mutually beneficial relationships.

WHAT CREATES CONFLICT?

Explain what feeds conflict.

Social-psychological studies have identified several ingredients of conflict. What's striking (and what simplifies our task) is that these ingredients are common to all levels of social conflict, whether intergroup (us versus them) or interpersonal (me versus us).

Social Dilemmas

Many problems that threaten our future—nuclear arms, climate change, overpopulation, depleting fish stocks, natural-resource depletion—arise as various parties pursue their self-interests, ironically, to their collective detriment. One individual may think, "It would cost me a lot to buy expensive greenhouse emission controls. Besides, the greenhouse gases I personally generate are trivial." Many others reason similarly, and the result is a warming climate, melting ice cover, rising seas, and more extreme weather.

Individually rewarding choices become collectively punishing. We therefore have a dilemma: How can we reconcile individual self-interest with communal well-being?

To isolate and study that dilemma, social psychologists have used laboratory games that expose the heart of many real social conflicts. "Social psychologists who study conflict are in much the same position as the astronomers," noted conflict researcher Morton Deutsch (1999). "We cannot conduct true experiments with large-scale social events. But we can identify the conceptual similarities between the large scale and the small, as the astronomers have between the planets and Newton's apple. That is why the games people play as subjects in our laboratory may advance our understanding of war, peace, and social justice."

Let's consider two examples of a **social trap**—a situation when conflicting parties are caught in mutually destructive behavior: the Prisoner's Dilemma and the Tragedy of the Commons.

THE PRISONER'S DILEMMA

This dilemma derives from an anecdote concerning two suspects being questioned separately by the district attorney (DA) (Rapoport, 1960). The DA knows they are jointly guilty but has only enough evidence to convict them of a lesser offense. So the DA creates an incentive for each one to confess privately:

- If Prisoner A confesses and Prisoner B doesn't, the DA will grant immunity to A and will use A's confession to convict B of a maximum offense (and vice versa if B confesses and A doesn't).
- If both confess, each will receive a moderate sentence.
- If neither prisoner confesses, each will be convicted of a lesser crime and receive a light sentence.

The matrix of Figure 1 summarizes the choices. If you were a prisoner faced with such a dilemma, with no chance to talk to the other prisoner, would you confess?

Many people say they would confess to be granted immunity, even though mutual *non*confession elicits lighter sentences than mutual confession. Perhaps this is because (as shown in the Figure 1 matrix) no matter what the other prisoner decides, each is better off confessing than being convicted individually. If the other also confesses, the sentence is moderate rather than severe. If the other does not confess, one goes free.

University students have faced variations of the Prisoner's Dilemma, with the choices being to defect or to cooperate, and the outcomes not being prison terms but chips, money, or grade points. As Figure 2 illustrates, on any given decision, a person is better off defecting (because such behavior exploits the other's cooperation or protects against the other's exploitation). However—and here's the rub—by not cooperating, both parties end up far worse off than if they had trusted each other and thus had gained a joint profit. This dilemma often traps each one in a maddening predicament in which both realize they *could* mutually profit. But unable to communicate, and mistrusting each other, they

FIGURE :: 1

The Classic Prisoner's Dilemma

In each box, the number above the diagonal is prisoner A's outcome. Thus, if both prisoners confess, both get five years. If neither confesses, each gets a year. If one confesses, that prisoner is set free in exchange for evidence used to convict the other of a crime bringing a 10-year sentence. If you were one of the prisoners, unable to communicate with your fellow prisoner, would you confess?

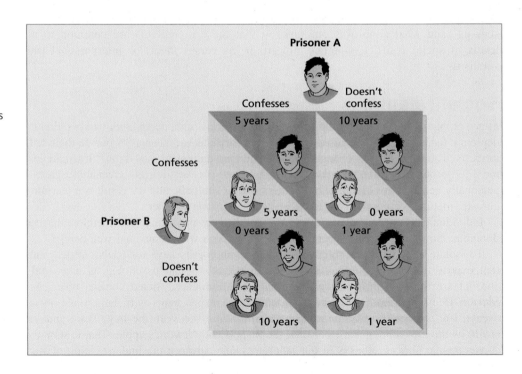

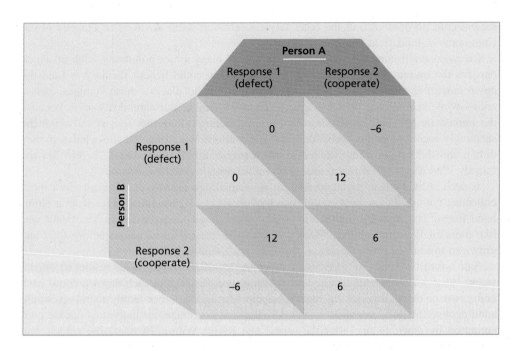

FIGURE :: 2

Laboratory Version of the Prisoner's Dilemma

The numbers represent some reward, such as money. In each box, the number above the diagonal lines is the outcome for person A. Unlike the classic Prisoner's Dilemma (a one-shot decision), most laboratory versions involve repeated plays.

often become "locked in" to not cooperating. Outside the university, examples abound: seemingly intractable and costly conflicts between Israelis and Palestinians over borders, U.S. Republicans and Democrats over taxation and deficits, and professional athletes and team owners over pay.

Punishing another's lack of cooperation might seem like a smart strategy, but in the laboratory it can have counterproductive effects (Dreber et al., 2008). Punishment typically triggers retaliation, which means that those who punish tend to escalate conflict, worsening their outcomes, while nice guys finish first. What punishers see as a defensive reaction, recipients see as an aggressive escalation (Anderson et al., 2008). When hitting back, they may hit harder while seeing themselves as merely returning tit for tat. In one experiment, London volunteers used a mechanical device to press back on another's finger after receiving pressure on their own. While seeking to reciprocate with the same degree of pressure, they typically responded with 40 percent more force. Thus, touches soon escalated to hard presses, much like a child saying "I just *touched* him, and then he *hit* me!" (Shergill et al., 2003).

THE TRAGEDY OF THE COMMONS

Many social dilemmas involve more than two parties. Climate change stems from deforestation and from the carbon dioxide emitted by vehicles, furnaces, and coal-fired power plants. Each car contributes infinitesimally to the problem, and the harm is diffused over many people. To model such social predicaments, researchers have developed laboratory dilemmas that involve multiple people.

A metaphor for the insidious nature of social dilemmas is what ecologist Garrett Hardin (1968) called the **Tragedy of the Commons.** He derived the name from the centrally located grassy pasture in old English towns.

In today's world the "commons" can be air, water, fish, cookies, or any shared and limited resource. If all use the resource in moderation, it may replenish itself as rapidly as it's harvested. The grass will grow, the fish will reproduce, and the cookie jar will be restocked. If not, there occurs a tragedy of the commons. Imagine 100 farmers surrounding a commons capable of sustaining 100 cows. When each grazes one cow, the common feeding ground is optimally used. But then a farmer reasons, "If I put a second cow in the pasture, I'll double my output, minus the mere 1 percent overgrazing" and adds a

Tragedy of the Commons
The "commons" is any shared resource, including air, water, energy sources, and food supplies. The tragedy occurs when individuals consume more than their share, with the cost of their doing so dispersed among all, causing the ultimate collapse—the tragedy—of the commons.

second cow. So does each of the other farmers. The inevitable result? The Tragedy of the Commons—a mud field and famished cows.

Likewise, environmental pollution is the sum of many minor pollutions, each of which benefits the individual polluters much more than they could benefit themselves (and the environment) if they stopped polluting. We litter public places—dorm lounges, parks, zoos—while keeping our personal spaces clean. We deplete our natural resources because the immediate personal benefits of, for instance, taking a long, hot shower outweigh the seemingly inconsequential costs. Whalers knew others would exploit the whales if they didn't, and that taking a few whales would hardly diminish the species. Therein lies the tragedy. *Everybody's business (conservation) becomes nobody's business.*

Is such individualism uniquely American? Kaori Sato (1987) gave students in a more collective culture, Japan, opportunities to harvest—for actual money—trees from a simulated forest. The students shared equally the costs of planting the forest. The result was like those in Western cultures. More than half the trees were harvested before they had grown to the most profitable size.

Sato's forest reminds me [DM] of our home's cookie jar, which was restocked once a week. What we *should* have done was conserve cookies so that each day we could each enjoy two or three. But lacking regulation and fearing that other family members would soon deplete the resource, what we actually did was maximize our individual cookie consumption by downing one after the other. The result: Within 24 hours the cookie glut would end, the jar sitting empty for the rest of the week.

When resources are not partitioned, people often consume more than they realize (Herlocker et al., 1997). As a bowl of mashed potatoes is passed around a table of 10, the first few diners are more likely to scoop out a disproportionate share than when a platter of 10 chicken drumsticks is passed.

The Prisoner's Dilemma and the Tragedy of the Commons games have several similar features.

THE FUNDAMENTAL ATTRIBUTION ERROR

First, both games tempt people to *explain their own behavior situationally* ("I had to protect myself against exploitation by my opponent") and to explain their partners' behavior dispositionally ("she was greedy," "he was untrustworthy"). Most never realize that their counterparts are viewing them with the same fundamental attribution error (Gifford & Hine, 1997; Hine & Gifford, 1996).

When Muslims have killed Americans, Western media have attributed the killings to evil dispositions—to the primitive, fanatical, hateful terrorists. When an American soldier killed 16 Afghans, including 9 children, he was said to be experiencing financial stress, suffering marital problems, and frustrated by being passed over for a promotion (Greenwald, 2012). Violence explanations vary by whether the act is by or toward one's side.

EVOLVING MOTIVES

Second, *motives often change.* At first, people are eager to make some easy money, then to minimize their losses, and finally to save face and avoid defeat (Brockner et al., 1982; Teger, 1980). These shifting motives are strikingly similar to the shifting motives during the buildup of the 1960s Vietnam War. At first, President Johnson's speeches expressed concern for democracy, freedom, and justice. As the conflict escalated, his concern became protecting America's honor and avoiding the national humiliation of losing a war.

OUTCOMES NEED NOT SUM TO ZERO

non-zero-sum games
Games in which outcomes need not sum to zero. With cooperation, both can win; with competition, both can lose (also called *mixed-motive situations*).

Third, most real-life conflicts, like the Prisoner's Dilemma and the Tragedy of the Commons, are **non-zero-sum games.** The two sides' profits and losses need not add up to zero. Both can win; both can lose. Each game pits the immediate interests of individuals against the well-being of the group. Each is a diabolical social trap that shows how, even when each individual behaves rationally, harm can result. No malicious person planned for the earth's atmosphere to be warmed by a carbon dioxide blanket.

Not all self-serving behavior leads to collective doom. In a plentiful commons—as in the world of the eighteenth-century capitalist economist Adam Smith (1776, p. 18)—individuals who seek to maximize their own profit may also give the community what it needs: "It is not from the benevolence of the butcher, the brewer, or the baker, that we expect our dinner," he observed, "but from their regard to their own interest."

RESOLVING SOCIAL DILEMMAS

In real-life situations, many people approach commons dilemmas with a cooperative outlook and expect similar cooperation from others, thus enabling their collective betterment (Krueger et al., 2012; Ostrom, 2014). Research with laboratory dilemmas has identified several ways to further encourage such mutual betterment (Gifford & Hine, 1997; Nowak, 2012).

REGULATION.   If taxes were entirely voluntary, how many would pay their full share? Modern societies do not depend on charity to pay for schools, parks, and social and military security. We also develop rules to safeguard our common good. Fishing and hunting have long been regulated by local seasons and limits; at the global level, an International Whaling Commission sets an agreed-upon "harvest" that enables whales to regenerate. Likewise, where fishing industries, such as the Alaskan halibut fishery, have implemented "catch shares"—guaranteeing each fisher a percentage of each year's allowable catch—competition and overfishing have been greatly reduced (Costello et al., 2008).

In everyday life, however, regulation has costs—costs of administering and enforcing the regulations, costs of diminished personal freedom. A volatile political question thus arises: At what point does a regulation's cost exceed its benefits?

> "Like the old buffalo hunters, fishermen have a personal incentive to make as much as they can this year, even if they're destroying their own profession in the process."
> —John Tierney,
> "Where the Tuna Roam," 2006

SMALL IS BEAUTIFUL.   There is another way to resolve social dilemmas: Make the group small. In a small commons, each person feels more responsible and effective (Kerr, 1989). As a group grows larger, people become more likely to think, "I couldn't have made a difference anyway"—a common excuse for noncooperation (Kerr & Kaufman-Gilliland, 1997).

In small groups, people also feel more identified with a group's success. Residential stability also strengthens communal identity and procommunity behavior (Oishi et al., 2007). On the Pacific Northwest island where I [DM] grew up, our small neighborhood shared a communal water supply. On hot summer days when the reservoir ran low, a light came on, signaling our 15 families to conserve. Recognizing our responsibility to one another, and feeling that our conservation really mattered, each of us conserved. Never did the reservoir run dry. In a much larger commons—say, a city—voluntary conservation is less successful.

> "For that which is common to the greatest number has the least care bestowed upon it."
> —Aristotle

Small is cooperative. On Scotland's Isle of Muck, Constable Lawrence MacEwan has had an easy time policing the island's 33 residents. Over his 40 years on the job, there was never a crime (*Scottish Life,* 2001). In 2010, a row between two friends who had been drinking at a wedding became the first recorded crime in 50 years, but the next morning, they shook hands and all was well (Cameron, 2010). In 2015, the nearby island of Canna experienced its "crime of the century" (its first crime since the 1960s) when thieves stole crafts, food, and money from its shop. The shop was left unlocked so that fishing people resting at the pier overnight could buy what they needed, paying via an "honesty box."
Catherine Karnow

Evolutionary psychologist Robin Dunbar (1992, 2010) notes that tribal villages and clans often have averaged about 150 people—enough to afford mutual support and protection but not more people than one can monitor. This seemingly natural group size is also, he believes, the optimum size for business organizations, religious congregations, and military fighting units.

COMMUNICATION.   To resolve a social dilemma, people must communicate. In the laboratory as in real life, group communication sometimes degenerates into threats and name-calling (Deutsch & Krauss, 1960). More often, communication enables cooperation (Bornstein et al., 1988, 1989). Discussing the dilemma forges a group identity, which enhances concern for everyone's welfare. It devises group norms and expectations and pressures members to follow them. Even just imagining group discussion can increase cooperation (Meleady et al., 2013). But especially when people are face-to-face, it enables them to commit themselves to cooperation (Bouas & Komorita, 1996; Drolet & Morris, 2000; Kerr et al., 1994, 1997; Pruitt, 1998). Humans, thanks to full-blown language, are the most cooperative, reciprocally helpful species (Nowak, 2012).

A clever experiment by Robyn Dawes (1980a, 1994) illustrates the importance of communication. Imagine that an experimenter offered you and six strangers a choice: You can each have $6, or you can donate your $6 to the others. If you give away your money, the experimenter will double your gift. No one will be told whether you chose to give or keep your $6. Thus, if all seven give, everyone pockets $12. If you alone keep your $6 and all the others give theirs, you pocket $18. If you give and the others keep, you pocket nothing. In this experiment, cooperation is mutually advantageous, but it requires risk. Dawes found that, without discussion, about 30 percent of people gave. With discussion, in which they could establish trust and cooperation, about 80 percent gave.

Open, clear, forthright communication between two parties reduces mistrust. Without communication, those who expect others not to cooperate will usually refuse to cooperate themselves (Messé & Sivacek, 1979; Pruitt & Kimmel, 1977). One who mistrusts is almost sure to be uncooperative (to protect against exploitation). Noncooperation, in turn, feeds further mistrust ("What else could I do? It's a dog-eat-dog world"). In experiments, communication reduces mistrust, enabling people to reach agreements that lead to their common betterment.

CHANGING THE PAYOFFS.   Laboratory cooperation rises when experimenters change the payoff matrix to reward cooperation and punish exploitation (Balliet et al., 2011). Changing payoffs also helps resolve actual dilemmas. In some cities, freeways clog and skies collect smog because people prefer the convenience of driving by themselves to work. Each knows that one more car does not add noticeably to the congestion and pollution. To alter the personal cost-benefit calculations, many cities now give carpoolers and electric cars incentives, such as designated freeway lanes or reduced tolls.

APPEALING TO ALTRUISTIC NORMS.   We have seen that increasing bystanders' feelings of responsibility for others boosts altruism. Will appeals to altruistic motives similarly prompt people to act for the common good?

The evidence is mixed. On the one hand, just *knowing* the dire consequences of noncooperation has little effect. People may realize that their self-serving choices are mutually destructive, yet continue to make them. People know that climate change is underway, yet continue buying gas-slurping SUVs. As we have seen many times in this book, attitudes sometimes fail to influence behavior. *Knowing* what is good does not necessarily lead to *doing* what is good.

Still, most people do adhere to norms of social responsibility, reciprocity, equity, and keeping one's commitments (Kerr, 1992). The problem is how to tap such feelings. One way is

"My own belief is that Russian and Chinese behavior is as much influenced by suspicion of our intentions as ours is by suspicion of theirs. This would mean that we have great influence on their behavior— that, by treating them as hostile, we assure their hostility."

—U.S. Senator J. William Fulbright, 1971

To change behavior, many cities have changed the payoff matrix. Fast carpool-only lanes increase the benefits of carpooling and clean air vehicles, and the costs of driving alone.
TIM MCCAIG/Getty Images

through the influence of a charismatic leader who inspires others to cooperate (De Cremer, 2002). In China, those who were educated during Mao's "planned economy" era—an era that emphasized equal wealth distribution—make more cooperative social dilemma game choices than those who were not (Zhu et al., 2013).

Another way is by defining situations in ways that invoke cooperative norms. In one experiment, only a third of participants cooperated in a simulation labeled the "Wall Street Game." Two-thirds did so when the same social dilemma was labeled the "Community Game" (Liberman et al., 2004).

Communication can also activate altruistic norms. When permitted to communicate, participants in laboratory games frequently appeal to the social-responsibility norm: "If you defect on the rest of us, you're going to have to live with it for the rest of your life" (Dawes et al., 1977). So researcher Robyn Dawes (1980a) and his associates gave participants a short sermon about group benefits, exploitation, and ethics. Then the participants played a dilemma game. The sermon worked: People chose to forgo immediate personal gain for the common good.

Could such appeals work in large-scale dilemmas? In the 1960s struggle for civil rights, many marchers willingly agreed, for the sake of the larger group, to suffer harassment, beatings, and jail. In wartime, people make great personal sacrifices for the good of their group. As Winston Churchill said of the Battle of Britain, the actions of the Royal Air Force pilots were genuinely altruistic: A great many people owed a great deal to those who flew into battle knowing there was a high probability—70 percent for those on a standard tour of duty—that they would not return (Levinson, 1950).

To summarize, we can minimize destructive entrapment in social dilemmas by establishing rules that regulate self-serving behavior, by keeping groups small, by enabling people to communicate, by changing payoffs to make cooperation more rewarding, and by invoking compelling altruistic norms.

> "Never in the field of human conflict was so much owed by so many to so few."
> —Sir Winston Churchill, House of Commons, August 20, 1940

Competition

Hostilities often arise when groups compete for scarce jobs, housing, or resources. When interests clash, conflict erupts. Feeling threatened, such as by economic or terrorist threats, predicts Dutch citizens' increased right-wing authoritarianism (Onraet et al., 2014). And reminders that ethnic minorities are becoming a majority in California shifted White Americans' views (regardless of political party) in a more conservative direction (Craig & Richeson, 2014).

To experiment on competition's effect, we could randomly divide people into two groups, have the groups compete for a scarce resource, and note what happens. That is precisely what Muzafer Sherif (1966) and his colleagues did in a dramatic series of experiments with typical 11- and 12-year-old boys. The inspiration for those experiments dated back to Sherif's witnessing, as a teenager, Greek troops invading his Turkish province in 1919.

> They started killing people right and left. [That] made a great impression on me. There and then I became interested in understanding why these things were happening among human beings. . . . I wanted to learn whatever science or specialization was needed to understand this intergroup savagery. (quoted by Aron & Aron, 1989, p. 131)

After studying the social roots of savagery, Sherif introduced the seeming essentials into several three-week summer camping experiences. In one study, he divided 22 unacquainted Oklahoma City boys into two groups, took them to a Boy Scout camp in separate buses, and settled them in bunkhouses about a half-mile apart at Oklahoma's Robber's Cave State Park. For most of the first week, each group was unaware of the other's existence. By cooperating in various activities—preparing meals, camping out, fixing up a swimming hole, building a rope bridge—each group soon became close-knit. They gave themselves names: "Rattlers" and "Eagles." Typifying the good feeling, a sign appeared in one cabin: "Home Sweet Home."

Group identity thus established, the stage was set for the conflict. Near the first week's end, the Rattlers discovered the Eagles "on 'our' baseball field." When the camp staff then proposed a tournament of competitive activities between the two groups (baseball games,

Competition kindles conflict. In competition-fostering situations, groups act more competitively than do individuals.
Muzafer Sherif

Little-known fact: How did Sherif unobtrusively observe the boys without inhibiting their behavior? He became the camp maintenance man (Williams, 2002).

tugs-of-war, cabin inspections, treasure hunts, and so forth), both groups responded enthusiastically. This was win-lose competition. The spoils (medals, knives) would all go to the tournament victor.

The result? The camp degenerated into open warfare. It was like a scene from William Golding's novel *Lord of the Flies,* which depicts the social disintegration of boys marooned on an island. In Sherif's study, the conflict began with each side calling the other names during the competitive activities. Soon it escalated to dining hall "garbage wars," flag burnings, cabin ransackings, even fistfights. Asked to describe the other group, the boys said they were "sneaky," "smart alecks," "stinkers," but referring to their own group as "brave," "tough," "friendly." It was a tough experience, driving some of the boys to bedwetting, running away, homesickness, and later recollections of an unhappy experience (Perry, 2014).

The win-lose competition had produced intense conflict, negative images of the outgroup, and strong ingroup cohesiveness and pride. Group polarization no doubt exacerbated the conflict. In competition-fostering situations, groups behave more competitively than do individuals (Wildschut et al., 2003, 2007). Even after hearing tolerance-advocating messages, ingroup discussion often exacerbates dislike of the conflicting group (Paluck, 2010).

All this occurred without any cultural, physical, or economic differences between the two groups, and with boys who were their communities' "cream of the crop." Sherif noted that, had we visited the camp at that point, we would have concluded these "were wicked, disturbed, and vicious bunches of youngsters" (1966, p. 85). Actually, their evil behavior was triggered by an evil situation. Fortunately, as we will see, Sherif not only made strangers into enemies; he then also made the enemies into friends.

Perceived Injustice

"That's unfair!" "What a ripoff!" "We deserve better!" Such comments typify conflicts bred by perceived injustice.

But what is "justice"? According to some social-psychological theorists, people perceive justice as equity—the distribution of rewards in proportion to individuals' contributions (Walster et al., 1978). If you and "Jamie" have a relationship (employer-employee, teacher-student, husband-wife, colleague-colleague), it is equitable if

$$\frac{\text{My outcomes}}{\text{My inputs}} = \frac{\text{Your outcomes}}{\text{Your inputs}}$$

"Do unto others 20% better than you would expect them to do unto you, to correct for subjective error."
—Linus Pauling, 1962

If you contribute more and benefit less than Jamie does, you will feel exploited and irritated; Jamie may feel exploitative and guilty. Chances are, though, that you will be more sensitive to the inequity than Jamie will be (Greenberg, 1986; Messick & Sentis, 1979).

We may agree with the equity principle's definition of justice yet disagree on whether our relationship is equitable. If two people are colleagues, what will each consider a relevant input? The older person may favor basing pay on seniority, the other on current productivity. Given such a disagreement, whose definition is likely to prevail? Those with social power usually convince themselves and others that they deserve what they're getting (Mikula, 1984). This has been called a "golden" rule: Whoever has the gold makes the rules.

Critics argue that equity is not the only conceivable definition of justice. (Pause a moment: Can you imagine any other?) Edward Sampson (1975) argued that equity theorists wrongly assume that the economic principles that guide Western, capitalist nations are universal. Some noncapitalist cultures define justice not as equity but as *equality* or even *fulfillment of need:* "From each according to his abilities, to each according to his needs" (Karl Marx). Compared with individualistic Americans, people socialized under the influence of collectivist cultures, such as China and India, have defined justice more as equality or need fulfillment (Hui et al., 1991; Leung & Bond, 1984).

On what basis *should* rewards be distributed? Merit? Equality? Need? Some combination of those? Political philosopher John Rawls (1971) invited us to consider a future in which our own place on the economic ladder is unknown. Which standard of justice would we prefer?

Misperception

Recall that conflict is a *perceived* incompatibility of actions or goals. Many conflicts contain but a small core of truly incompatible goals; the bigger problem is the misperceptions of the other's motives and goals. The Eagles and the Rattlers did indeed have some genuinely incompatible aims. But their perceptions subjectively magnified their differences (Figure 3).

In earlier chapters we considered the seeds of such misperception:

- *Self-serving bias* leads individuals and groups to accept credit for their good deeds and shirk responsibility for bad deeds.
- A tendency to *self-justify* inclines people to deny the wrong of their evil acts. ("You call that hitting? I hardly touched him!")
- Thanks to the *fundamental attribution error,* each side sees the other's hostility as reflecting an evil disposition.
- One then filters the information and interprets it to fit one's *preconceptions.*
- Groups frequently *polarize* these self-serving, self-justifying, biasing tendencies.
- One symptom of *groupthink* is the tendency to perceive one's own group as moral and strong, and the opposition as evil and weak. Acts of terrorism that in most people's eyes are despicable brutality are seen by others as "holy war."
- Indeed, the mere fact of being in a group triggers an *ingroup bias.*
- Negative *stereotypes* of the outgroup, once formed, are often resistant to contradictory evidence.

So it should not surprise us, though it should sober us, to discover that people in conflict form distorted images of one another. Wherever in the world you live, was it not true that when your country was last at war it clothed itself in moral virtue? that it prepared for war by demonizing the enemy? that most of its people accepted their government's case for war and rallied 'round its flag? Show social psychologists Ervin Staub and Daniel Bar-Tal (2003) a group in intractable conflict and they will show you a group that

- sees its own goals as supremely important,
- takes pride in "us" and devalues "them,"

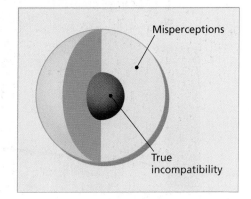

FIGURE :: 3

Many conflicts contain a core of truly incompatible goals surrounded by a larger exterior of misperceptions.

- believes itself victimized,
- elevates patriotism, solidarity, and loyalty to their group's needs, and
- celebrates self-sacrifice and suppresses criticism.

Although one side to a conflict may indeed be acting with greater moral virtue, the point is that enemy images are predictable. Even the types of misperception are intriguingly predictable.

MIRROR-IMAGE PERCEPTIONS

To a striking degree, the misperceptions of those in conflict are mutual. People in conflict attribute similar virtues to themselves and vices to the other. When the American psychologist Urie Bronfenbrenner (1961) visited the Soviet Union in 1960 and conversed with many ordinary citizens in Russian, he was astonished to hear them saying the same things about America that Americans were saying about Russia. The Russians said that the U.S. government was militarily aggressive; that it exploited and deluded the American people; that in diplomacy, it was not to be trusted. "Slowly and painfully, it forced itself upon one that the Russians' distorted picture of us was curiously similar to our view of them—a mirror image."

When two sides have clashing perceptions, at least one is misperceiving the other. And when such misperceptions exist, noted Bronfenbrenner, "It is a psychological phenomenon without parallel in the gravity of its consequences . . . for *it is characteristic of such images that they are self-confirming.*" If A expects B to be hostile, A may treat B in such a way that B fulfills A's expectations, thus beginning a vicious circle (Kennedy & Pronin, 2008). Morton Deutsch (1986) explained:

> You hear the false rumor that a friend is saying nasty things about you; you snub him; he then badmouths you, confirming your expectation. Similarly, if the policymakers of East and West believe that war is likely and either attempts to increase its military security vis-à-vis the other, the other's response will justify the initial move.

Negative **mirror-image perceptions** have been an obstacle to peace in many places:

- Both sides of the Arab-Israeli conflict insisted that "we" are motivated by our need to protect our security and our territory, whereas "they" want to obliterate us and gobble up our land. "We" are the indigenous people here, "they" are the invaders. "We" are the victims; "they" are the aggressors" (Bar-Tal, 2004, 2013; Heradstveit, 1979; Kelman, 2007). Given such intense mistrust, negotiation is difficult.
- Terrorism is in the eye of the beholder. In the Middle East, a public opinion survey found 98 percent of Palestinians agreeing that the killing of 29 Palestinians by

mirror-image perceptions
Reciprocal views of each other often held by parties in conflict; for example, each may view itself as moral and peace-loving and the other as evil and aggressive.

Self-confirming, mirror-image perceptions are a hallmark of intense conflict.
John Powell/TopFoto/The Image Works

an assault-rifle-bearing Israeli at a mosque constituted terrorism, and 82 percent *dis*agreed that the killing of 21 Israeli youths by a Palestinian suicide-bombing constituted terrorism (Kruglanski & Fishman, 2006). Israelis likewise have responded to violence with intensified perceptions of Palestinian evil intent (Bar-Tal, 2004, 2013).

- People, regardless of their intelligence, also display a "myside bias." In one experiment, American students were much more likely to favor banning an accident-prone German car from American roads than a comparably accident-prone American car from German roads (Stanovich et al., 2013). Even torture seems more morally justified when "we" rather than "they" do it (Tarrant et al., 2012).

Such conflicts, notes Philip Zimbardo (2004a), engage "a two-category world—of good people, like US, and of bad people, like THEM." "In fact," note Daniel Kahneman and Jonathan Renshon (2007), all the biases uncovered in 40 years of psychological research are conducive to war. They "incline national leaders to exaggerate the evil intentions of adversaries, to misjudge how adversaries perceive them, to be overly sanguine when hostilities start, and overly reluctant to make necessary concessions in negotiations."

Opposing sides in a conflict tend to exaggerate their differences. On issues related to abortion and politics, partisans perceive exaggerated differences from their adversaries—who actually agree with them more often than they supposed (Chambers et al., 2006). On immigration and affirmative action, proponents aren't as liberal and opponents aren't as conservative as their adversaries suppose (Sherman et al., 2003). Opposing sides also tend to have a "bias blind spot," notes Cynthia McPherson Frantz (2006). They see their own understandings as not biased by their liking or disliking for others; but those who disagree with them seem unfair and biased.

From exaggerated perceptions of the other's position arise culture wars. Ralph White (1996, 1998) reports that the Serbs started the war in Bosnia partly out of an exaggerated fear of the relatively secularized Bosnian Muslims, whose beliefs they wrongly associated with Middle Eastern Islamic fundamentalism and fanatical terrorism. Resolving conflict involves abandoning such exaggerated perceptions and coming to understand the other's mind. But that isn't easy, notes Robert Wright (2003): "Putting yourself in the shoes of people who do things you find abhorrent may be the hardest moral exercise there is."

Group conflicts are often fueled by an illusion that the enemy's top leaders are evil but their people, though controlled and manipulated, are pro-us. This *evil-leader–good people* perception characterized Americans' and Russians' views of each other during the Cold War. The United States entered the Vietnam War believing that in areas dominated by the Communist Vietcong "terrorists," many of the people were allies-in-waiting. As suppressed information later revealed, those beliefs were mere wishful thinking. In 2003 the United States began the Iraq War presuming the existence of "a vast underground network that would rise in support of coalition forces to assist security and law enforcement" (Phillips, 2003). Alas, the network didn't materialize, and the resulting postwar security vacuum enabled looting, sabotage, and persistent attacks on American forces.

"The American people are good, but the leaders are bad."

—Baghdad Grocer Adul Gesan after 1998 American Bombing of Iraq

SIMPLISTIC THINKING

When tension rises—as happens during an international crisis—rational thinking becomes more difficult (Janis, 1989). Views of the enemy become more simplistic and stereotyped, and seat-of-the-pants judgments become more likely. Even the mere expectation of conflict can serve to freeze thinking and impede creative problem solving (Carnevale & Probst, 1998). Social psychologist Philip Tetlock (1988) observed inflexible thinking when he analyzed the complexity of Russian and American rhetoric since 1945. During the Berlin blockade, the Korean War, and the Russian invasion of Afghanistan, political statements became simplified into stark, good-versus-bad terms.

Researchers have also analyzed political rhetoric preceding the outset of major wars, surprise military attacks, Middle Eastern conflicts, and revolutions (Conway et al., 2001). In nearly every case, attacking leaders displayed increasingly simplistic we-are-good/they-are-bad thinking immediately prior to their aggressive action. But shifts *away* from

research
CLOSE-UP
Misperception and War

Most research that we report in this book offers numerical data drawn from laboratory or survey observations of people's behavior, thoughts, and attitudes. But there are other ways to do research. Some social psychologists, especially in Europe, analyze natural human discourse; they study written texts or spoken conversation to glimpse how people interpret and construct the events of their lives (Edwards & Potter, 2005). Others have analyzed human behavior in historical contexts, as did Irving Janis (1972) in exploring groupthink in historical fiascoes and Philip Tetlock (2005) in exploring the judgment failures of supposed political experts.

In what was arguably social psychology's longest career, Ralph K. White, legendary for his late 1930s studies of democratic versus autocratic leadership (with pioneering social psychologists Kurt Lewin and Ronald Lippitt), published in 2004—at age 97—a capstone article summarizing his earlier analyses (1968, 1984, 1986) of how misperceptions feed war. In reviewing 10 wars from the past century, White reported that each was marked by at least one of three misperceptions: *underestimating* the strength of one's enemy, *rationalizing* one's own motives and behavior, and, especially, *demonizing* the enemy.

Underestimating one's adversary, he observed, emboldened Hitler to attack Russia, Japan to attack the United States, and the United States to enter the Korean and Vietnam wars. And rationalization of one's own actions and demonization of the adversary are the hallmark of war. In the early twenty-first century, as the United States and Iraq talked of war, each said the other was "evil." To George W. Bush, Saddam Hussein was a "murderous tyrant" and a "madman" who threatened the civilized world with weapons of mass destruction. To Iraq's government, the Bush government was a "gang of evil" (Preston, 2002).

The truth need not lie midway between such clashing perceptions. Yet "valid perception is an antidote to hate," concluded White as he reflected on his lifetime as a peace psychologist. Empathy—accurately perceiving the other's thoughts and feelings—is "one of the most important factors for preventing war. . . . Empathy can help two or more nations avoid the dangers of misperception that lead to the wars most would prefer not to fight."

simplistic rhetoric typically preceded new U.S.-Russian agreements, reported Tetlock. His optimism was confirmed when President Reagan in 1988 traveled to Moscow to sign the American-Russian intermediate-range nuclear force (INF) treaty, and then Gorbachev visited New York and told the United Nations that he would remove 500,000 Soviet troops from Eastern Europe:

> I would like to believe that our hopes will be matched by our joint effort to put an end to an era of wars, confrontation and regional conflicts, to aggressions against nature, to the terror of hunger and poverty as well as to political terrorism. This is our common goal and we can only reach it together.

SHIFTING PERCEPTIONS

If misperceptions accompany conflict, they should appear and disappear as conflicts wax and wane. And they do, with startling regularity. The same processes that create the enemy's image can reverse that image when the enemy becomes an ally. Thus, the "bloodthirsty, cruel, treacherous, buck-toothed little Japs" of World War II soon became—in North American minds (Gallup, 1972) and in the media—our "intelligent, hard-working, self-disciplined, resourceful allies."

The Germans, who after two world wars were hated, then admired, and then again hated, were once again admired—apparently no longer plagued by what earlier was presumed to be cruelty in their national character. So long as Iraq was attacking unpopular Iran, even while using chemical weapons to massacre its own Kurds, many nations supported it. Our enemy's enemy is our friend. When Iraq ended its war with Iran and invaded oil-rich Kuwait, Iraq's behavior suddenly became "barbaric." Images of our enemies change with amazing ease.

The extent of misperceptions during conflict provides a chilling reminder that people need not be insane or abnormally malicious to form distorted images of their antagonists. When we experience conflict with another nation, another group, or simply a roommate or a parent, we readily misperceive our own motives as good and the other's as evil. And just as readily, our antagonists form a mirror-image perception of us.

So, with antagonists trapped in a social dilemma, competing for scarce resources, or perceiving injustice, the conflict continues until something enables both parties to peel away their misperceptions and work at reconciling their actual differences. Good advice, then, is this: When in conflict, do not assume that the other fails to share your values and morality. Rather, compare perceptions, assuming that the other perceives the situation differently.

SUMMING UP: What Creates Conflict?

- Whenever two or more people, groups, or nations interact, their perceived needs and goals may conflict. Many social dilemmas arise as people pursue individual self-interest to their collective detriment. Two laboratory games, the Prisoner's Dilemma and the *Tragedy of the Commons,* exemplify such dilemmas. In real life we can avoid such traps by establishing rules that regulate self-serving behavior; by keeping social groups small so people feel responsibility for one another; by enabling communication, thus reducing mistrust; by changing payoffs to make cooperation more rewarding; and by invoking altruistic norms.

- When people compete for scarce resources, human relations often sink into prejudice and hostility. In his famous experiments, Muzafer Sherif found that win-lose competition quickly made strangers into enemies, triggering outright warfare even among normally upstanding boys.

- *Conflicts* also arise when people perceive injustice. According to equity theory, people define justice as the distribution of rewards in proportion to one's contributions. Conflicts occur when people disagree on the extent of their contributions and thus on the equity of their outcomes.

- Conflicts frequently contain a small core of truly incompatible goals, surrounded by a thick layer of misperceptions of the adversary's motives and goals. Often, conflicting parties have *mirror-image perceptions.* When both sides believe "We are peace-loving—they are hostile," each may treat the other in ways that provoke confirmation of its expectations. International conflicts are sometimes also fed by an evil leader–good people illusion.

HOW CAN PEACE BE ACHIEVED?

Explain the processes that enable the achievement of peace.

We have seen how conflicts are ignited by social traps, competition, perceived injustices, and misperceptions. Although the picture is grim, it is not hopeless. Sometimes closed fists become open arms as hostilities evolve into friendship. Social psychologists have focused on four peacemaking strategies, which we can remember as the four Cs of peacemaking: contact, cooperation, communication, and conciliation.

"We know more about war than we do about peace—more about killing than we know about living."

—General Omar Bradley, 1893–1981, Former U.S. Army Chief of Staff

Contact

Might putting two conflicting individuals or groups into close contact enable them to know and like each other? Perhaps not: We have seen how negative expectations can bias judgments and create self-fulfilling prophecies. When tensions run high, contact may fuel a fight.

But we have also seen that proximity—and the accompanying interaction, anticipation of interaction, and mere exposure—boosts liking. And we noted how blatant racial prejudice declined following desegregation, showing that *attitudes follow behavior.* If this social-psychological principle now seems obvious, remember: That's how things usually seem after you know them. To the U.S. Supreme Court in 1896, the idea that desegregated behavior might reduce prejudicial attitudes was anything but obvious. What seemed obvious at the time was "that legislation is powerless to eradicate racial instincts" *(Plessy v. Ferguson).*

DOES CONTACT PREDICT ATTITUDES?

In general, contact predicts tolerance. In a painstaking analysis, researchers assembled data from 516 studies of 250,555 people in 38 nations (Tropp & Pettigrew, 2005a; Pettigrew & Tropp, 2008, 2011). In 94 percent of studies, *increased contact predicted decreased prejudice.* This is especially so for majority group attitudes toward minorities (Durrheim et al., 2011; Gibson & Claassen, 2010).

Newer studies confirm the correlation between contact and positive attitudes:

- The more interracial contact South African Blacks and Whites have, the less prejudice they feel, and the more sympathetic their policy attitudes are to those of the other group (Dixon et al., 2007, 2010; Tredoux & Finchilescu, 2010).
- The more friendly contact Blacks and Whites have with one another, the better their attitudes toward one another—and toward other outgroups, such as Hispanics (Tausch et al., 2010). Ditto for South African Coloured and White teens (Swart et al., 2011).
- The more contact straight people have with gays and lesbians, the more accepting they become (Collier et al., 2012; Smith et al., 2009). Who you know matters.
- The more contact Dutch adolescents have with Muslims, the more accepting of Muslims they are (González et al., 2008).
- Even vicarious indirect contact, via story reading or imagination, or through a friend's having an outgroup friend, tends to reduce prejudice (Bilewicz & Kogan, 2014; Crisp et al., 2011; Turner et al., 2007a, b, 2008, 2010). Those who read the Harry Potter books—with their themes of supportive contacts with stigmatized groups—have better attitudes toward immigrants, homosexuals, and refugees (Vezzali et al., 2014). This indirect contact effect, also called "the extended-contact effect," can spread more positive attitudes through a peer group (Christ et al., 2010).
- For White students, having a Black roommate improves racial attitudes and leads to greater comfort with those of another race (Gaither & Sommers, 2013). Other potent connections with a single outgroup member, such an interracial adoption or having a gay child, similarly links people with the outgroup and reduces implicit prejudice (Gulker & Monteith, 2013). Even an outgroup person's physical touch—a cue to warmth and friendship—lessens automatic prejudice (Seger et al., 2014).

In the United States, segregation and expressed prejudice have diminished together since the 1960s. But was interracial contact the *cause* of these improved attitudes? Were those who actually experienced desegregation affected by it?

DOES DESEGREGATION IMPROVE RACIAL ATTITUDES?

School desegregation produced measurable benefits, such as leading more Blacks to attend and succeed in college (Stephan, 1988). Does desegregation of schools, neighborhoods, and workplaces also produce favorable *social* results? The evidence is mixed.

On the one hand, many studies conducted during and shortly after desegregation found Whites' attitudes toward Blacks improving markedly. Whether the people were department store clerks and customers, merchant marines, government workers, police officers, neighbors, or students, racial contact led to diminished prejudice (Amir, 1969; Pettigrew, 1969). For example, near the end of World War II, the U.S. Army partially desegregated some of its rifle companies (Stouffer et al., 1949). When asked their opinions of such desegregation, 11 percent of the White soldiers in segregated companies approved. Of those in desegregated companies, 60 percent approved. They exhibited "system justification"—the human tendency to approve the way things are.

When Morton Deutsch and Mary Collins (1951) took advantage of a made-to-order natural experiment, they observed similar results. In accord with state law, New York City desegregated its public housing units; it assigned families to apartments without regard to race. In a similar development across the river in Newark, New Jersey, Blacks and Whites were assigned to separate buildings. When surveyed, White women in the desegregated development were far more likely to favor interracial housing and to say their attitudes toward Blacks had improved. Exaggerated stereotypes had wilted in the face of reality. As one woman put it, "I've really come to like it. I see they're just as human as we are."

Such findings influenced the Supreme Court's 1954 decision to desegregate schools and helped fuel the 1960s civil rights movement (Pettigrew, 1986, 2004). Yet initial studies of the effects of school desegregation were less encouraging. After reviewing all the available studies, Walter Stephan (1986) concluded that racial attitudes had been little affected by desegregation. For Blacks, the noticeable effect of desegregated schooling was less on attitudes than on their increased likelihood of attending integrated (or predominantly White) colleges, living in integrated neighborhoods, and working in integrated settings.

Thus, we can see that sometimes desegregation improves racial attitudes, and sometimes—especially when there is anxiety or perceived threat (Pettigrew, 2004)—it doesn't. Such disagreements excite the scientist's detective spirit. What explains the difference? So far, we've been lumping all kinds of desegregation together. Actual desegregation occurs in many ways and under vastly different conditions.

WHEN DOES DESEGREGATION IMPROVE RACIAL ATTITUDES?

Given that "mere exposure" can produce liking (recall the "Attraction" chapter), might exposure to other-race faces produce increased liking for other-race strangers? Indeed yes, Leslie Zebrowitz and her colleagues (2008) discovered, when exposing White participants to Asian and Black faces. Might the frequency of interracial contact also be a factor? Indeed it seems to be. Researchers have gone into dozens of desegregated schools and observed with whom children of a given race eat, talk, and loiter. Race influences contact. Whites have disproportionately associated with Whites, Blacks with Blacks (Schofield, 1982, 1986).

The same self-imposed segregation was evident in a South African desegregated beach, as John Dixon and Kevin Durrheim (2003) discovered when they recorded the location of Black, White, and Indian beachgoers one midsummer (December 30th) afternoon (Figure 4). Desegregated neighborhoods, cafeterias, and restaurants, too, may fail to produce integrated interactions (Clack et al., 2005; Dixon et al., 2005a,b). "Why are all the Black kids sitting together?" people may wonder (a question that could as easily be asked of the White kids). One naturalistic study observed 119 class sessions of 26 University of Cape Town tutorial groups, which averaged 6 Black and 10 White students per group (Alexander & Tredoux, 2010). On average, the researchers calculated, 71 percent of Black students would have needed to change seats to achieve a fully integrated seating pattern.

Even within the same race, likes tend to self-segregate. That's what University of Ulster (Northern Ireland) researchers discerned when noting the lecture hall seating patterns of Catholic and Protestant students (Orr et al., 2012).

In one study that tracked the attitudes of more than 1,600 European students, contact reduced prejudice. But prejudice also minimized contact (Binder et al., 2009). Prejudice, however, is not the only obstacle to contact. Anxiety also helps explain why participants in interracial relationships (when students are paired as roommates or as partners in an experiment) may engage in less intimate self-disclosure than those in same-race relationships (Johnson et al., 2009; Trail et al., 2009).

Efforts to facilitate contact sometimes help, but sometimes fall flat. "We had one day when some of the Protestant schools came over," explained one Catholic youngster after a Northern Ireland school exchange (Cairns & Hewstone, 2002). "It was supposed to be

FIGURE :: 4

Desegregation Needn't Mean Contact

After this Scottburgh, South Africa, beach became "open" and desegregated in the new South Africa, Blacks (represented by red dots), Whites (blue dots), and Indians (yellow dots) tended to cluster with their own race.

Source: From Dixon & Durrheim, 2003, Lancaster University

like . . . mixing, but there was very little mixing. It wasn't because we didn't want to; it was just really awkward." The lack of mixing stems partly from "pluralistic ignorance." Many Whites and Blacks say they would like more contact but misperceive that the other does not reciprocate their feelings. (See "Research Close-Up: Relationships That Might Have Been," and "The Inside Story: Nicole Shelton and Jennifer Richeson on Cross-Racial Friendships.")

FRIENDSHIP. The encouraging older studies of store clerks, soldiers, and housing project neighbors involved considerable interracial contact, more than enough to reduce the anxiety that marks initial intergroup contact. Other studies show similar benefits when they involve prolonged, personal contact—between Black and White prison inmates, between Black and White girls in an interracial summer camp, between Black and White university roommates, and between Black, Coloured, and White South Africans (Al Ramiah & Hewstone, 2013; Beelmann & Heinemann, 2014). The same has been true of intergroup contact programs in Northern Ireland, Cyprus, and Bosnia (Hewstone et al., 2014). One program that brought Israeli and Palestinian youth to a 3-week camp in the United States produced significant and sustained improvement in intergroup attitudes (Schroeder & Risen, 2014).

So how does intergroup contact reduce prejudice? It does so, report contact researchers Ananthi Al Ramiah and Miles Hewstone (2013) by

- reducing anxiety (more contact brings greater comfort),
- increasing empathy (contact helps people put themselves in the others' shoes),
- enhancing knowledge (enabling people to discover their similarities), and
- decreasing perceived threats (alleviating overblown fears and increasing trust).

Among American students who have studied in Germany or in Britain, the more their contact with host country people, the more positive their attitudes (Stangor et al., 1996). Exchange students' hosts also are changed by the experience; they become more likely to see things from the visitor's cultural perspective (Vollhardt, 2010).

research
CLOSE-UP

Perhaps you can recall a time when you really would have liked to reach out to someone. Maybe it was someone to whom you felt attracted. But doubting that your feelings were reciprocated, you didn't risk rebuff. Or maybe it was someone of another race whom you wanted to welcome to the open seat at your dining hall or library table. But you worried that the person might be wary of sitting with you. It's likely that on some such occasions the other person shared your wish to connect but assumed that your distance signified indifference or even prejudice. Alas, thanks to "pluralistic ignorance"—shared false impressions of another's feelings—you passed like ships in the night.

Studies by University of Manitoba psychologist Jacquie Vorauer (2001, 2005; Vorauer & Sakamoto, 2006) illuminate this phenomenon. In new relationships, people often overestimate the transparency of their feelings, Vorauer reports. Presuming that their feelings are leaking out, they experience the "illusion of transparency." Thus, they may assume that their body language conveys their romantic interest, when actually the intended recipient never gets the message. If the other person shares the positive feelings, and is similarly overestimating his or her own transparency, then the possible relationship is quenched.

The same phenomenon, Vorauer reports, often occurs with low-prejudice people who would love more friendships with those outside their racial or social group. If Whites presume that Blacks think them prejudiced, and if Blacks presume that Whites stereotype them, both will feel anxious about making the first move. Such anxiety is "a central factor" in South Africa's "continuing informal segregation," reports Gillian Finchilescu (2005). Seeking to replicate and extend Vorauer's work, Nicole Shelton and Jennifer Richeson (2005; Richeson & Shelton, 2012) undertook a coordinated series of surveys and behavioral tests.

In their first study, University of Massachusetts White students viewed themselves as having more-than-average interest in cross-racial contacts and friendships, and they perceived White students in general as more eager for such than were Black students. Black students had mirror-image views—seeing themselves as more eager for such than were White students. "I want to have friendships across racial lines," thought the typical student. "But those in the other racial group don't share my desire."

Would this pluralistic ignorance generalize to a specific setting? To find out, Shelton and Richeson's second study asked White Princeton students to imagine how they would react upon entering their dining hall and noticing several Black (or White) "students who live near you

sitting together." How interested would you be in joining them? And how likely is it that one of them would beckon you to join them? Again, Whites believed that they, more than those of the other race, would be interested in the contact.

And how do people explain failures to make interracial contact? In their third study, Shelton and Richeson invited Princeton White and Black students to contemplate a dining hall situation in which they notice a table with familiar-looking students of the other race, but neither they nor the seated students reach out to the other. The study participants, regardless of race, attributed their own inaction in such a situation primarily to fear of rejection, and more often attributed the seated students' inaction to lack of interest. In a fourth study at Dartmouth University, Shelton and Richeson replicated this study with similar results.

Would this pluralistic ignorance phenomenon extend to other real-life settings, and to contact with a single other person? In Study 5, Shelton and Richeson invited Princeton students, both Black and White, to a study of "friendship formation." After participants had filled out some background information, the experimenter took their picture, attached it to background information, ostensibly took it to the room of a supposed fellow participant, and then returned with the other person's sheet and photo—showing a person of the same sex but the other race. The participants were then asked, "To what extent are you concerned about being accepted by the other participant?" and "How likely is it that the other person won't want you as a friend?" Regardless of their race, the participants guessed that they, more than the other-race fellow participant, were interested in friendship but worried about rejection.

Do these social misperceptions constrain actual interracial contact? In a sixth study, Shelton and Richeson confirmed that White Princeton students who were most prone to pluralistic ignorance—to presuming that they feared interracial rejection more than did Black students—were also the most likely to experience diminishing cross-racial contacts in the ensuing seven weeks.

Vorauer, Shelton, and Richeson are not contending that misperceptions alone impede romances and cross-racial friendships. But misperceptions do restrain people from risking an overture. Understanding this phenomenon—recognizing that others' coolness may actually reflect motives and feelings similar to our own—may help us reach out to others, and sometimes to transform potential friendships into real ones.

THE inside STORY

Nicole Shelton and Jennifer Richeson on Cross-Racial Friendships

We noticed that both White and ethnic minority students in our classes often indicated that they genuinely wanted to interact with people outside of their ethnic group but were afraid that they would not be accepted. However, they assumed that members of other groups simply did not want to connect. This sounded very much like Dale Miller's work on pluralistic ignorance. Over the course of a few weeks, we designed a series of studies to explore pluralistic ignorance during interracial interactions.

Since the publication of our article, we have had researchers tell us that we should use our work in new student orientation sessions in order to reduce students' fears about reaching across racial lines. We are delighted that when we present this work in our courses, students of all racial backgrounds tell us that it indeed has opened their eyes about making the first move to develop interracial friendships.

Nicole Shelton
Princeton University
Courtesy of Nicole Shelton

Jennifer Richeson
Northwestern University
Courtesy of Jennifer Richeson

"Group salience" (visibility) also helps bridge divides between people. If you forever think of that friend solely as an individual, your affective ties may not generalize to other members of the friend's group (Miller, 2002). Ideally, then, we should form trusting friendships across group lines but also recognize that the friend represents those in another group (Brown et al., 2007).

We are especially likely to befriend dissimilar people when their outgroup identity is initially minimized. If our liking for our new friends is then to generalize to others, their group identity must at some point become salient. So, to reduce prejudice and conflict, we had best initially minimize group diversity, then acknowledge it, then transcend it.

Surveys of nearly 4,000 Europeans reveal that friendship is a key to successful contact: If you have a minority group friend, you become much more likely to express sympathy and support for the friend's group, and even somewhat more support for immigration by that group. It's true of West Germans' attitudes toward Turks, French people's attitudes toward Asians and North Africans, Netherlanders' attitudes toward Surinamers and Turks, British attitudes toward West Indians and Asians, and Northern Ireland Protestants' and Catholics' attitudes toward each other (Brown et al., 1999; Hamberger & Hewstone, 1997; Paolini et al., 2004; Pettigrew, 1997).

EQUAL-STATUS CONTACT. The social psychologists who advocated desegregation never claimed that all contact would improve attitudes. Much as positive contact boosts liking, negative contact increases *disliking* (Barlow et al., 2012; Stark et al., 2013). Positive contact is more commonplace, but negative experiences have greater effect (Graf et al., 2014; Paolini et al., 2014).

Social psychologists had expected poor results when contacts were competitive, unsupported by authorities, and unequal (Pettigrew, 1988; Stephan, 1987). Before 1954 many prejudiced Whites had frequent contacts with Blacks—as shoeshine men and domestic workers. As we have seen, such unequal contacts breed attitudes that merely justify the continuation of inequality. So it's important that the contact be **equal-status contact,** like that between the store clerks, the soldiers, the neighbors, the prisoners, and the summer campers.

equal-status contact
Contact on an equal basis. Just as a relationship between people of unequal status breeds attitudes consistent with their relationship, so do relationships between those of equal status. Thus, to reduce prejudice, interracial contact should ideally be between persons equal in status.

Cooperation

Although equal-status contact can help, it is sometimes not enough. It didn't help when Muzafer Sherif stopped the Eagles versus Rattlers competition and brought the groups together for noncompetitive activities, such as watching movies, shooting off fireworks, and eating. By that time, their hostility was so strong that mere contact only provided opportunities for taunts and attacks. When an Eagle was bumped by a Rattler, his fellow Eagles urged him to "brush off the dirt." Desegregating the two groups hardly promoted their social integration.

Given entrenched hostility, what can a peacemaker do? Think back to the successful and the unsuccessful desegregation efforts. The army's racial mixing of rifle companies didn't just bring Blacks and Whites into equal-status contact, it made them interdependent. Together, they were fighting a common enemy, striving toward a shared goal.

Does that suggest a second factor that predicts whether the effect of desegregation will be favorable? Does competitive contact divide and *cooperative* contact unite? Consider what happens to people who together face a common predicament. In conflicts at all levels, from couples to rival teams to nations, *shared threats* and *common goals* breed unity.

COMMON EXTERNAL THREATS BUILD COHESIVENESS

Together with others, have you ever been caught in a blizzard, punished by a teacher, or persecuted and ridiculed because of your social, racial, or religious identity? If so, you may recall feeling close to those with whom you shared the predicament. Perhaps previous social barriers fell as you helped one another dig out of the snow or struggled to cope with your common enemy. Survivors of shared pain or more extreme crises, such as a bombing, also often report a spirit of cooperation and solidarity rather than all-for-themselves panic (Bastian et al., 2014; Drury et al., 2009).

Such friendliness is common among those who experience a shared threat. John Lanzetta (1955) observed this when he put four-man groups of naval ROTC cadets to work on problem-solving tasks and then began informing them over a loudspeaker that their answers were wrong, their productivity inexcusably low, their thinking stupid. Other groups did not receive this harassment. Lanzetta observed that the group members under duress became friendlier to one another, more cooperative, less argumentative, less competitive. They were in it together. And the result was a cohesive spirit. Recent experiments confirm a silver lining of mistreatment by a boss: those mistreated become more cohesive (Stoverink et al., 2014). Misery loves company.

Having a common enemy unified the groups of competing boys in Sherif's camping experiments—and in many subsequent experiments (Dion, 1979). Just being reminded of an outgroup (say, a rival school) heightens people's responsiveness to their own group (Wilder & Shapiro, 1984). To perceive discrimination against one's racial or religious group is to feel more bonded and identified with such (Craig & Richeson, 2012; Martinovic & Verkuyten, 2012; Ramos et al., 2012). When keenly conscious of who "they" are, we also know who "we" are.

When facing a well-defined external threat during wartime, we-feeling soars. The membership of civic organizations mushrooms (Putnam, 2000). Shared threats also produce a political "rally 'round the flag" effect (Lambert et al., 2011), Children and youth who survive war exposure later display a more cooperative spirit toward their in-group (Bauer et al., 2014). After September 11, 2001, "old racial antagonisms . . . dissolved," reported the *New York Times* (Sengupta, 2001). "I just thought of myself as Black," said 18-year-old Louis Johnson, reflecting on life before 9/11. "But now I feel like I'm an American, more than ever." In New York City, even divorce rates dropped in the aftermath of 9/11 (Hansel et al., 2011). One sampling of conversation on 9/11, and another of New York Mayor Giuliani's press conferences before and after 9/11, found a doubled rate of the word "we" (Liehr et al., 2004; Pennebaker & Lay, 2002).

"I couldn't help but say to [Mr. Gorbachev], just think how easy his task and mine might be in these meetings that we held if suddenly there was a threat to this world from some other species from another planet. [We'd] find out once and for all that we really are all human beings here on this earth together."

—Ronald Reagan,
December 4, 1985, Speech

Shared predicaments trigger cooperation, as these Walmart workers on strike in Germany demonstrate.
AP Images/FRANK AUGSTEIN

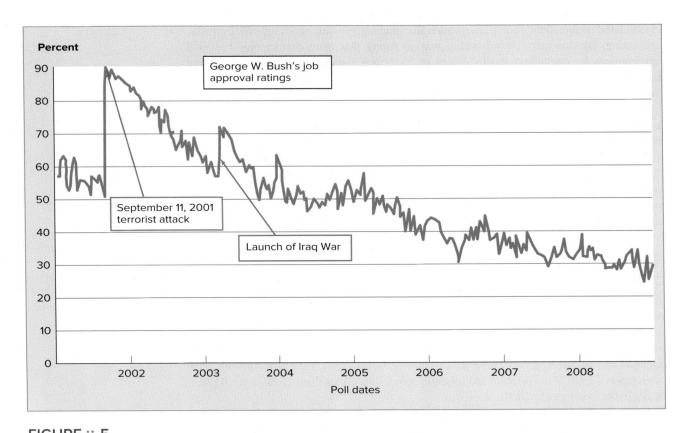

FIGURE :: 5

External Threats Breed Internal Unity

As the ups and downs of President George Bush's approval ratings illustrate, national conflicts mold public attitudes (Gallup, 2006).

George W. Bush's job performance ratings reflected this threat-bred spirit of unity. In the public eye, the mediocre-seeming president of 9/10 had become the exalted president of 9/12—"our leader" in the fight against "those who hate us." Thereafter, his ratings gradually declined but then jumped again as the war in Iraq began (Figure 5).

Even just imagining or fearing the extinction of one's group often serves to strengthen ingroup solidarity (Wohl et al., 2010). Likewise, just imagining the shared climate change threat reduced international antagonisms (Pyszczynski et al., 2012). Leaders may therefore *create* a threatening external enemy as a technique for building group cohesiveness. George Orwell's novel *1984* illustrates the tactic: The leader of the protagonist nation uses border conflicts with the other two major powers to lessen internal strife. From time to time the enemy shifts, but there is always an enemy. Indeed, the nation seems to *need* an enemy. For the world, for a nation, for a group, having a common enemy is powerfully unifying. Thus, we can expect that Protestant-Catholic religious differences that feel great in Northern Ireland or South America will feel more negligible to those living under Islamic regimes. Likewise, Sunni and Shia Islamic differences that feel great in Iraq will not seem so great to Muslims in countries where both must cope with anti-Muslim attitudes.

Might the world likewise find unity if facing a common enemy? In 1987, U.S. President Ronald Reagan observed, "In our obsession with antagonisms of the moment, we often forget how much unites all the members of humanity. Perhaps we need some outside, universal threat to recognize this common bond." Two decades later, Al Gore (2007) agreed, suggesting that, with the specter of climate change, "We—all of us—now face a universal threat. Though it is not from outside this world, it is nevertheless cosmic in scale." (To consider these social dynamics in sports rivalries, see "Focus on: Why Do We Care Who Wins?")

focus
ON   Why Do We Care Who Wins?

Why, for sports fans everywhere, does it matter who wins? Why does it matter to Bostonians whether two dozen multimillionaire temporary Red Sox employees, most born in other states or countries, win the World Series? During the annual NCAA basketball "March Madness," why do perfectly normal adults become insanely supportive of their team, and depressed when it loses? And why for that ultimate sporting event, World Cup Football, do soccer fans worldwide dream of their country victorious?

The roots of rivalry run deep. There's something primal at work when the crowd erupts as the two rivals take the field or the floor. There's something tribal at work during the ensuing passion, all in response to the flights of a mere leather sphere. Our ancestors, living in a world where neighboring tribes occasionally raided and pillaged one another's camps, knew that there was safety in solidarity. (Those who didn't band together left fewer descendants.) Whether hunting, defending, or attacking, more hands were better than two. Dividing the world into "us" and "them" entails significant costs, such as racism and war, but also provides the benefits of communal solidarity. To identify us and them, our ancestors—not so far removed from today's rabid fans—dressed or painted themselves in group-specific costumes and colors. Sports and warfare, notes evolutionary psychologist Benjamin Winegard (2010), are mostly done by males associated with geographical areas and wearing group-identifying uniforms. Both use war-relevant skills (running, tackling, throwing). And both offer rewards to the victors.

As social animals, we live in groups, cheer on our groups, kill for our groups, die for our groups. We also define ourselves by our groups. Our self-concept—our sense of who we are—consists not only of our personal attributes and attitudes but also of our social identity. Our social identities—our knowing who "we" are—strengthens self-concept and pride, especially when perceiving that "we" are superior. Lacking a positive individual identity, many youths find pride, power, and identity in gangs. Many patriots define themselves by their national identities.

The group definition of who we *are* also implies who we are *not*. Social-psychological experiments reveal that being formed into groups—even arbitrary groups—promotes ingroup bias. Cluster people into groups defined by nothing more than their birth date or even the last digit of their driver's license and they'll feel a certain kinship with their number mates and will show them favoritism. So strong is our group consciousness that "we" seem better than "they" even when "we" and "they" are defined randomly.

Group solidarity soars when people face a common enemy. As Muzafer Sherif's Robber's Camp experiment vividly demonstrated, competition creates enemies. Fueled by competition and unleashed by the anonymity of a crowd, passions can culminate in sport's worst moments—fans taunting opponents, screaming at umpires, even pelting referees with beer bottles.

Group identification soars further with success. Fans find self-respect by their personal achievements but also, in at least small measure, by their association with the victorious athletes when their team wins. Queried after a big football victory, university students commonly report that "*we* won" (Cialdini et al., 1976). They bask in reflected glory. Asked the outcome after a defeat, students more often distance themselves from the team by saying, "*They* lost."

Ironically, we often reserve our most intense passions for rivals most similar to us. Freud long ago recognized that animosities formed around small differences: "Of two neighbouring towns, each is the other's most jealous rival; every little canton looks down upon the others with contempt. Closely related races keep one another at arm's length; the South German cannot endure the North German, the Englishman casts every kind of aspersion upon the Scot, the Spaniard despises the Portuguese."

To today's non-Muslims, antagonist Sunni and Shia Muslims seem pretty similar (both revere the Qur'an, follow Muhammad, and pray to Allah). Likewise, to non-Christians, Northern Ireland's formerly combative Protestants and Catholics (both followers of the same Prince of

Group identity feeds, and is fed by, competition.
AP Images/MARTIN MEISSNER

(continued)

Peace) seemed religiously and ethnically so similar. But no matter our similarities to those near us, our attention focuses on our differences.

As an occasional resident of Scotland, I've witnessed many examples of the *Xenophobe's Guide to the Scots* observation—that Scots divide non-Scots "into two main groups: (1) The English; (2) The Rest." As rabid Chicago Cubs fans are happy if either the Cubs win or the White Sox lose, so ardent New Zealand soccer fans root for New Zealand and whoever is playing Australia (Halberstadt et al., 2006). Rabid fans of Scottish soccer likewise rejoice in either a Scotland victory or an England defeat. "Phew! They Lost," rejoiced one Scottish tabloid front-page headline

after England's 1996 Euro Cup defeat—by Germany, no less. To a sports fan, few things are so sweet as an archrival's misfortune. Both a rival's failure and a favored team's success activate pleasure-associated brain areas (Cikara et al., 2011).

Numerical minorities, such as the Scots in Britain, are especially conscious of their social identities. The 5 million Scots are more conscious of their national identity vis-à-vis the neighboring 51 million English than vice versa. Likewise, the 4 million New Zealanders are more conscious of their identity vis-à-vis the 23 million Australians, and they are more likely to root for Australia's sports opponents (Halberstadt et al., 2006).

SUPERORDINATE GOALS FOSTER COOPERATION

superordinate goal

A shared goal that necessitates cooperative effort; a goal that overrides people's differences from one another.

Closely related to the unifying power of an external threat is the unifying power of **superordinate goals,** goals that unite all in a group and require cooperative effort. To promote harmony among his warring campers, Sherif introduced such goals. He created a problem with the camp water supply, necessitating both groups' cooperation to restore the water. Given an opportunity to rent a movie, one expensive enough to require the joint resources of the two groups, they again cooperated. When a truck "broke down" on a camp excursion, a staff member casually left the tug-of-war rope nearby, prompting one boy to suggest that they all pull the truck to get it started. When it started, a backslapping celebration ensued over their victorious "tug-of-war against the truck."

After working together to achieve such superordinate goals, the boys ate together and enjoyed themselves around a campfire. Friendships sprouted across group lines. Hostilities plummeted (Figure 6). On the last day, the boys decided to travel home together on one bus. During the trip they no longer sat by groups. As the bus approached Oklahoma City and home, they, as one, spontaneously sang "Oklahoma" and then bade their friends farewell. With isolation and competition, Sherif made strangers into bitter enemies. With superordinate goals, he made enemies into friends.

Are Sherif's experiments mere child's play? Or can pulling together to achieve superordinate goals be similarly beneficial with conflicting adults? Robert Blake and

FIGURE :: 6

After competition, the Eagles and the Rattlers rated each other unfavorably. After they worked cooperatively to achieve superordinate goals, hostility dropped sharply.
Source: Data from Sherif, 1966, p. 84.

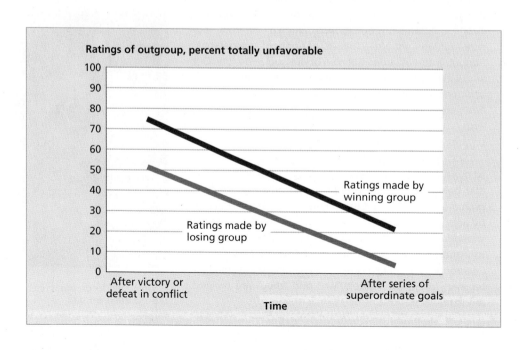

Ratings of outgroup, percent totally unfavorable

Ratings made by winning group

Ratings made by losing group

After victory or defeat in conflict

After series of superordinate goals

Time

Jane Mouton (1979) wondered. So in a series of two-week experiments involving more than 1,000 executives in 150 different groups, they re-created the essential features of the situation experienced by the Rattlers and the Eagles. Each group first engaged in activities by itself, then competed with another group, and then cooperated with the other group in working toward jointly chosen superordinate goals. Their results provided "unequivocal evidence that adult reactions parallel those of Sherif's younger subjects."

Extending those findings, John Dovidio, Samuel Gaertner, and their collaborators (2005, 2009) report that working cooperatively has especially favorable effects under conditions that lead people to define a new, inclusive group that dissolves their former subgroups. Old feelings of bias against another group diminish when members of the two groups sit alternately around a table (rather than on opposite sides), give their new group a single name, and then work together under conditions that foster a good mood. "Us" and "them" become "we." To combat Germany, Italy, and Japan during World War II, the United States and the former USSR, along with other nations, formed one united group named the Allies. So long as the superordinate goal of defeating a common enemy lasted, so did supportive U.S. attitudes toward the Russians. From Amazon tribes to European countries, peace arises when groups become interconnected and interdependent and develop an overarching social identity (Fry et al., 2012).

Promoting "common ingroup identity." The banning of gang colors and the common European practice of school uniforms—an increasing trend in the United States, as well—aim to change "us" and "them" to "we."
Ian Shaw/Getty Images

Economic interdependence through international trade also motivates peace. "Where goods cross frontiers, armies won't," noted Michael Shermer (2006). With so much of China's economy now interwoven with Western economies, their economic interdependence diminishes the likelihood of war between China and the West.

The cooperative efforts by the Rattlers and the Eagles ended in success. Would the same harmony have emerged if the water had remained off, the movie unaffordable, the truck still stalled? Likely not. Experiments with university students confirmed that *successful* cooperation between two groups boosts their attraction for each other. If previously conflicting groups *fail* in a cooperative effort, however, and if conditions allow them to attribute their failure to each other, the conflict may worsen (Worchel et al., 1977, 1978, 1980). Sherif's groups were already feeling hostile to each other. Thus, failure to raise sufficient funds for the movie might have been attributed to one group's "stinginess" and "selfishness." That would have exacerbated rather than alleviated their conflict. Unity is fed by striving for and reaching superordinate goals.

COOPERATIVE LEARNING IMPROVES RACIAL ATTITUDES

So far we have noted the modest social benefits when desegregation is unaccompanied by the emotional bonds of friendship and by equal-status relationships. And we have noted the dramatic social benefits of successful, cooperative contacts between members of rival groups. Several research teams therefore wondered: Without compromising academic achievement, could we promote interracial friendships by replacing competitive learning situations with cooperative ones? Given the diversity of their methods—all involving students on integrated study teams, sometimes in competition with other teams—the results are striking and heartening.

Are students who participate in existing cooperative activities, such as interracial athletic teams and class projects, less prejudiced? In one experiment, White youth on two- to three-week Outward Bound expeditions (involving intimate contact and cooperation) expressed improved attitudes toward Blacks a month after the expedition *if* they had been randomly assigned to an interracial expedition group (Green & Wong, 2008).

Robert Slavin and Nancy Madden (1979) analyzed survey data from 2,400 students in 71 American high schools and found similarly encouraging results. Those of different races who play and work together are more likely to report having friends of another race and to express positive racial attitudes. Charles Green and his colleagues (1988) confirmed this in a study of 3,200 Florida middle-school students. Compared with students at traditional, competitive schools, those at schools with interracial "learning teams" had more positive racial attitudes.

From such correlational findings, can we conclude that cooperative interracial activity improves racial attitudes? To find out, we experiment. Randomly designate some students, but not others, to work together in racially mixed groups. Slavin (1985; Slavin et al., 2003, 2009) and his colleagues divided classes into interracial teams, each composed of four or five students from all achievement levels. Team members sat together, studied a variety of subjects together, and at the end of each week competed with the other teams in a class tournament. All members contributed to their team's score by doing well, sometimes by competing with other students whose recent achievements were similar to their own, sometimes by competing with their own previous scores. Everyone had a chance to succeed. Moreover, team members were motivated to help one another prepare for the weekly tournament—by drilling each other on fractions, spelling, or historical events—whatever was the next event. Rather than isolating students from one another, team competition brought them into closer contact and drew out mutual support.

Another research team, led by Elliot Aronson (2004; Aronson & Gonzalez, 1988), elicited similar group cooperation with a "jigsaw" technique. In experiments in Texas and California elementary schools, the researchers assigned children to racially and academically diverse 6-member groups. The subject was then divided into six parts, with each student becoming the expert on his or her part. In a unit on Chile, one student might be the expert on Chile's history, another on its geography, another on its culture. First, the various "historians," "geographers," and so forth got together to master their material. Then they returned to the home groups to teach it to their classmates. Each group member held, so to speak, a piece of the jigsaw.

Self-confident students therefore had to listen to and learn from reticent students who, in turn, soon realized they had something important to offer their peers. Other research teams have devised additional methods for cooperative learning. Studies (148 of them across eleven countries) show that adolescents, too, have more positive peer relationships and may even achieve more when working cooperatively rather than competitively (Roseth et al., 2008).

What can we conclude from all this research? With cooperative learning, students learn not only the material but other lessons. Cooperative learning, said Slavin and Cooper (1999),

Interracial cooperation—on athletic teams, in class projects and extracurricular activities—melts differences and improves racial attitudes. White teen athletes who play cooperative team sports (such as basketball) with Black teammates express more liking and support for Blacks than do their counterparts involved in individual sports (such as wrestling) (Brown et al., 2003).
Wavebreak Media ltd/Alamy

Cooperation and peace. Researchers have identified more than 40 peaceful societies—societies where people live with no, or virtually no, recorded instances of violence. An analysis of 25 of these societies, including the Amish shown here, reveals that most base their worldviews on cooperation rather than competition (Bonta, 1997).
Jim Herrmann/Bettmann/Corbis

promotes "the academic achievement of all students while simultaneously improving inter-group relations." Aronson reported that "children in the interdependent, jigsaw classrooms grow to like each other better, develop a greater liking for school, and develop greater self-esteem than children in traditional classrooms" (1980, p. 232).

Cross-racial friendships also begin to blossom. The exam scores of minority students improve (perhaps because academic achievement is now peer supported). After the experiments are over, many teachers continue using cooperative learning (D. W. Johnson et al., 1981; Slavin, 1990). "It is clear," wrote race-relations expert John McConahay (1981), that cooperative learning "is the most effective practice for improving race relations in deseg-regated schools that we know of to date."

Should we have "known it all along"? At the time of the 1954 Supreme Court decision, Gordon Allport spoke for many social psychologists in predicting that "Prejudice . . . may be reduced by equal status contact between majority and minority groups in the pursuit of common goals" (1954, p. 281). Cooperative learning experiments confirmed Allport's insight, making Robert Slavin and his colleagues (1985, 2003) optimistic: "Thirty years after Allport laid out the basic principles operationalized in cooperative learning methods, we finally have practical, proven methods for implementing contact theory in the deseg-regated classroom. . . . Research on cooperative learning is one of the greatest success stories in the history of educational research."

To sum up, cooperative, equal-status contacts exert a positive influence on boy campers, industrial executives, college students, and schoolchildren. Does the principle extend to all levels of human relations? Are families unified by pulling together to farm the land, restore an old house, or sail a sloop? Are communal identities forged by barn raisings, group sing-ing, or cheering on the football team? Is international understanding bred by international collaboration in science and space, by joint efforts to feed the world and conserve resources, by friendly personal contacts between people of different nations? Indications are that the answer to all of those questions is *yes* (Brewer & Miller, 1988; Desforges et al., 1991, 1997; Deutsch, 1985, 1994). Thus, an important challenge facing our divided world is to identify and agree on our superordinate goals and to structure cooperative efforts to achieve them.

GROUP AND SUPERORDINATE IDENTITIES

In everyday life, we often reconcile multiple identities (Gaertner et al., 2000, 2001). We acknowledge our subgroup identity (as parent or child) and then transcend it (sensing our superordinate identity as a family). Pride in our ethnic heritage can complement our larger

"This was truly an exciting event. My students and I had found a way to make desegregation work the way it was intended to work!"
—Elliot Aronson,
"Drifting My Own Way," 2003

For an example of effective desegregation, see "Focus On: Branch Rickey, Jackie Robinson, and the Integration of Baseball."

focus
ON

On April 10, 1947, a nineteen-word announcement forever changed the face of baseball and put social-psychological principles to the test: "The Brooklyn Dodgers today purchased the contract of Jackie Roosevelt Robinson from the Montreal Royals. He will report immediately." Five days later, Robinson became the first African American since 1887 to play major league baseball. In the fall, Dodger fans realized their dreams of going to the World Series. Robinson, after enduring racial taunts, beanballs, and spikes, was voted *Sporting News* rookie of the year, and in a poll finished second to Bing Crosby as the most popular man in America. Baseball's racial barrier was forever broken.

Motivated by both his Methodist morality and a drive for baseball success, Major League baseball executive Branch Rickey had been planning the move for some time, reported social psychologists Anthony Pratkanis and Marlene Turner (1994a,b). Three years earlier, Rickey had been asked by the sociologist-chair of the Mayor's Committee on Unity to desegregate his team. His response was to ask for time (so the hiring would not be attributed to pressure) and for advice on how best to do it. In 1945 Rickey was the only owner voting against keeping Blacks out of baseball. In 1947 he made his move using these principles identified by Pratkanis and Turner:

- *Create a perception that change is inevitable.* Leave little possibility that protest or resistance can turn back the clock. The team's radio announcer, Red Barber, a traditional southerner, recalled that in 1945 Rickey took him to lunch and explained very slowly and strongly that his scouts were searching for "the first black player I can put on the white Dodgers. I don't know who he is or where he is, but, he is coming." An angered Barber at first intended to quit, but in time decided to accept the inevitable and keep the world's "best sports announcing job." Rickey was equally matter-of-fact with the players in 1947, offering to trade any player who didn't want to play with Robinson.

- *Establish equal-status contact with a superordinate goal.* One sociologist explained to Rickey that when relationships focus on an overarching goal, such as winning the pennant, "the people involved would adjust appropriately." One of the players who had been

initially opposed later helped Robinson with his hitting, explaining, "When you're on a team, you got to pull together to win."

- *Puncture the norm of prejudice.* Rickey led the way, but others helped. Team leader, shortstop Pee Wee Reese, a southerner, set a pattern of sitting and eating with Robinson. One day in Cincinnati, as the crowd was hurling slurs—"get the nigger off the field"—Reese left his shortstop position, walked over to Robinson at first base, smiled and spoke to him, and then—with a hushed crowd watching—put his arm around Robinson's shoulder.

- *Cut short the spiral of violence by practicing nonviolence.* Rickey, wanting "a ballplayer with guts enough not to fight back," role-played for Robinson the kind of insults and dirty play he would experience and gained Robinson's commitment not to return violence with violence. When Robinson was taunted and spiked, he left the responses to his teammates. Team cohesion was thereby increased.

Robinson and Bob Feller later became the first players in baseball history elected to the Hall of Fame in their first year of eligibility. As he received the award, Robinson asked three persons to stand beside him: his mother, his wife, and his friend Branch Rickey.

Jackie Robinson and Branch Rickey
AP Images/JH

communal or national identity. Being mindful of our *multiple* social identities enables social cohesion (Brewer & Pierce, 2005; Crisp & Hewstone, 1999, 2000). "I am many things, some of which you are, too."

But in ethnically diverse cultures, how do people balance their ethnic identities with their national identities? They may have a "bicultural" or "omnicultural" identity, one that identifies with both the larger culture and one's own ethnic and religious culture

TABLE :: 1 Ethnic and Cultural Identity

	Identification with Ethnic Group	
Identification with Majority Group	**Strong**	**Weak**
Strong	Bicultural	Assimilated
Weak	Separated	Marginal

(*Source:* Adapted from Phinney, 1990).

(Moghaddam, 2009, 2010; Phinney, 1990). "In many ways, I am like everyone around me, but I also affirm my own cultural heritage." Thus, ethnically conscious Asians living in England may also feel strongly British (Hutnik, 1985). French Canadians who identify with their ethnic roots may or may not also feel strongly Canadian (Driedger, 1975). Americans who retain a strong sense of their "Cubanness" (or of their Mexican or Puerto Rican heritage) may also feel strongly American (Roger et al., 1991). As W. E. B. DuBois (1903, p. 17) explained in *The Souls of Black Folk,* "The American Negro [longs] . . . to be both a Negro and an American."

Over time, identification with a new culture often grows. Former East and West Germans come to see themselves as "German" (Kessler & Mummendey, 2001). The children of Chinese immigrants to Australia and the United States feel their Chinese identity somewhat less keenly, and their new national identity more strongly, than do immigrants who were born in China (Rosenthal & Feldman, 1992). Often, however, the *grand*children of immigrants feel more comfortable identifying with their ethnicity (Triandis, 1994).

Researchers have wondered whether pride in one's group competes with identification with the larger culture. We evaluate ourselves partly in terms of our social identities. Seeing our own group (our school, our employer, our family, our race, our nation) as good helps us feel good about ourselves. A positive ethnic identity can therefore contribute to positive self-esteem. So can a positive mainstream culture identity. "Marginal" people, who have neither a strong ethnic nor a strong mainstream cultural identity (Table 1), often have low self-esteem. Bicultural people, who affirm both identities, typically have a strongly positive self-concept (Phinney, 1990; Sam & Berry, 2010). Often, they alternate between their two cultures, adapting their language and behavior to whichever group they are with (LaFromboise et al., 1993).

Debate continues over the ideals of multiculturalism (celebrating differences) versus assimilation (meshing one's values and habits with the prevailing culture). Compared with university minority students, those in the majority racial group—whether White or Black—have been more likely to favor assimilation. They more often agree, for example, that "there should be a single center on campus for all students, rather than separate cultural centers for students of different racial groups" (Hehman et al., 2012).

On one side of the multiculturalism vs. assimilation debate, are those who believe, as the Department of Canadian Heritage (2006) has declared, that "multiculturalism ensures that all citizens can keep their identities, can take pride in their ancestry and have a sense of belonging. Acceptance gives Canadians a feeling of security and self-confidence, making them open to and accepting of diverse cultures." On the other side are those who

> "Most of us have overlapping identities which unite us with very different groups. We can love what we are, without hating what—and who—we are not. We can thrive in our own tradition, even as we learn from others, and come to respect their teachings."
> —Kofi Annan,
> Nobel Peace Prize Lecture, 2001

Diversity within unity: Scottish *and* British. With the establishment of its own Parliament and the rise of the Scottish National Party, Scottish identity has strengthened. Yet in 2014, Scots voted also to retain their British identity, as part of the United Kingdom.
Rex Features

concur with Britain's Commission for Racial Equality chair, Trevor Phillips (2004), in worrying that multiculturalism separates people. Experiments by Jacquie Vorauer and Stacey Sasaki (2011) showed that in threatening situations, highlighting multicultural differences enhanced hostility. Focusing on differences prompted people to attend and attach meaning to outgroup members' threatening behaviors. An alternative common values view inspired the Rwandan government to declare "there is no ethnicity here. We are all Rwandan." In the aftermath of Rwanda's ethnic bloodbath, government documents and government-controlled radio and newspapers have ceased mentioning Hutu and Tutsi (Lacey, 2004).

In the space between multiculturalism and assimilation lies "diversity within unity," an omnicultural perspective advocated by cultural psychologist Fathali Moghaddam (2009, 2010) and by sociologist Amitai Etzioni and others (2005): "It presumes that all members of a given society will fully respect and adhere to those basic values and institutions that are considered part of the basic shared framework of the society. At the same time, every group in society is free to maintain its distinct subculture—those policies, habits, and institutions that do not conflict with the shared core."

By forging unifying ideals, immigrant countries such as the United States, Canada, and Australia have avoided ethnic wars. In these countries, Irish and Italians, Swedes and Scots, Asians and Africans seldom kill in defense of their ethnic identities. Nevertheless, even the immigrant nations struggle between separation and wholeness, between people's pride in their distinct heritage and unity as one nation, between acknowledging the reality of diversity and questing for shared values. The ideal of diversity within unity forms the United States motto: *E pluribus unum.* Out of many, one.

Communication

Conflicting parties have other ways to resolve their differences. When husband and wife, or labor and management, or nation X and nation Y disagree, they can **bargain** with each other directly. They can ask a third party to **mediate** by making suggestions and facilitating their negotiations. Or they can **arbitrate** by submitting their disagreement to someone who will study the issues and impose a settlement.

BARGAINING

If you want to buy or sell a new car, are you better off adopting a tough bargaining stance—opening with an extreme offer so that splitting the difference will yield a favorable result? Or are you better off beginning with a sincere "good-faith" offer?

Experiments suggest no simple answer. On the one hand, those who demand more will often get more. Robert Cialdini, Leonard Bickman, and John Cacioppo (1979) provide a typical result: In a control condition, they approached various Chevrolet dealers and asked the price of a new Monte Carlo sports coupe. In an experimental condition, they approached other dealers and first struck a tougher bargaining stance, asking for and rejecting a price on a *different* car ("I need a lower price than that. That's a lot"). When they then asked the price of the Monte Carlo, exactly as in the control condition, they received offers that averaged some $200 lower.

Tough bargaining may lower the other party's expectations, making the other side willing to settle for less (Yukl, 1974). But toughness can sometimes backfire. Many a conflict is not over a pie of fixed size but over a pie that shrinks if the conflict continues. A time delay is often a lose-lose scenario. When a strike is prolonged, both labor and management lose. Being tough is another potential lose-lose scenario. If the other party responds with an equally tough stance, both may be locked into positions from which neither can back down without losing face. In the weeks before the 1991 Persian Gulf War, the first President Bush threatened, in the full glare of publicity, to "kick Saddam's ass." Saddam Hussein, no less macho, threatened to make "infidel" Americans "swim in their own blood." After such belligerent statements, it was difficult for each side to evade war and save face. As this illustrates, although tough and even angry bargaining may sometimes gain more time or money, it can backfire when the negotiation concerns values—personal beliefs about what's important in life (Harinck & Van Kleef, 2012).

bargaining
Seeking an agreement to a conflict through direct negotiation between parties.

mediation
An attempt by a neutral third party to resolve a conflict by facilitating communication and offering suggestions.

arbitration
Resolution of a conflict by a neutral third party who studies both sides and imposes a settlement.

MEDIATION

A third-party mediator may offer suggestions that enable conflicting parties to make concessions and still save face (Pruitt, 1998). If my concession can be attributed to a mediator, who is gaining an equal concession from my antagonist, neither of us will be viewed as weakly caving in.

TURNING WIN-LOSE INTO WIN-WIN. Mediators also help resolve conflicts by facilitating constructive communication. Their first task is to help the parties rethink the conflict and gain information about the others' interests. Typically, people on both sides have a competitive "win-lose" orientation: They are successful if their opponent is unhappy with the result, and unsuccessful if their opponent is pleased (Thompson et al., 1995). The mediator aims to replace this win-lose orientation with a cooperative "win-win" orientation, by prodding both sides to set aside their conflicting demands and instead to think about each other's underlying needs, interests, and goals.

A classic win-win story concerns two sisters who quarreled over an orange (Follett, 1940). Finally they compromised and split the orange in half, whereupon one sister squeezed her half for juice while the other used the peel on her half to make a cake. If the sisters had each explained *why* they wanted the orange, they very likely would have agreed to share it, giving one sister all the juice and the other all the peel. This is an example of an **integrative agreement** (Pruitt & Lewis, 1975, 1977). Compared with compromises, in which each party sacrifices something important, integrative agreements are more enduring. Because they are mutually rewarding, they also lead to better ongoing relationships (Pruitt, 1986).

integrative agreements
Win-win agreements that reconcile both parties' interests to their mutual benefit.

UNRAVELING MISPERCEPTIONS WITH CONTROLLED COMMUNICATIONS. Communication often helps reduce self-fulfilling misperceptions. Perhaps you can recall experiences similar to that of this college student:

> Often, after a prolonged period of little communication, I perceive Martha's silence as a sign of her dislike for me. She, in turn, thinks that my quietness is a result of my being mad at her. My silence induces her silence, which makes me even more silent . . . until this snowballing effect is broken by some occurrence that makes it necessary for us to interact. And the communication then unravels all the misinterpretations we had made about one another.

The outcome of such conflicts often depends on *how* people communicate their feelings. Psychologists Ian Gotlib and Catherine Colby (1988) offer advice on how to avoid destructive quarrels and how to have good quarrels (Table 2). Children, for example, can learn that conflict is normal, that people can learn to get along with those who are different, that most disputes can be resolved with two winners, and that nonviolent communication strategies are an alternative to a world of bullies and victims. This "violence prevention

TABLE :: 2 How Couples Can Argue Constructively

Do Not	Do
• evade the argument, give the silent treatment, or walk out on it	• clearly define the issue and repeat the other's arguments in your own words
• use your intimate knowledge of the other person to hit below the belt and humiliate	• divulge your positive and negative feelings
• bring in unrelated issues	• welcome feedback about your behavior
• feign agreement while harboring resentment	• clarify where you agree and disagree and what matters most to each of you
• tell the other party how she or he is feeling	• ask questions that help the other find words to express the concern
• attack indirectly by criticizing someone or something the other person values	• wait for spontaneous explosions to subside, without retaliating
• undermine the other by intensifying his or her insecurity or threatening disaster	• offer positive suggestions for mutual improvement

Communication facilitators work to break down barriers, as in this diversity training exercise for teenagers. In work organizations, too, diversity training can improve attitudes (Kalinoski et al., 2013).

Mark Antman/The Image Works

"[There is] a psychological barrier between us, a barrier of suspicion, a barrier of rejection; a barrier of fear, of deception, a barrier of hallucination. . . ."

—Egyptian President Anwar Al-Sadat, to the Israeli Knesset, 1977

Trust, like other social behaviors, is also a biological phenomenon. Social neuroscientists have found that individuals with lowered levels of serotonin, the brain neurotransmitter, become more likely to see a low offer in a laboratory game as unfair, and to reject it (Bilderbeck et al., 2014; Colzato et al., 2013; Crockett et al., 2008). Infusions of the hormone oxytocin have something of an opposite effect, increasing people's trust of strangers in laboratory games (Zak, 2008).

The McGraw-Hills Companies inc

curriculum . . . is not about passivity," noted Deborah Prothrow-Stith (1991, p. 183). "It is about using anger not to hurt oneself or one's peers, but to change the world."

David Johnson and Roger Johnson (1995, 2000, 2003) put first-grade through ninth-grade children through about a dozen hours of conflict resolution training in six schools, with heartening results. Before the training, most students were involved in daily conflicts—put-downs and teasing, playground turn-taking conflicts, conflicts over possessions—conflicts that nearly always also resulted in a winner and a loser. After training, the children more often found win-win solutions, better mediated friends' conflicts, and retained and applied their new skills in and out of school throughout the school year. When implemented with a whole student body, the result is a more peaceful student community and increased academic achievement.

Conflict researchers report that a key factor is *trust* (Balliet & Van Lange, 2013). If you believe the other person is well intentioned, you are more likely to divulge your needs and concerns. Lacking trust, you may fear that being open will give the other party information that might be used against you. Even simple behaviors can enhance trust. In experiments, negotiators who were instructed to mimic the others' mannerisms, as naturally empathic people often do, elicited more trust and greater discovery of compatible interests and mutually satisfying deals (Maddux et al., 2008).

When the two parties mistrust each other and communicate unproductively, a third-party mediator—a marriage counselor, a labor mediator, a diplomat—sometimes helps. Often the mediator is someone trusted by both sides. In the 1980s it took an Algerian Muslim to mediate the conflict between Iran and Iraq, and the pope to resolve a geographical dispute between Argentina and Chile (Carnevale & Choi, 2000).

After coaxing the conflicting parties to rethink their perceived win-lose conflict, the mediator often has each party identify and rank its goals. When goals are compatible, the ranking procedure makes it easier for each to concede on less-important goals so that both achieve their chief goals (Erickson et al., 1974; Schulz & Pruitt, 1978). South Africa achieved internal peace when Black and White South Africans granted each other's top priorities—replacing apartheid with majority rule and safeguarding the security, welfare, and rights of Whites (Kelman, 1998).

When labor and management both believe that management's goal of higher productivity and profit is compatible with labor's goal of better wages and working conditions, they can begin to work for an integrative win-win solution. If workers will forgo benefits that are moderately beneficial to them but very costly to management (perhaps company-provided dental care), and if management will forgo moderately valuable arrangements that workers very much resent (perhaps inflexible working hours), both sides may gain (Ross & Ward, 1995). Rather than seeing itself as making a concession, each side can see the negotiation as an effort to exchange bargaining chips for things more valued.

When the parties then convene to communicate directly, they are usually not set loose in the hope that, eyeball-to-eyeball, the conflict will resolve itself. In the midst of a threatening, stressful conflict, emotions often disrupt the ability to understand the other party's point of view. Although happiness and gratitude can increase trust, anger decreases it (Dunn & Schweitzer, 2005). Communication may thus become most difficult just when it is most needed (Tetlock, 1985).

The mediator will often structure the encounter to help each party understand and feel understood by the other. The mediator may ask the conflicting parties to restrict their arguments to statements of fact, including statements of how they feel and how they respond when the other acts in a given way: "I enjoy music. But when you play it loud, I find it hard to concentrate. That makes me crabby." To increase empathy, the mediator may ask people to reverse roles and argue the other's position or to imagine and explain what the other person is experiencing (Yaniv, 2012). The mediator may have them restate one another's positions before replying with their own: "It annoys you when I play my music and you're trying to study."

Experiments show that taking the other's perspective and inducing empathy decreases stereotyping and increases cooperation (Batson & Moran, 1999; Galinsky & Moskowitz, 2000; Todd et al., 2011). Hearing an outgroup person criticizing their own group—as when Israeli Jews heard a Palestinian criticizing Palestinians—opens people to the outgroup's perspective (Saguy & Halperin, 2014). It helps to humanize rather than demonize the other. Older people often find that easier to do, by having the wisdom to appreciate multiple perspectives and the limits of knowledge (Grossmann et al., 2010). Sometimes our elders are older, wiser, and better able to navigate social conflicts.

Neutral third parties may also suggest mutually agreeable proposals that would be dismissed—"reactively devalued"—if offered by either side. A nuclear disarmament proposal that Americans dismissed when attributed to the former Soviet Union seemed more acceptable when attributed to a neutral third party (Stillinger et al., 1991). Likewise, people will

"Adversarial collaboration"—turning rivals into teammates. Groups with conflicting ideas may want to lay out where they agree, identify points of disagreement, and jointly propose solutions to those points.
Photononstop/Alamy

often reactively devalue a concession offered by an adversary ("they must not value it"); the same concession may seem more than a token gesture when suggested by a third party.

These peacemaking principles—based partly on laboratory experiments, partly on practical experience—have helped mediate both international and industrial conflicts (Blake & Mouton, 1962, 1979; Fisher, 1994; Wehr, 1979). One small team of Arab and Jewish Americans, led by social psychologist Herbert Kelman (1997, 2010), has conducted workshops bringing together influential Arabs and Israelis. Kelman and colleagues counter misperceptions and have participants seek creative solutions for their common good. Isolated, the participants are free to speak directly to their adversaries without fear that their constituents are second-guessing what they are saying. The result? Those from both sides typically come to understand the other's perspective and how the other side responds to their own group's actions.

ARBITRATION

Some conflicts are so intractable, the underlying interests so divergent, that a mutually satisfactory resolution is unattainable. Conflicting claims to Jerusalem as the capital of an independent Palestine versus a secure Israel have, so far, proven intractable. In a divorce dispute over custody of a child, both parents cannot enjoy full custody. In those and many other cases (disputes over tenants' repair bills, athletes' wages, and national territories), a third-party mediator may—or may not—help resolve the conflict.

If not, the parties may turn to *arbitration* by having the mediator or another third party *impose* a settlement. Disputants usually prefer to settle their differences without arbitration so that they retain control over the outcome. Neil McGillicuddy and others (1987) observed this preference in an experiment involving disputants coming to a dispute settlement center. When people knew they would face an arbitrated settlement if mediation failed, they tried harder to resolve the problem, exhibited less hostility, and thus were more likely to reach agreement.

In cases where differences seem large and irreconcilable, the prospect of arbitration may cause the disputants to freeze their positions, hoping to gain an advantage when the arbitrator chooses a compromise. To combat that tendency, some disputes, such as those involving salaries of individual baseball players, are settled with "final-offer arbitration," in which the third party chooses one of the two final offers. Final-offer arbitration motivates each party to make a reasonable proposal.

Typically, however, the final offer is not as reasonable as it would be if each party, free of self-serving bias, saw its own proposal through others' eyes. Negotiation researchers report that most disputants are made stubborn by "optimistic overconfidence" (Kahneman & Tversky, 1995). Successful mediation is hindered when, as often happens, both parties believe they have a two-thirds chance of winning a final-offer arbitration (Bazerman, 1986, 1990).

Conciliation

Sometimes tension and suspicion run so high that even communication, let alone resolution, becomes all but impossible. Each party may threaten, coerce, or retaliate against the other. Unfortunately, such acts tend to be reciprocated, escalating the conflict. So, would a strategy of appeasing the other party by being unconditionally cooperative produce a satisfying result? Often not. In laboratory games, those who are 100 percent cooperative often are exploited. Politically, a one-sided pacifism is usually out of the question.

GRIT

Social psychologist Charles Osgood (1962, 1980) advocated a third alternative, one that is conciliatory yet strong enough to discourage exploitation. Osgood called it "graduated and reciprocated initiatives in tension reduction." He nicknamed it **GRIT,** a label that suggests the determination it requires. GRIT aims to reverse the "conflict spiral" by triggering reciprocal de-escalation. To do so, it draws upon social-psychological concepts, such as the norm of reciprocity and the attribution of motives.

GRIT requires one side to initiate a few small de-escalatory actions, after *announcing a conciliatory intent*. The initiator states its desire to reduce tension, declares each conciliatory act before making it, and invites the adversary to reciprocate. Such announcements

GRIT
Acronym for "graduated and reciprocated initiatives in tension reduction"—a strategy designed to de-escalate international tensions.

create a framework that helps the adversary correctly interpret what otherwise might be seen as weak or tricky actions. They also bring public pressure to bear on the adversary to follow the reciprocity norm.

Next, the initiator establishes credibility and genuineness by carrying out, exactly as announced, several verifiable *conciliatory acts*. This intensifies the pressure to reciprocate. Making conciliatory acts diverse—perhaps offering medical help, closing a military base, and lifting a trade ban—keeps the initiator from making a significant sacrifice in any one area and leaves the adversary freer to choose its own means of reciprocation. If the adversary reciprocates voluntarily, its own conciliatory behavior may soften its attitudes.

GRIT *is* conciliatory. But it is not "surrender on the installment plan." The remaining aspects of the plan protect each side's self-interest by *maintaining retaliatory capability*. The initial conciliatory steps entail some small risk but do not jeopardize either one's security; rather, they are calculated to begin edging both sides down the tension ladder. If one side takes an aggressive action, the other side reciprocates in kind, making clear it will not tolerate exploitation. Yet the reciprocal act is not an overresponse that would re-escalate the conflict. If the adversary offers its own conciliatory acts, these, too, are matched or even slightly exceeded. Morton Deutsch (1993) captured the spirit of GRIT in advising negotiators to be "'firm, fair, and friendly': *firm* in resisting intimidation, exploitation, and dirty tricks; *fair* in holding to one's moral principles and not reciprocating the other's immoral behavior despite his or her provocations; and *friendly* in the sense that one is willing to initiate and reciprocate cooperation."

Does GRIT really work? In a lengthy series of experiments at Ohio University, Svenn Lindskold and his associates (1976 to 1988) found "strong support for the various steps in the GRIT proposal." In laboratory games, announcing cooperative intent *does* boost cooperation. Repeated conciliatory or generous acts *do* breed greater trust (Klapwijk & Van Lange, 2009; Shapiro, 2010). Maintaining an equality of power *does* protect against exploitation.

Lindskold was not contending that the world of the laboratory experiment mirrors the more complex world of everyday life. Rather, experiments enable us to formulate and verify powerful theoretical principles, such as the reciprocity norm and the self-serving bias. As Lindskold (1981) noted, "It is the theories, not the individual experiments, that are used to interpret the world."

REAL-WORLD APPLICATIONS

GRIT-like strategies have occasionally been tried outside the laboratory, with promising results. During the Berlin crisis of the early 1960s, U.S. and Russian tanks faced each other barrel to barrel. The crisis was defused when the Americans pulled back their tanks step-by-step. At each step, the Russians reciprocated. Similarly, in the 1970s, small concessions by Israel and Egypt (for example, Israel allowing Egypt to open up the Suez Canal, Egypt allowing ships bound for Israel to pass through) helped reduce tension to a point where the negotiations became possible (Rubin, 1981).

To many, the most significant attempt at GRIT was the so-called Kennedy experiment (Etzioni, 1967). On June 10, 1963, President Kennedy gave a major speech, "A Strategy for Peace." He noted that "Our problems are man-made . . . and can be solved by man," and then announced his first conciliatory act: The United States was stopping all atmospheric nuclear tests and would not resume them unless another country did. Kennedy's entire speech was published in the Soviet press. Five days later Premier Khrushchev reciprocated, announcing he had halted production of strategic bombers. There soon followed further reciprocal gestures: The United States agreed to sell wheat to Russia, the Russians agreed to a "hot line" between the two countries, and the two countries soon achieved a test-ban treaty. For a time, these conciliatory initiatives eased relations between the two countries.

Might conciliatory efforts also help reduce tension between individuals? There is every reason to expect so. When a relationship is strained and communication nonexistent, it sometimes takes only a conciliatory gesture—a soft answer, a warm smile, a gentle touch—for both parties to begin easing down the tension ladder, to a rung where contact, cooperation, and communication again become possible.

"I am not suggesting that principles of individual behavior can be applied to the behavior of nations in any direct, simpleminded fashion. What I am trying to suggest is that such principles may provide us with hunches about international behavior that can be tested against experience in the larger arena."
—Charles E. Osgood, 1966

SUMMING UP: How Can Peace Be Achieved?

- Although conflicts are readily kindled and fueled by social dilemmas, competition, and misperceptions, some equally powerful forces, such as contact, cooperation, communication, and conciliation, can transform hostility into harmony. Despite some encouraging early studies, other studies show that mere contact (such as mere desegregation in schools) has little effect upon racial attitudes. But when contact encourages emotional ties with individuals identified with an outgroup, and when it is structured to convey *equal status,* hostilities often lessen.

- Contacts are especially beneficial when people work together to overcome a common threat or to achieve a *superordinate goal.* Taking their cue from experiments on *cooperative contact,* several research teams have replaced competitive classroom learning situations with opportunities for cooperative learning, with heartening results.

- Conflicting parties often have difficulty communicating. A third-party mediator can promote communication by prodding the antagonists to replace their competitive win-lose view of their conflict with a more cooperative win-win orientation. Mediators can also structure communications that will peel away misperceptions and increase mutual understanding and trust. When a negotiated settlement is not reached, the conflicting parties may defer the outcome to an *arbitrator,* who either dictates a settlement or selects one of the two final offers.

- Sometimes tensions run so high that genuine communication is impossible. In such cases, small conciliatory gestures by one party may elicit reciprocal conciliatory acts by the other party. One such conciliatory strategy, graduated and reciprocated initiatives in tension reduction *(GRIT),* aims to alleviate tense international situations. Those who mediate tense labor-management and international conflicts sometimes use another peacemaking strategy. They instruct the participants, as this chapter instructed you, in the dynamics of conflict and peacemaking in the hope that understanding can help former adversaries establish and enjoy peaceful, rewarding relationships.

POSTSCRIPT:
The Conflict Between Individual and Communal Rights

"This is the age of the individual."

—President Ronald Reagan, Address on Wall Street, 1982

Many social conflicts are a contest between individual and collective rights. One person's right to own handguns conflicts with a neighborhood's right to safe streets. One person's right to smoke conflicts with others' rights to a smoke-free environment. One industrialist's right to do unregulated business conflicts with a community's right to clean air.

Hoping to blend the best of individualist and collectivist values, some social scientists have advocated a communitarian synthesis that aims to balance individual rights with the collective right to communal well-being. Communitarians welcome incentives for individual initiative and appreciate why Marxist economies have crumbled. "If I were, let's say, in Albania at this moment," said communitarian sociologist Amitai Etzioni (1991), "I probably would argue that there's too much community and not enough individual rights." But communitarians also question the other extreme—rugged individualism and self-indulgence of the 1960s ("Do your own thing"), the 1970s (the "Me decade"), the 1980s ("Greed is good"), the 1990s ("Follow your bliss"), the 2000s ("An Army of One"), and the 2010s ("Never compromise"). Unrestrained personal freedom, they say, destroys a culture's social fabric; unregulated commercial freedom, they add, has plundered our shared environment.

During the last half-century, Western individualism has intensified. Parents have become more likely to prize independence and self-reliance in their children and are less concerned with obedience (Alwin, 1990; Remley, 1988; Park et al., 2014). Children more often have uncommon names (Twenge et al., 2010). Clothing and grooming styles have become more diverse, personal freedoms have increased, and common values have waned (Putnam, 2000; Schlesinger, 1991).

Communitarians are not advocating a nostalgia trip—a return, for example, to the more restrictive and unequal gender roles of the 1950s. Rather, they propose a middle ground between the individualism of the West and the collectivism of the East, between the macho independence traditionally associated with males and the caregiving connectedness traditionally associated with females, between concerns for individual rights and for communal well-being, between liberty and fraternity, between me-thinking and we-thinking.

As with luggage searches at airports, smoking bans on planes, and sobriety checkpoints and speed limits on highways, societies accept some adjustments to individual rights in order to protect the public good. Environmental restraints on individual freedoms (to pollute, to hunt whales, to deforest) similarly exchange certain short-term liberties for long-term communal gain. Some individualists warn that such constraints on individual liberties may plunge us down a slippery slope leading to the loss of more important liberties. If today we let them search our luggage, tomorrow they'll be knocking down the doors of our houses. If today we censor cigarette ads or pornography on television, tomorrow they'll be removing books from our libraries. If today we ban handguns, tomorrow they'll take our hunting rifles. In protecting the interests of the majority, do we risk suppressing the basic rights of minorities? Communitarians reply that if we don't balance concern for individual rights with concern for our collective well-being, we risk worse civic disorder, which in turn *will* fuel cries for an autocratic crackdown.

This much is sure: As the conflict between individual and collective rights continues, cross-cultural and gender scholarship can illuminate alternative cultural values and make visible our own assumed values.

Social Psychology in the Clinic

CHAPTER

14

Mark Bowden/Getty Images

> "Life does not consist mainly, or even largely, of facts and happenings. It consists mainly of the storm of thoughts that are forever blowing through one's mind."
>
> —Mark Twain, 1835–1910

What influences the accuracy of clinical judgments?

What cognitive processes accompany behavior problems?

What are some social-psychological approaches to treatment?

How do social relationships support health and well-being?

Postscript: Enhancing happiness

Throughout this book, we have linked laboratory and life by relating social psychology's principles and findings to everyday happenings. In these chapters, we recall many of these principles and apply them in practical contexts. "Social Psychology in the Clinic" applies social psychology to evaluating and promoting mental and physical health. "Social Psychology in Court" explores the social thinking of, and social influences on, jurors and juries. "Social Psychology and the Sustainable Future" explores how social psychological principles might help avert the ecological crisis that threatens to engulf us as a result of increasing population, consumption, and climate change.

If you are a typical college student, you occasionally feel mildly depressed. Perhaps you have at times felt dissatisfied with life, discouraged about the future, sad, lacking appetite and energy, unable to concentrate, perhaps even wondering if life is worth living. Maybe disappointing grades have jeopardized your career goals. Perhaps the breakup of a relationship has left you downcast. At such times, you may fall into self-focused brooding that only worsens your feelings. In one survey of American collegians, 31 percent reported that during the last school year they had at some point felt "so depressed it was difficult to function" (ACHA, 2009), and 33 percent said they "felt overwhelmed by all I had to do" (Eagan et al., 2014). For 13 percent of adult American men and 22 percent of women, life's down times are not just temporary blue moods in response to bad events; rather, they define a major depressive episode that lasts for weeks without any obvious cause—and thus a diagnosis of depression (Pelham, 2009).

Among the many thriving areas of applied social psychology is one that relates social psychology's concepts to depression; to other problems, such as loneliness, anxiety, and physical illness; and to happiness and well-being. This bridge-building research between social psychology and **clinical psychology** seeks answers to four important questions:

clinical psychology
The study, assessment, and treatment of people with psychological difficulties.

- As laypeople or as professional psychologists, how can we improve our judgments and predictions about others?
- How do the ways in which we think about self and others fuel problems such as depression, loneliness, anxiety, and ill health?
- How might people reverse these maladaptive thought patterns?
- What part do close, supportive relationships play in health and happiness?

WHAT INFLUENCES THE ACCURACY OF CLINICAL JUDGMENTS?

Identify influences on social judgment that affect clinicians' judgments of clients. Describe biases that clinicians and their clients should be wary of.

A parole board talks with a convicted rapist and ponders whether to release him. A clinical psychologist ponders whether her patient is seriously suicidal. A physician notes a patient's symptoms and decides whether to recommend an invasive test. A school social worker ponders whether a child's overheard threat was a macho joke, a onetime outburst, or a signal indicating a potential school assassin.

All these professionals must decide whether to make their judgments subjectively or objectively. Should they listen to their subjective gut instincts, their hunches, their inner wisdom? Or should they rely on the objective wisdom embedded in formulas, statistical analyses, and computerized predictions?

In the contest between heart and head, most psychological clinicians vote with their hearts. They listen to the whispers from their experience, a still small voice that clues them. They prefer not to let cold calculations decide the futures of warm human beings. As Figure 1 indicates, they are far more likely than nonclinical (and more research-oriented) psychologists to welcome nonscientific "ways of knowing." Feelings trump formulas.

Clinical judgments are also *social* judgments, notes social-clinical psychologist James Maddux (2008). The social construction of mental illness works like this, he says: Someone observes a pattern of atypical or unwanted thinking and acting. A powerful group sees

FIGURE :: 1

Clinical Intuition

When Narina Nunez, Debra Ann Poole, and Amina Memon (2003) surveyed a national sample of clinical and nonclinical psychologists, they discovered "two cultures"—one mostly skeptical of "alternative ways of knowing," the other mostly accepting.

Source: From Nunez, Poole, & Memon, 2003.

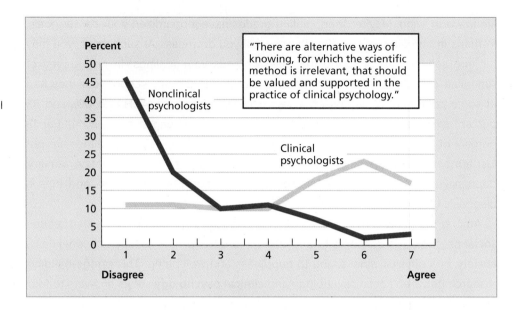

the desirability or profitability of diagnosing and treating this problem, and thus gives it a name. News about this "disease" spreads, and people begin seeing it in themselves or family members. And thus is born Body Dysmorphic Disorder (for those preoccupied with an appearance defect), Oppositional Defiant Disorder (for toddlers throwing tantrums), Hypoactive Sexual Desire Disorder (for those not wanting sex often enough), or Orgasmic Disorder (for those having orgasms too seldom or too soon). "The science of medicine is not diminished by acknowledging that the notions of *health* and *illness* are socially constructed," notes Maddux, "nor is the science of economics diminished by acknowledging that the notions of *poverty* and *wealth* are socially constructed."

As social phenomena, clinical judgments are vulnerable to illusory correlations, overconfidence bred by hindsight, and self-confirming diagnoses (Garb, 2005; Maddux, 1993). Let's see why alerting mental health workers to how people form impressions (and misimpressions) might help avert serious misjudgments (McFall, 1991, 2000).

Illusory Correlations

It's tempting to see illusory correlations where none exist. If we expect two things to be associated—if, for example, we believe that premonitions predict events—it's easy to perceive illusory correlations. Even when shown random data, we may notice and remember instances when premonitions and events are coincidentally related and soon forget all the instances when premonitions aren't borne out and when events happen without a prior premonition.

Clinicians, like all of us, may perceive illusory correlations. Imagine that Mary, a mental health worker, expects particular responses to Rorschach inkblots to be more common among people with a sexual disorder. Might she, in reflecting on her experience, believe she has witnessed such associations?

To discover when such a perception is an illusory correlation, psychological science offers a simple method: Have one clinician administer and interpret the test. Have another clinician assess the same person's traits or symptoms. Repeat this process with many people. Are test outcomes in fact correlated with reported symptoms? Some tests are indeed predictive. Others, such as the Rorschach inkblots and the Draw-a-Person test, have correlations far weaker than their users suppose (Lilienfeld et al., 2000, 2005).

Why, then, do clinicians continue to express confidence in uninformative or ambiguous tests? Pioneering experiments by Loren Chapman and Jean Chapman (1969, 1971) helped us see why. They invited college students and professional clinicians to study some test performances and diagnoses. If the students or clinicians *expected* a particular association,

"To free a man of error is to give, not to take away. Knowledge that a thing is false is a truth."

—Arthur Schopenhauer, 1788–1860

they generally *perceived* it. For example, clinicians who believed that only suspicious people draw peculiar eyes on the Draw-a-Person test perceived such a relationship—even when shown cases in which suspicious people drew peculiar eyes less often than nonsuspicious people. If they believed in a connection, they were more likely to notice confirming instances.

In fairness to clinicians, illusory thinking also occurs among political analysts, historians, sportscasters, personnel directors, stockbrokers, and many other professionals, including research psychologists. As researchers, we have often been unaware of the shortcomings of our theoretical analyses. We so eagerly presume that our idea of truth is *the* truth that, no matter how hard we try, we cannot see our own errors. We have read dozens of reviews of our own manuscripts and have been reviewers for dozens of others. Our experience is that it is far easier to spot someone else's sloppy thinking than to perceive our own.

"No one can see his own errors."

—Psalm 19:12

Hindsight and Overconfidence

If someone we know commits suicide, how do we react? One common reaction is to think that we, or those close to the person, should have been able to predict and therefore to prevent the suicide: "We should have known!" In hindsight, we can see the suicidal signs and the pleas for help. One experiment gave participants a description of a depressed person. Some participants were told that the person subsequently committed suicide; other participants were not told this. Compared with those not informed of the suicide, those who had been informed became more likely to say they "would have expected" it (Goggin & Range, 1985). Moreover, they viewed the victim's family more negatively. After a tragedy, an I-should-have-known-it-all-along phenomenon can leave family, friends, and therapists feeling guilty.

David Rosenhan (1973) and seven associates provided a striking example of error-prone after-the-fact explanations. To test mental health workers' clinical insights, they each made an appointment with a different mental hospital admissions office and complained of "hearing voices." Apart from giving false names and vocations, they reported their life histories and emotional states honestly and exhibited no further symptoms. Most were diagnosed with schizophrenia and remained hospitalized for two to three weeks. Hospital clinicians then searched for early incidents in the pseudopatients' life histories and hospital behavior that "confirmed" and "explained" the diagnosis. Rosenhan tells of one pseudopatient who truthfully explained to the interviewer that he had a close childhood relationship with his mother but was rather remote from his father. During adolescence and beyond, however, his father became a close friend while his relationship with his mother cooled. His present relationship with his wife was characteristically close and warm. Apart from occasional angry exchanges, friction was minimal. The children had rarely been spanked.

The interviewer, "knowing" the person suffered schizophrenia, explained the problem this way:

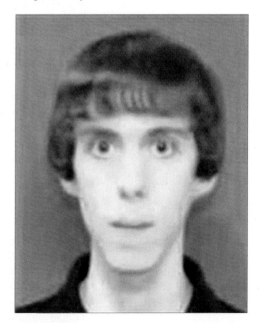

> This white 39-year-old male . . . manifests a long history of considerable ambivalence in close relationships, which begins in early childhood. A warm relationship with his mother cools during his adolescence. A distant relationship to his father is described as becoming very intense. Affective stability is absent. His attempts to control emotionality with his wife and children are punctuated by angry outbursts and, in the case of the children, spankings. And while he says that he has several good friends, one senses considerable ambivalence embedded in those relationships also.

Rosenhan later told some staff members (who had heard about his controversial experiment but doubted such mistakes could occur in their hospital) that during the next three months one or more pseudopatients

20/20 hindsight. *After* school shootings, people look back and see signs of the coming violence—the drug use, the easy access to guns, the social isolation, the ill-temper. Before the blood is spilled, as when Adam Lanza was on the verge of killing 20 Connecticut schoolchildren and six adults, it's nearly impossible to pick the to-be-violent youth out from among the hordes of similarly troubled teens.
infuklo-171/Insight/Corbis

would seek admission to their hospital. After the three months, he asked the staff to guess which of the 193 patients admitted during that time were really pseudopatients. Of the 193 new patients, 41 were believed by at least one staff member to be pseudopatients. Actually, there were none.

Self-Confirming Diagnoses

So far we've seen that mental health clinicians sometimes perceive illusory correlations and that hindsight explanations can err. A third possible problem with clinical judgment is that patients may supply information that fulfills clinicians' expectations. To get a feel for how this phenomenon might be tested experimentally, imagine yourself on a blind date with someone who has been told that you are an uninhibited, outgoing person. To see whether this is true, your date slips questions into the conversation, such as "Have you ever done anything crazy in front of other people?" As you answer such questions, will you reveal a different "you" than if your date thought you were shy and reserved?

In a clever series of experiments, Mark Snyder (1984), in collaboration with William Swann and others, gave University of Minnesota students some hypotheses to test concerning individuals' traits. Their finding: People often test for a trait by looking for information that confirms it. As in the blind-date example, if people are trying to find out if someone is an extravert, they often solicit instances of extraversion ("What would you do if you wanted to liven things up at a party?"). Testing for introversion, they are more likely to ask, "What factors make it hard for you to really open up to people?" In response, those probed for extraversion *seem* more sociable, and those probed for introversion seem more shy. Our assumptions about another help elicit the behavior we expect.

At Indiana University, Russell Fazio and his colleagues (1981) reproduced this finding and also discovered that those asked the "extraverted" questions later perceived themselves as actually more outgoing than those asked the introverted questions. Moreover, they really became noticeably more outgoing. An accomplice of the experimenter later met each participant in a waiting room and 70 percent of the time guessed correctly from the person's behavior which condition the person had come from.

Given such experiments, can you see why confirmation bias can lead to misdiagnoses, and the behaviors of people undergoing psychotherapy come to fit their therapists' theories (Mendel et al., 2011; Whitman et al., 1963)? When Harold Renaud and Floyd Estess (1961) conducted life-history interviews of 100 healthy, successful adult men, they were startled to discover that their subjects' childhood experiences were loaded with "traumatic events," tense relations with certain people, and bad decisions by their parents—the very factors usually used to explain psychiatric problems. If therapists go fishing for traumas in early childhood experiences, they will often find them.

"As is your sort of mind, so is your sort of search: You'll find what you desire."

—Robert Browning, 1812–1889

Clinical Intuition Versus Statistical Prediction

Not surprisingly, given these hindsight- and diagnosis-confirming tendencies, most clinicians and interviewers express more confidence in their intuitive assessments than in statistical data (such as using past grades and aptitude scores to predict success in graduate or professional school). Yet when researchers pit statistical prediction against intuitive prediction, the statistics usually win. Statistical predictions are indeed unreliable. But human intuition—even expert intuition—is even more unreliable (Faust & Ziskin, 1988; Meehl, 1954; Swets et al., 2000).

Three decades after demonstrating the superiority of statistical over intuitive prediction, Paul Meehl (1986) found the evidence stronger than ever:

> There is no controversy in social science which shows [so many] studies coming out so uniformly in the same direction as this one . . . When you are pushing 90 investigations, predicting everything from the outcome of football games to the diagnosis of liver disease and when you can hardly come up with a half dozen studies showing even a weak tendency in favor of the clinician, it is time to draw a practical conclusion.

One University of Minnesota research team conducted an all-encompassing digest ("meta-analysis") of 134 studies predicting human behavior or making psychological or medical diagnoses and prognoses (Grove et al., 2000). In only 8 of the studies did clinical prediction surpass "mechanical" (statistical) prediction. In 8 times as many (63 studies), statistical prediction fared better. (The rest were a virtual draw.) Ah, but would clinicians fare differently when given the opportunity for a firsthand clinical interview? Yes, report the researchers: Allowed interviews, the clinicians fared substantially *worse*. "It is fair to say that 'the ball is in the clinicians' court,'" the researchers concluded. "Given the overall deficit in clinicians' accuracy relative to mechanical prediction, the burden falls on advocates of clinical prediction to show that clinicians' predictions are more [accurate or cost-effective]."

Daniel Kahneman (2011, p. 223) notes that we now have some 200 studies comparing clinical and statistical prediction, most of which favor the latter, the rest a draw. These include efforts to predict

- *medical outcomes*—cancer patients' longevity, hospital stays, cardiac diagnoses, babies' susceptibility to sudden infant death syndrome,
- *economic outcomes*—new business success, credit risks, career satisfaction,
- *government agency outcomes*—foster parent assessments, juvenile offender re-offense, violent behavior, and
- *miscellaneous other outcomes*—football winners, Bordeaux wine prices.

What if we combined statistical prediction with clinical intuition? What if we gave professional clinicians the statistical prediction of someone's future academic performance or risk of parole violation or suicide and asked them to refine or improve on the prediction? Alas, in the few studies where that has been done, prediction was better if the "improvements" were ignored (Dawes, 1994).

Why then do so many clinicians continue to interpret Rorschach inkblot tests and offer intuitive predictions about parolees, suicide risks, and likelihood of child abuse? Partly out of sheer ignorance, said Meehl, but also partly out of "mistaken conceptions of ethics":

> If I try to forecast something important about a college student, or a criminal, or a depressed patient by inefficient rather than efficient means, meanwhile charging this person or the taxpayer 10 times as much money as I would need to achieve greater predictive accuracy, that is not a sound ethical practice. That it feels better, warmer, and cuddlier to me as predictor is a shabby excuse indeed.

Such words are shocking. Did Meehl (who did not completely dismiss clinical expertise) underestimate experts' intuitions? To see why his findings are apparently valid, consider the assessment of human potential by graduate admissions interviewers. Dawes (1976) explained why statistical prediction is so often superior to an interviewer's intuition when predicting certain outcomes such as graduate school success:

> What makes us think that we can do a better job of selection by interviewing (students) for a half hour, than we can by adding together relevant (standardized) variables, such as undergraduate GPA, GRE score, and perhaps ratings of letters of recommendation? The most reasonable explanation to me lies in our overevaluation of our cognitive capacity. And it is really cognitive conceit. Consider, for example, what goes into a GPA. Because for most graduate applicants it is based on at least 3½ years of undergraduate study, it is a composite measure arising from a minimum of 28 courses and possibly, with the popularity of the quarter system, as many as 50 . . . Yet you and I, looking at a folder or interviewing someone for a half hour, are supposed to be able to form a better impression than one based on 3½ years of the cumulative evaluations of 20–40 different professors. . . . Finally, if we do wish to ignore GPA, it appears that the only reason for doing so is believing that the candidate is particularly brilliant even though his or her record may not show it. What better evidence for such brilliance can we have than a score on a carefully devised aptitude test? Do we really think we are better equipped to assess such aptitude than is the Educational Testing Service, whatever its faults?

"A very bright young man who is likely to succeed in life. He is intelligent enough to achieve lofty goals as long as he stays on task and remains motivated."

—Probation Officer's Clinical Intuition in Response to Eric Harris's "Homicidal Thoughts"—2½ Months Before He Committed the Columbine High School Massacre.

"The effect of Meehl's work on clinical practice in the mental health area can be summed up in a single word: Zilch. He was honored, elected to the presidency of [the American Psychological Association] at a very young age in 1962, recently elected to the National Academy of Sciences, and ignored."

—Robyn M. Dawes, 1989

focus
ON
A Physician's View: The Social Psychology of Medicine

Reading this book helps me understand the human behaviors I observe in my work as a cancer specialist and as medical director of a large staff of physicians. A few examples:

Reviews of medical records illustrate the "I-knew-it-all-along phenomenon." Physician reviewers who assess the medical records of their colleagues often believe, in hindsight, that problems such as cancer or appendicitis should clearly have been recognized and treated much more quickly. Once you know the correct diagnosis, it's easy to look back and interpret the early symptoms accordingly.

For many physicians I have known, the intrinsic motives behind their entering the profession—to help people, to be scientifically stimulated—soon become "overjustified" by the high pay. Before long, the joy is lost. The extrinsic rewards become the reason to practice, and the physician, having lost the altruistic motives, works to increase "success," measured in income.

"Self-serving bias" is ever present. We physicians gladly accept personal credit when things go well. When they don't—when the patient is misdiagnosed or doesn't get well or dies—we attribute the failure elsewhere. We were given inadequate information or the case was ill-fated from the beginning.

I also observe many examples of "belief perseverance." Even when presented with the documented facts about, say, how AIDS is transmitted, people will strangely persist in wrongly believing that it is just a "gay" disease or that they should fear catching it from mosquito bites. It makes me wonder: How can I more effectively persuade people of what they need to know and act upon?

Indeed, as I observe medical attitudes and decision making I feel myself submerged in a giant practical laboratory of social psychology. To understand the goings-on around me, I find social psychological insights invaluable and would strongly advise premed students to study the field.

Burton F. VanderLaan
Grand Rapids, Michigan
Courtesy of Dr. Burton F VanderLaan

The bottom line, contended Dawes (2005) after three decades pressing his point, is that, lacking evidence, using clinical intuition rather than statistical prediction "is simply unethical."

When evaluating clients, mental health workers, like all of us, are vulnerable to cognitive illusions.
Robin Nelson/PhotoEdit

When considering valid behavioral predictors, psychologists can offer useful predictions. Such was the case when psychologists Melissa Dannelet and Carl Redick assessed Maurice Clemmon, who was in a Tacoma, Washington, jail on rape and assault charges. Based partly on "previous violence, young age at first violent incident, relationship instability and prior supervision failure," Dannelet and Redick predicted that Clemmons was at "risk for future dangerous behavior and for committing future criminal acts jeopardizing public safety and security due to past illicit behaviors" (AP, 2009). Six weeks later, after being released on bond, Clemmons came upon four police officers working on their laptops in a coffee shop, and shot and killed them.

Implications for Better Clinical Practice

Professional clinicians are human; they are "vulnerable to insidious errors and biases," concluded James Maddux (1993). They are, as we have seen,

- frequently the victims of illusory correlation.
- too readily convinced of their own after-the-fact analyses.
- unaware that erroneous diagnoses can be self-confirming.
- likely to overestimate their clinical intuition.

The implications for mental health workers are easily stated: Be mindful that clients' verbal agreement with what you say does not prove its validity. Beware of the tendency to see relationships that you expect to see or that are supported by striking examples readily available in your memory. Rely on your notes more than on your memory. Recognize that hindsight is seductive: It can lead you to feel overconfident and sometimes to judge yourself too harshly for not having foreseen outcomes. Guard against the tendency to ask questions that assume your preconceptions are correct; consider opposing ideas and test them, too (Garb, 1994).

> "'I beseech ye in the bowels of Christ, think that ye may be mistaken.' I shall like to have that written over the portals of every church, every school, and every courthouse, and, may I say, of every legislative body in the United States."
>
> —Judge Learned Hand, 1951, Echoing Oliver Cromwell's 1650 Plea to the Church of Scotland

---

SUMMING UP: What Influences the Accuracy of Clinical Judgments?

- As psychiatrists and *clinical psychologists* diagnose and treat their clients, they may perceive illusory correlations.

- Hindsight explanations of people's difficulties are sometimes too easy. Indeed, after-the-fact explaining can breed overconfidence in clinical judgment.

- In interaction with clients, erroneous diagnoses are sometimes self-confirming because interviewers tend to seek and recall information that verifies what they are looking for.

- Research on the errors that so easily creep into intuitive judgments illustrates the need for rigorous testing of intuitive conclusions and the use of statistics to make predictions.

- The scientific method cannot answer all questions and is itself vulnerable to bias. Thankfully, however, it can help us sift truth from falsehood if we are aware of the biases that tend to cloud judgments that are made "from the heart."

WHAT COGNITIVE PROCESSES ACCOMPANY BEHAVIOR PROBLEMS?

Describe the cognitive processes that accompany psychological disorders.

Let's next consider how people's thinking affects their feelings. What are the memories, attributions, and expectations of depressed, lonely, shy, or illness-prone people?

Depression

People who feel depressed tend to think in negative terms. They view life through the dark glasses of low self-esteem (Kuster et al., 2012; Sowislo & Orth, 2012). With seriously depressed people—those who are feeling worthless, lethargic, indifferent toward friends and family, and unable to sleep or eat normally—the negative thinking is self-defeating. Their intensely pessimistic outlook leads them to magnify every bad experience and minimize every good one. They may view advice to "count your blessings" or "look on the bright side" as hopelessly unrealistic. As one depressed young woman reported, "The real me is worthless and inadequate. I can't move forward with my work because I become frozen with doubt" (Burns, 1980, p. 29).

DISTORTION OR REALISM?

Are all depressed people unrealistically negative? To find out, Lauren Alloy and Lyn Abramson (1979; Alloy et al., 2004) studied college students who were either mildly depressed or not depressed. They had the students press a button and observe whether the button controlled a light coming on. Surprisingly, the depressed students were quite accurate in estimating their degree of control. It was the nondepressives whose judgments were distorted; they exaggerated their control. Despite their self-preoccupation, mildly depressed people also are more attuned to others' feelings and often more accurate in their memories and judgments (Forgas, 2014; Harkness et al., 2005). They even excel at estimating time intervals (Kornbrot et al., 2013).

depressive realism

The tendency of mildly depressed people to make accurate rather than self-serving judgments, attributions, and predictions.

This surprising phenomenon of **depressive realism,** nicknamed the "sadder-but-wiser" effect," shows up in various judgments of one's control or skill (Ackermann & DeRubeis, 1991; Alloy et al., 1990). Shelley Taylor (1989, p. 214) explains:

> Normal people exaggerate how competent and well liked they are. Depressed people do not. Normal people remember their past behavior with a rosy glow. Depressed people [unless severely depressed] are more evenhanded in recalling their successes and failures. Normal people describe themselves primarily positively. Depressed people describe both their positive and their negative qualities. Normal people take credit for successful outcomes and tend to deny responsibility for failure. Depressed people accept responsibility for both success and failure. Normal people exaggerate the control they have over what goes on around them. Depressed people are less vulnerable to the illusion of control. Normal people believe to an unrealistic degree that the future holds a bounty of good things and few bad things. Depressed people are more realistic in their perceptions of the future. In fact, on virtually every point on which normal people show enhanced self-regard, illusions of control, and unrealistic visions of the future, depressed people fail to show the same biases. "Sadder but wiser" does indeed appear to apply to depression.

"Life is the art of being well deceived."

—William Hazlitt, 1778–1830

explanatory style

One's habitual way of explaining life events. A negative, pessimistic, depressive explanatory style attributes failure to stable, global, and internal causes.

Underlying the thinking of depressed people are their attributions of responsibility. Consider: If you fail an exam and blame yourself, you may conclude that you are stupid or lazy; consequently, you may feel depressed. If you attribute the failure to an unfair exam or to other circumstances beyond your control, you may feel angry. In more than 100 studies of 15,000 participants, depressed people have been more likely than nondepressed people to exhibit a negative **explanatory style** (Haeffel et al., 2008; Peterson & Steen, 2002; Sweeney et al., 1986). As shown in Figure 2, this explanatory style attributes failure

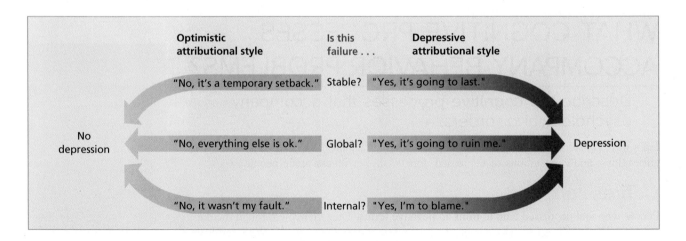

FIGURE :: 2

Depressive Explanatory Style

Depression is linked with a negative, pessimistic way of explaining and interpreting failures.

and setbacks to causes that are *stable* ("It's going to last forever"), *global* ("It's going to affect everything I do"), and *internal* ("It's all my fault"). The result of this pessimistic, overgeneralized, self-blaming thinking, say Abramson and her colleagues (1989), is a depressing sense of hopelessness.

IS NEGATIVE THINKING A CAUSE OR A RESULT OF DEPRESSION?

The cognitive accompaniments of depression raise a chicken-and-egg question: Do depressed moods cause negative thinking, or does negative thinking cause depression?

DEPRESSED MOODS CAUSE NEGATIVE THINKING. Our moods color our thinking. When we *feel* happy, we *think* happy. We see and recall a good world. But let our mood turn gloomy, and our thoughts switch to a different track. Off come the rose-colored glasses; on come the dark glasses. Now the bad mood primes our recollections of negative events (Bower, 1987; Johnson & Magaro, 1987). Our relationships seem to sour, our self-images tarnish, our hopes dim, others seem more sinister (Brown & Taylor, 1986; Mayer & Salovey, 1987). As depression increases, memories and expectations plummet.

When depression lifts, thinking brightens (Barnett & Gotlib, 1988; Kuiper & Higgins, 1985). Thus, *currently* depressed people recall their parents as having been rejecting and punitive. But *formerly* depressed people recall their parents in the same positive terms as do never-depressed people (Lewinsohn & Rosenbaum, 1987). Thus, when you hear depressed people trashing their parents, remember: *Moods modify memories.*

By studying Indiana University basketball fans, Edward Hirt and his colleagues (1992) demonstrated that even a temporary bad mood can darken our thinking. After the fans were either depressed by watching their team lose or elated by a victory, the researchers asked them to predict the team's future performance, and their own. After a loss, people offered bleaker assessments not only of the team's future but also of their own likely performance at throwing darts, solving anagrams, and getting a date. When things aren't going our way, it may seem as though they never will.

> "To the man who is enthusiastic and optimistic, if what is to come should be pleasant, it seems both likely to come about and likely to be good, while to the indifferent or depressed man it seems the opposite."
>
> —Aristotle,
> *The Art of Rhetoric,* 4th century B.C.

THE inside STORY

Shelley Taylor on Positive Illusions

Some years ago, I was conducting interviews with people who had cancer for a study on adjustment to intensely stressful events. I was surprised to learn that, for some people, the cancer experience actually seemed to have brought benefits, as well as the expected liabilities. Many people told me that they thought they were better people for the experience, they felt they were better adjusted to cancer than other people, they believed that they could exert control over their cancer in the future, and they believed their futures would be cancer-free, even when we knew from their medical histories that their cancers were likely to recur.

As a result, I became fascinated by how people can construe even the worst of situations as good, and I've studied these "positive illusions" ever since. Through our research, we learned quickly that you don't have to experience a trauma to demonstrate positive illusions. Most people, including the majority of college students, think of themselves as somewhat better than average, as more in control of the circumstances around them than may actually be true, and as likely to experience more positive future outcomes in life than may be realistic. These illusions are not a sign of maladjustment—quite the contrary. Good mental health may depend on the ability to see things as somewhat better than they are and to find benefits even when things seem most bleak.

Shelley Taylor
UCLA
Courtesy of Shelley Taylor

Stresses challenge some people and defeat others. Researchers have sought to understand the "explanatory style" that makes some people more vulnerable to depression.
Punchstock Uppercut Images

A depressed mood also affects behavior. When depressed, we tend to be withdrawn, glum, and quick to complain. Depressed people are realistic in thinking that others don't appreciate their behavior; their pessimism and bad moods can trigger social rejection (Carver et al., 1994; Strack & Coyne, 1983).

Depressed behavior can also trigger depression in others. College students who have depressed roommates tend to become a little depressed themselves (Burchill & Stiles, 1988; Joiner, 1994; Sanislow et al., 1989). In dating couples, too, depression is often contagious (Katz et al., 1999). Better news comes from a study that followed nearly 5,000 residents of one Massachusetts city for 20 years. Happiness also is contagious. When surrounded by happy people, people often become happier (Fowler & Christakis, 2008).

We can see, then, that being depressed has cognitive and behavioral effects. Does it also work the other way around: Does depression have cognitive *origins?*

NEGATIVE THINKING CAUSES DEPRESSED MOODS. Depression is natural when experiencing severe stress—losing a job, getting divorced or rejected, or suffering any experience that disrupts our sense of who we are and why we are worthy human beings. The brooding that comes with this short-term depression can be adaptive. Much as nausea and pain protect the body from toxins, so depression protects us, by slowing us down, causing us to reassess, and then redirecting our energy in new ways (Andrews & Thomson, 2009, 2010; Watkins, 2008). Insights gained during times of depressed inactivity may later result in better strategies for interacting with the world.

Although all of us may be temporarily depressed by bad events, some people are more enduringly depressed. Depression-prone people respond to bad events with intense rumination and self-blame (Mor & Winquist, 2002; Pyszczynski et al., 1991). Their self-esteem fluctuates more rapidly up with boosts and down with threats (Butler et al., 1994).

Why are some people so affected by *minor* stresses? Evidence suggests that when stress-induced rumination is filtered through a negative explanatory style, the frequent outcome is depression (Robinson & Alloy, 2003). Colin Sacks and Daphne Bugental (1987) asked some young women to get acquainted with a stranger who sometimes acted cold and unfriendly, creating an awkward social situation. Unlike optimistic women, those with a pessimistic explanatory style—who characteristically offer stable, global, and internal attributions for bad events—reacted to the social failure by feeling depressed. Moreover, they then behaved more antagonistically toward the next people they met. Their negative thinking led to a negative mood, which led to negative behavior.

Such depressing rumination is more common among women, reported the late Susan Nolen-Hoeksema (2003). When trouble strikes, men tend to act, women tend to think—and often to "overthink," she observed. And that helps explain why, beginning in adolescence, women worldwide have, compared with men, a nearly doubled risk of depression (Bromet et al., 2011; CDC, 2014).

Outside the laboratory, studies of children, teenagers, and adults confirm that those with the pessimistic explanatory style more often become depressed when bad things happen. One study monitored university students every six weeks for two-and-a-half years (Alloy et al., 1999). One percent of those who began college with optimistic thinking styles had a first depressive episode, as did 17 percent of those with pessimistic thinking styles. "A recipe for severe depression is preexisting pessimism encountering failure," noted Martin Seligman (1991, p. 78).

Researcher Peter Lewinsohn and his colleagues (1985) assembled these findings into a coherent psychological understanding of depression. The negative self-image, attributions, and expectations of a depressed person are, they reported, an essential link in a vicious circle that is triggered by negative experience—perhaps academic or vocational failure, family conflict, or social rejection (Figure 3). Such ruminations cre-

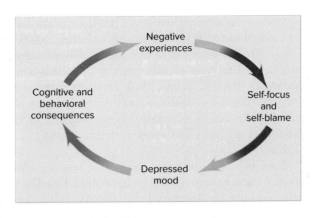

FIGURE :: 3

The Vicious Circle of Depression

ate a depressed mood that alters how a person thinks and acts, which then fuels further negative experiences, self-blame, and depressed mood. In experiments, mildly depressed people's moods brighten when a task diverts their attention to something external (Nix et al., 1995). Depression is therefore *both* a cause and a result of negative cognitions.

Martin Seligman (1991, 1998, 2002) believes that self-focus and self-blame help explain the high levels of depression in today's Western world. He contends that the decline of religion and family, plus the growth of individualism, breeds hopelessness and self-blame when things don't go well. Failed courses, careers, and marriages produce despair when we stand alone, with nothing and no one to fall back on. If, as a macho *Fortune* ad declared, you can "make it on your own," on "your own drive, your own guts, your own energy, your own ambition," then whose fault is it if you *don't* make it? In non-Western cultures, where close-knit relationships and cooperation are the norm, major depression is less common and less tied to guilt and self-blame over perceived personal failure. In Japan, for example, depressed people instead tend to report feeling shame over letting down their family or co-workers (Draguns, 1990).

These insights into the thinking style linked with depression have prompted social psychologists to study thinking patterns associated with other problems. How do those who are plagued with excessive loneliness, shyness, or substance abuse view themselves? How well do they recall their successes and their failures? And to what do they attribute their ups and downs?

Loneliness

If depression is the common cold of psychological disorders, then loneliness is the headache. Loneliness is a painful awareness that our social relationships are less numerous or meaningful than we desire. Social connectedness and identity helps protect people from depression (Cruwys et al., 2014). Yet in modern cultures, close social relationships *are* less numerous. One national survey revealed a one-third drop, over two decades, in the number of people with whom Americans can discuss "important matters." Moreover, the number of Americans living alone is up from 5 percent in the 1920s to 27 percent in 2013 (Henderson, 2014).

Like depression, loneliness is also genetically influenced; identical twins are much more likely than fraternal twins to share moderate to extreme loneliness (Bartels et al., 2008; Boomsma et al., 2006).

FEELING LONELY AND EXCLUDED

But loneliness need not coincide with aloneness. One can feel lonely in the middle of a party. "In America, there is loneliness but no solitude," lamented Mary Pipher (2003). "There are crowds but no community." In Los Angeles, observed her daughter, "There are 10 million people around me but nobody knows my name." Lacking social connections, and feeling lonely (or when made to feel so in an experiment), people may compensate by seeing humanlike qualities in things, animals, and supernatural beings, with which they find companionship (Epley et al., 2008).

One can be utterly alone—as I [DM] am while writing these words in the solitude of an isolated turret office at a British university 5,000 miles from home—without feeling lonely. To feel lonely is to feel excluded from a group, unloved by those around you, unable to share your private concerns, different and alienated from those in your surroundings (Beck & Young, 1978; Davis & Franzoi, 1986). Having lonely acquaintances increases the chance that you feel lonely (Cacioppo et al., 2009). Loneliness tends to run in social clusters, as its negative thoughts and behaviors spread. Small wonder, then, that loneliness increases one's risk of future depression, pain, and fatigue (Jaremka et al., 2013).

Loneliness also increases the risk of health problems. Loneliness affects stress hormones, immune activity, and inflammation. Loneliness therefore puts people at increased risk not only for depression and suicide, but also high blood pressure, heart disease, cognitive decline, and sleep impairment (Cacioppo et al., 2014). A digest of data from more than 300,000 people in 148 studies showed that social isolation increased the risk of death about as much as smoking, and more than obesity or inactivity (Holt-Lunstad et al., 2010). Even brief social contacts—small talk with neighbors or Facebook connections—can decrease loneliness and its health risks (Deters & Mehl, 2013; Steptoe et al., 2013).

Loneliness—which may be evoked by an icy stare or a cold shoulder—feels, quite literally, cold. When recalling an experience of exclusion, people estimate a lower room temperature than when thinking of being included. After being excluded in a little ball game, people show a heightened preference for warm foods and drinks (Zhong & Leonardelli, 2008).

Such feelings can be adaptive. Loneliness signals people to seek social connections, which facilitate survival. Even when loneliness triggers nostalgia—a longing for the past—it serves to remind people of their social connections (Zhou et al., 2008).

PERCEIVING OTHERS NEGATIVELY

Like depressed people, chronically lonely people seem caught in a vicious circle of self-defeating social thinking and social behaviors. They have some of the negative explanatory style of the depressed; they perceive their interactions as making a poor impression, blame themselves for their poor social relationships, and see most things as beyond their control (Anderson et al., 1994; Christensen & Kashy, 1998; Snodgrass, 1987). Moreover, they perceive others in negative ways. When paired with a stranger of the same gender or with a first-year college roommate, lonely students are more likely to perceive the other person negatively (Jones et al., 1981; Wittenberg & Reis, 1986). Ironically, report Danu Stinson and her co-researchers (2011), socially insecure people therefore often behave in ways that produce the very social rejection they fear. As Figure 4 illustrates, loneliness, depression, and shyness sometimes feed one another.

These negative views may both reflect and color the lonely person's experience. Believing in their social unworthiness and feeling pessimistic about others inhibit lonely people from acting to reduce their loneliness. Lonely people often find it hard to introduce themselves, make phone calls, and participate in groups

FIGURE :: 4

The Interplay of Chronic Shyness, Loneliness, and Depression

Solid arrows indicate primary cause-effect direction, as summarized by Jody Dill and Craig Anderson (1999). Dotted lines indicate additional effects.

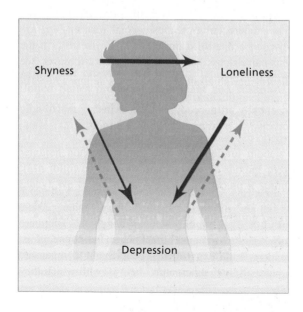

(Nurmi et al., 1996, 1997; Rook, 1984; Spitzberg & Hurt, 1987). Yet, like mildly depressed people, they are attuned to others and skilled at recognizing emotional expression (Gardner et al., 2005).

Anxiety and Shyness

Shyness is social anxiety marked by self-consciousness and worry about what others think (Anderson & Harvey, 1988; Asendorpf, 1987; Carver & Scheier, 1986). Being interviewed for a much-wanted job, dating someone for the first time, stepping into a roomful of strangers, performing before an important audience, or giving a speech (one of the most common phobias) can make almost anyone feel anxious. But some people feel anxious in almost any situation in which they may feel they are being evaluated, even having lunch with a co-worker. For these people, anxiety is more a personality trait than a temporary state.

Shyness (self-consciousness in social situations) is a form of social anxiety.
INGKUYKL0352-Ingram Publishing

DOUBTING OUR ABILITY IN SOCIAL SITUATIONS

What causes us to feel anxious in social situations? Why are some people shackled in the prison of their own social anxiety? Barry Schlenker and Mark Leary (1982, 1985; Leary & Kowalski, 1995) answer those questions by applying self-presentation theory. Self-presentation theory assumes that we are eager to present ourselves in ways that make a good impression. Thus, *we feel social anxiety when we are motivated to impress others but have self-doubts.* This simple principle helps explain a variety of research findings, each of which may ring true in your experience. We feel most anxious when we are

- with powerful, high-status people—people whose impressions of us matter.
- in an evaluative context, such as when making a first interview.
- self-conscious (as shy people often are), with our attention focused on ourselves and how we are coming across.
- focused on something central to our self-image, as when a college professor presents research before peers at a professional convention.
- in novel or unstructured situations, such as a first school dance or first formal dinner, where we are unsure of the social rules.

For most people, the tendency in all such situations is to be cautiously self-protective: to talk less; to avoid topics that reveal one's ignorance; to be guarded about oneself; to be unassertive, agreeable, and smiling. Ironically, such anxious concern with making a good impression often makes a bad impression (Broome & Wegner, 1994; Meleshko & Alden, 1993). With time, however, shy people often become well liked. Their lack of egotism, their modesty, sensitivity, and discretion wear well (Gough & Thorne, 1986; Paulhus & Morgan, 1997; Shepperd et al., 1995).

OVERPERSONALIZING SITUATIONS

Compared with unshy people, shy, self-conscious people (whose numbers include many adolescents) see incidental events as somehow relevant to themselves (Fenigstein, 1984; Fenigstein & Vanable, 1992). Shy, anxious people overpersonalize situations, a tendency that breeds anxious concern and, in extreme cases,

When a person is eager to impress important people, social anxiety is natural.
Shannon Fagan/Image Source

paranoia. They are especially prone to "the spotlight effect"—they overestimate the extent to which other people are watching and evaluating them. If their hair won't comb right or they have a facial blemish, they assume everyone else notices and judges them accordingly. Shy people may even be conscious of their self-consciousness. They wish they could stop worrying about blushing, about what others are thinking, or about what to say next.

To reduce social anxiety, some people turn to alcohol. Alcohol lowers anxiety and reduces self-consciousness (Hull & Young, 1983). Thus, chronically self-conscious people are especially likely to drink following a failure. If recovering from alcoholism, they are more likely than those low in self-consciousness to relapse when they again experience stress or failure.

Symptoms as diverse as anxiety and alcohol abuse can serve a self-handicapping function. Labeling oneself as anxious, shy, depressed, or under the influence of alcohol can provide an excuse for failure (Snyder & Smith, 1986). Behind a barricade of symptoms, the person's ego stands secure. "Why don't I date? Because I'm shy, so people don't easily get to know the real me." The symptom is an unconscious strategic ploy to explain away negative outcomes.

What if we were to remove the need for such a ploy by providing people with a handy alternative explanation for their anxiety and therefore for possible failure? Would a shy person no longer need to be shy? That is precisely what Susan Brodt and Philip Zimbardo (1981) found when they brought shy and not-shy college women to the laboratory and had them converse with a handsome male who posed as another participant. Before the conversation, the women were cooped up in a small chamber and blasted with loud noise. Some of the shy women (but not others) were told that the noise would leave them with a pounding heart, a common symptom of social anxiety. Thus, when these women later talked with the man, they could attribute their pounding hearts and any conversational difficulties to the noise, not to their shyness or social inadequacy. Compared with the shy women who were not given this handy explanation for their pounding hearts, these women were no longer so shy. They talked fluently once the conversation got going and asked questions of the man. In fact, unlike the other shy women (whom the man could easily spot as shy), these women were to him indistinguishable from the not-shy women.

Health, Illness, and Death

In the industrialized world, at least half of all deaths are linked with behavior—with consuming cigarettes, alcohol, drugs, and harmful foods; with reactions to stress; with lack of exercise and not following a doctor's advice. The interdisciplinary field of **behavioral medicine** studies these behavioral contributions to illness. Psychology's contribution to this interdisciplinary science is its subfield, **health psychology.** Health psychologists study how people respond to illness symptoms and how emotions and explanations influence health.

REACTIONS TO ILLNESS

How do people decide whether they are ill? How do they explain their symptoms? What influences their willingness to seek and follow treatment?

NOTICING SYMPTOMS.   Chances are you have recently experienced at least one of these physical complaints: headache, stomachache, nasal congestion, sore muscles, ringing in the ears, excess perspiration, cold hands, racing heart, dizziness, stiff joints, and diarrhea or constipation (Pennebaker, 1982). Are such symptoms meaningless? Or are you coming down with something that requires medical attention? Hardly a week goes by without our playing doctor by self-diagnosing some symptom.

Noticing and interpreting our body's signals is like noticing and interpreting how a car is running. Most of us cannot tell whether a car needs an oil change merely by listening to its engine. Similarly, most of us are not astute judges of our heart rate, blood-sugar level, or

behavioral medicine
An interdisciplinary field that integrates and applies behavioral and medical knowledge about health and disease.

health psychology
The study of the psychological roots of health and illness. Offers psychology's contribution to behavioral medicine.

blood pressure. People guess their blood pressure based on how they feel, which often is unrelated to their actual blood pressure (Baumann & Leventhal, 1985). Furthermore, the early signs of many illnesses, including cancer and heart disease, are subtle and easy to miss.

EXPLAINING SYMPTOMS: AM I SICK?   With more serious aches and pains, the questions become more specific—and more critical. Does the small cyst match our idea of a malignant lump? Is the abdominal ache bad enough to be appendicitis? Is the pain in the chest area merely—as many heart attack victims suppose—a muscle spasm? Indeed, reports the National Institutes of Health, most heart attack victims wait too long before seeking medical help. What factors influence how we explain symptoms?

After we notice symptoms, we interpret them using familiar disease schemas (Bishop, 1991). In medical schools, this can have amusing results. As part of their training, medical students learn the symptoms associated with various diseases. Because they also experience various symptoms, they sometimes attribute their symptoms to recently learned disease schemas. ("Maybe this wheeze is the beginning of pneumonia.") Psychology students (as you may have experienced) are likewise prone to this effect as they read about psychological disorders.

DO I NEED TREATMENT?   When people notice a symptom and interpret it as possibly serious, several factors influence their decision to seek medical care. People more often seek treatment if they believe their symptoms have a physical rather than a psychological cause (Bishop, 1987). They may delay seeking help, however, if they feel embarrassed, if they think the likely benefits of medical attention won't justify the cost and inconvenience, or if they want to avoid a possibly devastating diagnosis.

The U.S. National Center for Health Statistics (NCHS) reports a gender difference in decisions to seek medical treatment: Compared with men, women report more symptoms, use more prescription and nonprescription drugs, and visit physicians 67 percent more often for preventive care (NCHS, 2008, 2010). Women also visit psychotherapists 50 percent more often (Olfson & Pincus, 1994).

So, are women more often sick? Apparently not. In fact, men may be more disease prone. Among other problems, men have higher rates of hypertension, ulcers, and cancer, as well as shorter life expectancies. So why are women more likely to see a doctor? Perhaps women are more attentive to their internal states. Perhaps they are less reluctant to admit "weakness" and seek help (Bishop, 1984).

Patients are more willing to follow treatment instructions when they have warm relationships with their doctors, when they help plan their treatment, and when options are framed attractively. People are more likely to elect an operation when given "a 40 percent chance of surviving" than when given "a 60 percent chance of not surviving" (Rothman & Salovey, 1997; Wilson et al., 1987). Such "gainframed" messages also persuade more people to use sunscreen, eschew cigarettes, and get HIV tests (Detweiler et al., 1999; Salovey et al., 2002; Schneider et al., 2000). Better to tell people that "sunscreen maintains healthy, young-looking skin" than to tell them that "not using sunscreen decreases your chances of healthy, young-looking skin." Framing a desired exercise program as minutes per day, rather than hours per week, similarly increases people's willingness to commit to it (Peetz et al., 2011).

EMOTIONS AND ILLNESS

Do our emotions predict our susceptibility to heart disease, stroke, cancer, and other ailments (Figure 5)? Consider the following.

Heart disease has been linked with a competitive, impatient, and—the aspect that matters most—*anger-prone* personality (Chida & Steptoe, 2009; Kupper & Denollet, 2007). Under stress, reactive, anger-prone "Type A" people secrete more of the stress hormones believed to accelerate the buildup of plaque in the heart's arteries.

Depression also increases the risk of various ailments. Depressed people are more vulnerable to heart disease, even after controlling for differences in smoking and other disease-related factors (Boehm et al., 2011; Whang et al., 2009). The year after a heart attack, depressed people have a doubled risk of further heart problems

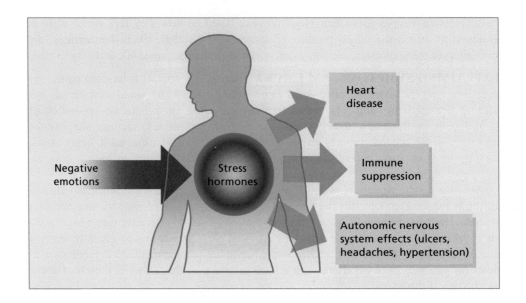

(Frasure-Smith et al., 1995, 1999, 2005). The association between depression and heart disease may result from stress-related inflammation of the arteries (O'Donovan et al., 2012). Stress hormones enhance protein production that contributes to inflammation, which helps fight infections. But inflammation also can exacerbate asthma, clogged arteries, and depression. The bottom line: Anger, depression, and stress are heartfelt emotions.

George Vaillant (1997) witnessed the effect of distress when he followed a group of male Harvard alumni from midlife (age 52) into old age. Of those who never abused alcohol, used tranquilizers, or saw a psychiatrist, only 5 percent had died by age 75. Of those who had done any of the three, 38 percent had died.

OPTIMISM AND HEALTH

Stories abound of people who take a sudden turn for the worse when something makes them lose hope, or who suddenly improve when hope is renewed. As cancer attacks the liver of 9-year-old Jeff, his doctors fear the worst. But Jeff remains optimistic. He is determined to grow up to be a cancer research scientist. One day Jeff is elated. A specialist who has taken a long-distance interest in his case is planning to stop off while on a cross-country trip. There is so much Jeff wants to tell the doctor and to show him from the diary he has kept since he got sick. On the anticipated day, fog blankets his city. The doctor's plane is diverted to another city, from which the doctor flies on to his final destination. Hearing the news, Jeff cries quietly. The next morning, pneumonia and fever have developed, and Jeff lies listless. By evening he is in a coma. The next afternoon he dies (Visintainer & Seligman, 1983).

Understanding the links between attitudes and disease requires more than dramatic true stories. If hopelessness coincides with cancer, we are left to wonder: Does cancer breed hopelessness, or does hopelessness also hinder resistance to cancer? To resolve this chicken-and-egg riddle, researchers have (1) experimentally created hopelessness by subjecting organisms to uncontrollable stresses and (2) correlated a hopeless explanatory style with future illnesses.

STRESS AND ILLNESS. The clearest indication of the effects of hopelessness—*learned helplessness*—comes from experiments that subject animals to mild but uncontrollable electric shocks, loud noises, or crowding. Such experiences do not cause diseases such as cancer, but they do lower the body's resistance. Rats injected with live cancer cells more often develop and die of tumors if they also receive inescapable shocks (rather than escapable shocks or no shocks). Moreover, compared with juvenile rats given controllable shocks, those given uncontrollable shocks are twice as likely in adulthood to develop tumors if given cancer cells and another round of shocks (Visintainer & Seligman, 1985). Animals that have learned helplessness react more passively, and blood tests reveal a weakened immune response.

It's a big leap from rats to humans. But a growing body of evidence reveals that people who undergo highly stressful experiences become more vulnerable to disease (Segerstrom & Miller, 2004). Stress doesn't make us sick, but it does divert energy from our disease-fighting immune system, leaving us more vulnerable to infections and malignancy (Cohen, 2002, 2004). The death of a spouse, the stress of a space flight landing, even the strain of an exam week have all been associated with depressed immune defenses (Jemmott & Locke, 1984).

Consider the following:

- Stress magnifies the severity of respiratory infections and of symptoms experienced by volunteers who are knowingly infected with a cold virus (Cohen et al., 2003, 2006, 2012; Pedersen et al., 2010).

- Newlywed couples who became angry while discussing problems suffered more immune system suppression the next day (Kiecolt-Glaser et al., 1993). When people are stressed by marital conflict, laboratory puncture wounds take a day or two longer to heal (Kiecolt-Glaser et al., 2005). Studies in eleven countries following 6.5 million lives through time reveal that, among men and younger adults, divorce increases the ensuing risk of early death (Sbarra et al., 2011).

- Work stress can literally be disheartening. In one study that followed 17,415 middle-aged American women, researchers found that significant work stress predicted an 88 percent increased risk of heart attacks (Slopen et al., 2010). In Denmark, a study of 12,116 female nurses found that those reporting "much too high" work pressures had a 40 percent increased risk of heart disease (Allesøe et al., 2010).

- Stress increases the production of inflammation-producing proteins. Those who experience social stress, including children reared in abusive families, are therefore more prone to inflammation responses (Dickerson et al., 2009; Miller et al., 2011). Inflammation fights infections, but persistent inflammation contributes to asthma, clogged arteries, and depression. Researchers have even discovered molecular, "epigenetic" mechanisms by which stress, in some people, activates genes that control inflammation (Cole et al., 2010).

EXPLANATORY STYLE AND ILLNESS. If uncontrollable stress affects health, depresses immune functioning, increases inflammation, and generates a passive, hopeless resignation, then will people who exhibit such pessimism be more vulnerable to illness? Indeed, a pessimistic style of explaining bad events (saying, "It's going to last, it's going to undermine everything, and it's my fault") makes illness more likely (Carver et al., 2010). Christopher Peterson and Martin Seligman (1987) studied the press quotations of 94 members of baseball's Hall of Fame and gauged how often they offered pessimistic (stable, global, internal) explanations for bad events, such as losing big games. Those who routinely did so tended to die at somewhat younger ages. Optimists—who offered stable, global, and internal explanations for *good* events— usually outlived the pessimists.

Other studies have followed lives through time:

- Harvard graduates who expressed the most optimism in 1946 were the healthiest when restudied 34 years later (Peterson et al., 1988).

- One Dutch research team followed 941 older adults for nearly a decade (Giltay et al., 2004, 2007). Among those in the upper optimism quartile only 30 percent died, compared with 57 percent of those in the lower optimism quartile.

- Catholic nuns who expressed the most positive feelings at an average age of 22 outlived their more dour counterparts by an average 7 years over the ensuing half-century and more (Danner et al., 2001).

The Delany sisters, who lived to 104 and 106, attributed their longevity to a positive outlook on life.
Marianne Barcellona/Getty Images

The healing power of positive belief is evident in the well-known *placebo effect,* referring to the healing power of *believing* that one is getting an effective treatment. (If you *think* a treatment is going to be effective, it just may be—even if it's actually inert.) But every silver lining has a cloud. Optimists may see themselves as invulnerable and thus fail to take sensible precautions; for example, those who smoke cigarettes optimistically underestimate the risks involved (Segerstrom et al., 1993). And when things go wrong in a big way—when the optimist encounters a devastating illness—adversity can be shattering. Optimism is good for health. But even optimists have a mortality rate of 100 percent.

SUMMING UP: What Cognitive Processes Accompany Behavior Problems?

- Social psychologists are actively exploring the attributions and expectations of depressed, lonely, socially anxious, and physically ill people. Depressed people have a negative *explanatory style,* interpreting negative events as being stable, global, and internally caused. Despite their more negative judgments, mildly depressed people in laboratory tests tend to be surprisingly realistic. Depression can be a vicious circle in which negative thoughts elicit self-defeating behaviors, and vice versa.

- Loneliness involves feelings of isolation or not fitting in, and is common in individualistic societies. Like depression, it can be a vicious circle in which feelings of aloofness lead to socially undesirable behaviors.

- Most people experience anxiety in situations where they are being evaluated, but shy individuals are extremely prone to anxiety even in friendly, casual situations. This can be another vicious circle in which anxious feelings elicit awkward, off-putting behavior.

- The mushrooming field of *health psychology* is exploring how people decide they are ill, how they explain their symptoms, and when they seek and follow treatment. It also is exploring the effects of negative emotions and the links among illness, stress, and a pessimistic explanatory style.

WHAT ARE SOME SOCIAL-PSYCHOLOGICAL APPROACHES TO TREATMENT?

Describe treatments that aim to undo the maladaptive thought patterns we have considered to be linked with problems ranging from serious depression to extreme shyness to physical illness.

There is no social-psychological therapy. But therapy is a social encounter, and social psychologists have suggested how their principles might be integrated into existing treatment techniques (Forsyth & Leary, 1997; Strong et al., 1992). Consider three approaches:

- To promote internal changes, change one's external behavior.
- Break negative, self-defeating thought-behavior cycles.
- Attribute improvements to one's own self-control, rather than the treatment.

Inducing Internal Change Through External Behavior

Our actions affect our attitudes. The roles we play, the things we say and do, and the decisions we make influence who we are.

Consistent with this attitudes-follow-behavior principle, several psychotherapy techniques prescribe action:

- Behavior therapists try to shape behavior on the theory that the client's inner disposition will also change after the behavior changes.
- Across varied studies, people who were asked to publicly advocate some healthy behavior (such as exercise or restrained eating and drinking) experienced dissonance—and later changed their behavior—when reminded of their own past behaviors (Freijy & Kothe, 2013).
- In assertiveness training, the individual may first role-play assertiveness in a supportive context, then gradually implement assertive behaviors in everyday life.
- Rational-emotive therapy assumes that we generate our own emotions; clients receive "homework" assignments to talk and act in new ways that will generate new emotions: Challenge that overbearing relative. Stop telling yourself you're an unattractive person and ask someone out.
- Self-help groups subtly induce participants to behave in new ways in front of the group—to express anger, cry, act with high self-esteem, express positive feelings.

All these techniques share a common assumption: If we cannot directly control our feelings by sheer willpower, we can influence them indirectly through our behavior.

Experiments confirm that what we say about ourselves can affect how we feel. Those engaged in doing kind acts over a 4-week period become happier (Alden & Trew, 2013). Those induced to present themselves in self-enhancing (rather than self-deprecating) ways later feel better about themselves (Jones et al., 1981; Rhodewalt & Agustsdottir, 1986). Public displays—whether upbeat or downbeat—carry over to later self-esteem. Saying is believing, even when we talk about ourselves.

In this experiment and many others, people internalized their behavior most when they perceive some choice. For example, Pamela Mendonca and Sharon Brehm (1983) invited one group of overweight children who were about to begin a weight-loss program to choose the treatment they preferred. Then they reminded them periodically that they had chosen their treatment. Other children who simultaneously experienced the same 8-week program were given no choice. Those who felt responsible for their treatment had lost more weight both at the end of the 8-week program and 3 months later.

Breaking Vicious Circles

If depression, loneliness, and social anxiety maintain themselves through a vicious circle of negative experiences, negative thinking, and self-defeating behavior, it should be possible to break the circle at any of several points—by changing the environment, by training the person to behave more constructively, or by reversing negative thinking. And it is. Several therapy methods help free people from depression's vicious circle.

SOCIAL SKILLS TRAINING

Depression, loneliness, and shyness are not just problems in someone's mind. Being around a depressed person can be irritating and depressing. As lonely and shy people suspect, they may indeed come across poorly in social situations. How ironic that the more that self-preoccupied people seek to make a good impression, the more their effort may backfire (Lun et al., 2011). Those who instead focus on supporting others often enjoy others' regard in return.

In these cases, social skills training may help. By observing and then practicing new behaviors in safe situations, the person may develop the confidence to behave more effectively in other situations. As the person begins to enjoy the rewards of behaving more skillfully, a more positive self-perception develops. Frances Haemmerlie and Robert Montgomery (1982, 1984, 1986) demonstrated this in several heartwarming studies with shy, anxious college students. Those who are inexperienced and nervous around those of the other sex may say to themselves, "I don't date much, so I must be socially inadequate, so I shouldn't try reaching out to anyone." To reverse this negative sequence, Haemmerlie and Montgomery enticed such students into pleasant interactions with people of the other sex.

In one experiment, college men completed social anxiety questionnaires and then came to the laboratory on two different days. Each day they enjoyed 12-minute conversations with each of six young women. The men thought the women were also participants. Actually, the women were confederates who had been asked to carry on a natural, positive, friendly conversation with each of the men.

The effect of these two-and-a-half hours of conversation was remarkable. As one participant wrote afterward, "I had never met so many girls that I could have a good conversation with. After a few girls, my confidence grew to the point where I didn't notice being nervous like I once did." Such comments were supported by a variety of measures. Unlike men in a control condition, those who experienced the conversations reported considerably less female-related anxiety when retested one week and six months later. Placed alone in a room with an attractive female stranger, they also became much more likely to start a conversation. Outside the laboratory they began dating occasionally.

Haemmerlie and Montgomery note that not only did all this occur without any counseling, it may very well have occurred *because* there was no counseling. Having behaved successfully on their own, the men could now perceive themselves as socially competent. Although 7 months later the researchers did debrief the participants, by that time the men had presumably enjoyed enough social success to maintain their internal attributions for success. "Nothing succeeds like success," concluded Haemmerlie (1987)—"as long as there are no external factors present that the client can use as an excuse for that success!"

EXPLANATORY STYLE THERAPY

The vicious circles that maintain depression, loneliness, and shyness can be broken by social skills training, by positive experiences that alter self-perceptions, *and* by changing negative thought patterns. Some people have good social skills, but their experiences with hypercritical friends and family have convinced them otherwise. For such people it may be enough to help them reverse their negative beliefs about themselves and their futures.

Among the cognitive therapies with this aim is an *explanatory style therapy* proposed by social psychologists (Abramson, 1988; Gillham et al., 2000; Masi et al., 2011).

One such program taught depressed college students to change their typical attributions. Mary Anne Layden (1982) first described the advantages of explaining outcomes as does the typical nondepressed person (by accepting credit for successes and seeing how circumstances can make things go wrong). After assigning a variety of tasks, she helped the students see how they typically interpreted success and failure. Then came the treatment phase: Layden instructed them to keep a diary of daily successes and failures, noting how they contributed to their own successes and noting external reasons for their failures. When retested after a month of this attributional retraining and compared with an untreated control group, their self-esteem had risen and their attributional style had become more positive. The more their explanatory style improved, the more their depression lifted. By changing their attributions, they had changed their emotions.

Maintaining Change Through Internal Attributions for Success

Two of the principles considered so far—that internal change may follow behavior change and that changed self-perceptions and self-attributions can help break a vicious circle—converge on a corollary principle: After improvement is achieved, it endures best if people attribute it to factors under their own control rather than to a treatment program.

As a rule, coercive techniques trigger the most dramatic and immediate behavior changes (Brehm & Smith, 1986). By making the unwanted behavior extremely costly or embarrassing and the healthier behavior extremely rewarding, a therapist may achieve impressive results. The problem, as 50 years of social-psychological research reminds us, is that coerced changes in behavior soon wane.

Consider the experience of Marta, who is concerned with her mild obesity and frustrated with her inability to do anything about it. Marta is considering several commercial weight-control programs. Each claims it achieves the best results. She chooses one and is ordered onto a strict 1,200-calorie-a-day diet. Moreover, she is required to record and report her calorie intake each day and to come in once a week and be weighed so she and her instructor can know precisely how she is doing. Confident of the program's value and not wanting to embarrass herself, Marta adheres to the program and is delighted to find the unwanted pounds gradually disappearing. As she reaches her target weight, Marta thinks, "This unique program really does work!"

Sadly, however, after graduating from the program, Marta experiences the fate of most weight-control graduates (Jeffery et al., 2000): She regains the lost weight. On the street, she sees her instructor approaching. Embarrassed, she moves to the other side of the sidewalk and looks away. Alas, she is recognized by the instructor, who warmly invites her back into "the program." Admitting that the program achieved good results for her the first time, Marta grants her need of it and agrees to return, beginning a second round of yo-yo dieting.

Marta's experience typifies that of the participants in several weight-control experiments, including one by Janet Sonne and Dean Janoff (1979). Half the participants were led, like Marta, to attribute their changed eating behavior to the program. The others were led to credit their own efforts. Both groups lost weight during the program. But when reweighed 11 weeks later, those in the self-control condition had maintained the weight loss better. These people, like those in the shy-man-meets-women study described earlier, illustrate the benefits of self-efficacy. Having learned to cope successfully and believing that *they did it,* they felt more confident and were more effective.

Having emphasized what changed behavior and thought patterns can accomplish, we do well to remind ourselves of their limits. Social skills training and positive thinking cannot transform us into consistent winners who are always loved and admired. Bad things will still happen, and temporary depression, loneliness, and shyness are perfectly appropriate responses to bad events. It is when such feelings exist chronically and without any discernible cause that there is reason for concern and a need to change the self-defeating thoughts and behaviors.

Using Therapy as Social Influence

Psychologists more and more accept the idea that social influence—one person affecting another—is at the heart of therapy. Stanley Strong (1991) offered a prototypical example: A thirtyish woman comes to a therapist complaining of depression. The therapist gently probes her feelings and her situation. She explains her helplessness and her husband's demands. Although admiring her devotion, the therapist helps her see how she takes responsibility for her husband's problems. She protests. But the therapist persists. In time, she realizes that her husband may not be as fragile as she presumed. She begins to see how she can respect both her husband and herself. With the therapist, she plans strategies for each new week. At the end of a long stream of reciprocal influences between therapist and client, she emerges no longer depressed and equipped with new ways of behaving.

Analyses of psychotherapeutic influence have focused on how therapists establish credible expertise and trustworthiness, how their credibility enhances their influence, and how the interaction affects the client's thinking (McNeill & Stoltenberg, 1988; Neimeyer et al., 1991; Strong, 1968). Peripheral cues, such as therapist credibility, may open the door for ideas that the therapist can now get the client to think about. But the thoughtful central route to persuasion provides the most enduring attitude and behavior change. Therapists should therefore aim not to elicit a client's superficial agreement with their expert judgment but to change the client's own thinking.

Fortunately, most clients entering therapy are motivated to take the central route—to think deeply about their problems under the therapist's guidance. The therapist's task is to offer arguments and raise questions that elicit favorable thoughts. The therapist's insights matter less than the thoughts they evoke in the client. Questions such as "How do you respond to what I just said?" can stimulate the client's thinking.

Martin Heesacker (1989) illustrated how a therapist can help a client reflect with the case of Dave, a 35-year-old male graduate student. Having seen what Dave denied—an underlying substance abuse problem—the counselor drew on his knowledge of Dave, an intellectual person who liked hard evidence, in persuading him to accept the diagnosis and join a treatment-support group. The counselor said, "OK, if my diagnosis is wrong, I'll be glad to change it. But let's go through a list of the characteristics of a substance abuser to check out my accuracy." The counselor then went through each criterion slowly, giving Dave time to think about each point. As he finished, Dave sat back and exclaimed, "I don't believe it: I'm a damned alcoholic."

In his 1620 *Pensées*, the philosopher Pascal foresaw this principle: "People are usually more convinced by reasons they discover themselves than by those found by others." It's a principle worth remembering.

SUMMING UP: What Are Some Social-Psychological Approaches to Treatment?

- Changes in external behavior can trigger internal change.

- A self-defeating cycle of negative attitudes and behaviors can be broken by training more skillful behavior, by positive experiences that alter self-perceptions, and by changing negative thought patterns.

- Improved states are best maintained after treatment if people attribute their improvement to internal factors under their continued control rather than to the treatment program itself.

- Mental health workers also are recognizing that changing clients' attitudes and behaviors requires persuasion. Therapists, aided by their image as expert, trustworthy communicators, aim to stimulate healthier thinking by offering cogent arguments and raising questions.

HOW DO SOCIAL RELATIONSHIPS SUPPORT HEALTH AND WELL-BEING?

Identify evidence suggesting that supportive, close relationships—feeling liked, affirmed, and encouraged by intimate friends and family—predict both health and happiness.

Our relationships are fraught with stress. "Hell is others," wrote Jean-Paul Sartre. When Peter Warr and Roy Payne (1982) asked a representative sample of British adults what, if anything, had emotionally strained them the day before, "family" was their most frequent answer. And stress, as we have seen, aggravates health problems such as coronary heart disease, hypertension, and suppression of our disease-fighting immune system.

Still, on balance, close relationships are more likely to lead to health and happiness than to illness. Asked what prompted yesterday's times of pleasure, the same British sample, by an even larger margin, again answered "family." Close relationships provide our greatest heartaches, but also our greatest joys. As social animals, people need people.

Close Relationships and Health

Extensive investigations, each interviewing thousands of people across years, have reached a common conclusion: Close relationships predict health (Berkman, 1995; Pantell et al., 2013; Ryff & Singer, 2000). In one digest of 148 studies worldwide, researchers found that social connections predicted longer life. Those with ample social connections had survival rates (across the average 7.5-year study period) about 50 percent greater than those with meager connections (Holt-Lunstad et al., 2010).

Health risks are greater among lonely people, who often experience more stress, sleep less well, and are more likely to commit suicide (Cacioppo & Patrick, 2008). Compared with those who have few social ties, those who have close relationships with friends, kin, or other members of close-knit religious or community organizations are less likely to die prematurely. "It takes a village to raise a centenarian," notes Susan Pinker (2014). "Longevity is a team sport."

Across 139 countries worldwide, people who "have friends or family you can count on" are also much more likely to report being satisfied with their personal health (Kumar et al., 2012). In experiments, highly sociable people are even less susceptible to cold viruses (Figure 6; Cohen et al., 1997, 2003).

Married people likewise tend to live healthier, longer lives than their unmarried counterparts. The National Center for Health Statistics (2004) reports that people, regardless of age, sex, race, and income, tend to be healthier if married. Married folks experience less pain from headaches and backaches, suffer less stress, and drink and smoke less. One experiment subjected married women to the threat of electric ankle shocks as they lay in an fMRI brain scanning machine (Coan et al., 2006). Meanwhile, some of the women held their husband's hand, some held an anonymous person's hand, and some held no hand at all. While awaiting the shocks, the threat-responsive areas of the women's brains were less active if they held their husband's hand. Consistent with findings that it's happy and supportive marriages that are conducive to health (De Vogli et al., 2007), the soothing hand-holding benefit was greatest for those reporting the happiest marriages.

More than marriage per se, it's marital *quality* that predicts health. One study found that at age 50, a person's good marriage predicted healthy aging better than did low cholesterol level (Vaillant, 2002). And divorce increases risk of ill health, as evident in 32 studies of 6.5 million people (Sbarra et al., 2011). A recent summary of all available research concluded that the association between marriage quality and physical health "is

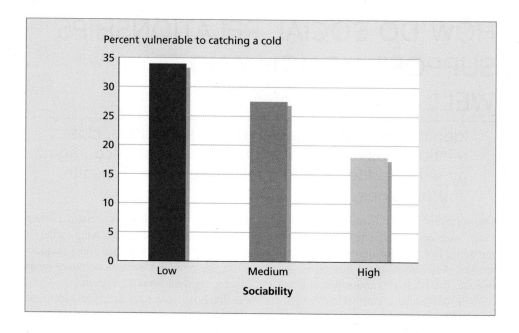

similar in size to associations between health behaviors (diet, physical activity) and health
outcomes" (Robles, 2015; Robles, et al., 2014). Moreover, over time, marital quality predicts future health (rather than the reverse).

But why? What mediates and explains an effect of marriage quality on health? Theodore Robles and others offer some possibilities:

- *Biological* mediators: our cardiovascular, hormonal, and immune systems respond
  to marital strain (Uchino et al., 2014). By contrast, social support calms us and
  reduces stress (Hostinar et al., 2014).
- *Social-cognitive* mediators: how spouses think about each other influences their
  emotional control and their anxiety and sadness.
- *Health* mediators: social support promotes healthier eating and better sleep,
  whereas marital tension increases unhealthy eating and substance use.

Giving social support also helps. In one five-year study of 423 elderly married couples,
those who gave the most social support (from rides and errands for friends and neighbors
to emotional support of their spouse) enjoyed greater longevity, even after controlling for
age, sex, initial health, and economic status (Brown et al., 2003). Especially among women,
suggests a Finnish study that tracked more than 700 people's illnesses, it is better to give
than only to receive (Väänänen et al., 2005).

Moreover, losing social ties heightens the risk of disease:

- A Finnish study of 96,000 newly widowed people found their risk of death
  doubled in the week following their partner's death (Kaprio et al., 1987).
- A National Academy of Sciences study revealed that recently widowed people
  become more vulnerable to disease and death (Dohrenwend et al., 1982).
- A study of 30,000 men revealed that when a marriage ends, men drink and smoke
  more and eat fewer vegetables and more fried foods (Eng et al., 2001).

CONFIDING AND HEALTH

So there is a link between social support and health. Why? Perhaps those who enjoy close
relationships eat better, exercise more, and smoke and drink less. Perhaps friends and
family help bolster our self-esteem. Perhaps a supportive network helps us evaluate and
overcome stressful events (Taylor et al., 1997). In more than 80 studies, social support has
been linked with better-functioning cardiovascular and immune systems (Uchino et al.,
1996). Thus, when we are wounded by someone's dislike or the loss of a job, a friend's

advice, help, and reassurance may indeed be good medicine (Cutrona, 1986; Rook, 1987). Even when the problem isn't mentioned, friends provide us with distraction and a sense that we're accepted, liked, and respected.

With someone we consider a close friend, we also may confide painful feelings. In one study, James Pennebaker and Robin O'Heeron (1984) contacted the surviving spouses of suicide or car accident victims. Those who bore their grief alone had more health problems than those who expressed it openly. When Pennebaker (1990) surveyed more than 700 college women, he found 1 in 12 reported a traumatic sexual experience in childhood. Compared with women who had experienced nonsexual traumas, such as parental death or divorce, the sexually abused women reported more headaches, stomach ailments, and other health problems, *especially if they had kept their abuse history secret.*

To isolate the confiding, confessional side of close relationships, Pennebaker asked the bereaved spouses to relate the upsetting events that had been preying on their minds. Those they first asked to describe a trivial event were physically tense. They stayed tense until they confided their troubles. Then they relaxed. Writing about personal traumas in a journal also seems to help. When volunteers in another experiment did so, they had fewer health problems during the next six months. One participant explained, "Although I have not talked with anyone about what I wrote, I was finally able to deal with it, work through the pain instead of trying to block it out. Now it doesn't hurt to think about it." Even if it's only "talking to my diary," and even if the writing is about one's future dreams and life goals, it helps to be able to confide (Burton & King, 2008; Lyubomirsky et al., 2006). In one experiment, writing therapy was as effective for 633 trauma victims as psychotherapy (van Emmerick et al., 2013). In everyday life, self-disclosures—when public and to accepting people—are healing (Kelly & Macready, 2009).

POVERTY, INEQUALITY, AND HEALTH

We have seen connections between health and a positive explanatory style. And we have seen connections between health and social support. Positive thinking and support together with health care and nutritional factors help explain why economic status correlates with longevity. In Scotland, the United States, Canada, and elsewhere, poorer people are at

> "Friendship is a sovereign antidote against all calamities."
> —Seneca, 5 B.C.–A.D. 65

Wealthy and healthy. A 2008 *Scotsman* article illustrated the striking disparity in life expectancy in lower-income Calton, on the east end of Glasgow, and in affluent Lenzie, eight miles away.
Spindrift Photo Agency

greater risk for premature death (Wilkinson & Pickett, 2009). At age 55, a rich American in the top income decile has a 10-year longer life expectancy than a poor American in the bottom income decile (Zumbrun, 2014). Poverty predicts perishing. Wealthy predicts healthy.

The correlation between poverty and ill health could run either way. Bad health isn't good for one's income. But most evidence indicates that the arrow runs from poverty toward ill health (Major et al., 2013; Sapolsky, 2005). So how *does* poverty "get under the skin"? The answers include (a) reduced access to quality health care, (b) unhealthier lifestyles (smoking is much more common among less-educated and lower-income people), and, to a striking extent, (c) increased stress. To be poor is to be at risk for increased stress, negative emotions, and a toxic environment (Adler & Snibbe, 2003; Chen, 2004; Gallo & Matthews, 2003). To be poor is to more often be sleep-deprived after working a second job, earning paychecks that don't cover the bills, commuting on crowded public transit, living in a high-pollution area, and doing hard labor that's controlled by someone else.

Poverty also helps explain a curious but oft-reported correlation between intelligence and health. Edinburgh University researcher Ian Deary (2005) and his colleagues observed this correlation after stumbling across data from an intelligence test administered on June 1, 1932, to virtually all Scots born in 1921. When they searched Scotland's death records, they found, as have researchers in other countries since, that "whether you live to collect your old-age pension depends in part on your IQ at age 11. You just can't keep a good predictor down."

Partly, the low-intelligence risk factor—which is roughly equivalent to that of obesity or high blood pressure, he reports—is due to the low-IQ persons having been less likely to cease smoking after its risks became known, and therefore more likely to die of lung cancer. Poverty-related stresses and lack of control also contribute, he notes.

People also die younger in regions with great income inequality (Kawachi et al., 1999; Lynch et al., 1998; See Figure 7). People in Britain and the United States have larger income disparities and lower life expectancies than people in Japan and Sweden. Where inequality has grown over the last decade, as in Eastern Europe and Russia, life expectancy has been at the falling end of the teeter-totter.

Is inequality merely an indicator of greater poverty? The mixed evidence indicates that poverty matters but that inequality matters, too. John Lynch and his colleagues (1998, 2000) report that people at every income level are at greater risk of early death if they live in a community with great income inequality. It's not just being poor, it's also *feeling* poor, relative to one's surroundings, that proves toxic. And that, Robert Sapolsky (2005) suggests, helps explain why the United States, which has the greatest income inequality of Westernized nations, has simultaneously ranked number 1 in the world on health care expenditures and number 29 on life expectancy.

Close Relationships and Happiness

Confiding painful feelings is good not only for the body but for the soul. That's the conclusion of studies showing that people are happier when supported by a network of friends and family.

Some studies, summarized in the "Self" chapter, compare people in a competitive, individualistic culture, such as the United States, Canada, and Australia, with those in collectivist cultures, such as Japan and many developing countries. Individualistic cultures offer independence, privacy, and pride in personal achievements. Collectivist cultures, with their tighter social bonds, offer protection from loneliness, alienation, divorce, and stress-related diseases.

FRIENDSHIPS AND HAPPINESS

Other studies compare individuals with few or many close relationships. Being attached to friends with whom we can share intimate thoughts has two effects, observed the seventeenth-century philosopher Francis Bacon. "It redoubleth joys, and cutteth griefs in half." So it seems from answers to a question asked of Americans by the National Opinion Research Center: "Looking back over the last six months, who are the people with whom you discussed matters important to you?" Compared with those who could name five or six such intimates, those who could name no such person were twice as likely to report being "not very happy."

"Woe to him who is alone when he falls and has not another to lift him up."

—Ecclesiastes 4:10b

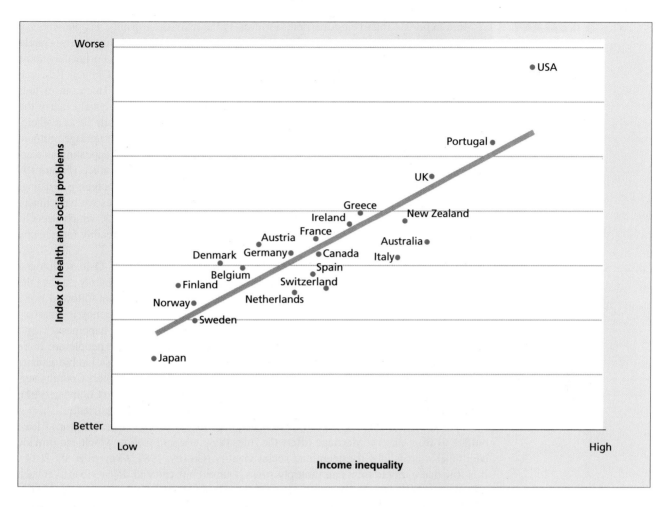

FIGURE :: 7

Social and physical health problems are greater in countries with high income inequality. This health problems index is a composite of lower life expectancy, infant mortality, obesity, teen births, mental illness, imprisonment, and lower levels of literacy, social -trust, and social mobility.
Source: Richard Wilkinson and Kate Pickett, *The Spirit Level: Why Greater Equality Makes Societies Stronger* (Penguin, 2009).

Other findings confirm the importance of social networks. In many experiments, others' acceptance has been gratifying, and their rejection painful—so much so that a pain reliever can help relieve the hurt (DeWall & Bushman, 2011). Across the life span, friendships foster self-esteem and well-being (Hartup & Stevens, 1997).

MARITAL ATTACHMENT AND HAPPINESS

For some 9 in 10 people worldwide, one eventual example of a close relationship has been marriage. Does marriage correlate positively with happiness? Or is there more happiness in the pleasure-seeking single life than in the "bondage," "chains," and "yoke" of marriage?

A mountain of data reveals that most people are happier attached than unattached. Survey after survey of many tens of thousands of Europeans and Americans has produced a consistent result: Compared with those single or widowed, and especially compared with those divorced or separated, married people report being happier and more satisfied with life (Gove et al., 1990; Inglehart, 1990). In National Opinion Research Center surveys of more than 50,000 Americans since 1972, for example, 23 percent of never-married adults, but 40 percent of married adults, have reported being "very happy." Lesbian couples, too, report greater well-being than those who are alone (Peplau & Fingerhut, 2007). There are multiple ways to satisfy the human need to belong (DePaulo, 2006). Nevertheless, there are few stronger predictors of happiness than a close, nurturing, equitable, intimate, lifelong companionship with one's best friend.

"The sun looks down on nothing half so good as a household laughing together over a meal."

—C. S. Lewis, "Membership," 1949

More important than being married, however, is the marriage's quality. People who say their marriages are satisfying—who find themselves still in love with their partners—rarely report being unhappy, discontented with life, or depressed (Robles, 2015). Fortunately, most married people *do* declare their marriages happy ones. In the National Opinion Research Center surveys, almost two-thirds say their marriages are "very happy." Three out of four say their spouses are their best friends. Four out of five people say they would marry the same people again. As a consequence, most such people feel quite happy with life as a whole.

Why are married people generally happier (as well as healthier)? Does marriage promote happiness, or does happiness promote marriage? Are happy people more appealing as marriage partners? Do depressed people more often stay single or suffer divorce (Figure 8)? Certainly, happy people are more fun to be with. They are also more outgoing, trusting, compassionate, and focused on others (Myers, 1993). Unhappy people, as we have noted, are more often socially rejected. Depression often triggers marital stress, which deepens the depression (Davila et al., 1997). So, positive, happy people do more readily form happy relationships.

But "the prevailing opinion of researchers," reported University of Oslo sociologist Arne Mastekaasa (1995), is that the marriage-happiness connection is "mainly due" to the beneficial effects of marriage. For example, a Rutgers University team that followed 1,380 New Jersey adults over 15 years concurs (Horwitz et al., 1997). The tendency for married people to be less depressed occurs even after controlling for premarital happiness.

Marriage enhances happiness for at least two reasons. First, married people are more likely to enjoy an enduring, supportive, intimate relationship and are less likely to suffer loneliness. No wonder male medical students in a study by UCLA's Robert Coombs survived medical school with less stress and anxiety if they were married (Coombs, 1991). A good marriage gives each partner a dependable companion, a lover, a friend.

There is a second, more prosaic, reason why marriage promotes happiness, or at least buffers us from misery. Marriage offers the roles of spouse and parent, which can provide additional sources of self-esteem and social identity (Crosby, 1987; Cruwys et al., 2014). It is true that multiple roles can multiply stress. Our circuits can and do overload. Yet each role also provides rewards, status, avenues to enrichment, and escape from stress faced in other parts of one's life. A self with many identities is like a mansion with many rooms. When fire struck one wing of Windsor Castle, most of the castle still remained for royals and tourists to enjoy. When our personal identity stands on several legs, it, too, holds up under the loss of any one. If we [DM and JT] mess up at work, well, we can tell ourselves that we're still good spouses and parents, and, in the final analysis, these parts of our identities are what matter most.

FIGURE :: 8

Marital Status and Depression

A National Institute of Mental Health survey of psychological disorders found depression rates two to four times greater for adults not married.
Source: Data from Robins & Regier, 1991, p. 72.

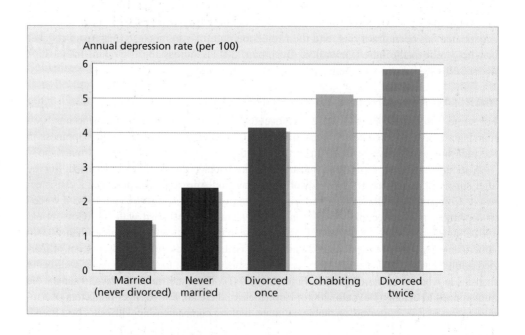

SUMMING UP: How Do Social Relationships Support Health and Well-Being?

- Health and happiness are influenced not only by social cognition but also by social relations. People who enjoy close, supportive relationships are at less risk for illness and premature death. Such relationships help people cope with stress, especially by enabling people to confide their intimate emotions.

- Close relationships also foster happiness. People who have intimate, long-term attachments with friends and family members cope better with loss and report greater happiness. Compared with unmarried adults, those who are married, for example, are much more likely to report being very happy and are at less risk for depression. This appears due both to the greater social success of happy people and to the well-being engendered by a supportive life companion.

POSTSCRIPT:
Enhancing Happiness

Several years ago I [DM] wrote a book, *The Pursuit of Happiness,* that reported key findings from new research studies of happiness. When the editors wanted to subtitle the book *What Makes People Happy?* I cautioned them: That's not a question this or any book can answer. What we have learned is simply what correlates with—and therefore predicts—happiness. Thus, the book's revised subtitle was *Who Is Happy—and Why?*

Nevertheless, in 400+ subsequent media interviews concerning happiness, the most frequent question has been "What can people do to be happy?" Without claiming any easy formula for health and happiness, I assembled 10 research-based points to ponder:

1. *Realize that enduring happiness doesn't come from "making it."* People adapt to changing circumstances—even to wealth or a disability. Thus, wealth is like health: Its utter absence breeds misery, but having it (or any circumstance we long for) doesn't guarantee happiness.

2. *Take control of your time.* Happy people feel in control of their lives, often aided by mastering their use of time. It helps to set goals and break them into daily aims. Although we often overestimate how much we will accomplish in any given day (leaving us frustrated), we generally underestimate how much we can accomplish in a year, given just a little progress every day.

3. *Act happy.* We can sometimes act ourselves into a frame of mind. Manipulated into a smiling expression, people feel better; when they scowl, the whole world seems to scowl back. So put on a happy face. Talk as if you feel positive self-esteem, are optimistic, and are outgoing. Going through the motions can trigger the emotions.

4. *Seek work and leisure that engage your skills.* Happy people often are in a zone called "flow"—absorbed in a task that challenges them without overwhelming them. The most expensive forms of leisure (sitting on a yacht) often provide less flow experience than gardening, socializing, or craft work.

5. *Join the "movement" movement.* An avalanche of research reveals that aerobic exercise not only promotes health and energy but also is an antidote for mild depression and anxiety. Sound minds reside in sound bodies.

6. *Give your body the sleep it wants.* Happy people live active, vigorous lives yet reserve time for renewing sleep and solitude. Many people suffer from a sleep debt, with resulting fatigue, diminished alertness, and gloomy moods.

7. *Give priority to close relationships.* Intimate friendships with those who care deeply about you can help you weather difficult times. Confiding is good for soul and body. Resolve to nurture your closest relationships: to *not* take those closest

to you for granted, to display to them the sort of kindness that you display to others, to affirm them, to share, and to play together. To rejuvenate your affections, resolve in such ways to *act* lovingly.

8. *Focus beyond the self.* Reach out to those in need. Happiness increases helpfulness. (Those who feel good do good.) But doing good also makes one feel good.

9. *Keep a gratitude journal.* Those who pause each day to reflect on some positive aspect of their lives (their health, friends, family, freedom, education, senses, natural surroundings, and so on) experience heightened well-being.

10. *Nurture your spiritual self.* For many people, faith provides a support community, a reason to focus beyond self, and a sense of purpose and hope. Study after study finds that actively religious people are happier and that they cope better with crises.

Social Psychology in Court

Scott Olson/Getty Images

"A courtroom is a battleground where lawyers compete for the minds of jurors."

—James Randi, 1999

On August 9, 2014, police officer Darren Wilson shot and killed 18-year-old Michael Brown in Ferguson, Missouri. Peaceful protests over Brown's death soon became heated, and Ferguson erupted into violence and rioting. At the center of the unrest was a question: Was Wilson justified in shooting Brown?

A grand jury convened in Ferguson in December 2014 did not indict Wilson, so he did not stand trial. The case featured several issues addressed in social psychology studies:

- Eyewitnesses provided varying accounts of Brown's behavior before he was shot. How influential is eyewitness testimony? How trustworthy are eyewitness recollections? What makes a credible witness?
- Darren Wilson is White and Michael Brown was Black. What impact do victims' and defendants' race, attractiveness, and social status have on jury judgments?

- The grand jury included three Blacks and nine Whites, and seven men and five women. Do jurors' characteristics bias their verdicts? If so, can lawyers use the jury selection process to stack a jury in their favor?

- During deliberations, how do jurors influence one another? Can a minority win over the majority? Do 12-member juries reach the same decisions as 6-member juries?

Such questions fascinate lawyers, judges, and defendants. They are questions to which social psychology can suggest answers, as law schools recognize by hiring professors of "law and social science," and as trial lawyers recognize when hiring psychological consultants.

We can think of a courtroom as a miniature social world, one that magnifies everyday social processes with major consequences for those involved. In criminal cases, psychological factors may influence decisions involving arrest, interrogation, prosecution, plea bargaining, sentencing, and parole. Whether or not a case reaches a jury verdict, the social dynamics of the courtroom matter. Let's therefore consider two sets of factors: (1) *eyewitness testimony* and its influence on jurors, and (2) characteristics of *jurors* as individuals and as a group.

HOW RELIABLE IS EYEWITNESS TESTIMONY?

Explain the accuracy of eyewitness testimony, its association (or not) with eyewitness confidence, its contamination by misinformation effects, and ways to increase eyewitness accuracy and educate jurors.

As the courtroom drama unfolds, jurors hear testimony, form impressions of the defendant, listen to instructions from the judge, and render a verdict. Let's take these steps one at a time, starting with eyewitness testimony.

Although never in trouble with the law, Kirk Bloodsworth was convicted for the sexual assault and slaying of a 9-year-old girl after five eyewitnesses identified him at his trial. During his 2 years on death row and 7 more under a sentence of life imprisonment, he maintained his innocence. Then DNA testing proved it was not his semen on the girl's underwear. Released from prison, he still lived under a cloud of doubt until in 2003, 19 years after his conviction, DNA testing identified the actual killer (Wells et al., 2006).

The Power of Persuasive Eyewitnesses

Vivid anecdotes and personal testimonies can be powerfully persuasive, often more so than compelling but abstract information. There's no better way to end an argument than to say, "I saw it with my own eyes!"

Memory researcher Elizabeth Loftus (1974, 1979a, 2011b) found that those who had "seen" were indeed believed, even when their testimony was shown to be useless. When students were presented with a hypothetical robbery–murder case with circumstantial evidence but no eyewitness testimony, only 18 percent voted for conviction. Other students received the same information but with the addition of a single eyewitness. Now, knowing that someone had declared, "That's the one!" 72 percent voted for conviction. For a third group, the defense attorney discredited that testimony (the witness had 20/400 vision and was not wearing glasses).

Did that discrediting reduce the effect of the testimony? In this case, not much: 68 percent still voted for conviction.

Later experiments revealed that discrediting may reduce somewhat the number of guilty votes (Whitley, 1987). But unless contradicted by another eyewitness, a vivid eyewitness account is difficult to erase from jurors' minds (Leippe, 1985). That helps explain why, compared with criminal cases lacking eyewitness testimony, those that have eyewitness testimony are more likely to produce convictions (Visher, 1987).

Can't jurors spot erroneous testimony? To find out, researchers staged hundreds of eye witnessed thefts of a calculator. Afterward, they asked each eyewitness to identify the culprit from a photo lineup. Other people, acting as jurors, observed the eyewitnesses being questioned and then evaluated their testimony. Are incorrect eyewitnesses believed less often than those who are accurate? As it happened, both correct and incorrect eyewitnesses were believed 80 percent of the time (Wells et al., 1979). That led the researchers to speculate that "human observers have absolutely no ability to discern eyewitnesses who have mistakenly identified an innocent person" (Wells et al., 1980).

In a follow-up experiment, the staged theft sometimes allowed witnesses a good long look at the thief and sometimes didn't. The jurors believed the witnesses more when conditions were good. But even when conditions were so poor that two-thirds of the witnesses had actually misidentified an innocent person, 62 percent of the jurors still usually believed the witnesses (Lindsay et al., 1981).

Later studies found that jurors are more skeptical of eyewitnesses whose memory of trivial details is poor—though these tend to be the most *accurate* witnesses (Wells & Leippe, 1981). Jurors think a witness who can remember that there were three pictures hanging in the room must have "really been paying attention" (Bell & Loftus, 1988, 1989). Actually, those who pay attention to surrounding details are *less* likely to attend to the culprit's face.

The persuasive power of three eyewitnesses sent Chicagoan James Newsome, who had never been arrested before, to prison on a life sentence for supposedly gunning down a convenience store owner. Fifteen years later he was released, after fingerprint technology revealed the real culprit to be Dennis Emerson, a career criminal who was 3 inches taller and had longer hair (*Chicago Tribune,* 2002).

When Eyes Deceive

Is eyewitness testimony often inaccurate? Stories abound of innocent people who have wasted away for years in prison because of the testimony of eyewitnesses who were sincerely wrong (Brandon & Davies, 1973; Doyle, 2005; Wells et al., 2006). Among the first 250 convictions overturned by DNA evidence, 76 percent were wrongful convictions influenced by mistaken eyewitnesses (Garrett, 2011a).

To assess the accuracy of eyewitness recollections, we need to learn their overall rates of "hits" and "misses." One way for researchers to gather such information is to stage crimes comparable to those in everyday life and then solicit eyewitness reports.

During the past century, this has been done many times in Europe and elsewhere, sometimes with disconcerting results (Sporer, 2008). For example, 141 students witnessed an "assault" on a professor at California State University, Hayward. Seven weeks later, when Robert Buckhout (1974) asked them to identify the assailant from a group of six photographs, 60 percent chose an innocent person. No wonder eyewitnesses to actual crimes sometimes disagree about what

"As it turned out, my battery of lawyers was no match for their battery of eyewitnesses."

© Joseph Mirachi/The New Yorker Collection/www.cartoonbank.com

Lie detection brain scans have, as yet, marginal validity. But such high-tech-seeming evidence can nevertheless seem credible to jurors (Gazzaniga, 2011; McCabe et al., 2011).

The innocent James Newsome (left) mistakenly identified by eyewitnesses, and the actual culprit (right).
Illinois Department of Corrections

they saw. Later studies have confirmed that eyewitnesses often are more confident than correct. In one study, students felt, on average, 74 percent sure of their later recollections of a classroom visitor but were only 55 percent correct (Bornstein & Zickafoose, 1999).

Three studies of live lineups conducted in England and Wales show remarkable consistency. Roughly 40 percent of witnesses identified the suspect. Forty percent made no identification. And, despite having been cautioned that the person they witnessed might not be in the lineup, 20 percent choose an innocent person (Valentine et al., 2003). Younger eyewitnesses, and those who had viewed the culprit for more than 1 minute at a distance of less than 5 meters (about 16 feet), were also more accurate than older eyewitnesses and those who viewed the person more briefly and from farther away (Horry et al., 2014).

Jurors find confident witnesses the most believable (Wells, Olson, & Charman, 2002; Wells, Memon & Penrod, 2006). Unless their credibility is punctured by an obvious error, confident witnesses seem more credible (Jules & McQuiston, 2013; Tenney et al., 2007). Confident witnesses are somewhat more accurate, especially when making quick and confident identifications soon after the event (Sauer et al., 2010; Sauerland & Sporer, 2009). In 57 percent of DNA exoneration cases that included eyewitness testimony, the eyewitnesses initially were uncertain (Garrett, 2011b). Jurors also have a difficult time interpreting statements of confidence—for example, what does "I'm fairly certain it's him?" mean? (Dodson & Dobolyi, 2015). Still, the overconfidence phenomenon affects witnesses, too. Under many conditions, witnesses that feel 90 to 100 percent confident tend to be approximately 75 to 90 percent accurate (Brewer & Wells, 2011). Moreover, some people—whether right or wrong—usually express themselves more assertively. That, says Michael Leippe (1994), explains why mistaken eyewitnesses are so often persuasive. Overall, a confident witness is not necessarily an accurate witness.

Eyewitness recall of detail is sometimes impressive. When John Yuille and Judith Cutshall (1986) studied accounts of a midafternoon murder on a busy Burnaby, British Columbia, street, they found that eyewitnesses' recall for detail was 80 percent accurate.

Errors sneak into our perceptions and our memories because our minds are not videotape machines. Many errors are understandable, as revealed by "change blindness" experiments in which people fail to detect that an innocent person entering a scene differs from another person exiting the scene (Davis et al., 2008). People are quite good at recognizing a pictured face when later shown the same picture alongside a new face. But researcher Vicki Bruce (1998) was surprised to discover that subtle differences in views, expressions, or lighting "are hard for human vision to deal with." We construct our memories based partly on what we perceived at the time and partly on our expectations, beliefs, and current knowledge (Figure 1).

The strong emotions that accompany witnessed crimes and traumas may further corrupt eyewitness memories. In one experiment, visitors wore heart rate monitors while in the London Dungeon's Horror Labyrinth. Those exhibiting the most emotion later made the most mistakes in identifying someone they had encountered (Valentine & Mesout, 2009).

One study documented the effect of stress on memory with more than 500 soldiers at survival schools—mock prisoner of war camps that were training the soldiers to withstand

FIGURE :: 1

Expectations Affect Perception
People will see what they expect in this image—either an old or a young woman.
New York Public Library/Getty Images.

deprivation of food and sleep, combined with intense, confrontational interrogation, resulting in a high heart rate and a flood of stress hormones. A day after release from the camp, when the participants were asked to identify their intimidating interrogators from a 15-person lineup, only 30 percent could do so, although 62 percent could recall a low-stress interrogator. Thus, concluded the researchers, "contrary to the popular conception that most people would never forget the face of a clearly seen individual who had physically confronted them and threatened them for more than 30 minutes, [many] were unable to correctly identify their perpetrator" (Morgan et al., 2004). We are most at risk for false recollections made with high confidence with faces of another race (Brigham et al., 2006; Meissner et al., 2005).

The Misinformation Effect

Can false memories be created? In a pioneering study on that question, Elizabeth Loftus and associates (1978) showed University of Washington students 30 slides depicting successive stages of an automobile–pedestrian accident. One critical slide showed a red Datsun stopped at a stop sign or a yield sign. Afterward they asked half the students, among other questions, "Did another car pass the red Datsun while it was stopped at the stop sign?" They asked the other half the same question, but with the words "stop sign" replaced by "yield sign." Later, all viewed both slides in Figure 2 and recalled which one

FIGURE :: 2

The Misinformation Effect

When shown one of these two pictures and then asked a question suggesting the sign from the other photo, most people later "remembered" seeing the sign they had never actually seen.
Source: From Loftus, Miller, & Burns (1978). Photos courtesy of Elizabeth Loftus.

they had seen previously. Those who had been asked the question consistent with what they had seen were 75 percent correct. Those previously asked the misleading question were only 41 percent correct; more often than not, they denied seeing what they had actually seen and instead "remembered" the picture they had never seen!

misinformation effect
Incorporating "misinformation" into one's memory of the event after witnessing an event and receiving misleading information about it.

Other studies of this **misinformation effect** found that after suggestive questions, witnesses may believe that a red light was actually green or that a robber had a mustache when he didn't (Loftus, 1979a, b, 2001). When questioning eyewitnesses, police and attorneys commonly ask questions framed by their own understanding of what happened. So it is troubling to discover how easily witnesses incorporate misleading information into their memories, especially when they believe the questioner is well informed, when shown fabricated evidence, when suggestive questions are repeated, or when they have discussed events with other witnesses (Frenda et al., 2011; Wade et al., 2010; Wright et al., 2009; Zaragoza & Mitchell, 1996). Fortunately, the misinformation effect can be reduced by warning witnesses, by explicitly saying that a piece of information was incorrect ("there was no stop sign") or implying it might be ("the police cadet was inexperienced at detailing observed crimes") (Blank & Launay, 2014; Echterhoff et al., 2005; Greene et al., 1982).

It also is troubling to realize that false memories feel and look like real memories. They can be as persuasive as real memories—convincingly sincere, yet sincerely wrong. This is true of young children (who are especially susceptible to misinformation) as well as adults. In one study, children were told once a week for 10 weeks, "Think real hard, and tell me if this ever happened to you: Can you remember going to the hospital with the mousetrap on your finger?" Remarkably, when later interviewed by a new adult who asked the same question, 58 percent of preschoolers produced false and often detailed stories about the fictitious event (Ceci & Bruck, 1993a, b, 1995). One boy explained that his brother had pushed him into a basement woodpile, where his finger got stuck in the trap. "And then we went to the hospital, and my mommy, daddy, and Colin drove me there, to the hospital in our van, because it was far away. And the doctor put a bandage on this finger."

Given such vivid stories, professional psychologists were often fooled. They could not reliably separate real from false memories—nor could the children. Told the incident never actually happened, some protested, "But it really did happen. I remember it!" Such findings raise the possibility of false accusations, as in alleged child sex abuse cases in which children's memories may have been contaminated by repeated suggestive questioning and in which there is no corroborating evidence. Given suggestive interview questions, most preschoolers and many older children will produce false reports, such as seeing a thief steal food in their day-care center (Bruck & Ceci, 1999, 2004).

In other studies, university students were asked to imagine childhood events, such as breaking a window or having a nurse remove a skin sample. This led one-fourth to recall that the imagined event actually happened (Garry et al., 1996; Mazzoni & Memom, 2003). This "imagination inflation" happens partly because visualizing something activates similar areas in the brain as does actually experiencing it (Gonsalves et al., 2004). Imagining inputs incorrect information.

Misinformation-induced false memories provide one explanation for a peculiar phenomenon: *false confessions* (Kassin et al., 2010; Lassiter, 2010; Loftus, 2011a). Among 250 closely studied cases in which DNA evidence cleared wrongfully convicted people, 16 percent involved false confessions (Garrett, 2011b). Many of these were *compliant confessions*—people who confessed when worn down and often sleep deprived ("If you will just tell us you accidentally rather than deliberately set the fire, you can go home.") Others were *internalized confessions*—ones apparently believed after people were fed misinformation. Confessions, even when coerced, can set off a chain reaction in a case. Police make more errors with evidence and eyewitness identifications when a suspect has confessed (Kassin et al., 2012). Sixty percent of judges will vote to convict a suspect who confessed, even if the confession was given under pressure and other evidence is weak (Wallace & Kassin, 2012).

After 43 hours of questioning by Italian police, the last 8 hours conducted overnight without food, water, or sleep, American exchange student Amanda Knox confessed to killing her roommate Meredith Kercher. She later recanted, and no physical evidence tied her to the crime. After 4 years in jail in Italy, she was acquitted in 2011 and returned home to the United States.
Federico Zirilli/AFP/Getty Images

It's tempting to believe that false confessions happen to other people, and that we ourselves would never do such a thing. Research suggests otherwise. In one experiment, researchers told students they had committed a crime, such as assault or theft as a young teen (in reality, none had ever had any police contact). After three interviews using memory-enhancing techniques such as visualization, an incredible 70 percent believed that they had actually committed a crime (Shaw & Porter, 2015).

Retelling

Retelling events commits people to their recollections, accurate or not. An accurate retelling helps them later resist misleading suggestions (Bregman & McAllister, 1982). Other times, the more we retell a story, the more we convince ourselves of a falsehood. Another study had eyewitnesses to a staged theft rehearse their answers to questions before taking the witness stand. Doing so increased the confidence of those who were wrong and thus made jurors who heard their false testimony more likely to convict the innocent person (Wells et al., 1981).

We often adjust what we say to please our listeners. Moreover, having done so, we come to believe the altered message. Imagine witnessing an argument that erupts into a fight in which one person injures the other. Afterward, the injured party sues. Before the trial, a smooth lawyer for one of the two parties interviews you. Might you slightly adjust your testimony, giving a version of the fight that supports this lawyer's client? If you did so, might your later recollections in court be similarly slanted?

Blair Sheppard and Neil Vidmar (1980) report that the answer to both questions is yes. At the University of Western Ontario, they had some students serve as witnesses to a fight and others as lawyers and judges. When interviewed by lawyers for the defendant, the witnesses later gave the judge testimony that was more favorable to the defendant. In a follow-up experiment, witnesses did not omit important facts from their testimony; they just changed their tone of voice and choice of words depending on whether they thought they were witnesses for the defendant or for the plaintiff (Vidmar & Laird, 1983). Even this was enough to bias the impressions of those who heard the testimony. So it's not only suggestive questions that can distort eyewitness recollections but also their own retellings, which may be adjusted subtly to suit their audience. How police officers and others respond to witness statements can also have an impact (see Research Close-up: Feedback to Witnesses).

"Witnesses probably ought to be taking a more realistic oath: 'Do you swear to tell the truth, the whole truth, or whatever it is you think you remember?'"
—Elizabeth F. Loftus, "Memory in Canadian Courts of Law," 2003

research
CLOSE-UP
Feedback to Witnesses

Eyewitness to a crime on viewing a lineup: "Oh, my God . . . I don't know . . . It's one of those two . . . but I don't know . . . Oh, man . . . the guy a little bit taller than number two . . . It's one of those two, but I don't know. . . ."

Months later at trial: "You were positive it was number two? It wasn't a maybe?"

Eyewitness's answer: "There was no maybe about it . . . was absolutely positive."

(*Missouri v. Hutching,* 1994, reported by Wells & Bradfield, 1998)

What explains witnesses misrecalling their original uncertainty? Gary Wells and Amy Bradfield (1998, 1999) wondered. Research had shown that one's confidence gains a boost from (a) learning that another witness has fingered the same person, (b) being asked the same question repeatedly, and (c) preparing for cross-examination (Lüüs & Wells, 1994; Shaw, 1996; Wells et al., 1981). Might the lineup interviewer's feedback also influence not just confidence but also recollections of earlier confidence ("I knew it all along")?

To find out, Wells and Bradfield conducted two experiments in which 352 Iowa State University students viewed a grainy security camera video of a man entering a store. Moments later, off camera, he murders a security guard.

The students then viewed the photo spread from the actual criminal case, minus the gunman's photo, and were asked to identify the gunman. All 352 students made a false identification, following which the experimenter gave confirming feedback ("Good. You identified the actual suspect"), disconfirming feedback ("Actually, the suspect was number _____"), or no feedback. Finally, all were later asked, "At the time that you identified the person in the photo spread, how certain were you that the person you identified from the photos was the gunman that you saw in the video?" (from 1, not at all certain, to 7, totally certain).

The experiment produced two striking results: First, the effect of the experimenter's casual comment was huge. In the confirming feedback condition, 58 percent of the eyewitnesses rated their certainty as 6 or 7 when making their initial judgments. This was 4 times the 14 percent who said the same in the no-feedback condition and 11 times the 5 percent in the disconfirming condition. What's striking is that those were their confident recollections *before* they received any feedback.

It wasn't obvious to the participants that their judgments were affected, because the second rather amazing finding is that when asked if the feedback had influenced their answers, 58 percent said no. Moreover, as a group, those who felt uninfluenced were influenced just as much as those who said they were (Figure 3).

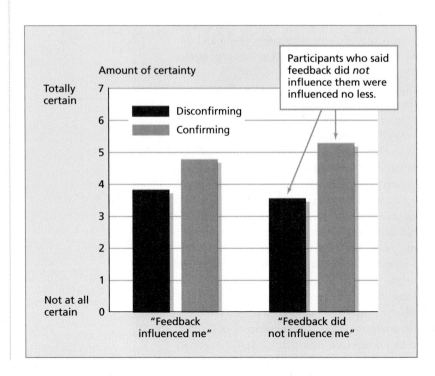

FIGURE :: 3

Recalled Certainty of Eyewitnesses' False Identification After Receiving Confirming or Disconfirming Feedback (Experiment 2)

Source: Data from Wells & Bradfield (1998).

This phenomenon—increased witness confidence after supportive feedback—is both big and reliable enough, across 21 studies of 7,000 participants, to have gained a name: the *post-identification feedback effect* (Douglass & Steblay, 2006; Smalarz & Wells, 2014; Steblay et al., 2014). It is understandable that eyewitnesses would be curious about the accuracy of their recollections, and that interrogators would want to satisfy their curiosity ("you did identify the actual suspect"). But the possible later effect of inflated eyewitness confidence points to the need to keep interrogators blind (ignorant) of which person is the suspect. Alternatively, witness certainty can be assessed before any feedback is given (Steblay et al., 2014).

The inability of eyewitnesses to appreciate the post-identification feedback effect points to a lesson that runs deeper than jury research. Again, we see why we need social psychological research. As social psychologists have so often found—recall Milgram's obedience experiments—simply asking people how they would act, or asking what explains their actions, sometimes gives us wrong answers. Benjamin Franklin was right: "There are three things extremely hard, steel, a diamond, and to know one's self." That is why we need not only surveys that ask people to explain themselves but also experiments in which we see what they actually do.

Reducing Error

Given these error-prone tendencies, what constructive steps can be taken to increase the accuracy of eyewitnesses and jurors? The U.S. Department of Justice convened a panel of researchers, attorneys, and law enforcement officers to hammer out *Eyewitness Evidence: A Guide for Law Enforcement* (Technical Working Group for Eyewitness Evidence, 1999; Wells et al., 2000). Their suggestions parallel many of those from a Canadian review of eyewitness identification procedures (Yarmey, 2003a). They include ways to (a) train police interviewers and (b) administer lineups. This "forensic science of mind" seeks to preserve rather than contaminate the eyewitness memory aspect of the crime scene.

TRAIN POLICE INTERVIEWERS

When Ronald Fisher and co-workers (1987, 1989, 2011) examined tape-recorded interviews of eyewitnesses conducted by experienced Florida police detectives, they found a typical pattern. Following an open-ended beginning ("Tell me what you recall"), the detectives would occasionally interrupt with follow-up questions, including questions eliciting terse answers ("How tall was he?").

The *Eyewitness Evidence* guide instructs interviewers to begin by allowing eyewitnesses to offer their own unprompted recollections. The recollections will be most complete if the interviewer jogs the memory by first guiding people to reconstruct the setting. Have them visualize the scene and what they were thinking and feeling at the time. Even showing pictures of the setting—of, say, the store checkout lane with a clerk standing where she was robbed—can promote accurate recall (Cutler & Penrod, 1988). After giving witnesses ample, uninterrupted time to report everything that comes to mind, the interviewer then jogs their memory with evocative questions ("Was there anything unusual about the voice? Was there anything unusual about the person's appearance or clothing?"). Such open-ended questions are better than those asking witnesses to focus on particular characteristics (such as hair color), which can lead them to forget other details (Camp et al., 2012).

When detectives were trained to question in this way, the eyewitnesses' information increased 25 to 50 percent without increasing the false memory rate (Fisher et al., 1989, 1994, 2011). A later meta-analysis of 46 published studies confirmed that this "cognitive interview" substantially increases details recalled, with no loss in accuracy (Memon et al., 2011). In response to such results, most police agencies in North America and Britain have adopted the cognitive interview procedure (Dando et al., 2009). (The procedure also shows promise for enhancing information gathered in oral histories and medical surveys.)

Accurate identifications tend to be automatic and effortless (Sauer et al., 2010). The right face just pops out. Eyewitnesses who made their identifications in fewer than 10 to 12 seconds were nearly 90 percent accurate; those taking longer were only about 50 percent accurate (Dunning & Perretta, 2002). Although other studies challenge a neat 10- to 12-second rule, they confirm that quicker identifications are generally more accurate (Weber et al., 2004). In an analysis of 640 eyewitness viewings of London police lineups, nearly 9 in 10 "fast" identifications were of the actual suspect, as were fewer than 4 in 10 slower identifications (Valentine et al., 2003). Similarly, witnesses who viewed a sequential lineup more than once were more likely to choose a "filler" photograph of an innocent person (Horry et al., 2012a). (Filler photographs are known as "foils.")

MINIMIZE FALSE LINEUP IDENTIFICATIONS

After a suburban Toronto department store robbery, the cashier involved could recall only that the culprit was not wearing a tie and was "very neatly dressed and rather good looking." When police put the good-looking Ron Shatford in a lineup with 11 unattractive men, the cashier readily identified him as the culprit. Only after he had served 15 months of a long sentence did another person confess, allowing Shatford to be retried and found not guilty (Doob & Kirshenbaum, 1973). Stacking the police lineup with dissimilar people can clearly promote misidentification.

If a suspect has a distinguishing feature—a tie, a tattoo, or an eye patch—false identifications are reduced by putting a similar feature on other lineup foils (Zarkadi et al., 2009). Suspects with angry expressions are also identified as the culprit more often, particularly if the foils have neutral or happy expressions (Flowe et al., 2014). Another way to reduce misidentifications is to remind witnesses that the person they saw may or may not be in the lineup—that reminder reduced wrong choices by 45 percent (Wells, 1984, 1993, 2005, 2008). Alternatively, give eyewitnesses a "blank" lineup that contains only foil pictures and screen out those who make false identifications. Those who do not make such errors turn out to be more accurate when they later face the actual lineup.

Mistakes also subside when witnesses make individual yes or no judgments in response to a *sequence* of people, as shown in dozens of studies in Europe, North America, Australia, and South Africa (Lindsay & Wells, 1985; Meissner et al., 2005; Steblay et al., 2001). A simultaneous lineup tempts people to pick the person who, among the lineup members, most resembles the perpetrator. Witnesses viewing just one suspect at a time are less likely to make false identifications, especially if they are not told in advance how many photos they will view (Horry et al., 2012b).

If witnesses view several photos or people simultaneously, they are more likely to choose whoever most resembles the culprit. (When not given a same-race lineup, witnesses may pick someone of the culprit's race, especially when it's a race different from their own [Wells & Olson, 2001].) With a "sequential lineup," eyewitnesses compare each person with their memory of the culprit and make an absolute decision—match or no-match (Goodsell et al., 2010; Gronlund, 2004a, b). One experiment randomly assigned crime eyewitnesses to view lineups simultaneously or sequentially. The sequential lineup reduced the misidentification of foils from 18 to 12 percent, with no reduction in accurate identifications of suspects (Wells et al., 2015).

These no-cost procedures make police lineups more like good experiments. They contain a *control group* (a no-suspect lineup or a lineup in which mock witnesses try to guess the suspect based merely on a general description). They have an experimenter who is *blind* to the hypothesis (and who therefore won't welcome an expected identification while asking, "Might it be anyone else?" in response to a different identification). Questions are *scripted and neutral,* so they don't subtly demand a particular response (the procedure doesn't imply the culprit is in the lineup). And they prohibit confidence-inflating post-lineup comments ("you got him") prior to trial testimony. Such procedures greatly reduce the natural human confirmation bias (having an idea and seeking confirming evidence). Lineups can also be effectively administered by computers (MacLin et al., 2005; Wells et al., 2015).

Although procedures such as double-blind testing are common in psychological science, they are still uncommon in criminal procedures (Wells & Olson, 2003). So it was when

Troy Davis was arrested for the 1989 killing of a Georgia police officer. The police showed some of the witnesses Davis's photo before they viewed the lineup. His lineup picture had a different background than the other photos. The lineup was administered by an officer who knew that Davis was the suspect. Later, 7 of the 9 witnesses against Davis recanted, with 6 saying the police threatened them if they did not identify Davis. The man who first told police that Davis was the shooter later confessed to the crime. Despite court appeals and pleas from the Pope, a former FBI director, and 630,000 others, in 2011, Georgia executed Troy Davis (*New York Times,* 2011).

Troy Davis (1968–2011). Despite error-prone procedures for screening eyewitness testimonies, the State of Georgia argued that Davis, who maintained his innocence to his last breath, was guilty of murder. Columbus Ledger-Enquirer/Getty Images

Mindful of all this research, New Jersey's attorney general has mandated statewide blind testing (to avoid steering witnesses toward suspects) and sequential lineups (to minimize simply comparing people and choosing the person who most resembles the one they saw commit a crime) (Kolata & Peterson, 2001; Wells et al., 2002). In 2011, the New Jersey Supreme Court, in response to research on eyewitness identification procedures, overhauled its state's rule for treating lineup evidence. By making it easier for defendants to challenge flawed evidence, the court attached consequences to the use of lineup procedures that are most likely to produce mistaken identifications (Goode & Schwartz, 2011). Oregon followed suit in 2012, requiring that judges consider factors that might limit an eyewitness's reliability and mandating that they rule out unreliable eyewitness evidence. The new rules followed a case in which Samuel Lawson was convicted of murdering a man and shooting that man's wife. Immediately after the shooting, the woman said she had not seen the shooter's face, and she did not identify Lawson in a photo lineup. Two years later, police told her that Lawson had been arrested for the shooting, and she then identified him. Lawson was convicted of the murder. After reviewing the research on eyewitness identification, however, the court (*Oregon v. Lawson*) overturned Lawson's conviction.

Researchers are also exploring the conditions under which "earwitness" testimony, based on voice recognition, is also vulnerable to error (Mullenix et al., 2011; Stevenage et al., 2011).

EDUCATE JURORS

Do jurors evaluate eyewitness testimony rationally? Do they understand how the circumstances of a lineup determine its reliability? Do they know whether or not to take an eyewitness's self-confidence into account? Do they realize how memory can be influenced—by earlier misleading questions, by stress at the time of the incident, by the interval between the event and the questioning, by whether the suspect is the same or a different race, by whether recall of other details is sharp or hazy? Studies in Canada, Great Britain, Norway, and the United States reveal that although juror knowledge seems on the increase, jurors fail to fully appreciate some of these factors, all of which are known to influence eyewitness testimony (Desmarais & Read, 2011; Magnussen et al., 2010; Wise & Safer, 2010). In one national survey, more than half mistakenly agreed that, "Human memory works like a video camera, accurately recording the events we see and hear so that we can review and inspect them later" (Loftus, 2011a).

To educate jurors, experts now are asked frequently (usually by defense attorneys) to testify about eyewitness testimony (Cutler & Kovera, 2011). Starting in 2012, New Jersey requires that jurors be instructed on factors that can influence eyewitness testimony: "human memory is not foolproof. Research has shown that human memory is not at all like a video recording . . . people may have greater difficulty identifying members of a different race . . . high levels of stress can reduce an eyewitness's ability to recall and make an accurate identification" (quoted in Schacter & Loftus, 2013). The aim is to offer jurors the sort of information you have been reading about to help them evaluate

TABLE :: 1 Influences on Eyewitness Testimony

Phenomenon	Eyewitness Experts Agreeing*	Jurors Agreeing*
Question wording. An eyewitness's testimony about an event can affected by how the questions put to that eyewitness are worded.	98%	85%
Lineup instructions. Police instructions can affect an eyewitness's willingness to make an identification.	98%	41%
Confidence malleability. An eyewitness's confidence can be influenced by factors that are unrelated to identification accuracy.	95%	50%
Mug-shot-induced bias. Exposure to mug shots of a suspect increases the likelihood that the witness will later choose that suspect in a lineup.	95%	59%
Postevent information. Eyewitnesses' testimony about an event often reflects not only what they actually saw but also information they obtained later on.	94%	60%
Attitudes and expectations. An eyewitness's perception and memory of an event may be affected by his or her attitudes and expectations.	92%	81%
Cross-race bias. Eyewitnesses are more accurate when identifying members of their own race than members of other races.	90%	47%
Accuracy versus confidence. An eyewitness's confidence is not a good predictor of his or her identification accuracy.	87%	38%

*"This phenomenon is reliable enough for psychologists to present it in courtroom testimony."

Source: Experts from S. M. Kassin, V. A. Tubb, H. M. Hosch, & A. Memon (2001). Jurors from T. R. Benton, D. F. Ross, E. Bradshaw, W. N. Thomas, & G. S. Bradshaw (2006).

the testimony of both prosecution and defense witnesses. Table 1, drawn from a survey of 64 researchers on eyewitness testimony, lists some of the most agreed-upon phenomena. A follow-up survey compared their understandings with those of 111 jurors sampled in Tennessee.

When taught the conditions under which eyewitness accounts are trustworthy, jurors become more discerning (Devenport et al., 2002; Pawlenko et al., 2013). Moreover, attorneys and judges are recognizing the importance of some of these factors when deciding when to ask for or permit suppression of lineup evidence (Stinson et al., 1996, 1997).

SUMMING UP: How Reliable Is Eyewitness Testimony?

- In hundreds of experiments, social psychologists have found that the accuracy of eyewitness testimony can be impaired by a host of factors involving the ways people form judgments and memories.

- Some eyewitnesses express themselves more assertively than others. The assertive witness is more likely to be believed, although assertiveness is actually a trait of the witness that does not reflect the certainty of the information.

- The human eye is not a video camera; it is vulnerable to variations in light, angle, and other changes that impair recognition of a face.

- When false information is given to a witness, the *misinformation effect* may result in the witness coming to believe that the false information is true.

- As the sequence of events in a crime is told repeatedly, errors may creep in and become embraced by the witness as part of the true account.

- To reduce such errors, interviewers are advised to let the witness tell what he or she remembers without interruption and to encourage the witness to visualize the scene of the incident and the emotional state the witness was in when the incident occurred.

- Educating jurors about the pitfalls of eyewitness testimony can improve the way testimony is received and, ultimately, the accuracy of the verdict.

WHAT OTHER FACTORS INFLUENCE JUROR JUDGMENTS?

Explain how defendants' attractiveness and similarity to jurors may bias jurors, and how faithfully jurors follow judges' instructions.

The Defendant's Characteristics

According to the famed trial lawyer Clarence Darrow (1933), jurors seldom convict a person they like or acquit one they dislike. He argued that the main job of the trial lawyer is to make a jury like the defendant. Was he right? And is it true, as Darrow also said, that "facts regarding the crime are relatively unimportant"?

Darrow overstated the case. One classic study of more than 3,500 criminal cases and 4,000 civil cases found that 4 times in 5 the judge agreed with the jury's decision (Kalven & Zeisel, 1966). Although both may have been wrong, the evidence usually is clear enough that jurors can set aside their biases, focus on the facts, and agree on a verdict (Saks & Hastie, 1978; Visher, 1987). Facts matter.

But facts are not all that matter. Communicators are more persuasive if they seem credible and attractive. Likewise, in courtrooms, high-status defendants often receive more leniency (McGillis, 1979).

Actual cases vary in so many ways—in the type of crime, in the status, age, gender, and race of the defendant—that it's difficult to isolate the factors that influence jurors. So experimenters have controlled such factors by giving mock jurors the same basic facts of a case while varying, for instance, the defendant's attractiveness or similarity to the jurors.

PHYSICAL ATTRACTIVENESS

The physical attractiveness stereotype holds that beautiful people seem like good people. Michael Efran (1974) wondered whether that stereotype would bias students' judgments of someone accused of cheating. He asked some of his University of Toronto students whether attractiveness should affect presumption of guilt. They answered, "No, it shouldn't." But did it? Yes. When Efran gave other students a description of the case with a photograph of either an attractive or an unattractive defendant, they judged the more attractive as less guilty and recommended a lesser punishment.

Other experimenters have confirmed that when the evidence is meager or ambiguous, justice is not blind to a defendant's looks (Maeder et al., 2015; Mazzella & Feingold, 1994). Baby-faced adults (people with large, round eyes and small chins) are judged as more naive and are found guilty more often of crimes of mere negligence but less often of intentional criminal acts (Berry & Zebrowitz-McArthur, 1988). If found guilty, unattractive people also strike people as more dangerous, especially if they are sexual offenders (Esses & Webster, 1988).

In a mammoth experiment conducted with BBC Television, Richard Wiseman (1998) showed viewers evidence about a burglary, with just one variation. Some viewers saw the defendant played by an actor who fit what a panel of 100 people judged as the stereotypical criminal—unattractive, crooked nose, small eyes. Among 64,000 people phoning in their verdict, 41 percent judged him guilty. British viewers elsewhere saw an attractive, baby-faced defendant with large blue eyes. Only 31 percent found him guilty.

To see if these findings extend to the real world, one study had police officers rate the physical attractiveness of 1,742 defendants appearing before 40 Texas judges in misdemeanor cases that were serious (such as forgery), moderate (such as harassment), or minor (such as public intoxication). In each type of case, the judges set higher bails and fines for less attractive defendants (Downs & Lyons, 1991; Figure 4). What explains this dramatic effect? Are unattractive people also lower in status? Are they more likely to flee or to commit another crime, as the judges perhaps suppose? Or do judges simply ignore the Roman statesman Cicero's advice: "The final good and the supreme duty of the wise man is to resist appearance."

FIGURE :: 4

Attractiveness and
Legal Judgments
Texas Gulf Coast judges set
higher bails and fines for less
attractive defendants.
Source: Data from Downs &
Lyons (1991).

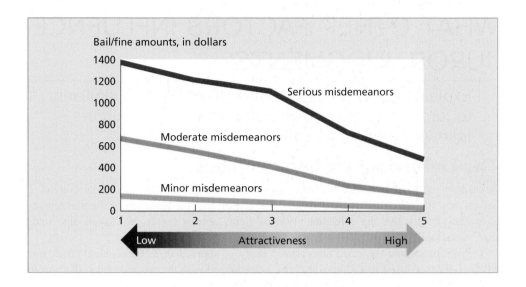

SIMILARITY TO THE JURORS

If Clarence Darrow was even partly right in his declaration that liking or disliking a defendant colors judgments, other factors that influence liking may also matter. Among such influences is the principle that similarity leads to liking. When people pretend they are jurors, they are indeed more sympathetic to a defendant who shares their attitudes, religion, race, or (in cases of sexual assault) gender (Selby et al., 1977; Towson & Zanna, 1983; Ugwuegbu, 1979). Juror racial bias is usually small, but jurors do exhibit some tendency to treat racial outgroups less favorably (Mitchell et al., 2005).

Some examples:

- In 1,748 small claims court cases in Israel, Jewish plaintiffs received more favorable outcomes when their cases were randomly assigned to Jewish judges, and Arab plaintiffs received more favorable outcomes when assigned to Arab judges (Shayo & Zussman, 2011).
- When a defendant's race fits a crime stereotype—say, a White defendant charged with embezzlement or a Black defendant charged with auto theft—mock jurors offer more negative verdicts and punishments (Jones & Kaplan, 2003; Mazzella & Feingold, 1994). Whites who espouse nonprejudiced views are more likely to demonstrate racial bias in trials in which race issues are not blatant (Sommers & Ellsworth, 2000, 2001).
- Australian students read evidence concerning a left- or right-wing person accused of a politically motivated burglary. The students judged less guilt when the defendant's political views were similar to their own (Amato, 1979).
- English-speaking participants were more likely to think someone accused of assault was not guilty if the defendant's testimony was in English rather than translated from Spanish or Thai (Stephan & Stephan, 1986).

A U.S. Sentencing Commission analysis of criminal convictions between 2007 and 2011 found that Black men received sentences 20 percent longer than those of White men in cases with the same seriousness and criminal history. Judges were also 25 percent less likely to show Black (vs. White) defendants leniency by giving a sentence shorter than suggested by federal sentencing guidelines (Palazzolo, 2013). Likewise, Blacks who kill Whites are more often sentenced to death than Whites who kill Blacks (Butterfield, 2001). Compared with killing a Black person, killing a White person is also three times as likely to lead (in one U.S. study) to a death sentence (Radelet & Pierce, 2011). As Craig Haney (1991) put it, "Blacks are overpunished as defendants or undervalued as victims, or both."

When neighborhood watch volunteer George Zimmerman (standing, above) fatally shot Black teen Trayvon Martin during a scuffle in 2012, he claimed self-defense and was not arrested until 6 weeks after the shooting, following a public outcry. Polls showed that 73 percent of Blacks believed Zimmerman would have been arrested sooner if Martin had been White, a view shared by only 35 percent of non-Blacks (Gallup, 2012). At his trial in 2013, Zimmerman was found not guilty, a verdict that 86 percent of Blacks, but only 30 percent of Whites, found dissatisfactory (Pew Research Center, 2013).
Source: The Guardian (UK)
POOL/Reuters/Corbis

In two studies, harsher sentences are also given those who look more stereotypically Black. Given similar criminal histories, Black and White inmates in Florida receive similar sentences—but within each race, those with more "Afrocentric" facial features are given longer sentences (Blair et al., 2004). Among Blacks convicted of murdering White victims over a 20-year period in Philadelphia, defendants whose appearance was more stereotypically Black were more likely to be sentenced to death (Eberhardt et al., 2006).

Ideally, jurors would leave their biases outside the courtroom and begin a trial with open minds. So implies the Sixth Amendment to the U.S. Constitution: "The accused shall enjoy the right to a speedy and public trial by impartial jury." In its concern for objectivity, the judicial system is similar to science. Both scientists and jurors are supposed to sift and weigh the evidence. Both the courts and science have rules about what evidence is relevant. Both keep careful records and assume that others given the same evidence would decide similarly.

When the evidence is clear and individuals focus on it (as when they reread and debate the meaning of testimony), their biases are indeed minimal (Kaplan & Schersching, 1980; Lieberman, 2011). The quality of the evidence matters more than the prejudices of the individual jurors.

The Judge's Instructions

All of us can recall courtroom dramas in which an attorney exclaimed, "Your honor, I object!" whereupon the judge sustains the objection and instructs the jury to ignore the other attorney's suggestive question or the witness's remark. How effective are such instructions?

Nearly all states in the United States now have "rape shield" statutes that prohibit or limit testimony

"You look like this sketch of someone who's thinking about committing a crime."

© David Sipress/The New Yorker Collection/www.cartoonbank.com

concerning the victim's prior sexual activity. Such testimony, though irrelevant to the case at hand, tends to make jurors more sympathetic to the accused rapist's claim that the woman consented to sex (Borgida, 1981; Cann et al., 1979). If such reliable, illegal, or prejudicial testimony is nevertheless slipped in by the defense or blurted out by a witness, will jurors follow a judge's instruction to ignore it? And is it enough for the judge to remind jurors, "The issue is not whether you like or dislike the defendant but whether the defendant committed the offense"?

Very possibly not. Several experimenters report that jurors show concern for due process (Fleming et al., 1999) but that they find it difficult to ignore inadmissible evidence, such as the defendant's previous convictions. In one study, University of Washington students heard a description of a grocery store robbery–murder and a summary of the prosecution's case and the defense's case. When the prosecution's case was weak, no one judged the defendant guilty. When a tape recording of an incriminating phone call made by the defendant was added to the weak case, approximately one-third judged the person guilty. The judge's instructions that the tape was not legal evidence and should be ignored did nothing to erase the effect of the damaging testimony (Sue et al., 1973).

Indeed, a judge's order to ignore testimony—"It must play no role in your consideration of the case. You have no choice but to disregard it"—can even boomerang, adding to the testimony's impact (Wolf & Montgomery, 1977). Perhaps such statements create **reactance** in the jurors. Or perhaps they sensitize jurors to the inadmissible testimony, as when we warn you not to notice your nose as you finish this sentence. Judges can more easily strike inadmissible testimony from the court records than from the jurors' minds. As trial lawyers sometimes say, "You can't unring a bell."

This is especially so with emotional information (Edwards & Bryan, 1997). Jurors are less able to ignore an emotionally provocative description of a defendant's record ("hacking up a woman") compared to a less emotional, dry legal description ("assault with a deadly weapon"). Even if jurors later claim to have ignored the inadmissible information, it may alter how they construe other information.

Pretrial publicity is also difficult for jurors to ignore (Steblay et al., 1999). In one large-scale experiment, 800 mock jurors saw incriminating news reports about the criminal record of a man accused of robbing a supermarket. Some heard the judge's instructions to disregard the pretrial publicity, and others did not. The effect of the judicial admonition? Nil. Those told to ignore it were just as likely to vote to convict (Kramer et al., 1990).

reactance
A motive to protect or restore one's sense of freedom. Reactance arises when someone threatens our freedom of action.

With a 24-hour news cycle, pretrial publicity often occurs before a jury is selected. Will jurors be biased by what they learned before they entered the courtroom? Although they deny being influenced, experiments have shown otherwise.
ZUMA Press, Inc./Alamy

People whose opinions are biased by pretrial publicity typically deny its effect on them, and that denial makes it difficult to eliminate biased jurors (Moran & Cutler, 1991). In experiments, even getting mock jurors to pledge their impartiality and their willingness to disregard prior information has not eliminated the pretrial publicity effect (Dexter et al., 1992).

Judges can hope, with some support from available research, that during deliberation, jurors who bring up inadmissible evidence will be chastised for doing so, thus limiting its influence on jury verdicts (London & Nunez, 2000). To minimize the effects of inadmissible testimony, judges also can forewarn jurors that certain types of evidence, such as a rape victim's sexual history, are irrelevant. Once jurors form impressions based on such evidence, a judge's admonitions have much less effect (Borgida & White, 1980; Kassin & Wrightsman, 1979). Thus, reports Vicki Smith (1991), a pretrial training session pays dividends. Teaching jurors legal procedures and standards of proof improves their understanding of the trial procedure and their willingness to withhold judgment until after they have heard all the trial information.

Better yet, judges could cut inadmissible testimony before the jurors hear it—by videotaping testimonies and removing the inadmissible parts. Live and videotaped testimonies have much the same impact as do live and videotaped lineups (Cutler et al., 1989; Miller & Fontes, 1979). Perhaps courtrooms of the future will have life-size television monitors. Videotaping not only enables the judge to edit out inadmissible testimony but also speeds up the trial and allows witnesses to talk about crucial events before memories fade.

Additional Factors

We have considered three courtroom factors—eyewitness testimony, the defendant's characteristics, and the judge's instructions. Researchers also study the influence of other factors. For example, does a severe potential punishment (for example, a death penalty) make jurors less willing to convict? Do experienced jurors' judgments differ from those of novice jurors? Are defendants judged more harshly when the *victim* is attractive or has suffered greatly? Research suggests that the answer to all three questions is yes (Kerr et al., 1978, 1981).

Experiments confirm that jurors' judgments of blame and punishment can be affected by the victim's characteristics—even when the defendant is unaware of such (Alicke & Davis, 1989; Enzle & Hawkins, 1992). Consider the 1984 case of the "subway vigilante" Bernard Goetz. When four teens asked Goetz for $5 on a New York subway, the frightened Goetz pulled out a loaded gun and shot each of them, leaving one partly paralyzed. When Goetz was charged with attempted homicide, there was an outcry of public support for him based partly on the disclosure that the youths had extensive criminal records and that three of them were carrying concealed, sharpened screwdrivers. Although Goetz didn't know any of this, he was acquitted of the attempted homicide charge and convicted only of illegal firearm possession.

SUMMING UP: What Other Factors Influence Juror Judgments?

- The facts of a case are usually compelling enough that jurors can lay aside their biases and render a fair judgment. When the evidence is ambiguous, however, jurors are more likely to interpret it with their preconceived biases and to feel sympathetic to a defendant who is attractive or similar to themselves.

- When jurors are exposed to damaging pretrial publicity or to inadmissible evidence, will they follow a judge's instruction to ignore it? In simulated trials, the judge's orders were sometimes followed, but often, especially when the judge's admonition came *after* an impression was made, they were not.

- Researchers have also explored the influence of other factors, such as the severity of the potential sentence and various characteristics of the victim.

WHAT INFLUENCES THE INDIVIDUAL JUROR?

│ Describe how verdicts depend on how the individual jurors process information.

Courtroom influences on "the average juror" are worth pondering. But no juror is the average juror; each carries into the courthouse individual attitudes and personalities. And when they deliberate, jurors influence one another. So two key questions are (1) How are verdicts influenced by individual jurors' characteristics? and (2) How are verdicts influenced by jurors' deliberations with each other?

Juror Comprehension

To gain insight into juror comprehension, researchers had mock jurors, sampled from courthouse jury pools, view reenactments of actual trials. In making their decisions, the jurors first constructed a story that made sense of all the evidence. After observing one murder trial, for example, some jurors concluded that a quarrel had made the defendant angry, triggering him to get a knife, search for the victim, and stab him to death. Others surmised that the frightened defendant picked up a knife that he used to defend himself when he later encountered the victim. When jurors begin deliberating, they often discover that others have constructed different stories (Pennington & Hastie, 1993). This implies—and research confirms—that jurors are best persuaded when attorneys present evidence in narrative fashion—a story. In felony cases, where the national conviction rate is 80 percent, the prosecution case more often than the defense case follows a narrative structure.

UNDERSTANDING INSTRUCTIONS

Next, the jurors must grasp the judge's instructions concerning the available verdict categories. For those instructions to be effective, jurors must first understand them. Study after study has found that many people do not understand the standard legalese of judicial instructions. Depending on the type of case, a jury may be told that the standard of proof is a "preponderance of the evidence," "clear and convincing evidence," or "beyond a reasonable doubt." Such statements may have one meaning for the legal community and different meanings in the minds of jurors (Kagehiro, 1990; Wright & Hall, 2007).

A judge may also remind jurors to avoid premature conclusions as they weigh each new item of presented evidence. But research with both college students and mock jurors chosen from prospective jury pools shows that warm-blooded human beings do form premature opinions, and those leanings do influence how they interpret new information (Carlson & Russo, 2001).

After observing actual cases and later interviewing the jurors, Stephen Adler (1994) found "lots of sincere, serious people who—for a variety of reasons—were missing key points, focusing on irrelevant issues, succumbing to barely recognized prejudices, failing to see through the cheapest appeals to sympathy or hate, and generally botching the job."

INCREASING JURORS' UNDERSTANDING

Understanding how jurors misconstrue judicial instructions is a first step toward better decisions. A next step might be giving jurors access to transcripts rather than forcing them to rely on their memories in processing complex information (Bourgeois et al., 1993). A further step would be devising and testing clearer, more effective ways to present information—a task on which several social psychologists have worked. For example, when a judge quantifies the required standard of proof (as, for instance, 51, 71, or 91 percent certainty), jurors understand and respond appropriately (Kagehiro, 1990). And surely there must be a simpler way to tell jurors, as required by the Illinois Death Penalty Act, not to impose the death sentence in murder cases when there are justifying circumstances: "If you do not unanimously find from your consideration of all the evidence that there are no mitigating factors sufficient to preclude imposition of a death sentence, then you should sign the verdict requiring the court to impose a sentence other than death" (Diamond, 1993). When jurors are given instructions rewritten into simple language, they are less susceptible to the judge's biases (Halverson et al., 1997; Smith & Haney, 2011).

Phoebe Ellsworth and Robert Mauro (1998) sum up the dismal conclusions of jury researchers: "Legal instructions are typically delivered in a manner likely to frustrate the most conscientious attempts at understanding. . . . The language is technical and . . . no attempt is made either to assess jurors' mistaken preconceptions about the law or to provide any kind of useful education." When jury instructions are instead written in more understandable "plain language," comprehension increases. Even better are instructions that define key terms, eliminate information irrelevant to the particular case, and use names instead of terms such as "the defendant" (Smith & Haney, 2011).

Jury Selection

Given the variations among individual jurors, can trial lawyers use the jury selection process to stack juries in their favor? Legal folklore suggests that sometimes they can. One president of the Association of Trial Lawyers of America boldly proclaimed, "Trial attorneys are acutely attuned to the nuances of human behavior, which enables them to detect the minutest traces of bias or inability to reach an appropriate decision" (Bigam, 1977). In actuality, attorneys, like all of us, are vulnerable to overconfidence. For example, they overestimate the likelihood of their meeting their goals (such as acquittal) in trial cases, and likely also of their ability to read jurors (Goodman-Delahunty et al., 2010).

Mindful that people's assessments of others are error prone, social psychologists doubt that attorneys come equipped with fine-tuned social Geiger counters. In some 6,000 American trials a year, consultants—some of them social scientists—help lawyers pick juries and plot strategy (Gavzer, 1997; Hutson, 2007; Miller, 2001).

Many trial attorneys have now used scientific jury selection to identify questions they can use to exclude those biased against their clients, and most have reported satisfaction with the results (Gayoso et al., 1991; Moran et al., 1994). Most jurors, when asked by a judge to "raise your hand if you've read anything about this case that would prejudice you," don't directly acknowledge their preconceptions. But if, for example, the judge allows an attorney to check prospective jurors' attitudes toward drugs, the attorney can often guess their verdicts in a drug-trafficking case (Moran et al., 1990). Likewise, people who acknowledge they "don't put much faith in the testimony of psychiatrists" are less likely to accept an insanity defense (Cutler et al., 1992).

Individuals react differently to specific case features. Racial prejudice becomes relevant in racially charged cases; gender seems linked with verdicts only in rape and battered-woman cases; belief in personal responsibility versus corporate responsibility relates to personal injury awards in suits against businesses (Ellsworth & Mauro, 1998).

Despite the excitement—and ethical concern—about scientific jury selection, experiments reveal that attitudes and personal characteristics are weak verdict predictors (Lieberman, 2011). There are "no magic questions to be asked of prospective jurors," cautioned Steven Penrod and Brian Cutler (1987). Researchers Michael Saks and Reid Hastie (1978) agreed: "The studies are unanimous in showing that evidence is a substantially more potent determinant of jurors' verdicts than the individual characteristics of jurors" (p. 68).

Ditto for judges. At her Senate confirmation hearing, the first Hispanic U.S. Supreme Court Justice, Sonia Sotomayor,

"Beware of the Lutherans, especially the Scandinavians; they are almost always sure to convict."

—Clarence Darrow, "How to Pick a Jury," 1936

© Dave Coverly/Speedbump.com

FIGURE :: 5

Hungry = harsh. After a food break (the dotted lines), Israeli judges became more likely, for a time, to approve prisoners' requests for parole (Danziger et al., 2011).

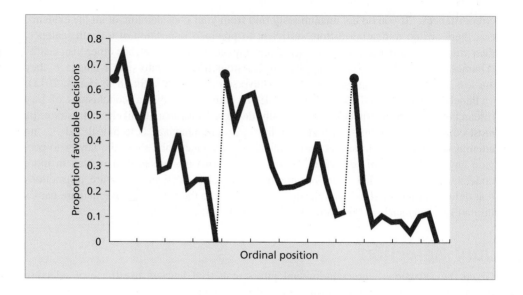

assured her skeptical questioners that she would follow the law without influence from her background and identity. But complete neutrality is an ideal that even judges seldom attain (as illustrated by the 5-to-4 Supreme Court vote that decided the contested 2000 U.S. presidential election for Republican George W. Bush, with conservative and liberal judges voting in opposition). Simple weariness can also color judges' judgments. In one study of 1,112 Israeli parole board hearings, judges granted parole to 65 percent of the prisoners when their cases were decided right after a lunch or snack break, with favorable decisions declining thereafter with time (Figure 5).

"Death-Qualified" Jurors

A *close* case can, however, be decided by who is selected for the jury. In criminal cases, people who do not oppose the death penalty—and who therefore are eligible to serve when a death sentence is possible—are more prone to favor the prosecution, to feel that courts coddle criminals, and to oppose protecting the constitutional rights of defendants (Bersoff, 1987). Simply put, these "death-qualified" jurors are more concerned with crime control and less concerned with due process of law. When a court dismisses potential jurors who have moral scruples against the death penalty, it constructs a jury that is more likely to vote guilty.

On this issue, social scientists are in "virtual unanimity . . . about the biasing effects of death qualification," reports Craig Haney (1993). The research record is "unified," reports Phoebe Ellsworth (1985, p. 46): "Defendants in capital-punishment cases do assume the extra handicap of juries predisposed to find them guilty." What is more, conviction-prone jurors tend also to be more authoritarian—more rigid, punitive, closed to mitigating circumstances, and contemptuous of those of lower status (Gerbasi et al., 1977; Luginbuhl & Middendorf, 1988; Moran & Comfort, 1982, 1986; Werner et al., 1982).

Because the legal system operates on tradition and precedent, such research findings only slowly alter judicial practice. In 1986, the U.S. Supreme Court, in a split decision, overturned a lower court ruling that death-qualified jurors are indeed a biased sample. Ellsworth (1989) believes the Court in this case disregarded the compelling and consistent evidence partly because of its "ideological commitment to capital punishment" and partly because of the havoc that would result if the convictions of thousands of people on death row had to be reconsidered. The solution, should the Court ever wish to adopt it for future cases, is to convene separate juries to (a) decide guilt in capital murder cases, and, given a guilty verdict, to (b) hear additional evidence on factors motivating the murder and to decide between death or imprisonment.

But a deeper issue is at stake here: whether the death penalty itself falls under the U.S. Constitution's ban on "cruel and unusual punishment." Canada, Australia, New Zealand, Western Europe, and most countries in South America prohibit capital punishment. There,

"The kind of juror who would be unperturbed by the prospect of sending a man to his death . . . is the kind of juror who would too readily ignore the presumption of the defendant's innocence, accept the prosecution's version of the facts, and return a verdict of guilty."

—*Witherspoon v. Illinois*, 1968

as in the United States, public attitudes tend to support the prevailing practice (Costanzo, 1997). But American pro-capital punishment attitudes seem to be softening. After reaching 80 percent in 1994, support fell to 63 percent in 2011 (Gallup, 2014).

In wrestling with the punishment, U.S. courts have considered whether courts inflict the penalty arbitrarily, whether they apply it with racial bias, and whether legal killing deters illegal killing. The social science answers to these questions are clear (Costanzo, 1997; Haney & Logan, 1994). Consider the deterrence issue. States with a death penalty do not have lower homicide rates. Homicide rates have not dropped when states have initiated the death penalty, and they have not risen when states have abolished it. When committing a crime of passion, people don't pause to calculate the consequences (which include life in prison without parole as another potent deterrent). Moreover, the death penalty is applied inconsistently (in Texas 40 times as often as in New York). And it is applied more often with poor defendants, who often receive a weak defense (*Economist,* 2000; Johnson & Johnson, 2001). Nevertheless, the Supreme Court has determined that admitting only death-qualified jurors provides a representative jury of one's peers and that "the death penalty undoubtedly is a significant deterrent."

Humanitarian considerations aside, say the appalled social scientists, what is the rationale for clinging to cherished assumptions and intuitions in the face of contradictory evidence? Why not put our cultural ideas to the test? If they find support, so much the better for them. If they crash against a wall of contradictory evidence, so much the worse for them. Such are the ideals of critical thinking that fuel both psychological science and civil democracy.

SUMMING UP: What Influences the Individual Juror?

- Social psychologists are interested in not only the interactions among witnesses, judges, and juries but also what happens within and between individual jurors. One major concern is jurors' ability to comprehend evidence, especially when it involves statistics indicating the probability that a given person committed the crime.

- Trial lawyers often use jury consultants to help them select jurors most sympathetic to their case. People who are aware of pretrial publicity, for example, may be disqualified from serving.

- In cases in which the death penalty may be applied, lawyers can disqualify any prospective juror who opposes the death penalty on principle. Social psychology research argues that this in itself produces a biased jury, but the Supreme Court has ruled otherwise.

HOW DO GROUP INFLUENCES AFFECT JURIES?

Explain how individual jurors' prejudgments coalesce into a group decision and what can influence the outcome.

Imagine a jury that has just finished a trial and has entered the jury room to begin its deliberations. Chances are approximately two in three that the jurors will *not* agree initially on a verdict. Yet, after discussion, 95 percent emerge with a consensus (Kalven & Zeisel, 1966). Group influence has occurred.

Are juries subject to the social influences that mold other decision groups—to patterns of majority and minority influence? To group polarization? To groupthink? Let's start with a simple question: If we knew the jurors' initial leanings, could we predict their verdict?

The law prohibits observing actual juries, so researchers simulate the jury process. They present a case to mock juries and have them deliberate as a real jury would. In a series of such studies, researchers tested various mathematical schemes for predicting group decisions, including decisions by mock juries (Davis et al., 1975, 1977, 1989; Kerr et al., 1976). Will some mathematical combination of initial decisions predict the final group decision? Davis and colleagues found that the scheme that predicts best varies with the nature of the case. But in several experiments, a "two-thirds-majority" scheme fared best: The group verdict was usually the alternative favored by at least two-thirds of the jurors at the outset. Without such a majority, a hung jury was likely.

Likewise, in a survey of juries, 9 in 10 reached the verdict favored by the majority on the first ballot (Kalven & Zeisel, 1966). Although we might fantasize about someday being the courageous lone juror who sways the majority, it seldom happens.

Minority Influence

Seldom, yet sometimes, what was initially a minority opinion prevails. A typical 12-person jury is like a typical small college class: The three quietest people rarely talk, and the three most vocal people contribute more than half the talking (Hastie et al., 1983). In one trial, the four jurors who favored acquittal persisted, were vocal, and eventually prevailed. From the research on minority influence, we know that jurors in the minority will be most persuasive when they are consistent, persistent, and self-confident. This is especially so if they can begin to trigger some defections from the majority (Gordijn et al., 2002; Kerr, 1981b).

Group Polarization

Jury deliberation shifts people's opinions in other intriguing ways as well. In experiments, deliberation often magnifies initial sentiments. For example, University of Kentucky students listened to a 30-minute tape of a murder trial and were asked to recommend a prison sentence. Groups with several students high in authoritarian attitudes initially recommended strong punishments (56 years) and after deliberation were even more punitive (68 years). The low-authoritarian groups were initially more lenient (38 years) and after deliberation became even more lenient lowering the sentence to 29 years (Bray & Noble, 1978). By contrast, group diversity often moderates judgments. Compared with Whites who judge Black defendants on all-White mock juries, those serving on racially mixed mock juries enter deliberation expressing more leniency and exhibit openness to a wider range of information (Sommers, 2006).

Confirmation of group polarization in juries comes from an ambitious study of 69 twelve-person mock juries. Each was shown a reenactment of an actual murder case, with roles played by an experienced judge and actual attorneys. Then they were given unlimited time to deliberate the case in a jury room. As Figure 6 shows, the evidence was incriminating:

FIGURE :: 6

Group Polarization in Juries

In highly realistic simulations of a murder trial, 828 Massachusetts jurors stated their initial verdict preferences, then deliberated the case for periods ranging from 3 hours to 5 days. Deliberation strengthened initial tendencies that favored the prosecution.
Source: From Hastie et al. (1983).

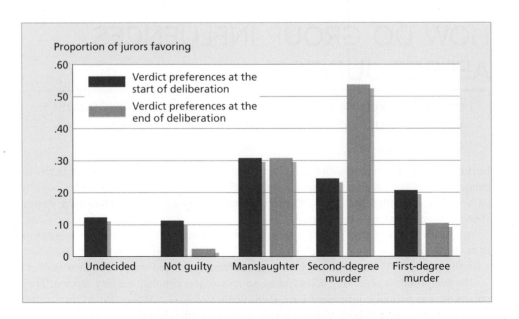

Before deliberation, four out of five jurors voted guilty but felt unsure enough that a weak verdict of manslaughter was their most popular preference. After deliberation, nearly all agreed the accused was guilty, and most now preferred a stronger verdict—second-degree murder (Hastie et al., 1983). Through deliberation, the jury's initial leanings had grown stronger—a classic example of group polarization. (For another example, see Research Close-up: Group Polarization in a Natural Court Setting).

research CLOSE-UP   Group Polarization in a Natural Court Setting

In simulated juries, deliberation often amplifies jurors' individual inclinations. Does such group polarization occur in actual courts? Cass Sunstein, David Schkade, and Lisa Ellman (2004) show us how researchers can harvest data from natural settings when exploring social psychological phenomena. Their data were 14,874 votes by judges on 4,958 three-judge U.S. circuit court panels. (On these federal "Courts of Appeals," an appeal is almost always heard by three of the court's judges.)

Sunstein and his colleagues first asked whether a judge's votes tended to reflect the ideology of the Republican or Democratic president who appointed them. Indeed, when voting on ideologically tinged cases involving affirmative action, environmental regulation, campaign finance, and abortion, Democratic-appointed judges more often supported the liberal position than did Republican-appointed judges. No surprise there. That's what presidents and their party members assume when seeking congressional approval of their kindred-spirited judicial nominees.

Would such tendencies be amplified when the panel had three judges appointed by the same party? Would three Republican-appointed judges be even more often conservative than the average Republican appointee? And would three Democratic-appointed judges be more

often liberal than the average Democrat appointee? Or would judges vote their convictions uninfluenced by their fellow panelists? Table 2 presents their findings.

Note that when three appointees from the same party formed a panel (RRR or DDD), they became more likely to vote their party's ideological preference than did the average individual judge. The polarization exhibited by like-minded threesomes was, the Sunstein team reported, "confirmed in many areas, including affirmative action, campaign finance, sex discrimination, sexual harassment, piercing the corporate veil, disability discrimination, race discrimination, and review of environmental regulations" (although not in the politically volatile cases of abortion and capital punishment, where judges voted their well-formed convictions).

Sunstein and colleagues offer an example: If all three judges "believe that an affirmative action program is unconstitutional, and no other judge is available to argue on its behalf, then the exchange of arguments in the room will suggest that the program is genuinely unconstitutional." This is group polarization in action, they conclude—an example of "one of the most striking findings in modern social science: Groups of like-minded people tend to go to extremes."

TABLE :: 2 Proportion of "Liberal" Voting by Individual Judges and by Three-Judge Panels

	Individual Judges' Votes		Individual Judges' Votes, by Panel Composition			
	Party					
Examples of Case Type	R	D	RRR	RRD	RDD	DDD
Campaign finance	.28	.46	.23	.30	.35	.80
Affirmative action	.48	.74	.37	.50	.83	.85
Environmental	.46	.64	.27	.55	.62	.72
Sex discrimination	.35	.51	.31	.38	.49	.75
Average across 13 case types	.38	.51	.34	.39	.50	.61

D, Democratic appointee; R, Republican appointee.

Leniency

In many experiments, one other curious effect of deliberation has surfaced: Especially when the evidence is not highly incriminating, jurors often become more lenient over the course of deliberations (MacCoun & Kerr, 1988). Even if only a bare majority initially favors finding the defendant not guilty, that bare majority will usually prevail (Stasser et al., 1981). Moreover, a minority that favors a not-guilty verdict stands a better chance of prevailing than one that favors conviction (Tindale et al., 1990).

Again, a survey of actual juries confirms the laboratory results. When the majority does not prevail, the shift is usually from guilty to not guilty (Kalven & Zeisel, 1966). When a judge disagrees with the jury's decision, it is usually because the jury acquits someone the judge would have convicted.

Might "informational influence" (stemming from others' persuasive arguments) account for the increased leniency? The "innocent-unless-proved-guilty" and "proof-beyond-a-reasonable-doubt" rules put the burden of proof on those who favor conviction. Perhaps this makes evidence of the defendant's innocence more persuasive. Or perhaps "normative influence" creates the leniency effect, as jurors who view themselves as fair-minded confront other jurors who are even more concerned with protecting a possibly innocent defendant.

"It is better that ten guilty persons escape than one innocent suffer."

—William Blackstone, 1769

Are Twelve Heads Better Than One?

When a problem has an objective right answer, group judgments surpass those by most individuals. Does the same hold true in juries? When deliberating, jurors exert normative pressure by trying to shift others' judgments by the sheer weight of their own. But they also share information, thus enlarging one another's understanding. So, does informational influence produce superior collective judgment?

The evidence, though meager, is encouraging. Groups recall information from a trial better than do their individual members (Vollrath et al., 1989). Deliberation also tends to cancel out certain biases and draws jurors' attention away from their own prejudgments and to the evidence. Twelve heads can be, it seems, better than one.

Are Six Heads as Good as Twelve?

In keeping with their British heritage, juries in the United States and Canada have traditionally been composed of 12 people whose task is to reach consensus—a unanimous verdict. However, in civil cases and state criminal cases not potentially involving a death

12-member juries are more diverse and deliberate longer than 6-member juries.
© bikeriderlondon/Shutterstock

penalty, the Supreme Court ruled in the early 1970s that courts could use 6-person juries. Do such juries operate the same as 12-person juries?

Many legal scholars and social psychologists argue that the answer is no (Saks, 1974, 1996). First, consider the statistics. For example, if 10 percent of a community's total jury pool is Black, then 72 percent of 12-member juries but only 47 percent of 6-member juries may be expected to have at least one Black person. So smaller juries may be less likely to include a community's diversity.

And if, in a given case, one-sixth of the jurors initially favor acquittal, that would be a single individual in a 6-member jury and 2 people in a 12-member jury. The Court assumed that, psychologically, the two situations would be identical. But as you may recall from our discussion of conformity, resisting group pressure is far more difficult for a minority of one than for a minority of two. Psychologically speaking, a jury split 10 to 2 is not equivalent to a jury split 5 to 1. Not surprisingly, then, 12-person juries are twice as likely as 6-person juries to have hung verdicts (Ellsworth & Mauro, 1998; Saks & Marti, 1997).

Jury researcher Michael Saks (1998) sums up the research findings: "Larger juries are more likely than smaller juries to contain members of minority groups, more accurately recall trial testimony, give more time to deliberation, hang more often, and appear more likely to reach 'correct' verdicts."

In 1978, after some of these studies were reported, the Supreme Court rejected Georgia's 5-member juries. Announcing the Court's decision, Justice Harry Blackmun drew upon both the logical and the experimental data to argue that 5-person juries would be less representative, less reliable, and less accurate (Grofman, 1980). Ironically, many of these data actually involved comparisons of 6- versus 12-member juries and thus also argued against the 6-member jury. But having made and defended a public commitment to the 6-member jury, the Court was not convinced that the same arguments applied (Tanke & Tanke, 1979).

From Lab to Life: Simulated and Real Juries

Perhaps while reading this chapter, you have wondered what some critics (Tapp, 1980; Vidmar, 1979) have wondered: Isn't there an enormous gulf between college students

Hung juries are rarely a problem. Among 59,511 U.S. federal court criminal trials during one 13-year period, 2.5 percent ended in a hung jury, as did a mere 0.6 percent of 67,992 federal civil trials (Saks, 1998).

"We have considered [the social science studies] carefully because they provide the only basis, besides judicial hunch, for a decision about whether smaller and smaller juries will be able to fulfill the purposes and functions of the Sixth Amendment."

—Justice Harry Blackmun, *Ballew v. Georgia*, 1978

Attorneys are using new technology to present crime stories in ways jurors can easily grasp, as in this computer simulation of a homicide generated on the basis of forensic evidence.
Courtesy of Alexander Jason

discussing a hypothetical case and real jurors deliberating a real person's fate? Indeed there is. It is one thing to ponder a pretend decision, given minimal information, and quite another to agonize over the complexities and profound consequences of an actual case. So Reid Hastie, Martin Kaplan, James Davis, Eugene Borgida, and others have asked their participants, who sometimes are drawn from actual juror pools, to view enactments of actual trials. The enactments are so realistic that sometimes participants forget the trial they are watching on television is staged (Thompson et al., 1981).

Student mock jurors become engaged, too. "As I eavesdropped on the mock juries," recalls researcher Norbert Kerr (1999), "I became fascinated by the jurors' insightful arguments, their mix of amazing recollections and memory fabrications, their prejudices, their attempts to persuade or coerce, and their occasional courage in standing alone. Here brought to life before me were so many of the psychological processes I had been studying! Although our student jurors understood they were only simulating a real trial, they really cared about reaching a fair verdict."

The U.S. Supreme Court (1986) debated the usefulness of jury research in its decision regarding the use of death-qualified jurors in capital punishment cases. Defendants have a constitutional "right to a fair trial and an impartial jury whose composition is not biased toward the prosecution." The dissenting judges argued that this right is violated when jurors include only those who accept the death penalty. Their argument, they said, was based chiefly on "the essential unanimity of the results obtained by researchers using diverse subjects and varied methodologies." The majority of the judges, however, declared their "serious doubts about the value of these studies in predicting the behavior of actual jurors." The dissenting judges replied that the courts have not allowed experiments with actual juries; thus, "defendants claiming prejudice from death qualification should not be denied recourse to the only available means of proving their case."

Researchers also defend the laboratory simulations by noting that the laboratory offers a practical, inexpensive method of studying important issues under controlled conditions (Dillehay & Nietzel, 1980; Kerr & Bray, 2005). As researchers have begun testing them in more realistic situations, findings from the laboratory studies have often held up quite well. No one contends that the simplified world of the jury experiment mirrors the complex world of the real courtroom. Rather, the experiments help us formulate theories with which we interpret the complex world.

Come to think of it, are these jury simulations any different from social psychology's other experiments, all of which create simplified versions of complex realities? By varying just one or two factors at a time in this simulated reality, the experimenter pinpoints how changes in one or two aspects of a situation can affect us. And that is the essence of social psychology's experimental method.

SUMMING UP: How Do Group Influences Affect Juries?

- Juries are groups, and they are swayed by the same influences that bear upon other types of groups. For example, the most vocal members of a jury tend to do most of the talking, and the quietest members say little.

- As a jury deliberates, opposing views may become more entrenched and polarized.

- Especially when evidence is not highly incriminating, deliberation may make jurors more lenient than they originally were.

- The 12-member jury is a tradition stemming from English Common Law. Researchers find that a jury this size allows for reasonable diversity among jurors, a

mix of opinions and orientations, and better recall of information.

- Researchers have also examined and questioned the assumptions underlying several recent U.S. Supreme Court decisions permitting smaller juries and non-unanimous juries.

- Simulated juries are not real juries, so we must be cautious in generalizing research findings to actual courtrooms. Yet, like all experiments in social psychology, laboratory jury experiments help us formulate theories and principles that we can use to interpret the more complex world of everyday life.

POSTSCRIPT:
Thinking Smart with Psychological Science

An intellectually fashionable idea, sometimes called "postmodernism," contends that truth is socially constructed; knowledge always reflects the cultures that form it. Indeed, as we have often noted in this book, we do often follow our hunches, our biases, our cultural bent. Social scientists are not immune to confirmation bias, belief perseverance, overconfidence, and the biasing power of preconceptions. Our preconceived ideas and values guide our theory development, our interpretations, our topics of choice, and our language.

Being mindful of hidden values within psychological science should motivate us to clean the cloudy spectacles through which we view the world. Mindful of our vulnerability to bias and error, we can steer between the two extremes—of being naive about a value-laden psychology that pretends to be value-neutral or of being tempted to an unrestrained subjectivism that dismisses evidence as nothing but collected biases. In the spirit of humility, we can put testable ideas to the test. If we think capital punishment does (or does not) deter crime more than other available punishments, we can utter our personal opinions, as has the U.S. Supreme Court. Or we can ask whether states with a death penalty have lower homicide rates, whether their rates have dropped after instituting the death penalty, and whether they have risen when abandoning the penalty.

As we have seen, the Court considered pertinent social science evidence when disallowing 5-member juries and ending school desegregation. But it has discounted research when offering opinions as to whether the death penalty deters crime, whether society views execution as what the U.S. Constitution prohibits ("cruel and unusual punishment"), whether courts inflict the penalty arbitrarily, whether they apply it with racial bias, and whether potential jurors selected by virtue of their accepting capital punishment are biased toward conviction.

Beliefs and values do guide the perceptions of judges as well as scientists and laypeople. And that is why we need to think smarter—to rein in our hunches and biases by testing them against available evidence. If our beliefs find support, so much the better for them. If not, so much the worse for them. That's the humble spirit that underlies both psychological science and everyday critical thinking.

Social Psychology and the Sustainable Future

Maxstock/Alamy RF

"Have always in view not only the present but also the coming generations, even those whose faces are yet beneath the surface of the ground—the unborn of the future Nation."

—*Gayanashagowa*, the Constitution of the Iroquois Nations (also known as "The Great Law of Peace")

Imagine yourself on a huge spaceship traveling through our galaxy. To sustain your community, a spacecraft biosphere grows plants and breeds animals. By recycling waste and managing resources, the mission has, until recently, been sustainable over time and across generations of people born onboard.

The spaceship's name is Planet Earth, and its expanding crew now numbers 7.3 billion. Alas, it increasingly consumes its resources at an unsustainable rate—50 percent beyond the spaceship's capacity. Thus, it takes the Earth a year and a half to regenerate what we use in a year (FootPrintNetwork.org, 2014). With the growing population and consumption have come deforestation, depletion of wild fish stocks, and climate destabilization. Some crew members are especially demanding. For all 7.3 billion to live the average American lifestyle would require four Planet Earths.

In 1960, the spaceship Earth carried 3 billion people and 127 million motor vehicles. Today, with more than 7 billion people, it has more than 1 billion motor vehicles. The greenhouse gases emitted by motor vehicles, along with the burning of coal and oil to generate electricity and heat homes and buildings, are changing the Earth's climate. To ascertain how much and how fast climate change is occurring, several thousand scientists worldwide have collaborated to create and review the evidence via the Intergovernmental Panel on Climate Change (IPCC). The past chair of its scientific assessment committee, John Houghton (2011), reports that their conclusions—supported by the national academies of science of the world's 11 most developed countries—are undergirded by the most "thoroughly researched and reviewed" scientific effort in human history.

As the IPCC (2014) and the American Association for the Advancement of Science (2014) report, and Figure 1 illustrates, converging evidence verifies climate change:

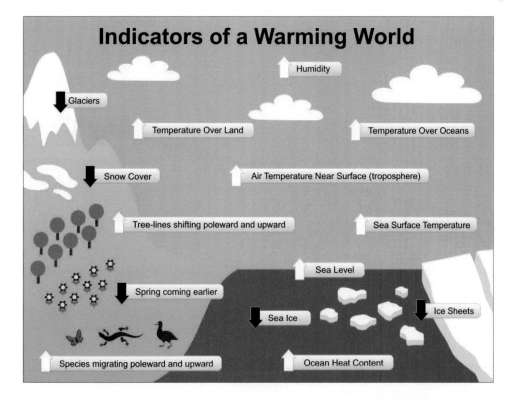

FIGURE :: 1

A synopsis of scientific indicators of global climate change.
Source: From John Cook (2010, and skepticalscience.com).

"The evidence is overwhelming: levels of greenhouse gases in the atmosphere are rising. Temperatures are going up. Springs are arriving earlier. Ice sheets are melting. Sea level is rising. The patterns of rainfall and drought are changing. Heat waves are getting worse as is extreme precipitation. The oceans are acidifying."

—American Association for the Advancement of Science (2014)

- *A warming greenhouse gas blanket is growing.* About half the carbon dioxide emitted by human activity since the Industrial Revolution (since 1750) remains in the atmosphere (Royal Society, 2010).

- There is now 39 percent more atmospheric carbon dioxide and 158 percent more atmospheric methane than before industrial times—and the increase has recently accelerated (World Meteorological Organization, 2011). As the permafrost thaws, methane gas release threatens to compound the problem (Carey, 2012).

- *Sea and air temperatures are rising.* The numbers—the facts—have no political leanings. The ten warmest years on record have all occurred since 1998 (NASA, 2014 Figure 2). If the world were not warming, random weather variations should produce equal numbers of record-breaking high and low temperatures. In reality,

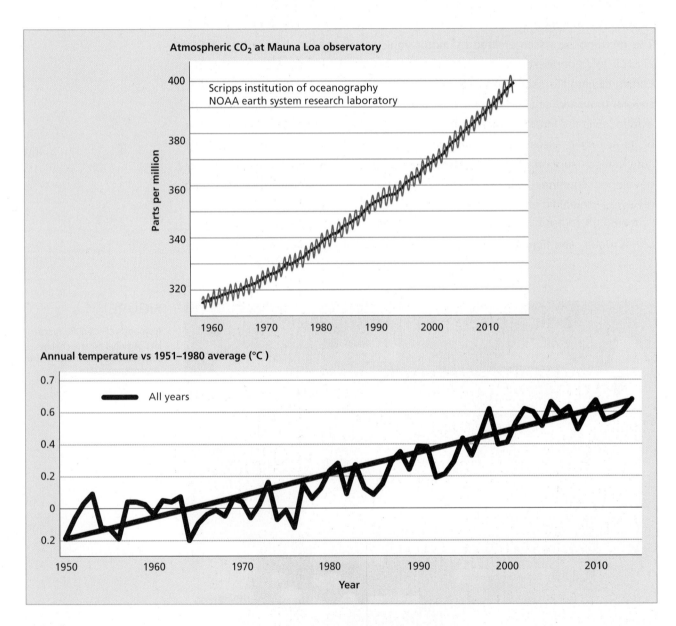

FIGURE :: 2

Global climate on steroids. As atmospheric CO_2 has risen, so have global temperatures.

Sources: (Top) http://www.esrl.noaa.gov/gmd/webdata/ccgg/trends/co2_data_mlo.png; (bottom) http://www.giss.nasa.gov/research/news/20150116/graph_gis_2014_lrg.pdf. (NASA/GSFC/Earth Observatory, NASA/GISS)

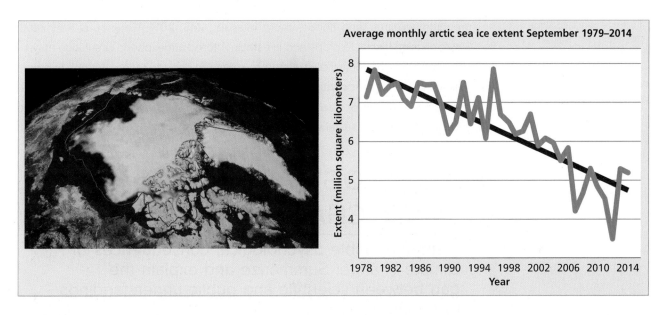

FIGURE :: 3

The shrinking ice cap. The National Snow and Ice Data Center and NASA show the September 2014, minimum Arctic ice sheet, compared with the average 1981–2010 minimum ice sheet. The figure depicts the shrinking September ice sheet year by year.

Source: (left) http://www.nasa.gov/press/2014/september/2014-arctic-sea-ice-minimum-sixth-lowest-on-record/#.VJW07P-AKA; (right) http://nsidc.org/arcticseaicenews/2014/10/2014-melt-season-in-review/.

NASA/Goddard Scientific Visualization Studio

record highs have been greatly outnumbering record lows—by about 5 to 1 in the United States, for example (Gillis, 2013). Australia has recently been experiencing three times as many record hot days as record cold days (Siegel, 2013).

- *Various plant and animal species are migrating.* In response to the warming world, they are creeping toward the poles and to higher elevations, with anticipated loss of biodiversity (Harley, 2011; Houghton, 2011).

- *Ice and snow packs are melting.* The late-summer Arctic ice cover has shrunk from nearly 3 million square miles in the late 1970s to 1.67 million square miles in 2011 (Figure 3). The West Antarctica and Greenland glacial ice sheets are also melting—faster than ever (Kerr, 2011). Most of the glaciers of Glacier National Park are now gone, with depleted summer melt and runoff for irrigation. Since 1979, Northern Hemisphere snow cover has shrunk 19.9 percent per decade (NOAA, 2014).

- *The seas are rising.* Projections of rising sea levels portend large problems for coastal and low-lying areas, including Pakistan, southern China, and Indian and Pacific Ocean islands (Houghton, 2011).

- *Extreme weather is increasing.* Any single weather event—a heat wave here, a hurricane there—cannot be attributed to climate change. Weird weather happens. But it is happening more often. Average annual weather-related losses (adjusted for inflation) have quadrupled—from $30 billion (1983–1992) to $131 billion (2004–2013), according to insurance giant Swiss Re (Borenstein, 2014). Moreover, climate scientists predict that global warming will make extreme weather events—heat waves, droughts, wildfires, and floods—more intense (AMS, 2014; Coumou & Rahmstorf, 2012), causing losses to crops and livestock. Altered atmospheric circulation may simultaneously bring record cold winters to some regions and record warmth to others (Palmer, 2014). As precipitation in a warming and wetter world falls more as rain and less as snow, the likely result will be more rainy season floods and less dry season snow and ice melt to sustain rivers.

PSYCHOLOGY AND CLIMATE CHANGE

Identify possible psychological consequences of climate change. Summarize and explain the gap between scientific and public understandings of climate change.

Throughout its history, social psychology has responded to human events—to the civil rights era with studies of stereotyping and prejudice, to years of civil unrest and increasing crime with studies of aggression, to the women's movement with studies of gender development and gender-related attitudes. If global climate change is now "the greatest problem the world faces" (Houghton, 2011), surely psychological science will more and more study the likely effects of climate change on human behavior, of public opinion about climate change, and of ways to modify the human sources of climate change. Such inquiry is under way.

Psychological Effects of Climate Change

It's a national security issue, say some: Terrorist bombs and climate change are both weapons of mass destruction. "If we learned that al Qaeda was secretly developing a new terrorist technique that could disrupt water supplies around the globe, force tens of millions from their homes and potentially endanger our entire planet, we would be aroused into a frenzy and deploy every possible asset to neutralize the threat," observed essayist Nicholas Kristof (2007). "Yet that is precisely the threat that we're creating ourselves, with our greenhouse gases." Consider the human consequences.

Is the weather getting weirder? In 2011, reported NOAA, the United States experienced a dozen billion-dollar weather disasters, sharply up from the more typical three or four. No single weather event, such as the massive Joplin, Missouri, tornado shown here, can be attributed to climate change. But climate scientists warn that global warming will produce increasing extreme weather events and increased human displacement and trauma.
Mario Tama/Getty Images

DISPLACEMENT AND TRAUMA

If temperatures increase by the expected 2° to 4° Celsius this century, the resulting changes in water availability, agriculture, disaster risk, and sea level will necessitate massive resettlement (de Sherbinin et al., 2011). When drought or floods force people to leave their land, shelter, and work, as when sub-Saharan African farming and grazing lands become desert, the frequent result is increased poverty and hunger, earlier death, and loss of cultural identity. If an extreme weather event or climate change disrupted your ties to a place and its people, you could expect to feel grief, anxiety, and a sense of loss (Doherty & Clayton, 2011). For social and mental health, climate matters.

CLIMATE AND CONFLICT

Got war? Blame the climate. Such is often the case. Many human maladies—from economic downturns to wars—have been traced to climate fluctuations (Zhang et al., 2011). When the climate changes, agriculture often suffers, leading to increased famine, epidemics, and overall misery. Poorer countries, with fewer resources, are especially vulnerable (Fischer & Van de Vliert, 2011). And when miserable, people become more prone to anger with their governments and with one another, leading to war. For social stability, climate matters.

One analysis of 60 quantitative studies revealed conflict spikes throughout history and across the globe. The conclusion: higher temperatures and rainfall extremes, such as drought and flood, predicted increased domestic violence, ethnic aggression, land invasions, and civil conflicts (Hsiang et al., 2013). The researchers project that a 2-degree Celsius temperature rise—as is predicted by 2040—could increase intergroup conflicts by more than 50 percent. Thus, the U.S. Department of Defense (2014) warns that climate change will likely increase poverty, instability, and social tensions—"conditions that can enable terrorist activity." The Military Advisory Board (2014) concurs that climate change is "a catalyst for conflict."

Studies both in the laboratory and in everyday life reveal that heat also amplifies short-term aggression. On hot days, neighborhood violence, and even batters hit by pitches in baseball games, become more frequent. Violence is also more common in hotter seasons of the year, hotter summers, hotter years, hotter cities, and hotter regions (Anderson & Delisi, 2010). Craig Anderson and his colleagues project that if a 4-degree-Fahrenheit (about 2°C) warming occurs, the United States will suffer at least 50,000 more serious assaults each year.

Public Opinion About Climate Change

Is the Earth getting hotter? Are humans responsible? Will it matter to our grandchildren? Yes, yes, and yes, say published climate scientists—97 percent of whom agree that climate change is occurring and is human caused (Anderegg et al., 2010). As one report in *Science* explained, "Almost all climate scientists are of one mind about the threat of global warming: It's real, it's dangerous, and the world needs to take action immediately" (Kerr, 2009).

Yet many folks don't know about that scientific consensus. In 2013, only 42 percent of Americans understood that "most scientists think global warming is happening" (AAAS, 2014). Fewer adults than most of us realize are completely dismissive of climate change (Leviston et al., 2013). In fact, in 2013, only 44 percent of Americans agreed that there is "solid evidence" of human-caused global warming (Pew, 2014). And in 2011, their doubts supported a 240 to 184 U.S. House of Representatives vote *defeating* a resolution stating that "climate change is occurring, is caused largely by human activities, and poses significant risks for public health and welfare" (McKibben, 2011).

The enormous gulf between the scientific and U.S. public understandings of climate change intrigues social psychologists. Why the gap? Why is global warming not a hotter topic? And what might be done to align scientific and public understandings?

PERSONAL EXPERIENCE AND THE AVAILABILITY HEURISTIC

By now, it's a familiar lesson: vivid and recent experiences often overwhelm abstract statistics. Despite knowing the statistical rarity of shark attacks and plane crashes, vivid images of such—being readily available in memory—often hijack our emotions and distort our judgments. We make our intuitive judgments under the influence of the availability heuristic—and thus we often fear the wrong things. If an airline misplaces our bag, we

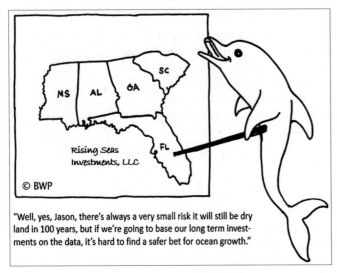

"Well, yes, Jason, there's always a very small risk it will still be dry land in 100 years, but if we're going to base our long term investments on the data, it's hard to find a safer bet for ocean growth."

Courtesy of Brett W. Pelham

"Global warming isn't real because I was cold today! Also great news: world hunger is over because I just ate."

—Stephen Colbert Tweet, November 18, 2014

likely will overweight our immediate experience; ignoring data on the airline's overall lost-bag rate, we belittle the airline. Our ancient brains come designed to attend to the immediate situation, not out-of-sight data and beyond-the-horizon dangers (Gifford, 2011).

Likewise, people will often scorn climate change in the face of a winter freeze. One climate skeptic declared a record East Coast blizzard "a coup de grace" for global warming (Breckler, 2010). In a May 2011 survey, 47 percent of Americans agreed that "The record snowstorms this winter in the eastern United States make me question whether global warming is occurring" (Leiserowitz et al., 2011b). But then after the ensuing blistering summer, 67 percent of Americans agreed that global warming worsened the "record high summer temperatures in the U.S. in 2011" (Leiserowitz, 2011). In studies in the United States and Australia, people have expressed more belief in global warming, and more willingness to donate to a global warming charity, on warmer-than-usual days than on cooler-than-usual days (Li et al., 2011; Zaval et al., 2014). After their vivid experiences of Hurricanes Irene and Sandy, New Jersey residents became more likely to agree with statements such as, "When humans interfere with nature it often produces disastrous consequences" (Rudman et al., 2013). As in so many life realms, our local experience distorts our global judgments. And as you've learned in this book, psychological science consistently teaches that hard data is more accurate than our own individual and sometimes distorted perceptions.

PERSUASION

Today's local weather may bias people's understanding of tomorrow's global warming. But that just begins to explain public skepticism about climate change. Resistance to climate science also stems from simple *misinformation* and from *motivated reasoning*.

MISINFORMATION.   People may discount climate threat because they are natural optimists or because they misinterpret uncertainty about the extent of temperature and sea level rise as uncertainty about the fact of climate change (Gifford, 2011). Especially in the United States, some groups seek to sow doubt about climate action by discrediting scientists and emphasizing the short-term costs of action rather than the long-term costs of inaction (CRED, 2014). People who doubt other scientific findings also tend to doubt the climate science consensus (Lewandowsky et al., 2013).

MOTIVATED REASONING.   Our desire to avoid negative emotions such as fear may motivate denial of climate threat. Moreover, we have a natural tendency to believe in and justify the way things are. We like our habitual ways of traveling, eating, and heating and cooling our spaces. Thus, when comfortable, we're motivated not to change the familiar status quo (Feygina et al., 2010; Kahan, 2014). And our natural confirmation bias may lead us to attend more to data that confirms our preexisting views. Thus, if a solution to a climate problem is unpalatable, people will tend to deny the problem itself (Campbell & Kay, 2014).

So, to overcome misinformation and motivated reasoning, how might climate educators apply social psychology's principles?

- *Connect the message to the audience's values.* Political values color people's views. In the United States in 2014, 68 percent of Democrats and 25 percent of Republicans viewed "global climate change" as a "major threat" (Pew, 2014). A Democrat-leaning audience might respond more to information about climate effects on the world's poor, and a Republican-leaning audience to information about how clean energy boosts national security by diminishing dependence on foreign energy.

- *Use credible communicators.* People are more open to messengers whose identities and affiliations are like their own—someone they trust and respect (CRED, 2014).

Mothers Against Drunk Driving succeeds by having mothers communicate with other mothers.

- *Think local.* Although climate change is a global issue, people respond more to threats that are near in place or time. In Australia, Texas, or California, the prospects of worsening drought may awaken concern. In Florida or the Netherlands, rising seas will seem more pertinent.

- *Make communications vivid and memorable.* Mindful of the availability heuristic, and of the effectiveness of cigarette warnings with graphic photos, make messages vivid. Rather than warn of "future climate change" explain that "the Earth has a fever."

- *Nudge people by using "green defaults."* Set printers to double-sided printing unless single-sided is chosen. Have building lights turn off when motion sensors do not detect a human presence. Offer a vegetarian entrée, with a meat option for those who wish (Scott et al., 2015).

- *Frame the risks effectively* (Bertolotti & Catellani, 2014). Rather than describe "a greenhouse effect," describe "a heat trapping blanket." Instead of a "theory" of climate change, offer "an understanding of how this works" (CRED, 2014). Instead of proposing a politically unpopular "carbon tax," suggest "carbon offsets." Liken the risk management to people's own decisions—buying fire insurance on their dwelling and liability insurance on their driving, and putting on seat belts—to spare themselves worst-case outcomes.

- *Frame energy savings in attention-getting ways.* An information sheet about energy savings might use long time periods. Instead of saying, "This Energy Star refrigerator will save you $120 a year on your electric bills, say it "will save you $2,400 in wasted energy bills over the next 20 years" (Hofmeister, 2010).

SUMMING UP: Psychology and Climate Change

- Scientists report that exploding population and increasing consumption and greenhouse gas emissions have together exceeded the Earth's carrying capacity. We now are seeing the predicted beginnings of global warming, melting polar ice, rising seas, and more extreme weather.

- Expected social consequences of climate change include human displacement and trauma and conflict stemming from competition over scarce resources.

- Social psychologists are also exploring the gap between scientific and public understandings of climate change. And they are suggesting ways to educate and persuade the public to support a sustainable future.

ENABLING SUSTAINABLE LIVING

Identify new technologies and strategies for reducing consumption that together may enable sustainable living.

What shall we do? Eat, drink, and be merry, for tomorrow is doom? Behave as so many participants have in prisoners' dilemma games, by pursuing self-interest to our collective detriment? ("Heck, on a global scale, my consumption is infinitesimal; it makes my life comfortable and costs the world practically nothing.") Wring our hands, dreading that fertility plus prosperity equals calamity, and vow never to bring children into a doomed world?

Those more optimistic about the future see two routes to sustainable lifestyles: (a) increasing technological efficiency and agricultural productivity, and (b) moderating consumption and population.

"No one made a greater mistake than he who did nothing because he could only do a little."

—Edmund Burke, 18th Century British Philosopher

Capturing light in a bottle. Illac Diaz inspects a new solar light bulb sealed into the corrugated roof of a Manila apartment.
JAY DIRECTO/Getty Images

New Technologies

With world population expected to grow another 2 billion by 2050—and with more and more people wanting to drive, eat, and live like North Americans—one of the world's great challenges is how to power our human future without polluting and warming it.

One component in a sustainable future is improved technologies. We have not only replaced incandescent bulbs with energy-saving ones, but replaced printed and delivered letters and catalogs with email and e-commerce, and replaced commuter miles driven with telecommuting.

Today's middle-aged adults drive cars that get twice the mileage and produce a twentieth of the pollution of the ones they drove as teenagers, and new hybrid and battery-driven cars offer even greater efficiency.

Plausible future technologies include diodes that emit light for 20 years; ultrasound washing machines that consume no water, heat, or soap; reusable and compostable plastics; cars running on fuel cells that combine hydrogen and oxygen and produce water exhaust; lightweight materials stronger than steel; roofs and roads that double as solar energy collectors; and heated and cooled chairs that provide personal comfort with less heating and cooling of rooms (N. Myers, 2000; Zhang et al., 2007).

Reducing Consumption

The second component of a sustainable future is controlling consumption. As today's poorer countries develop, consumption will increase. As it does, developed countries must consume less.

Thanks to family planning efforts, the world's population growth rate has decelerated, especially in developed nations. Even in less-developed countries, when food security has improved and women have become educated and empowered, birth rates have fallen. But if birth rates everywhere instantly fell to a replacement level of 2.1 children per woman, the lingering momentum of population growth, fueled by the bulge of younger humans, would continue for years to come. In 1960, after tens of thousands of years on the spaceship Earth, there were 3 billion people—which is also the number that demographers expect the human population to *grow* in just this century.

With this population size, humans have already overshot the Earth's carrying capacity, so consumption must become more sustainable. With our material appetites continually swelling—as more people seek personal computers, refrigeration, air-conditioning, jet travel—what can be done to moderate consumption by those who can afford to overconsume?

INCENTIVES

One way is through public policies that harness the motivating power of incentives (Swim et al., 2014). As a general rule, we get less of what is taxed, and more of what is rewarded. On jammed highways, vehicle lanes reward carpooling and penalize driving solo. Europe leads the way in incentivizing mass transit and bicycle use over personal vehicle use. In addition to the small vehicles incentivized by high fuel taxes, cities such as Vienna, Munich, Zurich, and Copenhagen have closed many city center streets to car traffic. London and Stockholm drivers pay congestion fees when entering the heart of the city. Amsterdam is a bicycle haven. Dozens of German cities have "environmental zones" where only low CO_2 cars may enter (Rosenthal, 2011).

THE inside STORY

While watching Al Gore's climate change movie, I had an epiphany. As I reflected on its message—that we must take action to avert impending climate change—I realized that psychology could help explain people's denial of climate change and could help motivate action. I then led an American Psychological Association task force that connected psychological research to understanding the human causes and responses to climate change. I was stunned by the attention given our report by the national press, government officials, and scholars worldwide.

What I learned refocused my career, with support from like-minded psychologists and fellow Pennsylvania State University researchers who study climate change and how we might avert or adapt to it. We have found, for example, that men are more open to masculine-framed policy persuasion; they prefer arguments that reference *leadership* over arguments that reference *care* for the planet. Our interdisciplinary team is also helping zoo and aquarium educators to communicate effectively about climate science.

Janet K. Swim
Pennsylvania State University
Courtesy of Pennsylvania State University

Some free-market proponents object to carbon taxes because they are taxes. Others respond that carbon taxes are simply payment for external damage to today's health and tomorrow's environment. If not today's CO_2 emitters, who should pay for the cost of tomorrow's more threatening floods, tornadoes, hurricanes, droughts, and sea rise? "Markets are truly free only when everyone pays the full price for his or her actions," contends Environmental Defense Fund economist Gernot Wagner (2011). "Anything else is socialism." (See "The Inside Story: Janet Swim on Psychology's Response to Climate Change.")

FEEDBACK

Another way to encourage greener homes and businesses is to harness the power of immediate feedback to the consumer by installing "smart meters" that provide a continuous readout of electricity use and its cost. Turn off a computer monitor or the lights in an empty room, and the meter displays the decreased wattage. Turn on the air-conditioning, and you immediately know the usage and cost. U.S. studies have shown that when an energy supplier sticks a "smiley" or "frowny" face on home energy bills when the consumer's energy use is less or more than the neighborhood average, energy use is reduced (Schultz et al., 2007; Van Vugt, 2009).

IDENTITY

In one survey, the top reason people gave for buying a Prius hybrid car was that it "makes a statement about me" (Clayton & Myers, 2009, p. 9). Indeed, argue Tom Crompton and Tim Kasser (2010), our sense of who we are—our identity—has profound implications for our climate-related behaviors. Does our social identity, the ingroup that defines our circle of concern, include only those around us now? Or does it encompass vulnerable people in places unseen, our descendants and others in the future, and even the creatures in the planet's natural environment?

Support for new energy policies will require a shift in public consciousness on the scale of the 1960s civil rights movement and the 1970s women's movement. Yale University environmental science dean James Gustave Speth (2008; 2012) has called for an enlarged identity—a "new consciousness"—in which people

- see humanity as part of nature.
- see nature as having intrinsic value that we must steward.
- value the future and its inhabitants as well as our present.

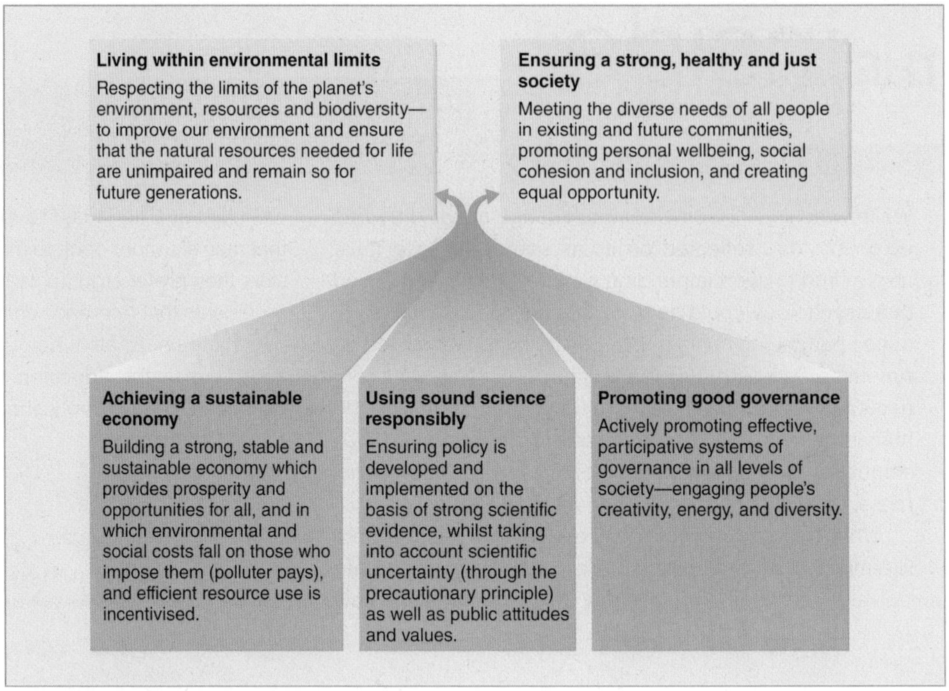

Living within environmental limits
Respecting the limits of the planet's environment, resources and biodiversity—to improve our environment and ensure that the natural resources needed for life are unimpaired and remain so for future generations.

Ensuring a strong, healthy and just society
Meeting the diverse needs of all people in existing and future communities, promoting personal wellbeing, social cohesion and inclusion, and creating equal opportunity.

Achieving a sustainable economy
Building a strong, stable and sustainable economy which provides prosperity and opportunities for all, and in which environmental and social costs fall on those who impose them (polluter pays), and efficient resource use is incentivised.

Using sound science responsibly
Ensuring policy is developed and implemented on the basis of strong scientific evidence, whilst taking into account scientific uncertainty (through the precautionary principle) as well as public attitudes and values.

Promoting good governance
Actively promoting effective, participative systems of governance in all levels of society—engaging people's creativity, energy, and diversity.

FIGURE :: 4

"Five Principles of Sustainable Development" in the U.K. government's Framework for Sustainable Development

The British government defines sustainable development as development that meets present needs without compromising future generations' abilities to meet their needs. "We want to live within environmental limits and achieve a just society, and we will do so by means of sustainable economy, good governance, and sound science." Social psychology's contribution will be to help influence behaviors that enable people to live within environmental limits and to enjoy personal and social well-being.
Source: www.sd-commission.org.uk.

- appreciate our human interdependence, by thinking "we" and not just "me."
- define quality of life in relational and spiritual rather than materialistic terms.
- value equity, justice, and the human community.

Is there any hope that human priorities might shift from accumulating money to finding meaning, and from aggressive consumption to nurturing connections? The British government's plan for achieving sustainable development includes an emphasis on promoting personal well-being and social health (Figure 4). Perhaps social psychology can help point the way to greater well-being, by suggesting *ways to reduce consumption*—and also by tracking *materialism,* by informing people that *economic growth does not automatically improve human morale,* and by helping people understand *why materialism and money fail to satisfy* and encouraging *alternative, intrinsic values.*

SUMMING UP: Enabling Sustainable Living

- Humanity can prepare for a sustainable future by increasing technological efficiency.
- We can also create incentives, give feedback, and promote identities that will support more sustainable consumption. Rapid cultural change has happened in the past 40 years, and there is hope that in response to the global crisis it can happen again.

THE SOCIAL PSYCHOLOGY OF MATERIALISM AND WEALTH

Explain social psychology's contribution to our understanding of changing materialism: To what extent do money and consumption buy happiness? And why do materialism and economic growth not bring enduringly greater satisfaction?

Despite the recent economic recession, life for most people in Western countries is good. Today the average North American enjoys luxuries unknown even to royalty in centuries past: hot showers, flush toilets, central air-conditioning, microwave ovens, jet travel, wintertime fresh fruit, big-screen digital television, e-mail, smartphones and Post-it notes. Does money—and its associated luxuries—*buy* happiness? Few of us would answer yes. But ask a different question—"Would a *little* more money make you a *little* happier?"—and most of us will say yes. There is, we believe, a connection between wealth and well-being. That belief feeds what Juliet Schor (1998) has called the "cycle of work and spend"—working more to buy more.

Increased Materialism

Although the Earth asks that we live more lightly upon it, materialism has surged, most clearly in the United States. Think of it as today's American dream: life, liberty, and the purchase of happiness. Evidence of rising materialism comes from the Higher Education Research Institute annual survey of nearly a quarter million entering collegians. The proportion considering it "very important or essential" that they become "very well-off financially" rose from 39 percent in 1970 to 82 percent in 2014 (Figure 5). Those proportions

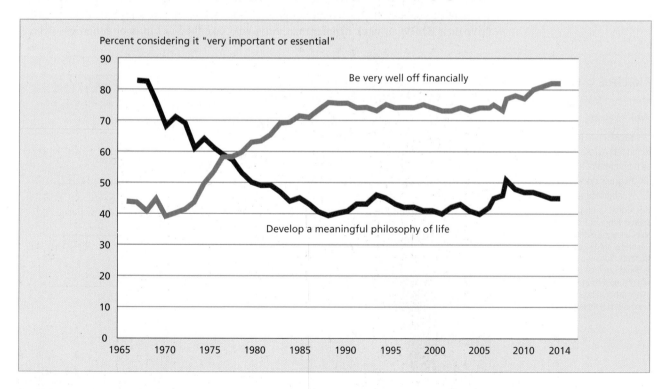

FIGURE :: 5

Changing materialism, from annual surveys of more than 200,000 entering U.S. collegians (total sample 13 million students)

Source: Data from Dey, Astin, & Korn, 1991, and subsequent annual reports.

virtually flip-flopped with those who considered it very important to "develop a meaning-ful philosophy of life." Materialism was up, spirituality down.

What a change in values! Among 19 listed objectives, new American collegians in most recent years have ranked becoming "very well-off financially" number 1. That outranks not only developing a life philosophy but also "becoming an authority in my own field," "helping others in difficulty," and "raising a family." The desire for material goods has also increased: Recent high school students (vs. those in the 1970s) were more likely to believe owning one's own home and having a new car every 2 to 3 years was important (Twenge & Kasser, 2013).

Wealth and Well-Being

Does unsustainable consumption indeed enable "the good life?" Does being well-off produce—or at least correlate with—psychological well-being? Would people be happier if they could exchange a simple lifestyle for one with palatial surroundings, ski vacations in the Alps, and executive-class travel? Would you be happier if you won a sweepstakes and could choose from its suggested indulgences: a 40-foot yacht, deluxe motor home, designer wardrobe, luxury car, or private housekeeper? Social-psychological theory and evidence offer some answers.

ARE WEALTHY COUNTRIES HAPPIER?

We can observe the traffic between wealth and well-being by asking, first, if rich nations are happier places. There is, indeed, some correlation between national wealth and well-being (measured as self-reported happiness and life satisfaction). The Scandinavians have been mostly prosperous and satisfied; the Bulgarians are neither (Figure 6). But after nations reached above $20,000 GDP per person, higher levels of national wealth are not predictive of increased life satisfaction.

ARE WEALTHIER INDIVIDUALS HAPPIER?

We can ask, second, whether within any given nation, rich people are happier. Are people who drive their BMWs to work happier than those who take the bus? In poor countries—where

FIGURE :: 6

National Wealth and Well-Being

Life satisfaction (on a 0 to 10 ladder) across 132 countries, as a function of national wealth (2005 gross domestic product (GDP), adjusted to the 2000 U.S. dollar value).
Source: From Di Tella & MacCullough (2008). (Technical note to economics students: Some economists prefer to display income on a log scale, which then indicates a more linear relationship between national income and happiness.)

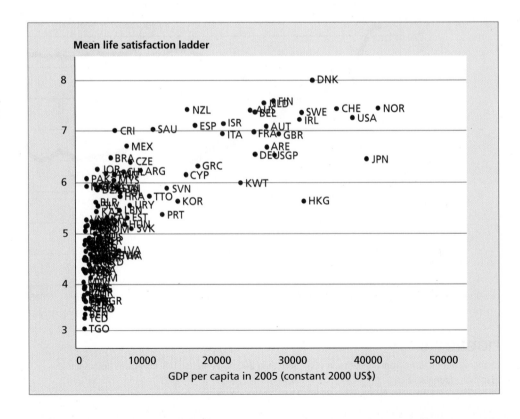

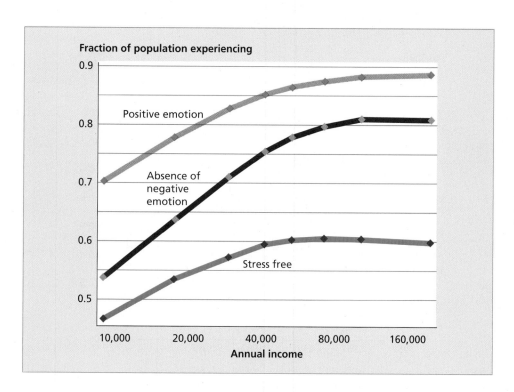

The Diminishing Effects of Increasing Income on Positive and Negative Feelings

Data from Gallup surveys of more than 450,000 Americans (Kahneman & Deaton, 2010). (Note: income is reported on a log scale, which tends to accentuate the appearance of correlation between income and well-being.)

low income threatens basic needs—being relatively well-off does predict greater well-being (Howell & Howell, 2008). In affluent countries, where most can afford life's necessities, affluence (and financial satisfaction) still matters—partly because people with more money perceive more control over their lives (Johnson & Krueger, 2006). But after a comfortable income level is reached, more and more money produces diminishing long-term returns. In Gallup surveys of more than 450,000 Americans during 2008 and 2009, daily positive feelings (the average of self-reported happiness, enjoyment, and frequent smiling and laughter) increased with income up to, but not beyond, $75,000 (Kahneman & Deaton, 2010). The same was true for the absence of negative feelings of worry and sadness (Figure 7). In worldwide Gallup surveys across 158 countries, financial satisfaction predicts life evaluation. But having one's psychological needs met (for respect, relationship, and empowerment) better predicts positive, happy feelings (Fischer & Boer, 2011; Ng & Diener, 2014; Tay & Diener, 2011). Even the super-rich—the *Forbes* 100 wealthiest Americans—have reported only slightly greater happiness than average (Diener et al., 1985).

IS THE WEALTHIER TWENTY-FIRST CENTURY HAPPIER?

We can ask, third, whether, over time, a culture's happiness rises with its affluence. Does our collective well-being float upward with a rising economic tide?

In 1957, as economist John Kenneth Galbraith was describing the United States as *The Affluent Society,* Americans' per-person income was (in 2009 dollars) less than $12,000. Today, as Figure 8 indicates, the United States is a triply affluent society. With increasing inequality, this rising tide has lifted the yachts faster than the dinghies. Yet, nearly all boats have risen. With double the spending power, thanks partly to the surge in married women's employment, we now own twice as many cars per person, eat out twice as often, and are supported by a whole new world of technology. Since 1960 we have also seen the proportion of households with dishwashers rise from 7 to 69 percent, with clothes dryers rise from 20 to 83 percent, and with air-conditioning rise from 15 to 89 percent (Bureau of the Census, 2013).

So, believing that it's "very important" to "be very well-off financially," and having become better off financially, are today's Americans happier? Are they happier with espresso coffee, smartphones, and suitcases on wheels than before?

FIGURE :: 8

Has Economic Growth Advanced Human Morale?

While inflation-adjusted income has risen, self-reported happiness has not.
Source: Happiness data from General Social Surveys, National Opinion Research Center, University of Chicago (and Niemi et al., 1989 for pre-1972 data). Income data from Bureau of the Census (1975) and *Economic Indicators.*

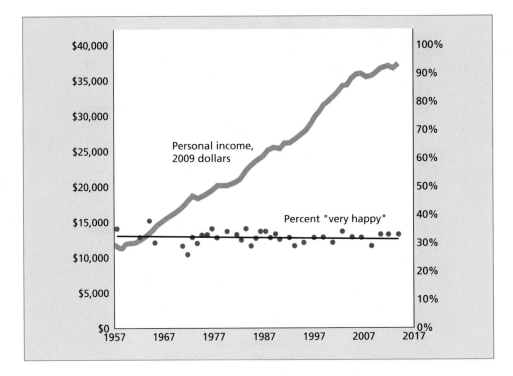

They are not. Since 1957 the number of Americans who say they are "very happy" has declined slightly: from 35 to 29 percent. Twice as rich and apparently no happier. The same has been true of many other countries as well (Easterlin et al., 2010). After a decade of extraordinary economic growth in China—from few owning a phone and 40 percent owning a color television to most people now having such things—Gallup surveys revealed a *decreasing* proportion of people satisfied "with the way things are going in your life today" (Burkholder, 2005; Davey & Rato, 2012; Easterlin et al., 2012).

The findings are startling because they challenge modern materialism: *Economic growth has provided no apparent boost to humans.* We excel at making a living but often fail at making a life. We celebrate our prosperity but yearn for purpose. We cherish our freedoms but long for connection.

Materialism Fails to Satisfy

It is striking that economic growth in affluent countries has failed to satisfy. It is further striking that individuals who strive most for wealth tend to live with lower well-being (Dittmar et al., 2014). This finding "comes through very strongly in every culture I've looked at," reported Richard Ryan (1999). Seek *extrinsic* goals—wealth, beauty, popularity, prestige, or anything else centered on external rewards or approval—and you may find anxiety, depression, and psychosomatic ills (Eckersley, 2005; Sheldon et al., 2004). Those who instead strive for *intrinsic* goals such as "intimacy, personal growth, and contribution to the community" experience a higher quality of life, concludes Tim Kasser (2000, 2002). Intrinsic values, Kasser (2011) adds, promote personal and social well-being and help immunize people against materialistic values. Those focused on close relationships, meaningful work, and concern for others enjoy inherent rewards that often prove elusive to those more focused on things or on their status and image.

Pause a moment and think: What is the most personally satisfying event that you experienced in the last month? Kennon Sheldon and his colleagues (2001) put that question (and similar questions about the last week and semester) to samples of university students. Then they asked them to rate the extent to which 10 different needs were met by the satisfying event. The students rated self-esteem, relatedness (feeling connected with others), and autonomy (feeling in control) as the emotional needs that most strongly accompanied the satisfying event. At the bottom of the list of factors predicting satisfaction were money and luxury.

Today's material comforts in China: people shopping for laptops and other increasingly valuable goods. Although living standards have risen, life satisfaction has not.
Wang Zhiyun/EyePress EPN/Newscom

People who identify themselves with expensive possessions experience fewer positive moods (Solberg et al., 2003). Such materialists tend to report a relatively large gap between what they want and what they have, and to enjoy fewer close, fulfilling relationships. Wealthier people also tend to savor life's simpler pleasures less (Quoidbach et al., 2010). Sipping tea with a friend, savoring a chocolate, or finishing a project may pale alongside the luxuries enabled by wealth.

People focused on extrinsic and material goals also "focus less on caring for the Earth," reports Kasser (2011). "As materialistic values go up, concern for nature tends to go down. . . . When people strongly endorse money, image, and status, they are less likely to engage in ecologically beneficial activities like riding bikes, recycling, and re-using things in new ways."

But why do yesterday's luxuries, such as air-conditioning, so quickly become today's requirements? Two principles drive this psychology of consumption: our ability to adapt and our need to compare.

"Why do you spend your money for that which is not bread, and your labor for that which does not satisfy?"
—Isaiah 55:2

OUR HUMAN CAPACITY FOR ADAPTATION

The **adaptation-level phenomenon** is our tendency to judge our experience (for example, of sounds, temperatures, or income) relative to a neutral level defined by our prior experience. We adjust our neutral levels—the points at which sounds seem neither loud nor soft, temperatures neither hot nor cold, events neither pleasant nor unpleasant—on the basis of our experience. We then notice and react to up or down changes from those levels.

Thus, as our achievements rise above past levels, we feel successful and satisfied. As our social prestige, income, or in-home technology improves, we feel pleasure. Before long, however, we adapt. What once felt good comes to register as neutral, and what formerly was neutral now feels like deprivation.

Would it ever, then, be possible to create a social paradise? Donald Campbell (1975b) answered no: If you woke up tomorrow to your utopia—perhaps a world with no bills, no ills, someone who loves you unreservedly—you would feel euphoric, for a time. Yet before long, you would recalibrate your adaptation level and again sometimes feel gratified (when achievements surpass expectations), sometimes feel deprived (when they fall below), and sometimes feel neutral.

To be sure, adaptation to some events, such as the death of a spouse, may be incomplete, as the sense of loss lingers (Diener et al., 2006). Yet, we generally underestimate our adaptive capacity. People have difficulty predicting the intensity and duration of their future positive and negative emotions (Wilson & Gilbert, 2003; Figure 9). The elation from getting what we want—riches, top exam scores, the Chicago Cubs winning the World Series—evaporates more rapidly than we expect.

adaptation-level phenomenon
The tendency to adapt to a given level of stimulation and thus to notice and react to changes from that level.

FIGURE :: 9

The Impact Bias

People generally overestimate the enduring impact of significant positive and negative life events. *Source:* Figure inspired by de Botton, 2004.

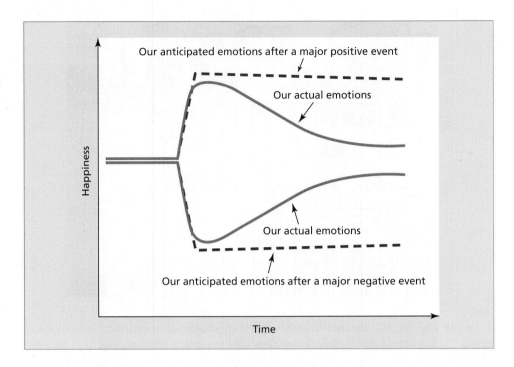

Our anticipated emotions after a major positive event

Our actual emotions

Happiness

Our actual emotions

Our anticipated emotions after a major negative event

Time

We also sometimes "miswant." When first-year university students predicted their satisfaction with various housing possibilities shortly before entering their school's housing lottery, they focused on physical features. "I'll be happiest in a beautiful and well-located dorm," many students seemed to think. But they were wrong. When contacted a year later, it was the social features, such as a sense of community, that predicted happiness, reported Elizabeth Dunn and her colleagues (2003). Other surveys and experiments have repeatedly confirmed that positive experiences leave us happier, especially experiences that build relationships, foster meaning and identity, and are not deflated by comparisons (Dunn & Norton, 2013; Gilovich & Kumar, 2015; Pchelin & Howell, 2014). The best things in life are not things.

OUR WANTING TO COMPARE

social comparison

Evaluating one's abilities and opinions by comparing oneself with others.

Much of life revolves around **social comparison,** a point made by the old joke about two hikers who meet a bear. One reaches into his backpack and pulls out a pair of sneakers. "Why bother putting those on?" asks the other. "You can't outrun a bear." "I don't have to outrun the bear," answers the first. "I just have to outrun you."

Similarly, happiness is relative to our comparisons with others, especially those within our own groups (Lyubomirsky, 2001; Zagefka & Brown, 2005). Whether we feel good or bad depends on whom we're comparing ourselves with. We are slow-witted or clumsy only when others are smart or agile. Let one professional athlete sign a new contract for $15 million a year and an $8-million-a-year teammate may now feel less satisfied. "Our poverty became a reality. Not because of our having less, but by our neighbors having more," recalled Will Campbell in *Brother to a Dragonfly.*

Social comparisons foster feelings.
© Barbara Smaller/The New Yorker Collection/www.cartoonbank.com

"O.K., if you can't see your way to giving me a pay raise, how about giving Parkerson a pay cut?"

Further feeding our luxury fever is the tendency to compare upward: As we climb the ladder of success or affluence, we mostly compare ourselves with peers who are at or above our current level, not with those who have less. People living in communities where some residents are very wealthy tend to feel envy and less satisfaction as they compare upward (Fiske, 2011b).

In developed and emerging economies worldwide, inequality has been growing. In the 34 Organisation for Economic Co-operation and Development 2014 countries, the richest 10 percent average 9.5 times the income of the poorest 10 percent. Countries with greater inequality not only have greater health and social problems, but also higher rates of mental illness (Pickett & Wilkinson, 2011). Likewise, U.S. states with greater inequality have higher rates of depression (Messias et al., 2011). And over time, years with more income inequality—and associated increases in perceived unfairness and lack of trust—correlate with less happiness among those with lower incomes (Oishi et al., 2011).

Although people often prefer the economic policies in place, a national survey found that Americans overwhelmingly preferred the income distribution on the right of Figure 10 (which, unbeknownst to the respondents, happened to be Sweden's income distribution) to the one on the left (which happened to be the United States' income distribution). Moreover, people preferred (in an ideal world) the top 20 percent income share ranging between 30 and 40 percent (rather than the actual 84 percent), with modest differences between Republicans and Democrats and between those making less than $50,000 and more than $100,000 (Norton & Ariely, 2011).

In a follow-up study that framed different questions—for example, asking Americans what percentage of people make less than $35,000—a different research team found them over-estimating both poverty and inequality (Chambers et al., 2014). But the story continues: In a another follow-up study of 55,238 people in 40 countries, Sorapop Kiatpongsan and Michael Norton (2014) once again found that people vastly *under*estimated inequality. Moreover, people's

Times of increased inequality tend, for many, to be times of diminished perceived fairness and happiness.
Marilyn Humphries/The Image Works

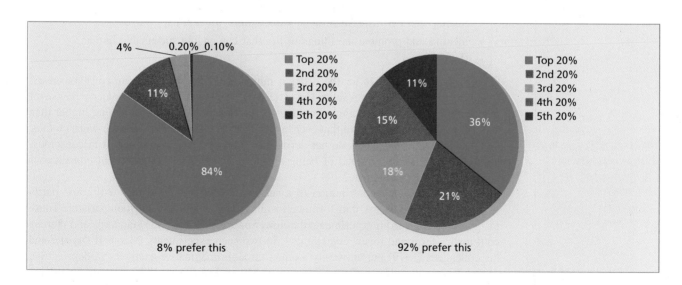

FIGURE :: 10

In an ideal society, what would be the level of income inequality? A survey of Americans provided a surprising consensus that a more equal distribution of wealth—like that shown on the right (which happened to be Sweden's distribution) would be preferable to the American status quo (shown on the left).
Source: Norton & Ariely, 2011.

ideal pay gaps between big company CEOs and unskilled workers are much smaller than actually exists. In the United States, for example, the actual pay ratio of S&P 500 CEOs to their unskilled workers (354:1) far exceeds the estimated ratio (30:1) and the ideal ratio (7:1). Their conclusion: "People all over the world and from all walks of life would prefer smaller pay gaps between the rich and poor." Informing people about the extent of income inequality increases their concern for the growing gaps, though not their support for income redistribution policies that would reduce inequality (Kuziemko et al., 2015).

Even in China, income inequality has grown. This helps explain why rising affluence has not produced increased happiness—there or elsewhere (Easterlin et al., 2012; Helliwell et al., 2013). Rising income inequality, noted Michael Hagerty (2000), makes for more people who have rich neighbors. Television's modeling of the lifestyles of the wealthy also serves to accentuate feelings of "relative deprivation" and desires for more (Schor, 1998).

The adaptation-level and social-comparison phenomena give us pause. They imply that the quest for happiness through material achievement requires continually expanding affluence. But the good news is that adaptation to simpler lives can also happen. If we shrink our consumption by choice or by necessity, we will initially feel a pinch, but the pain likely will pass. "Weeping may tarry for the night, but joy comes with the morning," reflected the Psalmist. Indeed, thanks to our capacity to adapt and to adjust comparisons, the emotional impact of significant life events—losing a job or even a disabling accident—dissipates sooner than most people suppose (Gilbert et al., 1998).

Toward Sustainability and Survival

As individuals and as a global society, we face difficult social and political issues. How might a democratic society induce people to adopt values that emphasize psychological well-being over materialism? How might a thriving market economy mix incentives for prosperity with restraints that preserve a habitable planet? To what extent can technological innovations, such as alternative energy sources, reduce our ecological footprints? And to what extent does the superordinate goal of preserving the Earth for our grandchildren call us each to limit our own liberties—our freedom to drive, burn, and dump whatever we wish?

A shift to postmaterialist values will gain momentum as people, governments, and corporations take these steps:

- Face the implications of population and consumption growth for climate change and environmental destruction
- Realize that extrinsic, materialist values make for *less* happy lives
- Identify and promote the things in life that can enable sustainable human flourishing

"If the world is to change for the better it must have a change in human consciousness," said Czech poet-president Vaclav Havel (1990). We must discover "a deeper sense of responsibility toward the world, which means responsibility toward something higher than self." If people were to believe that ever-bigger houses, closets full of seldom-worn clothes, and garages with luxury cars do not define the good life, then might a shift in consciousness become possible? Instead of being an indicator of social status, might conspicuous consumption become gauche?

Social psychology's contribution to a sustainable, flourishing future will come partly through its consciousness-transforming insights into adaptation and comparison. These insights also come from experiments that lower people's comparison standards and thereby cool luxury fever and renew contentment. In two such experiments, Marshall Dermer and his colleagues (1979) put university women through imaginative exercises in deprivation. After viewing depictions of the grimness of Milwaukee life in 1900, or after imagining and writing about being burned and disfigured, the women expressed greater satisfaction with their own lives.

In another experiment, Jennifer Crocker and Lisa Gallo (1985) found that people who five times completed the sentence "I'm glad I'm not a . . ." afterward felt less depressed and more satisfied with their lives than did those who completed sentences beginning

"All our wants, beyond those which a very moderate income will supply, are purely imaginary."

—Henry St. John, *Letter to Swift*, 1719

"I wish I were a. . . ." Realizing that others have it worse helps us count our blessings. "I cried because I had no shoes," says a Persian proverb, "until I met a man who had no feet." *Downward* social comparison facilitates contentment.

Downward comparison to a hypothetical worse-off self also enhances contentment. Minkyung Koo and her colleagues (2008) invited people to write about how they might never have met their romantic partner. Compared to others who wrote about meeting their partner, those who imagined not having the relationship expressed more satisfaction with it. Can you likewise imagine how some good things in *your* life might never have happened? It's very easy for me [DM] to imagine not having chanced into an acquaintance that led to an invitation to author this book. Just thinking about that reminds me to count my blessings.

Social psychology also contributes to a sustainable and survivable future through its explorations of the good life. If materialism does not enhance life quality, what does?

- *Close, supportive relationships.* Our deep need to belong is satisfied by close, supportive relationships. People who are supported by intimate friendships or a committed marriage are much more likely to declare themselves "very happy."

- *Faith communities* and voluntary organizations are often a source of such connections, as well as of meaning and hope. That helps explain a finding from National Opinion Research Center surveys of more than 50,000 Americans since 1972: 26 percent of those rarely or never attending religious services declared themselves very happy, as did 48 percent of those attending multiple times weekly. The high religiosity of most poor countries also enables their people to live with surprisingly high levels of meaning in life (Oishi & Diener, 2014).

- *Positive thinking habits.* Optimism, self-esteem, perceived control, and extraversion also mark happy experiences and happy lives. One analysis of 638 studies of 420,000+ people in 63 countries found that a sense of autonomy—feeling free and independent—consistently influences people's sense of well-being more than does wealth (Fischer & Boer, 2011).

- *Experiencing nature.* Carleton University students randomly assigned to a 17-minute nature walk near their campus ended up (to their and others' surprise) much happier than students who took a similar-length walk through campus walking tunnels (Nisbet & Zelenski, 2011). Japanese researchers report that "forest bathing"—walks in the woods—also help lower stress hormones and blood pressure (Phillips, 2011).

- *Flow.* Work and leisure experiences that engage one's skills mark happy lives. Between the anxiety of being overwhelmed and stressed, and the apathy of being underwhelmed and bored, notes Mihaly Csikszentmihalyi (1990, 1999), lies a zone in which people experience *flow*. Flow is an optimal state in which, absorbed in an activity, we lose consciousness of self and time. When people's experience is sampled using electronic pagers, they report greatest enjoyment not when they are mindlessly passive but when they are unselfconsciously absorbed in a mindful challenge. In fact, the less expensive (and generally more involving) a leisure activity, the *happier* people are while doing it. Most people are happier gardening than powerboating, talking to friends than watching TV. Low-consumption recreations prove most satisfying.

That is good news indeed. Those things that make for the genuinely good life—close relationships, social networks based on belief, positive thinking habits, engaging activity—are

The best things in life are not things. Research indicates that happiness grows more from spending on experiences than on stuff—especially when spent on anticipated and recollected experiences that foster relationships and identity, such as my hiking Scotland's West Highland Way with two of my children [DM] or spending time at the beach with mine [JT].
Courtesy of Dave Myers; Courtesy of Pam Davis

"We have failed to see how our economy, our environment and our society are all one. And that delivering the best possible quality of life for us all means more than concentrating solely on economic growth."

—Prime Minister Tony Blair, Foreword to *A Better Quality of Life*, 1999

enduringly sustainable. And that is an idea close to the heart of Jigme Singye Wangchuk, former King of Bhutan. "Gross national happiness is more important than gross national product," he said. Writing from the Center of Bhutan Studies in Bhutan, Sander Tideman (2003) explained: "Gross National Happiness . . . aims to promote real progress and sustainability by measuring the quality of life, rather than the mere sum of production and consumption." Now other nations, too, are assessing national quality of life. (See "Research Close-Up: Measuring National Well-Being.")

research CLOSE-UP Measuring National Well-Being

"A city is successful not when it's rich, but when its people are happy." So said Bogotá, Colombia, former mayor Enrique Peñalosa, in explaining his campaign to improve his city's quality of life—by building schools and increasing school enrollment 34 percent, building or rebuilding more than 1,200 parks, creating an effective transit system, and reducing the murder rate dramatically (Gardner & Assadourian, 2004).

Peñalosa's idea of national success is shared by a growing number of social scientists and government planners. In Britain, the New Economics Foundation (2009, 2011) has developed "National Accounts of Well-Being" that track national social health and has published a *Well-Being Manifesto for a Flourishing Society.* The foundation's motto: "We believe in economics as if people and the planet mattered." To assess national progress, they urge, we should measure not just financial progress but also the kinds of growth that enhance people's life satisfaction and happiness.

Andrew Oswald (2006), one of a new breed of economists who study the relationships between economic and psychological well-being, notes that "economists' faith in the value of growth is diminishing. That is a good thing and will slowly make its way into the minds of tomorrow's politicians."

Leading the way toward new ways of assessing human progress are the newly developed "Guidelines for National Indicators of Subjective Well-Being and Ill-Being" developed by University of Illinois psychologist Ed Diener (2005, 2013; Diener et al., 2008, 2009) and signed by four dozen of the world's leading researchers (Figure 11). It notes that "global measures of subjective well-being, such as assessments of life satisfaction and happiness, can be useful for policy debates," such as by detecting

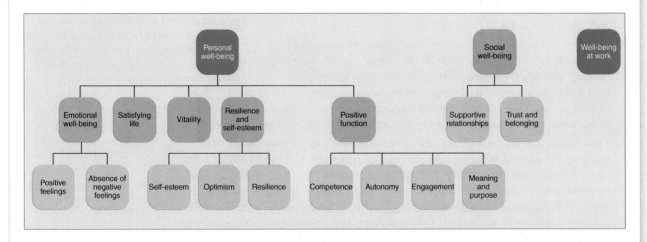

FIGURE :: 11

Components of Well-Being

In its 2009 *National Accounts of Well-Being* report, Britain's New Economic Foundation urges governments to "directly measure people's subjective well-being: their experiences, feelings and perceptions of how their lives are going." What matters, this think tank argues, is not so much the overall size of the economy as people's experienced quality of life. Categories for assessing national well-being include personal well-being, social well-being, and work-related well-being.

the human effects of any policy interventions. More specifically, questions are now available for assessing these indicators:

- *Positive emotions,* including those involving low arousal (contentment), moderate arousal (pleasure), and high arousal (euphoria), and those involving positive responses to others (affection) and to activities (interest and engagement).

- *Negative emotions,* including anger, sadness, anxiety, stress, frustration, envy, guilt and shame, loneliness, and helplessness. Measures may ask people to recall or record the frequency of their experiencing positive and negative emotions.

- *Happiness,* which often is taken to mean a general positive mood, such as indicated by people's answers to a widely used survey question: "Taking all things together, how would you say things are these days— would you say that you are very happy, pretty happy, or not too happy?"

- *Life satisfaction,* which engages people in appraising their life as a whole.

- *Domain satisfactions,* which invites people to indicate their satisfaction with their physical health, work, leisure, relationships, family, and community.

- *Quality of life,* a broader concept that includes one's environment and health, and one's perceptions of such.

Such well-being measures can assist governments as they debate economic and tax policies, family protection laws, health care, and community planning—a point now affirmed by 41 nations that now are assessing citizen well-being (Diener, 2013; Krueger & Stone, 2014).

Well-being indicators are also part of worldwide Gallup surveys of well-being in more than 150 countries encompassing more than 98 percent of the world's people. The surveys compare countries (revealing, for example, that people in some high-income countries such as Israel and Saudi Arabia report lower levels of positive emotion than people in some low-income countries such as Kenya and India). Gallup also is conducting a massive 25-year survey of the health and well-being of U.S. residents, with 250 interviewers conducting a thousand surveys a day, seven days a week. The result is a daily snapshot of American well-being—of people's happiness, stress, anger, sleep, money worries, laughter, socializing, work, and much more. Although the project was recently launched, researchers have already identified the best days of the year (weekends and holidays) and monitored the short-term emotional impact of economic ups and downs. And with some 350,000 respondents a year, any subgroup of 1 percent of the population will have 3,000+ respondents included, thus enabling researchers to compare people in very specific occupations, locales, religions, and ethnic groups.

SUMMING UP: The Social Psychology of Materialism and Wealth

- To judge from the expressed values of college students and the "luxury fever" that marked late-twentieth-century America, today's Americans—and to a lesser extent people in other Western countries—live in a highly materialistic age.

- People in rich nations report greater happiness and life satisfaction than those in poor nations (though with diminishing returns as one moves from moderately to very wealthy countries). Rich people within a country are somewhat happier than working-class people, though again more and more money provides diminishing returns (as evident in studies of the super-rich and of lottery winners). Does economic growth over time make people happier? Not at all, it seems from the slight decline in self-reported happiness and the increasing rate of depression during the post-1960 years of increasing affluence.

- Two principles help explain why materialism fails to satisfy: the *adaptation-level phenomenon* and *social comparison.* When incomes and consumption rise, we soon adapt. And comparing ourselves with others, we may find our relative position unchanged. Comparing upward breeds dissatisfaction, which helps explain the more frequent sense of unfairness and unhappiness in times and places of great inequality.

- To build a sustainable and satisfying future, we can individually seek and, as a society, promote close relationships, supportive social networks, positive thinking habits, and engaging activity.

POSTSCRIPT:
How Does One Live Responsibly
in the Modern World?

> We must recognize that . . . we are one human family and one Earth community with a common destiny. We must join together to bring forth a sustainable global society founded on respect for nature, universal human rights, economic justice, and a culture of peace. Towards this end, it is imperative that we, the peoples of the Earth, declare our responsibility to one another, to the greater community of life, and to future generations.

> —Preamble, The Earth Charter, www.earthcharter.org

Reading and writing about population growth, global warming, materialism, consumption, adaptation, comparison, and sustainability provokes my [DM's] reflection: Am I part of the answer or part of the problem? I can talk a good line. But do I walk my own talk?

If I'm to be honest, my record is mixed.

I ride a bike to work year-round. But I also flew 60,000 miles last year on fuel-guzzling jets.

I have insulated my 114-year-old home, installed an efficient furnace, and turned the winter daytime thermostat down to 68. But having grown up in a cool summer climate, I can't imagine living without my air-conditioning on sweltering summer days.

To control greenhouse gas production, I routinely turn off lights and the computer monitor when away from my office and have planted trees around my house. But I've helped finance South American deforestation with the coffee I've sipped.

I applauded in 1973 when the United States established an energy-conserving 55 mph national maximum speed limit and was disappointed when it was abandoned in 1995. But now that drivers on the highway around my town are back up to 70 mph, I drive no less than 70 mph—even with (blush) no other cars in sight.

At my house we recycle all our home paper, cans, and bottles. But each week we receive enough mail, newspapers, and periodicals to fill a 3-cubic-foot paper recycling bin.

Not bad, I tell myself. But it's hardly a bold response to the looming crisis. Our great-grandchildren will not thrive on this planet if all of today's 7.3 billion humans were to demand a similar-sized ecological footprint.

How, then, does one participate in the modern world, welcoming its beauties and conveniences, yet remain mindful of our environmental legacy? Even the leaders of the simpler-living movement—who, like me, flew gas-guzzling jets to our three conferences in luxurious surroundings—struggle with how to live responsibly in the modern world.

So what do you think? What regulations do you favor or oppose? Higher fuel-efficiency requirements for cars and trucks? Auto-pollution checks? Leaf-burning bans to reduce smog? If you live in a country where high fuel taxes motivate people to drive small, fuel-efficient cars, do you wish you could have the much lower fuel taxes and cheaper petrol that have enabled Americans to drive big cars? If you are an American, would you favor higher gasoline and oil taxes to help conserve resources and restrain climate change?

How likely is it that humanity will be able to curb global warming and resource depletion? If the biologist E. O. Wilson (2002) was right to speculate that humans evolved to commit themselves only to their small piece of geography, their own kin, and their own time, can we hope that our species will exhibit "extended altruism" by caring for our distant descendants? Will today's envied "lifestyles of the rich and famous" become gauche in a future where sustainability becomes necessity? Or will people's concern for themselves and for displaying the symbols of success always trump their concerns for their unseen great-grandchildren?

"The great dilemma of environmental reasoning stems from this conflict between short-term and long-term values."

—E. O. Wilson,
The Future of Life, 2002

Epilogue

If you have read this entire book, your introduction to social psychology is complete. In the Preface, we offered our hope that this book "would be at once solidly scientific and warmly human, factually rigorous and intellectually provocative." You, not us, are the judge of whether that goal has been achieved. But we can tell you that sharing the discipline has been a joy for us as your authors. If receiving our gift has brought you any measure of pleasure, stimulation, and enrichment, then our joy is multiplied.

A knowledge of social psychology, we do believe, has the power to restrain intuition with critical thinking, illusion with understanding, and judgmentalism with compassion. In these 16 chapters, we have assembled social psychology's insights into belief and persuasion, love and hate, conformity and independence. We have glimpsed incomplete answers to intriguing questions: How do our attitudes feed and get fed by our actions? What leads people sometimes to hurt and sometimes to help one another? What kindles social conflict, and how can we transform closed fists into helping hands? Answering such questions expands our minds. And, "once expanded to the dimensions of a larger idea," noted Oliver Wendell Holmes, the mind "never returns to its original size." Such has been our experience, and perhaps yours, as you, through this and other courses, become an educated person.

David G. Myers
davidmyers.org

Jean M. Twenge
jeantwenge.com

References

AAAS. (2014). *What we know: The reality, risks and response to climate change.* Washington, DC: The American Association for the Advancement of Science Climate Science Panel.

AAMC: American Association of Medical Colleges. (2014). Medical students, selected years, 1965–2014. Retrived March 26, 2015 from https://www.aamc.org/download/411782/data/2014_table1.pdf

ABA: American Bar Association. (2014). A current glance at women in the law. Retrieved March 26, 2015 from http://www.americanbar.org/content/dam/aba/marketing/women/current_glance_statistics_july2014.authcheckdam.pdf

Abbate, C. S., Isgro, A., Wicklund, R. A., & Boca, S. (2006). A field experiment on perspective-taking, helping, and self-awareness. *Basic and Applied Social Psychology, 28,* 283–287.

Abbey, A. (1987). Misperceptions of friendly behavior as sexual interest: A survey of naturally occurring incidents. *Psychology of Women Quarterly, 11,* 173–194.

Abbey, A. (1991). Misperception as an antecedent of acquaintance rape: A consequence of ambiguity in communication between women and men. In A. Parrot (Ed.), *Acquaintance rape.* New York: Wiley.

Abbey, A. (2011). Alcohol and dating risk factors for sexual assault: Double standards are still alive and well entrenched. *Psychology of Women Quarterly, 35,* 362–368.

ABC News. (2004, March 31). Bizarre hoax leads to strip searches (abcnews.go.com).

ABC News. (2004, December 28). Whistle-blower revealed abuse at Abu Ghraib prison (abcnews.go.com).

Abelson, R. (1972). Are attitudes necessary? In B. T. King & E. McGinnies (Eds.), *Attitudes, conflict and social change.* New York: Academic Press.

Abelson, R. P., Kinder, D. R., Peters, M. D., & Fiske, S. T. (1982). Affective and semantic components in political person perception. *Journal of Personality and Social Psychology, 42,* 619–630.

Abrams, D., Wetherell, M., Cochrane, S., Hogg, M. A., & Turner, J. C. (1990). Knowing what to think by knowing who you are: Self-categorization and the nature of norm formation, conformity and group polarization. *British Journal of Social Psychology, 29,* 97–119.

Abramson, L. Y. (Ed.). (1988). *Social cognition and clinical psychology: A synthesis.* New York: Guilford.

Abramson, L. Y., Metalsky, G. I., & Alloy, L. B. (1989). Hopelessness depression:

A theory-based subtype. *Psychological Review, 96,* 358–372.

Acevedo, B. P., Aron, A., Fisher, H. E., & Brown, L. L. (2012). Neural correlates of long-term intense romantic love. *Scan, 7,* 145–159.

Ackerman, J. M., Griskevicius, V., & Li, N. P. (2011). Let's get serious: Communicating commitment in romantic relationships. *Journal of Personality and Social Psychology, 100,* 1079–1094.

Ackermann, R., & DeRubeis, R. J. (1991). Is depressive realism real? *Clinical Psychology Review, 11,* 565–584.

Adachi, P. J. C., & Willoughby, T. (2011). The effect of violent video games on aggression: Is it more than just the violence? *Aggression and Violent Behavior, 16,* 55–62.

Adams, D. (Ed.). (1991). *The Seville statement on violence: Preparing the ground for the constructing of peace.* UNESCO.

Adams, G., Garcia, D. M., Purdie-Vaughns, V., & Steele, C. M. (2006). The detrimental effects of a suggestion of sexism in an instruction situation. *Journal of Experimental Social Psychology, 42,* 602–615.

Adams, J. M., & Jones, W. H. (1997). The conceptualization of marital commitment: An integrative analysis. *Journal of Personality and Social Psychology, 72,* 1177–1196.

Addis, M. E., & Mahalik, J. R. (2003). Men, masculinity, and the contexts of help seeking. *American Psychologist, 58,* 5–14.

Aderman, D., & Berkowitz, L. (1983). Self-concern and the unwillingness to be helpful. *Social Psychology Quarterly, 46,* 293–301.

Adler, N. E., Boyce, T., Chesney, M. A., Cohen, S., Folkman, S., Kahn, R. L., & Syme, S. L. (1993). Socioeconomic inequalities in health: No easy solution. *Journal of the American Medical Association, 269,* 3140–3145.

Adler, N. E., Boyce, T., Chesney, M. A., Cohen, S., Folkman, S., Kahn, R. L., & Syme, S. L. (1994). Socioeconomic status and health: The challenge of the gradient. *American Psychologist, 49,* 15–24.

Adler, N. E., & Snibbe, A. C. (2003). The role of psychosocial processes in explaining the gradient between socioeconomic status and health. *Current Directions in Psychological Science, 12,* 119–123.

Adler, R. P., Lesser, G. S., Meringoff, L. K., Robertson, T. S., & Ward, S. (1980). *The effects of television advertising on children.* Lexington, MA: Lexington Books.

Adler, S. J. (1994). *The jury.* New York: Times Books.

Adorno, T., Frenkel-Brunswik, E., Levinson, D., & Sanford, R. N. (1950). *The authoritarian personality.* New York: Harper.

AFP relaxnews. (2013). Young UK drivers overconfident of their abilities: Survey. March 13, 2013. https://sg.news.yahoo.com/young-uk-drivers-overconfident-abilities-survey-165114562.html.

Agerström, J., & Rooth, D-O. (2011). The role of automatic obesity stereotypes in real hiring discrimination. *Journal of Applied Psychology, 96,* 790–805.

Agthe, M., Spörrle, M., & Maner, J. K. (2011). Does being attractive always help? Positive and negative effects of attractiveness on social decision making. *Personality and Social Psychology Bulletin, 37,* 1042–1054.

Aiello, J. R., & Douthitt, E. Z. (2001). Social facilitation from Triplett to electronic performance monitoring. *Group Dynamics: Theory, Research, and Practice, 5,* 163–180.

Aiello, J. R., Thompson, D. E., & Brodzinsky, D. M. (1983). How funny is crowding anyway? Effects of room size, group size, and the introduction of humor. *Basic and Applied Social Psychology, 4,* 193–207.

Ainsworth, M. D. S. (1973). The development of infant-mother attachment. In B. Caldwell & H. Ricciuti (Eds.), *Review of child development research* (Vol. 3). Chicago: University of Chicago Press.

Ainsworth, M. D. S. (1979). Infant–mother attachment. *American Psychologist, 34,* 932–937.

Ainsworth, S. E., & Maner, J. K. (2012). Sex begets violence: Mating motives, social dominance, and physical aggression in men. *Journal of Personality and Social Psychology, 103,* 819–829.

Ajzen, I., & Fishbein, M. (1977). Attitude-behavior relations: A theoretical analysis and review of empirical research. *Psychological Bulletin, 84,* 888–918.

Ajzen, I., & Fishbein, M. (2005). The influence of attitudes on behavior. In D. Albarracin, B. T. Johnson, & M. P. Zanna (Eds.), *The handbook of attitudes.* Mahwah, NJ: Erlbaum.

Aknin, L. B., Barrington-Leigh, C., Dunn, E. W., Helliwell, J. F., Burns, J., Biswas-Diener, R., Kemeza, I., Nyende, P., Ashton-James, C. E., & Norton, M. I. (2013). Prosocial spending and well-being: Cross-cultural evidence for a psychological universal. *Journal of Personality and Social Psychology, 104,* 635–652.

Aknin, L. B., Fleerackers, A. L., & Hamlin, J. K. (2014). Can third-party observers detect the emotional rewards of generous spending? *The Journal of Positive Psychology, 9,* 198–203.

Akrami, N., Ekehammar, B., & Bergh, R. (2011). Generalized prejudice: Common and specific components. *Psychological Science, 22,* 57–59.

Albarracin, D., Johnson, B. T., Fishbein, M., & Muellerleile, P. A. (2001). Theories of reasoned action and planned behavior as models of condom use: A meta-analysis. *Psychological Bulletin, 127,* 142–161.

Alden, L. E., & Trew, J. L. (2013). If it makes you happy: Engaging in kind acts increases positive affect in socially anxious individuals. *Emotion, 13,* 64–75.

Alexander, L., & Tredoux, C. (2010). The spaces between us: A spatial analysis of informal segregation at a South African university. *Journal of Social Issues, 66,* 367–386.

Alicke, M. D., & Davis, T. L. (1989). The role of *a posteriori* victim information in judgments of blame and sanction. *Journal of Experimental Social Psychology, 25,* 362–377.

Alkhuzai, A. H., et al. (2008). Violence-related mortality in Iraq from 2002 to 2006. *New England Journal of Medicine, 358,* 484–493.

Allee, W. C., & Masure, R. M. (1936). A comparison of maze behavior in paired and isolated shell-parakeets (*Melopsittacus undulatus Shaw*) in a two-alley problem box. *Journal of Comparative Psychology, 22,* 131–155.

Allen, M. S., & Jones, M. V. (2014). The "home advantage" in athletic competitions. *Current Directions in Psychological Science, 23,* 48–53.

Allen, V. L., & Levine, J. M. (1969). Consensus and conformity. *Journal of Experimental Social Psychology, 5,* 389–399.

Allesøe, K., Hundrup, V. A., Thomsen, J. F., & Osler, M. (2010). Psychosocial work environment and risk of ischaemic heart disease in women: The Danish Nurse Cohort Study. *Occupational and Environmental Medicine, 67,* 318–322.

Alloy, L., Abramson, L. Y., Gibb, B. E., Crossfield, A. G., Pieracci, A. M., Spasojevic, J., & Steinberg, J. A. (2004). Developmental antecedents of cognitive vulnerability to depression: Review of findings from the cognitive vulnerability to depression project. *Journal of Cognitive Psychotherapy, 18,* 115–133.

Alloy, L. B., & Abramson, L. Y. (1979). Judgment of contingency in depressed and nondepressed students: Sadder but wiser? *Journal of Experimental Psychology: General, 108,* 441–485.

Alloy, L. B., Abramson, L. Y., Whitehouse, W. G., Hogan, M. E., Tashman, N. A., Steinberg, D. L., Rose, D. T., & Donovan, P. (1999). Depressogenic cognitive styles: Predictive validity, information processing and personality characteristics, and developmental origins. *Behaviour Research and Therapy, 37,* 503–531.

Alloy, L. B., Albright, J. S., Abramson, L. Y., & Dykman, B. M. (1990). Depressive realism and nondepressive optimistic illusions: The role of the self. In R. E. Ingram (Ed.), *Contemporary psychological approaches to depression: Theory, research and treatment.* New York: Plenum.

Allport, F. H. (1920). The influence of the group upon association and thought. *Journal of Experimental Psychology, 3,* 159–182.

Allport, G. W. (1954). *The nature of prejudice.* Cambridge, MA: Addison-Wesley.

Allport, G. W. (1958). *The nature of prejudice* (abridged). Garden City, NY: Anchor Books.

Allport, G. W., & Ross, J. M. (1967). Personal religious orientation and prejudice. *Journal of Personality and Social Psychology, 5,* 432–443.

Alquist, J. L., Ainsworth, S. E., & Baumeister, R. F. (2013). Determined to conform: Disbelief in free will increases in conformity. *Journal of Experimental Social Psychology, 49,* 80–86.

Al Ramiah, A., & Hewstone, M. (2013). Intergroup contact as a tool for reducing, resolving, and preventing intergroup conflict: Evidence, limitations, and potential. *American Psychologist, 68,* 527–542.

Altemeyer, R. (1988). *Enemies of freedom: Understanding right-wing authoritarianism.* San Francisco: Jossey-Bass.

Altemeyer, R. (1992). Six studies of right-wing authoritarianism among American state legislators. Unpublished manuscript, University of Manitoba.

Altman, I., & Vinsel, A. M. (1978). Personal space: An analysis of E. T. Hall's proxemics framework. In I. Altman & J. Wohlwill (Eds.), *Human behavior and the environment.* New York: Plenum.

Alwin, D. F. (1990). Historical changes in parental orientations to children. In N. Mandell (Ed.), *Sociological studies of child development* (Vol. 3). Greenwich, CT: JAI Press.

Alwin, D. F., Cohen, R. L., & Newcomb, T. M. (1991). *Political attitudes over the life span: The Bennington women after fifty years.* Madison: University of Wisconsin Press.

Amato, P. R. (1979). Juror-defendant similarity and the assessment of guilt in politically motivated crimes. *Australian Journal of Psychology, 31,* 79–88.

Ambady, N., Bernieri, F. J., & Richeson, J. A. (2000). Toward a histology of social behavior: Judgmental accuracy from thin slices of the behavioral stream. *Advances in Experimental Social Psychology, 32,* 201–271.

Ambady, N., & Rosenthal, R. (1992). Thin slices of expressive behavior as predictors of interpersonal consequences: A meta-analysis. *Psychological Bulletin, 111,* 256–274.

Ambady, N., & Rosenthal, R. (1993). Half a minute: Predicting teacher evaluations from thin slices of nonverbal behavior and physical attractiveness. *Journal of Personality and Social Psychology, 64,* 431–441.

American College Health Association. (2009). *American College Health Association-National College Health Assessment II: Reference group executive summary Fall 2008.* Baltimore: Author.

American Enterprises. (1992, January/February). *Women, men, marriages and ministers,* 106.

American Psychological Association. (2010). *Ethical principles of psychologists and code of conduct: 2010 amendments.* Washington, DC: Author (www.apa.org/ethics/code/index.asp).

American Society for Aesthetic Plastic Surgery. (2014). Cosmetic surgery national database statistics. http://www.surgery.org/sites/default/files/2014-Stats.pdf.

Amir, Y. (1969). Contact hypothesis in ethnic relations. *Psychological Bulletin, 71,* 319–342.

AMS. (2014). *Explaining extreme events of 2013 from a climate perspective.* American Meteorological Society (www2.ametsoc.org).

An, S., & Kang, H. (2013). Do online ad breaks clearly tell kids that advergames are advertisements that intend to sell things? *International Journal of Advertising, 32,* 655–678.

Anderegg, W. R. L., Prall, J. W., Harold, J., & Schneider, S. H. (2010). Expert credibility in climate change. *PNAS, 107,* 12107–12109.

Andersen, S. M. (1998). *Service learning: A national strategy for youth development. A position paper issued by the Task Force on Education Policy.* Washington, DC: Institute for Communitarian Policy Studies, George Washington University.

Andersen, S. M., & Chen, S. (2002). The relational self: An interpersonal social-cognitive theory. *Psychological Review, 109,* 619–645.

Anderson, C. (2011, August 2). Norway: War games and toys pulled from shelves. *New York Times* (www.nytimes.com).

Anderson, C. A. (2003). Video games and aggressive behavior. In D. Ravitch and J. P. Viteritti (Eds.), *Kids stuff: Marking violence and vulgarity in the popular culture.* Baltimore, MD: Johns Hopkins University Press.

Anderson, C. A. (2004). An update on the effects of violent video games. *Journal of Adolescence, 27,* 113–122.

Anderson, C. A., & Anderson, D. C. (1984). Ambient temperature and violent crime: Tests of the linear and curvilinear hypotheses. *Journal of Personality and Social Psychology, 46,* 91–97.

Anderson, C. A., Andrighetto, L., Bartholow, B. D., Begue, L., Boxer, P., Brockmyer, J. F., & . . . Warburton, W. (2015). Consensus on media violence effects: Comment on Bushman, Gollwitzer, and Cruz (2015). *Psychology of Popular Media Culture, 4,* 215–221.

Anderson, C. A., Benjamin, A. J., Jr., & Bartholow, B. D. (1998). Does the gun pull the trigger? Automatic priming effects of weapon pictures and weapon names. *Psychological Science, 9,* 308–314.

Anderson, C. A., & Buckley, K. E., & Carnagey, N. L. (2008). Creating your own hostile environment: A laboratory examination of trait aggressiveness and the violence escalation cycle. *Personality and Social Psychology Bulletin, 34,* 462–473.

Anderson, C. A., & Bushman, B. J. (1997). External validity of "trivial" experiments: The case of laboratory aggression. *Review of General Psychology, 1,* 19–41.

Anderson, C. A., & Delisi, M. (2010). Implications of global climate change for violence in developed and developing countries. In J. Forgas, A. Kruglanski, & K. Williams (Eds.), *Social Conflict and Aggression.* New York: Psychology Press.

Anderson, C. A., & Gentile, D. A. (2008). Media violence, aggression, and public policy. In E. Borgida & S. Fiske (Eds.), *Beyond common sense: Psychological science in the courtroom.* Malden, MA: Blackwell.

Anderson, C. A., Gentile, D. A., & Buckley, K. E. (2007). *Violent video game effects on children and adolescents: Theory, research, and public policy.* New York: Oxford University Press.

Anderson, C. A., & Harvey, R. J. (1988). Discriminating between problems in living: An examination of measures of depression, loneliness, shyness, and social anxiety. *Journal of Social and Clinical Psychology, 6,* 482–491.

Anderson, C. A., Lepper, M. R., & Ross, L. (1980). Perseverance of social theories: The role of explanation in the persistence of discredited information. *Journal of Personality and Social Psychology, 39,* 1037–1049.

Anderson, C. A., Lindsay, J. J., & Bushman, B. J. (1999). Research in the psychological laboratory: Truth or triviality? *Current Directions in Psychological Science, 8,* 3–9.

Anderson, C. A., Miller, R. S., Riger, A. L., Dill, J. C., & Sedikides, C. (1994). Behavioral and characterological attributional styles as predictors of depression and loneliness: Review, refinement, and test. *Journal of Personality and Social Psychology, 66,* 549–558.

Anderson, C. A., Shibuya, A., Ihori, N., Swing, E. L., Bushman, B. J., Sakamoto, A., Rothstein, C. R., & Saleen, M. (2010). Violent video game effects on aggression, empathy, and prosocial behavior in Eastern and Western countries: A meta-analytic review. *Psychological Bulletin, 136,* 151–173.

Anderson, C., Brion, S., Moore, D. A., & Kennedy, J. A. (2012). A status-enhancement account of overconfidence. *Journal of Personality and Social Psychology, 103,* 718–735.

Anderson, C., Keltner, D., & John, O. P. (2003). Emotional convergence between people over time. *Journal of Personality and Social Psychology, 84,* 1054–1068.

Anderson, C., & Kilduff, G. J. (2009). Why do dominant personalities attain influence in face-to-face groups? The competence-signaling effects of trait dominance. *Journal of Personality and Social Psychology, 96,* 491–503.

Anderson, C., Srivastava, S., Beer, J. S., Spataro, S. E., & Chatman, J. A. (2006). Knowing your place: Self-perceptions of status in face-to-face groups. *Journal of Personality and Social Psychology, 91,* 1094–1110.

Andrews, P. W., & Thomson, Jr., J. A. (2009). The bright side of being blue: Depression as an adaptation for analyzing complex problems. *Psychological Review, 116,* 620–654.

Andrews, P. W., & Thomson, Jr., J. A. (2010, January/February). Depression's evolutionary roots. *Scientific American Mind,* 57–61.

Anglemyer, A., Horvath, T., & Rutherford, G. (2014). The accessibility of firearms and risk for suicide and homicide victimization among household members: A systematic review and meta-analysis. *Annals of Internal Medicine, 160,* 101–110.

Anik, L., Aknin, L. B., Norton, M. I., Dunn, E. W., & Quoidbach, J. (2013). Prosocial bonuses increase employee satisfaction and team performance. *PLOS One, 8,* e75509.

Antonakis, J., & Dalgas, O. (2009). Predicting elections: Child's play! *Science, 323,* 1183.

AP. (2013, November 25). Man breaks woman's jump from Oakland stadium deck. Associated Press release.

AP: Associated Press. (2011). Storm gender debate rages in Canada as parents defend right to keep baby's sex a secret. May 27, 2011. Retrieved March 26, 2015 from: http://www.huffingtonpost.com/2011/05/27/storm-gender-debate-rages_n_868131.html

AP/Ipsos. (2006, May 4). Associated Press/Ipsos Poll data reported by personal correspondence with Michael Gross.

APA: American Psychiatric Association. (2012). Position statement on access to care for transgender and gender variant individuals. Retrieved March 26, 2015 from http://www.psychiatry.org/File%20Library/Learn/Archivcs/Position-2012-Transgender-Gender-Variant-Access-Care.pdf

Archer, D., Iritani, B., Kimes, D. B., & Barrios, M. (1983). Face-ism: Five studies of sex differences in facial prominence. *Journal of Personality and Social Psychology, 45,* 725–735.

Archer, J. (1991). The influence of testosterone on human aggression. *British Journal of Psychology, 82,* 1–28.

Archer, J. (2000). Sex differences in aggression between heterosexual partners: A meta-analytic review. *Psychological Bulletin, 126,* 651–680.

Archer, J. (2006). Testosterone and human aggression: An evaluation of the challenge hypothesis. *Neuroscience and Biobehavioral Reviews, 30,* 319–345.

Archer, J. (2009). Does sexual selection explain human sex differences? *Behavioral and Brain Sciences, 32,* 249–311.

Archer, R. L., & Cook, C. E. (1986). Personalistic self-disclosure and attraction: Basis for relationship or scarce resource. *Social Psychology Quarterly, 49,* 268–272.

Arendt, H. (1963). *Eichmann in Jerusalem: A report on the banality of evil.* New York: Viking.

Argyle, M., & Henderson M. (1985). *The anatomy of relationships.* London: Heinemann.

Argyle, M., Shimoda, K., & Little, B. (1978). Variance due to persons and situations in England and Japan. *British Journal of Social and Clinical Psychology, 17,* 335–337.

Arieff, A. (2011, August 22). It's not about the furniture: Cubicles, continued. *New York Times Opinionator* (www.nytimes.com).

Ariza, L. M. (2006, January). Virtual Jihad: The Internet as the ideal terrorism recruiting tool. *Scientific American,* 18–21.

Arkes, H. R. (1990). *Some practical judgment/decision making research.* Paper presented at the American Psychological Association convention.

Arkin, R. M., Appleman, A., & Burger, J. M. (1980). Social anxiety, self-presentation, and the self-serving bias in causal attribution. *Journal of Personality and Social Psychology, 38,* 23–35.

Arkin, R. M., & Burger, J. M. (1980). Effects of unit relation tendencies on interpersonal attraction. *Social Psychology Quarterly, 43,* 380–391.

Arkin, R. M., Lake, E. A., & Baumgardner, A. H. (1986). Shyness and self-presentation. In W. H. Jones, J. M. Cheek, & S. R. Briggs (Eds.), *Shyness: Perspectives on research and treatment.* New York: Plenum.

Armitage, C. J., & Conner, M. (2001). Efficacy of the theory of planned behaviour: A meta-analytic review. *British Journal of Social Psychology, 40,* 471–499.

Armor, D. A., & Sackett, A. M. (2006). Accuracy, error, and bias in predictions for real versus hypothetical events. *Journal of Personality and Social Psychology, 91,* 583–600.

Armor, D. A., & Taylor, S. E. (1996). Situated optimism: Specific outcome expectancies and self-regulation. In M. P. Zanna (Ed.), *Advances in experimental social psychology* (Vol. 30). San Diego: Academic Press.

Arms, R. L., Russell, G. W., & Sandilands, M. L. (1979). Effects on the hostility of spectators of viewing aggressive sports. *Social Psychology Quarterly, 42,* 275–279.

Aron, A., & Aron, E. (1989). *The heart of social psychology,* 2nd ed. Lexington, MA: Lexington Books.

Aron, A., & Aron, E. N. (1994). Love. In A. L. Weber & J. H. Harvey (Eds.), *Perspective on close relationships.* Boston: Allyn & Bacon.

Aron, A., Dutton, D. G., Aron, E. N., & Iverson, A. (1989). Experiences of falling in love. *Journal of Social and Personal Relationships, 6,* 243–257.

Aron, A., Fisher, H., Mashek, D. J., Strong, G., Li, H., & Brown, L. L. (2005). Reward, motivation, and emotion systems associated with early-stage intense romantic love. *Journal of Neurophysiology, 94,* 327–337.

Aron, A., Melinat, E., Aron, E. N., Vallone, R. D., & Bator, R. J. (1997). The experimental generation of interpersonal closeness: A procedure and some preliminary findings. *Personality and Social Psychology Bulletin, 23,* 363–377.

Aron, A., Norman, C. C., Aron, E. N., McKenna, C., & Heyman, R. E. (2000). Couples' shared participation in novel and arousing activities and experienced relationship quality. *Journal of Personality and Social Psychology, 78,* 273–284.

Aronson, E. (1980). *The social animal.* 3rd edition. New York: Freeman.

Aronson, E. (1988). *The social animal,* 5th edition. New York: Freeman.

Aronson, E. (2004). Reducing hostility and building compassion: Lessons from the jigsaw classroom. In A. G. Miller (Ed.), *The social psychology of good and evil.* New York: Guilford.

Aronson, E., Brewer, M., & Carlsmith, J. M. (1985). Experimentation in social psychology. In G. Lindzey & E. Aronson (Eds.), *Handbook of social psychology* (Vol. 1). Hillsdale, NJ: Erlbaum.

Aronson, E., & Gonzalez, A. (1988). Desegregation, jigsaw, and the Mexican-American experience. In P. A. Katz & D. Taylor (Eds.), *Towards the elimination of racism: Profiles in controversy.* New York: Plenum.

Arora, R. (2005). China's "Gen Y" bucks tradition. Gallup Poll, http://www.gallup.com/poll/15934/Chinas—Gen-Bucks-Tradition.aspx. Viewed online 1/22/09.

Arriaga, X. B. (2001). The ups and downs of dating: Fluctuations in satisfaction in newly formed romantic relationships. *Journal of Personality and Social Psychology, 80,* 754–765.

Arriaga, X. B., & Agnew, C. R. (2001). Being committed: Affective, cognitive, and conative components of relationship commitment. *Personality and Social Psychology Bulletin, 27,* 1190–1203.

Asch, S. E. (1946). Forming impressions of personality. *Journal of Abnormal and Social Psychology, 41,* 258–290.

Asch, S. E. (1955, November). Opinions and social pressure. *Scientific American,* pp. 31–35.

Asendorpf, J. B. (1987). Videotape reconstruction of emotions and cognitions related to shyness. *Journal of Personality and Social Psychology, 53,* 541–549.

Asher, J. (1987, April). Born to be shy? *Psychology Today, 56,* 56–64.

Ash, R. (1999). *The top 10 of everything 2000.* New York: DK Publishing.

Ashton-James, C., & Tracy, J. L. (2012). Pride and prejudice: How feelings about the self influence judgments of others. *Personality and Social Psychology Bulletin, 38,* 466–476.

Associated Press (AP). (2009, December 1). Psych report found Clemmons risk to public safety. *Associated Press.*

Associated Press. (2012). Judge blocks graphic images on cigarette packages. March 1, 2012 (http://www.nydailynews.com/life-style/health/judge-blocks-graphic-images-cigarette-packages-rules-extreme-warnings-violate-amendment-article-1.1031356).

Associated Press. (2012). Maria Hoefl-Riesch edges Lindsey Vonn. January 29, 2012. Retrieved April 1, 2015 from: http://espn.go.com/olympics/skiing/story/_/id/7516020/lindsey-vonn-denied-weekend-sweep-003-seconds

Associated Press. (2013, June 19). Boy, 13, allegedly murders sister, 5, while trying WWE wrestling moves he saw on TV, police say (http://www.huffingtonpost.com/2013/06/19/boy-murders-sister-wrestling_n_3467065.html).

Astin, A. W., Green, K. C., Korn, W. S., & Schalit, M. (1987). *The American freshman: National norms for Fall 1987.* Los Angeles: Higher Education Research Institute, UCLA.

Athota, V. S., & O'Connor, P. J. (2014). How approach and avoidance constructs of personality and trait emotional intelligence predict core human values. *Learning and Individual Differences, 31,* 51–58.

Auyeung, B., Lombardo, M. V., & Baron-Cohen, S. (2013). Prenatal and postnatal hormone effects on the human brain and cognition. *Pflugers Archiv-European Journal of Physiology, 465,* 557–571.

Averill, J. R. (1983). Studies on anger and aggression: Implications for theories of emotion. *American Psychologist, 38,* 1145–1160.

Axsom, D., Yates, S., & Chaiken, S. (1987). Audience response as a heuristic cue in persuasion. *Journal of Personality and Social Psychology, 53,* 30–40.

Azrin, N. H. (1967, May). Pain and aggression. *Psychology Today,* 27–33.

Baars, B. J., & McGovern, K. A. (1994). Consciousness. In V. Ramachandran (Ed.), *Encyclopedia of human behavior.* Orlando, FL: Academic Press.

Babad, E., Bernieri, F., & Rosenthal, R. (1991). Students as judges of teachers' verbal and nonverbal behavior. *American Educational Research Journal, 28,* 211–234.

Bachman, J. G., & O'Malley, P. M. (1977). Self-esteem in young men: A longitudinal analysis of the impact of educational and occupational attainment. *Journal of Personality and Social Psychology, 35,* 365–380.

Back, M. D., Schmukle, S. C., & Egloff, B. (2008). Becoming friends by chance. *Psychological Science, 19,* 439–440.

Bahrami, B., Olsen, K., Latham, P. E., Roepstorff, A., Rees, G., & Frith, C. D. (2010). Optimally interacting minds. *Science, 329,* 1081–1085.

Bailenson, J. N., Iyengar, S., Yee, N., & Collins, N. (2009). Facial similarity between voters and candidates causes influence. *Public Opinion Quarterly.*

Bailenson, J. N., & Yee, N. (2005). Digital chameleons: Automatic assimilation of nonverbal gestures in immersive virtual environments. *Psychological Science, 16,* 814–819.

Bailey, J. M., Kirk, K. M., Zhu, G., Dunne, M. P., & Martin, N. G. (2000). Do individual differences in sociosexuality represent genetic or environmentally contingent strategies? Evidence from the Australian Twin Registry. *Journal of Personality and Social Psychology, 78,* 537–545.

Baize, H. R., Jr., & Schroeder, J. E. (1995). Personality and mate selection in personal ads: Evolutionary preferences in a public mate selection process. *Journal of Social Behavior and Personality, 10,* 517–536.

Baker, L., & McNulty, J. K. (2010). Shyness and marriage: Does shyness shape even established relationships? *Personality and Social Psychology Bulletin, 36,* 665–676.

Baldwin, M. W., Keelan, J. P. R., Fehr, B., Enns, V., & Koh-Rangarajoo, E. (1996). Social-cognitive conceptualization of attachment working models: Availability and accessibility effects. *Journal of Personality and Social Psychology, 71,* 94–109.

Balliet, D., Mulder, L. B., & Van Lange, P. A. M. (2011). Reward, punishment, and cooperation: A meta-analysis. *Psychological Bulletin, 137,* 594–615.

Balliet, D., & Van Lange, P. A. M. (2013). Trust, conflict. and cooperation: A meta-analysis. *Psychological Bulletin, 139,* 1090–1112.

Balliet, D., Wu, J., & De Dreu, Carsten, K. W. (2014). Ingroup favoritism in cooperation: A meta-analysis. *Psychological Bulletin, 140,* 1556–1581.

Balsa, A. I., Homer, J. F., French, M. T., & Norton, E. C. (2010). Alcohol use and popularity: Social payoffs from conforming to peers' behavior. *Journal of Research on Adolescence, 21,* 559–568.

Banaji, M. R., & Greenwald, A. G. (2013). *Blindspot: Hidden biases of good people.* New York: Delacorte Press.

Bandura, A. (1979). The social learning perspective: Mechanisms of aggression. In H. Toch (Ed.), *Psychology of crime and criminal justice.* New York: Holt, Rinehart & Winston.

Bandura, A. (1997). *Self-efficacy: The exercise of control.* New York: Freeman.

Bandura, A. (2000). Social cognitive theory: An agentic perspective. *Annual Review of Psychology, 52,* 1–26.

Bandura, A. (2004). Swimming against the mainstream: The early years from chilly tributary to transformative mainstream. *Behaviour Research and Therapy, 42,* 613–630.

Bandura, A. (2008). Reconstrual of "free will" from the agentic perspective of social cognitive theory. In J. Baer, J. C. Kaufman, & R. F. Baumeister (Eds.), *Are we free? Psychology and free will.* New York: Oxford University Press.

Bandura, A., Pastorelli, C., Barbaranelli, C., & Caprara, G. V. (1999). Self-efficacy pathways to childhood depression. *Journal of Personality and Social Psychology, 76,* 258–269.

Bandura, A., Ross, D., & Ross, S. A. (1961). Transmission of aggression through imitation of aggressive models. *Journal of Abnormal and Social Psychology, 63,* 575–582.

Bandura, A., & Walters, R. H. (1959). *Adolescent aggression.* New York: Ronald Press.

Bandura, A., & Walters, R. H. (1963). *Social learning and personality development.* New York: Holt, Rinehart & Winston.

Banks, S. M., Salovey, P., Greener, S., Rothman, A. J., Moyer, A., Beauvais, J., & Epel, E. (1995). The effects of message framing on mammography utilization. *Health Psychology, 14,* 178–184

Barash, D. (1979). *The whisperings within.* New York: Harper & Row.

Barash, D. P. (2003, November 7). Unreason's seductive charms. *Chronicle of Higher Education* (www.chronicle.com/free/v50/i11/11b00601.htm).

Barber, B. M., & Odean, T. (2001a). Boys will be boys: Gender, overconfidence and common stock investment. *Quarterly Journal of Economics, 116,* 261–292.

Barber, B. M., & Odean, T. (2001b). The Internet and the investor. *Journal of Economic Perspectives, 15,* 41–54.

Barber, N. (2000). On the relationship between country sex ratios and teen pregnancy rates: A replication. *Cross-Cultural Research, 34,* 327–333.

Bargh, J. A. (2006). What have we been priming all these years? On the development, mechanisms, and ecology of nonconscious social behavior. *European Journal of Social Psychology, 36,* 147–168.

Bargh, J. A., & Chartrand, T. L. (1999). The unbearable automaticity of being. *American Psychologist, 54,* 462–479.

Bargh, J. A., & McKenna, K. Y. A. (2004). The Internet and social life. *Annual Review of Psychology, 55,* 573–590.

Bargh, J. A., McKenna, K. Y. A., & Fitzsimons, G. M. (2002). Can you see the real me? Activation and expression of the "true self" on the Internet. *Journal of Social Issues, 58,* 33–48.

Bargh, J. A., & Raymond, P. (1995). The naive misuse of power: Nonconscious sources of sexual harassment. *Journal of Social Issues, 51,* 85–96.

Bargh, J. A., Schwader, K. L., Hailey, S. E., Dyer, R. L., & Boothby, E. J. (2012). Automaticity in social-cognitive processes. *Trends in Cognitive Sciences, 16,* 593–605.

Bargh, J. A., & Shalev, I. (2012). The substitutability of physical and social warmth in daily life. *Emotion, 12,* 154–162.

Bar-Haim, Y., Ziv, T., Lamy, D., & Hodes, R. M. (2006). Nature and nurture in own-race face processing. *Psychological Science, 17,* 159–163.

Barlett, C. P., & Anderson, C. A. (2014). Bad news, bad times, and violence: The link between economic distress and aggression. *Psychology of Violence, 4,* 309–321.

Barlett, C. P., Harris, R. J., & Bruey, C. (2008). The effect of the amount of blood in a violence video game on aggression, hostility, and arousal. *Journal of Experimental Social Psychology, 44,* 539–546.

Barlow, F. K., Paolini, S., Pedersen, A., Hornsey, M. J., Radke, H. R. M., Harwood, J., Rubin, M., & Sibley, C. G. (2012). The contact caveat: Negative contact predicts increased prejudice more than positive contact predicts reduced prejudice. *Personality and Social Psychology Bulletin, 38,* 1629–1643.

Barnes, E. (2008, August 24). Scots heroine of Auschwitz who gave her life for young Jews. *Scotland on Sunday,* 3.

Barnes, R. D., Ickes, W., & Kidd, R. F. (1979). Effects of the perceived intentionality and stability of another's dependency on helping behavior. *Personality and Social Psychology Bulletin, 5,* 367–372.

Barnett, M. A., King, L. M., Howard, J. A., & Melton, E. M. (1980). *Experiencing negative affect about self or other: Effects on helping behavior in children and adults.* Paper presented at the Midwestern Psychological Association convention, Montreal, Quebec.

Barnett, P. A., & Gotlib, I. H. (1988). Psychosocial functioning and depression: Distinguishing among antecedents, concomitants, and consequences. *Psychological Bulletin, 104,* 97–126.

Baron-Cohen, S. (2004). The essential difference: Male and female brains and the truth about autism. New York: Basic Books.

Barongan, C., & Hall, G. C. N. (1995). The influence of misogynous rap music on sexual aggression against women. *Psychology of Women Quarterly, 19,* 195–207.

Baron, J., & Hershey, J. C. (1988). Outcome bias in decision evaluation. *Journal of Personality and Social Psychology, 54,* 569–579.

Baron, J., & Miller, J. G. (2000). Limiting the scope of moral obligations to help: A cross-cultural investigation. *Journal of Cross-Cultural Psychology, 31,* 703–725.

Baron, R. A. (1977). *Human aggression.* New York: Plenum.

Baron, R. A., Markman, G. D., & Bollinger, M. (2006). Exporting social psychology: Effects of attractiveness on perceptions of entrepreneurs, their ideas for new products, and their financial success. *Journal of Applied Social Psychology, 36,* 467–492.

Baron, R. S. (1986). Distraction-conflict theory: Progress and problems. In L. Berkowitz (Ed.), *Advances in experimental social psychology,* Orlando, FL: Academic Press.

Baron, R. S., Kerr, N. L., & Miller, N. (1992). *Group process, group decision, group action.* Pacific Grove, CA: Brooks/Cole.

Barry, D. (1995, January). Bored stiff. *Funny Times,* p. 5.

Barry, D. (1997, May). Can sanity be one of those gender things? *Times Daily,* May 27, 1997, p. 38.

Barry, D. (1998). *Dave Barry turns 50.* New York: Crown.

Bar-Tal, D. (2004). The necessity of observing real life situations: Palestinian-Israeli violence as a laboratory for learning about social behaviour. *European Journal of Social Psychology, 34,* 677–701.

Bar-Tal, D. (2013). *Intractable conflicts: Socio-psychological foundations and dynamics* New York: Cambridge University Press.

Bartels, M., Cacioppo, J. T., Hudziak, J. J., & Boomsma, D. I. (2008). Genetic and environmental contributions to stability in loneliness throughout childhood. *American Journal of Medical Genetics Part B, 147B,* 385–391.

Bartholomew, K., & Horowitz, L. (1991). Attachment styles among young adults: A test of a four-category model. *Journal of Personality and Social Psychology, 61,* 226–244.

Bartholow, B. C., & Heinz, A. (2006). Alcohol and aggression without consumption: Alcohol cues, aggressive thoughts, and hostile perception bias. *Psychological Science, 17,* 30–37.

Bartholow, B. D., Anderson, C. A., Carnagey, N. L., & Benjamin, A. J., Jr. (2004). Interactive effects of life experience and situational cues on aggression: The weapons priming effect in hunters and nonhunters. *Journal of Experimental Social Psychology, 41,* 48–60.

Bartholow, B. D., Bushman, B. J., & Sestir, M. A. (2006). Chronic violent video game exposure and desensitization: Behavioral and event-related brain potential data. *Journal of Experimental Social Psychology, 42(4),* 532–539.

Bartlett, C. P., & Rodeheffer, C. (2009). Effects of realism on extended violent and nonviolent video game play on aggressive thoughts, feelings, and physiological arousal. *Aggressive Behavior, 35,* 213–224.

Barzman, D. H., Mossman, D., Appel, K., Blom, T. J., Strawn, J. R., Ekhator, N. N., Patel, B., DelBello, M. P., Sorter, M., Kein, D., & Geracioti, T. D. (2013). The association between salivary hormone levels and children's inpatient aggression: A pilot study. *Psychiatry Quarterly, 84,* 475–484.

Barzun, J. (1975). *Simple and direct.* New York: Harper & Row, pp. 173–174.

Bassili, J. N. (2003). The minority slowness effect: Subtle inhibitions in the expression of views not shared by others. *Journal of Personality and Social Psychology, 84,* 261–276.

Bastian, B., & Haslam, N. (2006). Psychological essentialism and stereotype endorsement. *Journal of Experimental Social Psychology, 42,* 228–235.

Bastian, B., Jetten, J., Chen, H., Radke, H. R. M., Harding, J. F., & Fasoli, F. (2012). Losing our humanity: The self-dehumanizing consequences of social ostracism. *Personality and Social Psychology Bulletin, 39,* 156–169.

Bastian, B., Jetten, J., & Ferris, L. J. (2014). Pain as social glue: Shared pain increased cooperation. *Psychological Science, 25,* 2079–2085.

Bastian, B., Jetten, J., & Radke, H. R. M. (2012). Cyber-dehumanization: Violent video game play diminishes our humanity. *Journal of Experimental Social Psychology, 48,* 486–491.

Batson, C. D. (1983). Sociobiology and the role of religion in promoting prosocial behavior: An alternative view. *Journal of Personality and Social Psychology, 45,* 1380–1385.

Batson, C. D. (1999a). Behind the scenes. In D. G. Myers, *Social psychology,* 6th edition. New York: McGraw-Hill.

Batson, C. D. (1999b). *Addressing the altruism question experimentally.* Paper presented at the Templeton Foundation/Fetzer Institute Symposium on Empathy, Altruism, and Agape, Cambridge, MA.

Batson, C. D. (2001). Addressing the altruism question experimentally. In S. G. Post, L. B. Underwood, J. P. Schloss, & W. B. Hurlbut (Eds.), *Altruism and altruistic love: Science, philosophy, and religion in dialogue.* New York: Oxford University Press.

Batson, C. D. (2006). "Not all self-interest after all": Economics of empathy-induced altruism. In D. De Cremer, M. Zeelenberg, & J. K. Murnighan (Eds.), *Social psychology and economics.* Mahwah, NJ: Erlbaum.

Batson, C. D. (2011). *Altruism in humans.* New York: Oxford University Press.

Batson, C. D., Bolen, M. H., Cross, J. A., & Neuringer-Benefiel, H. E. (1986). Where is the altruism in the altruistic personality? *Journal of Personality and Social Psychology, 50,* 212–220.

Batson, C. D., Chao, M. C., & Givens, J. M. (2009). Pursuing moral outrage: Anger at torture. *Journal of Experimental Social Psychology, 45,* 155–160.

Batson, C. D., Coke, J. S., Jasnoski, M. L., & Hanson, M. (1978). Buying kindness: Effect of an extrinsic incentive for helping on perceived altruism. *Personality and Social Psychology Bulletin, 4,* 86–91.

Batson, C. D., Duncan, B. D., Ackerman, P., Buckley, T., & Birch, K. (1981). Is empathic emotion a source of altruistic motivation? *Journal of Personality and Social Psychology, 40,* 290–302.

Batson, C. D., Eklund, J. H., Chermok, V. L., Hoyt, J. L., & Ortiz, B. G. (2007). An additional antecedent of empathic concern: Valuing the welfare of the person in need. *Journal of Personality and Social Psychology, 93,* 65–74.

Batson, C. D., Fultz, J., & Schoenrade, P. A. (1987). Distress and empathy: Two qualitatively distinct vicarious emotions with different motivational consequences. *Journal of Personality, 55,* 19–40.

Batson, C. D., Harris, A. C., McCaul, K. D., Davis, M., & Schmidt, T. (1979). Compassion or compliance: Alternative dispositional attributions for one's helping behavior. *Social Psychology Quarterly, 42,* 405–409.

Batson, C. D., Kobrynowicz, D., Dinnerstein, J. L., Kampf, H. C., & Wilson, A. D. (1997). In a very different voice: Unmasking moral hypocrisy. *Journal of Personality and Social Psychology, 72,* 1335–1348.

Batson, C. D., Lishner, D. A., Carpenter, A., Dulin, L., Harjusola-Webb, S., Stocks, E. L., Gale, S., Hassan, O., & Sampat, B. (2003). ". . . As you would have them do unto you": Does imagining yourself in the other's place stimulate moral action? *Personality and Social Psychology Bulletin, 29,* 1190–1201.

Batson, C. D., & Moran, T. (1999). Empathy-induced altruism in a prisoner's dilemma. *European Journal of Social Psychology, 29,* 909–924.

Batson, C. D., Sympson, S. C., Hindman, J. L., Decruz, P., Todd, R. M., Jennings, G., & Burris, C. T. (1996). "I've been there, too": Effect on empathy of prior experience with a need. *Personality and Social Psychology Bulletin, 22,* 474–482.

Batson, C. D., & Thompson, E. R. (2001). Why don't moral people act morally? Motivational considerations. *Current Directions in Psychological Science, 10,* 54–57.

Batson, C. D., Thompson, E. R., & Chen, H. (2002). Moral hypocrisy: Addressing some alternatives. *Journal of Personality and Social Psychology, 83,* 330–339.

Batson, C. D., Thompson, E. R., Seuferling, G., Whitney, H., & Strongman, J. A. (1999). Moral hypocrisy: Appearing moral to oneself without being so. *Journal of Personality and Social Psychology, 77,* 525–537.

Batson, C. D., & Ventis, W. L. (1982). *The religious experience: A social psychological perspective.* New York: Oxford University Press.

Batson, C. D., & Weeks, J. L. (1996). Mood effects of unsuccessful helping: Another test of the empathy-altruism hypothesis. *Personality and Social Psychology Bulletin, 22,* 148–157.

Bauer, M., Cassar, A., Chytilová, J., & Henrich, J. (2014). War's enduring effects on the development of egalitarian motivations and in-group biases. *Psychological Science, 25,* 47–57.

Bauman, C. W., & Skitka, L. J. (2010). Making attributions for behaviors: The prevalence of correspondence bias in the general population. *Basic and Applied Social Psychology, 32,* 269–277.

Baumann, L. J., & Leventhal, H. (1985). "I can tell when my blood pressure is up, can't I?" *Health Psychology, 4,* 203–218.

Baumeister, R. (1996). Should schools try to boost self-esteem? Beware the dark side. *American Educator, 20,* 14–19, 43.

Baumeister, R. (2005). Rejected and alone. *The Psychologist, 18,* 732–735.

Baumeister, R. (2007). Is there anything good about men? Address to the American Psychological Association convention San Francisco, California.

Baumeister, R. F. (2010). *Is there anything good about men? How cultures flourish by exploiting men.* New York: Oxford University Press.

Baumeister, R. F., & Bratslavsky, E. (1999). Passion, intimacy, and time: Passionate love as a function of change in intimacy. *Personality and Social Psychology Review, 3,* 49–67.

Baumeister, R. F., Bratslavsky, E., Finkenauer, C., & Vohs, D. K. (2001). Bad is stronger than good. *Review of General Psychology, 5,* 323–370.

Baumeister, R. F., Bratslavsky, E., Muraven, M., & Tice, D. M. (1998). Ego depletion: Is the active self a limited resource? *Journal of Personality and Social Psychology, 74,* 1252–1265.

Baumeister, R. F., Campbell, J. D., Krueger, J. I., & Vohs, K. D. (2003). Does high self-esteem cause better performance, interpersonal success, happiness, or healthier lifestyles?

Psychological Science in the Public Interest, 4 (1), 1–44.

Baumeister, R. F., DeWall, C. N., Ciarocco, N. J., & Twenge, J. M. (2005). Social exclusion impairs self-regulation. *Journal of Personality and Social Psychology, 88,* 589–604.

Baumeister, R. F., & Exline, J. J. (2000). Self-control, morality, and human strength. *Journal of Social and Clinical Psychology, 19,* 29–42.

Baumeister, R. F., & Leary, M. R. (1995). The need to belong: Desire for interpersonal attachment as a fundamental human motivation. *Psychological Bulletin, 117,* 497–529.

Baumeister, R. F., & Scher, S. J. (1988). Self-defeating behavior patterns among normal individuals: Review and analysis of common self-destructive tendencies. *Psychological Bulletin, 104,* 3–22.

Baumeister, R. F., & Tierney, J. (2011). *Willpower: The rediscovery of humans' greatest strength.* New York: Penguin.

Baumeister, R. F., & Vohs, K. (2004). Sexual economics: Sex as female resource for social exchange in heterosexual interactions. *Personality and Social Psychology Bulletin, 8,* 339–363.

Baumeister, R. F., & Wotman, S. R. (1992). *Breaking hearts: The two sides of unrequited love.* New York: Guilford.

Baumgardner, A. H., & Brownlee, E. A. (1987). Strategic failure in social interaction: Evidence for expectancy disconfirmation process. *Journal of Personality and Social Psychology, 52,* 525–535.

Baumhart, R. (1968). *An honest profit.* New York: Holt, Rinehart & Winston.

Baxter, T. L., & Goldberg, L. R. (1987). Perceived behavioral consistency underlying trait attributions to oneself and another: An extension of the actor-observer effect. *Personality and Social Psychology Bulletin, 13,* 437–447.

Bayer, E. (1929). Beitrage zur zeikomponenten theorie des hungers. *Zeitschrift fur Psychologie, 112,* 1–54.

Bazerman, M. H. (1986, June). Why negotiations go wrong. *Psychology Today,* pp. 54–58.

Bazerman, M. H. (1990). *Judgment in managerial decision making,* 2nd edition. New York: John Wiley.

Bazzini, D., Curtin, L., Joslin, S., Regan, S., & Martz, D. (2010). Do animated Disney characters portray and promote the beauty-goodness stereotype? *Journal of Applied Social Psychology, 40,* 2687–2709.

BBC. (2008, November 21). Pirates "gained $150m this year" (news.bbc.co.uk).

Beach, S. R. H., Hurt, T. R., Fincham, F. D., Franklin, K. J., McNair, L. M., & Stanley, S. M. (2011). Enhancing marital enrichment through spirituality: Efficacy data for prayer focused relationship enhancement. *Psychology of Religion and Spirituality, 3,* 201–216.

Beals, K. P., Peplau, L. A., & Gable, S. L. (2009). Stigma management and well-being: The role of perceived social support, emotional processing, and suppression. *Personality and Social Psychology Bulletin, 35,* 867–879.

Beaman, A. L., Barnes, P. J., Klentz, B., & McQuirk, B. (1978). Increasing helping rates through information dissemination: Teaching pays. *Personality and Social Psychology Bulletin, 4,* 406–411.

Beaman, A. L., & Klentz, B. (1983). The supposed physical attractiveness bias against supporters of the women's movement: A meta-analysis. *Personality and Social Psychology Bulletin, 9,* 544–550.

Beaman, A. L., Klentz, B., Diener, E., & Svanum, S. (1979). Self-awareness and transgression in children: Two field studies. *Journal of Personality and Social Psychology, 37,* 1835–1846.

Beaman, L., Duflo, E., Pande, R., & Topalova, P. (2012). Female leadership raises aspirations and educational attainment for girls: A policy experiment in India. *Science, 335,* 582–586.

Bearak, B. (2010, July 9). South Africa braces for new attacks on immigrants. *New York Times* (www.nytimes.com).

Bearman, P. S., & Brückner, H. (2001). Promising the future: Virginity pledges and first intercourse. *American Journal of Sociology, 106,* 859–912.

Beaulieu, C. M. J. (2004). Intercultural study of personal space: A case study. *Journal of Applied Social Psychology, 34,* 794–805.

Beauvois, J. L., Courbet, D., & Oberle, D. (2012). The prescriptive power of the television host: A transposition of Milgram's obedience paradigm to the context of a TV game show. *European Review of Applied Psychology, 62,* 111–119.

Becatoros, E. (2012, November 13). On streets of Athens, racist attacks increase. Associated Press (news.yahoo.com).

Beck, A. T., & Young, J. E. (1978, September). College blues. *Psychology Today,* 80–92.

Beck, L. A., Pietrimonoco, P. R., DeBuse, C. J., Powers, S. I., Sayer, A. G. (2013). Spouses' attachment pairings predict neuroendocrine, behavioral, and psychological responses to marital conflict. *Journal of Personality and Social Psychology, 105,* 388–424.

Becker, D. V., Neel, R., Anderson, U. S. (2010). Illusory conjunctions of angry facial expressions follow intergroup biases. *Psychological Science, 21,* 938–940.

Becker, S. W., & Eagly, A. H. (2004). The heroism of women and men. *American Psychologist, 59,* 163–178.

Beelmann, A., & Heinemann, K. S. (2014). Preventing prejudice and improving intergroup attitudes: A meta-analysis of child and adolescent training programs.

Journal of Applied Developmental Psychology, 35, 10–24.

Begue, L., Bushman, B., Giancola, P., Subra, B., & Rosset, E. (2010). "There is no such thing as an accident," especially when people are drunk. *Personality and Social Psychology Bulletin, 36,* 1301–1304.

Bélanger-Gravel, A., Godin, G., & Amireault, S. (2013). A meta-analytic review of the effect of implementation intentions on physical activity. *Health Psychology Review, 7,* 23–54.

Bell, B. E., & Loftus, E. F. (1988). Degree of detail of eyewitness testimony and mock juror judgments. *Journal of Applied Social Psychology, 18,* 1171–1192.

Bell, B. E., & Loftus, E. F. (1989). Trivial persuasion in the courtroom: The power of (a few) minor details. *Journal of Personality and Social Psychology, 56,* 669–679.

Bell, P. A. (1980). Effects of heat, noise, and provocation on retaliatory evaluative behavior. *Journal of Social Psychology, 110,* 97–100.

Bell, P. A. (2005). Reanalysis and perspective in the heat-aggression debate. *Journal of Personality and Social Psychology, 89,* 71–73.

Bellah, R. N. (1995/1996, Winter). Community properly understood: A defense of "democratic communitarianism." *The Responsive Community,* pp. 49–54.

Bellezza, S., Gino, F., & Keinan, A. (2014). The red sneakers effect: Inferring status and competence from signals of nonconformity. *Journal of Consumer Research, 41,* 35–54.

Belluck, P. (2008, June 15). Gay couples find marriage is a mixed bag. *New York Times* (www.nytimes.com).

Belson, W. A. (1978). *Television violence and the adolescent boy.* Westmead, England: Saxon House, Teakfield Ltd.

Beltz, A. M., Swanson, J. L., & Berenbaum, S. A. (2011). Gendered occupational interests: Prenatal androgen effects on psychological orientation to Things versus People. *Hormones and Behavior, 60,* 313–317.

Bem, D. J. (1972). Self-perception theory. In L. Berkowitz (Ed.), *Advances in experimental social psychology* (Vol. 6). New York: Academic Press.

Bem, D. J., & McConnell, H. K. (1970). Testing the self-perception explanation of dissonance phenomena: On the salience of premanipulation attitudes. *Journal of Personality and Social Psychology, 14,* 23–31.

Benartzi, S., & Thaler, R. H. (2013). Behavioral economics and the retirement savings crisis. *Science, 339,* 1152–1153.

Benenson, J. F., Markovits, H., Fitzgerald, C., Geoffroy, D., Flemming, J., Kahlenberg, S. M., & Wrangham, R. W. (2009). Males' greater tolerance of same-sex peers. *Psychological Science, 20,* 184–190.

Benjamin, Jr., L. T., & Simpson, J. A. (2009). The power of the situation: The impact of Milgram's obedience studies on personality and social psychology. *American Psychologist, 64,* 12–19.

Bennett, D. (2010, January 31). *How "cognitive fluency" shapes what we believe, how we invest, and who will become a supermodel.* www.boston.com.

Bennett, R. (1991, February). Pornography and extrafamilial child sexual abuse: Examining the relationship. Unpublished manuscript, Los Angeles Police Department Sexually Exploited Child Unit.

Bennis, W. (1984). Transformative power and leadership. In T. J. Sergiovani & J. E. Corbally (Eds.), *Leadership and organizational culture.* Urbana: University of Illinois Press.

Benson, P. L., Dehority, J., Garman, L., Hanson, E., Hochschwender, M., Lebold, C., Rohr, R., & Sullivan, J. (1980). Intrapersonal correlates of nonspontaneous helping behavior. *Journal of Social Psychology, 110,* 87–95.

Benson, P. L., Karabenick, S. A., & Lerner, R. M. (1976). Pretty pleases: The effects of physical attractiveness, race, and sex on receiving help. *Journal of Experimental Social Psychology, 12,* 409–415.

Benton, S. L., Downey, R. G., Gilder, P. J., & Benton, S. A. (2008). College students' norm perception predicts reported use of protective behavioral strategies for alcohol consumption. *Journal of Studies on Alcohol and Drugs, 69,* 859–866.

Berg, J. H. (1984). Development of friendship between roommates. *Journal of Personality and Social Psychology, 46,* 346–356.

Berg, J. H. (1987). Responsiveness and self-disclosure. In V. J. Derlega & J. H. Berg (Eds.), *Self-disclosure: Theory, research, and therapy.* New York: Plenum.

Berg, J. H., & McQuinn, R. D. (1986). Attraction and exchange in continuing and noncontinuing dating relationships. *Journal of Personality and Social Psychology, 50,* 942–952.

Berg, J. H., & Peplau, L. A. (1982). Loneliness: The relationship of self-disclosure and androgyny. *Personality and Social Psychology Bulletin, 8,* 624–630.

Berger, J., Bradlow, E. T., Braumstein, A., & Zhang, Y. (2012). From Karen to Katie: Using baby names to understand cultural evolution. *Psychological Science, 23,* 1067–1073.

Berger, J., & Heath, C. (2008). Who drives divergence? Identity signaling, outgroup dissimilarity, and the abandonment of cultural tastes. *Journal of Personality and Social Psychology, 95,* 593–607.

Berger, J., & Le Mens, G. (2009). How adoption speed affects the abandonment of cultural tastes. *Proceedings of the National Academy of Sciences, 106,* 8146–8150.

Berger, J. M. (2014). Situational features in Milgram's experiment that kept his participants shocking. *Journal of Social Issues, 70,* 489–500.

Berglas, S., & Jones, E. E. (1978). Drug choice as a self-handicapping strategy in response to noncontingent success. *Journal of Personality and Social Psychology, 36,* 405–417.

Bergsieker, H. B., Leslie, L. M., Constantine, V. S., & Fiske, S. T. (2012). Stereotyping by omission: Eliminate the negative, accentuate the positive. *Journal of Personality and Social Psychology, 102,* 1214–1238.

Berkman, L. F. (1995). The role of social relations in health promotion. *Psychosomatic Medicine, 57,* 245–254.

Berkowitz, L. (1954). Group standards, cohesiveness, and productivity. *Human Relations, 7,* 509–519.

Berkowitz, L. (1968, September). Impulse, aggression and the gun. *Psychology Today,* 18–22.

Berkowitz, L. (1972). Social norms, feelings, and other factors affecting helping and altruism. In L. Berkowitz (Ed.), *Advances in experimental social psychology* (Vol. 6). New York: Academic Press.

Berkowitz, L. (1978). Whatever happened to the frustration-aggression hypothesis? *American Behavioral Scientists, 21,* 691–708.

Berkowitz, L. (1981, June). How guns control us. *Psychology Today,* 11–12.

Berkowitz, L. (1983). Aversively stimulated aggression: Some parallels and differences in research with animals and humans. *American Psychologist, 38,* 1135–1144.

Berkowitz, L. (1984). Some effects of thoughts on anti- and prosocial influences of media events: A cognitive-neoassociation analysis, *Psychological Bulletin, 95,* 410–427.

Berkowitz, L. (1987). Mood, self-awareness, and willingness to help. *Journal of Personality and Social Psychology, 52,* 721–729.

Berkowitz, L. (1989). Frustration-aggression hypothesis: Examination and reformulation. *Psychological Bulletin, 106,* 59–73.

Berkowitz, L. (1995). A career on aggression. In G. G. Brannigan & M. R. Merrens (Eds.), *The social psychologists: Research adventures.* New York: McGraw-Hill.

Berkowitz, L. (1998). Affective aggression: The role of stress, pain, and negative affect. In R. G. Geen & E. Donnerstein (Eds.), *Human aggression: Theories, research, and implications for social policy.* San Diego: Academic Press.

Berkowitz, L., & Geen, R. G. (1966). Film violence and the cue properties of available targets. *Journal of Personality and Social Psychology, 3,* 525–530.

Berkowitz, L., & LePage, A. (1967). Weapons as aggression-eliciting stimuli. *Journal of Personality and Social Psychology, 7,* 202–207.

Berndsen, M., Spears, R., van der Plight, J., & McGarty, C. (2002). Illusory correlation and stereotype formation: Making sense of group differences and cognitive biases. In C. McGarty, V. Y. Yzerbyt, & R. Spears (Eds.), *Stereotypes as explanations: The formation of meaningful beliefs about social groups.* New York: Cambridge University Press.

Bernhardt, P. C., Dabbs, J. M., Jr., Fielden, J. A., & Lutter, C. D. (1998). Testosterone changes during vicarious experiences of winning and losing among fans at sporting events. *Physiology and Behavior, 65,* 59–62.

Berns, G. S., Chappelow, J., Zink, C. F., Pagnoni, G., Martin-Skurski, M. E., & Richards, J. (2005). Neurobiological correlates of social conformity and independence during mental rotation. *Biological Psychiatry, 58,* 245–253.

Bernstein, M. J., Young, S. G., & Claypool, H. M. (2010). Is Obama's win a gain for Blacks? Changes in implicit racial prejudice following the 2008 election. *Social Psychology, 41,* 147–151.

Berry, D. S., & Zebrowitz-McArthur, L. (1988). What's in a face: Facial maturity and the attribution of legal responsibility. *Personality and Social Psychology Bulletin, 14,* 23–33.

Berscheid, E. (1981). An overview of the psychological effects of physical attractiveness and some comments upon the psychological effects of knowledge of the effects of physical attractiveness. In W. Lucker, K. Ribbens, & J. A. McNamera (Eds.), *Logical aspects of facial form (craniofacial growth series).* Ann Arbor: University of Michigan Press.

Berscheid, E. (2010). Love in the fourth dimension. *Annual Review of Psychology, 61,* 1–25.

Berscheid, E., Boye, D., & Walster (Hatfield), E. (1968). Retaliation as a means of restoring equity. *Journal of Personality and Social Psychology, 10,* 370–376.

Berscheid, E., Dion, K., Walster (Hatfield), E., & Walster, G. W. (1971). Physical attractiveness and dating choice: A test of the matching hypothesis. *Journal of Experimental Social Psychology, 7,* 173–189.

Berscheid, E., Graziano, W., Monson, T., & Dermer, M. (1976). Outcome dependency: Attention, attribution, and attraction. *Journal of Personality and Social Psychology, 34,* 978–989.

Berscheid, E., Walster, G. W., & Hatfield (was Walster), E. (1969). *Effects of accuracy and positivity of evaluation on liking for the evaluator.* Unpublished manuscript. Summarized by E. Berscheid and E. Walster (Hatfield) (1978), *Interpersonal attraction.* Reading, MA: Addison-Wesley.

Berscheid, E., & Walster (Hatfield), E. (1978). *Interpersonal attraction.* Reading, MA: Addison-Wesley.

Bersoff, D. N. (1987). Social science data and the Supreme Court: Lockhart as a case in point. *American Psychologist, 42,* 52–58.

Bertolotti, M., & Catellani, P. (2014). Effects of message framing in policy communication on climate change. *European Journal of Social Psychology, 44,* 474–486.

Bertrand, M., & Mullainathan, S. (2003). Are Emily and Greg more employable than Lakisha and Jamal? A field experiment on labor market discrimination. Massachusetts Institute of Technology, Department of Economics, Working Paper 03-22.

Besser, A., & Priel, B. (2005). The apple does not fall far from the tree: Attachment styles and personality vulnerabilities to depression in three generations of women. *Personality and Social Psychology Bulletin, 31,* 1052–1073.

Bettencourt, B. A., Dill, K. E., Greathouse, S. A., Charlton, K., & Mulholland, A. (1997). Evaluations of ingroup and outgroup members: The role of category-based expectancy violation. *Journal of Experimental Social Psychology, 33,* 244–275.

Bettencourt, B. A., & Kernahan, C. (1997). A meta-analysis of aggression in the presence of violent cues: Effects of gender differences and aversive provocation. *Aggressive Behavior, 23,* 447–456.

Bettencourt, B. A., Talley, A., Benjamin, A. J., & Valentine, J. (2006). Personality and aggressive behavior under provoking and neutral conditions: A meta-analytic review. *Psychological Bulletin, 132,* 751–777.

Bianchi, S. M., Milkie, M. A., Sayer, L. C., & Robinson, J. P. (2000). Is anyone doing the housework? Trends in the gender division of household labor. *Social Forces, 79,* 191–228.

Bickman, L. (1975). Bystander intervention in a crime: The effect of a mass-media campaign. *Journal of Applied Social Psychology, 5,* 296–302.

Bickman, L. (1979). Interpersonal influence and the reporting of a crime. *Personality and Social Psychology Bulletin, 5,* 32–35.

Bickman, L., & Green, S. K. (1977). Situational cues and crime reporting: Do signs make a difference? *Journal of Applied Social Psychology, 7,* 1–18.

Biernat, M. (1991). Gender stereotypes and the relationship between masculinity and femininity: A developmental analysis. *Journal of Personality and Social Psychology, 61,* 351–365.

Biernat, M., & Kobrynowicz, D. (1997). Gender- and race-based standards of competence: Lower minimum standards but higher ability standards for devalued groups. *Journal of Personality and Social Psychology, 72,* 544–557.

Bigam, R. G. (1977, March). Voir dire: The attorney's job. *Trial 13,* p. 3. Cited by G. Bermant & J. Shepard in "The voir dire examination, juror challenges, and adversary advocacy." In B. D. Sales (Ed.), *Perspectives in law and psychology, Vol. II: The trial process.* New York: Plenum, 1981.

Bilderbeck, A. C., Brown, G. D. A., Read, J., Woolrich, M., Cowen, P. J., Behrens, T. E. J., & Rogers, R. D. (2014). Serotonin and social norms: Tryptophan depletion impairs social comparison and leads to resource depletion in a multiplayer harvesting game. *Psychological Science, 25,* 1303–1313.

Bilewicz, M., & Kogan, A. (2014). Embodying imagined contact: Facial feedback moderates the intergroup consequences of mental simulation. *British Journal of Social Psychology, 53,* 387–395.

Billig, M., & Tajfel, H. (1973). Social categorization and similarity in intergroup behaviour. *European Journal of Social Psychology, 3,* 27–52.

Binder, J., Zagefka, H., Brown, R., Funke, F., Kessler, T., Mummendey, A., Maquil, A., Demoulin, S., & Leyens, J-P. (2009). Does contact reduce prejudice or does prejudice reduce contact? A longitudinal test of the contact hypothesis among majority and minority groups in three European countries. *Journal of Personality and Social Psychology, 96,* 843–856.

Biner, P. M. (1991). Effects of lighting-induced arousal on the magnitude of goal valence. *Personality and Social Psychology Bulletin, 17,* 219–226.

Bingenheimer, J. B., Brennan, R. T., & Earls, F. J. (2005). Firearm violence exposure and serious violent behavior. *Science, 308,* 1323–1326.

Binham, R. (1980, March–April). Trivers in Jamaica. *Science, 80,* 57–67.

BIS: Department for Business, Innovation, & Skills, UK. (2014). Women on boards: 6-month monitoring report October 2014. Retrieved March 27, 2015 from https://www.gov.uk/government/uploads/system/uploads/attachment_data/file/363077/bis-14-1121-women-on-boards-6-months-monitoring-report-october-2014.pdf

Bishop, B. (2008). *The big sort: Why the clustering of like-minded America is tearing us apart.* Boston: Houghton-Mifflin.

Bishop, G. D. (1984). Gender, role, and illness behavior in a military population. *Health Psychology, 3,* 519–534.

Bishop, G. D. (1987). Lay conceptions of physical symptoms. *Journal of Applied Social Psychology, 17,* 127–146.

Bishop, G. D. (1991). Understanding the understanding of illness: Lay disease representations. In J. A. Skelton & R. T. Croyle (Eds.), *Mental representation in health and illness.* New York: Springer-Verlag.

Björkqvist, K. (1994). Sex differences in physical, verbal, and indirect aggression: A review of recent research. *Sex Roles, 30,* 177–188.

Black, M. C., Basile, K. C., Breiding, M. J., Smith, S. G., Walters, M. L., Merrick, M. T., Chen, J., & Stevens, M. R. (2011). *The National Intimate Partner and Sexual Violence Survey (NISVS): 2010 Summary Report.* Atlanta, GA: National Center for Injury Prevention and Control, Centers for Disease Control.

Blair, C. A., Thompson, L. F., & Wuensch, K. L. (2005). Electronic helping behavior: The virtual presence of others makes a difference. *Basic and Applied Social Psychology, 27,* 171–178.

Blair, I. V., Judd, C. M., & Chapleau, K. M. (2004). The influence of Afrocentric facial features in criminal sentencing. *Psychological Science, 15,* 674–679.

Blaker, N. M., Rompa, I., Dessing, I. H., Vriend, A. F., Herschberg, C., & van Vugt, M. (2013). The height leadership advantage in men and women: Testing evolutionary psychology predictions about the perceptions of tall leaders. *Group Processes & Intergroup Relations, 16,* 17–27.

Blake, R. R., & Mouton, J. S. (1962). The intergroup dynamics of win-lose conflict and problem-solving collaboration in union-management relations. In M. Sherif (Ed.), *Intergroup relations and leadership.* New York: Wiley.

Blake, R. R., & Mouton, J. S. (1979). Intergroup problem solving in organizations: From theory to practice. In W. G. Austin and S. Worchel (Eds.), *The social psychology of intergroup relations.* Monterey, CA: Brooks/Cole.

Blanchard, F. A., & Cook, S. W. (1976). Effects of helping a less competent member of a cooperating interracial group on the development of interpersonal attraction. *Journal of Personality and Social Psychology, 34,* 1245–1255.

Blank, H., & Launay, C. (2014). How to protect eyewitness memory against the misinformation effect: A meta-analysis of post-warning studies. *Journal of Applied Research in Memory and Cognition, 3,* 77–88.

Blank, H., Nestler, S., von Collani, G., & Fischer, V. (2008). How many hindsight biases are there? *Cognition, 106,* 1408–1440.

Blanton, D. (2011, April 7). *Fox News poll: 24 percent believe Obama not born in U.S.* FoxNews.com.

Blanton, H., Jaccard, J., Christie, C., & Gonzales, P. M. (2007). Plausible assumptions, questionable assumptions and post hoc rationalizations: Will the real IAT please stand up? *Journal of Experimental Social Psychology, 43,* 399–409.

Blanton, H., Jaccard, J., Gonzales, P. M., & Christie, C. (2006). Decoding the implicit association test: Implications for criterion prediction. *Journal of Experimental Social Psychology, 42,* 192–212.

Blanton, H., Jaccard, J., Klick, J., Mellers, B., Mitchell, G., & Tetlock P. E. (2009). Strong claims and weak evidence: reassessing the predictive validity of the IAT. *Journal of Applied Psychology, 94,* 583–603.

Blanton, H., Pelham, B. W., DeHart, T., & Carvallo, M. (2001). Overconfidence as dissonance reduction. *Journal of Experimental Social Psychology, 37,* 373–385.

Blascovich, J., & Bailenson, J. (2011). *Infinite reality: Avatars, eternal life, new worlds, and the dawn of the virtual revolution.* New York: Morrow.

Blass, T. (1996). Stanley Milgram: A life of inventiveness and controversy. In G. A. Kimble, C. A. Boneau, & M. Wertheimer (Eds.). *Portraits of pioneers in psychology* (Vol. II). Washington, DC: American Psychological Association.

Blass, T. (1999). The Milgram paradigm after 35 years: Some things we now know about obedience to authority. *Journal of Applied Social Psychology, 29,* 955–978.

Blass, T. (2000). The Milgram paradigm after 35 years: Some things we now know about obedience to authority. In T. Blass (Ed.), *Obedience to authority: Current perspectives on the Milgram paradigm.* Mahwah, NJ: Erlbaum.

Bleske-Rechek, A., Remiker, M. W., & Baker, J. P. (2009). Similar from the start: Assortment in young adult dating couples and its link to relationship stability over time. *Individual Differences Research, 7,* 142–158.

Block, J., & Funder, D. C. (1986). Social roles and social perception: Individual differences in attribution and error. *Journal of Personality and Social Psychology, 51,* 1200–1207.

Bloom, P. (2010, May 6). The moral life of babies. *The New York Times Magazine* (www.nytimes.com).

Bodenhausen, G. V. (1990). Stereotypes as judgmental heuristics: Evidence of circadian variations in discrimination. *Psychological Science, 1,* 319–322.

Bodenhausen, G. V. (1993). Emotions, arousal, and stereotypic judgments: A heuristic model of affect and stereotyping. In D. M. Mackie & D. L. Hamilton (Eds.), *Affect, cognition, and stereotyping: Interactive processes in group perception.* San Diego: Academic Press.

Bodenhausen, G. V., & Macrae, C. N. (1998). Stereotype activation and inhibition. In R. S. Wyer, Jr., *Stereotype activation and inhibition: Advances in social cognition* (Vol. 11). Mahwah, NJ: Erlbaum.

Bodenhausen, G. V., Sheppard, L. A., & Kramer, G. F. (1994). Negative affect and social judgment: The differential impact of anger and sadness. *European Journal of Social Psychology, 24,* 45–62.

Boden, J. M., Fergusson, D. M., & Horwood, L. J. (2008). Does adolescent self-esteem predict later life outcomes? A test of the causal role of self-esteem. *Development and Psychopathology, 20,* 319–339.

Boehm, J. K., Peterson, C., Kivimaki, M., & Kubzansky, L. (2011). A prospective study of positive psychological well-being and coronary heart disease. *Health Psychology, 30,* 259–267.

Boer, D., Fischer, R., Strack, M., Bond, M. H., Lo, E., & Lam, J. (2011). How shared preferences in music create bonds between people: Values as the missing link. *Personality and Social Psychology Bulletin, 37,* 1159–1171.

Boggiano, A. K., & Ruble, D. N. (1985). Children's responses to evaluative feedback. In R. Schwarzer (Ed.), *Self-related cognitions in anxiety and motivation.* Hillsdale, NJ: Erlbaum.

Bond, C. F., Jr., DiCandia, C. G., & MacKinnon, J. R. (1988). Responses to violence in a psychiatric setting: The role of patient's race. *Personality and Social Psychology Bulletin, 14,* 448–458.

Bond, C. F., Jr., & Titus, L. J. (1983). Social facilitation: A meta-analysis of 241 studies. *Psychological Bulletin, 94,* 265–292.

Bond, M. H. (2004). Culture and aggression: From context to coercion. *Personality and Social Psychology Review, 8,* 62–78.

Bond, R. M., Fariss, C. J., Jones, J. J., Kramer, A. I., Marlow, C., Settle, J. E., & Fowler, J. H. (2012). A 61-million-person experiment in social influence and political mobilization. *Nature, 489,* 295–298.

Bond, R., & Smith, P. B. (1996). Culture and conformity: A meta-analysis of studies using Asch's (1952b, 1956) line judgment task. *Psychological Bulletin, 119,* 111–137.

Bonner, B. L., & Baumann, M. R. (2012). Leveraging member expertise to improve knowledge transfer and demonstrability in groups. *Journal of Personality and Social Psychology, 102,* 337–350.

Bonnot, V., & Croizet, J-C. (2007). Stereotype internalization and women's math performance: The role of interference in working memory. *Journal of Experimental Social Psychology, 43,* 857–866.

Bono, J. E., & Judge, T. A. (2004). Personality and transformational and transactional leadership: A meta-analysis. *Journal of Applied Psychology, 89,* 901–910.

Bonta, B. D. (1997). Cooperation and competition in peaceful societies. *Psychological Bulletin, 121,* 299–320.

Boomsma, D. I., Cacioppo, J. T., Slagboom, P. E., & Posthuma, D. (2006). Genetic linkage and association analysis for loneliness in Dutch twin and sibling pairs points to a region on chromosome 12q23-24. *Behavior Genetics, 36,* 137–146.

Borenstein, S. (2014, December 2). Hotter, weirder: How climate has changed Earth. Associated Press.

Borgida, E. (1981). Legal reform of rape laws. In L. Bickman (Ed.), *Applied social psychology annual* (Vol. 2, pp. 211–241). Beverly Hills, CA: Sage.

Borgida, E., & Brekke, N. (1985). Psycholegal research on rape trials. In A. W. Burgess (Ed.), *Rape and sexual assault: A research handbook.* New York: Garland.

Borgida, E., Locksley, A., & Brekke, N. (1981). Social stereotypes and social judgment. In N. Cantor & J. Kihlstrom (Eds.), *Cognition, social interaction, and personality.* Hillsdale, NJ: Erlbaum.

Borgida, E., & White, P. (1980). *Judgmental bias and legal reform.* Unpublished manuscript, University of Minnesota.

Bornstein, B. H., & Zickafoose, D. J. (1999). "I know I know it, I know I saw it": The stability of the confidence-accuracy relationship across domains. *Journal of Experimental Psychology: Applied, 5,* 76–88.

Bornstein, G., & Rapoport, A. (1988). Intergroup competition for the provision of step-level public goods: Effects of preplay communication. *European Journal of Social Psychology, 18,* 125–142.

Bornstein, G., Rapoport, A., Kerpel, L., & Katz, T. (1989). Within- and between-group communication in intergroup competition for public goods. *Journal of Experimental Social Psychology, 25,* 422–436.

Bornstein, R. F. (1989). Exposure and affect: Overview and meta-analysis of research, 1968–1987. *Psychological Bulletin, 106,* 265–289.

Bornstein, R. F. (1999). Source amnesia, misattribution, and the power of unconscious perceptions and memories. *Psychoanalytic Psychology, 16,* 155–178.

Bornstein, R. F., & D'Agostino, P. R. (1992). Stimulus recognition and the mere exposure effect. *Journal of Personality and Social Psychology, 63,* 545–552.

Bos, P. A., Terburg, D., & van Honk, J. (2010). Testosterone decreases trust in socially naïve humans. *Proceedings of the National Academy of Sciences, 107,* 11149–11150.

Bossard, J. H. S. (1932). Residential propinquity as a factor in marriage selection. *American Journal of Sociology, 38,* 219–224.

Bosson, J. K., & Michniewicz, K. S. (2013). Gender dichotimization at the level of ingroup identify: What it is, and why men use it more than women. *Journal of Personality and Social Psychology, 105,* 425–442.

Bothwell, R. K., Brigham, J. C., & Malpass, R. S. (1989). Cross-racial identification. *Personality and Social Psychology Bulletin, 15,* 19–25.

Botvin, G. J., Epstein, J. A., & Griffin, K. W. (2008). A social influence model of alcohol use for inner-city adolescents: Family drinking, perceived drinking norms, and perceived social benefits of drinking. *Journal of Studies on Alcohol and Drugs, 69,* 397–405.

Botvin, G. J., Schinke, S., & Orlandi, M. A. (1995). School-based health promotion: Substance abuse and sexual behavior. *Applied & Preventive Psychology, 4,* 167–184.

Botwin, M. D., Buss, D. M., & Shackelford, T. K. (1997). Personality and mate preferences: Five factors in mate selection and marital satisfaction. *Journal of Personality, 65,* 107–136.

Bouas, K. S., & Komorita, S. S. (1996). Group discussion and cooperation in social dilemmas. *Personality and Social Psychology Bulletin, 22,* 1144–1150.

Bouman, T., Zomeren, M., & Otten, S. (2014). Threat by association: Do distant intergroup threats carry-over into local intolerance? *British Journal of Social Psychology, 53,* 405–421.

Bourgeois, M. J., Horowitz, I. A., & Lee, L. F. (1993). Effects of technicality and access to trial transcripts on verdicts and information processing in a civil trial. *Personality and Social Psychology Bulletin, 19,* 219–226.

Bourke, M. L., & Hernandez, A. E. (2009). The 'Butner study' redux: A report of the incidence of hands-on child victimization by child pornography offenders. *Journal of Family Violence, 24,* 183–191.

Bowen, E. (1988, April 4). Whatever became of Honest Abe? *Time.*

Bowen, N. K., Wegmann, K. M., & Webber, K. C. (2013). Enhancing a brief writing intervention to combat stereotype threat among middle-school students. *Journal of Educational Psychology, 105,* 427–435.

Bower, G. H. (1987). Commentary on mood and memory. *Behavioral Research and Therapy, 25,* 443–455.

Bowlby, J. (1980). *Loss, sadness and depression, Vol. III of Attachment and loss.* London: Basic Books.

Boyatzis, C. J., Matillo, G. M., & Nesbitt, K. M. (1995). Effects of the "Mighty Morphin Power Rangers" on children's aggression with peers. *Child Study Journal, 25,* 45–55.

Boyce, C. J., Wood, A. M., Banks, J., Clark, A. E., & Brown, G. D. A. (2013). Money, well-being, and loss aversion: Does an income loss have a greater effect on well-being than an equivalent income gain? *Psychological Science, 24,* 2557–2562.

Boyes, A. D., & Fletcher, G. J. O. (2007). Metaperceptions of bias in intimate relationships. *Journal of Personality and Social Psychology, 92,* 286–306.

Bradley, W., & Mannell, R. C. (1984). Sensitivity of intrinsic motivation to reward procedure instructions. *Personality and Social Psychology Bulletin, 10,* 426–431.

Branas, C. C., Richmond, T. S., Culhane, D. P., Have, T. R. T., & Wiebe, D. J. (2009). Investigating the link between gun possession and gun assault. *American Journal of Public Health, 99,* 2034–2040.

Brandon, R., & Davies, C. (1973). *Wrongful imprisonment: Mistaken convictions and their consequences.* Hamden, CT: Archon Books.

Brand, R. J., Bonatsos, A., D'Orazio, R., & DeShong, H. (2012). What is beautiful is good, even online: Correlations between photo attractiveness and text attractiveness in men's online dating profiles. *Computers in Human Behavior. 28,* 166–170.

Brandt, M. J. (2011). Sexism and gender inequality across 57 societies. *Psychological Science, 22,* 1413–1418.

Brandt, M. J., IJzerman, H., Dijksterhuis, A., Farach, F. J., Geller, J., Giner-Sorolla, R., Grange, J. A., Perugini, M., Spies, J. R., & van't Veer, A. (2014). The replication recipe: What makes for a convincing replication? *Journal of Experimental Social Psychology, 50,* 217–224.

Branscombe, N. R., Schmitt, M. T., & Harvey, R. D. (1999). Perceiving pervasive discrimination among African Americans: Implications for group identification and well-being. *Journal of Personality and Social Psychology, 77,* 135–149.

Brauer, M., Judd, C. M., & Gliner, M. D. (1995). The effects of repeated expressions on attitude polarization during group discussions. *Journal of Personality and Social Psychology, 68,* 1014–1029.

Brauer, M., Judd, C. M., & Jacquelin, V. (2001). The communication of social stereotypes: The effects of group discussion and information distribution on stereotypic appraisals. *Journal of Personality and Social Psychology, 81,* 463–475.

Braverman, J. (2005). The effect of mood on detection of covariation. *Personality and Social Psychology Bulletin, 31,* 1487–1497.

Bray, R. M., & Noble, A. M. (1978). Authoritarianism and decisions of mock juries: Evidence of jury bias and group polarization. *Journal of Personality and Social Psychology, 36,* 1424–1430.

Breckler, S. J. (2010, April). In the heat of the moment. *Monitor on Psychology, 39.*

Bregman, N. J., & McAllister, H. A. (1982). Eyewitness testimony: The role of commitment in increasing reliability. *Social Psychology Quarterly, 45,* 181–184.

Brehm, J. W. (1956). Post-decision changes in desirability of alternatives. *Journal of Abnormal Social Psychology, 52,* 384–389.

Brehm, S., & Brehm, J. W. (1981). *Psychological reactance: A theory of freedom and control.* New York: Academic Press.

Brehm, S. S., & Smith, T. W. (1986). Social psychological approaches to psychotherapy and behavior change. In S. L. Garfield & A. E. Bergin (Eds.), *Handbook of psychotherapy and behavior change,* 3rd edition. New York: Wiley.

Brenner, S. N., & Molander, E. A. (1977, January–February). Is the ethics of business changing? *Harvard Business Review,* pp. 57–71.

Brescoll, V. L., Uhlmann, E. L., & Newman, G. E. (2013). The effects of system-justifying motives on endorsement of essentialist explanations for gender differences. *Journal of Personality and Social Psychology, 105,* 891–908.

Brethel-Haurwitz, K., & Marsh, A. A. (2014). Geographical differences in subjective well-being predict extraordinary altruism. *Psychological Science, 25,* 762–771.

Breuer, J., Scharkow, M., & Quandt, T. (2014). Sore losers? A reexamination of the frustration-aggression hypothesis for collocated video game play. Psychology of Popular Media Culture.

Brewer, M. B., & Gaertner, S. L. (2004). Toward reduction of prejudice: Intergroup contact and social categorization. In M. B. Brewer & M. Hewstone (Eds.), *Self and social identity.* Malden, MA: Blackwell.

Brewer, M. B., & Miller, N. (1988). Contact and cooperation: When do they work? In P. A. Katz & D. Taylor (Eds.), *Towards the elimination of racism: Profiles in controversy.* New York: Plenum.

Brewer, M. B., & Pierce, K. P. (2005). Social identity complexity and outgroup tolerance. *Personality and Social Psychology Bulletin, 31,* 428–437.

Brewer, M. B., & Silver, M. (1978). In-group bias as a function of task characteristics. *European Journal of Social Psychology, 8,* 393–400.

Brewer, N., & Wells, G. L. (2011). Eyewitness identification. *Current Directions in Psychological Science, 20,* 24–27.

Brigham, J. C., Bennett, L. B., Meissner, C. A., & Mitchell, T. L. (2006). The influence of race on eyewitness testimony. In R. Lindsay, M. Toglia, D. Ross, & J. D. Read (Eds.), *Handbook of eyewitness psychology.* Mahwah, NJ: Erlbaum.

Briñol, P., Petty, R. E., & Tormala, Z. L. (2004). Self-validation of cognitive responses to advertisements. *Journal of Consumer Research, 30,* 559–573.

Briñol, P., Petty, R. E., & Wagner, B. (2009). Body posture effects on self-evaluation: A self-validation approach. *European Journal of Social Psychology, 39,* 1053–1064.

Briñol, P., Tormala, Z. L., & Petty, R. E. (2002). *Source credibility as a determinant of self-validation effects in persuasion.* Poster presented at the European Association of Experimental Social Psychology, San Sebastian, Spain.

British Psychological Society. (2000). *Code of conduct, ethical principles and guidelines.* Leicester, UK: British Psychological Society (www.bps.org.uk/documents/Code.pdf).

Britt, T. W., & Garrity, M. J. (2006). Attributions and personality as predictors of the road rage response. *British Journal of Social Psychology, 45,* 127–147.

Brockner, J., Rubin, J. Z., Fine, J., Hamilton, T. P., Thomas, B., & Turetsky, B. (1982). Factors affecting entrapment in escalating conflicts: The importance of timing. *Journal of Research in Personality, 16,* 247–266.

Brock, S. E., Nickerson, A., & Serwacki, M. (2013). Youth gun violence fact sheet. National Association of School Psychologists (http://www.nasponline.org/resources/crisis_safety/Youth_Gun_Violence_Fact_Sheet.pdf).

Brodt, S. E., & Zimbardo, P. G. (1981). Modifying shyness-related social behavior through symptom misattribution. *Journal of Personality and Social Psychology, 41,* 437–449.

Bromet, E., & 21 others. (2011). Cross-national epidemiology of DSM-IV major depressive episode. *BMC Medicine, 9,* 90.

Bronfenbrenner, U. (1961). The mirror image in Soviet-American relations. *Journal of Social Issues, 17(3),* 45–56.

Brooks, D. (2005, August 10). All cultures are not equal. *New York Times* (www.nytimes.com).

Brooks, D. (2011, September 29). The limits of empathy. *New York Times* (www.nytimes.com).

Brooks, R. (2012). "Asia's missing women" as a problem in applied evolutionary psychology? *Evolutionary Psychology, 12,* 910–925.

Broome, A., & Wegner, D. M. (1994). Some positive effects of releasing socially anxious people from the need to please. Paper presented to the American Psychological Society convention.

Brown, D. E. (1991). *Human universals.* New York: McGraw-Hill.

Brown, D. E. (2000). Human universals and their implications. In N. Roughley (Ed.), *Being humans: Anthropological universality and particularity in transdisciplinary perspectives.* New York: Walter de Gruyter.

Brown, G. (2008). *Wartime courage: Stories of extraordinary bravery in World War II.* London: Bloomsbury.

Brown, H. J., Jr. (1990). *P.S. I love you.* Nashville: Rutledge Hill.

Brown, J. D., & Dutton, K. A. (1994). From the top down: Self-esteem and self-evaluation. Unpublished manuscript, University of Washington.

Brown, J. D., Novick, N. J., Lord, K. A., & Richards, J. M. (1992). When Gulliver travels: Social context, psychological closeness, and self-appraisals. *Journal of Personality and Social Psychology, 62,* 717–727.

Brown, J. D., & Taylor, S. E. (1986). Affect and the processing of personal information: Evidence for mood-activated self-schemata. *Journal of Experimental Social Psychology, 22,* 436–452.

Brown, R. (1965). *Social psychology.* New York: Free Press.

Brown, R. (1987). Theory of politeness: An exemplary case. Paper presented to the Society of Experimental Social Psychology meeting. Cited by R. O. Kroker & L. A. Wood (1992), Are the rules of address universal? IV: Comparison of Chinese, Korean, Greek, and German usage. *Journal of Cross-Cultural Psychology, 23,* 148–162.

Brown, R., Eller, A., Leeds, S., & Stace, K. (2007). Intergroup contact and intergroup attitudes: A longitudinal study. *European Journal of Social Psychology, 37,* 692–703.

Brown, R., Maras, P., Masser, B., Vivian, J., & Hewstone, M. (2001). Life on the ocean wave: Testing some intergroup hypotheses in a naturalistic setting. *Group Processes and Intergroup Relations, 4,* 81–97.

Brown, R. P., Charnsangavej, T., Keough, K. A., Newman, M. L., & Rentfrom, P. J. (2000). Putting the "affirm" into affirmative action: Preferential selection and academic performance. *Journal of Personality and Social Psychology, 79,* 736–747.

Brown, R. P., Osterman, L. L., & Barnes, C. D. (2009). School violence and the culture of honor. *Psychological Science, 20,* 1400–1405.

Brown, R., Vivian, J., & Hewstone, M. (1999). Changing attitudes through intergroup contact: The effects of group membership salience. *European Journal of Social Psychology, 29,* 741–764.

Brown, R., & Wootton-Millward, L. (1993). Perceptions of group homogeneity during group formation and change. *Social Cognition, 11,* 126–149.

Brown, S. L., Brown, R. M., House, J. S., & Smith, D. M. (2008). Coping with spousal loss: Potential buffering effects of self-reported helping behavior. *Personality and Social Psychology Bulletin, 34,* 849–861.

Brown, S. L., Nesse, R. M., Vinokur, A. D., & Smith, D. M. (2003). Providing social support may be more beneficial than receiving it. *Psychological Science, 14,* 320–327.

Brown, S. L., Smith, D. M., Schulz, R., Kabeto, M. U., Ubel, P. A., Poulin, M., Yi, J., Kim, C., & Langa, K. M. (2009). Caregiving behavior is associated with decreased mortality risk. *Psychological Science, 20,* 488–494.

Brown, V. R., & Paulus, P. B. (2002). Making group brainstorming more effective: Recommendations from an associative memory perspective. *Current Directions in Psychological Science, 11,* 208–212.

Brown, W. M., Price, M. E., Kang, J., Pound, N., Zhao, Y., & Yu, H. (2008). Fluctuating asymmetry and preferences for sex-typical bodily characteristics. *Proceedings of the National Academy of Sciences USA, 105,* 12938–12943.

Browning, C. R. (1992). *Ordinary men: Reserve Police Battalion 101 and the final solution in Poland.* New York: HarperCollins.

Bruce, V. (1998, July). Identifying people caught on video. *The Psychologist,* pp. 331–335.

Bruck, M., & Ceci, S. J. (1999). The suggestibility of children's memory. *Annual Review of Psychology, 50,* 419–439.

Bruck, M., & Ceci, S. J. (2004). Forensic developmental psychology: Unveiling four common misconceptions. *Current Directions in Psychological Science, 15,* 229–232.

Brückner, H., & Bearman, P. (2005). After the promise: The STD consequences of adolescent virginity pledges. *Journal of Adolescent Health, 36,* 271–278.

Bryan, C. J., Master, A., & Walton, G. M. (2014). "Helping" versus "being a helper": Invoking the self to increase helping in young children. *Child Development, 85,* 1836–1842.

Bryan, J. H., & Test, M. A. (1967). Models and helping: Naturalistic studies in aiding behavior. *Journal of Personality and Social Psychology, 6,* 400–407.

Buck, D. M., Plant, E. A., Ratcliff, J., Zielaskowski, K., & Boerner, P. (2013). Concern over the misidentification of sexual orientation: Social contagion and the avoidance of sexual minorities. *Journal of Personality and Social Psychology, 105,* 941–960.

Buckhout, R. (1974, December). Eyewitness testimony. *Scientific American,* pp. 23–31.

Buehler, R., Griffin, D., & Ross, M. (2002). Inside the planning fallacy: The causes and consequences of optimistic time predictions. In T. Gilovich, D. Griffin, & D. Kahneman (Eds.), *Heuristics and biases: The psychology of intuitive judgment.* Cambridge: Cambridge University Press.

Buffardi, L. E., & Campbell, W. K. (2008). Narcissism and social networking websites. *Personality and Social Psychology Bulletin, 34,* 1303–1314.

Bugental, D. B., & Hehman, J. A. (2007). Ageism: A review of research and policy implications. *Social Issues and Policy Review, 1,* 173–216.

Bui, N. H. (2012). False consensus in attitudes toward celebrities. *Psychology of Popular Media Culture, 1,* 236–243.

Bullock, J. (2006, March 17). *The enduring importance of false political beliefs.* Paper presented at the annual meeting of the Western Political Science Association, Albuquerque (www.allacademic.com/meta/p97459_index.html).

Burchill, S. A. L., & Stiles, W. B. (1988). Interactions of depressed college students with their roommates: Not necessarily negative. *Journal of Personality and Social Psychology, 55,* 410–419.

Bureau of Labor Statistics. (2014). American time use survey summary. June 18, 2014 (http://www.bls.gov/news.release/atus.nr0.htm).

Bureau of the Census. (2012). *The 2012 Statistical Abstract.* Washington, DC: Government Printing Office.

Bureau of the Census. (2013, September). Extended measures of well-being: Living conditions in the United States: 2011. www.census.gov/prod/2013pubs/p70-136.pdf.

Burger, J. M. (1987). Increased performance with increased personal control: A self-presentation interpretation. *Journal of Experimental Social Psychology, 23,* 350–360.

Burger, J. M. (2009, January). Replicating Milgram: Would people still obey today? *American Psychologist, 64,* 1–11.

Burger, J. M., Bender, T. J., Day, L., DeBolt, J. A., Guthridge, L., How, H. W., Meyer, M., Russell, K. A., & Taylor, S. (2014). The power of one: The relative influence of helpful and selfish models. *Social Influence,* in press.

Burger, J. M., & Burns, L. (1988). The illusion of unique invulnerability and the use of effective contraception. *Personality and Social Psychology Bulletin, 14,* 264–270.

Burger, J. M., & Cornelius, T. (2003). Raising the price of agreement: Public commitment and the lowball compliance procedure. *Journal of Applied Social Psychology, 33,* 923–934.

Burger, J. M., Girgis, Z. M., & Manning, C. C. (2011). In their own words: Explaining obedience to authority through an examination of participants' comments. *Social Psychological and Personality Science, 2,* 460–466.

Burger, J. M., & Guadagno, R. E. (2003). Self-concept clarity and the foot-in-the-door procedure. *Basic and Applied Social Psychology, 25,* 79–86.

Burger, J. M., Messian, N., Patel, S., del Prade, A., & Anderson, C. (2004). What a coincidence! The effects of incidental similarity on compliance. *Personality and Social Psychology Bulletin, 30,* 35–43.

Burger, J. M., & Palmer, M. L. (1991). Changes in and generalization of unrealistic optimism following experiences with stressful events: Reactions to the 1989 California earthquake. *Personality and Social Psychology Bulletin, 18,* 39–43.

Burger, J. M., & Pavelich, J. L. (1994). Attributions for presidential elections: The situational shift over time. *Basic and Applied Social Psychology, 15,* 359–371.

Burger, J. M., Sanchez, J., Imberi, J. E., & Grande, L. R. (2009). The norm of reciprocity as an internalized social norm: Returning favors even when no one finds out. *Social Influence, 4,* 11–17.

Burger, J. M., Soroka, S., Gonzago, K., Murphy, E., & Somervell, E. (2001). The effect of fleeting attraction on compliance to requests. *Personality and Social Psychology Bulletin, 27,* 1578–1586.

Burkett, J. P., & Young, L. J. (2012). The behavioral, anatomical and pharmacological parallels between social attachment, love, and addiction. *Psychopharmacology, 224,* 1–26.

Burkholder, R. (2003, February 14). Unwilling coalition? Majorities in Britain, Canada oppose military action in Iraq. *Gallup Poll Tuesday Briefing* (www.gallup.com/poll).

Burkholder, R. (2005, January 11). Chinese far wealthier than a decade ago, but are they happier? Gallup Poll (www.poll.gallup.com).

Burns, D. D. (1980). *Feeling good: The new mood therapy.* New York: Signet.

Burns, J. F. (2003a, April 13). Pillagers strip Iraqi museum of its treasure. *New York Times* (www.nytimes.com).

Burns, J. F. (2003b, April 14). Baghdad residents begin a long climb to an ordered city. *New York Times* (www.nytimes.com).

Burnstein, E. (2009). Robert B. Zajonc (1923–2008). *American Psychologist, 64,* 558–559.

Burnstein, E., Crandall, R., & Kitayama, S. (1994). Some neo-Darwinian decision rules for altruism: Weighing cues for inclusive fitness as a function of the biological importance of the decision. *Journal of Personality and Social Psychology, 67,* 773–789.

Burnstein, E., & Vinokur, A. (1977). Persuasive argumentation and social comparison as determinants of attitude polarization. *Journal of Experimental Social Psychology, 13,* 315–332.

Burnstein, E., & Worchel, P. (1962). Arbitrariness of frustration and its consequences for aggression in a social situation. *Journal of Personality, 30,* 528–540.

Burr, W. R. (1973). *Theory construction and the sociology of the family.* New York: Wiley.

Burson, K. A., Larrick, R. P., & Klayman, J. (2006). Skilled or unskilled, but still unaware of it: How perceptions of difficulty drive miscalibration in relative comparisons. *Journal of Personality and Social Psychology, 90,* 60–77.

Burton, C. M., & King, L. A. (2008). Effects of (very) brief writing on health: The two-minute miracle. *British Journal of Health Psychology, 13,* 9–14.

Bushman, B. J. (1993). Human aggression while under the influence of alcohol and other drugs: An integrative research review. *Current Directions in Psychological Science, 2,* 148–152.

Bushman, B. J. (1998). Priming effects of media violence on the accessibility of aggressive constructs in memory. *Personality and Social Psychology Bulletin, 24,* 537–545.

Bushman, B. J. (2002). Does venting anger feed or extinguish the flame? Catharsis, rumination, distraction, anger, and aggressive responding. *Personality and Social Psychology Bulletin, 28,* 724–731.

Bushman, B. J. (2005). Violence and sex in television programs do not sell products in advertisements. *Psychological Science, 16,* 702–708.

Bushman, B. J. (2007). That was a great commercial, but what were they selling? Effects of violence and sex on memory for products in television commercials. *Journal of Applied Social Psychology, 37,* 1784–1796.

Bushman, B. J., & Anderson, C. A. (1998). Methodology in the study of aggression: Integrating experimental and nonexperimental findings. In R. Geen & E. Donnerstein (Eds.), *Human aggression: Theories, research and implications for policy.* San Diego: Academic Press.

Bushman, B. J., & Anderson, C. A. (2001). Media violence and the American public: Scientific facts versus media misinformation. *American Psychologist, 56,* 477–489.

Bushman, B. J., & Anderson, C. A. (2002). Violent video games and hostile expectations: A test of the general aggression model. *Personality and Social Psychology Bulletin, 28,* 1679–1686.

Bushman, B. J., & Anderson, C. A. (2009). Comfortably numb: Desensitizing effects of violent media on helping others. *Psychological Science, 20,* 273–277.

Bushman, B. J., & Baumeister, R. F. (1998). Threatened egotism, narcissism, self-esteem, and direct and displaced aggression: Does self-love or self-hate lead to violence? *Journal of Personality and Social Psychology, 75,* 219–229.

Bushman, B. J., & Baumeister, R. F. (2002). Does self-love or self-hate lead to violence? *Journal of Research in Personality, 36,* 543–545.

Bushman, B. J., Baumeister, R. F., & Phillips, C. M. (2000). Do people aggress to improve their mood? Catharsis beliefs, affect regulation opportunity, and aggressive responding. *Journal of Personality and Social Psychology, 81,* 17–32.

Bushman, B. J., Baumeister, R. F., & Phillips, C. M. (2001). Do people aggress to improve their mood? Catharsis beliefs, affect regulation opportunity, and aggressive responding. *Journal of Personality and Social Psychology, 81,* 17–32.

Bushman, B. J., Baumeister, R. F., & Stack, A. D. (1999). Catharsis, aggression, and persuasive influence: Self-fulfilling or self-defeating prophecies? *Journal of Personality and Social Psychology, 76,* 367–376.

Bushman, B. J., Baumeister, R. F., Thomaes, S., Ryu, E., Begeer, S., & West, S. G. (2009). Looking again, and harder, for a link between low self-esteem and aggression. *Journal of Personality,* published online February 2, 2009.

Bushman, B. J., Bonacci, A. M., Pedersen, W. C., Vasquez, E. A., & Miller, N. (2005). Chewing on it can chew you up: Effects of rumination on triggered displaced aggression. *Journal of Personality and Social Psychology, 88,* 969–983.

Bushman, B. J., & Geen, R. G. (1990). Role of cognitive-emotional mediators and individual differences in the effects of media violence on aggression. *Journal of Personality and Social Psychology, 58,* 156–163.

Bushman, B. J., Gollwitzer, M., & Cruz, C. (2015). There is broad consensus: Media researchers agree that violent media increase aggression in children, and pediatricians and parents concur. *Psychology of Popular Media Culture, 4,* 200–214.

Bushman, B. J., & Huesmann, L. R. (2014). Twenty-five years of research on violence in digital games and aggression revisited. *European Psychologist, 19,* 47–55.

Bushman, B. J., Moeller, S. J., & Crocker, J. (2011). Sweets, sex, or self-esteem? Comparing the value of self-esteem boosts with other pleasant rewards. *Journal of Personality, 79,* 993–1012.

Bushman, B. J., Wang, M. C., & Anderson, C. A. (2005a). Is the curve relating temperature to aggression linear or curvilinear? Assaults and temperature in Minneapolis reexamined. *Journal of Personality and Social Psychology, 89,* 62–66.

Bushman, B. J., Wang, M. C., & Anderson, C. A. (2005b). Is the curve relating temperature to aggression linear or curvilinear? A response to Bell (2005) and to Cohn and Rotton (2005). *Journal of Personality and Social Psychology, 89,* 74–77.

Bushman, B. J., & Whitaker, J. L. (2010). Like a magnet: Catharsis beliefs attract angry people to violent video games. *Psychological Science, 21,* 790–792.

Buss, D. M. (1984). Toward a psychology of person-environment (PE) correlation: The role of spouse selection. *Journal of Personality and Social Psychology, 47,* 361–377.

Buss, D. M. (1985). Human mate selection. *American Scientist, 73,* 47–51.

Buss, D. M. (1989). Sex differences in human mate preferences: Evolutionary hypotheses tested in 37 cultures. *Behavioral and Brain Sciences, 12,* 1–49.

Buss, D. M. (1995a). Evolutionary psychology: A new paradigm for psychological science. *Psychological Inquiry, 6,* 1–30.

Buss, D. M. (1995b). Psychological sex differences: Origins through sexual selection. *American Psychologist, 50,* 164–168.

Buss, D. M. (1999). Behind the scenes. In D. G. Myers, *Social psychology,* 6th edition. New York: McGraw-Hill.

Buss, D. M. (2007). The evolution of human mating strategies: Consequences for conflict and cooperation. In S. W. Gangestad & J. A. Simpson (Eds.), *The evolution of mind: Fundamental questions and controversies.* New York: Guilford.

Buss, D. M. (2009). The great struggles of life: Darwin and the emergence of evolutionary psychology. *American Psychologist, 64,* 140–148.

Buss, D. M. (Ed.). (2005). *The handbook of evolutionary psychology.* New York: Wiley.

Butcher, S. H. (1951). *Aristotle's theory of poetry and fine art.* New York: Dover.

Butler, A. C., Hokanson, J. E., & Flynn, H. A. (1994). A comparison of self-esteem lability and low trait self-esteem as vulnerability factors for depression. *Journal of Personality and Social Psychology, 66,* 166–177.

Butler, D. M., & Broockman, D. E. (2011). Do politicians racially discriminate against constituents? A field experiment on state legislators. *American Journal of Political Science, 55,* 463–477.

Butler, J. L., & Baumeister, R. F. (1998). The trouble with friendly faces: Skilled performance with a supportive audience. *Journal of Personality and Social Psychology, 75,* 1213–1230.

Buttelmann, D., & Böhm, R. (2014). The ontogeny of the motivation that underlies in-group bias. *Psychological Science, 25,* 921–927.

Butterfield, F. (2001, April 20). Victims' race affects decisions on killers' sentence, study finds. *New York Times,* p. A10.

Butz, D. A., & Plant, E. A. (2006). Perceiving outgroup members as unresponsive: Implications for approach-related emotions, intentions, and behavior. *Journal of Personality and Social Psychology, 91,* 1066–1079.

Buunk, B. P., & Van Yperen, N. W. (1991). Referential comparisons, relational comparisons, and exchange orientation: Their relation to marital satisfaction. *Personality and Social Psychology Bulletin, 17,* 709–717.

Byrne, D. (1971). *The attraction paradigm.* New York: Academic Press.

Byrne, D., & Clore, G. L. (1970). A reinforcement model of evaluative responses. *Personality: An International Journal, 1,* 103–128.

Byrne, D., & Wong, T. J. (1962). Racial prejudice, interpersonal attraction, and assumed dissimilarity of attitudes. *Journal of Abnormal and Social Psychology, 65,* 246–253.

Byrnes, J. P., Miller, D. C., & Schafer, W. D. (1999). Gender differences in risk taking: A meta-analysis. *Psychological Bulletin, 125,* 367–383.

Cacioppo, J. T. (2007, October). The rise in collaborative science. *Association for Psychological Science Observer,* 52–53.

Cacioppo, J. T., & Cacioppo, S. (2014). Social relationships and health: The toxic effects of perceived social isolation. *Social and Personality Psychology Compass, 8,* 58–72.

Cacioppo, J. T., Cacioppo, S., Gonzaga, G. C., Ogburn, E. L., & VanderWeele, T. J. (2013). Marital satisfaction and break-ups differ across on-line and off-line meeting venues. *Proceedings of the National Academy of Sciences, 110,* 10135–10140.

Cacioppo, J. T., Claiborn, C. D., Petty, R. E., & Heesacker, M. (1991). General framework for the study of attitude change in psychotherapy. In C. R. Snyder & D. R. Forsyth (Eds.), *Handbook of social and clinical psychology.* New York: Pergamon.

Cacioppo, J. T., Fowler, J. H., & Christakis, N. A. (2009). Alone in the crowd: The structure and spread of loneliness in a large social network. *Journal of Personality and Social Psychology, 97,* 977–991.

Cacioppo, J. T., & Patrick, W. (2008). *Loneliness: Human nature and the need for social connection.* New York: Norton.

Cacioppo, J. T., & Petty, R. E. (1986). Social processes. In M. G. H. Coles, E. Donchin, & S. W. Porges (Eds.), *Psychophysiology.* New York: Guilford.

Cacioppo, J. T., Petty, R. E., Feinstein, J. A., & Jarvis, W. B. G. (1996). Dispositional differences in cognitive motivation: The life and times of individuals varying in need for cognition. *Psychological Bulletin, 119,* 197–253.

Cacioppo, J. T., Petty, R. E., & Morris, K. J. (1983). Effects of need for cognition on message evaluation, recall, and persuasion. *Journal of Personality and Social Psychology, 45,* 805–818.

Cacioppo, S., Capitanio, J. P., & Cacioppo, J. T. (2014). Toward a neurology of loneliness. *Psychological Bulletin, 140,* 1464–1504.

Cafferty, J. (2011, March 15). *Why is there no looting in Japan?* www.caffertyfile .blogs.cnn.com.

Cai, S., Kwan, V. S. Y., & Sedikides, C. (2011). The People's Republic of China: A culture of increasing narcissism. Unpublished manuscript.

Cairns, E., & Hewstone, M. (2002). The impact of peacemaking in Northern Ireland on intergroup behavior. In S. Gabi & B. Nevo (Eds.), *Peace education: The concept, principles, and practices around the world.* Mahwah, NJ: Erlbaum.

Caldwell, H. K., Lee, H.-J., MacBeth, A. H., & Young, W. S. (2008). Vasopressin: Behavioral roles of an "original" neuropeptide. *Progress in Neurobiology, 84,* 1–24.

Cameron, G. (2010, May 7). The Muck files. *The Scottish Sun* (www.thesun.co.uk/ scotsol).

Camp, G., Wesstein, H., & deBruin, A. B. H. (2012). Can questioning induce forgetting? Retrieval-induced forgetting of eyewitness information. *Applied Cognitive Psychology, 26,* 431–435.

Campbell, D. T. (1975a). The conflict between social and biological evolution and the concept of original sin. *Zygon, 10,* 234–249.

Campbell, D. T. (1975b). On the conflicts between biological and social evolution and between psychology and moral tradition. *American Psychologist, 30,* 1103–1126.

Campbell, E. Q., & Pettigrew, T. F. (1959). Racial and moral crisis: The role of Little Rock ministers. *American Journal of Sociology, 64,* 509–516.

Campbell, M. A. (2005). Cyberbulling: An old problem in a new guise? *Australian Journal of Guidance and Counselling, 15,* 68–76.

Campbell, T. H., & Kay, A. C. (2014). Solution aversion: On the relation between ideology and motivated disbelief. *Journal of Personality and Social Psychology, 107,* 809–824.

Campbell, W. K. (2005). *When you love a man who loves himself.* Chicago: Sourcebooks.

Campbell, W. K., Bosson, J. K., Goheen, T. W., Lakey, C. E., & Kernis, M. H. (2007). Do narcissists dislike themselves "deep down inside"? *Psychological Science, 18,* 227–229.

Campbell, W. K., & Foster, C. A. (2002). Narcissism and commitment in romantic relationships: An investment model analysis. *Personality and Social Psychology Bulletin, 28,* 484–495.

Campbell, W. K., & Sedikides, C. (1999). Self-threat magnifies the self-serving bias: A meta-analytic integration. *Review of General Psychology, 3,* 23–43.

Canadian Centre on Substance Abuse. (1997). *Canadian profile: Alcohol, tobacco, and other drugs.* Ottawa: Canadian Centre on Substance Abuse.

Canadian Psychological Association. (2000). *Canadian code of ethics for psychologists.* Ottawa: Canadian Psychological Association (www.cpa.ca/ ethics2000.html).

Canevello, A. & Crocker, J. (2011). Interpersonal goals, others' regard for the self, and self-esteem: The paradoxical consequences of self-image and compassionate goals. *European Journal of Social Psychology, 41,* 422–434.

Cann, A., Calhoun, L. G., & Selby, J. W. (1979). Attributing responsibility to the victim of rape: Influence of information regarding past sexual experience. *Human Relations, 32,* 57–67.

Canter, D., Breaux, J., & Sime, J. (1980). Domestic, multiple occupancy, and hospital fires. In D. Canter (Ed.), *Fires and human behavior.* Hoboken, NJ: Wiley.

Cantril, H., & Bumstead, C. H. (1960). *Reflections on the human venture.* New York: New York University Press.

Cantu, S. M., Simpson, J. A., Griskevicius, V., Weisberg, Y. J., Durante, K. M., & Beal, D. J. (2014). Fertile and selectively flirty: Women's behavior toward men changes across the ovulatory cycle. *Psychological Science, 25,* 431–438.

Caprioli, M., & Boyer, M. A. (2001). Gender, violence, and international crisis. *Journal of Conflict Resolution, 45,* 503–518.

Caputo, D., & Dunning, D. (2005). What you don't know: The role played by errors of omission in imperfect self-assessments. *Journal of Experimental Social Psychology, 41,* 488–505.

Carducci, B. J., Cosby, P. C., & Ward, D. D. (1978). Sexual arousal and interpersonal evaluations. *Journal of Experimental Social Psychology, 14,* 449–457.

Carey, J. (2012, November). Global warming faster than expected? *Scientific American,* 51–55.

Carli, L. L. (1999). Cognitive reconstruction, hindsight, and reactions to victims and perpetrators. *Personality and Social Psychology Bulletin, 25,* 966–979.

Carli, L. L., & Leonard, J. B. (1989). The effect of hindsight on victim derogation. *Journal of Social and Clinical Psychology, 8,* 331–343.

Carlo, G., Eisenberg, N., Troyer, D., Switzer, G., & Speer, A. L. (1991). The altruistic personality: In what contexts is it apparent? *Journal of Personality and Social Psychology, 61,* 450–458.

Carlsmith, J. M., & Gross, A. E. (1969). Some effects of guilt on compliance. *Journal of Personality and Social Psychology, 11,* 232–239.

Carlson, E. N., Vazire, S., & Oltmanns, T. F. (2011). You probably think this paper's about you: Narcissists' perceptions of their personality and reputation. *Journal of Personality and Social Psychology, 101,* 185–201.

Carlson, J., & Hatfield, E. (1992). *The psychology of emotion.* Fort Worth, TX: Holt, Rinehart & Winston.

Carlson, K. A., & Russo, J. E. (2001). Biased interpretation of evidence by mock jurors. *Journal of Experimental Psychology: Applied, 7,* 91–103.

Carlson, M., Charlin, V., & Miller, N. (1988). Positive mood and helping behavior: A test of six hypotheses. *Journal of Personality and Social Psychology, 55,* 211–229.

Carlson, M., Marcus-Newhall, A., & Miller, N. (1990). Effects of situational aggression cues: A quantitative review. *Journal of Personality and Social Psychology, 58,* 622–633.

Carlston, D. E., & Shovar, N. (1983). Effects of performance attributions on others' perceptions of the attributor. *Journal of Personality and Social Psychology, 44,* 515–525.

Carnagey, N. L., Anderson, C. A., & Bushman, B. J. (2007). The effect of video game violence on physiological desensitization to real-life violence. *Journal of Experimental Social Psychology, 43,* 489–496.

Carnaghi, A., Maass, A., & Fasoli, F. (2011). Enhancing masculinity by slandering homosexuals: The role of homophobic epithets in heterosexual gender identity. *Personality and Social Psychology Bulletin, 37,* 1655–1665.

Carnevale, P. J., & Choi, D-W. (2000). Culture in the mediation of international disputes. *International Journal of Psychology, 35,* 105–110.

Carnevale, P. J., & Probst, T. M. (1998). Social values and social conflict in creative problem solving and categorization. *Journal of Personality and Social Psychology, 74,* 1300–1309.

Carney, D. R., & Banaji, M. R. (2008). *First is best.* Unpublished manuscript, Harvard University.

Carney, D. R., Cuddy, A. J. C., & Yap, A. J. (2010). Power posing: Brief nonverbal displays affect neuroendocrine levels and risk tolerance. *Psychological Science, 21,* 1363–1368.

Carothers, B. J., & Reis, H. T. (2013). Men and women are from Earth: Examining the latent structure of gender. *Journal of Personality and Social Psychology, 104,* 385–407.

Carpenter, C. J. (2012). A meta-analysis and an experiment investigating the effects of speaker disfluency on persuasion. *Western Journal of Communication, 76,* 552–569.

Carpenter, J., Nida, S., Saylor, C., & Taylor, C. (2012, February). Consequences: Bullying versus ostracism in middle school students. Poster presented at the Southeastern Psychological Association annual conference, New Orleans, LA.

Carpenter, T. F., & Marshall, M. A. (2009). An examination of religious priming and intrinsic religious motivation in the moral hypocrisy paradigm. *Journal for the Scientific Study of Religion, 48,* 386–393.

Carpusor, A. G., & Loges, W. E. (2006). Rental discrimination and ethnicity in names. *Journal of Applied Social Psychology, 36,* 934–952.

Carré, J. M., & McCormick, C. M. (2008). In your face: Facial metrics predict aggressiveness behaviour in the laboratory and in varsity and professional hockey players. *Proceedings of the Royal Society B, 275,* 2651–2656.

Carré, J. M., McCormick, C. M., & Mondloch, C. J. (2009). Facial structure is a reliable cue of aggressive behavior. *Psychological Science, 20,* 1194–1198.

Carroll, D., Davey Smith, G., & Bennett, P. (1994, March). Health and socioeconomic status. *The Psychologist,* pp. 122–125.

Carroll, J. S., Padilla-Walker, L. M., Nelson, L. J., Olson, C. D., Barry, C. M., & Madsen, S. D. (2008). Generation XXX: Pornography acceptance and use among emerging adults. *Journal of Adolescent Research, 23,* 6–30.

Carroll, L. (2014). The Robin Williams effect: Could suicides follow star's death? NBCnews.com, August 12, 2014 (http:// www.nbcnews.com/storyline/robin- williams-death/ robin-williams-effect-could-suicides- follow-stars-death-n178961).

Carter, S. L. (1993). *Reflections of an affirmative action baby.* New York: Basic Books.

Carter, S., & Snow, C. (2004, May). *Helping singles enter better marriages using predictive models of marital success.* Presented at the American Psychological Society convention.

Cartwright, D. S. (1975). The nature of gangs. In D. S. Cartwright, B. Tomson, & H. Schwartz (Eds.), *Gang delinquency.* Monterey, CA: Brooks/Cole.

Carvallo, M., & Gabriel, S. (2006). No man is an island: The need to belong and dismissing avoidant attachment style. *Personality and Social Psychology Bulletin, 32,* 697–709.

Carver, C. S., Kus, L. A., & Scheier, M. F. (1994). Effect of good versus bad mood and optimistic versus pessimistic outlook on social acceptance versus rejection. *Journal of Social and Clinical Psychology, 13,* 138–151.

Carver, C. S., & Scheier, M. F. (1981). *Attention and self-regulation.* New York: Springer-Verlag.

Carver, C. S., & Scheier, M. F. (1986). Analyzing shyness: A specific application of broader self-regulatory principles. In W. H. Jones, J. M. Cheek, & S. R. Briggs (Eds.), *Shyness: Perspectives on research and treatment.* New York: Plenum.

Carver, C. S., Scheier, M. F., & Segerstrom, S. C. (2010). Optimism. *Clinical Psychology Review, 30,* 879–889.

Cash, T. F., & Janda, L. H. (1984, December). The eye of the beholder. *Psychology Today,* 46–52.

Caspi, A., & Herbener, E. S. (1990). Continuity and change: Assortative marriage and the consistency of personality in adulthood. *Journal of Personality and Social Psychology, 58,* 250–258.

Caspi, A., McClay, J., Moffitt, T., Mill, J., Martin, J., Craig, I. W., Taylor, A., & Poulton, R. (2002). Role of genotype in the cycle of violence in maltreated children. *Science, 297,* 851–854.

Caspi, A., Sugden, K., Moffitt, T. E., Taylor, A., Craig, I. W., Harrington, H. L., McClay, J., Mill, J., Martin, J., Braithwaite, A., & Poulton, R. (2003). Influence of life stress on depression: Moderation by a polymorphism in the 5-HTT gene. *Science, 30,* 386–389.

Cassidy, J. (2000). Adult romantic attachments: A developmental perspective on individual differences. *Review of General Psychology Special Issue: Adult attachment, 4,* 111–131.

Castelli, L., Arcuri, L., & Carraro, L. (2009). Projection processes in the perception of political leaders. *Basic and Applied Social Psychology, 31,* 189–196.

Castelli, L., Carraro, L., Tomelleri, S., & Amari, A. (2007). White children's alignment to the perceived racial attitudes of the parents: Closer to the mother than father. *British Journal of Developmental Psychology, 25,* 353–357.

Ceci, S. J., & Bruck, M. (1993a). Child witnesses: Translating research into policy.

Social Policy Report (Society for Research in Child Development), *7(3),* 1–30.

Ceci, S. J., & Bruck, M. (1993b). Suggestibility of the child witness: A historical review and synthesis. *Psychological Bulletin, 113,* 403–439.

Ceci, S. J., & Bruck, M. (1995). *Jeopardy in the courtroom: A scientific analysis of children's testimony.* Washington, DC: American Psychological Association.

Cemalcilar, Z., & Falbo, T. (2008). A longitudinal study of the adaptation of international students in the United States. *Journal of Cross-Cultural Psychology, 39,* 799–804.

Centers for Disease Control (CDC). (2008, Spring). Sexual violence: Facts at a glance. Author (www.cdc.gov/injury).

Chaiken, S. (1979). Communicator physical attractiveness and persuasion. *Journal of Personality and Social Psychology, 37,* 1387–1397.

Chaiken, S. (1980). Heuristic versus systematic information processing and the use of source versus message cues in persuasion. *Journal of Personality and Social Psychology, 39,* 752–766.

Chaiken, S., & Eagly, A. H. (1976). Communication modality as a determinant of message persuasiveness and message comprehensibility. *Journal of Personality and Social Psychology, 34,* 605–614.

Chaiken, S., & Eagly, A. H. (1983). Communication modality as a determinant of persuasion: The role of communicator salience. *Journal of Personality and Social Psychology, 45,* 241–256.

Chaiken, S., & Maheswaran, D. (1994). Neuristic processing can bias systematic processing: Effects of source credibility, argument ambiguity, and task importance on attitude judgment. *Journal of Personality and Social Psychology, 66,* 460–473.

Chambers, J. R., Baron, R. S., & Inman, M. L. (2006). Misperceptions in intergroup conflict: Disagreeing about what we disagree about. *Psychological Science, 17,* 38–45.

Chambers, J. R., Schlenker, B. R., & Collisson, B. (2012). Ideology and prejudice: The role of value conflicts. *Psychological Science, 24,* 140–149.

Chambers, J. R., Swan, L. K., & Heesacker, M. (2014). Better off than we know: Distorted perceptions of incomes and income inequality in America. *Psychological Science, 25,* 613–618.

Chambers, J. R., & Windschitl, P. D. (2004). Biases in social comparative judgments: The role of nonmotivated factors in above-average and comparative-optimism effects. *Psychological Bulletin, 130,* 813–838.

Champagne, F. A., & Mashoodh, R. (2009). Genes in context: Gene-environment interplay and the origins of individual differences in behavior. *Current Directions in Psychological Science, 18,* 127–131.

Champagne, F., Francis, D. D., Mar, A., & Meaney, M. J. (2003). Naturally occurring variations in maternal care in the rat as a mediating influence for the effects of environment on the development of individual differences in stress reactivity. *Physiology & Behavior, 79,* 359–371.

Chan, M. K. H., Louis, W. R., & Jetten, J. (2010). When groups are wrong and deviants are right. *European Journal of Social Psychology, 40,* 1103–1109.

Chance, J. E., & Goldstein, A. G. (1981). Depth of processing in response to own- and other-race faces. *Personality and Social Psychology Bulletin, 7,* 475–480.

Chance, J. E., & Goldstein, A. G. (1996). The other-race effect and eyewitness identification. In S. L. Sporer (Ed.), *Psychological issues in eyewitness identification* (pp. 153–176). Mahwah, NJ: Erlbaum.

Chandra, A., Mosher, W. D., & Copen, C. (2011, March). Sexual behavior, sexual attraction, and sexual identity in the United States: Data from the 2006–2008 National Survey of Family Growth. *National Health Statistics Reports,* Number 36 (Centers for Disease Control and Prevention).

Chapman, L. J., & Chapman, J. P. (1969). Genesis of popular but erroneous psychodiagnostic observations. *Journal of Abnormal Psychology, 74,* 272–280.

Chapman, L. J., & Chapman, J. P. (1971, November). Test results are what you think they are. *Psychology Today,* 18–22, 106–107.

Chartrand, T. L., & Bargh, J. A. (1999). The chameleon effect: The perception-behavior link and social interaction. *Journal of Personality and Social Psychology, 76,* 893–910.

Chatard, A., Guimond, S., & Selimbegovic, L. (2007). "How good are you in math?" The effect of gender stereotypes on students' recollection of their school marks. *Journal of Experimental Social Psychology, 43,* 1017–1024.

Check, J., & Malamuth, N. (1984). Can there be positive effects of participation in pornography experiments? *Journal of Sex Research, 20,* 14–31.

Chen, E. (2004). Why socioeconomic status affects the health of children: A psychosocial perspective. *Current Directions in Psychological Science, 13,* 112–115.

Chen, F. F., & Kenrick, D. T. (2002). Repulsion or attraction? Group membership and assumed attitude similarity. *Journal of Personality and Social Psychology, 83,* 111–125.

Chen, F. S., Minson, J. A., Schone, M., & Heinrichs, M. (2013). In the eye of the beholder: Eye contact increases resistance to persuasion. *Psychological Science, 24,* 2254–2261.

Chen, H. (2012). *Dark web: Exploring and data mining the dark side of the web.* New York: Springer.

Chen, H., Luo, S., Yue, G., Xu, D., & Zhaoyang, R. (2009). Do birds of a feather flock together in China? *Personal Relationships, 16,* 167–186.

Chen, L.-H., Baker, S. P., Braver, E. R., & Li, G. (2000). Carrying passengers as a risk factor for crashes fatal to 16- and 17-year-old drivers. *Journal of the American Medical Association, 283,* 1578–1582.

Chen, S., Boucher, H. C., & Tapias, M. P. (2006). The relational self revealed: Integrative conceptualization and implications for interpersonal life. *Psychological Bulletin, 132,* 151–179.

Chen, S. C. (1937). Social modification of the activity of ants in nest-building. *Physiological Zoology, 10,* 420–436.

Chen, Z., Williams, K. D., Fitness, J., & Newton, N. C. (2008). When hurt will not heal: Exploring the capacity to relive social and physical pain. *Psychological Science, 19,* 789–795.

Cheney, R. (2003, March 16). Comments on Face the Nation, CBS News.

Chiao, J. Y., Bowman, N. E., & Gill, H. (2008). The political gender gap: Gender bias in facial inferences that predict voting behavior. *PLoS One 3(10):* e3666. (doi:10.1371/journal.pone.0003666).

Chicago Tribune. (2002, September 30). When believing isn't seeing. www.chicagotribune.com.

Chida, Y., & Steptoe, A. (2009). The association of anger and hostility with future coronary heart disease: A meta-analytic review of prospective evidence. *Journal of the American College of Cardiology, 17,* 936–946.

Chodorow, N. J. (1978). *The reproduction of mother: Psychoanalysis and the sociology of gender.* Berkeley, CA: University of California Press.

Chodorow, N. J. (1989). *Feminism and psychoanalytic theory.* New Haven, CT: Yale University Press.

Choi, I., & Choi, Y. (2002). Culture and self-concept flexibility. *Personality & Social Psychology Bulletin, 28,* 1508–1517.

Choi, I., Nisbett, R. E., & Norenzayan, A. (1999). Causal attribution across cultures: Variation and universality. *Psychological Bulletin, 125,* 47–63.

Chou, H. G., & Edge, N. (2012). "They are happier and having better lives than I am": The impact of using Facebook on perceptions of others' lives. *Cyberpsychology, Behavior, and Social Networking, 15,* 117–121.

Chou, W. S., Prestin, A., & Kunath, S. (2014). Obesity in social media: A mixed methods analysis. *Translational Behavioral Medicine, 4,* 314–323.

Chow, R. M., & Galak, J. (2012). The effect of inequality frames on support for redistributive tax policies. *Psychological Science, 23,* 1467–1469.

Christakis, N. A., & Fowler, J. H. (2009). *Connected: The surprising power of social networks and how they shape our lives.* New York: Little, Brown.

Christensen, P. N., & Kashy, D. A. (1998). Perceptions of and by lonely people in initial social interaction. *Personality and Social Psychology Bulletin, 24,* 322–329.

Christ, O., Hewstone, M., Tausch, N., Wagner, U., Voci, A., Hughes, J., & Cairns, E. (2010). Direct contact as a moderator of extended contact effects: Cross-sectional and longitudinal impact on outgroup attitudes, behavioral intentions, and attitude certainty. *Personality and Social Psychology Bulletin, 36,* 1662–1674.

Chua, H. F., Boland, J. E., & Nisbett, R. E. (2005). Cultural variation in eye movements during scene perception. *Proceedings of the National Academy of Sciences, 102,* 12629–12633.

Chulov, M. (2014, December 11). ISIS: The inside story. *The Guardian* (www.theguardian.com).

Church, A. T., Aria, R. M., Rincon, B. C., Vargas-Flores, J. J., Ibanez-Eyes, J., Wang, L., Alvarez, J. M., Wang, C., & Ortiz, F. A. (2014). A four-culture study of self-enhancement and adjustment using the social relations model: Do alternative conceptualizations and indices make a difference? *Journal of Personality and Social Psychology, 106,* 997–1014.

Church, G. J. (1986, January 6). China. *Time,* pp. 6–19.

CIA. (2014, accessed April 23). Sex ratio. *The world fact book* (www.cia.gov).

CIA: Central Intelligence Agency. (2014). The World Factbook. Retrieved March 27, 2015 from: https://www.cia.gov/library/publications/the-world-factbook/geos/ja.html

Cialdini, R. B. (1984). *Influence: How and why people agree to things.* New York: William Morrow.

Cialdini, R. B. (1988). *Influence: Science and practice.* Glenview, IL: Scott, Foresman/Little, Brown.

Cialdini, R. B. (1991). Altruism or egoism? That is (still) the question. *Psychological Inquiry, 2,* 124–126.

Cialdini, R. B. (1995). A full-cycle approach to social psychology. In G. G. Brannigan & M. R. Merrens (Eds.), *The social psychologists: Research adventures.* New York: McGraw-Hill.

Cialdini, R. B. (2005). Basic social influence is underestimated. *Psychological Inquiry, 16,* 158–161.

Cialdini, R. B. (2008). *Influence: Science and practice,* 5th edition. Upper Saddle River, NJ: Prentice-Hall.

Cialdini, R. B., Bickman, L., & Caciopppo, J. T. (1979). An example of consumeristic social psychology: Bargaining tough in the new car showroom. *Journal of Applied Social Psychology, 9,* 115–126.

Cialdini, R. B., Borden, R. J., Thorne, A., Walker, M. R., Freeman, S., & Sloan, L. R. (1976). Basking in reflected glory: Three (football) field studies. *Journal of Personality and Social Psychology, 39,* 406–415.

Cialdini, R. B., Cacioppo, J. T., Bassett, R., & Miller, J. A. (1978). Lowball procedure for producing compliance: Commitment then cost. *Journal of Personality and Social Psychology, 36,* 463–476.

Cialdini, R. B., Demaine, L. J., Barrett, D. W., Sagarin, B. J., & Rhoads, K. L. V. (2003). *The poison parasite defense: A strategy for sapping a stronger opponent's persuasive strength.* Unpublished manuscript, Arizona State University.

Cialdini, R. B., & Schroeder, D. A. (1976). Increasing compliance by legitimizing paltry contributions: When even a penny helps. *Journal of Personality and Social Psychology, 34,* 599–604.

Cialdini, R. B., Vincent, J. E., Lewis, S. K., Catalan, J., Wheeler, D., & Danby, B. L. (1975). Reciprocal concessions procedure for inducing compliance: The door-in-the-face technique. *Journal of Personality and Social Psychology, 31,* 206–215.

Cicerello, A., & Sheehan, E. P. (1995). Personal advertisements: A content analysis. *Journal of Social Behavior and Personality, 10,* 751–756.

Cikara, M., Botvinick, M. M., & Fiske, S. T. (2011). Us versus them: Social identity shapes neural responses to intergroup competition and harm. *Psychological Science, 22,* 306–313.

Cikara, M., Bruneau, E. G., & Saxe, R. R. (2011). Us and them: Intergroup failures of empathy. *Current Directions in Psychological Science, 20,* 149–153.

Cikara, M., & Van Bavel, J. J. (2014). The neuroscience of intergroup relations: An integrative review. *Perspectives on Psychological Science, 9,* 245–274.

Cioffi, D., & Garner, R. (1998). The effect of response options on decisions and subsequent behavior: Sometimes inaction is better. *Personality and Social Psychology Bulletin, 24,* 463–472.

Clack, B., Dixon, J., & Tredoux, C. (2005). Eating together apart: Patterns of segregation in a multi-ethnic cafeteria. *Journal of Community and Applied Social Psychology, 15,* 1–16.

Clark, K., & Clark, M. (1947). Racial identification and preference in Negro children. In T. M. Newcomb & E. L. Hartley (Eds.), *Readings in social psychology.* New York: Holt.

Clark, M. S. (1984). Record keeping in two types of relationships. *Journal of Personality and Social Psychology, 47,* 549–557.

Clark, M. S. (1986). Evidence for the effectiveness of manipulations of desire for communal versus exchange relationships. *Personality and Social Psychology Bulletin, 12,* 414–425.

Clark, M. S., Lemay, E. P., Jr., Graham, S. M., Pataki, S. P., & Finkel, E. J. (2010). Ways of giving benefits in marriage: Norm use, relationship satisfaction, and attachment-related variability. *Psychological Science, 21,* 944–951.

Clark, M. S., & Mills, J. (1979). Interpersonal attraction in exchange and communal relationships. *Journal of Personality and Social Psychology, 37,* 12–24.

Clark, M. S., & Mills, J. (1993). The difference between communal and exchange relationships: What it is and is not. *Personality and Social Psychology Bulletin, 19,* 684–691.

Clark, M. S., Mills, J., & Corcoran, D. (1989). Keeping track of needs and inputs of friends and strangers. *Personality and Social Psychology Bulletin, 15,* 533–542.

Clark, M. S., Mills, J., & Powell, M. C. (1986). Keeping track of needs in communal and exchange relationships. *Journal of Personality and Social Psychology, 51,* 333–338.

Clark, R. D. (1990). The impact of AIDS on gender differences in willingness to engage in casual sex. *Journal of Applied Social Psychology, 20,* 771–782.

Clark, R. D., & Hatfield, E. (1989). Gender differences in receptivity to sexual offers. *Journal of Psychology and Human Sexuality, 2,* 39–55.

Clark, R. D., III. (1974). Effects of sex and race on helping behavior in a nonreactive setting. *Representative Research in Social Psychology, 5,* 1–6.

Clark, R. D., III, & Maass, S. A. (1988). The role of social categorization and perceived source credibility in minority influence. *European Journal of Social Psychology, 18,* 381–394.

Clarke, A. C. (1952). An examination of the operation of residual propinquity as a factor in mate selection. *American Sociological Review, 27,* 17–22.

Clayton, S., & Myers, G. (2009). *Conservation psychology: Understanding and promoting human care for nature.* Hoboken, NJ: Wiley-Blackwell.

Cleghorn, R. (1980, October 31). ABC News, meet the Literary Digest. *Detroit Free Press.*

Clevstrom, J., & Passariello, C. (2006, August 18). No kicks from "champagne." *Wall Street Journal,* A11.

Clifford, M. M., & Walster, E. H. (1973). The effect of physical attractiveness on teacher expectation. *Sociology of Education, 46,* 248–258.

CNN. (2007, October 6). Jury awards $6.1 million in McDonald's strip search case (www.cnn.com).

Coan, J. A., Schaefer, H. S., & Davidson, R. J. (2006). Lending a hand: Social regulation of the neural response to threat. *Psychological Science, 17,* 1032–1039.

Coates, B., Pusser, H. E., & Goodman, I. (1976). The influence of "Sesame Street" and "Mister Rogers' Neighborhood" on children's social behavior in the preschool. *Child Development, 47,* 138–144.

Coats, E. J., & Feldman, R. S. (1996). Gender differences in nonverbal correlates

of social status. *Personality and Social Psychology Bulletin, 22,* 1014–1022.

Cohen, D. (1996). Law, social policy, and violence: The impact of regional cultures. *Journal of Personality and Social Psychology, 70,* 961–978.

Cohen, D. (1998). Culture, social organization, and patterns of violence. *Journal of Personality and Social Psychology, 75,* 408–419.

Cohen, D., Nisbett, R. E., Bowdle, B. F., & Schwarz, N. (1996). Insult, aggression, and the Southern culture of honor: An "experimental ethnography." *Journal of Personality and Social Psychology, 70,* 945–960.

Cohen, E. E. A., Ejsmond-Frey, R., Knight, N., & Dunbar, R. I. M. (2009, September 15). Rowers' high: Behavioural synchrony is correlated with elevated pain thresholds. *Biology Letters.*

Cohen, E. G. (1980). Design and redesign of the desegregated school: Problems of status, power and conflict. In W. G. Stephan & J. R. Feagin (Eds.), *School desegregation: Past, present, and future.* New York: Plenum.

Cohen, G. L., Garcia, J., Apfel, N., & Master, A. (2006). Reducing the racial achievement gap: A social-psychological intervention. *Science, 313,* 1307–1310.

Cohen, G. L., Garcia, J., Purdie-Vaughns, V., Apfel, N., & Brzustoski, P. (2009). Recursive processes in self-affirmation: Intervening to close the minority achievement gap. *Science, 324,* 400–403.

Cohen, G. L., Steele, C. M., & Ross, L. D. (1999). The mentor's dilemma: Providing critical feedback across the racial divide. *Personality and Social Psychology Bulletin, 25,* 1302–1318.

Cohen, M., & Davis, N. (1981). *Medication errors: Causes and prevention.* Philadelphia: G. F. Stickley Co. Cited by R. B. Cialdini (1989), Agents of influence: Bunglers, smugglers, and sleuths. Paper presented at the American Psychological Association convention.

Cohen, R. (2011, January 13). Mohammed the Brit. *New York Times* (www.nytimes .com).

Cohen, S. (2002). Psychosocial stress, social networks, and susceptibility to infection. In H. G. Koenig & H. J. Cohen (Eds.), *The link between religion and health: Psychoneuroimmunology and the faith factor.* New York: Oxford University Press.

Cohen, S. (2004). Social relationships and health. *American Psychologist, 59,* 676–684.

Cohen, S., Alper, C. M., Doyle, W. J., Treanor, J. J., & Turner, R. B. (2006). Positive emotional style predicts resistance to illness after experimental exposure to rhinovirus or influenza A virus. *Psychosomatic Medicine, 68,* 809–815.

Cohen, S., Doyle, W. J., Skoner, D. P., Rabin, B. S., & Gwaltney, J. M., Jr. (1997). Social ties and susceptibility to the

common cold. *Journal of the American Medical Association, 277,* 1940–1944.

Cohen, S., Doyle, W. J., Turner, R., Alper, C. M., & Skoner, D. P. (2003). Sociability and susceptibility to the common cold. *Psychological Science, 14,* 389–395.

Cohen, S., Janicki-Deverts, D., Doyle, W. J., Miller, G. E., Frank, E., Rabin, B. S., & Turner, R. B. (2012). Chronic stress, glucocorticoid receptor resistance, inflammation, and disease risk. *PNAS Proceedings of the National Academy of Sciences of the United States of America, 109,* 5995–5999.

Cohn, E. G. (1993). The prediction of police calls for service: The influence of weather and temporal variables on rape and domestic violence. *Environmental Psychology, 13,* 71–83.

Cohn, E. G., & Rotton, J. (2005). The curve is still out there: A reply to Bushman, Wang, and Anderson (2005), Is the curve relating temperature to aggression linear or curvilinear? *Journal of Personality and Social Psychology, 89,* 67–70.

Coker, B. (2012). Seeking the opinions of others online: Evidence of evaluation overshoot. *Journal of Economic Psychology, 33,* 1033–1042.

Colarelli, S. M., Spranger, J. L., Hechanova, M. R. (2006). Women, power, and sex composition in small groups: An evolutionary perspective. *Journal of Organizational Behavior Special Issue: Darwinian Perspectives on Behavior in Organizations, 27,* 163–184.

Coleman, L. M., Jussim, L., & Abraham, J. (1987). Students' reactions to teachers' evaluations: The unique impact of negative feedback. *Journal of Applied Social Psychology, 17,* 1051–1070.

Cole, S. W., Arevalo, J. M. G., Takahashi, R., Sloan, E. K., Lutgendorf, S. K., Sood, A. K., Sheridan, J. F., & Seeman, T. E. (2010). Computational identification of gene-social environment interaction at the human IL6 locus. *PNAS, 107,* 5681–5686.

Collier, K. L., Bos, H. M. W., & Sandfort, T. G. M. (2012). Intergroup contact, attitudes toward homosexuality, and the role of acceptance of gender non-conformity in young adolescents. *Journal of Adolescence, 35,* 899–907.

Collins, N. L., & Miller, L. C. (1994). Self-disclosure and liking: A meta-analytic review. *Psychological Bulletin, 116,* 457–475.

Colman, A. M. (1991). Crowd psychology in South African murder trials. *American Psychologist, 46,* 1071–1079. See also Colman, A. M. (1991). Psychological evidence in South African murder trials. *The Psychologist, 14,* 482–486.

Colzato, L. S., Steenbergen, L., de Kwaadsteniet, E. W., Sellaro, R., Liepelt, R., & Hommel, B. (2013). Tryptophan promotes interpersonal trust. *Psychological Science, 24,* 2575–2577.

Comer, D. R. (1995). A model of social loafing in a real work group. *Human Relations, 48,* 647–667.

Comstock, G. (2008). A sociological perspective on television violence and aggression. *American Behavioral Scientist, 51,* 1184–1211.

Confer, J. C., Easton, J. A., Fleischman, D. S., Goetz, C. D., Lewis, D. M. G., Perilloux, C., & Buss, D. M. (2010). Evolutionary psychology: Controversies, questions, prospects, and limitations. *American Psychologist, 65,* 110–126

Conger, R. D., Cui, M., Bryant, C. M., & Elder, G. H. (2000). Competence in early adult romantic relationships: A developmental perspective on family influences. *Journal of Personality and Social Psychology, 79,* 224–237.

Contrada, R. J., Ashmore, R. D., Gary, M. L., Coups, E., Egeth, J. D., Sewell, A., Ewell, K., Goyal, T. M., & Chasse, V. (2000). Ethnicity-related sources of stress and their effects on well-being. *Current Directions in Psychological Science, 9,* 136–139.

Conway, F., & Siegelman, J. (1979). *Snapping: America's epidemic of sudden personality change.* New York: Delta Books.

Conway, L. G., III, Suedfeld, P., & Tetlock, P. E. (2001). Integrative complexity and political decisions that lead to war or peace. In D. J. Christie, R. V. Wagner, & D. Winter (Eds.), *Peace, conflict, and violence: Peace psychology for the 21st century.* Englewood Cliffs, NJ: Prentice-Hall.

Conway, M., & Ross, M. (1986). Remembering one's own past: The construction of personal histories. In R. Sorrentino & E. T. Higgins (Eds.), *Handbook of motivation and cognition.* New York: Guilford.

Cook, K. (2014). *Kitty Genovese: The murder, the bystanders, the crime that changed America.* New York: Norton.

Cooke, L., Chambers, L., Anez, E., Croker, H., Boniface, D., Yeomans, M., & Wardle, J. (2011). Eating for pleasure or profit: The effect of incentives on children's enjoyment of vegetables. *Psychological Science, 22,* 190–196.

Cooley, C. H. (1902). *Human nature and the social order.* New York: Schocken Books.

Coombs, R. H. (1991, January). Marital status and personal well-being: A literature review. *Family Relations, 40,* 97–102.

Cooper, H. (1983). Teacher expectation effects. In L. Bickman (Ed.), *Applied social psychology annual* (Vol. 4). Beverly Hills, CA: Sage.

Cooper, J. (1999). Unwanted consequences and the self: In search of the motivation for dissonance reduction. In E. Harmon-Jones & J. Mills (Eds.), *Cognitive dissonance: Progress on a pivotal theory in social psychology.* Washington, DC: American Psychological Association.

Correll, J., Park, B., Judd, C. M., & Wittenbrink, B. (2002). The police officer's dilemma: Using ethnicity to disambiguate potentially threatening individuals. *Journal of Personality and Social Psychology, 83,* 1314–1329.

Correll, J., Park, B., Judd, C. M., & Wittenbrink, B. (2007). The influence of stereotypes on decisions to shoot. *European Journal of Social Psychology, 37,* 1102–1117.

Costa-Lopes, R., Dovidio, J. F., Pereira, C., & Jost, J. T. (2013). Social psychological perspectives on the legitimation of social inequality: Past, present and future. *European Journal of Social Psychology, 43,* 229–237.

Costanzo, M. (1997). *Just revenge: Costs and consequences of the death penalty.* New York: St. Martin's.

Costanzo, M. (1998). *Just revenge.* New York: St. Martins.

Costello, C., Gaines, S. D., & Lynham, J. (2008). Can catch shares prevent fisheries' collapse? *Science, 321,* 1678–1682.

Coster, H. (2014, May 14). Peer pressure can be a lifesaver. *New York Times.*

Cota, A. A., & Dion, K. L. (1986). Salience of gender and sex composition of ad hoc groups: An experimental test of distinctiveness theory. *Journal of Personality and Social Psychology, 50,* 770–776.

Cotton, J. L. (1981). Ambient temperature and violent crime. Paper presented at the Midwestern Psychological Association convention, Chicago, IL.

Cotton, J. L. (1986). Ambient temperature and violent crime. *Journal of Applied Social Psychology, 16,* 786–801.

Cottrell, N. B., Wack, D. L., Sekerak, G. J., & Rittle, R. M. (1968). Social facilitation of dominant responses by the presence of an audience and the mere presence of others. *Journal of Personality and Social Psychology, 9,* 245–250.

Coulter, K. S., & Grewal, D. (2014). Name-letters and birthday-numbers: Implicit egotism effects in pricing. *Journal of Marketing, 78,* 102–120.

Coumou, D., & Rahmstorf, S. (2012). A decade of weather extremes. *Nature Climate Change, 2,* 491–496.

Courbet, D., Fourquet-Courbet, M. P., Kazan, R., & Intartaglia, J. (2014). The long-term effects of e-advertising: The influence of Internet pop-ups viewed at a low level of attention in implicit memory. *Journal of Computer-Mediated Communication, 19,* 274–293.

Cousins, N. (1978, September 16). The taxpayers revolt: Act two. *Saturday Review,* p. 56.

Cox, C. R., Van Enkevort, E. A., Hicks, J. A., Kahn-Weintraub, M., & Morin, A. (2014). The relationship between alcohol cues, alcohol expectancies, and physical balance. *Experimental and Clinical Psychopharmacology, 22,* 307–315

Coyne, S. M., & Archer, J. (2005). The relationship between indirect and physical aggression on television and in real life. *Social Development, 14,* 324–338.

Coyne, S. M., Nelson, D. A., Lawton, F., Haslam, S., Rooney, L., Titterington, L., & . . . Ogunlaja, L. (2008). The effects of viewing physical and relational aggression in the media: Evidence for a cross-over effect. *Journal of Experimental Social Psychology, 44,* 1551–1554.

Coyne, S. M., Ridge, R., Stevens, M., Callister, M., & Stockdale, L. (2012). Backbiting and bloodshed in books: Short-term effects of reading physical and relational aggression in literature. *British Journal of Social Psychology, 51,* 188–196.

Crabtree, S. (2002, January 22). Gender roles reflected in teen tech use. *Gallup Tuesday Briefing* (www.gallup.com).

Craig, M. A., & Richeson, J. A. (2012). Coalition or derogation? How perceived discrimination influences intraminority intergroup relations. *Journal of Personality and Social Psychology, 102,* 759–777.

Craig, M. A., & Richeson, J. A. (2014). On the precipice of a "majority-minority" America: Perceived status threat from the racial demographic shift affects White Americans' political ideology. *Psychological Science, 25,* 1189–1197.

Craig, W., & Harel, Y. (2004). Bullying, physical fighting, and victimization. In C. Currie (Ed.), *Young people's health in context: International report from the HSBC 2001/2 survey. WHO Policy Series: Health policy for children and adolescents issue 4.* Copenhagen: WHO Regional Office for Europe.

Crandall, C. S. (1988). Social contagion of binge eating. *Journal of Personality and Social Psychology, 55,* 588–598.

Crandall, C. S., & Eshleman, A. (2003). A justification–suppression model of the expression and experience of prejudice. *Psychological Bulletin, 129,* 414–446.

Crano, W. D., & Mellon, P. M. (1978). Causal influence of teachers' expectations on children's academic performance: A cross-legged panel analysis. *Journal of Educational Psychology, 70,* 39–49.

CRED. (2014). *Connecting on climate: A guide to effective climate change communication.* New York: Center for Research on Environmental Decisions, Earth Institute, Columbia University.

Crisp, R. J., Birtel, M. D., & Meleady, R. (2011). Mental simulations of social thought and action: Trivial tasks or tools for transforming social policy? *Current Directions in Psychological Science, 20,* 261–264.

Crisp, R. J., & Hewstone, M. (1999). Differential evaluation of crossed category groups: Patterns, processes, and reducing intergroup bias. *Group Processes & Intergroup Relations, 2,* 307–333.

Crisp, R. J., & Hewstone, M. (2000). Multiple categorization and social identity. In D. Capozza & R. Brown (Eds.), *Social identity theory: Trends in theory and research.* Beverly Hills, CA: Sage.

Critcher, C. R., & Dunning, D. (2013). Predicting persons' versus a person's goodness: Behavioral forecasts diverge for individuals versus populations. *Journal of Personality and Social Psychology, 104,* 28–44.

Crocker, J. (1981). Judgment of covariation by social perceivers. *Psychological Bulletin, 90,* 272–292.

Crocker, J. (2002). The costs of seeking self-esteem. *Journal of Social Issues, 58,* 597–615.

Crocker, J. (2011). Presidential address: Self-image and compassionate goals and construction of the social self: Implications for social and personality psychology. *Personality and Social Psychology Review, 15,* 394–407.

Crocker, J., & Gallo, L. (1985). The self-enhancing effect of downward comparison. Paper presented at the American Psychological Association convention, Los Angeles, California.

Crocker, J., Hannah, D. B., & Weber, R. (1983). Personal memory and causal attributions. *Journal of Personality and Social Psychology, 44,* 55–56.

Crocker, J., & Knight, K. M. (2005). Contingencies of self-worth. *Current Directions in Psychological Science, 14,* 200–203.

Crocker, J., & Luhtanen, R. (1990). Collective self-esteem and ingroup bias. *Journal of Personality and Social Psychology, 58,* 60–67.

Crocker, J., & Luhtanen, R. (2003). Level of self-esteem and contingencies of self-worth: Unique effects on academic, social, and financial problems in college students. *Personality and Social Psychology Bulletin, 29,* 701–712.

Crocker, J., & McGraw, K. M. (1984). What's good for the goose is not good for the gander: Solo status as an obstacle to occupational achievement for males and females. *American Behavioral Scientist, 27,* 357–370.

Crocker, J., & Park, L. E. (2004). The costly pursuit of self-esteem. *Psychological Bulletin, 130,* 392–414.

Crocker, J., Thompson, L. L., McGraw, K. M., & Ingerman, C. (1987). Downward comparison, prejudice, and evaluations of others: Effects of self-esteem and threat. *Journal of Personality and Social Psychology, 52,* 907–916.

Crocker, J., & Wolfe, C. (2001). Contingencies of self-worth. *Psychological Review.*

Crockett, M. J., Clark, L., Tabibnia, G., Lieberman, M. D., & Robbins, T. W. (2008). Serotonin modulates behavioral reactions to unfairness. *Science, 320,* 1739.

Crompton, T., & Kasser, T. (2010, July/August). Human identity: A missing link in environmental campaigning. *Environment Magazine,* pp. 23–33 (www .environmentmagazine.org).

Crosby, F., Bromley, S., & Saxe, L. (1980). Recent unobtrusive studies of black and white discrimination and prejudice: A literature review. *Psychological Bulletin, 87,* 546–563.

Crosby, F. J. (Ed.) (1987). *Spouse, parent, worker: On gender and multiple roles.* New Haven, CT: Yale University Press.

Crosby, J. R., & Monin, B. (2007). Failure to warn: How student race affects warnings of potential academic difficulty. *Journal of Experimental Social Psychology, 43,* 663–670.

Cross, C. P., Copping, L. T., & Campbell, A. (2011). Sex differences in impulsivity: A meta-analysis. *Psychological Bulletin, 137,* 97–130.

Cross, S. E., Liao, M-H., & Josephs, R. (1992). A cross-cultural test of the self-evaluation maintenance model. Paper presented at the American Psychological Association convention, Washington, DC.

Crossen, C. (1993). *Tainted truth: The manipulation of face in America.* New York: Simon & Schuster.

Croxton, J. S., Eddy, T., & Morrow, N. (1984). Memory biases in the reconstruction of interpersonal encounters. *Journal of Social and Clinical Psychology, 2,* 348–354.

Croyle, R. T., & Cooper, J. (1983). Dissonance arousal: Physiological evidence. *Journal of Personality and Social Psychology, 45,* 782–791.

Cruwys, T., Haslam, S. A., Dingle, G. A., Haslam, C., & Jetten, J. (2014). Depression and social identity: An integrative review. *Personality and Social Psychology Review, 18,* 215–238.

Csikszentmihalyi, M. (1990). *Flow: The psychology of optimal experience.* New York: Harper & Row.

Csikszentmihalyi, M. (1999). If we are so rich, why aren't we happy? *American Psychologist, 54,* 821–827.

Cuddy, A. J. C., & 23 others. (2009). Stereotype content model across cultures: Towards universal similarities and some differences. *British Journal of Social Psychology, 48,* 1–33.

Cullum, J., & Harton, H. C. (2007). Cultural evolution: Interpersonal influence, issue importance, and the development of shared attitudes in college residence halls. *Personality and Social Psychology Bulletin, 33,* 1327–1339.

Cunningham, J. D. (1981). Self-disclosure intimacy: Sex, sex-of-target, cross-national, and generational differences. *Personality and Social Psychology Bulletin, 7,* 314–319.

Cunningham, M. R., Shaffer, D. R., Barbee, A. P., Wolff, P. L., & Kelley, D. J. (1990). Separate processes in the relation of elation and depression to helping: Social versus personal concerns. *Journal of Experimental Social Psychology, 26,* 13–33.

Cutler, B. L., & Kovera, M. B. (2011). Expert psychological testimony. *Current Directions in Psychological Science, 20,* 53–57.

Cutler, B. L., Moran, G., & Narvy, D. J. (1992). Jury selection in insanity defense cases. *Journal of Research in Personality, 26,* 165–182.

Cutler, B. L., & Penrod, S. D. (1988). Context reinstatement and eyewitness identification. In G. M. Davies & D. M. Thomson (Eds.), *Context reinstatement and eyewitness identification.* New York: Wiley.

Cutler, B. L., Penrod, S. D., & Dexter, H. R. (1989). The eyewitness, the expert psychologist and the jury. *Law and Human Behavior, 13,* 311–332.

Cutrona, C. E. (1986). Behavioral manifestations of social support: A microanalytic investigation. *Journal of Personality and Social Psychology, 51,* 201–208.

Dabbs, J. M., Jr. (1992). Testosterone measurements in social and clinical psychology. *Journal of Social and Clinical Psychology, 11,* 302–321.

Dabbs, J. M., Jr. (2000). Heroes, rogues, and lovers: Testosterone and behavior. New York: McGraw-Hill.

Dabbs, J. M., Jr., Carr, T. S., Frady, R. L., & Riad, J. K. (1995). Testosterone, crime, and misbehavior among 692 male prison inmates. *Personality and Individual Differences, 18,* 627–633.

Dabbs, J. M., Jr., Riad, J. K., & Chance, S. E. (2001). Testosterone and ruthless homicide. *Personality and Individual Differences, 31,* 599–603.

Dabbs, J. M., Jr., Strong, R., & Milun, R. (1997). Exploring the mind of testosterone: A beeper study. *Journal of Research in Personality, 31,* 577–588.

D'Abreu, L. F., & Krahé, B. (2014). Predicting sexual aggression in male college students in Brazil. *Psychology of Men & Masculinity, 15,* 152–162.

Dalrymple, T. (2007). On evil. *New English Review* (www.newenglishreview.org).

Dambrun, M., Kamiejski, R., Haddadi, N., & Duarte, S. (2009). Why does social dominance orientation decrease with university exposure to the social sciences? The impact of institutional socialization and the mediating role of "geneticism." *European Journal of Social Psychology, 39,* 88–100.

Dambrun, M., & Vatiné, E. (2010). Reopening the study of extreme social behaviors: Obedience to authority within an immersive video environment. *European Journal of Social Psychology, 40,* 760–773.

Damon, W. (1995). *Greater expectations: Overcoming the culture of indulgence in America's homes and schools.* New York: Free Press.

Dando, C., Wilcock, R., & Milne, R. (2009). The cognitive interview: The efficacy of a modified mental reinstatement of context procedure for frontline police investigators. *Applied Cognitive Psychology, 23,* 138–147.

Danner, D. D., Snowdon, D. A., & Friesen, W. V. (2001). Positive emotions in early life and longevity: Findings from the Nun Study. *Journal of Personality and Social Psychology, 80,* 804–813.

Danziger, S., Levay, J., & Avnaim-Pesso, L. (2011). Extraneous factors in judicial decisions. *Proceedings of the National Academy of Sciences USA, 108,* 6889–6892.

Dardenne, B., Dumont, M., & Bollier, T. (2007). Insidious dangers of benevolent sexism: Consequences for women's performance. *Journal of Personality and Social Psychology, 93,* 764–779.

Darley, J., & Alter, A. (2009). Behavioral issues of punishment and deterrence. In E. Shafir (Ed.), *The behavioral foundations of policy.* Princeton, NJ: Princeton University Press.

Darley, J. M. (1995). Book review essay. *Political Psychology.*

Darley, J. M., & Batson, C. D. (1973). From Jerusalem to Jericho: A study of situational and dispositional variables in helping behavior. *Journal of Personality and Social Psychology, 27,* 100–108.

Darley, J. M., & Berscheid, E. (1967). Increased liking as a result of the anticipation of personal contact. *Human Relations, 20,* 29–40.

Darley, J. M., & Gross, P. H. (1983). A hypothesis-confirming bias in labelling effects. *Journal of Personality and Social Psychology, 44,* 20–33.

Darley, J. M., & Latané, B. (1968). Bystander intervention in emergencies: Diffusion of responsibility. *Journal of Personality and Social Psychology, 8,* 377–383.

Darrow, C. (1933), cited by E. H. Sutherland & D. R. Cressy, *Principles of criminology.* Philadelphia: Lippincott, 1966, 442.

Darwin, C. (1859/1988). *The origin of species.* Vol. 15 of *The Works of Charles Darwin,* edited by P. H. Barrett & R. B. Freeman. New York: New York University Press.

Dasgupta, N., & Rivera, L. M. (2006). From automatic antigay prejudice to behavior: The moderating role of conscious beliefs about gender and behavioral control. *Journal of Personality and Social Psychology, 91,* 268–280.

Dashiell, J. F. (1930). An experimental analysis of some group effects. *Journal of Abnormal and Social Psychology, 25,* 190–199.

Davey, G., & Rato, R. (2012). Subjective well-being in China: A review. *Journal of Happiness Studies, 13,* 333–346.

Davidson, R. J., Putnam, K. M., & Larson, C. L. (2000). Dysfunction in the neural circuitry of emotion regulation—A possible prelude to violence. *Science, 289,* 591–594.

Davies, M. F. (1997). Belief persistence after evidential discrediting: The impact of generated versus provided explanations on the likelihood of discredited outcomes. *Journal of Experimental Social Psychology, 33,* 561–578.

Davies, P. (2004, April 14). Into the 21st century. *Metaviews* (www.metanexus.net).

Davies, P. (2007). *Cosmic jackpot: Why our universe is just right for life.* Boston: Houghton-Mifflin.

Davila, J., Bradbury, T. N., Cohan, C. L., & Tochluk, S. (1997). Marital functioning and depressive symptoms: Evidence for a stress generation model. *Journal of Personality and Social Psychology, 73,* 849–861.

Davis, B. M., & Gilbert, L. A. (1989). Effect of dispositional and situational influences on women's dominance expression in mixed-sex dyads. *Journal of Personality and Social Psychology, 57,* 294–300.

Davis, C. G., Lehman, D. R., Silver, R. C., Wortman, C. B., & Ellard, J. H. (1996). Self-blame following a traumatic event: The role of perceived avoidability. *Personality and Social Psychology Bulletin, 22,* 557–567.

Davis, C. G., Lehman, D. R., Wortman, C. B., Silver, R. C., & Thompson, S. C. (1995). The undoing of traumatic life events. *Personality and Social Psychology Bulletin, 21,* 109–124.

Davis, D., Loftus, E. F., Vanous, S., & Cucciare, M. (2008). "Unconscious transference" can be an instance of "change blindness." *Applied Cognitive Psychology, 22,* 605–623.

Davis, J. A. (2004). Did growing up in the 1960s leave a permanent mark on attitudes and values? Evidence from the GSS. *Public Opinion Quarterly, 68,* 161–183.

Davis, J. H., Kameda, T., Parks, C., Stasson, M., & Zimmerman, S. (1989). Some social mechanics of group decision making: The distribution of opinion, polling sequence, and implications for consensus. *Journal of Personality and Social Psychology, 57,* 1000–1012.

Davis, J. H., Kerr, N. L., Atkin, R. S., Holt, R., & Meek, D. (1975). The decision processes of 6- and 12-person mock juries assigned unanimous and two-thirds majority rules. *Journal of Personality and Social Psychology, 32,* 1–14.

Davis, J. H., Kerr, N. L., Stasser, G., Meek, D., & Holt, R. (1977). Victim consequences, sentence severity, and decision process in mock juries. *Organizational Behavior and Human Performance, 18,* 346–365.

Davis, J. H., Stasson, M. F., Parks, C. D., Hulbert, L., Kameda, T., Zimmerman, S. K., & Ono, K. (1993). Quantitative decisions by groups and individuals: Voting procedures and monetary awards by mock civil juries. *Journal of Experimental Social Psychology, 29,* 326–346.

Davis, J. L., & Rusbult, C. E. (2001). Attitude alignment in close relationships. *Journal of Personality and Social Psychology, 81,* 65–84.

Davis, K. E. (1985, February). Near and dear: Friendship and love compared. *Psychology Today,* pp. 22–30.

Davis, K. E., & Jones, E. E. (1960). Changes in interpersonal perception as a means of reducing cognitive dissonance. *Journal of Abnormal and Social Psychology, 61,* 402–410.

Davis, L., & Greenlees, C. (1992). *Social loafing revisited: Factors that mitigate—and reverse—performance loss.* Paper presented at the Southwestern Psychological Association convention, Austin, Texas.

Davis, M. H., & Franzoi, S. L. (1986). Adolescent loneliness, self-disclosure, and private self-consciousness: A longitudinal investigation. *Journal of Personality and Social Psychology, 51,* 595–608.

Dawes, R. (1998, October). The social usefulness of self-esteem: A skeptical view. *Harvard Mental Health Letter,* pp. 4–5.

Dawes, R. M. (1976). Shallow psychology. In J. S. Carroll & J. W. Payne (Eds.), *Cognition and social behavior.* Hillsdale, NJ: Erlbaum.

Dawes, R. M. (1980a). Social dilemmas. *Annual Review of Psychology, 31,* 169–193.

Dawes, R. M. (1980b). You can't systematize human judgment: Dyslexia. In R. A. Shweder (Ed.), *New directions for methodology of social and behavioral science: Fallible judgment in behavioral research.* San Francisco: Jossey-Bass.

Dawes, R. M. (1990). The potential nonfalsity of the false consensus effect. In R. M. Hogarth (Ed.), *Insights in decision making: A tribute to Hillel J. Einhorn.* Chicago: University of Chicago Press.

Dawes, R. M. (1994). *House of cards: Psychology and psychotherapy built on myth.* New York: Free Press.

Dawes, R. M. (2005). The ethical implications of Paul Meehl's work on comparing clinical versus actuarial prediction methods. *Journal of Clinical Psychology, 61,* 1245–1255.

Dawes, R. M., McTavish, J., & Shaklee, H. (1977). Behavior, communication, and assumptions about other people's behavior in a commons dilemma situation. *Journal of Personality and Social Psychology, 35,* 1–11.

Dawkins, R. (1976). *The selfish gene.* New York: Oxford University Press.

Dawkins, R. (1993). Gaps in the mind. In P. Cavalieri & P. Singer (Eds.), *The Great Ape Project: Equality beyond Humanity.* London: Fourth Estate, 80–87.

Dawson, N. V., Arkes, H. R., Siciliano, C., Blinkhorn, R., Lakshmanan, M., & Petrelli, M. (1988). Hindsight bias: An impediment to accurate probability estimation in clinicopathologic conferences. *Medical Decision Making, 8,* 259–264.

Dearden, J., & Payne, J. (2009). Alcohol and homicide in Australia. *Trends & issues in crime and criminal justice* no. 372. Canberra: Australian Institute of Criminology. http://www.aic.gov.au/publications/current series/tandi/361-380/tandi372.aspx

Deary, I. J. (2005). Intelligence, health and death. *Psychologist, 18,* 610–613.

Deary, I. J., Batty, G. D., & Gale, C. R. (2008). Bright children become enlightened adults. *Psychological Science, 19,* 1–6.

De Assis, S., Warri, A., Cruz, M. I., Laja, O., Tian, Y., Zhang, B., Wang, Y., Huang, T. H., & Hilakivi-Clarke, L. (2012). High-fat or ethinyl-oestradiol intake during pregnancy increases mammary cancer risk in several generations of offspring. *Nature Communications, 3,* doi:10.1038/ncomms2058.

Deaton, A. (2009). Religion and wellbeing. Unpublished manuscript, Princeton University.

Deaux, K., & LaFrance, M. (1998). Gender. In D. Gilbert, S. Fiske, & G. Lindzey (Eds.), *The handbook of social psychology,* 4th ed. Hillsdale, NJ: Erlbaum.

DeBruine, L. M. (2002). Facial resemblance enhances trust. *Proceedings of the Royal Society of London, 269,* 1307–1312.

DeBruine, L. M. (2004). Facial resemblance increases the attractiveness of same-sex faces more than other-sex faces. *Proceedings of the Royal Society of London, B, 271(1552),* 2085–2090.

Decety, J., & Cowell, J. M. (2014). Friends or foes: Is empathy necessary for moral behavior? *Perspectives on Psychological Science, 9,* 525–537.

Decety, J., & Sommerville, J. A. (2003). Shared representations between self and other: A social cognitive neuroscience view. *Trends in Cognitive Sciences, 7,* 527–533.

Dechêne, A., Stahl, C., Hansen, J., & Wänke, M. (2010). The truth about the truth: A meta-analysis review of the truth effect. *Personality and Social Psychology Review, 14,* 238–257.

Deci, E. L., & Ryan, R. M. (1985). Intrinsic motivation and self-determination in human behavior. New York: Plenum.

Deci, E. L., & Ryan, R. M. (1991). A motivational approach to self: Integration in personality. In R. Dienstbier (Ed.) *Perspectives on motivation: Nebraska Symposium on Motivation* (Vol. 38, pp. 237–288). Lincoln, NE: University of Nebraska Press.

Deci, E. L., & Ryan, R. M. (2008). Facilitating optimal motivation and psychological well-being across life's domains. *Canadian Psychology, 49,* 14–23.

Deci, E. L., & Ryan, R. M. (2012). Self-determination theory. In P. A. Van Lange, A. W. Kruglanski, & E. T. Higgins (Eds.), *Handbook of theories of social psychology (Vol. 1).* Thousand Oaks, CA: Sage.

Deci, E. L., & Ryan, R. M. (Eds.) (2002). *Handbook of self-determination research.* Rochester, NY: University of Rochester Press.

De Cremer, D. (2002). Charismatic leadership and cooperation in social dilemmas: A matter of transforming motives? *Journal of Applied Social Psychology, 32,* 997–1016.

de Hoogh, A. H. B., den Hartog, D. N., Koopman, P. L., Thierry, H., van den Berg, P. T., van der Weide, J. G., & Wilderom, C. P. M. (2004). Charismatic leadership, environmental dynamism, and performance. *European Journal of Work and Organisational Psychology, 13,* 447–471.

de Hoog, N., Stroebe, W., & de Wit, J. F. (2007). The impact of vulnerability to and severity of a health risk on processing and acceptance of fear-arousing communications: A meta-analysis. *Review of General Psychology, 11,* 258–285.

De Houwer, J., Thomas, S., & Baeyens, F. (2001). Associative learning of likes and dislikes: A review of 25 years of research on human evaluative conditioning. *Psychological Bulletin, 127,* 853–869.

Dehue, F., Bolman, C., & Vollink, T. (2008). Cyberbulling: Youngsters' experiences and parental perception. *Cyberpsychology & Behavior, 11,* 217–223.

de Lange, M. A., Debets, L. W., Ruitenburg, K., & Holland, R. W. (2012). Making less of a mess: Scent exposure as a tool for behavioral change. *Social Influence, 7,* 90–97.

Delgado, J. (1973). In M. Pines, *The brain changers.* New York: Harcourt Brace Jovanovich.

DeLisi, M., Vaughn, M. G., Gentile, D. A., Anderson, C. A., & Shook, J. J. (2013). Violent video games, delinquency, and youth violence: New evidence. *Youth Violence and Juvenile Justice, 11,* 132–142.

Demoulin, S., Saroglou, V., & Van Pachterbeke, M. (2008). Infra-humanizing others, supra-humanizing gods: The emotional hierarchy. *Social Cognition, 26,* 235–247.

Denissen, J. J. A., Penke, L., Schmitt, D. P., & van Aken, M. A. G. (2008). Self-esteem reactions to social interactions: Evidence for sociometer mechanisms across days, people, and nations. *Journal of Personality and Social Psychology, 95,* 181–196.

Dennett, D. (2005, December 26). Spiegel interview with evolution philosopher Daniel Dennett: Darwinism completely refutes intelligent design. *Der Spiegel* (www.service.dspiegel.de).

Denrell, J. (2008). Indirect social influence. *Science, 321,* 47–48.

Denrell, J., & Le Mens, G. (2007). Interdependent sampling and social influence. *Psychological Review, 114,* 398–422.

Denson, T. F., Pedersen, W. C., & Miller, N. (2006). The displaced aggression questionnaire. *Journal of Personality and Social Psychology, 90,* 1032–1051.

Denson, T. F., Pedersen, W. C., Ronquillo, J., & Nandy, A. S. (2009). The angry brain: Neural correlates of anger, angry rumination, and aggressive personality. *Journal of Cognitive Neuroscience, 21,* 734–744.

Department of Canadian Heritage. (2006). What is multiculturalism? (www.pch.gc.ca).

DePaulo, B. (2006). *Singled out: How singles are stereotyped, stigmatized, and ignored, and still live happily ever after.* New York: St. Martin's.

Derks, B., Inzlicht, M., & Kang, S. (2008). The neuroscience of stigma and stereotype threat. *Group Processes and Intergroup Relations, 11,* 163–181.

Derlega, V., Metts, S., Petronio, S., & Margulis, S. T. (1993). *Self-disclosure.* Newbury Park, CA: Sage.

Dermer, M., Cohen, S. J., Jacobsen, E., & Anderson, E. A. (1979). Evaluative judgments of aspects of life as a function of vicarious exposure to hedonic extremes. *Journal of Personality and Social Psychology, 37,* 247–260.

Dermer, M., & Pyszczynski, T. A. (1978). Effects of erotica upon men's loving and liking responses for women they love. *Journal of Personality and Social Psychology, 36,* 1302–1309.

Desforges, D. M., Lord, C. G., Pugh, M. A., Sia, T. L., Scarberry, N. C., & Ratcliff, C. D. (1997). Role of group representativeness in the generalization part of the contact hypothesis. *Basic and Applied Social Psychology, 19,* 183–204.

Desforges, D. M., Lord, C. G., Ramsey, S. L., Mason, J. A., Van Leeuwen, M. D., West, S. C., & Lepper, M. R. (1991). Effects of structured cooperative contact on changing negative attitudes toward stigmatized social groups. *Journal of Personality and Social Psychology, 60,* 531–544.

de Sherbinin, A., & 17 others. (2011). Preparing for resettlement associated with climate change. *Science, 334,* 456–457.

Desmarais, S. L., & Read, J. D. (2011). After 30 years, what do we know about what jurors know? A meta-analytic review of lay knowledge regarding eyewitness factors. *Law and Human Behavior, 35,* 200–210.

DeSteno, D., Petty, R. E., Wegener, D. T., & Rucker, D. D. (2000). Beyond valence in the perception of likelihood: The role of emotion specificity. *Journal of Personality and Social Psychology, 78,* 397–416.

Deters, F. G., & Mehl, M. R. (2013). Does posting Facebook status updates increase or decrease loneliness? An online social networking experiment. *Social Psychological and Personality Science, 4,* 579–586.

Detweiler, J. B., Bedell, B. T., Salovey, P., Pronin, E., & Rothman, A. J. (1999). Message framing and sunscreen use: Gain-framed messages motivate beach-goers. *Health Psychology, 18,* 189–196.

Deutsch, M. (1985). *Distributive justice: A social psychological perspective.* New Haven: Yale University Press.

Deutsch, M. (1986). Folie à deux: A psychological perspective on Soviet-American relations. In M. P. Kearns (Ed.), *Persistent patterns and emergent structures in a waning century.* New York: Praeger.

Deutsch, M. (1993). Educating for a peaceful world. *American Psychologist, 48,* 510–517.

Deutsch, M. (1994). Constructive conflict resolution: Principles, training, and research. *Journal of Social Issues, 50,* 13–32.

Deutsch, M. (1999). Behind the scenes. In D. G. Myers, *Social Psychology,* 6th edition. New York: McGraw-Hill.

Deutsch, M., & Collins, M. E. (1951). *Interracial housing: A psychological evaluation of a social experiment.* Minneapolis: University of Minnesota Press.

Deutsch, M., & Gerard, H. B. (1955). A study of normative and informational social influence upon individual judgment. *Journal of Abnormal and Social Psychology, 51,* 629–636.

Deutsch, M., & Krauss, R. M. (1960). The effect of threat upon interpersonal bargaining. *Journal of Abnormal and Social Psychology, 61,* 181–189.

Devenport, J. L., Stinson, V., Cutler, B. L., & Kravitz, D. A. (2002). How effective are the cross-examination and expert testimony safeguards? Jurors' perceptions of the suggestiveness and fairness of biased lineup procedures. *Journal of Applied Psychology, 87,* 1042–1054.

Devine, P. A., Brodish, A. B., & Vance, S. L. (2005). Self-regulatory processes in interracial interactions: The role of internal and external motivation to respond without prejudice. In J. P. Forgas, K. D. Williams, & S. M. Laham (Eds.), *Social motivation: Conscious and unconscious processes.* New York: Cambridge University Press.

Devine, P. G. (1989). Stereotypes and prejudice: Their automatic and controlled components. *Journal of Personality and Social Psychology, 56,* 5–18.

Devine, P. G., Evett, S. R., & Vasquez-Suson, K. A. (1996). Exploring the interpersonal dynamics of intergroup contact. In R. Sorrentino & E. T. Higgins (Eds.), *Handbook of motivation and cognition: The interpersonal content* (Vol. 3). New York: Guilford.

Devine, P. G., Forscher, P. S., Austin, A. J., & Cox, W. T. L. (2012). Long-term reduction in implicit race bias: A prejudice habit-breaking intervention. *Journal of Experimental Social Psychology, 48,* 1267–1278.

De Vogli, R., Chandola, T., & Marmot, M. G. (2007). Negative aspects of close relationships and heart disease. *Archives of Internal Medicine, 167,* 1951–1957.

Devos-Comby, L., & Salovey, P. (2002). Applying persuasion strategies to alter HIV-relevant thoughts and behavior. *Review of General Psychology, 6,* 287–304.

Devries, K. M., & 13 others. (2013). The global prevalence of intimate partner violence against women. *Science, 340,* 1527.

De Waal, F. (2014a, September). One for all. *Scientific American,* 69–71.

De Waal, F. (2014b). *The Bonobo and the atheist: In search of humanism among the primates.* New York: Norton.

DeWall, C., MacDonald, G., Webster, G. D., Masten, C. L., Baumeister, R. F., Powell, C., & . . . Eisenberger, N. I. (2010). Acetaminophen reduces social pain: Behavioral and neural evidence. *Psychological Science, 21,* 931–937.

DeWall, C. N., Baumeister, R. F., Stillman, T. F., & Gailliot, M. T. (2007). Violence restrained: Effects of self-regulation and its depletion on aggression. *Journal of Experimental Social Psychology, 43,* 62–76.

DeWall, C. N., & Bushman, B. J. (2011). Social acceptance and rejection: The sweet and the bitter. *Current Directions in Psychological Science, 20,* 256–260.

DeWall, C. N., Bushman, B. J., Giancola, P. R., & Webster, G. D. (2010). The big, the bad, and the boozed-up: Weight moderates the effect of alcohol on aggression. *Journal of Experimental Social Psychology, 46,* 619–623.

DeWall, C. N., Lambert, N. M., Slotter, E. B., Pond, R. S., Deckman, T., Finkel, E. J., Luchies, L. B., & Fincham, F. D. (2011). So far away from one's partner, yet so close to romantic alternatives: Avoidant attachment, interest in alternatives, and infidelity. *Journal of Personality and Social Psychology, 101,* 1302–1316.

DeWall, C. N., Maner, J. K., & Rouby, D. A. (2009). Social exclusion and early-stage interpersonal perception: Selective attention to signs of acceptance. *Journal of Personality and Social Psychology, 96,* 729–741.

DeWall, C. N., Pond, R. S., Jr., Campbell, W. K., & Twenge, J. M. (2011). Tuning in to psychological change: Linguistic markers of psychological traits and emotions over time in popular U.S. song lyrics. *Psychology of Aesthetics, Creativity, and the Arts, 5,* 200–207.

Dexter, H. R., Cutler, B. L., & Moran, G. (1992). A test of voir dire as a remedy for the prejudicial effects of pretrial publicity. *Journal of Applied Social Psychology, 22,* 819–832.

DeYoung, C. G., Peterson, J. B., & Higgins, D. M. (2002). Higher-order factors of the Big Five predict conformity: Are there neuroses of health? *Personality and Individual Differences, 33,* 533–552.

de Zavala, A. G., Cichocka, A., & Iskra-Golec, I. (2013). Collective narcissism moderates the effect of in-group image threat on intergroup hostility. *Journal of Personality and Social Psychology, 104,* 1019–1039.

de Zavala, A. G., Cichocka, A., Orehek, E., & Abdollahi, A. (2012). Intrinsic religiosity reduces intergroup hostility under mortality salience. *European Journal of Social Psychology, 42,* 451–461.

Diamond, J. (1996, December). The best ways to sell sex. *Discover,* 78–86.

Diamond, S. S. (1993). Instructing on death: Psychologists, juries, and judges. *American Psychologist, 48,* 423–434.

Dickerson, S. S., Gable, S. L., Irwin, M. R., Aziz, N., & Kemeny, M. E. (2009). Social-evaluative threat and proinflammatory cytokine regulation: An experimental laboratory investigation. *Psychological Science, 20,* 1237–1243.

Dicum, J. (2003, November 11). Letter to the editor. *New York Times,* p. A20.

Diekman, A. B., Brown, E. R., Johnston, A. M., & Clark, E. K. (2010). Seeking congruity between goals and roles: A new look at why women opt out of science, technology, engineering, and mathematics careers. *Psychological Science, 21,* 1051–1057.

Diekman, A. B., McDonald, M., & Gardner, W. L. (2000). Love means never having to be careful: The relationship between reading romance novels and safe sex behavior. *Psychology of Women Quarterly, 24,* 179–188.

Diekmann, K. A., Samuels, S. M., Ross, L., & Bazerman, M. H. (1997). Self-interest and fairness in problems of resource allocation: Allocators versus recipients. *Journal of Personality and Social Psychology, 72,* 1061–1074.

Diener, E. (1976). Effects of prior destructive behavior, anonymity, and group presence on deindividuation and aggression. *Journal of Personality and Social Psychology, 33,* 497–507.

Diener, E. (1979). Deindividuation, self-awareness, and disinhibition. *Journal of Personality and Social Psychology, 37,* 1160–1171.

Diener, E. (1980). Deindividuation: The absence of self-awareness and self-regulation in group members. In P. Paulus (Ed.), *The psychology of group influence.* Hillsdale, NJ: Erlbaum.

Diener, E. (2005, December 1). Guidelines for national indicators of subjective well-being and ill-being. Department of Psychology, University of Illinois.

Diener, E. (2013). The remarkable changes in the science of well-being. *Perspectives on Psychological Science, 8,* 663–666.

Diener, E., Fraser, S. C., Beaman, A. L., & Kelem, R. T. (1976). Effects of deindividuation variables on stealing among Halloween trick-or-treaters. *Journal of Personality and Social Psychology, 33(2),* 178–183.

Diener, E., Horwitz, J., & Emmons, R. A. (1985). Happiness of the very wealthy. *Social Indicators, 16,* 263–274.

Diener, E., Kesebir, P., & Lucas, R. (2008). Benefits of accounts of well-being—for societies and for psychological science. *Applied Psychology, 57,* 37–53.

Diener, E., Lucas, R. E., & Schimmack, U. (2009). *Well-being for public policy.* Oxford, UK: Oxford University Press.

Diener, E., Lucas, R. E., & Scollon, C. N. (2006). Beyond the hedonic treadmill: Revising the adaptation theory of well-being. *American Psychologist, 61,* 305–314.

Diener, E., & Wallbom, M. (1976). Effects of self-awareness on antinormative behavior. *Journal of Research in Personality, 10,* 107–111.

Dienstbier, R. A., Roesch, S. C., Mizumoto, A., Hemenover, S. H., Lott, R. C., & Carlo, G. (1998). Effects of weapons on guilt judgments and sentencing recommendations for criminals. *Basic and Applied Social Psychology, 20,* 93–102.

Dijksterhuis, A., Smith, P. K., van Baaren, R. B., & Wigboldus, D. H. J. (2005). The unconscious consumer: Effects of environment on consumer behavior. *Journal of Consumer Psychology, 15,* 193–202.

Dillehay, R. C., & Nietzel, M. T. (1980). Constructing a science of jury behavior. In L. Wheeler (Ed.), *Review of personality and social psychology* (Vol. 1). Beverly Hills, CA: Sage.

Dill, J. C., & Anderson, C. A. (1999). Loneliness, shyness, and depression: The etiology and interrelationships of everyday problems in living. In T. Joiner and J. C. Coyne (Eds.) *The interactional nature of depression: Advances in interpersonal approaches.* Washington, DC: American Psychological Association.

Dindia, K., & Allen, M. (1992). Sex differences in self-disclosure: A meta-analysis. *Psychological Bulletin, 112,* 106–124.

Dion, K. K. (1972). Physical attractiveness and evaluations of children's transgressions. *Journal of Personality and Social Psychology, 24,* 207–213.

Dion, K. K., & Berscheid, E. (1974). Physical attractiveness and peer perception among children. *Sociometry, 37,* 1–12.

Dion, K. K., & Dion, K. L. (1985). Personality, gender, and the phenomenology of romantic love. In P. R. Shaver (Ed.) *Review of personality and social psychology* (Vol. 6). Beverly Hills, CA: Sage.

Dion, K. K., & Dion, K. L. (1991). Psychological individualism and romantic love. *Journal of Social Behavior and Personality, 6,* 17–33.

Dion, K. K., & Dion, K. L. (1993). Individualistic and collectivistic perspectives on gender and the cultural context of love and intimacy. *Journal of Social Issues, 49,* 53–69.

Dion, K. K., & Stein, S. (1978). Physical attractiveness and interpersonal influence. *Journal of Experimental Social Psychology, 14,* 97–109.

Dion, K. L. (1979). Intergroup conflict and intragroup cohesiveness. In W. G. Austin & S. Worchel (Eds.), *The social psychology of intergroup relations.* Monterey, CA: Brooks/Cole.

Dion, K. L. (1998). The social psychology of perceived prejudice and discrimination. Colloquium presentation, Carleton University, Ottawa, Ontario.

Dion, K. L., & Dion, K. K. (1988). Romantic love: Individual and cultural perspectives. In R. J. Sternberg & M. L. Barnes (Eds.), *The psychology of love.* New Haven, CT: Yale University Press.

Dishion, T. J., McCord, J., & Poulin, F. (1999). When interventions harm: Peer groups and problem behavior. *American Psychologist, 54,* 755–764.

Dittmar, H., Bond, R., Hurst, M., & Kasser, T. (2014). The relationship between materialism and personal well-being: A meta-analysis. *Journal of Personality and Social Psychology, 107,* 879–924.

Dixon, J., & Durrheim, K. (2003). Contact and the ecology of racial division: Some varieties of informal segregation. *British Journal of Social Psychology, 42,* 1–23.

Dixon, J., Durrheim, K., & Tredoux, C. (2005a). Beyond the optimal contact strategy: A reality check for the contact hypothesis. *American Psychologist, 60,* 697–711.

Dixon, J., Durrheim, K., & Tredoux, C. (2007). Intergroup contact and attitudes toward the principle and practice of racial equality. *Psychological Science, 18,* 867–872.

Dixon, J., Tredoux, C., & Clack, B. (2005b). On the micro-ecology of racial division: A neglected dimension of segregation. *South African Journal of Psychology, 35,* 395–411.

Dixon, J., Tropp, L. R., Durrheim, K., & Tredoux, C. (2010). "Let them eat harmony": Prejudice-reduction strategies and attitudes of historically disadvantaged groups. *Current Directions in Psychological Science, 19,* 76–80.

Dodson, C. S., & Dobolyi, D. G. (2015). Misinterpreting eyewitness expressions of confidence: The featural justification effect. *Law and Human Behavior,*

Doherty, T. J., & Clayton, S. (2011). The psychological impacts of global climate change. *American Psychologist, 66,* 265–276.

Dohrenwend, B., Pearlin, L., Clayton, P., Hamburg, B., Dohrenwend, B. P., Riley, M., & Rose, R. (1982). Report on stress and life events. In G. R. Elliott & C. Eisdorfer (Eds.), *Stress and human health: Analysis and implications of research* (A study by the Institute of Medicine/National Academy of Sciences). New York: Springer.

Dolinski, D. (2000). On inferring one's beliefs from one's attempt and consequences for subsequent compliance. *Journal of Personality and Social Psychology, 78,* 260–272.

Dolinski, D., & Nawrat, R. (1998). "Fear-then-relief" procedure for producing compliance: Beware when the danger is over. *Journal of Experimental Social Psychology, 34,* 27–50.

Dolinski, D., & Szczucka, K. (2012). Fear-then-relief-then-argument: How to sell goods using the EDTR technique of social influence. *Social Influence, 7,* 251–267.

Dollard, J., Doob, L., Miller, N., Mowrer, O. H., & Sears, R. R. (1939). *Frustration and aggression.* New Haven, CT: Yale University Press.

Dolnik, L., Case, T. I., & Williams, K. D. (2003). Stealing thunder as a courtroom tactic revisited: Processes and boundaries. *Law and Human Behavior, 27,* 265–285.

Dominus, S. (2012). What happened to the girls in Le Roy. *New York Times Magazine,* May 7, 2012. Retrieved March 28, 2015 from: http://www.nytimes.com/2012/03/11/magazine/teenage-girls-twitching-le-roy.html?_r=0

Donaldson, Z. R., & Young, L. J. (2008). Oxytocin, vasopressin, and the neurogenetics of sociality. *Science, 322,* 900–904.

Donnelly, K., Twenge, J. M., Clark, M. A., Shaikh, S. K., Beiler, A., & Carter, N. T. (2015). Americans' attitudes towards women's work and family roles, 1976–2013. *Psychology of Women Quarterly.*

Donnerstein, E. (1980). Aggressive erotica and violence against women. *Journal of Personality and Social Psychology, 39,* 269–277.

Donnerstein, E. (2011). The media and aggression: From TV to the Internet. In J. Forgas, A. Kruglanski, & K. Williams (Eds.) *The psychology of social conflict and aggression* (pp. 267–284). New York: Psychology Press.

Donnerstein, E., Linz, D., & Penrod, S. (1987). *The question of pornography.* London: Free Press.

Doob, A. N., & Kirshenbaum, H. M. (1973). Bias in police lineups—Partial remembering. *Journal of Police Science and Administration, 1,* 287–293.

Doob, A. N., & McLaughlin, D. S. (1989). Ask and you shall be given: Request size and donations to a good cause. *Journal of Applied Social Psychology, 19,* 1049–1056.

Doob, A. N., & Roberts, J. (1988). Public attitudes toward sentencing in Canada. In N. Walker & M. Hough (Eds.), *Sentencing and the public.* London: Gower.

D'Orlando, F. (2011). The demand for pornography. *Journal of Happiness Studies, 12,* 51–75.

Douglass, A. B., & Steblay, N. (2006). Memory distortion in eyewitnesses: A meta-analysis of the post-identification feedback effect. *Applied Cognitive Psychology, 20,* 859–869.

Douglass, F. (1845/1960). *Narrative of the life of Frederick Douglass, an American slave: Written by himself.* (B. Quarles, Ed.). Cambridge, MA: Harvard University Press.

Dovidio, J. F. (1991). The empathy-altruism hypothesis: Paradigm and promise. *Psychological Inquiry, 2,* 126–128.

Dovidio, J. F., Gaertner, S. L., Anastasio, P. A., & Sanitioso, R. (1992). Cognitive and motivational bases of bias: Implications of aversive racism for attitudes toward Hispanics. In S. Knouse, P. Rosenfeld, & A. Culbertson (Eds.), *Hispanics in the workplace.* Newbury Park, CA: Sage.

Dovidio, J. F., Gaertner, S. L., Hodson, G., Houlette, M., & Johnson, K. M. (2005). Social inclusion and exclusion: Recategorization and the perception of intergroup boundaries. In D. Abrams, M. A. Hogg, & J. M. Marques (Eds.), *The social psychology of inclusion and exclusion.* New York: Psychology Press.

Dovidio, J. F., Gaertner, S. L., & Saguy, T. (2009). Commonality and the complexity of "we": Social attitudes and social change. *Personality and Social Psychology Bulletin, 13,* 3–20.

Dovidio, J. R., Brigham, J. C., Johnson, B. T., & Gaertner, S. L. (1996). Stereotyping, prejudice, and discrimination: Another look. In N. Macrae, M. Hewstone, & C. Stangor (Eds.), *Stereotypes and stereotyping.* New York: Guilford.

Downs, A. C., & Lyons, P. M. (1991). Natural observations of the links between attractiveness and initial legal judgments. *Personality and Social Psychology Bulletin, 17,* 541–547.

Doyle, J. M. (2005). *True witness: Cops, courts, science, and the battle against misidentification.* New York: Palgrave Macmillan.

Draguns, J. G. (1990). Normal and abnormal behavior in cross-cultural perspective: Specifying the nature of their relationship. *Nebraska Symposium on Motivation 1989, 37,* 235–277.

Dreber, A., Rand, D. G., Fudenberg, D., & Nowak, M. A. (2008). Winners don't punish. *Nature, 452,* 348–351.

Driedger, L. (1975). In search of cultural identity factors: A comparison of ethnic students. *Canadian Review of Sociology and Anthropology, 12,* 150–161.

Driskell, J. E., & Mullen, B. (1990). Status, expectations, and behavior: A meta-analytic review and test of the theory. *Personality and Social Psychology Bulletin, 16,* 541–553.

Drolet, A. L., & Morris, M. W. (2000). Rapport in conflict resolution: Accounting for how face-to-face contact fosters mutual cooperation in mixed-motive conflicts. *Journal of Experimental Social Psychology, 36,* 26–50.

Drury, J., Cocking, C., & Reicher, S. (2009). Everyone for themselves? A comparative study of crowd solidarity among emergency survivors. *British Journal of Social Psychology, 48,* 487–506.

Drydakis, N. (2009). Sexual orientation discrimination in the labour market. *Labour Economics, 16,* 364–372.

Dryer, D. C., & Horowitz, L. M. (1997). When do opposites attract? Interpersonal complementarity versus similarity. *Journal of Personality and Social Psychology, 72,* 592–603.

DuBois, W. E. B. (1903/1961). *The souls of black folk.* Greenwich, CT: Fawcett Books.

Duck, J. M., Hogg, M. A., & Terry, D. J. (1995). Me, us and them: Political identification and the third-person effect in the 1993 Australian federal election. *European Journal of Social Psychology, 25,* 195–215.

Duffy, M. (2003, June 9). Weapons of mass disappearance. *Time,* pp. 28–33.

Dunbar, R. (1992). Neocortex size as a constraint on group size in primates. *Journal of Human Evolution, 22,* 469–493.

Dunbar, R. (2010, December 25). You've got to have (150) friends. *New York Times* (www.nytimes.com).

Duncan, B. L. (1976). Differential social perception and attribution of intergroup violence: Testing the lower limits of stereotyping of blacks. *Journal of Personality and Social Psychology, 34,* 590–598.

Dunfield, K. A., & Kuhlmeier, V. A. (2010). Intention-mediated selective helping in infancy. *Psychological Science, 21,* 523–527.

Dunham, Y., Chen, E. E., & Banaji, M. R. (2013). Two signatures of implicit intergroup attitudes: Developmental invariance and early enculturation. *Psychological Science, 24,* 860–868.

Dunkel, C. S. (2014). Sharing in childhood as precursor to support for national health insurance. *Basic and Applied Social Psychology, 36,* 515–519.

Dunlosky, J., & Rawson, K. A. (2012). Overconfidence produces underachievement: Inaccurate self evaluations undermine students' learning and retention. *Learning and Instruction, 22,* 271–280.

Dunn, E., & Ashton-James, C. (2008). On emotional innumeracy: Predicted and actual affective response to grand-scale tragedies. *Journal of Experimental Social Psychology, 44,* 692–698.

Dunn, E., & Norton, M. (2013). *Happy money: The science of smarter spending.* New York: Simon & Schuster.

Dunn, E. W., Aknin, L. B., & Norton, M. I. (2008). Spending money on others promotes happiness. *Science, 319,* 1687–1688.

Dunn, E. W., Wilson, T. D., & Gilbert, D. T. (2003). Location, location, location: The misprediction of satisfaction in housing lotteries. *Personality and Social Psychology Bulletin, 29,* 1421–1432.

Dunning, D. (1995). Trait importance and modifiability as factors influencing self-assessment and self-enhancement motives. *Personality and Social Psychology Bulletin, 21,* 1297–1306.

Dunning, D. (2005). *Self-insight: Roadblocks and detours on the path to knowing thyself.* London: Psychology Press.

Dunning, D. (2006). Strangers to ourselves? *The Psychologist, 19,* 600–603.

Dunning, D., Meyerowitz, J. A., & Holzberg, A. D. (1989). Ambiguity and self-evaluation. *Journal of Personality and Social Psychology, 57,* 1082–1090.

Dunning, D., Perie, M., & Story, A. L. (1991). Self-serving prototypes of social categories. *Journal of Personality and Social Psychology, 61,* 957–968.

Dunning, D., & Perretta, S. (2002). Automaticity and eyewitness accuracy: A 10- to 12-second rule for distinguishing accurate from inaccurate positive identifications. *Journal of Applied Psychology, 87,* 951–962.

Dunning, D., & Sherman, D. A. (1997). Stereotypes and tacit inference. *Journal of Personality and Social Psychology, 73,* 459–471.

Dunn, J. R., & Schweitzer, M. E. (2005). Feeling and believing: The influence of emotion on trust. *Journal of Personality and Social Psychology, 88,* 736–748.

Dunn, M., & Searle, R. (2010). Effect of manipulated prestige-car ownership on both sex attractiveness ratings. *British Journal of Psychology, 101,* 69–80.

Durante, K. M., Li, N. P., & Haselton, M. G. (2008). Changes in women's dress across the ovulatory cycle: Naturalistic and laboratory task-based evidence. *Personality and Social Psychology Bulletin, 34,* 1451–1460.

Durrheim, K., Tredoux, C., Foster, D., & Dixon, J. (2011). Historical trends in South African race attitudes. *South African Journal of Psychology, 41,* 263–278.

Dutton, D. (2006, January 13). Hardwired to seek beauty. *The Australian* (www.theastralian.news.com.au).

Dutton, D. G. (1971). Reactions of restaurateurs to blacks and whites violating restaurant dress regulations. *Canadian Journal of Behavioural Science, 3,* 298–302.

Dutton, D. G. (1973). Reverse discrimination: The relationship of amount of perceived discrimination toward a minority group and the behavior of majority group members. *Canadian Journal of Behavioural Science, 5,* 34–45.

Dutton, D. G., & Aron, A. P. (1974). Some evidence for heightened sexual attraction under conditions of high anxiety. *Journal of Personality and Social Psychology, 30,* 510–517.

Dutton, D. G., Boyanowsky, E. O., & Bond, M. H. (2005). Extreme mass homicide: From military massacre to genocide. *Aggression and violent behavior, 10,* 437–473.

Dutton, D. G., & Lake, R. A. (1973). Threat of own prejudice and reverse discrimination in interracial situations. *Journal of Personality and Social Psychology, 28,* 94–100.

Duval, S., Duval, V. H., & Neely, R. (1979). Self-focus, felt responsibility, and helping behavior. *Journal of Personality and Social Psychology, 37,* 1769–1778.

Dye, M. W. G., Green, C. S., & Bavelier, D. (2009). Increasing speed of processing with action video games. *Current Directions in Psychological Science, 18,* 321–326.

Eagan, K., Lozano, J. B., Hurtado, S., & Case, M. H. (2014). *The American Freshman: National Norms Fall 2013.* Los Angeles: Higher Education Research Institute, UCLA.

Eagan, K., Stolzenberg, E. B., Ramirez, J. J., Aragon, M. C., Suchard, M. R., & Hurtado, S. (2014). *The American freshman: National norms Fall 2014.* Los Angeles: Higher Education Research Institute, UCLA.

Eagan, K., Stolzenberg, E. B., Ramirez, J. J., Aragon, M. C., Suchard, M. R., & Hurtado, S. (2015). *The American Freshman: National norms fall 2014.* Los Angeles: Higher Education Research Institute.

Eagly, A. H. (1987). Sex differences in social behavior: A social-role interpretation. Hillsdale, NJ: Erlbaum.

Eagly, A. H. (1994). Are people prejudiced against women? Donald Campbell Award invited address, American Psychological Association convention, Los Angeles, California.

Eagly, A. H. (2009). The his and hers of prosocial behavior: An examination of the social psychology of gender. *American Psychologist, 64,* 644–658.

Eagly, A. H., Ashmore, R. D., Makhijani, M. G., & Longo, L. C. (1991). What is beautiful is good, but . . . : A meta-analytic review of research on the physical attractiveness stereotype. *Psychological Bulletin, 110,* 109–128.

Eagly, A. H., & Chaiken, S. (1993). *The psychology of attitudes.* San Diego: Harcourt Brace Jovanovich.

Eagly, A. H., & Chaiken, S. (1998). Attitude structure and function. In D. Gilbert, S. Fiske, & G. Lindzey (Eds.), *The handbook of social psychology,* 4th edition. New York: McGraw-Hill.

Eagly, A. H., & Chaiken, S. (2005). Attitude research in the 21st century: The current state of knowledge. In D. Albarracin, B. T. Johnson, & M. P. Zanna (Eds.), *The handbook of attitudes.* Mahwah, NJ: Erlbaum.

Eagly, A. H., & Crowley, M. (1986). Gender and helping behavior: A meta-analytic review of the social psychological literature. *Psychological Bulletin, 100,* 283–308.

Eagly, A. H., Diekman, A. B., Johannesen-Schmidt, M. C., & Koenig, A. M. (2004). Gender gaps in sociopolitical attitudes: A social psychological analysis. *Journal of Personality and Social Psychology, 87,* 796–816.

Eagly, A. H., & Wood, W. (2013). The nature-nurture debates: 25 years of challenges in understanding the psychology of gender. *Perspective on Psychological Science, 8,* 340–357.

Easterbrook, M., & Vignoles, V. (2015). When friendship formation goes down the toilet: Design features of share accommodation influence interpersonal bonds and well-being. *British Journal of Social Psychology, 54,* 125–139.

Easterlin, R. A., McVey, L. A., Switek, M., Sawangfa, O., & Zweig, J. S. (2010). The happiness-income paradox revisited. *PNAS, 107,* 22463–22468.

Easterlin, R. A., Morgan, R., Switek, M., & Wang, F. (2012). China's life satisfaction, 1990–2010. *PNAS, 109,* 9670–9671.

Eastwick, P. W., & Finkel, E. J. (2008a). Speed-dating as a methodological innovation. *The Psychologist, 21,* 402–403.

Eastwick, P. W., & Finkel, E. J. (2008b). Sex differences in mate preferences revisited: Do people know what they initially desire in a romantic partner? *Journal of Personality and Social Psychology, 94,* 245–264.

Eastwick, P. W., Finkel, E. J., Krishnamurti, T., & Loewenstein, G. (2007). Mispredicting distress following romantic breakup: Revealing the time course of the affective forecasting error. *Journal of Experimental Social Psychology, 44,* 800–807.

Eastwick, P. W., & Hunt, L. L. (2014). Relational mate value: Consensus and uniqueness in romantic evaluations. *Journal of Personality and Social Psychology, 106,* 728–751.

Eastwick, P. W., Luchies, L. B., Finkel, E. J., & Hunt, L. L. (2014). The predictive validity of ideal partner preferences: A review and meta-analysis. *Psychological Bulletin, 140,* 623–665.

Eaton, A. A., Visser, P. S., Krosnick, J. A., & Anand, S. (2009). Social power and attitude strength over the life course. *Personality and Social Psychology Bulletin, 35,* 1646–1660.

Eberhardt, J. L. (2005). Imaging race. *American Psychologist, 60,* 181–190.

Eberhardt, J. L., Davies, P. G., Purdie-Vaughns, V. J., & Johnson, S. L. (2006). Looking deathworthy: Perceived stereotypicality of Black defendants predicts capital-sentencing outcomes. *Psychological Science, 17,* 383–386.

Eberle, D., Berens, G., & Li, T. (2013). The impact of interactive corporate social responsibility communication on corporate reputation. *Journal of Business Ethics, 118,* 731–746.

Echterhoff, G., Hirst, W., & Hussy, W. (2005). How eyewitnesses resist misinformation: Social postwarnings and the monitoring of memory characteristics. *Memory & Cognition, 33,* 770–782.

Ecker, U. K. H., Lewandowsky, S., Swire, B., & Chang, D. (2011). Correction false information in memory: Manipulating the strength of information encoding and its retraction. *Psychonomic Bulletin & Review, 18,* 570–578.

Eckersley, R. (2005, November 22). Is modern Western culture a health hazard? *International Journal of Epidemiology,* published online.

Economist. (2000, June 10). America's death-penalty lottery. *The Economist, 15.*

Edelson, M., Sharot, T., Dolan, R. J., & Dudai, Y. (2011). Following the crowd: brain substrates of long-term memory conformity. *Science, 333,* 108–111.

Edsall, T. B. (2011, December 5). The reinvention of political morality. *New York Times* (www.nytimes.com).

Edwards, C. P. (1991). Behavioral sex differences in children of diverse cultures: The case of nurturance to infants. In M. Pereira & L. Fairbanks (Eds.), *Juveniles: Comparative socioecology.* Oxford: Oxford University Press.

Edwards, D., & Potter, J. (2005). Discursive psychology, mental states and descriptions. In H. te Molder & J. Potter (Eds.), *Conversation and cognition.* New York: Cambridge University Press.

Edwards, K. (1990). The interplay of affect and cognition in attitude formation and change. *Journal of Personality and Social Psychology, 59,* 202–216.

Edwards, K., & Bryan, T. S. (1997). Judgmental biases produced by instructions to disregard: The (paradoxical) case of emotional information. *Personality and Social Psychology Bulletin, 23,* 849–864.

Efran, M. G. (1974). The effect of physical appearance on the judgment of guilt, interpersonal attraction, and severity of recommended punishment in a simulated jury task. *Journal of Research in Personality, 8,* 45–54.

Ehrenreich, S. E., Beron, K. J., Brinkley, D. Y., & Underwood, M. K. (2014). Family predictors of continuity and change in social and physical aggression from ages 9 to 18. *Aggressive Behavior, 40,* 421–439.

Ehrlich, P., & Feldman, M. (2003). Genes and cultures: What creates our behavioral phenome? *Current Anthropology, 44,* 87–95.

Eibach, R. P., & Ehrlinger, J. (2006). "Keep your eyes on the prize": Reference points and racial differences in assessing progress toward equality. *Personality and Social Psychology Bulletin, 32,* 66–77.

Eich, E., Reeves, J. L., Jaeger, B., & Graff-Radford, S. B. (1985). Memory for pain: Relation between past and present pain intensity. *Pain, 23,* 375–380.

Eisenberg, N. (2014, September). Is our focus becoming overly narrow? *Observer,* pp. 5, 46.

Eisenberg, N., Fabes, R. A., Schaller, M., Miller, P., Carlo, G., Poulin, R., Shea, C., & Shell, R. (1991). Personality and socialization correlates of vicarious emotional responding. *Journal of Personality and Social Psychology, 61,* 459–470.

Eisenberger, N. I., Lieberman, M. D., & Williams, K. D. (2003). Does rejection hurt? An fMRI study of social exclusion. *Science, 302,* 290–292.

Eisenberger, N. I., Way, B. M., Taylor, S. E., Welch, W. T., & Liberman, M. D. (2007). Understanding genetic risk for aggression: Clues from the brain's response to social exclusion. *Biological Psychiatry, 61,* 1100–1108.

Eisenberger, R., & Aselage, J. (2009). Incremental effects of reward on experienced performance pressure: Positive outcomes for intrinsic interest and creativity. *Journal of Organizational Behavior, 30,* 95–117.

Eisenberger, R., Rhoades, L., & Cameron, J. (1999). Does pay for performance increase or decrease perceived self-determination and intrinsic motivation? *Journal of Personality and Social Psychology, 77,* 1026–1040.

Eiser, J. R., Sutton, S. R., & Wober, M. (1979). Smoking, seat-belts, and beliefs about health. *Addictive Behaviors, 4,* 331–338.

Elder, G. H., Jr. (1969). Appearance and education in marriage mobility. *American Sociological Review, 34,* 519–533.

Ellemers, N., Van Rijswijk, W., Roefs, M., & Simons, C. (1997). Bias in intergroup perceptions: Balancing group identity with social reality. *Personality and Social Psychology Bulletin, 23,* 186–198.

Elliot, A. J., & Devine, P. G. (1994). On the motivational nature of cognitive dissonance: Dissonance as psychological discomfort. *Journal of Personality and Social Psychology, 67,* 382–394.

Elliott, J. (2010, May 24). Souder: I'm happy that abstinence vid with mistress now defines me. *TPMMuckraker* (tpmmuckraker.talkingpointsmemo.com).

Elliott, L. (1989, June). Legend of the four chaplains. *Reader's Digest,* pp. 66–70.

Ellis, B. J., & Symons, D. (1990). Sex difference in sexual fantasy: An evolutionary psychological approach. *Journal of Sex Research, 27,* 490–521.

Ellis, H. D. (1981). Theoretical aspects of face recognition. In G. H. Davies, H. D. Ellis, & J. Shepherd (Eds.), *Perceiving and remembering faces.* London: Academic Press.

Ellis, L., Hershberger, S., Field, E., Wersinger, S., Pellis, S., Geary, D., Palmer, C., Hoyenga, K., Hetroni, A., & Karadi, K. (2008). *Sex differences: Summarizing more than a century of*

scientific research. New York: Psychology Press.

Ellison, P. A., Govern, J. M., Petri, H. L., & Figler, M. H. (1995). Anonymity and aggressive driving behavior: A field study. *Journal of Social Behavior and Personality, 10,* 265–272.

Ellsworth, P. (1985, July). Juries on trial. *Psychology Today,* 44–46.

Ellsworth, P. (1989, March 6). Supreme Court ignores social science research on capital punishment. Quoted by *Behavior Today,* pp. 7–8.

Ellsworth, P. C., & Mauro, R. (1998). Psychology and law. In D. Gilbert, S. T. Fiske, & G. Lindzey (Eds.), *Handbook of social psychology,* 4th edition. New York: McGraw-Hill.

Elms, A. (2009). Obedience lite. *American Psychologist, 64,* 32–36.

Elms, A. C. (1995). Obedience in retrospect. *Journal of Social Issues, 51,* 21–31.

Elson, M., & Ferguson, C. J. (2014). Twenty-five years of research on violence in digital games and aggression: Empirical evidence, perspectives, and a debate gone astray. *European Psychologist, 19,* 33–46.

Emswiller, T., Deaux, K., & Willits, J. E. (1971). Similarity, sex, and requests for small favors. *Journal of Applied Social Psychology, 1,* 284–291.

Eng, P. M., Kawachi, I., Fitzmaurice, G., & Rimm, E. B. (2001). Effects of marital transitions on changes in dietary and other health behaviors in men. Paper presented to the American Psychosomatic Society meeting.

Engemann, K. M., & Owyang, M. T. (2003, April). So much for that merit raise: The link between wages and appearance. *The Regional Economist* (www.stlouisfed.org).

Engs, R., & Hanson, D. J. (1989). Reactance theory: A test with collegiate drinking. *Psychological Reports, 64,* 1083–1086.

Ennis, R., & Zanna, M. P. (1991). Hockey assault: Constitutive versus normative violations. Paper presented at the Canadian Psychological Association convention.

Environics Research Group. (2006). Eave 11: The health effects of tobacco and health warning messages on cigarette packages, survey of youth. Toronto (Canada): Environics Research Group.

Enzle, M. E., & Hawkins, W. L. (1992). A priori actor negligence mediates a posteriori outcome. *Journal of Experimental Social Psychology, 28(2),* 169–185.

Epley, N., Akalis, S., Waytz, A., & Cacioppo, J. T. (2008). Creating social connection through inferential reproduction: Loneliness and perceived agency in gadgets, gods, and greyhounds. *Psychological Science, 19,* 114–120.

Epley, N., & Huff, C. (1998). Suspicion, affective response, and educational benefit as a result of deception in psychology research. *Personality and Social Psychology Bulletin, 24,* 759–768.

Epley, N., Savitsky, K., & Kachelski, R. A. (1999, September/October). What every skeptic should know about subliminal persuasion. *Skeptical Inquirer,* pp. 40–45.

Epley, N., & Whitchurch, E. (2008). Mirror, mirror on the wall: Enhancement in self-recognition. *Personality and Social Psychology Bulletin, 34,* 1159–1170.

Epstein, J. A., & Botvin, G. J. (2008). Media refusal skills and drug skill refusal techniques: What is their relationship with alcohol use among inner-city adolescents? *Addictive Behavior, 33,* 528–537.

Epstude, K., & Roese, N. J. (2008). The functional theory of counterfactual thinking. *Personality and Social Psychology Review, 12,* 168–192.

Erickson, B., Holmes, J. G., Frey, R., Walker, L., & Thibaut, J. (1974). Functions of a third party in the resolution of conflict: The role of a judge in pretrial conferences. *Journal of Personality and Social Psychology, 30,* 296–306.

Erickson, B., Lind, E. A. Johnson, B. C., & O'Barr, W. M. (1978). Speech style and impression formation in a court setting: The effects of powerful and powerless speech. *Journal of Experimental Social Psychology, 14,* 266–279.

Erikson, E. H. (1963). *Childhood and society.* New York: Norton.

Ernst, M. O. (2010). Decisions made better. *Science, 329,* 1022–1023.

Eron, L. D. (1987). The development of aggressive behavior from the perspective of a developing behaviorism. *American Psychologist, 42,* 425–442.

Eron, L. D., & Huesmann, L. R. (1980). Adolescent aggression and television. *Annals of the New York Academy of Sciences, 347,* 319–331.

Eron, L. D., & Huesmann, L. R. (1984). The control of aggressive behavior by changes in attitudes, values, and the conditions of learning. In R. J. Blanchard & C. Blanchard (Eds.), *Advances in the study of aggression* (Vol. 1). Orlando, FL: Academic Press.

Eron, L. D., & Huesmann, L. R. (1985). The role of television in the development of prosocial and antisocial behavior. In D. Olweus, M. Radke-Yarrow, and J. Block (Eds.), *Development of antisocial and prosocial behavior.* Orlando, FL: Academic Press.

Escobar-Chaves, S. L., & Anderson, C. A. (2008). Media and risky behaviors. *The Future of Children, 18,* 147–180.

Escobar-Chaves, S. L., Tortolero, S. R., Markham, C. M., Low, B. J., Eitel, P., & Thickstun, P. (2005). Impact of the media on adolescent sexual attitudes and behaviors. *Pediatrics, 116,* 303–326.

Esser, J. K. (1998, February–March). Alive and well after 25 years. A review of groupthink research. *Organizational Behavior and Human Decision Processes, 73,* 116–141.

Esses, V. M., Haddock, G., & Zanna, M. P. (1993a). Values, stereotypes, and emotions as determinants of intergroup attitudes. In D. Mackie & D. Hamilton (Eds.), *Affect, cognition and stereotyping: Interactive processes in intergroup perception.* San Diego, CA: Academic Press.

Esses, V. M., Haddock, G., & Zanna, M. P. (1993b). The role of mood in the expression of intergroup stereotypes. In M. P. Zanna & J. M. Olson (Eds.), *The psychology of prejudice: The Ontario symposium* (Vol. 7). Hillsdale, NJ: Erlbaum.

Esses, V. M., & Webster, C. D. (1988). Physical attractiveness, dangerousness, and the Canadian criminal code. *Journal of Applied Social Psychology, 18,* 1017–1031.

Etzioni, A. (1967). The Kennedy experiment. *The Western Political Quarterly, 20,* 361–380.

Etzioni, A. (1991, May–June). The community in an age of individualism (interview). *The Futurist,* pp. 35–39.

Etzioni, A. (1993). *The spirit of community.* New York: Crown.

Etzioni, A. (2005). The diversity within unity platform. Washington, DC: The Communitarian Network.

Evans, G. W. (1979). Behavioral and physiological consequences of crowding in humans. *Journal of Applied Social Psychology, 9,* 27–46.

Evans, G. W., Lepore, S. J., & Allen, K. M. (2000). Cross-cultural differences in tolerance for crowding: Fact or fiction? *Journal of Personality and Social Psychology, 79,* 204–210.

Evans, G. W., Lepore, S. J., & Schroeder, A. (1996). The role of interior design elements in human responses to crowding. *Journal of Personality and Social Psychology, 70,* 41–46.

Evans, R. I., Smith, C. K., & Raines, B. E. (1984). Deterring cigarette smoking in adolescents: A psycho-social-behavioral analysis of an intervention strategy. In A. Baum, J. Singer, & S. Taylor (Eds.), *Handbook of psychology and health: Social psychological aspects of health* (Vol. 4). Hillsdale, NJ: Erlbaum.

Exline, J. J., Zell, A. L., Bratslavsky, E., Hamilton, M., & Swenson, A. (2012). People-pleasing through eating: Sociotropy predicts greater eating in response to perceived social pressure. *Journal of Social and Clinical Psychology, 31,* 169–193.

Fabrigar, L. R., & Petty, R. E. (1999). The role of the affective and cognitive bases of attitudes in susceptibility to affectively and cognitively based persuasion. *Personality and Social Psychology Bulletin, 25,* 363–381.

Fachner, G., & Carter, S. (2015). *Collaborative reform initiative: An assessment of deadly force in the Philadelphia Police Department.* Washington, DC: Office of Community Oriented Policing Services, U.S. Department of Justice.

Falk, A., Kuhn, A., & Zweimüller, J. (2011). Unemployment and right-wing extremist crime. *Scandinavian Journal of Economics, 113,* 260–285.

Falk, C. F., Heine, S. J., Yuki, M., & Takemura, K. (2009). Why do Westerners self-enhance more than East Asians? *European Journal of Personality, 23,* 183–203.

Farb, N. A. S., Segal, Z. V., Mayberg, H., Bean, J., & McKeon, D. (2007). Attending to the present: Mindfulness meditation reveals distinct neural modes of self-reference. *Social Cognitive and Affective Neuroscience, 2,* 313–322.

Farquhar, J. W., Maccoby, N., Wood, P. D., Alexander, J. K., Breitrose, H., Brown, B. W., Jr., Haskell, W. L., McAlister, A. L., Meyer, A. J., Nash, J. D., & Stern, M. P. (1977, June 4). Community education for cardiovascular health. *Lancet,* 1192–1195.

Farrelly, M. C., Davis, K. C., Duke, J., & Messeri, P. (2009). Sustaining "truth": Changes in youth tobacco attitudes and smoking intentions after three years of a national antismoking campaign. *Health Education Research, 24,* 42–48.

Farrelly, M. C., Healton, C. G., Davis, K. C., Messeri, P., Hersey, J. C., & Haviland, M. L. (2002). Getting to the truth: Evaluating national tobacco countermarketing campaigns. *American Journal of Public Health, 92,* 901–907.

Farris, C., Treat, T. A., Viken, R. J., & McFall, R. M. (2008). Perceptual mechanisms that characterize gender differences in decoding women's sexual intent. *Psychological Science, 19,* 348–354.

Farwell, L., & Weiner, B. (2000). Bleeding hearts and the heartless: Popular perceptions of liberal and conservative ideologies. *Personality and Social Psychology Bulletin, 26,* 845–852.

Faulkner, S. L., & Williams, K. D. (1996). *A study of social loafing in industry.* Paper presented at the Midwestern Psychological Association convention, Chicago, Illinois.

Faust, D., & Ziskin, J. (1988). The expert witness in psychology and psychiatry. *Science, 241,* 31–35.

Fay, A. J., & Maner, J. K. (2014). When does heat promote hostility? Person by situation interactions shape the psychological effects of haptic sensations. *Journal of Experimental Social Psychology, 50,* 210–16.

Fazio, R. (1987). Self-perception theory: A current perspective. In M. P. Zanna, J. M. Olson, & C. P. Herman (Eds.), *Social influence: The Ontario symposium* (Vol. 5). Hillsdale, NJ: Erlbaum.

Fazio, R. H., Effrein, E. A., & Falender, V. J. (1981). Self-perceptions following social interaction. *Journal of Personality and Social Psychology, 41,* 232–242.

Fazio, R. H., Zanna, M. P., & Cooper, J. (1977). Dissonance versus self-perception: An integrative view of each theory's proper domain of application. *Journal of Experimental Social Psychology, 13,* 464–479.

Fazio, R. H., Zanna, M. P., & Cooper, J. (1979). On the relationship of data to theory: A reply to Ronis and Greenwald. *Journal of Experimental Social Psychology, 15,* 70–76.

FBI. (2013, November 25). Latest hate crime statistics. Washington, DC: Federal Bureau of Investigation (www.fbi.gov).

FBI: Federal Bureau of Investigation. (2012). Uniform Crime Reports, 2011.

FBI: Federal Bureau of Investigation. (2013). National Incident-Based Reporting System, Uniform Crime Reports. http://www.fbi.gov/about-us/cjis/ucr/nibrs/2013/data-tables

FBI: Federal Bureau of Investigation. (2014). Uniform Crime Reports, 2013. Retrieved March 27, 2015 from: http://www.fbi.gov/about-us/cjis/ucr/crime-in-the-u.s/2013/crime-in-the-u.s.-2013/tables/table-35/table_35_five_year_arrest_trends_by_sex_2013.xls

Feather, N. T. (2005). Social psychology in Australia: Past and present. *International Journal of Psychology, 40,* 263–276.

Feeney, J., Peterson, C., & Noller, P. (1994). Equity and marital satisfaction over the family life cycle. *Personality Relationships, 1,* 83–99.

Feeney, J. A. (1996). Attachment, caregiving, and marital satisfaction. *Personal Relationships, 3,* 401–416.

Feeney, J. A., & Noller, P. (1990). Attachment style as a predictor of adult romantic relationships. *Journal of Personality and Social Psychology, 58,* 281–291.

Feinberg, J. M., & Aiello, J. R. (2006). Social facilitation: A test of competing theories. *Journal of Applied Social Psychology, 36,* 1–23.

Feinberg, M., & Willer, R. (2011). Apocalypse soon? Dire messages reduce belief in global warming by contradicting just-world beliefs. *Psychological Science, 22,* 34–38.

Feinberg, M., Willer, R., & Keltner, D. (2012). Flustered and faithful: Embarrassment as a signal of prosociality. *Journal of Personality and Social Psychology, 102,* 81–97.

Feingold, A. (1988). Matching for attractiveness in romantic partners and same-sex friends: A meta-analysis and theoretical critique. *Psychological Bulletin, 104,* 226–235.

Feingold, A. (1990). Gender differences in effects of physical attractiveness on romantic attraction: A comparison across five research paradigms. *Journal of Personality and Social Psychology, 59,* 981–993.

Feingold, A. (1991). Sex differences in the effects of similarity and physical attractiveness on opposite-sex attraction. *Basic and Applied Social Psychology, 12,* 357–367.

Feingold, A. (1992b). Good-looking people are not what we think. *Psychological Bulletin, 111,* 304–341.

Fein, S., & Hilton, J. L. (1992). Attitudes toward groups and behavioral intentions toward individual group members: The impact of nondiagnostic information. *Journal of Experimental Social Psychology, 28,* 101–124.

Fein, S., & Spencer, S. J. (1997). Prejudice as self-image maintenance: Affirming the self through derogating others. *Journal of Personality and Social Psychology, 73,* 31–44.

Feldman, R. S., & Prohaska, T. (1979). The student as Pygmalion: Effect of student expectation on the teacher. *Journal of Educational Psychology, 71,* 485–493.

Feldman, R. S., & Theiss, A. J. (1982). The teacher and student as Pygmalions: Joint effects of teacher and student expectations. *Journal of Educational Psychology, 74,* 217–223.

Felson, R. B. (2000). A social psychological approach to interpersonal aggression. In V. B. Van Hasselt & M. Hersen (Eds.), *Aggression and violence: An introductory text.* Boston: Allyn & Bacon.

Fenigstein, A. (1984). Self-consciousness and the overperception of self as a target. *Journal of Personality and Social Psychology, 47,* 860–870.

Fenigstein, A., & Vanable, P. A. (1992). Paranoia and self-consciousness. *Journal of Personality and Social Psychology, 62,* 129–138.

Fennis, B. M., & Aarts, H. (2012). Revisting the agentic shift: Weakening personal control increases susceptibility to social influence. *European Journal of Social Psychology, 42,* 824–831.

Ferguson, C. J., & Kilburn, J. (2010). Much ado about nothing: The misestimation and overinterpretation of violent video game effects in Eastern and Western nations: Comment on Anderson et al. (2010). *Psychological Bulletin, 136,* 174–178.

Fergusson, D. M., Horwood, L. J., & Shannon, F. T. (1984). A proportional hazards model of family breakdown. *Journal of Marriage and the Family, 46,* 539–549.

Ferriday, C., Vartanian, O., & Mandel, D. R. (2011). Public but not private ego threat triggers aggression in narcissists. *European Journal of Social Psychology, 41,* 564–568.

Ferriman, K., Lubinski, D., & Benbow, C. P. (2009). Work preferences, life values, and personal views of top math/science graduate students and the profoundly gifted: Developmental changes and gender differences during emerging adulthood and parenthood. *Journal of Personality and Social Psychology, 97,* 517–522.

Feshbach, S. (1980). *Television advertising and children: Policy issues and alternatives.* Paper presented at the American Psychological Association convention.

Festinger, L. (1954). A theory of social comparison processes. *Human Relations, 7,* 117–140.

Festinger, L. (1957). *A theory of cognitive dissonance.* Stanford: Stanford University Press.

Festinger, L., & Carlsmith, J. M. (1959). Cognitive consequences of forced compliance. *Journal of Abnormal and Social Psychology, 58,* 203–210.

Festinger, L., & Maccoby, N. (1964). On resistance to persuasive communications. *Journal of Abnormal and Social Psychology, 68,* 359–366.

Festinger, L., Pepitone, A., & Newcomb, T. (1952). Some consequences of deindividuation in a group. *Journal of Abnormal and Social Psychology, 47,* 382–389.

Festinger, L., Riecken, H. W., & Schachter, S. (1956). *When prophecy fails.* Minneapolis: University of Minnesota Press.

Feygina, I., Jost, J. T., & Goldsmith, R. E. (2010). System justification, the denial of global warming, and the possibility of "system-sanctioned change." *Personality and Social Psychology Bulletin, 36,* 326–338.

Feynman, R. (1967). *The character of physical law.* Cambridge, MA: MIT Press.

Fichter, J. (1968). *America's forgotten priests: What are they saying?* New York: Harper.

Fiedler, F. E. (1987, September). When to lead, when to stand back. *Psychology Today,* 26–27.

Fincham, F. D., & Bradbury, T. N. (1993). Marital satisfaction, depression, and attributions: A longitudinal analysis. *Journal of Personality and Social Psychology, 64,* 442–452.

Fincham, F. D., Lambert, N. M., & Beach, S. R. H. (2010). Faith and unfaithfulness: Can praying for your partner reduce infidelity? *Journal of Personality and Social Psychology, 99,* 649–659.

Finchilescu, G. (2005). Meta-stereotypes may hinder inter-racial contact. *South African Journal of Psychology, 35,* 460–472.

Finkel, E., & Fitzsimmons, G. (2013). When helping hurts. *New York Times* (www.nytimes.com).

Finkel, E. J., & Campbell, W. K. (2001). Self-control and accommodation in close relationships: An interdependence analysis. *Journal of Personality and Social Psychology, 81,* 263–277.

Finkel, E. J., Eastwick, P. W., Karney, B. R., Reis, H. T., & Sprecher, S. (2012). Online dating: A critical analysis from the perspective of psychological science. *Psychological Science,* in press.

Finkel, E. J., Hui, C. M., Carswell, K. L., & Larson, G. M. (2014). The suffocation of marriage: Climbing Mount Maslow without enough oxygen. *Psychological Inquiry, 25,* 1–41.

Finkel, E. J., Slotter, E. B., Luchies, L. B., Walton, G. M., & Gross, J. J. (2013).

A brief intervention to promote conflict reappraisal preserves marital quality over time. *Psychological Science, 24,* 1595–1601.

Fischer, P., & Greitemeyer, T. (2006). Music and aggression: The impact of sexual-aggressive song lyrics on aggression-related thoughts, emotions, and behavior toward the same and the opposite sex. *Personality and Social Psychology Bulletin, 32,* 1165–1176.

Fischer, P., & Greitemeyer, T. (2010). A new look at selective-exposure effects: An integrative model. *Current Directions in Psychological Science, 19,* 384–389.

Fischer, P., Krueger, J., Greitemeyer, T., Kastenmüller, A., Vogrincic, C., Frey, D., Heene, M., Wicher, M., & Kainbacher, M. (2011). The bystander-effect: A meta-analytic review on bystander intervention in dangerous and non-dangerous emergencies. *Psychological Bulletin, 137,* 517–537.

Fischer, R., & Boer, D. (2011). What is more important for national well-being: Money or autonomy? A meta-analysis of well-being, burnout, and anxiety across 63 societies. *Journal of Personality and Social Psychology, 101,* 164–184.

Fischer, R., & Chalmers, A. (2008). Is optimism universal? A meta-analytical investigation of optimism levels across 22 nations. *Personality and Individual Differences, 45,* 378–382.

Fischer, R., & Van de Vliert, E. (2011). Does climate undermine subjective well-being? A 58-nation study. *Personality and Social Psychology Bulletin, 37,* 1031–1041.

Fischhoff, B. (1982). Debiasing. In D. Kahneman, P. Slovic, & A. Tversky (Eds.), *Judgment under uncertainty: Heuristics and biases.* New York: Cambridge University Press.

Fischhoff, B., & Bar-Hillel, M. (1984). Diagnosticity and the base rate effect. *Memory and Cognition, 12,* 402–410.

Fishbein, M., & Ajzen, I. (1974). Attitudes toward objects as predictive of single and multiple behavioral criteria. *Psychological Review, 81,* 59–74.

Fisher, G. H. (1968). Ambiguity of form: Old and new. *Perception and Psychophysics, 4,* 189–192.

Fisher, H. (1994, April). The nature of romantic love. *Journal of NIH Research,* 59–64.

Fisher, K., Egerton, M., Gershuny, J. I., & Robinson, J. P. (2007). Gender convergence in the American Heritage Time Use Study (AHTUS). *Social Indicators Research, 82,* 1–33.

Fisher, R. J. (1994). Generic principles for resolving intergroup conflict. *Journal of Social Issues, 50,* 47–66.

Fisher, R. P., Geiselman, R. E., & Amador, M. (1989). Field test of the cognitive interview: Enhancing the recollection of actual victims and witnesses of crime. *Journal of Applied Psychology, 74,* 722–727.

Fisher, R. P., Geiselman, R. E., & Raymond, D. S. (1987). Critical analysis of police interview techniques. *Journal of Police Science and Administration, 15,* 177–185.

Fisher, R. P., McCauley, M. R., & Geiselman, R. E. (1994). Improving eyewitness testimony with the Cognitive Interview. In D. F. Ross, J. D. Read, & M. P. Toglia (Eds.), *Adult eyewitness testimony: Current trends and developments.* Cambridge, UK: Cambridge University Press.

Fisher, R. P., Milne, R., & Bull, R. (2011). Interviewing cooperative witnesses. *Current Directions in Psychological Science, 20,* 20–23.

Fisher, T. D., Moore, Z. T., & Pittinger, M. J. (2012). Sex on the brain? An examination of frequency of sexual cognitions as a function of gender, erotophilia, and social desirability. *Journal of Sex Research, 49,* 69–77.

Fiske, S. T. (1989). Interdependence and stereotyping: From the laboratory to the Supreme Court (and back). Invited address, American Psychological Association convention, New Orleans, Louisiana.

Fiske, S. T. (1992). Thinking is for doing: Portraits of social cognition from daguerreotype to laserphoto. *Journal of Personality and Social Psychology, 63,* 877–889.

Fiske, S. T. (1999). Behind the scenes. In D. G. Myers, *Social psychology,* 6th edition. New York: McGraw-Hill.

Fiske, S. T. (2004). Mind the gap: In praise of informal sources of formal theory. *Personality and Social Psychology Review, 8,* 132–137.

Fiske, S. T. (2011a, January 27). *One word: Plasticity.* Presentation to the Society of Personality and Social Psychology Presidential Symposium: Visions for the next decade of personality and social psychology, San Antonio, TX.

Fiske, S. T. (2011b). *Envy up, scorn down: How status divides us.* New York: Sage Foundation.

Fiske, S. T., Bersoff, D. N., Borgida, E., Deaux, K., & Heilman, M. E. (1991). Social science research on trial: The use of sex stereotyping research in Price Waterhouse *v.* Hopkins. *American Psychologist, 46,* 1049–1060.

Fiske, S. T., Harris, L. T., & Cuddy, A. J. C. (2004). Why ordinary people torture enemy prisoners. *Science, 306,* 1482–1483.

Fiske, S. T., & Hauser, R. M. (2014). Protecting human research participants in the age of big data. *Proceedings of the National Academic of Sciences, 111,* 13675–13676 (www.pnas.org).

Fiske, S. T., Xu, J., Cuddy, A. C., & Glick, P. (1999). (Dis)respecting versus (Dis)liking: Status and interdependence predict ambivalent stereotypes of competence and warmth. *Journal of Social Issues, 55,* 473–489.

Flay, B. R., Ryan, K. B., Best, J. A., Brown, K. S., Kersell, M. W., d'Avernas, J. R., & Zanna, M. P. (1985). Are social-psychological smoking prevention programs effective? The Waterloo study. *Journal of Behavioral Medicine, 8,* 37–59.

Fleming, M. A., Wegener, D. T., & Petty, R. E. (1999). Procedural and legal motivations to correct for perceived judicial biases. *Journal of Experimental Social Psychology, 35,* 186–203.

Fletcher, G. J. O., Fincham, F. D., Cramer, L., & Heron, N. (1987). The role of attributions in the development of dating relationships. *Journal of Personality and Social Psychology, 53,* 481–489.

Fletcher, G. J. O., Simpson, J. A., Thomas, G., & Giles, L. (1999). Ideals in intimate relationships. *Journal of Personality and Social Psychology, 76,* 72–89.

Fletcher, G. J. O., Tither, J. M., O'Loughlin, C., Friesen, M., & Overall, N. (2004). Warm and homely or cold and beautiful? Sex differences in trading off traits in mate selection. *Personality and Social Psychology Bulletin, 30,* 659–672.

Fletcher, G. J. O., & Ward, C. (1989). Attribution theory and processes: A cross-cultural perspective. In M. H. Bond (Ed.), *The cross-cultural challenge to social psychology.* Newbury Park, CA: Sage.

Flowe, H. D., Klatt, T., & Colloff, M. F. (2014). Selecting fillers on emotional appearance improves lineup identification accuracy. *Law and Human Behavior, 38,* 509–519.

Foa, U. G., & Foa, E. B. (1975). *Resource theory of social exchange.* Morristown, NJ: General Learning Press.

Fogelman, E. (1994). *Conscience and courage: Rescuers of Jews during the Holocaust.* New York: Doubleday Anchor.

Follett, M. P. (1940). Constructive conflict. In H. C. Metcalf & L. Urwick (Eds.), *Dynamic administration: The collected papers of Mary Parker Follett.* New York: Harper.

FootPrintNetwork.org. (2014). World footprint: Do we fit on the planet? Global Footprint Network.

Ford, R. (2008). Is racial prejudice declining in Britain? *British Journal of Sociology, 59,* 609–636.

Ford, T. E. (1997). Effects of stereotypical television portrayals of African-Americans on person perception. *Social Psychology Quarterly, 60,* 266–278.

Ford, T. E., Boxer, C. F., Armstrong, J., & Edel, J. R. (2008). More than "just a joke": The prejudice-releasing function of sexist humor. *Personality and Social Psychology Bulletin, 34,* 159–170.

Forgas, J. P. (1999). Behind the scenes. In D. G. Myers (Ed.), *Social psychology,* 6th edition. New York: McGraw-Hill.

Forgas, J. P. (2007). When sad is better than happy: Negative affect can improve the quality and effectiveness of persuasive messages and social influence strategies. *Journal of Experimental Social Psychology, 43,* 513–528.

Forgas, J. P. (2008). Affect and cognition. *Perspectives on Psychological Science, 3,* 94–101.

Forgas, J. P. (2010). Affective influences on the formation, expression, and change of attitudes. In J. P. Forgas, J. Cooper, & W. D. Crano (Eds.), *The psychology of attitudes and attitude change.* New York: Psychology Press.

Forgas, J. P. (2011). Affect and global versus local processing: The processing benefits of negative affect for memory, judgments, and behavior. *Psychological Inquiry, 21,* 216–224.

Forgas, J. P. (2013). Don't worry, be sad! On the cognitive, motivational, and interpersonal benefits of negative mood. *Current Directions in Psychological Science, 22,* 225–232.

Forgas, J. P. (2014, June 4). Four ways sadness may be good for you. www.greatergood.berkeley.edu.

Forgas, J. P., Bower, G. H., & Krantz, S. E. (1984). The influence of mood on perceptions of social interactions. *Journal of Experimental Social Psychology, 20,* 497–513.

Forgas, J. P., Dunn, E., & Granland, S. (2008). Are you being served . . . ? An unobtrusive experiment of affective influences on helping in a department store. *European Journal of Social Psychology, 38,* 333–342.

Forgas, J. P., Goldenberg, L. & Unkelbach, C. (2009). Can bad weather improve your memory? An unobtrusive field study of natural mood effects on real-life memory. *Journal of Experimental Social Psychology,* 254–259.

Forgas, J. P., & Moylan, S. (1987). After the movies: Transient mood and social judgments. *Personality and Social Psychology Bulletin, 13,* 467–477.

Form, W. H., & Nosow, S. (1958). *Community in disaster.* New York: Harper.

Forscher, P. S., & Devine, P. G. (2014). Breaking the prejudice habit: Automaticity and control in the context of a long-term goal. In J. W. Sherman, B. Gawronski, & Y. Trope (Eds.), *Dual-process theories of the social mind.* (pp. 468–482). New York: Guilford Press.

Forster, E. M. (1976). *Aspects of the novel* (Ed. O. Stallybrass). Harmondsworth: Penguin. (Original work published 1927.)

Forsyth, D. R., Kerr, N. A., Burnette, J. L., & Baumeister, R. F. (2007). Attempting to improve the academic performance of struggling college students by bolstering their self-esteem: An intervention that backfired. *Journal of Social and Clinical Psychology, 26,* 447–459.

Forsyth, D. R., & Leary, M. R. (1997). Achieving the goals of the scientist-practitioner model: The seven interfaces of social and counseling psychology. *The Counseling Psychologist, 25,* 180–200.

Foss, R. D. (1978). *The role of social influence in blood donation.* Paper presented at the American Psychological Association convention, Toronto, Ontario.

Foster, C. A., Witcher, B. S., Campbell, W. K., & Green, J. D. (1998). Arousal and attraction: Evidence for automatic and controlled processes. *Journal of Personality and Social Psychology, 74,* 86–101.

Fournier, R., & Tompson, T. (2008, September 20). Poll: Racial views steer some white Dems away from Obama. Associated Press via news.yahoo.com (data from www.knowledgenetworks.com survey for AP-Yahoo in partnership with Stanford University).

Fowler, J. H., & Christakis, N. A. (2008). Dynamic spread of happiness in a large social network: Longitudinal analysis over 20 years in the Framingham Heart Study. *British Medical Journal, 337* (doi: 10.1136/bmj.a2338).

Fraley, R. C., Griffin, B. N., Belsky, J., & Roisman, G. I. (2012). Developmental antecedents of political ideology: A longitudinal investigation from birth to age 18 years. *Psychological Science, 23,* 1425–1431.

Frank, R. (1999). *Luxury fever: Why money fails to satisfy in an era of excess.* New York: Free Press.

Frankel, A., & Snyder, M. L. (1987). Egotism among the depressed: When self-protection becomes self-handicapping. Paper presented at the American Psychological Association convention, New York, NY.

Franklin, B. J. (1974). Victim characteristics and helping behavior in a rural southern setting. *Journal of Social Psychology, 93,* 93–100.

Frantz, C. M. (2006). I AM being fair: The bias blind spot as a stumbling block to seeing both sides. *Basic and Applied Social Psychology, 28,* 157–167.

Frasure-Smith, N., & Lespérance, F. (2005). Depression and coronary heart disease: Complex synergism of mind, body, and environment. *Current Directions in Psychological Science, 14,* 39–43.

Frasure-Smith, N., Lesperance, F., Juneau, M., Talajic, M., & Bourassa, M. G. (1999). Gender, depression, and one-year prognosis after myocardial infarction. *Psychosomatic Medicine, 61,* 26–37.

Frasure-Smith, N., Lesperance, F., & Talajic, M. (1995). The impact of negative emotions on prognosis following myocardial infarction: Is it more than depression? *Health Psychology, 14,* 388–398.

Frederick, D. A., & Haselton, M. G. (2007). Why is muscularity sexy? Tests of the fitness indicator hypothesis. *Personality and Social Psychology Bulletin, 8,* 1167–1183.

Freedman, J. L. (1965). Long-term behavioral effects of cognitive dissonance. *Journal of Experimental Social Psychology, 1,* 145–155.

Freedman, J. L., Birsky, J., & Cavoukian, A. (1980). Environmental determinants of behavioral contagion: Density and number. *Basic and Applied Social Psychology, 1,* 155–161.

Freedman, J. L., & Fraser, S. C. (1966). Compliance without pressure: The foot-in-the-door technique. *Journal of Personality and Social Psychology, 4,* 195–202.

Freedman, J. L., & Perlick, D. (1979). Crowding, contagion, and laughter. *Journal of Experimental Social Psychology, 15,* 295–303.

Freedman, J. L., & Sears, D. O. (1965). Warning, distraction, and resistance to influence. *Journal of Personality and Social Psychology, 1,* 262–266.

Freeman, M. A. (1997). Demographic correlates of individualism and collectivism: A study of social values in Sri Lanka. *Journal of Cross-Cultural Psychology, 28,* 321–341.

Freijy, T., & Kothe, E. J. (2013). Dissonance-based interventions for health behaviour change: A systematic review. *British Journal of Health Psychology, 18,* 310–337.

French, J. R. P. (1968). The conceptualization and the measurement of mental health in terms of self-identity theory. In S. B. Sells (Ed.), *The definition and measurement of mental health.* Washington, DC: Department of Health, Education, and Welfare. (Cited by M. Rosenberg, 1979, *Conceiving the self.* New York: Basic Books.)

Frenda, S. J., Nichols, R. M., & Loftus, E. F. (2011). Current issues and advances in misinformation research. *Current Directions in Psychological Science, 20,* 20–23.

Freund, B., Colgrove, L. A., Burke, B. L., & McLeod, R. (2005). Self-rated driving performance among elderly drivers referred for driving evaluation. *Accident Analysis and Prevention, 37,* 613–618.

Frey, B. S., Savage, D. A., & Torgler, B. (2010). Interaction of natural survival instincts and internalized social norms exploring the Titanic and Lusitania disasters. *Proceedings of the National Academy of Sciences USA, 107,* 4862–4865.

Friebel, G., & Seabright, P. (2011). Do women have longer conversations? Telephone evidence of gendered communication strategies. *Journal of Economic Psychology, 32,* 348–356.

Friedman, H. S., Riggio, R. E., & Casella, D. F. (1988). Nonverbal skill, personal charisma, and initial attraction. *Personality and Social Psychology Bulletin, 14,* 203–211.

Friedman, T. L. (2003, June 4). Because we could. *New York Times* (www.nytimes .com).

Friedrich, L. K., & Stein, A. H. (1973). Aggressive and prosocial television programs and the natural behavior of preschool children. *Monographs of the Society of Research in Child Development, 38* (4, Serial No. 151).

Friedrich, L. K., & Stein, A. H. (1975). Prosocial television and young children: The effects of verbal labeling and role playing on learning and behavior. *Child Development, 46,* 27–38.

Frieze, I. H., Olson, J. E., & Russell, J. (1991). Attractiveness and income for men and women in management. *Journal of Applied Social Psychology, 21,* 1039–1057.

Frisell, T., Lichtenstein, P., & Långström, N. (2011). Violent crime runs in families: A total population study of 12.5 million individuals. *Journal of Research in Psychiatry and the Allied Sciences, 41,* 97–105.

Froming, W. J., Walker, G. R., & Lopyan, K. J. (1982). Public and private self-awareness: When personal attitudes conflict with societal expectations. *Journal of Experimental Social Psychology, 18,* 476–487.

Fry, D. P. (2012). Life without war. *Science, 336,* 879–884.

Fulgoni, G. M., & Mörn, M. (2009). Whither the click?: How online advertising works. *Journal of Advertising Research, 49,* 134–142.

Fuller, S. R., & Aldag, R. J. (1998). Organizational Tonypandy: Lessons from a quarter century of the groupthink phenomenon. *Organizational Behavior and Human Decision Processes, 73,* 163–185.

Fultz, J., Batson, C. D., Fortenbach, V. A., McCarthy, P. M., & Varney, L. L. (1986). Social evaluation and the empathy-altruism hypothesis. *Journal of Personality and Social Psychology, 50,* 761–769.

Fumento, M. (2014). Runaway hysteria: The Toyota panic, with the federal government's seal of approval. *Skeptical Inquirer, 38*(5), 42–49.

Furnham, A. (1982). Explanations for unemployment in Britain. *European Journal of Social Psychology, 12,* 335–352.

Furnham, A., & Gunter, B. (1984). Just world beliefs and attitudes towards the poor. *British Journal of Social Psychology, 23,* 265–269.

Fürst, G., Ghisletta, P., & Lubart, T. (2014). Toward an integrative model of creativity and personality: Theoretical suggestions and preliminary empirical testing. *Journal of Creative Behavior.*

Gabbiadini, A., Riva, P., Andrighetto, L., Volpato, C., & Bushman, B. J. (2014). Interactive effect of moral disengagement and violent video games on self-control, cheating, and aggression. *Social Psychological and Personality Science, 5,* 451–458.

Gable, S. L., Gonzaga, G. C., & Strachman, A. (2006). Will you be there for me when things go right? Supportive responses to positive event disclosures. *Journal of Personality and Social Psychology, 91,* 904–917.

Gabrenya, W. K., Jr., Wang, Y.-E., & Latané, B. (1985). Social loafing on an optimizing task: Cross-cultural differences among Chinese and Americans. *Journal of Cross-Cultural Psychology, 16,* 223–242.

Gabriel, S., & Gardner, W. L. (1999). Are there "his" and "hers" types of interdependence? The implications of gender differences in collective versus relational interdependence for affect, behavior, and cognition. *Journal of Personality and Social Psychology, 77,* 642–655.

Gaebelein, J. W., & Mander, A. (1978). Consequences for targets of aggression as a function of aggressor and instigator roles: Three experiments. *Personality and Social Psychology Bulletin, 4,* 465–468.

Gaertner, L., Iuzzini, J., Witt, M. G., & Oriña, M. M. (2006). Us without them: Evidence for an intragroup origin of positive in-group regard. *Journal of Personality and Social Psychology, 90,* 426–439.

Gaertner, L., Sedikides, C., & Chang, K. (2008). On pancultural self-enhancement: Well-adjusted Taiwanese self-enhance on personally valued traits. *Journal of Cross-Cultural Psychology, 39,* 463–477.

Gaertner, L., Sedikides, C., & Graetz, K. (1999). In search of self-definition: Motivational primacy of the individual self, motivational primacy of the collective self, or contextual primacy? *Journal of Personality and Social Psychology, 76,* 5–18.

Gaertner, S. L. (1973). Helping behavior and racial discrimination among liberals and conservatives. *Journal of Personality and Social Psychology, 25,* 335–341.

Gaertner, S. L. (1975). The role of racial attitudes in helping behavior. *Journal of Social Psychology, 97,* 95–101.

Gaertner, S. L., & Bickman, L. (1971). Effects of race on the elicitation of helping behavior. *Journal of Personality and Social Psychology, 20,* 218–222.

Gaertner, S. L., & Dovidio, J. F. (1977). The subtlety of white racism, arousal, and helping behavior. *Journal of Personality and Social Psychology, 35,* 691–707.

Gaertner, S. L., & Dovidio, J. F. (1986). The aversive form of racism. In J. F. Dovidio & S. L. Gaertner (Eds.), *Prejudice, discrimination, and racism.* Orlando, FL: Academic Press.

Gaertner, S. L., & Dovidio, J. F. (2005). Understanding and addressing contemporary racism: From aversive racism to the Common Ingroup Identity Model. *Journal of Social Issues, 61,* 615–639.

Gaertner, S. L., Dovidio, J. F., Nier, J. A., Banker, B. S., Ward, C. M., Houlette, M., & Loux, S. (2000). The common ingroup identity model for reducing intergroup bias: Progress and challenges. In D. Capozza & R. Brown (Eds.), *Social identity processes: Trends in theory and research.* London: Sage.

Gaertner, S. L., Mann, J., Murrell, A., & Dovidio, J. F. (2001). Reducing intergroup bias: The benefits of recategorization. In M. A. Hogg & D. Abrams (Eds.), *Intergroup relations: Essential readings.* Philadelphia: Psychology Press.

Gailliot, M. T., & Baumeister, R. F. (2007). Self-regulation and sexual restraint. Dispositionally and temporarily poor self-regulatory abilities contribute to failures at restraining sexual behavior. *Personality and Social Psychology Bulletin, 33,* 173–186.

Gaither, S. E., & Sommers, S. R. (2013). Living with an other-race roommate shapes Whites' behavior in subsequent diverse settings. *Journal of Experimental Social Psychology, 49,* 272–276.

Gal, D., & Rucker, D. D. (2010). When in doubt, shout! paradoxical influences of doubt on proselytizing. *Psychological Science, 21,* 1701–1707.

Galinsky, A. D., & Moskowitz, G. B. (2000). Perspective-taking: Decreasing stereotype expression, stereotype accessibility, and in-group favoritism. *Journal of Personality and Social Psychology, 78,* 708–724.

Galinsky, E., Aumann, K., & Bond, J. T. (2009). *Times are changing: Gender and generation at work and at home.* New York: Families and Work Institute.

Gallagher, K. M., & Updegraff, J. A. (2012). Health message framing effects on attitudes, intentions, and behavior: A meta-analytic review. *Annals of Behavioral Medicine, 43,* 101–116.

Gallo, L. C., & Matthews, K. A. (2003). Understanding the association between socioeconomic status and physical health: Do negative emotions play a role? *Psychological Bulletin, 129,* 10–51.

Gallup. (1996). Gallup survey of scientists sampled from the 1995 edition of *American Men and Women of Science.* Reported by National Center for Science Education (www.ncseweb.org).

Gallup, G. G., Jr., & Frederick, D. A. (2010). The science of sex appeal: An evolutionary perspective. *Journal of General Psychology, 14,* 240–250.

Gallup, G. G., Jr., & Frederick, M. J., & Pipitone, R. N. (2008). Morphology and behavior: Phrenology revisited. *Review of General Psychology, 12,* 297–304.

Gallup, G. H. (1972). *The Gallup poll: Public opinion 1935–1971* (Vol. 3, pp. 551, 1716). New York: Random House.

Gallup, G. H., Jr., & Jones, T. (1992). *The saints among us.* Harrisburg, PA: Morehouse.

Gallup Organization. (2003, June 16). Americans still think Iraq had weapons of mass destructions before war. (http://www.gallup.com/poll/8623/americans-still-think-iraq-had-weapons-mass-destruction-before-war.aspx)

Gallup Organization. (2003, July 8). *American public opinion about Iraq.* Gallup Poll News Service (www.gallup.com).

Gallup Organization. (2013). Same-sex marriage support solidifies above 50% in U.S. Retrieved April 1, 2015 from: http://www.gallup.com/poll/162398/sex-marriage-support-solidifies-above.aspx

Gallup Polls. (2012). Blacks, Nonblacks hold sharply different views of Trayvon Martin case. http://www.gallup.com/poll/153776/blacks-nonblacks-hold-sharply-different-views-martin-case.aspx.

Gallup Polls. (2014). Death Penalty. http://www.gallup.com/poll/1606/death-penalty.aspx.

Gangestad, S. W., Simpson, J. A., & Cousins, A. J. (2004). Women's preferences for male behavioral displays change across the menstrual cycle. *Psychological Science, 15,* 203–207.

Gangestad, S. W., & Snyder, M. (2000). Self-monitoring: Appraisal and reappraisal. *Psychological Bulletin, 126,* 530–555.

Gangestad, S. W., & Thornhill, R. (1997). Human sexual selection and developmental stability. In J. A. Simpson & D. T. Kenrick (Eds.), *Evolutionary social psychology.* Mahwah, NJ: Erlbaum.

Garb, H. N. (1994). Judgment research: Implications for clinical practice and testimony in court. *Applied and Preventive Psychology, 3,* 173–183.

Garb, H. N. (2005). Clinical judgment and decision making. *Annual Review of Clinical Psychology, 1,* 67–89.

Garcia-Marques, T., Mackie, D. M., Claypool, H. M., & Garcia-Marques, L. (2004). Positivity can cue familiarity. *Personality and Social Psychology Bulletin, 30,* 585–593.

Gardner, G., & Assadourian, E. (2004). Rethinking the good life. Chapter 8 in *State of the World 2004.* Washington, DC: WorldWatch Institute.

Gardner, W. L., Pickett, L., Jefferis, V., & Knowles, M. (2005). On the outside looking in: Loneliness and social monitoring. *Personality and Social Psychology Bulletin, 31,* 1549–1560.

Garneau, C., Olmstead, S. B., Pasley, K., & Fincham, F. D. (2013). The role of family structure and attachment in college student hookups. *Archives of Sexual Behavior, 42,* 1473–1486.

Garrett, B. L. (2011a, August 31). Procedures that defy science. *New York Times* (www.nytimes.com).

Garrett, B. L. (2011b, April 12). Getting it wrong: Convicting the innocent. *Slate* (www.slate.com).

Garry, M., Manning, C. G., Loftus, E. F., & Sherman, S. J. (1996). Imagination inflation: Imagining a childhood event inflates confidence that it occurred. *Psychonomic Bulletin & Review, 3,* 208–214.

Garver-Apgar, C. E., Gangestad, S. W., Thornhill, R., Miller, R. D., & Olp, J. J. (2006). Major histocompatibility complex alleles, sexual responsivity, and unfaithfulness in romantic couples. *Psychological Science, 17,* 830–834.

Gates, G. J. (2011, April). *How many people are lesbian, gay, bisexual, and transgender?* Los Angeles: The William Institute, UCLA School of Law.

Gates, M. F., & Allee, W. C. (1933). Conditioned behavior of isolated and grouped cockroaches on a simple maze. *Journal of Comparative Psychology, 15,* 331–358.

Gati, I., & Perez, M. (2014). Gender differences in career preferences from 1990 to 2010: Gaps reduced but not eliminated. *Journal of Counseling Psychology, 61,* 63–80.

Gaucher, D., Friesen, J., & Kay, A. C. (2011). Evidence that gendered wording in job advertisements exists and sustains gender inequality. *Journal of Personality and Social Psychology, 101,* 109–128.

Gaunt, R. (2006). Couple similarity and marital satisfaction: Are similar spouses happier? *Journal of Personality, 74,* 1401–1420.

Gavanski, I., & Hoffman, C. (1987). Awareness of influences on one's own judgments: The roles of covariation detection and attention to the judgment process. *Journal of Personality and Social Psychology, 52,* 453–463.

Gavzer, B. (1997, January 5). Are trial consultants good for justice? *Parade,* 20.

Gawande, A. (2002). *Complications: A surgeon's notes on an imperfect science.* New York: Metropolitan Books, Holt.

Gawronski, B., & Bodenhausen, G. V. (2006). Associative and propositional processes in evaluation: An integrative review of implicit and explicit attitude change. *Psychological Bulletin, 132,* 692–731.

Gayoso, A., Cutler, B. L., & Moran, G. (1991). *Assessing the value of social scientists as trial consultants: A consumer research approach.* Unpublished manuscript, Florida International University.

Gazzaniga, M. (1998). *The mind's past.* Berkeley, CA: University of California Press.

Gazzaniga, M. (2008). *Human: The science behind what makes us unique.* New York: Ecco.

Gazzaniga, M. S. (1985). *The social brain: Discovering the networks of the mind.* New York: Basic Books.

Gazzaniga, M. S. (1992). *Nature's mind: The biological roots of thinking, emotions, sexuality, language, and intelligence.* New York: Basic Books.

Gazzaniga, M. S. (2011, April). Neuroscience in the courtroom. *Scientific American,* 54–59.

Gebauer, J. E., Riketta, M., Broemer, P., & Maio, G. R. (2008). "How much do you like your name?" An implicit measure of global self-esteem. *Journal of Experimental Social Psychology, 44,* 1346–1354.

Geenen, N. Y. R., Hohelüchter, M., Langholf, V., & Walther, E. (2014). The beneficial effects of prosocial spending on happiness: Work hard, make money, and spend it on others? *The Journal of Positive Psychology, 9,* 204–208.

Geen, R. G. (1998). Aggression and antisocial behavior. In D. Gilbert, S. Fiske, & G. Lindzey (Eds.), *Handbook of social psychology,* 4th edition. New York: McGraw-Hill.

Geen, R. G., & Gange, J. J. (1983). Social facilitation: Drive theory and beyond. In H. H. Blumberg, A. P. Hare, V. Kent, & M. Davies (Eds.), *Small groups and social interaction* (Vol. 1). London: Wiley.

Geen, R. G., & Thomas, S. L. (1986). The immediate effects of media violence on behavior. *Journal of Social Issues, 42(3),* 7–28.

Geers, A. L., Handley, I. M., & McLarney, A. R. (2003). Discerning the role of optimism in persuasion: The valence-enhancement hypothesis. *Journal of Personality and Social Psychology, 85,* 554–565.

Gelfand, M. J. & 44 others. (2011). Differences between tight and loose cultures: A 33-nation study. *Science, 332,* 1100–1104.

Gentile, B. C., Twenge, J. M., & Campbell, W. K. (2009). Birth cohort differences in self-esteem, 1988–2008: A cross-temporal meta-analysis. Unpublished manuscript.

Gentile, B., Twenge, J. M., & Campbell, W. K. (2010). Birth cohort differences in self-esteem, 1988–2008: A cross-temporal meta-analysis. *Review of General Psychology, 14,* 261–268.

Gentile, B., Twenge, J. M., Freeman, E. C., & Campbell, W. K. (2012). The effect of social networking websites on positive self-views: An experimental investigation. *Computers in Human Behavior, 28,* 1929–1933.

Gentile, D. A. (2004, May 14). Quoted by K. Laurie in *Violent games* (ScienCentral.com).

Gentile, D. A., & Anderson, C. A. (2003). Violent video games: The newest media violence hazard. In D. A. Gentile (Ed.), *Media violence and children.* Westport, CT: Ablex.

Gentile, D. A., & Anderson, C. A. (2011). Don't read more into the Supreme Court's ruling on the California video game law. Iowa State University press release, June 30, 2011. www.psychology.iastate.edu/faculty/caa/Multimedia/VGV-SC-OpEdDDAGCAA.pdf.

Gentile, D. A., & Bushman, B. J. (2012). Reassessing media violence effects using a risk and resilence approach to understanding aggression. *Psychology of Popular Media Culture, 1,* 138–151.

Gentile, D. A., Lynch, P. J., Linder, J. R., & Walsh, D. A. (2004). The effects of violent video game habits on adolescent hostility, aggressive behaviors, and school performance. *Journal of Adolescence, 27,* 5–22.

Gentile, D. A., Saleem, M., & Anderson, C. A. (2007). Public policy and the effects of media violence on children. *Social Issues and Policy Review, 1,* 15–61.

George, D., Carroll, P., Kersnick, R., & Calderon, K. (1998). Gender-related patterns of helping among friends. *Psychology of Women Quarterly, 22,* 685–704.

Gerard, H. B. (1999). A social psychologist examines his past and looks to the future. In A. Rodrigues & R. Levine (Eds.), *Reflections on 100 years of experimental social psychology.* New York: Basic Books.

Gerard, H. B., Wilhelmy, R. A., & Conolley, E. S. (1968). Conformity and group size. *Journal of Personality and Social Psychology, 8,* 79–82.

Gerbasi, K. C., Zuckerman, M., & Reis, H. T. (1977). Justice needs a new blindfold: A review of mock jury research. *Psychological Bulletin, 84,* 323–345.

Gerber, A. S., & Green, D. P. (1999). Does canvassing increase voter turnout? A field experiment. *Proceedings of the National Academic of Sciences of the United States of America, 96,* 10939–10942.

Gerbner, G. (1994). The politics of media violence: Some reflections. In C. Hamelink & O. Linne (Eds.), *Mass communication research: On problems and policies.* Norwood, NJ: Ablex.

Gerbner, G., Gross, L., Signorielli, N., Morgan, M., & Jackson-Beeck, M. (1979). The demonstration of power: Violence profile No. 10. *Journal of Communication, 29,* 177–196.

Gergen, K. E. (1982). *Toward transformation in social knowledge.* New York: Springer-Verlag.

Gerrig, R. J., & Prentice, D. A. (1991, September). The representation of fictional information. *Psychological Science, 2,* 336–340.

Gershoff, E. T. (2002). Corporal punishment by parents and associated child behaviors and experiences: A meta-analytic and theoretical review. *Psychological Bulletin, 128,* 539–579.

Gerstenfeld, P. B., Grant, D. R., & Chiang, C.-P. (2003). Hate online: A content analysis of extremist Internet sites. *Analyses of Social Issues and Public Policy, 3,* 29–44.

Gesch, C. B., Hammond, S. M., Hampson, S. E., Eves, A., & Crowder, M. J. (2002). Influence of supplementary vitamins, minerals and essential fatty acids on the antisocial behavior of young adult prisoners. Randomised, placebo-controlled trial. *British Journal of Psychiatry, 181,* 22–28.

Ghumman, S., & Barnes, C. M. (2013). Sleep and prejudice: A resource recovery approach. *Journal of Applied Social Psychology, 43,* E166–E178.

Giancola, P. R., & Corman, M. D. (2007). Alcohol and aggression: A test of the attention-allocation model. *Psychological Science, 18,* 649–655.

Gibbons, F. X. (1978). Sexual standards and reactions to pornography: Enhancing behavioral consistency through self-focused attention. *Journal of Personality and Social Psychology, 36,* 976–987.

Gibbons, F. X., & Wicklund, R. A. (1982). Self-focused attention and helping behavior. *Journal of Personality and Social Psychology, 43,* 462–474.

Gibson, J. I., & Claassen, C. (2010). Racial reconciliation in South Africa: Interracial contact. *Journal of Social Issues, 66,* 255–272.

Gibson, S. (2013). Milgram's obedience experiments: A rhetorical analysis. *British Journal of Social Psychology, 52,* 290–309.

Gifford, R. (2011). The dragons of inaction: Psychological barriers that limit climate change mitigation and adaptation. *American Psychologist, 66,* 290–302.

Gifford, R., & Hine, D. W. (1997). Toward cooperation in commons dilemmas. *Canadian Journal of Behavioural Science, 29,* 167–179.

Gigerenzer, G. (2004). Dread risk, September 11, and fatal traffic accidents. *Psychological Science, 15,* 286–287.

Gigerenzer, G. (2007). *Gut feelings: The intelligence of the unconscious.* New York: Viking.

Gigerenzer, G. (2010). *Rationality for mortals: How people cope with uncertainty.* New York: Oxford University Press.

Gigerenzer, G., & Gaissmaier, W. (2011). Heuristic decision making. *Annual Review of Psychology, 62,* 451–482.

Gigone, D., & Hastie, R. (1993). The common knowledge effect: Information sharing and group judgment. *Journal of Personality and Social Psychology, 65,* 959–974.

Gilbert, D. T., & Ebert, J. E. J. (2002). Decisions and revisions: The affective forecasting of escapable outcomes. Unpublished manuscript, Harvard University.

Gilbert, D. T., Giesler, R. B., & Morris, K. A. (1995). When comparisons arise. *Journal of Personality and Social Psychology, 69,* 227–236.

Gilbert, D. T., & Hixon, J. G. (1991). The trouble of thinking: Activation and application of stereotypic beliefs. *Journal of Personality and Social Psychology, 60,* 509–517.

Gilbert, D. T., & Jones, E. E. (1986). Perceiver-induced constraint: Interpretations of self-generated reality. *Journal of Personality and Social Psychology, 50,* 269–280.

Gilbert, D. T., Krull, D. S., & Malone, P. S. (1990). Unbelieving the unbelievable: Some problems in the rejection of false information. *Journal of Personality and Social Psychology, 59,* 601–613.

Gilbert, D. T., Lieberman, M. D., Morewedge, C. K., & Wilson, T. D. (2004). The peculiar longevity of things not so bad. *Psychological Science, 15,* 14–19.

Gilbert, D. T., & Malone, P. S. (1995). The correspondence bias. *Psychological Bulletin, 117,* 21–38.

Gilbert, D. T., Pinel, E. C., Wilson, T. D., Blumberg, S. J., & Wheatley, T. P. (1998). Immune neglect: A source of durability bias in affective forecasting. *Journal of Personality and Social Psychology, 75,* 617–638.

Gilbert, D. T., Tafarodi, R. W., & Malone, P. S. (1993). You can't not believe everything you read. *Journal of Personality and Social Psychology, 65,* 221–233.

Gilbert, D. T., & Wilson, T. D. (2000). Miswanting: Some problems in the forecasting of future affective states. In J. Forgas (Ed.), *Feeling and thinking: The role of affect in social cognition.* Cambridge, England: Cambridge University Press.

Gildersleeve, K., Haselton, M. G., & Fales, M. R. (2014). Do women's mate preferences change across the ovulatory cycle? A meta-analytic review. *Psychological Bulletin. 140,* 1205–1259.

Gillath, O. M., Shaver, P. R., Baek, J.-M., & Chun, D. S. (2008). Genetic correlates of adult attachment. *Personality and Social Psychology Bulletin, 34,* 1396–1405.

Gillham, J. E., Shatte, A. J., Reivich, K. J., & Seligman, M. E. P. (2000). Optimism, pessimism, and explanatory style. In E. C. Chang (Ed.), *Optimism and pessimism.* Washington, DC: APA Books.

Gilligan, C. (1982). *In a different voice: Psychological theory and women's development.* Cambridge, MA: Harvard University Press.

Gilligan, C., Lyons, N. P., & Hanmer, T. J. (Eds.) (1990). *Making connections: The relational worlds of adolescent girls at Emma Willard School.* Cambridge, MA: Harvard University Press.

Gillis, J. (2013, January 8). Not even close: 2012 was hottest ever in U.S. *New York Times* www.nytimes.com).

Gillis, J. S., & Avis, W. E. (1980). The male-taller norm in mate selection. *Personality and Social Psychology Bulletin, 6,* 396–401.

Gilovich, T., & Douglas, C. (1986). Biased evaluations of randomly determined gambling outcomes. *Journal of Experimental Social Psychology, 22,* 228–241.

Gilovich, T., & Eibach, R. (2001). The fundamental attribution error where it really counts. *Psychological Inquiry, 12,* 23–26.

Gilovich, T., Kerr, M., & Medvec, V. H. (1993). Effect of temporal perspective on subjective confidence. *Journal of Personality and Social Psychology, 64,* 552–560.

Gilovich, T., & Kumar, A. (2015). We'll always have Paris: The hedonic payoff from experiential and material investments. In M. Zanna & J. Olson (Eds.), *Advances in Experimental Social Psychology, 51,* in press. New York: Elsevier.

Gilovich, T., & Medvec, V. H. (1994). The temporal pattern to the experience of regret. *Journal of Personality and Social Psychology, 67,* 357–365.

Gilovich, T., Medvec, V. H., & Savitsky, K. (2000). The spotlight effect in social judgment: An egocentric bias in estimates of the salience of one's own actions and appearance. *Journal of Personality and Social Psychology, 78,* 211–222.

Gilovich, T., Savitsky, K., & Medvec, V. H. (1998). The illusion of transparency: Biased assessments of others' ability to read one's emotional states. *Journal of Personality and Social Psychology, 75,* 332–346.

Gilsdorf, E. (2013). Why we need violent video games. Cognoscenti, January 17, 2013. http://cognoscenti.wbur.org/2013/01/17/video-games-ethan-gilsdorf

Giltay, E. J., Geleijnse, J. M., Zitman, F. G., Buijsse, B., & Kromhout, D. (2007). Lifestyle and dietary correlates of dispositional optimism in men: The Zutphen Elderly Study. *Journal of Psychosomatic Research, 63,* 483–490.

Giltay, E. J., Geleijnse, J. M., Zitman, F. G., Hoekstra, T., & Schouten, E. G. (2004). Dispositional optimism and all-cause and cardiovascular mortality in a prospective cohort of elderly Dutch men and women. *Archives of General Psychiatry, 61,* 1126–1135.

Gini, G., Pozzoli, T., & Hymel, S. (2014). Moral disengagement among children and youth: A meta-analytic review of links to aggressive behavior. *Aggressive Behavior, 40,* 56–68.

Gino, F., Ayal, S., & Ariely, D. (2009). Contagion and differentiation in unethical behavior: The effect of one bad apple on the barrel. *Psychological Science, 20,* 393–398.

Ginsburg, B., & Allee, W. C. (1942). Some effects of conditioning on social dominance and subordination in inbred strains of mice. *Physiological Zoology, 15,* 485–506.

Gladwell, M. (2003, March 10). Connecting the dots: The paradoxes of intelligence reform. *New Yorker,* pp. 83–88.

Glasman, L. R., & Albarracin, D. (2006). Forming attitudes that predict future behavior: A meta-analysis of the attitude-behavior relation. *Psychological Bulletin, 132,* 778–822.

Glass, D. C. (1964). Changes in liking as a means of reducing cognitive discrepancies between self-esteem and aggression. *Journal of Personality, 32,* 531–549.

Gleason, M. E. J., Iida, M., Bolger, N., & Shrout, P. E. (2003). Daily supportive equity in close relationships. *Personality and Social Psychology Bulletin, 29,* 1036–1045.

Glick, P., & Fiske, S. T. (1996). The ambivalent sexism inventory: Differentiating hostile and benevolent sexism. *Journal of Personality and Social Psychology, 70,* 491–512.

Glick, P., & Fiske, S. T. (2007). Sex discrimination: The psychological approach. In F. J. Crosby, M. S. Stockdale, & S. Ropp (Eds.), *Sex discrimination in the workplace: Multidisciplinary perspectives.* Malden, MA: Blackwell.

Glick, P., & Fiske, S. T. (2011). Ambivalent sexism revisited. *Psychology of Women Quarterly, 35,* 530–535.

Glick, P., Gangl, C., Gibb, S., Klumpner, S., & Weinberg, E. (2007). Defensive reactions to masculinity threat: More negative affect toward effeminate (but not masculine) gay men. *Sex Roles, 57,* 55–59.

GLSEN. (2012). The 2011 National School Climate Survey. New York: Gay, Lesbian & Straight Education Network (www.glsen.org).

Gluszek, A., & Dovidio, J. F. (2010). The way *they* speak: A social psychological perspective on the stigma of nonnative accents in communication. *Personality and Social Psychology Review, 14,* 214–237.

Gockel, C., Kerr, N. L., Seok, D-H., & Harris, D. W. (2008). Indispensability and group identification as sources of task motivation. *Journal of Experimental Social Psychology, 44,* 1316–1321.

Goel, S., Mason, W., & Watts, D. J. (2010). Real and perceived attitude agreement in social networks. *Journal of Personality and Social Psychology, 99,* 611–621.

Goethals, G. R., Messick, D. M., & Allison, S. T. (1991). The uniqueness bias: Studies of constructive social comparison. In J. Suls & T. A. Wills (Eds.), *Social comparison: Contemporary theory and research.* Hillsdale, NJ: Erlbaum.

Goetz, J. L., Keltner, D., & Simon-Thomas, E. (2010). Compassion: An evolutionary analysis and empirical review. *Psychological Bulletin, 136,* 351–374.

Goetz, S. M. M., Tang, L., Thomason, M. E., Diamond, M. P., Hariri, A. R., & Carre, J. M. (2014). Testosterone rapidly increases neural reactivity to threat in healthy men: A novel two-step pharmacological challenge paradigm *Biological Psychiatry, 76,* 324–331.

Goggin, W. C., & Range, L. M. (1985). The disadvantages of hindsight in the perception of suicide. *Journal of Social and Clinical Psychology, 3,* 232–237.

Goh, J. O., Chee, M. W., Tan, J. C., Venkatraman, V., Hebrank, A., Leshikar, E. D., Jenkins, L., Sutton, B. P., Gutchess, A. H., & Park, D. C. (2007). Age and culture modulate object processing and object-science binding in the ventral visual area. *Cognitive, Affective & Behavioral Neuroscience, 7,* 44–52.

Goldhagen, D. J. (1996). *Hitler's willing executioners.* New York: Knopf.

Goldman, S. K. (2012). Effects of the 2008 Obama presidential campaign on White racial prejudice. *Public Opinion Quarterly, 76,* 663–687.

Goldman, W., & Lewis, P. (1977). Beautiful is good: Evidence that the physically attractive are more socially skillful. *Journal of Experimental Social Psychology, 13,* 125–130.

Goldstein, A. P. (1994). Delinquent gangs. In A. P. Goldstein, B. Harootunian, and J. C. Conoley (Eds.), *Student aggression: Prevention, control, and replacement.* New York: Guilford.

Goldstein, A. P., Glick, B., & Gibbs, J. C. (1998). Aggression replacement training: A comprehensive intervention for aggressive youth (rev. ed.). Champaign, IL: Research Press.

Goldstein, J. H., & Arms, R. L. (1971). Effects of observing athletic contests on hostility. *Sociometry, 34,* 83–90.

Golomb, B. A., Evans, M. A., White, H. L., & Dimsdale, J. E. (2012). Trans fat consumption and aggression. *Plos ONE, 7,* doi:10.1371/journal.pone.0032175

Gómez, Á., Brooks, M. L., Buhrmeister, M. D., Váquez, A., Jetten, J., & Swann, Jr., W. B. (2011). On the nature of identity fusion: Insights into the construct and a new measure. *Journal of Personality and Social Psychology, 100,* 918–933.

Gonsalkorale, K., & Williams, K. D. (2006). The KKK would not let me play: Ostracism even by a despised outgroup hurts. *European Journal of Social Psychology, 36,* 1–11.

Gonsalves, B., Reber, P. J., Gitelman, D. R., Parrish, T. B., Mesulam, M-M., & Paller, K. A. (2004). Neural evidence that vivid imagining can lead to false remembering. *Psychological Science, 15,* 655–659.

Gonzaga, G. C., Campos, B., & Bradbury, T. (2007). Similarity, convergence, and relationship satisfaction in dating and married couples. *Journal of Personality and Social Psychology, 93,* 34–48.

Gonzaga, G. C., Keltner, D., Londahl, E. A., & Smith, M. D. (2001). Love and the commitment problem in romantic relations and friendship. *Journal of Personality and Social Psychology, 81,* 247–262.

Gonzales, A. L., & Hancock, J. T. (2011). Mirror, mirror on my Facebook wall: Effects of exposure to Facebook on self-esteem. *Cyberpsychology, Behavior, and Social Networking, 14,* 79–83.

González, K. V., Verkuyten, M., Weesie, J., & Poppe, E. (2008). Prejudice towards Muslims in the Netherlands: Testing integrated threat theory. *British Journal of Social Psychology, 47,* 667–685.

Goode, E., & Schwartz, J. (2011, August 28). Police lineups start to face fact: Eyes can lie. *New York Times* (www.nytimes.com).

Goodhart, D. E. (1986). The effects of positive and negative thinking on performance in an achievement situation.

Journal of Personality and Social Psychology, 51, 117–124.

Goodman-Delahunty, J., Granhag, P. A., Hartwig, M., & Loftus, E. F. (2010). Insightful or wishful: Lawyers' ability to predict case outcomes. *Psychology, Public Policy, and Law, 16,* 133–157.

Goodman, J. D. (2012, November 28). Photo of officer giving boots to barefoot man warms hearts online. *New York Times* (www.nytimes.com).

Goodsell, C. A., Gronlund, S. D., & Carlson, C. A. (2010). Exploring the sequential lineup advantage using WITNESS. *Law and Human Behavior, 34,* 445–459.

Gordijn, E. H., De Vries, N. K., & De Dreu, C. K. W. (2002). Minority influence on focal and related attitudes: Change in size, attributions and information processing. *Personality and Social Psychology Bulletin, 28,* 1315–1326.

Gordon, R. A. (1996). Impact of ingratiation on judgments and evaluations: A meta-analytic investigation. *Journal of Personality and Social Psychology, 71,* 54–70.

Gore, A. (2007, July 1). Moving beyond Kyoto. *New York Times* (www.nytimes.com).

Gorman, J. (2012, December 17). Ancient bones tell a story of compassion. *New York Times* (www.nytimes.com).

Gortmaker, S. L., Must, A., Perrin, J. M., Sobol, A. M., & Dietz, W. H. (1993). Social and economic consequences of overweight in adolescence and young adulthood. *New England Journal of Medicine, 329,* 1008–1012.

Gotlib, I. H., & Colby, C. A. (1988). How to have a good quarrel. In P. Marsh (Ed.), *Eye to eye: How people interact.* Topsfield, MA: Salem House.

Gottlieb, J., & Carver, C. S. (1980). Anticipation of future interaction and the bystander effect. *Journal of Experimental Social Psychology, 16,* 253–260.

Gottman, J. (with N. Silver). (1994). *Why marriages succeed or fail.* New York: Simon & Schuster.

Gottman, J. (2005, April 14). The mathematics of love. *Edge,* No. 159 (www.edge.org).

Gottman, J. M. (1998). Psychology and the study of marital processes. *Annual Review of Psychology, 49,* 169–197.

Gough, H. G., & Thorne, A. (1986). Positive, negative, and balanced shyness. In W. H. Jones, J. M. Cheek, & S. R. Briggs (Eds.), *Shyness: Perspectives on research and treatment.* New York: Plenum.

Gough, S. (2003, November 3). My journey so far (www.nakedwalk.alivewww.co.uk/about_me.htm).

Gouldner, A. W. (1960). The norm of reciprocity: A preliminary statement. *American Sociological Review, 25,* 161–178.

Gove, W. R., Style, C. B., & Hughes, M. (1990). The effect of marriage on the well-being of adults: A theoretical analysis. *Journal of Family Issues, 11,* 4–35.

Graf, S., Paolini, S., & Rubin, M. (2014). Negative intergroup contact is more influential, but positive intergroup contact is more common: Assessing contact prominence and contact prevalence in five Central European countries. *European Journal of Social Psychology, 44,* 536–547.

Graham, J., Nosek, B. A., & Haidt, J. (2012, December 12). The moral stereotypes of liberals and conservatives: Exaggeration of differences across the political spectrum. *PLoS ONE 7*: e50092.

Granberg, D., & Bartels, B. (2005). On being a lone dissenter. *Journal of Applied Social Psychology, 35,* 1849–1858.

Granstrom, K., & Stiwne, D. (1998). A bipolar model of groupthink: An expansion of Janis's concept. *Small Group Research, 29,* 32–56.

Grant, A. (2013, July 20). Why men need women. *New York Times* (www.nytimes.com).

Grant, A. M. (2013). Rethinking the extraverted sales ideal: The ambivert advantage. *Psychological Science, 24,* 1024–1030.

Gray, J. D., & Silver, R. C. (1990). Opposite sides of the same coin: Former spouses' divergent perspectives in coping with their divorce. *Journal of Personality and Social Psychology, 59,* 1180–1191.

Greeley, A. M. (1991). *Faithful attraction.* New York: Tor Books.

Greeley, A. M., & Sheatsley, P. B. (1971). Attitudes toward racial integration. *Scientific American, 225*(6), 13–19.

Green, A. R., Carney, D. R., Pallin, D. J., Ngo, L. H., Raymond, K. L., Iezzoni, L. I., & Banaji, M. R. (2007). Implicit bias among physicians and its prediction of thrombolysis decisions for Black and White patients. *Journal of General Internal Medicine, 22,* 1231–1238.

Green, C. W., Adams, A. M., & Turner, C. W. (1988). Development and validation of the school interracial climate scale. *American Journal of Community Psychology, 16,* 241–259.

Green, D. P., Glaser, J., & Rich, A. (1998). From lynching to gay bashing: The elusive connection between economic conditions and hate crime. *Journal of Personality and Social Psychology, 75,* 82–92.

Green, D. P., & Wong, J. S. (2008). Tolerance and the contact hypothesis: A field experiment. In E. Borgida (Ed.), *The political psychology of democratic citizenship.* London: Oxford University Press.

Green, M. C., Strange, J. J., & Brock, T. C. (Eds.) (2002). *Narrative impact: Social and cognitive foundations.* Mahwah, NJ: Erlbaum.

Greenaway, K. H., Louis, W. R., Hornsey, M. J., & Jones, J. M. (2014). Perceived control qualifies the effects of threat on prejudice. *British Journal of Social Psychology, 53,* 422–442.

Greenberg, J. (1986). Differential intolerance for inequity from organizational and individual agents. *Journal of Applied Social Psychology, 16,* 191–196.

Greenberg, J. (2008). Understanding the vital human quest for self-esteem. *Perspectives on Psychological Science, 3,* 48–55.

Greenberg, J., Landau, M. J., & Arndt, J. (2013). Mortal cognition: Viewing self and the world from the precipice. In Carlston, D. E. (Ed.) *The Oxford handbook of social cognition.* (pp. 680–701) New York: Oxford University Press.

Greenberg, J., Pyszczynski, T., Solomon, S., Rosenblatt, A., Veeder, M., Kirkland, S., & Lyon, D. (1990). Evidence for terror management theory II: The effects of mortality salience on reactions to those who threaten or bolster the cultural worldview. *Journal of Personality and Social Psychology, 58,* 308–318.

Greenberg, J., Schimel, J., Martens, A., Solomon, S., & Pyszczynski, T. (2001). Sympathy for the devil: Evidence that reminding whites of their mortality promotes more favorable reactions to white racists. *Motivation and Emotion, 25,* 113–133.

Greene, E., Flynn, M. S., & Loftus, E. F. (1982). Inducing resistance to misleading information. *Journal of Verbal Learning & Verbal Behavior, 21,* 207–219.

Greenfield, P. M. (2009). Linking social change and developmental change: Shifting pathways of human development. *Developmental Psychology, 45,* 401–408.

Greenfield, P. M. (2013). The changing psychology of culture from 1800 through 2000. *Psychological Science, 24,* 1722–1731.

Greenwald, A. G. (1975). On the inconclusiveness of crucial cognitive tests of dissonance versus self-perception theories. *Journal of Experimental Social Psychology, 11,* 490–499.

Greenwald, A. G. (1980). The totalitarian ego: Fabrication and revision of personal history. *American Psychologist, 35,* 603–618.

Greenwald, A. G. (1992). New look 3: Unconscious cognition reclaimed. *American Psychologist, 47,* 766–779.

Greenwald, A. G., Banaji, M. R., & Nosek, B. A. (2015). Statistically small effects of the Implicit Association Test can have societally large effects. *Journal of Personality and Social Psychology,* in press.

Greenwald, A. G., Nosek, B. A., & Banaji, M. R. (2003). Understanding and using the implicit association test: I. An improved scoring algorithm. *Journal of Personality and Social Psychology, 85,* 197–216.

Greenwald, A. G., & Pettigrew, T. F. (2014). With malice toward none and charity for some: Ingroup favoritism enables discrimination. *American Psychologist, 69,* 669–684.

Greenwald, A. G., & Schuh, E. S. (1994). An ethnic bias in scientific citations. *European Journal of Social Psychology, 24,* 623–639.

Greenwald, G. (2012, March 19). Discussing the motives of the Afghan shooter: The contrast is glaring in how we talk about violence by Americans versus violence toward Americans. *Salon* (www.salon.com).

Greitemeyer, T. (2009). Stereotypes of singles: Are singles what we think? *European Journal of Social Psychology, 39,* 368–383.

Greitemeyer, T. (2009a). Effects of songs with prosocial lyrics on prosocial thoughts, affect, and behavior. *Journal of Experimental Social Psychology, 45,* 186–190.

Greitemeyer, T. (2009b). Effects of songs with prosocial lyrics on prosocial behavior: Further evidence and a mediating mechanism. *Personality and Social Psychology Bulletin, 35,* 1500–1511.

Greitemeyer, T. (2009c). Effects of songs with prosocial lyrics on prosocial thoughts, affect, and behavior. *Journal of Experimental Social Psychology, 45,* 186–190.

Greitemeyer, T. (2011). Exposure to music with prosocial lyrics reduces aggression: First evidence and test of the underlying mechanism. *Journal of Experimental Social Psychology, 47,* 28–36.

Greitemeyer, T. (2014). Intense acts of violence during video game play make daily life aggression appear innocuous: A new mechanism why violent video games increase aggression. *Journal of Experimental Social Psychology, 50,* 52–56.

Greitemeyer, T., Agthe, M., Turner, R., & Gschwendtner, C. (2012). Acting prosocially reduces retaliation: Effects of prosocial video games on aggressive behavior. *European Journal of Social Psychology, 42,* 235–242.

Greitemeyer, T., & McLatchie, N. (2011). Denying humanness to others: A newly discovered mechanism by which violent video games increase aggressive behavior. *Psychological Science, 22,* 659–665.

Greitemeyer, T., & Osswald, S. (2010). Effects of prosocial video games on prosocial behavior. *Journal of Personality and Social Psychology, 98,* 211–221.

Greitemeyer, T., Osswald, S., & Brauer, M. (2010). Playing prosocial video games increases empathy and decreases Schadenfreude. *Emotion, 10,* 796–802.

Griffith, S. (2012). Hold the extra burgers and fries when people pleasers arrive. Think blog. February 1, 2012 (blog.case.edu).

Griffitt, W. (1970). Environmental effects on interpersonal affective behavior.

Ambient effective temperature and attraction. *Journal of Personality and Social Psychology, 15,* 240–244.

Griffitt, W. (1987). Females, males, and sexual responses. In K. Kelley (Ed.), *Females, males, and sexuality: Theories and research.* Albany: State University of New York Press.

Griffitt, W., & Veitch, R. (1971). Hot and crowded: Influences of population density and temperature on interpersonal affective behavior. *Journal of Personality and Social Psychology, 17,* 92–98.

Griggs, R. (2014). Coverage of the Stanford Prison Experiment in introductory psychology textbooks. *Teaching of Psychology, 41,* 195–203.

Griskevicius, V., Tybur, J. M., Gangestad, S. W., Perea, E. F., Shapiro, J. R., & Kenrick, D. T. (2009). Aggress to impress: Hostility as an evolved context-dependent strategy. *Journal of Personality and Social Psychology, 96,* 980–994.

Griskevicius, V., Tybur, J. M., Sundie, J. M., Cialdini, R. B., Miller, G. F., & Kenrick, D. T. (2007). Blatant benevolence and conspicuous consumption: When romantic motives elicit strategic costly signals. *Journal of Personality and Social Psychology, 93,* 85–102.

Groenenboom, A., Wilke, H. A. M., & Wit, A. P. (2001). Will we be working together again? The impact of future interdependence on group members' task motivation. *European Journal of Social Psychology, 31,* 369–378.

Grofman, B. (1980). The slippery slope: Jury size and jury verdict requirements—Legal and social science approaches. In B. H. Raven (Ed.), *Policy studies review annual* (Vol. 4). Beverly Hills, CA: Sage.

Gronlund, S. D. (2004a). Sequential lineups: Shift in criterion or decision strategy? *Journal of Applied Psychology, 89,* 362–368.

Gronlund, S. D. (2004b). Sequential lineup advantage: Contributions of distinctiveness and recollection. *Applied Cognitive Psychology, 19,* 23–37.

Gross, A. E., & Crofton, C. (1977). What is good is beautiful. *Sociometry, 40,* 85–90.

Gross, J. T. (2001). *Neighbors: The destruction of the Jewish community in Jedwabne, Poland.* Princeton: Princeton University Press.

Gross, T. F. (2009). Own-ethnicity bias in the recognition of Black, East Asian, Hispanic, and White faces. *Basic and Applied Social Psychology, 31,* 128–135.

Grossmann, I., Na, J., Varnum, M. E. W., Park, D. C., Kitayama, S., & Nisbett, R. E. (2010). Reasoning about social conflicts improves into old age. *PNAS, 107,* 7246–7250.

Grossman, S. (2014, February 16). 1 in 4 Americans apparently unaware the Earth orbits the Sun. Time.com. (http://time.com/7809/1-in-4-americans-thinks-sun-orbits-earth/).

Grote, N. K., & Clark, M. S. (2001). Perceiving unfairness in the family: Cause or consequence of marital distress? *Journal of Personality and Social Psychology, 80,* 281–293.

Grove, J. R., Hanrahan, S. J., & McInman, A. (1991). Success/failure bias in attributions across involvement categories in sport. *Personality and Social Psychology Bulletin, 17,* 93–97.

Grove, W. M., Zald, D. H., Lebow, B. S., Snitz, B. E., & Nelson, C. (2000). Clinical versus mechanical prediction: A meta-analysis. *Psychological Assessment, 12,* 19–30.

Grube, J. W., Kleinhesselink, R. R., & Kearney, K. A. (1982). Male self-acceptance and attraction toward women. *Personality and Social Psychology Bulletin, 8,* 107–112.

Gruder, C. L. (1977). Choice of comparison persons in evaluating oneself. In J. M. Suls & R. L. Miller (Eds.), *Social comparison processes.* Washington, DC: Hemisphere.

Gruendl, M. (2005, accessed December 14). Beautycheck (www.beautycheck.de).

Gruman, J. C., & Sloan, R. P. (1983). Disease as justice: Perceptions of the victims of physical illness. *Basic and Applied Social Psychology, 4,* 39–46.

Grunberger, R. (1971). *The 12-year Reich: A social history of Nazi Germany, 1933–1945.* New York: Holt, Rinehart & Winston.

Guéguen, N. (2013). Handshaking and compliance with a request: A door-to-door setting. *Social Behavior and Personality, 41,* 1585–1588.

Guéguen, N. (2014). Door-in-the-Face technique and delay to fulfill the final request: An evaluation with a request to give blood. *The Journal of Psychology: Interdisciplinary And Applied, 148,* 569–576

Guéguen, N., Jacob, C., & Meineri, S. (2011). Effects of the Door-in-the-Face technique on restaurant customers' behavior. *International Journal of Hospitality Management, 30,* 759–761.

Guéguen, N., Marchand, M., Pascual, A., & Lourel, M. (2008). Foot-in-the-door technique using a courtship request: A field experiment. *Psychological Reports, 103,* 529–534.

Guerin, B. (1993). *Social facilitation.* Paris: Cambridge University Press.

Guerin, B. (1994). What do people think about the risks of driving? Implications for traffic safety interventions. *Journal of Applied Social Psychology, 24,* 994–1021.

Guerin, B. (1999). Social behaviors as determined by different arrangements of social consequences: Social loafing, social facilitation, deindividuation, and a modified social loafing. *The Psychological Record, 49,* 565–578.

Guimond, S., Dambrun, N., Michinov, N., & Duarte, S. (2003). Does social dominance generate prejudice? Integrating individual and contextual determinants of intergroup cognitions. *Journal of Personality and Social Psychology, 84,* 697–721.

Guiness, O. (1993). *The American hour: A time of reckoning and the once and future role of faith.* New York: Free Press.

Gulker, J. E., & Monteith, M. J. (2013). Intergroup boundaries and attitudes: The power of a single potent link. *Personality and Social Psychology Bulletin, 39,* 943–955.

Gupta, U., & Singh, P. (1982). Exploratory study of love and liking and type of marriages. *Indian Journal of Applied Psychology, 19,* 92–97.

Gutierres, S. E., Kenrick, D. T., & Partch, J. J. (1999). Beauty, dominance, and the mating game: Contrast effects in self-assessment reflect gender differences in mate selection. *Journal of Personality and Social Psychology, 25,* 1126–1134.

Gutmann, D. (1977). The cross-cultural perspective: Notes toward a comparative psychology of aging. In J. E. Birren & K. Warner Schaie (Eds.), *Handbook of the psychology of aging.* New York: Van Nostrand Reinhold.

Ha, T., van denBerg, J. E. M., Engels, R. C., & Lichtwarck-Aschoff, A. (2012). Effects of attractiveness and status in dating desire in homosexual and heterosexual men and women. *Archives of Sexual Behavior, 41,* 673–682.

Hacker, H. M. (1951). Women as a minority group. *Social Forces, 30,* 60–69.

Hackman, J. R. (1986). The design of work teams. In J. Lorsch (Ed.), *Handbook of organizational behavior.* Englewood Cliffs, NJ: Prentice-Hall.

Hadden, J. K. (1969). *The gathering storm in the churches.* Garden City, NY: Doubleday.

Haddock, G., Maio, G. R., Arnold, K., & Huskinson, T. (2008). Should persuasion be affective or cognitive? The moderating effects of need for affect and need for cognition. *Personality and Social Psychology Bulletin, 34,* 769–778.

Haddock, G., & Zanna, M. P. (1994). Preferring "housewives" to "feminists." *Psychology of Women Quarterly, 18,* 25–52.

Haeffel, G. J., Gibb, B. E., Metalsky, G. I., Alloy, L. B., Abramson, L. Y., Hankin, B. L., Joiner, T. E., Jr., & Swendsen, J. D. (2008). Measuring cognitive vulnerability to depression: Development and validation of the cognitive style questionnaire. *Clinical Psychology Review, 28,* 824–836.

Haemmerlie, F. M. (1987). Creating adaptive illusions in counseling and therapy using a self-perception theory perspective. Paper presented at the Midwestern Psychological Association, Chicago.

Haemmerlie, F. M., & Montgomery, R. L. (1982). Self-perception theory and unobtrusively biased interactions: A treatment for heterosocial anxiety. *Journal of Counseling Psychology, 29,* 362–370.

Haemmerlie, F. M., & Montgomery, R. L. (1984). Purposefully biased interventions: Reducing heterosocial anxiety through self-perception theory. *Journal of*

Personality and Social Psychology, 47, 900–908.

Haemmerlie, F. M., & Montgomery, R. L. (1986). Self-perception theory and the treatment of shyness. In W. H. Jones, J. M. Cheek, & S. R. Briggs (Eds.), *A sourcebook on shyness: Research and treatment.* New York: Plenum.

Hafer, C. L., & Rubel, A. N. (2015). The why and how of defending belief in a just world. *Advances in Experimental Social Psychology, 51,* 41–96.

Hagerty, M. R. (2000). Social comparisons of income in one's community: Evidence from national surveys of income and happiness. *Journal of Personality and Social Psychology, 78,* 764–771.

Haidt, J. (2003). The moral emotions. In R. J. Davidson (Ed.), *Handbook of affective sciences.* Oxford: Oxford University Press.

Haidt, J. (2006). *The happiness hypothesis: Finding modern truth in ancient wisdom.* New York: Basic Books.

Haidt, J. (2011, January 27). *The bright future of post-partisan social psychology.* Presentation to the Society of Personality and Social Psychology presidential symposium: Visions for the next decade of personality and social psychology. San Antonio, TX. Available at people.virginia.edu/~jdh6n/postpartisan.html.

Haines, M. P. (1996). A social norms approach to preventing binge drinking at colleges and universities. Higher Education Center for Alcohol and Other Drug Prevention. (http://www.socialnormsresources.org/pdf/socnormapproach.pdf).

Halberstadt, A. G., & Saitta, M. B. (1987). Gender, nonverbal behavior, and perceived dominance: A test of the theory. *Journal of Personality and Social Psychology, 53,* 257–272.

Halberstadt, J. (2006). The generality and ultimate origins of the attractiveness of prototypes. *Personality and Social Psychology Review, 10,* 166–183.

Halberstadt, J., O'Shea, R. P., & Forgas, J. (2006). Outgroup fanship in Australia and New Zealand. *Australian Journal of Psychology, 58,* 159–165.

Hald, G. M., & Malamuth, N. N. (2015). Experimental effects of exposure to pornography: The moderating effect of personality and mediating effect of sexual arousal. *Archives of Sexual Behavior, 44,* 99–109.

Halevy, N., Berso, Y., & Galinsky, A. D. (2011). The mainstream is not electable: When vision triumphs over representativeness in leader emergence and effectiveness. *Personality and Social Psychology Bulletin, 37,* 893–904.

Halford, J. T., & Hsu, H-C. (2014). Beauty is wealth: CEO appearance and shareholder value, http://sfs.org/wp-content/uploads/2014/03/BEAUTY-IS-WEALTH1.pdf.

Halko, M-L., Kaustia, M., & Alanko, E. (2012). The gender effect in risky asset holdings. *Journal of Economic Behavior and Organization, 83,* 66–81.

Hall, C. C., Zhao, J., & Shafir, E. (2014). Self-affirmation among the poor: Cognitive and behavioral implications. *Psychological Science, 25,* 619–625.

Hall, D. L., Matz, D. C., & Wood, W. (2010). Why don't we practice what we preach? A meta-analytic review of religious racism. *Personality and Social Psychology Review, 14,* 126–139.

Hall, J. A. (1984). *Nonverbal sex differences: Communication accuracy and expressive style.* Baltimore: Johns Hopkins University Press.

Hall, J. A. (2006). Nonverbal behavior, status, and gender: How do we understand their relations? *Psychology of Women Quarterly, 30,* 384–391.

Hall, J. A., Coats, E. J., & LeBeau, L. S. (2005). Nonverbal behavior and the vertical dimension of social relations: A meta-analysis. *Psychological Bulletin, 131,* 898–924.

Hall, J. A., & Pennington, N. (2013). Self-monitoring, honesty, and cue use on Facebook: The relationship with user extraversion and conscientiousness. *Computers in Human Behavior, 29,* 1556–1564.

Hall, J. A., Rosip, J. C., LeBeau, L. S., Horgan, T. G., & Carter, J. D. (2006). Attributing the sources of accuracy in unequal-power dyadic communication: Who is better and why? *Journal of Experimental Social Psychology, 42,* 18–27.

Hall, T. (1985, June 25). The unconverted: Smoking of cigarettes seems to be becoming a lower-class habit. *Wall Street Journal,* pp. 1, 25.

Halpern, D. F. (2010). How neuromythologies support sex role stereotypes. *Science, 330,* 1320–1321.

Halverson, A. M., Hallahan, M., Hart, A. J., & Rosenthal, R. (1997). Reducing the biasing effects of judges' nonverbal behavior with simplified jury instruction. *Journal of Applied Psychology, 82,* 590–598.

Hamberger, J., & Hewstone, M. (1997). Inter-ethnic contact as a predictor of blatant and subtle prejudice: Tests of a model in four West European nations. *British Journal of Social Psychology, 36,* 173–190.

Hamblin, R. L., Buckholdt, D., Bushell, D., Ellis, D., & Feritor, D. (1969). Changing the game from get the teacher to learn. *Transaction,* January, 20–25, 28–31.

Hamermesh, D. S. (2011). *Beauty pays: Why attractive people are more successful.* Princeton, NJ: Princeton University Press.

Hamilton, D. L., & Gifford, R. K. (1976). Illusory correlation in interpersonal perception: A cognitive basis of stereotypic judgments. *Journal of Experimental Social Psychology, 12,* 392–407.

Hamilton, D. L., & Rose, T. L. (1980). Illusory correlation and the maintenance of stereotypic beliefs. *Journal of Personality and Social Psychology, 39,* 832–845.

Hammond, M. D., & Overall, N. C. (2013). Men's hostile sexism and biased perceptions of intimate partners: Fostering dissatisfaction and negative behavior in close relationships. *Personality and Social Psychology Bulletin, 39,* 1585–1599.

Hampson, R. B. (1984). Adolescent prosocial behavior: Peer-group and situational factors associated with helping. *Journal of Personality and Social Psychology, 46,* 153–162.

Hampton, K., Rainie, L., Lu, W., Dwyer, M., Shin, I., & Purcell, K. (2014, August 26). Social media and the 'spiral of silence.' Pew Research Internet Project (www.pewinternet.org).

Haney, C. (1991). The fourteenth amendment and symbolic legality: Let them eat due process. *Law and Human Behavior, 15,* 183–204.

Haney, C. (1993). Psychology and legal change. *Law and Human Behavior, 17,* 371–398.

Haney, C., & Logan, D. D. (1994). Broken promise: The Supreme Court's response to social science research on capital punishment. *Journal of Social Issues, 50,* 75–101.

Haney, C., & Zimbardo, P. (1998). The past and future of U.S. prison policy: Twenty-five years after the Stanford Prison Experiment. *American Psychologist, 53,* 709–727.

Haney, C., & Zimbardo, P. G. (2009). Persistent dispositionalism in interactionist clothing: Fundamental attribution error in explaining prison abuse. *Personality and Social Psychology Bulletin, 35,* 807–814.

Hansel, T. C., Nakonezny, P. A., & Rodgers, J. L. (2011). Did divorces decline after the attacks on the World Trade Center? *Journal of Applied Social Psychology, 41,* 1680–1700.

Hansen, D. E., Vandenberg, B., & Patterson, M. L. (1995). The effects of religious orientation on spontaneous and nonspontaneous helping behaviors. *Personality and Individual Differences, 19,* 101–104.

Hansen, J., & Wänke, M. (2009). Liking what's familiar: The importance of unconscious familiarity in the mere-exposure effect. *Social Cognition, 27,* 161–182.

Harbaugh, W. T., Mayr, U., & Burghart, D. R. (2007). Neural responses to taxation and voluntary giving reveal motives for charitable donations. *Science, 316,* 1622–1625.

Harber, K. D. (1998). Feedback to minorities: Evidence of a positive bias. *Journal of Personality and Social Psychology, 74,* 622–628.

Harber, K. D., Stafford, R., & Kennedy, K. A. (2010). The positive feedback bias as a response to a self-image threat. *Journal of Social Psychology, 49,* 207–218.

Hardin, G. (1968). The tragedy of the commons. *Science, 162*, 1243–1248.

Hardy, C., & Latané, B. (1986). Social loafing on a cheering task. *Social Science, 71*, 165–172.

Hardy, C. L., & Van Vugt, M. (2006). Nice guys finish first: The competitive altruism hypothesis. *Personality and Social Psychology Bulletin, 32*, 1402–1413.

Harinck, F., & Van Kleef, G. A. (2012). Be hard on the interests and soft on the values: Conflict issue moderates the effects of anger in negotiations. *British Journal of Social Psychology, 51*, 741–752.

Haritos-Fatouros, M. (1988). The official torturer: A learning model for obedience to the authority of violence. *Journal of Applied Social Psychology, 18*, 1107–1120.

Haritos-Fatouros, M. (2002). *Psychological origins of institutionalized torture.* New York: Routledge.

Harkins, S. G. (1981). *Effects of task difficulty and task responsibility on social loafing.* Presentation to the First International Conference on Social Processes in Small Groups, Kill Devil Hills, North Carolina.

Harkins, S. G., & Jackson, J. M. (1985). The role of evaluation in eliminating social loafing. *Personality and Social Psychology Bulletin, 11*, 457–465.

Harkins, S. G., Latané, B., & Williams, K. (1980), Social loafing: Allocating effort or taking it easy? *Journal of Experimental Social Psychology, 16*, 457–465.

Harkins, S. G., & Petty, R. E. (1982). Effects of task difficulty and task uniqueness on social loafing. *Journal of Personality and Social Psychology, 43*, 1214–1229.

Harkins, S. G., & Petty, R. E. (1987). Information utility and the multiple source effect. *Journal of Personality and Social Psychology, 52*, 260–268.

Harkness, K. L., Sabbagh, M. A., Jacobson, J. A., Chowdrey, N. K., & Chen, T. (2005). Enhanced accuracy of mental state decoding in dysphoric college students. *Cognition & Emotion, 19*, 999–1025.

Harley, C. D. G. (2011). Climate change, keystone predation, and biodiversity loss. *Science, 334*, 1124–1127.

Harmon-Jones, E., & Allen, J. J. B. (2001). The role of affect in the mere exposure effect: Evidence from psychophysiological and individual differences approaches. *Personality and Social Psychology Bulletin, 27*, 889–898.

Harmon-Jones, E., Gerdjikov, T., & Harmon-Jones, C. (2008). The effect of induced compliance on relative left frontal cortical activity: A test of the action-based model of dissonance. *European Journal of Social Psychology, 38*, 35–45.

Harries, K. D., & Stadler, S. J. (1988). Heat and violence: New findings from Dallas field data, 1980–1981. *Journal of Applied Social Psychology, 18*, 129–138.

Harris, C. R., Jenkins, M., & Glaser, D. (2006). Gender differences in risk assessment: Why do women take fewer risks than men? *Judgment and Decision Making, 1*, 48–63.

Harris, J. R. (1996). Quoted from an article by Jerome Burne for the *Manchester Observer* (via Harris: 72073.1211@ CompuServe.com).

Harris, J. R. (1998). *The nurture assumption.* New York: Free Press.

Harris, J. R. (2007). *No two alike: Human nature and human individuality.* New York: Norton.

Harris, L. T., & Fiske, S. T. (2006). Dehumanizing the lowest of the low: Neuroimaging responses to extreme out-groups. *Psychological Science, 17*(10), 847–853.

Harris, M. J., & Rosenthal, R. (1985). Mediation of interpersonal expectancy effects: 31 meta-analyses. *Psychological Bulletin, 97*, 363–386.

Harris, M. J., & Rosenthal, R. (1986). Four factors in the mediation of teacher expectancy effects. In R. S. Feldman (Ed.), *The social psychology of education.* New York: Cambridge University Press.

Harrison, A. A. (1977). Mere exposure. In L. Berkowitz (Ed.), *Advances in experimental social psychology* (Vol. 10, pp. 39–83). New York: Academic Press.

Hart, A. J., & Morry, M. M. (1997). Trait inferences based on racial and behavioral cues. *Basic and Applied Social Psychology, 19*, 33–48.

Hart, A. J., Whalen, P. J., Shin, L. M., & others. (2000, August). Differential response in the human amygdala to racial outgroup vs. ingroup face stimuli. *Neuroreport: For Rapid Communication of Neuroscience Research, 11*, 2351–2355.

Hart, W., Albarracin, D., Eagly, A. H., Brechan, I., Lindberg, M. J., & Merrill, L. (2009). Feeling validated versus being correct: A meta-analysis of selective exposure to information. *Psychological Bulletin, 135*, 555–588.

Hartup, W. W., & Stevens, N. (1997). Friendships and adaptation in the life course. *Psychological Bulletin, 121*, 355–370.

Harvey, J. H., & Omarzu, J. (1997). Minding the close relationship. *Personality and Social Psychology Review, 1*, 224–240.

Hasan, Y., Begue, L., & Bushman, B. J. (2012). Viewing the world through "blood-red tinted glasses": The hostile expectation bias mediates the link between violent video game exposure and aggression. *Journal of Experimental Social Psychology, 48*, 953–956.

Hasan, Y., Begue, L., Scharkow, M., & Bushman, B. J. (2013). The more you play, the more aggressive you become: A long-term experimental study of cumulative violent video game effects on hostile expectations and aggressive behavior. *Journal of Experimental Social Psychology, 49*, 224–227.

Haselton, M. G., & Buss, D. M. (2000). Error management theory: A new perspective on biases in cross-sex mind reading. *Journal of Personality and Social Psychology, 78*, 81–91.

Haselton, M. G., & Gildersleeve, K. (2011). Can men detect ovulation? *Current Directions in Psychological Science, 20*, 87–92.

Haselton, M. G., & Nettle, D. (2006). The paranoid optimist: An integrative evolutionary model of cognitive biases. *Personality and Social Psychology Review, 10*, 47–66.

Haslam, N., & Kashima, Y. (2010). The rise and rise of social psychology in Asia: A bibliometric analysis. *Asian Journal of Social Psychology, 13*, 202–207.

Haslam, S. A. (2014). Making good theory practical: Five lessons for an applied social identity approach to challenges of organizational, health, and clinical psychology. *British Journal of Social Psychology, 53*, 1–20.

Haslam, S. A., Adarves-Yorno, I., & Postmes, T. (2014, July/August). Creative is collective. *Scientific American Mind*, pp. 31–35.

Haslam, S. A., & Reicher, S. (2007). Beyond the banality of evil: Three dynamics of an interactionist social psychology of tyranny. *Personality and Social Psychology Bulletin, 33*, 615–622.

Haslam, S. A., & Reicher, S. D. (2012). Contesting the "nature" of conformity: What Milgram and Zimbardo's studies really show. *PLoS Biology, 10*, e1001426.

Haslam, S. A., Reicher, S. D., & Platow, M. J. (2010). *The new psychology of leadership: Identity, influence and power.* London: Psychology Press.

Hass, R. G., Katz, I., Rizzo, N., Bailey, J., & Eisenstadt, D. (1991). Cross-racial appraisal as related to attitude ambivalence and cognitive complexity. *Personality and Social Psychology Bulletin, 17*, 83–92.

Hastie, R., Penrod, S. D., & Pennington, N. (1983). *Inside the jury.* Cambridge, MA: Harvard University Press.

Hatfield, E. (1988). Passionate and compassionate love. In R. J. Sternberg & M. L. Barnes (Eds.), *The psychology of love.* New Haven, CT: Yale University Press.

Hatfield, E., Cacioppo, J. T., & Rapson, R. (1992). The logic of emotion: Emotional contagion. In M. S. Clark (Ed.), *Review of Personality and Social Psychology.* Newbury Park, CA: Sage.

Hatfield, E., & Rapson, R. L. (1987). Passionate love: New directions in research. In W. H. Jones & D. Perlman (Eds.), *Advances in personal relationships*, Vol. 1. Greenwich, CT: JAI.

Hatfield, E., & Sprecher, S. (1986). *Mirror, mirror: The importance of looks in everyday life.* Albany, NY: SUNY Press.

Hatfield, E., Traupmann, J., Sprecher, S., Utne, M., & Hay, J. (1985). Equity and intimate relations: Recent research. In

W. Ickes (Ed.), *Compatible and incompatible relationships.* New York: Springer-Verlag.

Hatfield, E., & Walster, G. W. (1978). *A new look at love.* Reading, MA: Addison-Wesley. (Note: originally published as Walster, E., & Walster, G. W.)

Hatfield (Walster), E., Aronson, V., Abrahams, D., & Rottman, L. (1966). Importance of physical attractiveness in dating behavior. *Journal of Personality and Social Psychology, 4,* 508–516.

Hatzenbuehler, M. L. (2014). Structural stigma and the health of lesbian, gay, and bisexual populations. *Current Directions in Psychological Science, 23,* 127–132.

Hatzfeld, J. (2005). *Machete season: The killers in Rwanda speak.* New York: Farrar, Straus and Giroux.

Hatzfeld, J. (2007). *Machete season: The killers in Rwanda speak.* New York: Farrar, Straus and Giroux.

Haugtvedt, C. P., & Wegener, D. T. (1994). Message order effects in persuasion: An attitude strength perspective. *Journal of Consumer Research, 21,* 205–218.

Hauser, M. (2006). *Moral minds: How nature designed our universal sense of right and wrong.* New York: Ecco.

Hauser, M. (2009). It seems biology (not religion) equals morality. *The Edge* (www.edge.org).

Havas, D. A., Glenberg, A. M., Gutowski, K. A., Lucarelli, M. J., & Davidson, R. J. (2010). Cosmetic use of Botulinum Toxin-A affects processing of emotional language. *Psychological Science, 21,* 895–900.

Havel, V. (1990). *Disturbing the peace.* New York: Knopf.

Hawkley, L. C., Williams, K. D., & Cacioppo, J. T. (2011). Responses to ostracism across adulthood. *Social, Cognitive, and Affective Neuroscience, 6,* 234–243.

Hazan, C. (2004). Intimate attachment/ capacity to love and be loved. In C. Peterson & M. E. P. Seligman (Eds.), *The values in action classification of strengths and virtues.* Washington, DC: American Psychological Association.

Hazan, C., & Shaver, P. R. (1994). Attachment as an organizational framework for research on close relationships. *Psychological Inquiry, 5,* 1–22.

He, Y., Ebner, N. C., & Johnson, M. K. (2011). What predicts the own-age bias in face recognition memory? *Social Cognition, 29,* 97–109.

Headey, B., & Wearing, A. (1987). The sense of relative superiority—central to well-being. *Social Indicators Research, 20,* 497–516.

Hearold, S. (1986). A synthesis of 1043 effects of television on social behavior. In G. Comstock (Ed.), *Public communication and behavior* (Vol. 1). Orlando, FL: Academic Press.

Hedge, A., & Yousif, Y. H. (1992). Effects of urban size, urgency, and cost on

helpfulness: A cross-cultural comparison between the United Kingdom and the Sudan. *Journal of Cross-Cultural Psychology, 23,* 107–115.

Heesacker, M. (1989). Counseling and the elaboration likelihood model of attitude change. In J. F. Cruz, R. A. Goncalves, & P. P. Machado (Eds.), *Psychology and education: Investigations and interventions.* (Proceedings of the International Conference on Interventions in Psychology and Education, Porto, Portugal, July 1987.) Porto, Portugal: Portugese Psychological Association.

Hegarty, P., Watson, N., Fletcher, L., & McQueen, G. (2010). When gentlemen are first and ladies are last: Effects of gender stereotypes on the order of romantic partners' names. *British Journal of Social Psychology, 50,* 21–35.

Hehman, E., Gaertner, S. L., Dovidio, J. F., Mania, E. W., Guerra, R., Wilson, D. C., & Friel, B. M. (2012). Group status drives majority and minority integration preferences. *Psychological Science, 23,* 46–52.

Heider, F. (1958). *The psychology of interpersonal relations.* New York: Wiley.

Heine, S. J., & Hamamura, T. (2007). In search of East Asian self-enhancement. *Personality and Social Psychology Review, 11,* 4–27.

Heine, S. J., Kitayama, S., Lehman, D. R., Takata, T., Ide, E., Leung, C., & Matsumoto, H. (2001). Divergent consequences of success and failure in Japan and North America: An investigation of self-improving motivations and malleable selves. *Journal of Personality and Social Psychology, 81,* 599–615.

Heine, S. J., & Lehman, D. R. (1997). The cultural construction of self-enhancement: An examination of group-serving biases. *Journal of Personality and Social Psychology, 72,* 1268–1283.

Heine, S. J., Lehman, D. R., Markus, H. R., & Kitayama, S. (1999). Is there a universal need for positive self-regard? *Psychological Review, 106,* 766–794.

Heine, S. J., Takemoto, T., Moskalenko, S., Lasaleta, J., & Heinrich, J. (2008). Mirrors in the head: Cultural variation in objective self-awareness. *Personality and Social Psychology Bulletin, 34,* 879–887.

Helliwell, J., Layard, R., & Sachs, J. (Eds.) (2013). World happiness report. New York: The Earth Institute, Columbia University.

Hellman, P. (1980). *Avenue of the righteous of nations.* New York: Atheneum.

Helweg-Larsen, M., Cunningham, S. J., Carrico, A., & Pergram, A. M. (2004). To nod or not to nod: An observational study of nonverbal communication and status in female and male college students. *Psychology of Women Quarterly, 28,* 358–361.

Helzer, E. G., & Dunning, D. (2012). Why and when peer prediction is superior to

self-prediction: The weight given to future aspiration versus past achievement. *Journal of Personality and Social Psychology Bulletin, 103,* 38–53.

Henderson, T. (2014, September 28). More Americans living alone, Census says. *Washington Post.* (www.WashingtonPost.com). See also, U.S. Census Bureau, "Fact for features: Unmarried and Single Americans Week, Sept. 21–27, 2014.

Henderson-King, E. I., & Nisbett, R. E. (1996). Anti-black prejudice as a function of exposure to the negative behavior of a single black person. *Journal of Personality and Social Psychology, 71,* 654–664.

Hendrick, S. S., & Hendrick, C. (1995). Gender differences and similarities in sex and love. *Personal Relationships, 2,* 55–65.

Hendrick, S. S., Hendrick, C., & Adler, N. L. (1988). Romantic relationships: Love, satisfaction, and staying together. *Journal of Personality and Social Psychology, 54,* 980–988.

Hennenlotter, A., Dresel, C., Castrop, F., Ceballos Baumann, A., Wohschlager, A., & Haslinger, B. (2008). The link between facial feedback and neural activity within central circuitries of emotion: New insights from Botulinum Toxin-induced denervation of frown muscles. *Cerebral Cortex, 19,* 537–542.

Hennigan, K. M., Del Rosario, M. L., Health, L., Cook, T. D., Wharton, J. D., & Calder, B. J. (1982). Impact of the introduction of television on crime in the United States: Empirical findings and theoretical implications. *Journal of Personality and Social Psychology, 42,* 461–477.

Henrich, J., Heine, S. J., & Norenzayan, A. (2010). The weirdest people in the world? *Behavioral and Brain Sciences, 33,* 61–135.

Henrich, J., McElreath, R., Barr, A., Ensminger, J., Barrett, C., Bolyanatz, A., Cardenas, J. C., Gurven, M., Gwako, E., Henrich, N., Lerorogol, C., Marlowe, F., Tracer, D., & Ziker, J. (2006). Costly punishment across human societies. *Science, 312,* 1767–1770.

Henry, P. J. (2008a). College sophomores in the laboratory redux: Influences of a narrow data base on social psychology's view of the nature of prejudice. *Psychological Inquiry, 19,* 49–71.

Henry, P. J. (2008b). Student sampling as a theoretical problem. *Psychological Inquiry, 19,* 114–126.

Henry, P. J. (2009). Low-status compensation: A theory for understanding the role of status in cultures of honor. *Journal of Personality and Social Psychology, 97,* 451–466.

Henslin, M. (1967). Craps and magic. *American Journal of Sociology, 73,* 316–330.

Hepach, R., Vaish, A., & Tomasello, M. (2012). Young children are intrinsically motivated to see others helped. *Psychological Science, 23*, 967–972.

Hepper, E. G., & Carnelley, K. B. (2012). The self-esteem roller coaster: Adult attachment moderates the impact of daily feedback. *Personal Relationships, 19*, 504–520.

Hepworth, J. T., & West, S. G. (1988). Lynchings and the economy: A time-series reanalysis of Hovland and Sears (1940), *Journal of Personality and Social Psychology, 55*, 239–247.

Heradstveit, D. (1979). *The Arab-Israeli conflict: Psychological obstacles to peace* (Vol. 28). Oslo, Norway: Universitetsforlaget. Distributed by Columbia University Press. Reviewed by R. K. White (1980), *Contemporary Psychology, 25*, 11–12.

Herbenick, D., Reece, M., Schick, V., Sanders, S. A., Dodge, B., & Fortenberry, J. D. (2010). Sexual behaviors, relationships, and perceived health among adult women in the United States: Results from a national probability sample. *Journal of Sexual Medicine, 7* (suppl 5), 277–290.

Herlocker, C. E., Allison, S. T., Foubert, J. D., & Beggan, J. K. (1997). Intended and unintended overconsumption of physical, spatial, and temporal resources. *Journal of Personality and Social Psychology, 73*, 992–1004.

Hernandez, I., & Preston, J. L. (2013). Disfluency disrupts the confirmation bias. *Journal of Experimental Social Psychology, 49*, 178–182.

Herring, D. R., White, K. R., Jabeen, L. N., Hinojos, M., Terrazas, G., Reyes, S. M., & . . . Crites, S. J. (2013). On the automatic activation of attitudes: A quarter century of evaluative priming research. *Psychological Bulletin, 139*, 1062–1089.

Herzog, S. M., & Hertwig, R. (2009). The wisdom of many in one mind: Improving individual judgments with dialectical bootstrapping. *Psychological Science, 20*, 231–237.

Hewstone, M. (1990). The "ultimate attribution error"? A review of the literature on intergroup causal attribution. *European Journal of Social Psychology, 20*, 311–335.

Hewstone, M. (1994). Revision and change of stereotypic beliefs: In search of the elusive subtyping model. In S. Stroebe & M. Hewstone (Eds.), *European review of social psychology* (Vol. 5). Chichester, England: Wiley.

Hewstone, M., & Fincham, F. (1996). Attribution theory and research: Basic issues and applications. In M. Hewstone, W. Stroebe, & G. M. Stephenson (Eds.), *Introduction to social psychology: A European perspective.* Oxford, UK: Blackwell.

Hewstone, M., Hantzi, A., & Johnston, L. (1991). Social categorisation and person memory: The pervasiveness of race as an organizing principle. *European Journal of Social Psychology, 21*, 517–528.

Hewstone, M., Hopkins, N., & Routh, D. A. (1992). Cognitive models of stereotype change: Generalization and subtyping in young people's views of the police. *European Journal of Social Psychology, 22*, 219–234.

Hewstone, M., Lolliot, S., Swart, H., Myers, E., Voci, A., Al Ramiah, A., & Cairns, E. (2014). Intergroup contact and intergroup conflict. *Peace and Conflict: Journal of Peace Psychology, 20*, 39–53.

Higgins, E. T., & McCann, C. D. (1984). Social encoding and subsequent attitudes, impressions and memory: "Context-driven" and motivational aspects of processing. *Journal of Personality and Social Psychology, 47*, 26–39.

Higgins, E. T., & Rholes, W. S. (1978). Saying is believing: Effects of message modification on memory and liking for the person described. *Journal of Experimental Social Psychology, 14*, 363–378.

Hilmert, C. J., Kulik, J. A., & Christenfeld, N. J. S. (2006). Positive and negative opinion modeling: The influence of another's similarity and dissimilarity. *Journal of Personality and Social Psychology, 90*, 440–452.

Hine, D. W., & Gifford, R. (1996). Attributions about self and others in commons dilemmas. *European Journal of Social Psychology, 26*, 429–445.

Hines, M. (2004). *Brain gender.* New York: Oxford University Press.

Hinkle, S., Brown, R., & Ely, P. G. (1992). Social identity theory processes: Some limitations and limiting conditions. *Revista de Psicologia Social*, pp. 99–111.

Hinsz, V. B. (1990). Cognitive and consensus processes in group recognition memory performance. *Journal of Personality and Social Psychology, 59*, 705–718.

Hinsz, V. B., Tindale, R. S., & Vollrath, D. A. (1997). The emerging conceptualization of groups as information processors. *Psychological Bulletin, 121*, 43–64.

Hirschman, R. S., & Leventhal, H. (1989). Preventing smoking behavior in school children: An initial test of a cognitive-development program. *Journal of Applied Social Psychology, 19*, 559–583.

Hirsh, J. B., Kang, S. K., & Bodenhausen, G. V. (2012). Personalized persuasion: Tailoring persuasive appeals to recipients' personality traits. *Psychological Science, 23*, 578–581.

Hirt, E. R., Zillmann, D., Erickson, G. A., & Kennedy, C. (1992). Costs and benefits of allegiance: Changes in fans' self-ascribed competencies after team victory versus defeat. *Journal of Personality and Social Psychology, 63*, 724–738.

Hitsch, G. J., Hortacsu, A., & Ariely, D. (2006, February). *What makes you click? Mate preferences and matching outcomes in online dating.* MIT Sloan Research Paper No. 4603-06 (ssrn.com/abstract =895442).

Hobden, K. L., & Olson, J. M. (1994). From jest to antipathy: Disparagement humor as a source of dissonance-motivated attitude change. *Basic and Applied Social psychology, 15*, 239–249.

Hodges, B. H., & Geyer, A. L. (2006). A nonconformist account of the Asch experiments: Values, pragmatics, and moral dilemmas. *Personality and Social Psychology Review*, 102–119.

Hodgson, T. L., Guala, F., Miller, T., & Summers, I. (2012). Limbic and prefrontal activity during conformity and violation of norms in a coordination game. *Journal of Neuroscience, Psychology, and Economics, 5*, 1–17.

Hoffman, L. W. (1977). Changes in family roles, socialization, and sex differences. *American Psychologist, 32*, 644–657.

Hoffman, M. L. (1981). Is altruism part of human nature? *Journal of Personality and Social Psychology, 40*, 121–137.

Hofling, C. K., Brotzman, E., Dairymple, S., Graves, N., & Pierce, C. M. (1966). An experimental study in nurse-physician relationships. *Journal of Nervous and Mental Disease, 143*, 171–180.

Hofmann, W., De Houwer, J., Perugini, M., Baeyens, F., & Crombez, G. (2010). Evaluative conditioning in humans: A meta-analysis. *Psychological Review, 136*, 390–421.

Hofmeister, B. (2010). Bridging the gap: Using social psychology to design market interventions to overcome the energy efficiency gap in residential energy markets. *Southeastern Environmental Law Journal, 19*, pp. 1ff. Available at SSRN: http://ssrn.com/abstract51892906.

Hogan, R., Curphy, G. J., & Hogan, J. (1994). What we know about leadership: Effectiveness and personality. *American Psychologist, 49*, 493–504.

Hogg, M. (2014). From uncertainty to extremism: Social categorization and identity formation. *Current Directions in Psychological Science, 23*, 338–342.

Hogg, M. A. (1992). *The social psychology of group cohesiveness: From attraction to social identity.* London: Harvester Wheatsheaf.

Hogg, M. A. (2001). A social identity theory of leadership. *Personality and Social Psychology Review, 5*, 184–200.

Hogg, M. A. (2010). Human groups, social categories, and collective self: Social identity and the management of self-uncertainty. In R. M. Arkin, K. C. Oleson, & P. J. Carroll (Eds.), *Handbook of the uncertain self.* New York, NY, US: Psychology Press, 2010.

Hogg, M. A., & Hains, S. C. (1998). Friendship and group identification: A new look at the role of cohesiveness in groupthink. *European Journal of Social Psychology, 28*, 323–341.

Hogg, M. A., Hains, S. C., & Mason, I. (1998). Identification and leadership in small groups: Salience, frame of reference, and leader stereotypicality effects on leader evaluations. *Journal of Personality and Social Psychology, 75,* 1248–1263.

Hogg, M. A., Turner, J. C., & Davidson, B. (1990). Polarized norms and social frames of reference: A test of the self-categorization theory of group polarization. *Basic and Applied Social Psychology, 11,* 77–100.

Hollander, E. P. (1958). Conformity, status, and idiosyncrasy credit. *Psychological Review, 65,* 117–127.

Holland, R. W., Hendriks, M., & Aarts, H. (2005). Smells like clean spirit: Nonconscious effect of scent on cognition and behavior. *Psychological Science, 16,* 689–693.

Holland, R. W., Meertens, R. M., & Van Vugt, M. (2002). Dissonance on the road: Self-esteem as a moderator of internal and external self-justification strategies. *Personality and Social Psychology Bulletin, 28,* 1712–1724.

Holmberg, D., & Holmes, J. G. (1994). Reconstruction of relationship memories: A mental models approach. In N. Schwarz & S. Sudman (Eds.), *Autobiographical memory and the validity of retrospective reports.* New York: Springer-Verlag.

Holmes, J. G., & Rempel, J. K. (1989). Trust in close relationships. In C. Hendrick (Ed.), *Review of personality and social psychology* (Vol. 10). Newbury Park, CA: Sage.

Holoien, D. S., & Fiske, S. T. (2013). Downplaying positive impressions: Compensation between warmth and competence in impression management. *Journal of Experimental Social Psychology, 49,* 33–41.

Holt-Lunstad, J., Smith, T. B., & Layton, J. B. (2010). Social relationships and mortality risk: A meta-analytic review. *PLoS Medicine, 7*(7): e1000316.

Holtgraves, T. (1997). Styles of language use: Individual and cultural variability in conversational indirectness. *Journal of Personality and Social Psychology, 73,* 624–637.

Holtzworth, A., & Jacobson, N. S. (1988). An attributional approach to marital dysfunction and therapy. In J. E. Maddux, C. D. Stoltenberg, & R. Rosenwein (Eds.), *Social processes in clinical and counseling psychology.* New York: Springer-Verlag.

Hong, S., & Park, H. S. (2012). Computer-mediated persuasion in online reviews: Statistical versus narrative evidence. *Computers in Human Behavior, 28,* 906–919.

Honigman, R. J., Phillips, K. A., & Castle, D. J. (2004). A review of psychosocial outcomes for patients seeking cosmetic surgery. *Plastic and Reconstructive Surgery, 113,* 1229–1237.

Hoorens, V. (1993). Self-enhancement and superiority biases in social comparison. In W. Stroebe & M. Hewstone (Eds.), *European review of social psychology* (Vol. 4). Chichester: Wiley.

Hoorens, V. (1995). Self-favoring biases, self-presentation and the self-other

asymmetry in social comparison. *Journal of Personality, 63,* 793–819.

Hoorens, V., & Nuttin, J. M. (1993). Overvaluation of own attributes: Mere ownership or subjective frequency? *Social Cognition, 11,* 177–200.

Hoorens, V., Nuttin, J. M., Herman, I. E., & Pavakanun, U. (1990). Mastery pleasure versus mere ownership: A quasi-experimental cross-cultural and cross-alphabetical test of the name letter effect. *European Journal of Social Psychology, 20,* 181–205.

Hoorens, V., Smits, T., & Shepperd, J. A. (2008). Comparative optimism in the spontaneous generation of future life-events. *British Journal of Social Psychology, 47,* 441–451.

Hoover, C. W., Wood, E. E., & Knowles, E. S. (1983). Forms of social awareness and helping. *Journal of Experimental Social Psychology, 19,* 577–590.

Hooykaas, R. (1972). *Religion and the rise of modern science.* Grand Rapids, MI: Eerdmans.

Hormuth, S. E. (1986). Lack of effort as a result of self-focused attention: An attributional ambiguity analysis. *European Journal of Social Psychology, 16,* 181–192.

Horner, V., Carter, J. D., Suchak, M., & de Waal, F. B. M. (2011). Spontaneous prosocial choice by chimpanzees. *Proceedings of the National Academy of Sciences (PNAS), 108,* 13847–13851.

Horner, V., Proctor, D., Bonnie, K. E., Whiten, A., & de Waal, F. B. M. (2010). Prestige affects cultural learning in chimpanzees. *PLoS One, 5,* e10625 (www .plosone.org).

Hornstein, H. (1976). *Cruelty and kindness.* Englewood Cliffs, NJ: Prentice-Hall.

Horry, R., Halford, P., Brewer, N., Milne, R., & Bull, R. (2014). Archival analyses of eyewitness identification test outcomes: What can they tell us about eyewitness memory? *Law and Human Behavior, 38,* 94–108.

Horry, R., Memon, A., Wright, D. B., & Milne, R. (2012a). Predictors of eyewitness identification decisions from video lineups in England: A field study. *Law and Human Behavior, 36,* 257–265.

Horry, R., Palmer, M. A., & Brewer, N. (2012b). Backloading in the sequential lineup prevents within-lineup criterion shifts that undermine eyewitness identification performance. *Journal of Experimental Psychology: Applied, 18,* 346–360.

Horwitz, A. V., White, H. R., & Howell-White, S. (1997). Becoming married and mental health: A longitudinal study of a cohort of young adults. *Journal of Marriage and the Family, 58,* 895–907.

Hostinar, C. E., Sullivan, R. M., & Gunnar, M. R. (2014). Psychobiological mechanisms underlying the social buffering of the hypothalamic-pituitary-adrenocortical axis: A review of animal

models and human studies across development. *Psychological Bulletin, 140,* 256–282.

Houghton, J. (2011). Global warming, climate change and sustainability: A challenge to scientists, policymakers and religious believers. Cambridge, England: The International Society for Science and Religion (www.issr.org.uk/latest-news/global-warming).

House, R. J., & Singh, J. V. (1987). Organizational behavior: Some new directions for I/O psychology. *Annual Review of Psychology, 38,* 669–718.

Houston, V., & Bull, R. (1994). Do people avoid sitting next to someone who is facially disfigured? *European Journal of Social Psychology, 24,* 279–284.

Hovland, C. I., Lumsdaine, A. A., & Sheffield, F. D. (1949). *Experiments on mass communication. Studies in social psychology in World War II* (Vol. III). Princeton, NJ: Princeton University Press.

Hovland, C. I., & Sears, R. (1940). Minor studies of aggression: Correlation of lynchings with economic indices. *Journal of Psychology, 9,* 301–310.

Howard, D. J. (1997). Familiar phrases as peripheral persuasion cues. *Journal of Experimental Social Psychology, 33,* 231–243.

Howard, J. (2013). I went after guns. Obama can, too. *New York Times,* January 16, 2013.

Howell, R. T., & Howell, C. J. (2008). The relation of economic status to subjective well-being in developing countries: A meta-analysis. *Psychological Bulletin, 134,* 536–560.

Hoyle, R. H. (1993). Interpersonal attraction in the absence of explicit attitudinal information. *Social Cognition, 11,* 309–320.

Hsiang, S. M., Burke, M., & Miguel, E. (2013). Quantifying the influence of climate on human conflict. *Science, 341,* 1212.

Huang, C., & Park, D. (2012). Cultural influences on Facebook photographs. *International Journal of Psychology,* 1–10.

Huang, J., Su, S., Zhou, L., & Liu, X. (2013). Attitude toward the viral ad: Expanding traditional advertising models to interactive advertising. *Journal of Interactive Marketing, 27,* 36–46.

Huang, Y., Kendrick, K. M., & Yu, R. (2014). Conformity to the opinions of other people lasts for no more than 3 days. *Psychological Science, 25,* 1388–1393.

Huddy, L., & Virtanen, S. (1995). Subgroup differentiation and subgroup bias among Latinos as a function of familiarity and positive distinctiveness. *Journal of Personality and Social Psychology, 68,* 97–108.

Huesmann, L. R., Lagerspetz, K., & Eron, L. D. (1984). Intervening variables in the TV violence-aggression relation: Evidence from two countries. *Developmental Psychology, 20,* 746–775.

Huesmann, L. R., Moise-Titus, J., Podolski, C-L., & Eron, L. D. (2003). Longitudinal relations between children's exposure to TV violence and their aggressive and violent behavior in young adulthood: 1977–1992. *Developmental Psychology, 39,* 201–222.

Hüffmeier, J., Krumm, S., Kanthak, J., & Hertel, G. (2012). "Don't let the group down": Facets of instrumentality moderate the motivating effects of groups in a field experiment. *European Journal of Social Psychology, 42,* 533–538.

Hugenberg, K., & Bodenhausen, G. V. (2003). Facing prejudice: Implicit prejudice and the perception of facial threat. *Psychological Science, 14,* 640–643.

Hui, C. H., Triandis, H. C., & Yee, C. (1991). Cultural differences in reward allocation: Is collectivism the explanation? *British Journal of Social Psychology, 30,* 145–157.

Hull, J. G., Brunelle, T. J., Prescott, A. T., & Sargent, J. D. (2014). A longitudinal study of risk-glorifying video games and behavioral deviance. *Journal of Personality and Social Psychology, 107,* 300–325.

Hull, J. G., Levenson, R. W., Young, R. D., & Sher, K. J. (1983). Self-awareness-reducing effects of alcohol consumption. *Journal of Personality and Social Psychology, 44,* 461–473.

Hull, J. G., & Young, R. D. (1983). The self-awareness-reducing effects of alcohol consumption: Evidence and implications. In J. Suls & A. G. Greenwald (Eds.), *Psychological perspectives on the self* (Vol. 2). Hillsdale, NJ: Erlbaum.

Human, L. J., Biesanz, J. C., Prisotto, K. L., & Dunn, E. W. (2012). Your best self helps reveal your true self: Positive self-presentation leads to more accurate personality impressions. *Social Psychological and Personality Science, 3,* 23–30.

Hundhammer, T., & Mussweiler, T. (2012). How sex puts you in gendered shoes: Sexuality-priming leads to gender-based self-perception and behavior. *Journal of Personality and Social Psychology, 103,* 176–193.

Hunt, A. R. (2000, June 22). Major progress, inequities cross three generations. *Wall Street Journal,* A9, A14.

Hunt, M. (1990). *The compassionate beast: What science is discovering about the humane side of humankind.* New York: William Morrow.

Hunt, P. J., & Hillery, J. M. (1973). Social facilitation in a location setting: An examination of the effects over learning trials. *Journal of Experimental Social Psychology, 9,* 563–571.

Hunt, R., & Jensen, J. (2007). The experiences of young gay people in Britain's schools. Stonewall (www.stonewall.org.uk).

Huston, T. L., & Chorost, A. F. (1994). Behavioral buffers on the effect of negativity on marital satisfaction: A longitudinal study. *Personal Relationships, 1,* 223–239.

Huston, T. L., Niehuis, S., & Smith, S. E. (2001). The early marital roots of conjugal distress and divorce. *Current Directions in Psychological Science, 10,* 116–119.

Hutnik, N. (1985). Aspects of identity in a multi-ethnic society. *New Community, 12,* 298–309.

Hutson, M. (2007, March/April). Unnatural selection. *Psychology Today,* 90–95.

Hvistendahl, M. (2009). Making every baby girl count. *Science, 323,* 1164–1166.

Hvistendahl, M. (2010). Has China outgrown the one-child policy? *Science, 329,* 1458–1461.

Hvistendahl, M. (2011). *Unnatural selection: Choosing boys over girls, and the consequences of a world full of men.* New York: PublicAffairs.

Hyde, J. S. (2005). The gender similarities hypothesis. *American Psychologist, 60,* 581–592.

Hyman, H. H., & Sheatsley, P. B. (1956 & 1964). Attitudes toward desegregation. *Scientific American, 195(6),* 35–39, and *211(1),* 16–23.

Ickes, B. (1980). *On disconfirming our perceptions of others.* Paper presented at the American Psychological Association convention.

Ickes, W., Layden, M. A., & Barnes, R. D. (1978). Objective self-awareness and individuation: An empirical link. *Journal of Personality, 46,* 146–161.

Ickes, W., Patterson, M. L., Rajecki, D. W., & Tanford, S. (1982). Behavioral and cognitive consequences of reciprocal versus compensatory responses to preinteraction expectancies. *Social Cognition, 1,* 160–190.

Ickes, W., Snyder, M., & Garcia, S. (1997). Personality influences on the choice of situations. In R. Hogan, J. Johnson, & S. Briggs (Eds.), *Handbook of Personality Psychology.* San Diego: Academic Press.

Imai, Y. (1994). Effects of influencing attempts on the perceptions of powerholders and the powerless. *Journal of Social Behavior and Personality, 9,* 455–468.

Imhoff, R., & Banse, R. (2009). Ongoing victim suffering increases prejudice: The case of secondary anti-Semitism. *Psychological Science, 20,* 1443–1447.

Imhoff, R., Dotsch, R., Bianchi, M., Banse, R., & Wigboldus, D. (2011). Facing Europe: Visualizing spontaneous ingroup projection. *Psychological Science, 22,* 1583–1590.

Imhoff, R., & Erb, H. (2009). What motivates nonconformity? Uniqueness seeking blocks majority influence. *Personality And Social Psychology Bulletin, 35,* 309–320.

Inbar, Y., & Lammers, J. (2012). Political diversity in social and personality

psychology. *Perspectives on Psychological Science, 7,* 496–503.

Indo-Asian News Service. (2013, March 13). Child killed after imitating TV hanging scene (http://www.ndtv.com/article/cities/child-killed-after-imitating-tv-hanging-scene-346554).

Ingham, A. G., Levinger, G., Graves, J., & Peckham, V. (1974). The Ringelmann effect: Studies of group size and group performance. *Journal of Experimental Social Psychology, 10,* 371–384.

Inglehart, R. (1990). *Culture shift in advanced industrial society.* Princeton, NJ: Princeton University Press.

Inglehart, R., & Welzel, C. (2005). *Modernization, cultural change, and democracy: The human development sequence.* New York: Cambridge University Press.

Innis, M. (2014, June 11). Australia's graphic cigarette pack warnings appear to work. *New York Times.*

International Parliamentary Union. (2011). *Women in national parliaments: Situation as of 30 November 2011.* Author (www.ipu.org).

International Telecommunications Union. (2014). *ICT Facts and Figures 2014,* http://www.itu.int/en/ITU-D/Statistics/Pages/stat/default.aspx.

Inzlicht, M., Gutsell, J. N., & Legault, L. (2012). Mimicry reduces racial prejudice. *Journal of Experimental Social Psychology, 48,* 361–365.

Inzlicht, M., McKay, L., & Aronson, J. (2006). Stigma as ego depletion: How being the target of prejudice affects self-control. *Psychological Science, 17,* 262–269.

IPCC. (2014). *Climate change 2014: Impacts, adaptation, and vulnerability.* Geneva: Intergovernmental Panel on Climate Change (www.ipcc.ch).

IPU: Inter-Parliamentary Union. (2015). Women in national parliaments. Retrieved March 27, 2015 from http://www.ipu.org/wmn-e/world.htm

Ireland, M. E., & Pennebaker, J. W. (2010). Language style matching in writing: Synchrony in essays, correspondence, and poetry. *Journal of Personality and Social Psychology, 99,* 549–571.

Ireland, M. E., Slatcher, R. B., Eastwick, P. W., Scissors, L. E., Finkel, E. J., & Pennebaker, J. W. (2011). Language style matching predicts relationship initiation and stability. *Psychological Science, 22,* 39–44.

Isen, A. M., Clark, M., & Schwartz, M. F. (1976). Duration of the effect of good mood on helping: Footprints on the sands of time. *Journal of Personality and Social Psychology, 34,* 385–393.

Isen, A. M., & Means, B. (1983). The influence of positive affect on decision-making strategy. *Social Cognition, 2,* 28–31.

Isen, A. M., Shalker, T. E., Clark, M., & Karp, L. (1978). Affect, accessibility of material in memory, and behavior: A cognitive loop. *Journal of Personality and Social Psychology, 36,* 1–12.

Iso-Ahola, S. E. (2013). Exercise: Why it is a challenge for both the nonconscious and conscious mind. *Psychological Bulletin, 17,* 93–110.

Isozaki, M. (1984). The effect of discussion on polarization of judgments. *Japanese Psychological Research, 26,* 187–193.

ISR Newsletter. (1975). Institute for Social Research, University of Michigan, 3(4), 4–7.

Ito, T. A., Miller, N., & Pollock, V. E. (1996). Alcohol and aggression: A meta-analysis on the moderating effects of inhibitory cues, triggering events, and self-focused attention. *Psychological Bulletin, 120,* 60–82.

Iyengar, S., & Westwood, S. J. (2014). Fear and loathing across party lines: New evidence on group polarization. *American Journal of Political Science,* in press.

Jackman, M. R., & Senter, M. S. (1981). Beliefs about race, gender, and social class different, therefore unequal: Beliefs about trait differences between groups of unequal status. In D. J. Treiman & R. V. Robinson (Eds.), *Research in stratification and mobility* (Vol. 2). Greenwich, CT: JAI Press.

Jackson, J. J., Thoemmes, F., Jonkmann, K., Lüdtke, O., & Trautwien, U. (2012). Military training and personality trait development: Does the military make the man, or does the man make the military? *Psychological Science, 23,* 270–277.

Jackson, J. M., & Latané, B. (1981). All alone in front of all those people: Stage fright as a function of number and type of co-performers and audience. *Journal of Personality and Social Psychology, 40,* 73–85.

Jackson, J. W., Kirby, D., Barnes, L., & Shepard, L. (1993). Institutional racism and pluralistic ignorance: A cross-national comparison. In M. Wievorka (Ed.), *Racisme et modernite.* Paris: Editions la Découverte.

Jackson, L. A., Hunter, J. E., & Hodge, C. N. (1995). Physical attractiveness and intellectual competence: A meta-analytic review. *Social Psychology Quarterly, 58,* 108–123.

Jacobs, R. C., & Campbell, D. T. (1961). The perpetuation of an arbitrary tradition through several generations of a laboratory microculture. *Journal of Abnormal and Social Psychology, 62,* 649–658.

Jacoby, S. (1986, December). When opposites attract. *Reader's Digest,* 95–98.

Jaffe, Y., Shapir, N., & Yinon, Y. (1981). Aggression and its escalation. *Journal of Cross-Cultural Psychology, 12,* 21–36.

Jaffe, Y., & Yinon, Y. (1983). Collective aggression: The group-individual paradigm in the study of collective antisocial behavior. In H. H. Blumberg, A. P. Hare, V. Kent, & M. Davies (Eds.), *Small groups and social interaction* (Vol. 1). Cambridge: Wiley.

Jagel, K. (2014, February 12). Poll results: Barack Obama birth. YouGov.com, (https://today.yougov.com/news/2014/02/12/poll-results-barack-obama-birth/).

James, W. (1890, reprinted 1950). *The principles of psychology* (Vol. 2). New York: Dover.

James, W. (1899). Talks to teachers on psychology: And to students on some of life's ideals. New York: Holt, 1922, p. 33. Cited by W. J. McKeachie, Psychology in America's bicentennial year. *American Psychologist, 31,* 819–833.

James, W. (1902, reprinted 1958). *The varieties of religious experience.* New York: Mentor Books.

Jamieson, D. W., Lydon, J. E., Stewart, G., & Zanna, M. P. (1987). Pygmalion revisited: New evidence for student expectancy effects in the classroom. *Journal of Educational Psychology, 79,* 461–466.

Jamieson, J. P. (2010). The home field advantage in athletics: A meta-analysis. *Journal of Applied Social Psychology, 40,* 1819–1848.

Janes, L. M., & Olson, J. M. (2000). Jeer pressure: The behavioral effects of observing ridicule of others. *Personality and Social Psychology Bulletin, 26,* 474–485.

Jang, K. L., Dick, D. M., Wolf, H., Livesley, W. J., & Paris, J. (2005). Psychosocial adversity and emotional instability: An application of gene-environment interaction models. *European Journal of Personality, 19,* 359–372.

Janis, I. L. (1971, November). Groupthink. *Psychology Today,* 43–46.

Janis, I. L. (1972). *Victims of groupthink.* New York: Houghton Mifflin.

Janis, I. L. (1982). Counteracting the adverse effects of concurrence-seeking in policy-planning groups: Theory and research perspectives. In H. Brandstatter, J. H. Davis, & G. Stocker-Kreichgauer (Eds.), *Group decision making.* New York: Academic Press.

Janis, I. L. (1989). Crucial decisions: Leadership in policymaking and crisis management. New York: Free Press.

Janis, I. L., & Mann, L. (1977). *Decision-making: A psychological analysis of conflict, choice and commitment.* New York: Free Press.

Jankowiak, W. R., & Fischer, E. F. (1992). A cross-cultural perspective on romantic love. *Ethnology, 31,* 149–155.

Jaremka, L. M., Fagundes, C. P., Glaser, R., Bennett, J. M., Malarkey, W. B., & Kiecolt-Glaser, J. (2013). Loneliness predicts pain, depression, and fatigue: Understanding the role of immune dysregulation. *Psychoneuroendocrinology, 38,* 1310–1317.

Jaremka, L. M., Gabriel, S., & Carvallo, M. (2011). What makes us feel the best also makes us feel the worst: The emotional impact of independent and interdependent experiences. *Self and Identity, 10,* 44–63.

Jason, L. A., Rose, T., Ferrari, J. R., & Barone, R. (1984). Personal versus impersonal methods for recruiting blood donations. *Journal of Social Psychology, 123,* 139–140.

Jeffery, R. W., Drewnowski, A., Epstein, L. H., Stunkard, A. J., Wilson, G. T., Wing, R. R., & Hill, D. R. (2000). Long-term maintenance of weight loss: Current status. *Health Psychology, 19,* No. 1 (Supplement), 5–16.

Jelalian, E., & Miller, A. G. (1984). The perseverance of beliefs: Conceptual perspectives and research developments. *Journal of Social and Clinical Psychology, 2,* 25–56.

Jellison, J. M., & Green, J. (1981). A self-presentation approach to the fundamental attribution error: The norm of internality. *Journal of Personality and Social Psychology, 40,* 643–649.

Jemmott, J. B., III., & Locke, S. E. (1984). Psychosocial factors, immunologic mediation, and human susceptibility to infectious diseases: How much do we know? *Psychological Bulletin, 95,* 78–108.

Jeong, S-H., & Hwang, Y. (2012). Does multitasking increase or decrease persuasion? Effects of multitasking on comprehension and counterarguing. *Journal of Communication, 62,* 571–587.

Jervis, R. (1985). Perceiving and coping with threat: Psychological perspectives. In R. Jervis, R. N. Lebow, & J. Stein (Eds.), *Psychology and deterrence.* Baltimore: Johns Hopkins University Press.

Jetten, J., Hornsey, M. J., & Adarves-Yorno, I. (2006). When group members admit to being conformist: The role of relative intragroup status in conformity self-reports. *Personality and Social Psychology Bulletin, 32,* 162–173.

Jiang, L. C., Bazarova, N. N., & Hancock, J. T. (2013). From perception to behavior: Disclosure reciprocity and the intensification of intimacy in computer-mediated communication. *Communication Research, 40,* 125–143.

Johnson, A. L., Crawford, M. T., Sherman, S. J., Rutchick, A. M., Hamilton, D. L., Ferreira, M. B., & Petrocelli, J. V. (2006). A functional perspective on group memberships: Differential need fulfillment in group typology. *Journal of Experimental Social Psychology, 42,* 707–719.

Johnson, C. S., Olson, M. A., & Fazio, R. H. (2009). Getting acquainted in interracial interactions: Avoiding intimacy but approaching race. *Personality and Social Psychology Bulletin, 35,* 557–571.

Johnson, D. J., & Rusbult, C. E. (1989). Resisting temptation: Devaluation of alternative partners as a means of maintaining commitment in close relationships. *Journal of Personality and Social Psychology, 57,* 967–980.

Johnson, D. W., & Johnson, R. T. (1995). Teaching students to be peacemakers: Results of five years of research. *Peace and Conflict: Journal of Peace Psychology, 1,* 417–438.

Johnson, D. W., & Johnson, R. T. (2000). The three Cs of reducing prejudice and discrimination. In S. Oskamp (Ed.), *Reducing prejudice and discrimination.* Mahwah, NJ: Erlbaum.

Johnson, D. W., & Johnson, R. T. (2003). Student motivation in co-operative groups: Social interdependence theory. In R. M. Gillies & A. F. Ashman (Eds.), *Co-operative learning: The social and intellectual outcomes of learning in groups.* New York: Routledge.

Johnson, D. W., Maruyama, G., Johnson, R., Nelson, D., & Skon, L. (1981). Effects of cooperative, competitive, and individualistic goal structures on achievement: A meta-analysis. *Psychological Bulletin, 89,* 47–62.

Johnson, E. J., & Goldstein, D. (2003). Do defaults save lives? *Science, 302,* 1338–1339.

Johnson, J. A. (2007, June 26). Not so situational. Commentary on the SPSP listserv (spsp-discuss@stolaf.edu).

Johnson, J. D., Jackson, L. A., & Gatto, L. (1995). Violent attitudes and deferred academic aspirations: Deleterious effects of exposure to rap music. *Basic and Applied Social Psychology, 16,* 27–41.

Johnson, J. D., Trawalter, S., & Dovidio, J. F. (2000). Converging interracial consequences of exposure to violent rap music on stereotypical attributions of Blacks. *Journal of Experimental Social Psychology, 36,* 233–251.

Johnson, J. G., Cohen, P., Smailes, E. M., Kasen, S., & Brook, J. S. (2002). Television viewing and aggressive behavior during adolescence and adulthood. *Science, 295,* 2468–2471.

Johnson, J. L., & Johnson, C. F. (2001). Poverty and the death penalty. *Journal of Economic Issues, 2,* 517–523.

Johnson, M. H., & Magaro, P. A. (1987). Effects of mood and severity on memory processes in depression and mania. *Psychological Bulletin, 101,* 28–40.

Johnson, M. K., Rowatt, W. C., Barnard-Brak, L. M., Patock-Peckham, J. A., LaBouff, J. P., & Carlisle, R. D. (2011). A mediational analysis of the role of right-wing authoritarianism and religious fundamentalism in the religiosity-prejudice link. *Personality and Individual Differences, 50,* 851–856.

Johnson, R. D., & Downing, L. L. (1979). Deindividuation and valence of cues: Effects of prosocial and antisocial behavior. *Journal of Personality and Social Psychology, 37,* 1532–1538.

Johnson, W., & Krueger, R. F. (2006). How money buys happiness: Genetic and environmental processes linking finances and life satisfaction. *Journal of Personality and Social Psychology, 90,* 680–691.

Johnston, L. D., O'Malley, P. M., Miech, R. A., Bachman, J. G., & Schulenberg, J. E. (2015). Monitoring the Future national results on adolescent drug use: Overview of key findings, 2014. Ann Arbor, Mich.: Institute for Social Research, the University of Michigan.

Joiner, T. E., Jr. (1994). Contagious depression: Existence, specificity to depressed symptoms, and the role of reassurance seeking. *Journal of Personality and Social Psychology, 67,* 287–296.

Joinson, A. N. (2001). Self-disclosure in computer-mediated communication: The role of self-awareness and visual anonymity. *European Journal of Social Psychology, 31,* 177–192.

Joly-Mascheroni, R. M., Senju, A., & Shepherd, A. J. (2008). Dogs catch human yawns. *Biology Letters, 4,* 446–448.

Jones, C. R., Fazio, R. H., & Olson, M. A. (2009). Implicit misattribution as a mechanism underlying evaluative conditioning. *Journal of Personality and Social Psychology, 96,* 933–948.

Jones, C. S., & Kaplan, M. F. (2003). The effects of racially stereotypical crimes on juror decision-making and information-processing strategies. *Basic and Applied Social Psychology, 25,* 1–13.

Jones, E. E. (1964). *Ingratiation.* New York: Appleton-Century-Crofts.

Jones, E. E. (1976). How do people perceive the causes of behavior? *American Scientist, 64,* 300–305.

Jones, E. E., & Davis, K. E. (1965). From acts to dispositions: The attribution process in person perception. In L. Berkowitz (Ed.), *Advances in experimental social psychology* (Vol. 2). New York: Academic Press.

Jones, E. E., & Harris, V. A. (1967). The attribution of attitudes. *Journal of Experimental Social Psychology, 3,* 2–24.

Jones, E. E., & Nisbett, R. E. (1971). *The actor and the observer: Divergent perceptions of the causes of behavior.* Morristown, NJ: General Learning Press.

Jones, E. E., Rhodewalt, F., Berglas, S., & Skelton, J. A. (1981). Effects of strategic self-presentation on subsequent self-esteem. *Journal of Personality and Social Psychology, 41,* 407–421.

Jones, J. M. (1988). *Piercing the veil: Bi-cultural strategies for coping with prejudice and racism.* Invited address at the national conference "Opening Doors: An Appraisal of Race Relations in America," University of Alabama, June 11.

Jones, J. M. (2003, April 4). *Blacks show biggest decline in support for war compared with 1991.* Gallup Poll (www.gallup.com).

Jones, J. M. (2003). TRIOS: A psychological theory of the African legacy in American culture. *Journal of Social Issues, 59,* 217–242.

Jones, J. M. (2004). TRIOS: A model for coping with the universal context of racism? In G. Philogène (Ed.), *Racial identity in context: The legacy of Kenneth B. Clark.* Washington, DC: American Psychological Association.

Jones, J. M. (2012, December 6). Most in U.S. say gay/lesbian bias is a serious problem. Gallup Poll (www.gallup.com).

Jones, J. M. (2014, March 13). In U.S., most do not see global warming as a serious threat. Gallup Organization (http://www.gallup.com/poll/167879/not-global-warming-serious-threat.aspx).

Jones, J. T., & Cunningham, J. D. (1996). Attachment styles and other predictors of relationship satisfaction in dating couples. *Personal Relationships, 3,* 387–399.

Jones, J. T., Pelham, B. W., Carvallo, M., & Mirenberg, M. C. (2004). How do I love thee? Let me count the Js: Implicit egotism and interpersonal attraction. *Journal of Personality and Social Psychology, 87,* 665–683.

Jones, J. T., Pelham, B. W., & Mirenberg, M. C. (2002). Name letter preferences are not merely mere exposure: Implicit egotism as self-regulation. *Journal of Experimental Social Psychology, 38,* 170–177.

Jones, L. L., & Brunell, A. B. (2014). Clever and crude but not kind: Narcissism, self-esteem, and the self-reference effect. *Memory, 22,* 307–322.

Jones, W. H., Carpenter, B. N., & Quintana, D. (1985). Personality and interpersonal predictors of loneliness in two cultures. *Journal of Personality and Social Psychology, 48,* 1503–1511.

Josephson, W. L. (1987). Television violence and children's aggression: Testing the priming, social script, and disinhibition predictions. *Journal of Personality and Social Psychology, 53,* 882–890.

Jost, J. T., Kay, A. C., & Thorisdottir, H. (Eds.) (2009). *Social and psychological bases of ideology and system justification.* New York: Oxford University Press.

Jourard, S. M. (1964), *The transparent self.* Princeton, NJ: Van Nostrand.

Judd, C. M., Blair, I. V., & Chapleau, K. M. (2004). Automatic stereotypes vs. automatic prejudice: Sorting out the possibilities in the Payne (2001) weapon paradigm. *Journal of Experimental Social Psychology, 40,* 75–81.

Judge, T. A., LePine, J. A., & Rich, B. L. (2006). Loving yourself abundantly: Relationship of the narcissistic personality to self and other perceptions of workplace deviance, leadership, and task and contextual performance. *Journal of Applied Psychology, 91,* 762–776.

Jugert, P., Cohrs, J., & Duckitt, J. (2009). Inter- and intrapersonal processes underlying authoritarianism: The role of social conformity and personal need for structure. European *Journal of Personality, 23,* 607–621.

Jules, S. J., & McQuiston, D. E. (2013). Speech style and occupational status affect assessments of eyewitness testimony. *Journal of Applied Social Psychology, 43,* 741–748.

Jussim, L. (1986). Self-fulfilling prophecies: A theoretical and integrative review. *Psychological Review, 93,* 429–445.

Jussim, L. (2005). Accuracy in social perception: Criticisms, controversies, criteria, components and cognitive processes. *Advances in Experimental Social Psychology, 37,* 1–93.

Jussim, L. (2012). *Social perception and social reality: Why accuracy dominates bias and self-fulfilling prophecy.* New York: Oxford University Press.

Jussim, L., & Harber, K. D. (2005). Teacher expectations and self-fulfilling prophecies: Knowns and unknowns, resolved and unresolved controversies. *Personality and Social Psychology Review, 9,* 131–155.

Jussim, L., McCauley, C. R., & Lee, Y-T. (1995). Introduction: Why study stereotype accuracy and innaccuracy? In Y. T. Lee, L. Jussim, & C. R. McCauley (Eds.), *Stereotypes accuracy: Toward appreciating group differences.* Washington, DC: American Psychological Association.

Jussim, L., Robustelli, S. L., & Cain, T. R. (2009). Teacher expectations and self-fulfilling prophecies. In K. R. Wenzel & A. Wigfield (Eds.), *Handbook of motivation at school.* New York: Routledge/Taylor & Francis.

Juvonen, J., & Graham, S. (2014). Bullying in schools: The power of bullies and the plight of victims. *Annual Review of Psychology, 65,* 159–185.

Kagan, J. (1989). Temperamental contributions to social behavior. *American Psychologist, 44,* 668–674.

Kagan, J. (2009). Historical selection. *Review of General Psychology, 13,* 77–88.

Kagehiro, D. K. (1990). Defining the standard of proof in jury instructions. *Psychological Science, 1,* 194–200.

Kahan, D. M. (2014). Making Climate-Science Communication Evidence-Based—All the Way Down, In M. Boykoff & D. Crow (Eds.), *Culture, Politics and Climate Change.* New York: Routledge Press.

Kahan, D. M., Jenkins-Smith, H., & Braman, D. (2010). Cultural cognition of scientific consensus. *Journal of Risk Research, 14,* 147–174.

Kahan, D. M., Jenkins-Smith, H., & Braman, D. (2011). Cultural cognition of scientific consensus. *Journal of Risk Research, 14,* 147–174.

Kahan, D. M., Peters, E., Dawson, E. C., & Slovic, P. (2014). Motivated numeracy and enlightened self-government. The Cultural Cognition Project, Yale University, Working Paper No. 116.

Kahle, L. R., & Berman, J. (1979). Attitudes cause behaviors: A cross-lagged panel analysis. *Journal of Personality and Social Psychology, 37,* 315–321.

Kahlor, L., & Morrison, D. (2007). Television viewing and rape myth

acceptance among college women. *Sex Roles, 56,* 729–739.

Kahn, M. W. (1951). The effect of severe defeat at various age levels on the aggressive behavior of mice. *Journal of Genetic Psychology, 79,* 117–130.

Kahneman, D. (2011). *Thinking, fast and slow.* New York: Farrar, Straus, and Giroux.

Kahneman, D., & Deaton, A. (2010). High income improves evaluation of life but not emotional well-being. *PNAS, 107,* 16489–16493.

Kahneman, D., & Miller, D. T. (1986). Norm theory: Comparing reality to its alternatives. *Psychological Review, 93,* 75–88.

Kahneman, D., & Renshon, J. (2007, January/February). Why hawks win. *Foreign Policy* (www.foreignpolicy.com).

Kahneman, D., & Snell, J. (1992). Predicting a changing taste: Do people know what they will like? *Journal of Behavioral Decision Making, 5,* 187–200.

Kahneman, D., & Tversky, A. (1979). Intuitive prediction: Biases and corrective procedures. *Management Science, 12,* 313–327.

Kahneman, D., & Tversky, A. (1995). Conflict resolution: A cognitive perspective. In K. Arrow, R. Mnookin, L. Ross, A. Tversky, & R. Wilson (Eds.), *Barriers to the negotiated resolution of conflict.* New York: Norton.

Kaiser, C. R., & Pratt-Hyatt, J. S. (2009). Distributing prejudice unequally: Do Whites direct their prejudice toward strongly identified minorities? *Journal of Personality and Social Psychology, 96,* 432–445.

Kalenkoski, C. M., Ribar, D. C., & Stratton, L. S. (2009). *How do adolescents spell time use?* Institute for the Study of Labor, Bonn, Germany, Discussion Paper 4374.

Kalick, S. M. (1977). *Plastic surgery, physical appearance, and person perception.* Unpublished doctoral dissertation, Harvard University. Cited by E. Berscheid in An overview of the psychological effects of physical attractiveness and some comments upon the psychological effects of knowledge of the effects of physical attractiveness. In W. Lucker, K. Ribbens, & J. A. McNamera (Eds.), *Logical aspects of facial form* (craniofacial growth series). Ann Arbor: University of Michigan Press, 1981.

Kalinoski, Z. T., Steele-Johnson, D., Peyton, E. J., Leas, K. A., Steinke, J., & Bowling, N. A. (2013). A meta-analytic evaluation of diversity training outcomes. *Journal of Organizational Behavior, 34,* 1076–1104.

Kalven, H., Jr., & Zeisel, H. (1966). *The American jury.* Chicago: University of Chicago Press.

Kameda, T., & Sugimori, S. (1993). Psychological entrapment in group decision making: An assigned decision

rule and a groupthink phenomenon. *Journal of Personality and Social Psychology, 65,* 282–292.

Kammer, D. (1982). Differences in trait ascriptions to self and friend: Unconfounding intensity from variability. *Psychological Reports, 51,* 99–102.

Kamphuis, J., Meerlo, P., Koolhaas, J. M., & Lancel, M. (2012). Poor sleep as a potential causal factor in aggression and violence. *Sleep Medicine, 13,* 327–334.

Kanagawa, C., Cross, S. E., & Markus, H. R. (2001). "Who am I?" The cultural psychology of the conceptual self. *Personality and Social Psychology Bulletin, 27,* 90–103.

Kanazawa, S., & Kovar, J. L. (2004). Why beautiful people are more intelligent. *Intelligence, 32,* 227–243.

Kandel, D. B. (1978). Similarity in real-life adolescent friendship pairs. *Journal of Personality and Social Psychology, 36,* 306–312.

Kanekar, S., & Nazareth, A. (1988). Attributed rape victim's fault as a function of her attractiveness, physical hurt, and emotional disturbance. *Social Behaviour, 3,* 37–40.

Kanten, A. B., & Teigen, K. H. (2008). Better than average and better with time: Relative evaluations of self and others in the past, present, and future. *European Journal of Social Psychology, 38,* 343–353.

Kaplan, M. F. (1989). Task, situational, and personal determinants of influence processes in group decision making. In E. J. Lawler (Ed.), *Advances in group processes* (Vol. 6). Greenwich, CT: JAI Press.

Kaplan, M. F., & Schersching, C. (1980). Reducing juror bias: An experimental approach. In P. D. Lipsitt & B. D. Sales (Eds.), *New directions in psycholegal research* (pp. 149–170). New York: Van Nostrand Reinhold.

Kaplan, M. F., Wanshula, L. T., & Zanna, M. P. (1993). Time pressure and information integration in social judgment: The effect of need for structure. In O. Svenson & J. Maule (Eds.), *Time pressure and stress in human judgment and decision making.* Cambridge, England: Cambridge University Press.

Kaprio, J., Koskenvuo, M., & Rita, H. (1987). Mortality after bereavement: A prospective study of 95,647 widowed persons. *American Journal of Public Health, 77,* 283–287.

Karau, S. J., & Williams, K. D. (1993). Social loafing: A meta-analytic review and theoretical integration. *Journal of Personality and Social Psychology, 65,* 681–706.

Karau, S. J., & Williams, K. D. (1997). The effects of group cohesiveness on social loafing and compensation. *Group Dynamics: Theory, Research, and Practice, 1,* 156–168.

Karberg, J. C., & James, D. J. (2005). Substance dependence, abuse, and treatment of jail inmates, 2002. Bureau of Justice Statistics Special Report. Washington, DC: U.S. Department of Justice.

Karna, A., Voeten, M., Little, T. D., Poskiparta, E., Kalijonen, A., & Salmivalli, C. (2011). A large-scale evaluation of the KiVa antibullying program. *Child Development, 82,* 311–330.

Karney, B. R., & Bradbury, T. N. (1995). The longitudinal course of marital quality and stability: A review of theory, method, and research. *Psychological Bulletin, 118,* 3–34.

Karney, B. R., & Bradbury, T. N. (1997). Neuroticism, marital interaction, and the trajectory of marital satisfaction. *Journal of Personality and Social Psychology, 72,* 1075–1092.

Karpen, S. C., Jia, L., & Rydell, R. J. (2012). Discrepancies between implicit and explicit attitude measures as an indicator of attitude strength. *European Journal of Social Psychology, 42,* 24–29.

Karremans, J. C., Frankenhis, W. E., & Arons, S. (2010). Blind men prefer a low waist-to-hip ratio. *Evolution and Human Behavior, 31,* 182–186.

Kasen, S., Chen, H., Sneed, J., Crawford, T., & Cohen, P. (2006). Social role and birth cohort influences on gender-linked personality traits in women: A 20-year longitudinal analysis. *Journal of Personality and Social Psychology, 91,* 944–958.

Kashima, E. S., & Kashima, Y. (1998). Culture and language: The case of cultural dimensions and personal pronoun use. *Journal of Cross-Cultural Psychology, 29,* 461–486.

Kashima, Y., & Kashima, E. S. (2003). Individualism, GNP, climate, and pronoun drop: Is individualism determined by affluence and climate, or does language use play a role? *Journal of Cross-Cultural Psychology, 34,* 125–134.

Kasser, T. (2000). Two versions of the American dream: Which goals and values make for a high quality of life? In E. Diener and D. Rahtz (Eds.), *Advances in quality of life: Theory and research.* Dordrecht, Netherlands: Kluwer.

Kasser, T. (2002). *The high price of materialism.* Cambridge, MA: MIT Press.

Kasser, T. (2011). High price of materialism. Animated video. Center for the New American Dream (www .newdream.org).

Kassin, S. M., Bogart, D., & Kerner, J. (2012). Confessions that corrupt: Evidence from the DNA exoneration case files. *Psychological Science, 23,* 41–45.

Kassin, S. M., Drizin, S. A., Grisso, T., Gudjonsson, G. H., Leo, R. A., & Redlich, A. D. (2010). Police-induced confessions: Risk factors and recommendations. *Law and Human Behavior, 34,* 3–38.

Kassin, S. M., Goldstein, C. C., & Savitsky, K. (2003). Behavioral

confirmation in the interrogation room: On the dangers of presuming guilt. *Law and Human Behavior, 27,* 187–203.

Kassin, S. M., & Wrightsman, L. S. (1979). On the requirements of proof: The timing of judicial instruction and mock juror verdicts. *Journal of Personality and Social Psychology, 37,* 1877–1887.

Katz, E. (1957). The two-step flow of communication: An up-to-date report on a hypothesis. *Public Opinion Quarterly, 21,* 61–78.

Katz, I., Cohen, S., & Glass, D. (1975). Some determinants of cross-racial helping behavior. *Journal of Personality and Social Psychology, 32,* 964–970.

Katz, J., Beach, S. R. H., & Joiner, T. E., Jr. (1999). Contagious depression in dating couples. *Journal of Social and Clinical Psychology, 18,* 1–13.

Katz-Wise, S. L., & Hyde, J. S. (2012). Victimization experiences of lesbian, gay, and bisexual individuals: A meta-analysis. *Journal of Sex Research, 49,* 142–167.

Katz-Wise, S. L., Priess, H. A., & Hyde, J. S. (2010). Gender-role attitudes and behavior across the transition to parenthood. *Developmental Psychology, 46,* 18–28.

Katzer, C., Fetchenhauer, D., & Belschak, F. (2009). Cyberbullying: Who are the victims? A comparison of victimization in Internet chatrooms and victimization in school. *Journal of Media Psychology, 21,* 25–36.

Katzev, R., Edelsack, L., Steinmetz, G., & Walker, T. (1978). The effect of reprimanding transgressions on subsequent helping behavior: Two field experiments. Personality and Social Psychology Bulletin, 4, 126–129.

Katzev, R., & Wang, T. (1994). Can commitment change behavior? A case study of environmental actions. *Journal of Social Behavior and Personality, 9,* 13–26.

Kaufman, J., & Zigler, E. (1987). Do abused children become abusive parents? *American Journal of Orthopsychiatry, 57,* 186–192.

Kawachi, I., Kennedy, B. P., & Wilkinson, R. G. (1999). Crime: Social disorganization and relative deprivation. *Social Science and Medicine, 48,* 719–731.

Kawakami, K., Dovidio, J. F., Moll, J., Hermsen, S., & Russin, A. (2000). Just say no (to stereotyping): Effects of training in the negation of stereotypic associations on stereotype activation. *Journal of Personality and Social Psychology, 78,* 871–888.

Kawakami, K., Dunn, E., Kiarmali, F., & Dovidio, J. F. (2009). Mispredicting affective and behavioral responses to racism. *Science, 323,* 276–278.

Kawakami, K., Williams, A., Sidhu, D., Choma, B. L., Rodriguez-Bailón, R., Cañadas, E., Chung, B. L., & Hugenberg, K. (2014). An eye for the I: Preferential attention to the eyes of

ingroup members. *Journal of Personality and Social Psychology, 107,* 1–20.

Kay, A. C., Baucher, D., Peach, J. M., Laurin, K., Friesen, J., Zanna, M. P., & Spencer, S. J. (2009). Inequality, discrimination, and the power of the status quo: Direct evidence for a motivation to see the way things are as the way they should be. *Journal of Personality and Social Psychology, 97,* 421–434.

Kay, A. C., Day, M. V., Zanna, M. P., & Nussbaum, A. D. (2013). The insidious (and ironic) effects of positive stereotypes. *Journal of Experimental Social Psychology, 49,* 287–291.

Kay, A. C., & Eibach, R. P. (2013). Compensatory control and its implications for ideological extremism. *Journal of Social Issues, 69,* 564–585.

Keating, J. L., Van Boven, L., & Judd, C. (2013). Polarization blindness: Underestimating the effect of group discussion on political polarization. Paper presented to the Association for Psychological Science convention, Washington, D.C.

Keating, J. P., & Brock, T. C. (1974). Acceptance of persuasion and the inhibition of counterargumentation under various distraction tasks. *Journal of Experimental Social Psychology, 10,* 301–309.

Keller, E. B., & Berry, B. (2003). *The influentials: One American in ten tells the other nine how to vote, where to eat, and what to buy.* New York: Free Press.

Keller, J., & Dauenheimer, D. (2003). Stereotype threat in the classroom: Dejection mediates the disrupting threat effect on women's math performance. *Personality and Social Psychology Bulletin, 29,* 371–381.

Kellerman, J., Lewis, J., & Laird, J. D. (1989). Looking and loving: The effects of mutual gaze on feelings of romantic love. *Journal of Research in Personality, 23,* 145–161.

Kellermann, A. L. (1997). Comment: Gunsmoke—changing public attitudes toward smoking and firearms. *American Journal of Public Health, 87,* 910–912.

Kellermann, A. L., Rivara, F. P., Rushforth, N. B., Banton, J. G., Reay, D. T., Francisco, J. T., Locci, A. B., Prodzinski, J., Hackman, B. B., & Somes, G. (1993). Gun ownership as a risk factor for homicide in the home. *New England Journal of Medicine, 329,* 1984–1991.

Kelley, H. H., & Stahelski, A. J. (1970). The social interaction basis of cooperators' and competitors' beliefs about others. *Journal of Personality and Social Psychology, 16,* 66–91.

Kelly, A. E., & Macready, D. E. (2009). Why disclosing to a confidant can be so good (or bad) for us. In W. & T. Afifi (Eds.), Uncertainty and information regulation in interpersonal contexts:

Theories and applications (pp. 384–402). New York: Routledge.

Kelly, D. J., Liu, S., Ge, L., Quinn, P. C., Slater, A. M., Lee, K., Liu, Q., & Pascalis, O. (2007). Cross-race preferences for same-race faces extended beyond the African versus Caucasian contrast in 3-month-old infants. *Infancy, 11,* 87–95.

Kelly, D. J., Quinn, P. C., Slater, A. M., Lee, K., Ge, L., & Pascalis, O. (2007). The other-race effect develops during infancy: Evidence of perceptual narrowing. *Psychological Science, 18,* 1084–1089.

Kelly, D. J., Quinn, P. C., Slater, A. M., Lee, K., Gibson, A., Smith, M., Ge, L., & Y Pascalis, O. (2005). Three-month-olds, but not newborns prefer own-race faces. *Developmental Science, 8,* F31–F36.

Kelman, H. C. (1997). Group processes in the resolution of international conflicts: Experiences from the Israeli-Palestinian case. *American Psychologist, 52,* 212–220.

Kelman, H. C. (1998). Building a sustainable peace: The limits of pragmatism in the Israeli-Palestinian negotiations. Address to the American Psychological Association convention, San Francisco, California.

Kelman, H. C. (2007). The Israeli-Palestinian peace process and its vicissitudes: Insights from attitude theory. *American Psychologist, 62,* 287–303.

Kelman, H. C. (2010). Looking back at my work on conflict resolution in the Middle East. *Peace and Conflict: Journal of Peace Psychology, 16,* 361–387.

Kendrick, R. V., & Olson, M. A. (2012). When feeling right leads to being right in the reporting of implicitly-formed attitudes, or how I learned to stop worrying and trust my gut. *Journal of Experimental Social Psychology, 48,* 1316–1321.

Kennedy, J. A., Anderson, C., & Moore, D. A. (2013). When overconfidence is revealed to others: Testing the status-enhancement theory of overconfidence. *Organizational Behavior and Human Decision Processes, 122,* 266–279.

Kennedy, J. F. (1956). *Profiles in courage.* New York: Harper.

Kennedy, K. A., & Pronin, E. (2008). When disagreement gets ugly: Perceptions of bias and the escalation of conflict. *Personality and Social Psychology Bulletin, 34,* 833–848.

Kenny, D. A., & Acitelli, L. K. (2001). Accuracy and bias in the perception of the partner in a close relationship. *Journal of Personality and Social Psychology, 80,* 439–448.

Kenny, D. A., & Nasby, W. (1980). Splitting the reciprocity correlation. *Journal of Personality and Social Psychology, 38,* 249–256.

Kenrick, D. T. (1987). Gender, genes, and the social environment: A biosocial interactionist perspective. In P. Shaver & C. Hendrick (Eds.), *Sex and gender: Review of personality and social psychology* (Vol. 7). Beverly Hills, CA: Sage.

Kenrick, D. T., Gutierres, S. E., & Goldberg, L. L. (1989). Influence of popular erotica on judgments of strangers and mates. *Journal of Experimental Social Psychology, 25,* 159–167.

Kenrick, D. T., & MacFarlane, S. W. (1986). Ambient temperature and horn-honking: A field study of the heat/aggression relationship. *Environment and Behavior, 18,* 179–191.

Kenrick, D. T., Nieuweboer, S., & Buunk, A. P. (2009). Universal mechanisms and cultural diversity: Replacing the blank slate with a coloring book. In M. Schaller, A. Norenzayan, S. Heine, T. Yamagishi, & T. Kameda (Eds.), *Evolution, culture, and the human mind.* New York: Psychology Press.

Kenrick, D. T., & Trost, M. R. (1987). A biosocial theory of heterosexual relationships. In K. Kelly (Ed.), *Females, males, and sexuality.* Albany: State University of New York Press.

Kenworthy, J. B., Hewstone, M., Levine, J. M., Martin, R., & Willis, H. (2008). The phenomenology of minority-majority status: Effects of innovation in argument generation. *European Journal of Social Psychology, 38,* 624–636.

Kern, M. L., & Sap, M. (2014, February). *Do you feel what I feel? Cultural variations in linguistic expressions of emotion.* Symposium talk presented at the 16th annual meeting of the Society of Personality and Social Psychology, Long Beach, CA.

Kerr, N. (1999). Behind the scenes. In D. G. Myers (Ed.), *Social psychology,* 6th edition. New York: McGraw-Hill.

Kerr, N. L. (1978). Severity of prescribed penalty and mock jurors' verdicts. *Journal of Personality and Social Psychology, 36,* 1431–1442.

Kerr, N. L. (1981b). Social transition schemes: Charting the group's road to agreement. *Journal of Personality and Social Psychology, 41,* 684–702.

Kerr, N. L. (1983). Motivation losses in small groups: A social dilemma analysis. *Journal of Personality and Social Psychology, 45,* 819–828.

Kerr, N. L. (1989). Illusions of efficacy: The effects of group size on perceived efficacy in social dilemmas. *Journal of Experimental Social Psychology, 25,* 287–313.

Kerr, N. L. (1992). Norms in social dilemmas. In D. Schroeder (Ed.), *Social dilemmas: Psychological perspectives.* New York: Praeger.

Kerr, N. L., Atkin, R. S., Stasser, G., Meek, D., Holt, R. W., & Davis, J. H. (1976). Guilt beyond a reasonable doubt: Effects of concept definition and assigned decision rule on the judgments of mock jurors. *Journal of Personality and Social Psychology, 34,* 282–294.

Kerr, N. L., & Bray, R. M. (2005). Simulation, realism, and the study of the jury. In N. Brewer & K. D. Williams (Eds.), *Psychology and law: An empirical perspective.* New York: Guilford.

Kerr, N. L., & Bruun, S. E. (1981). Ringelmann revisited: Alternative explanations for the social loafing effect. *Personality and Social Psychology Bulletin, 7,* 224–231.

Kerr, N. L., Garst, J., Lewandowski, D. A., & Harris, S. E. (1997). That still, small voice: Commitment to cooperate as an internalized versus a social norm. *Personality and Social Psychology Bulletin, 23,* 1300–1311.

Kerr, N. L., Harmon, D. L., & Graves, J. K. (1982). Independence of multiple verdicts by jurors and juries. *Journal of Applied Social Psychology, 12,* 12–29.

Kerr, N. L., & Kaufman-Gilliland, C. M. (1994). Communication, commitment, and cooperation in social dilemmas. *Journal of Personality and Social Psychology, 66,* 513–529.

Kerr, N. L. & Kaufman-Gilliland, C. M. (1997). ". . . and besides, I probably couldn't have made a difference anyway": Justification of social dilemma defection via perceived self-inefficacy. *Journal of Experimental Social Psychology, 33,* 211–230.

Kerr, N. L., & MacCoun, R. J. (1985). The effects of jury size and polling method on the process and product of jury deliberation. *Journal of Personality and Social Psychology, 48,* 349–363.

Kerr, N. L., Messé, L. A., Seok, D.-H., Sambolec, E. J., Lount, R. B., Jr., & Park, E. S. (2007). Psychological mechanisms underlying the Köhler motivation gain. *Personality and Social Psychology Bulletin, 33,* 828–841.

Kerr, R. A. (2009). Amid worrisome signs of warming, 'climate fatigue' sets in. *Science, 326,* 926–928.

Kerr, R. A. (2011). Antarctic ice's future still mired in its murky past. *Science, 333,* 401.

Kesebir, S., & Oishi, S. (2010). A spontaneous self-reference effect in memory: Why some birthdays are harder to remember than others. *Psychological Science, 21,* 1525–1531.

Kessler, T., & Mummendey, A. (2001). Is there any scapegoat around? Determinants of intergroup conflicts at different categorization levels. *Journal of Personality and Social Psychology, 81,* 1090–1102.

Kiatponsong, S., & Norton, M. (2014). How much (more) should CEOs make? A universal desire for more equal pay. *Perspectives on Psychological Science, 9,* 587–593.

Kiecolt-Glaser, J. K., Loving, T. J., Stowell, J. R., Malarkey, W. B., Lemeshow, S., Dickinson, S. L., & Glaser, R. (2005). Hostile marital interactions, proinflammatory cytokine production, and wound healing. *Archives of General Psychiatry, 62,* 1377–1384.

Kiecolt-Glaser, J. K., Malarkey, W. B., Chee, M., Newton, T., Cacioppo, J. T., Mao, H-Y., & Glaser, R. (1993). Negative behavior during marital conflict is associated with immunological down-regulation. *Psychosomatic Medicine, 55,* 395–409.

Kihlstrom, J. F. (1994). The social construction of memory. Address to the American Psychological Society convention., Washington, DC.

Kihlstrom, J. F., & Cantor, N. (1984). Mental representations of the self. In L. Berkowitz (Ed.), *Advances in experimental social psychology* (Vol. 17). New York: Academic Press.

Kille, D. R., Forest, A. L., & Wood, J. V. (2013). Tall, dark, and stable: Embodiment motivates mate selection preferences. *Psychological Science, 24,* 112–114.

Kim, H., & Markus, H. R. (1999). Deviance of uniqueness, harmony or conformity? A cultural analysis. *Journal of Personality and Social Psychology, 77,* 785–800.

Kim, H. S., & Sherman, D. K. (2007). "Express yourself": Culture and the effect of self-expression on choice. *Journal of Personality and Social Psychology, 92,* 1–11.

Kimmel, A. J. (1998). In defense of deception. *American Psychologist, 53,* 803–805.

Kinder, D. R., & Sears, D. O. (1985). Public opinion and political action. In G. Lindzey & E. Aronson (Eds.), *The handbook of social psychology,* 3rd edition. New York: Random House.

Kingdon, J. W. (1967). Politicians' beliefs about voters. *The American Political Science Review, 61,* 137–145.

Kingston, D. A., Fedoroff, P., Firestone, P., Curry, S., & Bradford, J. M. (2008). Pornography use and sexual aggression: The impact of frequency and type of pornography use on recidivism among sexual offenders. *Aggressive Behavior, 34,* 341–351.

Kingston, D. A., Malamuth, N. M., Fedoroff, P., & Marshall, W. L. (2009). The importance of individual differences in pornography use: Theoretical perspectives and implications for treating sexual offenders. *Journal of Sex Research, 46,* 216–232.

Kinias, Z., Kim, H. S., Hafenbrack, A. C., & Lee, J. J. (2014). Standing out as a signal to selfishness: Culture and devaluation of non-normative characteristics. *Organizational Behavior and Human Decision Processes, 124,* 190–203.

Kinnier, R. T., & Metha, A. T. (1989). Regrets and priorities at three stages of life. *Counseling and Values, 33,* 182–193.

Kinzler, K. D., Shutts, K., Dejesus, J., & Spelke, E. S. (2009). Accent trumps race in guiding children's social preferences. *Social Cognition, 27,* 623–634.

Kitayama, S. (1999). Behind the scenes. In D. G. Myers (Ed.), *Social psychology,* 6th ed. New York: McGraw-Hill.

Kitayama, S., & Karasawa, M. (1997). Implicit self-esteem in Japan: Name letters and birthday numbers. *Personality and Social Psychology Bulletin, 23,* 736–742.

Kitayama, S., & Markus, H. R. (2000). The pursuit of happiness and the realization of sympathy: Cultural patterns of self, social relations, and well-being. In E. Diener & E. M. Suh (Eds.), *Subjective well-being across cultures.* Cambridge, MA: MIT Press.

Kite, M. E. (2001). Changing times, changing gender roles: Who do we want women and men to be? In R. K. Unger (Ed.), *Handbook of the psychology of women and gender.* New York: Wiley.

Klaas, E. T. (1978). Psychological effects of immoral actions: The experimental evidence. *Psychological Bulletin, 85,* 756–771.

Klapwijk, A., & Van Lange, P. A. M. (2009). Promoting cooperation and trust in "noisy" situations: The power of generosity. *Journal of Personality and Social Psychology, 96,* 83–103.

Klauer, K. C., & Voss, A. (2008). Effects of race on responses and response latencies in the weapon identification task: A test of six models. *Personality and Social Psychology Bulletin, 34,* 1124–1140.

Kleck, R. E., & Strenta, A. (1980). Perceptions of the impact of negatively valued physical characteristics on social interaction. *Journal of Personality and Social Psychology, 39,* 861–873.

Kleiman, T., & Hassin, R. R. (2013). When conflicts are good: Nonconscious goal conflicts reduce confirmatory thinking. *Journal of Personality and Social Psychology, 105,* 374–387.

Kleinfield, N. R., Rivera, R., & Kovaleski, S. F. (2013). Newtown killer's obsessions, in chilling detail. *New York Times,* March 28, 2013, A1.

Klein, J. G. (1991). Negative effects in impression formation: A test in the political arena. *Personality and Social Psychology Bulletin, 17,* 412–418.

Kleinke, C. L. (1977). Compliance to requests made by gazing and touching experimenters in field settings. *Journal of Experimental Social Psychology, 13,* 218–223.

Klein, O., Snyder, M., & Livingston, R. W. (2004). Prejudice on the stage: Self-monitoring and the public expression of group attitudes. *British Journal of Social Psychology, 43,* 299–314.

Klein, R. A., & 50 others (2014). Investigating variation in replicability: A "many labs" replication project. *Social Psychology, 45,* 142–152.

Klein, W. M., & Kunda, Z. (1992). Motivated person perception: Constructing justifications for desired beliefs. *Journal of Experimental Social Psychology, 28,* 145–168.

Klentz, B., Beaman, A. L., Mapelli, S. D., & Ullrich, J. R. (1987). Perceived physical attractiveness of supporters and nonsupporters of the women's movement: An attitude-similarity-mediated error (AS-ME). *Personality and Social Psychology Bulletin, 13,* 513–523.

Klinesmith, J., Kasser, T., & McAndrew, F. T. (2006). Guns, testosterone, and aggression. *Psychological Science, 17(7),* 568–571.

Klopfer, P. H. (1958). Influence of social interaction on learning rates in birds. *Science, 128,* 903.

Knewtson, H. S., & Sias, R. W. (2010). Why Susie owns Starbucks: The name letter effect in security selection. *Journal of Business Research, 63,* 1324–1327.

Kniffin, K. M., Wansink, B., Grisevicius, V., & Wilson, D. S. (2014). Beauty is in the in-group of the beholded: Intergroup differences in the perceived attractiveness of leaders. *Leadership Quarterly, 25,* 1143–1153.

Knight, G. P., Guthrie, I. K., Page, M. C., & Fabes, R. A. (2002). Emotional arousal and gender differences in aggression: A meta-analysis. *Aggressive Behavior, 28,* 366–393.

Knight, J. A., & Vallacher, R. R. (1981). Interpersonal engagement in social perception: The consequences of getting into the action. *Journal of Personality and Social Psychology, 40,* 990–999.

Knowles, E. D., & Peng, K. (2005). White selves: Conceptualizing and measuring a dominant-group identity. *Journal of Personality and Social Psychology, 89,* 223–241.

Knowles, E. S. (1983). Social physics and the effects of others: Tests of the effects of audience size and distance on social judgment and behavior. *Journal of Personality and Social Psychology, 45,* 1263–1279.

Knox, R. E., & Inkster, J. A. (1968). Postdecision dissonance at post-time. *Journal of Personality and Social Psychology, 8,* 319–323.

Koehler, D. J. (1991). Explanation, imagination, and confidence in judgment. *Psychological Bulletin, 110,* 499–519.

Koenig, A. M., & Eagly, A. H. (2014). Evidence for the social role theory of stereotype content: Observations of groups' roles shape stereotypes. *Journal of Personality and Social Psychology, 107,* 371–392.

Koenig, A. M., Eagly, A. H., Mitchell, A. A., & Ristikari, T. (2011). Are leader stereotypes masculine? A meta-analysis of three research paradigms. *Psychological Bulletin, 137,* 616–642.

Koenig, L. B., McGue, M., & Iacono, W. G. (2008). Stability and change in religiousness during emerging adulthood. *Developmental Psychology, 44,* 531–543.

Koestner, R., & Wheeler, L. (1988). Self-presentation in personal advertisements: The influence of implicit notions of attraction and role expectations. *Journal of Social and Personal Relationships, 5,* 149–160.

Kolata, G., & Peterson, I. (2001, July 21). New way to insure eyewitnesses can ID the right bad guy. *New York Times* (www .nytimes.com).

Kolivas, E. D., & Gross, A. M. (2007). Assessing sexual aggression: Addressing the gap between rape victimization and perpetration prevalence rates. *Aggression and Violent Behavior, 12,* 315–328.

Konrad, A. M., Ritchie, J. E., Jr., Lieb, P., & Corrigall, E. (2000). Sex differences and similarities in job attribute preferences: A meta-analysis. *Psychological Bulletin, 126,* 593–641.

Konrath, S., Au, J., & Ramsey, L. R. (2012). Cultural differences in face-ism: Male politicians have bigger heads in more gender-equal cultures. *Psychology of Women Quarterly, 36,* 476–487.

Konrath, S. H., Chopik, W. J., Hsing, C. K., & O'Brien, E. (2014). Changes in adult attachment styles in American college students over time: A meta-analysis. *Personality and Social Psychology Review, 18,* 326–348.

Konrath, S. H., O'Brien, E. H., & Hsing, C. (2011). Changes in dispositional empathy in American college students over time: A meta-analysis. *Personality & Social Psychology Review, 15,* 180–198.

Konrath, S., Meier, B. P., & Bushman, B. J. (2014). Development and validation of the single item narcissism scale (SINS). *Plos One.* DOI: 10.1371/journal. pone.0103469

Koo, M., Algoe, S. B., Wilson, T. D., & Gilbert, D. T. (2008). It's a wonderful life: Mentally subtracting positive events improves people's affective states, contrary to their affective forecasts. *Journal of Personality and Social Psychology, 95,* 1217–1224.

Koole, S. L., Dijksterhuis, A., & van Knippenberg, A. (2001). What's in a name? Implicit self-esteem and the automatic self. *Journal of Personality and Social Psychology, 80,* 669–685.

Koomen, W., & Dijker, A. J. (1997). Ingroup and outgroup stereotypes and selective processing. *European Journal of Social Psychology, 27,* 589–601.

Koop, C. E. (1987). Report of the Surgeon General's workshop on pornography and public health. *American Psychologist, 42,* 944–945.

Koppel, M., Argamon, S., & Shimoni, A. R. (2002). Automatically categorizing written texts by author gender. *Literary and Linguistic Computing, 17,* 401–412.

Koriat, A., Lichtenstein, S., & Fischhoff, B. (1980). Reasons for confidence. *Journal of Experimental Social Psychology: Human Learning and Memory, 6,* 107–118.

Kornbrot, D. E., Msetfi, R. M., & Grimwood, M. J. (2013). Time perception and depressive realism: Judgment type,

psychophysical functions and bias. *PLoS ONE, 8,* e71585.

Korn, J. H., & Nicks, S. D. (1993). The rise and decline of deception in social psychology. Poster presented at the American Psychological Society convention.

Kouchaki, M., & Wareham, J. (2015). Excluded and behaving unethically: Social exclusion, physiological responses, and unethical behavior. *Journal of Applied Psychology, 100,* 547–556.

Kowalski, R. M., Guimetti, G. W., Schroeder, A. N., & Lattanner, M. R. (2014). Bullying in the digital age: A critical review and meta-analysis of cyberbulling research among youth. *Psychological Bulletin, 140,* 1073–1137.

Krackow, A., & Blass, T. (1995). When nurses obey or defy inappropriate physician orders: Attributional differences. *Journal of Social Behavior and Personality, 10,* 585–594.

Kraft, T. L., & Pressman, S. D. (2012). Grin and bear it: The influence of manipulated facial expression on the stress response. *Psychological Science, 23,* 1372–1378.

Krahe, B., Busching, R., & Moller, I. (2012). Media violence use and aggression among German adolescents: Associations and trajectories of change in a three-wave longitudinal study. *Psychology of Popular Media Culture, 1,* 152–166.

Krahe, B., Moller, I., Huesmann, L. R., Kirwil, L., Felber, J., & Berger, A. (2010). Desensitization to media violence: Links with habitual media violence exposure, aggressive cognitions, and aggressive behavior. *Journal of Personality and Social Psychology, 100,* 630–646.

Kramer, A. D. I., & Chung, C. K. (2011). Dimensions of self-expression in Facebook status updates. Proceedings of the Fifth International AAAI Conference on Weblogs and Social Media (www.aaai.org).

Kramer, A. D. I, Guillory, J. E., & Hancock, J. T. (2014). Experimental evidence of massive-scale emotional contagion through social networks. *Proceedings of the National Academy of Sciences, 111,* 8788–8790.

Kramer, A. E. (2008, August 32). Russia's collective farms: Hot capitalist property. *New York Times* (www.nytimes.com).

Kramer, G. P., Kerr, N. L., & Carroll, J. S. (1990). Pretrial publicity, judicial remedies, and jury bias. *Law and Human Behavior, 14,* 409–438.

Kraus, M. W., & Keltner, D. (2013). Social class rank, essentialism, and punitive judgment. *Journal of Personality and Social Psychology, 105,* 247–261.

Kraus, M. W., Piff, P. K., Mendoza-Denton, R., Rheinschmidt, M. L., & Keltner, D. (2012). Social class, solipsism, and contextualism: How the rich are different from the poor. *Psychological Review, 119,* 546–572.

Kraus, S. J. (1995). Attitudes and the prediction of behavior: A meta-analysis of the empirical literature. *Personality and Social Psychology Bulletin, 21,* 58–75.

Kraut, R. E. (1973). Effects of social labeling on giving to charity. *Journal of Experimental Social Psychology, 9,* 551–562.

Kravitz, D. A., & Martin, B. (1986). Ringelmann rediscovered: The original article. *Journal of Personality and Social Psychology, 50,* 936–941.

Krebs, D. (1970). Altruism—An examination of the concept and a review of the literature. *Psychological Bulletin, 73,* 258–302.

Krebs, D. (1975). Empathy and altruism. *Journal of Personality and Social Psychology, 32,* 1134–1146.

Krebs, D. (1998). The evolution of moral behaviors. In C. Crawford & D. L. Krebs (Eds.), *Handbook of evolutionary psychology: Ideas, issues, and applications.* Mahwah, NJ: Erlbaum.

Krendl, A. C., Richeson, J. A., Kelley, W. M., & Heatherton, T. F. (2008). The negative consequences of threat: A functional magnetic resonance imaging investigation of the neural mechanisms underlying women's underperformance in math. *Psychological Science, 19,* 168–175.

Krisberg, K. (2004). Successful "truth" anti-smoking campaign in funding jeopardy: New commission works to save campaign. *Medscape* (www.medscape .com).

Kristof, N. D. (2007, August 16). The big melt. *New York Times* (www.nytimes .com).

Krizan, Z., & Suls, J. (2008). Losing sight of oneself in the above-average effect: When egocentrism, focalism, and group diffuseness collide. *Journal of Experimental Social Psychology, 44,* 929–942.

Kroeper, K. M., Sanchez, D. T., & Himmelstein, M. S. (2014). Heterosexual men's confrontation of sexual prejudice: The role of precarious manhood. *Sex Roles, 70,* 1–13.

Kroger, R. O., & Wood, L. A. (1992). Are the rules of address universal? IV: Comparison of Chinese, Korean, Greek, and German usage. *Journal of Cross-Cultural Psychology, 23,* 148–162.

Krosnick, J. A., & Alwin, D. F. (1989). Aging and susceptibility to attitude change. *Journal of Personality and Social Psychology, 57,* 416–425.

Krosnick, J. A., & Schuman, H. (1988). Attitude intensity, importance, and certainty and susceptibility to response effects. *Journal of Personality and Social Psychology, 54,* 940–952.

Kross, E., Verduyn, P., Demiralp, E., Park, J., Lee, D. S., Lin, N., Shablack, H., Jonides, J., & Ybarra, O. (2013). Facebook use predicts declines in subjective well-being in young adults. *Plos One, 8,* e69841.

Krueger, A. B., & Malečková, J. (2009). Attitudes and action: Public opinion and the occurrence of international terrorism. *Science, 325,* 1534–1536.

Krueger, A. B., & Stone, A. A. (2014). Progress in measuring subjective well-being: Moving toward national indicators and policy evaluations. *Science, 346,* 42–43.

Krueger, J., & Clement, R. W. (1994a). Memory-based judgments about multiple categories: A revision and extension of Tajfel's accentuation theory. *Journal of Personality and Social Psychology, 67,* 35–47.

Krueger, J., & Clement, R. W. (1994b). The truly false consensus effect: An ineradicable and egocentric bias in social perception. *Journal of Personality and Social Psychology, 67,* 596–610.

Krueger, J. I., DiDonato, T. E., & Freestone, D. (2012). Social projection can solve social dilemmas. *Psychological Inquiry, 23,* 1–27.

Krueger, J. I., & Funder, D. C. (2003a). Towards a balanced social psychology: Causes, consequences and cures for the problem-seeking approach to social behavior and cognition. *Behavioral and Brain Sciences, 27*(3), 313–327.

Krueger, J. I., & Funder, D. C. (2003b). Social psychology: A field in search of a center. *Behavioral and Brain Sciences, 27*(3), 361–367.

Krueger, J., & Rothbart, M. (1988). Use of categorical and individuating information in making inferences about personality. *Journal of Personality and Social Psychology, 55,* 187–195.

Krueger, R. F., Hicks, B. M., & McGue, M. (2001). Altruism and antisocial behavior: Independent tendencies, unique personality correlates, distinct etiologies. *Psychological Science, 12,* 397–402.

Kruger, J., & Dunning, D. (1999). Unskilled and unaware of it: How difficulties in recognizing one's own incompetence lead to inflated self-assessments. *Journal of Personality and Social Psychology, 77,* 1121–1134.

Kruger, J., & Gilovich, T. (1999). "I cynicism" in everyday theories of responsibility assessment: On biased assumptions of bias. *Journal of Personality and Social Psychology, 76,* 743–753.

Kruger, J., Gordon, C. L., & Kuban, J. (2006). Intentions in teasing: When "just kidding" just isn't good enough. *Journal of Personality and Social Psychology, 90,* 412–425.

Kruger, J., Wirtz, D., & Miller, D. T. (2005). Counterfactual thinking and the first instinct fallacy. *Journal of Personality and Social Psychology, 88,* 725–735.

Kruglanski, A. W., Chen, X., Dechesne, M., Fishman, S., & Orehek E. (2009). Fully committed: Suicide bombers' motivation and the quest for personal significance. *Political Psychology, 30,* 331–357.

Kruglanski, A. W., & Fishman, S. (2006). The psychology of terrorism: "Syndrome" versus "tool" perspective. *Journal of Terrorism and Political Violence, 18(2),* 193–215.

Kruglanski, A. W., & Gigerenzer, G. (2011). Intuitive and deliberate judgments are based on common principles. *Psychological Review, 118,* 97–109.

Kruglanski, A. W., & Golec de Zavala, A. (2005). Individual motivations, the group process and organizational strategies in suicide terrorism. *Psychology and Sociology (Psycologie et sociologie).*

Kruglanski, A. W., & Webster, D. M. (1991). Group members' reactions to opinion deviates and conformists at varying degrees of proximity to decision deadline and of environmental noise. *Journal of Personality and Social Psychology, 61,* 212–225.

Krull, D. S., Loy, M. H.-M., Lin, J., Wang, C.-F., Chen, S., & Zhao, X. (1999). The fundamental fundamental attribution error: Correspondence bias in individualist and collectivist cultures. *Personality and Social Psychology Bulletin, 25,* 1208–1219.

Kubany, E. S., Bauer, G. B., Pangilinan, M. E., Muroka, M. Y., & Enriquez, V. G. (1995). Impact of labeled anger and blame in intimate relationships. *Journal of Cross-Cultural Psychology, 26,* 65–83.

Kubota, J. T., Li, J., Bar-David, E., Banaji, M. R., & Phelps, E. A. (2013). The price of racial bias: Intergroup negotiations in the ultimatum game. *Psychological Science, 24,* 2498–2504.

Kugihara, N. (1999). Gender and social loafing in Japan. *Journal of Social Psychology, 139,* 516–526.

Kuiper, N. A., & Higgins, E. T. (1985). Social cognition and depression: A general integrative perspective. *Social Cognition, 3,* 1–15.

Kulig, J. W. (2012). What's in a name? Our false uniqueness! *British Journal of Social Psychology, 52,* 173–179.

Kull, S. (2003, June 4). Quoted in "Many Americans unaware WMD have not been found." Program on International Policy Attitudes (http://pipa.org/whatsnew/html/new_6_04_03.html).

Kumar, S., Calvo, R., Avendano, M., Sivaramakrishnan, K., & Berkman, L. F. (2012). Social support, volunteering and health around the world: Cross-national evidence from 139 countries. *Social Science and Medicine, 74,* 696–706.

Kumkale, G. T., & Albarracin, D. (2004). The sleeper effect in persuasion: A meta-analytic review. *Psychological Bulletin, 130,* 143–172.

Kunda, Z., & Oleson, K. C. (1995). Maintaining stereotypes in the face of disconfirmation: Constructing grounds for subtyping deviants. *Journal of Personality and Social Psychology, 68,* 565–579.

Kunda, Z., & Oleson, K. C. (1997). When exceptions prove the rule: How extremity of deviance determines the impact of deviant examples on stereotypes. *Journal of Personality and Social Psychology, 72,* 965–979.

Kunda, Z., & Spencer, S. J. (2003). When do stereotypes come to mind and when do they color judgment? A goal-based theoretical framework for stereotype activation and application. *Psychological Bulletin, 129,* 522–544.

Kunkel, D. (2001, February 4). Sex on TV. Menlo Park, CA: Henry J. Kaiser Family Foundation (www.kff.org).

Kunst-Wilson, W. R., & Zajonc, R. B. (1980). Affective discrimination of stimuli that cannot be recognized. *Science, 207,* 557–558.

Kupper, N., & Denollet, J. (2007). Type D personality as a prognostic factor in heart disease: Assessment and mediating mechanisms. *Journal of Personality Assessment, 89,* 265–276.

Kurzman, D. (2004). *No greater glory: The four immortal chaplains and the sinking of the Dorchester in World War II.* New York: Random House.

Kuster, F., Orth, U., & Meier, L. L. (2012). Rumination mediates the prospective effect of low self-esteem on depression: A five-wave longitudinal study. *Personality and Social Psychology Bulletin, 38,* 747–759.

Kutner, L., & Olson, C. K. (2008). *Grand theft childhood: The surprising truth about violent video games and what parents can do* (pp. 111–137). New York: Simon & Schuster.

Kuziemko, I., Norton, M. I., Saez, E., Stantcheva, S. (2015). How elastic are preferences for redistribution? Evidence from randomized survey experiments. *American Economic Review,* in press.

Lacey, M. (2004, April 9). A decade after massacres, Rwanda outlaws ethnicity. *New York Times* (www.nytimes.com).

LaFrance, M. (1985). Does your smile reveal your status? *Social Science News Letter, 70* (Spring), 15–18.

LaFrance, M., Hecht, M. A., & Paluck, E. L. (2003). The contingent smile: A meta-analysis of sex differences in smiling. *Psychological Bulletin, 129,* 305–334.

LaFromboise, T., Coleman, H. L. K., & Gerton, J. (1993). Psychological impact of biculturalism: Evidence and theory. *Psychological Bulletin, 114,* 395–412.

Lagerspetz, K. (1979). Modification of aggressiveness in mice. In S. Feshbach & A. Fraczek (Eds.), *Aggression and behavior change.* New York: Praeger.

Lagerspetz, K. M. J., Bjorkqvist, K., Berts, M., & King, E. (1982). Group aggression among school children in three schools. *Scandinavian Journal of Psychology, 23,* 45–52.

Lai, C. K., & 23 others (2014). Reducing implicit racial preferences: I. A comparative investigation of 17 interventions. *Journal of Experimental Psychology: General, 143,* 1765–1785.

Laird, J. D. (1974). Self-attribution of emotion: The effects of expressive behavior on the quality of emotional experience. *Journal of Personality and Social Psychology, 29,* 475–486.

Laird, J. D. (1984). The real role of facial response in the experience of emotion: A reply to Tourangeau and Ellsworth, and others. *Journal of Personality and Social Psychology, 47,* 909–917.

Lakin, J. L., & Chartrand, T. L. (2003). Using nonconscious behavioral mimicry to create affiliation and rapport. *Psychological Science, 14,* 334–339.

Lakin, J. L., Chartrand, T. L., & Arkin, R. M. (2008). I am too just like you: Nonconscious mimicry as an automatic behavioral responses to social exclusion. *Psychological Science, 19,* 816–821.

Lalonde, R. N. (1992). The dynamics of group differentiation in the face of defeat. *Personality and Social Psychology Bulletin, 18,* 336–342.

Lalwani, A. K., Shavitt, S., & Johnson, T. (2006). What is the relation between cultural orientation and socially desirable responding? *Journal of Personality and Social Psychology, 90,* 165–178.

Lamal, P. A. (1979). College student common beliefs about psychology. *Teaching of Psychology, 6,* 155–158.

Lamb, C. S., & Crano, W. D. (2014). Parents' beliefs and children's marijuana use: Evidence for a self-fulfilling prophecy effect. *Addictive Behaviors, 39,* 127–132.

Lambert, A. J., Schott, J. P., & Scherer, L. (2011). Threat, politics, and attitudes: Toward a greater understanding of rally-'round-the-flag effects. *Current Directions in Psychological Science, 20,* 343–348.

Lambert, N. M., DeWall, C. N., Bushman, B. J., Stillman, T. F., Fincham, F. D., & Pond, R. S. (2011). Lashing out in lust: Effect of pornography on nonsexual, physical aggression against relationship partners. Unpublished manuscript, Florida State University.

Lambert, N. M., Fincham, F. D., LaVallee, D. C., & Brantley, C. W. (2012). Praying together and staying together: Couple prayer and trust. *Psychology of Religion and Spirituality, 4,* 1–9.

Landau, M. J., Solomon, S., Greenberg, J., Cohen, F., Pyszczynski, T., Arndt, J., Miller, C. H., Ogilvie, D. M., & Cook, A. (2004). Deliver us from evil: The effects of mortality salience and reminders of 9/11 on support for President George W. Bush. *Personality and Social Psychology Bulletin, 30,* 1136–1150.

Landberg, J., & Norstrom, T. (2011). Alcohol and homicide in Russia and the United States: A comparative analysis. *Journal of Studies on Alcohol and Drugs, 72,* 723–730.

Landers, A. (1969, April 8). Syndicated newspaper column. April 8, 1969. Cited by L. Berkowitz in The case for bottling up rage. *Psychology Today,* September, 1973, 24–31.

Landers, A. (1985, August). Is affection more important than sex? *Reader's Digest,* pp. 44–46.

Lane, D. J., Gibbons, F. X., O'Hara, R. E., & Gerrard, M. (2011). Standing out from the crowd: How comparison to prototypes can decrease health-risk behavior in young adults. *Basic and Applied Social Psychology, 33,* 228–238.

Langer, E. J. (1977). The psychology of chance. *Journal for the Theory of Social Behavior, 7,* 185–208.

Langer, E. J., & Imber, L. (1980). The role of mindlessness in the perception of deviance. *Journal of Personality and Social Psychology, 39,* 360–367.

Langford, D. J., Crager, S. E., Shehzad, Z., Smith, S. B., Sotocinal, S. G., Levenstadt, J. S., Chanda, M. L., Levitin, D. J., & Mogil, J. S. (2006). Social modulation of pain as evidence for empathy in mice. *Science, 312,* 1967–1970.

Langlois, J. H., Kalakanis, L., Rubenstein, A. J., Larson, A., Hallam, M., & Smoot, M. (2000). Maxims or myths of beauty? A meta-analytic and theoretical review. *Psychological Bulletin, 126,* 390–423.

Langlois, J. H., Kalakanis, L., Rubenstein, A., Larson, A., Hallam, M., & Smoot, M. (1996). *Maxims and myths of beauty: A meta-analytic and theoretical review.* Paper presented at the American Psychological Society convention, San Francisco, CA.

Langlois, J. H., & Roggman, L. A. (1990). Attractive faces are only average. *Psychological Science, 1,* 115–121.

Langlois, J. H., Roggman, L. A., Casey, R. J., Ritter, J. M., Rieser-Danner, L. A., & Jenkins, V. Y. (1987). Infant preferences for attractive faces: Rudiments of a stereotype? *Developmental Psychology, 23,* 363–369.

Langlois, J. H., Roggman, L. A., & Musselman, L. (1994). What is average and what is not average about attractive faces? *Psychological Science, 5,* 214–220.

Lankford, A. (2009). Promoting aggression and violence at Abu Ghraib: The U.S. military's transformation of ordinary people into torturers. *Aggression and Violent Behavior, 14,* 388–395.

Lanzetta, J. T. (1955). Group behavior under stress. *Human Relations, 8,* 29–53.

Larrick, R. P., Timmerman, T. A., Carton, A. M., & Abrevaya, J. (2011). Temper, temperature, and temptation: Heat-related retaliation in baseball. *Psychological Science, 22,* 423–428.

Larsen, R. (2009). The contributions of positive and negative affect to emotional well-being. *Psychological Topics, 18,* 247–266.

Larsen, R. J., & Diener, E. (1987). Affect intensity as an individual difference characteristic: A review. *Journal of Research in Personality, 21,* 1–39.

Larson, J. R., Jr., Foster-Fishman, P. G., & Keys, C. B. (1994). Discussion of shared and unshared information in decision-making groups. *Journal of Personality and Social Psychology, 67,* 446–461.

Larsson, K. (1956). *Conditioning and sexual behavior in the male albino rat.* Stockholm: Almqvist & Wiksell.

Larwood, L. (1978). Swine flu: A field study of self-serving biases. *Journal of Applied Social Psychology, 18,* 283–289.

Lassiter, G. D. (2010). Psychological science and sound public policy: Video recording of custodial interrogations. *American Psychologist, 65,* 768–779.

Lassiter, G. D., Diamond, S. S., Schmidt, H. C., & Elek, J. K. (2007). Evaluating videotaped confessions. *Psychological Science, 18,* 224–226.

Lassiter, G. D., & Dudley, K. A. (1991). The *a priori* value of basic research: The case of videotaped confessions. *Journal of Social Behavior and Personality, 6,* 7–16.

Lassiter, G. D., Geers, A. L., Handley, I. M., Weiland, P. E., & Munhall, P. J. (2002). Videotaped interrogations and confessions: A simple change in camera perspective alters verdicts in simulated trials. *Journal of Applied Psychology, 87,* 867–874.

Lassiter, G. D., & Irvine, A. A. (1986). Videotaped confessions: The impact of camera point of view on judgments of coercion. *Journal of Applied Social Psychology, 16,* 268–276.

Lassiter, G. D., & Munhall, P. J. (2001). The genius effect: Evidence for a nonmotivational interpretation. *Journal of Experimental Social Psychology, 37,* 349–355.

Lassiter, G. D., Munhall, P. J., Berger, I. P., Weiland, P. E., Handley, I. M., & Geers, A. L. (2005). Attributional complexity and the camera perspective bias in videotaped confessions. *Basic and Applied Social Psychology, 27,* 27–35.

Latané, B., & Dabbs, J. M., Jr. (1975). Sex, group size and helping in three cities. *Sociometry, 38,* 180–194.

Latané, B., & Darley, J. M. (1968). Group inhibition of bystander intervention in emergencies. *Journal of Personality and Social Psychology, 10,* 215–221.

Latané, B., & Darley, J. M. (1970). *The unresponsive bystander: Why doesn't he help?* New York: Appleton-Century-Crofts.

Latané, B., & Nida, S. (1981). Ten years of research on group size and helping. *Psychological Bulletin, 89,* 308–324.

Latané, B., & Rodin, J. (1969). A lady in distress: Inhibiting effects of friends and strangers on bystander intervention. *Journal of Experimental Social Psychology, 5,* 189–202.

Latané, B., Williams, K., & Harkins. S. (1979). Many hands make light the work: The causes and consequences of social loafing. *Journal of Personality and Social Psychology, 37,* 822–832.

Laughlin, P. R. (1996). Group decision making and collective induction. In E. H. Witte & J. H. Davis (Eds.), *Understanding group behavior: Consensual action by small groups.* Mahwah, NJ: Erlbaum.

Laughlin, P. R., & Adamopoulos, J. (1980). Social combination processes and individual learning for six-person cooperative groups on an intellective task. *Journal of Personality and Social Psychology, 38,* 941–947.

Laughlin, P. R., Hatch, E. C., Silver, J. S., & Boh, L. (2006). Groups perform better than the best individuals on letters-to-numbers problems: Effects of group size. *Journal of Personality and Social Psychology, 90,* 644–651.

Laughlin, P. R., Zander, M. L., Knievel, E. M., & Tan, T. K. (2003). Groups perform better than the best individuals on letters-to-numbers problems: Informative equations and effective strategies. *Journal of Personality and Social Psychology, 85,* 684–694.

Laumann, E. O., Gagnon, J. H., Michael, R. T., & Michaels, S. (1994). *The social organization of sexuality: Sexual practices in the United States.* Chicago: University of Chicago Press.

Lawler, A. (2003a). Iraq's shattered universities. *Science, 300,* 1490–1491.

Lawler, A. (2003b). Mayhem in Mesopotamia. *Science, 301,* 582–588.

Lawler, A. (2003c). Ten millennia of culture pilfered amid Baghdad chaos. *Science, 300,* 402–403.

Lawson, T. J. (2010). The social spotlight increases blindness to change blindness. *Basic and Applied Social Psychology, 32,* 360–368.

Layden, M. A. (1982). Attributional therapy. In C. Antaki & C. Brewin (Eds.), *Attributions and psychological change: Applications of attributional theories to clinical and educational practice.* London: Academic Press.

Layous, K., Nelson, S. K., Oberle, E., Schonert-Reichl, K. A., & Lyubomirsky, S. (2012). Kindness counts: Prompting prosocial behavior in preadolescents boosts peer acceptance and well-being. *Plos One, 7,* e51380.

Lazarsfeld, P. F. (1949). *The American soldier—an expository review. Public Opinion Quarterly, 13,* 377–404.

Lazer, D., & others. (2009). Computational social science. *Science, 323,* 721–723.

Leach, J. K., & Patall, E. A. (2013). Maximizing and counterfactual thinking in academic major decision making. *Journal of Career Assessment, 21,* 414–429.

Leaper, C., & Ayres, M. M. (2007). A meta-analytic review of gender variations in adults' language use: Talkativeness, affiliative speech, and assertive speech. *Personality and Social Psychology Review, 11,* 328–363.

Leaper, C., & Robnett, R. D. (2011). Women are more likely than men to use tentative language, aren't they? A meta-analysis testing for gender differences and moderators. *Psychology of Women Quarterly, 35,* 129–142.

Leary, M. (1994). *Self-presentation: Impression management and interpersonal behavior.* Pacific Grove, CA: Brooks/Cole.

Leary, M. R. (1998). The social and psychological importance of self-esteem. In R. M. Kowalski & M. R. Leary (Eds.), *The social psychology of emotional and behavioral problems.* Washington, DC: American Psychological Association.

Leary, M. R. (2004a). *The curse of the self: Self-awareness, egotism, and the quality of human life.* New York: Oxford University Press.

Leary, M. R. (2004b). The self we know and the self we show: Self-esteem, self-presentation, and the maintenance of interpersonal relationships. In M. Brewer & M. Hewstone (Eds.), *Emotion and motivation.* Malden, MA: Usishers.

Leary, M. R. (2007). Motivational and emotional aspects of the self. *Annual Review of Psychology, 58,* 317–344.

Leary, M. R. (2010). Affiliation, acceptance, and belonging: The pursuit of interpersonal connection. In S. T. Fiske, D. T. Gilbert, & G. Lindzey (Eds.), *Handbook of social psychology,* 5th edition. Hoboken, NJ: Wiley.

Leary, M. R. (2012). Sociometer theory. In P. A. M., Van Lange, A. W. Kruglanski, and E. T. Higgins (Eds.), *Handbook of theories of social psychology (Vol. 2),* pp. 151–159. Thousand Oaks, CA: Sage.

Leary, M. R. (2012). Sociometer theory. In P. A. M., Van Lange, A. W. Kruglanski, and E. T. Higgins (Eds.), *Handbook of theories of social psychology (Vol. 2),* pp. 151–159. Thousand Oaks, CA: Sage.

Leary, M. R., & Kowalski, R. M. (1995). *Social anxiety.* New York: Guilford.

Leary, M. R., Nezlek, J. B., Radford-Davenport, D., Martin, J., & McMullen, A. (1994). Self-presentation in everyday interactions: Effects of target familiarity and gender composition. *Journal of Personality and Social Psychology, 67,* 664–673.

LeDoux, J. (2002). *Synaptic self: How our brains become who we are.* New York: Viking.

LeDoux, J. (2014). Low roads and higher order thoughts in emotion. *Cortex: A Journal Devoted to the Study of the Nervous System and Behavior, 59,* 214–215.

Lee, F., Hallahan, M., & Herzog, T. (1996). Explaining real-life events: How culture and domain shape attributions. *Personality and Social Psychology Bulletin, 22,* 732–741.

Lee, I.-C., Pratto, F., & Johnson, B. T. (2011). Intergroup consensus/disagreement in support of group-based hierarchy: An examination of socio-structural and psycho-cultural factors. *Psychological Bulletin, 137,* 1029–1064.

Lee, R. Y.-P., & Bond, M. H. (1996). *How friendship develops out of personality and values: A study of interpersonal attraction in Chinese culture.* Unpublished manuscript, Chinese University of Hong Kong.

Lee, S. H., Rotman, J. D., & Perkins, A. W. (2014). Embodied cognition and social consumption: Self-regulating temperature through social products and behaviors. *Journal of Consumer Psychology, 24,* 234–240.

Lee, S. K., Benavides, P., Heo, Y. H., & Park, S. W. (2014). Narcissism increase among college students in Korea: A cross-temporal meta-analysis (1999–2014). *Korean Journal of Psychology: General, 33,* 609–625.

Lee, S., Rogge, R. D., & Reis, H. T. (2010). Assessing the seeds of relationship decay: Using implicit evaluations to detect the early stages of disillusionment. *Psychological Science, 21,* 857–864.

Lee, S. W. S., & Schwarz, N. (2012). Bidirectionality, mediation, and moderation of metaphorical effects: The embodiment of social suspicion and fishy smells. *Journal of Personality and Social Psychology, 103,* 737–749.

Légal, J., Chappé, J., Coiffard, V., & Villard-Forest, A. (2012). Don't you know that you want to trust me? Subliminal goal priming and persuasion. *Journal of Experimental Social Psychology, 48,* 358–360.

Legate, N., DeHaan, C. R., Weinstein, N., & Ryan, R. M. (2013). Hurting you hurts me too: The psychological costs of complying with ostracism. *Psychological Science, 24,* 583–588.

Legrain, P. (2003, May 9). Cultural globalization is not Americanization. *Chronicle of Higher Education* (www .chronicle.com/free).

Lehman, D. R., Lempert, R. O., & Nisbett, R. E. (1988). The effects of graduate training on reasoning: Formal discipline and thinking about everyday-life events. *American Psychologist, 43,* 431–442.

Leippe, M. R. (1985). The influence of eyewitness nonidentification on mock-jurors. *Journal of Applied Social Psychology, 15,* 656–672.

Leippe, M. R. (1994). The appraisal of eyewitness testimony. In D. F. Ross, J. D. Read, & M. P. Toglia (Eds.), *Adult eyewitness testimony: Current trends and developments.* New York: Cambridge University Press.

Leiserowitz, A. (2011, November 17). Do Americans connect climate change and extreme weather events? E-mail of Yale/ GMU survey, from Yale Project on Climate Change Communication.

Leiserowitz, A., Maibach, E., Roser-Renouf, C., & Smith, N. (2011b). *Climate change in the American mind: Americans' global warming beliefs and attitudes in May 2011.* Yale University and George Mason University. New Haven, CT: Yale Project on Climate Change Communication.

Lemay, E. P., Jr., Clark, M. S., & Greenberg, A. (2010). What is beautiful is good because what is beautiful is desired: Physical attractiveness stereotyping as projection of interpersonal goals. *Personality and Social Psychology Bulletin, 36,* 339–353.

Lemyre, L., & Smith, P. M. (1985). Intergroup discrimination and self-esteem in the minimal group paradigm. *Journal of Personality and Social Psychology, 49,* 660–670.

Lenhart, A. (2010, April 20). *Teens, cell phones and texting.* Pew Internet and American Life Project. Pew Research Center (www.pewresearch.org).

Lenhart, A. (2012). Teens, smartphones & texting. Pew Research Internet Project, http://www.pewinternet.org/2012/03/19/teens-smartphones-texting/

Lenton, A. P., & Francesconi, M. (2010). How humans cognitively manage an abundance of mate options. *Psychological Science, 21,* 528–533.

Leodoro, G., & Lynn, M. (2007). The effect of server posture on the tips of Whites and Blacks. *Journal of Applied Social Psychology, 37,* 201–209.

Leone, C., & Hawkins, L. B. (2006). Self-monitoring and close relationships. *Journal of Personality, 74,* 739–778.

Lepper, M. R., & Greene, D. (Eds.) (1979). *The hidden costs of reward.* Hillsdale, NJ: Erlbaum.

Lerner, M. J. (1980). *The belief in a just world: A fundamental delusion.* New York: Plenum.

Lerner, M. J., & Miller, D. T. (1978). Just world research and the attribution process: Looking back and ahead. *Psychological Bulletin, 85,* 1030–1051.

Lerner, M. J., & Simmons, C. H. (1966). Observer's reaction to the "innocent victim": Compassion or rejection? *Journal of Personality and Social Psychology, 4,* 203–210.

Lerner, M. J., Somers, D. G., Reid, D., Chiriboga, D., & Tierney, M. (1991). Adult children as caregivers: Egocentric biases in judgments of sibling contributions. *The Gerontologist, 31,* 746–755.

Lerner, R. M., & Frank, P. (1974). Relation of race and sex to supermarket helping behavior. *Journal of Social Psychology, 94,* 201–203.

Leshner, A. I. (2005, October). Science and religion should not be adversaries. *APS Observer* (www.psychologicalscience .org).

Leung, K., & Bond, M. H. (1984). The impact of cultural collectivism on reward allocation. *Journal of Personality and Social Psychology, 47,* 793–804.

Leung, K., & Bond, M. H. (2004). Social axioms: A model of social beliefs in multi-cultural perspective. In M. P. Zanna (Ed.), *Advances in Experimental Social Psychology.* San Diego, CA: Academic Press.

Levav, J., & Fitzsimons, G. J. (2006). When questions change behavior: The role of ease of representation. *Psychological Science, 17,* 207–213.

Levesque, M. J., Nave, C. S., & Lowe, C. A. (2006). Toward an understanding of gender differences in inferring sexual interest. *Psychology of Women Quarterly, 30,* 150–158.

Levin, S., Matthews, M., Guimond, S., Sidanius, J., Pratto, F., Kteily, N., Pitpitan, E. V., & Dover, T. (2011). Assimilation, multiculturalism, and colorblindness: Mediated and moderated relationships between social dominance orientation and prejudice. *Journal of Experimental Social Psychology, 47,* 208–214.

Levine, J. M. (1989). Reaction to opinion deviance in small groups. In P. Paulus (Ed.), *Psychology of group influence: New perspectives.* Hillsdale, NJ: Erlbaum.

Levine, M., & Crowther, S. (2008). The responsive bystander: How social group membership and group size can encourage as well as inhibit bystander intervention. *Journal of Personality and Social Psychology, 95,* 1429–1439.

Levine, R. (2003). *The power of persuasion: How we're bought and sold.* New York: Wiley.

Levine, R. V., Martinez, T. S., Brase, G., & Sorenson, K. (1994). Helping in 36 U.S. cities. *Journal of Personality and Social Psychology, 67,* 69–82.

Levine, R. V., & Norenzayan, A. (1999). The pace of life in 31 countries. *Journal of Cross-Cultural Psychology, 30,* 178–205.

Levinson, H. (1950). *The science of chance: From probability to statistics.* New York: Rinehart.

Leviston, Z., Walker, I., & Morwinski, S. (2013). Your opinion on climate change might not be as common as you think. *Nature Climate Change, 3,* 334–337.

Levitan, L. C., & Visser, P. S. (2008). The impact of the social context on resistance to persuasion: Effortful versus effortless responses to counter-attitudinal information. *Journal of Experimental Social Psychology, 44,* 640–649.

Levy-Leboyer, C. (1988). Success and failure in applying psychology. *American Psychologist, 43,* 779–785.

Levy, S. R., Stroessner, S. J., & Dweck, C. S. (1998). Stereotype formation and endorsement: The role of implicit theories. *Journal of Personality and Social Psychology, 74,* 1421–1436.

Lewandowski, G. W., & Bizzoco, N. M. (2007). Addition through subtraction: Growth following the dissolution of a low-quality relationship. *Journal of Positive Psychology, 2,* 40–54.

Lewandowski, G. W., Jr., Aron, A., & Gee, J. (2007). Personality goes a long way: The malleability of opposite-sex physical attractiveness. *Personal Relationships, 14,* 571–585

Lewandowsky, S., Ecker, U. K. H., Seifert, C. M., Schwarz, N., & Cooke, J. (2012).

Misinformation and its correction: Continued influence and successful debasing. *Psychological Science in the Public Interest, 13,* 106–131.

Lewandowsky, S., Oberauer, K., & Gignac, G. E. (2013). NASA faked the moon landing—therefore, (climate) science is a hoax: An anatomy of the motivated rejection of science. *Psychological Science, 24,* 622–633.

Lewicki, P. (1985). Nonconscious biasing effects of single instances on subsequent judgments. *Journal of Personality and Social Psychology, 48,* 563–574.

Lewis, C. S. (1952). *Mere Christianity.* New York: Macmillan.

Lewis, C. S. (1974). *The horse and his boy.* New York: Collier Books.

Lewis, D. O. (1998). *Guilty by reason of insanity.* London: Arrow.

Lewis, M. B., & Bowler, P. J. (2009). Botulinum toxin cosmetic therapy correlates with a more positive mood. *Journal of Cosmetic Dermatology, 8,* 24–26.

Lewis, R. J., Derlega, V. J., Clarke, E., & Kuang, J. C. (2006). Stigma consciousness, social constraints, and lesbian well-being. *Journal of Counseling Psychology, 53,* 48–56.

Lewis, R. S., Goto, S. G., & Kong, L. L. (2008). Culture and context: East Asian American and European American differences in P3 event-related potentials and self-construal. *Personality and Social Psychology Bulletin, 34,* 623–634.

Lewinsohn, P. M., Hoberman, H., Teri, L., & Hautziner, M. (1985). An integrative theory of depression. In S. Reiss & R. Bootzin (Eds.), *Theoretical issues in behavior therapy.* New York: Academic Press.

Lewinsohn, P. M., & Rosenbaum, M. (1987). Recall of parental behavior by acute depressives, remitted depressives, and nondepressives. *Journal of Personality and Social Psychology, 52,* 611–619.

Leyens, J.-P., Cortes, B., Demoulin, S., Dovidio, J. F., Fiske, S. T., Gaunt, R., Paladino, M-P., Rodriquez-Perez, A., Rodriquez-Torrez, R., & Vaes, J. (2003). Emotional prejudice, essentialism, and nationalism. *European Journal of Social Psychology, 33,* 703–717.

Leyens, J.-P., Demoulin, S., Vaes, J., Gaunt, R., & Paladino, M. P. (2007). Infra-humanization: The wall of group differences. *Social Issues and Policy Review, 1,* 139–172.

Li, C. (2010). Primacy effect or recency effect? A long-term memory test of Super Bowl commercials. *Journal of Consumer Behaviour, 9,* 32–44.

Li, N. P., Bailey, J. M., Kenrick, D. T., & Linsenmeier, J. A. W. (2002). The necessities and luxuries of mate preferences: Testing the tradeoffs. *Journal of Personality and Social Psychology, 82,* 947–955.

Li, T., & Chan, D. K-S. (2012). How anxious and avoidant attachment affect romantic relationship quality differently: A meta-analytic review. *European Journal of Social Psychology, 42,* 406–419.

Li, Y., Johnson, E. J., & Zaval, L. (2011). Local warming: Daily temperature change influences belief in global warming. *Psychological Science, 22,* 454–459.

Li, Y., Li, H., Decety, J., & Lee, K. (2013). Experiencing a natural disaster alters children's altruistic giving. *Psychological Science, 24,* 1686–1695.

Liberman, V., Samuels, S. M., & Ross, L. (2004). The name of the game: Predictive power of reputations vs. situational labels in determining Prisoner's Dilemma game moves. *Personality and Social Psychology Bulletin, 30,* 1175–1185.

Lichtblau, E. (2005, August 24). Profiling report leads to a demotion. *New York Times* (www.nytimes.com).

Lichtenstein, S., & Fischhoff, B. (1980). Training for calibration. *Organizational Behavior and Human Performance, 26,* 149–171.

Lieberman, J. D. (2011). The utility of scientific jury selection: Still murky after 30 years. *Current Directions in Psychological Science, 20,* 48–52.

Liehr, P., Mehl, M. R., Summers, L. C., & Pennebaker, J. W. (2004). Connecting with others in the midst of stressful upheaval on September 11, 2001. *Applied Nursing Research, 17,* 2–9.

Likowski, K. U., Muhlberger, A., Gerdes, A. B. M., Wieser, M. J., Pauli, P., & Weyers, P. (2012). Facial mimicry and the mirror neuron system: Simultaneous acquisition of facial electromyography and functional magnetic resonance imaging. *Frontiers in Human Neuroscience, 6,* Article 214, 1–10.

Lilienfeld, S. O., Fowler, K. A., Lohr, J. M., & Lynn, S. J. (2005). Pseudoscience, nonscience, and nonsense in clinical psychology: Dangers and remedies. In R. H. Wright & N. A. Cummings (Eds.), *Destructive trends in mental health: The well-intentioned path to harm.* New York: Routledge.

Lilienfeld, S. O., Wood, J. M., & Garb, H. N. (2000). The scientific status of projective techniques. *Psychological Science in the Public Interest, 1,* 27–66.

Lin, J-H. (2013). Do video games exert stronger effects on aggression than film? The role of media interactivity and identification on the association of violent content and aggressive outcomes. *Computers in Human Behavior, 29,* 535–543.

Lind, A., Hall, L., Breidegard, B., Balkenius, C., & Johansson, P. (2014). Speakers' acceptance of real-time speech exchange indicates that we use auditory feedback to specify the meaning of what we say. *Psychological Science, 25,* 1198–1205.

Lindsay, R. C. L., & Wells, G. L. (1985). Improving eyewitness identifications from lineups: Simultaneous versus sequential lineup presentation. *Journal of Applied Psychology, 70,* 556–564.

Lindsay, R. C. L., Wells, G. L., & Rumpel, C. H. (1981). Can people detect eyewitness-identification accuracy within and across situations? *Journal of Applied Psychology, 66,* 79–89.

Lindskold, S. (1981). The laboratory evaluation of GRIT: Trust, cooperation, aversion to using conciliation. Paper presented at the American Association for the Advancement of Science convention.

Lindskold, S., & Aronoff, J. R. (1980). Conciliatory strategies and relative power. *Journal of Experimental Social Psychology, 16,* 187–198.

Lindskold, S., Bennett, R., & Wayner, M. (1976). Retaliation level as a foundation for subsequent conciliation. *Behavioral Science, 21,* 13–18.

Lindskold, S., Betz, B., & Walters, P. S. (1986). Transforming competitive or cooperative climate. *Journal of Conflict Resolution, 30,* 99–114.

Lindskold, S., & Collins, M. G. (1978). Inducing cooperation by groups and individuals. *Journal of Conflict Resolution, 22,* 679–690.

Lindskold, S., & Finch, M. L. (1981). Styles of announcing conciliation. *Journal of Conflict Resolution, 25,* 145–155.

Lindskold, S., & Han, G. (1988). GRIT as a foundation for integrative bargaining. *Personality and Social Psychology Bulletin, 14,* 335–345.

Lindskold, S., Han, G., & Betz, B. (1986a). Repeated persuasion in interpersonal conflict. *Journal of Personality and Social Psychology, 51,* 1183–1188.

Lindskold, S., Han, G., & Betz, B. (1986b). The essential elements of communication in the GRIT strategy. *Personality and Social Psychology Bulletin, 12,* 179–186.

Lindskold, S., Walters, P. S., Koutsourais, H., & Shayo, R. (1981). Cooperators, competitors, and response to GRIT. Unpublished manuscript, Ohio University.

Linville, P. W., Fischer, G. W., & Fischhoff, B. (1992). AIDS risk perceptions and decision biases. In J. B. Pryor & G. D. Reeder (Eds.), *The social psychology of HIV infection.* Hillsdale, NJ: Erlbaum.

Linville, P. W., Fischer, G. W., & Salovey, P. (1989). Perceived distributions of the characteristics of in-group and out-group members: Empirical evidence and a computer simulation. *Journal of Personality and Social Psychology, 57,* 165–188.

Lippa, R. A. (2007). The preferred traits of mates in a cross-national study of heterosexual and homosexual men and women: An examination of biological and cultural influences. *Archives of Sexual Behavior, 36,* 193–208.

Lippa, R. A. (2008b). Sex differences in sex drive, sociosexuality, and height across 53 nations: Testing evolutionary and social structural theories. *Archives of Sexual Behavior* (www.springerlink.com/content/x754q0433g18hg81/).

Lippa, R. A. (2010). Sex differences in personality traits and gender-related occupational preferences across 53 nations: Testing evolutionary and social-environmental theories. *Archives of Sexual Behavior, 39,* 619–636.

Lit, L., Schweitzer, J. B., & Oberbauer, A. M. (2011). Handler beliefs affect scent detection dog outcomes. *Animal Cognition, 14,* 387–394.

Livingstone, S., & Haddon, L. (2009). *EU Kids Online; Final report.* LSE, London: EU Kids Online.

Livingston, R. W. (2001). What you see is what you get: Systematic variability in perceptual-based social judgment. *Personality and Social Psychology Bulletin, 27,* 1086–1096.

Livingston, R. W., & Drwecki, B. B. (2007). Why are some individuals not racially biased? Susceptibility to affective conditioning predicts nonprejudice toward Blacks. *Psychological Science, 18,* 816–823.

Locke, E. A., & Latham, G. P. (1990). Work motivation and satisfaction: Light at the end of the tunnel. *Psychological Science, 1,* 240–246.

Locke, E. A., & Latham, G. P. (2002). Building a practically useful theory of goal setting and task performance. *American Psychologist, 57,* 705–717.

Locke, E. A., & Latham, G. P. (2009). Has goal setting gone wild, or have its attackers abandoned good scholarship? *Academy of Management Perspectives, 23,* 17–23.

Locke, K. D., & Horowitz, L. M. (1990). Satisfaction in interpersonal interactions as a function of similarity in level of dysphoria. *Journal of Personality and Social Psychology, 58,* 823–831.

Locksley, A., Borgida, E., Brekke, N., & Hepburn, C. (1980). Sex stereotypes and social judgment. *Journal of Personality and Social Psychology, 39,* 821–831.

Locksley, A., Hepburn, C., & Ortiz, V. (1982). Social stereotypes and judgments of individuals: An instance of the base-rate fallacy. *Journal of Experimental Social Psychology, 18,* 23–42.

Lockwood, P. (2002). Could it happen to you? Predicting the impact of downward comparisons on the self. *Journal of Personality and Social Psychology, 87,* 343–358.

Loewenstein, G., & Schkade, D. (1999). Wouldn't it be nice? Predicting future feelings. In D. Kahneman, E. Diener, & N. Schwarz (Eds.), *Understanding well-being: Scientific perspectives on enjoyment and suffering* (pp. 85–105). New York: Russell Sage Foundation.

Lofland, J., & Stark, R. (1965). Becoming a worldsaver: A theory of conversion to a deviant perspective. *American Sociological Review, 30,* 862–864.

Loftin, C., McDowall, D., Wiersema, B., & Cottey, T. J. (1991). Effects of restrictive licensing of handguns on homicide and suicide in the District of Columbia. *New England Journal of Medicine, 325,* 1615–1620.

Loftus, E. F. (1974, December). Reconstructing memory: The incredible eyewitness. *Psychology Today,* 117–119.

Loftus, E. F. (1979a). *Eyewitness testimony.* Cambridge, MA: Harvard University Press.

Loftus, E. F. (1979b). The malleability of human memory. *American Scientist, 67,* 312–320.

Loftus, E. F. (2001, November). Imagining the past. *The Psychologist, 14,* 584–587.

Loftus, E. F. (2003). Make-believe memories. *American Psychologist, 58,* 867–873.

Loftus, E. F. (2007). Memory distortions: Problems solved and unresolved. In M. Garry & H. Hayne (Eds.), *Do justice and let the sky fall: Elizabeth Loftus and her contributions to science, law, and academic freedom.* Mahway, NJ: Erlbaum.

Loftus, E. F. (2011a, August 31). The risk of ill-informed juries. *New York Times* (www.nytimes.com).

Loftus, E. F. (2011b). How I got started: From semantic memory to expert testimony. *Applied Cognitive Psychology, 25,* 347–348.

Loftus, E. F., & Bernstein, D. M. (2005). Rich false memories: The royal road to success. In A. F. Healy (Ed.), *Experimental cognitive psychology and its applications.* Washington, DC: American Psychological Association.

Loftus, E. F., & Klinger, M. R. (1992). Is the unconscious smart or dumb? *American Psychologist, 47,* 761–765.

Loftus, E. F., Miller, D. G., & Burns, H. J. (1978). Semantic integration of verbal information into a visual memory. *Journal of Experimental Social Psychology: Human Learning and Memory, 4,* 19–31.

Logel, C., Walton, G. M., Spencer, S. J., Iserman, E. C., von Hippel, W., & Bell, A. E. (2009). Interacting with sexist men triggers social identity threat among female engineers. *Journal of Personality and Social Psychology, 96,* 1089–1103.

Lombardo, J. P., Weiss, R. F., & Buchanan, W. (1972). Reinforcing and attracting functions of yielding. *Journal of Personality and Social Psychology, 21,* 359–368.

London, K., & Nunez, N. (2000). The effect of jury deliberations on jurors' propensity to disregard inadmissible evidence. *Journal of Applied Psychology, 85,* 932–939.

London, P. (1970). The rescuers: Motivational hypotheses about Christians who saved Jews from the Nazis. In J. Macaulay & L. Berkowitz (Eds.), *Altruism and helping behavior.* New York: Academic Press.

Lonner, W. J. (1980). The search for psychological universals. In H. C. Triandis & W. W. Lambert (Eds.), *Handbook of cross-cultural psychology* (Vol. 1). Boston: Allyn & Bacon.

Lonner, W. J. (1989). The introductory psychology text and cross-cultural psychology: Beyond Ekman, Whorf, and biased I.Q. tests. In D. Keats, D. R. Munro, & L. Mann (Eds.), *Heterogeneity in cross-cultural psychology.*

Lonsdale, A. J., & North, A. C. (2011). Musical taste and the representativeness heuristic. *Psychology of Music, 40,* 131–142.

Lord, C. G., Desforges, D. M., Ramsey, S. L., Trezza, G. R., & Lepper, M. R. (1991). Typicality effects in attitude-behavior consistency: Effects of category discrimination and category knowledge. *Journal of Experimental Social Psychology, 27,* 550–575.

Losch, M. E., & Cacioppo, J. T. (1990). Cognitive dissonance may enhance sympathetic tonus, but attitudes are changed to reduce negative affect rather than arousal. *Journal of Experimental Social Psychology, 26,* 289–304.

Lott, A. J., & Lott, B. E. (1961). Group cohesiveness, communication level, and conformity. *Journal of Abnormal and Social Psychology, 62,* 408–412.

Lott, A. J., & Lott, B. E. (1974). The role of reward in the formation of positive interpersonal attitudes. In T. Huston (Ed.), *Foundations of interpersonal attraction.* New York: Academic Press.

Loughman, S., & Haslam, N. (2007). Animals and androids: Implicit associations between social categories and nonhumans. *Psychological Science, 18,* 116–121.

Lovett, F. (1997). Thinking about values (report of December 13, 1996 *Wall Street Journal* national survey). *The Responsive Community, 7*(2), 87.

Lowenstein, D. (2000, May 20). Interview. *The World* (www.cnn.com/TRANSCRIPTS/0005/20/stc.00.html).

Lowery, W. (2014, April 4). 91% of the time the better-financed candidate wins. *Washington Post* (http://www.washingtonpost.com/blogs/the-fix/wp/2014/04/04/think-money-doesnt-matter-in-elections-this-chart-says-youre-wrong/).

Loy, J. W., & Andrews, D. S. (1981). They also saw a game: A replication of a case study. *Replications in Social Psychology, 1*(2), 45–59.

Lubinski, D., & Benbow, C. P. (2006). Study of mathematically precocious youth after 35 years: Uncovering antecedents for math science expertise. *Perspectives on Psychological Science, 1,* 316–345.

Lücken, M., & Simon, B. (2005). Cognitive and affective experiences of minority and majority members: The role of group size, status, and power. *Journal of Experimental Social Psychology, 41,* 396–413.

Lueptow, L. B., Garovich, L., & Lueptow, M. B. (1995). The persistence of gender stereotypes in the face of changing sex roles: Evidence contrary to the sociocultural model. *Ethology and Sociobiology, 16,* 509–530.

Luginbuhl, J., & Middendorf, K. (1988). Death penalty beliefs and jurors' responses to aggravating and mitigating circumstances in capital trials. *Law and Human Behavior, 12,* 263–281.

Lumsden, A., Zanna, M. P., & Darley, J. M. (1980). *When a newscaster presents counter-additional information: Education or propaganda?* Paper presented at the Canadian Psychological Association annual convention.

Lun, J., Mesquita, B., & Smith, B. (2011). Self- and other-presentation styles in the Southern and Northern United States: An analysis of personal ads. *European Journal of Social Psychology, 41,* 435–445.

Luntz, F. (2003, June 10). Quoted by T. Raum, "Bush insists banned weapons will be found." Associated Press (story.news.yahoo.com).

Lutsky, L. A., Risucci, D. A., & Tortolani, A. J. (1993). Reliability and accuracy of surgical resident peer ratings. *Evaluation Review, 17,* 444–456.

Lüüs, C. A. E., & Wells, G. L. (1994). Determinants of eyewitness confidence. In D. F. Ross, J. D. Read, & M. P. Toglia (Eds.), *Adult eyewitness testimony: Current trends and developments* (pp. 348–362). New York: Cambridge University Press.

Lydon, J., & Dunkel-Schetter, C. (1994). Seeing is committing: A longitudinal study of bolstering commitment in amniocentesis patients. *Personality and Social Psychology Bulletin, 20,* 218–227.

Lykken, D. T. (1997). The American crime factory. *Psychological Inquiry, 8,* 261–270.

Lykken, D. T., & Tellegen, A. (1993). Is human mating adventitious or the result of lawful choice? A twin study of mate selection. *Journal of Personality and Social Psychology, 65,* 56–68.

Lynch, J. W., Kaplan, G. A., Pamuk, E. R., Cohen, R. D., Heck, K. E., Balfour, J. L., & Yen, I. H. (1998). Income inequality and mortality in metropolitan areas of the United States. *American Journal of Public Health, 88,* 1074–1080.

Lynch, J. W., Smith, G. D., Kaplan, G. A., & House, J. S. (2000). Income inequality and health: A neo-material interpretation. *British Medical Journal, 320,* 1200–1204.

Lyons, P. A., Kenworthy, J. B., & Popan, J. R. (2010). Ingroup identification and group-level narcissism as predictors of U.S. citizens' attitudes and behavior toward Arab immigrants. *Personality and Social Psychology Bulletin, 36,* 1267–1280.

Lyubomirsky, S. (2001). Why are some people happier than others? The role of cognitive and motivational processes in well-being. *American Psychologist, 56,* 239–249.

Lyubomirsky, S., Sousa, L., & Dickerhoof, R. (2006). The costs and benefits of writing, talking, and thinking about life's triumphs and defeats. *Journal of Personality and Social Psychology, 90,* 692–708.

Ma, D. S., Correll, J., Wittenbrink, B., Bar-Anan, Y., Sriram, N., & Nosek, B. A. (2013). When fatigue turns deadly: The association between fatigue and racial bias in the decision to shoot. *Basic and Applied Social Psychology, 35,* 515–524.

Ma, V., & Schoeneman, T. J. (1997). Individualism versus collectivism: A comparison of Kenyan and American self-concepts. *Basic and Applied Social Psychology, 19,* 261–273.

Maass, A. (1998). Personal communication from Universita degli Studi di Padova.

Maass, A. (1999). Linguistic intergroup bias: Stereotype perpetuation through language. In M. P. Zanna (Ed.), *Advances in Experimental Social Psychology, 31,* 79–121.

Maass, A., Milesi, A., Zabbini, S., & Stahlberg, D. (1995). Linguistic intergroup bias: Differential expectancies or in-group protection? *Journal of Personality and Social Psychology, 68,* 116–126.

Maass, A., Volparo, C., & Mucchi-Faina, A. (1996). Social influence and the verifiability of the issue under discussion: Attitudinal versus objective items. *British Journal of Social Psychology, 35,* 15–26.

Maccoby, E. E. (2002). Gender and group process: A developmental perspective. *Current Directions in Psychological Science, 11,* 54–58.

Maccoby, N. (1980). Promoting positive health behaviors in adults. In L. A. Bond & J. C. Rosen (Eds.), *Competence and coping during adulthood.* Hanover, NH: University Press of New England.

Maccoby, N., & Alexander, J. (1980). Use of media in lifestyle programs. In P. O. Davidson & S. M. Davidson (Eds.), *Behavioral medicine: Changing health lifestyles.* New York: Brunner/Mazel.

MacCoun, R. J., & Kerr, N. L. (1988). Asymmetric influence in mock jury deliberation: Jurors' bias for leniency. *Journal of Personality and Social Psychology, 54,* 21–33.

MacDonald, G., Zanna, M. P., & Holmes, J. G. (2000). An experimental test of the role of alcohol in relationship conflict. *Journal of Experimental Social Psychology, 36,* 182–193.

MacDonald, T. K., & Ross, M. (1997). Assessing the accuracy of predictions about dating relationships: How and why do lovers' predictions differ from those made by observers? Unpublished manuscript, University of Lethbridge.

Mack, D., & Rainey, D. (1990). Female applicants' grooming and personnel selection. *Journal of Social Behavior and Personality, 5,* 399–407.

Mackinnon, S. P., Jordan, C. H., & Wilson, A. E. (2011). Birds of a feather sit together: Physical similarity predicts seating choice. *Personality and Social Psychology Bulletin, 37,* 879–892.

MacLeod, C., & Campbell, L. (1992). Memory accessibility and probability judgments: An experimental evaluation of the availability heuristic. *Journal of Personality and Social Psychology, 63,* 890–902.

MacLin, O. H., Zimmerman, L. A., & Malpass, R. S. (2005). PC_Eyewitness and the sequential superiority effect: Computer based lineup administration. *Law and Human Behavior, 29,* 303–321.

Macrae, C. N., Alnwick, M. A., Milne, A. B., & Schloerscheidt, A. M. (2002). Person perception across the menstrual cycle: Hormonal influences on social-cognitive functioning. *Psychological Science, 13,* 532–536.

Macrae, C. N., & Bodenhausen, G. V. (2000). Social cognition: Thinking categorically about others. *Annual Review of Psychology, 51,* 93–120.

Macrae, C. N., & Bodenhausen, G. V. (2001). Social cognition: Categorical person perception. *British Journal of Psychology, 92,* 239–255.

Macrae, C. N., Bodenhausen, G. V., Milne, A. B., & Jetten, J. (1994). Out of mind but back in sight: Stereotypes on the rebound. *Journal of Personality and Social Psychology, 67,* 808–817.

Macrae, C. N., & Johnston, L. (1998). Help, I need somebody: Automatic action and inaction. *Social Cognition, 16,* 400–417.

Maddux, J. E. (1993). The mythology of psychopathology: A social cognitive view of deviance, difference, and disorder. *The General Psychologist, 29(2),* 34–45.

Maddux, J. E. (2008). Positive psychology and the illness ideology: Toward a positive clinical psychology. *Applied Psychology: An International Review, 57,* 54–70.

Maddux, J. E., & Gosselin, J. T. (2003). Self-efficacy. In M. R. Leary, & J. P. Tangney (Eds.), *Handbook of self and identity.* New York: Guilford.

Maddux, J. E., & Rogers, R. W. (1983). Protection motivation and self-efficacy: A revised theory of fear appeals and attitude change. *Journal of Experimental Social Psychology, 19,* 469–479.

Maddux, W. W., Galinsky, A. D., Cuddy, A. J. C., & Polifroni, M. (2008). When being a model minority is good . . . and bad: Realistic threat explains negativity towards Asian Americans. *Personality and Social Psychology Bulletin, 34,* 74–89.

Maddux, W. W., Galinsky, A. D., Cuddy, A. J. C., & Polifroni, M. (2008). When being a model minority is good . . . and bad: Realistic threat explains negativity towards Asian Americans. *Personality and Social Psychology Bulletin, 34,* 74–89.

Madera, J. M., Hebl, M. R., & Martin, R. C. (2009). Gender and letters of recommendation for academia: Agentic and communal differences. *Journal of Applied Psychology, 94,* 1591–1599.

Madon, S., Jussim, L., & Eccles, J. (1997). In search of the powerful self-fulfilling prophecy. *Journal of Personality and Social Psychology, 72,* 791–809.

Maeder, E. M., Yamamoto, S., & Saliba, P. (2015). The influence of defendant race and victim physical attractiveness on juror decision-making in a sexual assault trial. *Psychology, Crime & Law, 21,* 62–79.

Magnussen, S., Melinder, A., Stridbeck, U., & Raja, A. (2010). Beliefs about factors affecting the reliability of eyewitness testimony: A comparison of judges, jurors and the general public. *Applied Cognitive Psychology, 24,* 122–133.

Mahajan, N., & Wynn, K. (2012). Origins of "us" versus "Them": Prelinguistic infants prefer similar others. *Cognition, 124,* 227–233.

Maimaran, M., & Fishbach, A. (2014). If it's useful and you know it, do you eat? Preschoolers refrain from instrumental food. *Journal of Consumer Research, 41,* 642–655.

Major, B., Hunger, J. M., Bunyan, D. P., & Miller, C. T. (2014). The ironic effects of weight stigma. *Journal of Experimental Social Psychology, 51,* 74–80.

Major, B., Kaiser, C. R., & McCoy, S. K. (2003). It's not my fault: When and why attributions to prejudice protect self-esteem. *Personality and Social Psychology Bulletin, 29,* 772–781.

Major, B., Mendes, W. B., & Dovidio, J. F. (2013). Intergroup relations and health disparities: A social psychological perspective. *Health Psychology, 32,* 514–524.

Malahy, L. W., Rubinlicht, M. A., & Kaiser, C. R. (2009). Justifying inequality: A cross-temporal investigation of U.S. income disparities and just-world beliefs from 1973 to 2006. *Social Justice Research, 22,* 369–383.

Malamuth, N. M., & Check, J. V. P. (1981). The effects of media exposure on acceptance of violence against women: A field experiment. *Journal of Research in Personality, 15,* 436–446.

Malamuth, N. M., Haber, S., Feshbach, S., & others. (1980, March). *Journal of Research in Personality, 14,* 121–137.

Malka, A., Soto, C. J., Cohen, A. B., & Miller, D. T. (2011). Religiosity and social welfare: Competing influences of cultural conservatism and prosocial value orientation. *Journal of Personality, 79,* 763–792.

Malkiel, B. G. (2012). A random walk down Wall Street: The time-test strategy for successful investing. New York: W. W. Norton and Company.

Malle, B. F. (2006). The actor–observer asymmetry in attribution: A (surprising) meta-analysis. *Psychological Bulletin, 132,* 895–919.

Mallinckrodt, V., & Mizerski, D. (2007). The effects of playing an advergame on young children's perceptions, preferences, and requests. *Journal of Advertising, 36,* 87–100.

Maner, J. K., Gailliot, M. T., & Miller, S. L. (2009). The implicit cognition of relationship maintenance: Inattention to attractive alternatives. *Journal of Experimental Social Psychology, 45,* 174–179.

Maner, J. K., Miller, S. L., Schmidt, N. B., & Eckel, L. A. (2008). Submitting to defeat: Social anxiety, dominance threat, and decrements in testosterone. *Psychological Science, 19,* 764–768.

Manis, M., Cornell, S. D., & Moore, J. C. (1974). Transmission of attitude-relevant information through a communication chain. *Journal of Personality and Social Psychology, 30,* 81–94.

Manis, M., Nelson, T. E., & Shedler, J. (1988). Stereotypes and social judgment: Extremity, assimilation, and contrast. *Journal of Personality and Social Psychology, 55,* 28–36.

Manjoo, F. (2014, September 24). Exposing hidden bias at Google. *New York Times* (www.nytimes.com).

Mann, L. (1981). The baiting crowd in episodes of threatened suicide. *Journal of Personality and Social Psychology, 41,* 703–709.

Mannes, A. E., & Moore, D. A. (2013). A behavioral demonstration of overconfidence in judgment. *Psychological Science, 24,* 1190–1197.

Mannes, A. E., Soll, J. B., & Larrick, R. P. (2014). The wisdom of select crowds. *Journal of Personality and Social Psychology, 107,* 276–299.

Mar, R. A., & Oatley, K. (2008). The function of fiction is the abstraction and simulation of social experience. *Perspectives on Psychological Science, 3,* 173–192.

Marcus-Newhall, A., Pedersen, W. C., Carlson, M., & Miller, N. (2000). Displaced aggression is alive and well: A meta-analytic review. *Journal of Personality and Social Psychology, 78,* 670–689.

Marcus, S. (1974). Review of *Obedience to authority.* New York Times Book Review, January 13, 1–2.

Mares, M-L., & Braun, M. T. (2013). Effects of conflict in tween sitcoms on U.S. students' moral reasoning about social exclusion. *Journal of Children and Media, 7,* 428–445.

Marigold, D. C., Holmes, J. G., Wood, J. V., & Cavallo, J. V. (2014). You can't always give what you want: The challenge of providing social support to low self-esteem individuals. *Journal of Personality and Social Psychology, 107,* 56–80.

Marin-Garcia, E., Ruiz-Vargas, J. M., & Kapur, N. (2013). Mere exposure effect can be elicited in transient global amnesia. *Journal of Clinical and Experimental Neuropsychology, 35,* 1007–1014.

Markey, P. M., & Kurtz, J. E. (2006). Increasing acquaintanceship and complementarity of behavioral styles and personality traits among college roommates. *Personality and Social Psychology Bulletin, 32,* 907–916.

Markman, H. J., Floyd, F. J., Stanley, S. M., & Storaasli, R. D. (1988). Prevention of marital distress: A longitudinal investigation. *Journal of Consulting and Clinical Psychology, 56,* 210–217.

Markman, K. D., & McMullen, M. N. (2003). A reflection and evaluation model of comparative thinking. *Personality and Social Psychology Review, 7,* 244–267.

Marks, G., & Miller, N. (1987). Ten years of research on the false-consensus effect: An empirical and theoretical review. *Psychological Bulletin, 102,* 72–90.

Markus, H., & Wurf, E. (1987). The dynamic self-concept: A social psychological perspective. *Annual Review of Psychology, 38,* 299–337.

Markus, H. (2001, October 7). Culture and the good life. Address to the Positive Psychology Summit conference, Washington, DC.

Markus, H. R. (2005). On telling less than we can know: The too tacit wisdom of social psychology. *Psychological Inquiry, 16,* 180–184.

Markus, H. R., & Conner, A. (2011). The culture cycle. *The Edge* (www.edge.org).

Markus, H. R., & Conner, A. (2013). *Clash! 8 cultural conflicts that make us who we are.* New York: Hudson Street Press.

Markus, H. R., & Kitayama, S. (1991). Culture and the self: Implications for cognition, emotion, and motivation. *Psychological Review, 98,* 224–253.

Markus, H. R., & Kitayama, S. (1994). A collective fear of the collective: Implications for selves and theories of selves. *Personality and Social Psychology Bulletin, 20,* 568–579.

Markus, H. R., & Kitayama, S. (2010). Cultures and selves: A cycle of mutual constitution. *Perspectives on Psychological Science, 5,* 420–430.

Marsden, P., & Attia, S. (2005). A deadly contagion? *The Psychologist, 18,* 152–155.

Marsh, H. W., Kong, C-K., & Hau, K.-T. (2000). Longitudinal multilevel models of the big-fish-little-pond effect on academic self-concept: Counterbalancing contrast and reflected-glory effects in Hong Kong schools. *Journal of Personality and Social Psychology, 78,* 337–349.

Marsh, H. W., & O'Mara, A. (2008). Reciprocal effects between academic self-concept, self-esteem, achievement, and attainment over seven adolescent years: Unidimensional and multidimensional perspectives of self-concept. *Personality and Social Psychology Bulletin, 34,* 542–552.

Marshall, R. (1997). Variances in levels of individualism across two cultures and three social classes. *Journal of Cross-Cultural Psychology, 28,* 490–495.

Martens, A., & Kosloff, S. (2012). Evidence that killing escalates within-subjects in a bug-killing paradigm. *Aggressive Behavior, 38,* 170–174.

Martens, A., Kosloff, S., Greenberg, J., Landau, M. J., & Schmader, R. (2007). Killing begets killing: Evidence from a bug-killing paradigm that initial killing fuels subsequent killing. *Personality and Social Psychology Bulletin, 33,* 1251–1264.

Martens, A., Kosloff, S., & Jackson, L. E. (2010). Evidence that initial obedient killing fuels subsequent volitional killing beyond effects of practice. *Social Psychological and Personality Science, 1,* 268–273.

Martin, L. L., & Erber, R. (2005). The wisdom of social psychology: Five commonalities and one concern. *Psychological Inquiry, 16,* 194–202.

Martino, S. C., Collins, R. L., Kanouse, D. E., Elliott, M., & Berry, S. H. (2005). Social cognitive processes mediating the relationship between exposure to television's sexual content and adolescents' sexual behavior. *Journal of Personality and Social Psychology, 89,* 914–924.

Martinovic, B., & Verkuyten, M. (2012). Host national and religious identification among Turkish Muslims in Western Europe: The role of ingroup norms, perceived discrimination and value incompatibility. *European Journal of Social Psychology, 42,* 893–903.

Martin, R. C., Coyier, K. R., VanSistine, L. M., & Schroeder, K. L. (2013). Anger on the Internet: The perceived value of rant-sites. *Cyberpsychology, Behavior, and Social Networking, 16,* 119–122.

Martin, R., Hewstone, M., & Martin, P. Y. (2008). Majority versus minority influence: The role of message processing in determining resistance to counter-persuasion. *European Journal of Social Psychology, 38,* 16–34.

Martin, R., Martin, P. Y., Smith, J. R., & Hewstone, M. (2007). Majority versus minority influence and prediction of behavioural intentions and behaviour. *Journal of Experimental Social Psychology, 43,* 763–771.

Martin, S. J., Goldstein, N. J., & Cialdini, R. B. (2014). *The small big: Small changes that spark big influence.* New York: Grand Central Publishing.

Martins, N., & Wilson, B. J. (2012a). Mean on the screen: Social aggression in programs popular with children. *Journal of Communication, 62,* 991–1009.

Martins, N., & Wilson, B. J. (2012b). Social aggression on television and its relationship to children's aggression in the classroom. *Human Communication Research, 38,* 48–71.

Marty, M. (1988, December 1). Graceful prose: Your good deed for the day. *Context,* p. 2.

Maruyama, G., Rubin, R. A., & Kingbury, G. (1981). Self-esteem and educational achievement: Independent constructs with a common cause? *Journal* *of Personality and Social Psychology, 40,* 962–975.

Marvelle, K., & Green, S. (1980). Physical attractiveness and sex bias in hiring decisions for two types of jobs. *Journal of the National Association of Women Deans, Administrators, and Counselors, 44(1),* 3–6.

Marzoli, D., Custodero, M., Pagliara, A., & Tommasi, L. (2013). Sun-induced frowning fosters aggressive feelings. *Cognition and Emotion, 27,* 1513–1521.

Masi, C. M., Chen, H-Y., Hawkley, L. C., & Cacioppo, J. T. (2011). A meta-analysis of interventions to reduce loneliness. *Personality and Social Psychology Review, 15,* 219–266.

Massey, C., Simmons, J. P., & Armor, D. A. (2011). Hope over experience: Desirability and the persistence of optimism. *Psychological Science, 22,* 274–281.

Mastekaasa, A. (1995). Age variations in the suicide rates and self-reported subjective well-being of married and never-married persons. *Journal of Community & Applied Social Psychology, 5,* 21–39.

Mast, M. S., & Hall, J. A. (2006). Women's advantage at remembering others' appearance: A systematic look at the why and when of a gender difference. *Personality and Social Psychology Bulletin, 32,* 353–364.

Mastroianni, G. R., & Reed, G. (2006). Apples, barrels, and Abu Ghraib. *Sociological Focus, 39,* 239–250.

Masuda, T., Gonzalez, R., Kwan, L., & Nisbett, R. E. (2008). Culture and aesthetic preference: Comparing the attention to context of East Asians and Americans. *Personality and Social Psychology Bulletin, 34,* 1260–1275.

Masuda, T., & Kitayama, S. (2004). Perceiver-induced constraint and attitude attribution in Japan and the U.S.: A case for the cultural dependence of the correspondence bias. *Journal of Experimental Social Psychology, 40,* 409–416.

Mathieu, M. T., & Gosling, S. D. (2012). The accuracy or inaccuracy of affective forecasts depends on how accuracy is indexed: A meta-analysis of past studies. *Psychological Science, 23,* 161–162.

Maxwell, G. M. (1985). Behaviour of lovers: Measuring the closeness of relationships. *Journal of Personality and Social Psychology, 2,* 215–238.

Mayer, J. D., & Salovey, P. (1987). Personality moderates the interaction of mood and cognition. In K. Fiedler & J. Forgas (Eds.), *Affect, cognition, and social behavior.* Toronto: Hogrefe.

Mazur, A., & Booth, A. (1998). Testosterone and dominance in men. *Behavioral and Brain Sciences, 21,* 353–363.

Mazzella, R., & Feingold, A. (1994). The effects of physical attractiveness, race, socioeconomic status, and gender of

defendants and victims on judgments of mock jurors: A meta-analysis. *Journal of Applied Social Psychology, 24,* 1315–1344.

Mazzoni, G., & Memon, A. (2003). Imagination can create false autobiographical memories. *Psychological Science, 14,* 186–188.

McAlister, A., Perry, C., Killen, J., Slinkard, L. A., & Maccoby, N. (1980). Pilot study of smoking, alcohol and drug abuse prevention. *American Journal of Public Health, 70,* 719–721.

McAndrew, F. T. (2002). New evolutionary perspectives on altruism: Multilevel-selection and costly-signaling theories. *Current Directions in Psychological Science, 11,* 79–82.

McAndrew, F. T. (2009). The interacting roles of testosterone and challenges to status in human male aggression. *Aggression and Violent Behavior, 14,* 330–335.

McCabe, D., Castel, A., & Rhodes, M. (2011). The influence of fMRI lie detection evidence on juror decision-making. *Behavioral Sciences and the Law, 29,* 566–577.

McCann, C. D., & Hancock, R. D. (1983). Self-monitoring in communicative interactions: Social cognitive consequences of goal-directed message modification. *Journal of Experimental Social Psychology, 19,* 109–121.

McCarthy, J. (2014, May 21). Same-sex marriage support reaches new high at 55%. Gallup Poll (www.gallup.com).

McCarthy, J. F., & Kelly, B. R. (1978a). Aggression, performance variables, and anger self-report in ice hockey players. *Journal of Psychology, 99,* 97–101.

McCarthy, J. F., & Kelly, B. R. (1978b). Aggressive behavior and its effect on performance over time in ice hockey athletes: An archival study. *International Journal of Sport Psychology, 9,* 90–96.

McCauley, C. (1989). The nature of social influence in groupthink: Compliance and internalization. *Journal of Personality and Social Psychology, 57,* 250–260.

McCauley, C. (1998). Group dynamics in Janis's theory of groupthink: Backward and forward. *Organizational Behavior and Human Decision Processes, 73,* 142–163.

McCauley, C. R. (2002). Psychological issues in understanding terrorism and the response to terrorism. In C. E. Stout (Ed.) *The psychology of terrorism* (Vol 3). Westport, CT: Praeger/Greenwood.

McCauley, C. R., & Segal, M. E. (1987). Social psychology of terrorist groups. In C. Hendrick (Ed.), *Group processes and intergroup relations: Review of personality and social psychology* (Vol. 9). Newbury Park, CA: Sage.

McClintock, E. A. (2014). Beauty and status: The illusion of exchange in partner selection? *American Sociological Review, 79,* 575–604.

McClure, M. J., & Lydon, J. E. (2014). Anxiety doesn't become you: How attachment anxiety compromises relational opportunities. *Journal of Personality and Social Psychology, 106,* 89–111.

McConahay, J. B. (1981). Reducing racial prejudice in desegregated schools. In W. D. Hawley (Ed.), *Effective school desegregation.* Beverly Hills, CA: Sage.

McCrae, R. R., & Costa, Jr., P. T. (2008). The Five-Factor Theory of personality. In O. P. John, R. W., Robins, & L. A. Pervin (Eds.), *Handbook of personality: Theory and research* (3rd edition). New York: Guilford.

McCullough, J. L., & Ostrom, T. M. (1974). Repetition of highly similar messages and attitude change. *Journal of Applied Psychology, 59,* 395–397.

McDermott, R., Tingley, D. Cowden, J., Frazzetto, G., & Johnson, D. D. P. (2009). Monoamine oxidase A gene (MAOA) predicts behavioral aggression following provocation. *Proceedings of the National Academy of Sciences of the United States of America, 106,* 2118–2123.

McDermott, T. (2005). *Perfect soldiers: The hijackers: Who they were, why they did it.* New York: HarperCollins.

McDonald, M. M., Asher, B. D., Kerr, N. L., & Navarrete, C. D. (2011). Fertility and intergroup bias in racial and minimal-group contexts: Evidence for shared architecture. *Psychological Science, 22,* 860–865.

McFall, R. M. (1991). Manifesto for a science of clinical psychology. *The Clinical Psychologist, 44,* 75–88.

McFall, R. M. (2000). Elaborate reflections on a simple manifesto. *Applied and Preventive Psychology, 9,* 5–21.

McFarland, C., & Ross, M. (1985). *The relation between current impressions and memories of self and dating partners.* Unpublished manuscript, University of Waterloo.

McFarland, S., Brown, D., & Webb, M. (2013). "Identification with all humanity" as a moral concept and psychological construct. *Current Directions in Psychological Science, 22,* 192–196.

McFarland, S., & Carnahan, T. (2009). A situation's first powers are attracting volunteers and selecting participants: A reply to Haney and Zimbardo (2009). *Personality and Social Psychology Bulletin, 35,* 815–818.

McGillicuddy, N. B., Welton, G. L., & Pruitt, D. G. (1987). Third-party intervention: A field experiment comparing three different models. *Journal of Personality and Social Psychology, 53,* 104–112.

McGillis, D. (1979). Biases and jury decision making. In I. H. Frieze, D. Bar-Tal, & J. S. Carroll (Eds.), *New approaches to social problems.* San Francisco: Jossey-Bass.

McGlone, M. S., & Tofighbakhsh, J. (2000). Birds of a feather flock conjointly

(?): Rhyme as reason in aphorisms. *Psychological Science, 11,* 424–428.

McGlynn, R. P., Tubbs, D. D., & Holzhausen, K. G. (1995). Hypothesis generation in groups constrained by evidence. *Journal of Experimental Social Psychology, 31,* 64–81.

McGowan, P. O., Sasaki, A., D'Alessio, A. C., Dymov, S., Labonté, B., Szyl, M., Turecki, G., & Meaney, M. J. (2010). Epigenetic regulation of the glucocorticoid receptor in human brain associates with childhood abuse. *Nature Neuroscience, 12,* 342–348.

McGrath, J. E. (1984). *Groups: Interaction and performance.* Englewood Cliffs, NJ: Prentice-Hall.

McGraw, A. P., Mellers, B. A., & Tetlock, P. E. (2005). Expectations and emotions of Olympic athletes. *Journal of Experimental Social Psychology, 41,* 438–446.

McGregor, I., Newby-Clark, I. R., & Zanna, M. P. (1998). Epistemic discomfort is moderated by simultaneous accessibility of inconsistent elements. In E. Harmon-Jones and J. Mills (Eds.), *Cognitive dissonance theory 40 years later: A revival with revisions and controversies.* Washington, DC: American Psychological Association.

McGregor, I., Zanna, M. P., Holmes, J. G., & Spencer, S. J. (2001). Conviction in the face of uncertainty: Going to extremes and being oneself. *Journal of Personality and Social Psychology, 80,* 472–478.

McGrory, B. (2004, July 26). Not your father's Boston. *The Boston Globe,* p. D2.

McGuire, A. (2002, August 19). Charity calls for debate on adverts aimed at children. *The Herald* (Scotland), p. 4.

McGuire, W. J. (1964). Inducing resistance to persuasion: Some contemporary approaches. In L. Berkowitz (Ed.), *Advances in experimental social psychology* (Vol. 1). New York: Academic Press.

McGuire, W. J., McGuire, C. V., Child, P., & Fujioka, T. (1978). Salience of ethnicity in the spontaneous self-concept as a function of one's ethnic distinctiveness in the social environment. *Journal of Personality and Social Psychology, 36,* 511–520.

McGuire, W. J., McGuire, C. V., & Winton, W. (1979). Effects of household sex composition on the salience of one's gender in the spontaneous self-concept. *Journal of Experimental Social Psychology, 15,* 77–90.

McGuire, W. J., & Padawer-Singer, A. (1978). Trait salience in the spontaneous self-concept. *Journal of Personality and Social Psychology, 33,* 743–754.

McKelvie, S. J. (1995). Bias in the estimated frequency of names. *Perceptual and Motor Skills, 81,* 1331–1338.

McKelvie, S. J. (1997). The availability heuristic: Effects of fame and gender on the estimated frequency of male and female names. *Journal of Social Psychology, 137,* 63–78.

McKenna, F. P., & Myers, L. B. (1997). Illusory self-assessments—Can they be reduced? *British Journal of Psychology, 88,* 39–51.

McKenna, K. Y. A., & Bargh, J. A. (1998). Coming out in the age of the Internet: Identity demarginalization through virtual group participation. *Journal of Personality and Social Psychology, 75,* 681–694.

McKenna, K. Y. A., & Bargh, J. A. (2000). Plan 9 from cyberspace: The implications of the Internet for personality and social psychology. *Personality and Social Psychology Review, 4,* 57–75.

McKenna, K. Y. A., Green, A. S., & Gleason, M. E. J. (2002). What's the big attraction? Relationship formation on the Internet. *Journal of Social Issues, 58,* 9–31.

McKibben, B. (2011, May 23). A link between climate change and Joplin tornadoes? Never! *Washington Post* (www .washingtonpost.com).

McMillen, D. L., & Austin, J. B. (1971). Effect of positive feedback on compliance following transgression. *Psychonomic Science, 24,* 59–61.

McMillen, D. L., Sanders, D. Y., & Solomon, G. S. (1977). Self-esteem, attentiveness, and helping behavior. *Journal of Personality and Social Psychology, 3,* 257–261.

McNeill, B. W., & Stoltenberg, C. D. (1988). A test of the elaboration likelihood model for therapy. *Cognitive Therapy and Research, 12,* 69–79.

McNulty, J. K. (2010). When positive processes hurt relationships. *Current Directions in Psychological Science, 19,* 167–171.

McNulty, J. K., O'Mara, E. M., & Karney, B. R. (2008). Benevolent cognitions as a strategy of relationship maintenance: "Don't sweat the small stuff" . . . . But it is not all small stuff. *Journal of Personality and Social Psychology, 94,* 631–646.

McPherson, M., Smith-Lovin, L., & Cook, J. M. (2001). Birds of a feather: Homophily in social networks. *Annual Review of Sociology, 27,* 415–444.

Mead, G. H. (1934). *Mind, self, and society.* Chicago: University of Chicago Press.

Medin, D. L. (2011, September). Fields for psychology. APS *Observer,* pp. 5, 36.

Medvec, V. H., Madey, S. F., & Gilovich, T. (1995). When less is more: Counterfactual thinking and satisfaction among Olympic medalists. *Journal of Personality and Social Psychology, 69,* 603–610.

Medvec, V. H., & Savitsky, K. (1997). When doing better means feeling worse: The effects of categorical cutoff points on counterfactual thinking and satisfaction. *Journal of Personality and Social Psychology, 72,* 1284–1296.

Meehl, P. E. (1954). *Clinical vs. statistical prediction: A theoretical analysis and a review of evidence.* Minneapolis: University of Minnesota Press.

Meehl, P. E. (1986). Causes and effects of my disturbing little book. *Journal of Personality Assessment, 50,* 370–375.

Mehl, M. R., & Pennebaker, J. W. (2003). The sounds of social life: A psychometric analysis of students' daily social environments and natural conversations. *Journal of Personality and Social Psychology, 84,* 857–870.

Mehl, M. R., Vazire, S., Holleran, S. E., & Clark, C. S. (2010). Eavesdropping on happiness: Well-being is related to having less small talk and more substantive conversations. *Psychological Science, 21,* 539–541.

Meier, B. P., & Hinsz, V. B. (2004). A comparison of human aggression committed by groups and individuals: An interindividual-intergroup discontinuity. *Journal of Experimental Social Psychology, 40,* 551–559.

Meissner, C. A., & Brigham, J. C. (2001). Thirty years of investigating the own-race bias in memory for faces: A meta-analytic review. *Psychology, Public Policy, & Law, 7,* 3–35.

Meissner, C. A., Brigham, J. C., & Butz, D. A. (2005). Memory for own- and other-race faces: A dual-process approach. *Applied Cognitive Psychology, 19,* 545–567.

Melander, E. (2005), Gender equality and intrastate armed conflict. *International Studies Quarterly, 49,* 695–714.

Meleady, R., Hopthrow, T., & Crisp, R. J. (2013). Simulating social dilemmas: Promoting cooperative behavior through imagined group discussion. *Journal of Personality and Social Psychology, 104,* 839–853.

Meleshko, K. G. A., & Alden, L. E. (1993). Anxiety and self-disclosure: Toward a motivational model. *Journal of Personality and Social Psychology, 64,* 1000–1009.

Mellers, B., Hertwig, R., & Kahneman, D. (2001). Do frequency representations eliminate conjunction effects? An exercise in adversarial collaboration. *Psychological Science, 12,* 269–275.

Mellers, B., Ungar, L., Baron, J., Ramos, J., Gurcay, B., Fincher, K., Scott, S. E., Moore, D. Atanasov, P., Swift, S. A., Murray, T., Stone, E., & Tetlock, P. E. (2014). Psychological strategies for winning a geopolitical forecasting tournament. *Psychological Science, 25,* 1106–1115.

Meltzer, A. L., McNulty, J. K., Jackson, G. L., & Karney, B. R. (2014). Sex differences in the implications of partner physical attractiveness for the trajectory of marital satisfaction. *Journal of Personality and Social Psychology, 106,* 418–428.

Memon, A., Meissner, C. A., & Fraser, J. (2011). The cognitive interview: A meta-analytic review and study space analysis of the past 25 years. *Psychology, Public Policy, and Law, 16,* 340–372.

Mendel, R., Traut-Mattausch, E., Jonas, E., Leucht, S., Kane, J. M., Maino, K., Kissling, W., & Hamann, J. (2011). Confirmation bias: Why psychiatrists stick to wrong preliminary diagnoses. *Psychological Medicine, 41,* 2651–2659.

Mendonca, P. J., & Brehm, S. S. (1983). Effects of choice on behavioral treatment of overweight children. *Journal of Social and Clinical Psychology, 1,* 343–358.

Merari, A. (2002). *Explaining suicidal terrorism: Theories versus empirical evidence.* Invited address to the American Psychological Association, Chicago, Illinois.

Merikle, P. M., Smilek, D., & Eastwood, J. D. (2001). Perception without awareness: Perspectives from cognitive psychology. *Cognition, 79,* 115–134.

Merton, R. K. (1938; reprinted 1970). *Science, technology and society in seventeenth-century England.* New York: Fertig.

Merton, R. K. (1948). The self-fulfilling prophecy. *Antioch Review, 8,* 193–210.

Merton, R. K., & Kitt, A. S. (1950). Contributions to the theory of reference group behavior. In R. K. Merton & P. F. Lazarsfeld (Eds.), *Continuities in social research: Studies in the scope and method of the American soldier.* Glencoe, IL: Free Press.

Mesch, D. J., & Pactor, A. (2015). Women and philanthropy: A literature review. In T. Jung, S. Phillips, & J. Harlow (Eds.), *The Routledge companion to philanthropy.* New York: Routledge.

Mesmer-Magnus, J. R., & DeChurch, L. A. (2009). Information sharing and team performance: A meta-analysis. *Journal of Applied Psychology, 94,* 535–546.

Mesoudi, A. (2009). How cultural evolutionary theory can inform social psychology and vice versa. *Psychological Review, 116,* 929–952.

Messé, L. A., & Sivacek, J. M. (1979). Predictions of others' responses in a mixed-motive game: Self-justification or false consensus? *Journal of Personality and Social Psychology, 37,* 602–607.

Messias, E., Eaton, W. W., & Grooms, A. N. (2011). Income inequality and depression prevalence across the United States: An ecological study. *Psychiatric Services, 62,* 710–712.

Messick, D. M., & Sentis, K. P. (1979). Fairness and preference. *Journal of Experimental Social Psychology, 15,* 418–434.

Meyers, S. A., & Berscheid, E. (1997). The language of love: The difference a preposition makes. *Personality and Social Psychology Bulletin, 23,* 347–362.

Mezulis, A. H., Abramson, L. Y., Hyde, J. S., & Hankin, B. L. (2004). Is there a universal positivity bias in attributions? A meta-analytic review of individual, developmental, and cultural differences in the self-serving attributional bias. *Psychological Bulletin, 130,* 711–747.

Michaels, J. W., Blommel, J. M., Brocato, R. M., Linkous, R. A., & Rowe, J. S. (1982). Social facilitation and inhibition in a natural setting. *Replications in Social Psychology, 2,* 21–24.

Mickelson, K. D., Kessler, R. C., & Shaver, P. R. (1997). Adult attachment in a nationally representative sample. *Journal of Personality and Social Psychology, 73,* 1092–1106.

Miguel, E., & 18 others (2014). Promoting transparency in social science research. *Science, 343,* 30–31.

Mikula, G. (1984). Justice and fairness in interpersonal relations: Thoughts and suggestions. In H. Taijfel (Ed.), *The social dimension: European developments in social psychology* (Vol. 1). Cambridge: Cambridge University Press.

Mikulincer, M., Florian, V., & Hirschberger, G. (2003). The existential function of close relationships: Introducing death into the science of love. *Personality and Social Psychology Review, 7,* 20–40.

Mikulincer, M., & Shaver, P. R. (2001). Attachment theory and intergroup bias: Evidence that priming the secure base schema attenuates negative reactions to out-groups. *Journal of Personality and Social Psychology, 81,* 97–115.

Mikulincer, M., Shaver, P. R., Gillath, O., & Nitzberg, R. A. (2005). Attachment, caregiving, and altruism: Boosting attachment security increases compassion and helping. *Journal of Personality and Social Psychology, 89,* 817–839.

Milgram, A. (2000). My personal view of Stanley Milgram. In T. Blass (Ed.), *Obedience to authority: Current perspectives on the Milgram paradigm.* Mahwah, NJ: Erlbaum.

Milgram, S. (1965). Some conditions of obedience and disobedience to authority. *Human Relations, 18,* 57–76.

Milgram, S. (1974). *Obedience to authority.* New York: Harper and Row.

Milgram, S., Bickman, L., & Berkowitz, L. (1969). Note on the drawing power of crowds of different size. *Journal of Personality and Social Psychology, 13,* 79–82.

Military Advisory Board. (2014). *National security and the accelerating risks of climate change.* Arlington, VA: Center for Naval Analyses.

Millar, M. G. (2011). Predicting dental flossing behavior: The role of implicit and explicit responses and beliefs. *Basic and Applied Social Psychology, 33,* 7–15.

Miller, A. G. (1986). *The obedience experiments: A case study of controversy in social science.* New York: Praeger.

Miller, A. G. (2004). What can the Milgram obedience experiments tell us about the Holocaust? Generalizing from the social psychological laboratory. In A. G. Miller (Ed.), *The social psychology of good and evil.* New York: Guilford.

Miller, A. G. (2006). Exonerating harm-doers: Some problematic implications of social-psychological explanations. Paper presented to the Society of Personality and Social Psychology convention.

Miller, A. G., Ashton, W., & Mishal, M. (1990). Beliefs concerning the features of constrained behavior: A basis for the fundamental attribution error. *Journal of Personality and Social Psychology, 59,* 635–650.

Miller, C. E., & Anderson, P. D. (1979). Group decision rules and the rejection of deviates. *Social Psychology Quarterly, 42,* 354–363.

Miller, C. T., & Felicio, D. M. (1990). Person-positivity bias: Are individuals liked better than groups? *Journal of Experimental Social Psychology, 26,* 408–420.

Miller, D. W. (2001, November 23). Jury consulting on trial. *Chronicle of Higher Education,* A15, A16.

Miller, G. (2011, April 29). Using the psychology of evil to do good. *Science, 332,* 530–532.

Miller, G., Tybur, J. M., & Jordan, B. D. (2007). Ovulatory cycle effects on tip earnings by lap dancers: Economic evidence for human estrus? *Evolution and Human Behavior, 28,* 375–381.

Miller, G. E., Chen, E., & Parker, K. J. (2011). Psychological stress in childhood and susceptibility to the chronic diseases of aging: Moving toward a model of behavioral and biological mechanisms. *Psychological Bulletin, 137,* 959–997.

Miller, G. R., & Fontes, N. E. (1979). *Videotape on trial: A view from the jury box.* Beverly Hills, CA: Sage.

Miller, J. G. (1984). Culture and the development of everyday social explanation. *Journal of Personality and Social Psychology, 46,* 961–978.

Miller, N. (2002). Personalization and the promise of contact theory. *Journal of Social Issues, 58,* 387–410.

Miller, N., & Campbell, D. T. (1959). Recency and primacy in persuasion as a function of the timing of speeches and measurements. *Journal of Abnormal and Social Psychology, 59,* 1–9.

Miller, N., & Marks, G. (1982). Assumed similarity between self and other: Effect of expectation of future interaction with that other. *Social Psychology Quarterly, 45,* 100–105.

Miller, N., Pedersen, W. C., Earleywine, M., & Pollock, V. E. (2003). A theoretical model of triggered displaced aggression. *Personality and Social Psychology Review, 7,* 75–97.

Miller, P. A., & Eisenberg, N. (1988). The relation of empathy to aggressive and externalizing/antisocial behavior. *Psychological Bulletin, 103,* 324–344.

Miller, P. A., Kozu, J., & Davis, A. C. (2001). Social influence, empathy, and prosocial behavior in cross-cultural perspective. In W. Wosinska, R. B. Cialdini, D. W. Barrett, & J. Reykowski (Eds.), *The practice of social influence in multiple cultures.* Mahwah, NJ: Erlbaum.

Miller, P. J. E., Niehuis, S., & Huston, T. L. (2006). Positive illusions in marital relationships: A 13-year longitudinal study. *Personality and Social Psychology Bulletin, 32,* 1579–1594.

Miller, P. J. E., & Rempel, J. K. (2004). Trust and partner-enhancing attributions in close relationships. *Personality and Social Psychology Bulletin, 30,* 695–705.

Miller, R. L., Brickman, P., & Bolen, D. (1975). Attribution versus persuasion as a means for modifying behavior. *Journal of Personality and Social Psychology, 31,* 430–441.

Miller, R. S. (1997). Inattentive and contented: Relationship commitment and attention to alternatives. *Journal of Personality and Social Psychology, 73,* 758–766.

Miller, R. S., & Schlenker, B. R. (1985). Egotism in group members: Public and private attributions of responsibility for group performance. *Social Psychology Quarterly, 48,* 85–89.

Miller, R. S., & Simpson, J. A. (1990). *Relationship satisfaction and attentiveness to alternatives.* Paper presented at the American Psychological Association convention, Boston, MA.

Miller, S. L., Zielaskowski, K., & Plant, E. A. (2012). The basis of shooter biases: Beyond cultural stereotypes. *Personality and Social Psychology Bulletin, 38,* 1358–1366.

Millett, K. (1975, January). The shame is over. *Ms.,* 26–29.

Mills, B. M. (2014). Social pressure at the plate: Inequality aversion, status, and mere exposure. *Managerial and Decision Economics, 35,* 387–403.

Milyavskaya, M., Gingras, I., Mageau, G. A., Koestner, R., Gagnon, H., Fang, J., & Boiché, J. (2009). Balance across contexts: Importance of balanced need satisfaction across various life domains. *Personality and Social Psychology Bulletin, 35,* 1031–1045.

Mims, P. R., Hartnett, J. J., & Nay, W. R. (1975). Interpersonal attraction and help volunteering as a function of physical attractiveness. *Journal of Psychology, 89,* 125–131.

Min, K. S., & Arkes, H. R. (2012). When is difficult planning good planning? The effects of scenario-based planning on optimistic prediction bias. *Journal of Applied Social Psychology, 42,* 2701–2729.

Minard, R. D. (1952). Race relationships in the Pocohontas coal field. *Journal of Social Issues, 8(1),* 29–44.

Mirsky, S. (2009, January). What's good for the group. *Scientific American,* 51. motive. *Journal of Experimental Social Psychology, 24,* 163–181.

Mishna, F. (2004). A qualitative study of bullying from multiple perspectives. *Children & Schools, 26,* 234–247.

Mishna, F., Cook, C., Gadallo, T., Daciuk, J., & Solomon, S. (2010). Cyberbullying behaviors among middle and high school students. *American Journal of Orthopsychiatry, 80,* 362–374.

Mita, T. H., Dermer, M., & Knight, J. (1977). Reversed facial images and the mere-exposure hypothesis. *Journal of Personality and Social Psychology, 35,* 597–601.

Mitchell, G. (2012). Revisiting truth or triviality: The external validity of research in the psychological laboratory. *Perspectives on Psychological Science, 7,* 109–117.

Mitchell, T. L., Haw, R. M., Pfeifer, J. E., & Meissner, C. A. (2005). Racial bias in mock juror decision-making: A meta-analytic review of defendant treatment. *Law and Human Behavior, 29,* 621–637.

Mitchell, T. R., & Thompson, L. (1994). A theory of temporal adjustments of the evaluation of events: Rosy prospection and rosy retrospection. In C. Stubbart, J. Porac, & J. Meindl (Eds.), *Advances in managerial cognition and organizational information processing.* Greenwich, CT: JAI Press.

Mitchell, T. R., Thompson, L., Peterson, E., & Cronk, R. (1997). Temporal adjustments in the evaluation of events: The "rosy view." *Journal of Experimental Social Psychology, 33,* 421–448.

Miyake, A., Kost-Smith, L., Finkelstein, N. D., Pollock, S. J., Cohen, G. L., & Ito, T. A. (2010). Reducing the gender achievement gap in college science: A classroom study of values affirmation. *Science, 330,* 1234–1237.

Moffitt, T., & 12 others. (2011). A gradient of childhood self-control predicts health, wealth, and public safety. *PNAS, 108(7):* 2693–2698.

Moffitt, T., Caspi, A., Sugden, K., Taylor, A., Craig, I. W., Harrington, H., McClay, J., Mill, J., Martin, J., Braithwaite, A., & Poulton, R. (2003). Influence of life stress on depression: Moderation by a polymorphism in the 5-HTT gene. *Science, 301,* 386–389.

Moghaddam, F. M. (2005). The staircase to terrorism: A psychological exploration. *American Psychologist, 60,* 161–169.

Moghaddam, F. M. (2009). Omniculturalism: Policy solutions to fundamentalism in the era of fractured globalization. *Culture and Psychology, 15,* 337–347.

Moghaddam, F. M. (2010). *The new global insecurity.* New York: Praeger.

Mohr, H., Pritchard, J., & Lush, T. (2010, May 29). BP has been good at downplaying disaster. *Associated Press.*

Mojzisch, A., & Schulz-Hardt, S. (2010). Knowing others' preferences degrades the quality of group decisions. *Journal of Personality and Social Psychology, 98,* 784–808.

Moller, I., & Krahe, B. (2008). Exposure to violent video games and aggression in German adolescents: A longitudinal analysis. *Aggressive Behavior, 34,* 1–14.

Moller, I., Krahe, B., Busching, R., & Krause, C. (2012). Efficacy of an intervention to reduce the use of media violence and aggression: An experimental evaluation with adolescents in Germany. *Journal of Youth and Adolescence, 41,* 105–120.

Montag, C., Weber, B., Trautner, P., Newport, B., Markett, S., Walter, N. T., Felten, A., & Reuter, M. (2012). Does excessive play of violent first-person-shooter-video-games dampen brain activity in response to emotional stimuli? *Biological Psychology, 89,* 107–111.

Monteith, M. J. (1993). Self-regulation of prejudiced responses: Implications for progress in prejudice-reduction efforts. *Journal of Personality and Social Psychology, 65,* 469–485.

Montoya, R. M. (2008). I'm hot, so I'd say you're not: The influence of objective physical attractiveness on mate selection. *Personality and Social Psychology Bulletin, 34,* 1315–1331.

Montoya, R. M., & Horton, R. S. (2012). A meta-analytic investigation of the processes underlying the similarity-attraction effect. *Journal of Social and Personal Relationships, 30,* 64–94.

Montoya, R. M., & Insko, C. A. (2008). Toward a more complete understanding of the reciprocity of liking effect. *European Journal of Social Psychology, 38,* 477–498.

Moody, K. (1980). *Growing up on television: The TV effect.* New York: Times Books.

Moons, W. G., & Mackie, D. M. (2007). Thinking straight while seeing red: The influence of anger on information processing. *Personality and Social Psychology Bulletin, 33,* 706–720.

Moons, W. G., Mackie, D. M., & Garcia-Marques, T. (2009). The impact of repetition-induced familiarity on agreement with weak and strong arguments. *Journal of Personality and Social Psychology, 96,* 32–44.

Moor, B. G., Crone, E. A., & van der Molen, M. W. (2010). The heartbrake of social rejection: Heart rate deceleration in response to unexpected peer rejection. *Psychological Science, 21,* 1326–1333.

Moore, D. A., & Swift, S. A. (2011). The three faces of overconfidence in organizations. In D. De Cremer, R. van Dick, & J. K. Murnighan (Eds.), *Social psychology and organizations.* New York: Routledge/Taylor & Francis.

Moore, D. L., & Baron, R. S. (1983). Social facilitation: A physiological analysis. In J. T. Cacioppo & R. Petty (Eds.), *Social psychophysiology.* New York: Guilford.

Moore, D. W. (2003, March 18). Public approves of Bush ultimatum by more than 2-to-1 margin. Gallup News Service (www.gallup.com).

Moore, D. W. (2004a, March 23). The civil unions vs. gay marriage proposals. *Gallup Tuesday Briefing* (www.gallup.com).

Moore, D. W. (2004b, April 20). Ballot order: Who benefits? *Gallup Poll Tuesday Briefing* (www.gallup.com).

Mor, N., & Winquist, J. (2002). Self-focused attention and negative affect:

A meta-analysis. *Psychological Bulletin, 128,* 638–662.

Morales, A. C., Wu, E. C., & Fitzsimons, G. J. (2012). How disgust enhances the effectiveness of fear appeals. *Journal of Marketing Research, 44,* 383–393.

Morales, L. (2011, May 27). *U.S. adults estimate that 25% of Americans are gay or lesbian.* www.gallup.com.

Moran, G., & Comfort, J. C. (1982). Scientific juror selection: Sex as a moderator of demographic and personality predictors of impaneled felony juror behavior. *Journal of Personality and Social Psychology, 43,* 1052–1063.

Moran, G., & Comfort, J. C. (1986). Neither "tentative" nor "fragmentary": Verdict preference of impaneled felony jurors as a function of attitude toward capital punishment. *Journal of Applied Psychology, 71,* 146–155.

Moran, G., & Cutler, B. L. (1991). The prejudicial impact of pretrial publicity. *Journal of Applied Social Psychology, 21,* 345–367.

Moran, G., Cutler, B. L., & De Lisa, A. (1994). Attitudes toward tort reform, scientific jury selection, and juror bias: Verdict inclination in criminal and civil trials. *Law and Psychology Review, 18,* 309–328.

Moran, G., Cutler, B. L., & Loftus, E. F. (1990). Jury selection in major controlled substance trials: The need for extended voir dire. *Forensic Reports, 3,* 331–348.

Morano, M. (2013, September 25). Der Spiegel Poll: Only 39% of German fear global warming – down from 62% in 2006. Climate Depot (http://www.climatedepot .com/2013/09/25/der-spiegel-poll-only-39- of-germans-fear-global-warming-down- from-62-in-2006/).

Morgan, C. A., III, Hazlett, G., Doran, A., Garrett, S., Hoyt, G., Thomas, P., Baranoski, M., & Southwick, & S. M. (2004). Accuracy of eyewitness memory for persons encountered during exposure to highly intense stress. *International Journal of Law and Psychiatry, 27,* 265–279.

Morgan, G. S., Mullen, E., & Skitka, L. J. (2010). When values and attributions collide: Liberals' and conservatives' values motivate attributions for alleged misdeeds. *Personality and Social Psychology Bulletin, 36,* 1241–1254.

Mori, K., & Mori, H. (2009). Another test of the passive facial feedback hypothesis: When your face smiles, you feel happy. *Perceptual and Motor Skills, 109,* 1–3.

Morling, B., & Lamoreaux, M. (2008). Measuring culture outside the head: A meta-analysis of individualism- collectivism in cultural products. *Personality and Social Psychology Bulletin, 12,* 199–221.

Morris, W. N., & Miller, R. S. (1975). The effects of consensus-breaking and consensus-preempting partners on reduction of conformity. *Journal of Experimental Social Psychology, 11,* 215–223.

Morrow, L. (1983, August 1). All the hazards and threats of success. *Time,* 20–25.

Moscatelli, S., Albarello, F., Prati, F., & Rubini, M. (2014). Badly off or better off than them? The impact of relative deprivation and relative gratification on intergroup discrimination. *Journal of Personality and Social Psychology, 107,* 248–264.

Moscovici, S. (1985). Social influence and conformity. In G. Lindzey & E. Aronson (Eds.), *The handbook of social psychology,* 3rd edition. Hillsdale, NJ: Erlbaum.

Moscovici, S. (1988). Notes towards a description of social representations. *European Journal of Social Psychology, 18,* 211–250.

Moscovici, S. (2001). Why a theory of social representation? In K. Deaux & G. Philogène (Eds.), *Representations of the social: Bridging theoretical traditions.* Malden, MA: Blackwell.

Moscovici, S., Lage, S., & Naffrechoux, M. (1969). Influence of a consistent minority on the responses of a majority in a color perception task. *Sociometry, 32,* 365–380.

Moscovici, S., & Zavalloni, M. (1969). The group as a polarizer of attitudes. *Journal of Personality and Social Psychology, 12,* 124–135.

Moskowitz, T. J., & Wertheim, L. J. (2011). *Scorecasting: The hidden influences behind how sports are played and games are won.* New York: Crown Archetype.

Motherhood Project. (2001, May 2). *Watch out for children: A mothers' statement to advertisers.* Institute for American Values (www.watchoutforchildren.org).

Moutsiana, C., Fearon, P., Murray, L., Cooper, P., Goodyer, I., Johnstone, T., & Halligan, S. (2014). Making an effort to feel positive: Insecure attachment in infancy predicts the neural underpinnings of emotion regulation in adulthood. *Journal of Child Psychology and Psychiatry, 55,* 999–1008.

Moyer, K. E. (1976). *The psychobiology of aggression.* New York: Harper & Row.

Moyer, K. E. (1983). The physiology of motivation: Aggression as a model. In C. J. Scheier & A. M. Rogers (Eds.), *G. Stanley Hall Lecture Series* (Vol. 3). Washington, DC: American Psychological Association.

Moynihan, D. P. (1979). Social science and the courts. *Public Interest, 54,* 12–31.

Muehlenhard, C. L. (1988). Misinterpreted dating behaviors and the risk of date rape. *Journal of Social and Clinical Psychology, 6,* 20–37.

Mueller, C. M., & Dweck, C. S. (1998). Praise for intelligence can undermine children's motivation and performance. *Journal of Personality and Social Psychology, 75,* 33–52.

Mueller, C. W., Donnerstein, E., & Hallam, J. (1983). Violent films and prosocial behavior. *Personality and Social Psychology Bulletin, 9,* 83–89.

Mujcic, R., & Frijters, P. (2014, December). Still not allowed on the bus: It matters if you're Black or White. Working paper, University of Queensland.

Mukherjee, A., & Dube, L. (2012). Mixing emotions: The use of humor in fear advertising. *Journal of Consumer Behaviour, 11,* 147–161.

Mullen, B. (1986). Atrocity as a function of lynch mob composition: A self-attention perspective. *Personality and Social Psychology Bulletin, 12,* 187–197.

Mullen, B. (1986a). Atrocity as a function of lynch mob composition: A self-attention perspective. *Personality and Social Psychology Bulletin, 12,* 187–197.

Mullen, B. (1986b). Stuttering, audience size, and the other-total ratio: A self-attention perspective. *Journal of Applied Social Psychology, 16,* 139–149.

Mullen, B., Anthony, T., Salas, E., & Driskell, J. E. (1994). Group cohesiveness and quality of decision making: An integration of tests of the groupthink hypothesis. *Small Group Research, 25,* 189–204.

Mullen, B., & Baumeister, R. F. (1987). Group effects on self-attention and performance: Social loafing, social facilitation, and social impairment. In C. Hendrick (Ed.), *Group processes and intergroup relations: Review of personality and social psychology* (Vol. 9). Newbury Park, CA: Sage.

Mullen, B., Bryant, B., & Driskell, J. E. (1997). Presence of others and arousal: An integration. *Group Dynamics: Theory, Research, and Practice, 1,* 52–64.

Mullen, B., & Copper, C. (1994). The relation between group cohesiveness and performance: An integration. *Psychological Bulletin, 115,* 210–227.

Mullen, B., Copper, C., & Driskell, J. E. (1990). Jaywalking as a function of model behavior. *Personality and Social Psychology Bulletin, 16,* 320–330.

Mullen, B., & Goethals, G. R. (1990). Social projection, actual consensus and valence. *British Journal of Social Psychology, 29,* 279–282.

Mullen, B., & Riordan, C. A. (1988). Self- serving attributions for performance in naturalistic settings: A meta-analytic review. *Journal of Applied Social Psychology, 18,* 3–22.

Mullenix, J. W., Ross, A., Smith, C., Kuykendall, K., Conard, J., & Barb, S. (2011). Typicality effects on memory for voice: Implications for earwitness testimony. *Applied Cognitive Psychology, 25,* 29–34.

Muller, S., & Johnson, B. T. (1990). *Fear and persuasion: A linear relationship?* Paper presented at the Eastern Psychological Association convention.

Mullin, C. R., & Linz, D. (1995). Desensitization and resensitization to violence against women: Effects of exposure to sexually violent films on judgments of domestic violence victims. *Journal of Personality and Social Psychology, 69,* 449–459.

Munoz-Rivas, M. J., Grana, J. L., O'Leary, K. D., & Gonzalez, M. P. (2007). Aggression in adolescent dating relationships: Prevalence, justification, and health consequences. *Journal of Adolescent Health, 40,* 298–304.

Munro, G. D., Ditto, P. H., Lockhart, L. K., Fagerlin, A., Gready, M., & Peterson, E. (1997). *Biased assimilation of sociopolitical arguments: Evaluating the 1996 U.S. presidential debate.* Unpublished manuscript, Hope College.

Muraven, M., Baumeister, R. F., & Tice, D. M. (1999). Longitudinal improvement of self-regulation through practice: Building self-control strength through repeated exercise. *Journal of Social Psychology, 139,* 446–457.

Muraven, M., Tice, D. M., & Baumeister, R. F. (1998). Self-control as a limited resource: Regulatory depletion patterns. *Journal of Personality and Social Psychology, 74,* 774–790.

Murphy, C. (1990, June). New findings: Hold on to your hat. *The Atlantic,* pp. 22–23.

Murray, D. R., & Schaller, M. (2012). Threat(s) and conformity deconstructed: Perceived threat of infectious disease and its implications for conformist attitudes and behavior. *European Journal of Social Psychology, 42,* 180–188.

Murray, D. R., Trudeau, R., & Schaller, M. (2011). On the origins of cultural differences in conformity: Four tests of the pathogen prevalence hypothesis. *Personality and Social Psychology Bulletin, 37,* 318–329.

Murray, G. R., & Schmitz, J. D. (2011). Caveman politics: Evolutionary leadership preferences and physical stature. *Social Science Quarterly, 92,* 1215–1235.

Murray, K. E., & Marx, D. M. (2013). Attitudes toward unauthorized immigrants, authorized immigrants, and refugees. *Cultural Diversity and Ethnic Minority Psychology, 19,* 332–341.

Murray, S. L., Gellavia, G. M., Rose, P., & Griffin, D. W. (2003). Once hurt, twice hurtful: How perceived regard regulates daily marital interactions. *Journal of Personality and Social Psychology, 84,* 126–147.

Murray, S. L., & Holmes, J. G. (1997). A leap of faith? Positive illusions in romantic relationships. *Personality and Social Psychology Bulletin, 23,* 586–604.

Murray, S. L., Holmes, J. G., Gellavia, G., Griffin, D. W., & Dolderman, D. (2002). Kindred spirits? The benefits of egocentrism in close relationships. *Journal of Personality and Social Psychology, 82,* 563–581.

Murray, S. L., Holmes, J. G., & Griffin, D. W. (1996a). The benefits of positive illusions: Idealization and the construction of satisfaction in close relationships. *Journal of Personality and Social Psychology, 70,* 79–98.

Murray, S. L., Holmes, J. G., & Griffin, D. W. (1996b). The self-fulfilling nature of positive illusions in romantic relationships: Love is not blind, but prescient. *Journal of Personality and Social Psychology, 71,* 1155–1180.

Murray, S. L., Holmes, J. G., & Griffin, D. W. (2000). Self-esteem and the quest for felt security: How perceived regard regulates attachment processes. *Journal of Personality and Social Psychology, 78,* 478–498.

Murstein, B. L. (1986). *Paths to marriage.* Newbury Park, CA: Sage.

Muson, G. (1978, March). Teenage violence and the telly. *Psychology Today,* 50–54.

Myers, D. G. (1978). Polarizing effects of social comparison. *Journal of Experimental Social Psychology, 14,* 554–563.

Myers, D. G. (1993). *The pursuit of happiness.* New York: Avon.

Myers, D. G. (2000). The funds, friends, and faith of happy people. *American Psychologist, 55,* 56–67.

Myers, D. G. (2000a). *The American paradox: Spiritual hunger in an age of plenty.* New Haven, CT: Yale University Press.

Myers, D. G. (2000b). The funds, friends, and faith of happy people. *American Psychologist, 55,* 56–67.

Myers, D. G. (2001, December). Do we fear the right things? *American Psychological Society Observer,* p. 3.

Myers, D. G. (2010). Group polarization. In J. Levine & M. Hogg (Eds.), *Encyclopedia of group processes and intergroup relations.* Thousand Oaks, CA: Sage.

Myers, D. G., & Bishop, G. D. (1970). Discussion effects on racial attitudes. *Science, 169,* 778–789.

Myers, J. E., Madathil, J., & Tingle, L. R. (2005). Marriage satisfaction and wellness in India and the United States: A preliminary comparison of arranged marriages and marriages of choice. *Journal of Counseling and Development, 83,* 183–190.

Myers, J. N. (1997, December). Quoted by S. A. Boot, Where the weather reigns. *World Traveler, 86,* 88, 91, 124.

Myers, N. (2000). Sustainable consumption: The meta-problem. In B. Heap & J. Kent (Eds.), *Towards sustainable consumption: A European perspective.* London: The Royal Society.

Na, J., & Kitayama, S. (2011). Spontaneous trait inference is culture-specific: Behavioral and neural evidence. *Psychological Science, 22,* 1025–1032.

Nadler, A. (1991). Help-seeking behavior: Psychological costs and instrumental benefits. In M. S. Clark (Ed.), *Prosocial behavior.* Newbury Park, CA: Sage.

Nadler, A., & Fisher, J. D. (1986). The role of threat to self-esteem and perceived control in recipient reaction to help: Theory development and empirical validation. In L. Berkowitz (Ed.), *Advances in Experimental Social Psychology* (Vol. 19). Orlando, FL: Academic Press.

Nadler, A., Goldberg, M., & Jaffe, Y. (1982). Effect of self-differentiation and anonymity in group on deindividuation. *Journal of Personality and Social Psychology, 42,* 1127–1136.

Nadler, J. T., & Clark, M. H. (2011). Stereotype threat: A meta-analysis comparing African Americans to Hispanic Americans. *Journal of Applied Social Psychology, 41,* 872–890.

Nagar, D., & Pandey, J. (1987). Affect and performance on cognitive task as a function of crowding and noise. *Journal of Applied Social Psychology, 17,* 147–157.

Nail, P. R., MacDonald, G., & Levy, D. A. (2000). Proposal of a four-dimensional model of social response. *Psychological Bulletin, 126,* 454–470.

Nair, H., Manchanda, P., & Bhatia, T. (2008, May). *Asymmetric social interactions in physician prescription behavior: The role of opinion leaders.* Stanford University Graduate School of Business Research Paper No. 1970 (ssrn.com/abstract 5 937021).

Narang, P., Paladugu, A., Manda, S. R., Smock, W., Cosnay, C., & Lippmann, S. (2010). Do guns provide safety? At what cost? *Southern Medical Journal, 103,* 151–153.

Nario-Redmond, M. R. (2010). Cultural stereotypes of disabled and non-disabled men and women: Consensus for global category representations and diagnostic domains. *British Journal of Social Psychology, 49,* 471–488.

NASA. (2014, January 21). NASA finds 2013 sustained long-term climate warming trend, www.nasa.gov.

National Center for Health Statistics. (2004, December 15). Marital status and health: United States, 1999–2002 (by Charlotte A. Schoenborn). *Advance Data from Vital and Human Statistics,* No. 351. Centers for Disease Control and Prevention.

National Center for Health Statistics. (2008, August 6). National ambulatory medical care survey: 2006 summary. *National Health Statistics Report,* No. 3 (by D. K. Cherry, E. Hing, D. A. Woodwell, & E. A. Rechtsteiner). Centers for Disease Control and Prevention: National Center for Health Statistics (www.cdc.gov/nchs/data/nhsr/nhsr003.pdf).

National Safety Council. (2014). Traffic injury FAQ's. Retrieved April 1, 2015 from: http://www.nsc.org/learn/safety-knowledge/Pages/injury-facts-traffic-injury-faqs.aspx

Navarrete, C. D., McDonald, M. M., Molina, L. E., & Sidanius, J. (2010). Prejudice at the nexus of race and gender:

An outgroup male target hypothesis. *Journal of Personality and Social Psychology, 98,* 933–945.

NCADD–National Council of Alcoholism and Drug Dependence. (2014). Alcohol and crime (https://ncadd.org/learn-about-alcohol/alcohol-and-crime).

NCHS. (2010). National ambulatory medical care survey: 2010 summary tables. National Health Statistics Report, National Center for Health Statistics, Table 11 (www.cdc.gov/nchs/data/ahcd/namcs_summary/2010_namcs_web_tables.pdf).

Neal, D. T., & Chartrand, T. L. (2011). Embodied emotion perception: Amplifying and dampening facial feedback modulates emotion perception accuracy. *Social Psychological and Personality Science, 2,* 673–678.

Neff, K. D. (2011). Self-compassion, self-esteem, and well-being. *Social and Personality Psychology Compass, 5,* 1–12.

Neff, L. A., & Karney, B. R. (2005). To know you is to love you: The implications of global adoration and specific accuracy for marital relationships. *Journal of Personality and Social Psychology, 88,* 480–497.

Neimeyer, G. J., MacNair, R., Metzler, A. E., & Courchaine, K. (1991). Changing personal beliefs: Effects of forewarning, argument quality, prior bias, and personal exploration. *Journal of Social and Clinical Psychology, 10,* 1–20.

Nelson, L. D., & Morrison, E. L. (2005). The symptoms of resource scarcity: Judgments of food and finances influence preferences for potential partners. *Psychological Science, 16,* 167–173.

Nelson, L. J., & Miller, D. T. (1995). The distinctiveness effect in social categorization: You are what makes you unusual. *Psychological Science, 6,* 246.

Nelson, L., & LeBoeuf, R. (2002). *Why do men overperceive women's sexual intent? False consensus vs. evolutionary explanations.* Paper presented to the annual meeting of the Society for Personality and Social Psychology, Savannah, GA.

Nelson, T. E., Acker, M., & Manis, M. (1996). Everyday base rates (sex stereotypes): Potent and resilient. *Journal of Personality and Social Psychology, 59,* 664–675.

Nelson, T. E., Biernat, M. R., & Manis, M. (1990). Everyday base rates (sex stereotypes): Potent and resilient. *Journal of Personality and Social Psychology, 59,* 664–675.

Nemeth, C. (1979). The role of an active minority in intergroup relations. In W. G. Austin and S. Worchel (Eds.), *The social psychology of intergroup relations.* Monterey, CA: Brooks/Cole.

Nemeth, C., & Chiles, C. (1988). Modelling courage: The role of dissent in fostering independence. *European Journal of Social Psychology, 18,* 275–280.

Nemeth, C. J. (1997). Managing innovation: When less is more. *California Management Review, 40,* 59–74.

Nemeth, C. J. (1999). Behind the scenes. In D. G. Myers (Ed.), *Social psychology,* 6th edition. New York: McGraw-Hill.

Nemeth, C. J. (2011). Minority influence theory. In P. Van Lange, A. Kruglanski, & E. T. Higgins (Eds.), *Handbook of theories in social psychology.* New York: Sage.

Nemeth, C. J., Brown, K., & Rogers, J. (2001a). Devil's advocate versus authentic dissent: Stimulating quantity and quality. *European Journal of Social Psychology, 31,* 1–13.

Nemeth, C. J., Connell, J. B., Rogers, J. D., & Brown, K. S. (2001b). Improving decision making by means of dissent. *Journal of Applied Social Psychology, 31,* 48–58.

Nemeth, C. J., & Ormiston, M. (2007). Creative idea generation: Harmony versus stimulation. *European Journal of Social Psychology, 37,* 524–535.

Nemeth, C. J., Personnaz, B., Personnaz, M., & Goncalo, J. A. (2004). The liberating role of conflict in group creativity: A study in two countries. *European Journal of Social Psychology, 34,* 365–374.

Nemeth, C., & Wachtler, J. (1974). Creating the perceptions of consistency and confidence: A necessary condition for minority influence. *Sociometry, 37,* 529–540.

Nestler, S., Blank, H., & Egloff, B. (2010). Hindsight ≠ hindsight: Experimentally induced dissociations between hindsight components. *Journal of Experimental Psychology: Learning, Memory, and Cognition, 36,* 1399–1413.

Neumann, R., & Strack, F. (2000). Approach and avoidance: The influence of proprioceptive and exteroceptive cues on encoding of affective information. *Journal of Personality and Social Psychology, 79,* 39–48.

New Economic Foundation. (2009). National accounts of well-being: Bring real wealth onto the balance sheet. London: New Economics Foundation (www.neweconomics.org).

New Economic Foundation. (2011). Measuring our progress: The power of well-being. London: New Economics Foundation (www.neweconomics.org).

Newcomb, T. M. (1961). *The acquaintance process.* New York: Holt, Rinehart & Winston.

Newell, B., & Lagnado, D. (2003). Think-tanks, or think *tanks. The Psychologist, 16,* 176.

Newman, L. S. (1993). How individualists interpret behavior: Idiocentrism and spontaneous trait inference. *Social Cognition, 11,* 243–269.

Newman, M. L., Groom, C. J., Handelman, L. D., & Pennebaker, J. W. (2008). Gender differences in language use: An analysis of 14,000 text samples. *Discourse Processes, 45,* 211–236.

Newport, F. (2001, February 21). Americans see women as emotional and affectionate, men as more aggressive: Gender specific stereotypes persist in recent Gallup poll. (www.Gallup.com).

Newport, F. (2011). Americans prefer boys to girls, just as they did in 1941. www.gallup.com.

Newport, F. (2013, July 25). In U.S. 87% approve of Black-White marriage, vs. 4% in 1958. Gallup Poll (www.gallup.com).

Newport, F. (2014). In U.S., 42% believe creationist view of human origins. Gallup Organization. Retrieved March 27, 2015 from http://www.gallup.com/poll/170822/believe-creationist-view-human-origins.aspx

Newport, F., Moore, D. W., Jones, J. M., & Saad, L. (2003, March 21). Special release: American opinion on the war. *Gallup Poll Tuesday Briefing* (www.gallup.com/poll/tb/goverpubli/s0030325.asp).

Newton, P., & Meyer, D. (2013). Exploring the attitudes-action gap in household resource consumption: Does 'environmental lifestyle' segmentation align with consumer behaviour? *Sustainability, 5,* 1211–1233.

New York Times. (2010, April 25). Questions surround a delay in help for a dying man. www.nytimes.com.

New York Times. (2011, September 20). A grievous wrong. www.nytimes.com.

Ng, W., & Diener, E. (2014). What matters to the rich and the poor? Subjective well-being, financial satisfaction, and postmaterialist needs across the world. *Journal of Personality and Social Psychology, 107,* 326–338.

Nicholson, C. (2007, January). Framing science: Advances in theory and technology are fueling a new era in the science of persuasion. *APS Observer* (www.psychologicalscience.org).

Nicholson, I. (2011). "Torture at Yale": Experimental subjects, laboratory torment, and the "rehabilitiation" of Milgram's "Obedience to authority." *Theory and Psychology, 21,* 737–761.

Nie, N. H., & Erbring, L. (2000, February 17). *Internet and society: A preliminary report.* Stanford, CA: Stanford Institute for the Quantitative Study of Society.

Nielsen company. (2010). *U.S. homes add even more TV sets in 2010. Television Audience Report, 2009.* April 28, 2010.

Nielsen company. (2011, April). State of the media: Trends in TV viewing–2011 TV upfronts (http://www.nielsen.com/content/dam/corporate/us/en/newswire/uploads/2011/04/State-of-the-Media-2011-TV-Upfronts.pdf).

Nielsen, M. E. (1998). *Social psychology and religion on a trip to Ukraine.* Retrieved from http://psychwww.com/psyrelig/ukraine/index.htm)

Niemi, R. G., Mueller, J., & Smith, T. W. (1989). *Trends in public opinion: A compendium of survey data.* New York: Greenwood Press.

Nigbur, D., Lyons, E., & Uzzell, D. (2010). Attitudes, norms, identity and environmental behaviour: Using an expanded theory of planned behaviour to predict participation in a kerbside recycling programme. *British Journal of Social Psychology, 49,* 259–284.

Nigro, G. N., Hill, D. E., Gelbein, M. E., & Clark, C. L. (1988). Changes in the facial prominence of women and men over the last decade. *Psychology of Women Quarterly, 12,* 225–235.

Nijstad, B. A., & Stroebe, W. (2006). How the group affects the mind: A cognitive model of idea generation in groups. *Personality and Social Psychology Review, 10,* 186–213.

Nijstad, B. A., Stroebe, W., & Lodewijkx, H. F. M. (2006). The illusion of group productivity. A reduction of failures explanation. *European Journal of Social Psychology, 36,* 31–48.

Nisbet, E. K., & Zelenski, J. M. (2011). Underestimating nearby nature: Affective forecasting errors obscure the happy path to sustainability. *Psychological Science, 22,* 1101–1106.

Nisbett, R. (2003). *The geography of thought: How Asians and Westerners think differently . . . and why.* New York: Free Press.

Nisbett, R. E. (1990). Evolutionary psychology, biology, and cultural evolution. *Motivation and emotion, 14,* 255–263.

Nisbett, R. E. (1993). Violence and U.S. regional culture. *American Psychologist, 48,* 441–449.

Nisbett, R. E., Fong, G. T., Lehman, D. R., & Cheng, P. W. (1987). Teaching reasoning. *Science, 238,* 625–631.

Nisbett, R. E., & Masuda, T. (2003). Culture and point of view. *Proceedings of the National Academy of Sciences, 100,* 11163–11170.

Nisbett, R. E., & Ross, L. (1980). *Human inference: Strategies and shortcomings of social judgment.* Englewood Cliffs, NJ: Prentice-Hall.

Nix, G., Watson, C., Pyszczynski, T., & Greenberg, J. (1995). Reducing depressive affect through external focus of attention. *Journal of Social and Clinical Psychology, 14,* 36–52.

NOAA. (2014, July 12). 2013 state of the climate: Snow in the Northern Hemisphere. National Oceanic and Atmospheric Administration (www .climate.gov).

Noble, T. (2003). Nobody left to hate. *EQ Australia, 4,* 8–9.

Nocera, J. (2012, December 7). It's hard to be a hero. *New York Times* (www.nytimes .com).

Nock, M. K., Park, J. M., Finn, C. T., Deliberto, T. L., Dour, H. J., & Banaji, M. R. (2010). Measuring the suicidal mind: Implicit cognition predicts suicidal behavior. *Psychological Science, 21,* 511–517.

Noguchi, K., Albarracín, D., Durantini, M. R., & Glasman, L. R. (2007). Who

participates in which health promotion programs? A meta-analysis of motivations underlying enrollment and retention in HIV-Prevention interventions. *Psychological Bulletin, 133,* 955–975.

Nolan, S. A., Flynn, C., & Garber, J. (2003). Prospective relations between rejection and depression in young adolescents. *Journal of Personality and Social Psychology, 85,* 745–755.

Nolen-Hoeksema, S. (2003). *Women who think too much: How to break free of overthinking and reclaim your life.* New York: Holt.

Noller, P. (1996). What is this thing called love? Defining the love that supports marriage and family. *Personal Relationships, 3,* 97–115.

Noller, P., & Fitzpatrick, M. A. (1990). Marital communication in the eighties. *Journal of Marriage and Family, 52,* 832–843.

NORC. (1996). General Social Survey. National Opinion Research Center (sda. berkeley.edu/sdaweb/analysis/?dataset= gss12)

Nordgren, L. F., Banas, K., & MacDonald, G. (2011). Empathy gaps for social pain: Why people underestimate the pain of social suffering. *Journal of Personality and Social Psychology, 100,* 120–128.

Nordgren, L. F., van Harreveld, F., & van der Pligt, J. (2009). The restraint bias: How the illusion of self-restraint promotes impulsive behavior. *Psychological Science, 20,* 1523–1528.

Norem, J. K. (2000). Defensive pessimism, optimism, and pessimism. In E. C. Chang (Ed.), *Optimism and pessimism.* Washington, DC: APA Books.

Norem, J. K., & Cantor, N. (1986). Defensive pessimism: Harnessing anxiety as motivation. *Journal of Personality and Social Psychology, 51,* 1208–1217.

Norenzayan, A., & Heine, S. J. (2005). Psychological universals: What are they and how can we know? *Psychological Bulletin, 131,* 763–784.

North, A. C., Hargreaves, D. J., & McKendrick, J. (1997). In-store music affects product choice. *Nature, 390,* 132.

Norton, M. I., & Ariely, D. (2011). Building a better America—One wealth quintile at a time. *Perspectives on Psychological Science, 6,* 9–12.

Norton, M. I., Frost, J. H., & Ariely, D. (2007). Less is more: The lure of ambiguity, or why familiarity breeds contempt. *Journal of Personality and Social Psychology, 92,* 97–105.

Nosek, B. A. (2007). Implicit-explicit relations. *Current Directions in Psychological Science, 16,* 65–69.

Nosek, B. A., Hawkins, C. B., & Frazier, R. S. (2011). Implicit social cognition: From measures to mechanisms. *Trends in Cognitive Sciences, 15,* 152–159.

Notarius, C., & Markman, H. J. (1993). *We can work it out.* New York: Putnam.

Novelli, D., Drury, J., & Reicher, S. (2010). Come together: Two studies concerning the impact of group relations on 'personal space.' *British Journal of Social Psychology, 49,* 223–236.

Nowak, M. A. (2012, July). Why we help. *Scientific American,* 34–39.

Nowak, M. A., & Highfield, R. (2011). *Supercooperators: Altruism, evolution, and why we need each other to succeed.* New York: Free Press.

Nunez, N., Poole, D. A., & Memon, A. (2003). Psychology's two cultures revisited: Implications for the integration of science with practice. *Scientific Review of Mental Health Practice, 2,* 8–19.

Nurmi, J-E., & Salmela-Aro, K. (1997). Social strategies and loneliness: A prospective study. *Personality and Individual Differences, 23,* 205–215.

Nurmi, J-E., Toivonen, S., Salmela-Aro, K., & Eronen, S. (1996). Optimistic, approach-oriented, and avoidance strategies in social situations: Three studies on loneliness and peer relationships. *European Journal of Personality, 10,* 201–219.

Nuttin, J. M., Jr. (1987). Affective consequences of mere ownership: The name letter effect in twelve European languages. *European Journal of Social Psychology, 17,* 318–402.

Nyhan, B., & Reifler, J. (2008). *When corrections fail: The persistence of political misperceptions.* Unpublished manuscript, Duke University.

Oaten, M., & Cheng, K. (2006a). Improved self-control: The benefits of a regular program of academic study. *Basic and Applied Social Psychology, 28,* 1–16.

O'Brien, E., Konrath, S. H., Grühn, D., & Hagen, A. (2013). Empathic concern and perspective taking: Linear and quadratic effects of age across the adult life span. *The Journals Of Gerontology: Series B: Psychological Sciences And Social Sciences, 68B,* 168–175.

Oceja, L. (2008). Overcoming empathy-induced partiality: Two rules of thumb. *Basic and Applied Social Psychology, 30,* 176–182.

O'Connor, A. (2004, May 14). Pressure to go along with abuse is strong, but some soldiers find strength to refuse. *New York Times* (www.nytimes.com).

Oddone-Paolucci, E., Genuis, M., & Violato, C. (2000). A meta-analysis of the published research on the effects of pornography. In C. Violata (Ed.), *The changing family and child development.* Aldershot, England: Ashgate Publishing.

O'Dea, T. F. (1968). Sects and cults. In D. L. Sills (Ed.), *International encyclopedia of the social sciences* (Vol. 14). New York: Macmillan.

O'Donovan, A., Neylan, T. C., Metzler, T., & Cohen, B. E. (2012). Lifetime exposure to traumatic psychological stress is associated with elevated inflammation in the heart and soul study. *Brain, Behavior, and Immunity, 26,* 642–649.

Ohbuchi, K., & Kambara, T. (1985). Attacker's intent and awareness of outcome, impression management, and retaliation. *Journal of Experimental Social Psychology, 21,* 321–330.

O'Hegarty, M., Pederson, L. L., Yenokyan, G., Nelson, D., & Wortley, P. (2007). Young adults' perceptions of cigarette warning labels in the United States and Canada. *Preventing Chronic Disease: Public Health Research, Practice, and Policy, 30,* 467–473.

Ohtaki, P. (1999, March 24). *Internment-camp reporter makes homecoming visit.* Associated Press. Reprinted in P. T. Ohtaki (Ed.), *It was the right thing to do!* (Self-published collection of Walt and Mildred Woodward–related correspondence and articles).

Oishi, S., & Diener, E. (2014). Residents of poor nations have a greater sense of meaning in life than residents of wealthy nations. Psychological Science, *25,* 422–430.

Oishi, S., Kesebir, S., & Diener, E. (2011). Income inequality and happiness. *Psychological Science, 22,* 1095–1100.

Oishi, S., Rothman, A. J., Snyder, M., Su, J., Zehm, K., Hertel, A. W., Gonzales, M. H., & Sherman, G. D. (2007). The socioecological model of procommunity action: The benefits of residential stability. *Journal of Personality and Social Psychology, 93,* 831–844.

O'Keefe, D. J., & Jensen, J. D. (2011). The relative effectiveness of gain-framed and loss-framed persuasive appeals concerning obesity-related behaviors: Meta-analytic evidence and implications. In R. Batra, P. A. Keller, & V. J. Strecher (Eds.), *Leveraging consumer psychology for effective health communications: The obesity challenge* (pp. 171–185). Armonk, NY: Sharpe.

Okimoto, T. G., & Brescoll, V. L. (2010). The price of power: Power seeking and backlash against female politicians. *Personality and Social Psychology Bulletin, 36,* 923–936.

O'Leary, K. D., Christian, J. L., & Mendell, N. R. (1994). A closer look at the link between marital discord and depressive symptomatology. *Journal of Social and Clinical Psychology, 13,* 33–41.

Olfson, M., & Pincus, H. A. (1994). Outpatient therapy in the United States: II. Patterns of utilization. *American Journal of Psychiatry, 151,* 1289–1294.

Oliner, S. P., & Oliner, P. M. (1988). *The altruistic personality: Rescuers of Jews in Nazi Europe.* New York: Free Press.

Olson, I. R., & Marshuetz, C. (2005). Facial attractiveness is appraised in a glance. *Emotion, 5,* 498–502.

Olson, J. M., & Cal, A. V. (1984). Source credibility, attitudes, and the recall of past behaviours. *European Journal of Social Psychology, 14,* 203–210.

Olson, J. M., Roese, N. J., & Zanna, M. P. (1996). Expectancies. In E. T. Higgins & A. W. Kruglanski (Eds.), *Social psychology: Handbook of basic principles* (pp. 211–238). New York: Guilford.

Olson, K. R., Dunham, Y., Dweck, C. S., Spelke, E. S., & Banaji, M. R. (2008). Judgments of the lucky across development and culture. *Journal of Personality and Social Psychology, 94,* 757–776.

Olweus, D. (1979). Stability of aggressive reaction patterns in males: A review. *Psychological Bulletin, 86,* 852–875.

Olweus, D., & Breivik, K. (2013). The plight of victims of school bullying: The opposite of well-being. In B. A. Asher, F. Casas, I. Frones, & J. E. Korbin, (Eds.), *International Handbook of Child Well-Being.* Heidelberg, Germany: Springer.

Omoto, A. M., & Snyder, M. (2002). Considerations of community: The context and process of volunteerism. *American Behavioral Scientist, 45,* 846–867.

Onraet, E., Dhont, K., & Van Hiel, A. (2014). The relationships between internal and external threats and right-wing attitudes: A three-wave longitudinal study. *Personality and Social Psychology Bulletin, 40,* 712–725.

Opotow, S. (1990). Moral exclusion and injustice: An introduction. *Journal of Social Issues, 46,* 1–20.

Oppenheimer, D. M., & Trail, T. E. (2010). Why leaning to the left makes you lean to the left: Effect of spatial orientation on political attitudes. *Social Cognition, 28,* 651–661.

Orenstein, P. (2003, July 6). Where have all the Lisas gone? *New York Times* (www .nytimes.com).

Organisation for Economic Co-operation and Development. (2014, December). Focus on inequality and growth, www .oecd.org.

Orgaz, C., Estévez, A., & Matute, H. (2013). Pathological gamblers are more vulnerable to the illusion of control in a standard associative learning task. Frontiers in Psychology, 4doi:10.3389/fpsyg.2013.00306

Oriña, M. M., Collins, W. A., Simpson, J. A., Salvatore, J. E., Haydon, K. C., & Kim, J. S. (2011). Developmental and dyadic perspectives on commitment in adult romantic relationships. *Psychological Science, 22,* 908–915.

Orive, R. (1984). Group similarity, public self-awareness, and opinion extremity: A social projection explanation of deindividuation effects. *Journal of Personality and Social Psychology, 47,* 727–737.

Ornstein, R. (1991). *The evolution of consciousness: Of Darwin, Freud, and cranial fire: The origins of the way we think.* New York: Prentice-Hall.

Orr, R., McKeown, S., Cairns, E., & Stringer, M. (2012). Examining non-racial segregation: A micro-ecological approach. *British Journal of Social Psychology, 51,* 717–723.

Ortega, R., Elipe, P., Mora-Merchan, J. A., Genta, M. L., Brighi, A., Guarini, A., Smith, P. K., Thompson, F., & Tippett, N. (2012). The emotional impact of bullying and cyberbullying on victims: A European Cross-national study. *Aggressive Behavior, 38,* 342–356.

Orth, U., & Robins, R. W. (2013). Understanding the link between low self-esteem and depression. *Current Directions in Psychological Science, 22,* 455–460.

Osborne, D., & Sibley, C. G. (2013). Through rose-colored glasses: System-justifying beliefs dampen the effects of relative deprivation on well-being and political mobilization. *Personality and Social Psychology Bulletin, 39,* 991–1004.

Osborne, J. W. (1995). Academics, self-esteem, and race: A look at the underlying assumptions of the disidentification hypothesis. *Personality and Social Psychology Bulletin, 21,* 449–455.

Osgood, C. E. (1962). *An alternative to war or surrender.* Urbana, IL: University of Illinois Press.

Osgood, C. E. (1980). GRIT: A strategy for survival in mankind's nuclear age? Paper presented at the Pugwash Conference on New Directions in Disarmament, Racine, WI.

Oskamp, S. (1991). Curbside recycling: Knowledge, attitudes, and behavior. Paper presented at the Society for Experimental Social Psychology meeting, Columbus, OH.

Osofsky, M. J., Bandura, A., & Zimbardo, P. G. (2005). The role of moral disengagement in the execution process. *Law and Human Behavior, 29,* 371–393.

Osterhouse, R. A., & Brock, T. C. (1970). Distraction increases yielding to propaganda by inhibiting counterarguing. *Journal of Personality and Social Psychology, 15,* 344–358.

Ostrom, E. (2014). Do institutions for collective action evolve? *Journal of Bioeconomics, 16,* 3–30.

Ostrom, T. M., & Sedikides, C. (1992). Out-group homogeneity effects in natural and minimal groups. *Psychological Bulletin, 112,* 536–552.

Oswald, A. (2006, January 19). The hippies were right all along about happiness. *Financial Times, 15.*

Oswald, F. L., Mitchell, G., Blanton, H., Jaccard, J., & Tetlock, P. E. (2013). Predicting ethnic and racial discrimination: A meta-analysis of IAT criterion studies. *Journal of Personality and Social Psychology, 105,* 171–192.

Otten, M., & Jonas, K. J. (2013). Out of the group, out of control? The brain responds to social exclusion with changes in cognitive control. *Scan, 8,* 789–794.

Ouellette, J. A., & Wood, W. (1998). Habit and intention in everyday life: The multiple processes by which past behavior predicts future behavior. *Psychological Bulletin, 124,* 54–74.

Oxfam International (2005, December). Oxfam tsunami accountability report. (https://www.oxfam.org/sites/www.oxfam.org/files/tsunami_0.pdf).

Oyserman, D., Coon, H. M., & Kemmelmeier, M. (2002a). Rethinking individualism and collectivism: Evaluation of theoretical assumptions and meta-analyses. *Psychological Bulletin, 128,* 3–72.

Oyserman, D., Kemmelmeier, M., & Coon, H. M. (2002b). Cultural psychology, a new look: Reply to Bond (2002), Fiske (2002), Kitayama (2002), and Miller (2002). *Psychological Bulletin, 128,* 110–117.

Packer, D. J. (2008). Identifying systematic disobedience in Milgram's obedience experiments: A meta-analytic review. *Perspectives on Psychological Science, 3(4),* 301–304.

Packer, D. J. (2009). Avoiding groupthink: Whereas weakly identified members remain silent, strongly identified members dissent about collective problems. *Psychological Science, 20,* 546–548.

Padgett, V. R. (1989). Predicting organizational violence: An application of 11 powerful principles of obedience. Paper presented at the American Psychological Association convention.

Page, S. E. (2007). *The difference: How the power of diversity creates better groups, firms, schools, and societies.* Princeton, NJ: Princeton University Press.

Palazzolo, J. (2013). Racial gap in men's sentencing. Wall Street Journal, February 14, 2013. http://www.wsj.com/articles/SB10001424127887324432004578304463789858002.

Pallak, S. R., Murroni, E., & Koch, J. (1983). Communicator attractiveness and expertise, emotional versus rational appeals, and persuasion: A heuristic versus systematic processing interpretation. *Social Cognition, 2,* 122–141.

Palmer, D. L. (1996). Determinants of Canadian attitudes toward immigration: More than just racism? *Canadian Journal of Behavioural Science, 28,* 180–192.

Palmer, E. L., & Dorr, A. (Eds.) (1980). *Children and the faces of television: Teaching, violence, selling.* New York: Academic Press.

Palmer, T. (2014). Record-breaking winters and global climate change. *Science, 344,* 803.

Paluck, E. L. (2010). Is it better not to talk? Group polarization, extended contact, and perspective taking in Eastern Democratic Republic of Congo. *Personality and Social Psychology Bulletin, 36,* 1170–1185.

Pandey, J., Sinha, Y., Prakash, A., & Tripathi, R. C. (1982). Right–left political ideologies and attribution of the causes of poverty. *European Journal of Social Psychology, 12,* 327–331.

Pantell, M., Rehkopf, D., Jutte, D., Syme, S. L., Balmes, J., & Adler, N. (2013). Social isolation: A predictor of mortality comparable to traditional clinical risk factors. *American Journal of Public Health, 103,* 2056–2062.

Paolini, S., Harwood, J., Rubin, M., Husnu, S., Joyce, N., Hewstone, M. (2014). Positive and extensive intergroup contact in the past buffers against the disproportionate impact of negative contact in the present. *European Journal of Social Psychology, 44,* 548–562.

Paolini, S., Hewstone, M., Cairns, E., & Voci, A. (2004). Effects of direct and indirect cross-group friendships on judgments of Catholics and Protestants in Northern Ireland: The mediating role of an anxiety-reduction mechanism. *Personality and Social Psychology Bulletin, 30,* 770–786.

Pape, R. A. (2003, September 22). Dying to kill us. *New York Times* (www.nytimes.com).

Parachin, V. M. (1992, December). Four brave chaplains. *Retired Officer Magazine,* 24–26.

Parashar, U. D., Gibson, C. J., Bresse, J. S., & Glass, R. I. (2006). Rotavirus and severe childhood diarrhea. *Emerging Infectious Diseases, 12,* 304–306.

Pardini, D. A., Raine, A., Erickson, K., & Loeber, R. (2014). Low amygdala volume in men is associated with childhood aggression, early psychopathic traits, and future violence. *Biological Psychiatry, 75,* 73–80.

Park, A., Ickes, W., & Robinson, R. L. (2014). More f#!%ing rudeness: Reliable personality predictors of verbal rudeness and other ugly confrontational behaviors. *Journal of Aggression, Conflict, and Peace Research, 6,* 26–43.

Park, B., & Rothbart, M. (1982). Perception of out-group homogeneity and levels of social categorization: Memory for the subordinate attributes of in-group and out-group members. *Journal of Personality and Social Psychology, 42,* 1051–1068.

Park, H., Coello, J. A., & Lau, A. S. (2014). Child socialization goals in East Asian versus Western nations from 1989 to 2010: Evidence for social change in parenting. *Parenting: Science and Practice, 14,* 69–91.

Park, J., Malachi, E., Sternin, O., & Tevet, R. (2009). Subtle bias against Muslim job applicants in personnel decisions. *Journal of Applied Social Psychology, 39,* 2174–2190.

Park, L. E., Streamer, L., Huang, L., & Galinsky, A. D. (2013). Stand tall, but don't put your feet up: Universal and culturally-specific effects of expansive postures on power. *Journal of Experimental Social Psychology, 49,* 965–971.

Pascarella, E. T., & Terenzini, P. T. (1991). *How college affects students: Findings and insights from twenty years of research.* San Francisco: Jossey-Bass.

Patten, E., & Parker, K. (2012). A gender reversal on career aspirations (http://www.pewsocialtrends.org/2012/04/19/a-gender-reversal-on-career-aspirations/).

Patterson, D. (1996). *When learned men murder.* Bloomington, IN: Phi Delta Kappan.

Patterson, G. R., Chamberlain, P., & Reid, J. B. (1982). A comparative evaluation of parent training procedures. *Behavior Therapy, 13,* 638–650.

Patterson, G. R., Littman, R. A., & Bricker, W. (1967). Assertive behavior in children: A step toward a theory of aggression. *Monographs of the Society of Research in Child Development* (Serial No. 113), *32,* 5.

Patterson, M. L. (2008). Back to social behavior: Mining the mundane. *Basic and Applied Social Psychology, 30,* 93–101.

Patterson, M. L., Iizuka, Y., Tubbs, M. E., Ansel, J., Tsutsumi, M., & Anson, J. (2007). Passing encounters east and west: Comparing Japanese and American pedestrian interactions. *Journal of Nonverbal Behavior, 31,* 155–166.

Patterson, T. E. (1980). The role of the mass media in presidential campaigns: The lessons of the 1976 election. *Items, 34,* 25–30. Social Science Research Council, 605 Third Avenue, New York, NY 10016.

Paulhus, D. (1982). Individual differences, self-presentation, and cognitive dissonance: Their concurrent operation in forced compliance. *Journal of Personality and Social Psychology, 43,* 838–852.

Paulhus, D. L. (1998). Interpersonal and intrapsychic adaptiveness of trait self-enhancement: A mixed blessing? *Journal of Personality and Social Psychology, 74,* 1197–1208.

Paulhus, D. L., & Lim, D. T. K. (1994). Arousal and evaluative extremity in social judgments: A dynamic complexity model. *European Journal of Social Psychology, 24,* 89–99.

Paulhus, D. L., & Morgan, K. L. (1997). Perceptions of intelligence in leaderless groups: The dynamic effects of shyness and acquaintance. *Journal of Personality and Social Psychology, 72,* 581–591.

Paulhus, D. L., Westlake, B. G., Calvez, S. S., & Harms, P. D. (2013). Self-presentation style in job interviews: The role of personality and culture. *Journal of Applied Social Psychology, 43,* 2042–2059.

Paulhus, D. L., & Williams, K. M. (2002). The Dark Triad of personality: Narcissism, Machiavellianism and psychopathy. *Journal of Research in Personality, 36,* 556–563.

Paulus, P. B., & Coskun, H. (2012). Group creativity: Understanding collaborative creativity processes. In J. M. Levine (Ed.), *Group processes.* Boca Raton, FL: Psychology Press.

Paulus, P. B., Dzindolet, M., & Kohn, N. W. (2011). Collaborative creativity—Group creativity and team innovation. In M. D. Mumford (Ed.), *Handbook of organizational creativity.* New York: Elsevier.

Paulus, P. B., Kohn, N. W., & Arditti, L. E. (2011). Effect of quantity and quality instructions on brainstorming. *Journal of Creative Behavior, 45,* 38–46.

Paulus, P. B., & Korde, R. (2014). How to get the most creativity and innovation out of groups and teams. In K. Thomas & J. Chan (Eds.), *Handbook of Research on Creativity.* Northhampton, MA: Edward Elgar Publishing.

Paulus, P. B., Larey, T. S., & Dzindolet, M. T. (2000). Creativity in groups and teams. In M. Turner (Ed.), *Groups at work: Advances in theory and research.* Hillsdale, NJ: Hampton.

Paulus, P. B., Larey, T. S., & Ortega, A. H. (1995). Performance and perceptions of brainstormers in an organizational setting. *Basic and Applied Social Psychology, 17,* 249–265.

Pawlenko, N. B., Safer, M. A., Wise, R. A., & Holfeld, B. (2013). A teaching aid for improving jurors' assessments of eyewitness accuracy. *Applied Cognitive Psychology, 27,* 190–197.

Payne, B. K. (2001). Prejudice and perception: The role of automatic and controlled processes in misperceiving a weapon. *Journal of Personality and Social Psychology, 81,* 181–192.

Payne, B. K. (2006). Weapon bias: Split-second decisions and unintended stereotyping. *Current Directions in Psychological Science, 15,* 287–291.

Payne, B. K., Krosnick, J. A., Pasek, J., Lelkes, Y., Akhtar, O., & Tompson, T. (2010). Implicit and explicit prejudice in the 2008 American presidential election. *Journal of Experimental Social Psychology, 46,* 367–374.

Pchelin, P., & Howell, R. T. (2014). The hidden cost of value-seeking: People do not accurately forecast the economic benefits of experiential purchases. *The Journal of Positive Psychology, 9,* 322–334.

Pedersen, A., & Walker, I. (1997). Prejudice against Australian Aborigines: Old-fashioned and modern forms. *European Journal of Social Psychology, 27,* 561–587.

Pedersen, A., Zachariae, R., & Bovbjerg, D. H. (2010). Influence of psychological stress on upper respiratory infection—A meta-analysis of prospective studies. *Psychosomatic Medicine, 72,* 823–832.

Pedersen, W. C., Bushman, B. J., Vasquez, E. A., & Miller, N. (2008). Kicking the (barking) dog effect: The moderating role of target attributes on triggered displaced aggression. *Personality and Social Psychology Bulletin, 34,* 1382–1395.

Pedersen, W. C., Gonzales, C., & Miller, N. (2000). The moderating effect of trivial triggering provocation on displaced aggression. *Journal of Personality and Social Psychology, 78,* 913–927.

Peetz, J., & Buehler, R. (2009). Is there a budget fallacy? The role of savings goals in the prediction of personal spending.

Personality and Social Psychology Bulletin, 35, 1579–1591.

Peetz, J., Buehler, R., & Britten, K. (2011). Only minutes a day: Reframing exercise duration affects exercise intentions and behavior. *Basic and Applied Social Psychology, 33,* 118–127.

Pegalis, L. J., Shaffer, D. R., Bazzini, D. G., & Greenier, K. (1994). On the ability to elicit self-disclosure: Are there gender-based and contextual limitations on the opener effect? *Personality and Social Psychology Bulletin, 20,* 412–420.

Pelham, B., & Carvallo, M. (2011). The surprising potency of implicit egotism: A reply to Simonsohn. *Journal of Personality and Social Psychology, 101,* 25–30.

Pelham, B., & Crabtree, S. (2008, October 8). *Worldwide, highly religious more likely to help others: Pattern holds throughout the world and across major religions.* Gallup Poll (www.gallup.com).

Pelham, B. W. (2009, October 22). About one in six Americans report history of depression. www.gallup.com.

Pelham, B. W., Mirenberg, M. C., & Jones, J. T. (2002). Why Susie sells seashells by the seashore: Implicit egotism and major life decisions. *Journal of Personality and Social Psychology, 82,* 469–487.

Pelonero, C. (2014). *Kitty Genovese: A true account of a public murder and its private consequences.* New York: Skyhorse.

Pennebaker, J. (1990). *Opening up: The healing power of confiding in others.* New York: William Morrow.

Pennebaker, J. W. (1982). *The psychology of physical symptoms.* New York: Springer-Verlag.

Pennebaker, J. W. (2011). *The secret life of pronouns: What our words say about us.* New York: Bloomsbury Press.

Pennebaker, J. W., & Lay, T. C. (2002). Language use and personality during crises: Analyses of Mayor Rudolph Giuliani's press conferences. *Journal of Research in Personality, 36,* 271–282.

Pennebaker, J. W., & O'Heeron, R. C. (1984). Confiding in others and illness rate among spouses of suicide and accidental death victims. *Journal of Abnormal Psychology, 93,* 473–476.

Penner, L. A. (2002). Dispositional and organizational influences on sustained volunteerism: An interactionist perspective. *Journal of Social Issues, 58,* 447–467.

Penner, L. A., Dertke, M. C., & Achenbach, C. J. (1973). The "flash" system: A field study of altruism. *Journal of Applied Social Psychology, 3,* 362–370.

Pennington, N., & Hastie, R. (1993). The story model for juror decision making. In R. Hastie (Ed.), *Inside the juror: The psychology of juror decision making.* New York: Cambridge University Press.

Penrod, S., & Cutler, B. L. (1987). Assessing the competence of juries. In I. B. Weiner & A. K. Hess (Eds.), *Handbook of forensic psychology.* New York: Wiley.

Pentland, A. (2010). To signal is human. *American Scientist, 98,* 204–211.

Penton-Voak, I. S., Jones, B. C., Little, A. C., Baker, S., Tiddeman, B., Burt, D. M., & Perrett, D. I. (2001). Symmetry, sexual dimorphism in facial proportions and male facial attractiveness. *Proceedings of the Royal Society of London, 268,* 1–7.

Peplau, L. A., & Fingerhut, A. W. (2007). The close relationships of lesbians and gay men. *Annual Review of Psychology, 58,* 405–424.

Pereira, C., Vala, J., & Costa-Lopes, R. (2010). From prejudice to discrimination: The legitimizing role of perceived threat in discrimination against immigrants. *European Journal of Social Psychology, 40,* 1231–1250.

Perilloux, H. K., Webster, G. D., & Gaulin, S. J. C. (2010). Signals of genetic quality and maternal investment capacity: The dynamic effects of fluctuating asymmetry and waist-to-hip ratio on men's ratings of women's attractiveness. *Social Psychology and Personality Science, 1,* 34–42.

Perls, F. S. (1972). Gestalt therapy [interview]. In A. Bry (Ed.), *Inside psychotherapy.* New York: Basic Books.

Perls, F. S. (1973, July). *Ego, hunger and aggression: The beginning of Gestalt therapy.* Random House, 1969. Cited by Berkowitz in The case for bottling up rage. *Psychology Today, 24–30.*

Perrett, D. (2010). *In your face: The new science of human attraction.* New York: Palgrave Macmillan.

Perry, A., Rubinsten, O., Peled, L., & Shamay-Tsoory, S. G. (2013). Don't stand so close to me: A behavioral and ERP study of preferred interpersonal distance. *NeuroImage, 83,* 761–769.

Perry, G. (2013). *Behind the Shock Machine: The Untold Story of the Notorious Milgram Psychology Experiments.* New York: New Press.

Perry, G. (2014). The view from the boys. *Psychologist, 27,* 834–836.

Persico, N., Postlewaite, A., & Silverman, D. (2004). The effect of adolescent experience on labor market outcomes: The case of height. *Journal of Political Economy, 112,* 1019–1053.

Pessin, J. (1933). The comparative effects of social and mechanical stimulation on memorizing. *American Journal of Psychology, 45,* 263–270.

Pessin, J., & Husband, R. W. (1933). Effects of social stimulation on human maze learning. *Journal of Abnormal and Social Psychology, 28,* 148–154.

Peters, E., Romer, D., Slovic, P., Jamieson, K. H., Whasfield, L., Mertz, C. K., & Carpenter, S. M. (2007). The impact and acceptability of Canadian-style cigarette warning labels among U.S. smokers and nonsmokers. *Nicotine and Tobacco Research, 9,* 473–481.

Petersen, J. L., & Hyde, J. S. (2011). Gender differences in sexual attitudes and behaviors: A review of meta-analytic results and large datasets. *Journal of Sex Research, 48,* 149–165.

Peterson, C., Bishop, M. P., Fletcher, C. W., Kaplan, M. R., Yesko, E. S., Moon, C. H., et al. (2001). Explanatory style as a risk factor for traumatic mishaps. *Cognitive Therapy and Research, 25,* 633–649.

Peterson, C. K., & Harmon-Jones, E. (2012). Anger and testosterone: Evidence that situationally-induced anger relates to situationally-induced testosterone. *Emotion, 12,* 899–902.

Peterson, C., & Seligman, M. E. P. (1987). Explanatory style and illness. *Journal of Personality, 55,* 237–265.

Peterson, C., Seligman, M. E. P., & Vaillant, G. E. (1988). Pessimistic explanatory style is a risk factor for physical illness: A thirty-five-year longitudinal study. *Journal of Personality and Social Psychology, 55,* 23–27.

Peterson, C., & Steen, T. A. (2002). Optimistic explanatory style. In C. R. Snyder & S. J. Lopez (Ed.), *Handbook of positive psychology.* London: Oxford University Press.

Peterson, E. (1992). *Under the unpredictable plant.* Grand Rapids, MI: Eerdmans.

Peterson, J. L., & Zill, N. (1981). Television viewing in the United States and children's intellectual, social, and emotional development. *Television and Children, 2(2),* 21–28.

Petraitis, J. M., Lampman, C. B., Boeckmann, R. J., & Falconer, E. M. (2014). Sex differences in the attractiveness of hunter-gatherer and modern risks. *Journal of Applied Social Psychology, 44,* 442–453.

Petrocelli, J. V., Percy, E. J., Sherman, S. J., & Tormala, Z. L. (2011). Counterfactual potency. *Journal of Personality and Social Psychology, 100,* 30–46.

Pettigrew, T. F. (1958). Personality and socio-cultural factors in intergroup attitudes: A cross-national comparison. *Journal of Conflict Resolution, 2,* 29–42.

Pettigrew, T. F. (1969). Racially separate or together? *Journal of Social Issues, 2,* 43–69.

Pettigrew, T. F. (1979). The ultimate attribution error: Extending Allport's cognitive analysis of prejudice. *Personality and Social Psychology Bulletin, 55,* 461–476.

Pettigrew, T. F. (1980). Prejudice. In S. Thernstrom et al. (Eds.), *Harvard encyclopedia of American ethnic groups.* Cambridge, MA: Harvard University Press.

Pettigrew, T. F. (1986). The intergroup contact hypothesis reconsidered. In M. Hewstone & R. Brown (Eds.), *Contact and conflict in intergroup encounters.* Oxford: Blackwell.

Pettigrew, T. F. (1988). Advancing racial justice: Past lessons for future use. Paper for the University of Alabama conference "Opening Doors: An appraisal of Race Relations in America."

Pettigrew, T. F. (1997). Generalized intergroup contact effects on prejudice. *Personality and Social Psychology Bulletin, 23,* 173–185.

Pettigrew, T. F. (2004). Intergroup contact: Theory, research, and new perspectives. In J. A. Banks & C. A. McGee Banks (Eds.), *Handbook of research on multicultural education.* San Francisco: Jossey-Bass.

Pettigrew, T. F. (2006). A two-level approach to anti-immigrant prejudice and discrimination. In R. Mahalingam (Ed.), *Cultural psychology of immigrants.* Mahwah, NJ: Erlbaum.

Pettigrew, T. F., Christ, O., Wagner, U., Meertens, R. W., van Dick, R., & Zick, A. (2008). Relative deprivation and intergroup prejudice. *Journal of Social Issues, 64,* 385–401.

Pettigrew, T. F., Jackson, J. S., Brika, J. B., Lemaine, G., Meertens, R. W., Wagner, U., & Zick, A. (1998). Outgroup prejudice in western Europe. *European Review of Social Psychology, 8,* 241–273.

Pettigrew, T. F., & Tropp, L. R. (2008). How does intergroup contact reduce prejudice? Meta-analytic tests of three mediators. *European Journal of Social Psychology, 38,* 922–934.

Pettigrew, T. F., & Tropp, L. R. (2011). *When groups meet: The dynamics of intergroup contact.* New York: Psychology Press.

Pettigrew, T. F., Wagner, U., & Christ, O. (2010). Population ratios and prejudice: Modeling both contact and threat effects. *Journal of Ethnic and Migration Studies, 36,* 635–650.

Petty, R. E., Barden, J., & Wheeler, S. C. (2009). The Elaboration Likelihood Model of persuasion: Developing health promotions for sustained behavioral change. In R. J. DiClemente, R. A. Crosby, & M. C. Kegler (Eds.), *Emerging theories in health promotion practice and research,* 2nd ed. San Francisco: Jossey-Bass.

Petty, R. E., & Briñol, P. (2008). Persuasion: From single to multiple to metacognitive processes. *Perspectives on Psychological Science, 3,* 137–147.

Petty, R. E., & Cacioppo, J. T. (1986). *Communication and persuasion: Central and peripheral routes to attitude change.* New York: Springer-Verlag.

Petty, R. E., Cacioppo, J. T., & Goldman, R. (1981). Personal involvement as a determinant of argument-based persuasion. *Journal of Personality and Social Psychology, 41,* 847–855.

Petty, R. E., Haugtvedt, C. P., & Smith, S. M. (1995). Elaboration as a determinant of attitude strength: Creating attitudes that are persistent, resistant, and predictive of behavior. In R. E. Petty & J. A. Krosnick (Eds.), *Attitude strength: Antecedents and consequences.* Hillsdale, NJ: Erlbaum.

Petty, R. E., Schumann, D. W., Richman, S. A., & Strathman, A. J. (1993). Positive mood and persuasion: Different roles for affect under high and low elaboration conditions. *Journal of Personality and Social Psychology, 64,* 5–20.

Petty, R. E., & Wegener, D. T. (1998). Attitude change: Multiple roles for persuasion variables. In D. Gilbert, S. Fiske, & G. Lindzey (Eds.), *Handbook of social psychology,* 4th edition. New York: McGraw-Hill.

Pew Research Center. (2003). *Views of a changing world 2003. The Pew Global Attitudes Project.* Washington, DC: Pew Research Center for the People and the Press (people-press.org/reports/pdf/185.pdf).

Pew Research Center. (2006, March 30). *America's immigration quandary.* Pew Research Center (www.peoplepress.org).

Pew Research Center. (2007b, July 18). *Modern marriage: "I like hugs. I like kisses. But what I really love is help with the dishes."* Pew Research Center (pewresearch.org).

Pew Research Center. (2008). *Video Gamers Galore (*pewresearch.org/databank/dailynumber/?NumberID5787).

Pew Research Center. (2010). Gender equality universally embraced, but inequalities acknowledged. Global Attitudes Project (http://www.pewglobal.org/files/2010/07/Pew-Global-Attitudes-2010-Gender-Report-July-1-12-01AM-EDT-NOT-EMBARGOED.pdf).

Pew Research Center. (2010d, August 19). Growing number of Americans say Obama is a Muslim. Pew Research Center (www.pewresearch.org).

Pew Research Center. (2011, January 27). *The future of the global Muslim population: Projections for 2010–2030.* www.pewforum.org.

Pew Research Center. (2011, July 21). *Muslim-Western tensions persist: Common concerns about Islamic extremism.* Pew Global Attitudes Project (www.pewresearch.org).

Pew Research Center. (2012, June 4). Section 8: Values about immigration and race. Pew Research Center for the People & the Press (www.people-press.org).

Pew Research Center. (2013). Big racial divide over Zimmerman verdict. July 22, 2013.

Pew Research Center. (2013). Modern parenthood. March 13, 2013 (http://www.pewsocialtrends.org/2013/03/14/modern-parenthood-slideshow/modernparenthood/).

Pew Research Center. (2013, June 13). A survey of LGBT Americans. Pew Research Center (www.pewsocialtrends.org).

Pew Research Center. (2014). Global views on morality. Pew Research Global Attitudes Project (www.pewglobal.org).

Pew Research Center. (2014). The Web at 25 in the U.S., http://www.pewinternet.org/2014/02/27/the-web-at-25-in-the-u-s/.

Pew Research Center. (2014, January 27). Climate change: Key data points from Pew research. Washington, DC: Pew Research Center (www.pewresearch.org).

Pew Research Center. (2014, August 28). As new dangers loom, more think the U.S.

does "too little" to solve world problems. Pew Research Center for the People & the Press (www.people-press.org).

Pfaff, D. W. (2014). *The altruistic brain: How we are natural good.* New York: Oxford University Press.

Pfaff, L. A., Boatwright, K. J., Potthoff, A. L., Finan, C., Ulrey, L. A., & Huber, D. M. (2013). Perceptions of women and men leaders following 360-degree feedback evaluations. *Performance Improvement Quarterly, 26,* 35–56.

Phelan, J. E., & Rudman, L. A. (2010). Reactions to ethnic deviance: The role of backlash in racial stereotype maintenance. *Journal of Personality and Social Psychology, 99,* 265–281.

Phillips, A. L. (2011). A walk in the woods. *American Scientist, 69,* 301–302.

Phillips, D. L. (2003, September 20). Listening to the wrong Iraqi. *New York Times* (www.nytimes.com).

Phillips, T. (2004, April 3). Quoted by T. Baldwin & D. Rozenberg, "Britain 'must scrap multiculturalism.'" *The Times,* p. A1.

Phinney, J. S. (1990). Ethnic identity in adolescents and adults: Review of research. *Psychological Bulletin, 108,* 499–514.

Pichon, I., Boccato, G., & Saroglou, V. (2007). Nonconscious influences of religion on prosociality: A priming study. *European Journal of Social Psychology, 37,* 1032–1045.

Pickett, K., & Wilkinson, R. (2011). *The spirit level: Why greater equality makes societies stronger.* New York: Bloomsbury.

Piliavin, J. A. (2003). Doing well by doing good: Benefits for the benefactor. In C. L. M. Keyes & J. Haidt (Eds.), *Flourishing: Positive psychology and the life well-lived.* Washington, DC: American Psychological Association.

Piliavin, J. A., Evans, D. E., & Callero, P. (1982). Learning to "Give to unnamed strangers": The process of commitment to regular blood donation. In E. Staub, D. Bar-Tal, J. Karylowski, & J. Reykawski (Eds.), *The development and maintenance of prosocial behavior: International perspectives.* New York: Plenum.

Piliavin, J. A., & Piliavin, I. M. (1973). *The Good Samaritan: Why does he help?* Unpublished manuscript, University of Wisconsin.

Pincus, J. H. (2001). *Base instincts: What makes killers kill?* New York: Norton.

Pinel, E. C. (1999). Stigma consciousness: The psychological legacy of social stereotypes. *Journal of Personality and Social Psychology, 76,* 114–128.

Pinel, E. C. (2002). Stigma consciousness in intergroup contexts: The power of conviction. *Journal of Experimental Social Psychology, 38,* 178–185.

Pinel, E. C. (2004). You're just saying that because I'm a woman: Stigma consciousness and attributions to discrimination. *Self and Identity, 3,* 39–51.

Pinker, S. (1997). *How the mind works.* New York: Norton.

Pinker, S. (2002). *The blank slate.* New York: Viking.

Pinker, S. (2008). *The sexual paradox: Men, women, and the real gender gap.* New York: Scribner.

Pinker, S. (2011, September 27). A history of violence. *The Edge* (www.edge.org).

Pinker, S. (2014). *The village effect: How face-to-face contact can make us healthier, happier, and smarter.* New York: Spiegel & Grau.

Pipher, M. (2003). *The middle of everywhere: The world's refugees come to our town.* Houghton Mifflin Harcourt: Boston.

Place, S. S., Todd, P. M., Penke, L., & Asendorpf, J. B. (2009). The ability to judge the romantic interest of others. *Psychological Science, 20,* 22–26.

Plant, E. A., Goplen, J., & Kunstman, J. W. (2011). Selective responses to threat: The roles of race and gender in decisions to shoot. *Personality and Social Psychology, 37,* 1274–1281.

Platek, S. M., & Singh, D. (2010). Optimal waist-to-hip ratios in women activate neural reward centers in men. *PLoS One, 5(2),* e9042.

Platow, M. J., Haslam, S. A., Both, A., Chew, I., Cuddon, M., Goharpey, N., Måurer, J., Rosini, S., Tsekouras, A., & Grace, D. M. (2004). "It's not funny if *they're* laughing": Self-categorization, social influence, and responses to canned laughter. *Journal of Experimental Social Psychology, 41,* 542–550.

Plaut, V. C., Adams, G., & Anderson, S. L. (2009). Does attractiveness buy happiness? "It depends on where you're from." *Personal Relationships, 16,* 619–630.

Plaut, V. C., Markus, H. R., & Lachman, M. E. (2002). Place matters: Consensual features and regional variation in American wellbeing and self. *Journal of Personality and Social Psychology, 83,* 160–184.

Plaut, V. C., Markus, H. R., Treadway, J. R., & Fu, A. S. (2012). The cultural construction of self and well-being: A tale of two cities. *Personality and Social Psychology Bulletin, 38,* 1644–1658.

Plomin, R., & Daniels, D. (1987). Why are children in the same family so different from one another? *Behavioral and Brain Sciences, 10,* 1–60.

Polk, M., & Schuster, A. M. H. (2005). *The looting of the Iraq museum, Baghdad: The lost legacy of ancient Mesopotamia.* New York: Harry N. Abrams.

Pomazal, R. J., & Clore, G. L. (1973). Helping on the highway: The effects of dependency and sex. *Journal of Applied Social Psychology, 3,* 150–164.

Pond, R. S., DeWall, C. N., Lambert, N. M., Deckman, T., Bonser, I. M., & Fincham, F. D. (2012). Repulsed by violence: Disgust sensitivity buffers trait, behavioral, and daily aggression. *Journal of Personality and Social Psychology, 102,* 175–188.

Poniewozik, J. (2003, November 24). All the news that fits your reality. *Time,* p. 90.

Pooley, E. (2007, May 28). The last temptation of Al Gore. *Time,* 31–37.

Poon, K-T., Chen, Z., & DeWall, C. N. (2013). Feeling entitled to more: Ostracism increases dishonest behavior. *Personality and Social Psychology Bulletin, 39,* 1227–1239.

Poortinga, W., Pidgeon, N. F., Capstick, S., & Aoyagi, M. (2013, September 19). Public attitudes to nuclear power and climate change in Britain two years after the Fukushima accident. UK Energy Research Centre (www.ukerc.ac.uk/support/tiki-download_file.php?fileId=3371).

Popenoe, D. (2002). *The top ten myths of divorce.* Unpublished manuscript, National Marriage Project, Rutgers University.

Pornpitakpan, C. (2004). The persuasiveness of source credibility: A critical review of five decades' evidence. *Journal of Applied Social Psychology, 34,* 243–281.

Post, J. M. (2005). The new face of terrorism: Socio-cultural foundations of contemporary terrorism. *Behavioral Sciences and the Law, 23,* 451–465.

Postmes, T., & Spears, R. (1998). Deindividuation and antinormative behavior: A meta-analysis. *Psychological Bulletin, 123,* 238–259.

Postmes, T., Spears, R., & Cihangir, S. (2001). Quality of decision making and group norms. *Journal of Personality and Social Psychology, 80,* 918–930.

Pratkanis, A. R., Greenwald, A. G., Leippe, M. R., & Baumgardner, M. H. (1988). In search of reliable persuasion effects: III. The sleeper effect is dead. Long live the sleeper effect. *Journal of Personality and Social Psychology, 54,* 203–218.

Pratkanis, A. R., & Turner, M. E. (1994a). The year cool Papa Bell lost the batting title: Mr. Branch Rickey and Mr. Jackie Robinson's plea for affirmative action. *Nine: A Journal of Baseball History and Social Policy Perspectives, 2,* 260–276.

Pratkanis, A. R., & Turner, M. E. (1994b). Nine principles of successful affirmative action: Mr. Branch Rickey, Mr. Jackie Robinson, and the integration of baseball. *Nine: A Journal of Baseball History and Social Policy Perspectives, 3,* 36–65.

Pratkanis, A. R., & Turner, M. E. (1996). The proactive removal of discriminatory barriers: Affirmative action as effective help. *Journal of Social Issues, 52,* 111–132.

Pratt, M. W., Pancer, M., Hunsberger, B., & Manchester, J. (1990). Reasoning about the self and relationships in maturity: An integrative complexity analysis of individual differences. *Journal of Personality and Social Psychology, 59,* 575–581.

Pratto, F. (1996). Sexual politics: The gender gap in the bedroom, the cupboard, and the cabinet. In D. M. Buss & N. M. Malamuth (Eds.), *Sex, power, conflict: Evolutionary and feminist perspectives.* New York: Oxford University Press.

Pratto, F., Sidanius, J., Stallworth, L. M., & Malle, B. F. (1994). Social dominance orientation: A personality variable predicting social and political attitudes. *Journal of Personality and Social Psychology, 67,* 741–763.

Pratto, F., Stallworth, L. M., & Sidanius, J. (1997). The gender gap: Differences in political attitudes and social dominance orientation. *British Journal of Social Psychology, 36,* 49–68.

Prentice, D. A. (2012). Liberal norms and their discontents. *Perspectives on Psychological Science, 7,* 516–518.

Prentice, D. A., & Carranza, E. (2002). What women and men should be, shouldn't be, are allowed to be, and don't have to be: The contents of prescriptive gender stereotypes. *Psychology of Women Quarterly, 26,* 269–281.

Prentice-Dunn, S., & Rogers, R. W. (1980). Effects of deindividuating situational cues and aggressive models on subjective deindividuation and aggression. *Journal of Personality and Social Psychology, 39,* 104–113.

Prentice-Dunn, S., & Rogers, R. W. (1989). Deindividuation and the self-regulation of behavior. In P. B. Paulus (Ed.), *Psychology of group influence,* 2nd edition. Hillsdale, NJ: Erlbaum.

Preston, J. (2002, November 14). Threats and responses: Baghdad. Iraq tells the U.N. arms inspections will be permitted. *New York Times* (www.nytimes.com).

Preston, J. L., & Ritter, R. S. (2013). Different effects of religion and God on prosociality with the ingroup and outgroup. *Personality and Social Psychology Bulletin, 39,* 1471–1483.

Preston, S. D. (2013). The origins of altruism in offspring care. *Psychological Bulletin, 139,* 1305–1341.

Price, G. H., Dabbs, J. M., Jr., Clower, B. J., & Resin, R. P. (1974). *At first glance—Or, is physical attractiveness more than skin deep?* Paper presented at the Eastern Psychological Association convention. Cited by K. L. Dion & K. K. Dion (1979). Personality and behavioral correlates of romantic love. In M. Cook & G. Wilson (Eds.), *Love and attraction.* Oxford: Pergamon.

Prinsen, S., de Ridder, D. T. D., & de Vet, E. (2013). Eating by example: Effects of environmental cues on dietary decisions. *Appetite, 70,* 1–5.

Prinstein, M. J., & Cillessen, A. N. (2003). Forms and functions of adolescent peer aggression associated with high levels of peer status. *Merrill-Palmer Quarterly, 49,* 310–342.

Pritchard, I. L. (1998). The effects of rap music on aggressive attitudes toward women. Master's thesis, Humboldt State University.

Prohaska, V. (1994). "I know I'll get an A": Confident overestimation of final course grades. *Teaching of Psychology, 21,* 141–143.

Pronin, E. (2008). How we see ourselves and how we see others. *Science, 320,* 1177–1180.

Pronin, E., Berger, J., & Molouki, S. (2007). Alone in a crowd of sheep: Asymmetric perceptions of conformity and their roots in an introspection illusion. *Journal of Personality and Social Psychology, 92,* 585–595.

Pronin, E., Lin, D. Y., & Ross, L. (2002). The bias blind spot: Perceptions of bias in self versus others. *Personality and Social Psychology Bulletin, 28,* 369–381.

Pronin, E., & Ross, L. (2006). Temporal differences in trait self-ascription: When the self is seen as an other. *Journal of Personality and Social Psychology, 90,* 197–209.

Prothrow-Stith, D. (with M. Wiessman) (1991). *Deadly consequences.* New York: HarperCollins.

Prot, S., & 18 others. (2014). Long-term relations among prosocial-media use, empathy, and prosocial behavior. *Psychological Science, 25,* 358–368.

Provine, R. R. (2005). Yawning. *American Scientist, 93,* 532–539.

Pruitt, D. G. (1986). Achieving integrative agreements in negotiation. In R. K. White (Ed.), *Psychology and the prevention of nuclear war.* New York: New York University Press.

Pruitt, D. G. (1998). Social conflict. In D. Gilbert, S. T. Fiske, & G. Lindzey (Eds.), *Handbook of social psychology,* 4th edition. New York: McGraw-Hill.

Pruitt, D. G., & Kimmel, M. J. (1977). Twenty years of experimental gaming: Critique, synthesis, and suggestions for the future. *Annual Review of Psychology, 28,* 363–392.

Pruitt, D. G., & Lewis, S. A. (1975). Development of integrative solutions in bilateral negotiation. *Journal of Personality and Social Psychology, 31,* 621–633.

Pruitt, D. G., & Lewis, S. A. (1977). The psychology of integrative bargaining. In D. Druckman (Ed.), *Negotiations: A social-psychological analysis.* New York: Halsted.

Pryor, J. B., DeSouza, E. R., Fitness, J., Hutz, C., Kumpf, M., Lubbert, K., Pesonen, O., & Erber, M. W. (1997). Gender differences in the interpretation of social-sexual behavior: A cross-cultural perspective on sexual harassment. *Journal of Cross-Cultural Psychology, 28,* 509–534.

Pryor, J. H., Hurtado, S., DeAngelo, L., Blake, L. P., & Tran, S. (2010). *The American freshman: National norms fall 2010.* Los Angeles: Higher Education Research Institute, UCLA.

Pryor, J. H., Hurtado, S., Sharkness, J., & Korn, W. S. (2007). *The American freshman: National norms for fall 2007.* Los Angeles: Higher Education Research Institute, UCLA.

Przybylski, A. K., Rigby, C. S., & Ryan, R. M. (2010). A motivational model of video game engagement. *Review of General Psychology, 14,* 154–166.

PTC: Parents Television Council. (2013). Media violence: An examination of violence, graphic violence, and gun violence in the media (2012–2013). http://w2.parentstv.org/MediaFiles/PDF/Studies/VStudy_dec2013.pdf

Public Opinion. (1984, August/September). *Vanity Fair,* p. 22.

Puhl, R. M., & Heuer, C. A. (2009). The stigma of obesity: A review and update. *Obesity, 17,* 941–964.

Puhl, R. M., & Heuer, C. A. (2010). Obesity stigma: Important considerations for public health. *American Journal of Public Health, 100,* 1019–1028.

Purvis, J. A., Dabbs, J. M., Jr., & Hopper, C. H. (1984). The "opener": Skilled user of facial expression and speech pattern. *Personality and Social Psychology Bulletin, 10,* 61–66.

Putnam, R. (2000). *Bowling alone.* New York: Simon & Schuster.

Putnam, R. (2006, July 3). You gotta have friends: A study finds that Americans are getting lonelier. *Time,* p. 36.

Pyszczynski, T., Abdollahi, A., Solomon, S., Greenberg, J., Cohen, F., & Weise, D. (2006). Mortality salience, martyrdom, and military might: The great Satan versus the axis of evil. *Personality and Social Psychology Bulletin, 32,* 525–537.

Pyszczynski, T., & Greenberg, J. (1987). Self-regulatory perseveration and the depressive self-focusing style: A self-awareness theory of reactive depression. *Psychological Bulletin, 102,* 122–138.

Pyszczynski, T., Hamilton, J. C., Greenberg, J., & Becker, S. E. (1991). Self-awareness and psychological dysfunction. In C. R. Snyder & D. O. Forsyth (Eds.), *Handbook of social and clinical psychology: The health perspective.* New York: Pergamon.

Pyszczynski, T., Motyl, M., Vail, Kenneth E., I., II, Hirschberger, G., Arndt, J., & Kesebir, P. (2012). Drawing attention to global climate change decreases support for war. *Peace and Conflict: Journal of Peace Psychology, 18,* 354–368.

Qirko, H. N. (2004). "Fictive kin" and suicide terrorism. *Science, 304,* 49–50.

Quartz, S. R., & Sejnowski, T. J. (2002). *Liars, lovers, and heroes: What the new brain science reveals about how we become who we are.* New York: Morrow.

Quist, M. C., Watkins, C. D., Smith, F. G., Little, A. C., Debruine, L. M., & Jones, B. C. (2012). Sociosexuality predicts women's preferences for symmetry in men's faces. *Archives of Sexual Behavior, 41,* 1415–1421.

Quoidbach, J., Dunn, E., Petrides, K., & Mikolajczak, M. (2010). Money giveth, money taketh away: The dual effect of wealth on happiness. *Psychological Science, 21,* 759–763.

Quoidbach, J., & Dunn, E. W. (2010). Personality neglect: The unforeseen impact of personal dispositions on emotional life. *Psychological Science, 21,* 1783–1786.

Rabinovich, A., Morton, T. A., & Birney, M. E. (2012). Communicating climate science: The role of perceived communicator's motives. *Journal of Environmental Psychology, 32,* 11–28.

Radelet, M. L., & Pierce, G. L. (2011). Race and death sentencing in North Carolina, 1980–2007. *North Carolina Law Review, 89,* 2119–2159.

Rafferty, R., & Vander Ven, T. (2014). "I hate everything about you": A qualitative examination of cyberbullying and on-line aggression in a college sample. *Deviant Behavior, 35,* 364–377.

Raine, A. (1993). *The psychopathology of crime: Criminal behavior as a clinical disorder.* San Diego, CA: Academic Press.

Raine, A. (2005). The interaction of biological and social measures in the explanation of antisocial and violent behavior. In D. M. Stoff & E. J. Susman (Eds.), *Developmental psychobiology of aggression.* New York: Cambridge University Press.

Raine, A. (2008). From genes to brain to antisocial behavior. *Current Directions in Psychological Science, 17,* 323–328.

Raine, A., Lencz, T., Bihrle, S., LaCasse, L., & Colletti, P. (2000). Reduced prefrontal gray matter volume and reduced autonomic activity in antisocial personality disorder. *Archives of General Psychiatry, 57,* 119–127.

Raine, A., Stoddard, J., Bihrle, S., & Buchsbaum, M. (1998). Prefrontal glucose deficits in murderers lacking psychosocial deprivation. *Neuropsychiatry, Neuropsychology, & Behavioral Neurology, 11,* 1–7.

Rains, S. A. (2013). The nature of psychological reactance revisited: A meta-analytic review. *Human Communication Research, 39,* 47–73.

Rajagopal, P., Raju, S., & Unnava, H. R. (2006). Differences in the cognitive accessibility of action and inaction regrets. *Journal of Experimental Social Psychology, 42,* 302–313.

Rajecki, D. W., Bledsoe, S. B., & Rasmussen, J. L. (1991). Successful personal ads: Gender differences and similarities in offers, stipulations, and outcomes. *Basic and Applied Social Psychology, 12,* 457–469.

Ramirez, J. M., Bonniot-Cabanac, M-C., & Cabanac, M. (2005). Can aggression provide pleasure? *European Psychologist, 10,* 136–145.

Rammstedt, B., & Schupp, J. (2008). Only the congruent survive—Personality similarities in couples. *Personality and Individual Differences, 45,* 533–535.

Ramos, M. R., Cassidy, C., Reicher, S., & Haslam, S. A. (2012). A longitudinal investigation of the rejection–identification hypothesis. *British Journal of Social Psychology, 51,* 642–660.

Randler, C., & Kretz, S. (2011). Assortative mating in morningness-eveningness. *International Journal of Psychology, 46,* 91–96.

Randler, C., & Vollmer, C. (2013). Aggression in young adults–A matter of short sleep and social jetlag? *Psychological Reports: Disability and Trauma, 113,* 754–765.

Rank, S. G., & Jacobson, C. K. (1977). Hospital nurses' compliance with medication overdose orders: A failure to replicate. *Journal of Health and Social Behavior, 18,* 188–193.

Rapoport, A. (1960). *Fights, games, and debates.* Ann Arbor: University of Michigan Press.

Rappoport, L., & Kren, G. (1993). Amoral rescuers: The ambiguities of altruism. *Creativity Research Journal, 6,* 129–136.

Rateau, P., Moliner, P., Guimelli, C., & Abric, J. (2012). Social representation theory. In P. A. Van Lange, A. W. Kruglanski, & E. T. Higgins (Eds.), *Handbook of theories of social psychology (Vol 2).* Thousand Oaks, CA: Sage.

Ratliff, K. A., & Nosek, B. A. (2010). Creating distinct implicit and explicit attitudes with an illusory correlation paradigm. *Journal of Experimental Social Psychology, 46,* 721–728.

Rawls, J. (1971). *A theory of justice.* Cambridge, MA: Belknap Press of Harvard University Press.

Rawn, C. D., & Vohs, K. D. (2011). People use self-control to risk personal harm: An intra-interpersonal dilemma. *Personality and Social Psychology Review, 15,* 267–289.

Ray, D. G., Mackie, D. M., Rydell, R. J., & Smith, E. R. (2008). Changing categorization of self can change emotions about outgroups. *Journal of Experimental Social Psychology, 44,* 1210–1213.

Reed, D. (1989, November 25). Video collection documents Christian resistance to Hitler. Associated Press release in *Grand Rapids Press,* pp. B4, B5.

Regan, D. T., & Cheng, J. B. (1973). Distraction and attitude change: A resolution. *Journal of Experimental Social Psychology, 9,* 138–147.

Regan, D. T., & Fazio, R. (1977). On the consistency between attitudes and behavior: Look to the method of attitude formation. *Journal of Experimental Social Psychology, 13,* 28–45.

Regan, P. C. (1998). What if you can't get what you want? Willingness to compromise ideal mate selection standards as a function of sex, mate value, and relationship context. *Personality and Social Psychology Bulletin, 24,* 1294–1303.

Reicher, S. D., Haslam, S. A. (2011). Culture of shock. *Scientific American Mind,* November/December 2011, 57–61.

Reicher, S. D., Haslam, S. A., & Smith, J. R. (2012). Working toward the experimenter: Reconceptualizing obedience within the Milgram paradigm as identification-based followership. *Perspectives on Psychological Science, 7,* 315–324.

Reicher, S., Spears, R., & Postmes, T. (1995). A social identity model of deindividuation phenomena. In W. Storebe & M. Hewstone (Eds.), *European review of social psychology* (Vol. 6). Chichester, UK: Wiley.

Reid, C. A., Davis, J. L., & Green, J. D. (2013). The power of change: Interpersonal attraction as a function of attitude similarity and attitude alignment. *Journal of Social Psychology, 153,* 700–719.

Reid, P., & Finchilescu, G. (1995). The disempowering effects of media violence against women on college women. *Psychology of Women Quarterly, 19,* 397–411.

Reijntjes, A., Thomaes, S., Kamphuis, J. H., Bushman, B. J., de Castro, B. O., & Telch, M. J. (2011). Explaining the paradoxical rejection–aggression link: The mediating effects of hostile intent attributions, anger, and decreases in state self-esteem on peer rejection-induced aggression on youth. *Personality and Social Psychology Bulletin, 37,* 955–963.

Reiner, W. G., & Gearhart, J. P. (2004). Discordant sexual identity in some genetic males with cloacal exstrophy assigned to female sex at birth. *New England Journal of Medicine, 350,* 333–341.

Reis, H. T., & Aron, A. (2008). Love: Why is it, why does it matter, and how does it operate? *Perspectives on Psychological Science, 3,* 80–86.

Reis, H. T., Maniaci, M. R., Caprariello, P. A., Eastwick, P. W., & Finkel, E. J. (2011). Familiarity does indeed promote attraction in live interaction. *Journal of Personality and Social Psychology, 101,* 557–570.

Reis, H. T., Nezlek, J., & Wheeler, L. (1980). Physical attractiveness in social interaction. *Journal of Personality and Social Psychology, 38,* 604–617.

Reis, H. T., & Shaver, P. (1988). Intimacy as an interpersonal process. In S. Duck (Ed.), *Handbook of personal relationships: Theory, relationships and interventions.* Chichester, UK: Wiley.

Reis, H. T., Smith, S. M., Carmichael, C. L., Caprariello, P. A., Tsa, F.-F., Rodrigues, A., & Maniaci, M. R. (2010). Are you happy for me? How sharing positive events with others provides personal and interpersonal benefits. *Journal of Personality and Social Psychology, 99,* 311–329.

Reis, H. T., Wheeler, L., Spiegel, N., Kernis, M. H., Nezlek, J., & Perri, M. (1982). Physical attractiveness in social interaction: II. Why does appearance affect social experience? *Journal of Personality and Social Psychology, 43,* 979–996.

Reisenzein, R. (1983). The Schachter theory of emotion: Two decades later. *Psychological Bulletin, 94,* 239–264.

Reitzes, D. C. (1953). The role of organizational structures: Union versus neighborhood in a tension situation. *Journal of Social Issues, 9(1),* 37–44.

Remley, A. (1988, October). From obedience to independence. *Psychology Today,* 56–59.

Renaud, H., & Estess, F. (1961). Life history interviews with one hundred normal American males: "Pathogenecity" of childhood. *American Journal of Orthopsychiatry, 31,* 786–802.

Reynolds, J., Stewart, M., MacDonald, R., & Sischo, L. (2006). Have adolescents become too ambitious? High school seniors' educational and occupational plans, 1976 to 2000. *Social Problems, 53,* 186–206.

Reysen, S., Landau, M. J., & Branscombe, N. R. (2012) Copycatting as a threat to public identity. *Basic and Applied Social Psychology, 34,* 226–235.

Rhodes, G. (2006). The evolutionary psychology of facial beauty. *Annual Review of Psychology, 57,* 199–226.

Rhodes, G., Sumich, A., & Byatt, G. (1999). Are average facial configurations attractive only because of their symmetry? *Psychological Science, 10,* 52–58.

Rhodes, M. G., & Anastasi, J. S. (2012). The own-age bias in face recognition: A meta-analytic and theoretical review. *Psychological Bulletin, 138,* 146–174.

Rhodewalt, F. (1987). Is self-handicapping an effective self-protective attributional strategy? Paper presented at the American Psychological Association convention.

Rhodewalt, F., & Agustsdottir, S. (1986). Effects of self-presentation on the phenomenal self. *Journal of Personality and Social Psychology, 50,* 47–55.

Rhodewalt, F., Saltzman, A. T., & Wittmer J. (1984). Self-handicapping among competitive athletes: The role of practice in self-esteem protection. *Basic and Applied Social Psychology, 5,* 197–209.

Rholes, W. S., Newman, L. S., & Ruble, D. N. (1990). Understanding self and other: Developmental and motivational aspects of perceiving persons in terms of invariant dispositions. In E. T. Higgins & R. M. Sorrentino (Eds.), *Handbook of motivation and cognition: Foundations of social behavior* (Vol. 2). New York: Guilford.

Rice, B. (1985, September). Performance review: The job nobody likes. *Psychology Today,* pp. 30–36.

Rice, M. E., & Grusec, J. E. (1975). Saying and doing: Effects on observer performance. *Journal of Personality and Social Psychology, 32,* 584–593.

Richards, Z., & Hewstone, M. (2001). Subtyping and subgrouping: Processes for the prevention and promotion of stereotype change. *Personality and Social Psychology Review, 5,* 52–73.

Richardson, D. S. (2005). The myth of female passivity: Thirty years of revelations about female aggression. *Psychology of Women Quarterly, 29,* 238–247.

Richardson, J. D., Huddy, W. P., & Morgan, S. M. (2008). The hostile media effect, biased assimilation, and perceptions of a presidential debate. *Journal of Applied Social Psychology, 38,* 1255–1270.

Richardson, L. F. (1960). Generalized foreign policy. *British Journal of Psychology Monographs Supplements,* 23. Cited by A. Rapoport in *Fights, games, and debates* (p. 15). Ann Arbor: University of Michigan Press.

Richardson, M., Abraham, C., & Bond, R. (2012). Psychological correlates of university students' academic performance: A systematic review and meta-analysis. *Psychological Bulletin, 138,* 353–387.

Richeson, J. A., & Shelton, J. N. (2012). Stereotype threat in interracial interactions. In M. Inzlicht & T. Schmader (eds.), *Stereotype threat: Theory, process, and application,* 231–245. New York, NY, US: Oxford University Press.

Richeson, J. A., & Trawalter, S. (2008). The threat of appearing prejudiced, and race-based attentional biases. *Psychological Science, 19,* 98–102.

Ridge, R. D., & Reber, J. S. (2002). "I think she's attracted to me": The effect of men's beliefs on women's behavior in a job interview scenario. *Basic and Applied Social Psychology, 24,* 1–14.

Riek, B. M., Mania, E. W., & Gaertner, S. L. (2013). Reverse subtyping: The effects of prejudice level on the subtyping of counterstereotypic outgroup members. *Basic and Applied Social Psychology, 35,* 409–417.

Riess, M., Rosenfeld, P., Melburg, V., & Tedeschi, J. T. (1981). Self-serving attributions: Biased private perceptions and distorted public descriptions. *Journal of Personality and Social Psychology, 41,* 224–231.

Rietzschel, E. F., Nijstad, B. A., & Stroebe, W. (2006). Productivity is not enough: A comparison of interactive and nominal brainstorming groups on idea generation and selection. *Journal of Experimental Social Psychology, 42,* 244–251.

Riggs, J. M. (1992). Self-handicapping and achievement. In A. K. Boggiano & T. S. Pittman (Eds.), *Achievement and motivation: A social-developmental perspective.* New York: Cambridge University Press.

Rijnbout, J. S., & McKimmie, B. M. (2012). Deviance in group decision making: Group-member centrality alleviates negative consequences for the group. *European Journal of Social Psychology, 42,* 915–923.

Riordan, C. A. (1980). *Effects of admission of influence on attributions and attraction.* Paper presented at the American Psychological Association convention, Montreal, Quebec.

Risen, J. L., & Critcher, C. R. (2011). Visceral fit: While in a visceral state, associated states of the world seem more likely. *Journal of Personality and Social Psychology, 100,* 777–793.

Risen, J. L., Gilovich, T., & Dunning, D. (2007). One-shot illusory correlations and stereotype formation. *Personality and Social Psychology Bulletin, 33,* 1492–1502.

Riva, P., Romero Lauro, L. J., DeWall, C. N., & Bushman, B. J. (2012). Buffer the pain away: Stimulating the right ventrolateral prefrontal cortex reduces pain following social exclusion. *Psychological Science, 23,* 1473–1475.

Riva, P., Williams, K. D., Torstrick, A. M., & Montali, L. (2014). Orders to shoot (a camera): Effects of ostracism on obedience. *Journal of Social Psychology, 154,* 208–216.

Riva, P., Wirth, J. H., & Williams, K. D. (2011). The consequences of pain: The social and physical overlap on psychological responses. *European Journal of Social Psychology, 41,* 681–687.

Robberson, M. R., & Rogers, R. W. (1988). Beyond fear appeals: Negative and positive persuasive appeals to health and self-esteem. *Journal of Applied Social Psychology, 18,* 277–287.

Robertson, I. (1987). *Sociology.* New York: Worth Publishers.

Robertson, L. A., McAnally, H. M., & Hancox, R. J. (2013). Childhood and adolescent television viewing and antisocial behavior in early adulthood. *Pediatrics, 131,* 439–446.

Robins, L., & Regier, D. (Eds.). (1991). *Psychiatric disorders in America.* New York: Free Press.

Robins, R. W., & Beer, J. S. (2001). Positive illusions about the self: Short-term benefits and long-term costs. *Journal of Personality and Social Psychology, 80,* 340–352.

Robins, R. W., Mendelsohn, G. A., Connell, J. B., & Kwan, V. S. Y. (2004). Do people agree about the causes of behavior? A social relations analysis of behavior ratings and causal attributions. *Journal of Personality and Social Psychology, 86,* 334–344.

Robinson, M. D., & Ryff, C. D. (1999). The role of self-deception in perceptions of past, present, and future happiness. *Personality and Social Psychology Bulletin, 25,* 595–606.

Robinson, M. S., & Alloy, L. B. (2003). Negative cognitive styles and stress-reactive rumination interact to predict depression: A prospective study. *Cognitive Therapy and Research, 27,* 275–291.

Robinson, T. N., Wilde, M. L., Navracruz, L. C., Haydel, F., & Varady, A. (2001). Effects of reducing children's television and video game use on aggressive behavior. *Archives of Pediatric and Adolescent Medicine, 155,* 17–23.

Robles, T. F. (2015). Marital quality and health: Implications for marriage in the 21st century. *Current Directions in Psychological Science, 23,* 427–432.

Robles, T. F., Slatcher, R. B., Trombello, J. M., & McGinn, M. M. (2014). Marital quality and health: A meta-analytic review. *Psychological Bulletin, 140,* 140–187.

Roccas, S., Sagiv, L., Schwartz, S.H., & Knafo, A. (2002). The Big Five personality factors and personal values. *Personality and Social Psychology Bulletin, 28,* 789–801.

Rochat, F. (1993). How did they resist authority? Protecting refugees in Le Chambon during World War II. Paper presented at the American Psychological Association convention.

Rochat, F., & Modigliani, A. (1995). The ordinary quality of resistance: From Milgram's laboratory to the village of Le Chambon. *Journal of Social Issues, 51,* 195–210.

Roehling, M. V. (2000). Weight-based discrimination in employment: psychological and legal aspects. *Personnel Psychology, 52,* 969–1016.

Roehling, M. V., Roehling, P. V., & Odland, I. M. (2008). Investigating the validity of stereotypes about overweight employees. *Group and Organization Management, 23,* 392–424.

Roehling, M. V., Roehling, P. V., & Pichler, S. (2007). The relationship between body weight and perceived weight-related employment discrimination: The role of sex and race. *Journal of Vocational Behavior, 71,* 300–318.

Roehling, P. V., Roehling, M. V., Johnston, A., Brennan, A., & Drew, A. (2010). Weighty decisions: The effect of weight bias on the selection and election of U.S. political candidates. Unpublished manuscript, Hope College.

Roehling, P. V., Roehling, M. V., Vandlen, J. D., Blazek, J., & Guy, W. C. (2009). Weight discrimination and the glass ceiling effect among top U.S. male and female CEOs. *Equal Opportunities International, 28,* 179–196.

Roese, N. J., & Hur, T. (1997). Affective determinants of counterfactual thinking. *Social Cognition, 15,* 274–290.

Roese, N. J., & Vohs, K. D. (2012). Hindsight bias. *Perspectives on Psychological Science, 7,* 411–426.

Roese, N. L., & Olson, J. M. (1994). Attitude importance as a function of repeated attitude expression. *Journal of Experimental Social Psychology, 66,* 805–818.

Roger, L. H., Cortes, D. E., & Malgady, R. B. (1991). Acculturation and mental health status among Hispanics: Convergence and new directions for research. *American Psychologist, 46,* 585–597.

Rogers, C. R. (1980). *A way of being.* Boston: Houghton Mifflin.

Rogers, C. R. (1985, February). Quoted by Michael A. Wallach and Lise Wallach in "How psychology sanctions the cult of the self." *Washington Monthly,* 46–56.

Rogers, R. W., & Prentice-Dunn, S. (1981). Deindividuation and anger-mediated interracial aggression: Unmasking regressive racism. *Journal of Personality and Social Psychology, 41,* 63–73.

Rohrer, J. H., Baron, S. H., Hoffman, E. L., & Swander, D. V. (1954). The stability of autokinetic judgments. *Journal of Abnormal and Social Psychology, 49,* 595–597.

Rokeach, M., & Mezei, L. (1966). Race and shared beliefs as factors in social choice. *Science, 151,* 167–172.

Romer, D., Gruder, D. L., & Lizzadro, T. (1986). A person-situation approach to altruistic behavior. *Journal of Personality and Social Psychology, 51,* 1001–1012.

Roney, J. R. (2003). Effects of visual exposure to the opposite sex: Cognitive aspects of mate attraction in human males. *Personality and Social Psychology Bulletin, 29,* 393–404.

Rook, K. S. (1984). Promoting social bonding: Strategies for helping the lonely and socially isolated. *American Psychologist, 39,* 1389–1407.

Rook, K. S. (1987). Social support versus companionship: Effects on life stress, loneliness, and evaluations by others. *Journal of Personality and Social Psychology, 52,* 1132–1147.

Rooth, D-O. (2007). Implicit discrimination in hiring: Real-world evidence. IZA Discussion Paper No. 2764, University of Kalmar, Institute for the Study of Labor (IZA).

Rosander, M., & Eriksson, O. (2012). Conformity on the Internet—the role of task difficulty and gender differences. *Computers in Human Behavior, 28,* 1587–1595.

Rose, A. J., & Rudolph, K. D. (2006). A review of sex differences in peer relationship processes: Potential trade-offs for the emotional and behavioral development of girls and boys. *Psychological Bulletin, 132,* 98–131.

Rosenbaum, M. E. (1986). The repulsion hypothesis: On the nondevelopment of relationships. *Journal of Personality and Social Psychology, 51,* 1156–1166.

Rosenberg, L. A. (1961). Group size, prior experience and conformity. *Journal of Abnormal and Social Psychology, 63,* 436–437.

Rosenberg, T. (2010). The opt-out solution. *New York Times* (www.nytimes.com).

Rosenblatt, A., & Greenberg, J. (1988). Depression and interpersonal attraction: The role of perceived similarity. *Journal of Personality and Social Psychology, 55,* 112–119.

Rosenblatt, A., & Greenberg, J. (1991). Examining the world of the depressed: Do depressed people prefer others who are depressed? *Journal of Personality and Social Psychology, 60,* 620–629.

Rosenbloom, S. (2008, January 3). Putting your best cyberface forward. New York Times, Style section. www.nytimes.com/2008/01/03/fashion/03impression.html

Rosenfeld, D., Folger, R., & Adelman, H. F. (1980). When rewards reflect competence: A qualification of the overjustification effect. *Journal of Personality and Social Psychology, 39,* 368–376.

Rosenhan, D. L. (1970). The natural socialization of altruistic autonomy. In J. Macaulay & L. Berkowitz (Eds.), *Altruism and helping behavior.* New York: Academic Press.

Rosenhan, D. L. (1973). On being sane in insane places. *Science, 179,* 250–258.

Rosenthal, D. A., & Feldman, S. S. (1992). The nature and stability of ethnic identity in Chinese youth: Effects of length of residence in two cultural contexts. *Journal of Cross-Cultural Psychology, 23,* 214–227.

Rosenthal, E. (2011, June 26). Europe stifles drivers in favor of alternatives. *New York Times* (www.nytimes.com).

Rosenthal, R. (1985). From unconscious experimenter bias to teacher expectancy effects. In J. B. Dusek, V. C. Hall, & W. J. Meyer (Eds.), *Teacher expectancies.* Hillsdale, NJ: Erlbaum.

Rosenthal, R. (1991). Teacher expectancy effects: A brief update 25 years after the Pygmalion experiment. *Journal of Research in Education, 1,* 3–12.

Rosenthal, R. (2002). Covert communication in classrooms, clinics, courtrooms, and cubicles. *American Psychologist, 57,* 839–849.

Rosenthal, R. (2003). Covert communication in laboratories, classrooms, and the truly real world. *Current Directions in Psychological Science, 12,* 151–154.

Rosenthal, R. (2006). Applying psychological research on interpersonal expectations and covert communication in classrooms, clinics, corporations, and courtrooms. In S. I. Donaldson, D. E. Berger, & K. Pezdek (Eds.), *Applied psychology: New frontiers and rewarding careers.* Mahwah, NJ: Erlbaum.

Rosenthal, R. (2008). Introduction, methods, results, discussion: The story of a career. In R. Levin, A. Rodriques, & L. Zelezny (Eds.), *Journeys in social psychology: Looking back to inspire the future.* New York: Psychology Press.

Rosenthal, R., & Jacobson, L. (1968). *Pygmalion in the classroom: Teacher expectation and pupils' intellectual development.* New York: Holt, Rinehart & Winston.

Rosenzweig, M. R. (1972). Cognitive dissonance. *American Psychologist, 27,* 769.

Roseth, C. J., Johnson, D. W., & Johnson, R. T. (2008). Promoting early adolescents' achievement and peer relationships: The effects of cooperative, competitive, and individualistic goal structures. *Psychological Bulletin, 134,* 223–246.

Ross, L. (1977). The intuitive psychologist and his shortcomings: Distortions in the attribution process. In L. Berkowitz (Ed.), *Advances in experimental social psychology* (Vol. 10). New York: Academic Press.

Ross, L. (1981). The "intuitive scientist" formulation and its developmental implications. In J. H. Havell & L. Ross (Eds.), *Social cognitive development: Frontiers and possible futures.* Cambridge, England: Cambridge University Press.

Ross, L. (1988). Situationist perspectives on the obedience experiments. Review of A. G. Miller's *The obedience experiments. Contemporary Psychology, 33,* 101–104.

Ross, L., Amabile, T. M., & Steinmetz, J. L. (1977). Social roles, social control, and biases in social-perception processes. *Journal of Personality and Social Psychology, 35,* 485–494.

Ross, L., & Anderson, C. A. (1982). Shortcomings in the attribution process: On the origins and maintenance of erroneous social assessments. In D. Kahneman, P. Slovic, & A. Tversky (Eds.), *Judgment under uncertainty: Heuristics and biases.* New York: Cambridge University Press.

Ross, L., & Ward, A. (1995). Psychological barriers to dispute resolution. In M. P. Zanna (Ed.), *Advances in experimental social psychology* (Vol. 27). San Diego: Academic Press.

Ross, M., & Fletcher, G. J. O. (1985). Attribution and social perception. In G. Lindzey & E. Aronson (Eds.), *The Handbook of Social Psychology,* 3rd edition. New York: Random House.

Ross, M., McFarland, C., & Fletcher, G. J. O. (1981). The effect of attitude on the recall of personal histories. *Journal of Personality and Social Psychology, 40,* 627–634

Ross, M., & Sicoly, F. (1979). Egocentric biases in availability and attribution. *Journal of Personality and Social Psychology, 37,* 322–336.

Rossi, A. S., & Rossi, P. H. (1990). *Of human bonding: Parent-child relations across the life course.* Hawthorne, NY: Aldine de Gruyter.

Rossiter, J. R., & Smidts, A. (2012). Print advertising: Celebrity presenters. *Journal of Business Research, 65,* 874–879.

Roszell, P., Kennedy, D., & Grabb, E. (1990). Physical attractiveness and income attainment among Canadians. *Journal of Psychology, 123,* 547–559.

Rotenberg, K. J., Gruman, J. A., & Ariganello, M. (2002). Behavioral

confirmation of the loneliness stereotype. *Basic and Applied Social Psychology, 24,* 81–89.

Rothbart, M., Fulero, S., Jensen, C., Howard, J., & Birrell, P. (1978). From individual to group impressions: Availability heuristics in stereotype formation. *Journal of Experimental Social Psychology, 14,* 237–255.

Rothbart, M., & Taylor, M. (1992). Social categories and social reality. In G. R. Semin & K. Fielder (Eds.), *Language, interaction and social cognition.* London: Sage.

Rothblum, E. D. (2007). Same-sex couples in legalized relationships: I do, or do I? Unpublished manuscript, Women's Studies Department, San Diego State University.

Rothman, A. J., & Salovey, P. (1997). Shaping perceptions to motivate healthy behavior: The role of message framing. *Psychological Bulletin, 121,* 3–19.

Rothschild, Z. K., Landau, M. J., Sullivan, D., & Keefer, L. A. (2012). A dual-motive model of scapegoating: Displacing blame to reduce guilt or increase control. *Journal of Personality and Social Psychology, 102,* 1148–1163.

Rotton, J., & Cohn, E. G. (2004). Outdoor temperature, climate control, and criminal assault: The spatial and temporal ecology of violence. *Environment and Behavior, 36,* 276–306.

Rotton, J., & Frey, J. (1985). Air pollution, weather, and violent crimes: Concomitant time-series analysis of archival data. *Journal of Personality and Social Psychology, 49,* 1207–1220.

Rotundo, M., Nguyen, D.-H., & Sackett, P. R. (2001). A meta-analytic review of gender differences in perceptions of sexual harassment. *Journal of Applied Psychology, 86,* 914–922.

Rowe, D. C., Almeida, D. M., & Jacobson, K. C. (1999). School context and genetic influences on aggression in adolescence. *Psychological Science, 10,* 277–280.

Rowe, D. C., Vazsonyi, A. T., & Flannery, D. J. (1994). No more than skin deep: Ethnic and racial similarity in developmental process. *Psychological Review, 101,* 396–413.

Roy, M. M., Christenfeld, N. J. S., & McKenzie, C. R. M. (2005). Underestimating the duration of future events: Memory incorrectly used or memory bias? *Psychological Bulletin, 131,* 738–756.

Royal Society. (2010, September). *Climate change: A summary of the science.* London: The Royal Society.

Rubin, J. Z. (1986). Can we negotiate with terrorists: Some answers from psychology. Paper presented at the American Psychological Association convention, Washington, DC.

Rubin, L. B. (1985). *Just friends: The role of friendship in our lives.* New York: Harper & Row.

Rubin, R. B. (1981). Ideal traits and terms of address for male and female college

professors. *Journal of Personality and Social Psychology, 41,* 966–974.

Rubin, Z. (1973). *Liking and loving: An invitation to social psychology.* New York: Holt, Rinehart & Winston.

Rudman, L. A., McLean, M. C., & Bunzl, M. (2013). When truth is personally inconvenient, attitudes change: The impact of extreme weather on implicit support for green politicians and explicit climate-change beliefs. *Psychological Science, 14,* 2290–2296.

Rudman, L. A., & Mescher, K. (2012). Of animals and objects: Men's implicit dehumanization of women and likelihood of sexual aggression. *Personality and Social Psychology Bulletin, 38,* 734–746.

Rudolph, U., Roesch, S. C., Greitenmeyer, T., & Weiner, B. (2004). A meta-analytic review of help-giving and aggression from an attributional perspective: Contributions to a general theory of motivation. *Cognition and Emotion, 18,* 815–848.

Ruiter, R. A. C., Abraham, C., & Kok, G. (2001). Scary warnings and rational precautions: A review of the psychology of fear appeals. *Psychology and Health, 16,* 613–630.

Ruiter, R. A. C., Kessels, L. T. E., Peters, G-J. Y., & Kok, G. (2014). Sixty years of fear appeal research: Current state of the evidence. *International Journal of Psychology, 49,* 63–70.

Ruiter, S., & De Graaf, N. D. (2006). National context, religiosity, and volunteering: Results from 53 countries. *American Sociological Review, 71,* 191–210.

Rule, B. G., Taylor, B. R., & Dobbs, A. R. (1987). Priming effects of heat on aggressive thoughts. *Social Cognition, 5,* 131–143.

Rule, N. (2014) Snap-judgment science. APS Observer, May-June 2014. Retrieved April 1, 2015 from: http://www .psychologicalscience.org/index.php/ publications/observer/2014/may-june-14/ snap-judgment-science.html

Rule, N. O., Rosen, K. S., Slepian, M. L., & Ambady, N. (2011). Mating interest improves women's accuracy in judging male sexual orientation. *Psychological Science, 22,* 881–886.

Rupp, H. A., & Wallen, K. (2008). Sex differences in response to visual sexual stimuli: A review. *Archives of Sexual Behavior, 37,* 206–218.

Rusbult, C. E., Johnson, D. J., & Morrow, G. D. (1986). Impact of couple patterns of problem solving on distress and nondistress in dating relationships. *Journal of Personality and Social Psychology, 50,* 744–753.

Rusbult, C. E., Martz, J. M., & Agnew, C. R. (1998). The investment model scale: Measuring commitment level, satisfaction level, quality of alternatives, and investment size. *Personal Relationships, 5,* 357–391.

Rusbult, C. E., Morrow, G. D., & Johnson, D. J. (1987). Self-esteem and problem-solving behaviour in close relationships. *British Journal of Social Psychology, 26,* 293–303.

Rushton, J. P. (1975). Generosity in children: Immediate and long-term effects of modeling, preaching, and moral judgment. *Journal of Personality and Social Psychology, 31,* 459–466.

Rushton, J. P. (1991). Is altruism innate? *Psychological Inquiry, 2,* 141–143.

Rushton, J. P., & Campbell, A. C. (1977). Modeling, vicarious reinforcement and extraversion on blood donating in adults: Immediate and long-term effects. *European Journal of Social Psychology, 7,* 297–306.

Rushton, J. P., Chrisjohn, R. D., & Fekken, G. C. (1981). The altruistic personality and the self-report altruism scale. *Personality and Individual Differences, 2,* 293–302.

Rushton, J. P., Fulker, D. W., Neale, M. C., Nias, D. K. B., & Eysenck, H. J. (1986). Altruism and aggression: The heritability of individual differences. *Journal of Personality and Social Psychology, 50,* 1192–1198.

Russell, B. (1930/1980). *The conquest of happiness.* London: Unwin Paperbacks.

Russell, G. W. (1983). Psychological issues in sports aggression. In J. H. Goldstein (Ed.), *Sports violence.* New York: Springer-Verlag.

Russell, N. J. C. (2011). Milgram's obedience to authority experiments: Origins and early evolution. *British Journal of Social Psychology, 50,* 140–162.

Russell, N. J. C., & Gregory, R. J. (2005). Making the undoable doable: Milgram, the Holocaust, and modern government. *American Review of Public Administration, 35,* 327–349.

Ryan, R. (1999, February 2). Quoted by A. Kohn, In pursuit of affluence, at a high price. *New York Times* (www.nytimes.com).

Ryckman, R. M., Robbins, M. A., Kaczor, L. M., & Gold, J. A. (1989). Male and female raters' stereotyping of male and female physiques. *Personality and Social Psychology Bulletin, 15,* 244–251.

Rydell, R. J., McConnell, A. R., & Beilock, S. L. (2009). Multiple social identities and stereotype threat: Imbalance, accessibility, and working memory. *Journal of Personality and Social Psychology, 96,* 949–966.

Rydell, R. J., Rydell, M. T., & Boucher, K. L. (2010). The effect of negative performance stereotypes on learning. *Journal of Personality and Social Psychology, 99,* 883–896.

Ryff, C. D., & Singer, B. (2000). Interpersonal flourishing: A positive health agenda for the new millennium. *Personality and Social Psychology Review, 4,* 30–44.

Saad, L. (2002, November 21). Most smokers wish they could quit. Gallup News Service (www.gallup.com/poll/releases/pr021121.asp).

Sabina, C. (2013). Individual and national level associations between economic deprivation and partner violence among college students in 31 national settings. *Aggressive Behavior, 39,* 247–256.

Sabini, J., & Silver, M. (1982). *Moralities of everyday life.* New York: Oxford University Press.

Sacks, C. H., & Bugental, D. P. (1987). Attributions as moderators of affective and behavioral responses to social failure. *Journal of Personality and Social Psychology, 53,* 939–947.

Sadler, M. S., Correll, J., Park, B., & Judd, C. M. (2012). The world is not Black and White: Racial bias in the decision to shoot in a multiethnic context. *Journal of Social Issues, 68,* 286–313.

Safer, M. A., Bonanno, G. A., & Field, N. P. (2001). It was never that bad: Biased recall of grief and long-term adjustment to the death of a spouse. *Memory, 9,* 195–204.

Sagarin, B. J., Cialdini, R. B., Rice, W. E., & Serna, S. B. (2002). Dispelling the illusion of invulnerability: The motivations and mechanisms of resistance to persuasion. *Journal of Personality and Social Psychology, 83,* 526–541.

Sagarin, B. J., Rhoads, K. v. L., & Cialdini, R. B. (1998). Deceiver's distrust: Denigration as a consequence of undiscovered deception. *Personality and Social Psychology Bulletin, 24,* 1167–1176.

Sageman, M. (2004). *Understanding terror networks.* Philadelphia: University of Pennsylvania Press.

Saguy, T., & Halperin, E. (2014). Exposure to outgroup members criticizing their own group facilitates intergroup openness. *Personality and Social Psychology Bulletin, 40,* 791–802.

Said, C. P., & Todorov, A. (2011). A statistical model of facial attractiveness. *Psychological Science, 22,* 1183–1190.

Saks, M. J. (1974). Ignorance of science is no excuse. *Trial, 10(6),* 18–20.

Saks, M. J. (1996). The smaller the jury, the greater the unpredictability. *Judicature, 79,* 263–265.

Saks, M. J. (1998). What do jury experiments tell us about how juries (should) make decisions? *Southern California Interdisciplinary Law Journal, 6,* 1–53.

Saks, M. J., & Hastie, R. (1978). *Social psychology in court.* New York: Van Nostrand Reinhold.

Saks, M. J., & Marti, M. W. (1997). A meta-analysis of the effects of jury size. *Law and Human Behavior, 21,* 451–467.

Sakurai, M. M. (1975). Small group cohesiveness and detrimental conformity. *Sociometry, 38,* 340–357.

Saleem, M. Anderson, C. A., & Gentile, D. A. (2012). Effects of prosocial, neutral, and violent video games on college students' affect. *Aggressive Behavior, 38,* 263–271.

Sales, S. M. (1972). Economic threat as a determinant of conversion rates in authoritarian and nonauthoritarian churches. *Journal of Personality and Social Psychology, 23,* 420–428.

Salganik, M. J., Dodds, P. S., & Watts, D. J. (2006). Experimental study of inequality and unpredictability in an artificial cultural market. *Science, 311,* 854–856.

Salmela-Aro, K., & Nurmi, J-E. (2007). Self-esteem during university studies predicts career characteristics 10 years later. *Journal of Vocational Behavior, 70,* 463–477.

Salmivalli, C. (2009). Bullying and the peer group: A review. *Aggression and Violent Behavior, 15,* 112–120.

Salmivalli, C., Kaukiainen, A., Kaistaniemi, L., & Lagerspetz, K. M. J. (1999). Self-evaluated self-esteem, peer-evaluated self-esteem, and defensive egotism as predictors of adolescents' participation in bullying situations. *Personality and Social Psychology Bulletin, 25,* 1268–1278.

Salovey, P., Mayer, J. D., & Rosenhan, D. L. (1991). Mood and healing: Mood as a motivator of helping and helping as a regulator of mood. In M. S. Clark (Ed.), *Prosocial behavior.* Newbury Park, CA: Sage.

Salovey, P., Schneider, T. R., & Apanovitch, A. M. (2002). Message framing in the prevention and early detection of illness. In J. P. Dillard & M. Pfau (Eds.), *The persuasion handbook: Theory and practice.* Thousand Oaks, CA: Sage.

Saltzstein, H. D., & Sandberg, L. (1979). Indirect social influence: Change in judgmental processor anticipatory conformity. *Journal of Experimental Social Psychology, 15,* 209–216.

Salvatore, J., Kuo, S. I., Steele, R. D., Simpson, J. A., & Collins, W. A. (2011). Recovering from conflict in romantic relationships: A developmental perspective. *Psychological Science, 22,* 376–383.

Sam, D. L., & Berry, J. W. (2010). Acculturation: When individuals and groups of different cultural backgrounds meet. *Perspectives on Psychological Science, 5,* 472–481.

Sampson, E. E. (1975). On justice as equality. *Journal of Social Issues, 31(3),* 45–64.

Sanchez, C. A. (2012). Enhancing visiospatial performance through video game training to increase learning in visiospatial science domains. *Psychonomic Bulletin & Review, 19,* 58–65.

Sancton, T. (1997, October 13). The dossier on Diana's crash. *Time,* 50–56.

Sande, G. N., Goethals, G. R., & Radloff, C. E. (1988). Perceiving one's own traits and others': The multifaceted self. *Journal of Personality and Social Psychology, 54,* 13–20.

Sanders, G. S. (1981a). Driven by distraction: An integrative review of social facilitation and theory and research. *Journal of Experimental Social Psychology, 17,* 227–251.

Sanders, G. S. (1981b). Toward a comprehensive account of social facilitation: Distraction/conflict does not mean theoretical conflict. *Journal of Experimental Social Psychology, 17,* 262–265.

Sanders, G. S., Baron, R. S., & Moore, D. L. (1978). Distraction and social comparison as mediators of social facilitation effects. *Journal of Experimental Social Psychology, 14,* 291–303.

Sanderson, C. A., & Cantor, N. (2001). The association of intimacy goals and marital satisfaction: A test of four mediational hypotheses. *Personality and Social Psychology Bulletin, 27,* 1567–1577.

Sani, F., Herrera, M., & Bowe, M. (2009). Perceived collective continuity and ingroup identification as defence against death awareness. *Journal of Experimental Social Psychology, 45,* 242–245.

Sani, F., Herrera, M., Wakefield, J. R. H., Boroch, O., & Gulyas, C. (2012). Comparing social contact and group identification as predictors of mental health. *British Journal of Social Psychology, 51,* 781–790.

Sanislow, C. A., III, Perkins, D. V., & Balogh, D. W. (1989). Mood induction, interpersonal perceptions, and rejection in the roommates of depressed, nondepressed-disturbed, and normal college students. *Journal of Social and Clinical Psychology, 8,* 345–358.

Sanitioso, R., Kunda, Z., & Fong, G. T. (1990). Motivated recruitment of autobiographical memories. *Journal of Personality and Social Psychology, 59,* 229–241.

Sanna, L. J., Parks, C. D., Meier, S., Chang, E. C., Kassin, B. R., Lechter, J. L., Turley-Ames, K. J., & Miyake, T. M. (2003). A game of inches: Spontaneous use of counterfactuals by broadcasters during major league baseball playoffs. *Journal of Applied Social Psychology, 33,* 455–475.

Sansone, C. (1986). A question of competence: The effects of competence and task feedback on intrinsic interest. *Journal of Personality and Social Psychology, 51,* 918–931.

Santos, A., Meyer-Lindenberg, A., & Deruelle, C. (2010). Absence of racial, but not gender, stereotyping in Williams syndrome children. *Current Biology, 20,* R307–R308.

Sapadin, L. A. (1988). Friendship and gender: Perspectives of professional men and women. *Journal of Social and Personal Relationships, 5,* 387–403.

Sapolsky, R. (2005, December). Sick of poverty. *Scientific American,* 93–99.

Sarnoff, I., & Sarnoff, S. (1989). *Love-centered marriage in a self-centered world.* New York: Schocken Books.

Sartre, J-P. (1946/1948). *Anti-Semite and Jew.* New York: Schocken Books.

Sasaki, J. Y., & Kim, H. S. (2011). At the intersection of culture and religion: A cultural analysis of religion's implications for secondary control and social affiliation. *Journal of Personality and Social Psychology, 101,* 401–414.

Sassenberg, K., Moskowitz, G. B., Jacoby, J., & Hansen, N. (2007). The carry-over effect of competition: The impact of competition on prejudice towards uninvolved outgroups. *Journal of Experimental Social Psychology, 43,* 529–538.

Sato, K. (1987). Distribution of the cost of maintaining common resources. *Journal of Experimental Social Psychology, 23,* 19–31.

Saucier, D. A., & Miller, C. T. (2003). The persuasiveness of racial arguments as a subtle measure of racism. *Personality and Social Psychology Bulletin, 29,* 1303–1315.

Saucier, D. A., Miller, C. T., & Doucet, N. (2005). Differences in helping Whites and Blacks: A meta-analysis. *Personality and Social Psychology Review, 9,* 2–16.

Saucier, G., Akers, L. G., Shen-Miller, S., Knežević, G., & Stankov, L. (2009). Patterns of thinking in militant extremism. *Perspectives on Psychological Science, 4,* 256–271.

Saucier, G., Thalmayer, A. G., & Bel-Bahar, T. S. (2014). Human attribute concepts: Relative ubiquity across twelve mutually isolated languages. *Journal of Personality and Social Psychology, 107,* 199–216.

Sauer, J., Brewer, N., Zweck, T., & Weber, N. (2010). The effect of retention interval on the confidence–accuracy relationship for eyewitness identification. *Law and Human Behavior, 34,* 337–347.

Sauerland, M., & Sporer, S. L. (2009). Fast and confident: Postdicting eyewitness identification accuracy in a field study. *Journal of Experimental Psychology: Applied, 15,* 46–62.

Savani, K., Stephens, N. M., & Markus, H. R. (2011). The unanticipated interpersonal and societal consequences of choice: Victim blaming and reduced support for the public good. *Psychological Science, 22,* 795–802.

Savitsky, K., Epley, N., & Gilovich, T. (2001). Do others judge us as harshly as we think? Overestimating the impact of our failures, shortcomings, and mishaps. *Journal of Personality and Social Psychology, 81,* 44–56.

Savitsky, K., & Gilovich, T. (2003). The illusion of transparency and the alleviation of speech anxiety. *Journal of Experimental Social Psychology, 39,* 618–625.

Savitsky, K., Van Voven, L., Epley, N., & Wright, W. M. (2005). The unpacking effect in allocations of responsibility for group tasks. *Journal of Experimental Social Psychology, 41,* 447–457.

Sax, L. J., Lindholm, J. A., Astin, A. W., Korn, W. S., & Mahoney, K. M. (2002). *The American freshman: National norms for Fall, 2002.* Los Angeles: Cooperative Institutional Research Program, UCLA.

Sbarra, D. A., Law, R. W., & Portley, R. M. (2011). Divorce and death: A meta-analysis and research agenda for clinical, social, and health psychology. *Perspectives on Psychological Science, 6,* 454–474.

Scalia, A. (2011). *Opinion of the Supreme Court of the United States, Brown v. Entertainment Merchants Association.* June 27, 2011.

Scarr, S. (1988). Race and gender as psychological variables: Social and ethical issues. *American Psychologist, 43,* 56–59.

Schachter, S. (1951). Deviation, rejection and communication. *Journal of Abnormal and Social Psychology, 46,* 190–207.

Schachter, S., & Singer, J. E. (1962). Cognitive, social and physiological determinants of emotional state. *Psychological Review, 69,* 379–399.

Schacter, D. L., & Loftus, E. F. (2013). Memory and law: What can cognitive neuroscience contribute? *Nature Neuroscience, 16,* 119–123.

Schafer, R. B., & Keith, P. M. (1980). Equity and depression among married couples. *Social Psychology Quarterly, 43,* 430–435.

Schaffner, P. E. (1985). Specious learning about reward and punishment. *Journal of Personality and Social Psychology, 48,* 1377–1386.

Schaffner, P. E., Wandersman, A., & Stang, D. (1981). Candidate name exposure and voting: Two field studies. *Basic and Applied Social Psychology, 2,* 195–203.

Schaller, M., & Cialdini, R. B. (1988). The economics of empathic helping: Support for a mood management motive. *Journal of Experimental Social Psychology, 24,* 163–181.

Schein, E. H. (1956). The Chinese indoctrination program for prisoners of war: A study of attempted brainwashing. *Psychiatry, 19,* 149–172.

Schiffenbauer, A., & Schiavo, R. S. (1976). Physical distance and attraction: An intensification effect. *Journal of Experimental Social Psychology, 12,* 274–282.

Schimel, J., Simon, L., Greenberg, J., Pyszczynski, T., Solomon, S., & Waxmonsky, J. (1999). Stereotypes and terror management: Evidence that mortality salience enhances stereotypic thinking and preferences. *Journal of Personality and Social Psychology, 77,* 905–926.

Schimmack, U., Oishi, S., & Diener, E. (2005). Individualism: A valid and important dimension of cultural differences between nations. *Personality and Social Psychology Review, 9,* 17–31.

Schirmer, A., The, K., Wang, S., Vijayakumar, R., Ching, A., Nithianantham, D., Escoffier, N., & Cheok, A. (2011). Squeeze me, but don't tease me: Human and mechanical touch enhance visual attention and emotion discrimination. *Social Neuroscience, 6,* 219–230.

Schkade, D. A., & Kahneman, D. (1998). Does living in California make people happy? A focusing illusion in judgments of life satisfaction. *Psychological Science, 9,* 340–346.

Schkade, D. A., & Sunstein, C. R. (2003, June 11). Judging by where you sit. *New York Times* (www.nytimes.com).

Schkade, D. A., Sunstein, C. R., & Hastie, R. (2007). What happened on deliberation day? *California Law Review, 95,* 915–940.

Schlenker, B. R., & Leary, M. R. (1982). Social anxiety and self-presentation: A conceptualization and model. *Psychological Bulletin, 92,* 641–669.

Schlenker, B. R., & Leary, M. R. (1985). Social anxiety and communication about the self. *Journal of Language and Social Psychology, 4,* 171–192.

Schlenker, B. R., & Weigold, M. F. (1992). Interpersonal processes involving impression regulation and management. *Annual Review of Psychology, 43,* 133–168.

Schlesinger, A., Jr. (1949). The statistical soldier. *Partisan Review, 16,* 852–856.

Schlesinger, A., Jr. (1991, July 8). The cult of ethnicity, good and bad. *Time,* 21.

Schlesinger, A. M., Jr. (1965). *A thousand days.* Boston: Houghton Mifflin. Cited by I. L. Janis (1972) in *Victims of groupthink.* Boston: Houghton Mifflin.

Schmader, T., Johns, M., & Forbes, C. (2008). An integrated process model of stereotype threat effects on performance. *Psychological Review, 115,* 336–356.

Schmiege, S. J., Klein, W. M. P., & Bryan, A. D. (2010). The effect of peer comparison information in the context of expert recommendations on risk perceptions and subsequent behavior. *European Journal of Social Psychology, 40,* 746–759.

Schmitt, D. P., & 128 others. (2004). Patterns and universals of adult romantic attachment across 62 cultural regions: Are models of self and of other pancultural constructs? *Journal of Cross-Cultural Psychology, 35,* 367–402.

Schmitt, D. P. (2003). Universal sex differences in the desire for sexual variety; tests from 52 nations, 6 continents, and 13 islands. *Journal of Personality and Social Psychology, 85,* 85–104.

Schmitt, D. P. (2005). Sociosexuality from Argentina to Zimbabwe: A 48-nation study of sex, culture, and strategies of human mating. *Behavioral and Brain Sciences, 28,* 247–311.

Schmitt, D. P. (2006). Evolutionary and cross-cultural perspectives on love: The influence of gender, personality, and local ecology on emotional investment in romantic relationships. In R. J. Sternberg (Ed.), *The psychology of love* (2nd ed.). New Haven, CT: Yale University Press.

Schmitt, D. P. (2007). Sexual strategies across sexual orientations: How personality traits and culture relate to sociosexuality among gays, lesbians, bisexuals, and heterosexuals. *Journal of Psychology and Human Sexuality, 18,* 183–214.

Schmitt, D. P., & Allik, J. (2005). Simultaneous administration of the Rosenberg Self-Esteem Scale in 53 nations: Exploring the universal and culture-specific features of global self-esteem. *Journal of Personality and Social Psychology, 89,* 623–642.

Schmitt, D. P., Realo, A., Voracek, M., & Allik, J. (2008). Why can't a man be more like a woman? Sex differences in Big Five personality traits across 55 cultures. *Journal of Personality and Social Psychology, 94,* 168–182.

Schmitt, M. T., Branscombe, N. R., Postmes, T., & Garcia, A. (2014). The consequences of perceived discrimination for psychological well-being: A meta-analytic review. *Psychological Bulletin, 140,* 921–948.

Schnall, S., & Laird, J. D. (2003). Keep smiling: Enduring effects of facial expressions and postures on emotional experience and memory. *Cognition and Emotion, 17,* 787–797.

Schnall, S., Roper, J., & Fessler, D. M. T. (2010). Elevation leads to altruistic behavior. *Psychological Science, 21,* 315–320.

Schneider, M. E., Major, B., Luhtanen, R., & Crocker, J. (1996). Social stigma and the potential costs of assumptive help. *Personality and Social Psychology Bulletin, 22,* 201–209.

Schneider, T. R., Salovey, P., Pallonen, U., Mundorf, N., Smith, N. F., & Steward, W. T. (2000). Visual and auditory message framing effects on tobacco smoking. *Journal of Applied Social Psychology, 31(4),* 667–682.

Schoeneman, T. J. (1994). Individualism. In V. S. Ramachandran (Ed.), *Encyclopedia of Human Behavior.* San Diego: Academic Press.

Schofield, J. (1982). *Black and white in school: Trust, tension, or tolerance?* New York: Praeger.

Schofield, J. W. (1986). Causes and consequences of the colorblind perspective. In J. F. Dovidio & S. L. Gaertner (Eds.), *Prejudice, discrimination, and racism.* Orlando, FL: Academic Press.

Scholl, A., & Sassenberg, K. (2014). Where could we stand if I had . . .? How social power impacts counterfactual thinking after failure. *Journal of Experimental Social Psychology, 53,* 51–61.

Schor, J. B. (1998). *The overworked American.* New York: Basic Books.

Schroeder, D. A., Dovidio, J. F., Sibicky, M. E., Matthews, L. L., & Allen, J. L. (1988). Empathic concern and helping behavior: Egoism or altruism: *Journal of Experimental Social Psychology, 24,* 333–353.

Schroeder, J., & Risen, J. L. (2014). Befriending the enemy: Outgroup friendship longitudinally predicts intergroup attitudes in a coexistence program for Israelis and Palestinians. *Group Processes and Intergroup Relations,* in press.

Schultz, P. W., Nolan, J. M., Cialdini, R. B., Goldstein, N. J., & Griskevicius, V. (2007). The constructive, destructive, and reconstructive power of social norms. *Psychological Science, 18,* 429–434.

Schulz-Hardt, S., Frey, D., Luthgens, C., & Moscovici, S. (2000). Biased information search in group decision making. *Journal of Personality and Social Psychology, 78,* 655–669.

Schulz, J. W., & Pruitt, D. G. (1978). The effects of mutual concern on joint welfare. *Journal of Experimental Social Psychology, 14,* 480–492.

Schuman, H., & Kalton, G. (1985). Survey methods. In G. Lindzey & E. Aronson (Eds.), *Handbook of Social Psychology* (Vol. 1). Hillsdale, NJ: Erlbaum.

Schuman, H., & Scott, J. (1989). Generations and collective memories. *American Sociological Review, 54,* 359–381.

Schumann, K., McGregor, I., Nash, K. A., & Ross, M. (2014). Religious magnanimity: Reminding people of their religious belief system reduces hostility after threat. *Journal of Personality and Social Psychology, 107,* 432–453.

Schwartz, H. A., Eichstaedt, J. C., Kern, M. L., Dziurzynski, L., Ramones, S. M., Agarwal, M., Shah, A., Kosinski, M., Stillwell, D., Seligman, M. E. P., & Ungar, L. H. (2013). *Personality, gender, and age in the language of social media:* The open-vocabulary approach. Plos One, DOI: 10.1371/journal.pone.0073791.

Schwartz, S. H. (1975). The justice of need and the activation of humanitarian norms. *Journal of Social Issues, 31(3),* 111–136.

Schwartz, S. H., & Gottlieb, A. (1981). Participants' post-experimental reactions and the ethics of bystander research. *Journal of Experimental Social Psychology, 17,* 396–407.

Schwartz, S. H., & Rubel, T. (2005). Sex differences in value priorities: Cross-cultural and multimethod studies. *Journal of Personality and Social Psychology, 89,* 1010–1028.

Schwarz, N., & Kurz, E. (1989). What's in a picture? The impact of face-ism on trait attribution. *European Journal of Social Psychology, 19,* 311–316.

Schwarz, N., Sanna, L. J., Skurnik, I., & Yoon, C. (2007). Metacognitive experiences and the intricacies of setting people straight: Implications for debiasing and public information campaigns. *Advances in Experimental Social Psychology, 39,* 127–161.

Schwarz, N., Strack, F., Kommer, D., & Wagner, D. (1987). Soccer, rooms, and the quality of your life: Mood effects on judgments of satisfaction with life in general and with specific domains. *Journal of Applied Social Psychology, 17,* 69–79.

Schwinger, M., Wirthwein, L., Lemmer, G., & Steinmayr, R. (2014). Academic self-handicapping and achievement: A meta-analysis. *Journal of Educational Psychology.*

Scott, B., Amel, E. L., Kroger, S. M., & Manning, C. (2015). *Psychology for sustainability,* 4th Edition. New York: Psychology Press.

Scott, J. P., & Marston, M. V. (1953). Nonadaptive behavior resulting from a series of defeats in fighting mice. *Journal of Abnormal and Social Psychology, 48,* 417–428.

Searcy, T. (2011). The new rules on dressing for success. CBS Moneywatch, November 8, 2011.

Sears, D. O. (1979). *Life stage effects upon attitude change, especially among the elderly.* Manuscript prepared for Workshop on the Elderly of the Future, Committee on Aging, National Research Council, Annapolis, MD, May 3–5.

Sears, D. O. (1986). College sophomores in the laboratory: Influences of a narrow data base on social psychology's view of human nature. *Journal of Personality and Social Psychology, 51,* 515–530.

Sedikides, C. (1993). Assessment, enhancement, and verification determinants of the self-evaluation process. *Journal of Personality and Social Psychology, 65,* 317–338.

Sedikides, C., Gaertner, L., & Toguchi, Y. (2003). Pancultural self-enhancement. *Journal of Personality and Social Psychology, 84,* 60–79.

Sedikides, C., Gaertner, L., & Vevea, J. L. (2005). Pancultural self-enhancement reloaded: A meta-analytic reply to Heine (2005). *Journal of Personality and Social Psychology, 89,* 539–551.

Sedikides, C., Meek, R., Alicke, M. D., & Taylor, S. (2014). Behind bars but above the bar: Prisoners consider themselves more prosocial than non-prisoners. *British Journal of Social Psychology, 53,* 396–403.

Segal-Caspi, L., Roccas, S., & Sagiv, L. (2012). Don't judge a book by its cover, revisited: Perceived and reported traits and values of attractive women. *Psychological Science, 23,* 1112–1116.

Segal, H. A. (1954). Initial psychiatric findings of recently repatriated prisoners of war. *American Journal of Psychiatry, 61,* 358–363.

Segall, M. H., Dasen, P. R., Berry, J. W., & Poortinga, Y. H. (1990). *Human behavior in global perspective: An introduction to cross-cultural psychology.* New York: Pergamon.

Segal, N. L. (1984). Cooperation, competition, and altruism within twin sets: A reappraisal. *Ethology and Sociobiology, 5,* 163–177.

Segal, N. L., & Hershberger, S. L. (1999). Cooperation and competition between twins: Findings from a Prisoner's Dilemma game. *Evolution and Human Behavior, 20,* 29–51.

Seger, C. R., Smith, E. R., Percy, E. J., & Conrey, F. R. (2014). Reach out and reduce prejudice: The impact of interpersonal touch on intergroup liking. *Basic and Applied Social Psychology, 36,* 51–58.

Segerstrom, S. C. (2001). Optimism and attentional bias for negative and positive stimuli. *Personality and Social Psychology Bulletin, 27,* 1334–1343.

Segerstrom, S. C., McCarthy, W. J., Caskey, N. H., Gross, T. M., & Jarvik, M. E. (1993). Optimistic bias among cigarette smokers. *Journal of Applied Social Psychology, 23,* 1606–1618.

Segerstrom, S., & Miller, G. E. (2004). Psychological stress and the human immune system: A meta-analytic study of 30 years of inquiry. *Psychological Bulletin, 130,* 601–630.

Seibt, B., & Forster, J. (2004). Stereotype threat and performance: How self-stereotypes influence processing by inducing regulatory foci. *Journal of Personality and Social Psychology, 87(1),* 38–56.

Seidel, E., Eickhoff, S. B., Kellermann, T., Schneider, F., Gur, R. C., Habel, U., & Birgit, D. (2010). Who is to blame? Neural correlates of causal attribution in social situations. *Social Neuroscience, 5,* 335–350.

Selby, J. W., Calhoun, L. G., & Brock, T. A. (1977). Sex differences in the social perception of rape victims. *Personality and Social Psychology Bulletin, 3,* 412–415.

Seligman, M. (1994). *What you can change and what you can't.* New York: Knopf.

Seligman, M. E. P. (1991). *Learned optimism.* New York: Knopf.

Seligman, M. E. P. (1998). The prediction and prevention of depression. In D. K. Routh & R. J. DeRubeis (Eds.), *The science of clinical psychology: Accomplishments and future directions.* Washington, DC: American Psychological Association.

Seligman, M. E. P. (2002). *Authentic happiness: Using the new positive psychology to realize your potential for lasting fulfillment.* New York: Free Press.

Sen, S., & Lerman, D. (2007). Why are you telling me this? An examination into negative consumer reviews on the Web. *Journal of Interactive Marketing, 21,* 76–94.

Senate Committee on the Judiciary. (1999, September 14) Children, violence, and the media: a report for parents and policy makers (http://www.indiana.edu/~cspc/ressenate.htm).

Sendén, M., Lindholm, T., & Sikström, S. (2014). Biases in news media as reflected by personal pronouns in evaluative contexts. *Social Psychology, 45,* 103–111.

Sengupta, S. (2001, October 10). Sept. 11 attack narrows the racial divide. *New York Times* (www.nytimes.com).

Sentyrz, S. M., & Bushman, B. J. (1998). Mirror, mirror, on the wall, who's the thinnest one of all? Effects of self-awareness on consumption of fatty, reduced-fat, and fat-free products. *Journal of Applied Psychology, 83,* 944–949.

Shaffer, D. R., Pegalis, L. J., & Bazzini, D. G. (1996). When boy meets girls (revisited): Gender, gender-role orientation, and prospect of future interaction as determinants of self-disclosure among same- and opposite-sex acquaintances. *Personality and Social Psychology Bulletin, 22,* 495–506.

Shah, A. K., & Oppenheimer, D. M. (2008). Heuristics made easy: An effort-reduction framework. *Psychological Bulletin, 134,* 207–222.

Shapiro, D. L. (2010). Relational identity theory: A systematic approach for transforming the emotional dimension of conflict. *American Psychologist, 65,* 634–645.

Shariff, A. F., Willard, A. K., Andersen, T., & Norenzayan, A. (2015). Religious priming: A meta-analysis with a focus on prosociality. *Personality and Social Psychology Review,* in press.

Sharot, T., Fleming, S. M., Yu, X., Koster, R., & Dolan, R. J. (2012). Is choice-induced preference change long lasting? *Psychological Science, 23,* 1123–1129.

Sharot, T., Velasquez, C. M., & Dolan, R. J. (2010). Do decisions shape preference? Evidence from blind chance. *Psychological Science, 21,* 1231–1235.

Sharpe, D., & Faye, C. (2009). A second look at debriefing practices: Madness in our method? *Ethics and Behavior, 19,* 432–447.

Shaver, P. R., & Hazan, C. (1993). Adult romantic attachment: Theory and evidence. In D. Perlman & W. Jones (Eds.), *Advances in personal relationships* (Vol. 4). Greenwich, CT: JAI.

Shaver, P. R., & Hazan, C. (1994). Attachment. In A. L. Weber & J. H. Harvey (Eds.), *Perspectives on close relationships.* Boston: Allyn & Bacon.

Shaver, P. R., & Mikulincer, M. (2011). An attachment-theory framework for conceptualizing interpersonal behavior. In L. M. Horowitz & S. Strack (Eds.), *Handbook of interpersonal psychology: Theory, research, assessment, and therapeutic interventions.* Hoboken, NJ: Wiley.

Shaw, J., & Porter, S. (2015). Constructing rich false memories of committing crime. *Psychological Science, 26,* 291–301.

Shaw, J. S., III. (1996). Increases in eyewitness confidence resulting from postevent questioning. *Journal of Experimental Psychology: Applied, 2,* 126–146.

Shaw, M. E. (1981). *Group dynamics: The psychology of small group behavior.* New York: McGraw-Hill.

Shayo, M., & Zussman, A. (2011). Judicial ingroup bias in the shadow of terrorism. *Quarterly Journal of Economics, 126,* 1447–1484.

Sheese, B. E., & Graziano, W. G. (2005). Deciding to defect: The effects of video-game violence on cooperative behavior. *Psychological Science, 16,* 354–357.

Sheldon, K. M., Elliot, A. J., Youngmee, K., & Kasser, T. (2001). What is satisfying about satisfying events? Testing 10 candidate psychological needs. *Journal of Personality and Social Psychology, 80,* 325–339.

Sheldon, K. M., & Niemiec, C. P. (2006). It's not just the amount that counts: Balanced need satisfaction also affects well-being. *Journal of Personality and Social Psychology, 91,* 331–341.

Sheldon, K. M., Ryan, R. M., Deci, E. L., & Kasser, T. (2004). The independent effects of goal contents and motives on well-being: It's both what you pursue and why you pursue it. *Personality and Social Psychology Bulletin, 30,* 475–486.

Shell, R. M., & Eisenberg, N. (1992). A developmental model of recipients' reactions to aid. *Psychological Bulletin, 111,* 413–433.

Shelton, J. N., & Richeson, J. A. (2005). Intergroup contact and pluralistic ignorance. *Journal of Personality and Social Psychology, 88,* 91–107.

Shen, H., Wan, F., & Wyer, R. S., Jr. (2011). Cross-cultural differences in the refusal to accept a small gift: The differential influence of reciprocity norms on Asians and North Americans. *Journal of Personality and Social Psychology, 100,* 271–281.

Sheppard, B. H., & Vidmar, N. (1980). Adversary pretrial procedures and testimonial evidence: Effects of lawyer's role and Machiavellianism. *Journal of Personality and Social Psychology, 39,* 320–322.

Shepperd, J. A. (2003). Interpreting comparative risk judgments: Are people personally optimistic or interpersonally pessimistic? Unpublished manuscript, University of Florida.

Shepperd, J. A., & Arkin, R. M. (1991). Behavioral other-enhancement: Strategically obscuring the link between performance and evaluation. *Journal of Personality and Social Psychology, 60,* 79–88.

Shepperd, J. A., Arkin, R. M., & Slaughter, J. (1995). Constraints on excuse making: The deterring effects of shyness and anticipated retest. *Personality and Social Psychology Bulletin, 21,* 1061–1072.

Shepperd, J. A., Grace, J., Cole, L. J., & Klein, C. (2005). Anxiety and outcome predictions. *Personality and Social Psychology Bulletin, 31,* 267–275.

Shepperd, J. A., Klein, W. M. P., Waters, E. A., & Weinstein, N. D. (2013). Taking stock of unrealistic optimism. *Perspectives on Psychological Science, 8,* 395–411.

Shepperd, J. A., & Taylor, K. M. (1999). Ascribing advantages to social comparison targets. *Basic and Applied Social Psychology, 21,* 103–117.

Shepperd, J. A., Waters, E., Weinstein, N. D., & Klein, W. M. P. (2015). A primer on unrealistic optimism. *Current Directions in Psychological Science,* in press.

Shergill, S. S., Bays, P. M., Frith, C. D., & Wolpert, D. M. (2003). Two eyes for an eye: The neuroscience of force escalation. *Science, 301,* 187.

Sherif, M. (1935). A study of some social factors in perception. *Archives of Psychology, 187.*

Sherif, M. (1937). An experimental approach to the study of attitudes. *Sociometry, 1,* 90–98.

Sherif, M. (1966). *In common predicament: Social psychology of intergroup conflict and cooperation.* Boston: Houghton Mifflin.

Sherif, M., & Sherif, C. W. (1969). *Social psychology.* New York: Harper & Row.

Sherman, D. K., Hartson, K. A., Binning, K. R., Purdie-Vaughns, V., Garcia, J., Taborsky-Barba, S., Tomassetti, S., Nussbaum, A. D., & Cohen, G. L. (2013). Deflecting the trajectory and changing the narrative: How self-affirmation affects academic performance and motivation under identity threat. *Journal of Personality and Social Psychology, 104,* 591–618.

Sherman, D. K., Nelson, L. D., & Ross, L. D. (2003). Naive realism and affirmative action: Adversaries are more similar than they think. *Basic and Applied Social Psychology, 25,* 275–289.

Sherman, J. W. (1996). Development and mental representation of stereotypes. *Journal of Personality and Social Psychology, 70,* 1126–1141.

Sherman, J. W., Kruschke, J. K., Sherman, S. J., Percy, E. J., Petrocelli, J. V., & Conrey, F. R. (2009). Attentional processes in stereotype formation: A common model for category accentuation and illusory correlation. *Journal of Personality and Social Psychology, 96,* 305–323.

Sherman, J. W., Lee, A. Y., Bessenoff, G. R., & Frost, L. A. (1998). Stereotype efficiency reconsidered: Encoding flexibility under cognitive load. *Journal of Personality and Social Psychology, 75,* 589–606.

Sherman, S. J., Cialdini, R. B., Schwartzman, D. F., & Reynolds, K. D. (1985). Imagining can heighten or lower the perceived likelihood of contracting a disease: The mediating effect of ease of imagery. *Personality and Social Psychology Bulletin, 11,* 118–127.

Shermer, M. (2006). Answer on World Question Center 2006. The Edge (www.edge.org).

Shestakova, A., Rieskamp, J., Tugin, S., Ossadtchi, A., Krutitskaya, J., & Klucharev, V. (2013). Electrophysiological precursors of social conformity. *Scan, 8,* 756–763.

Shih, M., Pittinsky, T. L., & Ambady, N. (1999). Stereotype susceptibility: Identity salience and shifts in quantitative performance. *Psychological Science, 10,* 80–83.

Shiller, R. (2005). *Irrational exuberance* (2nd edition). New York: Crown.

Shin, H., Dovidio, J. F., & Napier, J. L. (2013). Cultural differences in targets of stigmatization between individual- and group-oriented cultures. *Basic and Applied Social Psychology, 35,* 98–108.

Shipman, P. (2003). We are all Africans. *American Scientist, 91,* 496–499.

Short, J. F., Jr. (Ed.) (1969). *Gang delinquency and delinquent subcultures.* New York: Harper & Row.

Shostak, M. (1981). *Nisa: The life and words of a !Kung woman.* Cambridge, MA: Harvard University Press.

Shotland, R. L. (1989). A model of the causes of date rape in developing and close relationships. In C. Hendrick (Ed.), *Review of personality and social psychology* (Vol. 10). Beverly Hills, CA: Sage.

Shotland, R. L., & Stebbins, C. A. (1983). Emergency and cost as determinants of helping behavior and the slow accumulation of social psychological knowledge. *Social Psychology Quarterly, 46,* 36–46.

Shotland, R. L., & Straw, M. K. (1976). Bystander response to an assault: When a man attacks a woman. *Journal of Personality and Social Psychology, 34,* 990–999.

Showers, C., & Ruben, C. (1987). Distinguishing pessimism from depression: Negative expectations and positive coping mechanisms. Paper presented at the American Psychological Association convention, New York, NY.

Shrauger, J. S. (1975). Responses to evaluation as a function of initial self-perceptions. *Psychological Bulletin, 82,* 581–596.

Shriver, E. R., Young, S. G., Hugenberg, K., Bernstein, M. J., & Lanter, J. R. (2008, February). Class, race, and the face: Social context modulates the cross-race effect in face recognition. *Personality and Social Psychology Bulletin, 34,* 260–274.

Shutts, K., Kinzler, K. D., Katz, R. C., Tredoux, C., & Spelke, E. S. (2011). Race preferences in children: Insights from

South Africa. *Developmental Science, 14,* 1283–1291.

Sidanius, J., & Pratto, F. (1999). *Social dominance: An intergroup theory of social hierarchy and oppression.* New York: Cambridge University Press.

Sidanius, J., Pratto, F., & Bobo, L. (1994). Social dominance orientation and the political psychology of gender: A case of invariance? *Journal of Personality and Social Psychology, 67,* 998–1011.

Sidanius, J., Van Laar, C., Levin, S., & Sinclair, S. (2004). Ethnic enclaves and the dynamics of social identity on the college campus: The good, the bad, and the ugly. *Journal of Personality and Social Psychology, 87,* 96–110.

Siegel, M. (2013, March 4). Report blames climate change for extremes in Australia. *New York Times* (www.nytimes.com).

Sieverding, M., Decker, S., & Zimmerman, F. (2010). Information about low participation in cancer screening demotivates other people. *Psychological Science, 21,* 941–943.

Sigall, H. (1970). Effects of competence and consensual validation on a communicator's liking for the audience. *Journal of Personality and Social Psychology, 16,* 252–258.

Sigurdson, J. F., Wallander, J., & Sund, A. M. (2014). Is involvement in school bullying associated with general health and psychosocial adjustment outcomes in adulthood? *Child Abuse & Neglect, 38,* 1607–1617.

Silk, J. B., Alberts, S. C., & Altmann, J. (2003). Social bonds of female baboons enhance infant survival. *Science, 302,* 1231–1234.

Silke, A. (2003). Deindividuation, anonymity, and violence: Findings from Northern Ireland. *Journal of Social Psychology, 143,* 493–499.

Silva, K., Bessa, J., & de Sousa, L. (2012). Auditory contagious yawning in domestic dogs (canis familiaris): First evidence for social modulation. *Animal Cognition, 15,* 721–724.

Silverman, A. M., & Cohen, G. L. (2014). Stereotypes as stumbling-blocks: how coping with stereotypes threat affects life outcomes for people with physical disabilities. *Personality and Social Psychology Bulletin, 40,* 1330–1340.

Silver, M., & Geller, D. (1978). On the irrelevance of evil: The organization and individual action. *Journal of Social Issues, 34,* 125–136.

Silver, N. (2009, May 9). Bush may haunt Republicans for generations. *New York Times* (www.fivethirtyeight.com).

Silver, N. (2012). *The signal and the noise: Why so many predictions fail.* New York: Penguin.

Silvia, P. J. (2005). Deflecting reactance: The role of similarity in increasing compliance and reducing resistance. *Basic and Applied Social Psychology, 27,* 277–284.

Simon, H. A. (1957). *Models of man: Social and rational.* New York: Wiley.

Simon, P. (1996, April 17). American provincials. *Christian Century,* pp. 421–422.

Simon, R. (2011, June 28). SCOTUS: Violence OK. Sex? Maybe. Politico.com column (www.politco.com).

Simonsohn, U. (2011a). Spurious? Name similarity effects (implicit egotism) in marriage, job, and moving decisions. *Journal of Personality and Social Psychology,* in press.

Simonsohn, U. (2011b). Spurious also? Name-similarity effects (implicit egotism) in employment decisions. *Psychological Science, 22,* 1087–1089.

Simonton, D. K. (1994). *Greatness: Who makes history and why.* New York: Guilford.

Simpson, J. A. (1987). The dissolution of romantic relationships: Factors involved in relationship stability and emotional distress. *Journal of Personality and Social Psychology, 53,* 683–692.

Simpson, J. A., Gangestad, S. W., & Lerma, M. (1990). Perception of physical attractiveness: Mechanisms involved in the maintenance of romantic relationships. *Journal of Personality and Social Psychology, 59,* 1192–1201.

Simpson, J. A., Rholes, W. S., & Nelligan, J. S. (1992). Support seeking and support giving within couples in an anxiety-provoking situation: The role of attachment styles. *Journal of Personality and Social Psychology, 62,* 434–446.

Simpson, J. A., Rholes, W. S., & Phillips, D. (1996). Conflict in close relationships: An attachment perspective. *Journal of Personality and Social Psychology, 71,* 899–914.

Sinclair, S., Dunn, E., & Lowery, B. S. (2004). The relationship between parental racial attitudes and children's implicit prejudice. *Journal of Experimental Social Psychology, 41,* 283–289.

Singer, M. (1979). *Cults and cult members.* Address to the American Psychological Association convention.

Singer, T., Seymour, B., O'Doherty, J. P., Stephan, K. E., Dolan, R. J., & Frith, C. D. (2006). Empathic neural responses are modulated by the perceived fairness of others. *Nature, 439,* 466–469.

Singh, D. (1993). Adaptive significance of female physical attractiveness: Role of waist-to-hip ratio. *Journal of Personality and Social Psychology, 65,* 293–307.

Singh, D. (1995). Female judgment of male attractiveness and desirability for relationships: Role of waist-to-hip ratio and financial status. *Journal of Personality and Social Psychology, 69,* 1089–1101.

Singh, D., & Randall, P. K. (2007). Beauty is in the eye of the plastic surgeon: Waist-hip ratio (WHR) and women's attractiveness. *Personality and Individual Differences, 43,* 329–340.

Singh, R., & Ho, S. J. (2000). Attitudes and attraction: A new test of the attraction, repulsion and similarity-dissimilarity asymmetry hypotheses. *British Journal of Social Psychology, 39,* 197–211.

Singh, R., & Teoh, J. B. P. (1999). Attitudes and attraction: A test of two hypotheses for the similarity-dissimilarity asymmetry. *British Journal of Social Psychology, 38,* 427–443.

SIPRI (2014, accessed November 22). Recent trends. Stockholm International Peace Research Institute (www.sipri.org/research/armaments/milex).

Sissons, M. (1981). Race, sex, and helping behavior. *British Journal of Social Psychology, 20,* 285–292.

Sittser, G. L. (1994, April). Long night's journey into light. *Second Opinion,* pp. 10–15.

Sivarajasingam, V., Moore, S., & Shepherd, J. P. (2005). Winning, losing, and violence. *Injury Prevention, 11,* 69–70.

Six, B., & Eckes, T. (1996). Metaanalysen in der Einstellungs-Verhaltens-Forschung. *Zeitschrift fur Sozialpsychologie,* pp. 7–17.

Skaalvik, E. M., & Hagtvet, K. A. (1990). Academic achievement and self-concept: An analysis of causal predominance in a developmental perspective. *Journal of Personality and Social Psychology, 58,* 292–307.

Skinner, B. F. (1971). *Beyond freedom and dignity.* New York: Knopf.

Skitka, L. J. (1999). Ideological and attributional boundaries on public compassion: Reactions to individuals and communities affected by a natural disaster. *Personality and Social Psychology Bulletin, 25,* 793–808.

Skitka, L. J., Bauman, C. W., & Mullen, E. (2004). Political tolerance and coming to psychological closure following the September 11, 2001, terrorist attacks: An integrative approach. *Personality and Social Psychology Bulletin, 30,* 743–756.

Skitka, L. J., Bauyman, C. W., & Sargis, E. G. (2005). Moral conviction: Another contributor to attitude strength or something more? *Journal of Personality and Social Psychology, 88,* 895–917.

Skitka, L. J., & Tetlock, P. E. (1993). Providing public assistance: Cognitive and motivational processes underlying liberal and conservative policy preferences. *Journal of Personality and Social Psychology, 65,* 1205–1223.

Skurnik, I., Yoon, C., Park, D. C., & Schwarz, N. (2005). How warnings about false claims become recommendations. *Journal of Consumer Research, 31,* 713–724.

Slatcher, R. B., & Pennebaker, J. W. (2006). How do I love thee? Let me count the words: The social effects of expressive writing. *Psychological Science, 17,* 660–664.

Slater, M., Antley, A., Davison, A., Swapp, D., Guger, C., Barker, C., Pistrang, N., & Sanchez-Vives, M. V. (2006). A virtual reprise of the Stanley Milgram obedience experiments. *PloS One, 1(1):* e39 (DOI:10.1371/journal.pone.0000039).

Slavin, R. E. (1985). Cooperative learning: Applying contact theory in desegregated schools. *Journal of Social Issues, 41(3),* 45–62.

Slavin, R. E. (1990, December/January). Research on cooperative learning: Consensus and controversy. *Educational Leadership,* 52–54.

Slavin, R. E., & Cooper, R. (1999). Improving intergroup relations: Lessons learned from cooperative learning programs. *Journal of Social Issues, 55,* 647–663.

Slavin, R. E., Hurley, E. A., & Chamberlain, A. (2003). Cooperative learning and achievement: Theory and research. In W. M. Reynolds & G. E. Miller (Eds.), *Handbook of psychology: Educational psychology* (Vol. 7). New York: Wiley.

Slavin, R. E., Lake, C., & Groff, C. (2009). Effective programs in middle and high school mathematics: A best-evidence synthesis. *Review of Educational Research, 79,* 839–911.

Slavin, R. E., & Madden, N. A. (1979). School practices that improve race relations. *Journal of Social Issues, 16,* 169–180.

Slepian, M. L., Rule, N. O., & Ambady, N. (2012). Proprioception and person perception: Politicians and professors. *Personality and Social Psychology Bulletin, 38,* 1621–1628.

Slopen, N., Glynn, R. J., Buring, J., & Albert, M. A. (2010, November 23). Job strain, job insecurity, and incident cardiovascular disease in the Women's Health Study (Abstract 18520). *Circulation, A18520* (circ.ahajournals. org).

Slotow, R., Van Dyke, G., Poole, J., Page, B., & Klocke, A. (2000). Older bull elephants control young males. *Nature, 408,* 425–426.

Slotter, E. B., & Gardner, W. L. (2009). Where do you end and I begin? Evidence for anticipatory, motivated self-other integration between relationship partners. *Journal of Personality and Social Psychology, 96,* 1137–1151.

Slotter, E. B., Gardner, W. L., & Finkel, E. (2010). Who am I without you? The influence of romantic breakup on the self-concept. *Personality and Social Psychology Bulletin, 36,* 147–160.

Slovic, P. (1972). From Shakespeare to Simon: Speculations—and some evidence—about man's ability to process information. *Oregon Research Institute Research Bulletin, 12(2).*

Slovic, P. (2007). "If I look at the mass I will never act": Psychic numbing and genocide. *Judgment and Decision Making, 2,* 79–95.

Slovic, P., & Fischhoff, B. (1977). On the psychology of experimental surprises. *Journal of Experimental Psychology: Human Perception and Performance, 3,* 455–551.

Slovic, P., & Västfjäll, D. (2010). Affect, moral intuition, and risk. *Psychological Inquiry, 21,* 387–398.

Smalarz, L., & Wells, G. L. (2014). Post-identification feedback to eyewitnesses impairs evaluators' abilities to discriminate between accurate and mistaken testimony. *Law and Human Behavior, 38,* 194–202.

Smedley, J. W., & Bayton, J. A. (1978). Evaluative race-class stereotypes by race and perceived class of subjects. *Journal of Personality and Social Psychology, 3,* 530–535.

Smelser, N. J., & Mitchell, F. (Eds.) (2002). *Terrorism: Perspectives from the behavioral and social sciences.* Washington, DC: National Research Council, National Academies Press.

Smith, A. (1776). The wealth of nations. Book 1. Chicago: University of Chicago Press. (Republished, 1976.)

Smith, A. E., & Haney, C. (2011). Getting to the point: Attempting to improve juror comprehension of capital penalty phase instructions. *Law and Human Behavior, 35,* 339–350.

Smith, C., & Davidson, H. (2014). *The paradox of generosity: Giving we receive, grasping we lose.* New York: Oxford University Press.

Smith, C. T., De Houwer, J., & Nosek, B. A. (2013). Consider the source: Persuasion of implicit evaluations is moderated by source credibility. *Personality and Social Psychology Bulletin, 39,* 193–205.

Smith, D. E., Gier, J. A., & Willis, F. N. (1982). Interpersonal touch and compliance with a marketing request. *Basic and Applied Social Psychology, 3,* 35–38.

Smith, H. (1976) *The Russians.* New York: Balantine Books. Cited by B. Latané, K. Williams, & S. Harkins in "Many hands make light the work." *Journal of Personality and Social Psychology,* 1979, *37,* 822–832.

Smith, H. J., & Tyler, T. R. (1997). Choosing the right pond: The impact of group membership on self-esteem and group-oriented behavior. *Journal of Experimental Social Psychology, 33,* 146–170.

Smith, J. (2011, August 14). Lack of empathy made it easier to wreck and rob. *The Independent* (www.independent. co.uk).

Smith, L. G. E., & Postmes, T. (2011). The power of talk: Developing discriminatory group norms through discussion. *British Journal of Social Psychology, 50,* 193–215.

Smith, M. B. (1978). Psychology and values. *Journal of Social Issues, 34,* 181–199.

Smith, P. B. (2005). Is there an indigenous European social psychology? *International Journal of Psychology, 40,* 254–262.

Smith, P. B., & Tayeb, M. (1989). Organizational structure and processes. In M. Bond (Ed.), *The cross-cultural challenge to social psychology.* Newbury Park, CA: Sage.

Smith, R. H., Turner, T. J., Garonzik, R., Leach, C. W., Urch-Druskat, V., & Weston, C. M. (1996). Envy and Schadenfreude. *Personality and Social Psychology Bulletin, 22,* 158–168.

Smith, S. J., Axelton, A. M., & Saucier, D. A. (2009). The effects of contact on sexual prejudice: A meta-analysis. *Sex Roles, 61,* 178–191.

Smith, V. L. (1991). Prototypes in the courtroom: Lay representations of legal concepts. *Journal of Personality and Social Psychology, 61,* 857–872.

Smoreda, Z., & Licoppe, C. (2000). Gender-specific use of the domestic telephone. *Social Psychology Quarterly, 63,* 238–252.

Snodgrass, M. A. (1987). The relationships of differential loneliness, intimacy, and characterological attributional style to duration of loneliness. *Journal of Social Behavior and Personality, 2,* 173–186.

Snopes. (2008, accessed July 30). The naked truth (www.snopes.com/humor/iftrue/ pollster.asp).

Snyder, C. R. (1978). The "illusion" of uniqueness. *Journal of Humanistic Psychology, 18,* 33–41.

Snyder, C. R. (1980). The uniqueness mystique. *Psychology Today,* March, 86–90.

Snyder, C. R., & Smith, T. W. (1986). On being "shy like a fox": A self-handicapping analysis. In W. H. Jones et al. (Eds.), *Shyness: Perspectives on research and treatment.* New York: Plenum.

Snyder, M. (1983). The influence of individuals on situations: Implications for understanding the links between personality and social behavior. *Journal of Personality, 51,* 497–516.

Snyder, M. (1984). When belief creates reality. In L. Berkowitz (Ed.), *Advances in experimental social psychology* (Vol. 18). New York: Academic Press.

Snyder, M. (1987). *Public appearances/ private realities: The psychology of self-monitoring.* New York: Freeman.

Snyder, M. (1988). Experiencing prejudice firsthand: The "discrimination day" experiments. *Contemporary Psychology, 33,* 664–665.

Snyder, M., Grether, J., & Keller, K. (1974). Staring and compliance: A field experiment on hitch-hiking. *Journal of Applied Social Psychology, 4,* 165–170.

Snyder, M., & Haugen, J. A. (1994). Why does behavioral confirmation occur? A functional perspective on the role of the perceiver. *Journal of Experimental Social Psychology, 30,* 218–246.

Snyder, M., & Haugen, J. A. (1995). Why does behavioral confirmation occur? A functional perspective on the role of the target. *Personality and Social Psychology Bulletin, 21,* 963–974.

Snyder, M., & Ickes, W. (1985). Personality and social behavior. In G. Lindzey &

E. Aronson (Eds.), *Handbook of social psychology,* 3rd edition. New York: Random House.

Snyder, M., & Swann, W. B., Jr. (1976). When actions reflect attitudes: The politics of impression management. *Journal of Personality and Social Psychology, 34,* 1034–1042.

Snyder, M., Tanke, E. D., & Berscheid, E. (1977). Social perception and interpersonal behavior: On the self-fulfilling nature of social stereotypes. *Journal of Personality and Social Psychology, 35,* 656–666.

Solano, C. H., Batten, P. G., & Parish, E. A. (1982). Loneliness and patterns of self-disclosure. *Journal of Personality and Social Psychology, 43,* 524–531.

Solberg, E. C., Diener, E., & Robinson, M. D. (2003). Why are materialists less satisfied? In T. Kasser & A. D. Kanner (Eds.), Psychology and consumer culture: The struggle for a good life in a materialistic world. Washington, DC: APA Books.

Solberg, E. C., Diener, E., Wirtz, D., Lucas, R. E., & Oishi, S. (2002). Wanting, having, and satisfaction: Examining the role of desire discrepancies in satisfaction with income. *Journal of Personality and Social Psychology, 83,* 725–734.

Solnick, S., & Hemenway, D. (1998). Is more always better? A survey on positional concerns. *Journal of Economic Behaviour and Organization, 37,* 373–383.

Solnick, S. J., & Hemenway, D. (2012). The 'Twinkie Defense': The relationship between carbonated non-diet soft drinks and violence perpetration among Boston high school students. *Injury Prevention, 18,* 259–263.

Solomon, H., & Solomon, L. Z. (1978). *Effects of anonymity on helping in emergency situations.* Paper presented at the Eastern Psychological Association convention.

Solomon, H., Solomon, L. Z., Arnone, M. M., Maur, B. J., Reda, R. M., & Rother, E. O. (1981). Anonymity and helping. *Journal of Social Psychology, 113,* 37–43.

Somaiya, R. (2011, August 13). After British riots, conflicting answers as to "why." *New York Times* (www.nytimes.com).

Sommer, F., Leuschner, V., & Scheithauer, H. (2014). Bullying, romantic rejection, and conflicts with teachers: The crucial role of social dynamics in the development of school shootings—A systematic review. *International Journal of Developmental Science, 8,* 3–24.

Sommers, S. R. (2006). On racial diversity and group decision making: Identifying multiple effects of racial composition on jury deliberations. *Journal of Personality and Social Psychology, 90,* 597–612.

Sommers, S. R., & Ellsworth, P. C. (2000). Race in the courtroom: Perceptions of guilt and dispositional attributions.

Personality and Social Psychology Bulletin, 26, 1367–1379.

Sommers, S. R., & Ellsworth, P. C. (2001). White juror bias: An investigation of prejudice against Black defendants in the American courtroom. *Psychology, Public Policy, and Law, 7,* 201–229.

Sonne, J., & Janoff, D. (1979). The effect of treatment attributions on the maintenance of weight reduction: A replication and extension. *Cognitive Therapy and Research, 3,* 389–397.

Sorhagen, N. S. (2013). Early teacher expectations disproportionately affect poor children's high school performance. *Journal of Educational Psychology, 105,* 465–477.

Sorokowski, P., et al. (2011). Attractiveness of leg length: Report from 27 nations. *Journal of Cross-Cultural Psychology, 42,* 131–139.

Sowislo, J. F., & Orth, U. (2012). Does low self-esteem predict depression and anxiety? A meta-analysis of longitudinal studies. *Psychological Bulletin, 139,* 213–240.

Sowislo, J. F., & Orth, U. (2013). Does low self-esteem predict depression and anxiety? A meta-analysis of longitudinal studies. *Psychological Bulletin, 139,* 213–240.

Sparrell, J. A., & Shrauger, J. S. (1984). Self-confidence and optimism in self-prediction. Paper presented at the American Psychological Association convention, Toronto, ON, Canada.

Spears, R., Ellemers, N., & Doosje, B. (2009). Strength in numbers or less is more? A matter of opinion and a question of taste. *Personality and Social Psychology Bulletin, 35,* 1099–1111.

Spector, P. E. (1986). Perceived control by employees: A meta-analysis of studies concerning autonomy and participation at work. *Human Relations, 39,* 1005–1016.

Speer, A. (1971). *Inside the Third Reich: Memoirs* (P. Winston & C. Winston, trans.). New York: Avon Books.

Spence, A., & Townsend, E. (2007). Predicting behaviour towards genetically modified food using implicit and explicit attitudes. *British Journal of Social Psychology, 46,* 437–457.

Spencer, S. J., Fein, S., Wolfe, C. T., Fong, C., & Dunn, M. A. (1998). Automatic activation of stereotypes: The role of self-image threat. *Personality and Social Psychology Bulletin, 24,* 1139–1152.

Spencer, S. J., Steele, C. M., & Quinn, D. M. (1999). Stereotype threat and women's math performance. *Journal of Experimental Social Psychology, 3,* 4–28.

Speth, J. G. (2008). Foreword. In A. A. Leiserowitz & L. O. Fernandez, *Toward a new consciousness: Values to sustain human and natural communities.* New Haven: Yale School of Forestry & Environmental Studies.

Speth, J. G. (2012, May/June). America, the possible: A manifesto, Part II. *Orion Magazine* (www.OrionMagazine.org).

Spiegel, H. W. (1971). *The growth of economic thought.* Durham, NC: Duke University Press.

Spielmann, S. S., MacDonald, G., & Wilson, A. E. (2009). On the rebound: Focusing on someone new helps anxiously attached individuals let go of ex-partners. *Personality and Social Psychology Bulletin, 35,* 1382–1394.

Spitzberg, B. H., & Hurt, H. T. (1987). The relationship of interpersonal competence and skills to reported loneliness across time. *Journal of Social Behavior and Personality, 2,* 157–172.

Spitz, H. H. (1999). Beleaguered *Pygmalion:* A history of the controversy over claims that teacher expectancy raises intelligence. *Intelligence, 27,* 199–234.

Spivak, J. (1979, June 6). *Wall Street Journal.*

Sporer, S. L. (2008). Lessons from the origins of eyewitness testimony research in Europe. *Applied Cognitive Psychology, 22,* 737–757.

Sporer, S. L., & Horry, R. (2011). Recognizing faces from ethnic in-groups and out-groups: Importance of outer face features and effects of retention interval. *Applied Cognitive Psychology, 25,* 424–431.

Sporer, S. L., Trinkl, B., & Guberova, E. (2007). Matching faces. Differences in processing speed of out-group faces by different ethnic groups. *Journal of Cross-Cultural Psychology, 38,* 398–412.

Sprecher, S. (1987). The effects of self-disclosure given and received on affection for an intimate partner and stability of the relationship. *Journal of Personality and Social Psychology, 4,* 115–127.

Sprecher, S., Aron, A., Hatfield, E., Cortese, A., Potapova, E., & Levitskaya, A. (1994b). Love: American style, Russian style, and Japanese style. *Personal Relationships, 1,* 349–369.

Sprecher, S., Sullivan, Q., & Hatfield, E. (1994a). Mate selection preferences: Gender differences examined in a national sample. *Journal of Personality and Social Psychology, 66,* 1074–1080.

Sprecher, S., & Toro-Morn, M. (2002). A study of men and women from different sides of Earth to determine if men are from Mars and women are from Venus in their beliefs about love and romantic relationships. *Sex Roles, 46,* 131–147.

Srivastava, S., McGonigal, K. M., Richards, J. M., Butler, E. A., & Gross, J. J. (2006). Optimism in close relationships: How seeing things in a positive light makes them so. *Journal of Personality and Social Psychology, 91,* 143–153.

Stack, S. (2000). Media impacts on suicide: A quantitative review of 293 findings. *Social Science Quarterly, 81,* 957–71.

Stack, S. (2003). Media coverage as a risk factor in suicide. *Journal of Epidemiology and Community Health, 57,* 238–240.

Stajkovic, A., & Luthans, F. (1998). Self-efficacy and work-related performance: A meta-analysis. *Psychological Bulletin, 124,* 240–261.

Stalder, D. R. (2008). Revisiting the issue of safety in numbers: The likelihood of receiving help from a group. *Social Influence, 3,* 24–33.

Stangor, C., Jonas, K., Stroebe, W., & Hewstone, M. (1996). Influence of student exchange on national stereotypes, attitudes and perceived group variability. *European Journal of Social Psychology, 26,* 663–675.

Stangor, C., Lynch, L., Duan, C., & Glass, B. (1992). Categorization of individuals on the basis of multiple social features. *Journal of Personality and Social Psychology, 62,* 207–218.

Stanley, D. J., & Spence, J. R. (2014). Expectations for replications: Are yours realistic? *Perspectives on Psychological Science, 9,* 305–318.

Stanley, D., Phelps, E., & Banaji, M. (2008). The neural basis of implicit attitudes. *Current Directions in Psychological Science, 17,* 164–170.

Stanovich, K. E., & West, R. F. (2008). On the relative independence of thinking biases and cognitive ability. *Journal of Personality and Social Psychology, 94,* 672–695.

Stanovich, K. E., West, R. F., & Toplak, M. E. (2013). Myside bias, rational thinking, and intelligence. *Current Directions in Psychological Science, 22,* 259–264.

Stanton, S. J., Beehner, J. C., Saini, E. K., Kuhn, C. M., & LaBar, K. S. (2009). Dominance, politics, and physiology: Voters' testosterone changes on the night of the 2008 United States Presidential election. *PLoS One, 4(10),* e7543.

Stark, E., Kim, A., Miller, C., & Borgida, E. (2008). Effects of including a graphic warning label in advertisements for reduced-exposure products: Implications for persuasion and policy. *Journal of Applied Social Psychology, 38,* 281–293.

Starks, T. J., & Parsons, J. T. (2014). Adult attachment among partnered gay men: Patterns and associations with sexual relationship quality. *Archives of Sexual Behavior, 43,* 107–117.

Stark, T. H., Flache, A., & Veenstra, R. (2013). Generalization of positive and negative attitudes toward individuals to outgroup attitudes. *Personality and Social Psychology Bulletin, 39,* 608–622.

Stasser, G. (1991). Pooling of unshared information during group discussion. In S. Worchel, W. Wood, & J. Simpson (Eds.), *Group process and productivity.* Beverly Hills, CA: Sage.

Stasser, G., Kerr, N. L., & Bray, R. M. (1981). The social psychology of jury deliberations: Structure, process, and product. In N. L. Kerr & R. M. Bray (Eds.), *The psychology of the courtroom.* New York: Academic Press.

Statistics Canada. (2010). *Victims and persons accused of homicide, by age and sex.* Table 253-0003.

Staub, E. (1978). *Positive social behavior and morality: Social and personal influences* (Vol. 1). Hillsdale, NJ: Erlbaum.

Staub, E. (1989). *The roots of evil: The origins of genocide and other group violence.* Cambridge: Cambridge University Press.

Staub, E. (1991). Altruistic and moral motivations for helping and their translation into action. *Psychological Inquiry, 2,* 150–153.

Staub, E. (1996). Altruism and aggression in children and youth: Origins and cures. In R. Feldman (Ed.), *The psychology of adversity.* Amherst, MA: University of Massachusetts Press.

Staub, E. (1997a). Blind versus constructive patriotism: Moving from embeddedness in the group to critical loyalty and action. In D. Bar-Tal and E. Staub (Eds.), *Patriotism in the lives of individuals and nations.* Chicago: Nelson-Hall.

Staub, E. (1997b). *Halting and preventing collective violence: The role of bystanders.* Background paper for symposium organized by the Friends of Raoul Wallenberg, Stockholm, June 13–16.

Staub, E. (1999). Behind the scenes. In D. G. Myers, *Social psychology,* 6th edition. New York: McGraw-Hill.

Staub, E. (2003). *The psychology of good and evil: Why children, adults, and groups help and harm others.* New York: Cambridge University Press.

Staub, E. (2005a). The origins and evolution of hate, with notes on prevention. In R. J. Sternberg (Ed.), *The psychology of hate.* Washington, DC: American Psychological Association.

Staub, E. (2005b). The roots of goodness: The fulfillment of basic human needs and the development of caring, helping and nonaggression, inclusive caring, moral courage, active bystandership, and altruism born of suffering. In G. Carlo & C. P. Edwards (Eds.), *Moral motivation through the life span: Theory, research, applications. Nebraska Symposium on Motivation* (Vol. 51). Lincoln, NE: University of Nebraska Press.

Staub, E. (2015). *The roots of goodness and resistance to evil: Inclusive caring, moral courage, altruism born of suffering, active bystandership, and heroism.* New York: Oxford.

Staub, E., & Bar-Tal, D. (2003). Genocide, mass killing, and intractable conflict. In D. Sears, L. Huddy, & R. Jervis (Eds.), *Handbook of political psychology.* New York: Oxford University Press.

Stavrova, O., & Siegers, P. (2014). Religious prosociality and morality across cultures: How social enforcement of religion shapes the effects of personal religiosity on prosocial and moral attitudes and behaviors. *Personality and Social Psychology Bulletin, 40,* 315–333.

Steblay, N., Dysart, J. E., Fulero, S., & Lindsay, R. C. L. (2001). Eyewitness accuracy rates in sequential and simultaneous lineup presentations: A meta-analytic comparison. *Law and Human Behavior, 25,* 459–473.

Steblay, N. K., Wells, G. L., & Douglass, A. B. (2014). The eyewitness post-identification effect 15 years later: Theoretical and policy implications. *Psychology, Public Policy, and Law, 20,* 1–18.

Steblay, N. M. (1987). Helping behavior in rural and urban environments: A meta-analysis. *Psychological Bulletin, 102,* 346–356.

Steblay, N. M., Besirevic, J., Fulero, S. M., & Jimenez-Lorente, B. (1999). The effects of pretrial publicity on juror verdicts: A meta-analytic review. *Law and Human Behavior, 23,* 219–235.

Steele, C. M. (1988). The psychology of self-affirmation: Sustaining the integrity of the self. In L. Berkowitz (Ed.), *Advances in experimental social psychology* (Vol. 21). Orlando, FL: Academic Press.

Steele, C. M. (1997). A threat in the air: How stereotypes shape intellectual identity and performance. *American Psychologist, 52,* 613–629.

Steele, C. M. (2010). *Whistling Vivaldi: And other clues to how stereotypes affect us.* New York: Norton.

Steele, C. M., & Aronson, J. (1995). Stereotype threat and the intellectual test performance of African Americans. *Journal of Personality and Social Psychology, 69,* 797–811.

Steele, C. M., Southwick, L. L., & Critchlow, B. (1981). Dissonance and alcohol: Drinking your troubles away. *Journal of Personality and Social Psychology, 41,* 831–846.

Steele, C. M., Spencer, S. J., & Aronson, J. (2002). Contending with group image: The psychology of stereotype and social identity threat. In Zanna, M. P. (Ed.), *Advances in experimental social psychology, 34,* 379–440. San Diego: Academic Press.

Steele, C. M., Spencer, S. J., & Lynch, M. (1993). Self-image resilience and dissonance: The role of affirmational resources. *Journal of Personality and Social Psychology, 64,* 885–896.

Stefan, S., & David, D. (2013). Recent developments in the experimental investigation of the illusion of control. A meta-analytic review. *Journal of Applied Social Psychology, 43,* 377–386.

Steffen, P. R., & Masters, K. S. (2005). Does compassion mediate the intrinsic religion-health relationship? *Annals of Behavioral Medicine, 30,* 217–224.

Stegall, A. (2013, August 26). Investigators believe 8-year-old intentionally killed 90-year-old woman (http://www.wafb.com/story/23242078/investigators-believe-8-year-old-intentionally-killed-90-year-old-woman).

Stein, A. H., & Friedrich, L. K. (1972). Television content and young children's behavior. In J. P. Murray, E. A. Rubinstein, & G. A. Comstock (Eds.), *Television and social learning*. Washington, DC: Government Printing Office.

Stein, D. D., Hardyck, J. A., & Smith, M. B. (1965). Race and belief: An open and shut case. *Journal of Personality and Social Psychology, 1,* 281–289.

Steinhauer, J. (2015, January 2). Fight on guns is being taken to state ballots. *New York Times* (www.nytimes.com).

Stelter, B. (2008, November 25). Web suicide viewed live and reaction spur a debate. *New York Times* (www.nytimes.com).

Stelzl, M., Janes, L., & Seligman, C. (2008). Champ or chump: Strategic utilization of dual social identities of others. *European Journal of Social Psychology, 38,* 128–138.

Stenseng, F., Belsky, J., Skalicka, V., & Wichstrøm, L. (2014). Preschool social exclusion, aggression, and cooperation: A longitudinal evaluation of the need-to-belong and the social-reconnection hypotheses. *Personality and Social Psychology Bulletin, 40,* 1637–1647.

Stephan, C. W., & Stephan, W. G. (1986). Habla Ingles? The effects of language translation on simulated juror decisions. *Journal of Applied Social Psychology, 16,* 577–589.

Stephan, W. G. (1986). The effects of school desegregation: An evaluation 30 years after *Brown.* In R. Kidd, L. Saxe, & M. Saks (Eds.), *Advances in applied social psychology.* New York: Erlbaum.

Stephan, W. G. (1987). The contact hypothesis in intergroup relations. In C. Hendrick (Ed.), *Group processes and intergroup relations.* Newbury Park, CA: Sage.

Stephan, W. G. (1988). School desegregation: Short-term and long-term effects. Paper presented at the national conference "Opening Doors: An Appraisal of Race Relations in America," University of Alabama.

Stephens-Davidowitz, S. (2014, January 18). Google, tell me. Is my son a genius? *New York Times* (www.nytimes.com).

Stephens, N. M., Markus, H. R., & Townsend, S. S. M. (2007). Choice as an act of meaning: The case of social class. *Journal of Personality and Social Psychology, 93,* 814–830.

Steptoe, A., Shankar, A., Demakakos, P., & Wardle, J. (2013). Social isolation, loneliness, and all-cause mortality in older men and women. *PNAS Proceedings of the National Academy of Sciences of the United States of America, 110,* 5797–5801.

Sternberg, R. J. (1988). Triangulating love. In R. J. Sternberg & M. L. Barnes (Eds.), *The psychology of love.* New Haven, CT: Yale University Press.

Sternberg, R. J. (1998). *Cupid's arrow: The course of love through time.* New York: Cambridge University Press.

Sternberg, R. J. (2003). A duplex theory of hate and its development and its

application to terrorism, massacres, and genocide. *Review of General Psychology, 7,* 299–328.

Sternberg, R. J., & Grajek, S. (1984). The nature of love. *Journal of Personality and Social Psychology, 47,* 312–329.

Stevenage, S. V., Howland, A., & Tippelt, A. (2011). Interference in eyewitness and earwitness recognition. *Applied Cognitive Psychology, 25,* 112–118.

Stewart, K. D., & Bernhardt, P. C. (2010). Comparing Millennials to pre-1987 students and with one another. *North American Journal of Psychology, 12,* 579–602.

Stewart-Williams, S. (2007). Altruism among kin vs. nonkin: Effects of cost of help and reciprocal exchange. *Evolution and Human Behavior, 28,* 193–198.

Stillinger, C., Epelbaum, M., Keltner, D., & Ross, L. (1991). The "reactive devaluation" barrier to conflict resolution. Unpublished manuscript, Stanford University.

Stinson, D. A., Cameron, J. J., Wood, J. V., Gaucher, D., & Holmes, J. G. (2009). Deconstructing the "reign of error": Interpersonal warmth explains the self-fulfilling prophecy of anticipated acceptance. *Personality and Social Psychology Bulletin, 35,* 1165–1178.

Stinson, D. A., Logel, C., Shepherd, S., & Zanna, M. P. (2011). Rewriting the self-fulfilling prophecy of social rejection: Self-affirmation improves relational security and social behavior up to 2 months later. *Psychological Science, 22,* 1145–1149.

Stinson, V., Devenport, J. L., Cutler, B. L., & Kravitz, D. A. (1996). How effective is the presence-of-counsel safeguard? Attorney perceptions of suggestiveness, fairness, and correctability of biased lineup procedures. *Journal of Applied Psychology, 81,* 64–75.

Stinson, V., Devenport, J. L., Cutler, B. L., & Kravitz, D. A. (1997). How effective is the motion-to-suppress safeguard? Judges' perceptions of the suggestiveness and fairness of biased lineup procedures. *Journal of Personality and Social Psychology, 82,* 211–220.

Stirrat, M., & Perrett, D. I. (2010). Valid facial cues to cooperation and trust: Male facial width and trustworthiness. *Psychological Science, 21,* 349–354.

Stockdale, L. A., Coyne, S. M., Nelson, D. A., & Padilla-Walker, L. M. (2013). Read anything mean lately? Associations between reading aggression in books and aggressive behavior in adolescents. *Aggressive Behavior, 39,* 493–502.

Stocks, E. L., Lishner, D. A., & Decker, S. K. (2009). Altruism or psychological escape: Why does empathy promote prosocial behavior? *European Journal of Social Psychology, 39,* 649–665.

Stok, F. M., de Ridder, D. T. D., de Vet, E., & de Wit, J. B. F. (2013). Don't tell me what I should do, but what others do:

The influence of descriptive and injunctive peer norms on fruit consumption in adolescents. *British Journal of Health Psychology, 19,* 52–64.

Stone, A. L., & Glass, C. R. (1986). Cognitive distortion of social feedback in depression. *Journal of Social and Clinical Psychology, 4,* 179–188.

Stone, J. (2000, November 6). Quoted by Sharon Begley, The stereotype trap. *Newsweek.*

Stone, J., Lynch, C. I., Sjomeling, M., & Darley, J. M. (1999). Stereotype threat effects on Black and White athletic performance. *Journal of Personality and Social Psychology, 77,* 1213–1227.

Stone, L. (1977). *The family, sex and marriage in England, 1500–1800.* New York: Harper & Row.

Stoner, J. A. F. (1961). *A comparison of individual and group decisions involving risk.* Unpublished master's thesis, Massachusetts Institute of Technology. Cited by D. G. Marquis in Individual responsibility and group decisions involving risk, *Industrial Management Review, 3,* 8–23.

Storms, M. D., & Thomas, G. C. (1977). Reactions to physical closeness. *Journal of Personality and Social Psychology, 35,* 412–418.

Stouffer, S. A., Suchman, E. A., DeVinney, L. C., Star, S. A., & Williams, R. M., Jr. (1949). *The American soldier: Adjustment during army life* (Vol. 1.). Princeton, NJ: Princeton University Press.

Stout, J. G., Dasgupta, N., Hunsinger, M., & McManus, M. A. (2011). STEMing the tide: Using ingroup experts to inoculate women's self-concept in science, technology, engineering, and mathematics (STEM). *Journal of Personality and Social Psychology, 100,* 255–270.

Stoverink, A., Umphress, E., Gardner, R., & Miner, K. (2014). Misery loves company: Team dissonance and the influence of supervisor-focused interpersonal justice climate on team cohesiveness. *Journal of Applied Psychology, 99,* 1059–1073.

Stowell, J. R., Oldham, T., & Bennett, D. (2010). Using student response systems ("clickers") to combat conformity and shyness. *Teaching of Psychology, 37,* 135–140.

Strack, F., & Deutsch, R. (2004). Reflective and impulsive determinants of social behavior. *Personality and Social Psychology Review, 8(3),* 220–247.

Strack, F., Martin, L. L., & Stepper, S. (1988). Inhibiting and facilitating conditions of the human smile: A nonobtrusive test of the facial feedback hypothesis. *Journal of Personality and Social Psychology, 54,* 768–777.

Strack, S., & Coyne, J. C. (1983). Social confirmation of dysphoria: Shared and private reactions to depression. *Journal of Personality and Social Psychology, 44,* 798–806.

Straus, M. A., & Gelles, R. J. (1980). *Behind closed doors: Violence in the American family.* New York: Anchor/Doubleday.

Strick, M., Holland, R. W., van Baaren, R. B., & van Kippenberg, A. (2012). Those who laugh are defenseless: How humor breaks resistance to influence. *Journal of Experimental Psychology: Applied, 18,* 213–223.

Strick, M., van Baaren, R. B., Holland, R. W., & van Knippenberg, A. (2009). Humor in advertisements enhances product liking by mere association. *Journal of Experimental Psychology: Applied, 15,* 35–45.

Stroebe, W. (2012). The truth about Triplett (1898), but nobody seems to care. *Perspectives on Psychological Science, 7,* 54–57.

Stroebe, W., & Diehl, M. (1994). Productivity loss in idea-generating groups. In W. Stroebe & M. Hewstone (Eds.), *European review of social psychology* (Vol. 5). Chichester, UK: Wiley.

Stroessner, S. J., Hamilton, D. L., & Lepore, L. (1990). Intergroup categorization and intragroup differentiation: Ingroup-outgroup differences. Paper presented at the American Psychological Association convention, Boston, Massachusetts.

Stroessner, S. J., & Mackie, D. M. (1993). Affect and perceived group variability: Implications for stereotyping and prejudice. In D. M. Mackie & D. L. Hamilton (Eds.), *Affect, cognition, and stereotyping: Interactive processes in group perception.* San Diego: Academic Press.

Strong, S. R. (1968). Counseling: An interpersonal influence process. *Journal of Counseling Psychology, 17,* 81–87.

Strong, S. R. (1991). Social influence and change in therapeutic relationships. In C. R. Snyder & D. R. Forsyth (Eds.), *Handbook of social and clinical psychology.* New York: Pergamon.

Strong, S. R., Welsh, J. A., Corcoran, J. L., & Hoyt, W. T. (1992). Social psychology and counseling psychology: The history, products, and promise of an interface. *Journal of Personality and Social Psychology, 39,* 139–157.

Stroufe, B., Chaikin, A., Cook, R., & Freeman, V. (1977). The effects of physical attractiveness on honesty: A socially desirable response. *Personality and Social Psychology, 3,* 59–62.

Strube, M. J. (2005). What did Triplett really find? A contemporary analysis of the first experiment in social psychology. *American Journal of Psychology, 118,* 271–286.

Stulp, G., Buunk, A. P., Verhulst, S., & Pollet, T. V. (2013). Tall claims? Sense and nonsense about the importance of height of US Presidents. *Leadership Quarterly, 24,* 159–171.

Sue, S., Smith, R. E., & Caldwell, C. (1973). Effects of inadmissible evidence on the decisions of simulated jurors: A moral dilemma. *Journal of Applied Social Psychology, 3,* 345–353.

Suedfeld, P. (2000). Reverberations of the Holocaust fifty years later: Psychology's contributions to understanding persecution and genocide. *Canadian Psychology, 41,* 1–9.

Sullivan, D., Landau, M. J., Kay, A. C., & Rothschild, Z. K. (2012). Collectivism and the meaning of suffering. *Journal of Personality and Social Psychology, 103,* 1023–1039.

Suls, J., & Tesch, F. (1978). Students' preferences for information about their test performance: A social comparison study, *Journal of Applied Social Psychology, 8,* 189–197.

Summers, G., & Feldman, N. S. (1984). Blaming the victim versus blaming the perpetrator: An attributional analysis of spouse abuse. *Journal of Social and Clinical Psychology, 2,* 339–347.

Sun, C., Bridges, A., Wosnitzer, R., Scharrer, E., & Liberman, R. (2008). A comparison of male and female directors in popular pornography: What happens when women are at the helm? *Psychology of Women Quarterly, 32,* 312–325.

Sundie, J. M., Kenrick, D. T., Griskevicius, V., Tybur, J. M., Vohs, K. D., & Beal, D. J. (2011). Peacocks, porches, and Thorstein Veblen: Conspicuous consumption as a sexual signaling system. *Journal of Personality and Social Psychology, 100,* 664–680.

Sunstein, C. R. (2001). Republic.com. Princeton, NJ: Princeton University Press.

Sunstein, C. R. (2007a). Group polarization and 12 angry men. *Negotiation Journal, 23,* 443–447.

Sunstein, C. R. (2009). *Going to extremes: How like minds unite and divide.* New York: Oxford University Press.

Sunstein, C. R., & Hastie, R. (2008). *Four failures of deliberating groups.* Economics Working Paper Series, University of Chicago Law School (www.law.uchicago.edu).

Sunstein, C. R., Schkade, D., & Ellman, L. M. (2004). Ideological voting on federal courts of appeals: A preliminary investigation. *Virginia Law Review, 90,* 301–354.

Surowiecki, J. (2004). *The wisdom of crowds.* New York: Doubleday.

Su, R., Rounds, J., & Armstrong, P. I. (2009). Men and things, women and people: A meta-analysis of sex differences in interests. *Psychological Bulletin, 135,* 859–884.

Sussman, N. M. (2000). The dynamic nature of cultural identity throughout cultural transitions: Why home is not so sweet. *Personality and Social Psychology Review, 4,* 355–373.

Svenson, O. (1981). Are we all less risky and more skillful than our fellow drivers? *Acta Psychologica, 47,* 143–148.

Swaab, R. I., Schaerer, M., Anicich, E. M., Ronay, R., & Galinsky, A. D. (2014). The too-much-talent effect: Team interdependence determines when more talent is too much or not enough. *Psychological Science, 25,* 1581–1591.

Swami, V., Chan, F., Wong, V., Furnham, A., & Tovée, M. J. (2008). Weight-based discrimination in occupational hiring and helping behavior. *Journal of Applied Social Psychology, 38,* 968–981.

Swann, W. B., Jr. (1996). *Self-traps: The elusive quest for higher self-esteem.* New York: Freeman.

Swann, W. B., Jr. (1997). The trouble with change: Self-verification and allegiance to the self. *Psychological Science, 8,* 177–180.

Swann, W. B., Jr., Buhrmester, M. D., Gómez, A., Jetten, J., Bastian, B., Vázquez, A., Zhang, A. (2014a). What makes a group worth dying for? Identity fusion fosters perception of familial ties, promoting self-sacrifice. *Journal of Personality and Social Psychology, 106,* 912–926.

Swann, W. B., Jr., Chang-Schneider, C., & Angulo, S. (2007). Self-verification in relationships as an adaptive process. In J. Wood, A. Tesser, & J. Holmes (Eds.), *Self and relationships.* New York: Psychology Press.

Swann, W. B., Jr., Gómez, Ý., Buhrmester, M. D., López-Rodríguez, L., Jiménez, J., & Vázquez, A. (2014b). Contemplating the ultimate sacrifice: Identity fusion channels pro-group affect, cognition, and moral decision making. *Journal of Personality and Social Psychology, 106,* 713–727.

Swann, W. B., Jr., Jetten, J., Gómez, Ý., Whitehouse, H., & Bastian, B. (2012). When group membership gets personal: A theory of identity fusion. *Psychological Review, 119,* 441–456.

Swann, W. B., Jr., & Pelham, B. (2002, July–September). Who wants out when the going gets good? Psychological investment and preference for self-verifying college roommates. *Self and Identity, 1,* 219–233.

Swann, W. B., Jr., & Predmore, S. C. (1985). Intimates as agents of social support: Sources of consolation or despair? *Journal of Personality and Social Psychology, 49,* 1609–1617.

Swann, W. B., Jr., & Read, S. J. (1981). Acquiring self-knowledge: The search for feedback that fits. *Journal of Personality and Social Psychology, 41,* 1119–1128.

Swann, W. B., Jr., Rentfrow, P. J., & Gosling, S. D. (2003). The precarious couple effect: Verbally inhibited men 1 critical, disinhibited women 5 bad chemistry. *Journal of Personality and Social Psychology, 85,* 1095–1106.

Swann, W. B., Jr., Sellers, J. G., & McClarty, K. L. (2006). Tempting today, troubling tomorrow: The roots of the precarious couple effect. *Personality and Social Psychology Bulletin, 32,* 93–103.

Swann, W. B., Jr., Stein-Seroussi, A., & Giesler, R. B. (1992a). Why people self-verify. *Journal of Personality and Social Psychology, 62,* 392–401.

Swann, W. B., Jr., Stein-Seroussi, A., & McNulty, S. E. (1992b). Outcasts in a white lie society. The enigmatic worlds of people with negative self-conceptions. *Journal of Personality and Social Psychology, 62,* 618–624.

Swann, W. B., Jr., Wenzlaff, R. M., Krull, D. S., & Pelham, B. W. (1991). Seeking truth, reaping despair: Depression, self-verification and selection of relationship partners. *Journal of Abnormal Psychology, 101,* 293–306.

Swap, W. C. (1977). Interpersonal attraction and repeated exposure to rewarders and punishers. *Personality and Social Psychology Bulletin, 3,* 248–251.

Swart, H., Hewstone, M., Christ, O., & Voci, A. (2011). Affective mediators of intergroup contact: A three-wave longitudinal study in South Africa. *Journal of Personality and Social Psychology, 101,* 1221–1238.

Sweeney, J. (1973). An experimental investigation of the free rider problem. *Social Science Research, 2,* 277–292.

Sweeney, P. D., Anderson, K., & Bailey, S. (1986). Attributional style in depression: A meta-analytic review. *Journal of Personality and Social Psychology, 50,* 947–991.

Sweeny, K., Melnyk, D., Miller, W., & Shepperd, J. A. (2010). Information avoidance: Who, what, when, and why. *Review of General Psychology, 14,* 340–353.

Swets, J. A., Dawes, R. M., & Monahan, J. (2000). Psychological science can improve diagnostic decisions. *Psychological Science in the Public Interest, 1,* 1–26.

Swim, J., Borgida, E., Maruyama, G., & Myers, D. G. (1989). Joan McKay vs. John McKay: Do gender stereotypes bias evaluations? *Psychological Bulletin, 105,* 409–429.

Swim, J., Geiger, N., & Zawakzki, S. J. (2014). Psychology and energy-use reduction policies. *Policy Insights from the Behavioral and Brain Sciences, 1,* 180–188.

Swim, J. K. (1994). Perceived versus meta-analytic effect sizes: An assessment of the accuracy of gender stereotypes. *Journal of Personality and Social Psychology, 66,* 21–36.

Swim, J. K., Cohen, L. L., & Hyers, L. L. (1998). Experiencing everyday prejudice and discrimination. In J. K. Swim & C. Stangor (Eds.), *Prejudice: The target's perspective.* San Diego: Academic Press.

Swim, J. K., & Hyers, L. L. (1999). Excuse me—What did you just say?!: Women's public and private reactions to sexist remarks. *Journal of Experimental Social Psychology, 35,* 68–88.

Symons, D. (1979). *The evolution of human sexuality.* New York: Oxford University Press.

Szymkow, A., Chandler, J., IJzerman, H., Parzuchowski, M., & Wojciszke, B. (2013). Warmer hearts, warmer rooms: How positive communal traits increase estimates of ambient temperature. *Social Psychology, 44,* 167–176.

Tafarodi, R. W., Lo, C., Yamaguchi, S., Lee, W. W-S., & Katsura, H. (2004). The inner self in three countries. *Journal of Cross-Cultural Psychology, 35,* 97–117.

Tajfel, H. (1970, November). Experiments in intergroup discrimination. *Scientific American,* pp. 96–102.

Tajfel, H. (1981). *Human groups and social categories: Studies in social psychology.* London: Cambridge University Press.

Tajfel, H. (1982). Social psychology of intergroup relations. *Annual Review of Psychology, 33,* 1–39.

Tajfel, H., & Billig, M. (1974). Familiarity and categorization in intergroup behavior. *Journal of Experimental Social Psychology, 10,* 159–170.

Tamres, L. K., Janicki, D., & Helgeson, V. S. (2002). Sex differences in coping behavior: A meta-analytic review and an examination of relative coping. *Personality and Social Psychology Review, 6,* 2–30.

Tan, H. H., & Tan, M. L. (2008). Organizational citizenship behavior and social loafing: The role of personality, motives, and contextual factors. *Journal of Psychology, 142,* 89–108.

Tang, L., Jang, S., & Morrison, A. (2012). Dual-route communication of destination websites. *Tourism Management, 33,* 38–49.

Tang, S-H., & Hall, V. C. (1995). The overjustification effect: A meta-analysis. *Applied Cognitive Psychology, 9,* 365–404.

Tanke, E. D., & Tanke, T. J. (1979). Getting off a slippery slope: Social science in the judicial processes. *American Psychologist, 34,* 1130–1138.

Tannenbaum, M. B. (2013). Do scare tactics work? A meta-analytic test of fear appeal theories. Poster presented at the annual conference of the Association for Psychological Science, Washington, DC, May.

Tannen, D. (1990). *You just don't understand: Women and men in conversation.* New York: Morrow.

Tanner, R. J., Ferraro, R., Chartrand, T. L., Bettman, J. R., & Van Barren, R. (2008). Of chameleons and consumption: The impact of mimicry on choice and preferences. *Journal of Consumer Research, 34,* 754–766.

Tapp, J. L. (1980). Psychological and policy perspectives on the law: Reflections on a decade. *Journal of Social Issues, 36(2),* 165–192.

Tarrant, M., Branscombe, N. R., Warner, R. H., & Weston, D. (2012). Social identity and perceptions of torture: It's moral when we do it. *Journal of Experimental Social Psychology, 48,* 513–518.

Tarrant, M., Dazeley, S., & Cottom, T. (2009). Social categorization and empathy for outgroup members. *British Journal of Social Psychology, 48,* 427–446.

Tausch, N., Hewstone, M., Kenworthy, J. B., Psaltis, C., Schmid, K., Popan, J. R., Cairns, E., & Hughes, J. (2010). Secondary transfer effects of intergroup contact: Alternative accounts and underlying processes. *Journal of Personality and Social Psychology, 99,* 282–302.

Tavris, C., & Aronson, E. (2007). *Mistakes were made (but not by me): Why we justify foolish beliefs, bad decisions, and hurtful acts.* New York: Harcourt.

Tay, L., & Diener, E. (2011). Needs and subjective well-being around the world. *Journal of Personality and Social Psychology, 101,* 354–365.

Taylor, D. A., Gould, R. J., & Brounstein, P. J. (1981). Effects of personalistic self-disclosure. *Personality and Social Psychology Bulletin, 7,* 487–492.

Taylor, L. S., Fiore, A. T., Mendelsohn, G. A., & Cheshire, C. (2011). "Out of my league": A real-world test of the matching hypothesis. *Personality and Social Psychology Bulletin, 37,* 942–954.

Taylor, S. E. (1981). A categorization approach to stereotyping. In D. L. Hamilton (Ed.), *Cognitive processes in stereotyping and intergroup behavior.* Hillsdale, NJ: Erlbaum.

Taylor, S. E. (1989). *Positive illusions: Creative self-deception and the healthy mind.* New York: Basic Books.

Taylor, S. E. (2002). The tending instinct: How nurturing is essential to who we are and how we live. New York: Times Books.

Taylor, S. E., Crocker, J., Fiske, S. T., Sprinzen, M., & Winkler, J. D. (1979). The generalizability of salience effects. *Journal of Personality and Social Psychology, 37,* 357–368.

Taylor, S. E., & Fiske, S. T. (1978). Salience, attention, and attribution: Top of the head phenomena. In L. Berkowitz (Ed.), *Advances in experimental social psychology* (Vol. 11). New York: Academic Press.

Taylor, S. E., Fiske, S. T., Etcoff, N. L., & Ruderman, A. J. (1978). Categorical and contextual bases of person memory and stereotyping. *Journal of Personality and Social Psychology, 36,* 778–793.

Taylor, S. E., Lerner, J. S., Sherman, D. K., Sage, R. M., & McDowell, N. K. (2003b). Portrait of the self-enhancer: Well adjusted and well liked or maladjusted and friendless? *Journal of Personality and Social Psychology, 84,* 165–176.

Taylor, S. E., Repetti, R. L., & Seeman, T. (1997). Health psychology: What is an unhealthy environment and how does it get under the skin? *Annual Review of Psychology, 48,* 411–447.

Taylor, S. E., Saphire-Bernstein, S., & Seeman, T. E. (2010). Are plasma oxytocin in women and plasma vasopressin in men biomarkers of distressed pair-bond relationships? *Psychological Science, 21,* 3–7.

Taylor, S. P., & Chermack, S. T. (1993). Alcohol, drugs and human physical aggression. *Journal of Studies on Alcohol,* Supplement No. 11, 78–88.

Technical Working Group for Eyewitness Evidence. (1999). *Eyewitness evidence: A guide for law enforcement.* A research report of the U.S. Department of Justice, Office of Justice Programs, National Institute of Justice.

Tedeschi, J. T., Nesler, M., & Taylor, E. (1987). Misattribution and the bogus pipeline: A test of dissonance and impression management theories. Paper presented at the American Psychological Association convention.

Teger, A. I. (1980). *Too much invested to quit.* New York: Pergamon.

Teigen, K. H. (1986). Old truths or fresh insights? A study of students' evaluations of proverbs. *British Journal of Social Psychology, 25,* 43–50.

Teigen, K. H., Evensen, P. C., Samoilow, D. K., & Vatne, K. B. (1999). Good luck and bad luck: How to tell the difference. *European Journal of Social Psychology, 29,* 981–1010.

Telch, M. J., Killen, J. D., McAlister, A. L., Perry, C. L., & Maccoby, N. (1981). *Long-term follow-up of a pilot project on smoking prevention with adolescents.* Paper presented at the American Psychological Association convention.

Tenney, E. R., MacCoun, R. J., Spellman, B. A., & Hastie, R. (2007). Calibration trumps confidence as a basis for witness credibility. *Psychological Science, 18,* 46–50.

Tennov, D. (1979). *Love and limerence: The experience of being in love.* New York: Stein & Day.

Tesser, A., Martin, L., & Mendolia, M. (1995). The impact of thought on attitude extremity and attitude-behavior consistency. In R. E. Petty & J. A Krosnick (Eds.), *Attitude strength: Antecedents and consequences.* Hillsdale, NJ: Erlbaum.

Tesser, A., Millar, M., & Moore, J. (1988). Some affective consequences of social comparison and reflection processes: The pain and pleasure of being close. *Journal of Personality and Social Psychology, 54,* 49–61.

Tesser, A., Rosen, S., & Conlee, M. C. (1972). News valence and available recipient as determinants of news transmission. *Sociometry, 35,* 619–628.

Testa, M. (2002). The impact of men's alcohol consumption on perpetration of sexual aggression. *Clinical Psychology Review, 22,* 1239–1263.

Tetlock, P. E. (1983). Accountability and complexity of thought. *Journal of Personality and Social Psychology, 45,* 74–83.

Tetlock, P. E. (1985). Integrative complexity of American and Soviet foreign policy rhetoric: A time-series analysis. *Journal of Personality and Social Psychology, 49,* 1565–1585.

Tetlock, P. E. (1988). Monitoring the integrative complexity of American and Soviet policy rhetoric: What can be learned? *Journal of Social Issues, 44,* 101–131.

Tetlock, P. E. (2005). *Expert political judgment: How good is it? How can we know?* Princeton, NJ: Princeton University Press.

Tetlock, P. E. (2007). Psychology and politics: The challenges of integrating levels of analysis in social science. In E. T. Higgins & A. Kruglanski (Eds.), *Social psychology: Handbook of basic principles.* New York: Guilford.

Tetlock, P. E., Peterson, R. S., McGuire, C., Chang, S., & Feld, P. (1992). Assessing political group dynamics: A test of the groupthink model. *Journal of Personality and Social Psychology, 63,* 403–425.

Thakar, M., & Epstein, M. (2011, November 16). *How love emerges in arranged marriages: A follow-up cross-cultural study.* Paper presented to the National Council on Family Relations.

t'Hart, P. (1998). Preventing groupthink revisited: Evaluating and reforming groups in government. *Organizational Behavior and Human Decision Processes, 73,* 306–326.

Thelwall, M. (2008). Social networks, gender and friending: An analysis of MySpace member profiles. *Journal of the American Society for Information Science and Technology, 59,* 1321–1330.

Thomas, E. F., & McGarty, C. A. (2009). The role of efficacy and moral outrage norms in creating the potential for international development activism through group-based interaction. *British Journal of Psychology, 48,* 115–134.

Thomas, L. (1971). Notes of a biology watcher: A fear of pheromones. *New England Journal of Medicine, 285,* 292–293.

Thompson, D. (2014, June 19). The most popular social network for young people? Texting. The Atlantic, http://www.theatlantic.com/technology/archive/2014/06/facebook-texting-teens-instagram-snapchat-most-popular-social-network/373043/.

Thompson, D. V., & Malaviya, P. (2013). Consumer-generated ads: Does awareness of advertising co-creation help or hurt persuasion? *Journal of Marketing, 77,* 33–47.

Thompson, L. L., & Crocker, J. (1985). Prejudice following threat to the self-concept. Effects of performance expectations and attributions. Unpublished manuscript, Northwestern University.

Thompson, L., Valley, K. L., & Kramer, R. M. (1995). The bittersweet feeling of success: An examination of social perception in negotiation. *Journal of Experimental Social Psychology, 31,* 467–492.

Thompson, W. C., Cowan, C. L., & Rosenhan, D. L. (1980). Focus of attention mediates the impact of negative affect on altruism. *Journal of Personality and Social Psychology, 38,* 291–300.

Thompson, W. C., Fong, G. T., & Rosenhan, D. L. (1981). Inadmissible evidence and juror verdicts. *Journal of Personality and Social Psychology, 40,* 453–463.

Thomson, R., & Murachver, T. (2001). Predicting gender from electronic discourse. *British Journal of Social Psychology, 40,* 193–208 (and personal correspondence from T. Murachver, May 23, 2002).

Thornton, B., & Maurice, J. (1997). Physique contrast effect: Adverse impact of idealized body images for women. *Sex Roles, 37,* 433–439.

Tice, D. M., Butler, J. L., Muraven, M. B., & Stillwell, A. M. (1995). When modesty prevails: Differential favorability of self-presentation to friends and strangers. *Journal of Personality and Social Psychology, 69,* 1120–1138.

Tideman, S. (2003, undated). Announcement of Operationalizing Gross National Happiness conference, February 18–20, 2004. Distributed via the Internet.

Tidwell, N. D., & Eastwick, P. W. (2013). Sex differences in succumbing to sexual temptations: A function of impulse or control? *Personality and Social Psychology Bulletin, 39,* 1620–1633.

Tidwell, N. D., Eastwick, P. W., & Finkel, E. J. (2013). Perceived, not actual, similarity predicts initial attraction in a live romantic context: Evidence from the speed-dating paradigm. *Personal Relationships, 20,* 199–215.

Tiffert, S., & Vilnai-Yavetz, I. (2014). Gender differences in Facebook self-presentation: An international randomized study. *Computers in Human Behavior, 35,* 388–399.

Tilcsik, A. (2011). Pride and prejudice: Employment discrimination against openly gay men in the United States. *American Journal of Sociology, 117,* 586–626.

Time. (1994, November 7). Vox pop (poll by Yankelovich Partners Inc.), p. 21.

Timmerman, T. A. (2007). "It was a thought pitch": Personal, situational, and target influences on hit-by-pitch events across time. *Journal of Applied Psychology, 92,* 876–884.

Tindale, R. S., Davis, J. H., Vollrath, D. A., Nagao, D. H., & Hinsz, V. B. (1990). Asymmetrical social influence in freely interacting groups: A test of three models. *Journal of Personality and Social Psychology, 58,* 438–449.

Toburen, T., & Meier, B. P. (2010). Priming God-related concepts increases anxiety and task persistence. *Journal of Social and Clinical Psychology, 29,* 127–143.

Todd, A. R., Bodenhausen, G. V., Richeson, J. A., & Galinsky, A. D. (2011). Perspective taking combats automatic expressions of racial bias. *Journal of Personality and Social Psychology, 100,* 1027–1042.

Todorov, A. (2011). Evaluating faces on social dimensions. In A. Todorov, S. T. Fiske, & D. A. Prentice (Eds.), *Social neuroscience: Toward understanding the underpinnings of the social mind.* New York: Oxford University Press.

Todorov, A., Mandisodza, A. N., Goren, A., & Hall, C. C. (2005). Inferences of competence from faces predict election outcomes. *Science, 308,* 1623–1626.

Tomasello, M. (2009). *Why we cooperate.* Boston: MIT Press.

Tomasello, M. (2014). The ultra-social animal. *European Journal of Social Psychology, 44,* 187–194.

Toner, K., Leary, M. R., Asher, M. W., & Jongman-Sereno, K. (2013). Feeling superior is a bipartisan issue: Extremity (not direction) of political views predicts perceived belief superiority. *Psychological Science, 24,* 2454–2462.

Topolinski, S., Maschmann, I. T., Pecher, D., & Winkielman, P. (2014). Oral approach–avoidance: Affective consequences of muscular articulation dynamics. *Journal of Personality and Social Psychology, 106,* 885–896.

Tormala, Z. L., Brinol, P., & Petty, R. E. (2006). When credibility attacks: The reverse impact of source credibility on persuasion. *Journal of Experimental Social Psychology, 42,* 684–691.

Toronto News. (1977, July 26).

Totterdell, P., Kellett, S., Briner, R. B., & Teuchmann, K. (1998). Evidence of mood linkage in work groups. *Journal of Personality and Social Psychology, 74,* 1504–1515.

Towles-Schwen, T., & Fazio, R. H. (2006). Automatically activated racial attitudes as predictors of the success of interracial roommate relationships. *Journal of Experimental Social Psychology, 42,* 698–705.

Towson, S. M. J., & Zanna, M. P. (1983). Retaliation against sexual assault: Self-defense or public duty? *Psychology of Women Quarterly, 8,* 89–99.

Trail, T. E., Shelton, J. N., & West, T. V. (2009). Interracial roommate relationships: Negotiating daily interactions. *Personality and Social Psychology Bulletin, 35,* 671–684.

Trautwein, U., & Lüdtke, O. (2006). Self-esteem, academic self-concept, and achievement: How the learning environment moderates the dynamics of self-concept. *Journal of Personality and Social Psychology, 90,* 334–349.

Travis, L. E. (1925). The effect of a small audience upon eye-hand coordination. *Journal of Abnormal and Social Psychology, 20,* 142–146.

Tredoux, C., & Finchilescu, G. (2010). Mediators of the contact-prejudice relation amongst South African students on four university campuses. *Journal of Social Issues, 66,* 289–308.

Triandis, H. C. (1981). Some dimensions of intercultural variation and their implications for interpersonal behavior. Paper presented at the American Psychological Association convention.

Triandis, H. C. (1982). Incongruence between intentions and behavior: A review. Paper presented at the American Psychological Association convention.

Triandis, H. C. (1994). *Culture and social behavior.* New York: McGraw-Hill.

Triandis, H. C. (2000). Culture and conflict. *International Journal of Psychology, 55,* 145–152.

Triandis, H. C., Bontempo, R., Villareal, M. J., Asai, M., & Lucca, N. (1988). Individualism and collectivism: Cross-cultural perspectives on self-ingroup relationships. *Journal of Personality and Social Psychology, 54,* 323–338.

Trimble, D. E. (1993). *Meta-analysis of altruism and intrinsic and extrinsic religiousness.* Paper presented at the Eastern Psychological Association convention, Evanston, Illinois.

Triplett, N. (1898). The dynamogenic factors in pacemaking and competition. *American Journal of Psychology, 9,* 507–533.

Trolier, T. K., & Hamilton, D. L. (1986). Variables influencing judgments of correlational relations. *Journal of Personality and Social Psychology, 50,* 879–888.

Tropp, L. R., & Pettigrew, T. F. (2005a). Differential relationships between intergroup contact and affective and cognitive dimensions of prejudice. *Personality and Social Psychology Bulletin, 31,* 1145–1158.

Tropp, L. R., & Pettigrew, T. F. (2005b). Relationships between intergroup contact and prejudice among minority and majority status groups. *Psychological Science, 16,* 951–957.

Trost, M. R., Maass, A., & Kenrick, D. T. (1992). Minority influence: Personal relevance biases cognitive processes and reverses private acceptance. *Journal of Experimental Social Psychology, 28,* 234–254.

Trzesniewski, K. H., & Donnellan, M. B. (2010). Rethinking "Generation Me": A study of cohort effects from 1976–2006. *Perspectives in Psychological Science, 5,* 58–75.

Tsang, J-A. (2002). Moral rationalization and the integration of situational factors and psychological processes in immoral behavior. *Review of General Psychology, 6,* 25–50.

Turner, C. W., Hesse, B. W., & Peterson-Lewis, S. (1986). Naturalistic studies of the long-term effects of television violence. *Journal of Social Issues, 42(3),* 51–74.

Turner, J. C. (1981). The experimental social psychology of intergroup behaviour. In J. Turner & H. Giles (Eds.), *Intergroup behavior.* Oxford, England: Blackwell.

Turner, J. C. (1984). Social identification and psychological group formation. In H. Tajfel (Ed.), *The social dimensions: European developments in social psychology* (Vol. 2). London: Cambridge University Press.

Turner, J. C. (2000). Social identity. In A. E. Kazdin (Ed.), *Encyclopedia of Psychology, 7.* Washington, DC: American Psychological Association.

Turner, M. E., & Pratkanis, A. R. (1993). Effects of preferential and meritorious selection on performance: An examination of intuitive and self-handicapping perspectives. *Personality and Social Psychology Bulletin, 19,* 47–58.

Turner, M. E., & Pratkanis, A. R. (1994). Social identity maintenance prescriptions for preventing groupthink: Reducing identity protection and enhancing intellectual conflict. *International Journal of Conflict Management, 5,* 254–270.

Turner, M. E., & Pratkanis, A. R. (1997). Mitigating groupthink by stimulating constructive conflict. In C. K. W. De Dreu & E. Van de Vliert (Eds.), *Using conflict in organizations.* London: Sage.

Turner, M. E., Pratkanis, A. R., Probasco, P., & Leve, C. (1992). Threat cohesion and group effectiveness: Testing a social identity maintenance perspective on groupthink. *Journal of Personality and Social Psychology, 63,* 781–796.

Turner, N., Barling, J., & Zacharatos, A. (2002). Positive psychology at work. In C. R. Snyder & S. J. Lopez (Eds.), *The handbook of positive psychology.* New York: Oxford University Press.

Turner, R. N., & Crisp, R. J. (2010). Imagining intergroup contact reduces implicit prejudice. *British Journal of Social Psychology, 49,* 129–142.

Turner, R. N., Hewstone, M., & Voci, A. (2007a). Reducing explicit and implicit outgroup prejudice via direct and extended contact: The mediating role of self-disclosure and intergroup anxiety. *Journal of Personality and Social Psychology, 93,* 369–388.

Turner, R. N., Hewstone, M., Voci, A., Paolini, S., & Christ, O. (2007b). Reducing prejudice via direct and extended cross-group friendship. *European Review of Social Psychology, 18,* 212–255.

Turner, R. N., Hewstone, M., Voci, A., & Vonofakou, C. (2008). A test of the extended intergroup contact hypothesis: The mediating role of intergroup anxiety, perceived ingroup and outgroup norms, and inclusion of the outgroup in the self. *Journal of Personality and Social Psychology, 95,* 843–860.

Tutu, D. (1999). *No future without forgiveness.* New York: Doubleday.

Tversky, A. (1985, June). Quoted by Kevin McKean in Decisions, decisions, *Discover*, pp. 22–31.

Tversky, A., & Kahneman, D. (1973). Availability: A neuristic for judging frequency and probability. *Cognitive Psychology, 5,* 207–302.

Tversky, A., & Kahneman, D. (1974). Judgment under uncertainty: Heuristics and biases. *Science, 185(4157),* 1124–1131.

Tversky, A., & Kahneman, D. (1983). Extensional versus intuitive reasoning: The conjunction fallacy in probability judgment. *Psychological Review, 90,* 293–315.

Twenge, J. M. (1997). Changes in masculine and feminine traits over time: A meta-analysis. *Sex Roles, 36,* 305–325.

Twenge, J. M. (2009). Change over time in obedience: The jury's still out, but it might be decreasing. *American Psychologist, 64,* 28–31.

Twenge, J. M. (2013). Teaching Generation Me. *Teaching of Psychology, 40,* 66–69.

Twenge, J. M. (2014). *Generation me: Why today's young Americans are more confident, assertive, entitled—and more miserable than ever before.* (2nd Ed.) New York: Atria.

Twenge, J. M., Abebe, E. M., & Campbell, W. K. (2010). Fitting in or standing out: Trends in American parents' choices for children's names, 1880–2007. *Social Psychological and Personality Science, 1,* 19–25.

Twenge, J. M., Baumeister, R. F., Tice, D. M., & Stucke, T. S. (2001). If you can't join them, beat them: Effects of social exclusion on aggressive behavior. *Journal of Personality and Social Psychology, 81,* 1058–1069.

Twenge, J. M., & Campbell, W. K. (2008). Increases in positive self-views among high school students: Birth cohort changes in anticipated performance, self-satisfaction, self-liking, and self-competence. *Psychological Science, 19,* 1082–1086.

Twenge, J. M., & Campbell, W. K. (2009). *The narcissism epidemic: Living in the age of entitlement.* New York: Free Press.

Twenge, J. M., Campbell, W. K., & Gentile, B. (2012). Generational increases in agentic self-evaluations among American college students, 1966–2009. *Self and Identity, 11,* 409–427.

Twenge, J. M., Campbell, W. K., & Gentile, B. (2012). Male and female pronoun use in U.S. books reflects women's status, 1900–2008. *Sex Roles, 67,* 488–493.

Twenge, J. M., Campbell, W. K., & Gentile, B. (2013). Changes in pronoun use in American books and the rise of individualism, 1960–2008. *Journal of Cross-Cultural Psychology, 44,* 406–415.

Twenge, J. M., Catanese, K. R., & Baumeister, R. F. (2002). Social exclusion causes self-defeating behavior. *Journal of Personality and Social Psychology, 83,* 606–615.

Twenge, J. M., Catanese, K. R., & Baumeister, R. F. (2003). Social exclusion and the deconstructed state: Time perception, meaninglessness, lethargy, lack of emotion, and self-awareness. *Journal of Personality and Social Psychology, 85,* 409–423.

Twenge, J. M., & Foster, J. D. (2008). Mapping the scale of the narcissism epidemic: Increases in narcissism 2002–2007 within ethnic groups. *Journal of Research in Personality, 42,* 1619–1622.

Twenge, J. M., & Foster, J. D. (2010). Birth cohort increases in narcissistic personality traits among American college students, 1982–2009. *Social Psychological and Personality Science, 1,* 99–106.

Twenge, J. M., & Kasser, T. (2013). Generational changes in materialism and work centrality, 1976–2007: Associations with temporal changes in societal insecurity and materialistic role modeling. *Personality and Social Psychology Bulletin, 39,* 883–897.

Twenge. J. M., Sherman, R. A., & Wells, B. E. (2015). Changes in American adults' sexual behavior and attitudes, 1972–2012. *Archives of Sexual Behavior.*

Twenge, J. M., Zhang, L., Catanese, K. R., Dolan-Pascoe, B., Lyche, L. F., & Baumeister, R. F. (2007). Replenishing connectedness: Reminders of social activity reduce aggression after social exclusion. *British Journal of Social Psychology, 46,* 205–224.

Tykocinski, O. E., & Bareket-Bojmel, L. (2009). The lost e-mail technique: Use of an implicit measure to assess discriminatory attitudes toward two minority groups in Israel. *Journal of Applied Social Psychology, 39,* 62–81.

Tyler, J. M. (2012). Triggering self-presentation efforts outside of people's conscious awareness. *Personality and Social Psychology Bulletin, 38,* 619–627.

Tyler, T. R., & Lind, E. A. (1990). Intrinsic versus community-based justice models: When does group membership matter? *Journal of Social Issues, 46,* 83–94.

Tzeng, M. (1992). The effects of socioeconomic heterogamy and changes on marital dissolution for first marriages. *Journal of Marriage and the Family, 54,* 609–619.

Uchino, B. N., Cacioppo, J. T., & Kiecolt-Glaser, J. K. (1996). The relationship between social support and physiological processes: A review with emphasis on underlying mechanisms and implications for health. *Psychological Bulletin, 119,* 488–531.

Uchino, B. N., Smith, T. W., & Berg, C. A. (2014). Spousal relationship quality and cardiovascular risk: Dyadic perceptions of relationship ambivalence are associated with coronary-artery calcification. *Psychological Science, 25,* 1037–1042.

Uecker, J. E. (2008). Religion, pledging, and the premarital sexual behavior of married young adults. *Journal of Marriage and Family, 70,* 728–744.

Ugwuegbu, C. E. (1979). Racial and evidential factors in juror attribution of legal responsibility. *Journal of Experimental Social Psychology, 15,* 133–146.

Uleman, J. S. (1989). A framework for thinking intentionally about unintended thoughts. In J. S. Uleman & J. A. Bargh (Eds.), *Unintended thought: The limits of awareness, intention, and control.* New York: Guilford.

Uleman, J. S., Saribay, S. A., & Gonzalez, C. M. (2008). Spontaneous inferences, implicit impressions, and implicit theories. *Annual Review of Psychology, 59,* 329–360.

UNESCO. (2013, September). Adult and youth literacy. UIS Fact Sheet, No. 26. Paris: UNESCO Institute for Statistics.

Unger, R. K. (1979). *Whom does helping help?* Paper presented at the Eastern Psychological Association convention, April.

Unger, R. K. (1985). Epistomological consistency and its scientific implications. *American Psychologist, 40,* 1413–1414.

United Nations. (2011, November 17). Discriminatory laws and practices and acts of violence against individuals based on their sexual orientation and gender identity. Report of the United Nations High Commissioner for Human Rights.

United Nations. (2014). The world's women reports. Retrieved March 27, 2015 from: http://unstats.un.org/unsd/demographic/products/indwm/ww2005/tab5g.htm

United Nations (UN). (2010). *The world's women 2010 trends and statistics.* United Nations Department of Economic and Social Affairs. www.unstats.un.org

Unkelbach, C., & Memmert, D. (2010). Crowd noise as a cue in referee decisions contributes to the home advantage. *Journal of Sport & Exercise Psychology, 32,* 483–498.

Urbina, I. (2010, May 29). Documents show early worries about safety of rig. *New York Times* (www.nytimes.com).

U.S. Department of Defense. (2014). *Quadrennial defense review 2014.* Washington, DC: Secretary of Defense.

U.S. Supreme Court, *Plessy v. Ferguson.* (1986). Quoted by L. J. Severy, J. C. Brigham, & B. R. Schlenker, *A contemporary introduction to social psychology* (p. 126). New York: McGraw-Hill.

Uysal, A., Lin, H. L., & Knee, C. R. (2010). The role of need satisfaction in self-concealment and well-being. *Personality and Social Psychology Bulletin, 36,* 187–199.

Väänänen, A., Buunk, B. P., Kivimäke, M., Pentti, J., & Vahtera, J. (2005). When it is better to give than to receive: Long-term health effects of perceived reciprocity in support exchange. *Journal of Personality and Social Psychology, 89*, 176–193.

Vaillant, G. E. (1977). *Adaptation to life.* Boston: Little, Brown.

Vaillant, G. E. (1997). Report on distress and longevity. Paper presented to the American Psychiatric Association convention, Chicago, Illinois.

Vaillant, G. E. (2002). *Aging well: Surprising guideposts to a happier life from the landmark Harvard study of adult development.* Boston: Little, Brown.

Vala, J., Pereira, C., Oliveira Lima, M. E., & Leyens, J. (2012). Intergroup time bias and racialized social relations. *Personality and Social Psychology Bulletin, 38*, 491–504.

Valdesolo, P., & DeSteno, D. (2007). Moral hypocrisy: Social groups and the flexibility of virtue. *Psychological Science, 18*, 689–690.

Valdesolo, P., & DeSteno, D. (2008). The duality of virtue: Deconstructing the moral hypocrite. *Journal of Experimental Social Psychology, 44*, 1334–1338.

Valentine, K. A., Li, N. P., Penke, L., & Perrett, D. I. (2014). Judging a man by the width of his face: The role of facial ratios and dominance in mate choice at speed-dating events. *Psychological Science, 25*, 806–811.

Valentine, T., & Mesout, J. (2009). Eyewitness identification under stress in the London Dungeon. *Applied Cognitive Psychology, 23*, 151–161.

Valentine, T., Pickering, A., & Darling, S. (2003). Characteristics of eyewitness identification that predict the outcome of real lineups. *Applied Cognitive Psychology, 17*, 969–993.

Vallone, R. P., Griffin, D. W., Lin, S., & Ross, L. (1990). Overconfident prediction of future actions and outcomes by self and others. *Journal of Personality and Social Psychology, 58*, 582–592.

Vallone, R. P., Ross, L., & Lepper, M. R. (1985). The hostile media phenomenon: Biased perception and perceptions of media bias in coverage of the "Beirut Massacre." *Journal of Personality and Social Psychology, 49*, 577–585.

van Baaren, R. B., Holland, R. W., Karremans, R. W., & van Knippenberg, A. (2003a). *Mimicry and interpersonal closeness.* Unpublished manuscript, University of Nijmegen.

van Baaren, R. B., Holland, R. W., Kawakami, K., & van Knippenberg, A. (2004). Mimicry and prosocial behavior. *Psychological Science, 15*, 71–74.

van Baaren, R. B., Holland, R. W., Steenaert, B., & van Knippenberg, A. (2003b). Mimicry for money: Behavioral consequences of imitation. *Journal of Experimental Social Psychology, 39*, 393–398.

Van Bavel, J. J., & Cunningham, W. A. (2012). A social identity approach to person memory: Group membership, collective identification, and social role shape attention and memory. *Personality and Social Psychology Bulletin, 38*, 1566–1578.

VanDellen, M. R., Campbell, W. K., Hoyle, R. H., & Bradfield, E. K. (2011). Compensating, resisting, and breaking: A meta-analytic examination of reactions to self-esteem threat. *Personality and Social Psychology Review, 15*, 51–74.

Vandello, J. A., & Bosson, J. K. (2013). Hard won and easily lost: A review and synthesis of theory and research on precarious manhood. *Psychology of Men and Masculinity, 14*, 101–113.

Vandello, J. A., & Cohen, D. (1999). Patterns of individualism and collectivism across the United States. *Journal of Personality and Social Psychology, 77*, 279–292.

Vandello, J. A., Cohen, D., & Ransom, S. (2008). U.S. southern and northern differences in perceptions of norms about aggression: Mechanisms for the perpetuation of a culture of honor. *Journal of Cross-Cultural Psychology, 39*, 162–177.

Van Den Bergh, B., Schmitt, J., & Warlop, L. (2011). Embodied myopia. *Journal of Marketing Research, 48*, 1033–44.

Van der Plight, J., Eise, J. R., & Spears, R. (1987). Comparative judgments and preferences: The influence of the number of response alternatives. *British Journal of Social Psychology, 26*, 269–280.

Vanderslice, V. J., Rice, R. W., & Julian, J. W. (1987). The effects of participation in decision-making on worker satisfaction and productivity: An organizational simulation. *Journal of Applied Social Psychology, 17*, 158–170.

Van der Velde, S. W., Stapel, D. A., & Gordijn, E. H. (2010). Imitation of emotion: When meaning leads to aversion. *European Journal of Social Psychology, 40*, 536–542.

van de Ven, N. (2011). Supporters are not necessary for the home advantage: Evidence from same-stadium derbies and games without an audience. *Journal of Applied Social Psychology, 41*, 2785–2792.

van Dijk, W. W., Finkenauer, C., & Pollmann, M. (2008). The misprediction of emotions in track athletics: Is experience the teacher of all things? *Basic and Applied Social Psychology, 30*, 369–376.

van Dijk, W. W., Ouwerkerk, J. W., van Koningsbruggen, G. M., & Wesseling, Y. M. (2012). "So You Wanna Be a Pop Star?": Schadenfreude Following Another's Misfortune on TV. *Basic & Applied Social Psychology, 34*, 168–174.

van Emmerik, A. A., Reijntjes, A., & Kamphuis, J. H. (2013). Writing therapy for post-traumatic stress: A meta-analysis. *Psychotherapy and Psychosomatics, 82*, 82–88.

Vanman, E. J., Paul, B. Y., Kaplan, D. L., & Miller, N. (1990). Facial electromyography differentiates racial bias in imagined cooperative settings. *Psychophysiology, 27*, 563.

van Straaten, I., Engels, R. C. M. E., Finkenauer, C., & Holland, R. W. (2009). Meeting your match: How attractiveness similarity affects approach behavior in mixed-sex dyads. *Personality and Social Psychology Bulletin, 35*, 685–697.

van Veluw, S. J., & Chance, S. A. (2014). Differentiating between self and others: An ALE meta-analysis of fMRI studies of self-recognition and theory of mind. *Brain Imaging and Behavior, 8*, 24–38.

Van Vugt, M. (2009). Averting the Tragedy of the Commons: Using social psychological science to protect the environment. *Current Directions in Psychological Science, 18*, 169–173.

Van Vugt, M., & Spisak, B. R. (2008). Sex differences in the emergence of leadership during competitions within and between groups. *Psychological Science, 19*, 854–858.

Van Yperen, N. W., & Buunk, B. P. (1990). A longitudinal study of equity and satisfaction in intimate relationships. *European Journal of Social Psychology, 20*, 287–309.

Vargas, R. A. (2009, July 6). "City of Heroes" character "Twixt" becomes game's most hated outcast courtesy of Loyola professor. *The Times-Picayune* (www.nola.com).

Varnum, M. E. W. (2012). Conformity effect sizes are smaller on the frontier. *Journal of Cognition and Cultures, 12*, 359–364.

Varnum, M. E. W. (2013). Frontiers, germs, and nonconformist voting. *Journal of Cross-Cultural Psychology, 44*, 832–837.

Varnum, M. E. W., & Kitayama, S. (2011). What's in a name? Popular names are less common on frontiers. *Psychological Science, 22*, 176–183.

Vasquez, E. A., Denson, T. F., Pedersen, W. C., Stenstrom, D. M., & Miller, N. (2005). The moderating effect of trigger intensity on triggered displaced aggression. *Journal of Experimental Social Psychology, 41*, 61–67.

Vaughan, K. B., & Lanzetta, J. T. (1981). The effect of modification of expressive displays on vicarious emotional arousal. *Journal of Experimental Social Psychology, 17*, 16–30.

Vazire, S., & Mehl, M. R. (2008). Knowing me, knowing you: The accuracy and unique predictive validity of self-ratings and other-ratings of daily behavior. *Journal of Personality and Social Psychology, 95*, 1202–1216.

Vedantam, S. (2012). Partisan psychology: Why do people choose political loyalties over facts? May 9, 2012. http://www.npr.org/blogs/itsallpolitics/2012/05/09/152287372/partisan-psychology-why-are-people-partial-to-political-loyalties-over-facts

Vega, V., & Malamuth, N. M. (2007). Predicting sexual aggression: The role of pornography in the context of general and specific risk factors. *Aggressive Behavior, 33,* 104–117.

Verkuyten, M., & Maliepaard, M. (2013). A further test of the "party over policy" effect: Political leadership and ethnic minority policies. *Basic and Applied Social Psychology, 35,* 241–248.

Verkuyten, M., & Yildiz, A. A. (2007). National (dis)identification and ethnic and religious identity: A study among Turkish-Dutch Muslims. *Personality and Social Psychology, 33,* 1448–1462.

Verplanken, B. (1991). Persuasive communication of risk information: A test of cue versus message processing effects in a field experiment. *Personality and Social Psychology Bulletin, 17,* 188–193.

Vescio, T. K., Gervais, S. J., Snyder, M., & Hoover, A. (2005). Power and the creation of patronizing environments: The stereotype-based behaviors of the powerful and their effects on female performance in masculine domains. *Journal of Personality and Social Psychology, 88,* 658–672.

Veysey, B. M., & Messner, S. F. (1999). Further testing of social disorganization theory: An elaboration of Sampson and Groves's "Community structure and crime." *Journal of Research in Crime and Delinquency, 36,* 156–174.

Vezzali, L., Stathi, S., Giovannini, D., Capozza, D., & Trifiletti, E. (2014). The greatest magic of Harry Potter: Reducing prejudice. *Journal of Applied Social Psychology,* in press.

Vidmar, N. (1979). The other issues in jury simulation research. *Law and Human Behavior, 3,* 95–106.

Vidmar, N., & Laird, N. M. (1983). Adversary social roles: Their effects on witnesses' communication of evidence and the assessments of adjudicators. *Journal of Personality and Social Psychology, 44,* 888–898.

Viken, R. J., Treat, T. A., Bloom, S. L., & McFall, R. M. (2005). Illusory correlation for body type and happiness: Covariation bias and its relationship to eating disorder symptoms. *International Journal of Eating Disorders, 38,* 65–72.

Visher, C. A. (1987). Juror decision making: The importance of evidence. *Law and Human Behavior, 11,* 1–17.

Visintainer, M. A., & Seligman, M. E. (1983, July/August). The hope factor. *American Health,* 59–61.

Visintainer, M. A., & Seligman, M. E. P. (1985). Tumor rejection and early experience of uncontrollable shock in the rat. Unpublished manuscript, University of Pennsylvania. See also M. A. Visintainer et al. (1982), Tumor rejection in rats after inescapable versus escapable shock. *Science, 216,* 437–439.

Visser, P. S., & Krosnick, J. A. (1998). Development of attitude strength over the life cycle: Surge and decline. *Journal of Personality and Social Psychology, 75,* 1389–1410.

Visser, P. S., & Mirabile, R. R. (2004). Attitudes in the social context: The impact of social network composition on individual-level attitude strength. *Journal of Personality and Social Psychology, 87,* 779–795.

Vitelli, R. (1988). The crisis issue assessed: An empirical analysis. *Basic and Applied Social Psychology, 9,* 301–309.

Vogel, T., Kutzner, F., Fiedler, K., & Freytag, P. (2010). Exploiting attractiveness in persuasion: Senders' implicit theories about receivers' processing motivation. *Personality and Social Psychology Bulletin, 36,* 830–842.

Vohs, K. D., Baumeister, R. F., & Ciarocco, N. J. (2005). Self-regulation and self-presentation: Regulatory resource depletion impairs impression management and effortful self-presentation depletes regulatory resources. *Journal of Personality and Social Psychology, 88,* 632–657.

Vohs, K. D., Mead, N. L., & Goode, M. R. (2006). The psychological consequences of money. *Science, 314,* 1154–1156.

Vohs, K. D., Mead, N. L., & Goode, M. R. (2008). Merely activating the concept of money changes personal and interpersonal behavior. *Current Directions in Psychological Science, 17,* 208–212.

Vollhardt, J. R. (2010). Enhanced external and culturally sensitive attributions after extended intercultural contact. *British Journal of Social Psychology, 49,* 363–383.

Vollman, W. T. (2008). California. In M. Weiland & S. Wilsey (Eds.) *State by state: A panoramic portrait of America* (pp. 43–55). New York, NY: HarperCollins.

Vollrath, D. A., Sheppard, B. H., Hinsz, V. B., & Davis, J. H. (1989). Memory performance by decision-making groups and individuals. *Organizational Behavior and Human Decision Processes, 43,* 289–300.

von Hippel, F. N. (2011, March 22). It could happen here. *New York Times* (www.nytimes.com).

von Hippel, W., Silver, L. A., & Lynch, M. B. (2000). Stereotyping against your will: The role of inhibitory ability in stereotyping and prejudice among the elderly. *Personality and Social Psychology Bulletin, 26,* 523–532.

Vorauer, J. D. (2001). The other side of the story: Transparency estimation in social interaction. In G. Moskowitz (Ed.), *Cognitive social psychology: The Princeton symposium on the legacy and future of social cognition.* Mahwah, NJ: Erlbaum.

Vorauer, J. D. (2005). Miscommunications surrounding efforts to reach out across group boundaries. *Personality and Social Psychology Bulletin, 31,* 1653–1664.

Vorauer, J. D., Main, K. J., & O'Connell, G. B. (1998). How do individuals expect to be viewed by members of lower status groups? Content and implications of meta-stereotypes. *Journal of Personality and Social Psychology, 75,* 917–937.

Vorauer, J. D., & Quesnel, M. (2013). You don't really love me, do you? Negative effects of imagine-other perspective-taking on lower self-esteem individuals' relationship well-being. *Personality and Social Psychology Bulletin, 39,* 1428–1440.

Vorauer, J. D., & Ratner, R. K. (1996). Who's going to make the first move? Pluralistic ignorance as an impediment to relationship formation. *Journal of Social and Personal Relationships, 13,* 483–506.

Vorauer, J. D., & Sakamoto, Y. (2006). I thought we could be friends, but . . . Systematic miscommunication and defensive distancing as obstacles to cross-group friendship formation. *Psychological Science 17,* 326–331.

Vorauer, J. D., & Sasaki, S. J. (2010). In need of liberation or constraint? How intergroup attitudes moderate the behavioral implications of intergroup ideologies. *Journal of Experimental Social Psychology, 46,* 133–138.

Vorauer, J. D., & Sasaki, S. J. (2011). In the worst rather than the best of times; Effect of salient intergroup ideology in threatening intergroup interactions. *Journal of Personality and Social Psychology, 101,* 307–320.

VPC: Violence Policy Center. (2015). States with weak gun laws and higher gun ownership lead nation in gun deaths, new data for 2013 confirms. https://www.vpc.org/press/1501gundeath.htm

Vul, E., & Pashler, H. (2008). Measuring the crowd within: Probabilistic representations within individuals. *Psychological Science, 19,* 646–647.

Wade, K. A., Green, S. L., & Nash, R. A. (2010). Can fabricated evidence induce false eyewitness testimony? *Applied Cognitive Psychology, 24,* 899–908.

Wadsworth, T. (2014). Sex and the pursuit of happiness: How other people's sex lives are related to our sense of well-being. *Social Indicators Research, 116,* 115–135.

Wagner, G. (2011, September 7). Going green but getting nowhere. *New York Times* (www.nytimes.com).

Wagner, M. (2014, October 23). Nevada school knew 13-year-old was being bullied before suicide, didn't tell girl's parents: Lawsuit. *New York Daily News* (http://www.nydailynews.com/news/national/nev-school-didn-girl-parents-bullying-suicide-lawsuit-article-1.1984436).

Wagner, U., Christ, O., & Pettigrew, T. F. (2008). Prejudice and group-related behavior in Germany. *Journal of Social Issues, 64,* 403–416.

Wagstaff, G. F. (1983). Attitudes to poverty, the Protestant ethic, and political affiliation:

A preliminary investigation. *Social Behavior and Personality, 11,* 45–47.

Walinsky, A. (1995, July). The crisis of public order. *The Atlantic Monthly,* 39–54.

Walker, L. J., & Frimer, J. A. (2007). Moral personality of brave and caring exemplars. *Journal of Personality and Social Psychology, 93,* 845–860.

Walker, P. M., & Hewstone, M. (2008). The influence of social factors and implicit racial bias on a generalized own-race effect. *Applied Cognitive Psychology, 22,* 441–453.

Walker, R. (2004, December 5). The hidden (in plain sight) persuaders. *New York Times Magazine* (www.nytimes.com).

Wallace, D. B., & Kassin, S. M. (2012). Harmless error analysis: How do judges respond to confession errors? *Law and Human Behavior, 36,* 155–164.

Wallace, D. S., Paulson, R. M., Lord, C. G., & Bond, C. F., Jr. (2005). Which behaviors do attitudes predict? Meta-analyzing the effects of social pressure and perceived difficulty. *Review of General Psychology, 9,* 214–227.

Wallace, M. (1969, November 25). Transcript of Interview of Vietnam War Veteran on His Role in Alleged Massacre of Civilians at Songmy. *New York Times.*

Waller, J. (2002). *Becoming evil: How ordinary people commit genocide and mass killing.* New York: Oxford University Press.

Walster (Hatfield), E., Aronson, V., Abrahams, D., & Rottman, L. (1966). Importance of physical attractiveness in dating behavior. *Journal of Personality and Social Psychology, 4,* 508–516.

Walster (Hatfield), E., Walster, G. W., & Berscheid, E. (1978). *Equity: Theory and research.* Boston: Allyn & Bacon.

Walther, E., Weil, R., & Düsing, J. (2011). The role of evaluative conditioning in attitude formation. *Current Directions in Psychological Science, 20,* 190–196.

Walton, G. M. (2014). The new science of wise psychological interventions. *Current Directions in Psychological Science, 23,* 73–82.

Walum, H., Westberg, L., Heinningsson, S., Neiderhiser, J. M., Reiss, D., Igl, W., Ganiban, J. M., Spotts, E. L., Pedersen, N. L., Eriksson, E., & Lichtenstein, P. (2008). Genetic variation in the vasopressin receptor 1a gene (*AVPR1A*) associates with pair-bonding behavior in humans. *Proceedings of the National Academy of Sciences USA, 105,* 14153–14156.

Wang, J., Leu, J., & Shoda, Y. (2011). When the seemingly innocuous "stings": Racial microaggressions and their emotional consequences. *Personality and Social Psychology Bulletin, 37,* 1666–1678.

Ward, W. C., & Jenkins, H. M. (1965). The display of information and the judgment of contingency. *Canadian Journal of Psychology, 19,* 231–241.

Warnick, D. H., & Sanders, G. S. (1980). The effects of group discussion on eyewitness accuracy. *Journal of Applied Social Psychology, 10,* 249–259.

Warren, N. C. (2005, March 4). Personal correspondence from founder of eHarmony.com.

Warr, P., & Payne, R. (1982). Experiences of strain and pleasure among British adults. *Social Science and Medicine, 16,* 1691–1697.

Washington, K. N., & Hans, J. D. (2013). Romantic attachment among young adults: The effects of parental divorce and residential instability. *Journal of Divorce & Remarriage, 54,* 95–111.

Wason, P. C. (1960). On the failure to eliminate hypotheses in a conceptual task. *Quarterly Journal of Experimental Psychology, 12,* 129–140.

Waters, E. A., Klein, W. M. P., Moser, R. P., Yu, M., Waldron, W. R., McNeel, T. S., & Freedman, A. N. (2011). Correlates of unrealistic risk beliefs in a nationally representative sample. *Journal of Behavioral Medicine, 34,* 225–235.

Watkins, D., Akande, A., & Fleming, J. (1998). Cultural dimensions, gender, and the nature of self-concept: A fourteen-country study. *International Journal of Psychology, 33,* 17–31.

Watkins, D., Cheng, C., Mpofu, E., Olowu, S., Singh-Sengupta, S., & Regmi, M. (2003). Gender differences in self-construal: How generalizable are Western findings? *Journal of Social Psychology, 143,* 501–519.

Watkins, E. R. (2008). Constructive and unconstructive repetitive thought. *Psychological Bulletin, 134,* 163–206.

Watson, D. (1982, November). The actor and the observer: How are their perceptions of causality divergent? *Psychological Bulletin, 92,* 682–700.

Watson, D., Beer, A., & McDade-Montez, E. (2014). The role of active assortment in spousal similarity. *Journal of Personality, 82,* 116–129.

Watson, D., Klohnen, E. C., Casillas, A., Simms, E. N., Haig, J., & Berry, D. S. (2004). Match makers and deal breakers: Analyses of assortative mating in newlywed couples. *Journal of Personality, 72,* 1029–1068.

Watson, R. I., Jr. (1973). Investigation into deindividuation using a cross-cultural survey technique. *Journal of Personality and Social Psychology, 25,* 342–345.

Watt, S. E., & Badger, A. J. (2009). Effects of social belonging on homesickness: An application of the belongingness hypothesis. *Personality and Social Psychology Bulletin, 35,* 516–530.

Watt, S. E., & Larkin, C. (2010). Prejudiced people perceive more community support for their views: The role of own, media, and peer attitudes in perceived consensus. *Journal of Applied Social Psychology, 40,* 710–731.

Weary, G., Harvey, J. H., Schwieger, P., Olson, C. T., Perloff, R., & Pritchard, S. (1982). Self-presentation and the moderation of self-serving biases. *Social Cognition, 1,* 140–159.

Webb, T. L., & Sheeran, P. (2006). Does changing behavioral intentions engender behavior change? A meta-analysis of the experimental evidence. *Psychological Bulletin, 132,* 249–268.

Weber, N., Wells, G. L., & Semmler, C. (2004). Eyewitness identification accuracy and response latency: The unruly 10–12-second rule. *Journal of Experimental Psychology: Applied, 10,* 139–147.

Webley, K. (2009, June 15). Behind the drop in Chinese adoptions. *Time,* 55.

Wegner, D. M., & Erber, R. (1992). The hyperaccessibility of suppressed thoughts. *Journal of Personality and Social Psychology, 63,* 903–912.

Wehr, P. (1979). *Conflict regulation.* Boulder, CO: Westview.

Weichselbaumer, D. (2003). Sexual orientation discrimination in hiring. *Labour Economics, 10,* 629–642.

Weiner, B. (1980). A cognitive (attribution)–emotion–action model of motivated behavior: An analysis of judgments of help-giving. *Journal of Personality and Social Psychology, 39,* 186–200.

Weiner, B. (1981). The emotional consequences of causal ascriptions. Unpublished manuscript, UCLA.

Weiner, B. (1985). "Spontaneous" causal thinking. *Psychological Bulletin, 97,* 74–84.

Weiner, B. (1995). *Judgments of responsibility: A foundation for a theory of social conduct.* New York: Guilford.

Weiner, B. (2008). Reflections on the history of attribution theory and research: People, personalities, publications, problems. *Social Psychology, 39,* 151–156.

Weiner, B. (2010). The development of an attribution-based theory of motivation: A history of ideas. *Educational Psychologist, 45,* 28–36.

Weiner, B., Osborne, D., & Rudoph, U. (2011). An attributional analysis of reactions to poverty: The political ideology of the giver and the perceived morality of the receiver. *Personality and Social Psychology Review, 15,* 199–213.

Weinstein, N. D. (1980). Unrealistic optimism about future life events. *Journal of Personality and Social Psychology, 39,* 806–820.

Weinstein, N. D. (1982). Unrealistic optimism about susceptibility to health problems. *Journal of Behavioral Medicine, 5,* 441–460.

Weinstein, N., & Ryan, R. M. (2010). When helping helps: Autonomous motivation for prosocial behavior and its influence on well-being for the helper and recipient. *Journal of Personality and Social Psychology, 98,* 222–244.

Weis, R., & Cerankosky, B. C. (2010). Effects of video-game ownership on young boys' academic and behavioral functioning: A randomized, controlled study. *Psychological Science, 21,* 463–470.

Weisbuch, M., Pauker, K., & Ambady, N. (2009). The subtle transmission of race bias via televised nonverbal behavior. *Science, 326,* 1711–1714.

Weischelbaum, S., Lauinger, J., & Hutchinson, B. (2010, November 29). Brave local man makes it to work on time—after heroically saving man sprawled on No. 6 track. *New York Daily News* (www.articles.nydailynews.com).

Welch, D. T., Ordonez, L. D., Snyder, D. G., & Christian, M. S. (2015). The slippery slope: How small ethical transgressions pave the way for larger future transgressions. *Journal of Applied Psychology.* 100, 114–127.

Wells, B. M., & Skowronski, J. J. (2012). Evidence of choking under pressure on the PGA tour. *Basic and Applied Social Psychology, 34,* 175–182.

Wells, G. L. (1984). The psychology of lineup identifications. *Journal of Applied Social Psychology, 14,* 89–103.

Wells, G. L. (1993). What do we know about eyewitness identification? *American Psychologist, 48,* 553–571.

Wells, G. L. (2005). Helping experimental psychology affect legal policy. In N. Brewer & K. D. Williams (Eds.), *Psychology and law: An empirical perspective.* New York: Guilford.

Wells, G. L. (2008). Field experiments on eyewitness identification: Towards a better understanding of pitfalls and prospects. *Law and Human Behavior, 32,* 6–10.

Wells, G. L., & Bradfield, A. L. (1998). "Good, you identified the suspect": Feedback to eyewitnesses distorts their reports of the witnessing experience. *Journal of Applied Psychology, 83,* 360–376.

Wells, G. L., & Bradfield, A. L. (1999). Distortions in eyewitnesses' recollections: Can the postidentification-feedback effect be moderated? *Psychological Science, 10,* 138–144.

Wells, G. L., Ferguson, T. J., & Lindsay, R. C. L. (1981). The tractability of eyewitness confidence and its implications for triers of fact. *Journal of Applied Psychology, 66,* 688–696.

Wells, G. L., & Leippe, M. R. (1981). How do triers of fact enter the accuracy of eyewitness identification? Memory for peripheral detail can be misleading. *Journal of Applied Psychology, 66,* 682–687.

Wells, G. L., Lindsay, R. C. L., & Ferguson, T. (1979). Accuracy, confidence, and juror perceptions in eyewitness identification. *Journal of Applied Psychology, 64,* 440–448.

Wells, G. L., Lindsay, R. C. L., & Tousignant, J. P. (1980). Effects of expert psychological advice on human performance in judging the validity of

eyewitness testimony. *Law and Human Behavior, 4,* 275–285.

Wells, G. L., Malpass, R. S., Lindsay, R. C. L., Fisher, R. P., Turtle, J. W., & Fulero, S. M. (2000). Mistakes in eyewitness identification are caused by known factors. Collaboration between criminal justice experts and research psychologists may lower the number of errors. *American Psychologist, 55,* 581–598.

Wells, G. L., Memon, A., & Penrod, S. D. (2006). Eyewitness evidence: Improving its probative value. *Psychological Science in the Public Interest, 7,* 45–75.

Wells, G. L., & Olson, E. A. (2001). The other-race effect in eyewitness identification: What do we do about it? *Psychology, Public Policy and the Law, 7,* 230–246.

Wells, G. L., & Olson, E. A. (2003). Eyewitness testimony. *Annual Review of Psychology, 54,* 277–295.

Wells, G. L., Olson, E. A., & Charman, S. D. (2002). The confidence of eyewitnesses in their identifications from lineups. *Current Directions in Psychological Science, 11,* 151–154.

Wells, G. L., & Petty, R. E. (1980). The effects of overt head movements on persuasion: Compatibility and incompatibility of responses. *Basic and Applied Social Psychology, 1,* 219–230.

Wells, G. L., Steblay, N. K., & Dystart, J. E. (2015). Double-blind photo lineups using actual eyewitnesses: An experimental test of a sequential versus simultaneous lineup procedure. *Law and Human Behavior, 39,* 1–14.

Wenzlaff, R. M., & Prohaska, M. L. (1989). When misery prefers company: Depression, attributions, and responses to others' moods. *Journal of Experimental Social Psychology, 25,* 220–233.

Werner, C. M., Kagehiro, D. K., & Strube, M. J. (1982). Conviction proneness and the authoritarian juror: Inability to disregard information or attitudinal bias? *Journal of Applied Psychology, 67,* 629–636.

Werner, C. M., Stoll, R., Birch, P., & White, P. H. (2002). Clinical validation and cognitive elaboration: Signs that encourage sustained recycling. *Basic and Applied Social Psychology, 24,* 185–203.

West, S. G., & Brown, T. J. (1975). Physical attractiveness, the severity of the emergency and helping: A field experiment and interpersonal simulation. *Journal of Experimental Social Psychology, 11,* 531–538.

West, S. G., Whitney, G., & Schnedler, R. (1975). Helping a motorist in distress: The effects of sex, race, and neighborhood. *Journal of Personality and Social Psychology, 31,* 691–698.

Weyant, J. M. (1984). Applying social psychology to induce charitable donations. *Journal of Applied Social Psychology, 14,* 441–447.

Weyant, J. M., & Smith, S. L. (1987). Getting more by asking for less: The effects of request size on donations of charity. *Journal of Applied Social Psychology, 17,* 392–400.

Whang, W., Kubzansky, L, D., Kawachi, I., Rexrode, K. M., Kroenke, C. H., Glynn, R. J., Garan, H., & Albert, C. M. (2009). Depression and risk of sudden cardiac death and coronary heart disease in women. *Journal of the American College of Cardiology, 53,* 950–958.

Whatley, M. A., Webster, J. M., Smith, R. H., & others. (1999). The effect of a favor on public and private compliance: How internalized is the norm of reciprocity? *Basic and Applied Social Psychology, 21,* 251–261.

Wheeler, L., Koestner, R., & Driver, R. E. (1982). Related attributes in the choice of comparison others: It's there, but it isn't all there is. *Journal of Experimental Social Psychology, 18,* 489–500.

White, G. L. (1980). Physical attractiveness and courtship progress. *Journal of Personality and Social Psychology, 39,* 660–668.

White, G. L., & Kight, T. D. (1984). Misattribution of arousal and attraction: Effects of salience of explanations for arousal. *Journal of Experimental Social Psychology, 20,* 55–64.

White, J. W., & Kowalski, R. M. (1994). Deconstructing the myth of the nonaggressive woman. *Psychology of Women Quarterly, 18,* 487–508.

White, K., & Lehman, D. R. (2005). Culture and social comparison seeking: The role of self-motives. *Personality and Social Psychology Bulletin, 31,* 232–242.

White, L., & Edwards, J. (1990). Emptying the nest and parental well-being: An analysis of national panel data. *American Sociological Review, 55,* 235–242.

White, M. J., & Gerstein, L. H. (1987). Helping: The influence of anticipated social sanctions and self-monitoring. *Journal of Personality, 55,* 41–54.

White, R. E. (1984). *Fearful warriors: A psychological profile of U.S.-Soviet relations.* New York: Free Press.

White, R. K. (1968). *Nobody wanted war: Misperception in Vietnam and other wars.* New York: Doubleday.

White, R. K. (1986). *Psychology and the prevention of nuclear war.* New York: New York University Press.

White, R. K. (1996). Why the Serbs fought: Motives and misperceptions. *Peace and Conflict: Journal of Peace Psychology, 2,* 109–128.

White, R. K. (1998). American acts of force: Results and misperceptions. *Peace and Conflict, 4,* 93–128.

Whitechurch, E. R., Wilson, T. D., & Gilbert, D. T. (2011). "He loves me, he loves me not . . ."; Uncertainty can increase romantic attraction. *Psychological Science, 22,* 172–175.

Whitehead, A. N. (1911). *An introduction to mathematics*. New York: Henry Holt.

Whitley, B. E., Jr. (1987). The effects of discredited eyewitness testimony: A meta-analysis. *Journal of Social Psychology, 127,* 209–214.

Whitman, R. M., Kramer, M., & Baldridge, B. (1963). Which dream does the patient tell? *Archives of General Psychology, 8,* 277–282.

Whitson, J. A., & Galinsky, A. D. (2008). Lacking control increases illusory pattern perception. *Science, 322,* 115–117.

WHO: World Health Organization. (2014). Violence against women: Intimate partner and sexual violence against women. Fact sheet No. 239, November 2014. http://www.who.int/mediacentre/factsheets/fs239/en/

Wicker, A. W. (1969). Attitudes versus actions: The relationship of verbal and overt behavioral responses to attitude objects. *Journal of Social Issues, 25,* 41–78.

Widom, C. S. (1989). Does violence beget violence? A critical examination of the literature. *Psychological Bulletin, 106,* 3–28.

Wiebe, D. J. (2003). Homicide and suicide risks associated with firearms in the home: A national case-control study. *Annals of Emergency Medicine, 41,* 771–782.

Wiegman, O. (1985). Two politicians in a realistic experiment: Attraction, discrepancy, intensity of delivery, and attitude change. *Journal of Applied Social Psychology, 15,* 673–686.

Wiesel, E. (1985, April 6). The brave Christians who saved Jews from the Nazis. *TV Guide,* 4–6.

Wieselquist, J., Rusbult, C. E., Foster, C. A., & Agnew, C. R. (1999). Commitment, pro-relationship behavior, and trust in close relationships. *Journal of Personality and Social Psychology, 77,* 942–966.

Wike, R., & Grim, B. J. (2007, October 30). Widespread negativity: Muslims distrust Westerners more than vice versa. Pew Research Center (pewresearch.org).

Wikipedia. (2008, accessed July 30). Strip search prank call scam (en.wikipedia.org).

Wilder, D. A. (1977). Perception of groups, size of opposition, and social influence. *Journal of Experimental Social Psychology, 13,* 253–268.

Wilder, D. A. (1978). Perceiving persons as a group: Effect on attributions of causality and beliefs. *Social Psychology, 41,* 13–23.

Wilder, D. A. (1981). Perceiving persons as a group: Categorization and intergroup relations. In D. L. Hamilton (Ed.). *Cognitive processes in stereotyping and intergroup behavior.* Hillsdale, NJ: Erlbaum.

Wilder, D. A., & Shapiro, P. (1991). Facilitation of outgroup stereotypes by enhanced ingroup identity. *Journal of Experimental Social Psychology, 27,* 431–452.

Wilder, D. A., & Shapiro, P. N. (1984). Role of out-group cues in determining social identity. *Journal of Personality and Social Psychology, 47,* 342–348.

Wilder, D. A., & Shapiro, P. N. (1989). Role of competition-induced anxiety in limiting the beneficial impact of positive behavior by out-group members. *Journal of Personality and Social Psychology, 56,* 60–69.

Wildschut, T., Insko, C. A., & Pinter, B. (2007). Interindividual-intergroup discontinuity as a joint function of acting as a group and interacting with a group. *European Journal of Social Psychology, 37,* 390–399.

Wildschut, T., Pinter, B., Vevea, J. L., Insko, C. A., & Schopler, J. (2003). Beyond the group mind: A quantitative review of the interindividual-intergroup discontinuity effect. *Psychological Bulletin, 129,* 698–722.

Wilford, J. N. (1999, February 9). New findings help balance the cosmological books. *New York Times* (www.nytimes.com).

Wilkes, J. (1987, June). Murder in mind. *Psychology Today,* 27–32.

Wilkinson, G. S. (1990, February). Food sharing in vampire bats. *Scientific American, 262,* 76–82.

Wilkinson, R., & Pickett, K. (2009). *The spirit level: Why greater equality makes societies stronger.* London: Bloomsbury.

Wilkowski, B. M., & Robinson, M. D. (2008). The cognitive basis of trait anger and reactive aggression: An integrative analysis. *Personality and Social Psychology Bulletin, 12,* 3–21.

Willard, G., & Gramzow, R. H. (2009). Beyond oversights, lies, and pies in the sky: Exaggeration as goal projection. *Personality and Social Psychology Bulletin, 35,* 477–492.

Willems, S., Dedonder, J., & Van der Linden, M. (2010). The mere exposure effect and recognition depend on the way you look! *Experimental Psychology, 57,* 185–192.

Williams, A. L., Grogan, S., Clark-Carter, D., & Buckley, E. (2013). Appearance-based interventions to reduce ultraviolet exposure and/or increase sun protection intentions and behaviours: A systematic review and meta-analyses. *British Journal of Health Psychology, 18,* 182–217.

Williams, D. K., Bourgeois, M. J., & Croyle, R. T. (1993). The effects of stealing thunder in criminal and civil trials. *Law and Human Behavior, 17,* 597–609.

Williams, E. F., & Gilovich, T. (2008). Do people really believe they are above average? *Journal of Experimental Social Psychology, 44,* 1121–1128.

Williams, J. E., & Best, D. L. (1990). *Measuring sex stereotypes: A multination study.* Newbury Park, CA: Sage.

Williams, J. E., Satterwhite, R. C., & Best, D. L. (1999). Pancultural gender stereotypes revisited: The Five Factor model. *Sex Roles, 40,* 513–525.

Williams, J. E., Satterwhite, R. C., & Best, D. L. (2000). Five-factor gender stereotypes in 27 countries. Paper presented at the XV Congress of the International Association for Cross-Cultural Psychology, Pultusk, Poland.

Williams, K. D. (2001). *Ostracism: The power of silence.* New York: Guilford.

Williams, K. D. (2002). *Ostracism: The power of silence.* New York: Guilford.

Williams, K. D. (2007). Ostracism. *Annual Review of Psychology, 58,* 425–452.

Williams, K. D. (2009). Ostracism: A temporal need-threat model. *Advances in Experimental Social Psychology, 41,* 275–313.

Williams, K. D. (2011, January/February). The pain of exclusion. *Scientific American Mind,* 30–37.

Williams, K. D., Harkins, S., & Latané, B. (1981). Identifiability as a deterrent to social loafing: Two cheering experiments. *Journal of Personality and Social Psychology, 40,* 303–311.

Williams, K. D., Jackson, J. M., & Karau, S. J. (1992). In D. A. Schroeder (Ed.) *Social Dilemmas: Perspectives on Individuals and Groups.* Westport, CT: Greenwood Publishing Group, Inc.

Williams K. D., & Nida, S. A. (2009). Is ostracism worse than bullying? In Harris, M.J. (Ed.).

Williams, K. D., & Nida, S. A. (2011). Ostracism: Consequences and coping. *Current Directions in Psychological Science, 20,* 71–75.

Williams, K. D., Nida, S. A., Baca, L. D., & Latané, B. (1989). Social loafing and swimming: Effects of identifiability on individual and relay performance of intercollegiate swimmers. *Basic and Applied Social Psychology, 10,* 73–81.

Williams, M. J., & Eberhardt, J. L. (2008). Biological conceptions of race and the motivation to cross racial boundaries. *Journal of Personality and Social Psychology, 94,* 1033–1047.

Willis, F. N., & Hamm, H. K. (1980). The use of interpersonal touch in securing compliance. *Journal of Nonverbal Behavior, 5,* 49–55.

Willis, J., & Todorov, A. (2006). First impressions: Making up your mind after a 100-ms exposure to a face. *Psychological Science, 17,* 592–598.

Willoughby, T., Adachi, P. J. C., & Good, M. (2012). A longitudinal study of the association between violent video game play and aggression among adolescents. *Developmental Psychology, 48,* 1044–1057.

Wilson, A. E., & Ross, M. (2001). From chump to champ: People's appraisals of their earlier and present selves. *Journal of Personality and Social Psychology, 80,* 572–584.

Wilson, D. K., Kaplan, R. M., & Schneiderman, L. J. (1987). Framing of decisions and selections of alternatives in health care. *Social Behaviour, 2,* 51–59.

Wilson, D. S. (2015). *Does altruism exist? Culture, genes, and the welfare of others.* New Haven, CT: Yale University Press.

Wilson, D. S., & Wilson, E. O. (2008). Evolution for "the good of the group." *American Scientist, 96,* 380–389.

Wilson, D. W., & Donnerstein, E. (1979). *Anonymity and interracial helping.* Paper presented at the Southwestern Psychological Association convention, New York, New York.

Wilson, E. O. (1978). *On human nature.* Cambridge, MA: Harvard University Press.

Wilson, E. O. (2002, February). The bottleneck. *Scientific American, 286,* 83–91.

Wilson, G. (1994, March 25). Equal, but different. *The Times Higher Education Supplement, Times of London.*

Wilson, J. P., & Petruska, R. (1984). Motivation, model attributes, and prosocial behavior. *Journal of Personality and Social Psychology, 46,* 458–468.

Wilson, M. S., & Sibley, C. G. (2011). 'Narcissism creep?' Evidence for age-related differences in narcissism in the New Zealand general populations. *New Zealand Journal of Psychology, 40,* 89–95.

Wilson, R. S., & Matheny, A. P., Jr. (1986). Behavior-genetics research in infant temperament: The Louisville twin study. In R. Plomin & J. Dunn (Eds.), *The study of temperament: Changes, continuities, and challenges.* Hillsdale, NJ: Erlbaum.

Wilson, S. J., & Lipsey, M. W. (2005). The effectiveness of school-based violence prevention programs for reducing disruptive and aggressive behavior. Revised Report for the National Institute of Justice School Violence Prevention Research Planning Meeting, May 2005.

Wilson, S., Miller, G., & Horwitz, S. (2013, April 23). Boston bombing suspect cites U.S. wars as motivation, officials say. *Washington Post* (www.washingtonpost .com).

Wilson, T. D. (1985). Strangers to ourselves: The origins and accuracy of beliefs about one's own mental states. In J. H. Harvey & G. Weary (Eds.), *Attribution in contemporary psychology.* New York: Academic Press.

Wilson, T. D. (2002). *Strangers to ourselves: Discovering the adaptive unconscious.* Cambridge: Harvard University Press.

Wilson, T. D., Dunn, D. S., Kraft, D., & Lisle, D. J. (1989). Introspection, attitude change, and attitude-behavior consistency: The disruptive effects of explaining why we feel the way we do. In L. Berkowitz (Ed.), *Advances in experimental social psychology* (Vol. 22). San Diego: Academic Press.

Wilson, T. D., & Gilbert, D. T. (2003). Affective forecasting. *Advances in Experimental Social Psychology, 35,* 346–413.

Wilson, T. D., Lindsey, S., & Schooler, T. Y. (2000). A model of dual attitudes. *Psychological Review, 107,* 101–126.

Wiltze, A. (2010, September 15). Annual Arctic ice minimum reached. *ScienceNews* (www.sciencenews.org).

Winch, R. F. (1958). *Mate selection: A study of complementary needs.* New York: Harper & Row.

Winegard, B. (2010). The evolutionary significance of Red Sox Nation: Sports fandom as a by-product of coalitional psychology. *Evolutionary Psychology, 8,* 432–446.

Wines, M. (2005, September 23). Crime in South Africa grows more vicious. *New York Times* (www.nytimes.com).

Wingate, V. S., Minney, J. A., & Guadagno, R. E. (2013). Sticks and stones may break your bones, but words will always hurt you: A review of cyberbulling. *Social Influence, 8,* 87–106.

Winquist, J. R., & Larson, J. R., Jr. (2004). Sources of the discontinuity effect: Playing against a group versus being in a group. *Journal of Experimental Social Psychology, 40,* 675–682.

Winseman, A. L. (2005, March 8). *Invitations, donations up among engaged congregation members.* Gallup Poll (www. gallup.com).

Winter, F. W. (1973). A laboratory experiment of individual attitude response to advertising exposure. *Journal of Marketing Research, 10,* 130–140.

Wirth, J. H., Sacco, D. F., Hugenberg, K., & Williams, K. D. (2010). Eye gaze as relational evaluation: Averted eye gaze leads to feelings of ostracism and relational devaluation. *Personality and Social Psychology Bulletin, 36,* 869–882.

Wiseman, R. (1998, Fall). Participatory science and the mass media. *Free Inquiry,* 56–57.

Wise, R. A., & Safer, M. A. (2010). A comparison of what U.S. judges and students know and believe about eyewitness testimony. *Journal of Applied Social Psychology, 40,* 1400–1422.

Wisman, A., & Koole, S. L. (2003). Hiding in the crowd: Can mortality salience promote affiliation with others who oppose one's worldviews? *Journal of Personality and Social Psychology, 84,* 511–526.

Wispe, L. G., & Freshley, H. B. (1971). Race, sex, and sympathetic helping behavior: The broken bag caper. *Journal of Personality and Social Psychology, 17,* 59–65.

Wittenberg, M. T., & Reis, H. T. (1986). Loneliness, social skills, and social perception. *Personality and Social Psychology Bulletin, 12,* 121–130.

Wixon, D. R., & Laird, J. D. (1976). Awareness and attitude change in the forced-compliance paradigm: The importance of when. *Journal of Personality and Social Psychology, 34,* 376–384.

Wohl, M. J. A., Branscombe, N. R., & Reysen, S. (2010). Perceiving your group's future to be in jeopardy: Extinction threat induces collective angst and the desire to strengthen the ingroup. *Personality and Social Psychology Bulletin, 36,* 898–910.

Wohl, M. J. A., & Enzle, M. E. (2002). The deployment of personal luck: Sympathetic magic and illusory control in games of pure chance. *Personality and Social Psychology Bulletin, 28,* 1388–1397.

Wojciszke, B., Bazinska, R., & Jaworski, M. (1998). On the dominance of moral categories in impression formation. *Personality and Social Psychology Bulletin, 24,* 1251–1263.

Wolf, S., & Montgomery, D. A. (1977). Effects of inadmissible evidence and level of judicial admonishment to disregard on the judgments of mock jurors. *Journal of Applied Social Psychology, 7,* 205–219.

Wollmer, M. A., & 18 others (2012). Facing depression with botulinum toxin: A randomized controlled trial. *Journal of Psychiatric Research, 46,* 574–581.

Women on Words and Images. (1972). *Dick and Jane as victims: Sex stereotyping in children's readers.* Princeton: Women on Words and Images. Cited by C. Tavris & C. Offir (1977) in *The longest war: Sex differences in perspective* (p. 177). New York: Harcourt Brace Jovanovich.

Wondergem, T. R., & Friedmeier, M. (2012). Gender and ethnic differences in smiling: A yearbook photographs analysis from kindergarten through 12th grade. *Sex Roles, 67,* 403–411.

Wong, E. M., Ormiston, M. E., & Haselhuhn, M. P. (2011). A face only an investor could love: CEOs' facial structure predicts their firms' financial performance. *Psychological Science, 22,* 1478–1483.

Wood, J. V., Heimpel, S. A., & Michela, J. L. (2003). Savoring versus dampening: Self-esteem differences in regulating positive affect. *Journal of Personality and Social Psychology, 85,* 566–580.

Wood, J. V., Perunovic, W., & Lee, J. W. (2009). Positive self-statements: Power for some, peril for others. *Psychological Science, 20,* 860–866.

Wood, O. (2012). How emotional tugs trump rational pushes: The time has come to abandon a 100-year-old advertising model. *Journal of Advertising Research, 52,* 31–39.

Wood, W., & Eagly, A. H. (2002). A cross-cultural analysis of the behavior of women and men: Implications for the origins of sex differences. *Psychological Bulletin, 128,* 699–727.

Wood, W., & Eagly, A. H. (2007). Social structural origins of sex differences in human mating. In S. W. Gangestad & J. A. Simpson (Eds.), *The evolution of mind: Fundamental questions and controversies.* New York: Guilford.

Woodward, W., & Woodward, M. (1942, March 26). Not time enough, "Not Time Enough." Editorial, *Bainbridge Review,* p. 1.

Woodzicka, J. A., & LaFrance, M. (2001). Real versus imagined gender harassment. *Journal of Social Issues, 57*(1), 15–30.

Woolley, A. W., Chabris, C. F., Pentland, A., Hasmi, N., & Malone, T. W. (2010). Evidence for a collective intelligence factor in the performance of human groups. *Science, 330,* 686–688.

Worchel, S., Andreoli, V. A., & Folger, R. (1977). Intergroup cooperation and intergroup attraction: The effect of previous interaction and outcome of combined effort. *Journal of Experimental Social Psychology, 13,* 131–140.

Worchel, S., Axsom, D., Ferris, F., Samah, G., & Schweitzer, S. (1978). Deterrents of the effect of intergroup cooperation on intergroup attraction. *Journal of Conflict Resolution, 22,* 429–439.

Worchel, S., & Brown, E. H. (1984). The role of plausibility in influencing environmental attributions. *Journal of Experimental Social Psychology, 20,* 86–96.

Worchel, S., & Norvell, N. (1980). Effect of perceived environmental conditions during cooperation on intergroup attraction. *Journal of Personality and Social Psychology, 38,* 764–772.

Worchel, S., Rothgerber, H., Day, E. A., Hart, D., & Butemeyer, J. (1998). Social identity and individual productivity within groups. *British Journal of Social Psychology, 37,* 389–413.

Word, C. O., Zanna, M. P., & Cooper, J. (1974). The nonverbal mediation of self-fulfilling prophecies in interracial interaction. *Journal of Experimental Social Psychology, 10,* 109–120.

Workman, E. A., & Williams, R. L. (1980). Effects of extrinsic rewards on intrinsic motivation in the classroom. *Journal of School Psychology, 18,* 141–147.

World Bank. (2003, April 4). *Gender equality and the millennium development goals.* Washington, DC: Gender and Development Group, World Bank (www.worldbank.org/gender).

World Meteorological Organization. (2011, November). *WMO greenhouse gas bulletin: The state of greenhouse gases in the atmosphere based on global observations through 2010.* Geneva: World Meteorological Organization.

Worringham, C. J., & Messick, D. M. (1983). Social facilitation of running: An unobtrusive study. *Journal of Social Psychology, 121,* 23–29.

Wraga, M., Helt, M., Jacobs, E., & Sullivan, K. (2007). Neural basis of stereotype-induced shifts in women's mental rotation performance. *Social Cognitive and Affective Neuroscience, 2,* 12–19.

Wright, D. B., Boyd, C. E., & Tredoux, C. G. (2001). A field study of own-race bias in South Africa and England. *Psychology, Public Policy, & Law, 7,* 119–133.

Wright, D. B., & Hall, M. (2007). How a "reasonable doubt" instruction affects decisions of guilt. *Basic and Applied Social Psychology, 29,* 91–98.

Wright, D. B., Memom, A., Skagerberg, E. M., & Gabbert, F. (2009). When eyewitnesses talk. *Current Directions in Psychological Science, 18,* 174–178.

Wright, D. B., & Stroud, J. N. (2002). Age differences in lineup identification accuracy: People are better with their own age. *Law and Human Behavior, 26,* 641–654.

Wright, E. F., Lüüs, C. A., & Christie, S. D. (1990). Does group discussion facilitate the use of consensus information in making causal attributions? *Journal of Personality and Social Psychology, 59,* 261–269.

Wright, P. J. (2013). U.S. males and pornography, 1973–2010: Consumption, predictors, correlates. *Journal of Sex Research, 50,* 60–71.

Wright, R. (1998, February 2). Politics made me do it. *Time,* p. 34.

Wright, R. (2003, June 29). Quoted by Thomas L. Friedman, "Is Google God?" *New York Times* (www.nytimes.com).

Wright, R. (2003, September 11). Two years later, a thousand years ago. *New York Times* (www.nytimes.com).

Wrosch, C., & Miller, G. E. (2009). Depressive symptoms can be useful: Self-regulatory and emotional benefits of dysphoric mood in adolescence. *Journal of Personality and Social Psychology, 96,* 1181–1190.

Wrzesniewski, A., & Schwartz, B. (2014b, July 4). The secret of effective motivation. *New York Times* (www.nytimes.com).

Wrzesniewski, A., Schwartz, B., Cong, X., Kane, M., Omar, A, & Kolditz, T. (2014a). Multiple types of motives don't multiply the motivation of West Point cadets. *PNAS, 111,* 10990–109905.

Wu, B-P., & Chang, L. (2012). The social impact of pathogen threat: How disease salience influences conformity. *Personality and Individual Differences, 53,* 50–54.

Wu, S., Cheng, C. K., Feng, J., D'Angelo, L., Alain, C., & Spence, I. (2012). Playing a first-person shooter video game induces neuroplastic change. *Journal of Cognitive Neuroscience, 24,* 1286–1293.

Wylie, R. C. (1979). *The self-concept (Vol. 2): Theory and research on selected topics.* Lincoln, NE: University of Nebraska Press.

Yamagishi, T., Hashimoto, H., Cook, K. S., Kiyonari, T., Shinada, M., Mifune, N., Inukai, K., Takagishi, H., Horita, Y., & Li, Y. (2012). Modesty in self-presentation: A comparison between the USA and Japan. *Asian Journal of Social Psychology, 15,* 60–68.

Yamaguchi, S., Greenwald, A. G., Banaji, M. R., Murakami, F., Chen, D., Shiomura, K., Kobayashi, C., Cai, H., & Krendl, A. (2007). Apparent universality of positive implicit self-esteem. *Psychological Science, 18,* 498–500.

Yaniv, D. (2012). Dynamics of creativity and empathy in role reversal: Contributions from neuroscience. *Review of General Psychology, 16,* 70–77.

Yap, A. J., Wazlawek, A. S., Lucas, B. J., Cuddy, A. J. C., & Carney, D. R. (2013). The ergonomics of dishonesty: The effect of incidental posture on stealing, cheating, and traffic violations. *Psychological Science, 24,* 2281–2289.

Yarmey, A. D. (2003a). Eyewitness identification: Guidelines and recommendations for identification procedures in the United States and in Canada. *Canadian Psychology, 44,* 181–189.

Ybarra, M. L., Huesmann, L. R., Korchmaros, J. D., & Reisner, S. L. (2014). Cross-sectional associations between violent video and computer game playing and weapon carrying in a national cohort of children. *Aggressive Behavior, 40,* 345–358.

Ybarra, M. L., Mitchell, K. J., Hamburger, M., Diener-West, M., & Leaf, P. J. (2011). X-rated material and perpetration of sexually aggressive behavior among children and adolescents: Is there a link? *Aggressive Behavior, 37,* 1–18.

Ybarra, M. L., West, M. D., Markow, D., Leaf, P. J., Hamburger, M. & Boxer, P. (2008). Linkages between Internet and other media violence with seriously violent behavior by youth. *Pediatrics, 122,* 929–937.

Yelsma, P., & Athappilly, K. (1988). Marriage satisfaction and communication practices: Comparisons among Indian and American couples. *Journal of Comparative Family Studies, 19,* 37–54.

You, D., Maeda, Y., & Bebeau, M. J. (2011). Gender differences in moral sensitivity: A meta-analysis. *Ethics and Behavior, 21,* 263–282.

Young, L. (2009). Love: Neuroscience reveals all. *Nature, 457,* 148.

Young, S. G., Bernstein, M. J., & Hugenberg, K. (2010). When do own-group biases in face recognition occur? Encoding versus post-encoding. *Social Cognition, 28,* 240–250.

Younger, J., Aron, A., Parke, S., Chatterjee, N., & Mackey, S. (2010). Viewing pictures of a romantic partner reduces experimental pain: Involvement of neural reward systems. *PLoS One, 5*(10), e13309.

Yousif, Y., & Korte, C. (1995). Urbanization, culture, and helpfulness. *Journal of Cross-Cultural Psychology, 26,* 474–489.

Yovetich, N. A., & Rusbult, C. E. (1994). Accommodative behavior in close relationships: Exploring transformation of motivation. *Journal of Experimental Social Psychology, 30,* 138–164.

Yuchtman (Yaar), E. (1976). Effects of social-psychological factors on subjective economic welfare. In B. Strumpel (Ed.), *Economic means for human needs.* Ann Arbor: Institute for Social Research, University of Michigan.

Yuille, J. C., & Cutshall, J. L. (1986). A case study of eyewitness memory of a crime. *Journal of Applied Psychology, 71,* 291–301.

Yukl, G. (1974). Effects of the opponent's initial offer, concession magnitude, and concession frequency on bargaining behavior. *Journal of Personality and Social Psychology, 30,* 323–335.

Yzerbyt, V. Y., & Leyens, J-P. (1991). Requesting information to form an impression: The influence of valence and confirmatory status. *Journal of Experimental Social Psychology, 27,* 337–356.

Zadro, L., Boland, C., & Richardson, R. (2006). How long does it last? The persistence of the effects of ostracism in the socially anxious. *Journal of Experimental Social Psychology, 42,* 692–697.

Zagefka, H., & Brown, R. (2005). Comparisons and perceived deprivation in ethnic minority settings. *Personality and Social Psychology Bulletin, 31,* 467–482.

Zagefka, H., Noor, M., & Brown, R. (2013). Familiarity breeds compassion: Knowledge of disaster areas and willingness to donate money to disaster victims. *Applied Psychology: An International Review, 62,* 640–654.

Zagefka, H., Noor, M., Brown, R., De Moura, G. R., & Hopthrow, T. (2011). Donating to disaster victims: Responses to natural and humanly caused events. *European Journal of Social Psychology, 41,* 353–363.

Zajonc, R. B. (1965). Social facilitation. *Science, 149,* 269–274.

Zajonc, R. B. (1968). Attitudinal effects of mere exposure. *Journal of Personality and Social Psychology, 9,* Monograph Suppl. No. 2, part 2.

Zajonc, R. B. (1970, February). Brainwash: Familiarity breeds comfort. *Psychology Today, 32–35,* 60–62.

Zajonc, R. B. (1980). Feeling and thinking: Preferences need no inferences. *American Psychologist, 35,* 151–175.

Zajonc, R. B. (1998). Emotions. In D. Gilbert, S. T. Fiske, & G. Lindzey (Eds.), *Handbook of social psychology,* 4th edition. New York: McGraw-Hill.

Zajonc, R. B. (2000). *Massacres: Mass murders in the name of moral imperatives.* Unpublished manuscript, Stanford University.

Zakaria, F. (2008). We need a wartime president. *Newsweek* (www.newsweek.com).

Zaki, J., Schirmer, J., & Mitchell, J. P. (2011). Social influence modulates the neural computation of value. *Psychological Science, 22,* 894–900.

Zak, P. J. (2008, June). The neurobiology of trust. *Scientific American,* 88–95.

Zanna, M. P., & Olson, J. M. (1982). Individual differences in attitudinal relations. In M. P. Zanna, E. T. Higgins, & C. P. Herman, *Consistency in social behavior: The Ontario symposium* (Vol. 2). Hillsdale, NJ: Erlbaum.

Zaragoza, M. S., & Mitchell, K. J. (1996). Repeated exposure to suggestion and the creation of false memories. *Psychological Science, 7,* 294–300.

Zarkadi, T., Wade, K. A., & Stewart, N. (2009). Creating fair lineups for suspects with distinctive features. *Psychological Science, 20,* 1448–1453.

Zaval, L., Keenan, E. A., Johnson, E. J., & Weber, E. U. (2014). How warm days increase belief in global warming. *Nature Climate Change, 4,* 143–147.

Zebrowitz, L. A., Collins, M. A., & Dutta, R. (1998). The relationship between appearance and personality across the life span. *Personality and Social Psychology Bulletin, 24,* 736–749.

Zebrowitz, L. A., Olson, K., & Hoffman, K. (1993). Stability of babyfaceness and attractiveness across the life span. *Journal of Personality and Social Psychology, 64,* 453–466.

Zebrowitz, L. A., White, B., & Wieneke, K. (2008). Mere exposure and racial prejudice: Exposure to other-race faces increases liking for strangers of that race. *Social Cognition, 26,* 259–275.

Zebrowitz-McArthur, L. (1988). Person perception in cross-cultural perspective. In M. H. Bond (Ed.), *The cross-cultural challenge to social psychology.* Newbury Park, CA: Sage.

Zeelenberg, M., van der Pligt, J., & Manstead, A. S. R. (1998). Undoing regret on Dutch television: Apologizing for interpersonal regrets involving actions or inactions. *Personality and Social Psychology Bulletin, 24,* 1113–1119.

Zerjal, T. (2003). The genetic legacy of the Mongols. *The American Journal of Human Genetics, 72,* 717–721.

Zhang, D. D., Lee, H. F., Wong, C., Li, B., Pei, Q., Zhang, J., & An, Y. (2011). The causality analysis of climate change and large-scale human crisis. *PNAS, 108,* 17296–17301.

Zhang, Q., & Covey, J. (2014). Past and future implications of near-misses and their emotional consequences. *Experimental Psychology, 61,* 118–126.

Zhang, S., & Kline, S. L. (2009). Can I make my own decision? A cross-cultural study of perceived social network influence in mate selection. *Journal of Cross-Cultural Psychology, 40,* 3–23.

Zhang, Y. F., Wyon, D. P., Fang, L., & Melikov, A. K. (2007). The influence of heated or cooled seats on the acceptable ambient temperature range. *Ergonomics, 50,* 586–600.

Zhong, C.-B., Bohns, V. K., & Gino, F. (2010). Good lamps are the best police: Darkness increases dishonesty and self-interested behavior. *Psychological Science, 21,* 311–314.

Zhong, C.-B., & Leonardelli, G. F. (2008). Cold and lonely: Does social exclusion literally feel cold? *Psychological Science, 19,* 838–842.

Zhou, X., Sedikides, C., Wildschut, T., & Gao, D-G. (2008). Counteracting loneliness: On the restorative function of nostalgia. *Psychological Science, 19,* 1023–1029.

Zhu, L., Gigerenzer, G., & Huangfu, G. (2013). Psychological traces of China's socio-economic reforms in the ultimatum and dictator games. *PLOS ONE, 8,* e70769.

Zhu, W. X., Lu, L., & Hesketh, T. (2009). China's excess males, sex selective abortion, and one child policy: Analysis of data from 2005 national intercensus survey. *British Medical Journal (BMJ), 338,* b1211.

Zhu, Y., Zhang, L., Fan, L., & Han, S. (2007). Neural basis of cultural influence on self-representation. *NeuroImage, 34,* 1310–1316.

Zick, A., Pettigrew, T. F., & Wagner, U. (2008). Ethnic prejudice and discrimination in Europe. *Journal of Social Issues, 64,* 233–251.

Zillmann, D. (1988). Cognition-excitation interdependencies in aggressive behavior. *Aggressive Behavior, 14,* 51–64.

Zillmann, D. (1989). Aggression and sex: Independent and joint operations. In H. L. Wagner & A. S. R. Manstead (Eds.), *Handbook of psychophysiology: Emotion and social behavior.* Chichester: Wiley.

Zillmann, D. (1989). Effects of prolonged consumption of pornography. In D. Zillmann & J. Bryant (Eds.), *Pornography: Research advances and policy considerations.* Hillsdale, NJ: Erlbaum.

Zillmann, D., & Weaver, J. B. (2007). Aggressive personality traits in the effects of violence imagery on unprovoked impulsive aggression. *Journal of Research in Personality, 41,* 753–771.

Zillmann, D., & Weaver, J. B., III. (1999). Effects of prolonged exposure to gratuitous media violence on provoked and unprovoked hostile behavior. *Journal of Applied Social Psychology, 29,* 145–165.

Zillmer, E. A., Harrower, M., Ritzler, B. A., & Archer, R. P. (1995). *The quest for the Nazi personality: A psychological investigation of Nazi war criminals.* Hillsdale, NJ: Erlbaum.

Zimbardo, P. G. (1970). The human choice: Individuation, reason, and order versus deindividuation, impulse, and chaos. In W. J. Arnold & D. Levine (Eds.), *Nebraska symposium on motivation, 1969.* Lincoln: University of Nebraska Press.

Zimbardo, P. G. (1971). *The psychological power and pathology of imprisonment.* A statement prepared for the U.S. House of Representatives Committee on the Judiciary, Subcommittee No. 3: Hearings on Prison Reform, San Francisco, October 25.

Zimbardo, P. G. (1972). The Stanford prison experiment. A slide/tape presentation produced by Philip G. Zimbardo, Inc., P. O. Box 4395, Stanford, CA 94305.

Zimbardo, P. G. (2002, April). Nurturing psychological synergies. *APA Monitor, 5*, 38.

Zimbardo, P. G. (2004). A situationist perspective on the psychology of evil: Understanding how good people are transformed into perpetrators. In A. G. Miller (Ed.), *The social psychology of good and evil.* New York: Guilford.

Zimbardo, P. G. (2004a). A situationist perspective on the psychology of evil: Understanding how good people are transformed into perpetrators. In A. G. Miller (Ed.), *The social psychology of good and evil.* New York: Guilford.

Zimbardo, P. G. (2004b, May 3). Awful parallels: Abuse of Iraqi inmates and SPE. Comments to Social Psychology of Personality and Social Psychology listserv.

Zimbardo, P. G. (2007, September). Person x situation x system dynamics. *The Observer* (Association for Psychological Science), p. 43.

Zimmer, C. (2005, November). The neurobiology of the self. *Scientific American,* pp. 93–101.

Zitek, E. M., & Hebl, M. R. (2007). The role of social norm clarity in the influenced expression of prejudice over time. *Journal of Experimental Social Psychology, 43,* 867–876.

Zola-Morgan, S., Squire, L. R., Alvarez-Royo, P., & Clower, R. P. (1991). Independence of memory functions and emotional behavior. *Hippocampus, 1,* 207–220.

Zou, D., Jin, L., He, Y., & Xu, Q. (2014). The effect of the sense of power of Chinese consumers' uniqueness-seeking behavior. *Journal of International Consumer Marketing, 26,* 14–28.

Zuckerman, E. W., & Jost, J. T. (2001). What makes you think you're so popular? Self-evaluation maintenance and the subjective side of the "friendship paradox." *Social Psychology Quarterly, 64,* 207–223.

Zumbrun, J. (2014, April 18). The richer you are the older you'll get. *Wall Street Journal* (www.blogs.wsj.com).

Zuwerink, J. R., Monteith, M. J., Devine, P. G., & Cook, D. A. (1996). Prejudice toward blacks: With and without compunction? *Basic and Applied Social Psychology, 18,* 131–150.

Name Index

Subject Index/Glossary

A

ABCs of attitudes, 98
accentuation effect, 235
acceptance: Conformity that involves both acting and believing in accord with social pressure, 154–155. *See also* conformity
achievement. *See* performance or achievement
adaptation-level phenomenon: The tendency to adapt to a given level of stimulation and thus to notice and react to changes from that level, 521–522
additive tasks, 225
advertising. *See also* persuasion
inoculating children against, 215–216
advice, professional, values in, 9–10
affective forecasting, 40–41
age
of audience, in persuasion, 208–210
in own-age bias, 280
prejudice based on, 255
aggregation, principle of, 100
aggression: Physical or verbal behavior intended to hurt someone. In laboratory experiments, this might mean delivering electric shocks or saying something likely to hurt another's feelings, 296–332
approaches to reducing, 328–332
arousal in, 311–312
aversive incidents in, 309–311
as biological phenomenon, 299–303
cues for, 312–313
definition of, 137, 298
gender differences in, 137, 144
group influences on, 325–328
hormones in, 144
hostile vs. instrumental, 298–299
media influences on, 313–320
narcissism and, 46
in prejudice, 271–272
as response to frustration, 304–306
rewards of, 306
social learning in, 306–308, 330–331
television violence and, 22, 315–320
theories of, 299–309
types of, 298–299
video games and, 320–325
alcohol
and aggression, 301–302
and social anxiety, 462
altruism: A motive to increase another's welfare without conscious regard for one's self-interests, 376. *See also* helping
approaches to socializing, 406–410
vs. egoism, 379
empathy-induced, 388–391
genuine, 387–391
modeling, 396–397, 407–409
in resolution of social dilemmas, 418–419
in reward theory of helping, 378–379
androgynous: From *andro* (man) + *gyn* (woman)—thus mixing both masculine and feminine characteristics, 145
animals, culture and, 124
anonymity, in deindividuation, 230–231
anticipation of interaction, 338–339
anxiety, 461–462

anxious attachment: Attachments marked by anxiety or ambivalence. An insecure attachment style, 364–365
arbitration: Resolution of a conflict by a neutral third party who studies both sides and imposes a settlement, 440, 444
arousal
aggression and, 311–312
deindividuation and, 232
dissonance as, 118–119
passionate love and, 359–360
from presence of others, 220–224
in two-factor theory of emotion, 359–360
assertiveness training, 467
assimilation, 439–440
attachment, 363–365
styles of, 364–365
attacks, aggression influenced by, 310-311
attitude(s): A favorable or unfavorable evaluative reaction toward something or someone (often rooted in one's beliefs, and exhibited in one's feelings and intended behavior), 97–120. *See also* prejudice
ABCs of, 98
behavior affected by, 6, 97–102
behavior's effect on, evidence of, 103–108
behavior's effect on, theories on, 108–120
changing, 120
cognitive dissonance theory on, 109–113, 118–119
dual attitude system, 41
facial feedback effect and, 115–116
immoral acts and, 105–107
implicit vs. explicit, 41, 99–100
moral hypocrisy in, 98–99, 102
past, reconstruction of, 80–81
potency of, 101–102
principle of aggregation and, 100
racial prejudice and, 107
role playing and, 103–105
self-perception theory on, 109, 113–119
self-presentation theory on, 109, 118
social influences on, 99–100
social movements and, 107–108
in theory of planned behavior, 101
attitude inoculation: Exposing people to weak attacks upon their attitudes so that when stronger attacks come, they will have refutations available, 213–217
attitudes-follow-behavior principle. *See* attitude(s)
attraction, 337–357
gender differences in, 141–142
mutual liking in, 354–356
of opposites, 353–354
physical attractiveness in, 342–351
proximity in, 337–342
reward theory of, 356–357
similarity vs. complementarity in, 351–354
attractiveness: Having qualities that appeal to an audience. An appealing communicator (often someone similar to the audience) is most persuasive on matters of subjective preference, 195–196. *See also* physical attractiveness
attribution theory: The theory of how people explain others' behavior—for example, by

attributing it either to internal dispositions (enduring traits, motives, and attitudes) or to external situations, 82–89
cultural differences in, 88
depression and, 456–459
flattery and, 354–356
fundamental attribution error in, 84–89
group-serving bias and, 284–285
helping and, 383–384
maintaining change and, 469–470
misattribution in, 82–83
on mutual liking, 354–356
on prejudice, 283–286
self-serving bias and, 49–50
audience, in persuasion, 196, 208–212
authoritarian personality: A personality that is disposed to favor obedience to authority and intolerance of outgroups and those lower in status, 267
authority, closeness and legitimacy in obedience to, 166–168
autokinetic phenomenon: Self *(auto)* motion *(kinetic)*. The apparent movement of a stationary point of light in the dark, 156
automatic processing: "Implicit" thinking that is effortless, habitual, and without awareness; roughly corresponds to "intuition," 64–65
automatic racial prejudice, 260–262
availability heuristic: A cognitive rule that judges the likelihood of things in terms of their availability in memory. If instances of something come readily to mind, we presume it to be commonplace, 69–71
and climate change, 511–512
average
in physical attractiveness, 348–349
in principle of aggregation, 100
regression toward the, 74–75
aversive incidents, aggression influenced by, 309–311
avoidant attachment: Attachments marked by discomfort over, or resistance to, being close to others, 364–365

B

bad events
aggression influenced by, 309–311
power of, 355
self-serving bias in explaining, 49–50
bargaining: Seeking an agreement to a conflict through direct negotiation between parties, 440
baseball, integration of, 438
"beautiful is good" stereotype, 347, 348
behavioral confirmation: A type of self-fulfilling prophecy whereby people's social expectations lead them to behave in ways that cause others to confirm their expectations, 93–94
behavioral medicine: An interdisciplinary field that integrates and applies behavioral and medical knowledge about health and disease, 462